Eugene W. Smith

Arthur D. Frey

with thanks to the above

April 26, 1963

SAVANNAH (1961)
United States Government

World's first nuclear
powered merchant ship

Courtesy, States
Marine Lines, Inc.

PASSENGER SHIPS OF THE WORLD

PAST AND PRESENT

By

Eugene W. Smith

Published by

GEORGE H. DEAN COMPANY

74 India Street, Boston, Massachusetts, U.S.A.

CONTENTS

FOREWORD

The author's two previous books entitled "Trans-Atlantic Passenger Ships—Past and Present" and "Trans-Pacific Passenger Ships" are now out of print. When the stock of those two books had dwindled to a relatively few copies, it was then decided to bring out a new book of world-wide scope. This new volume is the result of that decision. Although this new book contains much of the material that appeared in the original publications, it has been completely revised and enlarged. Two additional major parts have been included to make the work eligible for the descriptive title of ocean-going passenger ships of the world, past and present.

The pictorial section of representative ships are arranged in chronological order to show the general development of design from the early days of steam to the present era. As steamship travel reached its peak during 1890–1914 period, a greater number of ship pictures of this time are shown.

In the fleet list, I have endeavored to include all the principal passenger ship lines engaged in the various services that come within the scope of this book.

The explanatory notes given in the back part of this volume are provided to answer some of the questions that arise in a work of this kind.

The appendix has been provided, in order to take care of the list of passenger ships that have been regularly employed in the shuttle service between California and Hawaii. It, also, includes a composite listing of all ship pictures that appear in the author's three published books. A general index has been added at the end of the book for cross-reference purposes.

The writer would like to take this opportunity of expressing his appreciation to the many people who so kindly supplied information. Among those that contributed much help, I should particularly like to mention Mr. Osgood Williams and Mr. Arthur D. Fay of The Peabody Museum of Salem, Massachusetts; to Mr. John L. Lochhead of The Mariners' Museum, Newport News, Virginia, who has been most helpful in providing scrapping dates of certain ships, and to Contre-Amiral M. Adams of France, and Mr. L. L. von Munching of the Netherlands, who have given much valuable data for this book. I am, also, much indebted to Professor John Haskell Kemble of Pomona College for his help in the preparation of the trans-Pacific passenger ship section.

My acknowledgments would be incomplete without expressing thanks to the steamship lines for their generosity and co-operation in supplying photographs to illustrate this book.

I have been very fortunate to live comparatively near the Peabody Museum of Salem. It was through their extraordinary sources of historical and statistical data, along with my own extensive files of facts, that enabled me to carry on with the project I set out to accomplish many years ago.

Inasmuch as the subject matter of this book covers the principal sea lanes of the world, one might wonder why the numerous coastal liners are not included. In the author's opinion it would be better not to add the coastal and the somewhat similar cross-channel type of passenger ship to this book, as they would make the already sizable volume too cumbersome. The ideal way to handle the matter would be to add a companion volume, as this method would provide a clear distinction between these two different kinds of services.

In closing I wish to convey my thanks to the many readers of my previous books, who by their support have made possible the feasibility of bringing out this new volume.

EUGENE WALDO SMITH

424 Lebanon Street
Melrose, Massachusetts
June 4, 1962.

PART I

TRANS-ATLANTIC PASSENGER SHIPS

PAST AND PRESENT

PART I

TRANS-ATLANTIC PASSENGER SHIPS

Past and Present

(North Atlantic Service)

*Asterisk denotes ship in service, 1962

Aachen (1895) North German Lloyd.
Built by "Vulkan", Stettin, Germany. Tonnage: 3,833.
Dimensions: 355' x 43'. Single-screw, 12½ knots. Triple
expansion engines. Two masts and one funnel. Sunk in the
Baltic as German naval auxiliary during the First World
War. Sister ship: **Crefeld.**

Abbotsford (1871) Red Star Line.
Built by Gourlay & Co., Dundee, Scotland. Tonnage: 2,554.
Dimensions: 345' x 37'. Single-screw, 10 knots. Compound
engines. Two masts and one funnel. Service: Liverpool-Philadelphia. Vessel later transferred to American Line. Sister
ship: **Kenilworth.**

Abyssinia (1870) Cunard Line.
Built by J. & G. Thomson, Ltd., Clydebank, Glasgow,
Scotland. Tonnage: 3,253. Dimensions: 363' x 42'. Single-
screw, 12½ knots. Inverted engines. Three masts and one
funnel. Iron hull. In Guion Line service 1880–84. During
1887–91 period was in Vancouver-Hong Kong trade. Destroyed by fire in mid-Atlantic in December 1891, with all
lives saved by German liner **Spree.** Sister ship: **Algeria.**
Note: The last pre-compound type engined steamships built
for the Atlantic trade.

Acadia (1840) Cunard Line.
Built by John Wood, Port Glasgow, Scotland. Tonnage:
1,154. Dimensions: 207' x 34'. Paddle-wheels, 9 knots.
Side lever engines. Three masts and one funnel. Wooden
hull. Sold to the German Federated States in 1849 and
converted to warship under name of **Erzherzog Johann.**
Renamed **Germania** in 1853. Scrapped in 1858. Sister
ships: **Britannia, Caledonia** and **Columbia.**

Acropolis (1890) Stephen D. Stephenidis.
Built by Harland & Wolff, Ltd., Belfast, Ireland. Tonnage:
5,083. Dimensions: 370' x 44'. Single-screw, 13 knots.

Triple expansion engines. Four masts and two funnels. Second funnel was added in 1921, so as to impress prospective customers. Employed as an immigrant carrier between Greece and New York, but soon sold to new owners due to lack of business. Renamed: (a) **Washington,** (b) **Great Canton.** Scrapped in Italy, 1924. Ex-**Kilpatrick,** ex-**Michigan.**

Adriatic (1857) Collins Line.
Built by George Steers, New York, N. Y. Tonnage: 3,670. Dimensions: 355′ x 50′. Paddle-wheels, 13½ knots. Oscillating engines. Two masts and two funnels. Launched, April 8, 1856. Note: The last trans-Atlantic paddle-wheel vessel to be built. Passengers: 316 first and 60 second. Maiden voyage New York-Liverpool, November 23, 1857. After the collapse of the Collins Line in 1861 she was laid up until sold to the Galway Line. Unsuccessful in the Galway Line service and was soon sold. Converted to sail in 1869. Resold in 1873 and used as a hulk at Bonny, West Africa. Broken up for scrap in 1885.

[handwritten margin note: "II v. Scotia of 1862"]

Adriatic (1872) White Star Line.
Built by Harland & Wolff, Ltd., Belfast, Ireland. Tonnage: 3,888. Dimensions: 437′ x 44′ (454′ o.l.). Single-screw, 15 knots. Compound engines. Four masts and one funnel. Iron hull. Launched, October 17, 1871. Maiden voyage: Liverpool-New York, April 11, 1872. Equipped with gas lights. Won the trans-Atlantic speed record in 1872. Made her final crossing in November 1897. Broken up by British shipbreakers in 1899. Sister ship: **Celtic.**

Adriatic (1906) White Star Line.
Built by Harland & Wolff, Ltd., Belfast, Ireland. Tonnage: 24,563. Dimensions: 709′ x 75′ (726′ o.l.). Twin-screw, 18 knots. Quadruple expansion engines. Four masts and two funnels. Launched, September 20, 1906. Maiden voyage: Liverpool-New York, May 8, 1907. A very steady and excellent type of passenger ship. Sold to Japanese shipbreakers in December 1934. Dismantled in Japan, 1935. Sister ship: **Baltic.** Note: The top superstructure differed considerably from the **Baltic.** However they were quite similar in other aspects. The general appearance also was similar to the **Cedric** and **Celtic.** The four liners comprised the White Star Line's "Big Four".

Africa (1850) Cunard Line.
Built by Robert Steele & Co., Greenock, Scotland. Tonnage: 2,227. Dimensions: 266′ x 40′. Paddle-wheels, 12 knots.

Side lever engines. Three masts and one funnel. Maiden voyage: October 26, 1850. Used as a floating barracks at Liverpool for the British Government in 1867. Sold out of Cunard Line service in 1868. Note: The last wooden ship to be used by the Cunard Line. Sister ship: **Asia.**

Alaska   (1881)   Guion Line.
Built by John Elder & Co., Glasgow, Scotland. Tonnage: 6,392. Dimensions: 500′ x 50′ (520′ o.l.). Single-screw, 17 knots. Compound engines. Four masts and two funnels. Iron hull. She won the Atlantic Blue Ribbon in April 1882, by crossing the Atlantic in 7 days, 6 hours, 43 minutes. The average speed was recorded at 16.10 knots. Made the last sailing of Guion Line in April 1894. Renamed: (a) **Magallanes** (1897) chartered, (b) **Alaska.** Sold for scrap in 1899. Resold as a hulk. Broken up for scrap in 1902.

Alaunia   (1913)   Cunard Line.
Built by Scott's Shipbuilding & Engineering Co., Greenock, Scotland. Tonnage: 13,405. Dimensions: 520′ x 64′ (540′ o.l.). Twin-screw, 16 knots. Quadruple expansion engines. Two masts and two funnels. Passengers: 520 second and 1,540 third class. Maiden voyage: Liverpool-Portland, December 3, 1913. Sunk by mine two miles from Royal Sovereign, October 19, 1916. Sister ship: **Andania.**

Alaunia   (1925)   Cunard Line.
Built by John Brown & Co., Clydebank, Glasgow, Scotland. Tonnage: 14,030. Dimensions: 519′ x 65′ (540′ o.l.). Twin-screw, 15 knots. Steam turbines. Two masts and one funnel. Passengers: 500 cabin, 1,200 third. Maiden voyage: Liverpool-Quebec-Montreal, July 24, 1925. Converted to British armed merchant cruiser in late 1939. Sold to British Royal Navy in December 1944; served as repair ship. Sister ships: **Ascania** and **Aurania.** Similar to **Andania** class. All were designed for the Canadian service.

Albania   (1900)   Cunard Line.
Built by Swan & Hunter, Newcastle, England. Tonnage: 7,682. Dimensions: 461′ x 52′. Twin-screw, 11 knots. Triple expansion engines. Four masts and one funnel. In Cunard Line fleet 1911-12. Sold to Bank Line in 1912. Renamed: **Poleric** (1912). Broken up for scrap in 1930. Ex-**Cairnrona** (1911), ex-**Consuelo** (1910).

Albania   (1920)   Cunard Line.
Built by Scott's Shipbuilding & Engineering Co., Greenock, Scotland. Tonnage: 12,768. Dimensions: 523′ x 64′ (539′

3

o.l.). Twin-screw, 15 knots. Steam turbines. Four masts
and one funnel. Passengers: 500 cabin. Maiden voyage:
Liverpool-New York, January 18, 1921. Laid up in 1925.
Renamed: **California** (1930). Became a war loss, August
11, 1941.

Albert Ballin (1923) Hamburg-American Line.
Built by Blohm & Voss, Hamburg, Germany. Tonnage:
20,815. Dimensions: 602′ x 72′. Twin-screw, 16 knots.
Steam turbines. Four masts and two funnels. Note: Later
re-engined, speed increased to 20 knots. In 1934 was
lengthened to 645 feet (21,131 tons). Sunk by mine off
Warnemunde in March 1945. Refloated in 1949. Renamed:
Hansa (1935), (b) **Sovetsky Sojus** (1950) Russian. Sister
ship: **Deutschland.** Similar to: **Hamburg** and **New York.**

Albertic (1923) White Star Line.
Built by Akt. Ges. "Weser", Bremen, Germany. Tonnage:
18,940. Dimensions: 590′ x 72′. Twin-screw, 16 knots.
Quadruple expansion engines. Two masts and two funnels.
Launched as the **Munchen** on March 23, 1920. Ceded to
Great Britain in 1920. Sold to Royal Mail Line in 1922.
Renamed: **Ohio** (1923), (b) **Albertic** (1927). Broken up
by Japanese shipbreakers in 1934.

Aleppo (1865) Cunard Line.
Built by J. & G. Thomson, Glasgow, Scotland. Tonnage:
2,143. Dimensions: 292′ x 38′. Single-screw, 11 knots. Inverted engines. Compound engines in 1880. Triple expansion engines, 1890. Two masts and one funnel. Iron hull.
Passengers: 46 cabin, 590 third. Scrapped in 1909. Similar
ships: **Malta, Palmyra, Tarifa** and **Tripoli.**

Alesia (1882) Fabre Line.
Built by G. Forrester & Co., Liverpool, England. Tonnage:
2,845. Dimensions: 328′ x 40′. Single-screw, 11 knots.
Compound engines. Three masts and one funnel. Sold in
1896. Sister ship: **Burgundia.**

Alesia (1906) Fabre Line.
Built by Blohm & Voss, Hamburg, Germany. Tonnage:
9,720. Dimensions: 475′ x 55′ (498′ o.l.). Twin-screw, 15
knots. Quadruple expansion engines. Two masts and one
funnel. Sold to Italian shipbreakers in October 1933. Ex-
Montreal (1928), ex-**Konig Friedrich Auguste** (1920).

Alexandra (1897) Wilson-Furness Line.
Built by Alexander Stephen & Sons, Ltd., Glasgow, Scotland.
Tonnage: 6,919. Dimensions: 475′ x 52′. Single-screw, 14

knots. Triple expansion engines. Four masts and one funnel. Renamed: **Menominee** (1898). Sister ships: **Boadicea, Cleopatra** and **Victoria.**

Alexandria   (1870)   Anchor Line.
Built by Robert Duncan & Co., Port Glasgow, Scotland. Tonnage: 2,017. Dimensions: 300' x 33'. Single-screw, 10 knots. Compound engines. Three masts and one funnel. Iron hull. Launched, September 14, 1870. Sold to other British owners in 1895. Sister ships: **Assyria, Castalia, Ismailia, Italia, Olympia** and **Trinacria.**

Alfonso XII   (1875)   Spanish Line.
Built by Wm. Denny & Bros., Dumbarton, Scotland. Tonnage: 2,915. Dimensions: 363' x 38'. Single-screw. Compound inverted engines. Owner listed as A. Lopez & Co. Out of service by 1885.

Alfonso XII   (1890)   Spanish Line.
Built by "Vulkan" Co., Stettin, Germany. Tonnage: 6,966. Dimensions: 463' x 51'. Single-screw, 18 knots. Triple expansion engines. Three masts and two funnels. Scrapped in Italy, 1926. Ex-**Meteoro** (1899), ex-**Havel** (1898).

Alfonso XIII   (1888)   Spanish Line.
Built by Wm. Denny & Bros., Dumbarton, Scotland. Tonnage: 5,000. Dimensions: 408' x 47'. Single-screw, 16 knots. Triple expansion engines. Four masts and one funnel. Sunk in the port of Santander in 1915. Sister ship: **Reina Maria Cristina.**

Alfonso XIII   (1891)   Spanish Line.
Built by Wm. Denny & Bros., Ltd., Dumbarton, Scotland. Tonnage: 7,815. Dimensions: 531' x 54'. Twin-screw, 17 knots. Triple expansion engines. Two masts and one funnel. Renamed: **Vasco Nunez de Balboa** (1923). Scrapped in Italy, 1927. Ex-**Oceana** (1916), ex-**Scot** (1905).

Alfonso XIII   (1923)   Spanish Line.
Built by Soc. Espanola de Construction Naval Yard, Bilbao, Spain. Tonnage: 10,551. Dimensions: 480' x 61' (500' o.l.). Twin-screw, 17 knots. Steam turbines. Two masts and one funnel. Renamed: **Habana** (1931). Sister ship: **Cristobal Colon.**

Algeria   (1870)   Cunard Line.
Built by J. & G. Thomson, Ltd., Glasgow, Scotland. Tonnage: 3,253. Dimensions: 361' x 41'. Single-screw, 12½

knots. Inverted engines. Three masts and one funnel. Iron hull. Maiden voyage Liverpool-New York, September 27, 1870. Vessel sold to builder as part payment for **Servia** and **Catalonia** in 1881. Resold to Guion Line. Renamed: **Pennland** (1881). Scrapped in Italy, 1903. Sister ship: **Abyssinia.**

Algeria (1891)   Anchor Line.
Built by D. & W. Henderson & Co., Glasgow, Scotland. Tonnage: 4,510. Dimensions: 375' x 46'. Single-screw, 12½ knots. Triple expansion engines. Two masts and one funnel. Built for Calcutta service. Later placed in Mediterranean-New York service. Renamed: **Cyrill** (1913), (b) **Virginia** (Italian). Scrapped in 1923. Sister ship: **Scindia.**

Algeria (1914)   Anchor Line.
Built by Reiherstieg, Hamburg, Germany. Tonnage: 8,156. Dimensions: 449' x 55'. Twin-screw, 15 knots. Quadruple expansion engines. Two masts and one funnel. Passengers: 417 cabin, 118 third. Renamed: **Toledo** (1922). Scrapped in 1934. Ex-**Kigoma** (1921).

Alice (1907)   Austro-American Line.
Built by Russell & Co., Port Glasgow, Scotland. Tonnage: 6,122. Dimensions: 415' x 49'. Twin-screw, 16 knots. Triple expansion engines. Two masts and one funnel. Maiden voyage Trieste-New York in 1907. Renamed: **Asia** (1917) Brazilian, **Asia** (1920) Fabre Line. Destroyed by fire in Red Sea, May 21, 1930. Sister ship: **Laura.**

Allemannia (1865)   Hamburg-American Line.
Built by Day, Summers & Co., Southampton, England. Tonnage: 2,619. Dimensions: 301' x 41'. Single-screw, 12½ knots. Inverted engines. Three masts and one funnel. Iron hull. Maiden voyage Hamburg-Southampton-New York, September 16, 1865. Sold to W. Hunter of Liverpool in 1883. Renamed: **Oxenholme** (British). Abandoned at sea in April 1894.

Aller (1886)   North German Lloyd.
Built by Fairfield Shipbuilding & Engineering Co., Glasgow, Scotland. Tonnage: 5,217. Dimensions: 437' x 48' (455' o.l.). Single-screw, 17 knots. First trans-Atlantic liner with triple expansion engines. Four masts and two funnels. Refitted with only two masts in 1897. Service: (a) Bremen-Southampton-New York, (b) Mediterranean-New York. Scrapped in 1904. Sister ships: **Saale** and **Trave.**

Alma   (1856)   Compagnie Franco-Americaine.
Built by Laird Bros., Birkenhead, England.   Tonnage:
2,010.   Dimensions: 279' x 36'.   Single-screw, 10 knots.   In-
verted engines.   Three masts and one funnel.   Maiden vouage:
Havre-New York, April 2, 1856.   Renamed: **China** (1858),
P. & O. Line.

Alps   (1853)   Cunard Line.
Built by Wm. Denny & Bros., Dumbarton, Scotland.   Ton-
nage: 1,440.   Single-screw, 9 knots.   Geared beam engines.
Three masts and one funnel.   Served as a transport in
Crimean War, 1854.   Sold to Spanish Government in 1859.
Sister ship: **Andes.**

Alsatia   (1876)   Anchor Line.
Built by Henderson & Co., Glasgow, Scotland.   Tonnage:
2,810.   Dimensions: 356' x 36'.   Single-screw, 13 knots.
Compound engines.   Triple expansion engines in 1886.   Two
masts and one funnel.   Iron hull.   Maiden voyage Glasgow-
New York, May 20, 1876.   Later in Mediterranean-New York
service.   Sold to Khedivial Mail Line in 1901.   Similar to:
Elysia and **Utopia.**

Alsatian   (1913)   Allan Line.
Built by Wm. Beardmore & Co., Glasgow, Scotland.   Tonnage: 18,481.   Dimensions: 571' x 72' (600' o.l.).   Quadruple-
screw, 19 knots.   Steam turbines.   Two masts and two funnels.
Launched, March 22, 1913.   First North Atlantic liner with
cruiser stern.   Passengers: 287 first, 504 second, 848 third.
Maiden voyage Liverpool-St. John, New Brunswick, January
17, 1914.   Acquired by Canadian Pacific Line in 1917.   Renamed: **Empress of France** (1919).   Sister ship: **Calgarian.**

America   (1848)   Cunard Line.
Built by Robert Steel & Co., Greenock, Scotland.   Tonnage:
1,825.   Dimensions: 251' x 38'.   Paddle-wheels, 10 knots.
Side lever engines.   Three masts and one funnel.   Wooden
hull.   Passengers: 140 cabin class.   Paddle-wheels were
32 feet in diameter, float boards 9 feet long.   Maiden voyage:
Liverpool-Halifax-New York, April 15, 1848.   Sold and converted to sailing ship in 1866.   Renamed: **Coalgacondor.**
Sister ships: **Canada, Europa** and **Niagara.**

America   (1863)   North German Lloyd.
Built by Caird & Co., Greenock, Scotland.   Tonnage: 2,752.
Dimensions: 328' x 40'.   Single-screw, 11 knots.   Inverted
engines.   Compound engines in 1872.   Speed increased to
14 knots.   Two masts and one funnel.   Iron hull.   Passengers:

76 first, 107 second, 480 third. Maiden voyage: Bremen-Southampton-New York, May 24, 1863. Sold to Italians in 1894 and renamed **Orazio.** Scrapped at Spezia in 1895. Running mates: **Deutschland, Hansa, Hermann, Union** and **Weser.**

America (1881) Fabre Line.
Built by T. Royden & Sons, Liverpool, England. Tonnage: 2,403. Dimensions: 328' x 40'. Single-screw, 11 knots. Compound engines. Three masts and one funnel. Iron hull. Made her final voyage to New York in 1907. Sold to Italian shipbreakers in April 1909. Ex-**Britannia** (1902). Sister ship: **Scotia.**

America (1884) National Line.
Built by J. & G. Thomson, Clydebank, Glasgow, Scotland. Tonnage: 5,528. Dimensions: 441' x 51' (459' o.l.). Single-screw, 18 knots. Compound engines. Two masts and two funnels. Steel hull. The only National Line trans-Atlantic record-breaker. Had seven boilers. Consumed 190 tons of coal per day. Sold to Italian Government in 1886 and converted into a cruiser-transport. Renamed **Trinacria** (1887). Vessel was finally fitted out as an Italian royal yacht. Scrapped in 1925.

America (1905) United States Line.
Built by Harland & Wolff, Ltd., Belfast, Ireland. Tonnage: 21,145. Dimensions: 668' x 74' (687' o.l.). Twin-screw, 18 knots. Quadruple expansion engines. Four masts and two funnels. First sailing as an American passenger liner, New York-Plymouth-Cherbourg-Bremen, June 22, 1921, for United States Mail Steamship Company. Laid up as a reserved transport in 1932. Commissioned as the troopship **Edmund B. Alexander** in 1941. Reconditioned in 1942 and a large single funnel replaced the original two. Scrapped at Baltimore in 1957. Ex-**Amerika** (1917).

America (1908) Navigazione Generale Italiana.
Built by Cantieri Nav. Riuniti, Muggiano, Italy. Tonnage: 8,996. Dimensions: 476' x 55'. Twin-screw, $16\frac{1}{2}$ knots. Triple expansion engines. Two masts and two funnels. Note: Originally owned and operated by La Veloce Line, making her maiden voyage Genoa-New York, May 20, 1909. Scrapped in 1928.

*America (1940) United States Lines.
Built by Newport News Shipbuilding & Drydock Co., Newport News, Virginia. Tonnage: 33,532. Dimensions:

660' x 93' (723' o.l.). Twin-screw, 23 knots. Steam turbines. Two masts and two funnels. Tonnage under American rule of measurement: 26,454. Keel laid August 22, 1938. Launched, August 31, 1939. Maiden voyage in the form of a cruise to the West Indies, August 10, 1940. Taken over by the United States Navy and commissioned **West Point,** June 15, 1941. Served as a troopship in World War II. Thoroughly reconditioned for passenger service in 1946. Made the trans-Atlantic crossing from Ambrose Light to Daunt's Lightship in 4 days, 22 hours, 22 minutes, at an average speed of 24.54 knots in November 1946. Passengers: First and tourist class, since December 1960. Renamed: (a) **West Point** (1941), (b) **America** (1946).

American Banker (1920)   American Merchant Lines.
Built by American International Shipbuilding Corp., Hog Island, Pennsylvania. Tonnage: 7,430. Dimensions: 436' x 58'. Single-screw, 15 knots. Steam turbines. Two masts and one funnel. Passengers: 80 tourist. Renamed: (a) **Ville d' Anvers** (1940), (b) **City of Athens** (1946), (c) **Protea** (1947), (d) **Arosa Kulm** (1952). Out of service. Ex-**Cantigny.** Sister ships: **American Farmer, American Importer, American Merchant, American Shipper, American Trader** and **American Traveler.** Twelve ships of this class were built, but several were taken over by the United States Government and are not included in the above group.

American Farmer (1920)   American Merchant Lines.
Built by American International Shipbuilding Corp., Hog Island, Pa. Tonnage: 7,430. Dimensions: 436' x 58' (448' o.l.). Single-screw, 15 knots. Steam turbines. Two masts and one funnel. Renamed: **Ville de Liege** (1940). Torpedoed and sunk by German submarine in April 1941. Ex-**Ourcq** (1924). Sister ships: See **American Banker.**

American Importer (1920)   American Merchant Lines.
Built by American International Shipbuilding Corp., Hog Island, Pa. Tonnage: 7,590. Dimensions: 436' x 58'. Single-screw, 15 knots. Steam turbines. Two masts and one funnel. Renamed: **Ville de Gand** (1940). Torpedoed and sunk in August 1940. Ex-**Somme.** Sister ships: See **American Banker.**

American Merchant (1920)   American Merchant Lines.
Built by American International Shipbuilding Corp., Hog Island, Pa. Tonnage: 7,430. Dimensions: 436' x 58'. Single-screw, 15 knots. Steam turbines. Two masts and one funnel.

Renamed: **Ville de Namur** (1940). Torpedoed and sunk in June 1940. Ex-**Aisne** (1924). Sister ships: See **American Banker.**

American Shipper   (1920)   American Merchant Lines.
Built by American International Shipbuilding Corp., Hog Island, Pa. Tonnage: 7,430. Dimensions: 436′ x 58′. Single-screw, 15 knots. Steam turbines. Two masts and one funnel. Renamed: **Ville de Mons** (1940). Torpedoed and sunk in September 1940. Ex-**Tours** (1924). Sister ships: See **American Banker.**

American Trader   (1920)   American Merchant Lines.
Built by American International Shipbuilding Corp., Hog Island, Pa. Tonnage: 7,430. Dimensions: 436′ x 58′. Single-screw, 15 knots. Steam turbines. Two masts and one funnel. Renamed: **Ville de Hasselt** (1940). Torpedoed and sunk in August 1940. Ex-**Marne** (1924). Sister ships: See **American Banker.**

American Traveler   (1920)   American Merchant Lines.
Built by American International Shipbuilding Corp., Hog Island, Pa. Tonnage: 7,555. Dimensions: 436′ x 58′. Single-screw, 15 knots. Steam turbines. Two masts and one funnel. Renamed: **Ville d'Arlon** (1940) Antwerp Navigation Co. Torpedoed and sunk in December 1940. Ex-**Cambrai.** Sister ships: See **American Banker.**

Amerika   (1872)   Thingvalla Line (Danish).
Built by Harland & Wolff, Ltd., Belfast, Ireland. Tonnage: 3,867. Dimensions: 437′ x 40′. Single-screw, 15 knots. Compound engines. Four masts and one funnel. Passengers: 150 first, 50 second, 800 third. Scrapped in 1898. Ex-**Celtic.**

Amerika   (1905)   Hamburg-American Line.
Built by Harland & Wolff, Ltd., Belfast, Ireland. Tonnage: 22,225. Dimensions: 668′ x 74′ (687′ o.l.). Twin-screw, 18 knots. Quadruple expansion engines. Four masts and two funnels. Passengers: 386 first, 150 second, 1,970 third. Maiden voyage Hamburg-New York, October 11, 1905. First voyage Hamburg-Boulogne-Southampton-Boston, June 10, 1914. Interned at Boston in 1914. Converted into an American troopship in 1917. Renamed: **America** (1917). Acquired by United States Mail Steamship Company in 1921. Transferred to United States Lines in 1921. Renamed: **Edmund B. Alexander** (1941). Note: See **America** for further details.

Amerique   (1864)   French Line.
   Built by Chantier de 1' Atlantique, St. Nazaire, France.
   Tonnage: 4,585. Dimensions: 394' x 43'. Single-screw, 13
   knots. Compound engines. Triple expansion engines in
   1892. Three masts and two funnels. Ran ashore at Sea-
   bright, New Jersey, January 7, 1877, and it was not until
   April 10th, that she was refloated. First Havre-Panama
   voyage, September 22, 1886. Electric lights installed in
   1888. Wrecked at Savanilla, Columbia, January 28, 1895.
   Ex-**Atlantique** (1873), ex-**Imperatrice Eugenie** (1870).

Amsterdam   (1879)   Holland-America Line.
   Built by Harland & Wolff, Ltd., Belfast, Ireland. Tonnage:
   3,664. Dimensions: 410' x 39'. Single-screw, 13 knots.
   Compound engines. Four masts and one funnel. Passengers:
   94 first and 638 third. Triple expansion engines in 1893.
   Renamed: **Amsterda** (1905). Scrapped in 1905. Ex-
   British Crown (1887).

Amsterdam   (1880)   Holland-America Line.
   Built by Archibald McMillan & Son, Dumbarton, Scotland.
   Tonnage: 2,949. Dimensions: 320' x 39'. Single-screw, 10
   knots. Compound engines. Two masts and one funnel.
   Iron hull. Passengers: 46 first, 648 third. Wrecked off
   Sable Island, July 30, 1884, with the loss of four lives.
   Sister ship: **Edam.**

Anchoria   (1874)   Anchor Line.
   Built by Barrow Shipbuilding Co., Barrow-in-Furness, Eng-
   land. Tonnage: 4,168. Dimensions: 408' x 40'. Single-screw,
   14 knots. Compound engines. Three masts and one funnel.
   Passengers: 200 first, 100 second, 800 third. Maiden voyage:
   Glasgow-New York, November 13, 1875. Vessel sold in 1906;
   German owners. Scrapped in 1922. Class: **Bolivia, Cir-
   cassia, Devonia** and **Ethiopia.**

Ancona   (1908)   Italia Line.
   Built by Workman, Clark & Co., Ltd., Belfast, Ireland.
   Tonnage: 8,210; increased to 8,885. Dimensions: 482' x 58'.
   Twin-screw, 16 knots. Triple expansion engines. Two masts
   and one funnel. Launched, September 19, 1907. Maiden
   voyage: Genoa-Naples-Palermo-New York, April 23, 1908.
   Torpedoed and sunk by Austrian submarine in Mediterranean, November 7, 1915, with the loss of 206 lives. Sister
   ships: **Taormina** and **Verona.**

Andania   (1913)   Cunard Line.
   Built by Scott's Shipbuilding & Engineering Co., Greenock,
   Scotland. Tonnage: 13,404. Dimensions: 520' x 64' (540'

o.l.). Twin-screw, 16 knots. Quadruple expansion engines. Two masts and two funnels. Maiden voyage England-Canada, July 17, 1913. Torpedoed and sunk near Rathlin Light, January 27, 1918, with the loss of seven lives. Sister ship: **Alaunia.** First Cunard liners designed for the Canadian service.

Andania   (1922)   Cunard Line.
Built by R. & W. Hawthorn, Leslie & Co., Newcastle, England. Tonnage: 13,950. Dimensions: 520′ x 65′ (540′ o.l.). Twin-screw, 15 knots. Steam turbines. Two masts and one funnel. Passengers: 500 cabin, 1,200 third. Converted to British armed merchant cruiser in 1939. Torpedoed and sunk near Iceland, June 15, 1940. Sister ships: **Antonia** and **Ausonia.** Similar ships: **Alaunia, Ascania** and **Aurania.** Note: All were built for the Canadian trade.

Andes   (1852)   Cunard Line.
Built by Wm. Denny & Bros., Dumbarton, Scotland. Tonnage: 1,440. Dimensions: 236′ x 33′. Single-screw, 9 knots. Geared beam engines. Three masts and one funnel. Clipper bow. Iron hull. Served as a transport in Crimean War, 1854. Sold to Spanish Government in 1859. Sister ship: **Alps.** Passengers: 62 first and 122 second.

Andrea Doria   (1953)   Italia Line.
Built by Soc. Anon. Ansaldo, Sestri Ponente, Genoa, Italy. Tonnage: 29,082. Dimensions: 656′ x 90′ (700′ o.l.). Twin-screw, 23 knots. Six steam turbines. Single mast and one funnel. Launched, June 16, 1951. Passengers: 218 first, 320 cabin, 703 tourist. Maiden voyage Genoa-New York, January 14, 1953. Due to an unfortunate collision with the Swedish-American liner **Stockholm,** this very attractive passenger ship sank 60 miles off Nantucket Island, on the morning of July 26, 1956. The collision occurred in calm foggy conditions at 11:22 P.M., July 25th, and the damage was extensive to both liners. Of those on board the **Andrea Doria** two were lost, 18 listed as missing and 29 others unaccounted, therefore presumed lost. The **Stockholm** sustained a loss of 5 lives. The wreck of the **Andrea Doria** lies in a depth of 225 feet of water. Sister ship: **Cristoforo Colombo.**

Anglia   (1861)   Galway Line.
Built by Martin Samuelson & Co., Hull, England. Tonnage: 2,913. Dimensions: 364′ x 40′. Paddle-wheels, 13 knots. Oscillating engines. Two masts and two funnels. In trans-

Atlantic service, 1863–64. Sold to the Turkish Government in 1866. Laid down as **Munster.**

Anglia (1869)   Anchor Line.
Built by Alexander Stephen & Sons, Ltd., Glasgow, Scotland. Tonnage: 2,253. Dimensions: 328' x 35'. Single-screw, 12 knots. Inverted type engines. Three masts and one funnel. Passengers: 100 first, 75 second, 600 third. Maiden voyage Glasgow-New York, January 28, 1870. Later in Mediterranean-New York service. Sunk in collision with barque **Trongate** off St. John's, Newfoundland, September 10, 1880, with no loss of life. Sister ships: **Australia** and **Cambria.**

Anglo-Saxon (1856)   Allan Line.
Built by Wm. Denny & Bros., Ltd., Dumbarton, Scotland. Tonnage: 1,673. Dimensions: 283' x 35'. Single-screw, 11 knots. Inverted engines. Three masts and one funnel. Iron hull. Laid down as **Saxon.** Maiden voyage: Liverpool-Quebec-Montreal, June 4, 1856. Wrecked off Cape Race, April 27, 1863, with the loss of 237 lives. Only 33 cabin, 103 steerage and 71 of the crew were saved. Sister ship: **North American.**

Angloman (1892)   Warren Line.
Built by Laird Bros., Birkenhead, England. Tonnage: 4,892. Dimensions: 403' x 45'. Single-screw, 11 knots. Triple expansion engines. Four masts and one funnel. Service: Liverpool-Boston. Wrecked near Holyhead. February 1897, with no loss of life.

*Antilles (1952)   French Line.
Built by Naval Dockyard, Brest, France. Tonnage: 20,419. Dimensions: 580' x 80' (599' o.l.). Twin-screw, 22 knots. Steam turbines. Two masts and one funnel. Launched in April 1951. Commenced service to the West Indies in May 1953. Passengers: 404 first, 285 cabin, 89 tourist. Sister ship: **Flandre.**

Antonio (1921)   Cunard Line.
Built by Vickers-Armstrong, Ltd., Barrow-in-Furness, England. Tonnage: 13,867. Dimensions: 519' x 65' (540' o.l.). Twin-screw, 15 knots. Steam turbines. Two masts and one funnel. Passengers: 500 cabin and 1,200 third. Maiden voyage: England-Canada, June 1, 1922. From 1928 onwards in   Liverpool-Glasgow-Belfast-Quebec-Montreal   service. Armed as merchant cruiser at beginning of World War II. Sold to British Royal Navy in March 1942. Later converted

to repair ship and renamed **Wayland.** Scrapped in Scotland, 1948.   Sister ships: **Andania** and **Ausonia.**   Similar: **Alaunia, Ascania** and **Aurania.**

Antonio Lopez   (1891)   Spanish Line.
Built by Wm. Denny & Bros., Ltd., Dumbarton, Scotland. Tonnage: 5,975. Dimensions: 430' x 50'. Single-screw, 13½ knots. Quadruple expansion engines. Two masts and one funnel. Passengers: 58 first, 38 second, 36 third. Scrapped at Cadiz in 1946. Ex-**Ruahine.**

Aquitania   (1914)   Cunard Line.
Built by John Brown & Co., Ltd., Clydebank, Glasgow, Scotland. Tonnage: 45,647. Dimensions: 868' x 97' (901' o.l.). Quadruple-screw, 24 knots. Steam turbines. Two masts and four funnels. Fourth funnel was a dummy. From keel to boat deck measured 92½ feet. Passengers: 597 first, 614 second, 2,052 third. Laid down in June 1911. Launched, April 23, 1913. Maiden voyage: Liverpool-New York, May 30, 1914. Converted to an armed merchant cruiser in August 1914. Served as a hospital ship, 1915–19. She was later put in service as a troopship. Returned to regular passenger service in June 1919, ports being Southampton, Cherbourg and New York. From 1939 to 1948 was used as a troopship. Returned to Cunard Line service in May 1948. Her final trans-Atlantic voyage was in November 1949. This outstanding luxury liner was broken up for scrap in the Gareloch in 1950. She had crossed the Atlantic approximately 600 times.

Arabia   (1852)   Cunard Line.
Built by Robert Steele & Son, Greenock, Scotland. Tonnage: 2,393. Dimensions: 285' x 40'. Paddle-wheels, 12 knots. Side lever engines. Two masts and two funnels. Passengers: 180 cabin. The last wooden vessel built for the Cunard Line. Maiden voyage: Liverpool-New York, January 1, 1853. Sold and converted into a sailing ship in 1864. Broken up for scrap some years later.

Arabia   (1896)   Hamburg-American Line.
Built by Harland & Wolff, Ltd., Belfast, Ireland. Tonnage: 5,456. Dimensions: 399' x 49'. Single-screw, 13 knots. Quadruple expansion engines. Two masts and one funnel. Renamed: (a) **Barcelona** (1899), (b) **Ancona** (1915) Italian Government, Scrapped in 1926.

Arabic   (1881)   White Star Line.
Built by Harland & Wolff, Ltd., Belfast, Ireland. Tonnage: 4,386. Dimensions: 430' x 42'. Single-screw, 13 knots.

Compound engines. Four masts and one funnel. Note: Laid down and launched as **Asiatic,** but was renamed **Arabic** while fitting out. See PART II. Renamed: **Spaarndam** (1890). Scrapped in 1901.

Arabic (1903) White Star Line.
Built by Harland & Wolff, Ltd., Belfast, Ireland. Tonnage: 15,801. Dimensions: 600' x 65' (615' o.l.). Twin-screw, 16 knots. Quadruple expansion engines. Four masts and one funnel. Launched, December 18, 1902. Maiden voyage Liverpool-New York, June 26, 1903. Made her first Liverpool-Boston sailing in 1905. Torpedoed and sunk off Southern Ireland, August 19, 1915, with the loss of 44 lives. Note: Laid down as **Minnewaska,** but renamed before completion.

Arabic (1908) White Star Line.
Built by A. G. "Weser", Bremen, Germany. Tonnage: 16,821. Dimensions: 590' x 69' (615' o.l.). Twin-screw, 17 knots. Quadruple expansion engines. Two masts and two funnels. First voyage as **Arabic,** Southampton-New York, September 7, 1921. From 1925 to 1929 in Red Star Line service; Antwerp-Southampton-New York. Broken up by Italian shipbreakers in 1932. Ex-**Berlin** (1921).

Arago (1855) New York & Havre SteamNavigation Co.
Built by Westervelt & McKay, New York, N. Y. Tonnage: 2,260. Dimensions: 280' x 42'. Paddle-wheels, 10½ knots. Oscillating engines. Two masts and two funnels. Wooden hull. Maiden voyage: New York-Southampton-Havre, June 2, 1855. Sold to Peruvian Government in 1869. Sister ship: **Fulton.**

Arcadia (1896) Hamburg-American Line.
Built by Harland & Wolff, Ltd., Belfast, Ireland. Tonnage: 5,454. Dimensions: 399' x 49'. Single-screw, 13 knots. Quadruple expansion engines. Two masts and one funnel. Vessel was seized by United States in 1917. Her name was not changed. Scrapped in 1926. Sister ship: **Arabia.**

Archimede (1881) Navigazione Generale Italiana.
Built by Alexander Stephen & Sons, Ltd., Glasgow, Scotland. Tonnage: 2,837. Dimensions: 350' x 40'. Single-screw, 12½ knots. Compound engines. Three masts and one funnel. Iron hull. Straight bow. Launched, November 23, 1881. Services: (a) Italy-New York, (b) Italy-South America. Sunk off Alexandria, March 5, 1905. Sister ships: **Gottardo, Indipendente, Vincenzo Florio** and **Washington.**

Arconia   (1897)   Russian American Line.
Built by Barclay, Curle & Co., Glasgow, Scotland. Tonnage:
4,603.   Dimensions: 368' x 47'.   Single-screw, 12 knots.
Triple expansion engines.   Two masts and one funnel.
Made her first Libau-New York voyage in 1906. Renamed:
(a) **Hittfeld** (1908), (b) **Ioannina** (1913). Torpedoed and
sunk off the Azores, December 15, 1917. Ex-**Juliette** (1906),
ex-**Dunolly Castle** (1905).

Arctic   (1849)   Collins Line.
Built by William H. Brown, New York, N. Y. Tonnage:
2,856.   Dimensions: 282' x 45'.   Paddle-wheels, 12½ knots.
Side lever engines.   Three masts and one funnel.   Wooden
hull.   Cost about $700,000 to build.   Maiden voyage: New
York-Liverpool, October 27, 1850.   This noted American
trans-Atlantic record-breaker was in collision with the small
French iron steamship **Vesta,** during a dense fog, 60 miles
off Cape Race, September 27, 1854, while on way to New
York with 233 passengers.   She sunk four hours later with
the loss of 322 lives.   Captain Luce, true to naval tradition
went down with his ship, but was rescued from the water and
landed at Quebec.   Sister ships: **Atlantic, Baltic** and
Pacific.

Argentina   (1905)   La Veloce Line.
Built by Fratelli Orlando, Leghorn, Italy. Tonnage: 4,985.
Dimensions: 394' x 47'.   Twin-screw, 14½ knots.   Triple
expansion engines.   Two masts and two funnels. Renamed:
(a) **Brasile,** (b) **Venezuela** (1912).   Lost at Casablanca,
March 7, 1920.

Argentina   (1907)   Austro-American Line.
Built by Russell & Co., Port Glasgow, Scotland. Tonnage:
5,526.   Dimensions: 390' x 48'.   Twin-screw, 15 knots.
Triple expansion engines.   Two masts and one funnel.
Launched in March 1907.   Maiden voyage: Trieste-South
America, October 31, 1907.   Later transferred to New York
service.   Note: Acquired by Cosulich Line 1920.   Sold to
Florio Line in 1926.

Argentina   (1913)   Spanish Line.
Built by Swan, Hunter & Wigham Richardson, Ltd.,
Wallsend-on-Tyne, England. Tonnage: 10,137. Dimensions:
480' x 61'.   Quadruple-screw, 17 knots.   Combination quadruple expansion engines and steam turbines.   Two masts
and one funnel.   Transferred to the South American service.
Sunk at Barcelona in 1937, but was later refloated and sold

for scrap. Ex-**Reina Victoria Eugenia** (1931). Sister ship:
Uruguay.

Argentina   (1913)   Home Lines.
Built by Cammell, Laird & Co., Ltd., Birkenhead, England.
Tonnage: 11,015. Dimensions: 512' x 61' (530' o.l.). Twin-
screw, 15 knots. Combination quadruple expansion engines
and steam turbines. Two masts and two funnels. First
voyage as **Argentina,** Genoa-South America, January 13,
1947. Later transferred to New York service. Sold to Zim
Israel Navigation Company in 1953. Renamed: **Jerusalem**
(1953), (a), (b) **Aliya** (1957) Zim Line. Scrapped in Italy,
1959. Ex-**Bergensfjord** (1947).

Argo   (1852)   Galway Line.
Built by C. J. Mare & Co., Blackwall, London, England.
Tonnage: 2,380. Dimensions: 254' x 39'. Single-screw, 9
knots. Three masts and one funnel. Clipper bow. Iron hull.
Built originally for General Screw Co. Maiden voyage:
Galway-New York, May 28, 1859. Wrecked at Trepassey
Bay, Newfoundland, June 28, 1859, with no loss of life.

Ariel   (1855)   Vanderbilt Line.
Built by Jeremiah Simonson, New York, N. Y. Tonnage:
1,736. Dimensions: 252' x 33'. Paddle-wheels 11 knots.
Beam engines. Two masts and one funnel. Maiden voyage:
New York-Southampton-Havre, August 11, 1855. Made her
last voyage for line in November 1859. Wrecked on a submerged rock off Yokohama, October 27, 1873.

Arizona   (1879)   Guion Line.
Built by John Elder & Co., Glasgow, Scotland. Tonnage:
5,147. Dimensions: 450' x 45' (465' o.l.). Single-screw, 16
knots. Compound engines. Four masts and two funnels.
Iron hull. Passengers: 140 first, 70 second, 140 third. Broke
the trans-Atlantic speed record in July 1879. Made news in
November 1879 by running at full speed into a huge iceberg
and miraculously was able to make the port of St. John's,
Newfoundland, where temporary repairs were completed.
No loss of life, and no one was injured by the mishap. First
Atlantic liner with a compound 3-crank engine. Her original
funnels were replaced by a large single funnel in 1898, and
also triple expansion engines installed. Placed in San
Francisco-Japan-China service. Taken over by United
States Government in 1898. Renamed: **Hancock** (1898).
Receiving ship at Brooklyn Navy yard 1903–1914. Troop-
ship during 1917–18. Scrapped in California, 1926.

*Arkadia   (1931)   Greek Line.
   Built by Vickers-Armstrongs, Ltd., Newcastle, England.
   Tonnage: 20,256. Dimensions: 553' x 76' (590' o.l.). Maximum beam 83'–6''. Quadruple-screw, 20 knots. Service
   speed: 18½ knots. Turbo-electric. Single mast and one
   funnel. Note: Her forepeak has been extended 14 feet to
   give a curved bow. Passengers: 50 first, 1,337 tourist. First
   voyage for Greek Line, Bremen to Quebec and Montreal,
   May 22, 1958. First call to Boston in March 1959. Ex-**New
   Australia** (1958), ex-**Monarch of Bermuda** (1950).

Armenian   (1895)   Leyland Line.
   Built by Harland & Wolff, Ltd., Belfast, Ireland. Tonnage:
   8,825. Dimensions: 512' x 59'. Single-screw, 14 knots.
   Triple expansion engines. Four masts and one funnel.
   Passengers: 60 first class. Served as a cargo ship only at a
   later date. Captured and sunk by German submarine 20
   miles from Trevose Head, June 28, 1915.

Arosa Kulm   (1920)   Arosa Line (Swiss).
   Built by American International Shipbuilding Corp., Hog
   Island, Pa. Tonnage: 8,929. Dimensions: 436' x 59'. Single-
   screw, 15 knots. Steam turbines. Two masts and one funnel.
   Passengers: 965 tourist. Note: Sailed under the Panamanian
   flag, though ownership was Swiss. First voyage Bremen-
   Halifax, March 1952. Service was discontinued in 1958.
   Scrapped in Belgian, 1959. Ex-**Protea** (1952), ex-**City of
   Athens** (1947), ex-**Ville d'Anvers** (1940), ex-**American
   Banker** (1926), ex-**Cantigny** (1924).

Arosa Sky   (1939)   Arosa Line.
   Built by Provencale de Construction Navale, La Ciotat,
   France. Tonnage: 17,321. Dimensions: 562' x 75' (594' o.l.).
   Triple-screw, 20 knots. Motorship. Two masts and one
   funnel. First voyage as **Arosa Sky**, Havre-Southampton-
   Halifax-New York, May 10, 1957. This attractive liner was
   sold to Costa Line of Genoa in 1958. Renamed: **Bianca C**
   (1958). Ex-**La Marseillaise** (1957). Launched as **Marechal
   Petain** in 1944. Completed in 1949 as **La Marsilllaise.**

Arosa Star   (1931)   Arosa Line.
   Built by Bethlehem Shipbuilding Corp., Quincy, Mass.
   Tonnage: 7,114. Dimensions: 413' x 59' (465' o.l.). Single-
   screw, 15 knots. Steam turbines. Single mast and one funnel.
   Reconditioned in 1954; new type bow fitted. Passengers:
   38 first and 768 tourist. First Bremen-Quebec sailing made
   in May 1954. Seized for debts in December 1958. Renamed:

18

Bahama Star (1960). Ex-**Puerto Rico** (1954), ex-**Borinquen** (1949).

Arosa Sun   (1930)   Arosa Line.

Built by Ateliers & Chantiers de la Loire, St. Nazaire, France. Tonnage: 20,126. Dimensions: 575′ x 68′ (597′ o.l.). Twin-screw, 18 knots. Motorship. Two masts and one funnel. Passengers: 100 first, 984 tourist. First voyage Trieste-Palermo-Naples-Lisbon-New York, July 14, 1955. Second voyage was Bremen-Southampton-Havre-Quebec, August 20, 1955. Vessel sold to other owners in 1960. Ex-**Felix Roussel** (1955).

Ascania   (1911)   Cunard Line.

Built by Swan, Hunter & Wigham Richardson, Ltd., Wallsend-on-Tyne, England.   Tonnage: 9,111.   Dimensions: 466′ x 56′ (482′ o.l.). Twin-screw, 13 knots. Triple expansion engines.   Two masts and two funnels.   Maiden voyage: London-Southampton-Quebec-Montreal,   May   23,   1911. Wrecked off Cape Ray, June 13, 1918, with no loss of life. Note: Laid down as the **Gerona** for the Thomson Line, but was purchased by Cunard Line before completion.

Ascania   (1925)   Cunard Line.

Built by Sir W. G. Armstrong, Whitworth & Co., Newcastle, England. Tonnage: 14,013. Dimensions: 520′ x 65′ (538′ o.l.). Twin-screw, 15 knots. Four steam turbines. Two masts and one funnel. Launched, December 20, 1923. Passengers: 500 cabin, 1,200 third class. Accommodation later was changed to 198 first class and 498 tourist. Maiden voyage: London-Southampton-Quebec-Montreal, May 22, 1925. Taken over by British Government for war service in 1939. Resumed regular service in December 1947. Broken up for scrap at Newport, Mon., 1957. Sister ships: **Alaunia** and **Aurania**. Similar to **Andania, Antonia** and **Ausonia.**

Asia   (1850)   Cunard Line.

Built by Robert Steele & Co., Greenock, Scotland. Tonnage: 2,227. Dimensions: 268′ x 45′ (290′ o.l.). Paddle-wheels, 12 knots. Side lever engines. Three masts and one funnel. Wooden hull. Clipper bow. Passengers: 160 cabin. Maiden voyage: Liverpool-Halifax-New York, May 18, 1850. Mizzen mast was later removed. Crossed from Liverpool to Halifax in 8 days, 17 hours. Made her last sailing for Cunard Line in May 1867. Sold and converted to sailing ship. Destroyed by fire at Bombay in 1877. Sister ship: **Africa.**

Asia   (1907)   Fabre Line.
Built by Russell & Co., Port Glasgow, Scotland. Tonnage:
6,122. Dimensions: 415′ x 49′. Twin-screw, 16 knots. Triple
expansion engines. Two masts and one funnel. Destroyed
by fire in the Red Sea, May 21, 1930. Vessel acquired by
Fabre Line in 1920. Ex-**Alice** (1917). Sister ship: **Braga.**

Assyria   (1871)   Anchor Line.
Built by Robert Duncan & Co., Port Glasgow, Scotland.
Tonnage: 2,023. Dimensions: 300′ x 33′. Single-screw, 10
knots. Compound engines. Three masts and one funnel.
Iron hull. Passengers: 100 first, 500 third. In service 1871–
94. Scrapped in 1894. Sister ships: **Alexandria, Castalia,
Ismailia, Italia, Olympia** and **Trinacria.**

Assyria   (1908)   Anchor Line.
Built by Frd. Krupp, Kiel, Germany. Tonnage: 8,072.
Dimensions: 449′ x 54′. Twin-screw, 13½ knots. Quadruple
expansion engines. Two masts and one funnel. Passengers:
240 cabin, 140 third. First voyage Glasgow-New York,
May 28, 1921. Sold to Portuguese owners in December 1929.
Renamed: **Colonial** (1929). Wrecked in 1950 after having
been sold for scrap. Ex-**Ypiranga** (1921).

Assyrian   (1880)   Allan Line.
Built by Earle's Shipbuilding & Engineering Co., Hull, England. Tonnage: 3,317. Dimensions: 360′ x 42′. Single-screw,
11 knots. Compound engines. Four masts and one funnel.
Last voyage Glasgow-Boston, July 24, 1901. Scrapped in
1902. Ex-**Assyrian Monarch** (1887).

Assyrian Monarch   (1880)   Monarch Line.
Built by Earle's Shipbuilding & Engineering Co., Ltd., Hull,
England. Tonnage: 3,317. Dimensions: 360′ x 42′. Single-
screw, 11 knots. Compound engines. Four masts and one
funnel. Steel hull. Passengers: 40 first, 1,000 third. Maiden
voyage London-New York, November 1880. Renamed:
Assyrian (1887) Allan Line.

Astoria   (1884)   Anchor Line.
Built by Wm. Denny & Bros., Ltd., Dumbarton, Scotland.
Tonnage: 5,086. Dimensions: 439′ x 46′. Single-screw, 14
knots. Triple expansion engines. Two masts and two funnels.
Clipper Bow. First voyage Glasgow-New York, December
28, 1899. Scrapped in 1911. Ex-**Tainui** (1899), ex-**Covadonga** (1899), ex-**Tainui** (1897).

Athenia   (1904)   Anchor-Donaldson Line.
Built by Vickers Sons & Maxim, Ltd., Barrow-in-Furness, England. Tonnage: 9,080. Dimensions: 478′ x 56′. Twin-screw, 13½ knots. Triple expansion engines. Four masts and one funnel. First voyage as passenger ship, Glasgow-St. John, March 25, 1905. Torpedoed and sunk near Inishtrahull, August 16, 1917, with the loss of 15 lives.

Athenia   (1923)   Anchor-Donaldson Line.
Built by Fairfield Shipbuilding & Engineering Co., Glasgow, Scotland. Tonnage: 13,465. Dimensions: 526′ x 66′. Twin-screw, 15½ knots. Steam turbines. Two masts and one funnel. Passengers: (a) 516 cabin, 1,000 third; (b) 314 cabin, 310 tourist, 928 third. Maiden voyage: Glasgow-Quebec-Montreal, April 21, 1923. Note: First ship to be sunk in World War II. It was on September 3, 1939, that she was torpedoed and sunk 200 miles west of the Hebrides. Total loss among her passengers and crew amounted to 112. Sister ship: **Letitia**.

Athinai   (1908)   Moraitis Line (Greek).
Built by Sir Raylton Dixon & Co., Middlebrough, England. Tonnage: 6,742. Dimensions: 420′ x 52′. Twin-screw, 15 knots. Triple expansion engines. Two masts and two funnels. In 1914 acquired by National Steam Navigation Company of Greece. Destroyed by fire in North Atlantic in 1915.

Atlanta   (1908)   Austro-American Line.
Built by Russell & Co., Port Glasgow, Scotland. Tonnage: 5,387. Dimensions: 385′ x 49′. Single-screw, 13 knots. Triple expansion engines. Two masts and one funnel. Owned and operated by Cosulich Line after First World War.

Atlantic   (1849)   Collins Line.
Built by William H. Brown, New York, N. Y. Tonnage: 2,856. Dimensions: 282′ x 45′. Paddle-wheels, 13 knots. Side lever engines. Three masts and one funnel. First steamship to have straight stem. Pioneer vessel of the Collins Line. Coal consumption about 87 tons per day. Maiden voyage: New York-Liverpool, April 27, 1850. Broke the trans-Atlantic speed record. After the complete collapse of the Collins Line in January 1858, the **Atlantic** and her sister ship **Baltic** were taken over by the United States Government for service in the Civil War. From 1866 to 1870 both served the short-lived North American Lloyd Company. The **Atlantic** was broken up for scrap at Cold Springs, N. Y. in 1871. Sister ships: **Arctic, Baltic** and **Pacific.**

Atlantic   (1870)   White Star Line.
Built by Harland & Wolff, Ltd., Belfast, Ireland. Tonnage: 3,707. Dimensions: 420' x 40'. Single-screw, 14 knots. Compound engines. Four masts and one funnel. Iron hull. Launched, December 1, 1870. Maiden voyage: Liverpool-New York, June 8, 1871. Wrecked off Meagher's Head near Halifax during a strong gale, April 1, 1873, with the loss of 546 lives. Sister ships: **Baltic, Oceanic** and **Republic.**

Atlantic   (1927)   Home Lines.
Built by Wm. Cramp & Sons Shipbuilding Co., Philadelphia, Pa. Tonnage: 20,553. Dimensions: 554' x 83'. Twin-screw, 22 knots. Steam turbines. Two masts and two funnels. Passengers: 173 first and 1,023 tourist. First voyage: Genoa-New York, May 14, 1949. Renamed: **Queen Frederica** (1955). Ex-**Matsonia** (1949), ex-**Malolo** (1937).

*Atlantic   (1953)   American Export Lines.
Built by Sun Shipbuilding & Drydock Co., Chester, Pa. Tonnage: 14,138. Dimensions: 564' x 76'. Single-screw, 20 knots. Steam turbines. Two masts and one funnel. Passengers: 40 first and 840 tourist. The **Atlantic** was formerly operated by Arnold Bernstein Line in trans-Atlantic passenger service. Entered American Export Lines service in May 1960. Note: Originally built as a fast freighter, but reconstructed as passenger carrier during 1957–58. Ex-**Badger Mariner** (1957).

Atlantique   (1865)   French Line.
Built by Chantier de l' Atlantique, St. Nazaire, France. Tonnage: 3,200. Dimensions: 355' x 43'. Paddle-wheels, 11½ knots. Side lever engines. Two masts and two funnels. Renamed: **Amerique** (1873). Wrecked at Savanilla in 1895. Ex-**Imperatrice Eugenie** (1870).

Atlas   (1860)   Cunard Line.
Built by J. & G. Thomson, Glasgow, Scotland. Tonnage: 1,794. Dimensions: 274' x 36'. Single-screw, 10 knots. Geared oscillating engines. Three masts and one funnel. Iron hull. Compound engines in 1873. Lengthened to 339 feet (2,393 tons) in 1873. Masts reduced to two. Scrapped in 1896. Sister ships: **Hecla, Kedar, Marathon, Olympus** and **Sidon.**

Augusta Victoria   (1888)   Hamburg-American Line.
Built by "Vulkan" Shipbuilding Co., Stettin, Germany. Tonnage: 7,661. Dimensions: 461' x 56' (480' o.l.). Twin-

screw, 18½ knots. Triple expansion engines. Three masts
and three funnels. Note: Lengthened to 522 feet (8,479 tons)
and reduced to two masts in 1897. Spelling of her name was
changed to **Auguste Victoria.** Sold to the Russians in
1904 and renamed **Kuban.** Served as an auxiliary cruiser
during the Russo-Japanese War. Scrapped in 1907. Running
mates: **Columbia, Furst Bismarck** and **Normannia.**

Augustus (1927) (a) Navigazione Generale Italiana, (b)
Italia Line.
Built by Societa Anonima Ansaldo, Sestri, Ponente, Italy.
Tonnage: 32,650. Dimensions: 666′ x 82′ (710′ o.l.). Quad-
ruple-screw, 19 knots. Motorship. Two masts and two
funnels. Largest motorship built to date. Launched, Decem-
ber 13, 1926. Maiden voyage: Genoa-Naples-Buenos Aires,
November 12, 1927. First voyage to New York, August 28,
1928. Liner was transferred to Italia Line in 1932. Con-
verted to Italian aircraft carrier in 1943. Renamed:
Sparviero (1943) Italian Navy. Scuttled by Germans at
Genoa in September 1944. Refloated in 1946; sold for scrap.
Broken up in 1951. Sister ship: **Roma.**

*****Augustus** (1952) Italia Line.
Built by Cantieri Riuniti Dell' Adriatico, Trieste, Italy.
Tonnage: 27,226. Dimensions: 649′ x 87′ (680′ o.l.). Twin-
screw, 21 knots. Motorship. Single mast and one funnel.
Passengers: 180 first, 288 cabin, 714 tourist. Maiden voyage:
Italy-Brazil-River Plate, March 1952. Transferred to North
Atlantic service in 1957. Sister ship: **Giulio Cesare.**

Aurania (1883) Cunard Line.
Built by J. & G. Thomson, Ltd., Clydebank, Glasgow,
Scotland. Tonnage: 7,269. Dimensions: 470′ x 57′ (485′
o.l.). Single-screw, 17½ knots. Compound engines. Three
masts and two funnels. Steel hull. Passengers: 480 cabin,
700 third. Maiden voyage: Liverpool-New York, June 23,
1883. Her displacement was 13,360 tons. Scrapped at Genoa
in 1905. Running mate: **Servia.**

Aurania (1915) Cunard Line.
Built by Swan, Hunter & Wigham Richardson, Ltd.,
Wallsend-on-Tyne, England. Tonnage: 13,400. Dimensions:
520′ x 64′. Twin-screw, 16 knots. Steam turbines. Two
masts and two funnels. Torpedoed 15 miles from Inishtrahull, February 4, 1918, with the loss of 8 lives. Similar
in appearance to **Andania** class.

Aurania (1924) Cunard Line.
Built by Swan, Hunter & Wigham Richardson, Ltd., Newcastle, England. Tonnage: 13,984. Dimensions: 519' x 65' (540' o.l.). Twin-screw, 15 knots. Four steam turbines. Two masts and one funnel. Passengers: 500 cabin, 1,200 third. Maiden voyage: Liverpool-New York, September 1924. Converted to armed merchant cruiser in 1939. Sold to the British Admiralty in 1942. Renamed: **Artifex** (1944) repair ship. Sister ships: **Alaunia** and **Ascania.** Similar to **Andania** class.

Ausonia (1909) Cunard Line.
Built by Swan, Hunter & Wigham Richardson, Ltd., Wallsend-on-Tyne, England. Tonnage: 8,153. Dimensions: 450' x 54'. Single-screw, 13 knots. Triple expansion engines. Four masts and one funnel. Maiden voyage: London-Southampton-Quebec-Montreal, May 16, 1911. Torpedoed and sunk 620 miles from the Fastnet, May 30, 1918, with the loss of 44 lives. Ex-**Tortona** (1911).

Ausonia (1921) Cunard Line.
Built by Sir W. G. Armstrong, Whitworth & Co., Newcastle, England. Tonnage: 13,912. Dimensions: 520' x 65' (538' o.l.). Twin-screw, 15 knots. Steam turbines. Two masts and one funnel. Maiden voyage: Liverpool-Quebec-Montreal June 22, 1922. London-Southampton-Quebec-Montreal service during 1923–39. Sold to British Admiralty in 1939 and converted to armed merchant cruiser. Reported still in service as **H.M.S. Ausonia.** Sister ships: **Andania** and **Antonia.** Similar to: **Ascania, Alaunia** and **Aurania.**

Austral (1881) Anchor Line.
Built by John Elder & Co., Glasgow, Scotland. Tonnage: 5,524. Dimensions: 456' x 48'. Single-screw, 15 knots. Compound engines. Four masts and two funnels. Note: Vessel was on charter from Orient Line. Made several sailings for Anchor Line, in 1884.

Australasian (1857) Cunard Line.
Built by J. & G. Thomson, Glasgow, Scotland. Tonnage: 2,902. Dimensions: 338' x 42'. Single-screw, 12 knots. Inverted engines. Three masts and two funnels. First Cunard iron screw steamship. Acquired from European & Australian Royal Mail Company in 1860. New single expansion engines installed in 1870. Renamed: **Calabria** (1870). Sold and converted to cable ship at later date. Scrapped in 1898.

Australia   (1870)   Anchor Line.
Built by Robert Duncan & Co., Port Glasgow, Scotland.
Tonnage: 2,243. Dimensions: 324′ x 35′. Single-screw, 12
knots. Inverted engines. Three masts and one funnel. Iron
hull. Maiden voyage: Glasgow-New York, March 11, 1870.
Compound engines in 1877. Broken up for scrap in 1895.
Sister ships: **Anglia** and **Cambria.**

Australia   (1881)   Hamburg-American Line.
Built by C. Mitchell & Co., Newcastle, England. Tonnage:
2,119.   Dimensions: 297′ x 37′.   Single-screw, 10 knots.
Compound engines. Iron hull. Acquired from Carr Line
(German) in 1888. Wrecked near Antwerp in 1902. Albert
Ballin developed the passenger business of the Carr Line,
which was later taken over by Hamburg-American Line.
Mr. Ballin by his unusual ability became head of the Ham-
burg-American Line.

Austria   (1857)   Hamburg-American Line.
Built by Caird & Co., Greenock, Scotland. Tonnage: 2,383.
Dimensions: 320′ x 40′. Single-screw, 10 knots. Geared
oscillating engines. Three masts and one funnel. Iron hull.
Destroyed by fire in North Atlantic, September 13, 1858,
with the loss of 471 lives. This unfortunate tragedy was
caused by hot iron dropping into a tar-bucket in one of the
steerages. It is considered the most terrible fire disaster the
North Atlantic has ever known. Sister ship: **Saxonia.**

Austrian   (1866)   Allan Line.
Built by Barclay, Curle & Co., Glasgow, Scotland. Tonnage:
2,682. Dimensions: 319′ x 38′. Single-screw, 11 knots. In-
verted engines. Three masts and one funnel. Iron hull.
Compound engines installed in 1875.   Triple expansion
engines in 1888. Maiden voyage: Liverpool-Quebec-Montreal,
July 18, 1867. Services: North Atlantic; South Atlantic.
Broken up for scrap in 1905. Running mates: **Moravian,
Nestorian** and **Peruvian.**

Avoca   (1891)   New York & Continental Line (British).
Built by Wm. Denny & Bros., Ltd., Dumbarton, Scotland.
Tonnage: 5,183. Dimensions: 420′ x 48′. Single-screw, 14
knots. Quadruple expansion engines. Three masts and one
funnel. First voyage for line was on March 31, 1908. Renamed: (a) **Uranium** (1909), (b) **Feltria** (1916) Cunard
Line. Torpedoed and sunk, May 5, 1917. Ex-**Atlanta,**
ex-**Avoca,** ex-**San Fernando,** ex-**Avoca.**

25

Baltic   (1850)   Collins Line.
Built by Brown & Bell, New York, N. Y. Tonnage: 2,856.
Dimensions: 282' x 45'. Paddle-wheels, 12½ knots. Side
lever engines. Three masts and one funnel. Wooden hull.
Mizzen mast was removed in 1853. Maiden voyage New
York-Liverpool, November 16, 1850. Passengers: 200 first
and 80 second. Note: Made the final sailing for the Collins
Line in 1858. Laid up during 1858–61. Served as a transport
during the American Civil War. Engines removed in 1870.
Converted into a sailing ship and used for the wheat trade.
Scrapped at Apple Island in Boston Harbor during 1880.
Sister ships: **Arctic, Atlantic** and **Pacific.** They were all
considered fast vessels for their time.

Baltic   (1871)   White Star Line.
Built by Harland & Wolff, Ltd., Belfast, Ireland. Tonnage:
3,707. Dimensions: 420' x 40' (437' o.l.). Single-screw, 14
knots. Compound engines. Four masts and one funnel.
Iron hull. Maiden voyage: Liverpool-New York, September
14, 1871. Broke the trans-Atlantic speed record in January
1873. Renamed: **Veendam** (1888). Foundered after
striking a submerged derelict, February 6, 1898. Sister ships:
Atlantic, Oceanic and **Republic.**

Baltic   (1904)   White Star Line.
Built by Harland & Wolff, Ltd., Belfast, Ireland. Tonnage:
23,884. Dimensions: 709' x 75' (726' o.l.). Twin-screw, 17
knots. Quadruple expansion engines. Four masts and two
funnels. Had a displacement of 40,000 tons. Largest liner
built to date. Cost about $4,000,000. Launched, November
21, 1903. Maiden voyage: Liverpool-New York, June 29,
1904. Broken up by Japanese shipbreakers in 1933. Running mates: **Adriatic, Cedric** and **Celtic.** Note: These
wonderful liners were known as "The Big Four."

Baltimore   (1868)   North German Lloyd.
Built by Caird & Co., Greenock, Scotland. Tonnage: 2,321.
Dimensions: 297' x 39'. Single-screw, 10 knots. Inverted
engines. Two masts and one funnel. Iron hull. Clipper bow.
Compound engines in 1881. Launched, August 3, 1868.
Passengers: 84 first and 600 third. Maiden voyage: Bremen-
Southampton-Baltimore, March 1, 1868. Scrapped in 1894.
Running mates: **Berlin, Leipzig** and **Ohio.**

Barbarossa   (1896)   North German Lloyd.
Built by Blohm & Voss, Hamburg, Germany. Tonnage:
10,984. Dimensions: 526' x 60'. Twin-screw, 15½ knots.

Quadruple expansion engines. Two masts and two funnels. Passengers: 226 first, 255 second, 1,600 third. Services: Interchangeable between New York and Australian trades. Renamed: **Mercury** (1917). Served as an American troopship in World War I. Scrapped in 1924. Similar ships: **Friedrich der Grosse** and **Konigin Luise.**

Barcelone   (1855)   Compagnie Franco-Americaine.
Built by Laird Bros., Birkenhead, England. Tonnage: 1,603. Dimensions: 270' x 35'. Single-screw, 10 knots. Horizontal engines. Three masts and one funnel. Iron hull. Clipper bow. Laid down as **Erie** for Canadian Steam Navigation Co. First voyage February 23, 1856. Renamed: **Behar** (1858) P. & O. Line.

Batavia   (1870)   Cunard Line.
Built by Wm. Denny & Bros., Ltd., Dumbarton, Scotland. Tonnage: 2,553. Dimensions: 327' x 39'. Single-screw, 12 knots. Compound engines. Two masts and one funnel. Iron hull. Clipper bow. Passengers: 150 cabin, 800 third. Maiden voyage: Liverpool-New York, May 10, 1870. Taken in trade as part payment for **Umbria** and **Etruria** in 1884 by John Elder & Co. Triple expansion engines in 1885. Speed increased to 14 knots. Ran for Canadian Pacific Line in 1887. Renamed: (a) **Tacoma** (1892), (b) **Shikotan Maru** (1913). Wrecked in 1924; dismantled for scrap. Running mate: **Parthia.**

Batavia   (1899)   Hamburg-American Line.
Built by Blohm & Voss, Hamburg, Germany. Tonnage: 11,464. Dimensions: 501' x 62'. Twin-screw, 12 knots. Quadruple expansion engines. Two masts and one funnel. Tonnage originally listed as 10,178. Renamed: (a) **Polonia** (1913), (b) **Batavia** (1913). Acquired by Messageries Maritimes in 1920. Scrapped in 1923. Sister ship: **Bulgaria.**

*****Batory**   (1936)   Gdynia-America Line.
Built by Cantieri Riuniti dell' Adriatico, Monfalcone, Italy. Tonnage: 14,287. Dimensions: 498' x 70' (525' o.l.). Twin-screw, 20 knots. Motorship. Two masts and two funnels. Launched, July 8, 1935. Maiden voyage: Gdynia-Copenhagen-New York, May 18, 1936. Became an Allied transport in 1939. First voyage after World War II, Gdynia-New York in May 1947. Placed in Gdynia-Bombay-Karachi service in August 1951. Returned to Gdynia-Montreal service in August 1957. Still in North Atlantic service 1961. Sister ship: **Pilsudski.**

Bavaria   (1856)   Hamburg-American Line.
   Built by Caird & Co., Greenock, Scotland. Tonnage: 2,273.
   Dimensions: 298′ x 39′.   Single-screw, 10 knots.   Geared
   oscillating engines. Three masts and one funnel. Iron hull.
   First voyage Hamburg-Southampton-New York, November
   1, 1858. Compound engines in 1871. Sold to Dominion Line
   in 1876; retained name. Destroyed by fire at sea while on
   voyage from New Orleans to Liverpool, February 6, 1877,
   with no loss of life. Sister ship: **Teutonia.**

Bavarian   (1899)   Allan Line.
   Built by Wm. Denny & Bros., Ltd., Dumbarton, Scotland.
   Tonnage: 10,376. Dimensions: 501′ x 59′.   Twin-screw, 16
   knots. Triple expansion engines. Two masts and one funnel.
   Passengers: 240 first, 220 second, 1,000 third.   Maiden
   voyage: Liverpool-Quebec-Montreal, August 24, 1899.
   Grounded near Montreal, November 3, 1905, and dismantled for scrap where she lay in 1907. Sister ship: **Tunisian.** The **Bavarian** was first ship in the Canadian trade
   to exceed 10,000 tons, also the first twin-screw Allan Line
   steamship.

*Begona   (1945)   Spanish Line.
   Built by Bethlehem-Fairfield Yard, Baltimore, Maryland.
   Tonnage: 10,139.   Dimensions: 455′ (o.l.) x 62′.   Single-
   screw, 16 knots. Steam turbines. Single mast and one funnel.
   Service: Europe-West Indies.   Large passenger capacity.
   Ex-**Castel Bianco** (1957), ex-**Castelbianco** (1952), ex-
   Vassar Victory (1947).

Belgenland   (1878)   Red Star Line.
   Built by Vickers, Sons & Maxim, Ltd., Barrow-in-Furness,
   England. Tonnage: 3,692. Dimensions: 403′ x 40′. Single-
   screw, 14 knots. Compound engines. Four masts and one
   funnel. Iron hull. Placed in Antwerp-New York service in
   1879.   Transferred to American Line in 1895, and used in
   their Liverpool-Philadelphia service. Renamed: **Venere**
   (1904) Italian. Sister ship: **Rhynland.**

Belgenland   (1917)   Red Star Line.
   Built by Harland & Wolff, Ltd., Belfast, Ireland. Tonnage:
   27,132.   Dimensions: 670′ x 78′ (696′ o.l.).   Triple-screw,
   17½ knots. Combination triple expansion engines and steam
   turbines. Two masts and three funnels. Passengers: 500
   first, 500 second, 1,500 third. Launched, December 31, 1914.
   Named **Belgic** in 1917, as cargo ship for White Star Line.
   First voyage as **Belgenland** April 14, 1923, Antwerp-

Southampton-New York. Transferred to Panama-Pacific Line in 1934. Renamed: **Columbia** (1934). Scrapped in Scotland, 1936.

Belgian (1855)   Allan Line.
Built by Caird & Co., Greenock, Scotland. Tonnage: 2,349. Dimensions: 324' x 40'. Single-screw, 12½ knots. Geared oscillating engines. Three masts and one funnel. Iron hull. In Allan Line service 1864–69. Sold to Dominion Line and used in their Gulf trade. Renamed: **Missouri** (1873). Wrecked near the Bahamas, October 1, 1873, with no loss of life. Ex-**Hammonia** (1864).

Belgic (1873)   White Star Line.
Built by Harland & Wolff, Ltd., Belfast, Ireland. Tonnage: 2,652. Dimensions: 370' x 36'. Single-screw, 12 knots. Compound engines. Four masts and one funnel. Iron hull. First London-New York voyage, July 9, 1874. Made four sailings to New York. Note: Placed in San Francisco-Hong Kong service in 1875. Sister ship: **Gaelic.**

Belgic (1917)   White Star Line.
Built by Harland & Wolff, Ltd., Belfast, Ireland. Tonnage: 24,547. Dimensions: 670' x 78'. Triple-screw, 17 knots. Triple expansion engines and steam turbines. Three masts and two funnels. After First World War was rebuilt as a large capacity passenger ship. A third funnel was added, a dummy, and also one mast removed. Renamed: (a) **Belgenland** (1921), (b) **Columbia** (1934). Scrapped in 1936.

Belgique (1855)   Compagnie Transatlantique Belge.
Built by Van Vlissingen, Amsterdam, Netherlands. Tonnage: 2,190. Dimensions: 381' x 37'. Single-screw, 10 knots. Inverted engines. Three masts and one funnel. Iron hull. Maiden voyage: Antwerp-Southampton-New York, December 31, 1855. Renamed: **Ireland** (British).

Belgravia (1882)   Anchor Line.
Built by D. & W. Henderson, Ltd., Glasgow, Scotland. Tonnage: 4,977. Dimensions: 400' x 45'. Single-screw, 13 knots. Compound engines. Two masts and one funnel. Iron hull. Built mainly for Indian service. Also in Liverpool-New York; Glasgow-New York; Mediterranean-New York services. Wrecked near St. John, New Brunswick, May 22, 1896.

Belgravia   (1899)   Hamburg-American Line.
  Built by Blohn & Voss, Hamburg, Germany.   Tonnage:
  11,439.   Dimensions: 501' x 62'   Twin-screw, 13 knots.
  Quadruple expansion engines.   Two masts and one funnel.
  Renamed: (a) **Riga** (1905), (b) **Transbalt** (Russian).

Belvedere   (1913)   Cosulich Line.
  Built by Cantieri Navali Triestino, Monfalcone, Italy.
  Tonnage: 7,420.   Dimensions: 419' x 51' (437' o.l.).   Single-
  screw, 13 knots.   Triple expansion engines.   Two masts and
  one funnel.   Originally built for Austro-American Line.   In
  1921 had accommodation for 144 cabin and 1,400 third class
  passengers.   Renamed: **Audacious** (1941) United States
  Government.   Scuttled off Normandy coast in June 1944, in
  order to help form a breakwater for the Allied invasion
  of France.

Berengaria   (1912)   Cunard Line.
  Built by A. G. "Vulkan", Hamburg, Germany.   Tonnage:
  52,226.   Dimensions: 883' x 98' (919' o.l.).   Quadruple-screw,
  23½ knots.   Steam turbines.   Two masts and three funnels.
  The aft funnel was a dummy.   Passengers: 970 first, 830
  second, 1,000 third.   First voyage for Cunard Line, Liverpool-
  New York, February 21, 1920.   Last voyage New York-
  Cherbourge-Southampton in March 1938.   Sold to British
  shipbreakers in November 1938.   Partly dismantled for
  scrap prior to World War II.   The remains towed to the
  Firth of Forth in 1946 and completely scrapped.   Ex-
  Imperator (1921).   Similar ships: **Vaterland** and **Bis-
  marck.**   Note: The **Bismarck** was never in service of
  Hamburg-American Line, as when completed she became
  the White Star Line **Majestic.**

Bergensfjord   (1913)   Norwegian-American Line.
  Built by Cammell, Laird & Co., Birkenhead, England.
  Tonnage: 11,013.   Dimensions: 512' x 61' (530' o.l.).   Twin-
  screw, 15/17 knots.   Quadruple expansion engines.   Two
  masts and two funnels.   Later converted to combination
  quadruple expansion engines and steam turbines.   Maiden
  voyage Oslo-Bergen-New York in September 1913.   Served
  as a troopship in World War II.   Renamed: (a) **Argentina**
  (1947) Home Lines, (b) **Jerusalem** (1953) Zim Lines, (c)
  Aliya (1957) Zim Lines.   Scrapped in 1959.   Sister ship:
  Kristianafjord.

*****Bergensfjord**   (1956)   Norwegian-America Line.
  Built by Swan, Hunter & Wigham Richardson, Ltd., Newcastle, England.   Tonnage: 18,739.   Dimensions: 545' x 72'

(578′ o.l.). Twin-screw, 20 knots. Motorship. Two masts and one funnel. Launched, July 18, 1955. Passengers: 100 first, 775 tourist. Maiden voyage: Oslo-Bergen-New York, May 30, 1956. Superstructure constructed of aluminum.

Berlin (1868) North German Lloyd.
Built by Caird & Co., Greenock, Scotland. Tonnage: 2,333. Dimensions: 297′ x 39′. Single-screw, 10 knots. Inverted engines. Two masts and one funnel. Compound expansion engines in 1882. Maiden voyage: Bremen-Southampton-Baltimore, April 1, 1868. Scrapped in 1895. Sister ships: **Baltimore, Leipzig** and **Ohio.**

Berlin (1875) American Line.
Built by Caird & Co., Greenock, Scotland. Tonnage: 5,526. Dimensions: 488′ x 44′. Single-screw, 16 knots. Compound engines. Re-engined in 1887 with triple expansion engines. Three masts and one funnel. Renamed: **Meade** (1898) United States Government. Scrapped in 1921. Ex-**City of Berlin** (1893).

Berlin (1908) North German Lloyd.
Built by A. G. "Weser", Bremen, Germany. Tonnage: 17,324. Dimensions: 590′ x 69′ (613′ o.l.). Twin-screw, 17 knots. Quadruple expansion engines. Two masts and two funnels. Passengers: 266 first, 246 second, 2,700 third. Mainly in Mediterranean-New York service. Ceded to Great Britain after First World War. Renamed: **Arabic** (1921).

Berlin (1925) North German Lloyd.
Built by Bremer Vulkan, Vegesack, Germany. Tonnage: 15,286. Dimensions: 549′ x 69′. Twin-screw, 16½ knots. Triple expansion engines. Two masts and two funnels. Note: Rescued a number of survivors from the sinking liner **Vestris,** which foundered on November 12, 1928. Sunk by a mine in Swinemunde Bay early in 1945. Salvaged by the Russians in 1949. Renamed **Admiral Nakhimov.**

*****Berlin** (1925) North German Lloyd.
Built by Armstrong, Whitworth & Co., Newcastle, England. Tonnage: 19,105. Dimensions: 553′ x 74′ (587′ o.l.). Twin-screw, 17 knots. Motorship. Two masts and two funnels. Passengers: 98 first, 725 tourist. Made her first voyage from Bremen to New York, January 8, 1955. Ex-**Gripsholm** (1955).

Birma (1894) Russian-American Line.
Built by Fairfield Shipbuilding Co., Glasgow, Scotland. Tonnage: 4,595. Dimensions: 415′ x 45′. Single-screw, 13½

knots. Triple expansion engines. Four masts and one funnel.
Renamed: (a) **Mitau** (1913), (b) **Josef Pilsudski** (1920),
(c) **Wilbo** (1922). Scrapped in Italy, 1924. Ex-**Arundel
Castle** (1905).

Birmania   (1882)   Navigazione Generale Italiana.
Built by Fratelli Orlando, Leghorn, Italy. Tonnage: 2,384.
Dimensions: 292' x 36'. Single-screw. Triple expansion
engines. Sunk in 1916.

Bismarck   (1921)   Hamburg-American Line.
Built by Blohm & Voss, Hamburg, Germany. Tonnage:
56,551. Dimensions: 915' x 100'. Quadruple-screw, 23½
knots. Steam turbines. Two masts and three funnels. Note:
Never in Hamburg-American Line service, as she was turned
over to the British upon completion. Renamed: (a) **Majestic**
(1922), (b) **Caledonia** (1936). See **Majestic** for further
details.

Blue Hen State   (1921)   United States Mail Steamship Co.
Built by New York Shipbuilding Co., Camden, New Jersey.
Tonnage: 10,533. Dimensions: 502' x 62'. Twin-screw, 14
knots. Triple expansion engines. Two masts and one funnel.
Maiden voyage: New York-Bremen-Danzig, June 1921.
Transferred to United States Lines in August 1921. Renamed:
(a) **President Garfield** (1922), (b) **President Madison**
(1940), (c) **Refuge** (1942) hospital ship.

Bluecher   (1901)   Hamburg-American Line.
Built by Blohm & Voss, Hamburg, Germany. Tonnage:
12,334. Dimensions: 525' x 62' (550' o.l.). Twin-screw, 16½
knots. Quadruple expansion engines. Two masts and two
funnels. Passengers: 390 first, 230 second, 550 third. Maiden
voyage: Hamburg-Southampton-New York, June 6, 1902.
Transferred to South American service in 1911. Renamed:
(a) **Leopoldina** (1917) Brazilian, (b) **Suffren** (1923) French.
Scrapped in Italy, 1929. Sister ship: **Moltke.**

Boadicea   (1898)   Atlantic Transport Line.
Built by Harland & Wolff, Ltd., Belfast, Ireland. Tonnage:
7,057. Dimensions: 486' x 52'. Single-screw, 14 knots.
Triple expansion engines. Four masts and one funnel.
Renamed: **Marquette** (1898). Sister ships: **Alexandra,
Cleopatra** and **Victoria.**

Bohemia   (1881)   Hamburg-American Line.
Built by A. & J. Inglis, Ltd., Glasgow, Scotland. Tonnage:
3,441. Dimensions: 351' x 41'. Single-screw, 11 knots. Com-

pound engines. Two masts and one funnel. Iron hull.
Accommodation for 100 first class and 1,200 steerage.
Renamed: (a) **Pompeji** (1898), (b) **Pompei** (1899). Running mates: **Rhaetia, Rugia** and **Moravia.**

Bohemian (1859)   Allan Line.
Built by Wm. Denny & Bros., Dumbarton, Scotland. Tonnage: 2,190. Dimensions: 298' x 38'. Single-screw, 10 knots. Inverted engines. Three masts and one funnel. Iron hull. Maiden voyage: Liverpool-Portland, Maine, November 16, 1859. Wrecked near Cape Elizabeth, February 22, 1864, with loss of 20 lives. Sister ships: **Hungarian, North Briton** and **Nova Scotian.**

Bohemian (1900)   Leyland Line.
Built by Alexander Stephen & Sons, Ltd., Glasgow, Scotland. Tonnage: 8,555. Dimensions: 512' x 58'. Single-screw, 14 knots. Triple expansion engines. Four masts and one funnel. Passengers: 60 first class. Maiden voyage: Liverpool-Boston, September 8, 1900. Wrecked off Halifax in 1920.

Bolivia (1873)   Anchor Line.
Built by Robert Duncan & Co., Port Glasgow, Scotland. Tonnage: 3,999. Dimensions: 400' x 40'. Single-screw, 13 knots. Compound engines. Triple expansion engines in 1891. Three masts and one funnel. Iron hull. Passengers: 200 first, 100 second, 800 third. Launched, October 25, 1873. Maiden voyage: Glasgow-New York, April 4, 1874. Scrapped at Genoa, Italy, 1905. Similar ships: **Anchoria, Circassia, Devonia** and **Ethiopia.**

Bologna (1905)   La Veloce Line.
Built by Harland & Wolff, Ltd., Belfast, Ireland. Tonnage: 4,680. Dimensions: 380' x 46'. Twin-screw, 14 knots. Triple expansion engines. Two masts and two funnels. Scrapped in 1928. Sister ship: **Siena.** Note: These vessels also served in the South American service.

Bonn (1895)   North German Lloyd.
Built by Germania Werft, Kiel, Germany. Tonnage: 3,969. Dimensions: 355' x 43'. Single-screw, 12½ knots. Triple expansion engines. Renamed: **Gregor.** Stranded in 1920.

Borussia (1855)   Hamburg-American Line.
Built by Caird & Co., Greenock, Scotland. Tonnage: 2,349. Dimensions: 278' x 38'. Single-screw, 10 knots. Overhead

oscillating engines. Three masts and one funnel. Iron hull.
Note: First steamship to be operated by Hamburg-American
Line. Maiden voyage: Hamburg-New York, June 1, 1856.
In trans-Atlantic service 1856–69. Sold to Mississippi &
Dominion Line in 1876. Foundered in the Atlantic on
December 2, 1879, with the loss of 165 lives. Sister ship:
Hammonia.

Bothnia (1874) Cunard Line.
Built by J. & G. Thomson, Ltd., Clydebank, Glasgow,
Scotland. Tonnage: 4,556. Dimensions: 420′ x 42′. Single-
screw, 15 knots. Compound engines. Three masts and one
funnel. Iron hull. Passengers: 300 cabin and 548 third.
Maiden voyage: Liverpool-New York, April 15, 1885. Trans-
ferred later to Boston service. Sold to Italian owners in 1898.
Scrapped at Marseilles in 1899. Sister ship: **Scythia.**

Braga (1907) Fabre Line.
Built by Russell & Co., Port Glasgow, Scotland. Tonnage:
6,122. Dimensions: 415′ x 49′. Twin-screw, 16½ knots.
Triple expansion engines. Two masts and one funnel.
Wrecked near Lipsa, Mediterranean, November 16, 1926.
Sister ship: **Asia.** Ex-**Europa** (1920), ex-**Laura** (1917).

Brandenburg (1901) North German Lloyd.
Built by Bremer Vulkan Co., Vegesack, Germany. Tonnage:
7,532. Dimensions: 429′ x 54′. Twin-screw, 13 knots.
Quadruple expansion engines. Two masts and one funnel.
Sold to Blue Funnel Line after World War I. Renamed:
Hecuba. Scrapped in Italy, December 1924. Sister ship:
Breslau.

Brasil (1905) Home Lines.
Built by Alexander Stephen & Sons, Ltd., Glasgow, Scotland.
Tonnage: 11,165. Dimensions: 517′ x 60′ (540′ o.l.). Triple-
screw, 17 knots. Steam turbines. Two masts and one funnel.
First voyage Genoa-South America, July 27, 1948. Later
transferred to New York service. Renamed: **Homeland**
(1951). Vessel sold and scrapped at Trieste in 1955. Ex-
Drottningholm (1948), ex-**Virginian** (1920).

Brasilia (1897) Hamburg-American Line.
Built by Harland & Wolff, Ltd., Belfast, Ireland. Tonnage:
10,222. Dimensions: 498′ x 62′. Twin-screw, 12 knots.
Quadruple expansion engines. Two masts and one funnel.
Renamed: **Norseman** (1900). Sunk by submarine in Mudros
harbor, but later was raised and broken up for scrap.

Brasile (1905) La Veloce Line.
 Built by Fratelli Orlando, Leghorn, Italy. Tonnage: 4,985.
 Dimensions: 394' x 47'. Twin-screw, 14½ knots. Triple
 expansion engines. Two masts and two funnels. Renamed:
 Venezuela (1912). Lost at Casablanca, March 7, 1920.
 Ex-**Argentina.**

Braunschweig (1873) North German Lloyd.
 Built by Caird & Co., Greenock, Scotland. Tonnage: 3,173.
 Dimensions: 351' x 39'. Single-screw, 12 knots. Compound
 engines. Two masts and one funnel. Iron hull. Launched,
 April 1, 1873. Maiden voyage: Bremen-Southampton-
 Baltimore, September 9, 1873. Made her final voyage to
 New York in 1896. Sold in 1897.

Brazilian (1890) Allan Line.
 Built by D. & W. Henderson & Co., Glasgow, Scotland.
 Tonnage: 3,046. Dimensions: 340' x 42'. Single-screw, 11
 knots. Triple expansion engines. Two masts and one funnel.
 Maiden voyage to South America in 1891. Transferred to
 London-Montreal service. Renamed: **Corcovado** (1910)
 Brazilian.

Bremen (1858) North German Lloyd.
 Built by Caird & Co., Greenock, Scotland. Tonnage: 2,551.
 Dimensions: 321' x 39'. Single-screw, 10½ knots. Inverted
 engines. Three masts and one funnel. Iron hull. Note:
 Pioneer steamship of the North German Lloyd. Maiden
 voyage: Bremen-New York, June 19, 1858. Made her last
 voyage for line in November 1873. Sold to British ship-
 owners in 1874 and converted to sail. Wrecked off San
 Francisco in 1882. Running mates: **New York** (identical),
 Hudson and **Weser.**

Bremen (1896) North German Lloyd.
 Built by F. Schichau, Danzig, Germany. Tonnage: 11,570.
 Dimensions: 550' x 60' (569' o.l.). Twin-screw, 15½ knots.
 Quadruple expansion engines. Two masts and two funnels.
 Lengthened from 525 to 550 feet in 1901. Tonnage had been
 10,525. Served also in Australian trade. Renamed: (a)
 Constantinople (1921), (b) **King Alexander** (1924). Sold
 for scrap to Italian shipbreakers in March 1926.

Bremen (1900) North German Lloyd.
 Built by "Vulkan", Stettin, Germany. Tonnage: 10,826.
 Dimensions: 523' x 60'. Twin-screw, 15½ knots. Quadruple
 expansion engines. Two masts and two funnels. First

voyage as **Bremen** from Bremen to New York, April 1923.
Renamed: **Karlsruhe** (1928). Scrapped in Germany, 1932.
Ex-**Pocahontas** (1923), ex **Prinzess Irene** (1917).

Bremen (1929) North German Lloyd.
Built by A. G. "Weser", Bremen, Germany. Tonnage:
51,656. Dimensions: 898' x 101' (938' o.l.). Quadruple-
screw, 28½ knots. Steam turbines. Two masts and two
funnels. Laid down in July 1927. Launched, August 16,
1928. Displacement of 52,000 tons. Passengers: 600 first,
500 second, 300 tourist, 600 third. Maiden voyage: Bremen-
Southampton-New York, July 16, 1929. Made the Atlantic
crossing in the record breaking time of 4 days, 17 hours, 42
minutes. Her average speed was 27.82 knots. Funnels were
later raised 15 feet on account of the smoke nuisance. At
the beginning of World War II the **Bremen** made a dash
from New York to Germany to avoid seizure. Succeeded in
eluding the British fleet during the epic flight, by selecting
the most northerly route, via north of Iceland, then along
the Norwegian coast down to Germany. Badly gutted by
fire during an air raid at Bremerhaven, March 18, 1941.
Subsequently broken up for scrap. Sister ship: **Europa.**

*****Bremen** (1939) North German Lloyd.
Built by Chantiers de Penhoet, St. Nazaire, France. Ton-
nage: 32,336. Dimensions: 656' x 87' (696' o.l.). Quadruple-
screw, 23 knots. Steam turbines. Two masts and one funnel.
Passengers: 216 first, 906 tourist. Purchased from the French
in September 1957. First voyage Bremen-Southampton-
Cherbourg-New York, July 9, 1959. Major alterations and
improvements were made before liner was put in North
German Lloyd service. Ex-**Pasteur** (1957). Note: See
Pasteur for additional information.

Breslau (1901) North German Lloyd.
Built by Bremer Vulkan Co., Vegesack, Germany. Tonnage:
7,524. Dimensions: 429' x 54'. Twin-screw, 12½ knots.
Quadruple expansion engines. Two masts and one funnel.
Renamed: **Bridgeport** (1917) United States transport.
Sister ships: **Brandenburg, Cassel,** and **Chemnitz.**

Bretagne (1922) French Line.
Built by Barclay, Curle & Co., Glasgow, Scotland. Tonnage:
10,171. Dimensions: 450' x 59'. Twin-screw, 14½ knots.
Steam turbines. Two masts and two funnels. Torpedoed and
sunk while bound from the West Indies to England, October
14, 1939. Ex-**Flandria** (1937).

Britannia   (1840)   Cunard Line.
Built by Robert Duncan & Co., Port Glasgow, Scotland. Tonnage: 1,139. Dimensions: 207′ x 34′ (228′ o.l.). Paddle-wheels, 9 knots. Side lever engines. Three masts and one funnel. Wooden hull. Four boilers; 741 I.H.P. Bunkers carried 640 tons of coal. Passengers: 115 cabin. Maiden voyage: Liverpool-Halifax-Boston, July 4, 1840. Note: The pioneer Cunarder to open up regular service. The **Unicorn** actually made the first crossing of the Atlantic, Liverpool-Halifax, May 16, 1840. Charles Dickens was a passenger on the **Britannia** in 1842. Sold to German Government in November 1848. Renamed: **Barbarossa** (1849). Trans-ferred to the Prussian Navy in 1852. Sunk as a target ship in 1880. Sister ships: **Acadia, Caledonia** and **Columbia.**

Britannia   (1863)   Anchor Line.
Built by Tod & McGregor, Glasgow, Scotland. Tonnage: 1,417. Dimensions: 255′ x 33′. Single-screw, 10½ knots. Inverted engines. Three masts and one funnel. Iron hull. Maiden voyage: Glasgow-Quebec-Montreal, July 8, 1863. Wrecked on the Isle of Arran, January 27, 1873, with no loss of life. Sister ship: **Caledonia.**

Britannia   (1881)   Fabre Line.
Built by T. Royden & Sons, Liverpool, England. Tonnage: 2,477. Dimensions: 328′ x 40′. Single-screw, 11 knots. Com-pound engines. Three masts and one funnel. Maiden voyage: Marseilles-New York, August 30, 1882. Renamed: **America** (1902). Scrapped in 1909. Sister ship: **Scotia.**

Britannic   (1874)   White Star Line.
Built by Harland & Wolff, Ltd., Belfast, Ireland. Tonnage: 5,004. Dimensions: 455′ x 45′ (468′ o.l.). Single-screw, 16 knots. Compound engines. Four masts and one funnel. Iron hull. Launched, February 3, 1874. Maiden voyage: Liverpool-New York, July 30, 1874. Note: First ship to exceed 5,000 tons, **Great Eastern** excepted. This famous and successful liner won the Atlantic speed record in November 1876. Scrapped in Germany, 1903. Sister ship: **Germanic.**

Britannic   (1914)   White Star Line.
Built by Harland & Wolff, Ltd., Belfast, Ireland. Tonnage: 48,158. Dimensions: 870′ x 94′ (903′ o.l.). Triple-screw, 22 knots. Combination quadruple expansion engines and steam turbine on center shaft. Had 29 boilers. Two masts and four funnels. Launched, February 26, 1914. From keel to navigating bridge 104 feet. Never in service for White

Star Line, as she was taken over by British Government upon completion. Largest British liner built prior to the **Queen Mary.** Sunk by mines laid by a submarine in Aegean Sea, November 21, 1916, with the loss of 21 lives. Note: Quite similar to the **Olympic** and **Titanic.**

Britannic (1930)   White Star Line.
Built by Harland & Wolff, Ltd., Belfast, Ireland. Tonnage: 26,840. Dimensions: 683′ x 82′ (712′ o.l.). Twin-screw, 18 knots. Motorship. Two masts and two funnels. Passengers: 479 cabin, 557 tourist, 605 third. Launched, August 6, 1929. Maiden voyage: Liverpool to New York, June 28, 1930. Merged with the Cunard service in 1934. Served as a troopship in World War II. Re-entered trans-Atlantic passenger service in May 1948. Made her final crossing in December, 1960. Scrapped in 1961. Sister ship: **Georgic.**

British Crown (1879)   American Line.
Built by Harland & Wolff, Ltd., Belfast, Ireland. Tonnage: 3,563. Dimensions: 410′ x 39′. Single-screw, 12 knots. Compound engines. Four masts and one funnel. Iron hull. Note: Built for British Shipowners Co., Ltd. In American Line service, 1880–1886. Made her first sailing for Anchor Line from London to Boston, February 10, 1886. Ran for Furness Line in 1887 on same route. Renamed: **Amsterdam** (1887). Sister ships: **British King** and **British Queen.**

British Empire (1878)   American Line.
Built by Harland & Wolff, Ltd., Belfast, Ireland. Tonnage: 3,361. Dimensions: 392′ x 39′. Single-screw, 12 knots. Compound engines. Four masts and one funnel. Accommodation for cabin class passengers. Built for British Shipowners Co. Renamed: (a) **Rotterdam** (1886), (b) **Edam** (1896).

British Empire (1902)   British Shipowners Co., Ltd.
Built by Palmers Shipbuilding & Iron Co., Newcastle, England. Tonnage: 9,001. Dimensions: 470′ x 56′. Twin-screw, 12 knots. Triple expansion engines. Four masts and one funnel. Renamed: (a) **Campania** (1906), (b) **Campanello** (1911), (c) **Flavia** (1916). Sister ships: **British Prince** and **British Princess.**

British King (1881)   American Line.
Built by Harland & Wolff, Ltd., Belfast, Ireland. Tonnage: 3,412. Dimensions: 410′ x 39′. Single-screw, 12 knots. Compound engines. Four masts and one funnel. Note: Built for British Shipowners Co. In service between Liverpool and

Philadelphia.   Renamed: (a) **Werkendam** (1889), (b)
Harbin. Sister ships: **British Crown,** and **British Queen.**

British Prince (1882) American Line.
 Built by Harland & Wolff, Ltd., Belfast, Ireland. Tonnage:
 3,871. Dimensions: 420' x 42'. Single-screw, 12 knots. Com-
 pound engines. Four masts and one funnel. Note: Built for
 British Shipowners Co. In American Line service 1882–94.
 Renamed: **Les Andes** (1895). Scrapped in 1919. Sister ship:
 British Princess.

British Prince (1899) British Shipowners Co., Ltd.
 Built by Palmers Shipbuilding & Iron Co., Newcastle, England. Tonnage: 9,203. Dimensions: 470' x 56'. Twin-screw,
 12½ knots. Triple expansion engines. Four masts and one
 funnel. Renamed: (a) **Sannio** (1906), (b) **Napoli** (1913).
 Sister ships: **British Empire** and **British Princess.**

British Princess (1882) American Line.
 Built by Harland & Wolff, Ltd., Belfast, Ireland. Tonnage:
 3,864.   Dimensions: 420' x 42'.   Single-screw, 12 knots.
 Compound engines. Four masts and one funnel. Built for
 British Shipowners Co. Renamed: **Les Alpes** (1895). Sister
 ship: **British Prince.**

British Princess (1899) British Shipowners Co., Ltd.
 Built by Palmers Shipbuilding & Iron Co., Newcastle, England. Tonnage: 6,950. Dimensions: 470' x 56'. Twin-screw,
 12½ knots. Triple expansion engines. Four masts and one
 funnel. Renamed: (a) **Lazio** (1906), (b) **Palermo** (1913).
 Sister ships: **British Empire** and **British Prince.**

British Queen (1838) British & American Steam Navigation
 Co.
 Built by Curling & Young, Limehouse, England. Tonnage:
 1,863. Dimensions: 245' x 40'. Paddle-wheels, 8½ knots.
 Side lever engines. Three masts and one funnel. Wooden
 hull. Laid down as **Royal Victoria.** Commenced her
 maiden voyage as the **British Queen** from London via
 Portsmouth to New York, July 11, 1839. Made a westward
 sailing in 13 days, 11 hours in 1840. Sold to Belgian Government in 1841. Scrapped in 1845. Running mate: **President.**

British Queen (1881) American Line.
 Built by Harland & Wolff, Ltd., Belfast, Ireland. Tonnage:
 3,412.   Dimensions: 410' x 39'.   Single-screw, 12 knots.
 Compound engines. Four masts and one funnel. Note: Built
 for British Shipowners Co. Used mainly in Liverpool-

Philadelphia service. Renamed: (a) **Obdam** (1889), (b) **McPherson** (1898), (c) **Brooklyn,** (d) **S. V. Luckenbach,** (e) **Onega.** Torpedoed and sunk in 1918. Sister ships: **British Crown** and **British King.**

Brooklyn (1869) Dominion Line.
Built by Tod & McGregor, Glasgow, Scotland. Tonnage: 4,215. Dimensions: 400' x 42'. Single-screw, 13 knots. Compound engines in 1879. Three masts and one funnel. Note: Lengthened from 354' to 400' in 1879. Grounded on Anticosti Island, November 8, 1885, with no loss of life. Ex-**City of Brooklyn** (1878).

Buenos Aires (1887) Spanish Line.
Built by Wm. Denny & Bros., Ltd., Dumbarton, Scotland. Tonnage: 5,311. Dimensions: 410' x 48'. Single-screw, 14 knots. Quadruple expansion engines. Three masts and one funnel. Scrapped in Spain, 1942. Sister ship: **Montevideo.**

Buenos Ayrean (1879) Allan Line.
Built by Wm. Denny & Bros., Ltd., Dumbarton, Scotland. Tonnage: 4,005. Dimensions: 385' x 42'. Single-screw, 12 knots. Two masts and one funnel. Note: The first trans-Atlantic steamship built of steel. The **Rotomahana** of the Union Steamship Company of New Zealand was the first ocean-going vessel built of steel. Maiden voyage Glasgow-Halifax-Boston, March 31, 1880. Also served in South American service. Broken up for scrap at Falmouth in 1911.

Buffalo (1885) Wilson Line.
Built by Palmers Shipbuilding & Iron Co., Newcastle, England. Tonnage: 4,431. Dimensions: 385' x 45'. Single-screw, 12 knots. Compound engines. Four masts and two funnels. Iron hull. Triple expansion engines installed later, increasing speed to 14 knots. Passengers: 30 first class. Made her final voyage to New York in 1901.

Bulgaria (1898) Hamburg-American Line.
Built by Blohm & Voss, Hamburg, Germany. Tonnage: 11,440. Dimensions: 501' x 62'. Twin-screw, 12 knots. Quadruple expansion engines. Two masts and one funnel. Tonnage originally 10,237. Renamed: (a) **Canada** (1913), (b) **Bulgaria** (1913), (c) **Hercules** (1917), **Philippines** (1919) United States Shipping Board. Scrapped in 1924.

Bulow (1906) North German Lloyd.
Built by J. C. Tecklenborg, Geestemunde, Germany. Tonnage: 8,980. Dimensions: 462' x 57' (478' o.l.). Twin-screw,

14 knots. Quadruple expansion engines. Two masts and one funnel. Services: Australia, South America, Far East and North Atlantic. Passengers: 106 first, 113 second, 1,426 third. Renamed: (a) **Tras-os-Montes** (1916), (b) **Nyassa** (1927).

Burgundia (1882)   Fabre Line.
Built by T. Royden & Sons, Liverpool, England. Tonnage: 2,908. Dimensions: 328′ x 40′. Single-screw, 11 knots. Compound engines. Three masts and one funnel. Iron hull. Broken up for scrap in France, 1906. Sister ship: **Alesia.**

Byron (1914)   Byron Steamship Co., Ltd.
Built by Cammell, Laird & Co., Birkenhead, England. Tonnage: 9,272. Dimensions: 470′ x 58′. Twin-screw, 17 knots. Quadruple expansion engines. Two masts and two funnels. Transferred to National Steam Navigation Co. of Greece in 1928. Scrapped in Italy, 1937. Ex-**Megali Hellas** (1923), ex-**Vasilefs Constantinos** (1920).

C. de Eizaguirre (1904)   Spanish Line.
Built by Sir Raylton Dixon & Co., Middlesbrough, England. Tonnage: 4,376. Dimensions: 375′ x 47′. Twin-screw, 13½ knots. Triple expansion engines. Two masts and one funnel. Destroyed by explosion off Capetown in 1917, with great loss of life. Ex-**Landana**, ex-**Leopoldville**. Sister ship: **Legazpi.**

C. F. Tietgen (1897)   Scandinavian American Line.
Built by Harland & Wolff, Ltd., Belfast, Ireland. Tonnage: 8,173. Dimensions: 469′ x 53′. Twin-screw, 14 knots. Triple expansion engines. Two masts and one funnel. Passenger acommodations of 1912: 200 first, 100 second 700 third. Renamed: **Dwinsk** (1913). Torpedoed and sunk in the Atlantic, June 18, 1918. Ex-**Rotterdam** (1906).

C. Lopez-y-Lopez (1891)   Spanish Line.
Built by Barclay, Curle & Co., Glasgow, Scotland. Tonnage: 4,170. Dimensions: 396′ x 43′. Single-screw, 14 knots. Triple expansion engines. Two masts and one funnel. Scrapped at Savona in 1930. Ex-**Westmount**, ex-**Asia**, ex-**Susan**, ex-**Susan II**, ex-**Lismore Castle** (1905).

Cairnrona (1900)   Thomson Line (British).
Built by Swan & Hunter, Wallsend-on-Tyne, Newcastle, England. Tonnage: 7,682. Dimensions: 461′ x 52′. Twin-screw, 11 knots. Triple expansion engines. Four masts and one funnel. Passengers: 50 first and 800 third. Service:

England-Canada. Renamed: (a) **Albania** (1911), (b) **Poleric** (1912). Sold to Japan in 1929.

Calabria   (1857)   Cunard Line.
Built by J. & G. Thomson, Ltd., Glasgow, Scotland. Tonnage: 3,321. Dimensions: 338' x 42'. Single-screw, 13 knots. New single expansion engines in 1870. Three masts and two funnels. Iron hull. Sold in 1876 and converted to cable ship under same name. Scrapped in 1898. Ex-**Australasian** (1869).

Calabria   (1901)   Anchor Line.
Built by D. & W. Henderson & Co., Glasgow, Scotland. Tonnage: 4,376. Dimensions: 376' x 47'. Single-screw, 13 knots. Triple expansion engines. Two masts and one funnel. Launched, April 9, 1901. Scrapped in 1923.

Caledonia   (1840)   Cunard Line.
Built by R. Wood, River Clyde, Scotland. Tonnage: 1,139. Dimensions: 207' x 34'. Paddle-wheels, 8½ knots. Side lever engines. Three masts and one funnel. Wooden hull. Maiden voyage: Liverpool-Halifax-Boston, September 19, 1840. Sold to Spanish Government in 1850. Wrecked on rocks near Havana in 1851. Sister ships: **Acadia, Britannia** and **Columbia.**

Caledonia   (1862)   Anchor Line.
Built by Tod & McGregor, Glasgow, Scotland. Tonnage: 1,681. Dimensions: 248' x 33'. Single-screw, 10 knots. Inverted engines. Three masts and one funnel. Clipper bow. Iron hull. Maiden voyage: Glasgow-Portland-New York, February 25, 1862. Ran aground on Cape Cod, Massachusetts, December 31, 1862. Refloated later and sold to T. Nickerson & Company of Boston. Rebuilt by the Atlantic Works at Boston. Renamed: **Concordia.** Sold to Australian owners at a later date. Wrecked in 1872.

Caledonia   (1863)   Anchor Line.
Built by Tod & McGregor, Glasgow, Scotland. Tonnage: 1,393. Dimensions: 262' x 33'. Single-screw, 10½ knots. Inverted type engines. Compound engines in 1872. Three masts and one funnel. Iron hull. Clipper bow. Maiden voyage: Glasgow-Portland-New York, December 11, 1863. Inaugurated Glasgow-Bombay service in 1875. Lengthened to 311 feet (2,125 tons) in 1872. Scrapped in 1898. Sister ship: **Britannia.**

Caledonia   (1904)   Anchor Line.
Built by D. & W. Henderson & Co., Glasgow, Scotland. Tonnage: 9,223. Dimensions: 500' x 58'. Twin-screw, 16 knots. Triple expansion engines. Two masts and two funnels. Maiden voyage: Glasgow-New York, March 25, 1905. Passenger accommodation as of 1912: 390 first, 376 second, 850 third. Torpedoed and sunk in Mediterranean, December 4, 1916. Running mates: **California, Cameronia** and **Columbia.**

Caledonia   (1925)   Anchor Line.
Built by Alexander Stephen & Sons, Ltd., Glasgow, Scotland. Tonnage: 17,046. Dimensions: 553' x 70' (578' o.l.). Twin-screw, 15½ knots. Speed increased to 17 knots in 1939. Steam turbines. Two masts and three funnels. Passengers: 264 first, 458 second, 620 third. Launched, April 22, 1925. Maiden voyage: Glasgow-New York, October 3, 1925. Converted to armed merchant cruiser in 1939. Renamed: **Scotstoun** (1939). Torpedoed and sunk in the North Atlantic, June 13, 1940. Sixter ship: **Transylvania.**

Calgarian   (1913)   Allan Line.
Built by Fairfield Shipbuilding & Engineering Co., Glasgow, Scotland. Tonnage: 17,515. Dimensions: 571' x 72' (600' o.l.). Quadruple-screw, 19½ knots. Steam turbines. Two masts and two funnels. Passengers: 280 first, 500 second, 900 third. Maiden voyage: Liverpool-Quebec, May 8, 1914. Employed as an armed merchant cruiser in First World War. Torpedoed and sunk by German submarine near Rathlin Island, March 1, 1918, with the loss of 49 lives. Sister ship: **Alsatian.** Note: They were the finest and fastest of the pre-war liners to Canada.

Calgaric   (1918)   White Star Line.
Built by Harland & Wolff, Ltd., Belfast, Ireland. Tonnage: 16,063. Dimensions: 550' x 67' (569 'o.l.). Triple-screw, 14½ knots. Triple expansion engines and steam turbine. Two masts and one funnel. First voyage as **Calgaric:** Liverpool-Quebec-Montreal, May 4, 1927. Vessel laid up in 1933. Scrapped in Scotland, 1935. Ex-**Orca** (1927).

California   (1872)   Anchor Line.
Built by Alexander Stephen & Sons, Ltd., Glasgow, Scotland. Tonnage: 3,410. Dimensions: 361' x 40'. Single-screw, 13 knots. Compound engines. Three masts and one funnel. Launched, March 12, 1872. Maiden voyage: Glasgow-New York, June 15, 1872. Services: North Atlantic, Mediter-

ranean, India. Broken up by Italian shipbreakers in 1905. Sister ship: **Victoria.**

Calfornia   (1907)   Anchor Line.
Built by D. & W. Henderson & Co., Glasgow, Scotland. Tonnage: 8,662. Dimensions: 470′ x 58′ (485′ o.l.). Twin-screw, 17 knots. Triple expansion engines. Two masts and two funnels. Torpedoed and sunk off the S.W. coast of Ireland, February 8, 1917, with the loss of 41 lives. Running mates: **Caledonia, Cameronia** and **Columbia.**

California   (1923)   Anchor Line.
Built by Alexander Stephen & Sons, Ltd., Glasgow, Scotland. Tonnage: 16,792. Dimensions: 553′ x 70′ (575′ o.l.). Twin-screw, 16 knots. Steam turbines. Two masts and one funnel. Launched, April 17, 1923. Maiden voyage: Glasgow-New York, August 26, 1923. Passengers: 265 first, 370 second, 1,150 third. Converted to British armed merchant cruiser in September 1939. Commissioned as troopship in 1942. Sunk by bombers in Bay of Biscay, July 11, 1943. Sister ship: **Tuscania.**

Californian   (1891)   Allan Line.
Built by Alexander Stephen & Sons, Ltd., Glasgow, Scotland. Tonnage: 4,244. Dimensions: 386′ x 46′. Single-screw, 13 knots. Triple expansion engines. Three masts and one funnel. First voyage as **California,** Liverpool-Portland, March 10, 1898. Stranded near Portland, February 25, 1900, later salved, sold and reconstructed as **Coamo,** sailing under the United States flag. Renamed: **Coamo** (1901). Scrapped in 1925. Ex-**State of California**   (1898).

Cambria   (1845)   Cunard Line.
Built by Robert Steele & Co., Greenock, Scotland. Tonnage: 1,422. Dimensions: 219′ x 35′. Paddle-wheels, 9½ knots. Side lever engines. Three masts and one funnel. Mizzen mast removed at later date. Maiden voyage: Liverpool-Halifax-Boston, January 4, 1845. Passengers: 110 cabin. Sold to Italy in 1860. Sister ship: **Hibernia.**

Cambria   (1869)   Anchor Line.
Built by Alexander Stephen & Sons, Ltd., Glasgow, Scotland. Tonnage: 1,997. Dimensions: 325′ x 35′. Single-screw, 12 knots. Inverted engines. Three masts and one funnel. Maiden voyage: Glasgow-New York, May 7, 1869. Wrecked off the Irish coast, October 19, 1870, with the loss of 196 lives. Sister ships: **Anglia** and **Australia.**

Cambroman   (1892)   Dominion Line.
Built by Laird Bros., Birkenhead, England.   Tonnage:
6,059.   Dimensions: 429' x 46'.   Single-screw, 13½ knots.
Triple expansion engines.   Four masts and one funnel.
Originally used as a cargo ship in Warren Line service.
Passenger accommodation installed in 1899.   Sold for scrap
in 1909.

Cameronia   (1910)   Anchor Line.
Built by D. & W. Henderson & Co., Glasgow, Scotland.
Tonnage: 10,963.   Dimensions: 515' x 62' (532' o.l.).   Twin-
screw, 17 knots.   Triple expansion engines.   Two masts and
two funnels.   Passengers: 250 first, 450 second, 1,000 third.
Maiden voyage: Glasgow-New York, September 9, 1911.
Converted to troopship in 1917.   Torpedoed and sunk with-
out warning 150 miles from Malta, April 15, 1917, with the
loss of a number of lives.   Running mates: **Caledonia,**
California and **Columbia.**   Note: None were identical.

Cameronia   (1920)   Anchor Line.
Built by Wm. Beardmore & Co., Glasgow, Scotland.   Tonnage: 16,297.   Dimensions: 552' x 70' (575' o.l.).   Twin-
screw, 15½ knots.   Steam turbines.   Two masts and one
funnel.   Launched, December 23, 1919.   Maiden voyage from
Liverpool to New York in May 1921.   Carried a total of
186,770 passengers from time she commenced maiden voyage
to August 1939.   Served as a troopship in World War II.
Torpedoed by aircraft in December 1942, but was able to
make port.   Reconditioned for the Australian immigrant
service in 1948.   Renamed: **Empire Clyde** (1953).   Broken
up by British shipbreakers in 1958.   Similar in appearance
to **Lancastria** of Cunard Line.

Campanello   (1902)   Uranium Steamship Co. (British).
Built by Palmers Shipbuilding & Iron Co., Newcastle, England.   Tonnage: 9,291.   Dimensions: 470' x 56'.   Twin-screw,
14 knots.   Triple expansion engines.   Four masts and one
funnel.   Renamed: **Flavia** (1916).   Torpedoed and sunk off
Tory Island, August 24, 1918.   Ex-**Campania** (1911), ex-
British Empire (1906).

Campania   (1893)   Cunard Line.
Built by Fairfield Shipbuilding & Engineering Co., Govan,
Glasgow, Scotland.   Tonnage: 12,950.   Dimensions: 598' x
65' (622' o.l.).   Twin-screw, 22 knots.   Triple expansion
engines.   Two masts and two funnels.   Launched, September
8, 1892.   Boilers: 13.   Furnaces: 100.   Consumed 20½ tons

of coal per hour to obtain 22 knots. 30,000 I.H.P. Displacement: 21,000 tons. From keel to top of funnels measured 130 feet; diameter of funnels 19 feet. First twin-screw Cunarder. Passengers: 600 first, 400 second, 1,000 third. Maiden voyage: Liverpool-New York, April 22, 1893. Set a trans-Atlantic speed record of 5 days, 17 hours, 27 minutes, on her return trip. Sold to shipbreakers in 1914. However was resold to the British Admiralty and converted into aircraft carrier. In collision with the battleship **Revenge,** November 5, 1918, in Firth of Forth, and as a result sunk. Sister ship: **Lucania.**

Campania   (1902)   Royal Line (British).
Built by Palmers Shipbuilding & Iron Co., Newcastle, England. Tonnage: 9,291. Dimensions: 470' x 56'. Twin-screw, 13 knots. Triple expansion engines. Four masts and one funnel. Note: Line was owned by Canadian Northern Steamships, Ltd. Previously had been in Navigazione Generale Italiana service. Renamed: **Campanello** (1911), (b) **Flavia** (1916). Torpedoed and sunk in August 1918. Ex-**British Empire** (1906).

Canada   (1848)   Cunard Line.
Built by Robert Steele & Co., Greenock, Scotland. Tonnage: 1,831. Dimensions: 251' x 38'. Paddle-wheels, 10 knots. Side lever engines. Three masts and one funnel. Wooden hull. Sold and converted to sailing ship in 1867. Renamed: **Mississippi.** In service to Mauritius until 1876. Sold to Calcutta owners in 1876. Scrapped in India, 1883. Sister ships: **America, Europa** and **Niagara.**

Canada   (1863)   National Line.
Built by Palmers Shipbuilding & Iron Co., Newcastle, England. Tonnage: 4,276. Dimensions: 391' x 41'. Single-screw, 12 knots. Compound engines. Three masts and one funnel. Lengthened from 342 to 391 feet in 1872. Scrapped in 1894. Ex-**Pennsylvania** (1872). Sister ship: **Greece.**

Canada   (1865)   French Line.
Built by Chantiers de l'Atlantique, St. ,Nazaire, France. Tonnage: 4,287. Dimensions: 354' x 43'. Single-screw, 13½ knots. Compound engines. Three masts and two funnels. Converted from paddle-wheels to screw propulsion in 1876. First voyage: Havre-New York, April 22, 1876. Transferred to Havre-Panama route in 1886. Scrapped in France, 1908. Ex-**Panama** (1876).

Canada   (1896)   Dominion Line.
Built by Harland & Wolff, Ltd., Belfast, Ireland. Tonnage: 9,415. Dimensions: 500' x 58' (514' o.l.). Twin-screw, 15 knots. Two masts and one funnel. First twin-screw steamship built for the Canadian service. Maiden voyage: Liverpool-Quebec-Montreal, November 1, 1896. Tonnage was originally listed as 8,806. Made a number of sailings to Boston. Scrapped in Italy, 1926.

Canada   (1898)   Austro-American Line.
Built by Blohm & Voss, Hamburg, Germany. Tonnage: 11,440. Dimensions: 501' x 62'. Twin-screw, 12 knots. Quadruple expansion engines. Two masts and one funnel. First voyage: Trieste-Canada in 1913. Renamed: (a) **Bulgaria,** (b) **Hercules,** (c) **Philippines.** Scrapped in 1924. Ex-**Bulgaria** (1913).

Canada   (1911)   Fabre Line.
Built by Forges & Chantiers de la Mediterranee, La Seyne, France. Tonnage: 9,684. Dimensions: 476' x 56'. Twin-screw, 15½ knots. Triple expansion engines. Two masts and two funnels. Launched, August 12, 1911. Sold to British shipbreakers in August 1952. Sister ship: **Sant' Anna.**

Canadian   (1854)   Allan Line.
Built by Wm. Denny & Bros., Ltd., Dumbarton, Scotland. Tonnage: 1,873. Dimensions: 278' x 34'. Single-screw, 11 knots. Inverted engines. Three masts and two funnels. Iron hull. Clipper bow. Note: Pioneer steamship for Allan Line. Cost about $250,000. Passengers: 80 first and 350 third. Maiden voyage: Liverpool-Quebec-Montreal, September 16, 1854. Wrecked in the St. Lawrence River near Quebec, June 1, 1856, with no loss of life. Sister ship: **Indian.**

Canadian   (1860)   Allan Line.
Built by Robert Steele & Co., Greenock, Scotland. Tonnage: 1,926. Single-screw, 10 knots. Inverted engines. Three masts and one funnel. Iron hull. Maiden voyage, June 4, 1860. Crushed by a field of ice at the entrance of the Straits of Belle Isle, June 4, 1861, with the loss of 34 lives.

Canadian   (1872)   Allan Line.
Built by T. Royden & Sons, Liverpool, England. Tonnage: 2,401. Dimensions: 349' x 35'. Single-screw, 11 knots. Compound engines. Three masts and one funnel. In various services, including South America. Made her first sailing to South America, November 11, 1876. Scrapped in 1903.

Canadian (1900) Leyland Line.
   Built by Hawthorn, Leslie & Co., Newcastle, England.
   Tonnage: 9,309. Dimensions: 530' x 59'. Single-screw, 13
   knots. Triple expansion engines. Four masts and one funnel.
   Passengers: 60 first class. Service: (a) Liverpool-New York,
   (b) Liverpool-Boston. Torpedoed and sunk without warning
   47 miles from Fastnet, with loss of one life.

Canberra (1913) Greek Line.
   Built by Alexander Stephen & Sons, Ltd., Glasgow, Scotland.
   Tonnage: 7,710. Dimensions: 410' x 57' (426' o.l.). Twin-
   screw, 17 knots. Quadruple expansion engines. Two masts
   and one funnel. Passengers: 64 first and 630 tourist. First
   voyage for Greek Line was in 1949. Note: Originally owned
   by Howard Smith Co., Ltd., and operated in the Australian
   coastal trade. Renamed **Espana** in December 1954; under
   ownership of Dominican Government.

Canopic (1900) White Star Line.
   Built by Harland & Wolff, Ltd., Belfast, Ireland. Tonnage:
   12,268. Dimensions: 578' x 59' (594' o.l.). Twin-screw, 16
   knots. Triple expansion engines. Two masts and one funnel.
   First voyage: Liverpool-Boston, January 14, 1904. Transferred to Mediterranean-New York service. Later in Canadian trade. Scrapped in 1925. Ex-**Commonwealth** (1903).

Caribia (1932) Hamburg-American Line.
   Built by Blohm & Voss, Hamburg, Germany. Tonnage:
   12,049. Dimensions: 497' x 65'. Twin-screw, 17 knots.
   Motorship. Two masts and one funnel. Passengers: 200
   first, 100 second, 100 third. Service: Hamburg-Central
   America-West Indies. Acquired by the Russians in 1946.
   Renamed: **Ilich** (Russian). Still in their service as of 1961.
   Sister ship: **Cordillera.**

Carinthia (1895) Cunard Line.
   Built by London & Glasgow Shipbuilding Co., Glasgow,
   Scotland. Tonnage: 5,598. Dimensions: 445' x 49'. Twin-
   screw, 14 knots. Triple expansion engines. Four masts and
   one funnel. Employed mainly as a cargo-cattle steamship.
   Wrecked near Point Gravois, Haiti, in 1900. Sister ship:
   Sylvania.

Carinthia (1925) Cunard Line.
   Built by Vickers, Armstrong, Ltd., Barrow-in-Furness,
   England. Tonnage: 20,277. Dimensions: 600' x 73' (624'
   o.l.). Twin-screw, 18 knots. Four steam turbines. Two

masts and one funnel. Laid down as **Servia**, but renamed **Carinthia** before launching. Passengers: 240 first, 460 second, 950 third. Maiden voyage: Liverpool-New York, August 22, 1925. Torpedoed and sunk by German submarine off coast of Northern Ireland, June 6, 1940. Sister ship: **Franconia** (nearly identical). Similar to **Laconia, Samaria** and **Scythia,** except bridge was isolated from main part with these lines.

*Carinthia (1956) Cunard Line.
Built by John Brown & Co., Ltd., Clydebank, Glasgow, Scotland. Tonnage: 21,947. Dimensions: 570′ x 80′ (608′ o.l.). Twin-screw, 20 knots. Four steam turbines. Single mast and one funnel. Passengers: 150 first and 700 tourist. Maiden voyage: Liverpool-Quebec-Montreal, June 26, 1957. Sister ships: **Ivernia, Saxonia** and **Sylvania.**

Carmania (1905) Cunard Line.
Built by John Brown & Co., Clydebank, Glasgow, Scotland. Tonnage: 19,566. Dimensions: 650′ x 72′ (678′ o.l.). Triple-screw, 18½ knots. Steam turbines. Two masts and two funnels. Navigating bridge 60 feet above water line and 90 feet from keel. First Cunarder to be fitted with steam turbines. A faster ship than her sister, which had reciprocating engines. Attained 20.4 knots during her trials. Passengers: 300 first, 350 second, 1,100 third. Converted to armed merchant cruiser in 1914. Engaged the armed German liner **Cap Trafalgar** off Trinidad Island, September 14, 1914, and after many shots had been fired the Hamburg-American liner was sunk. The **Carmania** had received 79 shell holes, but the damage was not severe enough to prevent her making port for repairs. In December 1918 she was placed back in trans-Atlantic service. Sold to British shipbreakers in November 1932. Sister ship: **Caronia.**

Carolina (1905) Austro-American Line.
Built by Russell & Co., Port Glasgow, Scotland. Tonnage: 4,713. Dimensions: 359′ x 48′. Single-screw, 14 knots. Triple expansion engines. Two masts and one funnel. Scrapped in 1925. Sister ship: **Francesca.**

Caroline (1908) French Line.
Built by Chantiers & Ateliers de Provence, Port Bouc, France. Tonnage: 6,698. Dimensions: 413′ x 52′. Twin-screw, 13 knots. Triple expansion engines. Two masts and one funnel. Launched, July 14, 1908. Passengers: 50 second and 46 third. In North Atlantic service in summer, West

Indies during winter season. Renamed: **Jacques Cartier** (1929). Scrapped in Italy, 1933–34.

Caronia (1905) Cunard Line.
Built by John Brown & Co., Glasgow, Scotland. Tonnage: 19,782. Dimensions: 650' x 72' (678' o.l.). Twin-screw, 18 knots. Quadruple expansion engines. Two masts and two funnels. Maiden voyage: Liverpool-New York, February 25, 1905. During her long successful career saw service in Liverpool-Boston-New York, Liverpool-Canadian trade and Mediterranean-New York route. From 1926 to 1931 in London-Havre-Southampton-New York service. Purchased by Japanese shipbreakers in 1932, and sailed to Japan under name of **Taiseiyo Maru.** Dismantled for scrap in 1933. Sister ship: **Carmania.**

*****Caronia** (1948) Cunard Line.
Built by John Brown & Co., Clydebank, Glasgow, Scotland Tonnage: 34,183. Dimensions: 687' x 91' (715' o.l.). Twin-screw, 24 knots. Steam turbines. Single mast and one funnel. Keel laid in February 1946. Height from keel to top of funnel 149 feet. Promenade deck 495 feet long. Christened by the then Princess Elizabeth at its launching, October 30, 1947. Maiden voyage: Southampton-New York, January 4, 1949. Passengers: 580 first class and 350 cabin. Has served in regular trans-Atlantic sailing, also as a cruise ship.

Carpathia (1903) Cunard Line.
Built by Swan & Hunter, Ltd., Newcastle, England. Tonnage: 13,603. Dimensions: 540' x 64' (558' o.l.). Twin-screw, 14 knots. Quadruple expansion engines. Four masts and one funnel. Passengers: 204 first and 1,500 third. Maiden voyage: Liverpool-Boston, May 5, 1903. Alternated between Mediterranean-New York and Liverpool-New York services. Note: She answered the S.O.S. call of the great luxury liner **Titanic** and succeeded in rescuing a large number of survivors. Her fame has continued to live through the years. The **Carpathia** was sunk by three torpedoes fired from a submarine, July 17, 1918, when 170 miles from Bishop Rock. The lives of five men were lost in the boiler room.

Carthaginian (1884) Allan Line.
Built by Govan Shipbuilding Co., Glasgow, Scotland. Tonnage: 4,444. Dimensions: 386' x 45'. Single-screw, 14 knots. Compound engines. Three masts and one funnel. Steel hull. Maiden voyage; Glasgow-Boston, December 6, 1884. Served

in a number of North Atlantic routes. Sunk by a mine near Inishtrahull, June 14, 1917.

Caserta (1904) Navigazione Generale Italiana.
Built by Sir W. G. Armstrong, Whitworth & Co., Newcastle, England. Tonnage: 7,028. Dimensions: 420' x 51'. Twin-screw, 14 knots. Triple expansion engines. Two masts and one funnel. Renamed: **Venezuela** (1923). Scrapped in 1928. Ex-**Mendoza.**

Caspian (1870) Allan Line.
Built by London & Glasgow Shipbuilding Co., Glasgow, Scotland. Tonnage: 2,747. Dimensions: 349' x 38'. Single-screw, 11 knots. Inverted engines. Compound engines in 1882. Three masts and one funnel. Iron hull. Maiden voyage: Liverpool-Quebec-Montreal, November 5, 1870. Final voyage Glasgow-Portland, March 20, 1897. Scrapped in 1897.

Cassandra (1906) Anchor-Donaldson Line.
Built by Scott's Shipbuilding & Engineering Co., Greenock, Scotland. Tonnage: 8,135. Dimensions: 455' x 53'. Twin-screw, 14 knots. Triple expansion engines. Two masts and one funnel. Passengers: 200 second and 1,000 third. Tonnage originally 7,396. Maiden voyage: Glasgow-Quebec-Montreal, September 22, 1906. Passenger accommodation removed in 1925. Renamed: (a) **Carmia** (b) **Drachtenstein** (Bernstein Line).

Cassel (1901) North German Lloyd.
Built by J. C. Tecklenborg, Geestemunde, Germany. Tonnage: 7,543. Dimensions: 428' x 54'. Twin-screw, 13 knots. Triple expansion engines. Two masts and one funnel. Renamed: **Marechal Gallieni** (1919). Sister ships: **Brandenburg, Breslau** and **Chemnitz.**

Castalia (1873) Anchor Line.
Built by Charles Connell & Co., Glasgow, Scotland. Tonnage: 2,201. Dimensions: 306' x 34'. Single-screw, 11 knots. Compound engines. Three masts and one funnel. Iron hull. Launched, December 17, 1872. Maiden voyage: Glasgow-New York, March 12, 1873. Placed in the Mediterranean-New York service at later date. Wrecked in the Mediterranean in 1884. Sister ships: **Alexandria, Assyria, Ismailia, Italia, Olympia** and **Trinacria.**

*Castel Felice (1930) "Sitmar" Line (Italian).
Built by Alexander Stephen & Sons, Ltd., Glasgow, Scotland. Tonnage: 12,150. Dimensions: 471' x 64' (493' o.l.). Twin-

screw, 16 knots. Steam turbines. Single mast and one funnel. Type: Tourist class passenger ship. First voyage: Bremen-Quebec, July 13, 1954. Services: (a) North Atlantic, (b) Italy-Brazil-Argentina, (c) Europe-Australia. Ex-**Karen** (1952), ex-**Kenya** (1951), ex-**Fairstone** (1950), **Kenya** (1949), ex-**Karen** (1949), ex-**Kenya** (1949).

Castilian   (1898)   Allan Line.
Built by Workman, Clark & Co., Belfast, Ireland. Tonnage: 7,441. Dimensions: 470' x 53'. Single-screw, 14 knots. Triple expansion engines. Two masts and one funnel. Maiden voyage: Liverpool-Halifax-Portland, Maine, February 23, 1899. While homeward bound was wrecked in Bay of Fundy, March 11, 1899, with no loss of life. A very brief life indeed.

Catalonia   (1881)   Cunard Line.
Built by J. & G. Thomson, Ltd., Glasgow, Scotland. Tonnage: 4,841. Dimensions: 429' x 43'. Single-screw, 12½ knots. Compound engines. Three masts and one funnel. Iron hull. Passengers: 200 cabin and 1,500 third. Maiden voyage: Liverpool-New York, August 6, 1881. Transferred to the Boston service in 1883. Scrapped in Italy, 1901. Running mates: **Cephalonia** and **Pavonia.**

Cataluna   (1883)   Spanish Line.
Built by Wm. Denny & Bros., Ltd., Dumbarton, Scotland. Tonnage: 3,665. Dimensions: 384' x 42'. Single-screw, 14 knots. Compound engines. Two masts and one funnel. Wrecked in 1923.

Cedric   (1903)   White Star Line.
Built by Harland & Wolff, Ltd., Belfast, Ireland. Tonnage: 21,227. Dimensions: 680' x 75' (697' o.l.). Twin-screw, 17 knots. Quadruple expansion engines. Four masts and two funnels. Launched, August 21, 1902. Passengers: 365 first, 160 second, 2,350 third. Maiden voyage: Liverpool-New York, February 11, 1903. Served as a troopship in World War I. Scrapped at Inverkeithing in 1932. Sister ship: **Celtic.** Similar to: **Adriatic** and **Baltic.** Note: Known as "The Big Four".

Celtic   (1872)   White Star Line.
Built by Harland & Wolff, Ltd., Belfast, Ireland. Tonnage: 3,888. Dimensions: 437' x 40'. Single-screw, 14 knots. Compound engines. Four masts and one funnel. Maiden voyage: Liverpool-New York, October 24, 1872. Renamed: **Amerika** (1891). Scrapped in 1898. Sister ship: **Adriatic.**

Celtic   (1901)   White Star Line.
Built by Harland & Wolff, Ltd., Belfast, Ireland. Tonnage: 20,904. Dimensions: 680' x 75' (697' o.l.). Twin-screw, 17 knots. Quadruple expansion engines. Four masts and two funnels. Note: First steamship to exceed 20,000 tons. Maiden voyage: Liverpool-New York, July 26, 1901. Passengers: 347 first, 160 second, 2,350 third. Converted to cabin class liner in 1928. Went aground in a dense fog at entrance to Queenstown harbor, December 10, 1928 and became a total loss. Dismantled by shipbreakers in 1933, as she was a danger to navigation. Sister ship: **Cedric.** Similar ships: **Adriatic** and **Baltic.** Note: These liners were noted for their steadiness in bad weather.

Centennial State   (1921)   United States Mail Line.
Built by New York Shipbuilding Co., Camden, New Jersey. Tonnage: 10,533. Dimensions: 502' x 62'. Twin-screw, 14 knots. Triple expansion engines. Two masts and one funnel. Maiden voyage: New York-Cobh-London, June 1921. Transferred to United States Lines in August 1921. Renamed: (a) **President Adams** (1922), (b) **President Grant** (1940). Sister ships: **Blue Hen State, Creole State, Granite State, Old North State, Panhandle State** and **Wolverine State.**

Cephalonia   (1882)   Cunard Line.
Built by Laird Bros., Birkenhead, England. Tonnage: 5,517. Dimensions: 430' x 46' (440' o.l.). Single-screw, 14 knots. Compound engines. Three masts and one funnel. Iron hull. Launched in May 1882. Maiden voyage: Liverpool-Boston, August 23, 1882. Passengers: 200 cabin, 1,500 third. Renamed: **Hailor** (1900). Chinese Eastern Railway (Russian). Sunk as a blockship at Port Arthur in 1904. Sister ship: **Pavonia.**

Cesare Battisti   (1920)   Transatlantica Italiana.
Built by Societa Anonima Ansaldo, Genoa, Italy. Tonnage: 8,331. Dimensions: 434' x 60'. Twin-screw, 14½ knots. Steam turbines. Two masts and two funnels. Blew up in Massaua Harbor, Eritrea, December 26, 1936. Note: Also in service to South America.

Cestrian   (1896)   Leyland Line.
Built by Harland & Wolff, Ltd., Belfast, Ireland. Tonnage: 8,776. Dimensions: 512' x 59'. Single-screw, 14 knots. Triple expansion engines. Four masts and one funnel. Passengers: 60 first class. Service: Liverpool-Boston. Tor-

pedoed and sunk without warning four miles from Skyro, June 24, 1917, with the loss of three lives.

Champlain (1932) French Line.
Built by Chantiers & Ateliers de St. Nazaire, Penhoet, France. Tonnage: 28,124. Dimensions: 606' x 83' (641' o.l.). Twin-screw, 20 knots. Steam turbines. Two masts and one funnel. Launched August 15, 1931. Dining saloon was two decks high and 65 feet long. Beam on promenade deck 86 feet, which extended for 350 feet. Passengers: 623 cabin, 308 tourist, 122 third class. Maiden voyage: Havre-New York, June 15, 1931. Sunk by magnetic mine off La Pallice, June 17, 1940.

Chateau Lafite (1881) Cie Bordelaise de Navigation (French).
Built by Oswald, Mordaunt & Co., Liverpool, England. Tonnage: 3,467. Dimensions: 366' x 41'. Single-screw, 12 knots. Compound engines. Two masts and one funnel. Scrapped in Italy, 1902.

Chateau Leoville (1881) Cie Bordelaise de Navigation Co.
Built by Sunderland Shipbuilding Co., Sunderland, England. Tonnage: 3,393. Dimensions: 365' x 41'. Single-screw, 12 knots. Compound engines. Three masts and one funnel. Iron hull. Sold in May 1888. Renamed: (a) **Connemara** (1888), (b) **Belgian King** (1896).

Chateau Margaux (1883) Cie Bordelaise de Navigation.
Built by Chantiers de la Gironde, Bordeaux, France. Tonnage: 4,176. Dimensions: 386' x 41'. Single-screw, 13 knots. Compound engines. Three masts and one funnel. Sunk in collision with British steamer **Manora** in English Channel, April 28, 1889, while under charter to French Line.

Chateau Yquem (1883) Cie Bordelaise de Navigation.
Built by Chantiers & Atel, de la Gironde, Bordeaux, France. Tonnage: 4,211. Dimensions: 386' x 41'. Single-screw, 13 knots. Compound engines. Three masts and one funnel. Launched, November 17, 1883. In service to South America. Renamed: **Gallia** (1900).

Chemnitz (1901) North German Lloyd.
Built by J. C. Tecklenborg, Geestemunde, Germany. Tonnage: 7,543. Dimensions: 428' x 54'. Twin-screw, 13 knots. Triple expansion engines. Two masts and one funnel. Service: Mainly in Europe-Baltimore. Acquired by Ellerman Wilson Line after World War I. Sold to Dutch shipbreakers

in November 1923.   Sister ships: **Cassel, Brandenburg** and **Breslau.**

Chester   (1873)   American Line.
Built by Caird & Co., Greenock, Scotland. Tonnage: 4,770. Dimensions: 444' x 44'. Single-screw, 15 knots. Compound engines. Three masts and two funnels. Iron hull. First voyage as **Chester** was from Southampton to New York, March 18, 1893. Renamed: **Sedgwick** (1898) United States Government,   (b)   **Arizona** (1905),   (c) **Napoletano.** Scrapped in 1907.

Chicago   (1866)   Guion Line.
Built by Palmers Shipbuilding & Iron Co., Jarrow-on-Tyne, England. Tonnage: 2,866. Dimensions: 335' x 42'. Single-screw, 10 knots. Inverted engines. Two masts and one funnel. Iron hull. Wrecked on a reef off Queenstown, January 12, 1868, with no loss of life. Sister ships: **Colorado, Manhattan** and **Minnesota.**

Chicago   (1908)   French Line.
Built by Ateliers & Chantiers de l'Atlantique, St. Nazaire, France. Tonnage: 9,350. Dimensions: 508' x 57'. Twin-screw, 16 knots. Triple expansion engines. Two masts and two funnels. Launched, November 5, 1907. Passengers: 358 second and 1,250 third. Maiden voyage: Havre-New York, May 30, 1908. Renamed: **Guadeloupe** (1928). Scrapped in France, 1936.

China   (1861)   Cunard Line.
Built by Robert Napier & Sons, Glasgow, Scotland. Tonnage: 2,539. Dimensions: 326' x 40'. Single-screw, 14 knots. Geared oscillating engines. Three masts and one funnel. Note: First screw-propelled steamship built for the Cunard Line. The first Cunarder to carry emigrants. Passengers: 150 cabin, 753 third class. Maiden voyage: Liverpool-New York, March 15, 1862. Compound engines in 1873. Final sailing for Cunard Line was Liverpool-New York, March 9, 1878. Renamed: **Magallanes** (1888) Spanish. Converted to sail (4 masted barque) and renamed Theodor in 1889. Left Tampa in March 1906, for Yokohama with a cargo of phosphates, and was lost in rather strange circumstances.

Chrobry   (1939)   Gdynia-American Line.
Built by Nakskov Skibsvaerft, Nakskov, Denmark. Tonnage: 11,442. Dimensions: 477' x 66' (505' o.l.). Twin-screw, 17 knots. Motorship. Two masts and one funnel. Designed

for South American service. Torpedoed and sunk during the battle at Narvick, Norway, May 1940. Sister ship: **Sobieski.**

Cimbria   (1867)   Hamburg-American Line.
Built by Caird & Co., Greenock, Scotland. Tonnage: 3,037. Dimensions: 329' x 40'. Single-screw, 12 knots. Inverted engines. Two masts and one funnel. Iron hull. Later re-engined with compound engines. Speed increased to 14 knots. Sunk in collision with the British steamship **Sultan** off the Dutch coast, January 19, 1883, with the loss of 389 lives. Sister ship: **Hammonia.**

Cincinnati   (1908)   Hamburg-American Line.
Built by Blohm & Voss, Hamburg, Germany. Tonnage: 16,339. Dimensions: 582' x 65' (600' o.l.). Twin-screw, 16 knots. Quadruple expansion engines. Four masts and two funnels. Passengers: 243 first, 210 second, 2,305 third. Commenced Hamburg-Boulogne-Southampton-Boston service in 1913. Renamed: **Covington** (1917) American troopship. Sunk by German submarine in North Atlantic, July 1, 1918. Sister ship: **Cleveland.**

Circassia   (1878)   Anchor Line.
Built by Vickers, Sons & Maxim, Ltd., Barrow-in-Furnace, England. Tonnage: 4,272. Dimensions: 399' x 42'. Single-screw, 13 knots. Compound engines. Three masts and one funnel. Maiden voyage: Glasgow-New York, July 11, 1878. Broken up in Germany in 1900. Running mates: **Anchoria, Bolivia, Devonia** and **Ethiopia.**

Circassia   (1903)   Anchor Line.
Built by D. & W. Henderson & Co., Glasgow, Scotland. Tonnage: 6,861. Dimensions: 450' x 55'. Single-screw, 15 knots. Triple expansion engines. Two masts and one funnel. Passengers: 60 cabin. Scrapped in 1931.

Circassian   (1857)   North Atlantic Steam Navigation Co.
Built by Robert Hickson & Co., Belfast, Ireland. Note: This firm later became known as Harland & Wolff, Ltd. Tonnage: 1,387. Dimensions: 242' x 39'. Single-screw, 9 knots. Three masts and one funnel. Iron hull. Maiden voyage: Liverpool-St. John's-Halifax-Portland, March 7, 1857. Employed by Galway Line in 1858. Served as a blockade runner in the Civil War. Converted to sail in 1874.

Circassian (1872) Allan Line.
Built by Robert Steele & Co., Greenock, Scotland. Tonnage:
3,724. Dimensions: 415' x 40'. Single-screw, 13½ knots.
Compound engines. Three masts and one funnel. Iron hull.
Passengers: 100 first and 850 third. Maiden voyage: Liverpool-Quebec-Montreal, April 24, 1873. In 1875 was lengthened
from 375 to 415 feet (tonnage increased from 3,211 to 3,724
tons). Scrapped in 1896.

Citta di Genova (1882) La Veloce Line.
Built by Wigham Richardson & Co., Newcastle, England.
Tonnage: 3,919. Dimensions: 390' x 42'. Single-screw.
Made her final Italy-New York voyage in 1906.

Citta di Milano (1897) La Veloce Line.
Built by N. Odero, Sestri, Ponente, Italy. Tonnage: 3,848.
Dimensions: 364' x 43'. Single-screw, 12 knots. Triple
expansion engines. Two masts and one funnel. Made her
final Italy-New York voyage in 1907. Renamed: **Albania**
(1914) Sitmar Line. Transferred to Lloyd Triestino in 1932.
Sister ship: **Citta di Torino.**

Citta di Napoli (1871) La Veloce Line.
Built by Harland & Wolff, Belfast, Ireland. Tonnage: 4,125.
Dimensions: 426' x 41'. Single-screw, 14 knots. Compound
engines. Four masts and one funnel. In Genoa-New York
service. Scrapped in Italy, 1910. Ex-**Vittoria** (1902), ex-
Maasdam (1902), ex-**Republic** (1889).

Citta di Torino (1898) La Veloce Line.
Built by N. Odero & Co., Genoa, Italy. Tonnage: 3,836.
Dimensions: 363' x 43'. Single-screw, 12 knots. Two masts
and one funnel. Made her final Italy-New York voyage in
1907. Renamed: **Constantinopoli** (1914) Sitmar Line.
Sister ship: **Citta di Milano.** Note: They were built for
the Italy-Central American service.

City of Antwerp (1867) Inman Line.
Built by Tod & McGregor, Glasgow, Scotland. Tonnage:
2,391. Dimensions: 332' x 39'. Single-screw, 12 knots. Three
masts and one funnel. Iron hull. Maiden voyage: Liverpool-
New York, February 20, 1867. Compound engines installed
in 1879. Tonnage increased to 3,032. Sold to Johnston Line.
Renamed: **Thanemore** (1879). Disappeared at sea on
voyage from Baltimore to Liverpool in November 1890,
with loss of 43 lives.

City of Baltimore   (1854)   Inman Line.
Built by Tod & McGregor, Glasgow, Scotland. Tonnage: 2,472. Dimensions: 321′ x 33′. Single-screw, 10 knots. Compound engines installed at later date. Three masts and one funnel. Iron hull. Sold to the Hall Line in 1874 and renamed **Fivaller.** Resold in 1882 to Spanish shipowners. Renamed: **Benicarlo.** Sister ship: **City of Washington.**

City of Baltimore   (1919)   Baltimore Mail Line.
Built by Bethlehem's Alameda Shipyard, California. Tonnage: 8,378. Dimensions: 486′ x 56′. Single-screw, 16½ knots. Steam turbines. Two masts and one funnel. Passengers: 83 in one class. First voyage: Baltimore-Southampton-Havre-Hamburg, July 2, 1931. Transferred to Panama-Pacific Line in 1938. Served as a troopship in World War II. Renamed: **Heywood** (1940) United States Government. After war laid up in the reserve fleet. Ex-**Steadfast** (1931). Sister ships: **City of Hamburg, City of Havre, City of Newport News** and **City of Norfolk.** Note: These sister ships were originally freighters. All were reconstructed and lengthened in 1931 by Federal Shipbuilding & Drydock Company, Kearny, N. J. The combination passenger-cargo liners were transferred from trans-Atlantic service to the New York-Panama Canal-California trade route in 1938. All were sold to the United States Government in 1940.

City of Berlin   (1875)   Inman Line.
Built by Caird & Co., Greenock, Scotland. Tonnage: 5,491. Dimensions: 488′ x 44′ (513′ o.l.). Single-screw, 16 knots. Compound engines. Three masts and one funnel. Iron hull. Launched October 27, 1874. Dining saloon measured 44′ x 43′. Coal consumption was 120 tons per day; 12 boilers; 36 furnaces. New triple expansion engines in 1887. Passengers: 202 cabin, 1,500 third class. Maiden voyage: Liverpool-New York, April 29, 1875. Renamed: (a) **Berlin** (1893), (b) **Meade** (1898) United States Government. In transport service to the Philippines. Nearly destroyed by fire in 1906. Rebuilt and used as a training ship at Boston. This trans-Atlantic record-breaker was scrapped at Philadelphia in 1921.

City of Boston   (1864)   Inman Line.
Built by Tod & McGregor, Glasgow, Scotland. Tonnage: 2,213. Dimensions: 313′ x 39′. Single-screw, 12 knots. Three masts and one funnel. Iron hull. Maiden voyage: Liverpool-New York, February 8, 1865. Disappeared between Halifax and Liverpool in January 1870. Loss of life amounted to 116 passengers and 61 crew.

City of Bristol   (1855)   Inman Line.
    Built by Caird & Co., Greenock, Scotland. Tonnage: 2,215.
    Dimensions: 304′ x 37′.   Single-screw, 10 knots.   Three
    masts and one funnel. Lengthened to 349 feet (2,655 tons)
    in 1871; compound engines installed. Vessel sold in 1880.
    Ex-**Etna** (1871).

City of Brooklyn   (1869)   Inman Line.
    Built by Tod & McGregor, Glasgow, Scotland. Tonnage:
    2,911.   Dimensions: 354′ x 43′.   Single-screw, 13 knots.
    Inverted engines. Three masts and one funnel. Iron hull.
    Renamed: **Brooklyn** (1878). Wrecked in 1885.

City of Brussels   (1869)   Inman Line.
    Built by Tod & McGregor, Glasgow, Scotland. Tonnage:
    3,081.   Dimensions: 390′ x 40′.   Single-screw, 14 knots.
    Horizontal trunk type engines. Three masts and one funnel.
    Iron hull. Note: Broke the trans-Atlantic speed record in
    December 1869. The first steamship to reduce the crossing
    to under 8 days. Altered by having another deck added in
    1872, increasing tonnage to 3,747. Compound engines in
    1876. Her career was suddenly ended when in collision with
    the steamer **Kirby Hall,** January 7, 1887. She sunk off the
    mouth of the Mersey, with the loss of life listed as ten.

City of Chester   (1873)   Inman Line.
    Built by Caird & Co., Greenock, Scotland. Tonnage: 4,560.
    Dimensions: 444′ x 42′. Single-screw, 15 knots. Compound
    engines. Three masts and two funnels. Iron hull. Passen-
    gers: 132 cabin, 1,310 third. Maiden voyage: Liverpool-
    New York, July 10, 1873. Transferred to American Line in
    1893. Renamed: (a) **Chester** (1893), (b) **Sedgwick** (1898),
    (c) **Arizona** (1905), (d) **Napoletano** (Italian). Scrapped
    in 1907. Sister ship: **City of Richmond.**

City of Chicago   (1883)   Inman Line.
    Built by Charles Connell & Co., Scotstoun, Glasgow, Scot-
    land. Tonnage: 5,202. Dimensions: 430′ x 45′. Single-screw,
    14 knots. Compound engines. Four masts and two funnels.
    Iron hull. Note: Laid down as the **Vancouver,** as she origi-
    nally was intended for the Dominion Line. Maiden voyage:
    Liverpool-New York, September 18, 1883.   Wrecked by
    stranding near Old Head of Kinsale, on south coast of Ire-
    land, July 1892. Ex-**Vancouver** (1883).

City of Cork   (1863)   Inman Line.
    Built by Wm. Denny & Bros., Dumbarton, Scotland. Ton-
    nage: 1,547. Dimensions: 265′ x 33′. Single-screw, 10 knots.

Three masts and one funnel. Iron hull. Maiden voyage: Liverpool-New York, March 1863. Sold to other owners in 1871.

City of Dublin   (1864)   Inman Line.
Built by Smith & Rodger, Glasgow, Scotland. Tonnage: 1,999. Dimensions: 318′ x 36′. Single-screw, 11 knots. Three masts and one funnel. Iron hull. Note: Laid down as **Hellespont,** but became **City of Dublin.** Sold to Dominion Line in 1880. Renamed: (a) **Quebec** (1873), (b) **Nautique** (1888). Compound engines installed in 1873. Foundered in North Atlantic in 1890.

City of Glasgow   (1850)   Inman Line.
Built by Tod & McGregor, Glasgow, Scotland. This firm later became known as D. & W. Henderson, Ltd. Tonnage: 1,609. Dimensions: 237′ x 34′. Single-screw, 8½ knots. Geared beam engines. Three masts and one funnel. Iron hull. Barque-rigged and carried an enormous amount of canvas. Had two beam engines geared to a single shaft with a propeller 12 feet in diameter. Note: Pioneer vessel of the Inman Line. She had three decks, with height between decks seven feet. Passengers: 130 cabin and 400 third class. Steerage added in 1852. Maiden voyage was in 1850. She sailed from Liverpool for New York on March 1, 1854, with 480 people on board, and was never heard of again.

City of Hamburg   (1919)   Baltimore Mail Line.
Built by Bethlehem Shipbuilding Corp., Alameda, California. Tonnage: 8,378. Dimensions: 493′ x 56′. Single-screw, 16 knots. Steam turbines. Two masts and one funnel. Service: Baltimore-Southampton-Havre-Hamburg. Renamed: (a) **City of San Francisco** (1938), (b) **William P. Biddle** (1941) United States transport. After World War II was laid up in the reserve fleet. Ex-**Eclipse** (1931). Note: See **City of Baltimore** for other information.

City of Havre   (1918)   Baltimore Mail Line.
Built by Bethlehem Shipbuilding Corp., Alameda, California. Tonnage: 8,378. Dimensions: 486′ x 56′. Single-screw, 16 knots. Steam turbines. Two masts and one funnel. Renamed: (a) **City of Los Angeles,** (b) **George F. Elliott** (United States Govt.). Sunk by Japanese aircraft off Guadalcanal, August 8, 1942. Ex-**Victorious.** Note: See **City of Baltimore.**

City of Limrick   (1855)   Inman Line.
   Built by Smith of Glasgow, Scotland. Tonnage: 1,529.
   Dimensions: 281' x 34'. Single-screw, 10 knots. Geared
   beam engines. Three masts and one funnel. Clipper bow.
   Iron hull. Lengthened to 331 feet (2,536 tons); also com-
   pound engines installed, 1870. Sold to Wm. Ross & Company
   (Thistle Line) in 1880. Listed as missing at sea in 1881,
   with the loss of 43 lives. Ex-**African** (1863) British.

City of Lincoln   (1866)   Thistle Line (W. H. Ross & Co.).
   Built by Palmers Shipbuilding & Iron Co., Newcastle, England. Tonnage: 3,185. Dimensions: 335' x 42'. Single-
   screw, 10 knots. Compound engines. Two masts and one
   funnel. Clipper bow. Iron hull. First sailing London-New
   York, October 18, 1881. Renamed: **Solis** (1884) Spanish.
   Name reverted back to **City of Lincoln** in 1885. Wrecked
   near Cape Town on August 15, 1902, with no loss of life.
   Ex-**Massachusetts** (1881) Warren Line, ex-**Manhattan**
   (1875) Guion Line.

City of Liverpool   (1880)   Thistle Line (W. H. Ross & Co.).
   Built by Richardson Duck of Stockton. Tonnage: 3,065.
   Dimensions: 340' x 40'. Single-screw, 12 knots. Compound
   engines. Three masts and one funnel. Service: London-New
   York. Sold in 1881. Renamed: (a) **Pacifique** (French), (b)
   Betty (1895). Scrapped in Italy, 1903.

City of Liverpool   (1881)   Thistle Line.
   Built by Wm. Doxford & Sons, Ltd., Sunderland, England.
   Tonnage: 3,514. Dimensions: 358' x 41'. Single-screw, 12
   knots. Compound engines. Three masts and one funnel.
   Renamed: **Arctique** (1882) French. Wrecked in Straits of
   Magellan in 1884; subsequently destroyed by fire.

City of London   (1863)   Inman Line.
   Built by Tod & McGregor, Glasgow, Scotland. Tonnage:
   2,765. Dimensions: 336' x 41'. Single-screw, 11 knots.
   Inverted type engines. Three masts and one funnel. Iron
   hull. Clipper bow. Lengthened to 374 feet in 1869. Tonnage
   originally 2,560 tons. Sold to Thistle Line in 1879. Compound engines in 1881. Disappeared at sea, November 1881,
   with the loss of 41 lives. Sister ship: **City of New York.**

City of Manchester   (1851)   Inman Line.
   Built by Tod & McGregor, Glasgow, Scotland. Tonnage:
   1,892. Dimensions: 265' x 37'. Single-screw, 9 knots. Geared
   beam engines. Three masts and one funnel. Iron hull. Maiden

voyage: Liverpool-Philadelphia, July 26, 1851. Vessel sold in 1871. Converted to sail. Wrecked in 1876.

City of Montreal   (1872)   Inman Line.
Built by Tod & McGregor, Glasgow, Scotland. Tonnage: 4,489. Dimensions: 419' x 44'. Single-screw, 12½ knots. Compound horizontal engines. Three masts and one funnel. New compound engines in 1876; also a second funnel installed. Destroyed by fire at sea in August 1887. Passengers and crew were rescued by **York City.**

City of New York   (1861)   Inman Line.
Built by Tod & McGregor, Glasgow, Scotland. Tonnage: 2,360. Dimensions: 326' x 40'. Single-screw, 12 knots. Horizontal trunk engines. Three masts and one funnel. Wrecked on Daunts Rock, Queenstown, March 29, 1864, with no loss of life. Sister ship: **City of London.**

City of New York   (1865)   Inman Line.
Built by Tod & McGregor, Glasgow, Scotland. Tonnage: 2,642. Dimensions: 321' x 40'. Single-screw, 12 knots. Horizontal trunk engines. Three masts and one funnel. Clipper bow. Iron hull. Maiden voyage: Liverpool-New York, June 7, 1865. Lengthened to 375 feet (3,523 tons) in 1871. Compound engines in 1877. Sold to Allan Line 1883. Renamed: **Norwegian.** Wrecked in 1902. Dismantled for scrap in 1903.

City of New York   (1888)   Inman Line.
Built by J. & G. Thomson, Ltd., Glasgow, Scotland. Tonnage: 10,499. Dimensions: 528' x 63' (560' o.l.). Twin-screw, 20 knots. Triple expansion engines. Three masts and three funnels. Launched in March 1888. Made 20.2 knots on her trials. One of the first steamships to be equipped with twin-screws. Note: The **Notting Hill** built in 1881 had twin-screws. Several of the early French Line steamers were converted from paddle-wheels to twin-screw prior to that date. Maiden voyage: Liverpool-New York, August 1, 1888. Renamed: (a) **New York** (1893), (b) **Harvard** (1898) United States Government, (c) **New York** (after Spanish-American War), (d) **Plattsburg** (1917) U. S. Govt., (e) **New York** (1920). Sold to Polish Navigation Company in 1921. Scrapped in Italy, 1923. Sister ship: **City of Paris.**

City of Newport News   (1919)   Baltimore Mail Line.
Built by Bethlehem Shipbuilding Co., Alameda, Calif. Tonnage: 8,378. Dimensions: 486' x 56'. Single-screw, 16½

knots. Steam turbines. Two masts and one funnel. Renamed: **Fuller** (1940) United States Govt. Laid up in the
reserve fleet after World War II. Broken up in 1957. Ex-
Archer (1931). Note: See **City of Baltimore.**

City of Norfolk   (1918)   Baltimore Mail Steamship Co.
Built by Bethlehem Shipbuilding Corp., Alameda, Calif.
Tonnage: 8,378. Dimensions: 486′ x 56′. Single-screw, 16½
knots. Steam turbines. Two masts and one funnel. Renamed:
Neville (1940) United States Govt. After war was laid up
in reserve fleet. Scrapped in United States, 1957. Ex-
Independence (1931). Note: See **City of Baltimore.**

City of Paris   (1866)   Inman Line.
Built by Tod & McGregor, Glasgow, Scotland. Tonnage:
2,651. Dimensions: 346′ x 40′ (359′ o.l.). Single-screw, 13½
knots. Horizontal trunk engines. Three masts and one
funnel. Clipper bow. Iron hull. Displacement of 6,411 tons.
Hurricane deck was 17 feet above water line. Maiden voyage:
Liverpool-New York, March 21, 1866. Lengthened to 398
feet (3,081 tons) in 1870. Compound engines in 1879.
Renamed: **Tonquin** (1884) French. Sunk after collision in
fog off Malaga in March 1885.

City of Paris   (1889)   Inman Line.
Built by J. & G. Thomson, Ltd., Glasgow, Scotland. Tonnage: 10,669. Dimensions: 527′ x 63′ (560′ o.l.). Twin-screw,
20 knots. Triple expansion engines. Three masts and three
funnels. Launched in October 1888. Made 21.95 knots
during trials. Nine boilers; 54 furnaces; 18,500 I.H.P. Steel
hull. Displacement of 17,270 tons. Passengers: 540 first,
200 second, 1,000 third. Maiden voyage: Liverpool-New
York, April 3, 1889. Trans-Atlantic record-breaker. Made
the crossing at an average speed of 20.2 knots in May 1889.
Renamed: (a) **Paris** (1893), (b) **Yale** (1898) U. S. Govt.,
(c) **Paris**, (d) **Philadelphia** (1901), (e) **Harrisburg** (1917)
U. S. Govt., (f) **Philadelphia** (1920). Scrapped in Italy,
1923. Sister ship: **City of New York.**

City of Philadelphia   (1853)   Inman Line.
Built by Tod & McGregor, Glasgow, Scotland. Tonnage:
2,168. Dimensions: 294′ x 39′. Single-screw, 10 knots.
Three masts and one funnel. Clipper bow. Iron hull. Maiden
voyage: Liverpool-Philadelphia, August 30, 1854. Wrecked
near Cape Race, September 9, 1854, with no loss of life.

City of Richmond   (1873)   Inman Line.
Built by Tod & McGregor, Glasgow, Scotland.   Tonnage:
4,623.   Dimensions: 441' x 43'.   Single-screw, 15 knots.   Compound engines.   Three masts and two funnels.   Iron hull.
Clipper bow.   Note: The first liner built with three funnels.
Passengers: 132 cabin, 1,310 third.   Maiden voyage: Liverpool-New York, September 4, 1873.   Made a fast crossing
from Sandy Hook to Fastnet Rock in 7 days, 23 hours in
1873.   Sold in 1891.   Sister ship: **City of Chester.**

City of Rome   (1881)   (a) Inman Line, (b) Anchor Line.
Built by Vickers, Sons & Maxim, Ltd., Barrow-in-Furness,
England.   Tonnage: 8,415.   Dimensions: 560' x 52' (586' o.l.).
Single-screw, 16 knots.   Compound engines.   Four masts and
three funnels.   Note: Considered by many as the most beautiful steamship ever built.   Passengers: 520 cabin, 810 third
class.   Ownership was transferred to the Anchor Line in 1882.
As a record breaker she proved a failure, but nevertheless
ran successfully for many years for the Anchor Line.   Triple
expansion engines were later installed to replace the original
engines. Broken up for scrap by German shipbreakers in 1902.

City of Washington   (1853)   Inman Line.
Built by Tod & McGregor, Glasgow, Scotland.   Tonnage:
2,381.   Dimensions: 319' x 40'.   Single-screw, 10 knots.
Three masts and one funnel.   First voyage for Inman Line
was from Liverpool to Philadelphia, November 5, 1856.
Lengthened to 358 feet (2,870 tons) in 1869.   Wrecked near
Cape Sable, Nova Scotia, July 7, 1873, with no loss of life.
Sister ship: **City of Baltimore.**

Ciudad de Cadiz   (1878)   Spanish Line.
Built by Lobnitz, Coulborn & Co., Renfrew, Scotland.   Tonnage: 3,202.   Dimensions: 363' x 38'.   Single-screw, 13 knots.
Triple expansion engines.   Two masts and one funnel.   Iron
hull.   Wrecked off Africa in 1924.

Cleopatra   (1852)   Canadian Steam Navigation Co.
Built by Wm. Denny & Bros., Dumbarton, Scotland.   Ton-
nage: 1,452.   Dimensions: 220' x 32'.   Single-screw, 9 knots.
Three masts and one funnel.   Iron hull.   Maiden voyage:
Liverpool-Quebec-Montreal, July 14, 1853.   Sold to African
Steamship Company in 1856.   Wrecked off Sierra Leone
in 1862.

Cleopatra   (1898)   Atlantic Transport Line.
Built by Earle's Shipbuilding & Engine Co., Hull, England.
Tonnage: 6,849.   Dimensions: 475' x 52'.   Single-screw, 13

knots. Triple expansion engines. Four masts and one funnel. Passengers: 120 first class. Built for Wilson & Furness-Leyland Line. Renamed: **Mohegan** (1898). Wrecked on October 14, 1898. Sister ships: **Alexandra, Boadicea** and **Victoria.**

*Cleopatra (1944) Khedivial Mail Line (Egyptian).
Built by Oregon Shipbuilding Corp., Portland, Oregon. Tonnage: 8,193. Dimensions: 439′ x 62′ (455′ o.l.). Single-screw, 14 knots. Steam turbines. Two masts and one funnel. Originally a Victory type freighter. Converted to passenger ship at Alexandria, Egypt. Passengers: 75 first class. Ex-**Khedive Ismail** (1956), ex-**United Victory** (1947). Sister ship: **Mohamed Ali El Kebir.**

Cleveland (1908) Hamburg-American Line.
Built by Blohm & Voss, Hamburg, Germany. Tonnage: 16,971. Dimensions: 588′ x 65′. Twin-screw, 16 knots. Quadruple expansion engines. Four masts and two funnels. Passengers: 239 first, 224 second, 2,391 third. Maiden voyage: Hamburg-Southampton-Cherbourg-New York, March 27, 1909. Note: Inaugurated a new service to Boston, along with the **Cincinnati** in May 1913. Renamed (a) **Mobile** (1917), (b) **King Alexander** (1920), (c) **Cleveland** (1923). Scrapped in Germany, 1933. Sister ship: **Cincinnati.**

Coblenz (1923) North German Lloyd.
Built by Akt. Ges. "Weser", Bremen, Germany. Tonnage: 9,449. Dimensions: 458′ x 57′. Twin-screw, 11 knots. Steam turbines. Two masts and one funnel. Sold to Italy in August 1935. Renamed: **Sicilia** (1935). Became a war casualty, April 4, 1943. Sister ships: **Fulda, Saarbrucken, Trier, Werra** and **Weser.**

Coburg (1908) North German Lloyd.
Built by Bremer Vulkan, Vegesack, Germany. Tounage: 6,750. Dimensions: 419′ x 54′. Single-screw, 12 knots. Quadruple expansion engines. Two masts and one funnel. Renamed: **Pocone.** Sister ship: **Eisenach.**

Colombie (1862) French Line.
Built by Caird & Co., Greenock, Scotland. Tonnage: 1,859. Dimensions: 280′ x 39′. Single-screw, 11 knots. Three masts and one funnel. Service: France-West Indies. Sold to ship-breakers in December 1897. Ex-**Floride** (1874).

*Colombie   (1931)   French Line.
Built by Ateliers & Chantiers de France, Dunkirk, France.
Tonnage: 13,391.   Dimensions: 488′ x 66′ (508′ o.l.).   Twin-
screw, 17 knots.   Steam turbines.   Two masts and two funnels.   Launched July 18, 1931.   Service: Havre-West Indies-
Central America.   Seized by United States Government at
Martinique during World War II.   Served as a troopship
until 1945, she was then converted to hospital ship and
renamed **Aleda E. Lutz**.   Returned to France in 1946.
Reconditioned and altered to single funnel.   Given accommodation for 192 first, 140 cabin and 246 tourist.   Tonnage now
listed as 13,808.   Ex-**Aleda E. Lutz** (1946),   ex-**Colombie**
(1945).

Colombo   (1917)   Navigazione Generale Italiana.
Built by Palmers Shipbuilding & Iron Co., Newcastle, England.   Tonnage: 12,003.   Dimensions: 518′ x 64′ (536′ o.l.).
Twin-screw, 17 knots.   Quadruple expansion engines.   Two
masts and two funnels.   First voyage as **Colombo** Genoa-
Naples-New York, November 1921.   Tonnage originally was
10,917.   Later placed in South American service.   Transferred to Lloyd Triestino in 1934.   Scuttled at Massawa,
Eritrea, April 4, 1941.   Ex-**San Gennaro** (1921).

Colorado   (1867)   Guion Line.
Built by Palmers Shipbuilding & Iron Co., Jarrow-on-Tyne-
England.   Tonnage: 2,927.   Dimensions: 330′ x 42′.   Single-
screw, 10 knots.   Inverted engines.   Two masts and one
funnel.   Iron hull.   Maiden voyage: Liverpool-New York,
January 14, 1868.   Sunk in collision in the Mersey River
with **Arabian** February 7, 1872.   The accident caused the
loss of six lives.   Sister ships: **Chicago, Manhattan** and
Minnesota.

Colorado   (1887)   Wilson Line (British).
Built by Earle's Shipbuilding & Engineering Co., Hull,
England.   Tonnage: 4,220.   Dimensions: 370′ x 44′.   Single-
screw, 14 knots.   Compound engines.   Three masts and one
funnel.   Iron hull.   Made her final voyage to New York
in 1905.

Columbia   (1840)   Cunard Line.
Built by Robert Steele & Son, Greenock, Scotland.   Tonnage:
1,155.   Dimensions: 207′ x 34′.   Paddle-wheels, 8½ knots.
Side lever engines.   Three masts and one funnel.   Maiden
voyage Liverpool-Halifax-Boston, January 5, 1841.   Wrecked

on Devil's Limit Rock, near Halifax, July 2, 1843, with no loss of life. Sister ships: **Acadia, Britannia** and **Caledonia.**

Columbia   (1861)   Galway Line.
Built by Martin Samuelson, Hull, England. Tonnage: 2,913. Dimensions: 364' x 40'. Paddle-wheels, 13 knots. Oscillating engines. Two masts and two funnels. Attained a speed of 13.9 knots during her trials, March 28, 1861. Maiden voyage from Galway to Boston, April 9, 1861. Sold to Turkish Government in 1866. Sister ships: **Anglia, Connaught** and **Hibernia.**

Columbia   (1866)   Anchor Line.
Built by Alexander Stephen & Son, Ltd., Glasgow, Scotland. Tonnage: 1,698. Dimensions: 283' x 33'. Single-screw, 10 knots. Inverted engines. Three masts and one funnel. Iron hull. Tonnage increased to 2,030; compound engines installed. Originally in Bombay service. Renamed: **Francesco Crispi** (1894) Italian. Wrecked on Shipwash in August 1898. Sister ship: **Hibernia.**

Columbia   (1889)   Hamburg-American Line.
Built by Laird Bros., Ltd., Birkenhead, England. Tonnage: 7,383. Dimensions: 463' x 55' (480' o.l.). Twin-screw, 18 knots. Triple expansion engines. Three masts and three funnels. Steel hull. Passengers: 220 first, 120 second, 800 third. Renamed: (a) **Rapido** (1898), (b) **Columbia** (1899), (c) **Terek** (1904). Note: Attained a speed of 20.5 knots during trials. Sold to Spanish Government in 1898 and renamed **Rapido.** After the Spanish-American War, she was put back in the Hamburg-American Line service. Sold to the Russian Volunteer Fleet in 1904. Scrapped in 1907. Running mates: **Auguste Victoria, Furst Bismarck** and **Normannia.**

Columbia   (1901)   Anchor Line.
Built by D. & W. Henderson & Co., Ltd., Glasgow, Scotland. Tonnage: 8,292. Dimensions: 485' x 56' (503' o.l.). Twin-screw, 15½ knots. Triple expansion engines. Two masts and three funnels. Renamed: (a) **Columbella** (1914), (b) **Columbia** (1919), (c) **Moreas** (1926). Note: Employed as a British armed merchant cruiser during World War I. Scrapped in Italy, 1929.

Columbia   (1908)   Austro-American Line.
Built by Russell & Co., Ltd., Port Glasgow, Scotland. Tonnage: 5,460. Dimensions: 400' x 52'. Single-screw, 13 knots.

Triple expansion engines. Two masts and one funnel. Acquired by Cosulich Line after First World War. Renamed: **Annoula.** Foundered off Cape Lookout, October 7, 1933 Sister ship: **Georgia.**

Columbia (1913)   Greek Line.
Built by Harland & Wolff, Ltd., Belfast, Ireland. Tonnage: 9,424. Dimensions: 450′ x 60′ (466′ o.l.). Triple-screw, 16 knots. Combination triple expansion engines and steam turbines. Two masts and one funnel. Passengers: 57 first and 727 tourist. Service: Bremen-Southampton-Quebec-Montreal. Scrapped in Japan, 1959. Ex-**Katoomba** (1949).

Columbus (1903)   Dominion Line.
Built by Harland & Wolff, Ltd., Belfast, Ireland. Tonnage: 15,378. Dimensions: 593′ x 59′. Twin-screw, 15 knots. Quadruple expansion engines. Four masts and one funnel. Maiden voyage: Liverpool-Boston, October 1, 1903. Renamed: **Republic** (1903).

Columbus (1914)   North German Lloyd.
Built by F. Schichau, Danzig, Germany. Tonnage: 34,356. Dimensions: 751′ x 83′. Twin-screw, 20 knots. Triple expansion engines. Two masts and two funnels. Launched, December 17, 1913. Never in service for North German Lloyd. Renamed: **Homeric** (1920).

Columbus (1922)   North German Lloyd.
Built by F. Schichau, Danzig, Germany. Tonnage: 32,354. Dimensions: 749′ x 83′ (775′ o.l.). Twin-screw, 19½ knots. Triple expansion engines. Two masts and two funnels. Steam turbines installed in 1929. Speed increased to 23 knots. Shorter funnels of greater diameter replaced the original ones. Maiden voyage: Bremen-New York in November 1923. Note: Her original name was **Hindenburg,** which identified her between 1914 to 1918. Scuttled and set on fire by her German crew off Cape May, New Jersey, December 19, 1939, so as to avoid capture by the British. Similar in appearance to the White Star liner **Homeric.**

Commonwealth (1900)   Dominion Line.
Built by Harland & Wolff, Ltd., Belfast, Ireland. Tonnage: 12,268. Dimensions: 578′ x 59′ (594′ o.l.). Twin-screw, 16 knots. Triple expansion engines. Two masts and one funnel. Maiden voyage: Liverpool-Boston, October 4, 1900. Transferred to the White Star Line in 1903. Renamed: **Canopic** (1903).

Connaught (1860)   Galway Line.
Built by Palmers Shipbuilding & Iron Co., Newcastle, England. Tonnage: 2,860. Dimensions: 360' x 40' (378' o.l.). Paddle-wheels, 13 knots. Oscillating engines. Two masts and two funnels. Iron hull. Launched, April 21, 1860. Maiden voyage: Galway-St. John's-Boston, July 11, 1860. Abandoned at sea, leaking and on fire 170 miles from Boston, October 6, 1860. There was no loss of life. Sister ships: **Anglia, Columbia** and **Hibernia.**

Constantinople (1896)   Greek Line.
Built by F. Schichau, Danzig, Germany. Tonnage: 11,570. Dimensions: 550' x 60'. Twin-screw, 15 knots. Quadruple expansion engines. Two masts and two funnels. Passengers: 345 first, 314 second, 1,700 third. Renamed: **King Alexander** (1924). Scrapped in Italy, 1926. Ex-**Bremen** (1920).

Constitution (1855)   Compagnie Transatlantique Belge.
Built by Van Vlissingen, Amsterdam, Netherlands. Tonnage: 2,160. Dimensions: 281' x 37'. Single-screw, 10 knots. Inverted engines. Three masts and one funnel. Maiden voyage: Antwerp-Southampton-New York, November 23, 1856. Renamed: (a) **Princess Charlotte** (1857), (b) **Canarias** (1862)   Foundered near the Azores, October 31, 1871. Sister ship: **Belgique.**

*Constitution (1951)   American Export Lines.
Built by Bethlehem Steel Co., Shipbuilding Division, Quincy, Mass. Tonnage: 30,293 (23,750 U.S.A. measurement). Dimensions: 637' x 89' (683' o.l.). Twin-screw, 25 knots. Steam turbines. One mast and two funnels. Service speed: 22 knots. Launched, September 16, 1950. Maiden voyage: New York-Mediterranean ports, June 21, 1951. Superstructure was enlarged in 1959. Passengers: 484 first, 350 cabin, 254 tourist. Sister ship: **Independence.**

Consuelo (1900)   Wilson Line.
Built by Swan & Hunter, Ltd., Wallsend-on-Tyne, England. Tonnage: 6,182. Dimensions: 461' x 52'. Twin-screw, 12 knots. Triple expansion engines. Four masts and one funnel. Renamed: (a) **Cairnrona** (1910), (b) **Albania** (1911), (c) **Poleric** (1912). Broken up for scrap in Japan, 1930.

Conte Biancamano (1925)   (a) Lloyd Sabaudo Line, (b) Italia Line.
Built by Wm. Beardmore & Co., Glasgow, Scotland. Tonnage: 24,416. Dimensions: 626' x 76' (650' o.l.). Twin-screw, 20 knots. Four steam turbines. Two masts and two funnels.

Launched, April 23, 1925. Maiden voyage: Genoa-Naples-New York, November 20, 1925. Transferred to South American service in 1932. Placed in the Far East service of Lloyd Triestino prior to World War II. Seized by United States at Colon in December 1941. Renamed: (a) **Hermitage** (1942), (b) **Conte Biacamano** (1947). Since World War II has been used in both the North Atlantic and South American trade. Sold to Italian shipbreakers in 1960. Sister ship: **Conte Grande.**

Conte di Savoia (1932) Italia Line.
Built by Cantieri Riuniti dell' Adriatico, Trieste, Italy. Tonnage: 48,502. Dimensions: 785′ x 96′ (814′ o.l.). Quadruple-screw, 28 knots. Steam turbines. Two masts and two funnels. Diameter of funnels 43′ x 23′. Equipped with three gyro-stabilizers to minimize her motion in a rough sea. Launched, October 28, 1931. Maiden voyage: Genoa-New York, November 30, 1932. Made the Genoa-New York crossing frequently in 6½ days. However, she was never quite as fast as her running mate the **Rex.** Sunk by aircraft in shallow water near Venice, September 11, 1943. Refloated in October 1945. For a time it was thought she would be rebuilt. This contemplated work never took place, and in 1950 was broken up for scrap at Monfalcone, Italy. Running mate: **Rex.**

*****Conte Grande** (1927) (a) Lloyd Sabaudo Line, (b) Italia Line.
Built by Stabilimento Tecnico, Trieste, Italy. Tonnage: 25,661. Dimensions: 624′ x 78′ (652′ o.l.). Twin-screw, 21 knots. Steam turbines. Two masts and two funnels. Launched, June 29, 1927. Maiden voyage: Genoa-Naples-New York, April 13, 1928. Transferred to South American service in 1932. Seized by Brazil in 1941. Later became an American troopship during World War II. Returned to South American service of Italia Line in 1949, after being reconditioned. Renamed: (a) **Monticello** (1941), (b) **Conte Grande** (1947). Withdrawn from Italia Line service in 1960. Placed in Lloyd Triestino service, December 1960. Sister ship: **Conte Biancamano.**

Conte Rosso (1922) Lloyd Sabaudo Line.
Built by Wm. Beardmore & Co., Glasgow, Scotland. Tonnage: 17,048. Dimensions: 570′ x 74′ (588′ o.l.). Twin-screw, 18½ knots. Four steam turbines. Two masts and two funnels. Passengers: 208 first, 268 second, 1,800 third. Maiden voyage: Genoa-Naples-New York, February 19, 1922. Transferred to South American service in 1928. Acquired

by Lloyd Triestino in 1932. Torpedoed and sunk by a British submarine off Sicily, May 24, 1941. Sister ship: **Conte Verde.**

Conte Verde   (1923)   Lloyd Sabaudo Line.
Built by Wm. Beardmore & Co., Glasgow, Scotland. Tonnage: 18,765. Dimensions: 570′ x 74′ (593′ o.l.). Twin-screw, 18½ knots. Steam turbines. Two masts and two funnels. Maiden voyage: Genoa-Naples-New York, April 21, 1923. Placed in service to South America in 1926. Transferred to the Far East service of Lloyd Triestino in 1932. Scuttled at Shanghai in 1943. Refloated by Japanese and converted to troopship. Sunk by United States aircraft in December 1944. Vessel was refloated in June 1949. Sold to Mitsui Line. Sister ship: **Conte Rosso.**

Continental   (1902)   Arnold Bernstein Line.
Built by Maryland Steel Co., Sparrows Point, Maryland. Tonnage: 10,005. Dimensions: 489′ x 58′. Twin-screw, 13 knots. Triple expansion engines. Two masts and one funnel. Passengers: 350. In New York-Plymouth-Antwerp service during 1948 season. Ex-**Tidewater** (1948), ex-**Permanente** (1946), ex-**Ancon** (1941), ex-**Shawmut.**

Coptic   (1881)   White Star Line.
Built by Harland & Wolff, Ltd., Belfast, Ireland. Tonnage: 4,384. Dimensions: 430′ x 42′. Single-screw, 15 knots. Compound engines. Four masts and one funnel. Triple expansion engines in 1894. Maiden voyage: Liverpool-New York, November 16, 1881. Transferred to trans-Pacific service in 1882. Renamed: (a) **Persia** (1906), (b) **Persia Maru** (1916). Broken up for scrap in 1926.

Corcovado   (1907)   Hamburg-American Line.
Tonnage: 8,374. Mainly in West Indies and Central American service. See PART III for details.

Cordillera   (1932)   Hamburg-American Line.
Built by Blohm & Voss, Hamburg, Germany. Tonnage: 12,055. Dimensions: 497′ x 65′. Twin-screw, 17 knots. Motorship. Two masts and one funnel. Built for the Hamburg-West Indies-Central America service. Suffered heavy damage at Swinemunde in May 1945. Sister ship: **Caribia.**

Corean   (1881)   Allan Line.
Built by Wm. Doxford & Sons, Ltd., Sunderland, England. Tonnage: 3,488. Dimensions: 360′ x 41′. Single-screw, 11 knots. Compound engines. Three masts and one funnel.

Iron hull. Maiden voyage: Glasgow-Quebec-Montreal, May 10, 1881. Scrapped in Italy, 1908. Sister ship: **Grecian.**

Corinthian (1856)   Allan Line.
Built by Wm. Denny & Bros., Dumbarton, Scotland. Tonnage: 1,517. Dimensions: 288' x 32'. Single-screw, 10 knots. Compound engines installed in 1870, when vessel was lengthened from 253 feet (1,214 tons) to 288 feet. Renamed: (a) **Genova** (1881), (b) **Foulazi Osmani** (Turkish), (c) **Sakaria.** Scrapped in 1912. Ex-**Damascus** (1870).

Corinthian (1899)   Allan Line.
Built by Workman, Clark & Co., Belfast, Ireland. Tonnage: 6,229. Dimensions: 430' x 54'. Single-screw, 12 knots. Triple expansion engines. Two masts and one funnel. Tonnage increased to 7,333 in 1908. Wrecked near Brier Island, Bay of Fundy, December 14, 1918. Sister ship: **Sicilian.**

Corsican (1907)   Allan Line.
Built by Barclay, Curle & Co., Ltd., Glasgow, Scotland. Tonnage: 11,419. Dimensions: 499' x 500'. Twin-screw, 16 knots. Triple expansion engines. Two masts and one funnel. Passengers: 208 first, 250 second, 1,000 third. Maiden voyage: Liverpool-St. John, New Brunswick, November 1907. Vessel was acquired by Canadian Pacific Line in 1917. Renamed: **Marvale** (1922). Similar ships: **Grampian** and **Hesperian.** Note: The **Corsican** was built to replace the **Bavarian,** which had been wrecked.

Covadonga (1884)   Spanish Line.
Built by Wm. Denny & Bros., Ltd., Dumbarton, Scotland. Tonnage: 5,161. Dimensions: 439' x 46'. Single-screw, 13 knots. Compound engines. Four masts and two funnels. Clipper bow. Renamed: (a) **Tainui** (1899), (b) **Astoria** (1899). Scrapped in 1911. Ex-**Tainui.**

*Covadonga (1953)   Spanish Line.
Built by Compania Euskalduna de Construction de Buques, Bilbao, Spain. Tonnage: 10,226. Dimensions: 464' x 62' (487' o.l.). Single-screw, 18 knots. Motorship. Launched as **Monastero de la Rabida.** Passengers: 105 first and 244 tourist. Maiden voyage: Bilbao-New York, August 27, 1953. Sister ship: **Guadalupe.**

Crefeld (1895)   North German Lloyd.
Built by "Vulkan", Stettin, Germany. Tonnage: 3,829. Dimensions: 355' x 43'. Single-screw, 12½ knots. Two

masts and one funnel. Renamed: **Espana No. 4** (Spanish Government).

Cretic (1902)   White Star Line.
   Built by Hawthorn, Leslie & Co., Newcastle, England. Tonnage: 13,507. Dimensions: 582' x 60' (601' o.l.). Twin-screw, 16 knots. Triple expansion engines. Four masts and one funnel. First voyage as **Cretic,** November 26, 1903, Liverpool-Boston. Renamed: **Devonian** (1923). Broken up for scrap in 1930. Ex-**Mayflower** (1903), ex-**Hanoverian** (1903).

Cristobal Colon (1866)   Spanish Line.
   Built by Palmers Shipbuilding & Iron Co., Jarrow-on-Tyne, England. Tonnage: 2,869. Dimensions: 335' x 42'. Single-screw, 10 knots. Two masts and one funnel. Purchased from Guion Line in 1875. Ex-**Minnesota.** Renamed: (a) **Savoie,** (b) **Savoia.**

Cristobal Colon (1923)   Spanish Line.
   Built by Sociedad Espanola de Construccion Naval, Ferrol, Spain. Tonnage: 10,833. Dimensions: 499' x 61'. Twin-screw, 17 knots. Four steam turbines. Two masts and one funnel. Wrecked near Bermuda, October 24, 1936. Sister ship: **Alfonso XIII.**

*Cristoforo Colombo (1953)   Italia Line.
   Built by Soc. Anon. Ansaldo, Sestri, Genoa, Italy. Tonnage: 29,083. Dimensions: 626' x 89' (697' o.l.). Twin-screw, 23 knots. Six steam turbines. Single mast and one funnel. Launched, May 10, 1953. Maiden voyage: Genoa-New York, July 15, 1954. Passengers: 300 first, 242 cabin, 703 tourist. Sister ship: **Andrea Doria.**

Cuba (1865)   Cunard Line.
   Built by Tod & McGregor, Glasgow, Scotland. Tonnage: 2,668. Dimensions: 338' x 42'. Single-screw, 12½ knots. Oscillating geared engines. Three masts and one funnel. On trials she did 13.6 knots. Iron hull. Passengers: 160 cabin. Maiden voyage: Liverpool-New York, December 3, 1864. Vessel was sold in 1876. Converted to a four-masted sailing ship; renamed **Earl of Beaconsfield.** Wrecked in 1887.

Cuba (1923)   French Line.
   Built by Swan, Hunter & Wigham Richardson, Ltd., Newcastle, England. Tonnage: 11,337. Dimensions: 476' x 62'. Twin-screw, 16 knots. Steam turbines. Two masts and two

funnels. Service: France-West Indies-Central America. She became a war casualty in the English Channel, April 6, 1945.

Cufic   (1888)   White Star Line.
  Built by Harland & Wolff, Ltd., Belfast, Ireland. Tonnage: 4,639. Dimensions: 430' x 45'. Single-screw, 13 knots. Triple expansion engines. Four masts and one funnel. Sold to Dominion Line in 1901. Renamed: (a) **Manxman**, (b) **Nuestra Senora de Guadalupe.** Lost in 1919.

Cymric   (1898)   White Star Line.
  Built by Harland & Wolff, Ltd., Belfast, Ireland. Tonnage: 13,096. Dimensions: 585' x 64' (599' o.l.). Twin-screw, 15 knots. Quadruple expansion engines. Four masts and one funnel. Launched in October 1897. Maiden voyage: Liverpool-New York, April 29, 1898. Torpedoed and sunk 140 miles from Foreland, May 8, 1916, with the loss of five lives.

Czar   (1912)   Russian-American Line.
  Built by Barclay, Curle & Co., Glasgow, Scotland. Tonnage: 6,503. Dimensions: 426' x 53'. Twin-screw, 16 knots. Quadruple expansion engines. Two masts and two funnels. Renamed: (a) **Estonia** (1921), (b) **Pulaski** (1930), (c) **Empire Penryn** (1946). Scrapped in 1949.

Czaritza   (1915)   Russian-American Line.
  Built by Barclay, Curle & Co., Glasgow, Scotland. Tonnage: 6,598. Dimensions: 440' x 53'. Twin-screw, 15½ knots. Quadruple expansion engines. Two masts and two funnels. Entered Archangel-New York service in 1915. Renamed: (a) **Lituania** (1921), (b) **Kosciuszko** (1930), (c) **Gdynia** (1940) Polish Navy, (d) **Empire Helford** (1946). Sold in December 1949; broken up for scrap in Germany.

Dakota   (1872)   Guion Line.
  Built by Palmers Shipbuilding & Iron Co., Jarrow-on-Tyne, England. Tonnage: 4,332. Dimensions: 400' x 43'. Single-screw, 15 knots. Compound engines. Two masts and one funnel. Iron hull. Launched, June 12, 1873. Maiden voyage: Liverpool-New York, July 21, 1875. Wrecked near Anglesey, Wales, May 9, 1877, with no loss of life. Sister ship: **Montana.**

Damascus   (1856)   Cunard Line.
  Built by Wm. Denny & Bros., Dumbarton, Scotland. Tonnage: 1,214. Dimensions: 253' x 31'. Single-screw, 10 knots. Two masts and two funnels. Iron hull. Inverted engines. Chartered to Allan Line in 1862. Purchased by Allan Line in 1865. Lengthened about 1870. Sold to Italian owners in

1879. Renamed: (a) **Corinthian** (1870), (b) **Genova** (1881), (c) **Foulazi Osmani,** (d) **Sakariah.**

Dania   (1889)   Hamburg-American Line.
   Built by Reihersteig Schiffswerfte, Hamburg, Germany.
   Tonnage: 3,898. Dimensions: 373' x 44'. Single-screw, 14
   knots. Compound engines. Two masts and one funnel.
   Passengers: 230 first and 1,000 third. Renamed: **Montserrat** (1900). Scrapped in 1927. Sister ships: **Russia**
   and **Scandia.**

Danmark   (1880)   Thingvalla Line (Danish).
   Built by C. Mitchell & Co., Newcastle, England. Tonnage:
   3,414. Dimensions: 340' x 40'. Single-screw, 11 knots.
   Compound engines. Three masts and one funnel. This emigrant ship foundered in mid-Atlantic, April 6, 1889, due to
   broken propeller shaft. Not one of the 735 persons aboard,
   of which 669 were passengers, was lost. The rescue was
   effected by the Atlantic Transport steamship **Missouri,** the
   entire company of passengers and crew of the **Danmark**
   being landed safely in the Azores several days later. Ex-**Jan
   Breydel** (1888). Similar ship: **Norge.**

Dante Alighieri   (1914)   Transatlantica Italiana.
   Built by Soc. Esercizio Baccini, Riva Trigoso, Genoa, Italy.
   Tonnage: 9,757. Dimensions: 483' x 59'. Twin-screw, 16
   knots. Quadruple expansion engines. Two masts and two
   funnels. Launched, November 28, 1914. Maiden voyage:
   Genoa-Naples-Palermo-New York, February 15, 1915.
   Renamed: **Asahi Maru** (1927). Scrapped in 1949. Sister
   ship: **Giuseppe Verdi.**

Darmstadt   (1890)   North German Lloyd.
   Built by Fairfield Shipbuilding & Engineering Co., Glasgow,
   Scotland. Tonnage: 5,012. Dimensions: 413' x 48'. Single-
   screw, 13 knots. Triple expansion engines. Two masts and
   one funnel. Passengers: 49 first, 38 second, 1,904 third.
   Services: Used in various trades. Made her final voyage to
   New York in 1910. Sold to the Turkish Government in 1911.
   Renamed: **Karadeniz** (Turkish). Sister ships: **Gera,
   Karlsruhe, Oldenburg, Stuttgart** and **Weimar.**

De Grasse   (1924)   French Line.
   Built by Cammell, Laird & Co., Birkenhead, England. Tonnage: 17,759. Dimensions: 552' x 71' (574' o.l.). Twin-screw,
   16 knots. Steam turbines. Two masts and two funnels.
   Launched, February 23, 1924. Passengers: 536 cabin, 410

third. Maiden voyage: Havre-New York, August 21, 1924. Scuttled by the Germans at Bordeaux in August 1944. Early in 1946 was raised and reconditioned for service. She was given a single funnel in the refit. Re-entered trans-Atlantic service July 1947. Transferred later to the West Indies trade. Sold to Canadian Pacific early in 1953, as a replacement for their fire-gutted **Empress of Canada.** Renamed: (a) **Empress of Australia** (1953), (b) **Venezuela** (1956).

De la Salle   (1924)   French Line.
Built by Barclay, Curle & Co., Glasgow, Scotland. Tonnage: 8,400. Dimensions: 440' x 56'. Twin-screw, 14 knots. Triple expansion engines. Two masts and two funnels. Launched, February 9, 1921. Maiden voyage was made in October 1921. Employed mainly in France-West Indies-Central American service. Torpedoed and sunk in Gulf of Benin, July 9, 1943. Sister ship: **Sinaia** (Fabre Line).

Delphic   (1897)   White Star Line.
Built by Harland & Wolff, Ltd., Belfast, Ireland. Tonnage: 8,273.   Dimensions: 475' x 55'.   Twin-screw, 11½ knots. Triple expansion engines. Four masts and one funnel. Torpedoed and sunk near Bishop Rock, August 16, 1917, with the loss of five lives.

Demerara   (1872)   Cunard Line.
Built by J. & G. Thomson, Ltd., Glasgow, Scotland. Tonnage: 1,904. Dimensions: 307' x 34'. Single-screw, 12 knots. Compound engines. Two masts and one funnel. Commenced a service to the West Indies, along with the **Trinidad,** in 1872. Transferred to Mediterranean trade at later date. Also used in service to Boston. Listed as missing in 1887. Sister ship: **Trinidad.**

Denmark   (1865)   National Line.
Built by M. Pearse & Co., Stockton, England. Tonnage: 2,870.   Dimensions: 343' x 42'.   Single-screw, 10 knots. Inverted engines. Three masts and one funnel. Launched in September 1865 as **Chilian** for West India & Pacific Line. Made her first voyage as **Denmark** from Liverpool to New York, May 9, 1866. Lengthened to 355 feet and other alterations in 1874. Tonnage increased to 3,725. Compound engines in 1880. Speed increased to 12 knots. Made her final voyage to New York in 1891. Scrapped in Italy, 1895.

Derfflinger (1907)   North German Lloyd.
Built by F. Schichau, Danzig, Germany. Tonnage: 9,144.
Dimensions: 463′ x 57′. Twin-screw, 14½ knots. Quad-
ruple expansion engines. Two masts and one funnel. Built
for Australia and Far East trades. Made a number of
Bremen-New York sailings. Note: Seized by the British in
October 1914 and renamed **Huntsgreen.** Vessel was resold
to North German Lloyd in 1923. Scrapped in Germany,
1933. Ex-**Huntsgreen** (1923), ex-**Derfflinger** (1914).
Sister ships: **Luetzow** and **Yorck.**

Deutschland (1866)   North German Lloyd.
Built by Caird & Co., Ltd., Greenock, Scotland. Tonnage:
2,873. Dimensions: 337′ x 40′. Single-screw, 11 knots.
Inverted engines. Two masts and one funnel. Iron hull.
Maiden voyage: Bremen-Southampton-New York, October
14, 1866. Compound engines in 1872. Wrecked on Goodwin
Sands, December 1875, with the loss of a number of lives.
Running mates: **America, Hansa, Herman, Union** and
Weser.

Deutschland (1899)   Hamburg-American Line.
Built by A. G. "Vulkan", Stettin, Germany. Tonnage:
16,502. Dimensions: 660′ x 67′ (686′ o.l.). Twin-screw, 23
knots. Quadruple expansion engines. Two masts and four
funnels. She had 16 boilers, 112 furnaces and developed
36,000 I.H.P. Building cost amounted to $3,200,000. Note:
The only Hamburg-American liner to hold the trans-Atlantic
speed record. Passengers: 690 first, 300 second, 280 third.
Maiden voyage: Hamburg-Plymouth-New York, July 4,
1900. Converted to cruise ship in 1910. Renamed: (a)
Victoria Luise (1911), (b) **Hansa** (1922). Scrapped in 1925.

Deutschland (1923)   Hamburg-American Line.
Built by Blohm & Voss, Hamburg, Germany. Tonnage:
20,607. Dimensions: 602 x 72′. Twin-screw, 16 knots.
Steam turbines. Four masts and two funnels. Passengers:
180 first, 400 second, 935 third. Maiden voyage: Hamburg-
Southampton-New York, March 27, 1924. Note: Lengthened
in 1933–34 to 645 feet (21,046 tons). Speed increased to 20
knots by new engines and new type bow to replace the
original straight stem. Sunk by Allied air attack off Neus-
tadt, May 3, 1945. Dismantled for scrap in 1948. Sister
ship: **Albert Ballin.** Note: The **New York** and **Hamburg**
were very similar, except they had only two masts.

Devonia   (1877)   Anchor Line.
Built by Barrow Shipbuilding Co., Barrow-in-Furness, England. Tonnage: 4,270. Dimensions: 400′ x 42′. Single-screw, 14 knots. Compound engines. Three masts and one funnel. Iron hull. Passengers: 200 first, 100 second, 800 third. Maiden voyage: Glasgow-New York, June 2, 1877. Broken up by shipbreakers at Hamburg in 1899. Running mates: **Anchoria, Bolivia, Circassia** and **Ethiopia.**

Devonian   (1900)   Leyland Line.
Built by Harland & Wolff, Ltd., Belfast, Ireland. Tonnage: 10,418. Dimensions: 552′ x 59′ (571′ o.l.). Single-screw, 14 knots. Triple expansion engines. Four masts and one funnel. Passengers: 135 first class. Torpedoed and sunk 20 miles from Tory Island, August 21, 1917, with the loss of two lives. Sister ship: **Winifredian.** Note: These cargo-passenger liners were in Liverpool-Boston service.

Devonian   (1902)   Leyland Line.
Built by Hawthorn, Leslie & Co., Newcastle, England. Tonnage: 13,507. Dimensions: 582′ x 60′. Twin-screw, 15 knots. Triple expansion engines. Four masts and one funnel. In Liverpool-Boston service. Broken up in Great Britain, 1930. Ex-**Cretic** (1923), ex-**Mayflower** (1903), ex-**Hanoverian** (1903).

Didam   (1891)   Holland-America Line.
Built by Nederlandsch Stoomvaart, Rotterdam, Netherlands. Tonnage: 2,751. Dimensions: 321′ x 40′. Single-screw, 12 knots. Triple expansion engines. Two masts and one funnel. In service Netherlands-New York or Baltimore, 1891–1895. Renamed: **Santarense** (1895). Sister ship: **Dubbeldam.**

Digby   (1913)   Furness-Warren Line.
Built by Irvine's Shipbuilding & Drydock Co., West Hartlepool, England. Tonnage: 3,960. Dimensions: 350′ x 50′. Single-screw, 13½ knots. Triple expansion engines. Two masts and one funnel. Passengers: 90 first class. Service: Liverpool-St. John's, Newfoundland-Halifax, Boston. Renamed: (a) **Dominica** (1925), (b) **Baltrover** (1936), (c) **Ionia** (1947).

Dominion   (1874)   Dominion Line.
Built by A. McMillan & Son, Dumbarton, Scotland. Tonnage: 3,175. Dimensions: 335′ x 38′. Single-screw, 11 knots. Compound engines. Three masts and one funnel. Passengers: 130 first and 1,000 third. Maiden voyage: Liverpool-

Quebec-Montreal, April 29, 1874. New triple expansion engines and boilers installed in 1890. Stranded at Berehaven, January 4, 1896. The wreck was broken up for scrap. Sister ship: **Ontario.**

Dominion   (1894)   Dominion Line.
Built by Harland & Wolff, Ltd., Belfast, Ireland. Tonnage: 7,036. Dimensions: 445' x 50'. Twin-screw, 13 knots. Triple expansion engines. Four masts and one funnel. Passengers: 200 first, 170 second, 750 third. Placed in the Liverpool-Quebec-Montreal service, May 7, 1898. Scrapped in 1922. Ex-**Prussia** (1898).

Donau   (1868)   North German Lloyd.
Built by Caird & Co., Greenock, Scotland. Tonnage: 3,073. Dimensions: 347' x 40'. Single-screw, 13 knots. Inverted engines. Two masts and one funnel. Iron hull. Launched, October 24, 1868. Compound engines in 1877. Speed increased to 14 knots. Sold to other shipowners in 1889. Destroyed by fire in North Atlantic on March 16, 1895. Vessel was abandoned. Sister ships: **Main** and **Rhein.**

Doric   (1923)   White Star Line.
Built by Harland & Wolff, Ltd., Belfast, Ireland. Tonnage: 16,484. Dimensions: 575' x 67' (601' o.l.). Twin-screw, 17 knots. Steam turbines. Two masts and two funnels. Launched, August 8, 1922. Passengers: 600 cabin, 1,700 third. Maiden voyage: Liverpool-Quebec-Montreal, July 6, 1923. Late in her career was used exclusively as a cruise ship. Seriously damaged in collision with French steamer **Formigny** during a dense fog off coast of Portugal, September 5, 1935. The **Doric** commenced to list, but was able to make the port of Vigo, and undergo temporary repairs. She left Tilbury dock on October 7, bound for the shipbreaker's yard where the work of reducing her to junk took almost a full year.

Dresden   (1889)   North German Lloyd.
Built by Bremer Vulkan, Vegesack, Germany. Tonnage: 4,580. Dimensions: 390' x 46'. Single-screw, 13 knots. Triple expansion engines. Two masts and one funnel. Passengers: 38 first, 20 second, 1,760. Services: North Atlantic, South America, Far East and Australia. Made a number of Bremen- New York, Baltimore voyages. Renamed: (a) **Helius** (1903), (b) **Tirimujghian** (Turkish). Sunk by the Russians during First World War.

Dresden   (1914)   North German Lloyd.
Built by Bremer Vulkan, Vegesack, Germany. Tonnage: 14,690. Dimensions: 550' x 67'. Twin-screw, 15 knots.

Quadruple expansion engines. Two masts and two funnels. Launched as the **Zeppelin** in June 1914, but completion was suspended until after the war. Finally completed in 1920 and turned over to the British. Sold to the Orient Line in 1920; renamed **Ormuz** of the Orient Line. Resold to her former owners the North German Lloyd in 1927 and given the name **Dresden.** Struck a submerged wreck off Norway, June 20, 1934, while on a cruise with 1,000 passengers. Four lives were lost during launching of lifeboats. Ex-**Ormuz** (1927), ex-**Zeppelin** (1921).

Drottningholm (1905) Swedish-American Line.
Built by Alexander Stephen & Sons, Ltd., Glasgow, Scotland. Tonnage: 11,182. Dimensions: 517' x 60' (538' o.l.). Triple-screw, 18 knots. Steam turbines. Two masts and one funnel. Passengers: 426 first, 286 second, 1,000 third. First voyage as **Drottningholm** from Gothenburg to New York, May 1920. New single reductioned geared steam turbines installed in 1922. Served as repatriation ship during World War II. Renamed: (a) **Brasil** (1948), (b) **Homeland** (1951). Scrapped in Italy, 1955. Ex-**Virginian** (1920).

Dubbeldam (1891) Holland-America Line.
Built by Bonn & Mees, Rotterdam, Netherlands. Tonnage: 2,831. Dimensions: 332' x 40'. Single-screw, 12 knots. Triple expansion engines. Two masts and one funnel. Passengers: 40 first and 464 third. Renamed: **Madeirense** (1895). Sister ship: **Didam.**

Duca d' Aosta (1908) Navigazione Generale Italiana.
Built by Cantieri Nav. Sicilani, Palermo, Italy. Tonnage: 7,804. Dimensions: 476' x 53'. Twin-screw, 16½ knots. Quadruple expansion engines. Two masts and two funnels. Launched, September 29, 1908. Maiden voyage: Genoa-Naples-New York, November 9, 1909. Served also in South American service. Scrapped in 1929. Sister ship: **Duca di Genova.**

Duca degli Abruzzi (1907) Navigazione Generale Italiana.
Built by Cantieri Nav. Riuniti, Spezia, Italy. Tonnage: 7,838. Dimensions: 475' x 53'. Twin-screw, 16½ knots. Quadruple expansion engines. Two masts and two funnels. Launched, May 5, 1907. Maiden voyage: Genoa-Naples-New York, February 3, 1908. Transferred later to South American service. Sold to Italian shipbreakers in May 1928. Broken up in 1929. Sister ship: **Principe Umberto.**

Duca di Galliera   (1883)   La Veloce Line.
    Built by Robert Napier & Sons, Glasgow, Scotland. Tonnage: 4,304. Dimensions: 400' x 44'. Single-screw, 14½ knots. Triple expansion engines. Three masts and two funnels. Scrapped in 1906. Ex-**Oaxaca**. Sister ship: **Duchessa di Genova.**

Duca di Genova   (1907)   Navigazione Generale Italiana.
    Built by Cantieri Nav. Riuniti, Spezia, Italy. Tonnage: 7,811. Dimensions: 475' x 53'. Twin-screw, 16½ knots. Quadruple expansion engines. Two masts and two funnels. Maiden voyage: Genoa-Naples-New York, October 7, 1908. Transferred to La Veloce Line in 1913. Made her final voyage to New York in 1916. Served in both the North Atlantic and the South American trades. Sunk near Cape Canet, February 6, 1918. Sister ship: **Duca d' Aosta.**

Duchess of Atholl   (1928)   Canadian Pacific Line.
    Built by Wm. Beardmore & Co., Glasgow, Scotland. Tonnage: 20,119. Dimensions: 581' x 75' (601' o.l.). Steam turbines. Two masts and two funnels. Passengers: 580 cabin, 480 tourist, 510 third. Launched in November 1927. Maiden voyage: Liverpool-Quebec-Montreal, July 13, 1928. Torpedoed and sunk in the South Atlantic, while bound from the Near East to England, October 10, 1942. Sister ships: **Duchess of Bedford, Duchess of Richmond** and **Duchess of York.**

Duchess of Bedford   (1928)   Canadian Pacific Line.
    Built by John Brown & Co., Clydebank, Glasgow, Scotland. Tonnage: 20,123. Dimensions: 581' x 75' (601' o.l.). Twin-screw, 18 knots. Steam turbines. Two masts and two funnels. Launched, January 25, 1928. Maiden voyage: Liverpool-Quebec-Montreal, June 1, 1928. Renamed: **Empress of France** (1948). Sister ships: **Duchess of Atholl, Duchess of Richmond** and **Duchess of York.**

Duchess of Richmond   (1928)   Canadian Pacific Line.
    Built by John Brown & Co., Clydebank, Glasgow, Scotland. Tonnage: 20,022. Dimensions: 581' x 75' (601' o.l.). Twin-screw, 18 knots. Steam turbines. Two masts and two funnels. Maiden voyage: Liverpool-St. John, N. B., March 15, 1929. Renamed: **Empress of Canada** (1947). Destroyed by fire at dock in Liverpool, January 25, 1953. Refloated in March 1954. Broken up for scrap in Italy, afterwards. Sister ships: **Duchess of Atholl, Duchess of Richmond** and **Duchess of York.**

Duchess of York   (1929)   Canadian Pacific Line.
  Built by John Brown & Co., Clydebank, Glasgow, Scotland.
  Tonnage: 20,021. Dimensions: 581' x 75' (601' o.l.). Twin-
  screw, 18 knots. Steam turbines. Two masts and two
  funnels. Launched, September 28, 1928. Maiden voyage:
  Liverpool-St. John, March 22, 1929. Regular service:
  Liverpool-Quebec-Montreal. Sunk by high flying Focke
  Wolfe bombers in the Atlantic, off the Spanish coast, July
  11, 1943, with the loss of 11 lives. Sister ships: **Duchess of
  Atholl, Duchess of Bedford** and **Duchess of Richmond.**

Duchessa di Genova   (1884)   La Veloce Line.
  Built by Robert Napier & Sons, Glasgow, Scotland. Tonnage: 4,304. Dimensions: 400' x 44'. Single-screw, 14½
  knots. Triple expansion engines. Three masts and two
  funnels. Services: Italy-South American; Italy-New York.
  First Genoa-New York sailing, March 17, 1901. Sold to
  other shipowners in 1905. Ex-**Mexico** (1887). Sister ship:
  Duca di Galliera.

Duilio   (1923)   Navigazione Generale Italiana.
  Built by S. A. Ansaldo, Sestri, Ponente, Italy. Tonnage:
  24,281. Dimensions: 602' x 76' (635' o.l.). Quadruple-screw,
  19 knots. Four steam turbines. Two masts and two funnels.
  Laid down, May 30, 1914. Launched, January 9, 1916.
  Maiden voyage: Genoa-Naples-New York, October 30, 1923.
  Passengers: 280 first, 670 second, 600 third. Transferred to
  South American route in 1928. Acquired by Lloyd Triestino
  in 1935. Served as an Italian hospital ship in World War II.
  Bombed and sunk at Trieste, July 10, 1944, while trying to
  escape from Allied forces in the closing days of the Italian
  invasion. Sister ship: **Giulio Cesare.**

Dwinsk   (1897)   Russian-American Line.
  Built by Harland & Wolff, Ltd., Belfast, Ireland. Tonnage:
  8,173. Dimensions: 469' x 53'. Twin-screw, 15 knots. Triple
  expansion engines. Two masts and one funnel. Note:
  Russian-American Line was owned by Russian East Asiatic
  Steamship Company. Service: Libau-New York. Torpedoed
  and sunk 400 miles from Bermuda, June 18, 1918, with the
  loss of 34 lives. Ex-**C. F. Tietgen** (1913), ex-**Rotterdam**
  (1906).

Edam   (1878)   Holland-America Line.
  Built by Harland & Wolff, Ltd., Belfast, Ireland. Tonnage:
  3,329. Dimensions: 389' x 37'. Single-screw, 12 knots.
  Compound engines. Four masts and one funnel. Iron hull.

Passengers: 70 first and 850 third. Service: Amsterdam-New York. Sold to Italian owners in 1899. Ex-**Rotterdam** (1896), ex-**British Empire** (1886).

Edam   (1880)   Holland-America Line.
Built by A. McMillan & Co., Dumbarton, Scotland. Tonnage: 2,950. Dimensions: 320' x 39'. Single-screw, 10 knots. Compound engines. Two masts and one funnel. Iron hull. Maiden voyage: Rotterdam-New York, October 29, 1881. In collision with steamship **Lepanto,** September 21, 1882, off Sandy Hook and subsequently sank.   Sister ship: **Amsterdam.**

Edam   (1883)   Holland-America Line.
Built by Nederlandsch Stoomvart Maats., Rotterdam, Netherlands.   Tonnage: 3,130.   Dimensions: 328' x 41'. Single-screw, 12 knots. Compound engines. Two masts and one funnel. Passengers: 50 first and 424 third. Steel hull. Sank after colliding with **Turkistan** off Isle of Wight, September 19, 1895, with no loss of life.

Edam   (1921)   Holland-America Line.
Built by Kon. Maats. de Schelde, Flushing, Netherlands. Tonnage: 8,871.   Dimensions: 450' x 58'.   Single-screw, 13 knots. Steam turbines. Two masts and two funnels. Passengers: Cabin and third class. Service: Rotterdam-Cuba-Mexico. Also made sailings to New York and Baltimore. At later date altered to single funnel. Arrived at Hong Kong, September 20, 1954, so as to be broken up for scrap. Sister ships: **Leerdam, Maasdam** and **Spaarndam.**

Edinburgh   (1855)   Glasgow & New York Steam Ship Co. (British).
Built by Tod & McGregor, Glasgow, Scotland. Tonnage: 2,197.   Dimensions: 301' x 40'.   Single-screw, 10 knots. Three masts and one funnel. Clipper bow. Iron hull. Maiden voyage: Glasgow-New York, December 28, 1855. Acquired by Inman Line in 1859. Converted to cable ship in 1870. Renamed: **Amsterdam.** Sold to Italy in 1887. Broken up for scrap in early 1890's.

Edison   (1896)   Byron Steamship Co. (Greek).
Built by "Vulkan", Stettin, Germany. Tonnage: 11,103. Dimensions: 523' x 60'. Twin-screw, 15 knots. Quadruple expansion engines. Two masts and two funnels. Passengers: 226 first, 255 second, 1,600 third. Service: Piraeus-New York. Scrapped in Italy, 1935. Ex-**Omar** (1924), ex-**Konigin Luise** (1920).

Egypt (1871) National Line (British).
Built by Liverpool Shipbuilding Co., Liverpool, England.
Tonnage: 4,670. Dimensions: 440' x 43'. Single-screw, 12½
knots. Compound engines. Four masts and two funnels.
Iron hull. Launched, February 9, 1871. Frequently made
voyage from Queenstown to Sandy Hook in nine days.
Tonnage at later date listed as 5,089. Burned and abandoned
at sea on July 19, 1890, with no loss of life. Similar ship:
Spain.

Egyptian Monarch (1881) Monarch Line (British).
Built by A. McMillan & Son, Dumbarton, Scotland. Ton-
nage: 3,916. Dimensions: 360' x 43'. Single-screw, 11 knots.
Compound engines. Four masts and one funnel. Passengers:
40 first and 1,000 third. Maiden voyage: London-New York,
June 4, 1881. Quadruple expansion engines in 1895. Re-
named: **Ohio.** Scrapped about 1904. Sister ship: **Persian
Monarch.**

Eider (1884) North German Lloyd.
Built by John Elder & Co., Glasgow, Scotland. Tonnage:
4,719. Dimensions: 430' x 47'. Single-screw, 17 knots.
Compound engines. Four masts and two funnels. Iron hull.
Maiden voyage: Bremen-Southampton-New York, March
17, 1884. Lost by stranding on the Isle of Wight, January
31, 1892, with no loss of life. The wreck was subsequently
broken up for scrap. Sister ship: **Ems.**

Eisenach (1908) North German Lloyd.
Built by Bremer Vulkan, Vegesack, Germany. Tonnage:
6,757. Dimensions: 419' x 54'. Single-screw, 12 knots.
Quadruple expansion engines. Two masts and one funnel.
Renamed: **Santarem.** Sister ship: **Coburg.**

Elbe (1881) North German Lloyd.
Built by John Elder & Co., Glasgow, Scotland. Tonnage:
4,897. Dimensions: 418' x 44' (440' o.l.). Single-screw, 17
knots. Compound engines. Four masts and two funnels.
Iron hull. Hurricane deck amidship was 180 feet long. It
was used as a promenade deck for first class passengers.
Maiden voyage: Bremen-Southampton-New York, June 24,
1881. Sunk by collision with steamer **Crathie** in North Sea,
January 30, 1895, and went down within a few minutes with
the loss of over 330 lives. Sister ships: **Fulda** and **Werra.**

Elysia (1873) Anchor Line (British).
Built by John Elder & Co., Glasgow, Scotland. Tonnage:
2,714. Dimensions: 351' x 35'. Single-screw, 13 knots.

Compound engines. Two masts and one funnel. Launched, June 28, 1873. Passengers: 100 first, 40 second, 500 third. Maiden voyage: Glasgow-New York, October 11, 1873. Sister ship: **Utopia.**

Empress of Australia   (1914)   Canadian Pacific Line.
Built by A. G. "Vulkan" Werke, Stettin, Germany. Tonnage: 21,833. Dimensions: 588′ x 75′ (615′ o.l.). Twin-screw, 19 knots. Steam turbines. Two masts and three funnels. Passengers: 400 first, 150 second, 630 third. Services: (a) Trans-Pacific, (b) Trans-Atlantic. Made her first Southampton-Cherbourg-Quebec-Montreal sailing in June 1927. Note: Launched as the **Tirpitz** (Hamburg-American Line), December 20, 1913. Construction work was held up during the first part of First World War, but in 1916 the Kaiser ordered her to be completed as a royal yacht in which to receive the Allied naval fleets in the event the Germans were victorious. However, such not being the case, this beautiful liner was ceded to Great Britain in 1919. Sold to Canadian Pacific Line in 1922. After being re-engined was able to make 22.4 knots. Sold to British shipbreakers in May 1952. Ex-**Empress of China** (only for a brief time), ex-**Tirpitz** (1922).

Empress of Australia   (1924)   Canadian Pacific Line.
Built by Cammell, Laird & Co., Birkenhead, England. Tonnage: 19,665. Dimensions: 552′ x 71′ (574′ o.l.). Twin-screw, 16 knots. Steam turbines. Two masts and one funnel. Passengers: 220 first, 444 tourist. Purchased as a replacement for the destroyed **Empress of Canada.** First voyage: Liverpool-Quebec-Montreal, April 28, 1953. Sold to Grimaldi Line. Renamed: **Venezuela** (1955). Ex-**De Grasse** (1953).

Empress of Britain   (1906)   Canadian Pacific Line.
Built by Fairfield Shipbuilding & Engineering Co., Glasgow, Scotland. Tonnage: 14,189. Dimensions: 548′ x 65′ (570′ o.l.). Twin-screw, 20 knots. Quadruple expansion engines. Two masts and two funnels. Passengers: 310 first, 350 second, 800 third. Maiden voyage: Liverpool-Quebec, May 5, 1906. Note: First "Empress" of the North Atlantic service. Made the Liverpool-Halifax run in 5 days, 18 hours, 18 minutes. Converted to auxiliary cruiser in World War I. Resumed regular service in March 1919. Service speed listed as 18 knots. Renamed: **Montroyal** (1924). Sold to Norwegian shipbreakers in April 1930. Sister ship: **Empress of Ireland.**

Empress of Britain (1931) Canadian Pacific Line.
Built by John Brown & Co., Clydebank, Glasgow, Scotland.
Tonnage: 42,348. Dimensions: 733' x 97' (758' o.l.). Quad-
ruple-screw, 24 knots. Steam turbines. Two masts and
three funnels. Top of masts were 208 feet above water line.
Funnels measured 27 feet across at widest part and 35 feet
fore and aft. Cost $15,000,000 to build. Passengers: 452
first, 260 tourist, 470 third. Laid down, November 28, 1928.
Launched, June 11, 1930. Maiden voyage: Southampton-
Cherbourg-Quebec, May 27, 1931. Spent much time as a
cruise ship. The largest Allied liner lost in World War II.
Disabled by German bombers off the Irish coast, October
26, 1940, and two days later, on the 28th, she was sunk by
German submarine "U-32" while being towed.

*Empress of Britain (1955) Canadian Pacific Line.
Built by Fairfield Shipbuilding & Engineering Co., Glasgow,
Scotland. Tonnage: 25,516. Dimensions: 600' x 85' (640'
o.l.). Twin-screw, 20 knots. Two steam turbines. Single
mast and one funnel. Laid down on September 30, 1953.
Launched, June 22, 1955. Maiden voyage: Liverpool-
Quebec-Montreal, April 19, 1956. Sister ship: **Empress of
England.** Similar to the new (1961) **Empress of Canada.**

Empress of Canada (1922) Canadian Pacific Line.
Built by Fairfield Shipbuilding Co., Glasgow, Scotland.
Tonnage: 21,517. Dimensions: 627' x 77' (653' o.l.). Twin-
screw, 20 knots. Eight steam turbines. Two masts and
three funnels. Note: In trans-Atlantic service for only a
short time, as she was transferred to the trans-Pacific trade.
Torpedoed and sunk, March 13, 1943.

Empress of Canada (1928) Canadian Pacific Line.
Built by John Brown & Co., Clydebank, Glasgow, Scotland.
Tonnage: 20,325. Dimensions: 581' x 75'. Twin-screw, 18
knots. Steam turbines. Two masts and two funnels. Speed
increased to 20 knots. Refitted after war service, 1946.
First voyage as **Empress of Canada** was in July 1947.
Accommodation for 400 first class and 300 tourist. Destroyed
by fire at her Liverpool dock, January 25, 1953. The cap-
sized burned out hulk was later refloated and in September
1954 was towed to Italy to be broken up for scrap. Ex-
Duchess of Richmond (1947). Sister ship: **Empress of
France.**

*Empress of Canada (1960) Canadian Pacific Line.
Built by Vickers-Armstrongs, Ltd., Walker-on-Tyne, Newcastle, England. Tonnage: 27,500. Dimensions: 650' x 86'.

Twin-screw, 21 knots. Steam turbines. Single mast and one funnel. Laid down, January 27, 1959. Launched, May 10, 1960. Passengers: 200 first and 860 tourist. Maiden voyage in spring of 1961. Running mates: **Empress of Britain** and **Empress of England.**

*Empress of England** (1957)   Canadian Pacific Line.
Built by Vickers-Armstrongs, Ltd., Newcastle, England. Tonnage: 25,585. Dimensions: 600' x 85' (640' o.l.). Twin-screw, 20 knots. Steam turbines. Single mast and one funnel. Launched, May 9, 1956. Maiden voyage; Liverpool-Quebec-Montreal, April 18, 1957. Passengers: 160 first, 898 tourist. Sister ship: **Empress of Britain.** Similar to: **Empress of Canada.**

Empress of France (1913)   Canadian Pacific Line.
Built by Wm. Beardmore & Co., Glasgow, Scotland. Tonnage: 18,357. Dimensions: 571' x 72' (600' o.l.). Quadruple-screw, 19½ knots. Steam turbines. Two masts and two funnels. Passengers: 287 first, 505 second, 848 third. First voyage as **Empress of France** Liverpool to Quebec, November 14, 1919. Made a world cruise from New York in 1923. Placed in trans-Pacific service in December 1928 for a year. Last voyage: Southampton-Quebec, October 2, 1931. Laid up until scrapped in 1935. Ex-**Alsatian** (1919).

Empress of France (1928)   Canadian Pacific Line.
Built by John Brown & Co., Clydebank, Glasgow, Scotland. Tonnage: 20,448. Dimensions: 581' x 75' (601' o.l.). Twin-screw, 18 knots. Steam turbines. Two masts and two funnels. Reconditioned in 1947 after war service. For a time it was thought that she would be given the name **Empress of India.** However this contemplated name change did not take place and instead was renamed **Empress of France.** Re-entered the Liverpool-Quebec-Montreal service on September 1, 1948. New modern funnels installed in 1958. Scrapped in 1961. Ex-**Duchess of Bedford** (1948). Sister ship: **Empress of Canada.**

Empress of India (1908)   Canadian Pacific Line.
Built by J. C. Tecklenborg, Geestemunde, Germany. Tonnage: 16,992. Dimensions: 590' x 68'. Twin-screw, 17 knots. Quadruple expansion engines. Two masts and two funnels. Made her first voyage as **Empress of India** in June 1922. Renamed: (a) **Montlaurier** (1922), (b) **Monteith** (June 1925), (c) **Montnairn** (September 1925). Sold for scrap in 1929. Ex-**Prinz Friedrich Wilhelm** (1921).

Empress of Ireland   (1906)   Canadian Pacific Line.
Built by Fairfield Shipbuilding & Engineering Co., Glasgow, Scotland.   Tonnage: 14,191.   Dimensions: 548′ x 65′ (570′ o.l.).   Twin-screw, 19 knots.   Quadruple expansion engines. Two masts and two funnels.   Passengers: 310 first, 350 second, 800 third.   Maiden voyage: Liverpool-Quebec, June 23, 1906.   Sunk in collision with the **Storstad** during a thick fog that prevailed on the St. Lawrence River, May 29, 1914. She went down within 15 minutes, with the loss of 1,024 lives.   Rated as one of the worst disasters on the Atlantic. Sister ship: **Empress of Britain.**

Empress of Scotland   (1905)   Canadian Pacific Line.
Built by A. G. "Vulkan", Stettin, Germany.   Tonnage: 25,160.   Dimensions: 677′ x 77′ (699′ o.l.).   Twin-screw, 18 knots.   Quadruple expansion engines.   Four masts and two funnels.   Acquired by Canadian Pacific Line in 1922 and reconditioned for their services.   Passengers: 459 first, 478 second, 536 third.   Sold for scrap in November 1930, but caught fire on December 10th, at the shipbreakers yard at Blyth.   A second fire broke out on May 6, 1931.   Completely dismantled by October 1931.   **Ex-Kaiserin Auguste Victoria.**

Empress of Scotland   (1930)   Canadian Pacific Line.
Built by Fairfield Shipbuilding & Engineering Co., Glasgow, Scotland.   Tonnage: 26,313.   Dimensions: 644′ x 83′ (666′ o.l.).   Twin-screw, 21 knots.   Steam turbines.   Two masts and three funnels.   Note: After war service was reconditioned in 1948 for trans-Atlantic trade.   First Liverpool-Quebec sailing was made in May 1950, completing the crossing from Greenock to Father Point, Quebec, in 5 days, 36 minutes. Sold to German owners in January 1958.   Renamed: **Hanseatic** (1958) Hamburg Atlantic Line.   **Ex-Empress of Japan** (1942).

Ems   (1884)   North German Lloyd.
Built by John Elder & Co., Glasgow, Scotland.   Tonnage: 4,933.   Dimensions: 430′ x 47′.   Single-screw, 16 knots. Compound engines.   Four masts and two funnels.   Maiden voyage: Bremen-Southampton-New York, June 2, 1884. Reduced to two masts in 1896.   Transferred to Mediterranean-New York service.   Renamed: **Lake Simcoe** (1901). Scrapped in 1904.   Sister ship: **Eider.**

England   (1865)   National Line (British).
Built by Palmer's Shipbuilding & Iron Co., Jarrow-on-Tyne-England.   Tonnage: 3,440.   Dimensions: 355′ x 42′.   Single,

screw, 10 knots. Inverted engines. Three masts and one funnel. Lengthened to 438 feet (4,898 tons) in 1873. Compound engines. Speed increased to 12 knots. Vessel was sold in 1896. Sister ship: **Scotland.**

Entella   (1883)   Navigazione Generale Italiana.
Built by Blackwood & Gordon, Port Glasgow, Scotland. Tonnage: 2,258. Dimensions: 299' x 37'. Single-screw, 12 knots. Compound engines. Two masts and one funnel. Iron hull. Vessel was acquired from Raggio & Company in 1885. Sold to Soc. Nazionale di Servizi Marittimi in 1910.

Ericsson   (1853)   Collins Line.
Built by Perrin, Stack & Patterson, New York, N. Y. Tonnage: 1,920. Dimensions: 254' x 40'. Paddle-wheels, 10 knots. Side lever engines. Two masts and four funnels arranged two abreast. Wooden hull. In Collins Line service 1856–1857. Served as a transport during the American Civil War.

Erie   (1868)   American Steamship Company of Boston.
Built by Jackman of Newburyport, Massachusetts. Tonnage: 3,000. Dimensions: 322' x 43'. Single-screw, 11 knots. Vertical geared engines. Three masts and two funnels. Wooden hull. Clipper bow. Sold to the United States & Brazil Mail Steamship Company in 1870. Destroyed by fire near Pernambuco, January 1, 1873. Sister ship: **Ontario.**
Note: These wooden steamers were built for service between Boston and Liverpool. The venture was not successful and so the ships were soon sold.

Erin   (1864)   National Line (British).
Built by Palmer's Shipbuilding & Iron Co., Jarrow-on-Tyne, England. Tonnage: 3,319. Dimensions: 370' x 41'. Single-screw, 10 knots. Inverted type engines. Three masts and one funnel. Clipper bow. Iron hull. Launched, June 18, 1864. Maiden voyage: Liverpool-New York, August 2, 1864. Tonnage increased to 3,956 in 1872. Lengthened to 413 feet (4,577 tons) in 1877. After compound engines had been installed speed was increased to $12\frac{1}{2}$ knots. Sailed from New York for England on December 31, 1889, with 72 people on board and was never heard of again. Sister ship: **Helvetia.**

Erria   (1932)   Danish East Asiatic Co.
Built by Nakskov Skibsvaerft, Nakskov, Denmark. Tonnage: 8,786. Dimensions: 440' x 62' (463' o.l.). Twin-screw,

15½ knots. Motorship. Four masts and no funnels. In Copenhagen-New York service, 1949–1951. Burned off Portland, Oregon, December 1951. Vessel was salved.

Espagne (1909)   French Line.
Built by Chantier & Ateliers de Provence, Port de Bouc, France. Tonnage: 11,155. Dimensions: 539' x 60'. Twin-screw, 15½ knots. Triple expansion engines. Two masts and two funnels. Launched, December 19, 1909. Passengers: 296 first, 106 second, 86 third. Maiden voyage: France-West Indies, October 5, 1910. She was also in the New York service. Scrapped in France, 1934.

Espana (1873)   Spanish Line.
Built by Robert Napier & Sons, Glasgow, Scotland. Tonnage: 2,679. Dimensions: 335' x 37'. Single-screw. Compound engines. Two masts and one funnel. Iron hull. Scrapped in 1898. Ex-**Edinburgh Castle** (1880).

Estonia (1889)   Russian-American Line.
Built by Harland & Wolff, Ltd., Belfast, Ireland. Tonnage: 4,250. Dimensions: 400' x 45'. Single-screw, 14 knots. Triple expansion engines. Four masts and one funnel. Destroyed by fire at sea in 1913. Ex-**Indien** (1907), ex-**Yorkshire** (1905).

Estonia (1912)   Baltic American Line (Danish).
Built by Barclay, Curle & Co., Glasgow, Scotland. Tonnage: 6,516. Dimensions: 425' x 53'. Twin-screw, 16 knots. Quadruple expansion engines. Two masts and two funnels. First Libau-New York sailing, in February 1921. Vessel sold to Polish Transatlantic Shipping Company (Gdynia-America Shipping Line) in 1930. Renamed: (a) **Pulaski** (1930), (b) **Empire Penryn** (1946). Broken up by British shipbreakers in 1949. Ex-**Czar** (1921).

Ethiopia (1873)   Anchor Line.
Built by Alexander Stephen & Sons, Ltd., Glasgow, Scotland. Tonnage: 4,005. Dimensions: 402' x 40'. Single-screw, 13½ knots. Compound engines. Three masts and one funnel. Passengers: 110 first, 110 second, 800 third. Launched, August 12, 1873. Maiden voyage: Glasgow-New York, December 13, 1873. Final voyage to New York in 1907. Sold for scrap in 1907. Sister ship: **Bolivia.**

Etna (1855)   Cunard Line.
Built by Caird & Co., Greenock, Scotland. Tonnage: 2,215. Dimensions: 304' x 37'. Single-screw, 11 knots. Geared

beam engines. Three masts and one funnel. Clipper bow.
Iron hull. Sold to Inman Line in 1860. Lengthened to 349
feet (2,655 tons) in 1871. Compound engines installed.
Renamed: **City of Bristol.** Vessel sold in 1880. Sister
ship: **Jura.**

Etruria   (1884)   Cunard Line.
Built by John Elder & Co., Glasgow, Scotland. (Later
became Fairfield Shipbuilding & Engineering Co.). Tonnage:
8,127. Dimensions: 501′ x 57′ (520′ o.l.). Single-screw, 19
knots. Compound engines. 14,500 I.H.P. Three masts and
two funnels. Steel hull. Passengers: 550 cabin, 800 third.
Accommodation later was changed to 550 first, 160 second
and 800 third. The last single-screw trans-Atlantic liner to
break the speed record. Maiden voyage: Liverpool-New
York, April 25, 1886. Broken up for scrap at Preston in
1909. Sister ship: **Umbria.**

Eugenia   (1906)   Austro-American Line.
Built by Russell & Co., Port Glasgow, Scotland. Tonnage:
4,903. Dimensions: 385′ x 49′. Single-screw, 13 knots.
Triple expansion engines. Two masts and one funnel.
Torpedoed and sunk in 1916.

Europa   (1848)   Cunard Line.
Built by John Wood, Port Glasgow, Scotland. Tonnage:
1,834. Dimensions: 251′ x 38′. Paddle-wheels, 10 knots.
Side lever engines. Three masts and one funnel. Clipper
bow. Wooden hull. Maiden voyage: Liverpool-Halifax-
Boston, July 15, 1848. Sold to new owners in 1867. Lengthened
and put back in service. Lost by stranding in 1874. Sister
ships: **America, Canada** and **Niagara.**

Europa   (1867)   Anchor Line.
Built by Alexander Stephen & Sons, Ltd., Glasgow, Scotland.
Tonnage: 1,746. Dimensions: 278′ x 34′. Single-screw, 10
knots. Inverted engines. Three masts and one funnel. Iron
hull. Compound engines in 1874. Maiden voyage: Glasgow-
New York, September 25, 1867. Lengthened to 338 feet
(2,277 tons) in 1874. Sunk in collision, July 17, 1878.

Europa   (1907)   Fabre Line (French).
Built by Russell & Co., Port Glasgow, Scotland. Tonnage:
6,122. Dimensions: 415′ x 49′. Twin-screw, 16 knots. Triple
expansion engines. Two masts and one funnel. Renamed:
Braga (1920). Ex-**Laura** (1917).

Europa   (1907)   La Veloce Line.
>   Built by Cantieri Navali Siciliani, Palermo, Italy. Tonnage: 7,870. Dimensions: 454' x 53'. Twin-screw, 15 knots. Triple expansion engines. Two masts and two funnels. Maiden voyage: Genoa-New York, May 1907. Transferred to Navigazione Generale Italiana in 1922. Also made voyages to South America. Scrapped in 1928.

Europa   (1923)   Incres Line (Arnold Bernstein Co.).
>   Built by Armstrong, Whitworth & Co., Newcastle, England. Tonnage: 16,576. Dimensions: 551' x 72' (570' o.l.). Twin-screw, 16 knots. Steam turbines. Two masts and one funnel. Commenced New York-Plymouth-Antwerp service, July 5, 1950. Renamed: **Nassau** (1951). In New York-Nassau cruise service. Ex-**Rimutaka** (1950), ex-**Mongolia** (1938).

Europa   (1930)   North German Lloyd.
>   Built by Blohm & Voss, Hamburg, Germany. Tonnage: 49,746. Dimensions: 890' x 102' (936' o.l.). Quadruple-screw, 28 knots. Steam turbines. Two masts and two funnels. Launched in August 1928. From keel to top of masts 236 feet. Funnels measured 50' x 21'. Cost $20,000,-000 to build. At one time carried an airplane that was launched from the ship by a catapult. Maiden voyage: Bremen-Southampton-New York, March 19, 1930. A serious fire had delayed her completion for about a year. She became a trans-Atlantic record breaker, by making the westward passage in 4 days, 17 hours, 6 minutes. Remained tied up in a German harbor throughout World War II. After the war was used as a troopship to bring back soldiers to the United States. The liner was turned over to the French in 1946. Renamed: **Liberte** (1946). While being reconditioned at Havre for service, she was torn from her moorings during a severe gale in December 1946, and sustained serious damage when she crashed into the sunken hulk of the former French luxury liner **Paris.** As a result her hull was ripped open and she sank in the water of the harbor, but was subsequently refloated and reconditioned at great cost. Commenced her maiden voyage as a French liner in August 1950. Note: See **Liberte** for additional information. Sister ship: **Bremen.**

Europe   (1864)   French Line.
>   Built by Scott's Shipbuilding & Engineering Co., Greenock, Scotland. Tonnage: 3,443. Dimensions: 350' x 42'. Paddle-wheels, 12 knots. Side lever engines. Two masts and two funnels. Iron hull. Lengthened to 394 feet (5,333 tons) in

1873. Altered to screw propulsion and mizzen mast added. Attained a speed of 14.8 knots on her new trials. Abandoned at sea while bound from Havre to New York, April 4, 1874, with no loss of life. Running mates: **Lafayette** and **Washington.**

European   (1866)   Allan Line.
Built by Malcolmson Bros., Waterford, Ireland. Tonnage: 2,708. Dimensions: 236' x 36'. Single-screw, 10 knots. Three masts and one funnel. Clipper bow. Iron hull. Compound engines in 1875. Note: Laid down as **Manhattan.** However was completed as **William Penn** in 1866. Purchased by Allan Line in 1869. Renamed: **European** (1869). In their service for only a brief time, as she was resold in 1872. She broke in two while entering dock at Birkenhead in 1875. Repaired and lengthened. Sold to new owners in 1884.

Evangeline   (1900)   Furness Withy & Co., Ltd.
Built by Alexander Stephen & Sons, Ltd., Glasgow, Scotland. Tonnage: 3,944. Dimensions: 371' x 45'. Single-screw, 14 knots. Triple expansion engines. Two masts and one funnel. Clipper bow. Passengers: 70 first, 24 second, 48 third. Maiden voyage was made from London to Halifax and St. John, N. B. in 1900. Sold to Lamport & Holt Company in 1901. Renamed: **Tennyson** (1901). Sister ship: **Loyalist.**

Excalibur   (1930)   American Export Lines.
Built by New York Shipbuilding Corp., Camden, N. J. Tonnage: 9,359. Dimensions: 450' x 61' (474' o.l.). Single-screw, 16 knots. Steam turbines. Two masts and one funnel. Passengers: 125 in one class. Service: New York-Mediterranean. Renamed: **Joseph Hewes** (1941). Torpedoed and sunk by enemy submarine off the coast of Morocco, November 11, 1942, during the North African invasion. Sister ships: **Excambion, Exochorda** and **Exeter.**

*Excalibur   (1944)   American Export Lines.
Built by Bethlehem Shipbuilding Corp., Sparrows Point, Maryland. Tonnage: 9,644. Dimensions: 451' x 66' (473' o.l.). Single-screw, 18 knots. Two steam turbines. Two masts and one funnel. Passengers: 125 first class. First voyage: New York-Mediterranean, September 24, 1948. Ex-**Duchess** (1948) United States Navy. Sister ships: **Excambion, Exeter** and **Exochorda.** Note: Originally designed and built as freighters, but were later converted

to combination passenger-freight carriers for the American Export Lines.

Excambion   (1931)   American Export Lines.
Built by New York Shipbuilding Corp., Camden, N. J. Tonnage: 9,360.   Dimensions: 450′ x 61′.   Single-screw, 16 knots.   Steam turbines.   Two masts and one funnel.   Renamed: **John Penn** (1941) United States Navy.   Sunk by Japanese torpedo bomber off Guadalcanal, August 13, 1943. Sister ships: **Exeter, Excalibur** and **Exochorda.**

Excambion   (1944)   American Export Lines.
Built by Bethlehem Shipbuilding Corp., Sparrows Point, Maryland.   Tonnage: 9,644.   Dimensions: 451′ x 66′ (473′ o.l.).   Steam turbines.   Two masts and one funnel.   Withdrawn from service recently.   Ex-**Queens** (1948).   Sister ships: **Excalibur, Exeter** and **Exochorda.**

Exeter   (1931)   American Export Lines.
Built by New York Shipbuilding Corp., Camden, N. J. Tonnage: 9,360.   Dimensions: 450′ x 61′.   Single-screw, 16 knots.   Steam turbines.   Two masts and one funnel.   Renamed **Edward Rutledge** (1941).   Torpedoed and sunk near Casablanca, November 12, 1942.   Sister ships: **Excalibur, Excambion** and **Exochorda.**

*Exeter   (1945)   American Export Lines.
Built by Bethlehem Shipbuilding Corp., Sparrows Point, Md.   Tonnage: 9,644.   Dimensions: 451′ x 66′ (473′ o.l.). Single-screw, 18 knots.   Steam turbines.   Two masts and one funnel.   Passengers: 124 first.   Ex-**Shelby** (1948).   Sister ships: **Excalibur, Excambion** and **Exochorda.**

Exochorda   (1931)   American Export Lines.
Built by New York Shipbuilding Corp., Camden, N.J. Tonnage: 9,359.   Dimensions: 450′ x 61′.   Single-screw, 16 knots.   Steam turbines.   Two masts and one funnel.   Service: New York-Mediterranean ports.   Renamed: (a) **Harry Lee** (1940) United States Navy, (b) **Tarsus** (1946) Turkish. Sister ships: **Excambion, Excalibur** and **Exeter.**

Exochorda   (1944)   American Export Lines.
Built by Bethlehem Shipbuilding Corp., Sparrows Point, Md.   Tonnage: 9,644.   Dimensions: 451′ x 66′ (473′ o.l.). Single-screw, 18 knots.   Steam turbines.   Two masts and one funnel. Note: Withdrawn from service recently. Ex-**Dauphin** (1948).   Sister ships: **Excalibur, Excambion** and **Exeter.**

Falstria   (1945)   East Asiatic Co. (Danish).
Built by Nakskov Skibsvaerft, Nakskov, Denmark. Tonnage: 6,993. Dimensions: 432' x 63' (453' o.l.). Single-screw, 15½ knots. Motorship. Four masts and no funnel. Launched in 1941. Commissioned in 1945. Passengers: 60. In Copenhagen-New York service, 1951. Resumed trans-Atlantic service in early summer of 1952. Transferred to the Far East service.

Feldmarschall Moltke   (1873)   North German Lloyd.
Built by Caird & Co., Greenock, Scotland. Tonnage: 3,060. Dimensions: 350' x 39'. Single-screw, 12 knots. Compound engines. Two masts and one funnel. Iron hull. Passengers: 144 first, 68 second, 502 third. Maiden voyage: Bremen-Southampton-Panama, September 7, 1873. Served also in Bremen-New York service. Renamed: (a) **Assam** (1875) P. & O. Line, (b) **Kaijo Maru** (1897) N. Y. K. Line.

Ferdinand de Lesseps   (1875)   French Line.
Built by A. & J. Inglis Co., Glasgow, Scotland. Tonnage: 2,920. Dimensions: 350' x 38'. Single-screw, 12 knots. Compound engines. Three masts and one funnel. Iron hull. Launched as **Stad Haarlem** (Royal Netherlands Line) on January 23, 1875. Purchased by French Line in 1879. Renamed: **Ferdinand de Lesseps** (1879). Services: (a) Marseilles-West Indies, (b) New York. Scrapped in France, 1911. Sister ship: **Ville de Marseille.**

Ferdinando Palasciano   (1899)   Navigazione Generale Italiana.
Built by A. G. "Vulkan", Stettin, Germany. Tonnage: 10,643. Dimensions: 499' x 60'. Twin-screw, 15½ knots. Quadruple expansion engines. Two masts and two funnels. First voyage: Genoa-Naples-New York in May 1920. Scrapped in 1926. Ex-**Konig Albert** (1920).

Finland   (1902)   Red Star Line.
Built by Wm. Cramp & Sons, Shipbuilding & Engineering Co., Philadelphia, Pa. Tonnage: 12,188. Dimensions: 560' x 60' (580' o.l.). Twin-screw, 16 knots. Triple expansion engines. Four masts and two funnels. Service: Antwerp-New York. Also served in American Line service. Transferred to Panama-Pacific Line late in 1923. Scrapped in 1927. Sister ships: **Kroonland, Vaderland** and **Zeeland.**

Flandre   (1914)   French Line.
Built by Chantiers de l'Atlantique, St. Nazaire, France. Tonnage: 8,503. Dimensions: 464' x 57' (480' o.l.). Quad-

ruple-screw, 17 knots. Compound engines and two low pressure steam turbines. Two masts and two funnels. Launched, October 31, 1913.   Service: France-West Indies-Central America.   Sunk by magnetic mine in the mouth of the Gironde, September 14, 1940.

*Flandre   (1951)   French Line.
Built by Ateliers & Chantiers de France, Dunkirk, France. Tonnage: 20,459. Dimensions: 568' x 80' (600' o.l.). Twin-screw, 22 knots. Steam turbines. Two masts and one funnel. Launched, October 31, 1951. Maiden voyage: Havre-New York, July 23, 1952, which ended in failure to machinery difficulties. She was returned to builder for extensive repairs. Resumed trans-Atlantic service in April 1953. Passengers: 232 first and 511 tourist. Sister ship: **Antilles.**

Flavia   (1902)   Cunard Line.
Built by Palmer's Shipbuilding & Iron Co., Jarrow-on-Tyne, Newcastle, England. Tonnage: 9,291. Dimensions: 470' x 56'.   Twin-screw, 12½ knots.   Triple expansion engines. Four masts and one funnel.   Torpedoed and sunk off Tory Island, August 24, 1918.   Ex-**Campanello** (1916), ex-**Campania** (1911), ex-**British Empire** (1906).

Florida   (1905)   Lloyd Italiano.
Built by Societa Esercizio Bacini, Riva Trigoso, Genoa, Italy. Tonnage: 5,018. Dimensions: 381' x 47'. Twin-screw, 14 knots.   Triple expansion engines. Two masts and two funnels. Maiden voyage September 13, 1905. Involved in serious collision off Martha's Vineyard, with the White Star liner **Republic,** January 23, 1909. Note: See **Republic** for detail account. The **Florida** also was in service to South America. Renamed: **Cavour** (1912) Ligure Brasiliana Line. Transferred to Transatlantica Italiana in 1914.   Sunk in collision, December 12, 1917.   Sister ships: **Indiana, Luisiana** and **Virginia.**

Floride   (1862)   French Line.
Built by Caird & Co., Greenock, Scotland. Tonnage: 2,706. Dimensions: 278' x 37'.   Single-screw, 11 knots.   Reciprocating engines.   Three masts and one funnel.   Renamed: **Colombie** (1874). Ex-**Floride.** Sister ship: **Louisiane.**

Floride   (1907)   French Line.
Built by Chantiers & Ateliers de Provence, Port de Bouc, France. Tonnage: 6,629. Dimensions: 413' x 52' (437' o.l.). Single-screw, 13 knots. Triple expansion engines. Two masts

and one funnel. Tonnage later increased to 7,029. Passengers: 50 first, 785 third. Launched, July 14, 1907. Maiden voyage: Havre-New York, November 30, 1907. Sunk by the German raider **Prinz Eitel Friedrich** off Dakar, February 14, 1915. Sister ship: **Caroline.**

Folia   (1907)   Cunard Line.
Built by Sir James Laing & Sons, Ltd., Sunderland, England. Tonnage: 6,560. Dimensions: 430' x 52'. Twin-screw, 14 knots. Triple expansion engines. Two masts and two funnels. Torpedoed and sunk near Ram Head, Yougal, March 11, 1917, with the loss of 7 lives. Ex-**Principello** (1916), ex-**Principe di Piemonte** (1913).

Fort Victoria   (1913)   Warren Line.
Built by Wm. Beardmore & Co., Glasgow, Scotland. Tonnage: 7,784. Dimensions: 411' x 56'. Twin-screw, 16 knots. Quadruple expansion engines. Two masts and one funnel. Note: Made several Liverpool-Boston voyages in 1920. She was later in service of the Furness-Bermuda Line. Ex-**Willochra** (1920). Note: See Part III.

France   (1865)   French Line.
Built by Chantier de l'Atlantique, St. Nazaire, France. Tonnage: 3,300. Dimensions: 355' x 43'. Paddle-wheels, 12 knots. Side lever engines. Two masts and two funnels. Launched, October 1, 1864. In France-West Indies service 1865–73. Lengthened to 395 feet (4,648) in 1874. Converted to screw propulsion; compound engines; also mizzen mast was added in 1874. Placed in Havre-New York service. Transferred back to West Indies trade in 1883. Broken up by French shipbreakers in 1910. Note: Vessel was listed as **La France** in some directories.

France   (1867)   National Line (British).
Built by T. Royden & Sons, Liverpool, England. Tonnage: 3,572. Dimensions: 385' x 42'. Single-screw, 12½ knots. Inverted engines. Three masts and one funnel. Clipper bow. Iron hull. Launched, July 4, 1867. Maiden voyage: Liverpool-New York, October 13, 1867. Vessel enlarged to 4,281 tons in 1875. Compound engines in 1880. Made her final voyage to New York in 1893. Sister ships: **England** and **Denmark.**

France   (1912)   French Line.
Built by Chantiers & Ateliers (Penhoet), St. Nazaire, France. Tonnage: 23,769. Dimensions: 690' x 75' (720' o.l.). Quad-

ruple-screw, 24 knots. Four steam turbines. Two masts and four funnels. Keel laid in February 1909. Launched, September 20, 1910. Passengers: 535 first, 440 second, 950 third. Maiden voyage: Havre-New York, April 20, 1912. During her speed trials made 25.9 knots. Noted as a very fast liner, and the nearest in speed to the **Lusitania** and **Mauretania** of that era. Made the run between Havre and New York in 5 days, 17 hours. In service during World War I, as **France IV** for the French Navy. Used as troopship, and also in role of hospital ship. Returned to passenger service in August 1919. Converted from coal to oil fuel in 1923. Laid up at Havre in September 1932. Broken up by Dunkirk shipbreakers in 1935.

*France   (1961)   French Line.
Built by Chantiers de l'Atlantique, St. Nazaire, France. Tonnage: 66,000. Dimensions: 1,035′ (o.l.) x 110′. Quadruple-screw, 31 knots. Steam turbines. Single-mast and two funnels. Keel laid October 7, 1957. Launched, May 11, 1960. The 8 boilers installed will develop a total of 160,000 H.P. Equipped with stabilizers, which should cut roll to less than two degrees. Attained a speed of 34.13 knots during her trials in November 1961. There are 11 decks. Accommodation for 500 first and 1,500 tourist. Maiden voyage: Havre– New York, February 3, 1962. It is quite possible this liner will be faster than either the **Queen Mary,** or **Queen Elizabeth.** However it is quite unlikely that she will be able to surpass the potential speed of the **United States.**

Francesca   (1905)   Austro-American Line.
Built by Russell & Co., Port Glasgow, Scotland. Tonnage: 4,996. Dimensions: 359′ x 48′. Single-screw, 14 knots. Triple expansion engines. Two masts and one funnel. Scrapped in 1925. Sister ship: **Carolina.**

Franconia   (1873)   Hamburg-American Line.
Built by Caird & Co., Greenock, Scotland. Tonnage: 3,181. Dimensions: 350′ x 39′. Single-screw, 11 knots. Compound engines. Two masts and one funnel. Iron hull. Sold to French Line in April 1878. Renamed: **Olinde-Rodrigues** (1878). Sister ship: **Rhenania.**

Franconia   (1911)   Cunard Line.
Built by Swan, Hunter & Wigham Richardson, Ltd., Newcastle, England. Tonnage: 18,150. Dimensions: 600′ x 71′ (625′ o.l.). Twin-screw, 17 knots. Quadruple expansion engines. Two masts and two funnels. Passengers: 300 first,

350 second, 2,200 third. Maiden voyage: Liverpool-Boston, February 25, 1911. Converted to troopship in 1915. Torpedoed and sunk 195 miles from Malta, October 4, 1916, with the loss of 12 lives. Sister ship: **Laconia.**

Franconia   (1923)   Cunard Line.
Built by John Brown & Co., Clydebank, Glasgow, Scotland. Tonnage: 20,175. Dimensions: 601′ x 73′ (624′ o.l.). Twin-screw, 16½ knots. Steam turbines. Two masts and one funnel. Maiden voyage: Liverpool-New York, June 23, 1923. Frequently used as a cruise ship. Served as a British troopship in World War II. Resumed regular service in June 1949. Much of her time since then was in Canadian service. Last sailing was from New York to Liverpool in November 1956. Broken up for scrap at Inverkeithing in 1957. Sister ship: **Carinthia.**

Frankfurt   (1869)   North German Lloyd.
Built by Caird & Co., Greenock, Scotland. Tonnage: 2,582. Dimensions: 310′ x 39′. Single-screw, 12 knots. Inverted type engines. Two masts and one funnel. Iron hull. Service: (a) Bremen-Havre-New Orleans, (b) Bremen-Southampton-New York. Compound engines in 1880. Sold to Newcastle owners in 1896. Resold to Spezia firm and employed as a coal carrier. Broken up by Italian shipbreakers in 1897. Note: The **Frankfurt** was one of a large class of similar North German Lloyd ships.

Frankfurt   (1899)   North German Lloyd.
Built by Tecklenborg, Geestemunde, Germany. Tonnage: 7,431. Dimensions: 429′ x 54′. Twin-screw, 13 knots. Triple expansion engines. Two masts and one funnel. Mainly in Bremen-Baltimore service. Ceded to Great Britain in 1919, and placed under management of White Star Line. Sold in 1922. Renamed: **Sarvistan.** Scrapped in Japan, 1931. Sister ships: **Hannover** and **Koln.**

Franklin   (1848)   New York & Havre Steam Navigation Co. (United States).
Built by Westervelt & McKay, New York, N. Y. Tonnage: 2,184. Dimensions: 263′ x 41′. Paddle-wheels, 10½ knots. Side lever engines. Three masts and one funnel. Clipper bow. Wooden hull. Maiden voyage: New York-Southampton-Havre, October 5, 1850. Cross the Atlantic in 12 days, 10 hours. Wrecked on Long Island, July 17, 1854, with no loss of life.

Frederik VIII (1913) Scandinavian-American Line (Danish). Built by A. G. "Vulkan", Stettin, Germany. Tonnage: 11,850. Dimensions: 523′ x 62′ (544′ o.l.). Twin-screw, 17 knots. Triple expansion engines. Two masts and two funnels. Maiden voyage: Copenhagen-Oslo-New York, February 5, 1914. Made her final voyage to New York in December 1935. Sold to Hughes Bolckow for scrap in September 1936 and was dismantled by 1937.

Friedrich der Grosse (1896) North German Lloyd. Built by Akt. Ges. "Vulkan", Stettin, Germany. Tonnage: 10,771. Dimensions: 523′ x 60′ (546′ o.l.). Twin-screw, 15 knots. Quadruple expansion engines. Two masts and two funnels. She was shifted between New York and Australian routes. Renamed: (a) **Huron** (1917), (b) **City of Honolulu** (1922). Note: During her first voyage as the reconditioned **City of Honolulu**, in October 1922, caught fire and after passengers and crew were removed she was sunk by gun fire as a navigation menace. The United States army transport **Thomas** brought the passengers to San Francisco. Sister ship: **Konigin Luise.**

Friesland (1889) Red Star Line. Built by J. & G. Thomson, Ltd., Glasgow, Scotland. Tonnage: 6,409. Dimensions: 437′ x 51′ (450′ o.l.). Single-screw, 15 knots. Triple expansion engines. Four masts and one funnel. Passengers: 226 first, 102 second, 600 third. Launched, August 15, 1889. Service: Antwerp-New York. Vessel was transferred to American Line in 1905. Renamed: **La Plata** (1910) Italian. Note: This clipper bow liner built of steel was scrapped in 1912.

Frisia (1872) Hamburg-American Line. Built by Caird & Co., Greenock, Scotland. Tonnage: 3,256. Dimensions: 350′ x 40′. Single-screw, 13 knots. Compound engines. Two masts and one funnel. Iron hull. Launched, March 30, 1872. Passengers: 90 first, 130 second, 600 third. Maiden voyage: Hamburg-Havre-New York, August 21, 1872. Also in Germany-West Indies service. Sold to British owners in 1887. Sister ship: **Thuringia.**

Fulda (1882) North German Lloyd. Built by John Elder & Co., Glasgow, Scotland. Tonnage: 4,816. Dimensions: 438′ x 46′ (455′ o.l.). Single-screw, 17 knots. Compound engines. 6,300 I.H.P. Four masts and two funnels. Iron hull. Passengers: 125 first, 130 second, 1,000 third. Maiden voyage: Bremen-Southampton-New

York, March 12, 1883. Transferred to Mediterranean-New York service in 1891. Note: After sustaining serious damage in drydock at Birkenhead in 1899, was broken up for scrap. Sister ship: **Werra.**

Fulda   (1924)   North German Lloyd.
Built by Akt. Ges. "Weser", Bremen, Germany. Tonnage: 9,492. Dimensions: 458' x 57'. Twin-screw, 13 knots. Motorship. Two masts and one funnel. Note: At later date converted to carry only freight, tonnage reduced to 7,744 tons. Sold to Japan in 1940. Renamed: **Teikoku Maru** (1940). Sister ships: **Coblenz, Saarbrucken, Trier, Werra** and **Weser.**

Fulton   (1855)   New York & Havre Steam Navigation Co.
Built by Smith & Dimon, New York, N. Y. Tonnage: 2,307. Dimensions: 280' x 41'. Paddle-wheels, 10 knots. Oscillating engines. Two masts and two funnels. Wooden hull. Continued in trans-Atlantic service until 1861, when she was chartered by the United States Government and used as a transport in the Civil War. Sold for scrap in March 1870. Sister ship: **Arago.**

Furnessia   (1880)   Anchor Line (British).
Built by Barrow Shipbuilding Co., Barrow-in-Furness, England. Tonnage: 5,495. Dimensions: 445' x 44'. Single-screw, 14 knots. Compound engines. Two masts and two funnels. Iron hull. Maiden voyage: Glasgow-New York, January 27, 1881. Converted to single funnel in 1891; re-engined with triple expansion type. Made her final voyage to New York in 1911. Broken up by British shipbreakers in 1912.

Furst Bismarck   (1890)   Hamburg-American Line.
Built by Akt. Ges. "Vulkan", Stettin, Germany. Tonnage: 8,874. Dimensions: 504' x 57' (520' o.l.). Twin-screw, 19 knots. Triple expansion engines. Two masts and three funnels. Steel hull. Power equipment: 9 boilers; 72 furnaces; 17,000 I.H.P. Passengers: 420 first, 172 second, 700 third. Maiden voyage: Hamburg-Southampton-New York, 1890. Renamed: (a) **Don** (1904) Russian, (b) **Moskva** (1906), (c) **Gaa** (1912) (Austro-Hungarian Navy), (d) **San Giusto** (1920). Scrapped in 1924. Running mates: **Normannia, Columbia** and **Auguste Victoria.**

Gallia   (1878)   Cunard Line.
Built by J. & G. Thomson, Ltd., Glasgow, Scotland. Tonnage: 4,809. Dimensions: 430' x 44'. Single-screw, 15 knots.

Compound engines. Three masts and one funnel. Iron hull. Passengers: 300 cabin and 1,200 third. Cost about $775,000. Maiden voyage: Liverpool-New York, April 5, 1879. Also served in the Liverpool-Boston service. Chartered to the Spanish Line in 1896, sailing under name of **Don Alvado de Bazan.** Vessel sold to Beaver Line in 1897. Resold to Allan Line. The **Gallia** was wrecked near Quebec in 1899. Refloated and sold to French shipbreakers in 1900.

Gallia   (1883)   Fabre Line.
Built by Chantiers de la Gironde, Bordeaux, France. Tonnage: 4,211. Dimensions: 386' x 41'. Single-screw, 14 knots. Compound engines. Three masts and one funnel. Iron hull. Made her first Atlantic crossing as the **Gallia** in May 1901. Sold to Italian shipbreakers in December 1910. Ex-**Chateau Yquem** (1901).

Garibaldi   (1906)   Transatlantica Italiana.
Built by Soc. Esercizio Bacini, Riva Trigoso, Italy. Tonnage: 5,191. Dimensions: 372' x 48' (381' o.l.). Twin-screw, $14\frac{1}{2}$ knots. Triple expansion engines. Two masts and two funnels. Sold to Tirrenia Line in 1926. A World War II casualty in May 1943. Ex-**Virginia** (1912).

Gascogne   (1924)   French Line.
Built by Newport News Shipbuilding & Drydock Co., Newport News, Va. Tonnage: 5,195. Dimensions: 375' x 54'. Single-screw, 18 knots. Two steam turbines. Two masts and one funnel. Service: France-West Indies. Sold to Messageries Maritimes at later date. Sold to Hong Kong shipbreakers in 1955. Ex-**George Washington** (1949). Owned by Eastern Steamship Lines.

Gdansk   (1900)   Polish American Navigation Corp.
Built by W. Cramp & Sons Co., Philadelphia, Pa. Tonnage: 6,135. Dimensions: 400' x 50'. Twin-screw, 14 knots. Triple expansion engines. Two masts and one funnel. Commenced service from New York to Danzig in 1921. Vessel was returned to trans-Pacific service in 1924. Name reverted back to **Sierra.** Scrapped in 1934. Ex-**Sierra** (1921).

Geiser   (1881)   Thingvalla Line (Danish).
Built by Burmeister & Wain, Copenhagen, Denmark. Tonnage: 2,831. Dimensions: 324' x 39'. Single-screw, 12 knots. Compound engines. Three masts and one funnel. Service: Copenhagen-Christiansand-New York. Sunk as a result of collision with **Thingvalla** off Sable Island, August 14, 1888, with the loss of over one hundred lives. Sister ship: **Island.**

Gellert   (1874)   Adler (Eagle) Line.
Built by Alexander Stephen & Sons, Ltd., Glasgow, Scotland.
Tonnage: 3,533.   Dimensions: 374′ x 40′.   Single-screw, 14
knots.   Compound engines.   Two masts and one funnel.
Note: See next paragraph.   Transferred to the Hamburg-
American Line upon completion.   Sister ships: **Goethe,
Herder, Klopstock, Lessing, Schiller** and **Wieland.**

Gellert   (1874)   Hamburg-American Line.
Built by Alexander Stephen & Sons, Ltd., Glasgow, Scotland.
Tonnage: 3,533.   Dimensions: 374′ x 40′.   Single-screw, 14
knots.   Compound engines.   Two masts and one funnel.
Note: Altered to two funnels in 1881.   Iron hull.   Passengers:
200 first and 800 third.   The Hamburg-American Line purchased the fleet of the Adler Line in 1875.   The **Gellert** made
her final voyage to New York in 1894.   Scrapped in 1895.

General von Steuben   (1922)   North German Lloyd.
Built by "Vulkan", Stettin, Germany.   Tonnage: 14,690.
Dimensions: 526′ x 65′ (551′ o.l.).   Twin-screw, 17 knots.
Triple expansion engines and steam turbines.   Two masts
and two funnels.   Renamed: **Steuben** (1938).   Torpedoed
and sunk by Russian submarine in the Baltic, February 20,
1945.   Ex-**Munchen** (1931).

General Werder   (1874)   North German Lloyd.
Built by Caird & Co., Greenock, Scotland.   Tonnage: 3,020.
Dimensions: 351′ x 39′.   Single-screw, 12 knots.   Compound
engines.   Two masts and one funnel.   Iron hull.   Passengers:
144 first, 68 second, 502 third.   Launched, March 4, 1874.
Maiden voyage: Bremen-Southampton-Baltimore, September 16, 1874.   Transferred to Germany-Far East service in
service in 1886.   Renamed: (a) **Midnight Sun** (1893) British
owners, (b) **Princess of Wales** (British).

George Washington   (1908)   North German Lloyd.
Built by "Vulkan" Werke, Stettin, Germany.   Tonnage:
25,570.   Dimensions: 699′ x 78′ (722′ o.l.).   Twin-screw, 19
knots.   Quadruple expansion engines.   Four masts and two
funnels.   Her highest masts were 193 feet above the keel.
Length of upper promenade deck was 328 feet.   Two elevators were installed.   Passengers: 520 first, 377 second, 2,000
third.   Maiden voyage: Bremen-Southampton-New York,
June 12, 1909.   Seized by the United States in 1917 and
converted to troopship.   After the war she was first employed
by United States Mail Steamship Company for a brief time.
Sold to United States Lines in 1921.   Thoroughly recon-

ditioned for their trans-Atlantic service. Laid up in the
Patuxent River, Maryland, in 1931. In 1940 was removed
from her moorings and outfitted as a troopship. Renamed:
Catlin (1941). Her name soon reverted back to **George
Washington.** From June 1942 to April 1943, she underwent
an extensive overhaul. New oil-burning boilers were installed
and original funnels replaced by a single modern one, which
changed her appearance greatly. Gutted by fire while laid
up at Baltimore, January 16, 1951. The hulk was broken
up soon afterwards.

George Washington (1908) United States Lines.
Tonnage: 23,788. Note: Listed above as **George Washington**
(1908) North German Lloyd.

Georgia (1908) Austro-American Line.
Built by Russell & Co., Port Glasgow, Scotland. Tonnage:
5,380. Dimensions: 400' x 52'. Single-screw, 13 knots.
Triple expansion engines. Two masts and one funnel.
Passengers: 8 first, 61 second, 820 third. After World War
I, she was taken over by Cosulich Line; name retained.
Renamed: (a) **Georgia C,** (b) **Hasshu Maru,** (c) **Daigen
Maru No. 3.** Sunk by submarine, February 26, 1944.
Sister ship: **Columbia.**

Georgic (1895) White Star Line.
Built by Harland & Wolff, Ltd., Belfast, Ireland. Tonnage:
10,077. Dimensions: 558' x 60'. Twin-screw, 13 knots.
Triple expansion engines. Four masts and one funnel.
Type of vessel: Cargo-cattle. Did not have accommodation
for passengers. Captured and sunk by the German raider
Mowe, 590 miles from Cape Race on December 10, 1916.

Georgic (1932) White Star Line.
Built by Harland & Wolff, Ltd., Belfast, Ireland. Tonnage:
27,759. Dimensions: 683' x 82' (712' o.l.). Twin-screw, 18
knots. Motorship. Two masts and two funnels. Keel laid,
November 29, 1929. Launched, November 12, 1931. Maiden
voyage: Liverpool to New York, June 25, 1932. In 1933
made the Atlantic crossing at average speed of 18.43 knots.
Transferred to London-New York route in 1935. Began
operating under Cunard-White Star Line merger in 1934.
Bombed and badly gutted by fire due to German air attack
in Suez Bay, July 14, 1941. Rebuilt by Harland & Wolff,
Ltd. at their Belfast yard. She was converted to permanent
troopship, and as such had only a single mast and one funnel.
After the war was put in the emigrant service. Chartered

by Cunard Line in 1950 to help out during the peak season of trans-Atlantic travel. Scrapped by British shipbreakers in 1956. Sister ship: **Britannic.**

Gera   (1890)   North German Lloyd.
Built by Fairfield Shipbuilding & Engineering Co., Glasgow, Scotland. Tonnage: 5,005. Dimensions: 413' x 47'. Single-screw, 13 knots. Triple expansion engines. Two masts and one funnel. Passengers: 49 first, 38 second, 1,900 third. Also served in South American service. Sold to Italian owners in 1908. Renamed: **Valparaiso** (1909). Sister ships: **Darmstadt, Karlsruhe, Oldenburg, Stuttgart** and **Weimar.**

Gerania   (1909)   Gerania Steamship Co. (Austrian).
Built by Northamberland Shipbuilding Co., Newcastle, England. Tonnage: 4,940. Dimensions: 390' x 52'. Single-screw, 11 knots. Triple expansion engines. Type: An emigrant carrier.

Gergovia   (1883)   Fabre Line.
Built by Scott's Shipbuilding Co., Greenock, Scotland. Tonnage: 2,024. Dimensions: 288' x 37'. Single-screw, 13 knots. Compound engines. Iron hull. Scrapped in 1924.

Germania   (1863)   Hamburg-American Line.
Built by Caird & Co., Greenock, Scotland. Tonnage: 2,123. Dimensions: 321' x 40'. Single-screw, 10 knots. Inverted engines. Three masts and one funnel. Iron hull. Launched, April 6, 1863. Maiden voyage: Hamburg-Southampton-New York, August 22, 1863. Wrecked off Cape Race, August 7, 1869, with no loss of life.

Germania   (1871)   Hamburg-American Line.
Built by Caird & Co., Greenock, Scotland. Tonnage: 2,876. Dimensions: 329' x 39'. Single-screw, 11 knots. Compound engines. Iron hull. Two masts and one funnel. Also in Germany-South America service. Wrecked off South American coast in 1876.

Germania   (1903)   Fabre Line.
Built by Chantiers & Ateliers de Provence, Port de Bouc, France. Tonnage: 5,103. Dimensions: 407' x 46'. Single-screw, 15 knots. Triple expansion engines. Two masts and two funnels. Launched, August 2, 1902. Made her final voyage to New York in 1912. Renamed: **Britannia** (1914).

Germanic   (1874)   White Star Line.
Built by Harland & Wolff, Ltd., Belfast, Ireland. Tonnage: 5,008. Dimensions: 455' x 45' (468' o.l.). Single-screw, 16 knots. Compound engines. 5,000 I.H.P. Four masts and two funnels. Iron hull. Launched, July 15, 1874. Maiden voyage: Liverpool-New York, May 20, 1875. Won the trans-Atlantic "Blue Ribbon" in February 1876. Renamed: (a) **Ottawa** (1905), (b) **Gul Djemal** (1910) Turkish. Torpedoed by a British submarine in the Sea of Marmora, May 3, 1915, but was later salved. Made several crossings to New York during 1920–21 for Turkish owners. Name changed to **Gulcemal** about 1928. Scrapped in 1950. Sister ship: **Britannic.**

Germany   (1868)   Allan Line.
Built by M. Pearse & Co., Stockton, England. Tonnage: 3,244. Dimensions: 343' x 42'. Single-screw, 10 knots. Inverted engines. Three masts and one funnel. Iron hull. Service: Liverpool-Quebec-Montreal. Wrecked near Bordeaux, December 3, 1872, with the loss of 30 lives.

Gerolstein   (1904)   Bernstein Line.
Built by Harland & Wolff, Ltd., Belfast, Ireland. Tonnage: 7,772. Dimensions: 453' x 56'. Twin-screw, 13½ knots. Quadruple expansion engines. Two masts and one funnel. Passenger accommodation installed in 1931. Vessel sold to H. C. Horn Company in June 1939. Renamed: **Consul Horn** (1939). Mined off Borkum in July 1942. Ex-**Mamari** (1929). Running mates: **Ilsenstein** and **Konigstein.**

Gerona   (1911)   Thomson Line (British).
Built by Swan, Hunter & Wigham Richardson, Ltd., Newcastle, England. Tonnage: 9,111. Note: Never in service for the Thomson Line, as she was transferred to the Cunard Line, upon completion. Renamed: **Ascania** (1911).

Gerty   (1903)   Austro-American Line.
Built by J. Readhead & Sons, South Shields, England. Tonnage: 4,212. Dimensions: 346' x 45'. Single-screw, 12 knots. Triple expansion engines. Two masts and one funnel. Maiden voyage: Trieste-New York, May 23, 1904. Acquired by Cosulich Line in 1919. Renamed: **City of Candia.** Scrapped in 1929. Sister ship: **Giulia.**

Giulia   (1904)   Austro-American Line.
Built by Russell & Co., Port Glasgow, Scotland. Tonnage: 4,337. Dimensions: 346' x 45'. Single-screw, 12 knots.

Triple expansion engines. Two masts and one funnel. Launched, May 16, 1904. In Cosulich Line service, 1919. Cargo shifted and vessel abandoned, March 21, 1923, while bound from Portland, Maine to Girgenti. Sister ship: **Gerty.**

Giulio Cesare (1920) Navigazione Generale Italiana.
Built by Swan, Hunter & Wigham Richardson, Ltd., Newcastle, England. Tonnage: 21,657. Dimensions: 602' x 76' (634' o.l.). Quadruple-screw, 19½ knots. Four steam turbines. Two masts and two funnels. Laid down, December 13, 1913. Launched, February 7, 1920. Maiden voyage: Genoa-Naples-South America, May 4, 1922. Delay in completion of liner was due to World War I. Services: (a) North Atlantic (b) South Atlantic. Transferred to Italia Line in 1932. Placed in South Africa service in 1933. Acquired by Lloyd Triestino in 1935. Capsized and sunk at Trieste in May 1945. The hulk was broken up for scrap in 1947. Sister ship: **Duilio.**

*****Giulio Cesare** (1951) Italia Line.
Built by Cantieri Riuniti Dell' Adriatico, Monfalcone, Italy. Tonnage: 27,694. Dimensions: 649' x 87' (680' o.l.). Twin-screw, 21 knots. Motorship. Single mast and one funnel. Keel laid, July 28, 1949. Launched, May 18, 1950. Maiden voyage from Italy to South America, October 27, 1951. Passengers: 180 first, 288 cabin, 714 tourist. Transferred to the North Atlantic service in 1956. Sister ship: **Augustus.**

Giuseppe Verdi (1915) Transatlantica Italiana.
Built by Soc. Esercizio Bacini, Riva Trigoso, Italy. Tonnage: 9,760. Dimensions: 505' x 59'. Twin-screw, 16½ knots. Quadruple expansion engines. Two masts and two funnels. Launched, August 2, 1915. Maiden voyage: Genoa-Naples-Palermo-New York, November 7, 1915. Renamed: **Yamato Maru** (1927). Torpedoed and sunk by American submarine, September 13, 1943. Sister ship: **Dante Alighieri.**

Glasgow (1851) Inman Line.
Built by Tod & McGregor, Glasgow, Scotland. Tonnage: 1,950. Dimensions: 262' x 36'. Single-screw, 10 knots. Four masts and one funnel. Iron hull. Made her first voyage Liverpool-New York in February 1860. In service 1860–1865. Purchased from Glasgow & New York Steam Ship Company in 1859. Burned off Nantucket, July 31, 1865, with no loss of life.

Gneisenau   (1903)   North German Lloyd.
Built by A. Ges. "Vulkan", Stettin, Germany. Tonnage: 8,081. Dimensions: 442' x 55'. Twin-screw, 13½ knots. Triple expansion engines. Two masts and one funnel. Built for Australia service. In trans-Atlantic service too. Renamed: **Citta di Genova** (1921). Sold to Italian shipbreakers in October 1930. Sister ships: **Roon** and **Scharnhorst.**

Goeben   (1906)   North German Lloyd.
Built by Akt. Ges. "Weser", Bremen, Germany. Tonnage: 8,792. Dimensions: 462' x 57'. Twin-screw, 14 knots. Quadruple expansion engines. Two masts and one funnel. Built for Australian and Far East services, but also used in the trans-Atlantic trade.   Renamed: **Roussillon** (1920). Scrapped in 1931. Sister ship: **Kleist.**

Goethe   (1872)   Adler (Eagle) Line.
Built by Robert Napier & Sons, Glasgow, Scotland. Tonnage: 3,408. Dimensions: 375' x 40'. Single-screw, 13½ knots. Compound engines. Two masts and one funnel. Iron hull. Converted to two funnels, at later date. Passengers: 90 first, 100 second, 800 third. Service: Hamburg-New York. Transferred to Hamburg-American Line in 1875. Services: (a) North Atlantic, (b) South America. Wrecked off Bahia in 1876. Sister ships: **Gellert, Herder, Klopstock, Lessing, Schiller** and **Wieland.**

Gothland   (1893)   Red Star Line.
Built by Harland & Wolff, Ltd., Belfast, Ireland. Tonnage: 7,669. Dimensions: 490' x 53'. Twin-screw, 14 knots. Triple expansion engines. Four masts and one funnel. Service: Antwerp-Philadelphia. Scrapped in Great Britain, 1926. Renamed: (a) **Gothic** (1907), (b) **Gothland** (1911), (c) **Gothic** (1913). Note: As the **Gothic** was in the New Zealand service.

Gottardo   (1883)   Navigazione Generale Italiana.
Built by Alexander Stephen & Sons, Ltd., Glasgow, Scotland. Tonnage: 2,847. Dimensions: 350' x 40'. Single-screw, 12 knots. Compound engines. Three masts and one funnel. Iron hull. Launched, November 23, 1881. Services: (a) Genoa-Naples-New York, (b) Italy-South America. Renamed **Memfi** (1903). Sold to Servizi Marittimi (Italian) in 1910. Sister ships: **Archimede, Indipendente, Vincenzo Florio** and **Washington.**

Graf Bismarck   (1871)   North German Lloyd.
   Built by Caird & Co., Greenock, Scotland. Tonnage: 2,406.
   Dimensions: 318' x 39'. Single-screw, 12 knots. Inverted
   engines. Two masts and one funnel. Launched, November
   9, 1870. Maiden voyage: Bremen-Southampton-Panama,
   May 7, 1871. In New York service, too. Compound engines
   in 1879. Speed increased to 14 knots. Made her final voyage
   to New York in 1890. Sold about 1896.

Graf Waldersee   (1898)   Hamburg-American Line.
   Built by Blohm & Voss, Hamburg, Germany. Tonnage:
   13,102. Dimensions: 561' x 62'. Twin-screw, 13½ knots.
   Quadruple expansion engines. Four masts and one funnel.
   Passengers: 162 first, 184 second, 2,200 third. Service:
   Hamburg-New York. Sold to British shipbreakers in July
   1921. Sister ships: **Patricia, Pennsylvania** and **Pretoria.**

Grampian   (1907)   (a) Allan Line, (b) Canadian Pacific Line.
   Built by Alexander Stephen & Sons, Ltd., Glasgow, Scotland.
   Tonnage: 10,920. Dimensions: 485' x 60'. Twin-screw, 15
   knots. Triple expansion engines. Two masts and one funnel.
   Passengers: 210 first, 250 second, 1,000 third. Service:
   Glasgow-Quebec-Montreal. Taken over by Canadian Pacific
   Line in 1917. Retained her name in their service. Vessel
   was laid up in 1922. Scrapped in 1926. Sister ship: **Hes-
   perian.** Similar to **Corsican.**

Great Britain   (1843)   Great Western Steamship Co.
   Built by Patterson of Bristol, England. Tonnage: 3,270.
   Dimensions: 274' x 48' (324' o.l.). Single-screw, 10 knots.
   Chain gearing type of engine. Six masts and one funnel.
   Later altered to two funnels placed close together and much
   shorter than original one. Six boilers, developed 1,500 I.H.P.
   Note: First trans-Atlantic screw steamer and also first to be
   built of iron. Clipper bow. Vessel grounded in September
   1846. Salved and sold in 1850. Served later in Australian
   trade. Converted to sailing ship. Finally in 1890 was used
   as a hulk at the Falkland Islands.

Great Eastern   (1858)   Great Eastern Steamship Co. (British).
   Built by Scott, Russell & Co., Millwall, London, England.
   Tonnage: 18,915. Dimensions: 680' x 82' (691' o.l.). Combination paddle-wheels and single-screw, 13 knots. Six
   masts and five funnels. Her oscillating engines developed
   5,000, while the horizontal engines produced 6,000 I.H.P.
   Breadth over paddle boxes 118 feet. Keel laid on May 1,
   1854. Launched, January 31, 1858. Her double hull was

built of iron. She was at first called **Leviathan,** but was
christened the **Great Eastern.** The cost of launching the
great ship exhausted the owner's funds, and she lay unfinished
for a year. She was sold to a newly formed company, which
was called Great Ship Company, and they had her completed.
Building cost amounted to about $5,000,000. The vessel
had been designed by Isambard Kingdom Brunel, but he
died prior to completion of her trials in September 1859.
Passengers: 800 first, 2,000 second and 1,200 third. Intended
originally for the Eastern trade, but when commissioned
was put in trans-Atlantic service. Maiden voyage to New
York commenced, June 17, 1860. Became cable-laying ship
in 1864. Scrapped in 1891.

Great Western   (1838)   Great Western Steamship Co.
Built by William Patterson, Bristol, England. Tonnage:
1,340. Dimensions: 212' x 35' (236' o.l.). Paddle-wheels,
8½ knots. Side lever engines. Four masts and one funnel.
Wooden hull. Clipper bow. Passengers: 128 aft (first class),
20 forward. Launched, July 19, 1837. Maiden voyage:
Bristol-New York, April 8, 1838. Note: The first steamship
to be built especially for trans-Atlantic service. Sold to
Royal Mail Steam Packet Company in 1847. Broken up
in 1857.

Grecian   (1879)   Allan Line.
Built by Wm. Doxford & Sons, Ltd., Sunderland, England.
Tonnage: 3,613. Dimensions: 360' x 40'. Single-screw, 11
knots. Compound engines. Three masts and one funnel.
Iron hull. Maiden voyage: Glasgow-Quebec-Montreal, April
21, 1880. Wrecked near Halifax, February 9, 1902, with no
loss of life. Sister ship: **Corean.**

Grecian Monarch   (1882)   Monarch Line (British).
Built by Earle's Shipbuilding & Engineering Co., Hull,
England. Tonnage: 4,364. Dimensions: 381' x 43' (400' o.l.).
Single-screw, 11 knots. Four masts and two funnels. Iron
hull. Passengers: 40 first, 60 second, 1,000 third. Maiden
voyage: London-New York, August 24, 1882. Renamed:
Pomeranian (1887).

Greece   (1863)   National Line (British).
Built by Palmer's Shipbuilding & Iron Co., Jarrow-on-Tyne,
England. Tonnage: 4,310. Dimensions: 391' x 41'. Single-
screw, 10 knots. Compound engines. Three masts and one
funnel. Iron hull. Transferred to London-New York
service in 1875. Broken up in 1896. Ex-**Virginia** (1872).
Sister ship: **Canada.**

Gripsholm   (1925)   Swedish-American Line.
Built by Sir W. G. Armstrong, Whitworth & Co., Newcastle, England. Tonnage: 17,716. Dimensions: 553' x 74' (574' o.l.). Twin-screw, 17 knots. Motorship. Two masts and two funnels. Note: The first trans-Atlantic liner with Diesel motors. Passengers: 127 first, 482 second, 948 third. Maiden voyage: Gothenburg-New York, November 21, 1925. She became famous as a repatriation ship during World War II. Resumed regular passenger service in March 1946. Tonnage increased to 19,105. Passengers: (post-war) 210 first and 710 tourist. Sold to German owners in 1954. Renamed: **Berlin** (1955).

*Gripsholm   (1956)   Swedish-American Line.
Built by Ansaldo, Genoa, Italy. Tonnage: 23,191. Dimensions: 550' x 81' (631' o.l.). Twin-screw, 20 knots. Motorship. Two masts and two funnels. Clipper bow. Laid down May 10, 1955. Launched, April 8, 1956. Maiden voyage: Gothenburg-New York, May 14, 1957. Passengers: 150 first and 612 tourist.

*Groote Beer   (1944)   Dutch Government. (Holland-America Line, Mgr.).
Built by Permanente Metals Corp., Richmond, Calif. Tonnage: 9,191. Dimensions: 440' x 62' (455' o.l.). Single-screw, 15 knots. Steam turbines. Two masts and one funnel. Passengers: 900. Vessel has been used on other routes too. Ex-**Costa Rica Victory** (1947).

Grosser Kurfurst   (1899)   North German Lloyd.
Built by F. Schichau, Danzig, Germany. Tonnage: 13,245. Dimensions: 560' x 62' (580' o.l.). Twin-screw, 16 knots. Quadruple expansion engines. Two masts and two funnels. Service: Interchangeable between New York and Australian routes. Renamed: (a) **Aeolus** (1917), (b) **City of Los Angeles** (1923). Scrapped in Japan, 1937.

*Guadalupe   (1953)   Spanish Line.
Built by Sociedad Espanola de Construccion Naval, Bilbao, Spain. Tonnage: 14,540. Dimensions: 464' x 62' (487' o.l.). Single-screw, 17 knots. Motorship. Single mast and one funnel. Launched as **Monasterio de Guadalupe** in May 1951. Maiden voyage: Spain, via Lisbon, to New York and Central America, March 21, 1953. Passengers: 105 first and 244 cabin. Sister ship: **Covadonga.**

Guadeloupe (1855) French Line.
Built by Laird & Co., Liverpool, England. Tonnage: 1,900. Dimensions: 265' x 37'. Single-screw, 13 knots. Service: France-West Indies. Sold to Norwegian owners in June 1889. Renamed: **Sorrento** (1889). Ex-**Tampico**, ex-**Imperator.** Sister ship: **Martinique.**

Guadeloupe (1906) French Line.
Built by Chantiers de l'Atlantique, St. Nazaire, France. Tonnage: 6,600. Dimensions: 432' x 52'. Twin-screw, 16 knots. Triple expansion engines. Two masts and two funnels. Launched, December 15, 1906. Service: France-West Indies-Central America. Captured by the famed merchant cruiser **Kronprinz Wilhelm,** February 23, 1915, but not sunk by the enemy until February 28. Sister ship: **Perou.**

Guadeloupe (1908) French Line.
Built by Chantiers de l'Atlantique, St. Nazaire, France. Tonnage: 10,502. Dimensions: 508' x 57'. Twin-screw, 16 knots. Triple expansion engines. Two masts and two funnels. Reconditioned in 1928. Service: France-West Indies-Colon. Scrapped in France, 1936. Ex-**Chicago** (1929).

Guglielmo Peirce (1907) Sicula Americana Line (Italian).
Built by Frd. Krupp, Kiel, Germany. Tonnage: 8,512. Dimensions: 448' x 55'. Twin-screw, 12 knots. Quadruple expansion engines. Two masts and one funnel. Service: Naples-New York. Renamed: (a) **Maria Cristina** (1926) Lloyd Sabaudo, (b) **Mouzinho** (Portuguese). Scrapped in 1954. Ex-**Corcovado** (1920), ex-**Sueh** (1919), ex-**Corcovado** (1919).

Gul Djemal (1874) Turkish Government.
Built by Harland & Wolff, Ltd., Belfast, Ireland. Tonnage: 5,122. Dimensions: 455' x 45'. Single-screw, 15 knots. Triple expansion engines. Four masts and two funnels. Torpedoed by British submarine in Sea of Marmora, May 3, 1915. She was later salvaged. Made voyages to New York during 1920–21. Renamed: **Gulcemal** in 1928. Scrapped in 1950.

Gulcemal (1874) Turkish Government.
Built by Harland & Wolff, Ltd., Belfast, Ireland. Tonnage: 5,122. Note: See **Gul Djemal** for information.

*Gumhuryat Misr (1928) Khedivial Mail Line (Egyptian).
Built by Cammell, Laird & Co., Birkenhead, England. Tonnage: 7,830. Dimensions: 419' x 59' (437' o.l.). Twin-screw,

14 knots. Steam turbines. Two masts and one funnel. First voyage: Alexandria-New York, March 5, 1954. Passengers: 118 first, 115 tourist. Ex-**Lady Nelson** (1954). Sister ship: **Mecca.**

H. H. Meier   (1892)   North German Lloyd.
Built by Sir W. G. Armstrong, Whitworth & Co., Newcastle, England. Tonnage: 5,140. Dimensions: 421' x 48'. Twin-screw, 13½ knots. Triple expansion engines. Three masts and one funnel. Steel hull. Maiden voyage: Bremen-Southampton-New York, December 25, 1892. In Germany-South American service, too. Renamed: **Manuel Calvo** (1901).

Habana   (1872)   Spanish Line.
Built by Oswald & Co., Sunderland, England. Tonnage: 2,678. Dimensions: 317' x 37'. Single-screw, 12 knots. Compound engines. Two masts and one funnel. Launched, August 22, 1872. Accommodation for 900 passengers in three classes. Scrapped in 1900. Ex-**Ernst Moritz Arndt** (1880).

*****Habana**   (1923)   Spanish Line.
Built by Soc. Espanola de Construccion Naval, Bilbao, Spain. Tonnage: 10,551. Dimensions: 480' x 61' (500' o.l.). Twin-screw, 17 knots. Four steam turbines. Two masts and one funnel. Note: After being gutted by fire during the Spanish Civil War, she was reconstructed as cargo ship. Less superstructure reduced tonnage to 8,279. When World War II ended, she was altered by Todd's shipyard at Brooklyn, N. Y. Returned to service in April 1947, with accommodation for 101 first class passengers. Tonnage as of 1960, 8,391. Ex-**Alfonso XIII** (1931).

Habsburg   (1875)   North German Lloyd.
Built by Earle's Shipbuilding & Engineering Co., Hull, England. Tonnage: 3,094. Dimensions: 351' x 39'. Single-screw, 12 knots. Compound engines. Two masts and one funnel. Iron hull. Passengers: 142 first, and 800 third. Launched, January 9, 1875. Maiden voyage: Bremen-South America, 1875. Services: (a) South America, (b) North America, (c) Australia. Triple expansion engines in 1891. Final voyage to New York in 1895. Sold to Italians in 1898. Scrapped in 1899. Sister ship: **Salier.**

Haiti   (1913)   French Line.
Built by Chantiers & Ateliers de Provence, Port Bouc, France. Tonnage: 6,288. Dimensions: 410' x 51'. Twin-

screw, 13 knots. Triple expansion engines. Two masts and two funnels. Service: France-West Indies-Central America. Renamed: **Marrakech.** Scrapped in 1951.

Hamburg (1899) Hamburg-American Line.
Built by "Vulkan", Stettin, Germany. Tonnage: 10,532. Dimensions: 499′ x 60′. Twin-screw, 16 knots. Quadruple expansion engines. Two masts and two funnels. Note: Originally in Far East service. Transferred to Hamburg-New York trade in 1904. She was later used in Mediterranean-New York service. Renamed: (a) **Red Cross** (1917), (b) **Powhatan** (1917), (c) **New Rochelle** (1920), (d) **Hudson** (1921), (e) **President Fillmore** (1922). Scrapped in United States, 1928.

Hamburg (1926) Hamburg-American Line.
Built by Blohm & Voss, Hamburg, Germany. Tonnage: 21,133. Dimensions: 602′ x 72′. Twin-screw, 16 knots. Steam turbines. Two masts and two funnels. Launched, November 14, 1925. Passengers: 222 first, 476 second, 456 third. Service: Hamburg-Southampton-Cherbourg-New York. Re-engined in 1930; speed increased to 20 knots. In 1933 was lengthened to 645 feet (22,117 tons). Sunk by a floating mine near Rugen Island, March 7, 1945. Salvage operations took about four years. Converted to whale oil refinery ship. Renamed: **Jurio Dolgoruki.** Sister ship: **New York.** Similar to: **Albert Ballin** and **Deutschland.**

Hammonia (1855) Hamburg-American Line.
Built by Caird & Co., Greenock, Scotland. Tonnage: 2,026. Dimensions: 280′ x 38′. Single-screw, 10 knots. Geared oscillating engines. Three masts and one funnel. Made her first Atlantic crossing from Hamburg to New York, July 1, 1856. Renamed: (a) **Belgian** (1864), (b) **Missouri** (1873). Wrecked, October 10, 1873. Sister ship: **Borussia.** Note: These vessels inaugurated regular steamship service for the Hamburg-American Line.

Hammonia (1867) Hamburg-American Line.
Built by Caird & Co., Greenock, Scotland. Tonnage: 3,035. Dimensions: 330′ x 40′. Single-screw, 12 knots. Inverted engines. Two masts and one funnel. Iron hull. Maiden voyage: Hamburg-Southampton-New York, March 2, 1867. Re-boilered in 1875. Speed increased to 13½ knots. Sold to Russian Volunteer Fleet in 1878. Renamed: **Moskva** (1878). Wrecked while on voyage between Odessa and Hankow, July 19, 1882. Sister ship: **Cimbria.**

Hammonia   (1882)   Hamburg-American Line.
Built by J. & G. Thomson, Clydebank, Glasgow, Scotland.
Tonnage: 3,969.   Dimensions: 373' x 45'.   Single-screw, 16
knots.   Compound engines.   Three masts and two funnels.
Steel hull.   Passengers: 150 first, 100 second, 700 third.
Renamed: **Versailles** (1889).   Scrapped in Italy, 1914.

Hannover   (1869)   North German Lloyd.
Built by Caird & Co., Greenock, Scotland.   Tonnage: 2,571.
Dimensions: 311' x 39'.   Single-screw, 12 knots.   Inverted
engines.   Two masts and one funnel.   Iron hull.   Compound
engines installed later.   Services: (a) Bremen-New Orleans,
(b) Bremen-New York.   Scrapped in 1894.

Hannover   (1899)   North German Lloyd.
Built by Wigham Richardson & Co., Newcastle, England.
Tonnage: 7,305.   Dimensions: 429' x 54'.   Twin-screw, 12½
knots.   Quadruple expansion engines.   Two masts and one
funnel.   Services: (a) Hamburg-Baltimore, (b) Hamburg-
New York.   Made her final voyage to New York in 1923.
Scrapped in 1929.   Sister ships: **Frankfurt** and **Koln.**

Hanoverian   (1882)   Allan Line.
Built by Wm. Doxford & Sons, Ltd., Sunderland, England.
Tonnage: 3,603.   Dimensions: 366' x 41'.   Single-screw, 11
knots.   Compound engines.   Three masts and one funnel.
Iron hull.   Maiden voyage: Glasgow-Quebec-Montreal, May
25, 1882.   Wrecked on coast of Newfoundland, September 2,
1885, with no loss of life.

Hanoverian   (1902)   Leyland Line (British).
Built by Hawthorn, Leslie & Co., Newcastle, England.
Tonnage: 13,507.   Dimensions: 582' x 60'.   Twin-screw, 15
knots.   Triple expansion engines.   Four masts and one funnel.
Renamed: (a) **Mayflower** (1903), (b) **Cretic** (1903),
Devonian (1923).

Hansa   (1861)   North German Lloyd.
Built by Caird & Co., Greenock, Scotland.   Tonnage: 2,992.
Dimensions: 328' x 42'.   Single-screw, 11 knots.   Inverted
engines.   Three masts and one funnel.   Clipper bow.   Iron
hull.   Maiden voyage: Bremen-Southampton-New York,
November 24, 1861.   Sold to British owners in 1879.   Compound engines in 1881.   Renamed: **Ludwig** (1883).   Listed
as missing in 1883.   Sister ship: **America.**

Hansa   (1899)   Hamburg-American Line.
  Built by "Vulkan", Stettin, Germany. Tonnage: 16,376.
Dimensions: 660' x 67'. Twin-screw, 16 knots. Quadruple
expansion engines. Two masts and two funnels. Passengers:
220 cabin, 664 third. Service: Hamburg-New York. Scrapped
in 1925. Ex-**Victoria Luise** (1922), ex-**Deutschland** (1911).

Hansa   (1923)   Hamburg-American Line.
  Built by Blohm & Voss, Hamburg, Germany. Tonnage:
21,131. Dimensions: 645' x 72'. Twin-screw, 20 knots.
Eight steam turbines. Four masts and two funnels. Sunk
by a mine in the Baltic, March 6, 1945. Raised by the
Russians in 1949. Renamed: **Sovetsky Sojus** (1950). Ex-
Albert Ballin (1935). Sister ship: **Deutschland.** Similar
to: **Hamburg** and **New York.**

*****Hanseatic**   (1930)   Hamburg-Atlantic Line (German).
  Built by Fairfield Shipbuilding & Engineering Co., Glasgow,
Scotland. Tonnage: 30,030. Dimensions: 672' o.l. x 83'.
Twin-screw, 20 knots. Steam turbines. Two masts and two
funnels. Passengers: 85 first, 1,167 tourist. Purchased by
Hamburg Atlantic Line in January 1958. Reconditioned at
Hamburg. First voyage: Germany to New York, July 21,
1958. Ex-**Empress of Scotland** (1958), ex-**Empress of
Japan** (1942).

Havel   (1890)   North German Lloyd.
  Built by "Vulkan", Stettin, Germany. Tonnage: 6,963.
Dimensions: 463' x 51'. Single-screw, 18 knots. Compound
engines. Three masts and two funnels. Iron hull. Passen-
gers: 244 first, 122 second, 460 third. Maiden voyage:
Bremen-Southampton-New York, February 2, 1891. Note:
The last Atlantic single-screw express steamship to be built.
Quadruple expansion engines installed in 1898. Sold to
Spanish Government in 1898. Renamed: (a) **Meteoro**
(1898), (b) **Alfonso XII** (1899). Scrapped in Italy, 1926.
Sister ship: **Spree.**

Haverford   (1901)   American Line.
  Built by John Brown & Co., Clydebank, Glasgow, Scotland.
Tonnage: 11,635. Dimensions: 531' x 59'. Twin-screw, 13½
knots. Triple expansion engines. Four masts and one funnel.
Passengers: 150 second and 1,700 third class. Services: (a)
Liverpool-Philadelphia, (b) Southampton-New York. In
White Star Line service, 1921–24. Scrapped in Italy, 1925.
Sister ships: **Merion.**

Hecla   (1860)   Cunard Line.

Built by Robert Napier & Sons, Glasgow, Scotland. Tonnage: 1,784. Dimensions: 274' x 36'. Single-screw, 10 knots. Geared oscillating engines. Compound engines in 1871. Three masts and one funnel. Iron hull. Passengers: 70 cabin, 800 third. Built for the Mediterranean service. Also in New York and Boston trade. Lengthened to 339 feet (2,421 tons), in 1871. Renamed: **Claris** (1882) Spanish, (b) **Conde de Vilana** (1888), (c) **Pedro Tercero** (1892), **Tiempo** (1895), (d) **Rio Negro** (1897). Scrapped in 1954. Sister ships: **Atlas, Kedar, Marathon, Olympus** and **Sidon.**

Hekla   (1884)   Thingvalla Line (Danish).

Built by Scott's Shipbuilding & Engineering Co., Greenock, Scotland. Tonnage: 3,258. Dimensions: 330' x 41'. Single-screw, 11 knots. Compound engines. 2,000 I.H.P. Three masts and one funnel. Iron hull. Transferred to Scandinavian American Line in 1898. Made her final voyage to New York in 1904. Renamed: (a) **Eduard Regel** (1905), (b) **Minsk** (1909). Scrapped in 1910.

Hellig Olav   (1902)   Scandinavian-American Line.

Built by Alexander Stephen & Sons, Ltd., Glasgow, Scotland. Tonnage: 9,939. Dimensions: 500' x 58' (515' o.l.). Twin-screw, 16 knots. Triple expansion engines. Two masts and one funnel. Passengers: 130 first, 140 second, 900 third. Service: Copenhagen-Oslo-New York. Final Atlantic crossing in 1931. Scrapped in 1934. Sister ships: **Oscar II** and **United States.**

Helvetia   (1864)   National Line (British).

Built by Palmer's Shipbuilding & Iron Co., Newcastle, England. Tonnage: 3,325. Dimensions: 371' x 41'. Single-screw, 10 knots. Inverted engines. Three masts and one funnel. Compound engines in 1874. Speed increased to 12 knots. Lengthened to 419 feet (4,588 tons) in 1877. Vessel sold to France in 1893. Abandoned off Cape Finisterre in April 1894, while on way to shipbreakers yard. Sister ship: **Erin.**

Herder   (1873)   (a) Adler (Eagle) Line, (b) Hamburg-American Line.

Built by Alexander Stephen & Son, Ltd., Glasgow, Scotland. Tonnage: 3,494. Dimensions: 375' x 40'. Single-screw, 14 knots. Compound engines. Two masts and one funnel. Iron hull. Maiden voyage: Hamburg-New York, January 8, 1874. Acquired by Hamburg-American Line in 1875.

Wrecked near Cape Race, October 10, 1882, with no loss of life. Running mates: **Gellet, Goethe, Lessing, Klopstock, Schiller** and **Wieland.**

Hermann   (1847)   Ocean Steam Navigation Co. (American). Built by Westervelt & MacKay, New York, N. Y. Tonnage: 1,734. Dimensions: 241′ x 40′. Paddle-wheels, 11 knots. Side lever engines. Three masts and one funnel. Clipper bow. Wooden hull. Maiden voyage: New York-Southampton-Bremen, March 21, 1848. Sold to Pacific Mail Steamship Company in 1858. Wrecked on Kwatzu Point, Japan, February 13, 1869. Sister ship: **Washington.**

Hermann   (1865)   North German Lloyd. Built by Caird & Co., Greenock, Scotland. Tonnage: 2,873. Dimensions: 337′ x 40′. Single-screw, 13½ knots. Compound engines. Two masts and one funnel. Iron hull. Passengers: 80 first, 120 second, 500 third. Service: Bremen-Southampton-New York. Originally had inverted engines; speed 11 knots. Made her final voyage to New York in 1893. Scrapped in 1896. Running mates: **America, Deutschland, Hansa, Union** and **Weser.**

Hesperian   (1908)   Allan Line (British). Built by Alexander Stephen & Sons, Ltd., Glasgow, Scotland. Tonnage: 10,920. Dimensions: 485′ x 60′. Twin-screw, 15 knots. Triple expansion engines. Two masts and one funnel. Passengers: 210 first, 250 second, 1,000 third. Service: Glasgow-Quebec-Montreal. Torpedoed and sunk 85 miles from Fastnet, September 4, 1915, with the loss of 32 lives. Sister ship: **Grampian.** Note: The **Corsican,** and the earlier liners **Bavarian** and **Tunisian** were quite similar in appearance.

Hibernia   (1843)   Cunard Line. Built by Robert Steele & Co., Greenock, Scotland. Tonnage: 1,422. Dimensions: 219′ x 35′. Paddle-wheels, 9½ knots. Side lever engines. Three masts and one funnel. Wooden hull. Maiden voyage: Liverpool-Halifax-Boston, April 19, 1843. Sold to Spanish Government in 1850. Renamed: **Habanois.** Sister ship: **Cambria.**

Hibernia   (1860)   Galway Line (British). Built by Palmer's Shipbuilding & Iron Co., Newcastle, England. Tonnage: 2,959. Dimensions: 361′ x 40′. Paddle-wheels, 12 knots. Two masts and two funnels. Iron hull. Maiden voyage: Liverpool-Galway-Boston, August 14, 1863.

Vessel sold to Telegraph Construction Maintenance Company in 1869. Converted to twin-screw. Wrecked near Aspinwall in 1870. Sister ships: **Anglia, Columbia** and **Connaught.**

Hibernia (1865) Anchor Line (British).
Built by Alexander Stephen & Sons, Ltd., Glasgow, Scotland. Tonnage: 1,615. Dimensions: 278′ x 33′. Single-screw, 10 knots. Inverted engines. Three masts and one funnel. Iron hull. Maiden voyage: Glasgow-New York, June 9, 1865. Foundered at sea on November 25, 1868, as a result of damaged propeller shaft. There was a loss of 66 lives. Sister ship: **Columbia.**

Hibernian (1861) Allan Line (British).
Built by Wm. Denny & Bros., Dumbarton, Scotland. Tonnage: 1,888. Dimensions: 280′ x 37′. Single-screw, 11 knots. Inverted engines. Three masts and one funnel. Iron hull. Clipper bow. Maiden voyage: Liverpool-Quebec-Montreal, May 23, 1861. Lengthened in 1871 to 351 feet (2,752 tons). Tonnage raised to 3,440 in 1884; reduced to two masts; compound engines installed. Scrapped in Germany, 1901. Sister ship: **Norwegian.** Note: First Atlantic steamships built with "spar decks" fore and aft, without bulwarks, an arrangement which added to the safety of the ships and also to the comfort of the passengers in bad weather.

Hohenstaufen (1874) North German Lloyd.
Built by Earle's Shipbuilding & Engineering Co., Hull, England. Tonnage: 3,098. Dimensions: 353′ x 39′. Single-screw, 12 knots. Compound engines. Two masts and one funnel. Passengers: 142 first and 800 third. Launched, September 24, 1873. Maiden voyage: Bremen-Southampton-New York, October 24, 1874. In South American service, too. Triple expansion engines in 1890. Speed increased to 14 knots. Transferred to Australian trade. Sold in 1900.

Hohenzollern (1873) North German Lloyd.
Built by Earle's Shipbuilding & Engineering Co., Hull, England. Tonnage: 3,288. Dimensions: 353′ x 39′. Single-screw, 12½ knots. Compound engines. Triple expansion engines in 1890. Two masts and one funnel. Iron hull. Passengers: 142 first, 800 third. Launched, May 24, 1873. Maiden voyage: Bremen-Southampton-Panama, December 7, 1873. Also in Bremen-New York service. Placed in Bremen-Far East trade in 1886. Sold in 1899 and broken up for scrap. Sister ship: **Habsburg.** Both vessels were also used in South American trade.

Hohenzollern   (1889)   North German Lloyd.
Built by "Vulkan", Stettin, Germany. Tonnage: 6,668.
Dimensions: 449' x 51'.   Single-screw, 16 knots.   Triple
expansion engines. Two masts and two funnels. Service:
Mediterranean-New York. Wrecked on Sardinia in 1908.
Ex-**Kaiser Wilhelm II** (1901).

Holland   (1858)   National Line (British).
Built by Palmers Shipbuilding & Iron Co., Newcastle, England. Tonnage: 3,847. Dimensions: 395' x 40'. Single-screw,
10 knots. Compound engines. Three masts and one funnel.
Iron hull. Service: London-New York. Note: First Atlantic
steamer with compound engines. Scrapped in 1894.   Ex-
Louisiana (1870), ex-**Hudson** (1863).

Holsatia   (1868)   Hamburg-American Line.
Built by Caird & Co., Greenock, Scotland. Tonnage: 3,134.
Dimensions: 341' x 40'. Single-screw, 13½ knots. Inverted
engines. Two masts and one funnel. Iron hull. Maiden
voyage: Hamburg-Southampton-New York, June 9, 1868.
Renamed: (a) **Rossija** (1878), (b) **Dnestr** (1893), (c)
Bloshif N5 (Russian). Sunk in 1916. Sister ships: **Silesia**
and **Westphalia.**

Homeland   (1905)   Home Lines.
Built by Alexander Stephen & Sons, Ltd., Glasgow, Scotland.
Tonnage: 11,055. Dimensions: 517' x 60' (538' o.l.). Triple-
screw, 17½ knots. Steam turbines. Two masts and one
funnel. Passengers: 48 first and 875 tourist. Made her first
voyage as **Homeland,** Hamburg-New York, June 16, 1951.
Transferred to Genoa-Naples-New York service in 1952.
Scrapped in Italy, 1955. Ex-**Brasil** (1951), ex-**Drottningholm** (1948), ex-**Virginian** (1920).

Homeric   (1914)   White Star Line.
Built by F. Schichau, Danzig, Germany. Tonnage: 34,356.
Dimensions: 751' x 83' (776' o.l.). Twin-screw, 20 knots.
Triple expansion engines. Two masts and two funnels.
Note: Launched as the **Columbus** for the North German
Lloyd, December 17, 1913. Construction was held up during
First World War. Completed in 1920 and turned over to the
British. Acquired by White Star Line and renamed **Homeric.**
Largest twin-screw liner built to date. Maiden voyage:
Southampton-Cherbourg-New York, February 15, 1922.
Passengers: 529 first, 488 second, 1,750 third. Towards the
end of her career was used as a cruise ship. Sold to Birtish
shipbreakers in February 1936. Ex-**Columbus** (1920).

*__Homeric__   (1931)   Home Lines.
   Built by Bethlehem Shipbuilding Corp., Quincy, Mass.
   Tonnage: 18,563. Dimensions: 605' x 79' (637' o.l.). Twin-
   screw, 20 knots. Steam turbines. Two masts and two funnels. Passengers: 147 first and 1,096 tourist. First voyage:
   Italy-New York, January 24, 1955. Transferred to South-
   hampton-Havre-Quebec service in May 1955 and, also, used
   as cruise ship to West Indies. Ex-__Mariposa__ (1954).

__Hudson__   (1858)   North German Lloyd.
   Built by Palmers Shipbuilding & Iron Co., Newcastle, England. Tonnage: 2,266. Dimensions: 307' x 40' (345' o.l.).
   Single-screw, 10 knots. Inverted engines. Three masts and
   two funnels. Clipper bow. Iron hull. Maiden voyage:
   Bremen-New York, September 11, 1858. Severely damaged
   by fire at Bremerhaven, November 2, 1858. Returned to
   her builder and subsequently rebuilt. Acquired by National
   Line in 1863. Renamed: (a) __Louisiana__ (1863), (b) __Holland__
   (1870). Sold for scrap in 1893. Sister ship: __Weser.__ Running
   mates: __Bremen__ and __New York.__

__Hudson__   (1899)   United States Mail Steamship Co.
   Built by "Vulkan", Stettin, Germany. Tonnage: 9,699.
   Dimensions: 499' x 60'. Twin-screw, 16 knots. Quadruple
   expansion engines. Two masts and two funnels. Commenced
   service in May 1921. Transferred to United States Lines in
   August 1921. Renamed: __President Fillmore__ (1922).
   Scrapped in 1928. Ex-__New Rochelle__ (1921), ex-__Powhatan__
   (1920), ex-__Hamburg__ (1916).

__Humboldt__   (1850)   New York & Havre Steam Navigation Co.
   Built by Westervelt & McKay, New York, N. Y. Tonnage:
   2,181. Dimensions: 292' x 40'. Paddle-wheels, 10½ knots.
   Side lever engines. Three masts and one funnel. Wooden
   hull. Maiden voyage: New York-Southampton-Havre, May
   6, 1851. Wrecked near Halifax in December 1853, with the
   loss of one life. Running mate: __Franklin.__

__Hungarian__   (1858)   Allan Line.
   Built by Wm. Denny & Bros., Dumbarton, Scotland. Ton-
   nage: 2,190. Dimensions: 298' x 38'. Single-screw, 10 knots.
   Inverted engines. Three masts and one funnel. Clipper
   bow. Iron hull. Maiden voyage: Liverpool-Quebec-Montreal,
   May 18, 1859. Made a fast passage from Quebec to Rock
   Light in 9 days, 6 hours, 35 minutes. Wrecked on Sable
   Island, Nova Scotia, February 1860, with the loss of 237

lives. Sister ships: **Bohemian, North Briton** and **Nova Scotian.**

Iberia   (1881)   Fabre Line.
Built by S. & H. Morton & Co., Leith, Scotland. Tonnage: 1,388. Dimensions: 255′ x 36′. Single-screw. Iron hull. Sunk off New York in collision with the Cunard liner **Umbria** in November 1888.

Idaho   (1869)   Guion Line (British).
Built by Palmers Shipbuilding & Iron Co., Newcastle, England. Tonnage: 3,132. Dimensions: 345′ x 43′. (360′ o.l.). Single-screw, 11 knots. Inverted engines. Two masts and one funnel. Maiden voyage: Liverpool-New York, April 13, 1869. Wrecked on coast of Wexford, June 1, 1878, with no loss of life. Sister ship: **Nevada.**

Ile de France   (1926)   French Line.
Built by Chantiers de Penhoet, St. Nazaire, France. Tonnage: 43,153. Dimensions: 763′ x 92′ (791′ o.l.). Quadruple-screw, 24 knots. Steam turbines. Two masts and three funnels. Launched, March 14, 1926. Passengers: 670 first, 408 second, 508 third. Maiden voyage: Havre-Plymouth-New York, June 22, 1927. Always a very popular liner. Her grand foyer was four decks high. After World War II was thoroughly reconditioned for trans-Atlantic service. Converted to two funnels. Accommodation altered to 448 first, 546 cabin, 268 tourist. Re-entered service in July 1949. Sold to Japanese shipbreakers late in 1958. Sailed from Havre for Osaka, February 26, 1959, under name of **Furanzu Maru.**

Illinois   (1851)   Vanderbilt Line.
Built by Smith & Dimon, New York, N. Y. Tonnage: 2,123. Dimensions: 368′ x 40′. Paddle-wheels, 11 knots. Oscillating engines. Three masts and two funnels. Wooden hull. Clipper bow. Purchased as a replacement for the **Ocean Queen.** Acquired by United States Government during the Civil War.

Illinois   (1873)   American Line.
Built by Wm. Cramp & Sons Shipbuilding & Engineering Co., Philadelphia, Pa. Tonnage: 3,104. Dimensions: 360′ x 42′. Single-screw, 13 knots. Compound engines. Two masts and one funnel. Maiden voyage: Philadelphia-Liverpool in January 1874. Made a fast Atlantic crossing from Queenstown to Cape Henlopen in 8 days, 10 hours, 34 minutes in October 1880. Transferred to Red Star Line's Antwerp-

Philadelphia service in 1892. Vessel sold in 1898. Renamed:
Supply (U. S. Government). Scrapped in 1928. Sister
ships: **Indiana, Ohio** and **Pennsylvania.**

Ilsenstein (1904) Bernstein Line.
Built by Workman, Clark & Co., Belfast, Ireland. Tonnage:
8,216. Dimensions: 447′ x 56′. Twin-screw, 13 knots. Triple
expansion engines. Two masts and one funnel. Passenger
accommodation fitted in 1931. Sold to Great Britain in
1939. Sunk as a blockship at Scapa Flow in 1940. Ex-
Matatua.

Imperator (1912) Hamburg-American Line.
Built by Vulkan Werkes, Hamburg, Germany. Tonnage:
51,969. Dimensions: 883′ x 98′ (919′ o.l.). Quadruple-screw,
23 knots. Four steam turbines. Two masts and three funnels. Her huge funnels were 69 feet high from desk level.
Had draft of 39 feet. Launched, May 23, 1912. Passengers:
700 first, 600 second, 1,000 third, 1,800 fourth class. Maiden
voyage: Hamburg-Southampton-Cherbourg-New York, June
18, 1913. She wrs ceded to Great Britain under treaty of
Versailles after First World War. Renamed: **Berengaria**
(1921). Similar ships: **Vaterland** and **Bismarck.**

Imperatrice Eugenie (1864) French Line.
Built by Chantiers de Penhoet, St. Nazaire, France. (Under
supervision of Scott's Shipbuilding Co.). Tonnage: 3,200.
Dimensions: 355′ x 44′. Paddle-wheels, 12 knots. Side lever
engines. Single-screw, 12 knots. Two masts and two funnels.
Iron hull. Launched, April 23, 1864. Maiden voyage: St.
Nazaire-Vera Cruz, April 23, 1864. Lengthened to 393 feet
(4,585 tons) in 1873; also converted to screw propulsion.
Mizzen mast installed. Renamed: (a) **Atlantique** (1870),
(b) **Amerique** (1873). Running mates: **Europe, France,
Lafayette, Nouveau Monde, Panama** and **Washington.**

*Independence (1950) American Export Lines.
Built by Bethlehem Steel Co., Shipbuilding Division, Quincy,
Mass. Tonnage: 30,293 (23,719 tons by American measure-
ment). Dimensions: 637′ x 89′ (683′ o.l.). Twin-screw, 25
knots. Four steam turbines. Two masts and two funnels.
Keel laid March 29, 1949. Launched June 3, 1950. Attained
a speed of 26.105 knots during her trials off Rockland, Maine,
December 1950. Maiden voyage: New York-Mediterranean,
February 10, 1951. Note: Superstructure enlarged in 1959.
Cost $25,000,000 to build. Sister ship: **Constitution.**

India   (1868)   Anchor Line (British).
    Built by Wm. Simons & Co., Renfrew, Scotland. Tonnage: 2,477.   Dimensions: 311' x 36'.   Single-screw, 12 knots. Inverted engines. Three masts and one funnel. Iron hull.   Maiden voyage: Glasgow-New York, February 5, 1869.   Transferred to Glasgow-Bombay service.   Later in Mediterranean-New York trade.   Scrapped in 1894.

Indian   (1855)   Allan Line.
    Built by Wm. Denny & Bros., Ltd., Dumbarton, Scotland. Tonnage: 1,764.   Dimensions: 278' x 34'.   Single-screw, 11 knots. Inverted engines. Three masts and two funnels. Clipper bow. Iron hull. Served as a transport in Crimean War.   First sailing: Liverpool-Quebec-Montreal, May 21, 1856.   Wrecked near Cape Race, November 21, 1859, with the loss of 27 lives.   Sister ship: **Canadian.**

Indiana   (1873)   American Line.
    Built by Wm. Cramp & Sons Shipbuilding & Engineering Co., Philadelphia, Pa. Tonnage: 3,335. Dimensions: 357' x 43'. Single-screw, 13 knots. Compound engines. Two masts and one funnel. Iron hull. Maiden voyage: Philadelphia-Liverpool in October 1873. Triple expansion engines in 1891. Acquired by Pacific Mail Steamship Company in 1898. Lost by stranding at Cape Tosco, Santa Margarita Island, Mexico, April 3, 1909. Sister ships: **Illinois, Ohio** and **Pennsylvania.**

Indiana   (1905)   Lloyd Italiano.
    Built by Soc. Esercizio Bacini, Riva Trigoso, Italy. Tonnage: 5,012.   Dimensions: 393' x 48'.   Twin-screw, 14½ knots. Triple expansion engines. Two masts and two funnels. Maiden voyage: Genoa-New York, November 1905. Transferred to Navigazione Generale Italiana in 1918. Renamed: **Romania** (1925). Scrapped in 1928. Sister ships: **Florida, Luisiana** and **Virginia.**

Indipendente   (1883)   Navigazione Generale Italiana.
    Built by Alexander Stephen & Sons, Ltd., Glasgow, Scotland. Tonnage: 2,837. Dimensions: 350' x 40'. Single-screw, 12 knots. Compound engines. Three masts and one funnel. Iron hull. Launched June 20, 1883. Service: Genoa-Naples-New York. Transferred to Italy-South American trade in 1888. Renamed: **Tebe** (1903). Acquired by Servizi Marittimi (Italian) in 1910. Sister ships: **Archimede, Gottardo, Vincenzo Florio** and **Washington.**

Infanta Isabel de Borbon   (1913)   Spanish Line.
   Built by Wm. Denny & Bros., Ltd., Dumbarton, Scotland.
   Tonnage: 10,348.   Dimensions: 481′ x 61′.   Triple-screw, 17
   knots, and low pressure steam turbine.   Two masts and one
   funnel.   Service: Spain-Cuba-Mexico; also made New York
   sailings.   Renamed: **Uruguay** (1931).   Transferred to South
   American service.   Sunk by air attack at Barcelona during
   Spanish Civil War; refloated later and broken up for scrap.
   Sister ship: **Reina Victoria Eugenia.**

Ioannina   (1897)   National Greek line.
   Built by Barclay, Curle & Co., Glasgow, Scotland.   Tonnage:
   4,167.   Dimensions: 368′ x 47′.   Single-screw, $12\frac{1}{2}$ knots.
   Triple expansion engines.   Two masts and one funnel.
   Service: Greece-New York.   Torpedoed and sunk by German
   submarine off the Azores, December 15, 1917, while bound
   from Piraeus to New York.   Ex-**Hittfeld** (1913), ex-**Arconia**
   (1908), ex-**Juliette** (1906), ex-**Dunolly Castle** (1905).

Iowa   (1864)   Anchor Line.
   Built by Malcolmson & Co., Waterford, England.   Tonnage:
   1,988.   Dimensions: 315′ x 34′.   Single-screw, 10 knots.
   Geared inverted engines.   Four masts and one funnel.   Iron
   hull.   Clipper bow.   Originally built for London & New York
   Line.   Made her first sailing for Anchor Line, Glasgow-New
   York, June 30, 1866.   Tonnage increased to 2,273 in 1873.
   Compound engines installed.   Renamed: **Macedonia**
   (December 1873).   Wrecked on Mull of Kintyre, May 29,
   1881, while on passage to Glasgow from New York.

Iowa   (1879)   Warren Line (British).
   Built by R. & J. Evans & Co., Liverpool, England.   Tonnage:
   4,329.   Dimensions: 378′ x 34′.   Single-screw, 11 knots.
   Compound engines.   Four masts and one funnel.   Iron hull.
   Maiden voyage from Liverpool to Boston in 1879.   Sunk as
   a result of collision with iceberg, February 22, 1891, with
   no loss of life.

Iowa   (1903)   Warren Line (British).
   Built by Harland & Wolff, Ltd., Belfast, Ireland.   Tonnage:
   8,370.   Dimensions: 500′ x 58′.   Twin-screw, 12 knots.   Triple
   expansion engines.   Five masts and one funnel.   Largest
   vessel owned by the Warren Line.   Renamed: **Bohemia**
   (1912) Hamburg-American Line.   Taken over by the United
   States in 1917 and renamed **Artemis.**   Became **Empire
   Bittern** in 1942.   Sunk as a blockship during Normandy
   landings.

Irene   (1905)   Austro-American Line.
Built by Craig, Taylor & Co., Stockton, England. Tonnage: 3,454. Dimensions: 326′ x 42′. Single-screw, 12 knots. Triple expansion engines. Renamed: **Toyen Maru.** Sister ship: **Virginia.**

Irishman   (1899)   Dominion Line.
Built by Harland & Wolff, Ltd., Belfast, Ireland. Tonnage: 9,510. Dimensions: 500′ x 62′. Twin-screw, 12 knots. Quadruple expansion engines. Four masts and one funnel. Renamed: **Michigan** (1903). Scrapped in Italy, 1926. Ex-**Monmouth** (1899).

*Irpinia   (1929)   Grimaldi-Siosa Line (Italian).
Built by Swan, Hunter & Wigham Richardson, Ltd., Newcastle, England. Tonnage: 12,279. Dimensions: 510′ x 67′ (536′ o.l.). Twin-screw, 16 knots. Steam turbines. Two masts and two funnels. Passengers: 185 first and 1,000 tourist. Service: Genoa-Naples-Palermo-Montreal. Ex-**Campana** (1955), ex-**Rio Jachal** (1946), ex-**Campana** (1943).

Isla de Panay   (1882)   Spanish Line.
Built by Scott's Shipbuilding & Engineering Co., Greenock, Scotland. Tonnage: 3,545. Dimensions: 362′ x 43′. Single-screw, 13½ knots. Triple expansion engines. Two masts and one funnel. Iron hull. Acquired by Spanish Line (Cia Trasatlantica) in 1887. Wrecked in 1929.

Island   (1882)   Thingvalla Line (Danish).
Built by Burmeister & Wain, Copenhagen, Denmark. Tonnage: 2,844. Dimensions: 313′ x 39′. Single-screw, 13½ knots. Compound engines. Three masts and one funnel. Iron hull. Passengers 50 first, 50 second, 900 third. Maiden voyage: Copenhagen-Christiansand-New York, September 7, 1882. Transferred to Scandinavian-American Line in 1898. Made her final voyage to New York in 1904. Scrapped in 1906. Sister ship: **Geiser.**

Ismailia   (1870)   Anchor Line.
Built by Robert Duncan, Greenock, Scotland. Tonnage: 1,630. Dimensions: 306′ x 34′. Single-screw, 10 knots. Compound engines. Three masts and one funnel. Iron hull. Sailed from New York on voyage to Glasgow, September 29, 1873, and was never heard of again. There was a loss of 52 lives. Sister ships: **Alexandria, Assyria, Castalia, Italia, Olympia** and **Trinacria.**

*Israel   (1955)   Zim Israel Navigation Co., Ltd.
Built by Deutsche Werft A. G., Hamburg, Germany. Tonnage: 9,831. Dimensions: 454′ x 65′ (501′ o.l.). Single-screw, 18½ knots. Steam turbines. Two masts and one funnel. Passengers: 313 (first and tourist). Note: First passenger liner to be built for Israel. Launched, March 4, 1955. Maiden voyage: Hamburg-Southampton-Haifa, September 24, 1955. First voyage: Haifa-New York, October 13, 1955. Sister ship: **Zion.**

Italia   (1872)   Anchor Line.
Built by Robert Duncan & Co., Port Glasgow, Scotland. Tonnage: 2,248.   Dimensions: 306′ x 34′.   Single-screw, 11 knots. Compound engines. Three masts and one funnel. Iron hull. Launched, July 24, 1872. Services: Various routes. Sold to Italians in 1898. Subsequently scrapped. Sister ships: **Alexandria, Assyria, Castalia, Ismailia, Olympia** and **Trinacria.**

Italia   (1889)   Hamburg-American Line.
Built by Armstrong, Mitchell & Co., Newcastle, England. Tonnage: 3,564.   Dimensions: 344′ x 43′.   Single-screw, 11 knots. Triple expansion engines. Two masts and one funnel. Accommodation for steerage passengers only. Renamed: (a) **Milano** (1889), (b) **Tenedos** (Deutsche Vevante Line). She was later sold to Turkey and converted to auxiliary cruiser. Sunk in 1915.

Italia   (1903)   Anchor Line (British).
Built by D. & W. Henderson & Co., Glasgow, Scotland. Tonnage: 4,806.   Dimensions: 400′ x 49′.   Single-screw, 14 knots. Triple expansion engines. Two masts and one funnel. Service: Mediterranean-New York. Passengers: 20 first and 1,400 third. Final voyage to New York in 1919.

Italia   (1905)   La Veloce Line (Italian).
Built by N. Odero & Co., Genoa, Italy. Tonnage: 5,203. Dimensions: 393′ x 47′. Twin-screw, 15 knots. Triple expansion engines. Two masts and two funnels. Transferred to: (a) Navigazione Generale Italiana, (b) Soc. Italiana di Servizi Marittimi, (c) Lloyd Triestino. A World War II casualty.

*Italia   (1928)   Home Lines.
Built by Blohm & Voss, Hamburg, Germany. Tonnage: 21,532. (16,777 by Panamanian measurement.) Dimensions: 594′ x 78′ (609′ o.l.).   Twin-screw, 17 knots.   Motorship.

Two masts and two funnels. Passengers: 680 (one class). Commenced her first voyage to South America in July 1948. Transferred to Genoa-New York service in June 1949. Placed in Hamburg-Southampton-Havre-Halifax-New York trade in March 1952. In 1959 was in the Europe-Quebec-Montreal service. Refitted at Genoa late in 1960 for new cruise service to Nassau. Ex-**John Ericsson** (1948), ex-**Kungsholm** (1942).

Italy   (1870)   National Line (British).
Built by John Elder & Co., Glasgow, Scotland. Tonnage: 4,341. Dimensions: 389' x 42'. Single-screw, 12 knots. Compound engines. Three masts and one funnel. Iron hull. Note: First trans-Atlantic steamship in which engines of the compound principle were applied. Launched, April 2, 1870. Maiden voyage: Liverpool-New York, July 13, 1870. Largest ship built to date, except **Great Eastern.** Scrapped in 1894.

Ivernia   (1900)   Cunard Line.
Built by Swan & Hunter, Ltd., Newcastle, England. Tonnage: 14,210. Dimensions: 580' x 64' (600' o.l.). Twin-screw, 16 knots. Quadruple expansion engines. Four masts and one funnel. Her very tall funnel was 106 feet high from the deck level. Maiden voyage: Liverpool-New York, April 14, 1900. Also served in Boston service. Transferred to Trieste-New York trade in 1912. Passengers: 164 first, 200 second, 1,600 third. Torpedoed and sunk 58 miles from Cape Matapan, January 1, 1917, with the loss of 36 lives. Sister ship: **Saxonia.** Each cost about $1,600,000 to build.

*****Ivernia**   (1955)   Cunard Line.
Built by John Brown & Co., Clydebank, Glasgow, Scotland. Tonnage: 21,717. Dimensions: 570' x 80' (608' o.l.). Twin-screw, 21 knots. Four steam turbines. Single mast and one funnel. Launched, December 14, 1954. Passengers: 110 first and 800 tourist. Maiden voyage: Scotland-Quebec-Montreal, July 1, 1955. Also has been used in New York service. Sister ships: **Carinthia, Saxonia** and **Sylvania.**

Jacques Cartier   (1908)   French Line.
Built by Chantiers & Atel. de Provence, Port de Bouc, France. Tonnage: 6,693. Dimensions: 413' x 52'. Twin-screw, 13 knots. Triple expansion engines. Two masts and one funnel. Service: Havre-New York. Scrapped in Italy, 1934. Ex-**Caroline** (1929).

Java (1865) Cunard Line.
Built by J. & G. Thomson, Ltd., Glasgow, Scotland. Tonnage: 2,697. Dimensions: 337' x 42'. Single-screw, 12½ knots. Inverted engines. Three masts and one funnel. Clipper bow. Iron hull. Consumed 85 tons of coal per day. Passengers: 160 cabin. Maiden voyage: Liverpool-New York, November 21, 1865. Compound engines in 1877. Renamed: (a) **Zeeland** (1878) Red Star Line, (b) **Lord Spencer** (1892); as sailing ship. Lost at sea under name of **Electrique** in 1895.

Jerusalem (1913) Zim Lines (Zim Israel Navigation Co.).
Built by Cammell, Laird & Co., Birkenhead, England. Tonnage: 11,015. Dimensions: 512' x'61' (530' o.l.). Twin-screw, 17 knots. Combination quadruple expansion engines and steam turbines. Two masts and two funnels. Passengers: 35 first, 435 tourist, 224 dormitory-housed. Renamed: **Aliya** (1957). Scrapped in Italy, 1959. Ex-**Argentina** (1952), ex-**Bergensfjord** (1946).

*Jerusalem (1957) Zim Lines (Zim Israel Navigation Co.).
Built by Deutsche Werft, Hamburg, Germany. Tonnage: 9,920. Dimensions: 488' x 65'. Twin-screw, 19 knots. Steam turbines. Single mast and one funnel. Note: Can be used as either a one or a two class liner. This very graceful liner is usually employed in Haifa-Marseilles service, but has made voyages to New York. Sister ship: **Theodor.**

John Bell (1854) (a) Anchor Line, (b) Allan Line.
Built by Alexander Stephen & Sons, Ltd., Glasgow, Scotland. Tonnage: 1,101. Dimensions: 231' x 33'. Single-screw, 9 knots. Inverted engines. Three masts and one funnel. Clipper bow. Iron hull. Maiden voyage: Glasgow-Quebec-Montreal, May 20, 1859. Accommodation for cabin and steerage passengers. Note: Vessel originally was built as a sailing ship. Sold to Allan Line in 1962. Renamed: **St. Patrick.** Engines removed in 1872. Renamed: **Diamant**

Joszef Pilsudski (1894) Polish Navigation Co.
Built by Fairfield Shipbuilding Co., Glasgow, Scotland. Tonnage: 4,588. Dimensions: 415' x 45'. Single-screw, 14 knots. Triple expansion engines. Four masts and one funnel. Service: Danzig-New York. Renamed: **Wilbo** (1924). Scrapped in Italy, 1924. Ex-**Mitau** (1921), ex-**Birma** (1913), ex-**Arundel Castle** (1905).

Juan Sebastian Elcano   (1928)   Spanish Line.
Built by Soc. Espanola de Constr. Naval, Bilbao, Spain.
Tonnage: 9,965.   Dimensions: 459' x 55'.   Twin-screw, 17
knots.   Four steam turbines.   Two masts and two funnels.
Passengers: 155 first, 82 second, 350 third.   Vessel was seized
by Russia in the Black Sea in 1939.   Renamed: **Volga**
(Russian Navy).   Sister ships: **Magallanes** and **Marques
de Comillas.**

Jura   (1854)   Cunard Line.
Built by J. & G. Thomson, Glasgow, Scotland.   Tonnage:
2,241.   Dimensions: 316' x 36'.   Single-screw, 11 knots.
Geared beam engines.   Three masts and one funnel.   Clipper
bow.   Iron hull.   In service 1856–1864.   Sold to Allan Line
in 1861.   Wrecked near Liverpool, November 3, 1864, with
no loss of life.   Sister ship: **Etna.**

Justicia   (1917)   British Government (Management of White
Star Line).
Built by Harland & Wolff, Ltd., Belfast, Ireland.   Tonnage:
32,120.   Dimensions: 740' x 86'.   Triple-screw, 18 knots.
Triple expansion engines and steam turbines.   Three masts
and two funnels.   Launched as the **Statendam** for Holland-
America Line in 1914.   However was requisitioned by the
British Government and converted to troopship.   Torpedoed
and sunk 20 miles from Skerryvore, Northern Ireland,
July 19, 1918, with the loss of ten lives.

Jutlandia   (1934)   East Asiatic Co. (Danish).
Built by Nakskov Skibsvaerft, Nakskov, Denmark.   Tonnage: 8,457.   Dimensions: 436' x 61' (460' o.l.).   Twin-screw,
16 knots.   Motorship.   Four masts and no funnel.   Passengers:
80 first class.   In trans-Atlantic service 1946–50.   Converted
to hospital ship for use in the Korean War.

Kaiser Franz Josef I   (1912)   Austro-American Line.
Built by Cantieri Navali Triestino, Monfalcone, Austria-
Hungaria.   Tonnage: 12,567.   Dimensions: 477' x 60'.   Twin-
screw, 18 knots.   Quadruple expansion engines.   Two masts
and two funnels.   Launched, September 11, 1911.   Maiden
voyage: Trieste-Buenos Aires in February 1912.   Transferred
to Trieste-New York service in May 1912.   Renamed:
(a) **Generale Diaz** (1919) Cosulich Line, (b) **Presidente
Wilson** (1920), (c) **Gange** (1929), (d) **Marco Polo** (1936).
Torpedoed and sunk in Mediterranean in 1942.

Kaiser Friedrich   (1898)   North German Lloyd.
Built by F. Schichau, Danzig, Germany. Tonnage, 12,481.
Dimensions: 581' x 63' (600' o.l.). Twin-screw, 21½ knots.
Quadruple expansion engines; 9 boilers; 72 furnaces; 225 lb.
steam pressure in boilers. Two masts and three funnels.
Maiden voyage: Bremen-Southampton-New York, May 12,
1898. Made her final sailing for North German Lloyd in
June 1899. Withdrawn from service and returned to builders
on account of the speed being unsatisfactory. The builders
in August 1899 announced that the liner was to sail as a
Hamburg-American steamship, who chartered the **Kaiser
Friedrich.** Sold to Cie Sud-Atlantique (French) in 1912.
Renamed: **Burdigala** (1912).   Torpedoed and sunk by
submarine in the Mediterranean, November 14, 1916.

Kaiser Wilhelm der Grosse   (1897)   North German Lloyd.
Built by "Vulkan", Stettin, Germany. Tonnage: 14,349.
Dimensions: 627' x 66' (648' o.l.). Twin-screw, 22½ knots.
Triple expansion engines; 14 boilers; 104 furnaces. Two
masts and four funnels. Launched March 4, 1897. Displacement of 23,760 tons. To obtain 22½ knots she consumed 22
tons of coal per hour. Passengers: 332 first, 343 second,
1,074 third.   Maiden voyage: Bremen-Southampton-New
York, September 19, 1897, doing the crossing in the record
time of 5 days, 22 hours, 45 minutes. Best days' run was
580 nautical miles. Involved in the great dock fire at
Hoboken, June 30, 1900, but managed to be towed away
from the blazing piers, thus escaping damage. Fitted out as
a commerce raider at beginning of First World War. As
such, she was destroyed by the gunfire of the British cruiser
Highflyer at Rio de Oro (Spanish Colony), August 27, 1914.
Running mates: **Kronprinz Wilhelm, Kaiser Wilhelm II**
and **Kronprinzessin Cecilie.**

Kaiser Wilhelm II   (1889)   **North German Lloyd.**
Built by "Vulkan", Stettin, Germany. Tonnage: 4,773.
Dimensions: 449' x 51'.   Single-screw, 16 knots.   Triple
expansion engines. Four masts and **two** funnels. Launched,
April 23, 1889. Passengers: 120 first, 80 second, 1,000 third.
Sank at pier in Genoa, June 5, 1893.   Refloated, recon-
ditioned and altered to two masts. Tonnage increased to
6,990. Renamed: **Hohenzollern** (1901). Wrecked in 1908.

Kaiser   Wilhelm   II   (1903)   North   German   Lloyd.
Built by "Vulkan", Stettin, Germany. Tonnage: 19,361.
Dimensions: 684' x 72' (706' o.l.). Twin-screw, 23½ knots.

Quadruple expansion engines; 42,000 I.H.P. Three masts and four funnels. Note: Largest express liner in the world built to date. Dining room was 108 feet by 69 feet wide. Height from keel to roof of smoking room was 72 feet high. Won the trans-Atlantic speed record in 1903. Her best days' run being 564 nautical miles. Passengers: 775 first, 343 second, 770 third. Maiden voyage: Bremen-Southampton-New York, April 14, 1903. Renamed: (a) **Agamemnon** (1917), (b) **Monticello** (1927) United States Government. Scrapped at Baltimore in 1940. Running mates: **Kronprinzessin Cecilie** (identical), **Kronprinz Wilhelm** and **Kaiser Wilhelm der Grosse.**

Kaiserin Auguste Victoria (1905)   Hamburg-American Line. Built by "Vulkan", Stettin, Germany. Tonnage: 24,581. Dimensions: 677′ x 77′ (699′ o.l.). Twin-screw, 18 knots. Quadruple expansion engines. Four masts and two funnels. Note: Launched as the largest ship in the world. Passengers: 472 first, 174 second, 1,820 third. Ceded to Great Britain after First World War. Served in Cunard Line fleet for a time. Acquired by Canadian Pacific Line in 1921. Renamed: **Empress of Scotland** (1921). Scrapped in 1934.

Kaiserin Maria Theresa (1890)   North German Lloyd. Built by "Vulkan", Stettin, Germany. Tonnage: 7,840. Dimensions: 528′ x 51′ (545′ o.l.). Twin-screw, 20 knots. Triple expansion engines. Two masts and three funnels. Note: As originally built this liner had three masts and two funnels; also was of single-screw. In 1899 lengthened from 463 feet to 528 feet, which raised her tonnage to 7,840. Made her first voyage as **Kaiserin Maria Theresa,** March 11, 1900. Renamed: **Ural** (1904) Russian. Sunk during the Russo-Japanese War at Battle of Tsushima, May 27, 1905. Ex-**Spree** (1899).

Kangaroo (1854)   (a) Inman Line, (b) Cunard Line. Built by Charles Hill & Sons, Bristol, England. Tonnage: 1,773. Dimensions: 257′ x 36′. Single-screw, 10 knots. Oscillating engines. Three masts and one funnel. Clipper bow. Iron hull. Purchased from Australian Pacific Mail Steam Packet Company in 1854. Acquired by Cunard Line in 1856. Converted to cable laying steamer in 1870. Renamed: **Selamet** (1888) Turkish. Note: Had originally been built for a Panama-Sydney service, but this idea failed to materialize.

Kansas (1882)   Warren Line (British). Built by C. Connell & Co., Glasgow, Scotland. Tonnage: 5,277. Dimensions: 436′ x 43′. Single-screw, 11 knots.

Compound engines. Four masts and one funnel. Iron hull.
Service: Liverpool-Boston. Sold in 1906.

Karlsruhe   (1889)   North German Lloyd.
Built by Fairfield Shipbuilding & Engineering Co., Glasgow,
Scotland. Tonnage: 5,057. Dimensions: 411' x 47'. Single-
screw, 13 knots. Triple expansion engines. Two masts and
one funnel. Passengers: 44 first, 36 second, 1,900 third.
Services: South America, Far East/Australia, North
Atlantic. Final voyage to New York in 1907. Sold to shipbreakers in 1908. Sister ships: **Gera, Darmstadt, Oldenburg, Stuttgart** and **Weimar.**

Karlsruhe   (1900)   North German Lloyd.
Built by "Vulkan", Stettin, Germany. Tonnage: 10,826.
Dimensions: 523' x 60'. Twin-screw, 15½ knots. Quadruple
expansion engines. Two masts and two funnels. Service:
Bremen-New York. Scrapped in Germany, 1932. Ex-
Bremen (1928), ex-**Pocahontas** (1922), ex-**Prinzess Irene**
(1917).

Kedar   (1860)   Cunard Line.
Built by Wm. Denny & Bros., Ltd., Dumbarton, Scotland.
Tonnage: 1,876. Dimensions: 275' x 36'. Single-screw,
10 knots. Geared oscillating engines. Three masts and one
funnel. Iron hull. Passengers: 40 cabin and 500 steerage.
Maiden voyage: Liverpool-New York, November 27, 1860.
Note: Also in other services. Compound engines in 1873.
Altered to two masts. Scrapped in Italy, 1897. Sister ships:
Atlas, Hecla, Marathon, Olympus and **Sidon.**

Kensington   (1894)   American Line.
Built by J. & G. Thomson, Ltd., Glasgow, Scotland. Tonnage: 8,669. Dimensions: 480' x 57'. Twin-screw, 15 knots.
Quadruple expansion engines. Four masts and one funnel.
Note: Named after a Philadelphia suburb. Maiden voyage:
Liverpool-Philadelphia, June 27, 1894. Passengers: 60 first
and 1,000 third. Ran for a time in Antwerp-New York
service, Red Star Line. Also used in Dominion Line service
for a period. Scrapped in Italy, 1910. Sister ship: **Southwark.**

Khedive Ismail   (1944)   Khedival Mail Line (Egyptian).
Built by Oregon Shipbuilding Corp., Portland, Oregon.
Tonnage: 8,193. Dimensions: 439' x 62' (455' o.l.). Single-
screw, 15½ knots. Steam turbines. Three masts and one
funnel. First sailing: Alexandria-New York, March 15, 1948.

Passengers: 100 first class. Renamed: **Cleopatra** (1956). Sister ship: **Mohamed Ali El Kebir.** **Ex-United Victory** (1948).

Kiautschou   (1900)   Hamburg-American Line.
Built by "Vulkan", Stettin, Germany. Tonnage: 10,911. Dimensions: 523′ x 60′. Twin-screw, 15½ knots. Quadruple expansion engines. Two masts and two funnels. Built for Far East service. Renamed: (a) **Prinzess Alice** (1903), (b) **Princess Matoika** (1917), (c) **President Arthur** (1922), (d) **City of Honolulu** (1923). Note: See **Prinzess Alice.**

King Alexander   (1896)   Byron Steamship Co. (Greek Line).
Built by F. Schichau, Danzig, Germany. Tonnage: 11,455. Dimensions: 550′ x 60′. Twin-screw, 15 knots. Quadruple expansion engines. Two masts and two funnels. Passengers: 345 first, 314 second, 1,700 third. Service: Piraeus-New York. Scrapped in Italy, 1929. Ex-**Constantinople** (1924), ex-**Bremen** (1921). Note: The **Bremen** was ceded to Great Britain after World War I.

King Alexander   (1908)   Greek Line.
Built by Blohm & Voss, Hamburg, Germany. Tonnage: 16,960. Dimensions: 588′ x 65′. Twin-screw, 16 knots. Quadruple expansion engines. Four masts and two funnels. Passengers: 250 first, 390 second, 2,550 third. Began Piraeus-New York service in 1920. Liner was acquired by United American Lines in 1923. Renamed: **Cleveland** (1923). Sold to Hamburg-American Line in 1926. Continued to use name **Cleveland.** Scrapped in 1933. Ex-**Mobile** (1920), ex-**Cleveland** (1917).

Kleist   (1906)   North German Lloyd.
Built by F. Schichau, Danzig, Germany. Tonnage: 8,959. Dimensions: 463′ x 57′. Twin-screw, 14½ knots. Quadruple expansion engines. Two masts and one funnel. Built for Far East and Australian trades. However made some North Atlantic crossings. Renamed: **Yoshino Maru** (1919). Sister ship: **Goeben.**

Klopstock   (1874)   Adler (Eagle) Line.
Built by J. & G. Thomson, Ltd., Glasgow, Scotland. Tonnage: 3,641. Dimensions: 377′ x 40′. Single-screw, 13 knots. Compound engines. Two masts and one funnel. Iron hull. Acquired by Hamburg-American Line in 1875. Sold to the French Line in 1876. Renamed: **Saint Germain** (1876). Running mates: **Gellert, Goethe, Herder, Lessing, Schiller** and **Wieland.**

Koln (1871)   North German Lloyd.
Built by Caird & Co., Greenock, Scotland. Tonnage: 2,555.
Dimensions: 311' x 39'. Single-screw, 12 knots. Inverted
engines. Two masts and one funnel. Iron hull. Launched,
August 11, 1870. Maiden voyage: Bremen-Southampton-
New Orleans, April 1, 1871. Also was used in service to
New York. Compound engines in 1884. Vessel sold in 1896.

Koln (1899)   North German Lloyd.
Built by J. C. Tecklenborg, Geestemunde, Germany. Ton-
nage: 7,409. Dimensions: 428' x 54'. Twin-screw, 12½
knots. Triple expansion engines Two masts and one funnel.
Mainly in the Baltimore and Gulf services. Renamed:
Amphion (1917) United States Government. Sister ships:
Frankfurt and **Hannover.**

Konig Albert (1899)   North German Lloyd.
Built by "Vulkan", Stettin, Germany. Tonnage: 10,484.
Dimensions: 499' x 60'. Twin-screw, 15½ knots. Quadruple
expansion engines. Two masts and two funnels. Services:
(a) Far East, (b) Bremen-New York, (c) Mediterranean-
New York. Renamed: **Ferdinando Palasciano** (1915).
Scrapped in 1926. Sister ship: **Hamburg.**

Konig Friedrich Auguste (1906)   Hamburg-American Line.
Built by Blohm & Voss, Hamburg, Germany. Tonnage:
9,462. Dimensions: 475' x 55' (498' o.l.). Twin-screw, 15½
knots. Quadruple expansion engines. Two masts and one
funnel. Mainly in Latin American service. At outbreak of
the First World War was in Hamburg, remaining there until
surrendered to the Allies in April 1919. Sold to Canadian
Pacific Line in 1920. Renamed: (a) **Montreal** (1920), (b)
Alesia (1928). Scrapped in Italy, 1933.

Konig Wilhelm I (1870)   North German Lloyd.
Built by Caird & Co., Greenock, Scotland. Tonnage: 2,550.
Dimensions: 312' x 39'. Single-screw, 12 knots. Inverted
engines. Two masts and one funnel. Iron hull. Maiden
voyage: Bremen-Southampton-Panama, March 7, 1871.
Also was used in Baltimore and New York trades. Wrecked
on Dutch coast, November 26, 1873, while bound from New
York to Bremen. All on board were rescued.

Konig Wilhelm II (1907)   Hamburg-American Line.
Built by "Vulkan", Stettin, Germany. Tonnage: 9,410.
Dimensions: 490' x 55'. Twin-screw, 15½ knots. Quadruple
expansion engines. Two masts and one funnel. Services:

(a) Hamburg-Buenos Aires, (b) Hamburg-West Indies. May have made some voyages to New York. Renamed: (a) **Madawaska**, (b) **General Ulysses S. Grant**, (c) **U. S. Grant.**

Konigin Luise   (1896)   North German Lloyd.
     Built by "Vulkan", Stettin, Germany. Tonnage: 10,711. Dimensions: 523' x 60' (544' o.l.). Twin-screw, 15½ knots. Quadruple expansion engines. Two masts and two funnels. Service: Interchangeable between Bremen-New York and Australian routes. Later served in Mediterranean-New York trade. Renamed: (a) **Omar** (1920), (b) **Edison** (1924). Scrapped in Italy, 1935. Sister ship: **Friedrich der Grosse.**

Konigstein   (1907)   Bernstein Line.
     Built by Swan, Hunter & Wigham Richardson, Ltd., Newcastle, England. Tonnage: 9,626. Dimensions: 459' x 59'. Twin-screw, 14 knots. Triple expansion engines. Two masts and one funnel. Passenger accommodation constructed in 1931. One class ship. Renamed: **Gandia** (1938). A World War II loss, January 22, 1942. Ex-**Arawa** (1933). Running mates: **Gerolstein** and **Ilsenstein.**

Kosciuszko   (1915)   Gydnia-America Line.
     Built by Barclay, Curle & Co., Glasgow, Scotland. Tonnage: 6,598. Dimensions: 440' x 53'. Twin-screw, 14 knots. Quadruple expansion engines. Two masts and two funnels. Service: Gdynia-Copenhagen-New York. Transferred to South American trade in 1936. Renamed: (a) **Gdynia** (1939) Polish Navy, (b) **Empire Helford** (1946) British. Ex-**Lituania** (1930), ex-**Czaritza** (1921). Similar ships: **Polonia** and **Pulaski.**

Kristianafjord   (1913)   Norwegian-American Line.
     Built by Cammell, Laird & Co., Birkenhead, England. Tonnage: 10,669. Dimensions: 512' x 61' (530' o.l.). Twin-screw, 15½ knots. Quadruple expansion engines. Two masts and two funnels. Maiden voyage: Oslo-Bergen-New York, June 4, 1913. Wrecked seven miles west of Cape Race, July 15, 1917. Sister ship: **Bergensfjord.**

Kronprinz Friedrich Wilhelm   (1871)   North German Lloyd.
     Built by Caird & Co., Greenock, Scotland. Tonnage: 2,387. Dimensions: 318' x 39'. Single-screw, 12 knots. Inverted engines. Two masts and one funnel. Maiden voyage: Bremen-Southampton-Panama, April 7, 1871. She was also used in New York service. Compound engines in 1875;

quadruple expansions as replacement in 1887. Disposed of in 1898.

Kronprinz Wilhelm (1901) North German Lloyd.
Built by "Vulkan", Stettin, Germany. Tonnage: 14,908. Dimensions: 637' x 66' (663' o.l.). Twin-screw, 23 knots. Quadruple expansion engines. Two masts and four funnels. Displacement of 21,300 tons. Averaged 23.34 knots on her trials; 36,000 I.H.P. Passengers: 593 first, 362 second, 696 third. Maiden voyage: Bremen-Southampton-New York, September 17, 1901. Broke the trans-Atlantic speed record. Note: If any liner ever had a story book career, the **Kronprinz Wilhelm** should rank very high for such an honor. Her remarkable exploits as an armed commerce raider during World War I were crammed with excitement and adventure. Her final service in the role of an American troopship, under the name **Von Steuben.** Scrapped in 1923. Running mates: **Kaiser Wilhelm II, Kronprinzessin Cecilie** and **Kaiser Wilhelm der Grosse.**

Kronprinzessin Cecilie (1906) North German Lloyd.
Built by "Vulkan", Stettin, Germany. Tonnage: 19,503. Dimensions: 685' x 74' (706' o.l.). Twin-screw, 23½ knots. Quadruple expansion engines. Three masts and four funnels. From keel to top of funnels was 131 feet high. Maiden voyage: Bremen-Southampton-New York, August 6, 1907. She never won the Atlantic speed record for those phenomenal liners the **Lusitania** and the **Mauretania** were put in service and won the Blue Ribbon before the German steamship had any opportunity to try and annex it. Vessel was seized by the United States in 1917. Torpedoed while being employed as the American troopship **Mount Vernon,** September 5, 1918. Managed to make port, but the lives of 36 were lost when it became necessary to close the water tight bulkheads of the engine room. Laid up after the war. Scrapped in 1940. Running mates: **Kaiser Wilhelm II** (identical), **Kronprinz Wilhelm** and **Kaiser der Grosse.**

Kroonland (1902) Red Star Line.
Built by Wm. Cramp & Sons Shipbuilding & Engineering Co., Philadelphia, Pa. Tonnage: 12,760. Dimensions: 560' x 60' (577' o.l.). Twin-screw, 15 knots. Triple expansion engines. Four masts and two funnels. Note: In various North Atlantic services, including the Antwerp-New York route. Transferred to Panama-Pacific Line in 1923. Scrapped in 1927. Sister ships: **Finland, Vaderland** and **Zeeland.**

Kungsholm   (1902)   Swedish-American Line.
Built by Harland & Wolff, Ltd., Belfast, Ireland. Tonnage: 12,528. Dimensions: 550' x 62'. Twin-screw, 15 knots. Triple expansion engines. Two masts and one funnel. First sailing Gothenburg-New York, March 1922. Renamed: **Noordam** (1925). Scrapped in 1928. Ex-**Noordam** (1923). Note: Under charter while in service for Swedish-American Line.

Kungsholm   (1928)   Swedish-American Line.
Built by Blohm & Voss, Hamburg, Germany. Tonnage: 20,223. Dimensions: 594' x 78' (609' o.l.). Twin-screw, 17 knots. Motorship. Two masts and two funnels. Passengers: 115 first, 490 second, 970 third. Maiden voyage: Gothenburg-New York, November 24, 1928. Her swimming pool was 44 feet long by 21 feet wide. Sold to United States Government in 1942. Renamed: (a) **John Ericsson** (1942), (b) **Italia** (1948). Note: After being severely burned at New York in 1947, the vessel was sold back to the Swedish-American Line. They promptly resold her to the Home Lines.

Kungsholm   (1953)   Swedish-American Line.
Built by De Schelde Koninklijke Maatschappij, Flushing, Netherlands. Tonnage: 22,071. Dimensions: 587' x 77'. Twin-screw, 19 knots. Motorship. Two masts and two funnels. Passengers: 176 first and 626 tourist. Entered Gothenburg-New York service in November 1953. This attractive liner was also designed for cruise service to the tropics. Running mates: **Gripsholm.**

Kursk   (1910)   Russian-American Line.
Built by Barclay, Curle & Co., Ltd., Glasgow, Scotland. Tonnage: 7,890. Dimensions: 450' x 56'. Twin-screw, 16 knots. Quadruple expansion engines. Two masts and two funnels. Service: Libau-New York. Renamed: **Polonia** (1921). Scrapped in 1939. Similar ships: **Czar** and **Czaritza.**

L' Aquitaine   (1890)   French Line.
Built by Fairfield Shipbuilding & Engineering Co., Glasgow, Scotland. Tonnage: 8,810. Dimensions: 500' x 57'. Twin-screw, 18 knots. Triple expansion engines. Three masts and two funnels. Passengers: 432 first, 162 second, 640 third. First voyage: Havre-New York, November 1899. Scrapped in 1906. Ex-**Patriota** (1899) Spanish, ex-**Normannia** (1898).

La Bourdonnais   (1904)   French Line.
Built by J. C. Tecklenborg, Geestemunde, Germany. Tonnage: 8,287. Dimensions: 453' x 55'. Twin-screw, 13 knots.

Triple expansion engines. Two masts and one funnel. Passengers: 122 cabin and 210 third. First Havre-New York voyage, April 2, 1921. Transferred to Bordeaux-New York service in 1923. Sold to Italian shipbreakers in October 1934. Ex-**Scharnhorst** (1921).

La Bourgogne (1886) French Line.
Built by Chantiers de la Mediterranee, La Seyne, France. Tonnage: 7,395. Dimensions: 495' x 52'. Single-screw, 17½ knots. Compound engines. Four masts and two funnels. Launched, October 8, 1885. Maiden voyage: Havre-New York, June 19, 1886. Converted to quadruple expansion engines in 1897. Note: The only one of the "quartet" that did not have two of the four original masts removed. In collision with British sailing ship **Cromartyshire** off Sable Island, July 4, 1898, and sunk with the loss of 549 lives. Sister ships: **La Bretagne, La Champagne** and **La Gascogne.**

La Bretagne (1886) French Line.
Built by Cie. Generale Transatlantica (Penhoet), St. Nazaire, France. Tonnage: 6,756. Dimensions: 495' x 51' (508' o.l.). Single-screw, 17 knots. Compound engines. Triple expansion engines in 1895. Steel hull. Four masts and two funnels. Number of masts reduced to two in 1895. Launched, September 9, 1885. Maiden voyage: Havre-New York, August 14, 1886. Passengers: 402 first, 60 second, 598 third. Sold to Compagnie de Navigation Sud-Atlantique for service to South America in 1912. Renamed: **Alesia** (1919). Scrapped in Italy, 1923. Sister ships: **La Bourgogne, La Champagne** and **La Gascogne.**

La Champagne (1885) French Line.
Built by Cie. Generale Transatlantique (Penhoet), St. Nazaire, France. Tonnage: 7,087. Dimensions: 493' x 51' (508' o.l.). Single-screw, 17 knots. Compound engines. Four masts and two funnels. Steel hull. Launched, May 15, 1885. Passengers: 390 first, 65 second, 600 third. Maiden voyage: Havre-New York, May 22, 1886. Two of her four masts were removed in 1896. Triple expansion engines installed at time of reconditioning. Transferred to Central American service in 1905. Wrecked off St. Nazaire, May 28, 1915. Sister ships: **La Bourgogne, La Bretagne** and **La Gascogne.**

La France (1865) French Line.
Built by Chantiers de l' Atlantique, St. Nazaire, France. Tonnage: 4,648. Note: This vessel is listed under name **France.**

La Gascogne   (1887)   French Line.
Built by Forges & Chantiers de la Mediterranee, La Seyne, France. Tonnage: 7,090. Dimensions: 495′ x 52′. Single-screw, 17 knots. Compound engines. Four masts and two funnels. Steel hull. Launched, January 5, 1886. Maiden voyage: Havre-New York, September 18, 1886. Quadruple expansion engines in 1894. Altered to two masts. Sold to Cie Sud-Atlantique for service to South America in 1912. She retained name. Broken up for scrap, 1920. Sister ships: **La Bourgogne, La Bretagne** and **La Champagne.**

La Guardia   (1944)   American Export Lines.
Built by Federal Shipbuilding & Drydock Co., Kearny, N. J. Tonnage: 17,951. Dimensions: 573′ x 75′ (622′ o.l.). Twin-screw, 20 knots. Steam turbines. Two masts and two funnels. Passengers: 157 first and 452 tourist. First voyage: New York-Naples-Genoa. May 27, 1949. Laid up in United States reserve fleet in 1953. Renamed: (a) **Leilani** (1956), (b) **President Roosevelt** (1961). Ex-**General W. P. Richardson** (1949).

La Lorraine   (1899)   French Line.
Built by Cie. Gen. Transatlantica, Penhoet, St. Nazaire, France. Tonnage: 11,146. Dimensions: 563′ x 60′ (580′ o.l.). Twin-screw, 21 knots. Triple expansion engines. Two masts and two funnels. Launched, September 20, 1899. Maiden voyage: Havre-New York, August 11, 1900. Passengers: 446 first, 116 second, 552 third. Served as armed merchant cruiser in First World War, under name **Lorraine II.** In 1919 was put back in service under her original name. Broken up for scrap at St. Nazaire, 1923. Sister ship: **La Savoie.**

La Navarre   (1892)   French Line.
Built by Cie. Generale Transatlantique, St. Nazaire (Penhoet), France. Tonnage: 6,648. Dimensions: 471′ x 50′. Twin-screw, 16 knots. Triple expansion engines. Two masts and two funnels. Launched, November 4, 1892. Maiden voyage: France-Mexico, November 21, 1893. Also in New York service. During her trials made 18.6 knots. Scrapped at Dunkirk, 1925.

La Normandie   (1882)   French Line.
Built by Vickers & Sons & Maxim, Ltd., Barrow-in-Furness, England. Tonnage: 6,283. Dimensions: 459′ x 49′. Single-screw, 16½ knots. Compound engines. Four masts and two funnels. Launched, October 28, 1882. Passengers: 205 first, 76 second, 800 third. Maiden voyage: Havre-New York,

May 5, 1883. Triple expansion engines in 1894; also two masts were removed. Transferred to West Indies and Central American service. Scrapped in Great Britain, 1912.

La Provence   (1905)   French Line.
Built by Chantiers & Ateliers de la St. Nazaire (Penhoet), France. Tonnage: 13,753. Dimensions: 602' x 64' (624' o.l.). Twin-screw, 21½ knots. Triple expansion engines. Two masts and two funnels. Launched, March 21, 1905. Passengers: 422 first, 132 second, 800 third. Maiden voyage: Havre-New York, April 21, 1906. Considered a fast liner when built. Converted to armed merchant cruiser and renamed **Provence II** in 1914. Torpedoed and sunk by submarine in Mediterranean, February 26, 1916, with great loss of life. She had been on voyage from Toulon to Salonica with a large number of troops.

La Savoie   (1900)   French Line.
Built by Cie. Gen. Translatantique (Penhoet), St. Nazaire, France. Tonnage: 11,168. Dimensions: 563' x 60' (580' o.l.). Twin-screw, 21 knots. Triple expansion engines. Two masts and two funnels. Launched, March 31, 1901. Passengers: 437 first, 118 second, 398 third. Maiden voyage: Havre-New York, August 31, 1901. Served as armed merchant cruiser in World War I. Sold to Dunkirk shipbreakers in November 1927. Sister ship: **La Lorraine.**

La Touraine   (1891)   French Line.
Built by Chantiers de Penhoet, St. Nazaire, France. Tonnage: 9,047. Dimensions: 520' x 56' (536' o.l.). Twin-screw, 19 knots. Triple expansion engines. Three masts and two funnels. Launched, March 21, 1890. Maiden voyage: Havre-New York, June 20, 1891. At later date one mast was removed. Made a fast crossing from Havre to New York in 6 days, 18 hours. Made her final voyage to New York in 1922. Scrapped in France, 1924.

Labrador   (1865)   French Line.
Built by Chantiers de l' Atlantique, St. Nazaire, France. Tonnage: 4,612. Dimensions: 393' x 44'. Single-screw, 13 knots. Compound engines. Three masts and two funnels. First voyage as **Labrador** from Havre to New York, November 20, 1875. Transferred to France-Panama service. Triple expansion engines in 1889. Broken up in Italy, 1905. Ex-**Nouveau Monde** (1873).

Labrador   (1891)   Dominion Line (British).
    Built by Harland & Wolff, Ltd., Belfast, Ireland. Tonnage:
4,737.   Dimensions: 401′ x 47′.   Single-screw, 15 knots.
Compound engines. Four masts and one funnel. Iron hull.
Passengers: 100 first, 50 second, 1,000 third. Maiden voyage:
Liverpool-Quebec-Montreal, August 20, 1891. Wrecked on
Skerryvore, Scotland, March 1, 1899, with no loss of life.

Laconia   (1912)   Cunard Line.
    Built by Swan, Hunter & Wigham Richardson, Ltd., New-
castle, England. Tonnage: 18,098. Dimensions: 600′ x 71′
(625′ o.l.).   Twin-screw, 17 knots.   Quadruple expansion
engines. Two masts and two funnels. From keel to top of
masts 200 feet; keel to top of deckhouse 90 feet high; height
of funnels above grate bars 140 feet. Maiden voyage: Liverpool-New York, January 20, 1912. Transferred to Boston
service.   Torpedoed and sunk 160 miles from Fastnet,
February 25, 1917, with the loss of 12 lives. Sister ship:
Franconia.

Laconia   (1922)   Cunard Line.
    Built by Swan, Hunter & Wigham Richardson, Ltd., New-
castle, England. Tonnage: 19,695. Dimensions: 601′ x 73′
(624′ o.l.).   Twin-screw, 16½ knots.   Six steam turbines.
Two masts and one funnel. Passengers: 350 first, 350 second,
1,500 third. Note: First British liner fitted with anti-rolling
tanks.   Maiden voyage: Southampton-New York, May 25,
1922. Transferred to Liverpool-New York route. Converted
to troopship in World War II. Torpedoed and sunk in South
Atlantic, September 12, 1942, while bound from Egypt to
England *via* Cape Town. Heavy loss of life resulted. Sister
ships: **Samaria** and **Scythia.** Similar to **Franconia** and
Carinthia.

Lafayette   (1864)   French Line.
    Built by Scott's Shipbuilding & Engineering Co., Greenock,
Scotland. Tonnage: 3,394. Dimensions: 343′ x 43′. Paddle-
wheels, 13½ knots. Side lever engines. Two masts and two
funnels.   Iron hull.   Launched, October 15, 1863.   Maiden
voyage: Havre-New York, August 24, 1864.   Served in
France-Panama service, too. Vessel was converted to twin-
screw at St. Nazaire in 1868. New single expansion engines
installed; mizzen mast added.   Converted to compound
engines after serious fire at Havre in 1871. Re-engined with
triple expansion engines in 1887. Sold for scrap in 1906.
Running mates: **Imperatrice Eugenie** and **Washington.**

Lafayette   (1915)   French Line.
Built by Chantiers & Ateliers de Provence, Port Bouc, France. Tonnage: 11,953. Dimensions: 546' x 64'. Quadruple expansion engines and steam turbines. Two masts and two funnels. During trials made 18.9 knots. Passengers: 336 first, 110 second, 90 third. Maiden voyage: Bordeaux-New York, November 3, 1915. Converted to hospital ship in 1916. Transferred to West Indies service after First World War. Renamed: **Mexique** (1928). Sunk by a mine in the Gironde, June 19, 1940.

Lafayette   (1930)   French Line.
Built by Chantiers de Penhoet, St. Nazaire, France. Tonnage: 25,178. Dimensions: 577' x 77' (613' o.l.). Quadruple-screw, 18 knots. Motorship. Two masts and one funnel. Launched, May 9, 1929. Maiden voyage: Havre-Plymouth-New York, May 17, 1930. Passengers: 591 cabin, 334 tourist, 142 third. Destroyed by fire while in drydock at Havre, May 5, 1938. The burned out hulk was dismantled at Rotterdam.

Lahn   (1887)   North German Lloyd.
Built by Fairfield Shipbuilding & Engineering Co., Glasgow, Scotland. Tonnage: 5,681. Dimensions: 448' x 49' (464' o.l.). Single-screw, 18½ knots. Triple expansion engines. Four masts and two funnels. Iron hull. Passengers: 224 first, 106 second, 700 third. Maiden voyage: Bremen-Southampton-New York in December 1887. Note: When new was the third fastest steamship on the Atlantic. At later date reduced to two masts. Placed in Mediterranean-New York trade at later date. Renamed: (a) **Russ** (1904) Russian, (b) **Dniestr.** Still in Russian hands as late as 1927.

Lake Champlain   (1874)   Beaver Line (British).
Built by London & Glasgow Shipbuilding Co., Glasgow, Scotland. Tonnage: 2,207. Dimensions: 321' x 35'. Single-screw, 12 knots. Compound engines. Three masts and one funnel. Iron hull. Maiden voyage: Liverpool-Quebec-Montreal, April 13, 1875. Stranded on Antrim coast, June 30, 1886, with no loss of life. She was later refloated, sold and renamed **Lismore.** Listed as missing in 1891. Sister ships: **Lake Megantic** and **Lake Nepigon.**

Lake Champlain   (1900)   Canadian Pacific Line.
Built by Barclay, Curle & Co., Glasgow, Scotland. Tonnage: 7,392. Dimensions: 446' x 52'. Twin-screw, 13 knots. Triple expansion engines. Four masts and one funnel. Passengers:

100 first, 80 second, 500 third. Service: Liverpool-Quebec-Montreal. Note: Vessel originally built for Beaver Line (Elder, Dempster & Co.), but was purchased by Canadian Pacific Line in 1903. Renamed: **Ruthenia** (1913) Canadian Pacific Line's Trieste-Quebec-Montreal route. Sold to British Government in 1914; converted into dummy battleship. Afterwards became a store ship. Later served as a naval oiler in the Far East. Captured by Japanese at Singapore in 1942. Renamed: **Choran Maru.** Retaken by British in 1945. Stranded in 1946, but subsequently refloated. Scrapped in Great Britain in 1949. Sister ship: **Lake Erie.**

Lake Erie (1900) Canadian Pacific Line.
Built by Barclay, Curle & Co., Glasgow, Scotland. Tonnage: 7,550. Dimensions: 446′ x 52′. Twin-screw, 13 knots. Triple exapansion engines. Four masts and one funnel. Note: Originally owned by Beaver Line (Elder, Dempster & Co.). Acquired by Canadian Pacific Line in 1903. Service: Liverpool-Montreal. Renamed: **Tyrolia** (1913) Canadian Pacific Line. Vessel taken over by British Government in 1914. Converted first to a dummy battleship. In 1915 served as a store ship. Renamed: (a) **Tyrolia** (1913), (b) **Aspenleaf** (1916), (c) **Prygona** (1921). Scrapped in Denmark, 1925. Sister ship: **Lake Champlain.**

Lake Huron (1881) Beaver Line (British).
Built by London & Glasgow Shipbuilding Co., Glasgow, Scotland. Tonnage: 4,040. Dimensions: 385′ x 42′. Single-screw, 13 knots. Compound engines. Three masts and one funnel. Iron hull. Maiden voyage: Liverpool-New York, November 9, 1881. During operating season in Liverpool-Quebec-Montreal trade. Stranded near Quebec in 1900 and was subsequently dismantled.

Lake Manitoba (1880) Beaver Line (British).
Built by J. & G. Thomson, Ltd., Glasgow, Scotland. Tonnage: 3,322. Dimensions: 355′ x 40′. Single-screw, 12 knots. Compound engines. Three masts and one funnel. Carried first, second and third class passengers. Stranded on Miquelon Island, June 14, 1885, with no loss of life. Sister ship: **Lake Winnipeg.**

Lake Manitoba (1901) (a) Beaver line, (b) Canadian Pacific Line.
Built by C. S. Swan & Hunter, Ltd., Newcastle, England. Tonnage: 9,674. Dimensions: 469′ x 56′. Twin-screw, 13

knots. Triple expansion engines. Four masts and one funnel. Launched, June 6, 1901. Maiden voyage: Liverpool-Quebec-Montreal, September 24, 1901. Passengers: 122 first, 130 second, 500 third. Note: Acquired by Canadian Pacific Line from Elder, Dempster & Co. (Beaver Line) in 1903. Renamed: **Iver Heath** (1920). Scrapped in 1924. Sister ship: **Lake Michigan.**

Lake Megantic   (1875)   Beaver Line (British).
Built by London & Glasgow Shipbuilding Co., Glasgow, Scotland. Tonnage: 2,219. Dimensions: 321′ x 35′. Single-screw, 12 knots. Compound engines. Three masts and one funnel. Iron hull. Maiden voyage: Liverpool-Quebec-Montreal, July 21, 1875. Wrecked on Anticosta Island, July 30, 1878, with no loss of life. Sister ships: **Lake Champlain** and **Lake Nepigon.**

Lake Megantic   (1884)   Beaver Line.
Built by Wm. Denny & Bros., Dumbarton, Scotland. Tonnage: 5,026. Dimensions: 439′ x 46′. Single-screw, 13 knots. Compound engines. Four masts and two funnels. Steel hull. Clipper bow. Note: In Beaver Line (Elder, Dempster & Co.) service during 1900–1903. Renamed: (a) **Port Henderson** (1905), (b) **Anapo** (1912) Italian, (c) **Porto Said** (1913) Italian. Torpedoed and sunk by submarine in December 1915. Ex-**Arawa** (1900), ex-**Colon** (1899), ex-**Arawa** (1896).

Lake Michigan   (1901)   Canadian Pacific Line.
Built by C. S. Swan & Hunter, Ltd., Newcastle, England. Tonnage: 9,240. Dimensions: 469′ x 56′. Twin-screw, 13 knots. Triple expansion engines. Four masts and one funnel. Note: Built for Beaver Line (Elder, Dempster & Co.), but transferred to Canadian Pacific Line in 1903. First voyage: Liverpool-Quebec-Montreal, May 26, 1903. Torpedoed and sunk by enemy submarine 93 miles from Eagle Island, April 16, 1918, with loss of one life. Sister ship: **Lake Manitoba.**

Lake Nepigon   (1875)   Beaver Line.
Built by London & Glasgow Shipbuilding Co., Glasgow, Scotland. Tonnage: 2,209. Dimensions: 321′ x 35′. Single-screw, 12 knots. Compound engines. Three masts and one funnel. Iron hull. Maiden voyage: Liverpool-Quebec-Montreal, April 27, 1875. Renamed: **Golden Fleece** (1895). Wrecked in the West Indies in 1896. Sister ships: **Lake Champlain** and **Lake Megantic.**

145

Lake Ontario   (1887)   Beaver Line.

Built by Harland & Wolff, Ltd., Belfast, Ireland. Tonnage: 4,502.   Dimensions: 374' x 43'.   Single-screw, 13 knots. Triple expansion engines.   Three masts and two funnels. Steel hull.   Note: The only Beaver Line steamship with a clipper bow.   Service: Liverpool-Canada.   Sold to Elder, Dempster & Company in 1899.   Broken up by Italian shipbreakers in 1905.

Lake Simcoe   (1884)   Beaver Line.

Built by John Elder & Co., Glasgow, Scotland. Tonnage: 4,912.   Dimensions: 430' x 47'.   Single-screw, 16 knots. Compound engines.   Two masts and two funnels.   Iron hull. First voyage: Liverpool-Quebec-Montreal, August 20, 1901. Note: The Beaver Line had her funnels lengthened and two of her four masts removed.   Scrapped in 1904.   Ex-**Ems** (1901).

Lake Superior   (1884)   Beaver Line.

Built by J. & G. Thomson, Ltd., Glasgow, Scotland. Tonnage: 4,562. Dimensions: 400' x 44'.   Single-screw, 13 knots. Compound engines.   Three masts and one funnel.   Service: Liverpool-Canada.   Purchased by Elder, Dempster & Company in 1899.   Wrecked near St. John, New Brunswick, March 31, 1902.   She was dismantled as she lay.

Lake Winnipeg   (1879)   Beaver Line

Built by J. & G. Thomson, Ltd., Glasgow, Scotland. Tonnage: 3,329. Dimensions: 355' x 40'.   Single-screw, 11 knots. Compound engines.   Three masts and one funnel.   Accommodation for first, second and third class passengers.   Service: Liverpool-Canada.   Triple expansion engines.   Speed increased to 13 knots.   Renamed: **Garbi** (1898) Turkish. Torpedoed and sunk during Turko-Italian War of 1912. Sister ship: **Lake Manitoba.**

Lancashire   (1889)   Dominion Line.

Built by Harland & Wolff, Ltd., Belfast, Ireland. Tonnage: 4,244.   Dimensions: 400' x 45'.   Single-screw, 14 knots. Triple expansion engines.   Four masts and one funnel. Chartered by Dominion Line for a short time.   Note: This former Bibby liner was sold to the Danish East Asiatic Company and operated by their Russian-American Line, as the **Kina**, in 1905.   Renamed: **Lituania** (1907).

Lancastria   (1922)   Cunard Line.

Built by Wm. Beardmore & Co., Glasgow, Scotland. Tonnage: 16,243.   Dimensions: 552' x 70' (579' o.l.).   Twin-screw,

16½ knots. Six steam turbines. Two masts and one funnel. Service: Regular London, Havre, Southampton to New York trade. At later date she was used as a cruise ship. Sunk by a bomb, which went right through her funnel and exploded in the boiler room, June 17, 1940. There was great loss of life, caused by this German aircraft bombing near St. Nazaire. Ex-**Tyrrhenia** (1924). Note: The Anchor liner **Cameronia** was nearly identical in appearance.

Lapland (1908)   Red Star Line (Belgium).
Built by Harland & Wolff, Ltd., Belfast, Ireland. Tonnage: 18,565.   Dimensions: 605′ x 70′.   Twin-screw, 18 knots. Quadruple expansion engines. Four masts and two funnels. Launched, June 27, 1908. Passengers: 450 first, 400 second, 1,500 third. Maiden voyage: Antwerp-Dover-New York in April 1909. Note: In White Star Line during 1914–1919 period. Resumed regular Antwerp-New York sailings in January 1920. Towards end of her career was used as a cruise ship. Broken up by Japanese shipbreakers in 1934.

Latvia   (1908)   Gdynia-America Line.
Built by Barclay, Curle & Co., Glasgow, Scotland. Tonnage: 8,596. Dimensions: 475′ x 57′. Twin-screw, 14 knots. Triple expansion engines. Four masts and two funnels. Service: Libau-New York. First operated under name of Baltic-American Line. This line was later to be known as Gdynia-America Line. Passengers: 51 first and 1,240 third class. Renamed: (a) **Fuso Maru** (1924), (b) **Huso Maru.** A World War II casualty. Ex-**Russ**, ex-**Rossija**, ex-**Russia** (1917). Running mates: **Estonia, Lituania** and **Polonia.**

Laura   (1907)   Austro-American Line.
Built by Russell & Co., Port Glasgow, Scotland. Tonnage: 6,122. Dimensions: 415′ x 49′. Twin-screw, 16 knots. Triple expansion engines. Two masts and one funnel. Service: Trieste-New York. Renamed: (a) **Europa** (1917), (b) **Braga** (1920). Wrecked in November 1926. Sister ship: **Alice.**

*Laurentia   (1945)   Donaldson Atlantic Line.
Built by Permanente Metals Corp., Richmond, Calif. Tonnage: 8,349. Dimensions: 411′ x 62′ (455′ o.l.). Single-screw, 15½ knots. Steam turbines. Two masts and one funnel. Type: Combination freighter-passenger ship. Accommodation for 55 first class passengers. Service: Glasgow-Canada. Ex-**Medina Victory** (1947). Sister ship: **Lismoria.**

Laurentian   (1872)   Allan Line (British).
Built by Robert Steele & Co., Greenock, Scotland. Tonnage: 4,522.   Dimensions: 400′ x 42′.   Single-screw, 14 knots.

Triple expansion engines. Two masts and one funnel. First voyage as **Laurentian**: Liverpool-Quebec-Montreal, May 27, 1893. New engines and boilers installed in 1893. Wrecked near Cape Race, September 6, 1909, with no loss of life. The loss occurred, while on voyage from Boston to Glasgow. Ex-**Polynesian** (1893).

Laurentic   (1909)   White Star Line.
Built by Harland & Wolff, Ltd., Belfast, Ireland. Tonnage: 14,892. Dimensions: 550′ x 67′ (565′ o.l.). Triple-screw, 17 knots. Triple expansion engines and steam turbines. Two masts and one funnel. Passengers: 230 first, 430 second, 1,000 third. Note: Laid down as the **Alberta** for the Dominion Line, but was transferred to White Star Line before completion. Maiden voyage: Liverpool-Quebec-Montreal, in April 1909. Sunk by a mine off the north coast of Ireland, January 25, 1917, with the loss of 350 lives. Sister ship: **Megantic**.

Laurentic   (1927)   White Star Line.
Built by Harland & Wolff, Ltd., Belfast, Ireland. Tonnage: 18,724. Dimensions: 578′ x 75′ (603′ o.l.). Triple-screw, 17 knots. Combination triple expansion engines and steam turbines. Two masts and two funnels. Maiden voyage: Liverpool-Quebec-Montreal, November 1927. Torpedoed and sunk on November 3, 1940.

Lazio   (1899)   Navigazione Generale Italiana.
Built by Palmer's Shipbuilding & Iron Co., Newcastle, England. Tonnage: 9,203. Dimensions: 470′ x 56′. Twin-screw, 13 knots. Triple expansion engines. Four masts and one funnel. Service: Genoa-Naples-New York. Renamed: **Palermo** (1913). Torpedoed and sunk in December 1916. Ex-**British Princess** (1906).

Leerdam   (1881)   Holland-America Line.
Built by Nederlandsch Stoomvaart, Rotterdam, Netherlands. Tonnage: 2,796. Dimensions: 321′ x 37′. Single-screw, 10 knots. Compound engines. Two masts and one funnel. Iron hull. Passengers: 44 first and 392 third. Note: **Built as De Nederlander** for Dutch owners. In service 1883–1899. Vessel sold in 1899.

Leerdam   (1921)   Holland-America Line.
Built by New Waterway Shipbuilding Co., Schiedam, Netherlands. Tonnage: 8,815. Dimensions: 450′ x 58′. Single-screw, 13 knots. Three steam turbines. Two masts

and two funnels. Passengers: 175 cabin and 800 third. Mainly in Rotterdam-Cuba-Mexico service. Altered to one funnel in 1934; passenger accommodation reduced to 30 cabin and 60 third. Final voyage Rotterdam-Baltimore in December 1952. Laid up until sold to shipbreakers. Scrapped in Japan, 1954. Sister ships: **Edam, Maasdam** and **Spaarndam.**

Legazpi (1904)   Spanish Line.
Built by Sir Raylton Dixon & Co., Middlesbrough, England. Tonnage: 4,349. Dimensions: 375' x 47'. Twin-screw, 12 knots. Triple expansion engines. Two masts and one funnel. Passengers: 114 first, 55 second, 20 third, 147 fourth. Destroyed by aircraft in 1937, during Spanish Civil War. Ex-**Zungeru,** ex-**Bruzellesville,** ex-**Zungeru.**

Leipzig (1869)   North German Lloyd.
Built by Caird & Co., Greenock, Scotland. Tonnage: 2,388. Dimensions: 300' x 39'. Single-screw, 10 knots. Inverted engines. Two masts and one funnel. Iron hull. Compound engines in 1883. Launched, February 13, 1869. Employed mainly in Baltimore service. In service 1869–1894. Made her final voyage to New York in 1890. Sold for scrap in 1894. Running mates: **Baltimore, Berlin** and **Ohio.**

Leon XIII (1888)   Spanish Line.
Built by A. & J. Inglis, Ltd., Glasgow, Scotland. Tonnage: 5,087. Dimensions: 410' x 46'. Single-screw, 14 knots. Triple expansion engines. Two masts and one funnel. Steel hull. Passengers: 117 first, 58 second, 60 third. Scrapped in 1930. Ex-**Isla de Cuba** (1895), ex-**Taroba** (1894).

Leon XIII (1890)   Spanish Line.
Built by Wm. Denny & Bros., Ltd., Dumbarton, Scotland. Tonnage: 5,206. Dimensions: 410' x 48'. Single-screw, 14 knots. Quadruple expansion engines. Three masts and one funnel. Renamed: (a) **Santiago** (1896), (b) **Jelunga** (1897), (c) **Jehangir** (1914). Scrapped in 1923. Ex-**Jelunga** (1894).

Leonardo de Vinci (1925)   Transatlantica Italiana.
Built by Ansaldo San Giorgio, Spezia, Italy. Tonnage: 7,515. Dimensions: 427' x 52'. Twin-screw, 14 knots. Steam turbines. Two masts and two funnels. Built for Italy-South American. Made some North Atlantic crossings. Renamed: (a) **Empire Clyde,** (b) **Maine.**

*Leonardo de Vinci (1960)   Italia Line.
Built by Ansaldo Sp. A. Cantieri Navale, Sestri, Genoa, Italy. Tonnage: 33,340. Dimensions: 761' (o.l.) x 92'.

Twin-screw, 23 knots. Steam turbines. Single mast and one funnel. Two sets of stabilizers. Largest Italian liner built since World War II. Laid down June 23, 1957. Launched December 7, 1958. Maiden voyage: Genoa-New York, June 30, 1960. Passengers: 413 first, 342 cabin, 571 tourist. Note: Designed so that at some future date she can be converted to nuclear propulsion.

Leopoldina (1901) French Line.
Built by Blohm & Voss, Hamburg, Germany. Tonnage: 12,334. Dimensions: 525' x 62'. Twin-screw, 16 knots. Quadruple expansion engines. Two masts and two funnels. Placed in Havre-New York service in 1920. Renamed: **Suffren** (1923) French Line. Scrapped in Italy, 1929. Ex-**Bluecher** (1917).

Lessing (1874) Hamburg-American Line.
Built by Alexander Stephen & Sons, Ltd., Glasgow, Scotland. Tonnage: 3,527. Dimensions: 374' x 39'. Single-screw, 14 knots. Compound engines. Two masts and one funnel. Note: The Adler (Eagle) Line was the original owner and operator. Maiden voyage: Hamburg-New York, May 28, 1874. Acquired by Hamburg-American Line in 1875. In 1882 rebuilt with two funnels. Sold to Messageries Maritimes in 1889. Renamed: **Nerthe.** Scrapped at Marseilles in 1897. Running mates: **Gellert, Goethe, Herder, Klopstock, Schiller** and **Wieland.**

Letitia (1912) Anchor-Donaldson Line.
Built by Scott's Shipbuilding & Engineering Co., Greenock, Scotland. Tonnage: 8,991. Dimensions: 470' x 56'. Twin-screw, 14½ knots. Triple expansion engines. Two masts and one funnel. Passengers: 300 second and 1,000 third. Lost by stranding near Halifax, August 1, 1917, while being used as a hospital ship. Note: Quite similar to her running mate the **Saturnia.**

Letitia (1925) Anchor-Donaldson Line.
Built by Fairfield Shipbuilding & Engineering Co., Glasgow, Scotland. Tonnage: 13,475. Dimensions: 525' x 66'. Twin-screw, 15½ knots. Steam turbines. Two masts and one funnel. Maiden voyage: Glasgow-Quebec-Montreal, April 1925. Renamed: (a) **Empire Brent** (1946), (b) **Captain Cook** (1952). Served as emigrant ship to Australia and New Zealand. Sold to British shipbreakers. Sister ship: **Athenia.**

Leviathan   (1914)   United States Lines.
Built by Blohm & Voss, Hamburg, Germany. Tonnage: 59,957. Dimensions: 907′ x 100′ (950′ o.l.). Quadruple-screw, 24 knots. Steam turbines. Two masts and three funnels. Note: Funnels 80 feet high from deck level. Height from keel to top of funnels 184 feet. From water line to funnel tops was 144 feet. From keel to top of mast 210 feet. First voyage as an American passenger liner was on July 4, 1923 from New York to Cherbourg and Southampton. With-drawn from service in 1934. Left New York for the ship-breakers yard at Rosyth, Scotland, January 25, 1938. Ex-**Vaterland** (1917). The tonnage of this great liner was listed as 54,282 tons gross, when under German ownership. Her tonnage under American rules of measurement was finally set at 48,943 tons. During her American trials in 1923 attained a speed of 27.07 knots for one hour.

Liberte   (1930)   French Line.
Built by Blohm & Voss, Hamburg, Germany. Tonnage: 51,839. Dimensions: 890′ x 102′ (936′ o.l.). Quadruple-screw, 27 knots. Twelve steam turbines. Two masts and two funnels. Note: Allocated to France in May 1946. Broke loose during a severe gale in December 1946, while in the process of being thoroughly reconditioned for trans-Atlantic service. She was driven against the sunken hulk of the former luxury liner **Paris**, and a large section of her hull was ripped open and she sank in the water of the harbor. Her re-entry into service was delayed for a number of months. Recon-struction was completed in 1950, at a total cost of about $19,500,000. First voyage: Havre-New York, August 17, 1950. New funnels were fitted in 1954. Passengers: 555 first, 497 cabin, 450 tourist. Sold to Italian shipbreakers, Decem-ber 30, 1961. Ex-**Europa** (1946).

Liguria   (1901)   Navigazione Generale Italiana.
Built by G. Ansaldo & Co., Sestri, Ponente, Italy. Tonnage: 5,127. Dimensions: 403′ x 46′. Single-screw, 14 knots. Triple expansion engines. Two masts and one funnel. Service: Genoa-Naples-New York. Sold to Russian Steam Navigation Company in 1911. Renamed: **Affon.** Scrapped in 1928. Sister ship: **Lombardia.**

*****Lismoria**   (1945)   Donaldson Atlantic Line.
Built by California Shipbuilding Corp., Los Angeles, Cali-fornia. Tonnage: 8,323. Dimensions: 441′ x 62′ (455′ o.l.). Single-screw, 15½ knots. Steam turbines. Two masts and one funnel. Passengers: 55 in one class. Commenced

Glasgow-Montreal service in October 1948.   **Ex-Taos Victory** (1948). Sister ship: **Laurentia.**

Lituania   (1889)   Russian American Line.
Built by Harland & Wolff, Ltd., Belfast, Ireland. Tonnage: 4,244.   Dimensions: 400′ x 45′.   Single-screw, 14 knots. Triple expansion engines.   Four masts and one funnel. Note: This line was founded by East Asiatic Company of Copenhagen. Ex-**Kina** (1907), ex-**Lancashire** (1905).

Lituania   (1915)   Baltic American Line.
Built by Barclay, Curle & Co., Glasgow, Scotland. Tonnage: 6,598. Dimensions: 440′ x 53′. Twin-screw, 14 knots. Quadruple expansion engines. Two masts and two funnels. Note: Line later became known as Gdynia-America Line. Began Libau-New York service in February 1921.   Renamed: **Kosciuszko** (1930), (b) **Empire Helford** (1946).   Ex-**Czaritza** (1921). Sold to German owners in 1950. Running mates: **Estonia, Latvia** and **Polonia.**

Liverpool   (1838)   Transatlantic Steam Ship Co.   (British).
Built by Humble & Milcrest, Liverpool, England. Tonnage: 1,150. Dimensions: 223′ x 30′. Paddle-wheels, 8 knots. Side lever engines. Three masts and two funnels. Clipper bow. Wooden hull.   Maiden voyage: Liverpool-New York, October 20, 1838, arriving at New York on November 23rd. Sold to P. & O. Line. Renamed: **Great Liverpool** (1840). Wrecked off Cape Finisterre, February 24, 1846.

Livonian   (1881)   Allan Line.
Built by Dobie & Co., Glasgow, Scotland. Tonnage: 4,162. Dimensions: 420′ x 47′. Twin-screw, 12 knots. Compound engines. Four masts and one funnel. First sailing: Glasgow-New York, July 28, 1897. Triple expansion engines in 1900. Later in Glasgow-Boston service. Sold to British Government in 1914. Used as a blockship in Dover Harbor, during First World War. Ex-**Ludgate Hill** (1897).

Lombardia   (1901)   Navigazione Generale Italiana.
Built by G. Ansaldo & Co., Sestri, Ponente, Italy. Tonnage: 5,127.   Dimensions: 403′ x 46′.   Single-screw, 14½ knots. Triple expansion engines. Two masts and one funnel. Service: Genoa-Naples-New York.   Also used in South American trade. Renamed: **Jerousalim** (1911) Russian. Sister ship: **Liguria.**

Lone Star State   (1921)   United States Lines.
Built by New York Shipbuilding Co., Camden, N. J. Tonnage: 13,869. Renamed: (a) **President Taft** (1922), (b) **President Harding** (1922). Note: See **President Harding** for information.

Louisiana   (1858)   National Line (British).
Built by Palmer's Shipbuilding & Iron Co., Newcastle, England. Tonnage: 2,266. Dimensions: 307' x 39'. Single-screw, 10 knots. Inverted engines. Three masts and one funnel. Clipper bow. Iron hull. Note: Lengthened to 395 feet (3,847 tons) in 1870. Compound engines installed. Renamed: **Holland** (1870). Scrapped in 1894. Ex-**Hudson** (1863).

Louisiane   (1862)   French Line.
Built by Caird & Co., Greenock, Scotland. Tonnage: 1,786. Dimensions: 280' x 38'. Single-screw, 11 knots. Three masts and one funnel. In collision with Messageries Maritimes steamer **Gironde** near Panillac, December 20, 1875, and subsequently sunk with the loss of 16 lives. Sister ship: **Floride.**

Loyalist   (1901)   Furness Withy & Co.
Built by Alexander Stephen & Sons, Ltd., Glasgow, Scotland. Tonnage: 3,909.   Dimensions: 371' x 45'.   Single-screw, 14 knots. Triple expansion engines. Two masts and one funnel. Clipper bow. Passengers: 70 first, 24 second, 48 third. Service: London-Halifax-St. John, N. B. Renamed: (a) **Byron** (1901), (b) **Santiago.** Sister ship: **Evangeline.**

Lucania   (1893)   Cunard Line.
Built by Fairfield Shipbuilding & Engineering Co., Glasgow, Scotland. Tonnage: 12,950. Dimensions: 600' x 65' (620' o.l.). Twin-screw, 22 knots. Triple expansion engines. Two masts and two funnels. Passengers: 600 first, 400 second, 1,000 third.   Maiden voyage: Liverpool-New York, September 2, 1893. Badly gutted by fire at her Liverpool dock, August 14, 1909. Despite the fact that her interior had been burned, she was able to make the shipbreakers yard by her own engines, and at a speed of 17 knots, remarkable for a vessel under such conditions. Broken up at Swansea during 1910. Sister ship: **Campania.**

Lucerne   (1878)   Allan Line.
Built by Laird Bros., Birkenhead, England. Tonnage: 1,925. Dimensions: 291' x 34'. Single-screw, 11 knots. Compound engines. Three masts and one funnel. Iron hull. Maiden

voyage: Glasgow-South America. Served much of her time in the trade between Glasgow-Quebec-Montreal, or Boston service. Sold to United States Government in 1898.

Ludgate Hill   (1881)   Allan Line.

Built by Dobie & Co., Glasgow, Scotland. Tonnage: 4,063. Dimensions: 420' x 47'. Twin-screw, 13 knots. Compound engines. Four masts and one funnel. Steel hull. Note: First Atlantic steamer built with twin-screws. However, the French Line paddle-wheel steamships built in 1864, were later converted to twin-screw when only about four years old. **Ludgate Hill** made her first voyage Glasgow-New York, July 28, 1897, as an Allan liner. She was formerly owned and operated by the Hill Line (British). Renamed: **Livonian** (1897).

Luetzow   (1908)   North German Lloyd.

Built by Akt. Ges. "Weser", Bremen, Germany. Tonnage: 8,826. Dimensions: 462' x 57'. Twin-screw, 14 knots. Quadruple expansion engines. Two masts and one funnel. Built for Australia and Far East services, but also made a number of North Atlantic sailings. At one time served in South American trade. Became the British **Huntsend** during World War I. Resold to North German Lloyd in 1924. Name changed back to **Luetzow.** Scrapped in 1932. Sister ships: **Derfflinger** and **Yorck.**

Luisiana   (1906)   Lloyd Italiano.

Built by Soc. Esercizio Bacini, Riva Trigoso, Italy. Tonnage: 4,983. Dimensions: 393' x 48'. Twin-screw, 14½ knots. Triple expansion engines. Two masts and two funnels. Commenced Genoa-New York service in April 1906. She also served in Italy-South American trade. Made her final voyage to New York in 1913. Sunk near Almeria in February 1917, while on voyage from Buenos Aires to Genoa. Sister ships: **Florida, Indiana** and **Virginia.**

Lusitania   (1871)   Beaver Line (Elder, Dempster & Co.).

Built by Laird Bros., Birkenhead, England. Tonnage: 3,832. Note: Taken on charter from the Orient Line for fifteen months. Served in Liverpool-Canada service. Wrecked near Cape Race, June 26, 1901, with no loss of life. See PART III for further information.

Lusitania   (1907)   Cunard Line.

Built by John Brown & Co., Clydebank, Glasgow, Scotland. Tonnage: 31,550. Dimensions: 762' x 87' (790' o.l.). Quadruple-screw, 26 knots. Steam turbines. 68,000 I.H.P. Two

masts and four funnels. Had eleven elevators. Passengers:
563 first, 464 second, 1,138 third. Maiden voyage: Liverpool-
New York, September 7, 1907. Note: Recaptured the trans-
Atlantic speed record for the British. She and her sister ship
Mauretania retained the "Blue Ribbon" for a number of
years. Torpedoed and sunk by German submarine near
Old Head of Kinsale, May 7, 1915, with the loss of 1,198
lives, as she went down in 18 minutes after being hit, while
on voyage from New York to England. Sister ship: **Mauretania.**

Lydian Monarch   (1881)   Wilson Line (British).
Built by A. McMillan & Son, Dumbarton, Scotland. Ton-
nage: 3,987. Dimensions: 360' x 43'. Single-screw, 12 knots.
Compound engines. Four masts and one funnel. Iron hull.
Note: Originally owned by Monarch Line (British), who sold
vessel to Wilson Line in 1887. Passengers: 40 first, 30 second,
1,000 third. Re-engined with triple expansions in 1893.
Renamed: **Ontario** (1893). Sister ship: **Persian Monarch.**

Maas   (1872)   Holland-American Line.
Built by Henderson, Coulborn & Co., Glasgow, Scotland.
Tonnage: 1,703. Dimensions: 255' x 35'. Single-screw, 10
knots. Compound engines. Two masts and one funnel. Iron
hull. Launched, August 19, 1872. Passengers: 8 first and
288 third. In Rotterdam-New York service, 1873–84. Renamed: **Maasdam** (1883). Sister ship: **Rotterdam.**

Maasdam   (1871)   Holland-America Line.
Built by Harland & Wolff, Ltd., Belfast, Ireland. Tonnage:
3,984. Dimensions: 420' x 40'. Single-screw, 15 knots.
Compound engines. Four masts and one funnel. Service:
Rotterdam-New York, 1889–1901. New triple expansion
engines and boilers installed in 1890. Renamed: **Vittoria**
(1902), (b) **Citta di Napoli** (1902). Scrapped in 1910.
Ex-**Republic** (1889).

Maasdam   (1872)   Holland-America Line.
Built by Henderson, Coulborn & Co., Glasgow, Scotland.
Tonnage: 1,703. Dimensions: 255' x 35'. Single-screw, 10
knots. Compound engines. Two masts and one funnel.
Destroyed by fire at sea, while on voyage to New York,
October 24, 1884. Ex-**Maas** (1883).

Maasdam   (1921)   Holland-American Line.
Built by Maats. Fyenoord, Rotterdam, Netherlands. Ton-
nage: 8,812. Dimensions: 450' x 58'. Single-screw, 13 knots.
Three steam turbines. Two masts and two funnels. Passen-

gers: 174 cabin, 800 third. Service: Rotterdam-Cuba-Mexico. Also made North Atlantic sailings to New York and Baltimore. Rebuilt with one funnel in 1934. Passenger accommodation changed to 30 cabin and 60 third class. Torpedoed and sunk in North Atlantic by German submarine, July 26, 1941, with the loss of two lives. Sister ships: **Edam, Leerdam** and **Spaarndam.**

*Maasdam (1952) Holland-America Line.
Built by N. V. Wilton, Fijenoord, Schiedam, Netherlands. Tonnage: 15,015. Dimensions: 474' x 69' (503' o.l.). Single-screw, 16½ knots. Two steam turbines on one propulsion shaft. Two masts and one funnel. Laid down December 19, 1950. Launched April 5, 1952. Maiden voyage: Rotterdam-New York, August 11, 1952. Passengers: 39 first and 836 tourist. Sister ship: **Ryndam.**

Macedonia (1864) Anchor Line (British).
Built by Malcolmson & Co., Waterford, England. Tonnage: 2,130. Dimensions: 315' x 34'. Single-screw, 10 knots. Compound engines. Four masts and one funnel. Iron hull. First voyage as **Macedonia,** Glasgow-New York, December 31, 1873. Also in Glasgow-Bombay and Mediterranean services. Wrecked on Mull of Kintyre, May 29, 1881, with no loss of life. Ex-**Iowa** (1873).

Macedonia (1912) National Greek Line.
Built by Sir James Laing & Sons, Ltd., Sunderland, England. Tonnage: 6,333. Dimensions: 422' x 51'. Twin-screw, 17 knots. Quadruple expansion engines. Two masts and two funnels. Maiden voyage: Greece-New York, April 5, 1912. Sunk as an armed Greek merchant cruiser in Syra harbor, during war against Turkey. In 1916 was refloated and sold to Dutch owners. Repaired at Wilton's yard in Rotterdam. Retained name of **Macedonia** when put back in service under the Dutch flag. Sold to Lloyd Latino in October 1921 and renamed **Pinzio.** Broken up by Italian shipbreakers in 1932.

Macoris (1902) French Line.
Built by Flensburger Schiffsbau Ges., Flensburg, Germany. Tonnage: 5,879. Dimensions: 413' x 48'. Twin-screw, 13 knots. Triple expansion engines. Two masts and one funnel. Service: France-West Indies-Central America. Sold for scrap in December 1934. Ex-**Burgermeister** (1919).

Madonna (1905)   Fabre Line (French).
Built by Swan, Hunter & Wigham Richardson, Ltd., New-castle, England. Tonnage: 5,633. Dimensions: 430' x 48'. Twin-screw, 15 knots. Triple expansion engines. Two masts and two funnels. Launched, January 23, 1905. Passengers: 54 first and 1,310 third. Attained a speed of 17.4 knots during her trials. Made her final voyage to New York in 1924. Sold for scrap in May 1934.

Magallanes (1928)   Spanish Line.
Built by Soc. Espanola de Construccion Naval, Cadiz, Spain. Tonnage: 9,689. Dimensions: 459' x 56'. Twin-screw, 17 knots. Steam turbines. Two masts and two funnels. Service: Spain-New York. Also has been employed in Spain-Havana-Vera Cruz-New Orleans service. Note: Converted from two funnels to a single one in 1941. Sold to Spanish shipbreakers in June 1957. Sister ships: **Juan Sebastian Elcano** and **Marques de Comillas.**

Magdalena (1928)   Hamburg-American Line.
Built by F. Schichau, Danzig, Germany. Tonnage: 9,779. Dimensions: 460' x 60'. Twin-screw, 15½ knots. Motorship. Two masts and two funnels. Note: Built for West Indies and Central America service. Heavily damaged by grounding from February until June 1934 at Little Curacao, Dutch West Indies. Rebuilt with new single funnel and no longer resembled her former sister ship **Orinoco.** Renamed: (a) **Iberia** (1934), (b) **Pobeda** (1946) Russian. This Russian liner (1961) is still in service. Probably used for cruises, and in Black Sea-Mediterranean services.

Main (1868)   North German Lloyd.
Built by Caird & Co., Greenock, Scotland. Tonnage: 2,893. Dimensions: 365' x 40'. Single-screw, 14 knots. Inverted engines. Compound engines in 1878. Two masts and one funnel. Maiden voyage: Bremen-Southampton-New York, November 28, 1868. Made her final sailing to New York in 1890. Sold to other owners in 1891. Sister ships: **Donau** and **Rhein.**

Main (1900)   North German Lloyd.
Built by Blohm & Voss, Hamburg, Germany. Tonnage: 10,067. Dimensions: 501' x 58' (520' o.l.). Twin-screw, 14 knots. Quadruple expansion engines. Four masts and one funnel. Tied up at Antwerp during 1914–18. Came into British hands in 1919. However, vessel was allotted to France. Continued using name of **Main.** Scrapped in 1925.

Sister ships: **Neckar** and **Rhein.**   Note: Carried second-class and a large number of steerage passengers in New York and Baltimore services.

Majestic   (1890)   White Star Line.
Built by Harland & Wolff, Ltd., Belfast, Ireland. Tonnage: 9,861. Dimensions: 566′ x 57′ (582′ o.l.). Twin-screw, 20 knots. Triple expansion engines. Three masts and two funnels. Launched, June 29, 1889. Cost $2,000,000 to build. Maiden voyage: Liverpool-New York, April 2, 1890. Broke the trans-Atlantic speed record. Her power plant contained 16 boilers and were heated by 76 furnaces, which enabled the engines to develop 17,500 indicated horse-power. Main and mizzen masts were removed in 1902, and an intermediate mast installed instead. She was retired from active service in 1912. However due to the tragic loss of the **Titanic** in April of that year, she was put back in service as a replacement. Broken up for scrap at Morecambe in 1914. Sister ship: **Teutonic.**

Majestic   (1921)   White Star Line.
Built by Blohm & Voss, Hamburg, Germany. Tonnage: 56,551. Dimensions: 915′ x 100′ (956′ o.l.). Quadruple-screw, 24 knots. Eight steam turbines. Two masts and three funnels. Note: Launched as the **Bismarck** (Hamburg-American Line) on June 20, 1914. However, was not completed until after the First World War. From keel to top of funnels 183 feet high. From keel to boat deck 102 feet. She had a draft of 38′-10″. When the liner was finished, she was handed over to the British Shipping Controller, who sold her to the White Star Line. Maiden voyage: Southampton-Cherbourg-New York, May 10, 1922. Made a fast Atlantic crossing in June 1922, at an average speed of 24.2 knots. Made her final sailing from New York, as an Atlantic liner, February 22, 1936. Acquired by the British Admiralty in 1936. Renamed: **Caledonia** (1936). Used as a training ship. Gutted by fire and sunk at Rosyth, September 29, 1939. The hulk was refloated, and subsequently broken up for scrap. Ex-**Bismarck** (1922).

Malta   (1865)   Cunard Line.
Built by J. & G. Thomson, Glasgow, Scotland. Tonnage: 2,244. Dimensions: 303′ x 38′. Single-screw, 11 knots. Inverted engines. Two masts and one funnel. Iron hull. Passengers: 40 cabin and 535 third. Compound engines in 1879. In various North Atlantic routes. Wrecked near

Land's End, Cornwall, October 15, 1889. Running mates: **Aleppo, Palmyra, Tarifa** and **Tripoli.**

Manchuria   (1904)   American Line.
Built by New York Shipbuilding Corp., Camden, N. J. Tonnage: 13,639. In New York-Hamburg service, 1919–1923. Running mate: **Mongolia.** Note: See **Manchuria** in PART II for additional information.

Manhattan   (1866)   Guion Line.
Built by Palmer's Shipbuilding & Iron Co., Jarrow-on-Tyne, Newcastle, England. Tonnage: 2,869. Dimensions: 335′ x 42′. Single-screw, 10 knots. Inverted engines. Re-engined with compounds in 1874. Two masts and one funnel. Clipper bow. Iron hull. Passengers: 72 first, 800 third. Maiden voyage: Liverpool-New York, August 1866. Sold to Warren Line in 1875 and used in their Liverpool-Boston service. Renamed: (a) **Massachusetts** (1875) Warren Line, (b) **Solis** (1884) Spanish, (c) **City of Lincoln** (1880). Wrecked near Cape Town, South Africa, August 15, 1902. Sister ships: **Chicago, Colorado** and **Minnesota.**

Manhattan   (1932)   United States Lines.
Built by New York Shipbuilding Corp., Camden, N. J. Tonnage: 24,289. Dimensions: 668′ x 86′ (705′ o.l.). Twin-screw, 21 knots. Steam turbines. Two masts and two funnels. Keel laid December 8, 1930. Launched on December 5, 1931. Cost about $10,500,000. Maiden voyage: New York-Plymouth-Hamburg, August 10, 1932. Passengers: 1,200 (cabin, tourist, third). Renamed: **Wakefield** (1941) United States troopship. Suffered extensive fire damage in a North Atlantic west-bound convoy, September 3, 1942. She was salvaged and towed to Boston, where she was rebuilt. Recommissioned as a troopship in April 1944. Since World War II has remained under government ownership. Laid up in the reserve fleet. Sister ship: **Washington.**

Manilla   (1873)   Navigazione Generale Italiana.
Built by Palmer's Shipbuilding & Iron Co., Newcastle, England. Tonnage: 3,910. Dimensions: 399′ x 42′. Single-screw, 12 knots. Compound engines. Three masts and one funnel. Iron hull. First Genoa-Naples-New York sailing, April 18, 1899. Sold to other Italian owners in 1905. Ex-**Whampoa** (1899).

Manitoba   (1892)   Atlantic Transport Line.
Built by Harland & Wolff, Ltd., Belfast, Ireland. Tonnage: 5,590. Dimensions: 445′ x 49′. Single-screw, 14 knots.

Four masts and one funnel. Passengers: 80 first. Service: London-New York. Renamed: **Logan** (1898) United States Government. Broken up for scrap in 1926. Sister ships: **Massachusetts, Mobile** and **Mohawk.**

Manitoban   (1865)   Allan Line.
Built by Laird Bros., Birkenhead, England. Tonnage: 2,975. Dimensions: 339′ x 35′. Single-screw, 11 knots. Compound engines. Three masts and one funnel. Iron hull. Commenced first sailing as Manitoban on June 25, 1872. Her last voyage was Glasgow-Boston, December 3, 1898. Scrapped in 1899. Ex-**Ottawa** (1872). Note: She was lengthened from 287 feet (1,810 tons) to 339 feet in 1872.

Manitou   (1898)   Atlantic Transport Line.
Built by Furness, Withy & Co., West Hartlepool, England. Tonnage: 6,849. Dimensions: 475′ x 52′. Single-screw, 14½ knots. Triple expansion engines. Four masts and one funnel. Passengers: 120 first class. Service: London-New York. Renamed: **Poland** (1920), (b) **Natale** (1925). Broken up for scrap, 1925. Ex-**Victoria** (1898). Sister ships: **Marquette, Menominee, Mesaba** and **Mohegan.**

Manuel Arnus   (1923)   Spanish Line.
Built by Soc. Espanola de Construccion Naval, Cadiz, Spain. Tonnage: 7,578. Dimensions: 435′ x 56′. Twin-screw, 13½ knots. Two steam turbines. Two masts and one funnel. The vessel was scuttled at Vera Cruz during Spanish Civil War. Refloated by Mexicans and subsequently sold to the United States Government. Sunk during bombardment practice in the Pacific, October 24, 1946, by U. S. War Department.

Manuel Calvo   (1892)   Spanish Line.
Built by Armstrong, Mitchell & Co., Newcastle, England. Tonnage: 5,617. Dimensions: 421′ x 48′. Twin-screw, 13½ knots. Triple expansion engines. Three masts and one funnel. Services: Spain-Latin America-Cuba. Laid up in 1936. Rebuilt as freighter in 1940. Renamed: **Drago** (1952) Spanish. Broken up in Spain, 1959. Ex-**H. H. Meier** (1901).

Marathon   (1860)   Cunard Line.
Built by Robert Napier & Sons, Glasgow, Scotland. Tonnage: 1,783. Dimensions: 274′ x 36′. Single-screw, 10 knots. Geared oscillating engines. Three masts and one funnel. Clipper bow. Iron hull. Lengthened to 336 feet (2,403 tons) in 1873. Re-engined with Compounds. One mast was elimi-

nated. Scrapped in Italy, 1898. Sister ships: **Atlas, Hecla, Kedar, Olympus** and **Sidon.** Mainly in Liverpool-New York, or Boston service.

Marburn (1900)   Canadian Pacific Line.
Built by Alexander Stephen & Sons, Ltd., Glasgow, Scotland. Tonnage: 10,743. Dimensions: 500' x 59'. Twin-screw, 16 knots. Triple expansion engines. Two masts and one funnel. First sailing as **Marburn,** Liverpool to St. John, New Brunswick, November 17, 1922. Sold to Italian shipbreakers in August 1928. Ex-**Tunisian** (1922).

Marco Minghetti (1876)   Navigazione Generale Italiana.
Built by J. & G. Thomson, Ltd., Glasgow, Scotland. Tonnage: 2,489. Dimensions: 350' x 36'. Single-screw, 13 knots. Triple expansion engines. Two masts and one funnel. Services: Italy-South America; Italy-New York. Made her final voyage to New York in 1906. Ex-**Loudoun Castle.**

Marglen (1898)   Canadian Pacific Line.
Built by Harland & Wolff, Ltd., Belfast, Ireland. Tonnage: 10,417. Dimensions: 515' x 59'. Twin-screw, 15 knots. Triple expansion engines. Two masts and one funnel. In England-Canada service. Sold to Italian shipbreakers in December 1926. Ex-**Scotian** (1922), ex-**Statendam** (1911).

Marine Falcon (1945)   United States Lines.
Built by Kaiser Co., Vancouver, Wash. Tonnage: 497' x 71'. Single-screw, 16 knots. Two steam turbines. Two masts and one funnel aft. A "C-4" type of freighter-passenger ship. In trans-Atlantic passenger service 1947–48. Sister ships: **Marine Flasher, Marine Jumper, Marine Marlin, Marine Perch, Marine Shark, Marine Tiger** and **Ernie Pyle.** Note: These odd looking combination cargo-passenger ships were employed by United States Lines under arrangements with the United States Maritime Commission during the 1946–49 period. They had accommodation for 550 tourist passengers.

Marloch (1904)   Canadian Pacific Line.
Built by Workman, Clark & Co., Belfast, Ireland. Tonnage: 10,687. Dimensions: 517' x 60' (540' o.l.). Triple-screw, 15 knots. Steam turbines. Two masts and one funnel. New steam turbines in 1922. Passengers: 418 cabin and 566 third class. First Atlantic voyage as **Marloch,** December 20, 1922. Broken up for scrap in 1930. Ex-**Victorian** (1922).

*Marques de Comillas   (1928)   Spanish Line.

Built by Soc. Espanola de Construccion Naval, Ferrol, Spain. Tonnage: 9,922.   Dimensions: 459′ x 55′ (466′ o.l.).   Twin-screw, 16 knots.   Steam turbines.   Two masts and two funnels.   Altered to single funnel in 1941.   Accommodation for 550 passengers after World War II.   Transferred from New York service to Bilbao-Havana-Vera Cruz-New Orleans trade in 1953.   Converted to single mast.   Scheduled to sail between Spain and Venezuela in the fall of 1961. Sister ships: **Juan Sebastian Elcano** and **Magallanes.**

Marquette   (1898)   (a) Atlantic Transport Line,   (b) Red Star Line.

Built by Alexander Stephen & Sons, Ltd., Glasgow, Scotland. Tonnage: 7,057.   Dimensions: 486′ x 52′.   Single-screw, 14½ knots.   Triple expansion engines.   Four masts and one funnel. Passengers: 132 first.   Placed in London-New York service in 1898.   Torpedoed and sunk without warning 36 miles from Salonica Bay, October 23, 1915, with the loss of 29 lives. Ex-**Boadicea** (1898). Sister ships: **Manitou, Menom-inee, Mesaba** and **Mohegan.**

Martello   (1884)   Wilson Line (British).

Built by Earle's Shipbuilding & Engineering Co., Hull, England. Tonnage: 3,709.   Dimensions: 370′ x 43′.   Single-screw, 12 knots.   Triple expansion engines.   Three masts and one funnel.   Iron hull.   First Atlantic steamship with triple expansion engines.   Final voyage to New York in 1899.   Vessel sold in 1909.

Martha Washington   (1908)   Austro-American Line.

Built by Russell & Co., Port Glasgow, Scotland. Tonnage: 8,347. Dimensions: 459′ x 58′. Twin-screw, 17 knots. Triple expansion engines. Two masts and two funnels. Launched, June 10, 1908. Note: Austro-American Line's finest liner when built. Maiden voyage: Trieste-New York, May 10, 1909. Seized by United States in 1917 and converted to troopship. Acquired by Cosulich Line in 1923. Placed in New York service. She was later employed in Italy-South American trade. Renamed: **Tel Aviv.** Burned in 1934 and subsequently broken up for scrap.

Martinique   (1855)   French Line.

Built by Laird & Co., Liverpool, England. Tonnage: 1,900. Dimensions: 265′ x 37′.   Single-screw, 13 knots.   Three masts and one funnel.   Service: France-West Indies-Central America.   Sold to shipbreakers in January 1893.   Ex-**Vera Cruz** (1863), ex-**Imperatrix.**

Martinique (1883) French Line.

Built by John Elder & Co., Glasgow, Scotland. Tonnage: 4,392. Dimensions: 380′ x 48′. Single-screw, 15 knots. Triple expansion engines. Two masts and one funnel. Iron hull. Service: France-West Indies-Central America. Sold to Italian shipbreakers in September 1931. Dismantled in 1932. Ex-**Norham Castle** (1903).

Marvale (1907) Canadian Pacific Line.

Built by Barclay, Curle & Co., Glasgow, Scotland. Tonnage: 11,438. Dimensions: 499′ x 61′. Twin-screw, 16 knots. Triple expansion engines. Two masts and one funnel. Service speed: 14½ knots. In Canadian service. Wrecked 20 miles west of Cape Race, May 21, 1923, with no loss of life. Ex-**Corsican** (1922).

Massachusetts (1892) Atlantic Transport Line.

Built by Harland & Wolff, Ltd., Belfast, Ireland. Tonnage: 5,590. Dimensions: 445′ x 49′. Twin-screw, 14 knots. Compound engines. Four masts and one funnel. Service: London-New York. Passengers: 80 first. Renamed: **Sheridan** (1898) United States Govt. Wrecked by stranding off Barnegat Light in 1910. Sister ships: **Manitoba, Mobile** and **Mohawk.**

Massilia (1891) Fabre Line (French).

Built by Gourlay Bros. & Co., Dundee, Scotland. Tonnage: 3,097. Dimensions: 340′ x 41′. Single-screw, 11 knots. Triple expansion engines. Two masts and one funnel. Steel hull. Launched, January 10, 1891. Service: Marseilles-New York. Sold to Italian shipbreakers in July 1911.

Massilia (1902) Anchor Line (British).

Built by Alexander Stephen & Sons, Ltd., Glasgow, Scotland. Tonnage: 5,156. Dimensions: 400′ x 49′. Single-screw, 12 knots. Triple expansion engines. Two masts and one funnel. Passengers: 70 first. Sold for scrap in March 1930.

Mauretania (1907) Cunard Line.

Built by Swan, Hunter & Wigham Richardson, Ltd., Wallsend-on-Tyne, Newcastle, England. Tonnage: 30,696. Dimensions: 762′ x 88′ (790′ o.l.). Quadruple-screw, 26 knots. Four steam turbines. Two masts and four funnels. Launched, September 20, 1906. Passengers: 563 first, 464 second, 1,138 third. Maiden voyage: Liverpool-New York, November 16, 1907. Held the trans-Atlantic speed record, along with her sister ship for a number of years. In June

1909 she made the eastward crossing in 4 days, 17 hours and 21 minutes. Rated at 68,000 shaft horse-power. Equipped with 23 double and 2 single ended boilers working at 200 lb. pressure. In September 1928, made the Cherbourg to Ambrose Light crossing in 5 days, 2 hours, 34 minutes, a remarkable feat for a twenty-two year old liner, especially as she was at the time equipped with her original "Parson's" steam turbines. The grand old ship was finally broken up by shipbreakers at Rosyth in 1935, thus ending the career of one of the most famous and successful of Atlantic liners. Sister ship: **Lusitania.**

*Mauretania   (1939)   Cunard Line.
Built by Cammell, Laird & Co., Ltd., Birkenhead, England. Tonnage: 35,738. Dimensions: 739′ x 89′ (771′ o.l.). Twin-screw, 22½ knots. Steam turbines. Two masts and two funnels. Launched, July 28, 1938. Maiden voyage: Liverpool-New York, June 17, 1939. Made just two voyages to New York before World War II. Employed as a troopship during the war. Resumed trans-Atlantic service in April 1947. Passengers: 470 first, 370 cabin, 300 tourist (as of 1960). Ports: Southampton-Havre-Cobh-New York. Crew of 600 members.

Mayflower   (1902)   Dominion Line.
Built by Hawthorn, Leslie & Co., Newcastle, England. Tonnage: 13,518. Dimensions: 582′ x 60′. Twin-screw, 16 knots. Triple expansion engines. Four masts and one funnel. First voyage as Mayflower Liverpool-Boston, April 9, 1903. Renamed: (a) **Cretic** (1903), (b) **Devonian** (1923). Broken up in 1930. Ex-**Hanoverian** (1903) Leyland Line.

*Media   (1947)   Cunard Line.
Built by John Brown & Co., Clydebank, Glasgow, Scotland. Tonnage: 13,345. Dimensions: 518′ x 70′ (531′ o.l.). Twin-screw, 18 knots. Steam turbines. Single mast and one funnel. Launched, December 12, 1946. Passengers: 250 in one class. Arrived in New York on maiden voyage, August 28, 1947. In regular service between Liverpool and New York. Sister ship: **Parthia.**

Megali Hellas   (1914)   National Greek Line.
Built by Cammell, Laird & Co., Birkenhead, England. Tonnage: 9,272. Dimensions: 470′ x 58′. Twin-screw, 17 knots. Quadruple expansion engines. Two masts and two funnels. Launched as **Vasilefs Constantinos** in June 1914. Construction was held up during World War I. Maiden

voyage from Piraeus to New York in 1920.   Renamed:
Byron (1924).   Scrapped in 1937.

Megantic   (1909)   White Star Line.
Built by Harland & Wolff, Ltd., Belfast, Ireland. Tonnage:
14,878. Dimensions: 550' x 67' (565' o.l.). Twin-screw, 17
knots. Quadruple expansion engines. Two masts and one
funnel. Note: Laid down as the **Albany** for the Dominion
Line, but like her sister ship was taken over by the White
Star Line. She was given the name **Megantic** (derived from
Lake Megantic in Quebec Province, Canada).   Maiden
voyage: Liverpool-Quebec-Montreal, June 16, 1909. Passengers: 230 first, 430 second, 1,000 third. Sold to Japanese
shipbreakers in January 1933; broken up during the year.
Sister ship: **Laurentic.** The first ships completed for the
White Star Line service to Canada.

Meknes   (1913)   French Line.
Built by Ch. & Atl. de St. Nazaire, France. Tonnage: 6,127.
Dimensions: 413' x 51'. Twin-screw, 13 knots. Two masts
and two funnels. Note: Always in Bordeaux-Casablanca
service. Torpedoed and sunk, July 24, 1940. Ex-**Puerto
Rico** (1929).

Melita   (1853)   Cunard Line.
Built by Wm. Denny & Bros., Dumbarton, Scotland. Ton-
nage: 1,254. Dimensions: 233' x 29'. Single-screw, 9 knots.
Two masts and one funnel. Clipper bow. Iron hull. In
Liverpool-New York service in 1860. Had been built for
Mediterranean trade. Sold to Warren Line. Destroyed by
fire at sea in September 1868, with no loss of life.

Melita   (1918)   Canadian Pacific Line.
Built by Barclay, Curle & Co., Glasgow, Scotland. Tonnage:
15,183. Dimensions: 520' x 67' (546' o.l.). Triple-screw, 16
knots. Triple expansion engines and one low pressure steam
turbine. Two masts and two funnels. Passengers: 550 cabin
and 1,200 third class. Placed in England-Canada service.
Sold to Italy in 1935. Renamed: **Liguria** (1935). First
employed as a transport during Italian invasion of Ethiopia.
Bombed at Tobruk in July 1940. Scuttled at Tobruk in
January 1941. Refloated in August 1950; towed to Italy to
be broken up for scrap. Sister ship: **Minnedosa.**

Memphis   (1871)   Dominion Line.
Built by A. McMillan & Son, Dumbarton, Scotland. Tonnage: 2,487. Dimensions: 327' x 38'. Single-screw, 12 knots.

Compound engines. Three masts and one funnel. Iron hull. Passengers: 80 cabin and 600 third. Services: Canadian in summer; New Orleans in winter. Stranded off Corunna, February 25, 1879. Sister ship: **Vicksburg.**

Mendoza   (1904)   Lloyd Italiano.
Built by Armstrong, Whitworth & Co., Newcastle, England. Tonnage: 6,847. Dimensions: 420' x 51'. Twin-screw, 14 knots. Triple expansion engines. Two masts and one funnel. Built Italy-South America service. Renamed: (a) **Caserta** (1914), (b) **Venezuela** (1923). Scrapped in 1928.

Menominee   (1897)   Atlantic Transport Line.
Built by Alexander Stephen & Sons, Ltd., Glasgow, Scotland. Tonnage: 6,919. Dimensions: 475' x 52'. Single-screw, 14½ knots. Triple expansion engines. Four masts and one funnel. Passengers: 130. Service: London-New York. Made her final voyage to Boston in 1914. Commissioned as a British troopship in 1915. Recondition after the war at Harland & Wolff, Ltd. Commenced service as a freighter between London and New York in 1920. Sold for scrap in January 1927. Ex-**Alexandra** (1898). Sister ships: **Manitou, Marquette, Mesaba** and **Mohegan.**

Merion   (1902)   American Line.
Built by John Brown & Co., Clydebank, Glasgow, Scotland. Tonnage: 11,612. Dimensions: 531' x 59' (547' o.l.). Twin-screw, 12 knots. Triple expansion engines. Four masts and one funnel. Maiden voyage: Liverpool-Boston, March 8, 1902, as a Dominion liner. Served in Dominion Line for only a brief time, then transferred to American Line. Converted to dummy battleship in World War I. Torpedoed and sunk in Aegean Sea, May 30, 1915. Sister ship: **Haverford.**

Mesaba   (1898)   Atlantic Transport Line
Built by Harland & Wolff, Ltd., Belfast, Ireland. Tonnage: 6,833. Dimensions: 482' x 52'. Single-screw, 13 knots. Triple expansion engines. Four masts and one funnel. Torpedoed and sunk in Irish Sea, September 1, 1918. Ex-**Winifreda** (1898). Sister ships: **Manitou, Marquette, Menominee** and **Mohegan.**

Metagama   (1915)   Canadian Pacific Line.
Built by Barclay, Curle & Co., Glasgow, Scotland. Tonnage: 12,420. Dimensions: 500' x 64'. Twin-screw, 16 knots. Quadruple expansion engines. Two masts and two funnels. Passengers: 520 cabin and 1,200 third class. Maiden voyage: Liverpool-St. John, New Brunswick, March 26, 1915.

Scrapped in Great Britain in 1934. Sister ship: **Missanabie.**
The first so called "Cabin" class steamships built for the
Canadian Pacific Line.

Meteoro   (1890)   Spanish Line.
Built by "Vulkan", Stettin, Germany. Tonnage: 6,966.
Dimensions: 463' x 51'. Single-screw, 18 knots. Triple
expansion engines. Three masts and two funnels. Renamed:
Alfonso XII (1899). Scrapped in 1926. Ex-**Havel** (1898).

Mexico   (1876)   Spanish Line.
Built by London & Glasgow Shipbuilding Co., Glasgow,
Scotland. Tonnage: 2,113. Dimensions: 331' x 34'. Single-
screw, 12 knots. Compound engines. Three masts. Iron hull.
Ex-**Trentham Hall.**

Mexico   (1884)   Compania Mexicana Transatlantica.
Built by Robert Napier & Sons, Glasgow, Scotland. Ton-
nage: 4,133. Dimensions: 400' x 44'. Single-screw, 14 knots.
Compound engines. Three masts and two funnels. Renamed:
Duchessa di Genova (1887). Sister ships: **Oaxaca** and
Tamaulipas. These attractive liners were placed in service
between Mexico and Spain. However, this Mexican company
did not last long, as the vessels were soon sold.

Mexique   (1915)   French Line.
Built by Chantiers & Ateliers de Provence, Port de Bouc,
France. Tonnage: 12,220. Dimensions: 546' x 64'. Quad-
ruple-screw, 16 knots. Combination Quadruple expansion
engines and two low pressure steam turbines. Two masts
and two funnels. Service: France-Mexico (Vera Cruz).
Sunk by magnetic mine in the Gironde, June 19, 1940.
Ex-**Lafayette** (1928).

Michigan   (1887)   Warren Line (British).
Built by Harland & Wolff, Ltd., Belfast, Ireland. Tonnage:
4,909. Dimensions: 400' x 47'. Single-screw, 11 knots.
Triple expansion engines. Four masts and one funnel. Steel
hull. Service: Liverpool-Boston. Acquired by British
Admiralty in 1914. Filled with ballast at Swansea in December 1915 and sent out to be sunk as a block-ship at Mundros.

Michigan   (1890)   Atlantic Transport Line.
Built by Harland & Wolff, Ltd., Belfast, Ireland. Tonnage:
3,722. Dimensions: 370' x 44'. Single-screw, 13½ knots.
Triple expansion engines. Four masts and one funnel.
Renamed: (a) **Kilpatrick,** (b) **Acropolis,** (c) **Washington,**

(d) **Great Canton.** Scrapped in Italy, 1924. Note: See **Acropolis** for additional information.

Milwaukee   (1897)   Canadian Pacific Line.
Built by Swan & Hunter, Ltd., Newcastle, England. Tonnage: 7,317. Dimensions: 470′ x 56′. Single-screw, 12 knots. Triple expansion engines. Two masts and one funnel. Note: Built for Beaver Line (Elder, Dempster & Co.). Launched, November 7, 1896. Placed in service to New Orleans. Also in London-Quebec-Montreal trade. Transferred to Canadian Pacific Line ownership in 1903. Torpedoed and sunk 260 miles from Fastnet, August 31, 1918, with the loss of one life. Sister ship: **Mount Royal.**

Milwaukee   (1929)   Hamburg-American Line.
Built by Blohm & Voss, Hamburg, Germany. Tonnage: 16,699. Dimensions: 546′ x 72′ (574′ o.l.). Twin-screw, 16 knots. Motorship. Two masts and two funnels. Passengers: 270 cabin, 287 tourist, 416 third. Service: Hamburg-Cobh-Halifax-New York. Employed also as a cruise ship. Ceded to Great Britain in 1945. Renamed: **Empire Waveney** (1945). Destroyed by fire at Liverpool on March 1, 1946. The gutted hulk was dismantled in 1947. Sister ship: **St. Louis.**

Minister Roon   (1873)   North German Lloyd.
Built by Caird & Co., Greenock, Scotland. Tonnage: 3,068. Dimensions: 350′ x 39′. Single-screw, 12 knots. Compound engines. Two masts and one funnel. Iron hull. Launched, June 16, 1873. Maiden voyage: Bremen-Southampton-Panama, October 7, 1873. In addition was in Bremen-New York service. Renamed: (a) **Siam** (1875) P. & O. Line, (b) **Yorihime Maru** (1897) Japanese. Sister ship: **Feldmarschall Moltke.**

Minneapolis   (1901)   Atlantic Transport Line.
Built by Harland & Wolff, Ltd., Belfast, Ireland. Tonnage: 13,448. Dimensions: 600′ x 65′ (616′ o.l.). Twin-screw, 16 knots. Quadruple expansion engines. Four masts and one funnel. Passengers: 250 first class. Maiden voyage: London-New York, May 10, 1900. Employed as a British troopship in World War I. Torpedoed and sunk 195 miles from Malta, March 23, 1916, with the loss of 12 lives. Sister ships: **Minnehaha, Minnetonka** and **Minnewaska.**

Minnedosa   (1918)   Canadian Pacific Line.
Built by Barclay, Curle & Co., Glasgow, Scotland. Tonnage: 13,972. (15,186 in 1925). Dimensions: 520′ x 67′ (546′ o.l.).

Triple-screw, 16½ knots.   Triple expansion engines and steam turbine. Two masts and two funnels. Reconditioned by Cammell, Laird & Co., at Birkenhead in 1925. Maiden voyage: Liverpool-St. John, New Brunswick, December 6, 1918. In regular service to Quebec and Montreal. Sold to Italy in 1935. Renamed: **Piemonte** (1935). She later served as the passenger liner **Piemonte** for Lloyd Triestino. Torpedoed and sunk at Messina in March 1944. Refloated in 1949, but found unfit for further service and was broken up for scrap. Sister ship: **Melita.** Note: The hulls of these passenger ships were laid down in 1914 for the Hamburg-American Line. However, when World War I commenced, construction was temporarily halted. The vessels were completed for the Canadian Pacific Line.

Minnehaha   (1900)   Atlantic Transport Line.
Built by Harland & Wolff, Ltd., Belfast, Ireland. Tonnage: 13,443.   Dimensions: 600' x 65'.   Twin-screw, 16 knots. Quadruple expansion engines. Four masts and one funnel. Passengers: 250 first class. Maiden voyage: London-New York, August 11, 1900. Grounded on Scilly Isles in April 1910, but was subsequently refloated and put back in service. Torpedoed and sunk 12 miles from Fastnet, September 7, 1917, with the loss of 43 lives. Sister ships: **Minneapolis, Minnetonka** and **Minnewaska.** Note: These liners had great cargo capacity.

Minnekahda   (1917)   Atlantic Transport Line.
Built by Harland & Wolff, Ltd., Belfast, Ireland. Tonnage: 17,281.   Dimensions: 620' x 66'.   Triple-screw, 16 knots. Triple expansion engines and one low pressure steam turbine. Four masts and one funnel. Note: Converted to emigrant carrier for 2,000 passengers. Ran in this type of service between Danzig and New York for the American Line. Transferred to Atlantic Transport Line in 1924. Converted to tourist class ship with accommodation for 750 passengers; placed in New York-London service. Broken up by shipbreakers at Dalmuir on the Clyde in 1936.

Minnesota   (1866)   (a) Guion Line, (b) Warren Line.
Built by Palmer's Shipbuilding & Iron Co., Newcastle, England.   Tonnage: 2,869.   Dimensions: 335' x 42'.   Single-screw, 10 knots. Inverted type engines. Two masts and one funnel. Clipper bow. Iron hull. Maiden voyage: Liverpool-New York, April 14, 1867. Sold to the Warren Line in 1875. Placed in their Liverpool-Boston service. Re-engined with

compounds. Renamed: **San Ignacio de Loyola** (1886). Spanish. Scrapped in 1908. Sister ships: **Chicago, Colorado** and **Manhattan.**

Minnesota (1901) Atlantic Transport Line.
Built by John Brown & Co., Clydebank, Glasgow, Scotland. Tonnage: 11,667. Dimensions: 561′ x 60′. Twin-screw, 15 knots. Quadruple expansion engines. Four masts and two funnels. Note: First voyage as the tourist class liner **Minnesota** was made in 1927 between London and New York. Sold to Thos. W. Ward, Ltd. for scrap in October 1929. Broken up in 1930. Ex-**Zeeland** (1927), ex-**Northland** (1920), **Zeeland** (1915).

Minnetonka (1902) Atlantic Transport Line.
Built by Harland & Wolff, Ltd., Belfast, Ireland. Tonnage: 13,440. Dimensions: 600′ x 65′ (616′ o.l.). Twin-screw, 16 knots. Quadruple expansion engines. Four masts and one funnel. Passengers: 250 first class. Maiden voyage: London-New York, July 12, 1902. Torpedoed and sunk without warning by the submarine "U-66", 40 miles from Malta, January 30, 1918, with the loss of 4 lives. Sister ships: **Minneapolis, Minnehaha** and **Minnewaska.**

Minnetonka (1924) Atlantic Transport Line.
Built by Harland & Wolff, Ltd., Belfast, Ireland. Tonnage: 21,716. Dimensions: 600′ x 80′ (624′ o.l.). Twin-screw, 16½ knots. Steam turbines. Two masts and one funnel. Launched, January 10, 1924. Passengers: 368 first class. Maiden voyage: London-New York, May 3, 1924. Transferred to Red Star Line's Antwerp-New York service in 1932. Not very successful, thus in 1934 was sold to British shipbreakers. Dismantled during 1935. Sister ship: **Minnewaska.** Note: They had the largest cargo capacity of any ship built to date.

Minnewaska (1894) Atlantic Transport Line.
Built by Harland & Wolff, Ltd., Belfast, Ireland. Tonnage: 5,713. Dimensions: 445′ x 50′. Twin-screw, 14 knots. Triple expansion engines. Two masts and one funnel. Passengers: 80 first class. Acquired by United States Government in 1898. Renamed: **Thomas** (1898). Sold for scrap in July 1928. Ex-**Persia** (1897) Hamburg-American Line. Sister ship: **Dominion.**

Minnewaska (1903) Atlantic Transport Line.
Built by Harland & Wolff, Ltd., Belfast, Ireland. Tonnage: 15,801. Dimensions: 600′ x 65′. Twin-screw, 16 knots.

Quadruple expansion engines. Four masts and one funnel. Launched as the **Minnewaska** on December 18, 1902. Upon completion entered trans-Atlantic service, as the **Arabic** of the White Star Line. Maiden voyage: Liverpool-New York, June 26, 1903. Note: See **Arabic** for additional information.

Minnewaska (1909) Atlantic Transport Line.
Built by Harland & Wolff, Ltd., Belfast, Ireland. Tonnage: 14,317. Dimensions: 600′ x 65′ (616′ o.l.). Twin-screw, 16 knots. Quadruple expansion engines. Four masts and one funnel. Passengers: 330 first class. Service: London-New York. Converted to British troopship in 1915. Sunk by a floating mine in Suda Bay, November 21, 1916, while transporting 1,800 troops. She was beached, but her bottom had been torn away by the mines and she became a total loss. Sister ships: **Minneapolis, Minnehaha** and **Minnetonka.**

Minnewaska (1923) Atlantic Transport Line.
Built by Harland & Wolff, Ltd., Belfast, Ireland. Tonnage: 21,716. Dimensions: 600′ x 80′ (626′ o.l.). Twin-screw, 16½ knots. Steam turbines. Two masts and one funnel. Launched, March 22, 1923. Passengers: 368 first class. Maiden voyage: London-New York, September 1, 1923. Transferred to Red Star Line service in 1932, and used as a tourist class ship. Broken up for scrap in Scotland, 1935. Sister ship: **Minnetonka.**

Missanabie (1914) Canadian Pacific Line.
Built by Barclay, Curle & Co., Glasgow, Scotland. Tonnage: 12,469. Dimensions: 500′ x 64′. Twin-screw, 15½ knots. Quadruple expansion engines. Two masts and two funnels. Passengers: 520 cabin, 1,200 third class. Maiden voyage: Liverpool-Quebec-Montreal, October 2, 1914. Torpedoed and sunk 52 miles from Daunts Rock (Cobh) on September 9, 1918, with the loss of 45 lives. Sister ship: **Metagama.** Note: First Canadian Pacific liners designed as a "cabin class" ship.

Mississippi (1871) Dominion Line.
Built by A. McMillan & Son, Dumbarton, Scotland. Tonnage: 2,129. Dimensions: 320′ x 35′. Single-screw, 11 knots. Compound engines. Two masts and one funnel. Iron hull. Passengers: 80 cabin, 600 third. Maiden voyage: Liverpool-Quebec-Montreal, May 4, 1872. Renamed: **Sicilia** (1888).

Mississippi (1903) Atlantic Transport Line.
Built by New York Shipbuilding Corp., Camden, New Jersey. Tonnage: 7,913. Dimensions: 490′ x 58′. Twin-

screw, 13 knots. Triple expansion engines. Four masts and one funnel. Renamed: (a) **Samland,** (b) **Belgic,** (c) **Samland.** Scrapped in 1931.

Missouri (1855) Dominion Line (British).
Built by Caird & Co., Greenock, Scotland. Tonnage: 2,259. Dimensions: 280′ x 38′. Single-screw, 10 knots. Three masts and one funnel. Wrecked on Bahamas, October 1, 1873. Ex-**Belgian,** ex-**Hammonia** (1864) Hamburg-American Line.

Mitau (1894) Russian-American Line.
Built by Fairfield Shipbuilding Co., Glasgow, Scotland. Tonnage: 4,588. Dimensions: 415′ x 45′. Single-screw, 14 knots. Triple expansion engines. Four masts and one funnel. Renamed: (a) **Joszef Pilsudski** (1921), (b) **Wilbo** (1924). Scrapped in 1924. Ex-**Birma** (1913), ex-**Arundel Castle** (1905).

Mobile (1893) Atlantic Transport Line.
Built by Harland & Wolff, Ltd., Belfast, Ireland. Tonnage: 5,780. Dimensions: 445′ x 49′. Twin-screw, 13½ knots. Triple expansion engines. Four masts and one funnel. Renamed: (a) **Sherman** (1898) United States Government, (b) **Calawaii** (1923). Scrapped in Japan, 1933. Sister ships: **Manitoba, Massachusetts,** and **Manitoba.**

*Mohamed Ali El Kebir (1944) Khedivial Mail Line.
Built by California Shipbuilding Corp., Los Angeles, California. Tonnage: 8,199. Dimensions: 439′ x 62′ (455′ o.l.). Single-screw, 15 knots. Steam turbines. Three masts and one funnel. Passengers: 75 first. Service: Mediterranean-New York. Ex-**Atchison Victory** (1948). Sister ship: **Khedive Ismail.** Note: Built as **Victory-**type cargo ships.

Mohawk (1892) Atlantic Transport Line.
Built by Harland & Wolff, Ltd., Belfast, Ireland. Tonnage: 5,678. Dimensions: 445′ x 49′. Twin-screw, 14 knots. Compound engines. 3,600 I.H.P. Four masts and one funnel. Iron hull. Passengers: 80 first. Service: London-New York. Renamed: (a) **Grant** (1898) United States Government, (b) **Chinook** U. S. Army dredge. Sister ships: **Manitoba, Massachusetts** and **Mobile.**

Mohegan (1892) Atlantic Transport Line.
Built by Earle's Shipbuilding & Engine Co., Hull, England. Tonnage: 6,889. Dimensions: 475′ x 52′. Single-screw, 13 knots. Triple expansion engines. Four masts and one funnel.

Service: London-New York. Passengers: 140 first class. Wrecked off the Lizard (Cornwall), October 14, 1898, while on her second voyage. There was a loss of over 100 lives. Ex-**Cleopatra** (1898). Note: Originally built for Wilson's & Furness-Leyland Line. Running mates: **Manitou, Marquette, Menominee** and **Mesaba.**

Moltke (1901) Hamburg-American Line.
Built by Blohm & Voss, Hamburg, Germany. Tonnage: 12,335. Dimensions: 525' x 62' (550' o.l.). Twin-screw, 16½ knots. Quadruple expansion engines. Two masts and two funnels. Passengers: 390 first, 230 second, 550 third. Built for the Far East service. Maiden voyage: Hamburg-Plymouth-New York, February 9, 1902. Transferred to Genoa-Naples-New York route in 1906. Made a number of North Atlantic sailings. Renamed: **Pesaro** (1915) Italian Government. In 1919 was placed in the service of Lloyd Sabaudo. Scrapped in 1926. Sister ship: **Bluecher.**

Mongolia (1904) American Line.
Built by New York Shipbuilding Corp., Camden, N. J. Tonnage: 13,639. In trans-Atlantic service 1920–24. Her sister ship **Manchuria** was also used in the New York-Hamburg trade. Note: See PART II (**Mongolia**) for details.

Mongolian (1891) Allan Line.
Built by D. & W. Henderson & Co., Glasgow, Scotland. Tonnage: 4,837. Dimensions: 400' x 45'. Single-screw, 13½ knots. Triple expansion engines. 4,000 I.H.P. Two masts and one funnel. Steel hull. Passengers: 100 first, 80 second, 1,000 third. In various North Atlantic services, including Boston and Quebec-Montreal. Torpedoed and sunk by submarine near Filey Brig, July 21, 1918, with the loss of 36 lives. Sister ship: **Numidian.**

Montana (1872) Guion Line (British).
Built by Palmer's Shipbuilding & Iron Co., Newcastle, England. Tonnage: 4,321. Dimensions: 400' x 43'. Single-screw, 11½ knots. Compound engines. Two masts and one funnel. Iron hull. Launched, November 14, 1872. Maiden voyage: July 7, 1875. Originally had accommodation for 200 first and 1,200 third class. This number was later reduced substantially. Wrecked on the Welsh coast, March 14, 1880, with no loss of life. Sister ship: **Dakota.**

Montcalm (1897) Canadian Pacific Line.
Built by Palmer's Shipbuilding & Iron Co., Newcastle, England. Tonnage: 5,505. Dimensions: 445' x 52'. Single-

screw, 13 knots. Triple expansion engines. Four masts and one funnel. Renamed: (a) **Crenella** (1916), (b) **Rey Alfonso** (1923), (c) **Anglo Norse** (1927), (d) **Polar Chief** (1935), (e) **Empire Chief** (1941). Broken up for scrap at Dalmuir in 1952. Sister ship: **Monterey.**

Montcalm   (1921)   Canadian Pacific Line.
Built by John Brown & Co., Clydebank, Glasgow, Scotland. Tonnage: 16,418. Dimensions: 549' x 70' (577' o.l.). Twin-screw, 17 knots. Steam turbines. Two masts and two funnels. Passengers: 540 cabin and 1,250 third. Maiden voyage: Liverpool-St. John, New Brunswick, January 17, 1922. New single-reductioned geared steam turbines in 1929. Renamed: **Wolfe** (1939) British armed merchant cruiser. Converted to depot-ship at later date. Scrapped in 1952. Sister ships: **Montclare** and **Montrose.**

Montclare   (1922)   Canadian Pacific Line.
Built by John Brown & Co., Clydebank, Glasgow, Scotland. Tonnage: 16,314. Dimensions: 549' x 70' (577' o.l.). Twin-screw, 17 knots. Six steam turbines. Two masts and two funnels.   Maiden voyage: Liverpool-Quebec-Montreal, August 18, 1922. Served first as an armed merchant cruiser in World War II. Sold to British Government in 1942. Converted to a submarine tender in 1946. She was not renamed by British Government. Scrapped in Great Britain, 1958. Sister ships: **Montcalm** and **Montrose.**

Monte Videan   (1887)   Allan Line (British).
Built by D. & W. Henderson & Co., Glasgow, Scotland. Tonnage: 3,076. Dimensions: 330' x 42'. Single-screw, 11 knots. Triple expansion engines. Two masts and one funnel. Steel hull. Launched, October 20, 1887. Maiden voyage: Glasgow-South America, November 29, 1887. Also was used in service to Quebec and Montreal. Passengers: 20 first and 800 third class. Scrapped in 1910. Sister ship: **Rosarian.**

Monteagle   (1899)   Canadian Pacific Line.
Built by Palmer's Shipbuilding & Iron Co., Jarrow-on-Tyne, Newcastle, England. Tonnage: 6,955. Dimensions: 445' x 52'. Single-screw, 13 knots. Triple expansion engines. Four masts and one funnel. Note: Originally built for Elder, Dempster & Co. Placed in Canadian Pacific service to Canada in 1903. Renamed: **Belton** (1923). Scrapped in Great Britain, 1926. Sister ship: **Montfort.**

Monterey   (1897)   Canadian Pacific Line.
Built by Palmer's Shipbuilding & Iron Co., Newcastle, England. Tonnage: 5,478. Dimensions: 445' x 52'. Single-screw, 13 knots. Triple expansion engines. Four masts and one funnel. Note: Originally owned by Elder, Dempster & Company. Acquired by Canadian Pacific Line in 1903. Wrecked in the St. Lawrence River in July 1903, with no loss of life. Sister ship: **Montcalm.**

Montevideo   (1889)   Spanish Line.
Built by Wm. Denny & Bros., Ltd., Dumbarton, Scotland. Tonnage: 5,205. Dimensions: 410' x 48'. Single-screw, 14½ knots. Quadruple expansion engines. Three masts and one funnel. Steel hull. Commenced Mediterranean-New York service about 1901. Scrapped in 1940.

Montezuma   (1899)   Canadian Pacific Line.
Built by Harland & Wolff, Ltd., Belfast, Ireland. Tonnage· 7,345. Dimensions: 485' x 59'. Single-screw, 12½ knots. Triple expansion engines. Four masts and one funnel. Note: Originally owned by Elder, Dempster & Co. Transferred to Canadian Pacific Line in 1903. Acquired by British Government in First World War. Renamed: **Oakleaf** (1916). Torpedoed and sunk, July 25, 1917, while being operated as converted oil tanker by Lane & MacAndrew. Sister ship: **Mount Temple.** Accommodation for 2,000 passengers in 1912.

Montfort   (1899)   Canadian Pacific Line.
Built by Palmer's Shipbuilding & Iron Co., Newcastle, England. Tonnage: 7,087. Dimensions: 445' x 52'. Single-screw, 12½ knots. Triple expansion engines. Four masts and one funnel. Note: Originally owned by Elder, Dempster & Co. Acquired by Canadian Pacific Line in 1903. Torpedoed and sunk 170 miles from Bishop's Rock, October 1, 1918, with the loss of 5 lives. Sister ship: **Monteagle.**

Montlaurier   (1908)   Canadian Pacific Line.
Built by J. C. Tecklenborg & Co., Geestemunde, Germany. Tonnage: 16,992. Dimensions: 590' x 68'. Twin-screw, 17 knots. Quadruple expansion engines. Two masts and two funnels. First voyage as **Montlaurier** in May 1923. Nearly destroyed by fire on April 15, 1925, while undergoing repairs in Cammell, Laird's yard at Birkenhead. Renamed: **Montnairn** (1925). Scrapped in 1931. Ex-**Empress of India** (1922), ex-**Prinz Friedrich Wilhelm** (1920).

Montnairn   (1908)   Canadian Pacific Line.
    Built by J. C. Tecklenborg & Co., Geestemunde, Germany.
    Tonnage: 17,282. Dimensions: 590′ x 68′ (613′ o.l.). Twin-
    screw, 17 knots. Quadruple expansion engines. Two masts
    and two funnels. Sold to Italian shipbreakers in December
    1929, but not dismantled until 1931.   Ex-**Montlaurier**
    (1925), ex-**Empress of India** (1922), ex-**Prinz Friedrich
    Wilhelm** (1920).

Montreal   (1879)   Dominion Line.
    Built by C. Connell & Co., Glasgow, Scotland. Tonnage:
    3,308. Dimensions: 329′ x 39′. Single-screw, 12 knots. Com-
    pound engines. Two masts and one funnel. Iron hull.
    Maiden voyage: Liverpool-Quebec-Montreal, October 27,
    1879. Wrecked on Belle Isle during a fog, August 4, 1889,
    with no loss of life. Sister ship: **Toronto.**

Montreal   (1896)   French Line.
    Built by Robert Napier & Sons, Ltd., Glasgow, Scotland.
    Tonnage: 3,342. Dimensions: 345′ x 44′. Single-screw, 12
    knots. Triple expansion engines. Two masts and one funnel.
    Service: West Indies. Sunk by submarine in Bay of Biscay,
    March 24, 1917. Ex-**Halifax**, (1912), ex-**Minho** (1903).
    Sister ship: **Quebec.**

Montreal   (1900)   Canadian Pacific Line.
    Built by Swan & Hunter, Ltd., Newcastle, England. Ton-
    nage: 8,644. Dimensions: 469′ x 56′. Twin-screw, 12½
    knots. Triple expansion engines. Four masts and one funnel.
    Formerly owned by Elder, Dempster & Co. Tonnage when
    employed as freighter was 6,870. Sunk in collision near
    Morecambe Bay in January 1918.

Montreal   (1906)   Canadian Pacific Line.
    Built by Blohm & Voss, Hamburg, Germany. Tonnage:
    9,720. Dimensions: 475′ x 55′. Twin-screw, 15 knots.
    Quadruple expansion engines. Two masts and one funnel.
    First voyage as **Montreal,** London-Quebec-Montreal, April
    1921. Vessel was laid up in November 1925. Renamed:
    Alesia (1928). Broken up for scrap in Italy 1933. Ex-**Konig
    Friedrich Auguste** (1921).

Montrose   (1897)   Canadian Pacific Line.
    Built by Sir Raylton Dixon & Co., Ltd., Middlesbrough,
    England. Tonnage: 7,207. Dimensions: 444′ x 52′. Twin-
    screw, 13 knots. Triple expansion engines. 3,800 I.H.P.
    Four masts and one funnel. Formerly owned by Elder,

Dempster & Co. As a freighter tonnage was 6,094. In 1912 listed passenger accommodation for 57 second and 1,700 third class. Service: England-Canada. Wrecked on Goodwin Sands in December 1914, with no loss of life.

Montrose (1922)   Canadian Pacific Line.
Built by Fairfield Shipbuilding & Engineering Co., Glasgow, Scotland. Tonnage: 16,402. Dimensions: 548' x 70' (576' o.l.). Twin-screw, 17 knots. Steam turbines. Two masts and two funnels. Passengers: 542 cabin and 1,268 third. Maiden voyage: Liverpool-Quebec-Montreal, May 5, 1922. New steam turbines in 1931. Renamed: **Forfar** (1939) British Admiralty. Torpedoed and sunk by submarine "U-99" on December 2, 1940. Sister ships: **Montcalm** and **Montclare.**

Montroyal (1906)   Canadian Pacific Line.
Built by Fairfield Shipbuilding & Engineering Co., Glasgow, Scotland. Tonnage: 15,646. Dimensions: 548' x 65' (570' o.l.). Twin-screw, 18 knots. Quadruple expansion engines. Two masts and two funnels. Passengers: 600 cabin and 800 third class. Services: Liverpool-Quebec-Montreal; Antwerp-Southampton-Cherbourg-Quebec. Sold to Norwegian shipbreakers in June 1930. Ex-**Empress of Britain** (1924).

Montserrat (1889)   Spanish Line.
Built by "Vulkan", Stettin, Germany. Tonnage: 4,147. Dimensions: 373' x 44'. Single-screw, 14 knots. Triple expansion engines. Two masts and one funnel. Scrapped in 1927. Ex-**Dania.**

*__Montserrat__ (1945)   Spanish Line.
Built by California Shipbuilding Corp., Los Angeles, Calif. Tonnage: 9,001. Dimensions: 439' x 62' (455' o.l.). Single-screw, 16 knots. Two steam turbines. Two masts and one funnel. Passengers: 708 tourist. Service: West Indies. Ex-**Castel Verde** (1957), ex-**Wooster Victory** (1950).

Moraitis (1907)   Moraitis Line (Greek).
Built by Priestman & Co., Sunderland, England. Tonnage: 6,045. Dimensions: 400' x 50'. Twin-screw, 13 knots. Triple expansion engines. Two masts and two funnels. Maiden voyage: Greece-New York, July 4, 1907. Renamed: **Themistocles** (1908) Greek.

Moravia (1883)   Hamburg-American Line.
Built by A. & J. Inglis, Glasgow, Scotland. Tonnage: 3,690. Dimensions: 360' x 40'. Single-screw, 10½ knots. 1,940

I.H.P. Two masts and one funnel. Iron hull. Wrecked on Sable Island, February 12, 1899, with no loss of life. Running mates: **Bohemia, Rhaetia** and **Rugia.**

Moravian (1864) Allan Line.
Built by Robert Steele & Co., Greenock, Scotland. Tonnage: 2,481. Dimensions: 320' x 38'. Single-screw, 11 knots. Inverted engines. Three masts and one funnel. Iron hull. Clipper bow. Maiden voyage: Liverpool-Portland, November 10, 1864. Lengthened to 389 feet (3,300 tons) in 1874. Re-engined with compounds. Wrecked off Nova Scotian coast, December 30, 1881, with no loss of life. Sister ships: **Austrian, Nestorian** and **Peruvian.**

Moreas (1901) Greek Line.
Built by D. & W. Henderson & Co., Glasgow, Scotland. Tonnage: 8,497. Dimensions: 485' x 56'. Twin-screw, 15 knots. Triple expansion engines. Two masts and three funnels. Passengers: 340 first, 220 second, 740 third. Service: Piraeus-New York. Scrapped in Italy, 1929. Ex-**Columbia** (1926).

Mosel (1872) North German Lloyd.
Built by Caird & Co., Greenock, Scotland. Tonnage: 3,200. Dimensions: 365' x 40'. Single-screw, 14 knots. Inverted engines. Two masts and one funnel. Iron hull. Launched, August 20, 1872. Maiden voyage: Bremen-Southampton-New York, January 4, 1873. Cost $500,000 to build. Had 8 metal lifeboats and 2 gigs. Compound engines in 1882. Wrecked near the Lizard in a thick fog, August 9, 1882. Sister ships: **Neckar** and **Oder.**

Mount Carroll (1921) United American Line.
Built by Merchant Shipbuilding Corp., Chester, Pa. Tonnage: 7,469. Dimensions: 440' x 57'. Single-screw, 14 knots. Steam turbines. Two masts and two funnels. Passengers: 585 third class. Service: New York-Hamburg. Renamed: (a) **Maunawili** (1925), (b) **Socrates** (1946). (c) **Southern Albatross** (1955), (d) **Portaritissa.** Scrapped in 1958. Sister ship: **Mount Clinton.**

Mount Clay (1904) United American Lines.
Built by "Vulkan", Stettin, Germany. Tonnage: 8,865. Dimensions: 488' x 55'. Twin-screw, 15 knots. Quadruple expansion engines. Two masts and two funnels. Accommodation for about 100 first and 1,000 in third class. First sailing as **Mount Clay,** New York to Hamburg, February

19, 1921. Scrapped in 1934. Ex-**De Kalb** (1921), ex-**Prinz Eitel Friedrich** (1917).

Mount Clinton   (1921)   United American Lines.

Built by Merchant Shipbuilding Corp., Chester, Pa. Tonnage: 7,510. Dimensions: 440′ x 57′. Single-screw, 14 knots. Steam turbines. Two masts and two funnels. Passengers: 585 third. Maiden voyage: New York-Hamburg, May 26, 1921. Renamed: (a) **Maunalei** (1925), (b) **Santa Rosa** (1948) Italian, (c) **Capo Manara** (1948) Italian. Scrapped in Japan, 1954. Sister ship: **Mount Carroll.**

Mount Royal   (1898)   Canadian Pacific Line.

Built by Swan & Hunter, Ltd., Newcastle, England. Tonnage: 7,998. Dimensions: 470′ x 56′. Single-screw, 12 knots. Triple expansion engines. Two masts and one funnel. Note: Originally owned by Elder, Dempster & Co., Ltd. Tonnage as cargo ship listed at 7,064. Sold to British Government in 1914. Renamed: **Mapleleaf** (1914), (b) **British Maple.** Scrapped in 1933. Sister ship: **Milwaukee.**

Mount Temple   (1901)   Canadian Pacific Line.

Built by Sir W. G. Armstrong, Whitworth & Co., Newcastle, England. Tonnage: 7,656. Dimensions: 485′ x 59′. Single-screw, 12½ knots. Triple expansion engines. Four masts and one funnel. Note: Formerly owned by Elder, Dempster & Co. Acquired by Canadian Pacific Line in 1903. Services: (a) Liverpool-Canada, (b) London-Antwerp-Canada. Tonnage listed as 9,792 in 1914. Captured and sunk by German raider **Mowe,** December 6, 1916, when 620 miles west of Fastnet. Sister ship: **Montezeuma.**

Munchen   (1889)   North German Lloyd.

Built by Fairfield Shipbuilding & Engineering Co., Glasgow, Scotland. Tonnage: 4,801. Dimensions: 390′ x 46′. Single-screw, 13 knots. Triple expansion engines. Two masts and one funnel. Steel hull. Passengers: 38 first, 20 second, 1,700 third. Services: Various trade routes. Made a number of New York voyages. Renamed: **Gregory Morch** (about 1903). Sister ship: **Dresden.**

Munchen   (1922)   North German Lloyd.

Built by "Vulkan" Werke, Stettin, Germany. Tonnage: 13,483. Dimensions: 526′ x 65′ (551′ o.l.). Twin-screw, 16 knots. Triple expansion engines. Two masts and two funnels. Note: Name also has been spelled as **Muenchen.** Maiden voyage: Bremen-New York, September 14, 1923.

Badly gutted by fire at her New York pier in 1930. Rebuilt in Germany in 1931. Her outward appearance was greatly changed by the reconstruction. Renamed: (a) **General von Steuben** (1931), (b) **Steuben** (1938). Sunk by Russian submarine in Baltic, February 1945. Only 1,000 of the 4,000 refugees on board survived. Sister ship: **Stuttgart.**

Munchen   (1923)   North German Lloyd.
Built by Akt. Ges. "Weser", Bremen, Germany. Tonnage: 18,940. Dimensions: 590' x 72'. Twin-screw, 16 knots. Quadruple expansion engines. Two masts and two funnels. Never in passenger service for North German Lloyd, as she was one of the many German ships turned over to the Allies after the First World War. Renamed: (a) **Ohio** (1923), (b) **Albertic** (1927).

Napoleon III   (1866)   French Line.
Built by Thomas Ironworks, London, England. Tonnage: 3,376. Dimensions: 363' x 43'. Paddle-wheels, 12 knots. Side lever engines. Two masts and two funnels. Passengers: 170 first, 100 second, 50 third. Iron hull. Launched, February 11, 1865. Maiden voyage: Havre-Brest-New York, April 26, 1866. Lengthened to 413 feet (3,950 tons) in 1873. Paddle-wheels replaced by single-screw propulsion, also compound engines installed and mizzen mast added. Renamed: **Ville du Havre** (1870). Sunk in collision with **Loch Earn,** November 22, 1873, with great loss of life.

Napoli   (1899)   "Italia" Soc. di Navigazione.
Built by Palmer's Shipbuilding & Iron Co., Newcastle, England. Tonnage: 9,203. Dimensions: 470' x 56'. Twin-screw, 12½ knots. Triple expansion engines. Four masts and one funnel. Transferred to Transoceanica in 1917. Sunk by collision in the North Atlantic in November 1918. Ex-**Sannio** (1913), ex-**British Prince** (1906).

Napoli   (1907)   Navigazione Generale Italiana.
Built by Sir James Laing & Sons, Ltd., Sunderland, England. Tonnage: 6,094. Dimensions: 406' x 51'. Twin-screw, 14 knots. Triple expansion engines. Two masts and three funnels. Service: Genoa-Naples-New York. Broken up for scrap in 1928. Ex-**San Giorgio** (1921).

Nazario Sauro   (1921)   Transatlantica Italiana.
Built by Societa Anonima Ansaldo, Genoa, Italy. Tonnage: 8,150. Dimensions: 447' x 52'. Twin-screw, 14 knots. Six steam turbines. Two masts and two funnels. Built for the Italy-South America trade. Made some sailings to New

York. She was later transferred to Lloyd Triestino (Italian). Became a World War II casualty, April 6, 1941. Sister ship: **Ammiraglio Bettolo.**

Nea Hellas   (1922)   Greek Line.
Built by Fairfield Shipbuilding & Engineering Co., Glasgow, Scotland. Tonnage: 16,991. Dimensions: 552' x 70' (578' o.l.). Twin-screw, 16 knots. Four steam turbines. Two masts and one funnel. Made her first Greece-New York sailing in 1939. Served as a British troopship in World War II. Resumed Piraeus-New York service in 1947. Note: This liner was sold to the General Steam Navigation Company of Greece in 1939. Due to the war she was taken over by the British for transport duties. In 1947 was turned over to the Greek Line. Renamed: **New York** (1955). Ex-**Tuscania** (1939).

Nebraska   (1867)   Guion Line (British).
Built by Palmer's Shipbuilding & Iron Co., Newcastle, England. Tonnage: 3,985. Dimensions: 367' x 42'. Single-screw, 11 knots. Inverted engines. Compound engines in 1875. Two masts and one funnel. Clipper bow. Maiden voyage: Liverpool-New York, June 7, 1867. Transferred to Warren Line service in 1876. Renamed: **Victoria** (1876). Scrapped in 1887.

Neckar   (1873)   North German Lloyd.
Built by Caird & Co., Greenock, Scotland. Tonnage: 3,122. Dimensions: 351' x 40'. Single-screw, 14 knots. Compound engines. Two masts and one funnel. Iron hull. Launched, November 10, 1873. Maiden voyage: Bremen-Southampton-New York, April 18, 1874. Placed in the Far East service in 1886. Made her final voyage to New York in 1895. Scrapped in 1896. Sister ships: **Mosel** and **Oder.**

Neckar   (1901)   North German Lloyd.
Built by J. C. Tecklenborg & Co., Geestemunde, Germany. Tonnage: 9,835. Dimensions: 499' x 58'. Twin-screw, 14 knots. Quadruple expansion engines. Four masts and one funnel. Services: Various. Passengers: 370 second and 3,000 third class. Renamed: (a) **Antigone** (1917), (b) **Potomac** (1920). Broken up by Dutch shipbreakers in 1928. Sister ships: **Main** and **Rhein.**

Nederland   (1873)   Red Star Line.
Built by Palmer's Shipbuilding & Iron Co., Newcastle, England. Tonnage: 2,950. Dimensions: 329' x 38'. Single-screw,

13 knots. Compound engines, aft. Three masts and one funnel. Iron hull. Launched, June 23, 1873. Funnel placed aft. Service: Antwerp-Philadelphia. Final voyage to New York in 1893. Scrapped in Italy, 1906. Sister ships: **Switzerland** and **Vaderland.**

Neptunia (1920) Greek Line.
Built by Nederlandsche Scheepsbouw, Amsterdam, Netherlands. Tonnage: 10,474. Dimensions: 506' x 59'. Twin-screw, 17 knots. Triple expansion engines. Single mast and one funnel. Passengers: 39 first and 727 tourist. In various trans-Atlantic services, including Piraeus-New York. Struck Daunts Rock on November 2, 1957. Due to the severe damage by grounding, she was sold to Dutch shipbreakers. Arrived at New Waterway by tow, March 7, 1958; subsequently broken up for scrap. Ex-**Johan de Witt** (1948).

Nestorian (1866) Allan Line.
Built by Barclay, Curle & Co., Glasgow, Scotland. Tonnage: 2,466. Dimensions: 320' x 38'. Single-screw, 11 knots. Inverted engines. Three masts and one funnel. Iron hull. Maiden voyage: Liverpool-Portland, Maine, January 31, 1867. Tonnage later increased to 2,726. Compound engines installed. Made her final voyage to Boston in 1897. Sold for scrap in 1897. Sister ships: **Austrian, Moravian** and **Peruvian.**

Neustria (1883) Fabre Line (French).
Built by Claparede & Co., Rouen, France. Tonnage: 2,926. Dimensions: 328' x 40'. Single-screw, 12 knots. Compound engines. Two masts and one funnel. Iron hull. Launched, August 19, 1883. Maiden voyage: Marseilles-New York, September 20, 1884. Left New York for Marseilles, October 27, 1908, and never heard of again.

Nevada (1868) Guion Line (British).
Built by Palmer's Shipbuilding & Iron Co., Newcastle, England. Tonnage: 3,125. Dimensions: 345' x 43'. Single-screw, 11 knots. Inverted engines. Two masts and one funnel. Iron hull. First straight stemmed vessel of the Guion Line. Maiden voyage: Liverpool-New York, February 2, 1869. Tonnage was increased to 3,617 in 1881. Compound engines installed. Sold to Dominion Line. Renamed: **Hamilton** (1893). Scrapped in 1896. Sister ship: **Idaho.**

New England (1898) Dominion Line.
Built by Harland & Wolff, Ltd., Belfast, Ireland. Tonnage: 12,099. Dimensions: 550' x 59' (566' o.l.). Twin-screw, 16

knots. Triple expansion engines. Two masts and one funnel. Passengers: 200 first, 200 second, 800 third. Maiden voyage: Liverpool-Boston, June 30, 1898. Renamed: (a) **Romanic** (1903), (b) **Scandinavian** (1912). Scrapped in 1923.

New York   (1851)   Glasgow & New York Steam Ship Co.
Built by Tod & McGregor, Glasgow, Scotland. Tonnage: 1,962. Dimensions: 262' x 36'. Single-screw, 10½ knots. Single funnel. Iron hull. Maiden voyage: Glasgow-New York, September 16, 1851. Made a fast Atlantic crossing for that date, of 12 days, 5 hours on the eastward course. Sold to Inman Line in 1859. Destroyed by fire off Nantucket, July 31, 1865.

New York   (1858)   North German Lloyd.
Built by Caird & Co., Greenock, Scotland. Tonnage: 2,674. Dimensions: 318' x 40'. Single-screw, 10½ knots. Inverted type engines. Three masts and one funnel. Clipper bow. Iron hull. Passengers: 60 first, 110 second, 400 third. Maiden voyage: Bremen-New York, August 14, 1858. Sold to British owners in 1873. Converted to sailing ship. Wrecked in 1891. Running mates: **Bremen** (identical), **Hudson** and **Weser.**

New York   (1888)   American Line.
Built by J. & G. Thomson, Ltd., Clydebank, Glasgow, Scotland. Tonnage: 10,499. Dimensions: 528' x 63' (560' o.l.). Twin-screw, 20 knots. Three masts and three funnels. Steel hull. Clipper bow. First voyage as **New York** Southampton-New York, March 11, 1893. New triple expansion engines installed in 1903. Reduced to two funnels. Renamed: (a) **Harvard** (1898), (b) **New York** (1899), (c) **Plattsburg** (1917) United States Government, (d) **New York** (1919) American Line. Liner sold to Polish Navigation Company in 1921. Scrapped at Genoa in 1923. Ex-**City of New York** (1893). Sister ship: **Philadelphia.**

*****New York**   (1922)   Greek Line.
Built by Fairfield Shipbuilding & Engineering Co., Glasgow, Scotland. Tonnage: 16,991. Dimensions: 552' x 70' (578' o.l). Twin-screw, 16 knots. Steam turbines. Two masts and one funnel. Passengers: 73 first, 1,173 tourist. Service: Bremer-haven-New York. Vessel laid up in 1960. Ex-**Nea Hellas** (1955), ex-**Tuscania** (1939).

New York   (1927)   Hamburg-American Line.
Built by Blohm & Voss, Hamburg, Germany. Tonnage: 21,455. Dimensions: 602' x 72'. Twin-screw, 16 knots.

Steam turbines. Two masts and two funnels. Maiden voyage: Hamburg-Southampton-Cherbourg-New York, May 13, 1927. Speed was increased to 20 knots by having new steam turbines installed in 1930. Note: Lengthened to 645 feet (23,337 tons) in 1934. Bombed and sunk by air attack at Kiel, April 3, 1945. Refloated and towed to Great Britain in 1949; subsequently broken up for scrap. Sister ship: **Hamburg.**

Newfoundland (1925) Warren Line (Furness, Withy & Co.).
Built by Vickers, Armstrong, Ltd., Newcastle, England. Tonnage: 6,791. Dimensions: 406' x 55' (423' o.l.). Twin-screw, 15 knots. Quadruple expansion engines. Two masts and one funnel. Passengers: 105 cabin and 80 third. Maiden voyage: Liverpool-St. John's, Newfoundland-Halifax-Boston, in January 1925. Bombed and sunk by enemy aircraft off Salerno, Italy, while serving as a hospital ship, September 13, 1943. Sister ship: **Nova Scotia.**

*****Newfoundland** (1947) Furness-Warren Line.
Built by Vickers-Armstrong, Ltd., Newcastle, England. Tonnage: 7,437. Dimensions: 423' x 61' (440' o.l.). Single-screw, 16 knots. Three steam turbines. Two masts and one funnel. Passengers: 75 first class and 80 tourist. Commenced her maiden voyage from Liverpool to St. John's, Halifax and Boston in February, 1948 Sister ship: **Nova Scotia.**

Niagara (1848) Cunard Line.
Built by Robert Steele & Co., Greenock, Scotland. Tonnage: 1,825. Dimensions: 251' x 38'. Paddle-wheels, 10 knots. Side lever engines. Three masts and one funnel. Wooden hull. Clipper bow. Passengers: 140 cabin. Maiden voyage: Liverpool-Halifax-Boston, May 20, 1848. Vessel sold to Glasgow shipbuilders in 1866 and converted to sailing ship. Wrecked near South Stack, June 6, 1875, with no loss of life. Sister ships: **America, Canada** and **Europa.**

Niagara (1908) French Line.
Built by Ateliers & Chantiers de la Loire, St. Nazaire, France. Tonnage: 9,614. Dimensions: 485' x 56' (504' o.l.). Twin-screw, 14½ knots. Triple expansion engines. Two masts and one funnel. First voyage as **Niagara** Havre-New York, March 26, 1910. In various services. Scrapped at Dunkirk in 1931. Ex-**Corse** (1910).

Nieuw Amsterdam (1906) Holland-America Line.
Built by Harland & Wolff, Ltd., Belfast, Ireland. Tonnage: 17,149. Dimensions: 600' x 68' (615' o.l.). Twin-screw, 16

knots. Quadruple expansion engines. Four masts and one funnel. Passengers: 417 first, 391 second, 2,300 third. Maiden voyage: Rotterdam-New York, April 7, 1906. The only trans-Atlantic passenger liner to keep regular sailings during World War I. Scrapped in Japan, 1932.

*Nieuw Amsterdam** (1938) Holland-America Line.
Built by Rotterdam Dry Dock Co., Rotterdam, Netherlands. Tonnage: 36,287. Dimensions: 713' x 88' (758' o.l.). Twin-screw, 21 knots. Steam turbines. Two masts and two funnels. Laid down on January 3, 1936. Launched, April 10, 1937. Cost $12,000,000 to build. Passengers: 552 first, 426 cabin, 209 tourist. Maiden voyage: Rotterdam-Boulogne-Southampton-New York, May 10, 1938. Reconditioned after having served as a troopship in World War II. Re-entered regular trans-Atlantic service in October 1947. Passenger accommodation in 1960 listed as: 574 first, 413 cabin, 207 tourist.

Noordam (1902) Holland-America Line.
Built by Harland & Wolff, Ltd., Belfast, Ireland. Tonnage: 12,531. Dimensions: 550' x 62'. Twin-screw, 15 knots. Triple expansion engines. Two masts and one funnel. Passengers: 286 first, 192 second, 1,800 third. Renamed: (a) **Kungsholm** (1923), (b) **Noordam** (1925). Note: As the **Kungsholm** was on charter to the Swedish-American Line. Sister ships: **Potsdam** and **Rijndam.**

*Noordam** (1939) Holland-America Line.
Built by Van P. Smit, Jr., Rotterdam, Netherlands. Tonnage: 10,726. Dimensions: 480' x 64' (502' o.l.). Twin-screw, 17 knots. Motorship. Two masts and one funnel. Maiden voyage: Rotterdam-New York, September 28, 1938. Served as troopship in World War II. Re-entered trans-Atlantic service in July 1946. Passengers: 150 first class. Sister ships: **Westerdam** and **Zaandam.**

Noordland (1884) Red Star Line.
Built by Laird Bros., Ltd., Birkenhead, England. Tonnage: 5,129. Dimensions: 400' x 47'. Single-screw, 13½ knots. 2,500 I.H.P. Compound engines. Four masts and one funnel. Service: Antwerp-New York. Transferred to American Line's Liverpool-Philadelphia service in 1901. Scrapped in 1908.

Nord America (1882) La Veloce Line (Italian).
Built by John Elder & Co., Glasgow. Tonnage: 4,920. Dimensions: 418' x 50'. Single-screw, 16 knots. Triple

expansion engines. Three masts and two funnels. Iron hull. Vessel was purchased for their South American service. Transferred to Italy-New York route in 1901. Wrecked near Arzilla, December 6, 1910. Ex-**Stirling Castle,** ex-**Nord America,** ex-**Stirling Castle** (1883) British.

Norge   (1881)   Thingvalla Line (Danish).
Built by Alexander Stephen & Sons, Ltd., Glasgow, Scotland. Tonnage: 3,318. Dimensions: 340′ x 40′. Single-screw, 13 knots. Compound engines. Three masts and one funnel. Iron hull. Passengers: 50 first, 150 second, 900 third. Acquired by Scandinavian-American Line in 1898. Wrecked near Rockall in June 1904, with great loss of life. Ex-**Pieter de Coninck** (1888) T. C. Engels & Co.

Normandie   (1935)   French Line.
Built by Chantiers & Ateliers de Penhoet, St. Nazaire, France. Tonnage: 79,280. Dimensions: 981′ x 117′9 (1,027 o.l.). Quadruple-screw, 30 knots. Steam turbines connected to electric motors. Two masts and three funnels. Laid down on January 26, 1931. Launched, November 29, 1932. Height from water line to top of foremast was 202 feet high. Passengers: 848 first, 670 tourist, 454 third. Maiden voyage: Havre-Southampton-New York, May 29, 1935. Her superstructure was enlarged in 1936, thus increasing tonnage to 82,799. The increased enclosed space made her the largest ship in the world. She broke the trans-Atlantic speed record with a time of 4 days, 3 hours, 14 minutes with an average speed of 31.37 knots. Her mammoth funnels measured 160 feet in circumference with the foremost one towering at a height of 145 feet. Main dining room was 300 feet by 43 feet, and three decks high with a seating capacity for 1,000 people. Liner was laid up in New York in August 1939, due to the war. Taken over by United States Government in December 1941. Renamed: **Lafayette.** Badly gutted by fire at her New York pier, February 9, 1942, and as fire progressed keeled over and sank. After a costly salvage job was eventually refloated. Towed to Port Newark in December 1946 and she was completely dismantled by October 1947.

Normannia   (1890)   Hamburg-American Line.
Built by Fairfield Shipbuilding & Engineering Co., Glasgow, Scotland. Tonnage: 8,250. Dimensions: 500′ x 57′ (520′ o.l.). Twin-screw, 18½ knots. Triple expansion engines. Two masts and three funnels. Steel hull. Passengers: 420 first, 170 second, 700 third. Maiden voyage: Hamburg-South-

ampton-New York in May 1890. Sold to Spanish Government in 1898. Renamed: (a) **Patriota** (1898), (b) **L'Aquitaine** (1899) French Line. Broken up for scrap in Great Britain, 1906. Running mates: **Furst Bismarck, Augusta Victoria** and **Columbia.**

Norseman   (1882)   (a) Dominion Line, (b) Warren Line.
Built by Laird Bros., Ltd., Birkenhead, England. Tonnage: 4,386. Dimensions: 392′ x 44′. Single-screw, 12 knots. Compound engines. Four masts and one funnel. Iron hull. Owner: British & North Atlantic Steam Navigation Company. Vessel on charter to Warren Line. Service: Liverpool-Boston. Wrecked at Marblehead, Mass., March 28, 1899. Subsequently refloated and towed to Boston. Eventually was broken up for scrap at Philadelphia.

Norseman   (1897)   Dominion Line (British).
Built by Harland & Wolff, Ltd., Belfast, Ireland. Tonnage: 10,750. Dimensions: 500′ x 62′. Twin-screw, 12½ knots. Quadruple expansion engines. Four masts and one funnel. Torpedoed and sunk by submarine in Mundros harbor in 1917. Ex-**Brasilia** (1900).

North American   (1856)   Allan Line (British).
Built by Wm. Denny & Bros., Ltd., Dumbarton, Scotland. Tonnage: 1,715. Dimensions: 283′ x 35′. Single-screw, 11 knots. Inverted engines. Three masts and one funnel. Clipper bow. Iron hull. Passengers: 75 first and 350 third. Service: Canadian; later in Baltimore trade. Sold and converted to sail in 1874. Sister ship: **Anglo-Saxon.**

North Briton   (1858)   Allan Line.
Built by Wm. Denny & Bros., Ltd., Dumbarton, Scotland. Tonnage: 2,190. Dimensions: 298′ x 38′. Single-screw, 11 knots. Inverted engines. Three masts and one funnel. Maiden voyage: Liverpool-Quebec-Montreal, September 8, 1858. Wrecked on Paraquet Island, November 5, 1861, with no loss of life. Sister ships: **Bohemian, Hungarian** and **Nova Scotian.**

North Star   (1853)   Vanderbilt Line.
Built by J. Simonson, New York, N. Y. Tonnage: 1,867. Dimensions: 270′ x 38′. Paddle-wheels, 11 knots. Beam engines. Two masts and two funnels. First New York-Southampton-Havre sailing, July 21, 1855. Note: This wooden hull steamship had been built as Commodore Vanderbilt's private yacht. Vessel was transferred to New York-

Panama service in 1859. Sold to Pacific Mail Steamship Company in 1867.

Norwegian (1861) Allan Line.
Built by Wm. Denny & Bros., Ltd., Dumbarton, Scotland. Tonnage: 1,888. Dimensions: 280′ x 37′. Single-screw, 11 knots. Inverted engines. Three masts and one funnel. Clipper bow. Iron hull. Maiden voyage: Liverpool-Quebec-Montreal, July 18, 1861. Wrecked on St. Paul Island, June 14, 1863, with no loss of life. Sister ship: **Hibernian.**

Norwegian (1865) Allan Line.
Built by Tod & McGregor, Glasgow, Scotland. Tonnage: 3,523. Dimensions: 375′ x 39′. Single-screw, 11 knots. Compound engines. Three masts and one funnel. Iron hull. First sailing as **Norwegian** Glasgow-Quebec-Montreal, June 12, 1884. Made her final voyage to New York in 1900. Ran aground in Little Cod Bay in 1903. Refloated and broken up for scrap in the Netherlands. Ex-**City of New York** (1884).

Notting Hill (1881) Twin Screw Line (British).
Built by Dobie & Co., Glasgow, Scotland. Tonnage: 3,920. Displacement of 6,210 tons. Dimensions: 420′ x 45′. Twin-screw, 12 knots. Compound engines. 2,800 I.H.P. Four masts and one funnel. Steel hull. Service: London-New York. Struck an iceberg on February 5, 1883, with no loss of life.

Nouveau Monde (1865) French Line.
Built by Chantiers de l' Atlantique, St. Nazaire, France. Tonnage: 3,200. Dimensions: 355′ x 45′. Paddle-wheels, 12 knots. Side lever engines. Two masts and two funnels. Iron hull. Launched, January 27, 1865. Service: France-West Indies. Lengthened to 393 feet (4,503 tons) in 1875. Also converted to single-screw and re-engined with compounds. Mizzen mast added. Renamed: **Labrador** (1875). Scrapped in 1905.

Nova Scotia (1926) Warren Line (Furness, Withy & Co.).
Built by Vickers, Armstrong, Ltd., Barrow-in-Furness, Newcastle, England. Tonnage: 6,796. Dimensions: 406′ x 55′ (423′ o.l.). Twin-screw, 15 knots. Quadruple expansion engines. Two masts and one funnel. Passengers: 105 cabin and 80 third. Maiden voyage: Liverpool-St. John's-Halifax-Boston in May 1926. Torpedoed and sunk by submarine off Lourenco Marques, December 4, 1942, with heavy loss of

life. She had on board at time a number of Italian prisoners of war. Sistership: **Newfoundland.**

Nova Scotia   (1947)   Furness-Warren Line.
Built by Vickers-Armstrong, Ltd., Newcastle, England. Tonnage: 7,438. Dimensions: 423′ x 61′ (440′ o.l.). Single-screw, 16 knots. Three steam turbines. Two masts and one funnel. Passengers: 75 first and 85 tourist. Maiden voyage: Liverpool-St. John's-Halifax-Boston, September 2, 1947. The Liverpool-Boston crossing takes about 12 days, due to discharging of cargo at scheduled ports. Sister ship: **Newfoundland.**

Nova Scotian   (1858)   Allan Line.
Built by Wm. Denny & Bros., Ltd., Dumbarton, Scotland. Tonnage: 2,190. Dimensions: 280′ x 38′. Single-screw, 10 knots. Inverted engines. Compound engines in 1873. Three masts and one funnel. Iron hull. Clipper bow. Passengers: 80 first, 370 third. Maiden voyage: Liverpool-Quebec-Montreal, June 2, 1858. Lengthened to 366 feet (3,305 tons) in 1873. Scrapped in 1893. Sister ships: **Bohemian, Hungarian** and **North Briton.**

Numidian   (1891)   Allan Line.
Built by D. & W. Henderson & Co., Glasgow, Scotland. Tonnage: 4,836. Dimensions: 400′ x 45′. Single-screw, 13½ knots. Triple expansion engines. Two masts and one funnel. Steel hull. Passengers: 100 first, 80 second, 1,000 third. Maiden voyage: Liverpool-Quebec-Montreal, August 20, 1891. Made her final voyage to Boston in 1914. In the First World War she was filled with cement and sunk, so as to block a channel against submarines. Sister ship: **Mongolian.**

Nurnburg   (1873)   North German Lloyd.
Built by Robert Steele & Co., Greenock, Scotland. Tonnage: 3,116. Dimensions: 351′ x 39′. Single-screw, 12 knots. Compound engines. Two masts and one funnel. Launched in September 1873. Maiden voyage: Bremen-Southampton-Baltimore, February 17, 1874. Sold for scrap, 1895.

Oaxaca   (1883)   Compania Mexicana Transatlantica.
Built by Robert Napier & Sons, Glasgow, Scotland. Tonnage: 4,133. Dimensions: 400′ x 44′. Single-screw, 14½ knots. Triple expansion engines. Three masts and two funnels. Steel hull. Home port: Vera Cruz, Mexico. Service: Mexico-Spain. Renamed: **Duca di Galliera** (1887). Sister ships: **Mexico** and **Tamaulipas.**

Obdam   (1880)   Holland-America Line.
   Built by Harland & Wolff, Ltd., Belfast, Ireland. Tonnage:
   3,699.   Dimensions: 410′ x 40′.   Single-screw, 12 knots.
   Compound engines. Four masts and one funnel. Iron hull.
   Service: Rotterdam-New York. Triple expansion engines
   installed in 1890. Speed increased to 14 knots. Passengers:
   80 first, 60 second, 800 third. Renamed: (a) **McPherson**
   (1898) United States Government, (b) **Brooklyn,** (c) **S. V.
   Luckenbach** (1905) Luckenbach Line, (d) **Onega** (1915).
   Torpedoed and sunk by a German submarine, September
   30, 1918. Ex-**British Queen** (1889). Sister ships: **Amsterdam** and **Werkendam.**

Ocean Queen   (1859)   Vanderbilt European Line.
   Built by Westervelt & McKay, New York, N. Y. Tonnage:
   2,801. Dimensions: 377′ x 42′. Paddle-wheels, 12 knots.
   Beam engines. Wooden hull. Two masts and two funnels.
   Note: Launched in 1857 as **Queen of the Pacific,** but pur-
   chased by Vanderbilt before completion and renamed
   Ocean Queen. Service: New York-Southampton-Havre.
   Sold to Pacific Mail Steamship Company in 1870. Scrapped
   in 1875.

Oceana   (1891)   Hamburg-American Line.
   Built by Wm. Denny & Bros., Ltd., Dumbarton, Scotland.
   Tonnage: 7,815. Dimensions: 531′ x 54′. Twin-screw, 16
   knots. Triple expansion engines. Two masts and two funnels. Clipper bow. Used mainly as a cruise ship, but made
   North Atlantic sailings, too. The Hamburg-American Line
   sold vessel to other owners in 1910. Renamed: (a) **Alfonso
   XIII** (1916), (b) **Vasco Nunez de Balboa** (1923). Scrapped
   in 1927. Ex-**Scot** (1906).

Oceania   (1907)   Austro-American Line.
   Built by Alexander Stephen & Sons, Ltd., Glasgow, Scotland. Tonnage: 5,497. Dimensions: 391′ x 50′. Twin-screw,
   15 knots. Triple expansion engines. Two masts and one
   funnel. Service: Trieste-New York. Blown up by the
   Austrians in October 1918, so as to keep her from being
   captured by the Italians.

Oceania   (1909)   La Veloce Line (Italian).
   Built by Cantieri Navali Riuniti, Spezia, Italy. Tonnage:
   9,000. Dimensions: 476′ x 55′. Twin-screw, 16 knots. Triple
   expansion engines. Two masts and two funnels. Passengers:
   100 first and 2,400 third. Maiden voyage: Genoa-New York,

December 1, 1909. Renamed: **Stampalia** (1913). Torpedoed and sunk on August 18, 1916.

Oceanic   (1870)   White Star Line.
Built by Harland & Wolff, Ltd., Belfast, Ireland. Tonnage: 3,808. Dimensions: 420′ x 42′ (432′ o.l.). Single-screw, 14½ knots. Compound tandem engines. 3,000 I.H.P. Four masts and one funnel. Displacement of 7,240 tons. Laid down in 1869. Launched, August 27, 1870. Passengers: 166 first and 1,000 third. Maiden voyage: Liverpool-New York, March 2, 1871. Note: Pioneer vessel of the White Star Line. Transferred to Pacific service in 1875. See PART II for additional information. Scrapped in England, 1896. Sister ships: **Atlantic, Baltic** and **Republic.**

Oceanic   (1899)   White Star Line.
Built by Harland & Wolff, Ltd., Belfast, Ireland. Tonnage: 17,274. Dimensions: 685′ x 68′ (704′ o.l.). Twin-screw, 21 knots. Triple expansion engines. Three masts and two funnels. Promenade deck was 400 feet long. Note: The first steamship to exceed the **Great Eastern** in length. Displacement of 28,500 tons. Cost $3,600,000 to build. Passengers: 410 first, 300 second, 1,000 third. Launched, January 14, 1899. Maiden voyage: Liverpool-New York, September 6, 1899. Made a westward passage in 5 days, 16 hours, 34 minutes. Converted to an armed merchant cruiser in August 1914. Stranded on Foula Island, September 8, 1914 and became a total loss. The wreck was broken up for scrap.

Oder   (1873)   North German Lloyd.
Built by Caird & Co., Greenock, Scotland. Tonnage: 3,265. Dimensions: 351′ x 39′. Single-screw, 14½ knots. Compound engines. Two masts and one funnel. Iron hull. Passengers: 90 first, 126 second, 680 third. Maiden voyage: Bremen-Southampton-New York, May 23, 1874. Transferred to Far East route in 1886. Wrecked at Socotra, May 30, 1887. Sister ships: **Mosel** and **Neckar.**

Ohio   (1869)   North German Lloyd.
Built by Caird & Co., Greenock, Scotland. Tonnage: 2,394. Dimensions: 301′ x 39′. Single-screw, 10 knots. Inverted engines. Two masts and one funnel. Iron hull. Maiden voyage: Bremen-Southampton-Baltimore, March 8, 1869. Re-engined with compounds by 1881. Sold to Argentine Government in 1894. Renamed: (a) **Amazzone** (1894), (b) **Rio Santa Cruz** (1897). Sister ship: **Leipzig.**

Ohio   (1873)   American (Keystone) Line.
  Built by Wm. Cramp & Sons, Shipbuilding & Engineering
  Co., Philadelphia, Pa. Tonnage: 3,104. Dimensions: 360' x
  42'. Single-screw, 13 knots. Compound engines. Two masts
  and one funnel. Iron hull. Passengers: 76 cabin and 875
  third class.   Maiden voyage: Philadelphia-Liverpool in
  August 1873.   Triple expansion engines in 1887.   Speed
  increased to 14 knots. Made some New York sailings. Sold
  to White Star Steamship Company of Seattle. Stranded in
  Finlayson Channel, British Columbia, August 26, 1909, with
  the loss of several lives. Sister ships: **Indiana, Illinois** and
  Pennsylvania. Owner: American Steamship Company.

Ohio   (1923)   Royal Mail Line (British).
  Built by Akt. Ges. "Weser", Bremen, Germany. Tonnage:
  18,940.   Dimensions: 590' x 72'.   Twin-screw, 17 knots.
  Quadruple expansion engines. Two masts and two funnels.
  Passengers: 230 first, 523 second, 690 third. Laid down as
  the **Munchen** for North German Lloyd. However never in
  their service, as the vessel was acquired by the British.
  Renamed **Ohio** in 1923. Maiden voyage: Hamburg-South-
  ampton-Cherbourg-New York, April 4, 1923.   Renamed:
  Albertic (1927). Scrapped in 1934.

Olbia   (1873)   Fabre Line (French).
  Built by Wm. Denny & Bros., Ltd., Dumbarton, Scotland.
  Tonnage: 2,623.   Dimensions: 350' x 36'.   Single-screw.
  Three masts and one funnel. Iron hull. Quadruple expansion
  engines installed in 1888. Sold to Italian owners in January
  1906. Ex-**Martaban.**

Old North State   (1920)   United States Lines.
  Built by New York Shipbuilding Co., Camden, N. J. Tonnage: 10,533.   Dimensions: 502' x 62' (522' o.l.).   Twin-
  screw, 14 knots. Triple expansion engines. Two masts and
  one funnel. Note: Originally in service of United States Mail
  Steamship Co. Taken over by United States Lines in August
  1921. Service: New York-London. Renamed: (a) **President
  Van Buren** (1922), (b) **President Fillmore** (1940), (c)
  Marigold (1942) hospital ship.

Oldenburg   (1890)   North German Lloyd.
  Built by Fairfield Shipbuilding & Engineering Co., Glasgow,
  Scotland. Tonnage: 5,006. Dimensions: 415' x 48'. Single-
  screw, 13 knots. Triple expansion engines. Two masts and
  one funnel. Passengers: 49 first, 38 second, 1,900 third.
  Services: Interchangeable between various North German

Lloyd routes. Made her final voyage to New York in 1907. Sold to Turkey in 1911. Renamed: **Karadeniz.** Sister ships: **Darmstadt, Gera, Karlsruhe, Stuttgart** and **Weimar.**

Olinde Rodrigues   (1873)   French Line.
Built by Caird & Co., Greenock, Scotland. Tonnage: 3,188. Dimensions: 350′ x 39′. Single-screw, 11 knots. Compound engines. Two masts and one funnel. Iron hull. Passengers: 150 first, 70 second, 164 third. Service: France-West Indies-Central America. Made some voyages to New York. Scrapped in France, 1905. Ex-**Franconia** (1878) Hamburg-American Line. Sister ship: **Saint Simon.**

Olympia   (1871)   Anchor Line (British).
Built by Charles Connell & Co., Scotstoun, Glasgow, Scotland. Tonnage: 2,210. Dimensions: 307′ x 34′. Single-screw, 11 knots. Compound engines. Three masts and one funnel. Iron hull. Passengers: 75 first, 150 second, 500 third. Launched, November 16, 1871. Maiden voyage: Glasgow-Halifax-St. John, New Brunswick, April 2, 1872. Placed in various services. Made her final voyage to New York in 1897. Vessel sold in 1898. Sister ships: **Alexandria, Assyria, Castalia, Ismailia, Italia** and **Trinacria.**

*Olympia   (1953)   Greek Line.
Built by Alexander Stephen & Sons, Ltd., Glasgow, Scotland. Tonnage: 22,979. Dimensions: 569′ x 79′ (611′ o.l.). Twin-screw, 21 knots. Steam turbines. Two masts and one funnel. (Tripod type foremast.) Launched, April 17, 1953. Maiden voyage: from Glasgow to Belfast, Liverpool, Southampton, Cobh, Halifax and New York, October 15, 1953. Placed in Piraeus-New York service. Passengers: 138 first and 1,167 tourist. Two swimming pools. Also used as a cruise ship in winter.

Olympic   (1911)   White Star Line.
Built by Harland & Wolff, Ltd., Belfast, Ireland. Tonnage: 45,324. Dimensions: 852′ x 92′ (882′ o.l.). Triple-screw, 23 knots. Triple expansion engines and one low pressure steam turbine. Two masts and four funnels. Laid down on December 16, 1908. Launched, October 20, 1910. Note: From keel to top of funnels 175 feet. Navigating bridge was 104 feet above keel. Displacement of 60,000 tons. Draft of 34½ feet. The promenade deck had an extreme breadth of 94 feet. The bower anchors weighed 7¾ tons each. The centre anchor weighed 15½ tons. Cost $7,500,000 to build. Passengers: 1,054 first, 510 second, 1,020 third. The crew

numbered 860. Maiden voyage: Southampton-New York, June 14, 1911. Rammed and holed by the British cruiser **Hawke,** September 20, 1911, but was not seriously damaged. After the sinking of the **Titanic,** her construction was altered. The changes increased her tonnage to 46,439. Served as a troopship in World War I. Thoroughly reconditioned in 1921, including conversion to burning oil fuel. She rammed and sunk the well-known lightship **Nantucket** off the New England coast, May 16, 1934, during a thick fog. The seven members of the lightship crew were lost. The great liner was withdrawn from service in March 1935 and sold to British shipbreakers later in the year. The scrapped hulk was finally dismantled in 1937. Sister ship: **Titanic.**

Olympus (1860)   Cunard Line.
Built by Robert Napier & Sons, Glasgow, Scotland. Tonnage: 1,794. Dimensions: 276' x 36'. Single-screw, 10 knots. Geared oscillating engines. Three masts and one funnel. Mizzen mast added in 1872. Iron hull. Passengers: 70 cabin and 900 third. Services: (a) Mediterranean, (b) New York. Lengthened to 338 feet (2,415 tons) in 1872. Scrapped in 1891. Sister ships: **Atlas, Hecla, Kedar, Marathon** and **Sidon.**

Ontario (1864)   National Line (British).
Built by Palmer's Shipbuilding & Iron Co., Newcastle, England. Tonnage: 3,325. Dimensions: 371' x 41'. Single-screw 10 knots. Inverted engines. Three masts and one funnel. Iron hull. Launched, September 3, 1864. Wrecked while steaming from her builder's yard at Newcastle to Liverpool, October 16, 1864. Thus she never made an Atlantic crossing. Sister ships: **Erin** and **Helvatia.**

Ontario (1868)   American Steamship Company of Boston.
Built by Jackman of Newburyport, Mass. Tonnage: 3,000. Dimensions: 322' x 43'. Single-screw, 12 knots. Vertical geared engines. Three masts and two funnels. Clipper bow. Wooden hull. Made only three voyages to Europe, as financial troubles overtook the company. Sister ship: **Erie.** Note: Both vessels sold to other owners. The **Ontario** was destroyed by fire in 1872.

Ontario (1874)   Dominion Line.
Built by Archibald McMillan & Son, Dumbarton, Scotland. Tonnage: 3,175. Dimensions: 335' x 38'. Single-screw, 11 knots. Compound engines. Three masts and one funnel.

Iron hull.   Maiden voyage: Liverpool-Quebec-Montreal, July 15, 1874. Transferred to Avonmouth service in 1885. Scrapped in 1896. Sister ship: **Dominion.**

Orbita   (1915)   Royal Mail Line (British).
Built by Harland & Wolff, Ltd., Belfast, Ireland. Tonnage: 15,495. Dimensions: 550' x 67' (569' o.l.). Triple-screw, 15 knots. Triple expansion engines and one low steam turbine. Two masts and one funnel. Passengers: 190 first, 221 second, 476 third. First voyage: Hamburg-Southampton-Cherbourg-New York, April 30, 1921. Employed in the North Atlantic passenger service 1921–1926. Returned to Pacific Steam Navigation Company. Scrapped in 1950. Note: See PART III for further information. Sister ships: **Orca** and **Orduna.**

Orca   (1918)   Royal Mail Line (British).
Built by Harland & Wolff, Ltd., Belfast, Ireland. Tonnage: 16,063.   Dimensions: 550' x 57'.   Triple-screw, 15 knots. Triple expansion engines and one low pressure steam turbine. Two masts and one funnel. Began trans-Atlantic service in January 1923. Renamed: **Calgaric** (1927). White Star Line. Scrapped in 1935. Note: The Royal Mail Line operated a North Atlantic passenger service to New York from 1921 to 1927. In this service they employed the liners **Orbita, Orca, Orduna, Oropesa** and **Ohio.**

Orduna   (1914)   Royal Mail Line (British).
Built by Harland & Wolff, Ltd., Belfast, Ireland. Tonnage: 15,507. Dimensions: 550' x 67'. Triple-screw, 15 knots. Triple expansion engines and steam turbine. Two masts and one funnel.   First Hamburg-Southampton-Cherbourg-New York sailing, May 28, 1921. Resold back to Pacific Steam Navigation Company in 1927. Scrapped in 1951. Sister ships: **Orbita** and **Orca.** Note: See **Orca** for additional information.

Oregon   (1883)   Guion Line (British).
Built by John Elder & Co., Glasgow, Scotland. Tonnage: 7,375. Dimensions: 501' x 54' (520' o.l.). Single-screw, 18½ knots. Compound engines. Four masts and two funnels. Iron hull.   Her 3-cylinder compound engines developed 13,575 indicated horse-power at 64 revolutions per minute. Maiden voyage: Liverpool-Queenstown-New York, October 7, 1883. She made the crossing (Queenstown-New York) in the record breaking time of 6 days, 10 hours, 10 minutes. The liner was sold to Cunard Line in June 1884. In collision with unknown schooner 18 miles east of Long Island, March

14, 1886. She subsequently sank, but all on board were rescued by the North German Lloyd steamship **Fulda.**

Oregon (1883) Dominion Line.
  Built by Charles Connell & Co., Glasgow, Scotland. Tonnage: 3,672. Dimensions: 360′ x 40′. Single-screw, 12½ knots. Compound engines. Four masts and one funnel. Iron hull. Maiden voyage: Liverpool-Halifax-Portland, March 15, 1883. Passengers: 80 first, 200 second, 1,200 third. Reduced to two masts at later date. Sold to Furness, Withy & Company in 1896. Scrapped in Italy, 1897. Sister ships: **Sarnia** and **Ottawa.**

Orione (1883) Navigazione Generale Italiana.
  Built by Robert Napier & Sons, Glasgow, Scotland. Tonnage: 4,161. Dimensions: 380′ x 42′. Single-screw, 16 knots. Compound engines. Triple expansion engines in 1891. Three masts and two funnels. Iron hull. Mainly in Italy-South American service. Vessel later sold to Societa Marittima Italiana. Sister ships: **Sirio** and **Perseo.**

Oropesa (1920) Royal Mail Line (British).
  Built by Cammell, Laird & Co., Birkenhead, England. Tonnage: 14,075. Dimensions: 530′ x 66′ (552′ o.l.). Twin-screw, 14 knots. Steam turbines. Two masts and one funnel. Passengers: 141 first, 131 second, 360 third. This South American liner made at least six North Atlantic crossings to New York. Liner was returned to Pacific Steam Navigation Company in 1923. Torpedoed and sunk by submarine in North Atlantic, January 16, 1941. Note: See **Orca** for additional information.

Oscar II (1901) Scandinavian-American Line.
  Built by Alexander Stephen & Sons, Ltd., Glasgow, Scotland. Tonnage: 10,012. Dimensions: 500′ x 58′ (515′ o.l.). Twin-screw, 16 knots. Triple expansion engines. 8,500 I.H.P. Two masts and one funnel. Passengers: 130 first, 140 second, 900 third. Service: Copenhagen-Oslo-New York. Scrapped in Great Britain, 1934. Sister ships: **Hellig Olav** and **United States.**

Oslofjord (1938) Norwegian-America Line.
  Built by "Weser", Bremen, Germany. Tonnage: 18,372. Dimensions: 563′ x 73′ (588′ o.l.). Twin-screw, 19 knots. Motorship. Two masts and two funnels. Maiden voyage: Oslo-Bergen-New York, June 4, 1938. Struck a mine off

the British Isles, December 13, 1940. She was beached, but became a total loss.

*Oslofjord (1949) Norwegian-America Line.
Built by Netherlands Dock & Engineering Co., Amsterdam, Netherlands. Tonnage: 16,844. Dimensions: 545′ x 72 (577′ o.l.). Twin-screw, 20 knots. Motorship (2 diesels). Two masts and one funnel. Launched, April 4, 1949. This beautiful liner attained a speed of 21.74 knots during her sea trials. Maiden voyage: Oslo-Copenhagen-Christiansand-Stavenger-Bergen-New York, November 26, 1949. Passengers: 260 first, 370 tourist. She was the largest passenger ship of the Norwegian merchant fleet built, until the new **Bergensfjord** (1956).

Ottawa (1874) Dominion Line.
Built by Harland & Wolff, Ltd., Belfast, Ireland. Tonnage: 5,008. Dimensions: 455′ x 45′. Single-screw, 16 knots. Triple expansion engines. Four masts and two funnels. Iron hull. In Liverpool-Canada service, 1905–1909. Renamed: (a) **Gul Djemal** (1911) Turkish, (b) **Gulcemal.** Scrapped in 1950. Ex-**Germanic** (1904) White Star Line.

Ottawa (1880) Dominion Line.
Built by Charles Connell & Co., Glasgow, Scotland. Tonnage: 3,712. Dimensions: 359′ x 40′. Single-screw, 12 knots. Compound engines. Four masts and one funnel. Iron hull. Wrecked near Quebec, November 22, 1880, with no loss of life. Sister ships: **Oregon** and **Sarnia.**

P. Caland (1874) Holland-America Line.
Built by Robert Napier & Sons, Glasgow, Scotland. Tonnage: 2,548. Dimensions: 350′ x 38′. Single-screw, 10 knots. Compound engines. Three masts and one funnel. Clipper bow. Iron hull. Passengers: 50 first and 600 third. Sold to Cosulich Line in 1897. Renamed: (a) **Ressel** (1897), (b) **Caramanie** (1899). Scrapped in 1910. Sister ship: **W. A. Scholten.**

P. de Satrustegui (1890) Spanish Line.
Built by A. & J. Inglis, Glasgow, Scotland. Tonnage: 4,671. Dimensions: 410′ x 46′. Single-screw, 15 knots. Triple expansion engines. Two masts and one funnel. Steel hull. Made her final voyage to New York in 1922. Scrapped in 1927. Ex-**Tara.**

Pacific   (1849)   Collins Line (American).
    Built by Brown & Bell, New York, N. Y. Tonnage: 2,856. Dimensions: 282' x 45'. Paddle-wheels, 12½ knots. Two side lever engines. Three masts and one funnel. Wooden hull. Cost $700,000 to build. Maiden voyage: New York-Liverpool, May 25, 1850. She captured the trans-Atlantic "Blue Ribbon" by raising the average speed on the New York to Liverpool crossing to 13.01 knots. The Collins Line kept the speed record for the next five years, with her sister ships the **Baltic** and the **Atlantic** being rated as the fastest vessels afloat during that period. The **Pacific** sailed from Liverpool, January 23, 1856, bound for New York, and was never heard of again. The loss of life was heavy, as she had on board 45 passengers and a crew of 141. Sister ships: **Arctic, Atlantic** and **Baltic.**

Palatia   (1893)   Hamburg-American Line.
    Built by "Vulkan", Stettin, Germany. Tonnage: 7,118. Dimensions: 460' x 52'. Twin-screw, 14 knots. Reciprocating engines. Four masts and one funnel. Accommodation for 2,500 third class passengers. Service: Hamburg-New York. Renamed: **Nikolaieff** (1904) Russian Navy. Sister ships: **Patria** and **Phoenicia.**

Palermo   (1899)   Navigazione Generale Italiana.
    Built by Palmer's Shipbuilding & Iron Co., Newcastle, England. Tonnage: 9,203. Dimensions: 470' x 56'. Twin-screw, 12½ knots. Triple expansion engines. Four masts and one funnel. First voyage as **Palermo,** Italy to Halifax and Boston, July 8, 1913. Torpedoed and sunk on December 2, 1916. Ex-**Lazio** (1913), (b) **British Princess** (1906).

Palermo   (1907)   Navigazione Generale Italiana.
    Built by Sir James Laing & Sons, Ltd., Sunderland, England. Tonnage: 6,094. Dimensions: 430' x 52'. Twin-screw, 52'. Twin-screw, 14 knots. Triple expansion engines. Two masts and two funnels. Service: Genoa-Naples-New York. Scrapped in 1928. Ex-**San Giovanni** (1921).

Palmyra   (1866)   Cunard Line.
    Built by Caird & Co., Greenock, Scotland. Tonnage: 2,044. Dimensions: 290' x 38'. Single-screw, 11 knots. Inverted engines. Two masts and one funnel. Iron hull. Clipper bow. Transferred later to Mediterranean service. Scrapped in 1897. Sister ships: **Aleppo, Malta, Tarifa** and **Tripoli.**

Panama   (1865)   French Line.
Built by Generale Transatlantique, St. Nazaire, France. Tonnage: 3,200. Dimensions: 354′ x 43′. Paddle-wheels, 12 knots. Side lever engines. Two masts and two funnels. Iron hull. Service: France-West Indies. In the 1870's was reconditioned and converted to single-screw. Compound engines installed. Speed increased to 13½ knots. Tonnage raised to 4,287. Renamed: **Canada** (1876). Scrapped in 1908.

Panama   (1875)   Spanish Line.
Built by London & Glasgow Shipbuilding Co., Glasgow, Scotland. Tonnage: 2,085. Dimensions: 331′ x 34′. Single-screw. Compound engines. Three masts and one funnel. Iron hull. Renamed: **Hooker** (1898) United States Government. Wrecked off Corregidor in 1899. Ex-**Branksome Hall** (1885).

Panhandle State   (1920)   United States Lines.
Built by New York Shipbuilding Co., Camden, N. J. Tonnage: 10,533. Dimensions: 502′ x 62′. Single-screw, 14 knots. Triple expansion engines. Two masts and one funnel. Accommodation for 78 first class passengers. Originally ran for United States Mail Steamship Company for brief time. In trans-Atlantic service 1921–1922. Renamed: (a) **President Monroe** (1922), (b) **President Buchanan** (1941), (c) **Emily H. M. Weder** (U. S. hospital ship).

Pannonia   (1904)   Cunard Line.
Built by John Brown & Co., Clydebank, Glasgow, Scotland. Tonnage: 9,851. Dimensions: 486′ x 59′ (501′ o.l.). Twin-screw, 14 knots. Triple expansion engines. Four masts and one funnel. Passengers: 40 first and 800 third class. Mainly in Mediterranean-New York, and London-New York services. Scrapped in 1922.

Parana   (1851)   Galway Line (British).
Built by M. Wigram, Southampton, England. Tonnage: 2,943. Dimensions: 305′ x 42′. Paddle-wheels, 11 knots. Side lever engines. Three masts and two funnels. Clipper bow. Wooden hull. Vessel was on charter from the Royal Mail Line. First trans-Atlantic sailing for Galway Line was made on June 27, 1860. She was soon returned to the Royal Mail Line.

Paris   (1889)   American Line.
Built by J. & G. Thomson, Ltd., Glasgow, Scotland. Tonnage: 10,669. Dimensions: 527′ x 63′ (560′ o.l.).   Twin-

screw, 20 knots. Triple expansion engines. Three masts and three funnels. Service: Southampton-New York. Stranded on Manacles Rock, Cornwall in May 1899, where she remained until refloated the following July. She was rebuilt with two funnels and quadruple expansion engines installed. Renamed **Philadelphia** and placed back in service, August 31, 1901. Scrapped in 1923. Note: Renamed: (a) **Yale** (1898) United States Government, (b) **Paris** (1899), (c) **Philadelphia** (1900), (d) **Harrisburg** (1917) United States Government, (e) **Philadelphia** (1919). Ex-**City of Paris** (1893). Sister ship: **New York.**

Paris   (1921)   French Line.
Built by Chantiers & Ateliers de Penhoet, St. Nazaire, France. Tonnage: 34,569. Dimensions: 735′ x 83′ (763′ o.l.). Quadruple-screw, 22 knots. Four steam turbines. Two masts and three funnels. Laid down in 1913. Launched, September 12, 1916. Completion was delayed due to the war. Maiden voyage from Havre to New York in June 1921. This luxury liner capsized at her pier in Havre, after being gutted by fire on April 18, 1939. Her burned out hulk remained for years in shallow water in same spot where she capsized.

Parisian   (1881)   Allan Line (British).
Built by Robert Napier & Sons, Glasgow, Scotland. Tonnage: 5,395. Dimensions: 441′ x 46′. Single-screw, 15 knots. Compound engines. Four masts and two funnels. Steel hull. Passengers: 150 first, 100 second, 1,000 third. Maiden voyage: Liverpool-Halifax-Boston, March 10, 1881. Re-engined with triple expansions in 1899 and also had her original funnels replaced with a single large one. Served in various North Atlantic routes, including Glasgow-New York run. Sold to Italian shipbreakers in January 1914, and soon afterwards was dismantled at Genoa.

Parthia   (1870)   Cunard Line.
Built by Wm. Denny & Bros., Ltd., Dumbarton, Scotland. Tonnage: 3,502. Dimensions: 360′ x 40′. Single-screw, 13 knots. Compound engines. Three masts and one funnel. Iron hull. Commenced her maiden voyage from Liverpool on December 17, 1870. Mainly in Liverpool-Boston service. Transferred to trans-Pacific service in 1887. Renamed: **Victoria** (1891). Acquired by Alaska Steamship Company in 1908. Converted to barge in 1954.

*Parthia   (1947)   Cunard Line.
Built by Harland & Wolff, Ltd., Belfast, Ireland. Tonnage: 13,362. Dimensions: 518′ x 70′ (531′ o.l.). Twin-screw, 17½

knots. Steam turbines. Single mast and one funnel. Passengers: 250 first class.   Maiden voyage: Liverpool-New
York, April 10, 1948. Note: The first Cunard Line vessel to
be built by Harland & Wolff, Ltd. Sister ship: **Media.**

Patria   (1882)   Fabre Line (French).
Built by "Vulkan", Stettin, Germany.   Tonnage: 4,053.
Dimensions: 358' x 42'. Single-screw, 11 knots. Compound
engines. Three masts and one funnel. First voyage Marseilles-
New York, November 25, 1895.   Sold to Italian owners in
1903. Scrapped in Italy, 1906. Ex-**Rugia** (1895).

Patria   (1893)   Hamburg-American Line.
Built by "Vulkan", Stettin, Germany.   Tonnage: 7,118.
Dimensions: 460' x 52'. Twin-screw, 13½ knots. Compound
engines. Four masts and one funnel. Accommodation for
2,500 steerage passengers. Service: Hamburg-New York.
Destroyed by fire in the English Channel, November 17, 1899,
with no loss of life. Sister ships: **Palatia** and **Phoenicia.**

Patria   (1913)   Fabre Line.
Built by Chantiers de la Mediterranee, La Seyne, France.
Tonnage: 11,885. Dimensions: 487' x 59' (512' o.l.). Twin-
screw, 16 knots. Triple expansion engines. Two masts and
three funnels. Launched, November 11, 1913. Service:
Marseilles-New York. Towards end of career was in Messageries Maritimes service. Sunk by an explosion in Haifa
Harbor, November 26, 1940. There was heavy loss of life
among the many emigrants on board. The sunken hulk was
later broken up for scrap. Sister ship: **Providence** (nearly
identical).

Patria   (1938)   Hamburg-American Line.
Built by Deutsche Werft, Hamburg, Germany. Tonnage:
16,595. Dimensions: 562' x 74' (589' o.l.). Twin-screw, 17
knots. Motorship. Two masts and one funnel. Service:
Hamburg-West Indies-Central America. Renamed: (a)
Empire Welland (1945), (b) **Rossia.** Still in Russian
service.

Patricia   (1899)   Hamburg-American Line.
Built by "Vulkan", Stettin, Germany. Tonnage: 13,424.
Dimensions: 560' x 62' (584' o.l.). Twin-screw, 13½ knots.
Quadruple expansion engines. Four masts and one funnel.
Passengers: 162 first, 184 second, 2,100 third. Tonnage listed
as 14,466 in 1914. Service: Hamburg-New York. Note: Used
by the United States War Department as a troopship. The

liner was later turned over to the British Shipping Controller, who chartered her to Ellerman Lines. Sold for scrap in November 1921. Broken up in 1922. Sister ships: **Graf Waldersee, Pennsylvania** and **Pretoria.**

Patris   (1909)   Greek Line (Embiricos Bros.).
Built by Northumberland Shipbuilding Co., Newcastle, England. Tonnage: 4,390. Dimensions: 370' x 47'. Twin-screw, 14 knots. Triple expansion engines. Two masts and two funnels. Passengers: 60 first and 1,300 third class. Maiden voyage: Greece-New York, April 2, 1909. Made her final voyage to New York in 1920. Renamed: **Claude Chappe** (1925). Scrapped in 1939.

Pavonia   (1882)   Cunard Line.
Built by J. & G. Thomson, Ltd., Glasgow, Scotland. Tonnage: 5,588. Dimensions: 430' x 46'. Single-screw, 14 knots. Compound engines. Three masts and one funnel. Iron hull. Passengers: 200 cabin, 1,500 third. Maiden voyage: Liverpool-New York, September 13, 1882. Placed in the Liverpool-Boston service. In February 1899 was damaged in heavy weather and had to be towed to England for repairs. Sold for scrap in 1900. Broken up in 1901. Running mates: **Cephalonia** (identical) and **Catalonia.**

Pellerin le la Touche   (1913)   French Line.
Built by Cantieri San Rocco, Trieste, Austria-Hungaria. Tonnage: 8,217. Dimensions: 452' x 56'. Twin-screw, 16 knots. Quadruple expansion engines. Two masts and two funnels. Service: France-West Indies-Central America. Sold to German shipbreakers in November 1936. Ex-**General Gallieni**, ex-**Marienbad.**

Peninsula State   (1922)   United States Lines.
Built by New York Shipbuilding Co., Camden, N. J. Tonnage: 13,869. Dimensions: 516' x 72' (535' o.l.). Twin-screw, 18 knots. Steam turbines. Two masts and one funnel. In service in 1922. Renamed: (a) **President Roosevelt** (1922), (b) **Joseph T. Dickman** (1941) U. S. troopship. Scrapped in 1948.

Pennland   (1870)   Red Star Line.
Built by J. & G. Thomson, Ltd., Clydebank, Glasgow, Scotland. (This shipbuilding yard is now known as John Brown & Co., Ltd.). Tonnage: 3,760. Dimensions: 361' x 41'. Single-screw, 13 knots. Compound engines. Three masts and one funnel. Iron hull. Service: Antwerp-New York.

Transferred to the Liverpool-Philadelphia service of the American Line in 1895. Scrapped at Genoa in 1903. Ex-**Algeria** (1881).

Pennland (1922) Red Star Line.
Built by Harland & Wolff, Ltd., Belfast, Ireland. Tonnage: 16,322. Dimensions: 575′ x 67′ (601′ o.l.). Triple-screw, 16 knots. Triple expansion engines and one steam turbine. Two masts and two funnels. Service: Antwerp-Southampton-New York. Liner was sold to Arnold Bernstein in 1935. Converted to tourist class ship (538 passengers). Resold to Holland-America Line about 1939. Bombed and sunk by German aircraft in the Gulf of Athens, April 25, 1941, while on way from Alexandria to Greece to evacuate British soldiers. Ex-**Pittsburg** (1925). Sister ship: **Westernland.**

Pennsylvania (1863) National Line (British).
Built by Palmer's Shipbuilding & Iron Co., Newcastle, England. Tonnage: 2,890. Dimensions: 342′ x 41′. Single-screw, 11 knots. Inverted engines. Three masts and one funnel. Iron hull. Clipper bow. Passengers: 100 first and 750 third. Maiden voyage: Liverpool-New York, February 16, 1864. Lengthened to 390 feet (4,276 tons) by Laird Bros., 1872. Re-engined with compounds. Renamed: **Canada** (1872). Scrapped in 1894.

Pennsylvania (1873) American Line.
Built by Wm. Cramp & Sons Shipbuilding Co., Philadelphia, Pa. Tonnage: 3,126. Dimensions: 360′ x 42′. Single-screw, 13 knots. Compound engines. Two masts and one funnel. Iron hull. Note: Known as the American (Keystone) Line. Absorbed later by the American Line. Passengers: 76 cabin and 875 third class. Third class quarters enlarged in the 1880's. Tonnage increased to 3,300. The **Pennsylvania** was the pioneer vessel of the line. Launched in August 1872. Maiden voyage: Philadelphia-Liverpool, May 22, 1873. Re-engined with triple expansions in 1891. Transferred to Antwerp-Philadelphia service of the Red Star Line in 1892. Sold to Pacific Mail Line in 1898. Destroyed by fire at Iquique Bay, Chile, November 12, 1918. Sister ships: **Illinois, Indiana** and **Ohio.**

Pennsylvania (1896) Hamburg-American Line.
Built by Harland & Wolff, Ltd., Belfast, Ireland. Tonnage: 13,333. Dimensions: 559′ x 62′. Twin-screw, 13½ knots. Quadruple expansion engines. Four masts and one funnel. Passengers: 160 first, 180 second, 2,200 third. Service:

Hamburg-New York.   Renamed: **Nansemond** (1917) United States troopship. Scrapped in 1924. Sister ships: **Graf Waldersee, Patricia** and **Pretoria.**   Note: Large passenger-cargo type steamships, which could carry more cargo on one voyage than the entire Hamburg-American Line sailing fleet of the 1850's in a whole year.

Pereire (1865)   French Line.
Built by Robert Napier & Sons, Glasgow, Scotland. Tonnage: 3,150. Dimensions: 363' x 46'. Single-screw, 13 knots. Inverted engines. Three masts and one funnel. Iron hull. Clipper bow. Launched, November 4, 1865. Note: Originally designed as a side-wheeler, but converted to single-screw on the stocks. In 1872 was reboilered, re-engined with compounds and given two funnels in place of original single stack. Services: (a) France-New York, (b) France-Central America. Sold and converted to sail in 1888. Renamed: **Lancing** (1888). Performed some very fast voyages as the sailing ship **Lancing.** Broken up by Italian shipbreakers in 1925. Sister ship: **Ville de Paris.**

Perou (1907)   French Line.
Built by Chantiers de l' Atlantique, St. Nazaire, France. Tonnage: 6,599. Dimensions: 432' x 52'. Twin-screw, 16 knots. Triple expansion engines. Two masts and two funnels. Launched, March 1, 1907. Service: France-West Indies-Central America. Scrapped in 1934. Sister ship: **Guadeloupe.**

Perseo (1883)   Navigazione Generale Italiana.
Built by Robert Napier & Sons, Ltd., Glasgow, Scotland. Tonnage: 4,158. Dimensions: 380' x 42'. Single-screw, 16 knots. Compound engines. Re-engined with triple expansions in 1891. Three masts and two funnels. In service to South America, too. Sister ships: **Orione** and **Sirio.**

Persia (1856)   Cunard Line.
Built by Robert Napier & Sons, Ltd., Glasgow, Scotland. Tonnage: 3,414. Dimensions: 360' x 45'. Paddle-wheels, 13½ knots. Side lever engines. Two masts and two funnels. Clipper bow. First Cunard Line paddle-steamer built of iron. Displacement of 7,130 tons. Length from her figurehead to taffrail was 390 feet. Passengers: 200 cabin and 50 second class. Maiden voyage: Liverpool-New York, January 26, 1856. Won the trans-Atlantic speed record in 1856. Became one of the most famous of trans-Atlantic liners. Sold

out of Cunard Line service in 1868. Broken up for scrap on the Thames in 1872. Sister ship: **Scotia.**

Persia (1894) Hamburg-American Line.
Built by Harland & Wolff, Ltd., Belfast, Ireland. Tonnage: 5,713. Dimensions: 445′ x 50′. Twin-screw, 13 knots. Reciprocating engines. Four masts and one funnel. Passengers: 60 first and 1,800 third. Service: Hamburg-New York. Renamed: (a) **Minnewaska** (1897), (b) **Thomas** (1898) U. S. Government. Sold for scrap in July 1928.

Persian Monarch (1880) (a) Monarch Line, (b) Wilson Line.
Built by A. McMillan & Son, Dumbarton, Scotland. Tonnage: 3,923. Dimensions: 360′ x 48′. Single-screw, 12 knots. Compound engines. Four masts and one funnel. Iron hull. Passengers: 40 first and 1,000 third. Maiden voyage: London-New York in April 1881. Went aground on Long Island, New York in 1894. Subsequently refloated and converted to a four-masted bark. Renamed: **May Flint** (1895). Finally sunk in San Francisco Bay in September 1900, by running onto the ram of the anchored **U. S. S. Iowa.** Sister ships: **Egyptian Monarch** and **Lydian Monarch.**

Perugia (1901) Anchor Line.
Built by D. & W. Henderson & Co., Glasgow, Scotland. Tonnage: 4,348. Dimensions: 375′ x 47′. Single-screw, 13 knots. Triple expansion engines. Two masts and one funnel. Placed in the Mediterranean-New York service in August 1901. Passengers: 20 first and 1,150 third class. In 1912 had capacity for 1,400 third class passengers. Sunk in the Mediterranean, December 4, 1916.

Peruvian (1863) Allan Line.
Built by Robert Steele & Co., Greenock, Scotland. Tonnage: 2,549. Dimensions: 312′ x 39′. Single-screw, 11 knots. Inverted engines. Three masts and one funnel. Clipper bow. Iron hull. Maiden voyage: Liverpool-Portland, Maine, March 31, 1864. Served on various North Atlantic routes. Lengthened to 373 feet (3,038 tons) in 1874. Re-engined with compounds. Note: A second funnel was added in 1891. Scrapped at Genoa in 1905. Sister ships: **Austrian, Moravian** and **Nestorian.**

Pesaro (1901) Lloyd Sabaudo Line.
Built by Blohm & Voss, Hamburg, Germany. Tonnage: 12,335. Dimensions: 525′ x 62′. Twin-screw, 15½ knots. Quadruple expansion engines. Two masts and two funnels.

Liner was seized by Italian Government in 1915. Renamed: **Pesaro** (Italian). First Genoa-Naples-New York sailing for Lloyd Sabaudo in 1919. Transferred to their Italy-South American route in 1922. Scrapped in 1926. Ex-**Moltke** (1915).

Petersburg   (1894)   Russian Volunteer Fleet.
Built by R. & W. Hawthorn, Leslie & Co., Newcastle, England. Tonnage: 5,432. Dimensions: 439′ x 52′. Twin-screw, 15 knots. Triple expansion engines. Three masts and two funnels. Steel hull. Made her first Libau-Rotterdam-New York voyage in October 1906. Renamed: (a) **Dniepr** (1904) Russian Navy, (b) **Petersburg** (1906). Running mates: **Moskva, Saratov** and **Smolensk.**

Philadelphia   (1889)   American Line.
Built by J. & G. Thomson, Ltd., Clydebank, Glasgow, Scotland. Tonnage: 10,786. Dimensions: 527′ x 63′ (560′ o.l.). Twin-screw, 19½ knots. Quadruple expansion engines. Three masts and two funnels. First voyage as **Philadelphia,** Southampton to New York, August 31, 1901. Served as a transport for the United States in First World War. Resumed regular service in March 1920. Scrapped in Italy, 1923. Ex-**Harrisburg** (1919) United States Government, ex-**Philadelphia** (1917), ex-**Paris** (1900), ex-**Yale** (1899), ex-**Paris** (1898), ex-**City of Paris** (1893). Sister ship: **New York.**

Phoenicia   (1894)   Hamburg-American Line.
Built by Blohm & Voss, Hamburg, Germany. Tonnage: 6,761. Dimensions: 460′ x 52′. Twin-screw, 13 knots. Compound engines. Four masts and one funnel. Accommodation for a very large number of steerage passengers. Service: Hamburg-New York. Sold to the Russian Navy in 1905 and renamed **Kronstadt.** Sold to France in 1921 and converted to repair ship. Renamed: **Vulcain.** Scrapped in 1937. Sister ships: **Palatia** and **Patria.**

Phoenician   (1864)   Allan Line.
Built by Barclay, Curle & Co., Glasgow, Scotland. Tonnage: 2,356. Dimensions: 335′ x 34′. Single-screw, 12 knots. Compound engines. Three masts and one funnel. Iron hull. First voyage as **Phoenician,** Glasgow-Quebec-Montreal, June 12, 1873. Note: Built as the **St. David** and placed in the Canadian service. Lengthened from 272 feet (1,516 tons) to 335 feet (2,356 tons) in 1873. Re-engined with compounds and name changed to **Phoenician.** Given quadruple expansion

engines in 1888, which made her the first North Atlantic steamship to be so equipped. Between 1889 and 1903 made voyages to South America. Broken up at Genoa for scrap in 1905. Ex-**St. David** (1873).

Pilsudski (1935) Gdynia-America Shipping Line.
   Built by Cantieri Riuniti dell' Adriatico, Monfalcone, Italy. Tonnage: 14,294. Dimensions: 398' x 70' (525' o.l.). Twin-screw, 20 knots. Motorship. Two masts and two funnels. Launched, December 11, 1934. Entered Gdynia-New York service in 1935. Passengers: 355 tourist and 404 third class. Torpedoed and sunk near the Humber River, November 26, 1939, while serving as an Allied armed merchant cruiser. Sister ship: **Batory.**

Pisa (1896) Hamburg-American Line.
   Built by Alexander Stephen & Sons, Ltd., Glasgow, Scotland. Tonnage: 4,959. Dimensions: 390' x 46'. Single-screw, 12 knots. Seized by United States Government in World War I. Renamed: **Ascutney.** Later chartered to Italy. Afterwards sold to Wynant Steamship Co.

Pittsburgh (1922) White Star Line.
   Built by Harland & Wolff, Ltd., Belfast, Ireland. Tonnage: 16,322. Dimensions: 575' x 67'. Twin-screw, 16 knots. Triple expansion engines and one steam turbine. Two masts and two funnels. Passengers: 600 cabin and 1,500 third class. First Liverpool-Philadelphia sailing was made in June 1922. Also in New York service. Renamed: **Pennland** (1923). Note: This vessel was laid down in 1913 for the American Line. However, she was taken over by White Star Line before launching. Sister ship: **Regina.**

Pocahontas (1900) United States Mail Steamship Co.
   Built by "Vulkan", Stettin, Germany. Tonnage: 10,881. Dimensions: 523' x 60'. Twin-screw, 15 knots. Quadruple expansion engines. Two masts and two funnels. First voyage: New York-Naples-Genoa, February 23, 1921. Note: This former German liner was seized by United States in 1917 and renamed **Pocahontas.** Acquired by the subject line in 1921 for trans-Atlantic service. Renamed: (a) **Bremen** (1922), (b) **Karlsruhe** (1928). Scrapped in 1932. Ex-**Prinzess Irene** (1917).

Poland (1898) Red Star Line (Belgian).
   Built by Furness, Withy & Co., West Hartlepool, England. Tonnage: 8,282. Single-screw, 13 knots. Triple expansion

engines. Four masts and one funnel. Passengers: 1,100 third class. Service: Hamburg-New York. Broken up for scrap in 1925. Ex-**Manitou** (1922), ex-**Victoria** (1898).

Polonia (1910) Gdynia-America Line.
Built by Barclay, Curle & Co., Glasgow, Scotland. Tonnage: 7,890. Dimensions: 450' x 56'. Twin-screw, 16 knots. Quadruple expansion engines. Two masts and two funnels. Service: Gdynia-Copenhagen-New York. Transferred to South American service in 1936. Scrapped in Italy, 1939. Note: The **Polonia** originally operated by Baltic American Line (Danish). Transferred to subject line in 1930. Running mates: **Kosciuszko** and **Pulaski.**

Polynesian (1872) Allan Line.
Built by Robert Steele & Co., Greenock, Scotland. Tonnage: 3,983. Dimensions: 400' x 42'. Single-screw, 13½ knots. Compound engines. Three masts and one funnel. Iron hull. Commenced service in October 1872. Tonnage increased to 4,522 tons gross in 1893, also re-engined with triple expansions. Renamed: **Laurentian.** Wrecked in 1909. Sister ship: **Sardinian.**

Pomeranian (1882) Allan Line.
Built by Earle's Shipbuilding & Engineering Co., Hull, England. Tonnage: 4,365. Dimensions: 381' x 43' (400' o.l.). Single-screw, 12 knots. Compound engines. Four masts and two funnels. Iron hull. Passengers: 40 first, 60 second, 1,000 third. First voyage as **Pomeranian** was from London to Montreal in September 1887. She was later converted to two masts and single funnel. Triple expansion engines in 1902. Torpedoed and sunk 9 miles from Portland Bill, April 15, 1918, with the loss of about 50 lives. Ex-**Grecian Monarch** (1887).

Pommerania (1873) Hamburg-American Line.
Built by Caird & Co., Greenock, Scotland. Tonnage: 3,382. Dimensions: 361' x 41'. Single-screw, 13½ knots. Compound engines. Two masts and one funnel. Iron hull. Launched, July 26, 1873. Passengers: 100 first, 70 second, 600 third. Placed in Hamburg-New York service. Sunk in collision off Folkestone, November 26, 1878, with the loss of 50 lives. Sister ship: **Suevia.**

Potomac (1901) United States Lines.
Built by J. C. Tecklenborg, Geestemunde, Germany. Tonnage: 9,709. Dimensions: 499' x 58'. Twin-screw, 14 knots.

Quadruple expansion engines. Four masts and one funnel. Scrapped in 1928. Ex-**Antigone** (1920), ex-**Neckar** (1917).

Potsdam   (1900)   Holland-America Line.
   Built by Blohm & Voss, Hamburg, Germany. Tonnage: 12,522. Dimensions: 547′ x 62′ (565′ o.l.). Twin-screw, 15 knots. Triple expansion engines. Two masts and one funnel. Passengers: 280 first, 210 second, 1,800 third. Maiden voyage: Rotterdam-New York, May 17, 1900. Renamed: (a) **Stockholm** (1915), (b) **Solglimt** (1928) converted whale factory ship. Captured in the Antarctic by the German raider **Pinguin** and taken to occupied France. Sunk at Cherbourg during World War II. Sister ships: **Noordam** and **Rijndam.**

President   (1840)   London Line (British & American Steam Navigation Co.
   Built by Curling & Young, Limehouse on the Thames, London, England. Dimensions: 243′ x 41′. Tonnage: 2,366. Paddle-wheels, 8 knots. Side lever engines. Three masts and one funnel. Wooden hull. Clipper bow. Launched, December 7, 1839. Maiden voyage: Liverpool-New York, August 1, 1840. Sailed from New York with a small number of passengers, March 11, 1841, and was never seen again.

President Adams   (1921)   United States Lines.
   Built by New York Shipbuilding Co., Camden, N. J. Tonnage: 10,533. Dimensions: 502′ x 62′ (522′ o.l.). Twin-screw, 14 knots. Triple expansion engines. Two masts and one funnel. Placed in New York-London service in 1921. Purchased by Dollar Line for their trans-Pacific service in 1924. Renamed: **President Grant** (1939). Lost by stranding in South Pacific, February 26, 1944. Ex-**Centennial State** (1922). Note: See **President Adams** in PART II.

President Arthur   (1900)   United States Lines.
   Built by Akt. Ges. "Vulkan", Stettin, Germany. Tonnage: 10,680. Dimensions: 523′ x 60′. Twin-screw, 16 knots. Quadruple expansion engines. Two masts and two funnels. Placed in trans-Atlantic service in 1922. Renamed: **City of Honolulu** (1924). Scrapped in 1933. Ex-**Princess Matoika** (1921), ex-**Prinzess Alice** (1917), ex-**Kiautschau** (1903).

President Fillmore   (1899)   United States Lines.
   Built by "Vulkan", Stettin, Germany. Tonnage: 10,532. Dimensions: 499′ x 60′. Twin-screw, 16 knots. Quadruple expansion engines. Two masts and two funnels. Commenced

service as the **President Fillmore** in 1922. Sold to Dollar
Line in 1924. Scrapped in 1928. Ex-**Hudson** (1922), ex-
New Rochelle (1921), ex-**Powhatan** (1920), ex-**Hamburg**
(1917).

President Garfield (1921)   United States Lines.
Built by New York Shipbuilding Co., Camden, N. J. Ton-
nage: 10,538. Dimensions: 502′ x 62′. Twin-screw, 14 knots.
Triple expansion engines. Two masts and one funnel.
Commenced service in August 1922. Purchased by Dollar
Line in 1924. Retained name of **President Garfield.**
Renamed: (a) **President Madison** (1940), (b) **Refuge**
(1942) hospital ship. Ex-**Blue Hen State** (1922).

President Grant (1907)   Hamburg-American Line.
Built by Harland & Wolff, Ltd., Belfast, Ireland. Tonnage:
18,072. Dimensions: 599′ x 68′ (615′ o.l.). Twin-screw, 14½
knots. Quadruple expansion engines. Six masts and one
funnel. Note: Launched as the **Servian**, October 8, 1903,
for Furness, Withy & Co., Ltd. However, before completion
she was sold to Hamburg-American Line. They changed her
name to **President Grant.** Maiden voyage: Hamburg-
Plymouth-New York, September 14, 1907. Accommodation
for 200 first, 150 second and 3,000 third class. In service as
a transport for the United States in World War I. Renamed:
Republic (1924). Reduced to four masts. Converted to
troopship in World War II, and then to hospital ship.
Scrapped in 1952. Sister ship: **President Lincoln.** Noted
for being the only six-masted liners on the Atlantic.

President Harding (1921)   United States Lines.
Built by New York Shipbuilding Co., Camden, N. J. Ton-
nage: 13,869. Dimensions: 516′ x 72′ (535′ o.l.). Twin-screw,
18 knots. Four steam turbines. Two masts and one funnel.
Passengers: 300 first and 325 third class. Commenced
service as **President Harding** in August 1922. Renamed:
Ville de Bruges (1939) Antwerp Navigation Co. Bombed
and sunk by Nazi aircraft in River Scheldt, May 14, 1940.
Ex-**President Taft** (1922), ex-**Lone Star State** (1922).
Sister ship: **President Roosevelt.**

President Lincoln (1907)   Hamburg-American Line.
Built by Harland & Wolff, Ltd., Belfast, Ireland. Tonnage:
18,162. Dimensions: 599′ x 68′ (615′ o.l.). Twin-screw, 14½
knots. Quadruple expansion engines. Six masts and one
funnel. Launched as the **Scotian**, December 19, 1903 for
Furness, Withy & Co., but was purchased by Hamburg-

American Line before completion and renamed **President Lincoln.** Passengers: 200 first, 150 second, 3,000 third. Maiden voyage: Hamburg-Plymouth-New York, June 1, 1907. Liner was seized by United States in 1917. Converted to transport. Torpedoed and sunk, May 31, 1918, while bound from France to New York. The lives of 26 were lost. Sister ship: **President Grant.**

President Monroe   (1920)   United States Lines.
Built by New York Shipbuilding Co., Camden, N. J. Tonnage: 10,533. Dimensions: 502′ x 62′ (522′ o.l.). Twin-screw, 14 knots. Triple expansion engines. Two masts and one funnel. First voyage as **President Monroe** from New York to London, May 1922. Purchased by Dollar Line in 1924. Retained same name. In 1940 was renamed **President Buchanan.** Converted to hospital ship in World War II and name changed to **Emily H. Weder.** Ex-**Panhandle State** (1922).

President Polk   (1921)   United States Lines.
Built by New York Shipbuilding Co., Camden, N. J. Tonnage: 10,500. Dimensions: 502′ x 62′ (522′ o.l.). Twin-screw, 14 knots. Triple expansion engines. Two masts and one funnel. First voyage as **President Polk** for United States Line was made in August 1922. The liner was purchased by Dollar Line in 1924. Renamed: **President Taylor** (1940). Stranded and abandoned off Canton Island, February 14, 1942. Ex-**Granite State** (1922).

President Roosevelt   (1922)   United States Lines.
Built by New York Shipbuilding Co., Camden, N. J. Tonnage: 13,869. Dimensions: 516′ x 72′ (535′ o.l.). Twin-screw, 19 knots. Steam turbines. Two masts and one funnel. First sailing as **President Roosevelt** in August 1922. Renamed: **Joseph T. Dickman** (1941) United States troopship. Scrapped in 1948. Ex-**President Pierce** (1922), ex-**Peninsula State** (1922). Sister ship: **President Harding.**

President Taft   (1922)   United States Lines.
Built by New York Shipbuilding Co., Camden, N. J. Tonnage: 13,869. First voyage as **President Taft** was in May 1922. Renamed: (a) **President Harding** (1922), (b) **Ville de Bruges** (1939). Ex-**Lone Star State** (1922).

President Van Buren   (1920)   United States Lines.
Built by New York Shipbuilding Co., Camden, N. J. Tonnage: 10,533. Dimensions: 502′ x 62′ (522′ o.l.). Twin-screw,

14 knots. Quadruple expansion engines. Two masts and one funnel. Made her first sailing for United States Lines in August 1922. Purchased by Dollar Line in 1924. Renamed: (a) **President Fillmore** (1940), (b) **Marigold** (1942) U. S. hospital ship.

Presidente Wilson   (1912)   Cosulich Line (Italian).
Built by Cantieri Navale Triestino, Monfalcone, Austria-Hungaria. Tonnage: 12,588. Dimensions: 477' x 60' (500' o.l.). Twin-screw, 18 knots. Quadruple expansion engines. Two masts and two funnels. Made her first voyage from Trieste to New York in 1920. She was later transferred to South American service. Renamed: (a) **Gange** (1929), (b) **Marco Polo** (1932). Scuttled by Germans at Spezia, May 12, 1944. Ex-**Generale Diaz** (1919), ex-**Kaiser Franz Josef I** (1919).

Pretoria   (1897)   Hamburg-American Line.
Built by Blohm & Voss, Hamburg, Germany. Tonnage: 13,234. Dimensions: 561' x 62'. Twin-screw, 13½ knots. Quadruple expansion engines. Four masts and one funnel. Service: Hamburg-New York. Passengers: 160 first, 190 second, 2,400 third class. After First World War was placed under control of British Shipping Controller, and then charted by the Ellerman Lines. Sold to British shipbreakers in November 1921. Sister ships: **Graf Waldersee, Patricia** and **Pennsylvania.** Note: All had very large cargo capacity, besides being able to transport large numbers of immigrants.

Pretorian   (1900)   Allan Line.
Built by Furness, Withy & Co., West Hartlepool, England. Tonnage: 6,436. Dimensions: 436' x 53'. Single-screw, 14 knots. Triple expansion engines. Two masts and one funnel. Maiden voyage: Liverpool-Quebec-Montreal in August 1901. Tonnage increased to 7,650 in 1908. Transferred to Canadian Pacific Line ownership in 1917. Sold for scrap in January 1926.

Preussen   (1886)   North German Lloyd.
Built by "Vulkan", Stettin, Germany. Tonnage: 5,295. Dimensions: 454' x 45'. Single-screw, 14½ knots. Reciprocating engines. Two masts and two funnels. Vessel lengthened in 1893. Built for the Bremen-Far East service. Sold to Italians in 1909. Broken up for scrap in 1910. Sister ships: **Bayern** and **Sachsen.**

Prince Albert (1857) Galway Line (British).
Built by J. Cockerill, Hoboken, Belgium. Tonnage: 2,028.
Dimensions: 286′ x 38′. Single-screw, 10 knots. Inverted
engines. Three masts and one funnel. Clipper bow. Iron
hull. Note: Laid down as **Duc de Brabant.** Began Galway-
New York service in July 1858. Made 14 voyages in all.
Withdrawn from service in 1861.

Princess Charlotte (1855) Compagnie Transatlantique Belge.
Built by Van Vlissingen, Amsterdam, Holland. Tonnage:
2,160. Dimensions: 281′ x 37′. Single-screw, 10 knots.
Inverted engines. Three masts and one funnel. Iron hull.
Clipper bow. Note: Launched as the **Constitution.** Renamed: **Princess Charlotte** in 1856. Sold to British owners
in 1857. Renamed: **Scotland** (1862). Sister ship: **Belgique.**
Note: The **Belgique** made the company's initial Atlantic
crossing late in 1856. The **Leopold I,** built in 1857, was the
last vessel to enter their short-lived service.

Princess Matoika (1900) United States Mail Steamship Co.
Built by "Vulkan", Stettin, Germany. Tonnage: 10,421.
Dimensions: 523′ x 60′. Twin-screw, 16 knots. Quadruple
expansion engines. Two masts and two funnels. First voy-
age as the **Princess Matoika** was from New York to Naples
and Genoa in March 1921. The vessel was taken over by
United States Lines in August 1921. Renamed: (a) **President
Arthur** (1922), (b) **City of Honolulu.** Broken up by
Japanese shipbreakers in 1933. Ex-**Prinzess Alice** (1917),
ex-**Kiautschou** (1904).

Principe di Piemonte (1907) Lloyd Sabaudo Line.
Built by Sir James Laing & Sons, Ltd., Sunderland, England.
Tonnage: 6,365. Dimensions: 430′ x 52′. Twin-screw, 14
knots. Triple expansion engines. Two masts and two funnels. Passengers: 120 first and 1,700 third. Maiden voyage:
Genoa-New York, June 19, 1907. Renamed: (a) **Principello**
(1913), (b) **Folia** (1916). Note: Cunard Line purchased the
Principello in May 1916. As the Cunarder **Folia** she was
torpedoed and sunk off Waterford, March 11, 1917, with the
loss of 7 lives. Sister ships: **Re d' Italia** and **Regina d' Italia.**

Principe di Udine (1908) Lloyd Sabaudo Line.
Built by Barclay, Curle & Co., Glasgow, Scotland. Tonnage:
7,794. Dimensions: 450′ x 55′. Twin-screw, 16½ knots.
Quadruple expansion engines. Two masts and two funnels.
Built for the Italy-South American service, but used in
Genoa-Naples-New York trade, too. Sold for scrap in

February 1929. Sister ship: **Tomaso di Savoia.** Note: These sister ships were an improved version of the **Re d' Italia** class.

Principe Umberto   (1909)   Navigazione Generale Italiana.
Built by Cantieri Navali Riuniti, Palermo, Italy. Tonnage: 7,838. Dimensions: 476' x 53'. Twin-screw, 16 knots. Quadruple expansion engines. Two masts and two funnels. Mainly used in Italy-South American service, but also made some New York sailings. Torpedoed and sunk in 1916. Sister ship: **Duca Degli Abruzzi.**

Principello   (1907)   Uranium Line (Canadian Northern Steamships, Ltd.).
Built by Sir James Laing & Sons, Ltd., Sunderland, England. Tonnage: 6,560. Dimensions: 430' x 52'. Twin-screw, 14 knots. Triple expansion engines. Two masts and two funnels. In Rotterdam-New York service, 1913–1914. Sold to Cunard Line in 1916. Renamed: **Folia** (1916). Torpedoed and sunk, March 11, 1917, with the loss of 7 lives. Ex-**Principe di Piemonte** (1913).

Principessa Jolanda   (1908)   Lloyd Italiano.
Built by Soc. Esercizio Bacini, Riva Trigosa, Italy. Tonnage: 9,200. Built for Italy-South American service. Never commissioned as she capsized while being launched on September 21, 1907. Only a fraction of her completed hull showed above the water and was subsequently broken up by shipbreakers. Sister ship: **Principessa Mafalda.** Note: See PART III.

*****Prins Willem Van Oranje**   (1953)   Oranje Line (Dutch).
Built by Boele's Shipbuilding & Engineering Co., Bolnes, Netherlands. Tonnage: 7,328. Dimensions: 440' x 62' (461' o.l.). Single-screw, 18 knots. Motorship. Two masts and one funnel. Passengers: 60 (one class). Service: Rotterdam-Antwerp-Southampton-Quebec-Montreal-Chicago. In winter season to Halifax and St. John, New Brunswick. Running mate: **Prinses Irene.** Note: The first liners to conduct regular passenger service between Europe and the Great Lakes.

*****Prinses Irene**   (1959)   Oranje Line (Dutch).
Built by De Merwede, Hardinxveld, Netherlands. Tonnage: 8,526. Dimensions: 420' x 61' (455' o.l.). Single-screw, 16½ knots. Two masts and one funnel. Launched, July 12, 1958. Passengers: 115 (one class ship). Maiden voyage:

Rotterdam-Southampton-Montreal, April 29, 1959. Made her first regular voyage to Chicago from Rotterdam, June 10, 1959. Running mate: **Prins Willem Van Oranje.** Note: A sister ship to the **Prinses Irene** is expected to be completed in 1961. She is to be known as **Prinses Margriet.**

Prinz Adalbert   (1902)   Hamburg-American Line.
Built by Bremer Vulkan, Vegesack, Germany. Tonnage: 6,030. Dimensions: 403' x 49'. Twin-screw, 13 knots. Quadruple expansion engines. Two masts and two funnels. Placed in Genoa-Naples-New York service in 1902. She also served on other North Atlantic routes. Made her final voyage to New York in 1914. Renamed: (a) **Princetown** (1914) British, (b) **Alesia** (1917) French. Torpedoed and sunk, September 6, 1917. Sister ship: **Prinz Oskar.**

Prinz Eitel Friedrich   (1902)   Hamburg-American Line.
Built by Flensburger Schiffsbau Ges., Flensburg, Germany. Tonnage: 4,650. Dimensions: 371' x 45'. Single-screw, 12½ knots. Quadruple expansion engines. Two masts and one funnel. In service to Central America. Renamed: (a) **Otsego** (1917), (b) **Ural** (1945).   Russian.

Prinz Friedrich Wilhelm   (1908)   North German Lloyd.
Built by J. C. Tecklenborg, Geestemunde, Germany. Tonnage: 17,082. Dimensions: 590' x 68' (613' o.l.). Twin-screw, 17 knots. Quadruple expansion engines. Two masts and two funnels. Passengers: 400 first, 300 second, 1,700 third. In the Bremen-Southampton-New York intermediate service. Renamed: (a) **Empress of India** (1920), (b) **Montlaurier** (1922), (c) **Montnairn** (1925). Scrapped in 1931.

Prinz Oskar   (1902)   Hamburg-American Line.
Built by Bremer Vulkan, Vegesack, Germany. Tonnage: 6,026. Dimensions: 403' x 49'. Twin-screw, 13 knots. Quadruple expansion engines. Two masts and two funnels. Placed first in the Genoa-Naples-New York service. After 1906 was used on the Genoa-Buenos Aires route, and also, in North Atlantic services. Seized by United States in 1917. Renamed: **Orion** (1917). Scrapped about 1928. Sister ship: **Prinz Adalbert.**

Prinz Sigismund   (1902)   Hamburg-American Line.
Built by Akt. Ges. "Neptun", Rostock, Germany. Tonnage: 4,689. Dimensions: 370' x 45'. Single-screw, 12½ knots. Quadruple expansion engines. Two masts and two funnels.

Commenced service to Central America, but later was transferred to the South American route. Seized by United States
in 1917. Renamed: **General W. C. Gorgas** (1917). After
the war the vessel was acquired by Panama Railroad Company, then sold to Libby, McNeill & Libby. She was handed
over to Russia in 1941. Renamed: **Mikhail Lomonosov.**

Prinzess Alice   (1900)   North German Lloyd.
Built by "Vulkan", Stettin, Germany. Tonnage: 10,911.
Dimensions: 523′ x 60′. Twin-screw, 15½ knots. Quadruple
expansion engines. Two masts and two funnels. Much of
her time was spent on the Far East route, but she made some
voyages to New York. Renamed: (a) **Princess Matoika**
(1917), (b) **President Arthur** (1921), (c) **City of Honolulu**
(1924). Note: As the **City of Honolulu** she was badly
damaged by fire while tied to her pier in 1930. She was laid
up until sold to Japanese shipbreakers in 1933. The **Prinzess
Alice** was purchased from Hamburg-American Line in 1903.
Ex-**Kiautschou** (1903). Sister ship: **Prinzess Irene.**

Prinzess Irene   (1900)   North German Lloyd.
Built by "Vulkan", Stettin, Germany. Tonnage: 10,881.
Dimensions: 523′ x 60′. Twin-screw, 15½ knots. Quadruple
expansion engines. Two masts and two funnels. Maiden
voyage: Bremen-Southampton-China-Japan. Mainly in the
Far Eastern trade, but she did make a number of voyages
to New York from Mediterranean ports, and the Hamburg-
New York route. Renamed: (a) **Pocahontas** (1917), (b)
Bremen (1922), (c) **Karlsruhe** (1928). Scrapped in 1932.
Sister ship: **Prinzess Alice.**

Prinzessin Victoria Luise   (1901)   Hamburg-American Line.
Built by Blohm & Voss, Hamburg, Germany. Tonnage:
4,409. Dimensions: 407′ x 47′. Twin-screw, 15 knots. Quadruple expansion engines. Two masts and two funnels.
Clipper bow. Note: Built as a cruise ship. Did make some
sailings to New York. Wrecked near Plum Point, Jamaica
in 1906.

Protea   (1920)   Incres Line.
Built by American International Shipbuilding Corp., Hog
Island, Pa. Tonnage: 7,450. Dimensions: 436′ x 58′. Single-
screw, 15 knots. Steam turbines. Two masts and one funnel.
Served in Antwerp-Plymouth-Montreal service for a brief
time. Renamed: **Arosa Kulm** (1952). Ex-**City of Athens**
(1947), ex-**Ville d' Anvers** (1946), ex-**American Banker**
(1940), ex-**Cantigny** (1924).

Providence   (1915)   Fabre Line (French).
  Built by Forges & Chantiers de la Mediterranee, La Seyne, France. Tonnage: 11,996. Dimensions: 511' x 59'. Twin-screw, 16 knots. Triple expansion engines. Two masts and three funnels. Launched, August 4, 1914. Maiden voyage: Marseilles-New York, June 1, 1920. Boston became a port of call at a later date. Transferred to Messageries Maritimes service in 1932. Broken up for scrap in 1952. Sister ship: **Patria.**

Prussia   (1894)   Hamburg-American Line.
  Built by Harland & Wolff, Ltd., Belfast, Ireland. Tonnage: 7,008. Dimensions: 445' x 50'. Twin-screw, 13½ knots. Compound engines. Two masts and one funnel. Service: Hamburg-New York. Tonnage was 5,965 originally. Re-named: **Dominion** (1897). Sister ship: **Persia.**

Prussian   (1869)   Allan Line (British).
  Built by A. & J. Inglis, Ltd., Glasgow, Scotland. Tonnage: 3,030. Dimensions: 340' x 40'. Single-screw, 11 knots. Inverted engines. Three masts and one funnel. Clipper bow. Iron hull. Maiden voyage: Liverpool-Portland, Maine, February 18, 1869. Re-engined with compounds in 1879. Served on other Allan Line routes, including the Boston run. Scrapped in Italy, 1898. Sister ship: **Scandinavian.**

Puerto Rico   (1913)   French Line.
  Built by Chantiers & Ateliers de St. Nazaire, France. Tonnage: 6,127. Dimensions: 413' x 51'. Twin-screw, 13 knots. Triple expansion engines. Two masts and two funnels. Service: France-West Indies. Renamed: **Meknes** (1929). Sister ship: **Haiti.**

Pulaski   (1912)   Gdynia-America Line.
  Built by Barclay, Curle & Co., Glasgow, Scotland. Tonnage: 6,516. Dimensions: 425' x 53'. Twin-screw, 15½ knots. Quadruple expansion engines. Two masts and two funnels. Service: Gdynia-Copenhagen-New York. Transferred to South American trade in 1936. Converted to transport in World War II. Renamed: **Empire Penryn** (1946). Scrapped in Great Britain, 1949. Ex-**Estonia** (1930), ex-**Czar** (1921). Running mates: **Kosciuszko** and **Polonia.**

Quaker City   (1854)   (a) North American Lloyd, (b) New York & Bremen Steamship Co.
  Built by Vaughn & Lynn, Philadelphia, Pa. Tonnage: 1,428. Dimensions: 227' x 36'. Paddle-wheels, 10 knots. Side lever

engines. Two masts and two funnels. Clipper bow. Wooden hull. Note: Vessel originally built for New York, Havana & Mobile Line. During the American Civil War she was employed as an armed cruiser, searching for blockade runners. She made a special pleasure cruise to the Holy Land and Europe in 1867. This may well be considered the world's first cruise ship. It is reported that Mark Twain wrote a large part of "The Innocents Abroad" while on board the **Quaker City,** during this special cruise. Vessel was sold to foreign owners in 1869. Renamed: (a) **Columbia** (1869), (b) **Mont Organise** (1870).

Quebec (1864) Dominion Line.
Built by Smith & Rodger, Glasgow, Scotland. Tonnage: 2,621. Dimensions: 318′ x 36′. Single-screw, 12 knots. Compound engines. Three masts and one funnel. Iron hull. Service: Liverpool-Quebec-Montreal, 1874–1888. Sold to French owners in 1888. Renamed: **Nautique** (1888). Foundered in North Atlantic, February 16, 1890. Ex-**City of Dublin** (1873).

Quebec (1896) French Line.
Built by Robert Napier & Sons, Ltd., Glasgow, Scotland. Tonnage: 3,342. Dimensions: 345′ x 44′. Single-screw, 12 knots. Triple expansion engines. Two masts and one funnel. In service to the West Indies. Mined and sunk in the Gironde, January 24, 1917. Ex-**Ebro** (1903). Sister ship: **Montreal.**

*Queen Elizabeth (1940) Cunard Line.
Built by John Brown & Co., Clydebank, Glasgow, Scotland. Tonnage: 83,673. Dimensions, 987′ x 118′ (1,031′ o.l.). Quadruple-screw, 31 knots. Steam turbines. 160,000 s.h.p. Two masts and two funnels. Keel laid on December 4, 1936. Launched, September 27, 1938. Note: Largest ship built to date. Promenade deck 724 feet long. Her funnels are 70 feet high from deck level. Commenced her first sailing from the Clyde, bound for New York, February 27, 1940. Her secret sailing was under British Government regulations, so as to lessen the danger of being sunk by the Nazi. Throughout World War II she served as a very valuable troopship, completing the long period of duty in March 1946. Reconditioned for passenger service. Passengers: 850 first, 720 cabin, 744 tourist. Commenced her first regular Southampton-New York voyage, October 16, 1946, making the crossing in four days, 16 hours, 18 minutes. This was not a record breaking passage, and not surpassing the time of her running mate,

the **Queen Mary,** but on this occasion no special effort was made to accomplish that feat. The liner is equipped with two sets of stabilizers. Passenger accommodation in 1960: 800 first, 650 cabin, 700 third. Running mate: **Queen Mary.**

***Queen Frederica** (1927) National Hellenic American Line. Built by Wm. Cramp & Sons Shipbuilding Co., Philadelphia, Pa. Tonnage: 20,553 (21,329 Greek measurement). Dimensions: 554′ x 83′ (582′ o.l.). Twin-screw, 22 knots. Steam turbines. Two masts and two funnels. Note: The above line is a subsidiary of the Home Lines. Passengers: 132 first, 116 cabin, 931 tourist. First voyage as **Queen Frederica,** January 29, 1955, Piraeus-New York. Late in 1960 the liner was refitted. Tourist class accommodation will be provided for about 1,150 passengers. Ex-**Atlantic** (1955), ex-**Matsonia** (1949), ex-**Malolo** (1937).

***Queen Mary** (1936) Cunard Line.
Built by John Brown & Co., Ltd., Clydebank, Glasgow, Scotland. Tonnage: 80,774. Dimensions: 975′ x 118′ (1,018′ o.l.). Quadruple-screw, 30 knots. Steam turbines. 200,000 s.h.p. Two masts and three funnels. Laid down in August 1930. Work was suspended in December 1931 due to the depression. Building was resumed in April 1934. Launched, September 26, 1934. Commenced her maiden voyage from Southampton to New York on May 27, 1936, making the run from Bishop Rock to Ambrose Lightship in 4 days and 27 minutes at an average speed of 30.14 knots. In 1938 she made a new eastward record by crossing in 3 days, 20 hours and 42 minutes. Note: From keel to masthead 234 feet. Foremost funnel 70 feet high from deck level; from keel to top of funnel 180 feet high. Diameter of funnels measure 30 feet. Length on water line 1,104 feet. Displacement before the war listed as 77,482 tons. Served as a troopship in World War II. Re-entered trans-Atlantic service in August 1947. The actual story of the naming of this wonderful luxury liner was revealed in the press. Sir Percy Bates, former head of the Cunard Line, told King George V of their decision to name the new ship "after one of Britain's most noble queens." The King, thinking they intended to name the liner after his wife, the Queen, expressed enthusiastic approval. The Cunard Line promptly fell in line with the King's thought, and the ship was christened **Queen Mary.** The company's previous intention was to name the vessel after Queen Victoria, in keeping with their established policy of using only names ending in "ia" for their ships. Passenger

accommodation as of 1960: 700 first, 680 cabin, 500 tourist. Running mate: **Queen Elizabeth.**

Re d'Italia   (1907)   Lloyd Sabaudo Line.
Built by Sir James Laing & Sons, Ltd., Sunderland, England. Tonnage: 6,237.   Dimensions: 430' x 52'.   Twin-screw, 14 knots.   Triple expansion engines.   Two masts and two funnels.   Passengers: 120 first and 1,700 third class.   Pioneer ship of Lloyd Sabaudo.   Maiden voyage: Italy-New York, April 12, 1907.   Made her final voyage to New York in 1922.   Transferred to Italy-South American route.   Sold for scrap in October 1928.   Sister ships: **Principe di Piemonte** and **Regina d' Italia.**

Re Vittorio   (1907)   Navigazione Generale Italiana.
Built by Cantieri Navali Odero & Co., Genoa, Italy.   Tonnage: 7,847.   Dimensions: 476' x 53'.   Twin-screw, 16½ knots.   Quadruple expansion engines.   Two masts and two funnels. Service: Mainly in Italy-South American trade, but made some New York voyages.   Sold for scrap in June 1928. Sister ship: **Regina Elena.**   Similar ships: **Duca d'Aosta** and **Duca degli Abruzzi.**

Regina   (1918)   White Star Line.
Built by Harland & Wolff, Ltd., Belfast, Ireland.   Tonnage: 16,289.   Dimensions: 575' x 67'.   Triple-screw, 16 knots. Triple expansion engines and one steam turbine.   Two masts and two funnels.   Built as a cargo ship for Dominion Line. However, converted to passenger liner.   First voyage as such was in March 1922.   Transferred to White Star Line.   Renamed: **Westernland** (1929).   Sister ship: **Pittsburgh.**

Regina d' Italia   (1907)   Lloyd Sabaudo Line.
Built by Sir James Laing & Sons, Ltd., Sunderland, England. Tonnage: 6,560.   Dimensions: 430' x 52'.   Twin-screw, 14 knots.   Triple expansion engines.   Two masts and two funnels.   Maiden voyage: Italy-New York, May 17, 1907. Transferred to South American service on her 4th voyage. She later reverted back to New York service.   Made her final sailing to New York in 1924.   Then shifted back to Italy-South American route.   Sold for scrap in October 1928. Sister ships: **Principe di Piemonte** and **Re d'Italia.**

Regina Elena   (1907)   Navigazione Generale Italiana.
Built by Cantieri Ligur. Ancon, Ancona, Italy.   Tonnage: 7,865.   Dimensions: 476' x 53'.   Twin-screw, 16 knots.   Quadruple expansion engines.   Two masts and two funnels.   Serv-

ice: Italy-South America. Probably made some New York sailings. Torpedoed and sunk in 1918. Sister ships: **Duca d'Aosta, Duca degli Abruzzi** and **Re Vittoria.**

Regina Margherita (1884) Navigazione Generale Italiana.
Built by A. McMillan & Son, Dumbarton, Scotland. Tonnage: 3,577. Dimensions: 396' x 42'. Single-screw, 16 knots. Compound engines. Two masts and two funnels. Clipper bow. A fine looking passenger ship. Service: Italy-South America. Made voyages to New York, also.

Reina Maria Cristina (1889) Spanish Line.
Built by Wm. Denny & Bros., Ltd., Dumbarton, Scotland. Tonnage: 4,818. Dimensions: 408' x 48'. Single-screw, 16 knots. Triple expansion engines. Four masts and one funnel. Clipper bow. Passengers: 248 first, 52 second, 42 third. Masts reduced to two at later date. Scrapped in 1931. Sister ship: **Alfonso XIII.**

Reina Victoria Eugenia (1913) Spanish Line.
Built by Swan, Hunter & Wigham Richardson, Ltd., Newcastle, England. Tonnage: 10,137. Dimensions: 480' x 61'. Quadruple-screw, 17 knots. Triple expansion engines and two low pressure steam turbines. Two masts and one funnel. Passengers: 250 first, 100 second, 75 third. Service: Spain-Cuba-Mexico; Spain-New York. Renamed: **Argentina** (1931). Sunk during Spanish Civil War. Subsequently refloated and scrapped. Sister ship: **Infanta Isabel de Borbon.**

Reliance (1920) Hamburg-American Line.
Built by J. C. Tecklenborg, Weser-munde, Germany. Tonnage: 19,802. Dimensions: 592' x 72' (618' o.l.). Triple-screw, 17 knots. Triple expansion engines and one steam turbine. Two masts and three funnels. Keel was laid in 1914 for the Hamburg-American Line, but construction was held up during World War I. She was to have been named **Johann Heinrich Burchard.** However, when completed in 1920, she was turned over to the Dutch and renamed **Limburgia.** Did not continue for long in the Royal Holland Lloyd fleet, as she soon afterwards was transferred to United States. Renamed: **Reliance** (1922) United American Lines. In 1926 the Hamburg-American Line became the owners, and as the **Reliance** continued in Hamburg-New York service. Passengers: 290 first, 320 second, 400 third. Besides being employed in regular trans-Atlantic service, she was used as a cruise ship. Gutted by fire at Hamburg in August

1938. The burned out hulk was sold to German shipbreakers in April 1940. Ex-**Limburgia** (1922), ex-**Johann Heinrich Burchard** (1920). Sister ship: **Resolute.**

Republic   (1871)   White Star Line.
Built by Harland & Wolff, Ltd., Belfast, Ireland. Tonnage: 3,707. Dimensions: 426′ x 41′ (437′ o.l.). Single-screw, 14 knots. Compound engines. Four masts and one funnel. Iron hull. Launched, July 4, 1871. Maiden voyage: Liverpool-New York, February 1, 1872. Renamed: (a) **Maasdam** (1889), (b) **Vittoria** (1902), (c) **Citta di Napoli** (1902). Scrapped in 1910. Sister ships: **Atlantic, Baltic** and **Oceanic.**

Republic   (1900)   White Star Line.
Built by Harland & Wolff, Ltd., Belfast, Ireland. Tonnage: 15,378. Dimensions: 570′ x 68′. Twin-screw, 16 knots. Quadruple expansion engines. Four masts and one funnel. Built as Dominion liner **Columbus** but was transferred almost at once to the White Star Line and renamed **Republic.** First voyage as **Republic** from Liverpool to Boston, December 17, 1903. Note: She was rammed by the Lloyd Italiano liner **Florida** on January 23, 1909, just south of Martha's Vineyard (not far from where the **Andrea Doria** sank), while navigating in a dense fog. The **Republic** sank quite rapidly, but the damaged Italian liner was able to rescue most of the survivors. However, four of the passengers on board the **Republic** were crushed to death in their cabins by the bow of the **Florida,** as it penetrated the hull. This tragedy marked the first notable occasion upon which the wireless was put to practical use in summoning aid for ships in distress. The S.O.S. was answered by no fewer than five liners, which steamed immediately to the assistance of the stricken vessel. These were the **Baltic, Furnessia, La Lorraine** and **New York,** all well-known trans-Atlantic passenger ships. The survivors were transferred from the crippled **Florida** to the **Baltic.** The severely damaged **Florida** had thirty feet of her bow doubled up into a space of five feet. Her collision bulkhead withstood the blow and thus prevented the ship from sinking. She was able to steam into New York harbor and later had her crushed bow replaced by a new one, the Morse Drydock & Repair Company of Brooklyn doing the work within 24 days for the sum of $39,500. The **Republic** was the largest liner lost at sea prior to the **Titanic.**

Republic   (1907)   United States Lines.
Built by Harland & Wolff, Ltd., Belfast, Ireland. Tonnage:
17,910.   Dimensions: 599′ x 68′.   Twin-screw, 14 knots.
Quadruple expansion engines. Four masts and one funnel.
The **Republic** had two of her original six masts removed.
First voyage as **Republic** New York-Plymouth-Cherbourg-
Bremen, April 29, 1924. Vessel was sold to United States
Government in 1934. Served as a troopship in World War II.
Converted to hospital ship in 1945.   Decommissioned as
hospital ship in February 1946. Transformed back to troop-
ship. Scrapped at Baltimore in 1952. Ex-**President Grant**
(1924), ex-**Servian.** Note: See **President Grant** for further
information.

Resolute   (1920)   Hamburg-American Line.
Built by Akt. Ges. "Weser", Bremen, Germany. Tonnage:
19,692. Dimensions: 590′ x 72′ (616′ o.l.). Triple-screw, 17
knots.   Triple expansion engines and steam turbine.   Two
masts and three funnels. Laid down as the **William O'
Swald** in 1914 for the Hamburg-American Line, but was not
completed until after World War I.   Commissioned as the
Brabantia in 1920, of Royal Holland Lloyd. Acquired by
United American Lines in 1922 and renamed **Resolute.**
Transferred to Hamburg-American Line in 1926.   Service:
Hamburg-Southampton-Cherbourg-New York.   Sold to the
Italian Government in August 1935. Renamed: **Lombardia**
(1935).   Bombed at Naples in August 1943. The hulk was
broken up for scrap in 1947. Ex-**Brabantia** (1922), ex-
William O'Swald (1920). Sister ship: **Reliance.**

Rex   (1932)   Italia Line.
Built by Societa Anonima Ansaldo, Sestri, Genoa, Italy.
Tonnage: 51,062. Dimensions: 833′ x 97′ (879′ o.l.). Quad-
ruple-screw, 28 knots. Quadruple expansion engines. Two
masts and two funnels. Keel laid for Navigazione Generale
Italiana on April 27, 1930.   During construction in 1932,
ownership was transferred to the newly formed "Italia" Line.
Commenced her maiden voyage from Genoa to New York,
September 27, 1932.   Had accommodation for 2,024 passengers, and her crew numbered 810 members. She was the
first Italian liner to break the trans-Atlantic speed record.
She made a run from Gibraltar to Ambrose Light in 4 days,
13 hours and 58 minutes, covering a distance of 3,181 nautical
miles and averaging 28.92 knots. From her keel to the navigating bridge the height was 120 feet. This great liner was
bombed and sunk by British aircraft, September 9, 1944,
while being towed to a new hiding place. The sunken hull

(near Trieste) was broken up for scrap in 1947. Indeed a pitiful sight when one remembers how majestic she appeared before the War. Running mate: **Conte di Savoia.**

Rhaetia   (1883)   Hamburg-American Line.
Built by Reiherstieg, Hamburg, Germany. Tonnage: 3,458. Dimensions: 351' x 43'. Single-screw, 11 knots. Compound engines. Steel hull. 2,000 I.H.P. Three masts and one funnel. Passengers: 100 first and 800 third. Sold to United States Government in 1895. Renamed: (a) **Cassius** (1895), (b) **Sumner** (U. S. Army). Wrecked off Atlantic City, New Jersey, in 1916. Running mates: **Rugia, Bohemia** and **Moravia.**

Rhaetia   (1904)   Hamburg-American Line.
Built by Bremer Vulkan, Vegesack, Germany. Tonnage: 6,600. Dimensions: 409' x 52'. Single-screw, 13 knots. Quadruple expansion engines. Two masts and one funnel. Services: Hamburg-Philadelphia; Europe-West Indies. Seized by United States in 1917. Renamed: (a) **Black Hawk** (1917), (b) **Black Arrow** (1919). Scrapped in 1924. Sister ship: **Rugia.**

Rhein   (1868)   North German Lloyd.
Built by Caird & Co., Greenock, Scotland. Tonnage: 3,075. Dimensions: 349' x 40'. Single-screw, 14 knots. Inverted engines. Two masts and one funnel. Iron hull. Maiden voyage: Bremen-Southampton-New York, October 3, 1868. Compound engines in 1878. Sold to British owners in 1893. Sister ships: **Donau** and **Main.**

Rhein   (1899)   North German Lloyd.
Built by Blohm & Voss, Hamburg, Germany. Tonnage: 10,058. Dimensions: 501' x 58' (520' o.l.). Twin-screw, 13½ knots. Quadruple expansion engines. Four masts and one funnel. Mainly in New York and Baltimore services. Vessel seized by United States Government in 1917. Renamed: **Susquehanna** (1917). Broken up for scrap in Japan during 1929. Sister ships: **Main** and **Neckar.**

Rhynland   (1879)   Red Star Line (Belgian).
Built by Vickers, Sons & Maxim, Ltd., Barrow-in-Furness, England. Tonnage: 3,689. Dimensions: 402' x 40'. Single-screw, 12½ knots. Compound engines. 1,600 I.H.P. Four masts and one funnel. Iron hull. Employed mainly in the Antwerp-New York service. Transferred to Liverpool-

Philadelphia service of American Line in 1895. Renamed: **Rhyna** (1906). Italian owners. Scrapped in 1906. Sister ship: **Belgenland.**

Richmond Hill   (1883)   Twin Screw Line (British).
Built by H. Murray & Co., Dumbarton, Scotland. Tonnage: 4,225. Dimensions: 420′ x 47′. Twin-screw, 12 knots. Compound engines. Four masts and one funnel. Steel hull. Maiden voyage: Glasgow-New York, July 25, 1883. Sold to Allan Line in 1897. Renamed: **Roumanian** (1897).

Rijndam   (1901)   Holland-America Line (Dutch).
Built by Harland & Wolff, Ltd., Belfast, Ireland. Tonnage: 12,529. Dimensions: 550′ x 62′ (570′ o.l.). Twin-screw, 15 knots. Triple expansion engines. Two masts and one funnel. Passengers: 280 first, 200 second, 1,800 third. Maiden voyage: Rotterdam-New York, October 10, 1901. Sold to Dutch shipbreakers in January 1929. Sister ships: **Noordam** and **Potsdam.**

Rochambeau   (1911)   French Line.
Built by Chantiers & Ateliers de St. Nazaire, Penhoet, France. Tonnage: 12,678. Dimensions: 559′ x 63′. Quadruple-screw, 15 knots. Triple expansion engines and steam turbines. Two masts and two funnels. Launched, March 2, 1911. Maiden voyage: Havre-New York, November 16, 1911. Sold for scrap to Gosselin & Dumouries at Dunkirk in May 1934.

Roma   (1902)   Fabre Line.
Built by Forges & Chantiers de la Mediterranean, La Seyne, France. Tonnage: 5,291. Dimensions: 411′ x 46′ (426′ o.l.). Single-screw, 14½ knots. Triple expansion engines. Two masts and two funnels. Launched, August 14, 1901. Had trial speed of 15.9 knots. Passengers: 50 first and 1,300 third. Made her final voyage to New York in 1927. Broken up for scrap in France, 1929.

Roma   (1926)   Navigazione Generale Italiana.
Built by Societa Anonima Ansaldo, Sestri, Ponente, Genoa, Italy. Tonnage: 32,583. Dimensions: 666′ x 82′ (705′ o.l.). Quadruple-screw, 21 knots. Steam turbines. Launched, February 26, 1926. From keel to navigating bridge 98 feet. Her 8 steam turbines were geared to four shafts. Fitted with 36 lifeboats. Had 13 watertight compartments. Maiden voyage: Genoa-Naples-New York, September 21, 1926. Transferred to "Italia" Line ownership in 1932. Acquired by the Italian Government early in World War II. Renamed:

Aquila (1943) Italian Navy. Bombed and sunk January 1945, conversion to aircraft-carrier had nearly been completed. Refloated after the war, but was subsequently broken up in Italy. Sister ship: **Augustus.**

*Roma (1943) Lauro Line (Italian).
Built by Seattle-Tacoma Shipbuilding Corp., Tacoma, Washington. Tonnage: 14,687. Dimensions: 468' x 69' (492' o.l.). Single-screw, 17 knots. Two steam turbines geared to single-screw propulsion shaft. Single mast and one funnel. Laid down as a "C-3" type freighter. Converted to passenger ship in 1950. Commenced Mediterranean-New York service in May 1953. Note: The Home Lines acted as their agent in U.S.A. Passengers: 95 first and 678 tourist. She is now (1960) sailing between Italy and Australia. Ex-**Atheling** (1950). Sister ship: **Sydney.** In Australian service.

Roman (1884) Warren Line (British).
Built by Laird Bros., Birkenhead, England. Tonnage: 4,572. Dimensions: 405' x 43'. Single-screw, 11½ knots. Compound engines. Four masts and one funnel. Iron hull. Service: Liverpool-Boston. Scrapped in 1910.

Romanic (1898) White Star Line.
Built by Harland & Wolff, Ltd., Belfast, Ireland. Tonnage: 11,394. Dimensions: 550' x 59'. Twin-screw, 16 knots. Triple expansion engines. Two masts and one funnel. First voyage as **Romanic,** Liverpool-Boston, November 19, 1903. She was later shifted to Mediterranean-New York service. Renamed: **Scandinavian** (1912). Scrapped in 1923. Ex-**New England** (1903).

Roon (1903) North German Lloyd.
Built by J. C. Tecklenborg, Geestemunde, Germany. Tonnage: 8,022. Dimensions: 453' x 55'. Twin-screw, 14½ knots. Triple expansion engines. Two masts and one funnel. Passengers: 100 first, 100 second, 1,700 third. Services: (a) Far East, (b) Australian, (c) trans-Atlantic. Surrendered to British Shipping Controller after First World War. Renamed: **Constantinoupolis** (1920) Greek. Sold for scrap in May 1925 and dismantled in Germany. Sister ships: **Gneisenau** and **Scharnhorst.**

Rosarian (1887) Allan Line.
Built by D. & W. Henderson, Ltd., Glasgow, Scotland. Tonnage: 3,077. Dimensions: 330' x 42'. Single-screw, 11 knots. Triple expansion engines. Two masts and one funnel. Steel hull. Commenced her maiden voyage from

Glasgow to South America, November 25, 1887. She was also used in North Atlantic service. Scrapped in 1910. Sister ship: **Monte Videan.**

Rotterdam (1872)   Holland-America Line.
Built by Henderson, Coulborn & Co., Glasgow, Scotland. Tonnage: 1,694.   Dimensions: 254' x 35'.   Single-screw, 10½ knots. Compound engines. Two masts and one funnel. Launched, June 6, 1872. Commenced Rotterdam-New York service in 1873. Took about 16 days to make the trans-Atlantic voyage. This iron hull steamer had accommodation for about 400 third class passengers. The **Rotterdam** was wrecked off the Dutch coast late in 1883. Sister ship: **Maas.** Note: Pioneer vessels of the Holland-America Line.

Rotterdam (1878)   Holland-America Line.
Built by Harland & Wolff, Ltd., Belfast, Ireland. Tonnage: 3,329.   Dimensions: 389' x 37'.   Single-screw, 13 knots. Compound engines. Four masts and one funnel. Iron hull. Designed as freighter for British Shipowners Company. Converted to passenger carrier. Passengers: 70 first and 850 third class. Renamed: **Edam** (1896). Sold to Italians for scrap in 1899.   Ex-**British Empire** (1886).

Rotterdam (1897)   Holland-America Line.
Built by Harland & Wolff, Ltd., Belfast, Ireland. Tonnage: 8,287.   Dimensions: 469' x 53' (485' o.l.).   Twin-screw, 15 knots. Triple expansion engines. Two masts and one funnel. Launched, February 18, 1897. Passengers: 200 first, 150 second, 2,000 third. First outstanding Holland-America Line passenger ship.   Commenced her maiden voyage from Rotterdam to New York in August 1897. Renamed: (a) **C. F. Tietgen** (1906), (b) **Dwinsk** (1914). Torpedoed and sunk by submarine in the North Atlantic, June 18, 1918.

Rotterdam (1908)   Holland-America Line.
Built by Harland & Wolff, Ltd., Belfast, Ireland. Tonnage: 24,149.   Dimensions: 650' x 77' (668' o.l.).   Twin-screw, 18 knots. Quadruple expansion engines. Two masts and two funnels. Equipped with three elevators. Passengers: 500 first, 580 second, 2,500 third. A fine type of liner for her era. Maiden voyage: Rotterdam-New York, June 13, 1908.   Ran ashore on Morant Cays, near Kingston, September 30, 1935, while on a cruise. However, she was refloated successfully and put back in service. Broken up by Dutch shipbreakers in 1940.

*Rotterdam (1959) Holland-America Line.
Built by Rotterdamsche Droogdok Maats. (Rotterdam Dry Dock Co.), Rotterdam, Netherlands. Tonnage: 38,645. Dimensions: 680' x 94' (748' o.l.). Twin-screw, 20½ knots. Six steam turbines. Single mast and twin (athwart) funnels, placed aft. Distinctively different in appearance to earlier Holland-America liners. Much aluminium used for her superstructure. Keel laid on December 14, 1956. Launched, September 13, 1958. Maiden voyage: Rotterdam-Havre-Southampton-New York, September 3, 1959. Passengers: 580 first, 800 tourist. When used as a cruise ship fitted for 730 one class passengers. Note: The largest Dutch passenger liner.

Roumanian (1883) Allan Line (British).
Built by Henry Murray & Co., Dumbarton, Scotland. Tonnage: 4,126. Dimensions: 420' x 47'. Single-screw, 12 knots. Compound engines. Four masts and one funnel. Steel hull. Tonnage increased to 4,225. Commenced her first voyage as **Roumanian** in August 1897. Sold to United States Government in 1898. Renamed: **Crook** (U. S. Army transport). Sold for scrap about 1920. Ex-**Richmond Hill** (1897).

Roussillon (1906) French Line.
Built by Akt. Ges. "Weser", Bremen, Germany. Tonnage: 8,800. Dimensions: 462' x 57'. Twin-screw, 14 knots. Quadruple expansion engines. Two masts and one funnel. Service: (a) Havre-New York, (b) Bordeaux-New York. Scrapped in 1931. Sister ship: **La Bourdonnais.** *ex Goeben*

Royal Edward (1908) Royal Line (British).
Built by Fairfield Shipbuilding & Engineering Co., Glasgow, Scotland. Tonnage: 11,117. Dimensions: 526' x 60' (545' o.l.). Triple-screw, 20 knots. Three steam turbines. Placed in Avonmouth-Quebec-Montreal service in May 1910. Converted to troopship in 1914. Torpedoed and sunk near Kamadeliusa, Aegean Sea, August 1915, with the loss of 935 lives. Ex-**Cairo** (1910). Sister ship: **Royal George.** Note: These liners were built originally for the Egyptian Mail Steamship Company (British) for a fast service between Marseilles and Alexandria. The service was unsuccessful and the vessels were laid up until sold to Canadian Northern Steamships, Ltd. (Royal Line).

Royal George (1907) Royal Line (British).
Built by Fairfield Shipbuilding & Engineering Co., Glasgow, Scotland. Tonnage: 11,146. Dimensions: 525' x 60' (545' o.l.).

Triple-screw, 20 knots. Three steam turbines. Two masts and two funnels. First sailing from Avonmouth to Quebec and Montreal, May 26, 1910. During First World War was sold to Cunard Line. Made her first regular passenger sailing for Cunard in February 1919. Sold for scrap in July 1922. Dismantled in Germany by 1923. Ex-**Heliopolis** (1910). Sister ship: **Royal Edward.**

Royal William   (1831)   Owner: Campbell (Canadian).
   Built by Black and Campbell, Quebec, Canada. Tonnage: 364. Dimensions: 160′ x 28′. Paddle-wheels, 6 knots. Side lever engines. Three masts and one funnel. Clipper bow. Wooden hull. Keel laid in September 1830. Launched, April 27, 1831. Note: The first Canadian steamer to cross the Atlantic. Never in regular trans-Atlantic service. Converted to hulk in 1840.

Royal William   (1838)   City of Dublin Steam Packet Co.
   Built by William & Thomas Wilson, Liverpool, England. Tonnage: 720. Dimensions: 145′ x 27′ (175′ o.l.). Paddle-wheels, 7½ knots. Side lever engines. Two masts and one funnel. Clipper bow. Wooden hull. Two boilers; 400 I.H.P. First Liverpool-New York voyage, July 5, 1838. Final trans-Atlantic sailing made in December 1838. Scrapped in 1888. (She was only on charter to the newly formed Trans-atlantic Steam Ship Company (British). She was returned to her owners and used in their cross-channel service.

Rugia   (1882)   Hamburg-American Line.
   Built by "Vulkan", Stettin, Germany. Tonnage: 4,053. Dimensions: 358′ x 42′. Single-screw, 11 knots. Compound engines. 2,000 I.H.P. Three masts and one funnel. Iron hull. Tonnage: Originally 3,500. Passengers: 100 first and 800 third. Renamed: **Patria** (1895). Broken up in Italy, 1906. Running mates: **Rhaetia** (identical), **Bohemia** and **Moravia.**

Rugia   (1905)   Hamburg-American Line.
   Built by Bremer Vulkan, Vegesack, Germany. Tonnage: 6,598. Dimensions: 409′ x 52′. Single-screw, 13 knots. Quadruple expansion engines. Two masts and one funnel. Services: (a) Hamburg-Philadelphia, (b) Germany-South America, (c) Germany-West Indies. Ceded to Great Britain after First World War. Sold back to Hamburg-American Line in 1922. Scrapped in 1933. Sister ships: **Rhaetia** and **Rhenania.**

Runic   (1889)   White Star Line.

Built by Harland & Wolff, Ltd., Belfast, Ireland. Tonnage: 4,833.   Dimensions: 430' x 45'.   Single-screw, 13 knots. Triple expansion engines. Four masts and one funnel. Type: Cargo-cattle vessel. Possibly carried third-class passengers. Renamed: (a) **Tampican** (1895), (b) **Imo** (1913), (c) **Guvernoren.**   Note: As **Imo** was in collision with French freighter **Mont Blanc** at Halifax, Nova Scotia, December 6, 1917. The **Mont Blanc** was being loaded with explosives at the time, and she exploded as the result of the collision, the explosion causing the following casualties: dead, 1,500; missing, 2,000; injured, 8,000; dwellings destroyed, 3,000; property loss, $30,000,000.   The **Imo**, after having been driven ashore, was refloated, repaired, and returned to service.   As **Guvernoren** she ran on the rocks when but 20 miles from her destination, Port Stanley, Falkland Islands, in 1921, and became a total loss. Sister ship: **Cufic.**

Russia   (1867)   Cunard Line.

Built by J. & G. Thomson, Ltd., Glasgow, Scotland. Tonnage: 2,959. Dimensions: 358' x 42'. Single-screw, 14 knots. Inverted engines. Three masts and one funnel. Clipper bow. Iron hull. Passengers: 235 first class; at later date increased to 430. Maiden voyage: Liverpool-New York, June 15, 1867. Won the Blue Ribbon of the Atlantic by crossing from New York to Queenstown in 8 days and 25 minutes. She failed to hold the speed record for any extended period, for in November 1867 she relinquished it to the new victor, the Inman liner **City of Paris.** Sold to Red Star Line in 1881. Renamed: **Waesland** (1881).   Note: See **Waesland** for additional information.

Russia   (1889)   Hamburg-American Line.

Built by Laird Bros., Birkenhead, England. Tonnage: 4,017. Dimensions: 374' x 44'. Single-screw, 13 knots. Triple expansion engines. Two masts and one funnel. Note: Vessel chartered to Trasatlantica Espanola in 1895 and renamed **Santa Barbara.** Returned to Hamburg-American Line in 1896, resumed her former name. Sold to the Russian Government in January 1899. Renamed: **Odessa** (1899). Scrapped about 1929.

Russia   (1908)   Russian-American Line.

Built by Barclay, Curle & Co., Glasgow, Scotland. Tonnage: 8,596. Dimensions: 475' x 57'. Twin-screw, 16 knots. Triple expansion engines. Four masts and two funnels. Began service between Libau and New York in 1908. Renamed:

(a) **Rossija** (1917), (b) **Russ,** (c) **Latvia** (1921), (d) **Fuso Maru** (1924), **Huso Maru** (1938). A World War II casualty.

Ruthenia (1900)   Canadian Pacific Line.
Built by Barclay, Curle & Co., Glasgow, Scotland. Tonnage: 7,392. Dimensions: 446' x 52'. Twin-screw, 13 knots. Triple expansion engines. Four masts and one funnel. Placed in Trieste-Quebec-Montreal service in April 1913. Converted to British transport in August 1914. Then transformed into a dummy battleship, and named her **King George V.** Afterwards used as a naval oiler in the Far East until 1929. Became an oil holder at Singapore. Captured by the Japanese and renamed **Choran Maru** in 1942. Scrapped in Scotland, 1949. Ex-**Lake Champlain** (1913). Sister ship: **Tyrolia.**

*Ryndam   (1951)   Holland-America Line.
Built by N. V. Wilton Fijenoord, Schiedam, Netherlands. Tonnage: 15,015. Dimensions: 481' x 69' (503' o.l.). Single-screw, 16½ knots. Two steam turbines on single screw shaft. Two masts and one funnel. Laid down on December 17, 1949. Launched, December 19, 1950. Originally was intended to be a freighter, but this plan was soon changed. Maiden voyage: Rotterdam-New York, July 16, 1951. Passengers: 39 first, 836 tourist. Sister ship: **Maasdam.** The **Ryndam** inaugurated regular passenger service to Quebec and Montreal in 1960.

Saale   (1886)   North German Lloyd.
Built by Fairfield Shipbuilding & Engineering Co., Glasgow, Scotland. Tonnage: 5,381. Dimensions: 428' x 47'. Single-screw, 18 knots. Compound engines. Four masts and two funnels. Reduced to two masts in 1895. Note: The shipbuilder was formerly known as John Elder & Co. Commenced Bremen-Southampton-New York service in 1886. Passengers: 150 first, 90 second, 1,000 third. The **Saale** was involved in the tragic North German Lloyd dock fire of June 30, 1900. She caught fire and was severely damaged, besides the awful loss of life that mounted to 109 lives. The gutted liner was sold to Luckenbach Line, which had it rebuilt as a freighter. They renamed her **J. L. Luckenbach** in 1902. New triple expansion engines installed. Subsequently renamed: (a) **Princess** (1921), (b) **Madison.** Scrapped in Italy, 1924. Sister ships: **Aller** and **Trave.**

Sachem   (1893)   Warren Line (British).
Built by Harland & Wolff, Ltd., Belfast, Ireland. Tonnage: 5,204.   Dimensions: 445' x 46'.   Single-screw, 13 knots.

Triple expansion engines. Four masts and one funnel. Note: A freighter that was refitted in 1913 to provide accommodation for 58 passengers. In Liverpool-Boston service 1913–1926. Scrapped in 1927.

Sachsen (1886) North German Lloyd.
Built by "Vulkan", Stettin, Germany. Tonnage: 5,026. Dimensions: 440′ x 45′. Single-screw, 14½ knots. Triple expansion engines. Two masts and one funnel. Steel hull. Vessel was lengthened in 1893 from 388 feet (4,580 tons) to 440 feet (5,026 tons). Sold to Italians in 1909. Sister ship: **Bayern.**

Sagamore (1892) Warren Line (British).
Built by Harland & Wolff, Ltd., Belfast, Ireland. Tonnage: 5,197. Dimensions: 430′ x 46′. Single-screw, 11 knots. Triple expansion engines. Four masts and one funnel. Service: Liverpool-Boston. Torpedoed and sunk 150 miles from the Fastnet, March 3, 1917, with the loss of 52 lives.

St. Andrew (1861) Allan Line (British).
Built by Barclay, Curle & Co., Glasgow, Scotland. Tonnage: 1,432. Dimensions: 253′ x 34′. Single-screw, 10 knots. Inverted type engines. Three masts and one funnel. Clipper bow. Iron hull. Maiden voyage: Glasgow-Quebec-Montreal, September 28, 1861. Lengthened to 322 feet (2,256 tons) in 1874. Re-engined with compounds. Renamed: **Waldensian** (1874). Scrapped in 1903. Sister ship: **St. George.**

St. David (1864) Allan Line.
Built by Barlcay, Curle & Co., Glasgow, Scotland. Tonnage: 1,516. Dimensions: 272′ x 34′. Single-screw, 10 knots. Inverted engines. Three masts and one funnel. Clipper bow. Iron hull. Maiden voyage: Liverpool-Quebec-Montreal, July 21, 1864. Lengthened to 335 feet (2,356 tons) in 1873. Re-engined with compounds. Renamed: **Phoenician** (1873).

St. George (1863) Allan Line.
Built by Robert Steele & Son, Greenock, Scotland. Tonnage: 1,468. Dimensions: 253′ x 34′. Single-screw, 10 knots. Inverted engines. Three masts and one funnel. Clipper bow. Iron hull. Maiden voyage: Glasgow-Quebec-Montreal, October 25, 1861. Wrecked near Seal Island on April 29, 1869, with no loss of life. Sister ship: **St. Andrew.**

St. Germain (1874) French Line.
Built by J. & G. Thomson, Ltd., Clydebank, Glasgow, Scotland. Tonnage: 3,641. Dimensions: 377′ x 40′. Single-screw, 14 knots. Compound engines. Two masts and one

funnel. Iron hull. Note: Name spelled as **Saint Germain**. Service: (a) France-New York, (b) France-Panama. Made her final voyage to New York in 1900. Scrapped in 1907. Ex-**Klopstock** (1876).

St. Laurent   (1866)   French Line.
Built by Chantier de l' Atlantique, St. Nazaire, France. Tonnage: 3,400. Dimensions: 355′ x 43′9. Single-screw, 12 knots. Inverted engines. Three masts and one funnel. Iron hull. Note: Name spelled as **Saint Laurent**. Laid down as paddle-wheel steamer, but altered to screw propulsion. Launched, April 19, 1866. During 1875–76 was re-engined with compounds and second funnel added. Service: (a) France-New York, (b) France-Panama. Tonnage listed as 3,945 tons in 1888. Her compounds were replaced with triple expansion. Scrapped in Italy, 1902.

St. Louis   (1854)   New York & Havre Steam Navigation Co.
Built at New York, N. Y. Tonnage: 1,621. Dimensions: 266′ x 35′. Paddle-wheels. Wooden hull. Maiden voyage: New York-Southampton-Havre, August 1, 1854. In trans-Atlantic service 1854–55.

St. Louis   (1895)   American Line.
Built by Wm. Cramp & Sons Shipbuilding & Engineering Co., Philadelphia, Pa. Tonnage: 11,629. Dimensions: 535′ x 63′ (554′ o.l.). Twin-screw, 21 knots. Quadruple expansion engines. 20,500 I.H.P. Two masts and two funnels. Steel hull. Launched November 12, 1894. Displacement of 16,000 tons. Equipped with ten boilers, which had a total of 64 furnaces. Passengers: 320 first, 210 second, 800 third. Maiden voyage: New York-Southampton, June 5, 1895. Renamed: (a) **Louisville** (1917) United States Government, (b) **St. Louis** (1920). Served as a troopship in First World War. She caught fire while refitting in 1920. The scuttled liner was refloated, but the rusting burned-out liner remained tied up in New York for four years. Finally towed to Italy to be dismantled by shipbreakers in 1925. 1924–25. Sister ship: **St. Paul.**

St. Louis   (1929)   Hamburg-American Line.
Built by Bremer Vulkan, Vegesack, Germany. Tonnage: 16,732. Dimensions: 543′ x 72′ (574′ o.l.). Twin-screw, 16 knots. Motorship. Two masts and two funnels. Passengers: 270 cabin, 287 tourist, 416 third. Service: Hamburg-Cobh-Halifax-New York. At times used as a cruise ship. Severely damaged by air attacks at German port in August 1944.

The battered liner was used as a hotel ship at Hamburg after the war, until broken up for scrap in 1950. Sister ship: **Milwaukee.**

St. Patrick   (1854)   Allan Line.
Built by Alexander Stephen & Sons, Ltd., Glasgow, Scotland. Tonnage: 1,208. Dimensions: 231' x 33'. Single-screw, 10 knots. Three masts and one funnel. Iron hull. Note: She was built as a sailing ship for John Bell. Acquired by Anchor Line in 1856 and engines were installed. First sailing for Allan Line as **St. Patrick** was in July 1863. Reconverted back to sail in 1875. Renamed: **Diamant.** Ex-**John Bell.**

St. Paul   (1895)   American Line.
Built by Wm. Cramp & Sons Shipbuilding & Engineering Co., Philadelphia, Pa. Tonnage: 11,629. Dimensions: 535' x 63'. Twin-screw, 21 knots. Quadruple expansion engines. Two masts and two funnels. Passengers: 220 first, 220 second, 800 third. Crew: 377 members. Note: Launched on April 10, 1895. Not in March 1895, when an attempt was made. Maiden voyage: New York-Southampton, October 9, 1895. Served as auxiliary cruiser during Spanish-American War. Sunk the British cruiser **Gladiator,** by colliding of the Isle of Wight during a storm, April 25, 1908. The **Gladiator** lost 27 men and the **St. Paul** underwent repairs before returning to service. As the United States transport Knoxville, during World War I, she capsized (April 1918) alongside a New York pier. Subsequently refloated and reconditioned for trans-Atlantic service. Made her re-entry New York-Cherbourg-Southampton run route, in March 1920. Scrapped in Germany, 1923. Sister ship: **St. Louis.**

Saint Simon   (1874)   French Line.
Built by Caird & Co., Greenock, Scotland. Tonnage: 3,133. Dimensions: 350' x 39'. Single-screw, 11 knots. Compound engines. Two masts and one funnel. Iron hull. Service: (a) France-West Indies and Central America, (b) France-New York. Scrapped in Italy, 1905. Ex-**Rhenania** (1878). Sister ship: **Olinde Rodrigues.**

Salier   (1875)   North German Lloyd.
Built by Earle's Shipbuilding & Engineering Co., Hull, England. Tonnage: 3,098. Dimensions: 354' x 39'. Single-screw, 13 knots. Compound engines. Two masts and one funnel. Iron hull. Launched, June 15, 1874. Maiden voyage: Bremen-Southampton-New York, September 8, 1875. Note: Pioneer North German Lloyd mail steamer to Australia.

Mainly employed on the Germany-Australia route. However was also used in Bremen-South American trade, besides making a number of New York sailings. Sunk in Bay of Biscay in December 1896, with great loss of life. Sister ship: **Habsburg.**

Samaria   (1868)   Cunard Line.
Built by J. & G. Thomson, Ltd., Clydebank, Glasgow, Scotland.   Tonnage: 2,605.   Dimensions: 320′ x 39′.   Single-screw, 12 knots. Inverted type engines. Two masts and one funnel.   Iron hull.   Passengers: 130 cabin and 800 third. Service: (a) Liverpool-New York, (b) Liverpool-Boston. Compound engines installed in 1878.   Scrapped in 1902. Sister ship: **Siberia.**

Samaria   (1921)   Cunard Line.
Built by Cammell, Laird & Co., Birkenhead, England. Tonnage: 19,597. Dimensions: 601′ x 73′ (624′ o.l.). Twin-screw, 16½ knots. Steam turbines. Two masts and one funnel. Launched, November 27, 1920. Passengers: 350 first, 350 second, 1,500 third. Maiden voyage: Liverpool-Boston, April 19, 1922. Converted to troopship in World War II. After the war had accommodation for 248 first class and 641 tourist passengers. Broken up by British ship-breakers in 1956. Sister ships: **Laconia** and **Scythia.** Similar ships: **Franconia** and **Carinthia.**

Samland   (1903)   Red Star Line.
Built by New York Shipbuilding Co., Camden, N. J. Tonnage: 9,748. Dimensions: 490′ x 58′. Twin-screw, 13 knots. Triple expansion engines. Four masts and one funnel. Mainly in Antwerp-Philadelphia service. Sold for scrap in April 1931. Ex-**Belgic,** ex-**Samland,** ex-**Mississippi** (7,913 tons).

San Augustin   (1882)   Spanish Line.
Built by Aitken & Mansel, Glasgow, Scotland. Tonnage: 2,332. Dimensions: 300′ x 38′. Single-screw. Compound engines. Iron hull. Service: West Indies. Stranded in Smith's Channel, Petagonia, 1900. Ex-**Venezuela,** ex-**Albano.**

San Carlos   (1917)   Spanish Line.
Built by Soc. Espanola Constr. Vaval, Cadiz, Spain. Tonnage: 2,488. Dimensions: 291′ x 40′. Twin-screw, 12½ knots. Steam turbines. Two masts and one funnel. Service: West Indies. Became a World War II casualty in January 1941. Sister ship: **Santa Isabel.**

San Gennaro   (1917)   Sicula Americana Line (Italian).
Built by Palmer's Shipbuilding & Iron Co., Newcastle, England. Tonnage: 10,917. Dimensions: 518′ x 64′ (536′ o.l.). Twin-screw, 17 knots. Quadruple expansion engines. Two masts and two funnels. Renamed: **Colombo** (1921). See **Colombo** for additional information.

San Giorgio   (1886)   Sicula Americana Line.
Built by Oswald, Mordaunt & Co., Southampton, England. Tonnage: 2,817. Dimensions: 307′ x 41′. Single-screw. Compound engines. Iron hull. Sold to Marittima Italiana. Wrecked on November 23, 1920.

San Giorgio   (1907)   Sicula Americana Line.
Built by Sir James Laing & Sons, Ltd., Sunderland, England. Tonnage: 6,392. Dimensions: 406′ x 51′. Twin-screw, 13½ knots. Triple expansion engines. Two masts and two funnels. Commenced maiden voyage from Palermo to New York in July 1907. Acquired by Transoceanica (Italian) in July 1907, but was not renamed. Renamed: **Napoli** (1921) Navigazione Generale Italiana. Running mates: **San Giovanni** and **San Guglielmo.**

San Giovanni   (1907)   Sicula Americana Line.
Built by Sir James Laing & Sons, Ltd., Sunderland, England. Tonnage: 6,592. Dimensions: 430′ x 52′. Twin-screw, 14 knots. Triple expansion engines. Two masts and two funnels. Commenced in Palermo to New York service in November 1907. Vessel acquired by Transoceanica (Italian) in 1917. Renamed: **Palermo** (1921). Scrapped in 1928. Running mates: **San Giorgio** and **San Guglielmo.**

San Giusto   (1890)   Cosulich Line.
Built by "Vulkan", Stettin, Germany. Tonnage: 8,430. Dimensions: 504′ x 57′. Twin-screw, 17 knots. Triple expansion engines. Two masts and three funnels. Employed as an emigrant carrier between Trieste and New York. Scrapped in Italy, 1924. Ex-**Gaa** (1920) Austria-Hungarian Navy submarine depot ship, ex-**Moskva** (troopship) Russian, ex-**Don** (cruiser), ex-**Furst Bismarck** (1904).

San Guglielmo   (1911)   Sicula Americana Line.
Built by D. & W. Henderson & Co., Glasgow, Scotland. Tonnage: 8,341. Dimensions: 470′ x 56′. Twin-screw, 15½ knots. Triple expansion engines. Two masts and two funnels. Launched, March 29, 1911. Maiden voyage: Palermo-Messina-Naples-New York, January 8, 1913. Transferred

to Transoceanica (Italian) in 1917. Made her final voyage to New York in 1916. Wrecked near Loano, January 18, 1918. She may have been dismantled in 1919. Running mates: **San Giorgio** and **San Giovanni.**

Sannio   (1899)   Navigazione Generale Italiana.
Built by Palmer's Shipbuilding Co., Jarrow-on-Tyne, Newcastle, England. Tonnage: 9,210. Dimensions: 470′ x 56′. Twin-screw, 12½ knots. Triple expansion engines. Four masts and one funnel. Made her first voyage as **Sannio** from Genoa to New York in 1906. Renamed: **Napoli** (1913). Sunk in North Atlantic due to collision in 1918. Ex-**British Prince** (1906). Sister ships: **Lazio** and **Campania.**

Sant' Anna   (1910)   Fabre Line (French).
Built by Forges & Chantiers de la Mediterranee, La Seyne, France. Tonnage: 9,350. Dimensions: 470′ x 56′. Twinscrew, 16 knots. Triple expansion engines. Two masts and two funnels. Launched, February 7, 1910. Passengers: 70 first, 150 second, 1,750 third. Maiden voyage: Marseilles-New York, July 26, 1910. Torpedoed and sunk in the Mediterranean, May 10, 1918. Sister ship: **Canada.**

Santa Isabel   (1916)   Spanish Line.
Built by Soc. Espanola de Constr. Naval, Cadiz, Spain. Tonnage: 2,488. Dimensions: 291′ x 40′. Twin-screw, 12½ knots. Steam turbines. Two masts and one funnel. Wrecked during storm near Villagarcia in 1921, with the loss of 214 lives. Sister ship: **San Carlos.**

Santiago   (1890)   Spanish Line.
Built by Wm. Denny & Bros., Ltd., Dumbarton, Scotland. Tonnage: 5,206. Dimensions: 410′ x 48′. Single-screw, 14 knots. Quadruple expansion engines. Three masts and one funnel. Renamed: (a) **Jelunga,** (b) **Jehangir.** Scrapped in 1923. Ex-**Leon XIII,** ex-**Jelunga.**

Santo Domingo   (1877)   Spanish Line.
Built by Robert Napier & Sons, Glasgow, Scotland. Tonnage: 2,911. Dimensions: 344′ x 39′. Single-screw, 13½ knots. Compound engines. Two masts and one funnel. Purchased from Castle Line in 1882. Wrecked off the Isle of Pines in July 1898. Dismantled for scrap. Ex-**Dublin Castle** (1882).

Saragossa   (1874)   Cunard Line.
Built by J. & G. Thomson, Ltd., Clydebank, Glasgow, Scotland. Tonnage: 2,166. Dimensions: 316′ x 35′. Single-screw, 11 knots. Compound engines. Two masts and one funnel.

Iron hull. Passengers: 74 cabin and 550 third. Maiden voyage: Liverpool-Boston, April 22, 1874. Transferred later to Mediterranean service. Scrapped in 1909.

Sarah Sands (1846) Sands & Company (British).

Built by James Hodgson, Liverpool, England. Tonnage: 1,400. Dimensions: 182′ x 32′ (215′ o.l.). Single-screw, 9 knots. Oscillating engines. Four masts and one funnel. Iron hull. Launched in September 1846. Maiden voyage: Liverpool-New York, January 20, 1847. Transferred to Pacific service in 1849. Mainly in San Francisco-Panama service for Pacific Mail Steamship Co. Also, in other services at later date. Wrecked near Bombay, April 7, 1869.

Sardegna (1902) Navigazione Generale Italiana.

Built by Esercizio Bacini, Riva Trigoso, Italy. Tonnage: 5,255. Dimensions: 418′ x 47′. Single-screw, 14 knots. Triple expansion engines. Two masts and one funnel. Service: Genoa-Naples-New York. Sold to Servizi Marittimi (Italian) in 1912. Sister ship: **Sicilia.**

Sardegna (1923) Italia Line.

Built by Bremer Vulkan, Vegesack, Germany. Tonnage: 11,452. Dimensions: 490′ x 61′. Twin-screw, 14 knots. Triple expansion engines. Two masts and two funnels. Transferred to Lloyd Triestino. Torpedoed and sunk, December 29, 1940. Ex-**Sierra Ventana** (1935).

Sardinian (1875) Allan Line.

Built by Robert Steele & Co., Greenock, Scotland. Tonnage: 4,376. Dimensions: 400′ x 42′. Single-screw, 13½ knots. Compound engines. Three masts and one funnel. Iron hull. Passengers: 120 first and 850 third. Maiden voyage: Liverpool-Quebec-Montreal, July 29, 1875. After the tragic fire of this vessel on May 10, 1878, which cost many lives, she was salved, refitted and returned to trans-Atlantic service. Triple expansion engines installed in 1897. Reduced to two masts. Served in various North Atlantic routes. Sold to Spanish owners in 1920, and used as a hulk at Vigo. Sister ship: **Polynesian.**

Sarmatian (1871) Allan Line.

Built by Robert Steele & Son, Greenock, Scotland. Tonnage: 3,647. Dimensions: 370′ x 42′. Single-screw, 13½ knots. Compound engines. Three masts and one funnel. Iron hull. First straight-stemmed Allan Line steamship. Passengers: 100 first and 850 third. Accommodation changed later to 200 first, 75 second, 850 third. Note: A very large percentage of ocean-going passenger liners during the course of their life had their accommodation changed one or more times. This is a fact that is well to keep in mind, when noting the number of passengers a given liner can accommodate, when listed in a book such as the author's. The **Sarmatian** was broken up for scrap at Rotterdam in 1908.

Sarnia   (1882)   Dominion Line (British).
Built by Charles Connell & Co., Glasgow, Scotland. Tonnage: 3,726. Dimensions: 360′ x 40′. Single-screw, 13 knots. Compound engines. 4,500 I.H.P. Four masts and one funnel. Iron hull. Passengers: 80 first, 60 second, 1,200 third class. Maiden voyage: Liverpool-Quebec-Montreal, September 7, 1882. Scrapped at Genoa in 1897. Sister ship: **Oregon.**

Saturnia   (1910)   Anchor-Donaldson Line.
Built by Charles Connell & Co., Glasgow, Scotland. Tonnage: 8,611. Dimensions: 456′ x 55′. Twin-screw, 14 knots. Triple expansion engines. Two masts and one funnel. Service: Glasgow-Quebec-Montreal. Accommodation for a total of 1,250 passengers. Sold to Italian shipbreakers in November 1928. Broken up during 1929. Similar in appearance to **Letitia** (of 1912).

*****Saturnia**   (1927)   (a) Cosulich Line, (b) Italia Line.
Built by Cantieri Riuniti Dell' Adriatico, Monfalcone, Italy. Tonnage: 23,940. Dimensions: 601′ x 79′ (630′ o.l.). Twin-screw, 19 knots. Motorship. Two masts and one funnel. Keel laid on May 30, 1925. Launched, December 29, 1925. Maiden voyage was from Trieste to South America in September 1927. Transferred to Trieste-New York service early in 1928. New diesel engines installed in 1935, which increased speed to 21 knots. During World War II was taken over by United States and converted to hospital ship. Renamed: (a) **Francis Y. Slanger** (1944) U. S. hospital ship, (b) **Saturnia** (Dec. 1946). Resumed trans-Atlantic service in August 1947. Accommodation for 1,600 passengers. Sister ship: **Vulcania.**

Savannah   (1819)   Owner: Colonel John Stevens (United States).
Built by Crocker & Fickett, New York, N. Y. Tonnage: 319. Dimensions: 98′ x 25′. Paddle-wheels, 6 knots. Inclined direct acting single cylinder engine, 90 indicated horsepower. Three masts and one funnel. Clipper bow. Wooden hull. Launched, August 22, 1818. Ran her trials in March 1819. Sailed from Savannah to Liverpool, via New York,

May 22, 1819. Arrived at her destination on June 20th. Note: The first steam-propelled vessel to cross any ocean. In making her historic crossing she used her steam engine for only a total of four days, out of the four weeks required to complete the voyage. An endeavor was made to sell the vessel in Europe, but no buyer was found and the **Savannah** soon sailed back to the United States. Henceforth she was used as a sailing ship between Savannah and New York. Wrecked on Long Island, November 5, 1821. As a postscript to the **Savannah** of 1819, it may be appropriate to state why the historic ship has been and still is noteworthy. It is mainly due to the thought that the **Savannah** symbolized a new idea, a venture that was revolutionary, because she demonstrated to many people that the power of steam could be used to enable a ship to cross the oceans of the world propelled by steam engines. The year is now 1961 and a new **Savannah** that will fly the flag of the United States is nearing completion. The new **Savannah** will be a ship of peace. During voyages to many lands she will endeavor to show to the peoples of the world that atomic energy can be used for the benefit of men. She can help to lead the way to a much better life for all nations. The author of this book stated the following thought in his "Trans-Atlantic Passenger Ships—Past and Present", published in 1947. "The possible future use of atomic power as a propelling force, when applied to ships can, if it may be done at reasonable cost, make the liner a swifter form of ocean travel." That desire and hope is now approaching fulfillment. The foundation for the atomic age was born in 1905. Albert Einstein published papers in that year dealing with the subject. His theories captured the imagination and attention of other scientists, and through the combined efforts of many, Albert Einstein's ideas have brought forth accomplishments. The new atomic powered **Savannah** is to be one of those accomplishments.

Savoia   (1897)   La Veloce Line (Italian).
Built by Navali Odero & Co., Foce, Genoa, Italy. Tonnage: 4,429. Dimensions: 462' x 45'. Twin-screw, 15½ knots. Triple expansion engines. Two masts and one funnel. Clipper bow. Steel hull. Her tall thin funnel placed somewhat aft. Lengthened in 1901. Tonnage increased to 5,082. Served also in Latin American trade. Sold for scrap in 1922. Sister ship: **Venezuela.**

Saxonia   (1857)   Hamburg-American Line.
Built by Caird & Co., Greenock, Scotland. Tonnage: 2,404. Dimensions: 317' x 49'. Single-screw, 10 knots. Geared

oscillating engines. Three masts and one funnel. Clipper
bow. Iron hull. Service: Hamburg-Southampton-New
York. Re-engined with compounds in 1871. Sold to the
Russian Volunteer Fleet in 1877. Renamed: **Nijni Novgorod**
(1878). Scrapped in 1895. Sister ship: **Austria.**

Saxonia (1900) Cunard Line.
Built by John Brown & Co., Clydebank, Glasgow, Scotland.
Tonnage: 14,197. Dimensions: 580' x 64' (600' o.l.). Twin-
screw, 16 knots. Quadruple expansion engines. Four masts
and one funnel. Distinctive liner, as she had the tallest funnel
ever fitted to a ship. Cost about $1,600,000 to build. Passen-
gers: 160 first, 200 second, 1,600 third. Maiden voyage:
Liverpool-Boston, May 22, 1900. Transferred to Trieste-
New York service in 1911. After the First World War she
was placed in the Liverpool-New York service. Sold to
Dutch shipbreakers in March 1925. Broken up by 1926.
Sister ship: **Ivernia.** Note: Her funnel too was of the same
height (106 feet high from deck level) as the **Saxonia's.**

*Saxonia (1954) Cunard Line.
Built by John Brown & Co., Clydebank, Glasgow, Scotland.
Tonnage: 21,637. Dimensions: 586' x 80' (608' o.l.). Twin-
screw, 21 knots. Four steam turbines geared to 2 screw
shafts. Launched, February 17, 1954. Passengers: 125 first
and 800 tourist. Commenced her maiden voyage from Liverpool to Quebec and Montreal, September 2, 1954. Transferred to the Liverpool-New York service in 1961. Sister
ships: **Carinthia, Ivernia** and **Sylvania.** Note: These
liners were designed for the Canadian service of the Cunard
Line.

Scandia (1889) Hamburg-American Line.
Built by "Vulkan", Stettin, Germany. Tonnage: 4,243.
Dimensions: 370' x 44'. Single-screw, 13½ knots. Compound engines. Two masts and one funnel. Passengers: 30
first and 1,400 third. Sold to United States Government in
1898. Renamed: **Warren** (1898). Scrapped in 1924. Sister
ships: **Dania** and **Russia.**

Scandinavian (1870) Allan Line.
Built by Robert Steele & Co., Glasgow, Scotland. Tonnage:
3,068. Dimensions: 338' x 40'. Single-screw, 11 knots.
Compound engines. Three masts and one funnel. Iron hull.
Clipper bow. Maiden voyage: Liverpool-Quebec-Montreal,
May 5, 1870. Served also on other North Atlantic routes.
Scrapped in 1899. Sister ship: **Prussian.**

Scandinavian   (1898)   Allan Line (British).
Built by Harland & Wolff, Ltd., Belfast, Ireland. Tonnage:
12,116.   Dimensions: 550′ x 59′.   Twin-screw, 14½ knots.
Triple expansion engines.   Two masts and one funnel.   Service: Glasgow-Quebec-Montreal.   Transferred to Canadian
Pacific Line in 1917.   Scrapped in 1923.   Ex-**Romanic**
(1912), ex-**New England** (1903).

Scanmail   (1919)   American Scantic Line.
Built by American International S.B. Corp., Hog Island,
Pa. Tonnage: 5,152. Dimensions: 390′ x 54′. Single-screw,
13 knots. Turbines. Two masts and one funnel. Ex-
Chickasaw (1932). Sister ships: **Scanpenn, Scanstates**
and **Scanyork.** Passengers: 90 cabin class. Originally built
as freighters.

Scharnhorst   (1904)   North German Lloyd.
Built by J. C. Tecklenborg & Co., Geestemunde, Germany.
Tonnage: 8,131. Dimensions: 453′ x 55′. Twin-screw, 13½
knots. Triple expansion engines. Two masts and one funnel.
Built for East of Suez service, but made some Bremen-New
York voyages. Liner taken over by the French in 1919.
Renamed: **La Bourdonnais** (1921).   Scrapped in 1934.
Sister ships: **Gneisenau** and **Roon.**

Schiedam   (1874)   Holland-America Line.
Built by A. McMillan & Son, Dumbarton, Scotland. Ton-
nage: 2,236. Dimensions: 301′ x 39′. Single-screw, 10 knots.
Compound engines. Two masts and one funnel. Iron hull.
Service: Netherlands-New York.   Renamed: **Miramar**
(1897) Austro-American Line. Ex-**San Marcos** (1877).

Schiller   (1872)   Adler (Eagle) Line.
Built by Caird & Co., Greenock, Scotland. Tonnage: 3,408.
Dimensions: 375′ x 40′. Single-screw, 14 knots. Compound
engines. Two masts and two funnels. Iron hull. Maiden
voyage: Hamburg-New York, February 5, 1874. Passengers:
100 first, 100 second, 800 third. Wrecked on the Scilly
Islands, May 7, 1875, with very heavy loss of life. Running
mates: **Gellert, Goethe, Herder, Klopstock, Lessing** and
Wieland.

Schleswig   (1903)   North German Lloyd.
Built by "Vulkan", Stettin, Germany. Tonnage: 6,955.
Dimensions: 450′ x 52′. Twin-screw, 13½ knots. Triple ex-
pansion engines. Two masts and one funnel. Designed for
Latin American service, but made a number of North At-
lantic voyages. Renamed: **General Duchesne** (1919).

Scotia (1862) Cunard Line.

Built by Robert Napier & Sons, Glasgow, Scotland. Tonnage: 3,871. Dimensions: 379' x 47' (400' o.l.). Paddle-wheels, 13½ knots. Side lever engines. Two masts and two funnels. Note: The last Cunard paddle-wheel steamer. Her 4,000 indicated horse-power engines were capable of driving the ship at 14 knots. This was the greatest power by paddle-wheel engines of trans-Atlantic steamships, also, could maintain the highest average speed. In December 1863 she made the Queenstown to New York passage in the record breaking time of 8 days and 3 hours. In June 1864 she attained an average speed of 14.54 knots for the Atlantic crossing. Made her final Liverpool-New York voyage, May 29, 1876. Sold in 1878. As the converted twin-screw cable laying vessel, she was wrecked off Guam in March 1904.

Scotia (1881) Fabre Line.

Built by S. & H. Morton & Co., Leith, Scotland. Tonnage: 2,492. Dimensions: 328' x 40'. Single-screw, 11 knots. Compound engines. Three masts and one funnel. Iron hull. Service: (a) Marseilles-New York, (b) France-South America, (c) France-New York. Went aground on Long Island in March 1887. Subsequently refloated, repaired and sold. Renamed: **Mars.** Wrecked in 1889. Sister ship: **Britannia.**

Scotia (1889) Anchor Line (British).

Built by D. & W. Henderson & Co., Glasgow, Scotland. Tonnage: 2,846. Dimensions: 310' x 40'. Single-screw, 11½ knots. Triple expansion engines. Two masts and one funnel. Steel hull. Service: Mediterranean-New York, also, in Bombay and Calcutta trade. Vessel sold in 1903. Renamed: (a) **Lytton,** (b) **Takao Maru.** Listed as missing in 1906.

Scotian (1898) Allan Line.

Built by Harland & Wolff, Ltd., Belfast, Ireland. Tonnage: 10,417. Dimensions: 515' x 59'. Twin-screw, 14 knots. Triple expansion engines. Two masts and one funnel. In the Quebec and Montreal trade. Transferred to Canadian Pacific Line in 1917. Renamed: **Marglen** (1922). Scrapped in 1927. Ex-**Statendam** (1910).

Scotland (1865) National Line (British).

Built by Palmer's Shipbuilding & Iron Co., Newcastle, England. Tonnage: 3,803. Single-screw, 11 knots. Inverted type engines. Three masts and one funnel. Clipper bow. Iron hull. Launched, February 11, 1865. Maiden voyage: Liverpool-New York, June 6, 1865. In collision with **Kate**

Dyer off Fire Island, New York, December 1, 1866, and was driven ashore where she subsequently broke up. There was no loss of life.

Scotsman   (1894)   Dominion Line.
Built by Harland & Wolff, Ltd., Belfast, Ireland. Tonnage: 6,041. Dimensions: 470' x 49'. Twin-screw, 13 knots. Triple expansion engines. Four masts and one funnel. Commenced her first trans-Atlantic sailing in November 1895. Wrecked near Belle Isle, September 22, 1899, with loss of several lives.

Scythia   (1875)   Cunard Line.
Built by J. & G. Thomson, Ltd., Clydebank, Glasgow, Scotland. Tonnage: 4,556. Dimensions: 420' x 42'. Single-screw, 13½ knots. Compound engines. 2,780 I.H.P. Three masts and one funnel. Iron hull. Maiden voyage: Liverpool-New York, May 1, 1875. Passengers: 340 cabin and 1,100 third. Served also in Boston trade. Scrapped in Italy, 1899. Sister ship: **Bothnia.**

Scythia   1920)   Cunard Line.
Built by Vickers, Armstrong, Ltd., Barrow-in-Furness, Newcastle, England. Tonnage: 19,761. Dimensions: 600' x 73' (624' o.l.). Twin-screw, 16½ knots. Steam turbines. Two masts and one funnel. Passengers: 350 first, 350 second, 1,600 third. Maiden voyage: Liverpool-New York, August 20, 1921. Commissioned as a troopship in World War II. Resumed trans-Atlantic service in October 1948. Reconditioned in 1950. Tonnage increased to 19,930. Accommodation for 245 first and 639 tourist class. Placed in England-Canada service. Scrapped in Scotland, 1958. Sister ships: **Laconia** and **Samaria.**

Sempione   (1877)   Navigazione Generale Italiana.
Built by Wm. Denny & Bros., Ltd., Dumbarton, Scotland. Tonnage: 3,149. Dimensions: 350' x 39'. Single-screw, 12 knots. Compound engines. Two masts and one funnel. Iron hull. Service: Genoa-Naples-New York. Sold to other owners and converted into a hulk, October 1902. Ex-**German** (1896).

Servia   (1881)   Cunard Line.
Built by J. & G. Thomson, Ltd., Glasgow, Scotland. Tonnage: 7,391. Dimensions: 515' x 52' (532' o.l.). Single-screw, 17 knots. Compound engines. 12,000 I.H.P. Three masts and two funnels. Launched, March 1, 1881. Attained a speed of 17.8 knots during her trials. First Cunarder to be

built of steel. Main dining saloon measured 74 feet by 49 feet wide, with a height of 8½ feet and could seat 350 passengers. She had 168 staterooms. Passengers: 450 first and 600 third. Officers and crew members numbered 200. Maiden voyage: Liverpool-New York, November 26, 1881. After completing her 171st round voyage in October 1901, she was sold to Thos. W. Ward, Ltd., well-known ship-breakers. Towed to Preston and dismantled for scrap.

*Seven Seas (1940) Europe-Canada Line (German).
Built by Sun Shipbuilding & Dry Dock Co., Chester, Pennsylvania. Tonnage: 12,575. Dimensions: 492' (o.l.) x 69'. Single-screw, 16 knots. Motorship. Single mast and one funnel. Originally designed as a "C-3" type freighter. Converted to aircraft carrier. After the war was rebuilt as an emigrant ship. Made her first voyage as **Seven Seas** in April 1955. Mainly in Bremen-Quebec-Montreal service. Passengers: 20 first and 980 tourist. Ex-**Nelly** (1953), ex-**Long Island** (1949), ex-**Mormacmail**. Note: The Europe-Canada Line is jointly owned by Holland-America Line and Royal Rotterdam Lloyd.

Seydlitz (1903) North German Lloyd.
Built by F. Schichau, Danzig, Germany. Tonnage: 7,942. Dimensions: 442' x 55'. Twin-screw, 14½ knots. Triple expansion engines. Two masts and one funnel. Passengers: 100 first, 100 second, 1,700 third. Services: (a) Germany-Australia-Far East, (b) Bremen-New York, (c) Bremen-Cuba. Scrapped in Germany, 1933. Sister ships: **Gneisenau, Scharnhorst and Zieten.**

Siberia (1867) Cunard Line.
Built by J. & G. Thomson, Ltd., Glasgow, Scotland. Tonnage: 2,498. Dimensions: 320' x 39'. Single-screw, 11½ knots. Inverted engines. Two masts and one funnel. Passengers: 100 cabin and 800 third class. Maiden voyage: Liverpool-New York, March 26, 1879. Sold to Spanish owners. Renamed: **Manila** (1880). Wrecked in 1886. Sister ship: **Samaria.** Note: Last Cunarders to be built with clipper bow.

Siberian (1884) Allan Line.
Built by Govan Shipbuilding Co., Ltd., Glasgow, Scotland. Tonnage: 3,846. Dimensions: 372' x 45'. Single-screw, 12 knots. Compound engines. Three masts and one funnel. Steel hull. Maiden voyage from Glasgow to Quebec and

Montreal in September 1884. Made her final voyage to United States in 1906. Scrapped in Falmouth in 1912.

Sicilian (1899) Allan Line.
Built by Workman, Clark & Co., Belfast, Ireland. Tonnage: 6,224. Dimensions: 430' x 54'. Single-screw, 12½ knots. Triple expansion engines. Four masts and one funnel. First served as a transport during the Boer War in South Africa. Commenced regular trans-Atlantic service in February 1901. Tonnage increased to 7,328 in 1908. Transferred to Canadian Pacific Line in 1917. Renamed: **Bruton** (1922). Scrapped in 1925. Sister ship: **Corinthian.**

Sicilian Prince (1889) Prince Line (British).
Built by Scott's Shipbuilding & Engineering Co., Greenock, Scotland. Tonnage: 2,784. Dimensions: 363' x 42'. Single-screw, 12 knots. Triple expansion engines. Two masts and one funnel. Clipper bow. Steel hull. Renamed: **Abbassieh** (1910). Ex-**Alvares Cabral** (1902), ex-**Mocambique.** Sister ship: **Napolitan Prince.**

Sidon (1861) Cunard Line.
Built by Wm. Denny & Bros., Dumbarton, Scotland. Tonnage: 1,853. Dimensions: 276' x 36'. Single-screw, 10 knots. Geared oscillating engines. Two masts and one funnel. Iron hull. First Liverpool-New York voyage was made in May 1863. Spent her final years in the Mediterranean service. Wrecked in 1885. Sister ships: **Atlas, Hecla, Kedar, Marathon** and **Olympus.**

Sierra Nevada (1922) North German Lloyd.
Built by "Vulkan", Stettin, Germany. Tonnage: 8,753. Dimensions: 439' x 56'. Twin-screw, 14 knots. Triple expansion engines. Two masts and two funnels. She was used mainly in the South American service, but did make sailings to New York. Renamed: **Madrid** (1925). Sunk by air attack, December 9, 1941.

Sierra Ventana (1923) North German Lloyd.
Built by Bremer Vulkan, Vegesack, Germany. Tonnage: 11,392. Dimensions: 490' x 61' (511' o.l.). Twin-screw, 14½ knots. Triple expansion engines. Two masts and two funnels. Designed for Bremen-South American route. Made several Bremen-New York sailings. Renamed: **Sardegna** (1935) Italian. A World War II casualty, December 29, 1940. Sister ships: **Sierra Cordoba** and **Sierra Morena.**

Silesia   (1869)   Hamburg-American Line.
Built by Caird & Co., Ltd., Greenock, Scotland. Tonnage: 3,156. Dimensions: 341' x 40'. Single-screw, 13 knots. Inverted type engines. Re-engined with compounds. Two masts and one funnel. Iron hull. Launched, April 14, 1869. Maiden voyage: Hamburg-Havre-New York, June 22, 1869. Renamed: (a) **Pacifica** (1887) British, (b) **Citta di Napoli** (1888) Italian, (c) **Montevideo** (1891) Italian. Sister ships: **Holsatia** and **Westphalia**.

Sinaia   (1924)   Fabre Line.
Built by Barclay, Curle & Co., Glasgow, Scotland. Tonnage: 8,567. Dimensions: 439' x 56'. Twin-screw, 14 knots. Triple expansion engines. Two masts and two funnels. Launched, August 19, 1922. Maiden voyage: Marseilles-New York, September 25, 1924. Scuttled by the Germans at Marseilles in August 1944. Refloated on December 9, 1946, but soon broken up for scrap. Sister ship: **De la Salle** (French Line).

Sirius   (1838)   British & American Steam Navigation Co.
Built by Robert Menzies & Son, Leith, Scotland. Tonnage: 703. Dimensions: 178' x 25'. Paddle-wheels, 8 knots. Side lever engines. Two masts and one funnel. Clipper bow. Wooden hull. Note: The first British steamship to cross the Atlantic. This pioneer steamship left Cork Harbor, April 4, 1838, bound for New York. She arrived at her destination on April 22. Wrecked in fog near Ballycotton Head, January 16, 1847.

Skaubryn   (1951)   Greek Line.
Built at Gothenburg, Sweden. Tonnage: 9,786. Dimensions: 458' (o.l.) x 57'. Single-screw, 16½ knots. Two masts and one funnel. Originally built for I. M. Skaugen, Oslo, Norway. Purchased by Greek Line and placed in Europe-Canada service in June 1957. Made her final trans-Atlantic sailing in September 1957. Transferred to Bremen-Australia service. Caught fire and was abandoned in the Indian Ocean, March 31, 1958, while on voyage to Australia. Foundered on April 6, while in tow.

Slavonia   (1903)   Cunard Line.
Built by Sir James Laing & Sons, Ltd., Sunderland, England. Tonnage: 10,606. Dimensions: 510' x 59'. Twin-screw, 13½ knots. Triple expansion engines. Two masts and one funnel. Service: Trieste-New York. Passengers: 40 first and 800 third class. Vessel laid down as **Yamuna** for British India Steam Navigation Co. Wrecked on Flores, Azores, June 10, 1909, with no loss of life. Running mate: **Pannonia**.

Smolensk (1898)   Russian Volunteer Fleet.
Built by J. & G. Thomson, Ltd., Clydebank, Glasgow, Scotland. Tonnage: 7,270. Dimensions: 487' x 58'. Twin-screw, 17 knots. Triple expansion engines. Two masts and three funnels. Passengers: 50 first, 36 second, 1,500 third. Scrapped in 1922. Ex-**Rion** (1906), ex-**Smolensk** (1904). Running mates: **Petersburg, Saratov** and **Moskva.**

Sobieski (1939)   Gdynia-American Line.
Built by Swan, Hunter & Wigham Richardson, Ltd., Newcastle, England. Tonnage: 11,030. Dimensions: 493' x 67' (511' o.l.). Twin-screw, 17 knots. Motorship. Two masts and one funnel. Built for the South American route. First trans-Atlantic sailing to New York in 1946. Vessel sold to Russia in March 1950. Renamed: **Gruzia** (1950). Still (1961) in service as Russian liner. Sister ship: **Chrobry.**

Sofia Hohenberg (1905)   Austro-American Line.
Built by Lloyd Austriaco, Trieste, Austria-Hungary. Tonnage: 5,491. Dimensions: 360' x 48'. Single-screw, 13 knots. Triple expansion engines. Two masts and one funnel. Launched in September 1905. Service: Trieste-New York. Transferred to Cosulich Line in 1919. Renamed: **Sofia** (1919). Made her final voyage to New York in 1921. Scrapped in 1929.

Solunto (1872)   I. & V. Florio (Italian).
Built by W. Watson, Sunderland, England. Tonnage: 1,933. Dimensions: 280' x 34'. Single-screw, 11 knots. Compound engines. Two masts and one funnel. Iron hull. Note: Vessel made an experimental Atlantic crossing with 23 passengers in June 1877. Began regular service for the line in 1880. Service: Palermo-New York.

Southland (1900)   White Star Line.
Built by John Brown & Co., Clydebank, Glasgow, Scotland. Tonnage: 11,899. Dimensions: 560' x 60'. Twin-screw, 15 knots. Quadruple expansion engines. Four masts and two funnels. In White Star Line service 1915–1917. Converted to transport. Torpedoed and sunk 140 miles from Tory Island, June 4, 1917, with the loss of 4 lives. Ex-**Vaterland** (1915).

Southwark (1893)   (a) American Line, (b) Dominion Line.
Built by Wm. Denny & Bros., Ltd., Dumbarton, Scotland. Tonnage: 8,607. Dimensions: 480' x 57'. Twin-screw, 15 knots. Quadruple expansion engines. Four masts and one

funnel. Note: Named after a Philadelphia suburb. Passengers: 60 first and 1,000 third. Broken up for scrap in 1912. Sister ship: **Kinsington.** They were transferred to Dominion Line in 1903.

Spaarndam   (1881)   Holland-America Line.
Built by Harland & Wolff, Ltd., Belfast, Ireland. Tonnage: 4,539.   Dimensions: 427′ x 41′9.   Single-screw, 15 knots. Compound engines. 3,000 I.H.P. Four masts and one funnel. Service: Rotterdam-New York. Made her final voyage to New York in 1900. Sold to British shipbreakers in 1901. Ex-**Arabic** (1890).

Spaarndam   (1922)   Holland-America Line.
Built by New Waterway Shipbuilding Co., Schiedam, Netherlands.   Tonnage: 8,857.   Dimensions: 450′ x 58′. Single-screw, 13 knots. Steam turbines. Two masts and two funnels. Altered to single funnel in 1934. Services: Rotterdam-Cuba-Mexico; also, Rotterdam-New York/Baltimore. Sunk by a magnetic mine off England. November 27, 1939, while bound from New Orleans to Antwerp and Rotterdam. Sister ships: **Edam, Leerdam** and **Maasdam.**

Spain   (1871)   National Line (British).
Built by Laird Bros., Ltd., Birkenhead, England. Tonnage: 4,512.   Dimensions: 426′ x 43′.   Single-screw, 13½ knots. Compound engines. Four masts and two funnels. Iron hull. Passengers: 120 first and 1,400 third. Maiden voyage: Liverpool-New York, August 16, 1871. Tonnage later increased to 5,089. Considered a fast liner for her time. Made a Cobh-New York crossing in 8 days, 13 hours, at an average speed of 13.6 knots. Made her final voyage from London to New York in November 1895. Scrapped in France, 1896. Sister ship: **Egypt** (not identical).

Spree   (1890)   North German Lloyd.
Built by "Vulkan", Stettin, Germany. Tonnage: 6,963. Dimensions: 463′ x 51′. Single-screw, 19 knots. Compound engines. 12,500 I.H.P. Three masts and two funnels. Note: Very attractive liner. Not quite fast enough to have won the trans-Atlantic speed record. Maiden voyage: Bremen-Southampton-New York, November 6, 1890. Rebuilt and lengthened to 528 feet (7,840 tons) 1898–99. Altered to twin-screw; new engines installed. Renamed: (a) **Kaiserin Maria Theresa** (1899), (b) **Ural** (1904) Russian. Sunk at the Battle of Tsushima in Sea of Japan, May 27, 1905. Sister ship: **Havel.**

*Srbija   (1944)   Yugoslav Line.
    Built by Rotterdam Dry Dock Co., Rotterdam, Netherlands.
    Tonnage: 6,634.   Dimensions: 446' x 60' (475' o.l.).   Single-
    screw, 15 knots.   Motorship.   Two masts and one funnel.
    Launched as **Crostafels** in 1944.   Service: Fiume-New York.
    Ex-**Drvar** (1949).

Stampalia   (1909)   La Veloce Line (Italian).
    Built by Cantieri Navali Riuniti, Spezia, Italy.   Tonnage:
    9,000.   Dimensions: 476' x 55'.   Twin-screw, 16 knots.   Triple
    expansion engines.   Two masts and two funnels.   Passengers:
    100 first and 2,400 third.   Torpedoed and sunk on August
    18, 1916.   Ex-**Oceania** (1913).

State of Alabama   (1873)   State Line (British).
    Built by T. Wingate & Co., Glasgow, Scotland.   Tonnage:
    2,313.   Dimensions: 321' x 36'.   Single-screw, 12 knots.
    Compound engines.   Three masts and one funnel.   Accommo-
    dation for 30 cabin, 50 second, and 200 third class.   Maiden
    voyage: Glasgow-New York, June 20, 1873.   Sold to Allan
    Line in 1891, but soon resold to a Glasgow firm.   Scrapped
    in 1902.   Ex-**Alabama** (1873).

State of California   (1891)   (a) State Line, (b) Allan Line.
    Built by Alexander Stephen & Sons, Ltd., Glasgow, Scotland.
    Tonnage: 4,275.   Dimensions: 385' x 46'.   Single-screw, 14
    knots.   Compound engines.   Three masts and one funnel.
    Built for State Line, but transferred to Allan Line upon com-
    pletion.   Maiden voyage: Glasgow-New York, August 14,
    1891.   Renamed: (a) **Californian** (1898), (b) **Coamo** (1901).
    Note: As the **Californian** stranded near Portland, February
    25, 1900.   Later salved; sold to American interest and re-
    named **Coamo.**

State of Florida   (1875)   State Line (British).
    Built by London & Glasgow Shipbuilding Co., Glasgow,
    Scotland.   Tonnage: 3,155.   Dimensions: 371' x 38'.   Single-
    screw, 13½ knots.   Compound engines.   Three masts and
    one funnel.   Iron hull.   Commenced service in October 1874.
    Passengers: 90 cabin, 30 second, 450 third.   Renamed: (a)
    Queen Margaret (1874), (b) **State of Florida** (1880).
    Sunk by collision at sea, April 18, 1884, with the loss of
    108 lives.

State of Georgia   (1873)   State Line (British).
    Built by London & Glasgow Shipbuilding Co., Glasgow,
    Scotland.   Tonnage: 2,490.   Dimensions: 330' x 36'.   Single-

screw, 13 knots. Compound engines. Three masts and one funnel. Iron hull. First voyage: Glasgow-New York, as **State of Georgia** in December 1873. Transferred to Allan Line service in 1891. Sold to other owners in 1893. Disappeared at sea with 32 on board in December 1896. Ex-**Georgia** (1873). Sister ships: **State of Indiana, State of Nevada, State of Pennsylvania** and **State of Virginia.**

State of Indiana (1874) State Line (British).
Built by T. Wingate Co., Glasgow, Scotland. Tonnage: 2,528. Dimensions: 329' x 36'. Single-screw, 13 knots. Compound engines. Three masts and one funnel. Iron hull. Service: Glasgow-New York. Sold to Allan Line in 1891; resold to the Turkish Navy in 1893 and renamed **Ismir.** Sister ships: See **State of Georgia.**

State of Louisiana (1872) State Line (British).
Built by T. Wingate & Co., Glasgow, Scotland. Tonnage: 1,869. Dimensions: 300' x 35'. Single-screw, 12 knots. Compound engines. Three masts and one funnel. Iron hull. Passengers: 30 cabin, 50 second, 200 third. Wrecked at Lough Larne, Ireland, December 24, 1878, while bound from Glasgow to New York. There was no loss of life. Ex-**Louisiana** (1873).

State of Nebraska (1880) State Line (British).
Built by London & Glasgow Shipbuilding Co., Glasgow, Scotland. Tonnage: 3,986. Dimensions: 385' x 43'. Single-screw, 13½ knots. Compound engines. Three masts and one funnel. Iron hull. Service: Glasgow-New York. Sold to Allan Line in 1891. Passengers: 175 first and 826 third class. Scrapped in 1902.

State of Nevada (1874) State Line (British).
Built by London & Glasgow Shipbuilding Co., Glasgow, Scotland. Tonnage: 2,488. Dimensions: 332' x 36'. Single-screw, 13 knots. Compound engines. Three masts and one funnel. Iron hull. Maiden voyage: Glasgow-New York, July 17, 1874. This line was absorbed with the Allan Line in 1891. Vessel was sold. Renamed: **Mekke** (1893) Turkish. Sister ships: See **State of Georgia.**

State of Pennsylvania (1873) State Line (British).
Built by London & Glasgow Shipbuilding Co., Glasgow, Scotland. Tonnage: 2,472. Dimensions: 332' x 36'. Single-screw, 13 knots. Compound engines. Three masts and one funnel. Iron hull. Service: Glasgow-New York. This line

merged with Allan Line in 1891. Renamed: **Medina** Turkish. Later was renamed **Marmora**. Ex-**Pennsylvania** (1873).

State of Virginia   (1873)   State Line (British).
Built by London & Glasgow Shipbuilding Co., Glasgow, Scotland. Tonnage: 2,472. Dimensions 331' x 34'. Single-screw, 13 knots. Compound engines. Three masts and one funnel. Iron hull. First voyage as **State of Virginia** from Glasgow to New York, January 2, 1874. Wrecked off Sable Island, July 15, 1879, with the loss of 9 lives. Ex-**Virginia** (1873). Sister ships: See **State of Georgia.**

Statendam   (1898)   Holland-America Line.
Built by Harland & Wolff, Ltd., Belfast, Ireland. Tonnage: 10,491. Dimensions: 515' x 59' (530' o.l.). Twin-screw, 15 knots. Triple expansion engines. Two masts and one funnel. Commenced her maiden voyage from Rotterdam to New York in August 1898. Renamed: (a) **Scotian** (1911), (b) **Marglen** (1922). Scrapped in Italy, 1927.

Statendam   (1917)   Holland-America Line.
Built by Harland & Wolff, Ltd., Belfast, Ireland. Tonnage: 32,234. Dimensions: 740' x 86'. Triple-screw, 18½ knots. Triple expansion engines and one low pressure steam turbine. Two masts and three funnels. Launched as the **Statendam** in 1914. However, due to the First World War she was taken over by the British Government. Completed as a troopship and renamed **Justicia**. Torpedoed and sunk by submarines, July 19, 1918, off North Ireland while bound for New York to embark troops. There was a loss of 10 lives.

Statendam   (1929)   Holland-America Line.
Built by Harland & Wolff, Ltd., Belfast, Ireland. Tonnage: 29,511. Dimensions: 670' x 81' (698' o.l.). Steam turbines. Two masts and three funnels. Launched at Belfast on September 11, 1924. Work was held up for a time, but eventually was towed to Rotterdam for completion. Maiden voyage: Rotterdam to New York, April 11, 1929. This flag-ship of the Holland-America Line was laid up in September 1939. During the Nazi invasion of the Netherlands, May 1940, she was destroyed by fire. The **Statendam** was among the several vessels that were in the port of Rotterdam at the time. Some of the bitterest fighting took place in the vicinity of the piers where the ships were tied. The **Statendam** was repeatedly hit by the crossfire from both sides of the river. The fire on board continued to blaze for five days and she became a total loss.

*__Statendam__   (1957)   Holland-America Line.
   Built by N. V. Wilton-Fijenoord, Schiedam, Netherlands.
   Tonnage: 24,294.   Dimensions: 578' x 79' (642' o.l.).   Twin-
   screw, 20 knots.   Four steam turbines.   Single mast and one
   funnel.   Built in drydock and was floated out in June 1956.
   Passengers: 84 first and 868 tourist.   Maiden voyage: Rotter-
   dam-Havre-Southampton-New York, February 6, 1957.
   Officers and crew numbered 437.   Besides regular trans-
   Atlantic service, she is used as a cruise ship.   Made a round-
   the-world voyage in 1958.   This liner has high standards for
   tourist class travel.   Every cabin is equipped with telephone.
   Air-conditioned throughout.

*__Stavangerfjord__   (1918)   Norwegian-America Line.
   Built by Cammell, Laird & Co., Birkenhead, England.   Tonnage: 13,156.   Dimensions: 532' x 64' (553' o.l.).   Twin-
   screw, 16 knots.   Quadruple expansion engines.   Two masts
   and two funnels.   Launched in May 1917.   Service: Oslo-
   Bergen-New York.   Converted later to quadruple expansion
   engines and low pressure steam turbines.   In World War II
   served as a troop hotel ship.   Resumed trans-Atlantic service
   in August 1945.   Passengers: 122 first, 222 cabin, 335 tourist.
   Tonnage: 14,015 (1960).   Note: One of the oldest passenger
   liners still in service.

__Steuben__   (1922)   North German Lloyd.
   Built by "Vulkan", Stettin, Germany.   Tonnage: 14,690.
   Dimensions: 526' x 65' (551' o.l.).   Twin-screw, 16 knots.
   Triple expansion engines and steam turbines.   Two masts and
   two funnels.   Sunk by a Russian submarine in the Baltic,
   February 10, 1945, while she had on board about 4,000
   refugees.   The loss of life was extremely high among the
   refugees.   Ex-__General von Steuben__ (1938), ex-__München__
   (1931).

__Stockholm__   (1900)   Swedish-American Line.
   Built by Blohm & Voss, Hamburg, Germany.   Tonnage:
   12,835.   Dimensions: 547' x 62'.   Twin-screw, 15 knots.
   Triple expansion engines.   Two masts and one funnel.   Passengers: 280 first, 210 second, 1,800 third.   Service: Gothenburg-New York.   Sold to other owners (Norwegian) in 1928,
   who had her converted into whaling factory vessel.   Renamed:
   __Solglimt__ (1929).   Captured by the Nazi auxiliary cruiser
   __Pinguin__ in the Antarctic.   She was moved to a French port.
   Scuttled by the Germans at Cherbourg in 1944.   Ex-__Potsdam__
   __(1915)__.

Stockholm   (1939)   Swedish-American Line.

Built by Cantieri Riuniti del Adriatico, Trieste, Italy. Tonnage: 28,000. Dimensions: 642' x 83'. Triple-screw, 19 knots. Motorship. Two masts and two funnels. Launched, May 31, 1938. Note: This beautiful liner when nearing completion was destroyed by fire, December 19, 1938. After a survey of the hull it was decided that the only thing which could be saved was the machinery. Work on a new identical hull was immediately begun. The replacement was also to be named **Stockholm.** Further facts given below.

Stockholm   (1940)   Swedish-American Line.

Built by Cantieri Riuniti del' Adriatico, Trieste, Italy. Tonnage: 28,000. Dimensions: 642' x 83'. Triple-screw, 19 knots. Motorship. Two masts and two funnels. Note: This liner was to replace the previous **Stockholm,** which was destroyed by fire in December 1938. The new ship was launched, March 10, 1940. However, she never was used as a passenger ship. Taken over by Italian Government, and converted to troopship. Renamed: **Sabaudia** (1942). Bombed and sunk at Trieste in July 1944. Subsequently refloated and broken up for scrap.

Stockholm   (1947)   Swedish-American Line.

Built by Gotaverken, Gothenburg, Sweden. Tonnage: 11,650. Dimensions: 510' x 69' (524' o.l.). Twin-screw, 19 knots. Motorship. Single mast and one funnel. Launched, September 9, 1946. Largest ship built to date in Sweden. Resembles a large yacht. Maiden voyage: Gothenburg-New York, February 21, 1948. Passengers: 113 first and 282 tourist. Superstructure was later enlarged, thus her passenger accommodation total was increased to 86 first and 500 tourist. Made the Atlantic crossing in 8 days. In collision near Nantucket with **Andrea Doria,** July 26, 1956. The **Stockholm** was laid up for repairs for several months, and did not resume service until December 1956. Sold to East Germany in late 1959. Renamed: **Volkerfreundschaft** (1960). Note: See **Andrea Doria** for detailed account of the collision.

Strassburg   (1872)   North German Lloyd.

Built by Caird & Co., Greenock, Scotland. Tonnage: 3,025. Dimensions: 351' x 39'. Single-screw, 14 knots. Inverted engines. Two masts and one funnel. Iron hull. Services: (a) Bremen-Southampton-New York, (b) Bremen-Havre-New Orleans. Re-engined with compounds in 1874. Made her final voyage to New York in 1893. Vessel later sold to Hamburg-American Line.

Stuttgart   (1889)   North German Lloyd.
    Built by Fairfield Shipbuilding & Engineering Co., Glasgow,
Scotland. Tonnage: 5,048. Dimensions: 415′ x 48′. Single-
screw, 13 knots. Triple expansion engines. Two masts and
one funnel. Steel hull. Made her final voyage to New York
in 1909. Scrapped in 1909. Sister ships: **Darmstadt, Gera,
Karlsruhe, Oldenburg** and **Weimar.**

Stuttgart   (1923)   North German Lloyd.
    Built by "Vulkan", Stettin, Germany. Tonnage: 13,387.
Dimensions: 526′ x 65′ (551′ o.l.). Twin-screw, 16 knots.
Triple expansion engines. Two masts and two funnels.
Service: Bremen-New York. Bombed and sunk by Allied air
attack on Gdynia, October 9, 1943. Sister ship: **Munchen.**

Sud America   (1868)   La Veloce Line (Italian).
    Built by Caird & Co., Greenock, Scotland. Tonnage: 3,185.
Dimensions: 339′ x 40′. Single-screw, 13 knots. Inverted
engines. Two masts and two funnels. Scrapped in 1901.
Ex-**Mentana** (1890), ex-**Provincia di Sao Paolo** (1889),
ex-**Atlantica** (1888), ex-**Westphalia** (1887). Note: The
Sud America served in both North Atlantic and South
American routes.

Suevia   (1874)   Hamburg-American Line.
    Built by Caird & Co., Greenock, Scotland. Tonnage: 3,624.
Dimensions: 360′ x 41′. Single-screw, 14 knots. Compound
engines. Two masts and one funnel. Iron hull. Launched,
June 1, 1874. Made her final voyage to New York in 1894.
Sold out of service in 1896 to owners in Algiers. Renamed:
Quatre Amis. Sold for scrap in October 1897. Sister ship:
Pommerania.

Suffren   (1901)   French Line.
    Built by Blohm & Voss, Hamburg, Germany. Tonnage:
10,622. Dimensions: 525′ x 62′. Twin-screw, 16 knots.
Quadruple expansion engines. Two masts and two funnels.
Commenced her first voyage as **Suffren** in May 1923. Passengers: 500 cabin and 250 third class. Broken up for scrap
in Italy, 1929. Ex-**Leopoldina** (1923), ex-**Bluecher** (1917).
Note: Also spelled as **Blucher.**

Susquehanna   (1899)   United States Lines.
    Built by Blohm & Voss, Hamburg, Germany. Tonnage:
9,959. Dimensions: 501′ x 58′. Twin-screw, 13½ knots.
Quadruple expansion engines. Four masts and one funnel.
Service: New York-Bremen. Final voyage was made in

August 1922. Sold for scrap to Japan in November 1928
Ex-**Rhein** (1917).

Switzerland   (1874)   Red Star Line (Belgian).
Built by Palmer's Shipbuilding & Iron Co., Jarrow-on-Tyne,
Newcastle, England. Tonnage: 2,957. Dimensions: 329' x
38'.   Single-screw, 13½ knots. Compound engines. Three
masts and one funnel. Engines and boilers were aft. Launched,
January 17, 1874. Service: Antwerp-Philadelphia. Made her
final voyage to New York in 1904.   Renamed: **Sansone**
(1907) Italian. Sister ships: **Nederland** and **Vaderland.**

*****Sydney**   (1944)   Lauro Line (Italian).
Built by Western Pipe & Steel Co., San Francisco, California.
Tonnage: 14,708. Dimensions: 468' x 69' (492' o.l.). Single-
screw, 17 knots. Two steam turbines. Single mast and one
funnel. Passengers: 100 first and 670 tourist. In Liverpool-
Quebec trade in 1953. Services: Genoa-Australia. Originally
in South America trade. Note: Built as a "C-3" type ship
hull. Converted to escort aircraft carrier for the British and
named **Fencer.** The Lauro Line purchased the ship and had
her converted into a passenger ship. Renamed: **Sydney** in
1953. Sister ship: **Roma.**

*****Sylvania**   (1957)   Cunard Line.
Built by John Brown & Co., Clydebank, Glasgow, Scotland.
Tonnage: 21,989. Dimensions: 570' x 80' (608' o.l.). Twin-
screw, 20 knots. Four steam turbines. Single mast and one
funnel. Launched, November 22, 1956. Commenced her
maiden voyage to Quebec and Montreal in June 1957. Passengers: 150 first, 700 tourist class. Built for the Canadian
service, as also were her sister ships: **Carinthia, Ivernia**
and **Saxonia.**

Tampico   (1855)   French Line.
Built by Laird Bros., Liverpool, England. Tonnage: 1,707.
Dimensions: 265' x 37'. Single-screw, 11 knots. Three masts
and one funnel.   Renamed: **Guadeloupe** (1869).   Ex-
Imperator. Sister ship: **Vera Cruz.** Note: They were used
in the West Indies service.

Taormina   (1908)   Lloyd Italiano.
Built by D. & W. Henderson & Co., Glasgow, Scotland.
Tonnage: 8,921. Dimensions: 482' x 58' (520' o.l.). Twin-
screw, 16½ knots. Triple expansion engines. Two masts
and one funnel. Originally built for "Italia" Line, and as
such, served in the service to South America. Commenced

Genoa-New York service for Lloyd Italiano in 1912. Transferred to Navigazione Generale Italiana in 1918. Scrapped in Italy, 1929. Sister ships: **Ancona** and **Verona.**

Tarifa (1865) Cunard Line.
Built by J. & G. Thomson, Glasgow, Scotland. Tonnage: 2,058. Dimensions: 292' x 38'. Single-screw, 11 knots. Inverted engines. Two masts and one funnel. Clipper bow. Iron hull. Service: (a) Liverpool-New York, (b) Liverpool-Boston. (c) Transferred to minor services. Scrapped in 1899. Sister ships: **Aleppo, Malta, Palmyra** and **Tripoli.**

Tarsus (1931) Turkish State Maritime.
Built by New York Shipbuilding Corp., Camden, N. J. Tonnage: 9,359. Dimensions: 453' x 61' (475' o.l.). Single-screw, 16 knots. Steam turbines. Two masts and one funnel. Service: (a) Istanbul-New York, (b) Other routes. Passengers: 190 first, 66 second, 210 third. Turkey's largest passenger ship to date. Destroyed by fire in Bosphorus in December 1960. She had caught fire by a blazing oil tanker that drifted towards her. Ex-**Harry Lee** (1948), ex-**Exochorda** (1940).

Tempest (1855) Anchor Line (British).
Built by Alexander Stephen & Sons, Ltd., Glasgow, Scotland. Tonnage: 866. Dimensions: 214' x 29'. Single-screw, 9 knots. Inverted engines. Three masts and one funnel. Iron hull. Clipper bow. Note: Converted from sail to steam in 1856. Pioneer steamship of the Anchor Line. Made her first voyage from Glasgow to New York in October 1856. Left New York with 150 passengers and crew on board, February 11, 1857, and was never heard of again.

Teresa (1900) Austro-American Line.
Built by Russell & Co., Port Glasgow, Scotland. Tonnage: 3,769. Dimensions: 344' x 49'. Single-screw. Triple expansion engines. Two masts and one funnel. Renamed: **Demokratia.** Not listed after 1933.

Teutonia (1856) Hamburg-American Line.
Built by Caird & Co., Greenock, Scotland. Tonnage: 2,034. Dimensions: 287' x 37'. Single-screw, 10 knots. Geared oscillating engines. Three masts and one funnel. Iron hull. Clipper bow. Originally built for Hamburg-Brazilian Steam Navigation Co. In Hamburg-American Line service, 1859–1867. Sold to Dominion Line in 1877; retained same name. Renamed: (a) **Regina** (1882), (b) **Piemontese** (1899), (c)

Regina (1890), (d) **Mentana** (1891).   Scrapped in 1894.
Sister ship: **Bavaria.**

Teutonic   (1889)   White Star Line.
Built by Harland & Wolff, Ltd., Belfast, Ireland. Tonnage:
9,686.   Dimensions: 565′ x 57′ (582′ o.l.).   Twin-screw, 20
knots.   Triple expansion engines.   19,500 I.H.P.   Three masts
and two funnels.   Steel hull.   Displacement of 16,740 tons.
She had 16 boilers, 76 furnaces.   Consumed 12 tons of coal
per hour to obtain a speed of 20 knots.   Passengers: 300 first,
190 second, 1,000 third.   She won the coveted Blue Ribbon
by beating all previous records by steaming from Queenstown to Sandy Hook in 5 days, 16 hours and 31 minutes,
thus averaging 20.43 knots for the trip.   Sold to Dutch shipbreakers in July 1921, but resold to Germany for scrap in
September 1921.   Sister ship: **Majestic.**   Note: These liners
were built at a cost of $2,000,000 each.

Texas   (1872)   Dominion Line (British).
Built by A. McMillan & Son, Dumbarton, Scotland. Ton-
nage: 2,818. Dimensions: 325′ x 36′. Single-screw, 11 knots.
Compound engines. Three masts and one funnel. Iron hull.
Passengers: 80 cabin and 600 third. Services: (a) Liverpool-
Boston, (b) Liverpool-Quebec-Montreal, (c) Liverpool Gulf
ports. Wrecked near Cape Race, June 4, 1894, with no loss
of life.

The Queen   (1864)   National Line (British).
Built by Laird Bros., Birkenhead, England. Tonnage: 4,471.
Dimensions: 381′ x 42′. Single-screw, 12½ knots. Inverted
engines. Re-engined with compounds in 1874. Three masts
and one funnel. In service 1865–1895. Sold in 1896. Probably broken up for scrap soon after. Note: Tonnage originally
was listed as 3,412. Structural changes increased vessel to
4,471 gross tons.

Themistocles   (1907)   Greek Line.
Built by J. Priestman & Co., Sunderland, England. Tonnage:
6,045. Dimensions: 400′ x 50′. Twin-screw, 13 knots. Triple
expansion engines. Two masts and two funnels. Service:
Greece-New York. Made her final voyage to New York in
1924. Ex-**Moraitis** (1908).

Thessaloniki   (1890)   Greek Line.
Built by Workman, Clark & Co., Belfast, Ireland. Tonnage:
4,682. Dimensions: 412′ x 46′. Single-screw, 12½ knots.
Triple expansion engines. Two masts and one funnel. Sank

after being abandoned in the North Atlantic in 1916. Ex-**City of Vienna** (1913).

Thingvalla (1874) Thingvalla Line.
  Built by Burmeister & Wain, Copenhagen, Denmark. Tonnage: 2,524. Dimensions: 301′ x 37′. Single-screw, 10 knots. Compound engines. Three masts and one funnel. Iron hull. Passengers: 50 first, 50 second, 900 third. Service: Copenhagen-New York. The Scandinavian-American Line acquired vessel in 1898. Made her final voyage to New York in 1900. Sold in November 1900. Renamed: **Aslaug** (Danish).

Thuringia (1870) Hamburg-American Line.
  Built by Caird & Co., Greenock, Scotland. Tonnage: 3,130. Dimensions: 350′ x 40′. Single-screw, 13½ knots. Inverted engines. Two masts and one funnel. Iron hull. Service: Hamburg-Southampton-New York. Sold to Russian Volunteer Fleet in 1878. Renamed: (a) **Petersburg** (1878), (b) **Berezan** (1893) Russian. Sister ship: **Frisia.**

Thuringia (1922) Hamburg-American Line.
  Built by Howaldtswerke, Kiel, Germany. Tonnage: 11,343. Dimensions: 473′ x 60′. Single-screw, 13 knots. Two steam turbines. Two masts and one funnel. Passengers: 150 cabin and 680 third. Service: Hamburg-New York. Entered the Hamburg-South American route in 1930 as the **General San Martin.** Transferred to Hamburg-South American Line ownership in 1936. The liner was surrendered to the British in 1945. Renamed: (a) **General San Martin** (1930), (b) **Empire Deben** (1945). Scrapped in 1949. Sister ship: **Westphalia.**

Timgad (1911) French Line.
  Built by Chantiers & Ateliers de Provence, Port Bouc, France. Tonnage: 5,232. Dimensions: 402′ x 51′. Twin-screw, 18 knots. Triple expansion engines. Two masts and two funnels. Service: In Marseilles-North Africa trade only. Scrapped in 1939. Sister ship: **Carthage.**

Tirpitz (1914) Hamburg-American Line.
  Built by "Vulkan", Stettin, Germany. Tonnage: 21,833. Dimensions: 588′ x 75′. Twin-screw, 19 knots. Steam turbines. Two masts and three funnels. Note: Never operated as a passenger ship for Hamburg-American Line, as she was turned over to the British upon completion. Renamed: (a) **Empress of China** (1922), (b) **Empress of Australia** (1922).

Titanic　(1911)　White Star Line.
　　Built by Harland & Wolff, Ltd., Belfast, Ireland. Tonnage: 46,329. Dimensions: 852′ x 92′ (882′ o.l.). Triple-screw, 21 knots. Two quadruple expansion engines on outside shafts and one low pressure steam turbine on center shaft. Two masts and four funnels. From keel to top of funnels 175 feet high. Keel laid on March 21, 1909. Launched, May 31, 1911. Cost $7,500,000 to build. She had 29 boilers and could make a speed of 23 knots. Displacement of 66,000 tons. Fourth funnel was a dummy, but it enhanced her appearance. This very famous luxury liner commenced her maiden voyage from Southampton to New York, April 10, 1912, with a reported 1,308 passengers and a crew of 898 officers and men. It was on the night of April 14, near midnight, that she struck a giant iceberg at full speed. The submerged part of the iceberg opened up five of the foremost water-tight compartments, thus dooming the liner with such severe damage to her hull. The **Titanic** did not remain afloat long, as she went down into the deep icy cold water of the North Atlantic at 2:20 A.M. on the morning that followed. The staggering loss of life amounted to 815 passengers and 688 of the crew. Sister ship: **Olympic.**

Tomaso di Savoia　(1907)　Lloyd Sabaudo Line.
　　Built by Barclay, Curle & Co., Glasgow, Scotland. Tonnage: 7,914. Dimensions: 450′ x 55′. Twin-screw, 16½ knots. Quadruple expansion engines. Two masts and two funnels. Passengers: 150 first and 1,700 third. Services: (a) Genoa-New York, (b) Genoa-South America. Made her final voyage to New York in 1915. Scrapped in 1928. Sister ship: **Principe di Udine.**

Toronto　(1880)　Dominion Line.
　　Built in Scotland. Tonnage: 3,315. Dimensions: 329′ x 39′. Single-screw, 13 knots. Compound engines. Two masts and one funnel. Service: Liverpool-Quebec-Montreal. Renamed: **Pina** (1894) Italian. Scrapped in 1897. Sister ship: **Montreal.**

Tortona　(1909)　Thomson Line (British).
　　Built by Swan, Hunter & Wigham Richardson, Ltd., Wallsend-on-Tyne, Newcastle, England. Tonnage: 8,153. Dimensions: 450′ x 54′. Single-screw, 13 knots. Triple expansion engines. Four masts and one funnel. Passengers: 50 first and 1,000 third class. Service: England-Canada. Renamed: **Ausonia** (1911) Cunard Line. Torpedoed and sunk in 1918.

Transylvania   (1914)   (a) Cunard Line, (b) Anchor Line.
  Built by Scott's Shipbuilding & Engineering Co., Greenock, Scotland. Tonnage: 14,315. Dimensions: 548' x 66' (565' o.l.). Twin-screw, 16 knots. Four steam turbines. Two masts and two funnels. Maiden voyage: Liverpool-New York, November 7, 1914. Transferred to Anchor Line in February 1915. Note: Liner had originally been intended for Mediterranean-New York service. This plan did not materialize. Designed for 270 first, 250 second, 1,900 third. Torpedoed and sunk near Cape Vado, Gulf of Genoa, May 4, 1917, with the loss of 413 lives. Sister ship: **Tuscania**. First Atlantic liners were geared steam turbines.

Transylvania   (1925)   Anchor Line.
  Built by Fairfield Shipbuilding & Engineering Co., Glasgow, Scotland. Tonnage: 16,923. Dimensions: 552' x 70' (575' o.l.). Twin-screw, 15½ knots. Steam turbines. Two masts and three funnels. Note: The first and third funnels were dummies. Launched, March 11, 1925. Maiden voyage: Glasgow-New York, September 12, 1925. Passengers: 264 first, 458 second, 620 third. Converted to armed merchant cruiser in September 1939. Torpedoed and sunk by German submarine in the North Atlantic, August 10, 1940. Sister ship: **Caledonia.**

Trave   (1886)   North German Lloyd.
  Built by Fairfield Shipbuilding & Engineering Co., Glasgow, Scotland. Tonnage: 5,262. Dimensions: 437' x 48'. Single-screw, 18 knots. Triple expansion engines. Four masts and two funnels. Steel hull. Passengers: 150 first, 90 second, 1,000 third. Services: (a) Bremen-Southampton-New York, (b) Mediterranean-New York. Sold for scrap in September 1908. Sister ships: **Aller** and **Saale.**

Trier   (1924)   North German Lloyd.
  Built by Akt. Ges. "Weser", Bremen, Germany. Tonnage: 9,415. Dimensions: 458' x 57'. Twin-screw, 13 knots. Triple expansion engines. Two masts and one funnel. Passengers: 100 cabin and 800 third. Service: Bremen-Montreal. Running mates in this Canadian trade were **Crefeld** and **Koln** during 1930. The **Trier** was sold to Turkey in 1936. Renamed: **Erkin.**

Trinacria   (1871)   Anchor Line (British).
  Built by Robert Duncan & Co., Port Glasgow, Scotland. Tonnage: 2,051. Increased to 2,256 in 1882 by alterations. Dimensions: 306' x 34'. Single-screw, 11 knots. Compound

engines. Three masts and one funnel. Iron hull. Passengers: 75 first, 100 second, 500 third. In various Anchor Line services. Wrecked off Corunna, Portugal, February 7, 1893. Sister ships: **Alexandria, Assyria, Castalia, Ismailia, Italia** and **Olympia.**

Tripoli (1864) Cunard Line.
Built by J. & G. Thomson, Glasgow, Scotland. Tonnage: 2,058. Dimensions: 280' x 38'. Single-screw, 11 knots. Inverted engines. Two masts and one funnel. Passengers: 50 first and 650 third. Built for Mediterranean trade, but also, made voyages to New York and Boston. Wrecked on Tuskar Rocks, May 17, 1872, with no loss of life. Running mates: **Aleppo, Malta, Palmyra** and **Tarifa.**

Tunisian (1900) Allan Line.
Built by Alexander Stephen & Sons, Ltd., Glasgow, Scotland. Tonnage: 10,576. Dimensions: 500' x 59'. Twin-screw, 16 knots. Triple expansion engines. Two masts and one funnel. Passengers: 240 first, 220 second, 1,000 third. Commenced her maiden voyage from Liverpool to Canada in April 1900. Transferred to Canadian Pacific Line during World War II. Renamed: **Marburn** (1922). Scrapped in 1928. Sister ship: **Bavarian.**

Tuscania (1915) Anchor Line.
Built by Alexander Stephen & Sons, Ltd., Glasgow, Scotland. Tonnage: 14,348. Dimensions: 548' x 66' (567' o.l.). Twin-screw, 17 knots. Steam turbines. Two masts and two funnels. Launched in September 1914. Passengers: 271 first, 246 second, 1,900 third. Maiden voyage: Glasgow-Liverpool-New York, February 6, 1915. Commissioned as a British troopship in First World War. Torpedoed and sunk 7 miles from Rathlin Light (Ireland), February 5, 1918, with the loss of 44 lives. Sister ship: **Transylvania.** Note: The Cunard Line had control of the Anchor Line during the period these sister ships existed. They had planned to use the liners in a joint Mediterranean-New York service.

Tuscania (1922) Anchor Line.
Built by Fairfield Shipbuilding & Engineering Co., Glasgow, Scotland. Tonnage: 16,991. Dimensions: 552' x 70' (575' o.l.). Twin-screw, 15½ knots. Four steam turbines. Two masts and one funnel. Launched, October 4, 1921. Passengers: 267 first, 377 second, 1,800 third. Maiden voyage: Glasgow-New York, September 16, 1922. Renamed: (a) **Nea Hellas** (1939), (b) **Tuscania** (1941) British troopship,

(c) **Nea Hellas** (1947), (d) **New York** (1955). Sister ship: **California.**

Tyrolia (1900) Canadian Pacific Line.
Built by Barclay, Curle & Co., Glasgow, Scotland. Tonnage: 7,535. Dimensions: 446′ x 52′. Twin-screw, 13 knots. Triple expansion engines. Four masts and one funnel. In Trieste-Quebec-Montreal service 1913–1914. Renamed: (a) **Aspenleaf** (1914), (b) **Prygona** (1919). Scrapped in 1925. Ex-**Lake Erie** (1913). Sister ship: **Ruthenia.**

Tyrrhenia (1922) Cunard Line.
Built by Wm. Beardmore & Co., Glasgow, Scotland. Tonnage: 16,243. Dimensions: 552′ x 70′. Twin-screw, 17 knots. Steam turbines. Two masts and two funnels. Originally laid down for the Anchor Line, but was transferred to Cunard Line ownership before launching. Maiden voyage: Glasgow-Quebec-Montreal, June 13, 1922. The name **Tyrrhenia** *was not popular.* It was changed to **Lancastria** in 1924. Note: See **Lancastria** for additional information.

Ultonia (1898) Cunard Line.
Built by Swan & Hunter, Ltd., Wallsend-on-Tyne, Newcastle, England. Tonnage: 10,402. Dimensions: 500′ x 57′. Twin-screw, 13 knots. Triple expansion engines. Four masts and one funnel. Maiden voyage: Liverpool-Boston, February 28, 1899. Transferred to Trieste-New York service in 1904. Torpedoed and sunk without warning 190 miles from Fastnet, June 27, 1917, with loss of one life.

Umbria (1884) Cunard Line.
Built by John Elder & Co., Govan, Glasgow, Scotland. Tonnage: 8,127. Dimensions: 501′ x 57′ (520′ o.l.). Single-screw, 19½ knots. Compound engines. 15,000 I.H.P. Three masts and two funnels. Steel hull. Note: The shipbuilder later became known as Fairfield Shipbuilding & Engineering Co., Ltd. The **Umbria** commenced her maiden voyage from Liverpool to New York on November 1, 1884. Won the trans-Atlantic speed record in May 1887 by making the westward crossing in 6 days, 4 hours, 42 minutes, averaging 18.89 knots for the run. She consumed 10 tons of coal per hour to obtain a speed of 19 knots. Scrapped in 1910. Sister ship: **Etruria.**

Umbria (1902) Navigazione Generale Italiana.
Built by Orlando, Leghorn, Italy. Tonnage: 5,021. Dimensions: 401′ x 46′. Single-screw, 14 knots. Quadruple expan-

sion engines. Two masts and one funnel. Built for the Italy-South American route. Made some Genoa-Naples-New York sailings. Renamed: (a) **Umbria** (1913) La Veloce Line, (b) **San Paulo** (1913) "Italia" Line, (c) **Umbria** (1914) Sitmar Line.

Unicorn (1836)   Cunard Line.
Built by Robert Steele & Son, Greenock, Scotland. Tonnage: 648. Dimensions: 163' x 23' (185' o.l.). Paddle-wheels, 8 knots. Side lever engines. Three masts and one funnel. Clipper bow. Wooden hull. Note: This vessel actually made the first sailing for the Cunard Line. She originally had been built as a three-masted schooner for G. & J. Burns, for service between Glasgow and Liverpool. However, she was purchased by the newly-formed British & North American Royal Mail Steam Packet Company, which afterwards became known as the Cunard Line. Commenced her first voyage as a Cunarder on May 16, 1840, taking 14 days to make the Liverpool-Halifax crossing. She carried 24 passengers, including Samuel Cunard's son Edward, on this pioneer voyage. The **Unicorn** was then transferred to the Gulf of St. Lawrence service. The vessel was sold in the mid-1840's. Later was used in coastal service of Pacific Ocean.

Union (1866)   North German Lloyd.
Built by Caird & Co., Greenock, Scotland. Tonnage: 2,873. Dimensions: 337' x 40'. Single-screw, 10½ knots. Inverted engines. Two masts and one funnel. Iron hull. Launched, October 27, 1866. Maiden voyage: Bremen-Southampton-New York in January 1867. Wrecked near Scotland, November 28, 1870, with no loss of life. Sister ships: **America, Deutschland, Hansa, Hermann** and **Weser.**

United Kingdom (1857)   Anchor Line (British).
Built by Robert Steele & Son, Greenock, Scotland. Tonnage: 1,264. Dimensions: 245' x 32'. Single-screw, 10 knots. Inverted engines. Three masts and one funnel. Clipper bow. Iron hull. Service: (a) Glasgow-Canada, (b) Glasgow-New York. Sailed from New York with 80 people bound for Glasgow, April 19, 1869, and was never heard of again.

United States (1848)   Black Ball Line (United States).
Built by William H. Webb, New York, N. Y. Tonnage: 1,857. Dimensions: 245' x 40'. Paddle-wheels, 10 knots. Side lever engines. Three masts and one funnel. Clipper hull. Wooden hull. Made her first voyage from New York to England in April 1848. Sold in 1849. Renamed: (a) **Hansa**

(1849) German, (b) **Indian Empire** (1858) British. Destroyed by fire at Deptford, England, while undergoing overhaul, July 23, 1862.

United States   (1860)   Anchor Line (British).
Built by Tod & McGregor, Glasgow, Scotland. Tonnage: 1,197. Dimensions: 250′ x 32′. Single-screw, 10 knots. Inverted engines. Three masts and one funnel. Clipper bow. Iron hull. Wrecked on Bird Rock in the Gulf of St. Lawrence, April 25, 1961.

United States   (1903)   Scandinavian-American Line (Danish).
Built by Alexander Stephen & Sons, Ltd., Glasgow, Scotland. Tonnage: 10,095. Dimensions: 500′ x 58′ (515′ o.l.). Twin-screw, 16 knots. Triple expansion engines. Two masts and one funnel. Service: Copenhagen-Oslo-New York. Passengers: 130 first, 140 second, 900 third. Withdrawn from service in 1934. Broken up for scrap in 1935. Sister ships: **Hellig Olav** and **Oscar II.**

*****United States**   (1952)   United States Lines.
Built by Newport News Shipbuilding & Dry Dock Co., Newport News, Va. Tonnage: 53,329. Dimensions: 916′ x 101′ (990′ o.l.). Quadruple-screw, 30 knots (service speed). Steam turbines. Single mast and two funnels. Her keel was laid in drydock, February 8, 1950. Floated out of drydock on June 23, 1951. Completed her builder's trials by May 16, 1952. Largest merchant ship built to date in America. From keel to top of forward funnel 175 feet high. From keel to top of superstructure is 122 feet. Twelve decks. Cost about $73,000,000 to build. Has capacity to transport 14,000 fully-equipped fighting men. Her beam of 101½ feet will permit passage of the liner through the Panama Canal locks. Passengers: 888 first, 524 cabin, 544 tourist class. Commenced her maiden voyage from New York to Havre and Southampton, at about noon on July 3, 1952. Her epic record-breaking North Atlantic crossing from Ambrose Lightship to Bishop Rock, was timed at 3 days, 10 hours, 40 minutes, with an average speed of 35.59 knots. This fast passage shattered by a wide margin the best previous record run of the former Blue Ribbon holder **Queen Mary.** On the fourth day of this historic eastward crossing, the **United States** steamed 833 miles in 23 hours, averaging 36.21 knots for the distance. Thus a century had passed since an American steamship had won the trans-Atlantic speed record. The return trip of the **United States** was equally as thrilling and

fast. The westward sailing commenced on July 10, and was completed in the short time of 3 days, 12 hours, at an average speed of 34.51 knots. Therefore, the eastward and westward speed records were broken by her famous maiden voyage. Her potential speed is greater than 36 knots. Note: Gross tonnage now (1961) listed as 51,987. As of 1960 had accommodation for a total of 1,725 passengers: first, cabin and tourist.

Uranium   (1891)   Uranium Line (British).
Built by Wm. Denny & Bros., Ltd., Dumbarton, Scotland. Tonnage: 5,189. Dimensions: 420′ x 48′. Single-screw, 14½ knots. Quadruple expansion engines. Three masts and one funnel. Service: Rotterdam-New York. Made her final voyage to New York in 1914. Renamed: **Feltria** (1916) British. Torpedoed and sunk, May 5, 1917. Ex-**Avoca** (1909), ex-**Atlanta**, ex-**Avoca**, ex-**San Fernando**, ex-**Avoca**.

Utopia   (1874)   Anchor Line (British).
Built by Robert Duncan & Co., Port Glasgow, Scotland. Tonnage: 2,731. Dimensions: 350′ x 35′. Single-screw, 12½ knots. Compound engines. Two masts and one funnel. Iron hull. Launched, February 14, 1874. Maiden voyage: Glasgow-New York in April 1874. Re-engined with triple expansions in 1891. Sank after being in collision in Gibraltar Bay, March 17, 1891, with the loss of 563 lives. Sister ship: **Elysia.**

Vaderland   (1873)   Red Star Line (Belgian).
Built by Palmer's Shipbuilding & Iron Co., Jarrow-on-Tyne, Newcastle, England. Tonnage: 2,748. Dimensions: 320′ x 38′. Single-screw, 13½ knots. Compound engines. Three masts and one funnel. Iron hull. Launched, August 21, 1872. Note: Pioneer steamship of the Red Star Line. Maiden voyage: Antwerp-Philadelphia, January 19, 1873. The engine and boiler rooms were aft. Sold to French owners in March 1889. Renamed: **Geographique.** Sister ships: **Nederland** and **Switzerland.**

Vaderland   (1900)   Red Star Line.
Built by John Brown & Co., Clydebank, Glasgow, Scotland. Tonnage: 11,899. Dimensions: 560′ x 60′ (580′ o.l.). Twin-screw, 15 knots. Quadruple expansion engines. Four masts and two funnels. Launched, July 12, 1900. Service: Antwerp-New York. Passengers: 340 first, 200 second, 600 third. Renamed: **Southland** (1915) British. Converted to troopship. Torpedoed and sunk 140 miles from Tory Island, June

4, 1917, with the loss of 4 lives. Sister ships: **Finland, Kroonland** and **Zeeland.**

Vancouver   (1883)   Dominion Line (British).
Built by Charles Connell & Co., Glasgow, Scotland. Tonnage: 5,232. Dimensions: 430' x 45'. Single-screw, 14 knots. Compound engines. Four masts and two funnels. Iron hull. Note: This vessel was built as the **Vancouver** for Dominion Line, but was purchased by Inman Line while in the course of construction. She was renamed **City of Chicago.**

Vancouver   (1884)   Dominion Line (British).
Built by Charles Connell & Co., Glasgow, Scotland. Tonnage: 5,141. Dimensions: 431' x 45'. Single-screw, 14 knots. Compound engines. Four masts and two funnels. Iron hull. Built as a replacement to the previous **Vancouver** that was sold to Inman Line. Triple expansion engines installed in 1893; also converted to single funnel. Scrapped in 1910.

Vandalia   (1871)   Hamburg-American Line.
Built by Caird & Co., Greenock, Scotland. Tonnage: 2,815. Dimensions: 330' x 39'. Single-screw, 11 knots. Compound engines. Two masts and one funnel. Iron hull. Launched, April 22, 1871. In Hamburg-West Indies service. Renamed: (a) **Kehrwieder** (1888) German, (b) **Polonia** (1895) German.

Vanderbilt   (1855)   Vanderbilt Line (United States).
Built by Jeremiah Simonson, New York, N. Y. Tonnage: 3,360. Dimensions: 340' x 49'. Paddle-wheels, 13 knots. Vertical beam engines. Two masts and two funnels. Wooden hull. Passengers: 350. Considered a fast vessel for her time. Acquired by United States Navy during the Civil War. Converted to sail in 1873. Renamed: **Three Brothers** (1873). Finally sold to the Anchor Line and used as a coal hulk in Gibraltar. Broken up for scrap in 1929.

Vasco Nunez de Balboa   (1891)   Spanish Line.
Built by Wm. Denny & Bros., Ltd., Dumbarton, Scotland. Tonnage: 8,063. Dimensions: 531' x 54'. Twin-screw, 16 knots. Triple expansion engines. Two masts and two funnels. Vessel was purchased by Spanish Line in 1916. Scrapped in Italy, 1927. Ex-**Alfonso XIII,** ex-**Oceana,** ex-**Scot** (1905).

Vasconia   (1899)   Fabre Line.
Built by Russell & Co., Port Glasgow, Scotland. Tonnage: 3,281. Dimensions: 348' x 45'. Single-screw. Sold to Scandinavian owners in April 1907. Ex-**Anaxo.**

Vasilefs Constantinos   (1914)   Greek Line.
Built by Cammell, Laird & Co., Birkenhead, England. Tonnage: 9,272. Dimensions: 470′ x 58′. Twin-screw, 17 knots. Quadruple expansion engines. Two masts and two funnels. Launched, June 9, 1914. Construction held up during the war. Her name was changed to **Megali Hellas.** Maiden voyage from Piraeus to New York in 1920. Renamed: **Byron** (1923). Sister ship: **Vasilissa Sophia.**

Vasilissa Sophia   (1914)   Greek Line.
Built by Cammell, Laird & Co., Birkenhead, England. Tonnage: 9,272. Dimensions: 470′ x 58′. Twin-screw, 17 knots. Quadruple expansion engines. Two masts and two funnels. Note: Never used as a trans-Atlantic passenger ship, because the British Government took possession of the liner when completed, in order to convert her to troopship. Renamed: **Leasowe Castle** (Union-Castle Line, management.) Torpedoed and sunk, May 26, 1918, with the loss of 101 lives. Sister ship: **Vasilefs Constantinos.**

Vaterland   (1914)   Hamburg-American Line.
Built by Blohm & Voss, Hamburg, Germany. Tonnage: 54,282. Dimensions: 907′ x 100′ (950′ o.l.). Quadruple-screw, 24 knots. Steam turbines. Two masts and three funnels. She had a draft of 39′6″. This very impressive looking liner commenced her maiden voyage: Hamburg-Southampton-Cherbourg-New York, May 14, 1914. Seized by the United States in 1917 and converted to troopship. Renamed: **Leviathan** (1917). Reconditioned for the United States Lines after the war. The **Leviathan** began her first sailing as an American passenger ship on July 4, 1923. Scrapped in 1938. Running mates: **Imperator** and **Bismarck** (Never in actual service under this name.)

Vaterland   (1940)   Hamburg-American Line.
Built by Blohm & Voss, Hamburg, Germany. Tonnage: 36,000. Launched in 1940. This interesting unfinished passenger liner was heavily damaged by air attacks on Hamburg during World War II. The bombed hulk was broken up for scrap in 1948.

Vedic   (1918)   White Star Line.
Built by Harland & Wolff, Ltd., Belfast, Ireland. Tonnage: 9,332. Dimensions: 460′ x 58′. Twin-screw, 13 knots. Steam turbines. Two masts and one funnel. Passengers: 1,250 third class. Mainly in Canadian trade. This odd looking vessel was scrapped in 1934.

Veendam   (1873)   Holland-American Line.
Built by Harland & Wolff, Ltd., Belfast, Ireland. Tonnage:
3,707.   Dimensions: 420′ x 40′.   Single-screw, 14 knots.
Compound engines. Four masts and one funnel. Iron hull.
Passengers: 150 first, 60 second, 800 third. Service: Rotter-
dam-New York. Foundered at sea after hitting a derelict,
February 6, 1898.   Fortunately there was no loss of life.
Ex-**Baltic** (1888).

Veendam   (1923)   Holland-American Line.
Built by Harland & Wolff, Ltd., Govan, Glasgow, Scotland.
Tonnage: 15,450. Dimensions: 550′ x 67′ (576′ o.l.). Twin-
screw, 15 knots. Four steam turbines. Two masts and two
funnels. Maiden voyage: Rotterdam-New York, April 18,
1923. Slightly damaged by fire at Rotterdam in May 1940.
The liner was seized by the Germans and used as a submarine-
tender in the Baltic, first at Gdynia, afterwards at Hamburg.
After the German surrender, the liner was salved and towed
to Amsterdam to be reconditioned. Re-entered trans-
Atlantic service early in 1947. Passengers: 222 first and 330
tourist. Scrapped at Baltimore in 1953. Sister ship: **Volendam.**

Venezia   (1907)   Fabre Line.
Built by Swan, Hunter & Wigham Richardson, Ltd., Wallsend-on-Tyne, Newcastle, England.   Tonnage: 6,707.
Dimensions: 457′ x 51′. Twin-screw, 15½ knots. Triple
expansion engines. Two masts and one funnel. Launched,
April 30, 1907. Passengers: 80 first and 1,800 third. Service:
Mainly Marseilles-New York. Destroyed by fire while on
voyage from Cuba to France, October 19, 1919. She was
under charter to the French Line at the time.

Venezuela   (1905)   French Line.
Built by Cantieri Liguria, Ancona, Italy. Tonnage: 4,772.
Dimensions: 394′ x 47′.   Twin-screw, 14 knots.   Triple
expansion engines. Two masts and two funnels. Lost at
Casablanca on March 7, 1920. Ex-**Brasilie** (1912), ex-
Argentina.

Vera Cruz   (1855)   French Line.
Built by Laird & Co., Liverpool, England. Tonnage: 1,739.
Dimensions: 265′ x 37′. Single-screw, 11 knots. Three masts
and one funnel. Renamed: **Martinique** (1869). Ex-
Imperatrix (1862). Sister ship: **Tampico.**

Verona   (1908)   Navigazione Generale Italiana.
Built by Workman, Clark & Co., Belfast, Ireland. Tonnage:
8,886. Dimensions: 482′ x 58′. Twin-screw, 16 knots. Triple

expansion engines. Two masts and one funnel. Made her first Genoa-New York sailing as a N.G.I. liner in 1913. Originally built for "Italia" Line. She also had been used in the Italy-South American service. Made her final voyage to New York in 1915. Sunk near Punta Pellaro, May 11, 1918. Sister ships: **Ancona** and **Taormina.**

Vicksburg (1871) Dominion Line (British).
Built by A. McMillan & Son, Dumbarton, Scotland. Tonnage: 2,484. Dimensions: 317' x 38'. Single-screw, 11 knots. Compound engines. Three masts and one funnel. Iron hull. Passengers: 80 first and 600 third. Mainly in England-Gulf trade. Struck an iceberg off Newfoundland, June 2, 1875 and sank with the loss of 47 lives. Sister ship: **Memphis.**

Victoria (1872) Anchor Line (British).
Built by Robert Duncan & Co., Port Glasgow, Scotland. Tonnage: 3,358. Dimensions: 360' x 40'. Single-screw, 13 knots. Compound engines. Three masts and one funnel. Iron hull. Passengers: 170 first, 100 second, 700 third. Launched, May 7, 1872. Maiden voyage: Glasgow-New York, November 2, 1872. Served on various Anchor Line routes. Made her final voyage to New York in 1904. Scrapped in Italy, 1905. Sister ship: **California.**

Victoria (1898) Wilson-Furness Line (British).
Built by Furness, Withy & Co., West Hartlepool, England. Tonnage: 6,849. Dimensions: 475' x 52'. Single-screw, 14 knots. Triple expansion engines. Four masts and one funnel. Service: London-New York. Renamed: (a) **Mantou** (1898), (b) **Poland,** (c) **Natale** (1925). Scrapped in 1925. Sister ship: **Alexandra.**

Victoria Luise (1899) Hamburg-American Line.
Built by "Vulkan", Stettin, Germany. Tonnage: 16,502. Dimensions: 660' x 67'. Twin-screw, 18 knots. Quadruple expansion engines. Two masts and four funnels. Note: Served as a cruise ship, but did make some Hamburg-New York sailings. As the **Victoria Luise,** had some of her boilers removed, thus reducing her speed to 16½ knots. Recovered in a deplorable condition at Hamburg after First World War. Reconditioned and converted to emigrant carrier. Renamed: **Hansa** (1922). Scrapped in 1925. Ex-**Deutschland** (1911).

Victorian (1895) Leyland Line (British).
Built by Harland & Wolff, Ltd., Belfast, Ireland. Tonnage: 8,825. Dimensions: 512' x 59'. Single-screw, 13 knots. Triple

expansion engines. Four masts and one funnel. Passengers: 60 first class. Service: Liverpool-Boston. Transferred to White Star Line in 1903. Renamed: **Russian** (1914). Torpedoed and sunk near Malta, December 14, 1916. Sister ships: **Armenian, Bohemian** and **Cestrian.**

Victorian (1904) Allan Line (British).
Built by Workman, Clark & Co., Belfast, Ireland. Tonnage: 10,629. Dimensions: 517′ x 60′ (540′ o.l.). Triple-screw, 19 knots. Steam turbines. Two masts and one funnel. Note: The first trans-Atlantic steamship to be fitted with steam turbines. Her keel was laid in June 1904. Launched in April 1904. Ran her trials in March 1905, reaching a speed of 19½ knots on the measured mile. Commenced her maiden voyage from Liverpool to Canada in April 1905. Passengers: 470 first, 240 second, 940 third. Ownership of this world famous liner was transferred to Canadian Pacific Line in 1917. Renamed: **Marloch** (1922). Scrapped in 1930. Sister ship: **Virginian.**

Vigo (1855) Compagnie Franco-Americaine.
Built by Laird Bros., Birkenhead, England. Tonnage: 1,610. Dimensions: 270′ x 36′. Single-screw, 10 knots. Horizontal engines. Three masts and one funnel. Clipper bow. Iron hull. First voyage as **Vigo** from Havre to New York in July 1856. Acquired by Inman Line in 1858. Enlarged to 1,950 tons. In Inman Line service until May 1861. Sold to United States Government. Sister ships: **Barcelona** and **Cadiz.**

Ville de Bordeaux (1870) French Line.
Built by Chantiers de l'Ocean, Bordeaux, France. Tonnage: 2,670. Dimensions: 289′ x 41′. Twin-screw, 12½ knots. Compound engines. Three masts and one funnel. Iron hull. Noted as a pioneer example of *twin-screw* steamship. Service: France-West Indies-Central America. Scrapped in 1899. Sister ships: **Ville de Brest** and **Ville de St. Nazaire.**

Ville de Brest (1870) French Line.
Built by Chantiers de l'Ocean, Bordeaux, France. Tonnage: 2,676. Dimensions: 284′ x 42′. Twin-screw, 12½ knots. Compound engines. Three masts and one funnel. Iron hull. Service: France-West Indies-Central America. Scrapped in 1899. Sister ships: **Ville de Bordeaux** and **Ville de St. Nazaire.**

Ville de Marseille (1874) French Line.
Built by A. & J. Inglis, Ltd., Glasgow, Scotland. Tonnage: 2,836. Dimensions: 349′ x 38′. Single-screw, 13 knots.

Compound engines. Three masts and one funnel. Iron hull. Commenced her maiden voyage from Marseilles to Panama, June 14, 1879. Scrapped at Genoa in 1902. **Ex-Stad Amsterdam** (1879). Sister ship: **Ferdinand de Lesseps.**

Ville de Paris   (1866)   French Line.
Built by Robert Napier & Sons, Glasgow, Scotland. Tonnage: 3,014. Dimensions: 344' x 43'. Single-screw, 13½ knots. Inverted type engines. Three masts and one funnel. Iron hull. Launched in December 1865. Maiden voyage: France-New York in May 1866. Note: Originally designed as paddle-wheel steamer, but converted to single-screw before launching date. Re-engined with compounds in 1874; a second funnel was added. Sold to German owners in June 1888 and converted to sailing barque. Renamed: **H. Bischoff.** Stranded in River Elbe and became a total loss, October 28, 1900. Sister ship: **Pereire.**

Ville de St. Nazaire   (1870)   French Line.
Built by Chantiers de l'Ocean, Bordeaux, France. Tonnage: 2,623. Dimensions: 285' x 41'. Twin-screw, 12½ knots. Compound engines. Three masts and one funnel. Service: France-West Indies-Central America (St. Nazaire-Vera Cruz). Foundered at sea off the Carolina coast, March 8, 1897, with heavy loss of life. Sister ships: **Ville de Bordeaux** and **Ville de Brest.**

Ville du Havre   (1866)   French Line.
Built by Thames Ironworks Co., Blackwall, London, England. Tonnage: 5,065. Dimensions: 413' x 43'. Single-screw, 13½ knots. Compound engines. Three masts and two funnels. Iron hull. Commenced service as **Ville du Havre** in 1873. Note: Prior to being renamed, she was converted from paddle-wheels to screw propulsion, and also, lengthened from 363 feet to 413 feet. Her side lever engines were replaced with compounds. Speed increased from 11½ knots to 13½ knots. Her span of life was very brief, as she was in collision with sailing ship **Loch Earn** in English Channel, November 22, 1873, while bound from New York to Havre. For only fifteen minutes did she remain afloat before plunging to the bottom, with the loss of life running well over 200. Ex-**Napoleon III.**

Vincenzo Florio   (1880)   Navigazione Generale Italiana.
Built by Alexander Stephen & Sons, Ltd., Glasgow, Scotland. Tonnage: 2,840. Dimensions: 352' x 38'. Single-screw, 12½ knots. Compound engines. Three masts and one funnel.

Clipper bow. Iron hull. Maiden voyage from Palermo to New York in 1880. Made her final voyage to New York in 1906. Transferred to Italy-South American route. Passengers: 20 first, 24 second and a large number of steerage passengers. Sister ships: **Archimede** and **Washington.**

Virginia   (1863)   National Line.
  Built by Palmer's Shipbuilding & Iron Co., Newcastle, England. Tonnage: 2,876. Dimensions: 325′ x 41′. Single-screw, 10 knots. Inverted engines. Three masts and one funnel. Iron hull. Clipper bow. Service: Liverpool-New York. Lengthened in 1872 to 391 feet (4,310 tons) and re-engined with compounds. Renamed: **Greece** (1872).

Virginia   (1906)   Austro-American Line.
  Built by Craig, Taylor & Co., Stockton, England. Tonnage: 3,563. Dimensions: 326′ x 42′. Single-screw, 12½ knots. Triple expansion engines. Two masts and one funnel. Renamed: **Kerlew.** Sister ship: **Irene.**

Virginia   (1906)   Lloyd Italiano.
  Built by Soc. Esercizio Bacini, Riva Trigoso, Italy. Tonnage: 5,181. Dimensions: 381′ x 48′. Twin-screw, 14½ knots. Triple expansion engines. Two masts and two funnels. Maiden voyage: Genoa-New York in October 1906. She was also in Italy-South America trade. Renamed: **Garibaldi** (1912). Bombed and sunk at Genoa in 1944. Sister ships: **Florida, Indiana** and **Luisiana.**

*Virginia de Churruca   (1949)   Spanish Line.
  Built by Union Naval de Levante, Valencia, Spain. Tonnage: 6,518. Dimensions: 374′ x 55′ (401′ o.l.). Single-screw, 16 knots. Motorship. Two masts and one funnel. Passengers: 65 first, 54 cabin, 82 tourist. Service: Mediterranean-Caribbean-Cuba-Central America. Sister ship: **Satrustegui.**

Virginian   (1905)   Allan Line (British).
  Built by Alexander Stephen & Sons, Ltd., Glasgow, Scotland. Tonnage: 10,754. Dimensions: 520′ x 60′ (540′ o.l.). Triple-screw, 19 knots. Three steam turbines. Two masts and one funnel. Attained a speed of 19.8 knots during her trials. Nine boilers. Steam pressure of 180 lbs. per sq. in. Consumed about 2,500 tons of coal per voyage. Maiden voyage: Liverpool-Canada, April 6, 1905. She broke the Liverpool-Rimouski speed record, as she made it in 5 days, 20 hours, 40 minutes. She and her sister ship **Victorian** remained the fastest liners in the Canadian trade, until the

new Canadian Pacific liners **Empress of Britain** and
Empress of Ireland entered the service. Ownership of the
Virginian was transferred to Canadian Pacific Line in 1917.
Renamed: (a) **Drottningholm** (1920), (b) **Brasil** (1948),
(c) **Homeland** (1951). Scrapped in Italy, 1955. Sister ship:
Victorian. Note: These popular ships were the first trans-
Atlantic liners to be equipped with steam turbines.

Vittoria   (1871)   La Veloce Line (Italian).
Built by Harland & Wolff, Ltd., Belfast, Ireland. Tonnage:
3,707. Dimensions: 420' x 40'. Single-screw, 14½ knots.
Compound engines. Four masts and one funnel. Iron hull.
Renamed: **Citta di Napoli** (1902). Scrapped in 1910. Ex-
Maasdam (1902), ex-**Republic** (1889).

Vladimir   (1895)   Russian Volunteer Fleet.
Built by Wm. Denny & Bros., Ltd., Dumbarton, Scotland.
Tonnage: 5,621. Dimensions: 432' x 49'. Twin-screw, 12½
knots. Triple expansion engines. Two masts and one funnel. Clipper bow. Made her final voyage to New York
in 1919.

Volendam   (1922)   Holland-America Line.
Built by Harland & Wolff, Ltd., Govan, Glasgow, Scotland.
Tonnage: 15,434. Dimensions: 550' x 67' (576' o.l.). Twin-
screw, 15 knots. Four steam turbines. Two masts and two
funnels. Passengers: 1,800 in three classes. Maiden voyage
from Rotterdam to New York, November 4, 1922. Torpedoed by German submarine off the Irish coast, August
30, 1940. However, she was able to make port and after ten
months of repair work re-entered service as a troopship.
Returned to the Holland-America Line after the war and
was reconditioned for further service. Made her final trans-
Atlantic voyage in November 1951. Accommodation provided for 250 first and 335 tourist class. Scrapped in 1952.
Sister ship: **Veendam.**

Volturno   (1906)   Canadian Northern Steamship Co.
Built by Fairfield Shipbuilding & Engineering Co., Glasgow,
Scotland. Tonnage: 3,602. Dimensions: 340' x 43'. Twin-
screw, 14 knots. Triple expansion engines. Two masts and
one funnel. Could accommodate 1,000 immigrants. First
sailing for the line was from Rotterdam to New York in
1910. Ran for the Uranium Line from 1910 to 1913. Destroyed by fire in the North Atlantic, October 9, 1913, with
the loss of 136 lives. The Cunarder **Carmania** was notable
among the ships that rescued the survivors.

*Vulcania   (1928)   (a) Cosulich Line, (b) Italia Line.
Built by Cantieri Riuniti dell' Adriatico, Monfalcone, Italy.
Tonnage: 23,970. Dimensions: 601' x 79' (631' o.l.). Twin-
screw, 19 knots. Motorship. Two masts and one funnel.
Launched, December 18, 1926. Maiden voyage: Trieste-
New York, December 19, 1928. Passengers: 1,700 in four
classes. New oil engines of 26,000 s.h.p. installed in 1935.
Speed increased to 21 knots. Converted to American troopship in World War II. The liner was returned to Italy early
in 1947. Reconditioned for trans-Atlantic service. Tonnage
increased to 24,496. Since resuming regular service she was
used on the Genoa-Naples-New York route until 1955, when
she was once again placed in the Trieste-New York trade.
Passengers: 240 first, 270 cabin, 860 tourist. Sister ship:
Saturnia. Note: Largest motorships built to date.

W. A. Scholten   (1874)   Holland-America Line.
Built by Robert Napier & Sons, Glasgow, Scotland. Tonnage: 2,529. Dimensions: 351' x 38'. Single-screw, 10 knots.
Compound engines. Three masts and one funnel. Clipper
bow. Iron hull. Launched, February 16, 1874. Passengers:
50 first and 600 third. Foundered in fog after collision with
British collier **Rosa Mary** in the English Channel, November 19, 1887, with the loss of about 130 lives. Sister ship:
P. Caland.

Waesland   (1867)   Red Star Line.
Built by J. & G. Thomson, Ltd., Clydebank, Glasgow, Scotland. Tonnage: 4,752. Dimensions: 435' x 42'. Single-screw,
14 knots. Compound engines. Four masts and one funnel.
Passengers: 100 first and 1,000 third. Lengthened in 1880.
Re-fitted with triple expansion engines in 1890. Vessel was
transferred to American Line's Liverpool-Philadelphia
service in 1895. Lost in collision with Houstan steamship
Harmonides off Anglesey in March 1902. Ex-**Russia** (1880).

Waldensian   (1861)   Allan Line.
Built by Barclay, Curle & Co., Glasgow, Scotland. Tonnage:
2,250.   Dimensions: 322' x 33'.   Single-screw, 10 knots.
Compound engines. Three masts and one funnel. Clipper
bow. Iron hull. First sailing made as **Waldensian** was
made from Glasgow to Portland, Maine in January 1874.
Later transferred to Glasgow-Boston route. Finally used in
service to South America. Scrapped at Genoa in 1903.
Ex-**St. Andrew.**

Washington   (1847)   Ocean Steam Navigation Co. (U.S.A.).
Built by Westervelt & MacKay, New York, N. Y. Tonnage:

1,640. Dimensions: 236' x 39'. Paddle-wheels, 10 knots. Side lever engines. Three masts and one funnel. Clipper bow. Wooden hull. Launched, January 31, 1847. Maiden voyage: New York-Southampton-Bremen, June 2, 1847. Vessel sold in 1858. Broken up for scrap at Rincon Point, San Francisco in 1864. Sister ship: **Hermann.**

Washington (1863) French Line.
Built by Scott's Shipbuilding & Engineering Co., Greenock, Scotland. Tonnage: 3,401. Dimensions: 345' x 43'9. Paddle-wheels, 12½ knots. Side lever engines. Two masts and two funnels. Iron hull. Launched, June 17, 1863. Maiden voyage: Havre-New York, June 15, 1864. Note: Inaugurated the French Line service. This pioneer paddle-wheel steamer was converted to twin-screw by Robert Napier & Sons, in 1868. Became the earliest known trans-Atlantic steamship to be equipped with twin-screws. A third mast was added. Re-engined with compounds in 1873. She was later transferred to the France-West Indies route. Broken up by shipbreakers at Marseilles in 1900. Sister ship: **Lafayette.**

Washington (1880) Navigazione Generale Italiana.
Built by Alexander Stephen & Sons, Ltd., Glasgow, Scotland. Tonnage: 2,814. Dimensions: 340' x 38'. Single-screw, 12 knots. Compound engines. Three masts and one funnel. Iron hull. Service: Genoa-New York. Transferred to Italy-South American route, though continued to make some voyages to New York. Triple expansion engines in 1896. Made her final voyage to New York in 1907. It is reported that she was transferred to La Veloce Line in 1904. Vessel sold to Soc. Nazionale di Servizi Marittimi in 1910. Sunk off Piombino in May 1915. Sister ships: **Gottardo, Indipendente, Archimede** and **Vincenzo Florio.**

Washington (1933) United States Lines.
Built by New York Shipbuilding Corp., Camden, N. J. Tonnage: 24,289. Dimensions: 668' x 86' (705' o.l.). Twin-screw, 21 knots. Steam turbines. Two masts and two funnels. Launched, August 20, 1932. Maiden voyage: New York-Plymouth-Hamburg, May 10, 1933. Passengers: 500 cabin, 500 tourist, 200 third. Employed as a troopship during World War II, transporting thousands of American soldiers overseas. Resumed trans-Atlantic service in February 1948. In her post-war service accommodation was provided for 1,100 passengers in a single class. This former luxury liner was returned to the United States Government service in

October 1951. Subsequently laid up in the reserved fleet. Sister ship: **Manhattan.**

*Waterman** (1945) Holland-America Line.
Built by Oregon Shipbuilding Corp., Portland, Oregon. Tonnage: 9,177. Dimensions: 440′ x 62′ (455′ o.l.). Single-screw, knots. Two steam turbines. Two masts and one funnel. Passengers: 900 in single class. Mainly operated in Rotterdam-New York service. Owned by Dutch Government, but operated under management of Holland-America Line. Ex-**La Grande Victory** (1947). Running mates: **Groote Beer** and **Zuiderkruis.**

Weimar (1891) North German Lloyd.
Built by Fairfield Shipbuilding & Engineering Co., Glasgow, Scotland. Tonnage: 4,996. Dimensions: 415′ x 48′. Single-screw, 13 knots. Triple expansion engines. Two masts and one funnel. Passengers: 50 first, 38 second, 1,900 third. Placed in various North German Lloyd services, including the South American route. Renamed: **Santiago** (1908), (b) **Armonia** (Chile). Torpedoed and sunk in 1918. Sister ships: See **Gera.**

Werkendam (1881) Holland-America Line.
Built by Harland & Wolff, Ltd., Belfast, Ireland. Tonnage: 3,639. Dimensions: 410′ x 39′. Single-screw, 14 knots. Compound engines. 2,000 I.H.P. Four masts and one funnel. Steel hull. Passengers: 80 first, 80 second, 800 third. Sold to Chinese Eastern Railway, which was under Russian ownership, in 1900. Renamed: **Harbin** (1900). Scuttled by the Russians to block the entrance to Port Arthur in March 1904. Ex-**British King** (1889). Sister ships: **Amsterdam** and **Obdam.**

Werra (1882) North German Lloyd.
Built by John Elder & Co., Glasgow, Scotland. Tonnage: 5,109. Dimensions: 438′ x 46′ (455′ o.l.). Single-screw, 17 knots. Compound engines. 6,400 I.H.P. Four masts and two funnels. Iron hull. Passengers: 125 first, 130 second, 1,000 third. Maiden voyage: Bremen-Southampton-New York in October 1882. Transferred to Mediterranean-New York route in 1891. Sold to Italian shipbreakers in September 1901. Broken up at Genoa in 1903. Sister ship: **Fulda.** Similar to the **Elbe.** Note: These passenger ships were of a group of nine express liners built in Scotland for the North German Lloyd. They did much towards giving the line a

mark of prestige, which the North German Lloyd has maintained through the years that followed.

Werra (1922) North German Lloyd.
Built by Akt. Ges. "Weser", Bremen, Germany. Tonnage: 9,476. Dimensions: 458' x 57'. Triple expansion engines. Two masts and one funnel. Vessel was sold to Italy in August 1935. Renamed: **Calabria** (1935). Torpedoed and sunk by submarine, December 8, 1940. Sister ships: **Coblenz, Fulda, Saarbrucken** and **Trier.**

Weser (1858) North German Lloyd.
Built by Palmer, Allport & Co., Newcastle, England. Tonnage: 2,266. Dimensions: 307' x 40'. Single-screw, 11 knots. Inverted engines. Three masts and two funnels. Clipper bow. Iron hull. Commenced her maiden voyage from Bremen to New York, December 4, 1851. The bad weather that prevailed at the time, damaged the vessel so badly that she was soon sold. Running mates: **Hudson** (identical), **Bremen** and **New York.** Note: This group of steamships inaugurated North German Lloyd service.

Weser (1867) North German Lloyd.
Built by Caird & Co., Greenock, Scotland. Tonnage: 2,871. Dimensions: 351' x 40'. Single-screw, 11½ knots. Inverted engines. Two masts and one funnel. Iron hull. Launched, March 19, 1867. Maiden voyage: Bremen-Southampton-New York, June 1, 1867. Re-engined with compounds in 1881. Speed increased to 13½ knots. Scrapped in 1896. Running mates: **America, Deutschland, Hansa, Hermann** and **Union.**

Weser (1922) North German Lloyd.
Built by Akt. Ges. "Weser", Bremen, Germany. Tonnage: 9,444. Dimensions: 458' x 57'. Twin-screw, 13 knots. Triple expansion engines. Two masts and one funnel. Service: Various routes, including South American trade. Scrapped at Bremen in 1933. Sister ship: See **Fulda.**

*Westerdam (1946) Holland-America Line.
Built by Wilton-Fijenoord, Schiedam, Netherlands. Tonnage: 12,149. Dimensions: 496' x 66' (518' o.l.). Twin-screw, 18 knots. Motorship. Two masts and one funnel. She had been scheduled to make her maiden voyage in 1940, but World War II prevented the sailing to be made. During hostilities she was sunk in the Dutch harbor three times by different methods, so as to keep the ship from being used.

The second and third time by Dutch Underground, so to prevent use by Germany. After the war she was completed and placed in service, arriving in New York on July 8, 1946. Passengers: 134 single class. Service: Rotterdam-New York. Sister ships: **Noordam** and **Zaandam.** Note: The **Westerdam** is not identical to either the **Noordam** and **Zaandam.** However, she is quite similar in appearance and general specifications.

Western Metropolis (1863) New York & Bremen Steamship Co. (U.S.A.).
Built by F. D. Tucker, Brooklyn, N. Y. Tonnage: 2,269. Dimensions: 284' x 41'. Paddle-wheels, 12 knots. Three masts and one funnel. Wooden hull. Vessel was completed in 1864. Commenced New York-Southampton-Bremen service in June 1867. Service ceased in 1868. Conversed to sail in 1878. Note: The last wooden paddle steamer to be built for trans-Atlantic service.

Westernland (1884) Red Star Line (Belgian).
Built by Laird Bros., Birkenhead, England. Tonnage: 5,736. Dimensions: 440' x 47'. Single-screw, 14½ knots. Compound engines. Four masts and two funnels. Steel hull. Note: One of the early steamships to be built of steel. She was built in a dry-dock. Placed in Antwerp-New York service. Transferred to the Liverpool-Philadelphia service of the American Line in 1901. Scrapped in 1912. Running mate: **Noordland.**

Westernland (1918) Red Star Line.
Built by Harland & Wolff, Ltd., Govan, Glasgow, Scotland. (Note: This shipbuilding yard formerly was known as London & Glasgow Engineering & Iron Shipbuilding Co.) Tonnage: 16,289. Dimensions: 575' x 67' (601' o.l.). Triple-screw, 16 knots. Triple expansion engines and one steam turbine. Two masts and two funnels. Passengers: 350 cabin, 350 tourist, 800 third class. In the mid-thirties was sold to Arnold Bernstein. Resold to Holland-America Line in 1939. Acquired by the British Government in World War II. Took part in the attack on Dakar, as flagship of General de Gaulle. Vessel sold to British Government in January 1943. Scrapped in Belgium in 1947. Ex-**Regina** (1929). Sister ship: **Pennland.**

Westphalia (1868) Hamburg-American Line.
Built by Caird & Co., Greenock, Scotland. Tonnage: 3,185. Dimensions: 339' x 40'. Single-screw, 12 knots. Inverted

engines. Two masts and one funnel. Iron hull. Maiden voyage: Hamburg-Southampton-New York, September 15, 1868. In 1878 was re-engined with compounds, which increased speed to 13½ knots, also converted to two funnels. Renamed: (a) **Atlantica** (1887), (b) **Provincia di Sao Paolo** (1888) Italian, (c) **Mentana** (1889), (d) **Sud America** (1890). Scrapped in 1901. Sister ships: **Holsatia** and **Silesia.**

Westphalia (1923) Hamburg-American Line.
   Built by Howaldswerke, Kiel, Germany. Tonnage: 11,343. Dimensions: 473′ x 60′. Single-screw, 13 knots. Two steam turbines. Two masts and one funnel. Passengers: 150 cabin and 680 third. Service: Hamburg-New York. Shifted to the South American route in 1930 and renamed **General Artigas.** Transferred to Hamburg-South American Line ownership in 1936. Destroyed by British aircraft during attack on Hamburg in 1943. Sister ship: **Thuringia.**

Wieland (1874) (a) Adler Line, (b) Hamburg-American Line.
   Built by Alexander Stephen & Sons, Ltd., Glasgow, Scotland. Tonnage: 3,504. Dimensions: 375′ x 40′. Single-screw, 14 knots. Compound engines. Two masts and one funnel. Second funnel added later. Iron hull. Passengers: 200 first and 800 third. Note: The Hamburg-American Line purchased the Adler (Eagle) Line fleet in 1875. Made her final voyage to New York in 1894. Scrapped in 1895. Running mates: **Gellert, Goethe, Herder, Lessing, Klopstock** and **Schiller.**

Willehad (1894) North German Lloyd.
   Built by Blohm & Voss, Hamburg, Germany. Tonnage: 4,761. Dimensions: 383′ x 46′. Twin-screw, 13 knots. Triple expansion engines. Two masts and one funnel. Originally owned by Roland Line. Commenced service as an emigrant and cargo carrier. Services: (a) Bremen-New York, (b) Bremen-Baltimore, (c) Bremen-Quebec-Montreal. Renamed **Wyandotte** (1917) United States Government. Scrapped at Baltimore in 1924. Sister ship: **Wittekind.**

Winifreda (1898) Wilson's & Furness-Leyland Line.
   Built by Harland & Wolff, Ltd., Belfast, Ireland. Tonnage: 6,833. Dimensions: 482′ x 52′. Single-screw, 13½ knots. Triple expansion engines. Four masts and one funnel. Passengers: 120 first class. Maiden voyage from London to New York in March 1898. Renamed: **Mesaba** (1898) Atlantic Transport Line.

Winifredian   (1899)   Leyland Line (British).
Built by Harland & Wolff, Ltd., Belfast, Ireland. Tonnage:
10,428.   Dimensions: 552′ x 59′ (571′ o.l.).   Single-screw,
14½ knots.   Triple expansion engines.   5,500 I.H.P.   Four
masts and one funnel.   Maiden voyage: Liverpool-Boston,
July 22, 1899.   Passengers: 135 first class.   Sold to Italian
shipbreakers in March 1929.   Sister ship: **Devonian.**   Note:
They had large cargo capacity.

Winnipeg   (1918)   French Line.
Built by Chantiers de France, Dunkirk, France.   Tonnage:
9,802.   Dimensions: 473′ x 59′.   Twin-screw, 13 knots.   Triple
expansion engines.   Four masts and one funnel.   Made some
trans-Atlantic voyages as a passenger ship.   Sunk by submarine on October 22, 1942.   Ex-**Paimpol** (1939), ex-
Winnipeg (1938), ex-**Jacques Cartier.**

Wisconsin   (1870)   Guion Line (British).
Built by Palmer's Shipbuilding & Iron Co., Jarrow-on-Tyne,
Newcastle, England.   Tonnage: 3,238.   Dimensions: 366′ x
43′.   Single-screw, 11½ knots.   Compound engines.   Two
masts and one funnel.   Iron hull.   Note: The earliest com-
pound-engined ships built for trans-Atlantic service.   Maiden
voyage: Liverpool-New York, October 22, 1892.   Tonnage
increased to 3,700 tons at later date.   Scrapped in 1893.
Sister ship: **Wyoming.**

Wittekind   (1894)   North German Lloyd.
Built by Blohm & Voss, Hamburg-Germany.   Tonnage:
4,755.   Dimensions: 383′ x 46′.   Twin-screw, 13 knots.   Triple
expansion engines.   Two masts and one funnel.   First placed
in Bremen-South American trade.   At later date was lengthened to 444 feet (5,640 tons).   Spent much time in the North
Atlantic service.   Renamed: (a) **Iroquois** (1917), (b)
Freedom (1919) United States.   Scrapped in 1924.   Sister
ship: **Willehad.**   Note: Originally built for Roland Line.

Wyoming   (1870)   Guion Line (British).
Built by Palmer's Shipbuilding & Iron Co., Newcastle, England.   Tonnage: 3,238.   Dimensions: 366′ x 43′.   Single-screw,
11½ knots.   Compound engines.   Two masts and one funnel.
Iron hull.   Maiden voyage: Liverpool-New York, November
25, 1870.   At later date tonnage increased to 3,700.   Scrapped
in 1893.   Sister ship: **Wisconsin.**   Note: The earliest com-
pound-engined steamships built for trans-Atlantic service.

Yorck   (1906)   North German Lloyd.
   Built by F. Schichau, Danzig, Germany. Tonnage: 8,976.
   Dimensions: 463' x 57'. Twin-screw, 14½ knots. Quadruple
   expansion engines. Two masts and one funnel. Built originally for Australia and Far East services. Made a number
   of North Atlantic crossings. Passengers: 95 first, 70 second,
   2,000 third. Made her final voyage to New York in 1929.
   Sold to Danzig shipbreakers in November 1932. Sister ships:
   Derfflinger and **Luetzow.**

Yorkshire   (1889)   Dominion Line (British).
   Built by Harland & Wolff, Ltd., Belfast, Ireland. Tonnage:
   4,269.   Dimensions: 400' x 45'.   Single-screw, 14 knots.
   Triple expansion engines. Four masts and one funnel. Note:
   This Bibby liner was in the Liverpool-Quebec-Montreal
   service of the Dominion Line only during 1898. Renamed:
   (a) **Indien** (1905), (b) **Estonia** (1907). Lost by fire at sea
   in 1913.

Ypiranga   (1908)   Hamburg-American Line.
   Built by Frd. Krupp, Kiel, Germany. Tonnage: 8,309.
   Dimensions: 448' x 58'. Twin-screw, 12 knots. Quadruple
   expansion engines. Two masts and one funnel. Built
   specially for the Hamburg-West Indies service. Vessel was
   taken over by the British after First World War. Renamed:
   (a) **Assyria** (1921), (b) **Colonial** (1929). Scrapped in 1950.
   Sister ship: **Corcovado.**

Zaandam   (1882)   Holland-America Line.
   Built by Nederlandsch Stoomvaart, Rotterdam, Netherlands.   Tonnage: 3,063.   Dimensions: 328' x 39'.   Single-
   screw, 10 knots. Compound engines. Two masts and one
   funnel. Iron hull. Passengers: 50 first and 400 third. Renamed: (a) **Styria** (Austrian), (b) **Julia Luckenbach**
   (1902). Lost in collision with the **Indrakuala,** Chesapeake
   Bay, January 3, 1913.

Zaandam   (1939)   Holland-America Line.
   Built by Wilton-Feyenoord, Rotterdam, Netherlands. Ton-
   nage: 10,909.   Dimensions: 480' x 64' (501' o.l.).   Twin-
   screw, 18 knots. Motorship. Two masts and one funnel.
   Maiden voyage: Rotterdam-New York, January 7, 1939.
   Note: The following is a classic example of being set adrift
   on a raft in an isolated area of a large ocean. The **Zaandam**
   was torpedoed without warning several hundred miles from
   Recife, Brazil, November 2, 1942, while bound from Cape
   Town to the United States.   She sank in less than ten

minutes. On board the liner had been a total of 299, of which 169 were passengers. Ultimately only 169 were to survive the ordeal. The most outstanding experience to occur among them was the account about five men who climbed onto a raft just after the doomed **Zaandam** went to the bottom of the ocean. For 83 days three of the five occupants of the raft survived the terrible strain of drifting in the open sea in all kinds of weather, for a distance of over 2,000 miles. Their meager supply of food and water was exhausted on the 16th day. During the remaining days on the raft they obtained only rain water and a few small fish and birds on which to subsist. It was the longest period of time that any human beings were known to survive the open sea. On the raft at the outset were, George Beasley, an American sailor who had been a passenger on the ill-fated vessel and he died 66 days later; also, Ensign James Maddox of the United States Navy who remained alive for 77 days. The remaining three were Basil Izzi of South Barre, Massachusetts, member of the American gun crew, on the **Zaandam,** an oiler named Cornelis van der Slot, of Rotterdam, and Nicko Hoogendam, a young lad from Vlaardingen. The three living skeletons were picked up by a United States Navy patrol ship on January 24, 1943. It is needless to say that rescue came none too soon for the nearly gone survivors. This somewhat lengthy recital in what is supposed to be a mere reference book is meant as a tribute to all who have either died or survived the terrific hardships of having been exposed to the fury of the elements on the open sea. Sister ship: **Noordam.**

Zeeland   (1865)   Red Star Line.
Built by J. & G. Thomson, Ltd., Clydebank, Glasgow, Scotland. Tonnage: 2,866. Dimensions: 337' x 42'. Single-screw, 12½ knots. Compound engines. Three masts and one funnel. Iron hull. Service: Antwerp-Philadelphia. Later sold and converted to sail. Renamed: **Electrique** (1889) French. Ex-**Java** (1877). Disappeared at sea in 1895.

Zeeland   (1901)   Red Star Line.
Built by John Brown & Co., Clydebank, Glasgow, Scotland. Tonnage: 11,905. Dimensions: 561' x 60' (580' o.l.). Twin-screw, 15 knots. Quadruple expansion engines. Four masts and two funnels. Service: Antwerp-New York. During 1910–1911 period ran for White Star Line. Renamed: (a) **Northland** (1915), (b) **Zeeland** (1919), (c) **Minnesota.** Sold for scrap in October 1929. Sister ships: **Finland, Kroonland** and **Vaterland.**

Zeppelin (1914) North German Lloyd.
Built by Bremer Vulkan Co., Vegesack, Germany. Tonnage: 14,588. Dimensions: 550' x 67'. Twin-screw, 18 knots. Quadruple expansion engines. Two masts and two funnels. Note: When completed was turned over to the British. Renamed: (a) **Ormuz**, (b) **Dresden.**

Zieten (1902) North German Lloyd.
Built by F. Schichau, Danzig, Germany. Tonnage: 8,043. Dimensions: 442' x 55'. Twin-screw, 13½ knots. Triple expansion engines. Two masts and one funnel. Passengers: 100 first, 100 second, 1,700 third. Interned at Mozambique, August 5, 1914. Requisitioned by the Portuguese Government in March 1916. Renamed: **Tungue** (1916). Torpedoed and sunk by a German submarine, November 27, 1917. Sister ship: **Seydlitz.**

*Zion (1956) Zim Israel Navigation Co.
Built by Deutsche Werft, Hamburg, Germany. Tonnage: 9,855. Dimensions: 454' x 65' (501' o.l.). Single-screw, 18½ knots. Two steam turbines. Two masts and one funnel. Launched, March 4, 1955. First voyage from Haifa to New York, March 9, 1956. Passengers: 313 (first and tourist). Liner is equipped with stabilizers. Sister ship: **Israel.** Note: First passenger liners to be built for Israel.

*Zuiderkruis (1944) Holland-America Line.
Built by Oregon Shipbuilding Corp., Portland, Oregon. Tonnage: 9,126. Dimensions: 440' x 62'. Single-screw, 15 knots. Steam turbines. Two masts and one funnel. Owned by the Dutch Government, but operated under Holland-America Line management. Service: Rotterdam-New York. Passengers: 800. Tourist class ship. Also, has made sailings to Canada. Ex-**Cranston Victory** (1951). Running mates: **Groote Beer** and **Waterman.**

PART II

TRANS-PACIFIC PASSENGER SHIPS

Past and Present

Note: The California-Hawaiian Passenger Ships (shuttle service) are listed in the APPENDIX. This method of classification is used, so as to set apart the subject liners from those vessels that have been employed in the trans-Pacific trade.

INTRODUCTION

Regular trans-Pacific passenger service was established by the Pacific Mail Steamship Company in 1867. Their wooden side-wheeler *Colorado* made the historic crossing from San Francisco to Yokohama in slightly under twenty-two days. However, long before this date irregular crossings of the Pacific Ocean had been made by steamships. A very early crossing was made by the paddle-wheel steamer *Golden Age*, which had been launched from the New York yard of William H. Brown in 1852. The 2,281 ton *Golden Age*, under ownership of the New York & Australian Navigation Company, sailed with a number of passengers from Sydney for Panama, via Tahiti, on May 11, 1854, completing her classical voyage in about a month. The Pacific Mail bought the *Golden Age* in 1854, and she remained in their service until 1875, then sold to Japanese owners and renamed *Hiroshima Maru*.

The first steamship to cross the Pacific Ocean was the 737 ton (net) American screw propelled *Monumental City*, built at Baltimore in 1850. This pioneer of the Pacific commenced her famous voyage from San Francisco on February 17, 1853, but did not reach Sydney, her destination, until April 23rd. The *Monumental City* did not remain afloat long, for on May 15, 1853, while on passage from Melbourne to Sydney, she was wrecked and as a result thirty-three lives were lost.

Among the early steamships which made only one or two trans-Pacific sailings, were the Pacific Mail steamers *Moses Taylor* and the *Henry Chauncey*, built in 1857 and 1864 respectively. Pictures of these two ships and of the *Golden Age*, which also never was in regular trans-Pacific service, are included in the pictorial section of this book in order to give a clearer description of the vessels which were in the Pacific trade during that era.

Although the direct Panama-New Zealand-Australia service, and also the European-New Zealand-Australia trade, via the Panama Canal, which developed many years later, does come within the scope of this volume, it is perhaps well to mention that mail service was established from Sydney to Panama on June 15, 1866, by the newly formed Panama, New Zealand & Australian Royal Mail Company. Their 1,501 ton screw steamer *Kaikoura*, built in 1865, made the initial sailing. Her running mates were the *Ruahine*, *Rakaia* and *Mataura*, steamships of a similar type and size. Since the opening of the Panama Canal, the service from European ports by the way of the Panama Canal to New Zealand and Australia, has had excellent tonnage. First-class liners, such as the recently built sister ships, *Rangitoto* and *Rangitane* of the New Zealand Shipping Company, have served in this important world trade route.

The Pacific Mail Steamship Company, a name which for many years was synonymous to Pacific ships and shipping, began to receive some competition from a new line sponsored by the famous White Star Line. The Occidental & Oriental Company was the name of this newly formed steamship line. The former trans-Atlantic liner *Oceanic*, which had made the White Star Line's first sailing, inaugurated the service from San Francisco to Japan and Hong Kong in 1879. This new enterprise never did achieve great success and the company gradually became less important. Their service was finally terminated in 1906.

The next great effort to win a place in the trade between North America and the Orient was made by the Canadian Pacific Railway in 1887. For this purpose they acquired the former Cunard liners *Abyssinia*, *Batavia* and *Parthia*. This new Vancouver-Yokohama-Hong Kong service was greatly improved in 1891, by replacing the older ships with their new yacht-like sister ships, *Empress of China*, *Empress of India* and *Empress of Japan*. Thus, the Canadian Pacific became a leading contender in the trans-Pacific passenger trade. In 1913 they brought out the large new sister ships *Empress of Asia* and *Empress of Russia*, liners which were definitely superior to any ship afloat in the Pacific at that time. After the First World War further improvements were ordered. The *Empress of Canada*, a 20 knot liner, was built in 1922 for the Pacific trade. However, the finest, largest and fastest passenger ship the Canadian Pacific has thus far had in Pacific service was a luxury liner built in 1930 and named *Empress of Japan*. On her maiden voyage from Vancouver to Yokohama, she broke the speed record for the run, by making it in 8 days, 6 hours, 27 minutes. Later she even bettered that record time. In 1941 the *Empress of Japan* was renamed *Empress of Scotland*, due to the fact that Japan had entered the war against the Allies. After World War II, this splendid liner was thoroughly reconditioned for their trans-Atlantic service. Without a doubt the Canadian Pacific Railway with its vast coverage of service is the greatest transportation organization in the world today.

The Union Steamship Company of New Zealand has long ranked high in shipping circles. Their subsidiary, named the Canadian Australian Royal Mail Line, has provided passenger service between New Zealand to Australia, Vancouver and San Francisco, via Suva and Honolulu, for many years. The first *Aorangi*, built in 1883 for the New Zealand Shipping Company, was chartered for the Canadian-Australasian Line in 1893. This notable ship when found to be suitable for the service was purchased outright. The *Miowera* was actually their first steamer to cross the Pacific, as she took the initial sailing from Sydney on May 23, 1893. The *Makura* and *Niagara*, the former built in 1908 and the latter in 1913, were among their finest ships prior to the First World War. The *Makura* was the largest vessel sailing between Sydney and San Francisco for quite a few years. In 1936, after a long and useful life, she was sold to Chinese shipbreakers for scrap. The larger *Niagara* ran in the Sydney-Vancouver service, and maintained the vital All Red mail route throughout the First World War. The popular liner continued in operation until World War II, and unfortunately became a war casualty in 1940. The Canadian-Australasian Line reached its acme of service when they entered their new *Aorangi* in 1924. This new luxury liner had the distinction of being the largest motor-ship built to date, and the first ship in the trade to have four propellers. During the Second World War the *Aorangi* was employed as a British troopship. After the war she re-entered the Sydney-Vancouver service. This noteworthy vessel is to be withdrawn permanently from service upon completion of voyage to Sydney in June 1953. This abandonment of passenger service by the Canadian-Australasian Line brings to a close another chapter of Pacific shipping.

It was announced that the Orient Line would extend two of its sailings in 1954, with calls at Auckland, Suva, Honolulu, Victoria, Vancouver and San Francisco. Therefore, the way was prepared for future passenger service between Australia, New Zealand and North America. Inasmuch as the Orient Line used their new superliner *Oronsay* in these experimental sailings, the scheduled extended trips did prove successful.

The American President Lines is an outgrowth of the equally famed Dollar Steamship Lines, which in turn gained substance in 1924 from the now defunct Pacific Mail Steamship Company. This lineage dates back to 1848, the year that the Pacific Mail was chartered. In 1938, at the request of the United States Government, the Dollar Steamship Lines was reorganized and renamed American President Lines. The new company continued the various services under government regulations until 1952, at which time the holdings of the line were purchased by the present backers of this renowned steamship line and governmental controls were relinquished. The large first-class passenger liners *President Cleveland* and *President Wilson* cater to their San Francisco-Orient service.

Their round-the-world passenger ship sailings are made by the smaller sister ships *President Monroe* and *President Polk*. The line had planned to extend the number of available passenger ships, and thus ordered three luxury liners shortly before the Korean War. However, the vessels were taken over by the United States Government before completion and converted to troopships.

Prior to 1926 the main passenger service of the Matson Navigation Company was carried on between California and Honolulu. In that year the Matson organization acquired the old Spreckles Line, officially known as the Oceanic Steamship Company. The Matson Line continued the former owner's service between San Francisco and Sydney. In 1932 they improved the service by building new tonnage, as replacements for the former "old-timers" of the Spreckles Line. The vastly superior liners were named *Mariposa* and *Monterey*. These fine sister ships remained in the Australian trade until World War II. The *Lurline* (identical in appearance to the above liners) had also been built in 1932. However, she was confined exclusively to their de luxe service between California and Honolulu. During the Second World War all three ships were requisitioned by the government and converted to troop carriers. After the war the *Lurline* was reconditioned and put back in her former service. On the other hand the *Mariposa* and *Monterey* were laid up for quite a length of time at Alameda, California, after their release from World War II duties. However, in due time both vessels were reactivated to regular service. The *Mariposa* was sold to the Home Lines late in 1953. After a thorough refit she was renamed *Homeric* and placed in Atlantic service. The *Monterey* was reconditioned and renamed *Matsonia*, in 1956. She then joined her sister ship *Lurline* in the California-Hawaii shuttle service, which now enables the Matson Line to provide frequent sailings in this famous trade.

The Japan Mail Steamship Company, English derivative of Nippon Yusen Kaisha and which is better known as the

N. Y. K. Line, inaugurated their passenger service to the United States in 1896. Prior to the Second World War this big steamship company was a leader in the trans-Pacific trade. The company owned a large number of fine passenger liners, many of which served in the Pacific. During the war all their services were terminated. So far the N. Y. K. Line has not re-entered the trans-Pacific passenger service. Unquestionably, this steamship company in time will once again regain the prominence which they occupied during the 1930's. Japan is a natural maritime nation and it can be expected her people will support the N. Y. K. in their effort to build a large merchant fleet.

In order to further clarify a previous paragraph in this introduction, which states that the Orient Line would extend two of its 1954 sailings to Vancouver and San Francisco, via the Pacific, it should now be mentioned that the inauguration was performed by the Orient liner *Oronsay*. Since that date a number of notable passenger ships of the Orient Line and P. & O. Line have been employed in this new trans-Pacific service. The subject liners are: *Arcadia, Canberra, Chusan, Himalaya, Iberia, Orcades, Oriana, Oronsay* and *Orsova*. A sizable fleet indeed! The ships in this new service sail under the joint management merger of the Peninsular & Oriental Steam Navigation Company and the Orient Line, known now as the P & O-Orient Lines. The last passenger ship to enter the new service is the super liner *Canberra*, largest British vessel built since the *Queen Elizabeth*, and also accommodation for more passengers than any other in the world. The *Canberra* left her home port of Southampton on June 2, 1961, calling at Gibraltar, Naples, Port Said, Aden, Colombo, Fremantle, Sydney, Auckland and Honolulu, while on way to San Francisco. It is quite evident that this new P & O-Orient Lines service has done much to increase the prestige of trans-Pacific passenger service. The above liners are listed with details in PART IV, as they are essentially ships built for the Australian and Far East services.

As the year 1961 comes to a close it is worth noting that there are three major lines handling the direct trans-Pacific passenger phase of the shipping business. Namely they are the American President Lines, Matson Navigation Company and the newly organized P & O-Orient Lines. Prospects are bright in this particular area of sea travel, as it has many attractions to offer the tourist.

The passenger service between Europe and New Zealand - Australia, via the Panama Canal route, is well provided for by several shipping lines. The *Rangitata, Rangitiki, Rangitane, Rangitoto,* and *Ruahine* are engaged in the trans-Pacific service, via Panama Canal for New Zealand Shipping Company. The sister ships *Athenic, Ceramic, Corinthic* and *Gothic* are also regularly employed in this trade for Shaw, Savill & Albion Company. This line also has in service the *Southern Cross,* which uses the Panama Canal in its voyage around-the-world. The famous Messageries Maritimes of France have been making good use of their *Caledonien* and *Tahitien* on the Marseilles-Tahiti-Sydney route. The Dutch have three outstanding passenger liners in a round-the-world service, via Panama Canal. They are the *Oranje* and *Johan van Oldenbarnevelt* of the Nederland Line and the *Willem Ruys,* a Rotterdam Lloyd vessel. The modern passenger ships *Argentina Maru* and *Brazil Maru* of Osaka Shosen Kaisha, pass through the Canal, while on their way from Japan to South America. This Japanese firm have the *Africa Maru, America Maru* and *Santos Maru,* as supporting liners in this particular service. Finally it should be noted that the American President Lines have been using the *President Monroe* and *President Polk* on their long established round-the-world service, via Panama Canal.

As part of this final summarization to trans-Pacific service in 1961, it is well to point out that the Matson Navigation Company have the relatively new sister ships *Mariposa* and *Monterey* in their San Francisco-New Zealand-Australia passenger service. The American President Lines now have in service the reconditioned liner *President Hoover*, formerly known as the *Panama*. This smaller passenger ship serves as a support to the larger liners *President Cleveland* and *President Wilson* in their first-class San Francisco-Orient trade. The ex-*La Guardia*, which originally ran in the New York-Mediterranean service for American Export Lines is now being refitted for the American President Lines. This thoroughly reconditioned passenger ship will commence her first trans-Pacific sailing early in 1962, as the *President Roosevelt*.

Of special interest is the 22,000 ton passenger ship now under construction for Shaw, Savill & Albion Company. She has been given the name *Northern Star* and when ready for service in 1962 will become the running mate to the line's *Southern Cross*. The exterior appearance of the *Northern Star* is even more radical than that of the *Southern Cross*, which similarly has her exhaust stack placed at the aft end of the ship. Accommodation will be for 1,400 passengers in a single class. Both liners will be employed on their round-the-world service, via Panama Canal. It is planned that each ship will make four of these voyages each year.

PART II
TRANS-PACIFIC PASSENGER SHIPS
PAST AND PRESENT

Note: An asterisk (*) denotes ship in trans-Pacific service in 1962.

Abyssinia (1870) CanadianPacific Line.
Built by J. & G. Thomson, Ltd., Clydebank, Glasgow. Tonnage: 3,651. Dimensions: 363' x 42'. Single-screw, 12½ knots. Three masts and one funnel. Iron hull. This former Cunarder was under charter to Canadian Pacific Line. In Vancouver-Hong Kong service, 1887–91. Destroyed by fire in mid-Atlantic in December 1891, with no loss of life. Note: Also listed under trans-Atlantic ships.

Africa Maru (1918) Osaka Line.
Built by Mitsubishi Zozen, Japan. Tonnage: 9,476. Dimensions: 475' x 61'. Twin-screw, 13 knots. Reciprocating engines. Two masts and one funnel . Torpedoed and sunk on October 20, 1942. Sister ships: **Arabia Maru, Arizona Maru, Hawaii Maru** and **Manila Maru.**

Alameda (1883) Oceanic Steamship Co.
Built by W. Cramp & Sons Co., Chester, Pa. Tonnage: 3,158. Dimensions: 314' x 41'. Single-screw, 15 knots. Triple expansion engines. Two masts and one funnel. Note: Later lengthened to 327 feet (3,709 tons). In San Francisco-Sydney service, 1885–1901; San Francisco-Honolulu, 1901–10. Sold to Alaska Steamship Co. in March 1910. Sister ship: **Mariposa.**

Alaska (1867) Pacific Mail Steamship Co.
Built by Henry Steers, Greenpoint, Long Island, New York. Tonnage: 4,011. Dimensions: 346' x 47'. Paddle-wheels. Wooden hull. Launched in March 1868. Reported to have cost $964,138 to build. Engaged in trans-Pacific service, 1871–79. Rebuilt as a hulk in 1879, and used as a store-ship at Acapulco until 1885. Her registry surrendered in 1882, when in use as coal hulk at Acapulco.

America (1868) Pacific Mail Steamship Co.
Built by Henry Steers, Greenpoint, Long Island, New York. Tonnage: 4,454. Dimensions: 363' x 49'. Paddle-wheels. One funnel and three masts. Wooden hull. Made her first trans-Pacific crossing from Hong Kong on September 18, 1869, arriving in San Francisco on October 20th. Had cost $1,017,942. Destroyed by fire in Yokohama Harbor on August 24, 1872, with loss of 59 lives.

America Maru   (1898)   Toyo Kisen Kaisha.
> Built by C. S. Swan & Hunter, Ltd., Newcastle, England. Tonnage: 6,307. Dimensions: 423′ x 51′. Twin-screw, 17 knots. Reciprocating engines. Two masts and two funnels. Clipper bow. Note: Later acquired by Osaka Line. Torpedoed and sunk by a United States submarine on March 6. 1944. Sister ships: **Hongkong Maru** and **Nippon Maru,**

Aorangi   (1883)   Canadian-Australian R. M. Steamship Co., Ltd., (Union Steamship Co. of New Zealand).
> Built by J. Elder & Co., Glasgow. Tonnage: 4,268. Dimensions: 389′ x 46′. Single-screw, 16 knots. Compound engines. Later re-engined with triple expansion engines. Three masts and one funnel. Sunk at Scapa Flow in 1915, with other ships, so as to block channel against submarines. In 1921 was raised and used as a hulk at Scapa Flow. Sister ships: **Ruapehu** and **Tongariro.**

Aorangi   (1924)   Union Steamship Co. of New Zealand.
> Built by Fairfield Shipbuilding and Engineering Co., Ltd., Glasgow. Tonnage: 17,491. Dimensions: 580′ x 72′ (600′ o.l.). Quadruple-screw, 18½ knots. Motorship. Two masts and two funnels. Passengers: 440 first, 300 second, 230 third. Largest British motorship built to date. Served as a troopship in World War II. Afterwards re-entered the trans-Pacific service. Sold to British shipbreakers in 1953.

Arabia Maru   (1918)   Osaka Line.
> Built by Mitsubishi, Zozen, Japan. Tonnage: 9,480. Dimensions: 475′ x 61′. Twin-screw, 13 knots. Reciprocating engines. Two masts and one funnel. Used on Hong Kong-Tacoma service until July 1931. Torpedoed and sunk on October 18, 1944. Sister ships: **Africa Maru, Arizona Maru, Hawaii Maru** and **Manila Maru.**

Arabic   (1881)   White Star Line (Occidental & Oriental Steamship Co.).
> Built by Harland & Wolff, Ltd., Belfast, Ireland. Tonnage: 4,368. Dimensions: 430′ x 42′. Single-screw. Four masts and one funnel. Steel hull. In San Francisco-Hong Kong service 1882–1885, 1888–1889. Note: Also was in trans-Atlantic service. Renamed: **Spaarndam.**

Arizona Maru   (1920)   Osaka Line.
> Built by Mitsubishi, Zozen, Japan. Tonnage: 9,684. Dimensions: 475′ x 61′. Twin-screw, 13 knots. Reciprocating engines. Two masts and one funnel. Sunk by aircraft on November 14, 1942. Sister ships: **Africa Maru, Arabia Maru, Hawaii Maru** and **Manila Maru.**

Asama Maru   (1929)   N. Y. K. Line.
Built by Mitsubishi Nagasaki Dockyard, Nagasaki, Japan.
Tonnage: 16,947. Dimensions: 560′ x 72′ (583′ o.l.). Quadruple-screw, 20 knots. Motorship. Two masts and two
funnels. Keel laid September 10, 1927. Launched October
30, 1928. Completed September 15, 1929. Made a trans-
Pacific crossing in 12 days, 3 hours and 22 minutes. Torpedoed and sunk on November 1, 1944. Running mates:
Tatsuta Maru and **Chichibu Maru.**

Asia   (1883)   Pacific Mail Steamship Co.
Built by Harland & Wolff, Ltd., Belfast, Ireland. Tonnage:
4,784. Dimensions: 440′ x 44′.   Single-screw, 15 knots.
Four masts and one funnel. Ex-**Doric** (1907). Note: Sold by
White Star Line to Asia Steamship Co. of London, and
operated on account of owners on commission basis by Pacific
Mail Steamship Co. Wrecked on Finger Rock, Taichow
Islands, off China Coast, on April 23, 1911.

Athenian   (1882)   Canadian Pacific Line.
Built by Aitken & Mansel, Glasgow, Scotland. Tonnage:
3,882. Dimensions: 365′ x 45′. Single-screw, 16 knots.
Three masts and one funnel. Iron hull. Note: Originally
owned by the Union Line and used in their service between
England and South Africa. Purchased by Canadian Pacific
Line in 1897 for Vancouver-Skagway trade. In Vancouver-
Hong Kong service, 1898–9, 1901–1907. Sold to Japanese
owners in 1907. Broken up in 1908. Sister ship: **Moor.**

Atsuta Maru   (1909)   N. Y. K. Line.
Built by Mitsubishi Dockyard, Nagasaki, Japan. Tonnage:
7,974.   Dimensions: 473′ x 54′.   Twin-screw, 15 knots.
Reciprocating engines. Two masts and one funnel. Com-
pleted March 3, 1909. Note: Transferred from the Japan-
European route to trans-Pacific service in September 1917,
remaining in same until March 1922, when put back on the
European trade. Torpedoed and sunk on November 30,
1942. Sister ships: **Kamo Maru, Hirano Maru, Mishima
Maru, Miyazaki Maru** and **Kitano Maru.**

Australia   (1875)   Oceanic Steamship Co.
Built by J. Elder & Co., Glasgow. Tonnage: 2,755. Dimensions: 376′ x 37′. Single-screw, 14 knots. Four masts and
one funnel. Note: Chartered by Pacific Mail Steamship Co.
from Elder, and used in San Francisco-Sydney service, 1876–
1885. Purchased from John Elder by Oceanic Steamship

Co. in 1886. In their San Francisco-Honolulu service, 1886–1901; San Francisco-Tahiti run, 1901–1902. Seized and confiscated by the Japanese Government at Yokohama on August 26, 1905. Sister ship: **Zealandia.**

Batavia (1870) Canadian Pacific Line.

Built by W. Denny & Bros., Dumbarton, Scotland. Tonnage: 2,553. Dimensions: 327' x 29'. Single-screw, 15 knots. Two masts and one funnel. Iron hull. Renamed: **Tacoma** (1892), (b) **Shikotan Maru.** Note: Originally operated on the Cunard trans-Atlantic service. In the Vancouver-Hong Kong service for Canadian Pacific Line, 1887–1891. Chartered to Upton Line, 1891–1892. Began service for Northern Pacific Steamship Co. in 1892 and renamed **Tacoma.** Used in their Tacoma-Hong Kong service. Served as U. S. Army transport, 1899–1900. Purchased by Northern Pacific Steamship Co. in 1901. (This was a subsidiary of Northern Pacific Railway, and was a different company from that which had previously operated her.) Transferred to Northwestern Improvement Co. (also a Northern Pacific Railway subsidiary) in 1902. Sold to Northwestern Commercial Co. in 1904. Used as blockade runner in Russo-Japanese War. Captured by Japanese and placed under their flag on March 14, 1905. Renamed: **Shikotan Maru** and engaged in Japanese and Chinese coasting trade. Ran aground in October 1924, and although subsequently refloated was broken up soon after. This ship is also listed under trans-Atlantic vessels.

Belgic (1873) White Star Line (Occidental and Oriental Steamship Co.).

Built by Harland & Wolff, Ltd., Belfast, Ireland. Tonnage: 2,652. Dimensions: 370' x 36'. Single-screw. Four masts and one funnel. Iron hull. Note: Chartered by O. & O. and in service San Francisco-Hong Kong, 1875–1883. Sold to Spanish owners in 1883 and renamed **Geofredo.** Wrecked in the Mersey in 1884. Sister ship: **Gaelic.**

Belgic (1885) White Star Line (Occidental and Oriental Steamship Co.).

Built by Harland & Wolff, Ltd., Belfast, Ireland. Tonnage: 4,212. Dimensions: 420' x 42'. Single-screw, 14 knots. Four masts and one funnel. Steel and iron hull. In service San Francisco-Hong Kong, 1885–1898. Sold to Atlantic Transport Co. and renamed **Mohawk** in 1899. Scrapped at Garston in 1903. Sister ship: **Gaelic.**

Chicago Maru (1910) Osaka Line.
Built by Kawasaki Dockyard Co., Ltd., Kobe, Japan.
Tonnage: 6,182. Dimensions: 419′ x 49′. Twin-screw, 13
knots. Reciprocating engines. Two masts and one funnel.
In the trans-Pacific Tacoma service. Torpedoed and sunk
on October 15, 1943. Running mates: **Seattle Maru** and
Tacoma Maru.

Chichibu Maru (1930) N. Y. K. Line.
Built by Yokohama Dock Co., Yokohama, Japan. Tonnage:
17,498. Dimensions: 560′ x 74′ (583′ o.l.). Twin-screw,
20 knots. Motorship. Two masts and one funnel. Laid
down February 6, 1928. Launched May 8, 1929. Completed March 10, 1930. Made her maiden voyage from
Yokohama to San Francisco in 12 days, 7 hours, 5 minutes.
Renamed: **Kamakura Maru** (1939). Running mates:
Asama Maru and **Tatsuta Maru.**

China (1866) Pacific Mail Steamship Co.
Built by Wm. H. Webb, New York, N. Y. Tonnage: 3,836.
Dimensions: 360′ x 47′. Paddle-wheels. Wooden hull.
Keel laid January 13, 1866. Commenced service in 1867.
In service San Francisco-Hong Kong, 1867–1879. Laid up,
1879–1883. Sold by Pacific Mail in 1883. Broken up in 1886.

China (1889) Pacific Mail Steamship Co.
Built by Fairfield Shipbuilding and Engineering Co., Ltd.,
Govan, Scotland. Tonnage: 5,060. Dimensions: 440′ x 48′.
Single-screw, 17 knots. Triple expansion engines. Four
masts and two funnels. Steel hull. Note: Built to replace
the **City of Tokio** lost in 1885. In service San Francisco-
Hong Kong and Manila, 1889–1915. Sold to Atlantic Trans-
port Co. in 1915, and then resold to China Mail Steamship
Co. In service San Francisco-Manila for China Mail, 1915–
1923. Broken up for scrap at Kowloon in 1925.

Chiyo Maru (1908) Toyo Kisen Kaisha. Built by Mitsu-
bishi Dockyard, Nagasaki, Japan. Tonnage: 13,431.
Dimensions: 558′ x 61′ (570′ o.l.). Triple-screw, 16 knots.
Turbines. Two masts and two funnels. Attained a speed
of about 20 knots on her trials. Lost on Tam Kan Island,
near eastern end of Lema Group, 20 miles south of Hong
Kong on March 31, 1916. Sister ships: **Shinyo Maru** and
Tenyo Maru.

City of Adelaide (1864) California, New Zealand and Austra-
lian Mail Steamship Co. (Australasian Steam Navigation Co.).
Built by J. & G. Thomson, Glasgow. Tonnage: 1,211.
Dimensions: 252′ x 28′. Single-screw.

City of Melbourne (1862) Australasian United Steam Navigation Co., Ltd.
   Built by J. & G. Thomson, Glasgow. Tonnage: 838. Dimensions: 250′ x 28′. Single-screw. In Sydney-San Francisco Service.

City of New York (1875) Pacific Mail Steamship Co.
   Built by J. Roach & Son, Chester, Pa. Tonnage: 3,019. Dimensions: 339′ x 40′. Single-screw. Compound engine. Three masts and one funnel. Iron hull. Wrecked on Point Bonita, San Francisco Bay on October 26, 1893. Sister ships: **City of San Francisco** and **City of Sydney.**

City of Peking (1874) Pacific Mail Steamship Co.
   Built by John Roach & Son, Chester, Pa. Tonnage: 5,080. Dimensions: 408′ x 47′. Single-screw, 15 knots. Compound engine. Four masts and two funnels. Iron hull. Launched March 18, 1874. Broken up in 1910. Sister ship: **City of Tokio.**

City of Rio de Janeiro (1878) Pacific Mail Steamship Co.
   Built by J. Roach & Son, Chester, Pa. Tonnage: 3,548. Dimensions: 345′ x 38′. Single-screw, 14 knots. Three masts and one funnel. Iron hull. Purchased by Pacific Mail in 1881. Had been built for United States and Brazil Mail Steamship Co. Wrecked on February 22, 1901, off Fort Point, San Francisco Bay, in a fog and sank with a loss of 131 passengers and crew.

City of San Francisco (1875) Pacific Mail Steamship Co.
   Built by J. Roach & Son, Chester, Pa. Tonnage: 3,009. Dimensions: 339′ x 40′. Single-screw, 14 knots. Compound engines. Three masts and one funnel. Iron hull. Made three round trips between San Francisco and Sydney during the 1875–1876 period. Wrecked June 5, 1877, on uncharted rock off Mexican coast. Sister ships: **City of New York** and **City of Sydney.**

City of Sydney (1875) Pacific Mail Steamship Co.
   Built by J. Roach & Son, Chester, Pa. Tonnage: 3,016. Dimensions: 339′ x 40′. Single-screw, 14 knots. Compound engines. Three masts and one funnel. Iron hull. Sold in 1915. Engines removed and then rigged as 6-masted barkentine. Burned for metal in 1930. Sister ships: **City of New York** and **City of San Francisco.**

City of Tokio   (1874)   Pacific Mail Steamship Co.
Built by J. Roach & Son, Chester, Pa. Tonnage: 5,079.
Dimensions: 408' x 47'. Single-screw, 15 knots. Compound
engines. Four masts and two funnels. Iron hull. Launched
May 13, 1874. Wrecked on June 24, 1885, on Honshu,
Japan. Sister ship: **City of Peking.**

Colima   (1873)   Pacific Mail Steaamship Co.
Built by John Roach, Chester, Pa. Tonnage: 2,905.
Dimensions: 299' x 39'. Single-screw. Two masts and one
funnel. Iron hull. Foundered off Manzanillo, Mexico on
May 27, 1895.

Colombia   (1915)   Pacific Mail Steamship Co.
Built by Nederland Schps. Maats, Amsterdam. Tonnage:
5,644. Dimensions: 379' x 48'. Single-screw, 14 knots.
Reciprocating engines. Two masts and one funnel. Pur-
chased by Pacific Mail in 1916. Entered trans-Pacific service
in 1917. Transferred to Panama Mail Steamship Co. in 1925.
Wrecked on coast of Lower California on September 13, 1931.
Sister ships **Ecuador** and **Venezuela.**

Colorado   (1864)   Pacific Mail Steamship Co.
Built by Wm. H. Webb, New York, N. Y. Tonnage: 3,728.
Dimensions: 340' x 45'. Paddle-wheels. Two masts and
one funnel. Wooden hull. Keel laid June 6, 1863. Launched
May 21, 1864. Cost about $750,000. Opened the service
to the Orient in 1867. Note: Later had three masts. Broken
up for scrap at San Francisco in 1879.

Colusa   (1913)   Pacific Mail Steamship Co.
Built by W. Hamilton & Co., Ltd., Port Glasgow, Scotland.
Tonnage: 6,003. Dimensions: 408' x 55'. Single-screw.
Four masts and one funnel. Steel hull. In the San Fran-
cisco-Manila-Singapore-Calcutta-Colombo service. Had
been chartered by Pacific Mail from W. R. Grace & Co.

Coptic   (1881)   White Star Line (Occidental and Oriental
Steamship Co.).
Built by Harland & Wolff, Ltd., Belfast, Ireland. Tonnage:
4,352. Dimensions: 430' x 42'. Single-screw, 15 knots.
Compound engines. Four masts and one funnel. Steel hull.
Sold to Pacific Mail in 1906. Owned by Persia Steamship
Co. of London and operated on commission basis by Pacific
Mail Steamship Co. Sold to Toyo Kisen Kaisha in 1915.
Renamed: (a) **Persia** (1907), (b) **Persia Maru** (1915).
Scrapped in 1925.

Creole State (1920) United States Shipping Board (Operated by Pacific Mail Steamship Co.).
Built by New York Shipbuilding Co., Camden, N. J. Tonnage: 10,533. Dimensions: 502′ x 62′ (522′ o.l.). Twin-screw, 14 knots. Reciprocating engines. Two masts and one funnel. Steel hull. Renamed: (a) **President Hayes** (1922), (b) **President Tyler.** Note: Operated for the United States Shipping Board between 1921–22. In San Francisco-Manila-East India service.

Dakota (1865) Pacific Mail Steamship Co.
Built by William H. Webb, Greenport, N. Y. Tonnage: 2,135. Dimensions: 270′ x 40′. Paddle-wheels. Two masts and one funnel. Wooden hull. Note: Built for North American Steamship Co. Purchased by Pacific Mail in 1873. Sold to Pacific Coast Steamship Co. in 1880. Condemned and sold by Pacific Coast Steamship Co. Broken up in 1886.

Dakota (1904) Great Northern Steamship Co.
Built by Eastern Shipbuilding Co., New London, Conn. Tonnage: 20,714. Dimensions: 622′ x 73′. Twin-screw, 14½ knots. Reciprocating engines. Four masts and one funnel. Steel hull. Made 17.1 knots on her trials in April 1905. Sailed on her maiden voyage on September 20, 1905. Wrecked on reef near Yokohama on March 3, 1907, with no loss of life. Sister ship: **Minnesota.**

Doric (1883) White Star Line (Occidental and Oriental Steamship Co.).
Built by Harland & Wolff, Ltd., Belfast, Ireland. Tonnage: 4,676. Dimensions: 440′ x 44′. Single-screw, 15 knots. Four masts and one funnel. Steel hull. Renamed: **Asia** (1907). Note: In service San Francisco-Hong Kong, 1896–1906. Sold to Pacific Mail Steamship Co. in 1906. Renamed **Asia** in 1907. Owned by Asia Steamship Co. of London, a subsidiary of Southern Pacific. Operated by Pacific Mail Steamship Co. Wrecked April 23, 1911 on Finger Rock, Taichow Island.

Ecuador (1915) Pacific Mail Steamship Co.
Built by Kon. Maats de Schelde, Flushing, Netherlands. Tonnage: 5,544. Dimensions: 380′ x 48′. Single-screw, 14 knots. Reciprocating engines. Two masts and one funnel. Renamed: **Santa Olivia.** Note: Purchased by Pacific Mail in 1916. In San Francisco-Hong Kong-Manila service, 1916–1921. Transferred to Panama Mail Steamship Co. in 1925. Sister ships: **Colombia** and **Venezuela.**

Empire State (1921) United States Shipping Board (Operated by Pacific Mail Steamship Co.).
Built by New York Shipbuilding Co., Camden, N. J. Tonnage: 14,127. Dimensions: 516′ x 72′ (535′ o.l.). Twin-screw, 17 knots. Turbines. Two masts and one funnel. Renamed: (a) **President Wilson** (1922), (b) **Maria Pipa** (1940), (c) **Cabo de Hornos** (1940). Note: Operated by Pacific Mail, 1921–1925. In San Francisco-Manila service. Sold by United States Shipping Board to Dollar Steamship Co. in 1925.

Empress of Asia (1913) Canadian Pacific Line.
Built by Fairfield Shipbuilding and Engineering Co., Ltd., Govan, Scotland. Tonnage: 16,909. Dimensions: 570′ x 68′ (590′ o.l.). Quadruple-screw, 20 knots. Turbines. Two masts and three funnels. Keel laid December 4, 1911. Launched November 23, 1912. Completed in May 1913. Made a trial speed of 21.43 knots. Did a trans-Pacific crossing from Yokohama in 9 days, 2 hours, 44 minutes in 1914. Sunk by enemy action off Singapore on February 5, 1942. Sister ship: **Empress of Russia.** Note: The first large liners to have cruiser sterns.

Empress of Australia (1914) Canadian Pacific Line.
Built by Vulcan Co., Stettin, Germany. Tonnage: 21,861. Dimensions: 589′ x 75′ (615′ o.l.). Twin-screw, 19 knots. Turbines. Two masts and three funnels. Note: Also listed under trans-Atlantic ships. Launched December 20, 1913. Completed in June 1922. In service Vancouver-Hong Kong, 1922–26. Took part in rescue work at Yokohama earthquake in 1925. Attained a trial speed of 17.2 knots in 1922, and after being re-engined in 1927 made 20.3 knots. Sold for scrap in 1952. Ex-**Empress of China,** ex-**Tirpitz** (1922).

Empress of Canada (1922) Canadian Pacific Line.
Built by Fairfield Shipbuilding and Engineering Co., Ltd., Govan, Scotland. Tonnage: 21,517. Dimensions: 627′ x 77′ (653′ o.l.). Twin-screw, 20 knots. Turbines. Two masts and three funnels. Launched August 17, 1920. Completed in April 1922. Attained a trial speed of 20.3 knots in 1922; after being re-engined in 1929 made 22.4 knots. Torpedoed and sunk on March 13, 1943, by an Italian submarine 390 miles S. of C. Palmas.

Empress of China (1890) Canadian Pacific Line.
Built by Naval Construction and Armaments Co., Ltd., Barrow, England. Tonnage: 5,947. Dimensions: 455′ x 51′

Twin-screw, 17 knots. Triple expansion engines. Three masts and two funnels. Steel hull. Launched March 25, 1891. Attained 19 knots on her trials. In service Vancouver-Hong Kong, 1891–1911. Wrecked near Yokohama in July 1911, with no loss of life. Later was refloated, but too badly damaged to be repaired and subsequently sold for scrap. Sister ships: **Empress of Japan** and **Empress of India**. Note: Beautiful yacht-like ships.

Empress of China (1914) Canadian Pacific Line.
Built by Vulcan Co., Stettin, Germany. Tonnage: 21,816. Dimensions: 589' x 75' (615) o.l.). Twin-screw, 19 knots. Turbines. Two masts and three funnels. Note: Used under name of **Empress of China** for only a brief time. Renamed **Empress of Australia**. Ex-**Tirpitz** (1922).

Empress of France (1913) Canadian Pacific Line.
Built by Wm. Beardmore & Co., Ltd., Glasgow. Tonnage: 18,388. Dimensions: 571' x 72' (590' o.l.). Quadruple-screw, 19½ knots. Turbines. Two masts and two funnels Note: Replaced **Empress of Canada** in Vancouver-Hong Kong service, 1928–1929. She was primarily a trans-Atlantic liner. Broken up for scrap in 1935. Ex-**Alsatian**.

Empress of India (1889) Canadian Pacific Line.
Built by Naval Construction and Armaments Co., Ltd., Barrow, England. Tonnage: 5,943. Dimensions: 455' x 51'. Twin-screw, 17 knots. Triple expansion engines. Three masts and two funnels. Launched August 30, 1890. Made 18.65 knots on her trials. In service Vancouver-Hong Kong, 1891–1914. Sold by Canadian Pacific in 1914 to Maharajah of Gwalior, who equipped her as a hospital ship, named **Loyalty**. Later sold to Scindia Steamship Company of Bombay, as **Loyalty**. Broken up for scrap in 1923. Sister ships: **Empress of China** and **Empress of Japan**.

Empress of Japan (1890) Canadian Pacific Line.
Built by Naval Construction and Armaments Co., Ltd., Barrow, England. Tonnage: 5,940. Dimensions: 455' x 51'. Twin-screw, 18 knots. Triple expansion engines. Three masts and two funnels. Steel hull. Launched December 13, 1890. Attained a speed of 18.91 knots on her trials. Held the trans-Pacific speed record for a number of years, until bettered by the **Empress of Russia**. In service Vancouver-Hong Kong, 1891–1914, 1915–1922. Served as auxiliary cruiser during the 1914–1915 period Scrapped in 1926. Sister ships: **Empress of China** and **Empress of India**.

304

Empress of Japan   (1930)   Canadian Pacific Line.
   Built by Fairfield Shipbuilding and Engineering Co., Ltd.
   Govan, Scotland.   Tonnage: 26,032.   Dimensions: 644′ x
   83′ (666′ o.l.). Twin-screw, 22 knots. Turbines. Two masts
   and three funnels. Her maximum trial speed was 22.38
   knots. Held the trans-Pacific speed record. Made the crossing from Yokohama to Vancouver in 8 days, 6 hours, 27
   minutes. From keel to navigating bridge 98 feet. She was
   launched on December 17, 1929. Completed in June 1930.
   Renamed: (a) **Empress of Scotland** (1942), (b) **Hanseatic**
   (1958). Note: See PART I.

Empress of Russia   (1913)   Canadian Pacific Line.
   Built by Fairfield Shipbuilding and Engineering Co., Ltd.,
   Govan, Scotland. Tonnage: 16,810. Dimensions: 570′ x 68′
   (590′ o.l.). Quadruple-screw, 20 knots. Turbines. Two
   masts and three funnels. Keel laid November 7, 1911.
   Launched August 28, 1912. Completed in March 1913.
   Her maximum trial speed was 21.178 knots. Cost about
   $2,500,000. Made a record trans-Pacific crossing from
   Yokohama to Race Rocks in 8 days, 18 hours, 31 minutes,
   at an average speed of 19.86 knots. Burned while refitting
   at Vickers-Armstrong Yard, Barrow-in-Furness, September
   8, 1945. The hulk was broken up for scrap in 1946. Sister
   ship: **Empress of Asia.**

Fushima Maru   (1914)   N. Y. K. Line.
   Built by Mitsubishi Dockyard, Nagasaki, Japan. Tonnage:
   10,936. Dimensions: 513′ x 63′. Twin-screw, 15½ knots.
   Reciprocating engines. Two masts and one funnel. Completed December 2, 1914. Note: Transferred from her
   regular Japan-European run to trans-Pacific service in
   September 1917, and not put back on the European trade
   until March 1922. Torpedoed and sunk on February 1, 1943.
   Sister ships: **Suwa Maru, Kashima Maru, Katori Maru**
   and **Yasaka Maru.**

Gaelic   (1872)   White Star Line; Occidental and Oriental
   Steamship Co.
   Built by Harland & Wolff, Belfast, Ireland. Tonnage: 2,652.
   Dimensions: 370′ x 36′. Single-screw. Four masts and one
   funnel. In service Liverpool-South America, London-New
   York, 1873–1875; chartered by Occidental and Oriental and
   in service San Francisco-Hong Kong, 1875–1883. Sold to
   Spanish owners in 1883 and renamed **Hugo.** Sold in 1896
   at Amsterdam with stranding damage and subsequently
   broken up.

Gaelic   (1885)   White Star Line; Occidental and Oriental Steamship Co.
Built by Harland & Wolff, Ltd., Belfast, Ireland. Tonnage: 4,206.   Dimensions: 420′ x 42′.   Single-screw, 14 knots. Four masts and one funnel. Sister ship: **Belgic.**

General Lee   (1908)   States Steamship Co.
Built by Workman, Clark & Co., Ltd., Belfast, Ireland. Tonnage: 4,732. Dimensions: 378′ x 49′. Single-screw, 14 knots. Reciprocating engines. Two masts and one funnel. Ex-**Cartago** (1932). Renamed: **Cartago** (1938). Sister ships: **General Pershing** and **General Sherman.** Note: These three liners entered the trans-Pacific (Portland-San Francisco-Japan-China-Philippines) service in 1933.

General Pershing   (1908)   States Steamship Co.
Built by Workman, Clark & Co., Ltd., Belfast, Ireland. Tonnage: 4,732. Dimensions: 378′ x 49′. Single-screw, 14 knots. Reciprocating engines. Two masts and one funnel. Ex-**Heredia** (1932). Renamed: **Heredia** (1938). Note: See **General Lee** for additional facts.

General Sherman   (1908)   States Steamship Co.
Built by Workman, Clark & Co., Ltd., Belfast, Ireland. Tonnage: 4,732. Dimensions: 378′ x 49′. Single-screw, 14 knots. Reciprocating engines. Two masts and one funnel. Ex-**Parismina** (1932). Renamed: **Parismina** (1938). Note: See **General Lee** for additional facts.

Golden State   (1921)   United States Shipping Board. (Operated by Pacific Mail Steamship Co.).
Built by Newport News Shipbuilding & Drydock Co., Newport News, Va. Tonnage: 14,123. Dimensions: 517′ x 72′ (539′ o.l.). Twin-screw, 17 knots. Turbines. Two masts and one funnel. Note: Operated by Pacific Mail, 1921–1925. Sold by United States Shipping Board to Dollar Steamship Company in 1925. Renamed: (a) **President Cleveland** (1922), (b) **Tasker H. Bliss.**

Granada   (1873)   Pacific Mail Steamship Co.
Built by Harlan & Hollingsworth, Wilmington, Delaware. Tonnage 2,572. Dimensions: 280′ x 40′. Single-screw. Two masts and one funnel. Iron hull. Wrecked June 22, 1889 on Point Tejupan, Mexico.

Granite State   (1921)   United States Shipping Board. (Operated by Pacific Mail Steamship Co.).
Built by New York Shipbuilding Co., Camden, N. J. Tonnage: 10,500. Dimensions: 502′ x 62′ (522′ o.l.). Twin-

screw, 14 knots. Reciprocating engines. Two masts and one funnel. In San Francisco-East Indies service, 1921–1922. Renamed: (a) **President Polk** (1922), (b) **President Taylor.**

Great Republic   (1866)   Pacific Mail Steamship Co.
Built by Henry Steers, Greenpoint, Long Island, N. Y. Tonnage: 3,881. Dimensions: 360′ x 47′. Paddle-wheels. Vertical beam engine. Three masts and one funnel. Wooden hull. Launched November 8, 1866. Cost $1,053,234. Note: First vessel of the company to be built for the San Francisco-Japan-China service. In San Francisco-Hong Kong service, 1867–1876. Sold to P. B. Cornwall in 1878. Wrecked on Sand Island, Columbia River Bar, April 19, 1879.

Hakata Maru   (1897)   N. Y. K. Line.
Built by D. & W. Henderson & Co., Glasgow, Scotland. Tonnage: 6,241. Dimensions: 445′ x 49′. Twin-screw, 13 knots. Reciprocating engines. Four masts and one funnel. Note: originally used on the Japan-European route. Later transferred to the Japan-Seattle service. Ships in this class were: **Kawachi Maru, Kanagawa Maru, Wakasa Maru, Kamakura Maru, Sanuki Maru, Inaba Maru, Tamba Maru, Bingo Maru, Sado Maru, Hitachi Maru** and **Awa Maru.**

Hawaii Maru   (1915)   Osaka Line.
Built by Mitsubishi Zozen, Japan. Tonnage: 9,482. Dimensions: 475′ x 61′. Twin-screw, 13 knots. Reciprocating engines. Two masts and one funnel. Torpedoed and sunk on December 2, 1944. Sister ships: **Africa Maru, Arabia Maru, Arizona Maru** and **Manila Maru.**

Heian Maru   (1930)   N. Y. K. Line.
Built by Osaka Iron Works, Osaka, Japan. Tonnage: 11,616. Dimensions: 510′ x 66′. Twin-screw, 18 knots. Motorship. Two masts and one funnel. Laid down June 19, 1929. Launched April 16, 1930. Completed November 24, 1930. Cost about $7,000,000. Sunk by United States naval plane on February 17, 1944. Sister ships: **Hikawa Maru** and **Hiye Maru.**

Hie Maru   (1930)   N. Y. K. Line.
Built by Yokohama Dock Co., Yokohama, Japan. Tonnage: 11,621. Dimensions: 511′ x 66′. Twin-screw, 18 knots. Motorship. Two masts and one funnel. Torpedoed and sunk on November 17, 1943. Ex-**Hiye Maru** (1938). Sister ships: **Hikawa Maru** and **Heian Maru.**

Hikawa Maru (1930) N. Y. K. Line.
  Built by Yokohama Dock Co., Yokohama, Japan. Tonnage: 11,622. Dimensions: 511′ x 66′. Twin-screw, 18 knots. Motorship. Two masts and one funnel. Laid down November 9, 1928. Launched September 30, 1929. Completed April 25, 1930. Reconditioned for passenger service between Japanese ports and Seattle, Portland and Vancouver in 1953. Accommodation for 34 first-class and 200 third-class passengers. The first Japanese liner to re-enter the trans-Pacific passenger trade since World War II. Note: The only Japanese trans-Pacific passenger ship to survive the Second World War. Withdrawn from service in 1961. Sister ships: **Hiye Maru** and **Heian Maru.**

Hiye Maru (1930) N. Y. K. ine.
  Built by Yokohama Dock Co., Yokohama, Japan. Tonnage: 11,622. Dimensions: 511′ x 66′. Twin-screw, 18 knots. Motorship. Laid down May 25, 1929. Launched February 12, 1930. Completed July 31, 1930. Renamed: **Hie Maru** (1938). Sister ships: **Hikawa Maru,** and **Heian Maru.**

Hongkong Maru (1898) Toyo Kisen Kaisha.
  Built by Sir J. Laing, Sunderland, England. Tonnage: 6,185. Dimensions: 431′ x 50′. Twin-screw, 17 knots. Recrocating engines. Two masts and two funnels. Clipper bow. Note: Later acquired by Osaka Line. Running mates: **America Maru** and **Nippon Maru.**

Hoosier State (1921) United States Shipping Board. (Operated by Pacific Mail Steamship Co.).
  Built by New York Shipbuilding Co., Camden, N. J. Tonnage: 14,187. Dimensions: 516′ x 72′ (535′ o.l.). Twin-screw, 17 knots. Turbines. Two masts and one funnel. In San Francisco-Manila service, 1921–1925. Sold by United States Shipping Board to Dollar Steamship Company in 1925. Renamed (a) **President Lincoln** (1922), (b) **Maria del Carmen** (1940), (c) **Cabo de Buena Esperanza.**

Iyo Maru (1901) N. Y. K. Line.
  Built by Mitsubishi Dockyard, Nagasaki, Japan. Tonnage: 6,320. Dimensions: 445′ x 49′. Twin-screw, 14 knots. Reciprocating engines. Two masts and one funnel. In Seattle-Japan service. Note: She was one of three ships which replaced the line's original vessels used in this service. For list of similar ships see **Hakata Maru.**

Japan   (1867)   Pacific Mail Steamship Co.
Built by Henry Steers, Greenpoint, Long Island, N. Y. Tonnage: 4,351.   Dimensions: 362′ x 49′.   Paddle-wheels. Vertical-beam engines.   Three masts and one funnel. Wooden hull. Launched December 17, 1867. Cost $1,049,434. In San Francisco-Hong Kong service, 1868–1874.   Burned at sea between Yokohama and Hong Kong during December 17–18, 1874.   Running mates: **America, China** and **Great Republic.**

Kaga Maru   (1901)   N. Y. K. Line.
Built by Mitsubishi Dockyard, Nagasaki, Japan. Tonnage: 6,301.   Dimensions: 445′ x 49′.   Twin-screw, 14 knots. Reciprocating engines. Two masts and one funnel. Completed in May 1901. In Seattle-Japan service. Note: For list of similar ships see **Hakata Maru.**

Kamakura Maru   (1930)   N. Y. K. Line.
Built by Yokohama Dock Co., Yokohama, Japan. Tonnage: 17,526.   Dimensions: 560′ x 74′.   Twin-screw, 19 knots. Motorship. Two masts and one funnel. Sunk by submarine on April 28, 1943, while on way from Manila to Singapore. A number of lives were lost. Ex-**Chichibu Maru** (1939). Running mates: **Asama Maru** and **Tatuta Maru.**

Kamo Maru   (1908)   N. Y. K. Line.
Built by Mitsubishi Dockyard, Nagasaki, Japan. Tonnage: 8,524.   Dimensions: 464′ x 54′.   Triple-screw, 15 knots. Reciprocating engines. Two masts and one funnel. Completed December 8, 1908. Note: One of several liners transferred from the Japan-European route to the trans-Pacific service in September 1917. It was not until March 1922 that they were returned to their original run. Torpedoed and sunk on July 3, 1944. Sister ships: **Hirano Maru, Mishima Maru, Miyazaki Maru, Atsuta Maru** and **Kitano Maru.**

Kanagawa Maru   (1896)   N. Y. K. Line.
Built by D. & W. Henderson & Co., Glasgow. Tonnage: 6,238.   Dimensions: 445′ x 49′.   Twin-screw, 13 knots. Reciprocating engines. Four masts and one funnel. Note: The first of twelve new vessels built for the Japan-European service.   Commenced her maiden voyage from Japan to Europe on May 14, 1898. Transferred to the trans-Pacific trade in June 1904, as also were **Iyo Maru** and **Shinano Maru.** See **Hakata Maru** for list of sister ships.

Kashima Maru   (1913)   N. Y. K. Line.
Built by Kawasaki Dockyard Co., Kobe, Japan. Tonnage: 10,559. Dimensions: 501' x 59'. Twin-screw, 14½ knots. Reciprocating engines. Two masts and one funnel. Completed October 1, 1913. Transferred from the Japan-European route to trans-Pacific service in September 1917, and not put back on her original run until March 1922. Renamed: **Kasima Maru.** Torpedoed and sunk on September 27, 1943. Sister ships: **Katori Maru, Suwa Maru, Yasaka Maru** and **Fushima Maru.**

Katori Maru   (1913)   N. Y. K. Line.
Built by Mitsubishi Dockyard, Nagasaki, Japan. Tonnage: 10,526. Dimensions: 500' x 59'. Triple-screw, 15½ knots. Reciprocating engines. Two masts and one funnel. Completed September 9, 1913. Transferred from the Japan-European service to the trans-Pacific run in September 1917, remaining on it until March 1922. Sunk by a Dutch submarine on December 23, 1941. Sister ships: **Fushima Maru, Kashima Maru, Suwa Maru** and **Yasaka Maru.**

Korea   (1901)   Pacific Mail Steamship Co.
Built by Newport News Shipbuilding & Drydock Co., Newport News, Va. Tonnage: 11,276. Dimensions: 551' x 63'. Twin-screw, 20 knots (service speed 16 knots). Quadruple expansion engines. Two masts and two funnels. Steel hull. The elliptical funnels were 14' x 10' and measured 108' high from fire grate to rim. In San Francisco-Hong Kong, Manila service of Pacific Mail, 1902–1915. Sold to Atlantic Transport Co. in 1915. Purchased by Toyo Kisen Kaisha in 1916. Renamed: **Korea Maru** (1916). Sold to be broken up in 1934. Sister ship: **Siberia.**

Korea Maru   (1901)   N. Y. K. Line.
Built by Newport News Shipbuilding & Drydock Co., Newport News, Va. Tonnage: 11,810. Dimensions: 551' x 63'. Twin-screw, 20 knots. Quadruple expansion engines. Two masts and two funnels. Formerly owned by Toyo Kisen Kaisha. Scrapped in 1934. Ex-**Korea.** Sister ship: **Siberia Maru.**

Lord of the Isles   (1870)   Mocondray Line.
Built by R. Napier & Sons, Glasgow. Tonnage: 2,477. Dimensions: 320' x 37'. Single-screw.

Macgregor   (1872)   Australian and American Mail Steamship Co.
Built by John Key and Kirkcaldy, Kinghorn. Tonnage:

2,167. Dimensions: 338′ x 34′. Single-screw. Compound engines. Four masts. Under charter. Operated by Pacific Mail Steamship Co. on their trans-Pacific route in 1873.

Maheno (1905) Union Steamship Co. of New Zealand. Built by W. Denny & Bros., Dumbarton, Scotland. Tonnage: 5,323. Dimensions: 400′ x 50′. Triple-screw, 17 knots. Turbines. Two masts and two funnels. Note: The first turbine steamship to cross the Pacific. Sold to Japan for scrap in 1935. However, broke from tow July 7, 1935, 60 miles S.E. of Sandy Cape, Sydney to Osaka. Drifted ashore July 9, on Ocean Beach, Fraser Island. The wreck was sold.

Maitai (1892) Union Steamship Company of New Zealand. Built by C. S. Swan & Hunter, Ltd., Newcastle, England. Tonnage: 3,393. Dimensions: 345′ x 42′. Single-screw. Three masts and one funnel. Wrecked at Raratonga in 1916. Ex-**Miowera**. Sister ship: **Warrimoo**.

Makura (1908) Union Steamship Co. of New Zealand. Built by Alexander Stephen & Sons, Ltd., Linthouse, Glasgow. Tonnage: 8,075. Dimensions: 450′ x 57′. Twinscrew, 17 knots. Reciprocating engines. Two masts and one funnel. Note: Entered the trans-Pacific service as the largest vessel in that trade. Converted from coal to oil fuel in 1924. Broken up by Chinese shipbreakers in 1936.

Manchuria (1904) Pacific Mail Steamship Co. Built by New York Shipbuilding Co., Camden, N. J. Tonnage: 13,638. Dimensions: 600′ x 65′. (616′ o.l.). Twinscrew, 16 knots. Quadruple expansion engines. Four masts and one funnel. Steel hull. In San Francisco-Hong Kong-Manila service, 1904–1915. Owned by E. H. Harriman and chartered by Pacific Mail during the 1904–1911 period. Purchased by Pacific Mail in 1911. Sold to Atlantic Transport Co. in 1915. Later in trans-Atlantic service for a time. Renamed: (a) **President Johnson** (1929), (b) **Santa Cruz** (1947). Broken up in Italy in 1952. Sister ship: **Mongolia**.

Manila Maru (1915) Osaka Line. Built by Mitsubishi Zozen, Japan. Tonnage: 9,518. Dimensions: 475′ x 61′. Twin-screw, 13 knots. Reciprocating engines. Two masts and one funnel. Torpedoed and sunk on November 25, 1944. Sister ships: **Africa Maru, Hawaii Maru, Arabia Maru** and **Arizona Maru**.

Manuka (1903) Union Steamship Co. of New Zealand. Built by Wm. Denny & Bros., Dumbarton, Scotland. Tonnage: 4,534. Dimensions: 368' x 47'. Twin-screw, 15 knots. Two masts and one funnel. Wrecked on December 16, 1929, at Long Point, New Zealand while bound from Melbourne to Wellington.

Marama (1907) Union Steamship Co. of New Zealand. Built by Caird & Co., Ltd., Greenock, Scotland. Tonnage: 6,437. Dimensions: 420' x 53'. Twin-screw, 16 knots. Reciprocating engines. Two masts and one funnel. Broken up for scrap in 1938.

Mararoa (1885) Union Steamship Co. of New Zealand. Built by Wm. Denny Bros., Dumbarton, Scotland. Tonnage: 2,598. Dimensions: 320' x 42'. Single-screw, 15 knots. Triple expansion engines. Two masts and one funnel. Note: The first vessel with triple expansion engines to cross the Pacific. Made a speed of 16.8 knots on her trials. Entered trans-Pacific service in 1885. Made only a few trips across the Pacific as she was much too small for the service. Scrapped in 1938.

Mariposa (1883) Oceanic Steamship Co. Built by W. Cramp & Sons, Philadelphia, Pa. Tonnage: 3,158. Dimensions: 314' x 41'. Single-screw, 15 knots. Reciprocating engines. Two masts and one funnel. Steel hull. Launched March 7, 1883. Attained a speed of 15½ knots on her trials. In San Francisco-Honolulu service, 1883–1885. In San Francisco-Tahiti trade during 1901–1912 period. Sold to Alaska Steamship Company in 1912. Lost on Straits Island Reef, Sumner Straits, Alaska in 1917. Sister ship: **Alameda.**

Mariposa (1932) Oceanic Steamship Co. Built by Bethlehem Steel Co., Shipyard Division, Quincy, Massachusetts. Tonnage: 18,017. Dimensions: 605' x 79' (631' o.l.). Twin-screw, 20½ knots. Turbines. Two masts and two funnels. Used as a troopship in World War II. Laid up at Alameda, California. Near the end of 1953 the Home Lines purchased the **Mariposa** for their Atlantic service. She was thoroughly reconditioned and in January 1955 commenced her first sailing as a Home liner under the new name of **Homeric.** Sister ships: **Monterey** and **Lurline.**

*****Mariposa** (1953) Matson Lines. Built by Bethlehem Shipbuilding Co., Quincy, Massachusetts. Tonnage: 14,812. Dimensions: 529' x 70'4 (563' o.l.). Single-screw, 20 knots. Two steam turbines. Single mast and one funnel. Note: Originally built as a "Mariner" type fast freighter. Converted to passenger ship at Portland, Oregon. Made a top speed of 24.6 knots during her trials. Passengers: 365 first class. Route: California-Australia, via South Sea Islands. Ex-**Pine Tree Mariner** (1956). Sister ship: **Monterey.**

Maunganui (1911) Union Steamship Co. of New Zealand. Built by Fairfield Shipbuilding and Engineering Co., Ltd., Govan, Scotland. Tonnage: 7,527. Dimensions: 430′ x 55′. Twin-screw, 17 knots. Reciprocating engines. Two masts and one funnel. Sold to Panamanian interests in 1947 and renamed **Cyrenia.**

Miike Maru (1888) N. Y. K. Line. Built by R. Thompson & Sons, Sunderland, England. Tonnage: 3,308. Dimensions: 320′ x 42′. Single-screw. Two masts and one funnel. Inaugurated their service from Kobe to Seattle on August 1, 1896.

Mikado (1873) Australian & American Mail Steamship Co. Built by Aitken & Mansel, Glasgow, Scotland. Tonnage: 3,034. Dimensions: 371′ x 36′ (386′ o.l.). Four masts, single-screw, compound engines. Note: D. R. Macgregor & Co. listed as owners of the vessel.

Minnesota (1904) Great Northern Steamship Co. Built by Eastern Shipbuilding Co., Groton, Conn. Tonnage: 20,718. Dimensions: 622′ x 73′. Twin-screw, 14½ knots. Reciprocating engines. Four masts and one funnel. Note: Largest ship on the Pacific when built. Commenced her maiden voyage on January 23 1905. Sold to German shipbreakers in June 1923. Sister ship: **Dakota.**

Miowera (1892) Huddart, Parker & Co. Built by C. S. Swan & Hunter, Ltd., Newcastle, England. Tonnage: 3,393. Dimensions: 345′ x 42′. Single-screw. Three masts and one funnel. Renamed: **Maitai.** Sister Ship: **Warrimoo.**

Moana (1897) Union Steamship Co. of New Zealand. Built by W. Denny & Bros., Dumbarton, Scotland. Tonnage: 3,915. Dimensions: 350′ x 44′. Single-screw, 16 knots. Two masts and one funnel. Broken up for scrap in New Zealand in 1927.

Moeraki (1902) Union Steamship Co. of New Zealand. Built by W. Denny & Bros., Dumbarton, Scotland. Ton-

nage: 4,392. Dimensions: 368' x 47'. Twin-screw, 15 knots.
Reciprocating engines. Two masts and one funnel. Broken
up for scrap in 1933.

Mongolia (1904)   Pacific Mail Steamship Co.
Built by New York Shipbuilding Co., Camden, N. J. Tonnage: 13,635. Dimensions: 600' x 65' (616' o.l.). Twin-
screw, 16 knots. Quadruple expansion engines. Four masts
and one funnel. On San Francisco-Hong Kong-Manila run,
1904–1915. Owned by E. H. Harriman, 1904–1911, chartered to Pacific Mail. Owned by Pacific Mail Steamship
Co., 1911–1915. Sold to Atlantic Transport Co. in 1915.
Later was in trans-Atlantic service for a time. To Panama
Pacific Line in 1923. Renamed: (a) **President Fillmore**
(1929), (b) **Panamanian** (1940). Broken up for scrap at
Shanghai in 1946. Sister ship: **Manchuria.**

Monowai (1890)   Union Steamship Co. of New Zealand.
Built by W. Denny & Bros., Dumbarton, Scotland. Tonnage: 3,433.   Dimensions: 330' x 42'.   Single-screw, 14
knots. Reciprocating engines. Two masts and one funnel.
Partially dismantled and sunk, so as to form a breakwater
at Gisborne, New Zealand, in 1926.

Monowai (1925)   Union Steamship Co. of New Zealand.
Built by Harland & Wolff, Ltd., Belfast, Ireland. Tonnage:
10,852.   Dimensions: 500' x 63'.   Twin-screw, 19 knots.
Reciprocating engines and turbines. Two masts and two
funnels. Still (1958) in service. Ex-**Razmak.**

Monteagle (1899)   Canadian Pacific Line.
Built by Palmer's Shipbuilding & Iron Co., Ltd., Jarrow-on-
Tyne, Newcastle, England. Tonnage: 6,163. Dimensions:
445' x 52'. Single-screw, 13 knots. Reciprocating engines.
Four masts and one funnel. Steel hull. Originally built for
Beaver Line's cattle and freight service, Bristol-Montreal.
In Vancouver-Hong Kong service, 1906–1922. Note: Also
served in transatlantic trade. Broken up for scrap in 1926.
Sister ship: **Montfort.**

Monterey (1932)   Oceanic Steamship Co. (Matson Line.)
Built by Bethlehem Steel Co., Shipyard Division, Quincy,
Massachusetts. Tonnage: 18,017. Dimensions: 605' x 79'
(631' o.l.). Twin-screw, 20½ knots. Turbines. Two masts
and two funnels. Built at a cost of $8,000,000. Served as an
American troopship in World War II. Laid up after the
war. Vessel was sold to United States Government in 1952.

She was later sold back to the Matson Line, who had her refitted for their California-Hawaii service. Renamed: **Matsonia** (1956). Sister ships: **Mariposa** and **Lurline.**

*Monterey (1952)   Matson Lines.
   Built by Bethlehem Sparrows Point Shipyard, Md. Tonnage: 14,799. Dimensions: 529′ x 70′ (563′ o.l.). Single-screw, 20 knots. Two steam turbines. Single mast and one funnel. Note: Originally built as a "Mariner" class freighter. Rebuilt as passenger ship for Matson Lines in 1956. Passengers: 365 first class. Route: California-Australia, via South Sea Islands. Ex-**Free State Mariner** (1956). Sister ship: **Mariposa.**

Nanking (1913)   China Mail Steamship Co. (United States).
   Built by New York Shipbuilding Co., Camden, N. J. Tonnage: 8,262. Dimensions: 423′ x 54′. Twin-screw, 17 knots. Triple expansion engines. Two masts and two funnels. Service: Trans-Pacific passenger trade. Renamed: **Emma Alexander** (1924). Vessel sold to British in 1941 after several years of idleness. Ex-**Congress.**

Nebraska (1865)   United States, New Zealand and Australia Mail Steamship Co.
   Built by Henry Steers, Williamsburg, N. Y. Tonnage: 2,143. Dimensions: 269′ x 40′. Paddle-wheels. Beam engines. Two masts and one funnel. Wooden hull. In service San Francisco-Sydney, 1871–1873. Purchased by Pacific Mail Steamship Co. in 1873. Sold to Goodall, Nelson & Perkins in 1875. Sold to be broken up for scrap in 1876. Register surrendered, vessel unfit for service and scrapped in January, 1878.

Nevada (1867)   United States, New Zealand and Australia Mail Steamship Co.
   Built by J. Simonson, Brooklyn, N. Y. Tonnage: 2,143. Dimensions: 281′ x 40′. Paddle-wheels, 12½ knots. Beam engines. Two masts and two funnels. Wooden hull. In service San Francisco-Sydney, 1871–1873. Purchased by Pacific Mail Steamship Co. in 1873. Placed on Yokohama-Shanghai branch line. Sold to Mitsu Bishi Mail Steamship Co. in 1875. Renamed: **Seikyo Maru.** Note: Originally built as the **Paou Shan.** Renamed the **Nevada in** 1866.

Niagara (1913)   Union Steamship Co. of New Zealand.
   Built by John Brown & Co., Ltd., Clydebank, Glasgow. Toinnage: 13,413. Dimensions: 524′ x 66′. Triple-screw,

18 knots. Two masts and two funnels. Note: The first ship with combination reciprocating engines and turbine to serve in the trans-Pacific trade. Held the honor for a number of years of being the largest passenger ship trading to Australia from North American Pacific ports. Did not serve as a troopship in the First World War, as her need in maintaining the mail service in this particular trade was too great. Note: This liner was actually operated by the Canadian-Australasian Line, a subsidiary of the above company. During the Second World War, she struck a mine and sunk NW of North Island, New Zealand, on June 19, 1940.

Nile   (1893)   Pacific Mail Steamship Co.
     Built by J. & G. Thomson, Ltd., Glasgow. Tonnage: 5,888. Dimensions: 420′ x 52′. Single-screw, 15 knots. Reciprocating engines. Three masts and two funnels. Steel hull. Note: Purchased from Royal Mail Line by Nile Steamship Co. of London, a Southern Pacific Line subsidiary, in 1911. Operated on commission basis by Pacific Mail Steamship Co. In service San Francisco-Hong Kong, 1912–1914. Sold to China Mail Steamship Co. in 1915. In service San Francisco-Hong Kong, Manila, 1916–1922. This former South American passenger liner was acquired for the purpose of replacing the **Asia,** which was wrecked in 1911.

Nippon Maru   (1898)   Toyo Kisen Kaisha.
     Built by Sir J. Laing, Sunderland, England. Tonnage: 6,178. Dimensions: 431′ x 50′. Twin-screw, 17 knots. Reciprocating engines. Two masts and two funnels. Later appeared with three masts. Sold to Chile. In 1929 was serving as a depot ship at Iquique. Renamed: **Renaico.** Running mates: **America Maru** and **Hongkong Maru.**

Nitta Maru   (1939)   N. Y. K. Line.
     Built by Mitsubishi Dockyard, Nagasaki, Japan. Tonnage: 17,150. Dimensions: 557′ x 73′ (590′ o.l.). Twin-screw, 22 knots. Turbines. Two masts and one funnel. Note: Designed and built for the Japan-European service, but never served on it as she was placed on the trans-Pacific route because of war conditions when completed. She set a trans-Pacific speed record for the Yokohama-San Francisco run in April 1941, doing 5,490 miles in 11 days, 18 hours, 42 minutes. During World War II was acquired by the Japanese Government and renamed. Sunk by United States submarine on December 4, 1943. Sister ships: **Yawata Maru** and **Kasuga Maru.**

Oceanic   (1870)   White Star Line; Occidental and Oriental Steamship Co.
Built by Harland & Wolff, Ltd., Belfast, Ireland. Tonnage: 3,808. Dimensions: 420' x 40'. Single-screw, 14½ knots. Compound engines. Four masts and one funnel. Iron hull. In service San Francisco-Hong Kong, 1875–1895. Broken up at London in 1896. Note: This famous pioneer White Star liner is also listed in the trans-Atlantic section.

Parthia   (1870)   Canadian Pacific Line.
Built by Wm. Denny & Bros., Ltd., Dumbarton, Scotland. Tonnage: 3,431. Dimensions: 360' x 41'. Single-screw, 13 knots. Two masts and one funnel. Renamed: **Victoria** (1892). Note: Built for the Cunard Line. Operated for the Canadian Pacific Railway on the Vancouver-Hong Kong route, 1887–1891. Placed on Tacoma-Hong Kong service for Northern Pacific Steamship Co., 1892–1899. In trans-Pacific service, 1900–1904. In service to Alaska since 1904.

Persia   (1881)   Pacific Mail Steamship Co.
Built by Harland & Wolff, Ltd., Belfast, Ireland. Tonnage: 4,356. Dimensions: 430' x 42'. Single-screw, 14 knots. Four masts and one funnel. Renamed: **Persia Maru.** Ex-**Coptic.**

Persia Maru   (1881)   Toyo Kisen Kaisha.
Built by Harland & Wolff, Ltd., Belfast, Ireland. Tonnage: 4,356. Dimensions: 430' x 42'. Single-screw, 14 knots. Four masts and one funnel. Broken up for scrap in 1915. Ex-**Persia,** ex-**Coptic.**

Peru   (1892)   Pacific Mail Steamship Co.
Built by Union Iron Works, San Francisco, California. Tonnage: 3,528. Dimensions: 336' x 45'. Single-screw. Two masts and one funnel. Steel hull. Sold to French owners in 1919.

President Adams   (1921)   Dollar Steamship Co.
Built by New York Shipbuilding Co., Camden, N. J. Tonnage: 10,533. Dimensions: 502' x 62' (522' o.l.). Twin-screw, 14 knots. Reciprocating engines. Two masts and one funnel. Renamed: **President Grant.** A unit of the Dollar fleet, 1924–1938. Stranded off New Guinea on February 26, 1944. Ex-**Centennial State.** Sister ships: **President Garfield, President Harrison, President Hayes, President Monroe, President Polk** and **President Van Buren.**

317

President Buchanan (1920) Dollar Steamship Co.
  Built by New York Shipbuilding Co., Camden, N. J. Tonnage: 10,533. Dimensions: 502′ x 62′ (522′ o.l.). Twinscrew, 14 knots. Reciprocating engines. Two masts and one funnel. Ex-**President Monroe**, ex-**Panhandle State.** Renamed: (a) **Emily H. M. Weder** (U.S. Army hospital ship), (b) **President Buchanan.** Now (1953) in the United States Government laid-up fleet Sister ships listed under **President Adams.**

President Cleveland (1921) Dollar Steamship Co.
  Built by Newport News Shipbuilding & Drydock Co., Newport News, Va. Tonnage: 14,123. Dimensions: 517′ x 72′ (539′ o.l.). Twin-screw, 17 knots. Turbines. Two masts and one funnel. Ex-**Golden State.** Renamed: **Tasker H. Bliss.** Torpedoed and sunk in the harbor at Fedala, French Morocco, on November 12, 1942, during the Allied invasion of North Africa. Note: See **President Jefferson** for list of sister ships.

*President Cleveland (1947) American President Lines.
  Built by Bethlehem Shipbuilding Co., Alameda Shipyard, Inc., Alameda, California. Tonnage: 15,359. Dimensions: 573′ x 75′ (609′ o.l.). Twin-screw, 18 knots. Turbo-electric. Two masts and two funnels. Accommodation for 326 firstclass and 506 third-class passengers. Sister ship: **President Wilson.** Note: The newest and finest liners on the trans-Pacific trade to date.

President Coolidge (1931) Dollar Steamship Co.
  Built by Newport News Shipbuilding & Drydock Co., Newport News, Va. Tonnage: 21,936. Dimensions: 615′ x 81′ (654′ o.l.). Twin-screw, 21 knots. Turbo-electric. Two masts and two funnels. Launched in October 1931. Struck a mine and sunk rapidly in channel at Espiritu Santo in the South Pacific, on October 26, 1942. Nearly all of the 5,000 officers and men on board were saved. Sister ship: **President Hoover.**

President Fillmore (1904) Dollar Steamship Co.
  Built by New York Shipbuilding Co., Camden, N. J. Tonnage: 15,575. Dimensions: 600′ x 65′ (616′ o.l.). Twinscrew, 16 knots. Quadruple expansion engines. Four masts and one funnel. Ex-**Mongolia** (1923). Renamed: **Panamanian.** Broken up at Shanghai in 1946. Sister ship: **President Johnson.**

President Garfield (1921) Dollar Steamship Co.
Built by New York Shipbuilding Co., Camden, N. J. Tonnage: 10,538. Dimensions: 502′ x 62′ (522′ o.l.). Twin-screw, 14 knots. Reciprocating engines. Two masts and one funnel. Ex-**Blue Hen State.** Renamed: (a) **President Madison,** (b) **Kenmore,** (c) **Refuge** (hospital ship). Scrapped in 1948. Note: See **President Adams** for list of sister ships.

President Grant (1921) American Mail Line.
Built by Bethlehem Shipbuilding Co., Alameda Shipyard, Inc., Alameda, Calif. Tonnage: 14,199. Dimensions: 517′ x 72′ (539′ o.l.). Twin-screw, 17 knots. Turbines. Two masts and one funnel. Ex-**Pine Tree State.** Renamed: **Harris.** Scrapped in 1948. Note: See **President Jefferson** for list of sister ships.

President Grant (1921) American President Lines.
Built by New York Shipbuilding Co., Camden, N. J. Tonnage: 10,533. Dimensions: 502′ x 62′ (522′ o.l.). Twin-screw, 14 knots. Reciprocating engines. Two masts and one funnel. Grounded on reef 70 miles from Milne Bay on February 27, 1944 and became a total loss. Ex-**President Adams,** ex-**Centennial State.** Note: Sister ships listed under **President Adams.**

President Harrison (1921) Dollar Steamship Co.
Built by New York Shipbuilding Co., Camden, N. J. Tonnage: 10,533. Dimensions: 502′ x 62′ (522′ o.l.). Twin-screw, 14 knots. Reciprocating engines. Two masts and one funnel. Captured by the Japanese on December 8, 1941. Sunk by an American submarine on September 12, 1944. Ex-**Wolverine State.** Sister ships listed under **President Adams.**

President Hayes (1920) Dollar Steamship Co.
Built by New York Shipbuilding Co., Camden, N. J. Tonnage: 10,533. Dimensions: 502′ x 62′ (522′ o.l.). Twin-screw, 14 knots. Reciprocating engines. Two masts and one funnel. Renamed: **President Tyler** (1940). Scrapped in 1957. Sister ships listed under **President Adams.** Ex-**Creole State** (1924).

President Hoover (1931) Dollar Steamship Co.
Built by Newport News Shipbuilding & Drydock Co., Newport News, Va. Tonnage: 21,936. Dimensions: 615′ x 81′ (654′ o.l.). Twin-screw, 21 knots. Turbo-electric. Two

masts and two funnels. Cost $8,000,000. Launched July 1930. Attained a speed of 22.2 knots on her trials in June 1931. Went aground on Hoishoto Island near Formosa on December 11, 1937. Attempts were made to salvage her, but this was given up in June 1938, and she was subsequently broken up by Japanese shipbreakers for scrap. Sister ship: **President Coolidge.**

*President Hoover   (1939)   American President Lines.
Built by Bethlehem Shipbuilding Co., Quincy, Mass. Tonnage: 10,603. Dimensions: 474′ x 64′ (493′ o.l.). Twin-screw, 16½ knots. Four steam turbines. Two masts and one funnel. Service: California-Japan, via Honolulu. Passengers: 202 first class. Ex-**Panama** (1957), ex-**James Parker** (1946), ex-**Panama** (1941).

President Jackson   (1921)   American Mail Line.
Built by Newport News Shipbuilding & Drydock Co., Newport News, Va. Tonnage: 14,124. Dimensions: 517′ x 72′ (539′ o.l.). Twin-screw, 17 knots. Turbines. Two masts and one funnel. Renamed: **Zeilin.** Scrapped in 1948. Ex-**Silver State.** Sister ships listed under **President Jefferson.**

President Jackson   (1941)   American President Lines.
Built by Newport News Shipbuilding & Drydock Co., Newport News, Va. Tonnage: 9,273. Dimensions: 465′ x 69′. Single-screw, 16½ knots. Turbines. Two masts and one funnel. Sister ships: **President Polk, President Monroe** and **President Van Buren.**

President Jefferson   (1920)   American Mail Line.
Built by New York Shipbuilding Co., Camden, N. J. Tonnage: 14,174. Dimensions: 516′ x 72′ (535′ o.l.). Twin-screw, 17 knots. Turbines. Two masts and one funnel. Ex-**Wenatchee.** Renamed: **Henry T. Allen.** Sister ships: **President Cleveland, President Grant, President Jackson, President Lincoln, President McKinley, President Madison, President Pierce, President Taft** and **President Wilson.** Note: The **President Harding** and **President Roosevelt** of the United States Lines were identical in appearance to the above liners; also were the Munson liners **American Legion, Southern Cross, Pan American** and **Western World.**

President Johnson   (1904)   Dollar Steamship Co.
Built by New York Shipbuilding Co., Camden, N. J. Tonnage: 15,543. Dimensions: 600′ x 65′ (616′ o.l.). Twin-

screw, 16 knots. Quadruple expansion engines. Four masts and one funnel. Note: Launched as the **Minnekahda** for the Atlantic Transport Line in May 1904. Sold before completion to Pacific Mail Steamship Co., renamed **Manchuria** and employed in their trans-Pacific service. In 1915 was bought by the International Mercantile Marine Co. and transferred to the Atlantic Transport Line. Put on the New York and London route. In 1920 used in the American Line's New York-Hamburg service. In Panama Pacific Line service New York-San Francisco, 1923–1929. Purchased by Dollar Steamship Co. in 1929 and renamed **President Johnson.** She was not one of the ships transferred to the newly formed American President Lines in 1938. Renamed: **Santa Cruz** (1947). Broken up for scrap in Italy in 1952. Ex-**Manchuria** (1929). Sister ship: **President Fillmore.**

President Lincoln (1921)   Dollar Steamship Co.
Built by New York Shipbuilding Co., Camden, N. J. Tonnage: 14,187. Dimensions: 516′ x 72′ (535′ o.l.). Twin-screw, 17 knots. Turbines. Two masts and one funnel. Ex-**Hoosier State.** Renamed: (a) **Maria del Carmen** (1940), (b) **Cabo de Buena Esperanza.** Sister ships listed under **President Jefferson.** Scrapped in 1958.

President Madison (1921)   American Mail Line.
Built by New York Shipbuilding Co., Camden, N. J. Tonnage: 14,187. Dimensions: 516′ x 72′ (535′ o.l.). Twin-screw, 17 knots. Turbines. Two masts and one funnel. Capsized in dock at Seattle on March 24, 1933. Refloated on April 13, 1933 and repairs completed in November 1934. Renamed: **President Quezon.** Stranded and sunk off Japan in January 1940. Ex-**Bay State.** Sister ships: listed under **President Jefferson.**

President Madison (1921)   Dollar Steamship Co.
Built by New York Shipbuilding Co., Camden, N. J. Tonnage: 10,538. Dimensions: 502′ x 62′ (522′ o.l.). Twin-screw, 14 knots. Reciprocating engines. Two masts and one funnel. Ex-**President Garfield,** ex-**Blue Hen State.** Renamed: (a) **Kenmore,** (b) **Refuge** (hospital ship). Scrapped in 1948. Sister ships listed under **President Adams.**

President McKinley (1921)   American Mail Line.
Built by New York Shipbuilding Co., Camden, N. J. Tonnage: 14,127. Dimensions: 516′ x 72′ (535′ o.l.). Twin-screw, 17 knots. Turbines. Two masts and one funnel.

Renamed: **J. Franklin Bell.** Scrapped in 1948. Ex-**Keystone State.** Sister ships listed under **President Jefferson.**

President Monroe (1920) Dollar Steamship Co.
Built by New York Shipbuilding Co., Camden, N. J. Tonnage: 10,533. Dimensions: 502' x 62' (522' o.l.). Twin-screw, 14 knots. Reciprocating engines. Two masts and one funnel. Renamed: (a) **President Buchanan,** (b) **Emily H. Weder** (hospital ship), (c) **President Buchanan.** Laid up now. Ex-**Panhandle State.** Sister ships listed under **President Adams.**

*****President Monroe** (1940) American President Lines.
Built by Newport News Shipbuilding & Drydock Co., Newport News, Va. Tonnage: 9,261. Dimensions: 465' x 69'. Single-screw, 16½ knots. Turbines. Two masts and one funnel. Accommodation for 96 first-class passengers. Sister ships: **President Jackson, President Polk** and **President Van Buren.**

President Pierce (1921) Dollar Steamship Co.
Built by Bethlehem Shipbuilding Corp., Sparrows Point, Maryland. Tonnage: 14,123. Dimensions: 517' x 72' (539' o.l.). Twin-screw, 17 knots. Turbines. Two masts and one funnel. Renamed: **Hugh L. Scott.** Sunk by the enemy off Casablanca in November 1942 as she participated in the Allied invasion of North Africa. Ex-**Hawkeye State.** Sister ships listed under **President Jefferson.**

President Polk (1921) Dollar Steamship Co.
Built by New York Shipbuilding Co., Camden, N. J. Tonnage: 10,500. Dimensions: 502' x 62' (522' o.l.). Twin-screw, 14 knots. Reciprocating engines. Two masts and one funnel. Renamed: **President Taylor.** Stranded and abandoned on February 14, 1942. Later destroyed by Japanese air attack. Ex-**Granite State.** Sister ships listed under **President Adams.**

*****President Polk** (1941) American President Lines.
Built by Newport News Shipbuilding & Drydock Co., Newport News, Va. Tonnage: 9,261. Dimensions: 465' x 69'. Single-screw, 16½ knots. Turbines. Two masts and one funnel. Accommodation for 96 first-class passengers. Cost approximately $3,600,000. Sister ships: **President Jackson, President Monroe** and **President Van Buren.**

*President Roosevelt (1944) American President Lines.
Built by Federal Shipbuilding & Drydock Co., Kearny, N. J.
Tonnage: 18,000. Dimensions: 573' x 75' (622' o.l.). Twin-
screw, 20 knots. Steam turbines. Two masts and two funnels. Note: Originally a P2-S2-R2 type American troopship.
Converted to passenger ship in 1949. Reverted back to
United States Government in 1951. Vessel was laid up in
1952. Reconditioned as a 600 passenger tourist class ship
in 1955 and placed under charter to the newly formed
Hawaiian Steamship Company, so as to run in the San
Francisco-Honolulu service. In 1961 was turned over to
shipbuilders to be rebuilt for the American President Lines
trans-Pacific trade. Renamed: **President Roosevelt** in
1961. She will commence regular service early in 1962.
Ex-**Leilani** (1960), ex-**La Guardia** (1956), ex-**General W.
P. Richardson** (1949). Note: See **La Guardia.**

President Taft (1921) Dollar Steamship Co.
Built by Bethlehem Shipbuilding Corp., Sparrows Point,
Maryland. Tonnage: 14,123. Dimensions: 517' x 72' (539'
o.l.). Twin-screw, 17 knots. Turbines. Two masts and one
funnel. Renamed: (a) **Willard A. Holbrook,** (b) **American Representative.** Ex-**Buckeye State.** Sister ships
listed under **President Jefferson.** Note: The **Willard A.
Holbrook** is now (1953) laid up in the reserve fleet.

President Taylor (1921) Dollar Steamship Co.
Built by New York Shipbuilding Corp., Camden, N. J.
Tonnage: 10,500. Dimensions: 502' x 62' (522' o.l.). Twin-
screw, 14 knots. Reciprocating engines. Two masts and
one funnel. Stranded and abandoned on February 14, 1942.
Later was destroyed by Japanese air attack. Ex-**President
Polk,** ex-**Granite State.**

President Tyler (1920) Dollar Steamship Co.
Built by New York Shipbuilding Co., Camden, N. J. Tonnage: 10,533. Dimensions: 502' x 62' (522' o.l.). Twin-
screw, 14 knots. Reciprocating engines. Two masts and
one funnel. Ex-**Howard A. McCurdy,** ex-**President
Tyler,** ex-**President Hayes,** ex-**Creole State.** Note: The
President Tyler is now (1953) laid up in the United States
Government reserve fleet. Sister ships listed under **President Adams.**

President Van Buren (1920) Dollar Steamship Co.
Built by New York Shipbuilding Co., Camden, N. J. Tonnage: 10,533. Dimensions: 502' x 62' (522' o.l.). Twin-

screw, 14 knots. Reciprocating engines. Two masts and one funnel. Renamed: (a) **President Fillmore,** (b) **Marigold** (hospital ship). Ex-**Old North State.** Sister ships listed under **President Adams.**

President Van Buren   (1941)   American President Lines.
Built by Newport News Shipbuilding & Drydock Co., Newport News, Va. Tonnage: 9,260. Dimensions: 465′ x 69′. Single-screw, 16½ knots. Turbines. Two masts and one funnel. Sister ships: **President Polk, President Jackson** and **President Monroe.**

President Wilson   (1921)   Dollar Steamship Co.
Built by New York Shipbuilding Co., Camden, N. J. Tonnage: 14,127. Dimensions: 516′ x 72′ (535′ o.l.). Twin-screw, 17 knots. Turbines. Two masts and one funnel. Renamed: (a) **Maria Pipa,** (b) **Cabo de Hornos** (1940). Scrapped in 1959. Ex-**Empire State.**

***President Wilson**   (1948)   American President Lines.
Built by Bethlehem Steel Co., Alameda Shipyard, Inc., Alameda, Calif. Tonnage: 15,359. Dimensions: 573′ x 75′ (609′ o.l.). Twin-screw, 18½ knots. Turbo-electric engines. Two masts and two funnels. Accommodation for 326 first-class and 506 third-class passengers. Sister ship: **President Cleveland.**

Ruapehu   (1883)   Union Steamship Co. of New Zealand.
Built by J. Elder & Co., Glasgow. Tonnage: 4,163. Dimensions: 389′ x 46′. Single-screw, 16 knots. Three masts and one funnel. Sold to British India Steam Navigation Co. about 1901. Renamed: **Gwalior.** Broken up for scrap in 1911. Sister ships: **Aorangi** and **Tongariro.**

San Pablo   (1884)   Occidental and Oriental Steamship Co. (Chartered from Pacific Improvement Co.).
Built by W. Cramp & Sons, Philadelphia, Pa. Tonnage: 4,064. Dimensions: 331′ x 42′. Single-screw. In Occidental and Oriental service San Francisco-Hong Kong, 1884–1888. Wrecked on reef, Turnabout Island, Formosa Channel in April 1888. Sister ship: **San Pedro.**

Santa Cruz   (1913)   Pacific Mail Steamship Co.
Built by W. Cramp & Sons, Philadelphia, Pa. Tonnage: 5,081. Dimensions: 384′ x 50′. Single-screw. Two masts and one funnel. Owned by W. R. Grace & Co. Chartered by Pacific Mail Steamship Co. In San-Francisco-Calcutta service, 1917–1920.

Seattle Maru (1909) Osaka Line.
Built by Kawasaki Dockyard Co., Ltd., Kobe, Japan.
Tonnage: 6,182. Dimensions: 419' x 49'. Twin-screw, 13
knots. Reciprocating engines. Two masts and one funnel.
One of the pioneer vessels to open the service between
Tacoma and Japan in 1909. Torpedoed and sunk on July 16,
1944. Sister ships: **Chicago Maru** and **Tacoma Maru.**

Shidzuoka Maru (1912) N. Y. K. Line.
Built by Mitsubishi Dockyard, Nagasaki, Japan. Tonnage:
6,568. Dimensions: 409' x 49'. Twin-screw, 14 knots.
Reciprocating engines. Two masts and one funnel. Com-
pleted May 14, 1912. In Seattle-Japan service. Sister ship:
Yokohama Maru.

Shinano Maru (1900) N. Y. K. Line.
Built by D. & W. Henderson & Co., Glasgow, Scotland.
Tonnage: 6,416. Dimensions: 445' x 49'. Twin-screw, 14
knots. Two masts and one funnel. In Japan-Seattle service.

Shinyo Maru (1911) Toyo Kisen Kaisha.
Built by Mitsubishi Dockyard, Nagasaki, Japan. Tonnage:
13,039. Dimensions: 558' x 61'. (570' o.l.). Triple-screw, 18
knots. Turbines. Two masts and two funnels. Note:
Transferred to N. Y. K. Line in 1926. Sister ships: **Tenyo
Maru** and **Chiyo Maru.** Broken up for scrap in 1936.

Siberia (1901) Pacific Mail Steamship Co.
Built by Newport News Shipbuilding & Drydock Co., New-
port News, Va. Tonnage: 11,785. Dimensions: 551' x 63'.
Twin-screw, 20 knots. Quadruple expansion engines. Two
masts and two funnels. Delivered in November 1902. In
service San Francisco-Hong Kong, Manila, 1903–1915.
Sold to Atlantic Transport Co. in 1915. Sold to Toyo Kisen
Kaisha in 1916. Renamed: **Siberia Maru.** Transferred to
N. Y. K. Line in 1926. Sold for scrap in 1934. Sister ship:
Korea.

Siberia Maru (1901) N. Y. K. Line.
Built by Newport News Shipbuilding & Drydock Co., Newport News, Va. Tonnage: 11,785. Dimensions: 551' x 63'.
Twin-screw, 16 knots. Quadruple expansion engines. Two
masts and two funnels. Scrapped in 1934. Note: For
further details see **Siberia.** Sister ship: **Korea Maru.**

Sierra (1900) Oceanic Steamship Co.
Built by W. Cramp & Sons Co., Philadelphia, Pa. Tonnage:
6,135. Dimensions: 400' x 50'. Twin-screw, 17 knots.

Reciprocating engines. Two masts and one funnel. Note: Originally had two funnels. In service San Francisco-Sydney, 1901–1907; San Francisco-Honolulu, 1910–1915; San Francisco-Sydney, 1915–1917. Sold to Green Star Steamship Co. in 1919. Renamed: **Gdansk.** Re-purchased (as **Gdansk**) from Polish American Navigation Corporation in 1923. In service San Francisco-Sydney, 1924–1932. Sold to Japanese shipbreakers in 1934. Sister ships: **Sonoma** and **Ventura.**

Sonoma   (1901)   Oceanic Steamship Co.
Built by W. Cramp & Sons Co., Philadelphia, Pa. Tonnage: 6,279. Dimensions: 400′ x 50′. Twin-screw, 17 knots. Reciprocating engines. Two masts and one funnel. Note: Originally had two funnels. In service San Francisco-Sydney, 1901–1907, 1912–1917, 1920–1932. Sold to Japanese shipbreakers in 1934. Sister ships: **Sierra** and **Ventura.**

Starbuck   (1881)   Pacific Mail Steamship Co.
Built by J. Laing, Sunderland, England. Tonnage: 2,157. Dimensions: 266′ x 36′. Single-screw. Iron hull. Purchased by Pacific Mail in 1886. In San Francisco-Hong Kong service. Wrecked off the coast of Nicaragua on February 28, 1898. Ex-**Oliveto.**

Suwa Maru   (1914)   N. Y. K. Line.
Built by Mitsubishi Dockyard, Nagasaki, Japan. Tonnage: 10,672. Dimensions: 516′ x 62′. Twin-screw, 15½ knots. Reciprocating engines. Two masts and one funnel. Completed September 11, 1914. Transferred from the Japan-European trade to the trans-Pacific service in September 1917. This change took place because of the prevailing war conditions at that time. She was not put back on the European run until March 1922. Sunk by a United States submarine on March 28, 1943. Sister ships: **Fushima Maru, Katori Maru, Kashima Maru** and **Yasaka Maru.**

Tacoma Maru   (1909)   Osaka Line.
Built by Kawasaki Dockyard Co., Ltd., Kobe, Japan. Tonnage: 6,178. Dimensions: 419′ x 49′. Twin-screw, 13 knots. Reciprocating engines. Two masts and one funnel. Sister ships: **Seattle Maru** and **Chicago Maru.** The vessels inaugurated the Osaka Line Tacoma-Japan service.

Tahiti   (1904)   Union Steamship Co. of New Zealand.
Built by Alexander Stephen & Sons, Ltd., Linthouse, Glasgow.   Tonnage: 7,898.   Dimensions: 460′ x 55′.   Twin-

screw, 17 knots. Triple expansion engines. Two masts and one funnel. Foundered in the Pacific, 450 miles from Rarotonga on August 18, 1930. Ex-**Port Kingston.**

Taiyo Maru   (1911)   Toyo Kisen Kaisha; N. Y. K. Line.
Built by Blohm & Voss, Hamburg, Germany. Tonnage: 14,457. Dimensions: 560′ x 65′. Twin-screw, 16 knots. Quadruple expansion engines. Two masts and two funnels. Ex-**Cap Finisterre.** Note: This former Hamburg-South America Line luxury ship commenced her maiden voyage on November 11, 1911. In 1919 was turned over to the Allies and allocated to the Japanese Government, later sold to Nippon Yusen Kaisha (N. Y. K. Line). Prior to that transfer, she had been operated by Toyo Kisen Kaisha. She was torpedoed and sunk on May 8, 1942. Note: The name **Taiyo Maru** means a great ocean liner.

Tartar   (1883)   Canadian Pacific Line.
Built by Aitken & Mansel, Glasgow, Scotland. Tonnage: 4,425. Dimensions: 376′ x 47′. Single-screw, 14½ knots. Three masts and one funnel. Iron hull. Purchased by Canadian Pacific in 1897. In trans-Pacific service, 1898–1899, 1900–1907. Sold to Japanese owners in 1907. Broken up for scrap in 1908. Note: Originally owned and operated by the Union Line for their South Africa service.

Tatsuta Maru   (1929)   N. Y. K. Line.
Built by Mitsubishi Dockyard, Nagasaki, Japan. Tonnage: 16,975. Dimensions: 560′ x 72′ (583′ o.l.). Quadruple-screw, 19 knots. Motorship. Two masts and two funnels. Laid down December 3, 1927. Launched April 12, 1929. Completed March 15, 1930. The running time for her maiden voyage from Yokohama to San Francisco was 12 days, 9 hours, 14 minutes. Renamed: **Tatuta Maru.** Running mates: **Asama Maru** and **Chichibu Maru.**

Tatuta Maru   (1929)   N. Y. K. Line.
Built by Mitsubishi Dockyard, Nagasaki, Japan. Tonnage: 16,975. Dimensions: 560′ x 72′ (583′ o.l.). Quadruple-screw, 19 knots. Motorship. Two masts and two funnels. Torpedoed and sunk on February 8, 1943, with all on board lost. Ex-**Tatsuta Maru** (1938). Running mates: **Asama Maru** and **Chichibu Maru.**

Tenyo Maru   (1908)   Toyo Kisen Kaisha.
Built by Mitsubishi Dockyard, Nagasaki, Japan. Tonnage: 13,398. Dimensions: 558′ x 61′ (570′ o.l.). Triple-screw,

16 knots (service speed). Turbines. Two masts and two funnels. Averaged 18.25 knots on one trip from Honolulu to San Francisco, attaining a top speed of nearly 20 knots. Transferred to N. Y. K. Line in 1926. Sold in 1933. Sister ships: **Shinyo Maru** and **Chiyo Maru.**

Tongariro (1883) Union Steamship Co. of New Zealand. Built by John Elder & Co., Glasgow. Tonnage: 4,163. Dimensions: 389' x 46'. Single-screw, 16 knots. Compound engines. Three masts and one funnel. She was sold to British India Steam Navigation Co. about 1901. Renamed: **Zibenghla.** Scrapped in 1910. Sister ships: **Aorangi** and **Ruapehu.**

Vancouver (1873) Pacific Mail Steamship Co. Built by Henderson at Renfrew, Scotland. Tonnage: 2,923. Dimensions: 349' x 37'. Single-screw. Compound engines. Iron hull. Three masts and one funnel. Note: Chartered, not owned, by Pacific Mail in 1875 for their China Line. Sailed from San Francisco for Hong Kong for Macondray & Co. on March 18, 1876. Purchased by Royal Mail Line in 1878. Renamed: **Tamar.** Out of Royal Mail Line service in 1897. Sister ship: **Vasco de Gama.** Scrapped in 1898.

Vasco de Gama (1873) Pacific Mail Steamship Co. Built by Henderson at Renfrew, Scotland. Tonnage: 2,912. Dimensions: 349' x 37'. Single-screw. Compound engines. Iron hull. Note: Chartered, not owned, by Pacific Mail Steamship Co. in 1875. In San Francisco-Hong Kong, and also United States coastwise services. Opened San Francisco-Sydney service for the Pacific Mail. When charter expired the vessel was turned over to Macondray & Co. in January 1876. She left San Francisco for Hong Kong for Macondray on March 30, 1876. Sold to Royal Mail Line in 1878. Renamed: **Trent.** Disposed of in 1897. Sister ship: **Vancouver.**

Venezuela (1915) Pacific Mail Steamship Co. Built by Nederland Schps. Maats, Amsterdam. Tonnage: 5,641. Dimensions: 380' x 48'. Single-screw, 14 knots. Reciprocating engines. Two masts and one funnel. Purchased by Pacific Mail Steamship Co. in 1916. At time of purchase could accommodate 111 cabin and 78 steerage passengers. Entered San Francisco-Hong Kong, Manila service in 1917. Transferred to Panama Mail Steamship Co. in 1925. Remained in trans-Pacific service until 1921, and then placed in the inter-coastal trade. Renamed: **Santa Isabel.** Sister ships: **Ecuador** and **Colombia.**

Ventura   (1900)   Oceanic Steamship Co.
   Built by W. Cramp & Sons Co., Philadelphia, Pa. Tonnage:
   6,282.   Dimensions: 400' x 50'.   Twin-screw, 17 knots.
   Triple expansion engines. Two masts and one funnel. Completed in December 1900. In San Francisco-Sydney service
   1901–1907, 1912–1917, 1920–1932. Sold to Japanese shipbreakers in 1934. Sister ships: **Sierra** and **Sonoma.**

Warrimoo   (1892)   Huddart, Parker & Co.
   Built by C. S. Swan & Hunter, Newcastle, England. Tonnage: 3,326. Dimensions: 345' x 42'. Single-screw. Three
   masts and one funnel. In trans-Pacific service for only a
   short time. Her usual route was between Melbourne and
   New Zealand ports. Sister ship: **Miowera.**

Wonga Wonga   (1854)   California, New Zealand & Australian
   Mail Steamship Co.
   Built at Glasgow, Scotland. Tonnage: 1,002. Dimensions:
   242' x 27'. Single-screw. Home port: Sydney, Australia.
   Scrapped in 1880.

Yamaguchi Maru   (1890)   N. Y. K. Line.
   Built by J. L. Thompson & Sons, Sunderland, England.
   Tonnage: 3,321. Dimensions: 362' x 41'. Single-screw, 13
   knots. One of the early Japanese vessels used on the Seattle-
   Japan service. Ex-**Pak Ling.**

Yawata Maru   (1939)   N. Y. K. Line.
   Built by Mitsubishi Dockyard, Nagasaki, Japan. Tonnage:
   16,500.   Dimensions: 557' x 73' (590' o.l.).   Twin-screw,
   22 knots. Turbines. Two masts and one funnel. Note:
   Taken over by the Japanese Government during World War
   II and converted to aircraft carrier. Renamed: **Unyo.**
   Sunk by submarine on September 16, 1944. Sister ships:
   Nitta Maru and **Kasaga Maru.** These fine liners were
   originally intended for the Japan-European route, but due to
   prevailing war conditions were put in the trans-Pacific
   service when completed.

Yokohama Maru   (1912)   N. Y. K. Line.
   Built by Kawasaki Dockyard Co., Kobe, Japan. Tonnage:
   6,147.   Dimensions: 406' x 49'.   Twin-screw, 14 knots.
   Reciprocating engines. Two masts and one funnel. Completed June 24, 1912. Built specially for the Japan-Seattle
   service. Sunk by aircraft on March 10, 1942. Sister ship:
   Shidzuoka Maru.

Zealandia   (1875)   Oceanic Steamship Co.

Built by J. Elder & Co., Glasgow, Scotland.   Tonnage: 2,489.   Dimensions: 377' x 37'.   Single-screw,   13   knots. Compound engines.   Four masts and one funnel.   Designed for San Francisco-New Zealand, Australia mail service. When completed could accommodate 170 first-class, 30 second-class and 100 third-class passengers.   Chartered by Pacific Mail Steamship Co. and entered their San Francisco-Sydney service in 1876.   Remained in it until 1885.   Purchased from the builder John Elder by Oceanic Steamship Co. in 1886.   In San Francisco-Honolulu service in 1901. Sold by Oceanic Steamship Co. after 1905.   Owned by Universal Transportation Co., when wrecked in the Atlantic in March 1917.   Sister ship: **Australia.**

PART II-A

TRANS-PACIFIC PASSENGER SHIPS
via PANAMA CANAL

Note: An asterisk (*) signifies ship in service in 1962.

The Panama Canal was opened to traffic in 1914.

*Africa Maru   (1951)   Osaka Shosen Kaisha.
Built by Central Japan Heavy Industries, Kobe, Japan.
Tonnage: 8,354. Dimensions: 473' x 61'. Twin-screw, 14
knots. Motorship. Two masts and one funnel. Passengers:
12 cabin, 532 third class. Route: Japan-South America, via
the Panama Canal. Note: Originally built as freighters with
accommodation for 12 passengers. Running mates: **America
Maru** and **Santos Maru.**

Akaroa   (1914)   Shaw, Savill & Albion Co.
Built by Harland & Wolff, Ltd., Belfast, Ireland. Tonnage:
15,128. Dimensions: 550' x 67' (569' o.l.). Triple-screw,
15 knots. Reciprocating engines and turbine. Two masts
and one funnel. Had accommodation for 200 passengers.
Note: Also was in the service to Australia via Capetown.
Ex-**Euripides** (1932). Sold to Belgian shipbreakers in 1954.

*America Maru   (1950)   Osaka Shosen Kaisha.
Built by Central Japan Heavy Industries, Kobe, Japan.
Tonnage: 8,343. Dimensions: 473' x 62'. Single-screw, 14
knots. Motorship. Two masts and one funnel. Passengers:
12 cabin and 524 third. Route: Japan-South America, via
Panama Canal. Originally had only accommodation for 12
cabin passengers.   Running mates: **Africa Maru** and
Santos Maru.

Arawa   (1907)   Shaw, Savill & Albion Co.
Built by Swan, Hunter & Wigham Richardson, Ltd., Wallsend-on-Tyne, England. Tonnage: 9,372. Dimensions:
459' x 59'. Twin-screw, 14 knots.   Two masts and one
funnel. Sold in 1928. Renamed: (a) **Konigstein** (1933),
(b) **Gandia** (1938). World War II casualty, January 22,
1942.

Arawa   (1922)   Shaw, Savill & Albion Co.
Built by Wm. Beardmore & Sons, Ltd., Dalmuir, Glasgow.
Tonnage: 14,462. Dimensions: 530' x 68'. Twin-screw,

15 knots. Turbines. Two masts and one funnel. Employed as an armed merchant cruiser at the beginning of World War II. Later was converted to troopship. Accommodation for 680 passengers. In service by way of Capetown to Australia and New Zealand in 1953. Scrapped in Great Britain, 1955. Ex-**Esperance Bay** (1936). Note: This liner was purchased from Aberdeen & Commonwealth Line in September 1936, and was a sister ship to the **Jervis Bay, Hobsons Bay, Largs Bay** and **Moreton Bay.**

***Argentina Maru**   (1958)   Osaka Shosen Kaisha.
     Built by Mitsubishi Heavy Industries, Kobe, Japan. Tonnage: 10,863. Dimensions: 513′ (o.l.) x 67′. Single-screw, 16½ knots. Steam turbines. Two masts and one funnel. During her trials made a top speed of 19½ knots. Route: Japan-South America, via the Panama Canal. Running mate: **Brazil Maru.** The first ocean-going passenger ships built in Japan since the war.

Athenic   (1901)   Shaw Savill Line.
     Built by Harland & Wolff, Ltd., Belfast, Ireland. Tonnage: 12,234. Dimensions: 500′ x 63′ (520′ o.l.). Twin-screw, 13 knots. Reciprocating engines. Four masts and one funnel. Sold to Norwegian owners and converted to whale-oil factory vessel. Renamed: **Pelagos.** Note: The **Athenic** was built for the White Star Line. Sister ships: **Corinthic** and **Ionic.**

***Athenic**   (1947)   Shaw, Savill & Albion Co.
     Built by Harland & Wolff, Ltd., Belfast, Ireland. Tonnage: 15,187. Dimensions: 538′ x 71′ (560′ o.l.). Twin-screw, 17 knots. Six steam turbines. Two masts and one funnel. Passengers: 85 first class. Service: England-New Zealand, via Panama Canal. Sister ships: **Ceramic, Corinthic** and **Gothic.**

***Brazil Maru**   (1954)   Osaka Shosen Kaisha.
     Built by Mitsubishi Heavy Industries, Kobe, Japan. Tonnage: 10,101. Dimensions: 476′ x 68′ (512′ o.l.). Motorship. Two masts and one funnel. Passengers: 12 first, 68 tourist, 902 third. Officers and crew, 118. Liner delivered to owners, July 10, 1954. Service: Japan-South America, via Panama Canal. Running mate: **Argentina Maru.**

***Caledonien**   (1952)   Messageries Maritimes (French).
     Built by Ateliers & Chantiers de France, Dunkirk, France. Tonnage: 12,712. Dimensions: 528′ x 67′. Twin-screw, 16

knots. Motorship. Two masts and one funnel. Passengers: 71 first, 84 tourist, 86 third. Service: Marseilles-New Caledonia-Australia, via Panama Canal. Sister ship: **Tahitien.**

*Ceramic   (1948)   Shaw, Savill & Albion Co.
Built by Cammell Laird & Co., Birkenhead, England. Tonnage: 15,896. Dimensions: 539' x 72' (560' o.l.). Twin-screw, 17 knots. Two sets of geared steam turbines. 18,400 S.H.P. at 125 r.p.m. Two masts and one funnel. Passengers: 85 first. Route: England-New Zealand, via Panama Canal. Sister ships: **Athenic, Ceramic** and **Gothic.**

Commissaire Ramel   (1920)   Messageries Maritimes.
Built by Soc. Provencale de Const. Navale, La Ciotat, France. Tonnage: 10,061. Dimensions: 478' x 59'. Single-screw, 14 knots. Triple expansion engines. Two masts and one funnel. Launched, March 20, 1920. Note: Built as freighter, but converted to passenger ship in 1925. Service: France-New Hebrides-Tahiti, via the Panama Canal. Sunk in Pacific by German A.M.C. **Tamesis,** September 17, 1940.

Corinthic   (1902)   Shaw Savill Line.
Built by Harland & Wolff, Ltd., Belfast, Ireland. Tonnage: 12,367. Dimensions: 500' x 63' (520' o.l.). Twin-screw, 13 knots. Reciprocating engines. Four masts and one funnel. Broken up for scrap in 1932. Note: Built for White Star Line. Sister ships: **Athenic** and **Ionic.**

*Corinthic   (1947)   Shaw, Savill & Albion Co.
Built by Cammell Laird & Co., Birkenhead, England. Tonnage: 15,682. Dimensions: 538' x 71' (559' o.l.). Twin-screw, 17 knots. Steam turbines. Two masts and one funnel. Passengers: 85 first class. Commenced service in April 1947. Route: England-New Zealand, via Panama Canal. Sister ships: **Athenic, Ceramic** and **Gothic.**

El Kantara   (1905)   Messageries Maritimes.
Built by Messageries Maritimes, La Ciotat, France. Tonnage: 6,879. Dimensions: 447' x 52'. Twin-screw, 12 knots. Triple expansion engines. Two masts and one funnel. The **El Kantara** inaugurated a Pacific service from France to Tahiti and New Hebrides, via the Panama Canal on April 24, 1923 for Messageries Maritimes. Prior to First World War this vessel was used in the Far East service.

Eridan   (1928)   Messageries Maritimes.
Built by Soc. Provecale de Const. Navale, La Ciotat, France. Tonnage: 9,927. Dimensions: 445' x 61'. Twin-screw, 16

knots. Motorship. Two masts and two funnels. Note: Had square shape funnels. Launched, June 3, 1928. Service: France-Tahiti-New Hebrides, via Panama Canal. The **Eridan** has also been used in the Far East route.

*Gothic   (1948)   Shaw, Savill & Albion Co.
Built by Swan, Hunter & Wigham Richardson, Ltd., Wallsend, Newcastle, England. Tonnage: 15,902. Dimensions: 539' x 72' (561' o.l.). Twin-screw, 18 knots. Steam turbines. Two masts and one funnel. Passengers: 85 first. Route: England-New Zealand, via Panama Canal. Sister ships: **Athenic, Ceramic** and **Corinthic.**

Ionic   (1902)   Shaw Savill Line.
Built by Harland & Wolff, Ltd., Belfast, Ireland. Tonnage: 12,352. Dimensions: 500' x 63' (520' o.l.). Twin-screw, 13 knots. Reciprocating engines. Four masts and one funnel. Note: Built for White Star Line. Broken up by Japanese shipbreakers in 1937. Sister ships: **Athenic** and **Corinthic.**

*Johan van Oldenbarnevelt   (1930)   Nederland Line.
Built by Netherland Shipbuilding Co. (Nederlandsche Scheepsbouw Maatschappij), Amsterdam, Netherlands. Tonnage: 20,314. Dimensions: 586' x 74' (605' o.l.). Twin-screw, 17 knots. Motorship. Single mast and two funnels. Passengers: 1,210 in single class. Service: Round-the-world, via Panama Canal. Note: Reconditioned in 1959 for round-the-world passenger trade. Originally built for the Netherlands-Suez-Dutch Indies service. See PART IV.

Louqsor   (1904)   Messageries Maritimes.
Built by Messageries Maritimes, La Ciotat, France. Tonnage: 6,879. Dimensions: 447' x 52'. Twin-screw, 13 knots. Triple expansion engines. Two masts and one funnel. Launched, April 9, 1904. Service: France-Tahiti-New Hebrides, via Panama Canal. Originally in Far East trade, Scrapped in Belgium, 1930.

Mahana   (1917)   Shaw, Savill & Albion Co.
Built by Workman, Clark, Ltd., Belfast, Ireland. Tonnage: 10,951. Dimensions: 500' x 63'. Twin-screw, 14 knots. Turbines. Two masts and one funnel. Had accommodation for 1,500 emigrants. Scrapped at Dalmuir in 1953.

Mataroa   (1922)   Shaw, Savill & Albion Co.
Built by Harland & Wolff, Ltd., Belfast, Ireland. Tonnage: 12,390. Dimensions: 500' x 63'. Twin-screw, 15 knots.

Turbines. Two masts and one funnel. Accommodation for 130 passengers. Scrapped at Faslane in 1957. Ex-**Diogenes**. Sister ship: **Tamaroa**.

Northern Star   (1962)   Shaw, Savill & Albion Co.
Built by Vickers-Armstrongs, Ltd., Walker-on-Tyne, Newcastle, England. Tonnage: 22,000. Dimensions: 650' x 82'. Twin-screw, 21 knots. Steam turbines. Single mast and one funnel aft. Launched in 1961. Maiden voyage scheduled later in 1962. Accommodation for 1,400 passengers in one class. Service: Round-the-world, via Panama Canal. Running mate: **Southern Cross**.

*Oranje   (1939)   Nederland Line.
Built by Netherlands Shipbuilding Co., Amsterdam, Netherlands. Tonnage: 20,551. Dimensions: 613' x 83' (656' o.l.). Triple screw, 21 knots. Motorship (3 Sulzer diesels). Single mast and one funnel. Passengers: 323 first and 626 tourist. Reconditioned for round-the-world service, via Panama Canal, commencing her first sailing in 1959. Running mate in this new Dutch service is the modernized **Johan van Oldenbarnevelt**. The **Oranje** originally was in Netherlands-Dutch Indies service.

Rangitane   (1929)   New Zealand Shipping Co., Ltd.
Built by John Brown & Co., Ltd., Clydebank, Glasgow. Tonnage: 16,733. Dimensions: 531' x 70' (552' o.l.). Twin-screw, 15 knots. Motorship. Two masts and two funnels. Torpedoed and sunk on November 26, 1940. Sister ships: **Rangitiki** and **Rangitata**.

*Rangitane   (1949)   New Zealand Shipping Co., Ltd.
Built by John Brown & Co., Ltd., Clydebank, Glasgow. Tonnage: 21,867. Dimensions: 587' x 78' (609' o.l.). Twin-screw, 17 knots. Motorship. Two masts and one funnel. Completed and delivered to owner in December 1949. Accommodation for 410 passengers. Sister ship: **Rangitoto**.

*Rangitata   (1929)   Shaw, Savill & Albion Co.
Built by John Brown & Co., Ltd., Clydebank, Glasgow. Tonnage: 16,969. Dimensions: 531' x 70' (552' o.l.). Twin-screw, 16 knots. Motorship. Two masts and two funnels. Employed as a troopship in World War II. Thoroughly reconditioned and re-engined after the war. Resumed service on October 1949. Accommodation for 430 passengers. Sister ships: **Rangitane** and **Rangitiki**.

*Rangitiki   (1929)   New Zealand Shipping Co., Ltd.
   Built by John Brown & Co., Ltd., Clydebank, Glasgow.
   Tonnage: 16,984. Dimensions: 531' x 70' (552' o.l.). Twin-
   screw, 16 knots. Motorship. Two masts and two funnels.
   Served as a troopship in World War II. Withdrawn from
   service in 1947 to be reconditioned and re-engined. Resumed
   service in September 1948. Accommodation for 430 passengers. Sister ships: **Rangitane** and **Rangitata.**

*Rangitoto   (1949)   New Zealand Shipping Co., Ltd.
   Built by Vickers-Armstrongs, Ltd., Walker-on-Tyne, England. Tonnage: 21,809. Dimensions: 587' x 78' (609' o.l.).
   Twin-screw, 17 knots. Motorship. Two masts and one
   funnel. Entered service in August 1949. Accommodation
   for 410 passengers. Note: Rangitoto is a small island in
   Waitemata Harbor, Auckland. Sister ship: **Rangitane.**

Remuera   (1911)   New Zealand Shipping Co., Ltd.
   Built by Wm. Denny & Bros., Ltd., Dumbarton, Scotland.
   Tonnage: 11,276. Dimensions: 485' x 62'. Twin-screw,
   15 knots. Reciprocating engines. Two masts and one
   funnel. Became a war loss on August 26, 1940. Sister ships:
   Rotorua and **Ruahine.**

Rimutaka   (1900)   New Zealand Shipping Co., Ltd.
   Built by Wm. Denny & Bros., Ltd., Dumbarton, Scotland.
   Tonnage: 8,997. Dimensions: 457' x 58'. Twin-screw, 13½
   knots. Triple expansion engines. Two masts and one funnel.
   Withdrawn from service in 1929. Sister ship: **Ruapehu.**

Rimutaka   (1923)   New Zealand Shipping Co., Ltd.
   Built by Sir W. G. Armstrong, Whitworth & Co., Ltd.,
   Newcastle-on-Tyne, England. Tonnage: 16,576. Dimensions: 551' x 72'. Twin-screw, 16 knots. Turbines. Two
   masts and one funnel. Note: Acquired from the P. & O.
   Line on an indefinite charter basis in 1938. Sold in January
   1950. Ex-**Mongolia** (1938). Renamed: (a) **Europa** (1950),
   (b) **Nassau** (1951).

Rotorua   (1911)   New Zealand Shipping Co., Ltd.
   Built by John Brown & Co., Ltd., Clydebank, Glasgow.
   Tonnage: 12,184. Dimensions: 526' x 61' (544' o.l.). Twin-
   screw, 14 knots. Reciprocating engines. Five masts and
   one funnel. Became a war casualty on December 11, 1940.
   Ex-**Shropshire.** Note: This steamship line owned an earlier
   Rotorua, which had been built in 1910. The vessel was
   11,130 tons, and a sister ship to the **Remuera** and **Ruahine.**

The **Rotorua** of 1910 was torpedoed and sunk in English Channel, near Start Point, on March 22, 1917.

Ruahine (1909) New Zealand Shipping Co., Ltd.
Built by Wm. Denny & Bros., Ltd., Dumbarton, Scotland. Tonnage: 10,839. Dimensions: 480′ x 60′. Twin-screw, 15 knots. Reciprocating engines. Two masts and one funnel. Sold to Italians in January 1949. Renamed: **Auriga** (1949). Scrapped in Italy, 1957. Sister ships: **Rotorua** and **Remuera.**

****Ruahine** (1951) New Zealand Shipping Co., Ltd.
Built by John Brown & Co., Ltd., Clydebank, Glasgow. Tonnage: 17,851. Dimensions: 563′ x 75′. Twin-screw, 17 knots. Motorship. Two masts and one funnel. Accommodation for 257 first-class passengers.

Ruapehu (1901) New Zealand Shipping Co., Ltd.
Built by Wm. Denny & Bros., Ltd., Dumbarton, Scotland. Tonnage: 8,887. Dimensions: 457′ x 58′. Twin-screw, 13 knots. Triple expansion engines. Three masts and one funnel. Sold to Italian shipbreakers in August 1931. Broken up for scrap during 1932. Ex-**Australasian,** ex-**Ruapehu.** Sister ship: **Rimutaka.**

Sagittaire (1929) Messageries Maritimes.
Built by Bremer Vulkan, Vegesack, Germany. Tonnage: 8,253. Dimensions: 473′ x 61′. Twin-screw, 14½ knots. Motorship. Two masts and one funnel. Passengers: 58 first and 107 second. Route: France-Tahiti-New Hebrides, via Panama Canal. Renamed: **Pacific Glory** (1954). Ex-**Washington** (1938) French Line.

****Santos Maru** (1952) Osaka Shosen Kaisha.
Built by Mitsubishi Heavy Industries, Kobe, Japan. Tonnage: 8,516. Dimensions: 475′ x 61′8. Single-screw, 14½ knots. Motorship. Two masts and one funnel. Passengers: 12 cabin, 50 second, 558 third. Route: Japan-South America, via Panama Canal. Running mates: **Africa Maru** and **America Maru.**

****Southern Cross** (1956) Shaw, Savill & Albion Co.
Built by Harland & Wolff, Ltd., Belfast, Ireland. Tonnage: 20,204. Dimensions: 560′ x 78′ (603′ o.l.). Twin-screw, 20 knots. Four steam turbines. Single mast and one funnel aft. During her trials she attained a speed of 21.3 knots. The profile of this passenger liner is unorthodox, but does give the viewer an interesting aspect of contrast with the past.

Launched, August 17, 1954.   Passengers: 1,100 tourist. Service: Round-the-world, via the Panama Canal. The new **Northern Star** will be her running mate in 1962.

*****Tahitien**   (1953)   Messageries Maritimes.
Built by Naval Dockyard, Brest, France. Tonnage: 12,614. Dimensions: 529′ x 67′ (549′ o.l.).   Twin-screw, 16 knots. Motorship. Two masts and one funnel. Commissioned in February 1953. Passengers: 71 first, 84 tourist, 86 third. Service: Marseilles-New Hebrides-New Caledonia-Australia, via Panama Canal. Sister ship: **Caledonien.**

Tainui   (1908)   Shaw Savill Line.
Built by Workman, Clark, Ltd., Belfast, Ireland. Tonnage: 9,957.   Dimensions: 477′ x 61′.   Twin-screw, 14 knots. Reciprocating engines. Two masts and one funnel. Converted to tourist class ship in 1932. Renamed: **Empire Trader** (1940). Became a war loss on February 23, 1943.

Tamaroa   (1922)   Shaw, Savill & Albion Co.
Built by Harland & Wolff, Ltd., Belfast, Ireland. Tonnage: 12,405.   Dimensions: 500′ x 63′.   Twin-screw, 15 knots. Turbines. Two masts and one funnel. Accommodation for 130 passengers. Scrapped at Blyth in 1957. Ex-**Sophocles.** Sister ship: **Mataroa.**

Ville d' Amiens   (1924)   Messageries Maritimes.
Built by North of Ireland Shipbuilding Co., Londonderry, Ireland. Tonnage: 7,350. Dimensions: 411′ x 53′. Single-screw. Triple expansion engines. Service: France-Tahiti-New Hebrides, via Panama Canal. Vessel was acquired from Cie Havraise Pen. de Navigation in 1928 and converted to passenger and cargo liner. Scrapped in France, 1953.

Ville de Verdun   (1921)   Messageries Maritimes.
Built by North of Ireland Shipbuilding Co., Londonderry, North Ireland. Tonnage: 7,209. Dimensions: 411′ x 53′. Single-screw. Triple expansion engines. Purchased in 1928 and converted to passenger-cargo liner for their France-Tahiti-New Hebrides, via Panama Canal service. Torpedoed and sunk off Formosa, October 17, 1942.

*****Willem Ruys**   (1947)   Rotterdam Lloyd.
Built by De Schelde, Flushing, Netherlands. Tonnage: 23,114. Dimensions: 580′ x 82′ (633′ o.l.). Twin-screw, 21½ knots. Eight Sulzer type diesels. Two masts and two funnels. Keel laid in January 1939, but remained unfinished during World War II. During her trials in November 1947, attained a speed of 24.6 knots. Originally in Rotterdam-Indonesia service. Commenced round-the-world via Panama Canal in 1959. Passengers: 275 first and 770 tourist.

PART III

LATIN AMERICAN PASSENGER SHIPS

Past and Present

PART III

LATIN AMERICAN PASSENGER SHIPS

Past and Present

Note: *Asterisk denotes ship in service, 1962.

Abangarez (1909) United Fruit Co.
Built by Workman, Clark & Co., Belfast, Ireland. Tonnage: 4,572. Dimensions: 378′ x 50′. Single-screw, 14 knots. Triple expansion engines. Two masts and one funnel. A large section of cabin superstructure was removed in the early 1930's. This change limited the ship to 12 passengers. Scrapped in California, 1948. Sister ships listed under **Metapan.**

Aconcagua (1872) Pacific Steam Navigation Co.
Built by John Elder & Co., Glasgow, Scotland. Tonnage: 4,106. Dimensions: 404′ x 41′. Single-screw, 14 knots. Compound inverted D.A. engines. Three masts and one funnel. Iron hull. Clipper bow. Entered service to Australia in 1880. Renamed: **Egypte** (1895). Similar ships: **Cotopaxi, Illimani** and **Sorata.**

Aconcagua (1922) Compania Sud Americana de Vapores (Chile).
Built by Scott's Shipbuilding & Engine Co., Greenock, Scotland. Tonnage: 7,290. Dimensions: 422′ x 56′. Twin-screw, 17 knots. Steam turbines. Two masts and one funnel. Renamed: **Khedive Ismail** (1935). Sister ship: **Teno.**

Aconcagua (1938) Compania Sud Americana de Vapores (Chile).
Built by Nakskov. Skibs., Nakskov, Denmark. Tonnage: 7,237. Dimensions: 414′ x 58′ (440′ o.l.). Single-screw, 15 knots. Motorship. Two masts and one funnel. Renamed: **Giresun** (Turkish). Sister ships: **Copiapo** and **Imperial.**

Adolf von Baeyer (1922) Stinnes Line (German).
Built by Marine-werft, Wilhelmshaven, Germany. Tonnage: 5,708. Dimensions: 409′ x 53′. Single-screw. Triple expansion engines. Two masts and one funnel. Renamed: **Peles** (1933) Rumanian. Sister ships: **Albert Vogler, Carl Legien** and **Emil Kirdorff.**

341

Advance   (1883)   (a) United States and Brazil Mail Steamship Co., (b) Panama Railroad Co.
Built by John Roach & Son, Chester, Pennsylvania. Tonnage: 2,603. Dimensions: 295' x 38'. Single-screw, 12 knots. Compound engines. Two masts and one funnel. Sister ships: **Alliance** and **Finance**.

Aeolus   (1899)   Munson Line.
Built by F. Schichau, Danzig, Germany. Tonnage: 12,642. Dimensions: 560' x 62'. Twin-screw, 15 knots. Quadruple expansion engines. Steam turbines installed in 1924. Two masts and two funnels. Renamed: **City of Los Angeles**. Ex-**Grosser Kurfurst** (1917).

Aidan   (1911)   Booth Line.
Built by Tyne Shipbuilding Co., Newcastle, England. Tonnage: 4,545. Dimensions: 375' x 50'. Single-screw, 11 knots. Triple expansion engines. Two masts and one funnel. Scrapped in 1936.

Alba   (1912)   Compagnie Sud-Atlantique (French).
Built by Bremer Vulkan, Vegesack, Germany. Tonnage: 8,324. Dimensions: 439' x 56'. Twin-screw, 12 knots. Triple expansion engines. Two masts and one funnel. Renamed: **Amerique**. Ex-**Sierra Ventana**.

Alban   (1914)   Booth Line.
Built by Caledon Shipbuilding & Engine Co., Dundee, Scotland. Tonnage: 5,223. Dimensions: 375' x 51'. Single-screw. Triple expansion engines. Two masts and one funnel. Renamed: **Zena** (Italian).

Albert Vogler   (1923)   Stinnes Line (German).
Built by Marine-werft, Wilhelmshaven, Germany. Tonnage: 5,708. Dimensions: 409' x 53'. Single-screw. Triple expansion engines. Two masts and one funnel. Renamed: **Suceava** (1933). Sister ship: **Adolf von Baeyer**. These vessels were later acquired by Hamburg-American Line.

*Alberto Dodero   (1951)   Dodero Line (Argentina).
Built by N. V. Konink. Maats De Schelde, Flushing, Netherlands. Tonnage: 11,521. Dimensions: 490' x 64' (523' o.l.). Twin-screw, 17 knots. Motorship. Two masts and one funnel. Sister ships: **Maipu** and **Yapeyu**.

Alcala   (1912)   Royal Mail Line (British).
Built by Workman, Clark & Co., Belfast, Ireland. Tonnage: 10,660. Dimensions: 495' x 60'. Twin-screw, 14 knots.

Quadruple expansion engines. Two masts and one funnel.
In service for Royal Mail Line only during 1913. Renamed:
Vauban (1913).   Ex-**Vauban** (1913).

Alcantara   (1913)   Royal Mail Line (British).
Built by Harland & Wolff, Ltd., Govan, Scotland. Tonnage:
15,831.   Dimensions: 570′ x 67′ (589′ o.l.).   Triple-screw,
16 knots. Two masts and one funnel. As an armed British
merchant cruiser, was in naval action with the German raider
Grief, February 29, 1916, and as a result of shell fire sank
with the loss of 69 lives. Sister ships: **Almanzora, Andes** and
Arlanza.

Alcantara   (1926)   Royal Mail Line (British).
Built by Harland & Wolff, Ltd., Belfast, Ireland. Tonnage:
22,181.   Dimensions: 630′ x 78′ (655′ o.l.).   Twin-screw, 18
knots. Motorship. Two masts and two funnels. Later had
only a single funnel. Diesel engines were replaced with steam
turbines in 1934.   Scrapped in Japan, 1958.   Sister ship:
Asturias.

*****Alcoa Cavalier**   (1947)   Alcoa Steamship Co.
Built by Oregon Shipbuilding Corp., Portland, Oregon.
Tonnage: 8,481.   Dimensions: 439′ x 62′.   Single-screw,
16½ knots.   Steam turbines.   Two masts and one funnel.
Sister ships: **Alcoa Clipper** and **Alcoa Corsair.**

*****Alcoa Clipper**   (1946)   Alcoa Steamship Co.
Built by Oregon Shipbuilding Corp., Portland, Oregon.
Tonnage: 8,481.   Dimensions: 439′ x 62′.   Single-screw,
16½ knots.   Steam turbines.   Two masts and one funnel.
Sister ships: **Alcoa Cavalier** and **Alcoa Corsair.**

*****Alcoa Corsair**   (1947)   Alcoa Steamship Co.
Built by Oregon Shipbuilding Corp., Portland, Oregon.
Tonnage: 8,481. Dimensions: 439′ x 62′ (455′ o.l.).   Single-
screw, 16½ knots.   Steam turbines.   Two masts and one
funnel. Sister ships: **Alcoa Cavalier** and **Alcoa Clipper.**

*****Alcoa Polaris**   (1941)   Alcoa Steamship Co.
Built by Consolidated Steel Corp., Wilmington, California.
Tonnage: 6,679.   Dimensions: 396′ x 60′.   Single-screw, 14
knots.   Steam turbines.   Two masts and one funnel.

Alesia   (1902)   Compagnie Sud-Atlantique (French).
Built by Bremer Vulkan, Vegesack, Germany.   Tonnage:
6,030.   Dimensions: 403′ x 49′.   Twin-screw, 13 knots.

Quadruple expansion engines. Two masts and one funnel. Torpedoed and sunk, September 6, 1917. Ex-**Princetown** (1917), **Prinz Adalbert.**

*Alessandro Volta   (1954)   Italia Line.
Built by Ateliers et Chantiers de la Loire, St. Nazaire, France. Tonnage: 8,086. Dimensions: 502′ x 64′. Twin-screw, 16 knots. Motorship. Two masts and one funnel. Ex-**Clement Ader** (1956). Sister ships: **Antonio Pacinotti** and **Galileo Ferraris.**

Algerie   (1901)   Transport Maritimes (French).
Built by Forges et Chantiers de la Mediterranee, Havre, France. Tonnage: 3,035. Dimensions: 397′ x 42′. Single-screw, 13½ knots. Triple expansion engines. Two masts and one funnel. Sunk by submarine in Mediterranean, 1916.

Alliance   (1886)   Panama Railroad Co.
Built by Delaware River Shipbuilding Co., Chester, Pa. Tonnage: 2,985. Dimensions: 303′ x 42′. Single-screw, 14 knots. Compound engines. In fleet 1895–1922. Vessel abandoned in 1925. Running mates: **Advance** and **Finance.**

Almanzora   (1914)   Royal Mail Line (British).
Built by Harland & Wolff, Ltd., Belfast, Ireland. Tonnage: 15,551. Dimensions: 570′ x 67′ (589′ o.l.). Triple-screw, 17 knots. Triple expansion engines. Two masts and one funnel. Scrapped in 1947. Sister ships: **Alcantara, Andes** and **Arlanza.**

Almeda Star   (1926)   Blue Star Line.
Built by Cammell Laird & Co., Ltd., Birkenhead, England. Tonnage: 12,848 (14,935 as altered). Dimensions: 512′ x 68′ (578′ as lengthened). Twin-screw, 16 knots. Steam turbines. Two masts and two funnels. Torpedoed and sunk by submarine, January 17, 1941. Ex-**Almeda.** Sister ships: **Arandora Star, Andalucia Star, Avelona Star** and **Avila Star.** Note: These sister ships were later altered. The **Avila Star** and **Andalucia Star** were the only ones alike when alterations were completed. The **Avelona Star** had one funnel removed and was used as a freighter.

Almirante   (1900)   Lloyd Brasileiro.
Built by Reiherstieg Schiffsw., Hamburg, Germany. Tonnage: 5,786. Dimensions: 411′ x 48′. Single-screw, 13 knots. Quadruple expansion engines. Two masts and one funnel. Ex-**Itu** (1926), ex-**Cap Roca** (1917).

Almirante   (1909)   Tropical Fruit Steamship Co.
   Built by Workman, Clark & Co., Belfast, Ireland. Tonnage: 5,010.   Dimensions: 378' x 50'.   Single-screw, 14 knots. Triple expansion engines. Two masts and one funnel. Sunk in collision, 1918. Sister ships listed under **Metapan.**

Almirante Jacequay   (1912)   Lloyd Brasileiro.
   Built by Reiherstieg Schiffsw., Hamburg, Germany. Tonnage: 6,079.   Dimensions: 392' x 52'.   Single-screw, 13 knots. Quadruple expansion engines. Two masts and one funnel.   Scrapped in 1956.   Ex-**General San Martin,** ex-**Edmund Wagenknecht,** ex-**Professor,** ex-**Professor Woermann.**

Alsace   (1889)   Transport Maritimes (French).
   Built by Wigham, Richardson & Co., Newcastle, England. Tonnage: 2,016.   Dimensions: 300' x 35'.   Single-screw, 13 knots. Triple expansion engines. Two masts and one funnel. Steel hull. Vessel was purchased in 1899. Scrapped in Italy, 1921.   Ex-**Rio de Janeiro,** ex-**Adelaide Lavarello.**

Alsina   (1921)   Transport Maritimes (French).
   Built by Swan, Hunter & Wigham Richardson, Ltd., Newcastle, England. Tonnage: 8,404.   Dimensions: 450' x 58'. Twin-screw, 15 knots. Steam turbines. Two masts and two funnels. Sunk by Allied air attack in 1941. Sister ship: **Mendoza.**

Amapala   (1924)   Standard Fruit Co.
   Built by Swan, Hunter & Wigham Richardson, Ltd., Newcastle, England. Tonnage: 4,148.   Dimensions: 350' x 50'. Single-screw, 15½ knots.   Triple expansion engines.   Two masts and one funnel. Became a World War II casualty in 1942. Sister ship: **Atlantida.**

Amasis   (1896)   Kosmos Steamship Co.
   Built by C. Connell & Co., Glasgow, Scotland. Tonnage: 4,552.   Dimensions: 370' x 46'.   Single-screw, 11 knots. Quadruple expansion engines. Two masts and one funnel. Renamed: (a) **Eichsfeld,** ex-**Archipelagos.**

Amasis   (1923)   (a) Kosmos Line, (b) Hamburg-American Line.
   Built by Bremer Vulkan, Vegesack, Germany. Tonnage: 7,129.   Dimensions: 438' x 55'.   Single-screw, 12 knots. Triple expansion engines. Two masts and one funnel. Torpedoed and sunk in Kattegat, 1940.

Amazon   (1851)   Royal Mail Line (British).
Built by R. & H. Green, Blackwall, London, England. Tonnage: 2,256. Paddle-wheels, 12 knots. Three masts and two funnels. Wooden hull. Clipper bow. Out of fleet in 1852.

Amazon   (1906)   Royal Mail Line (British).
Built by Harland & Wolff, Ltd., Belfast, Ireland. Tonnage: 10,037.   Dimensions: 513' x 60'.   Twin-screw, 15 knots. Quadruple expansion engines. Two masts and one funnel. Launched, February 24, 1906. Torpedoed and sunk without warning 30 miles from Malin Head on February 15, 1918. Sister ship: **Aragon.**

*****Amazon**   (1960)   Royal Mail Line (British).
Built by Harland & Wolff, Ltd., Belfast, Ireland. Tonnage: 20,348.   Dimensions: 540' x 78'.   (584' o.l.).   Twin-screw, 17 knots. Motorship. Single mast and one funnel. Sister ships: **Aragon** and **Arlanza.**

Amazonas   (1890)   Hamburg-South American Line.
Built by Blohm & Voss, Hamburg, Germany. Tonnage: 2,950.   Dimensions: 325' x 41'.   Single-screw, 12½ knots. Triple expansion engines. Renamed: (a) **Rio Gallegos** (1903), (b) **Amazonas** (1905), (c) Venetia (1905).   Torpedoed by a British submarine off mouth of River Ems, September 25, 1915; beached but became a total loss.

Amazone   (1896)   Messageries Maritimes.
Built by Messageries Maritimes, La Ciotat, France. Tonnage: 6,019.   Dimensions: 442' x 50'.   Twin-screw, 18½ knots. Triple expansion engines. Two masts and one funnel. Later was altered to single stack. Named **Amazone** in 1904 when transferred from Far East service to South Atlantic route. Returned to the Far East service in 1912. Scrapped in 1932.   Ex-**Laos** (1904).

Ambrose   (1903)   Booth Line.
Built by Sir Raylton Dixon & Co., Middlesbro, England. Tonnage: 4,594.   Dimensions: 387' x 47'.   Single-screw, 15 knots. Triple expansion engines. Two masts and one funnel. Accommodation for 149 first- and 134 third-class passengers. Vessel was taken over by British Admiralty in 1915.

America   (1908)   (a) La Veloce Line, (b) Navigazione Generale Italiana. Built by Cantieri Navali Riuniti, Muggiano, Italy. Tonnage: 8,996.   *Note: See PART I for details.*

American Legion   (1920)   Munson Line.
     Built by New York Shipbuilding Co., Camden, N. J. Tonnage: 13,736.   Dimensions: 516′ x 72′   (535′ o.l.).   Twinscrew, 17 knots. Steam turbines. Two masts and one funnel. Scrapped in 1948. Sister ships: **Pan America, Southern Cross** and **Western World.**

Amerigo Vespucci   (1949)   Italia Line.
     Built by Soc. Anon. Ansaldo, Genoa-Sestri, Italy. Tonnage: 9,774. Dimensions: 446′ x 62′ (485′ o.l.). Single-screw, 15½ knots. Motorship. Two masts and one funnel. Launched as **Giuseppe Majorana** in 1942. Commissioned in 1949. Sister ships: **Antoniotto Usodimare, Marco Polo, Sebastiano Caboto** and **Paolo Toscanelli.**

Amerique   (1879)   Fraissinet & Co. (French).
     Built by A. McMillan & Son, Dumbarton, Scotland. Tonnage: 2,008. Dimensions: 308′ x 36′. Single-screw. Compound engines. Iron hull.

Ammiraglio Bettolo   (1923)   Transatlantica Italiana.
     Built by G. Ansaldo & Co., Sestri Ponente, Italy. Tonnage: 8,139. Dimensions: 429′ x 52′. Twin-screw, 14 knots. Steam turbines. Two masts and two funnels. Renamed: **Kawsar.** Sister ship: **Nazario.**

Ammon   (1922)   (a) Kosmos Line, (b) Hamburg-American Line.
     Built by Bremer Vulkan, Vegesack, Germany. Tonnage: 7,134.   Dimensions: 438′ x 55′.   Single-screw, 12 knots. Triple expansion engines. Two masts and one funnel. Not listed after 1939.

Ancon   (1902)   Panama Railroad Co.
     Built by Maryland Steel Co., Sparrows Point, Maryland. Tonnage: 9,606.   Dimensions: 489′ x 58′.   Twin-screw, 13 knots. Triple expansion engines. Two masts and one funnel. Renamed: (a) **Permanente** (1941), (b) **Tidewater** (1946), (c) **Continental** (1948).   Sister ship: **Cristobal.**

*Ancon   (1939)   Panama Railroad Co.
     Built by Bethlehem Steel Co., Shipbuilding Division, Quincy, Mass. Tonnage: 10,021. Dimensions: 474′ x 64′ (493′ o.l.). Twin-screw, 16½ knots. Steam turbines. Two masts and one funnel. Sister ships: **Cristobal** and **Panama.**

Ancona   (1908)   "Italia" Societa Anonima di Navigazione.
     Tonnage: 8,885.   *Note: See PART I for details.*

Andalucia Star   (1927)   Blue Star Line.
　　Built by Cammell, Laird & Co., Birkenhead, England. Tonnage: 12,848. Dimensions: 512′ x 68′. As altered and lengthened: 14,943 tons, 578′ (597′ o.l.). Twin-screw, 16 knots. Steam turbines. Two masts and two funnels. Later used mainly as a cruise ship. Torpedoed and sunk, October 6, 1942. Ex-**Andalucia**. Sister ships: **Almeda Star, Arandora Star, Avelona Star** and **Avila Star.**

Andes   (1913)   (a) Pacific Steam Navigation Co., (b) Royal Mail Line.
　　Built by Harland & Wolff, Ltd., Belfast, Ireland. Tonnage: 15,620. Dimensions: 570′ x 67′ (589′ o.l.). Triple-screw, 17 knots. Triple expansion engines and steam turbine. Two masts and one funnel. Reconditioned at Belfast in 1930 for cruising. Renamed: **Atlantis** (1930). Scrapped in Great Britain, 1952. Sister ships: **Alcantara, Almanzora** and **Arlanza.**

*****Andes**   (1939)   Royal Mail Line (British).
　　Built by Harland & Wolff, Ltd., Belfast, Ireland. Tonnage: 25,689. Dimensions: 643′ x 83′ (669′ o.l.). Twin-screw, 21 knots. Steam turbines. Two masts and one funnel. Note: Completed in 1939, but did not enter regular service until January 1948, as she was taken over as a troopship upon completion.

Andrea C   (1942)   Giacoma Costa Line (Italian).
　　Built by Todd-California Shipbuilding Corp., Richmond, California. Tonnage: 7,867. Dimensions: 425′ x 57′ (442′ o.l.). Single-screw, 15 knots. Motorship. Two masts and one funnel.   Ex-**Ocean Virtue** (1948).

*****Anna C**   (1929)   "C" Line (Giacomo Costa fu Andrea).
　　Built by Lithgows, Ltd., Port Glasgow, Scotland. Tonnage: 11,736. Dimensions: 506′ x 64′ (516′ o.l.). Twin-screw, 18 knots. Motorship. Two masts and one funnel. Her original diesels were replaced in 1951. Ex-**Southern Prince** (1947).

Anselm   (1905)   Booth Line.
　　Built by Workman, Clark & Co., Belfast, Ireland. Tonnage: 5,450. Dimensions: 400′ x 50′. Single-screw, 14 knots. Triple expansion engines. Two masts and one funnel. Renamed: (a) **Comodoro Rivadavia** (1922), (b) **Rio Santa Cruz** (1944).

Anselm   (1935)   Booth Line.
> Built by Wm. Denny & Bros., Ltd., Dumbarton, Scotland. Tonnage: 5,954. Dimensions: 412′ x 55′. Single-screw, 14 knots. Steam turbines. Two masts and one funnel. Torpedoed and sunk by enemy submarine, July 5, 1941.

Antigua   (1932)   United Fruit Co.
> Built by Bethlehem Shipbuilding Corp., Quincy, Mass. Tonnage: 6,982. Dimensions: 415′ x 60′. Twin-screw, 18 knots. Two steam turbines connected to electric motors. Two masts and one funnel. Renamed: **Tortuga.** Sister ships: **Chiriqui, Peten, Quirigua, Talamanca** and **Veragua.**

Antisana   (1893)   Pacific Steam Navigation Co.
> Built by Harland & Wolff, Ltd., Belfast, Ireland. Tonnage: 3,584. Dimensions: 360′ x 42′. Single-screw, 13½ knots. Triple expansion engines. Two masts and one funnel. Renamed: **Basque** (1911). Scrapped in 1923. Class of: **Inca, Magellan** and **Sarmiento.**

Antonina   (1898)   Hamburg-American Line.
> Built by Blohm & Voss, Hamburg, Germany. Tonnage: 4,010. Dimensions: 361′ x 44′. Single-screw, 12 knots. Triple expansion engines. Vessel originally in Hamburg-South American Line fleet. Interned in Mexico in 1917. Resold to Germany. Renamed: (a) **Haimon,** (b) **Ancona,** (c) **Pirangy** (1928). Running mate: **La Plata.**

Antonio Delfino   (1921)   Hamburg-South American Line.
> Built by Akt. Ges. "Vulkan", Hamburg, Germany. Tonnage: 13,589. Dimensions: 499′ x 64. Twin-screw, 15 knots. Triple expansion engines. Two masts and one funnel. Renamed: (a) **Sierra Nevada,** (b) **Antonio Delfino** (1934), (c) **Empire Halladale** (1945). Note: Taken as a war prize at Copenhagen in May 1945 and renamed **Empire Halladale.** She then served as a troopship under Anchor Line management. Scrapped in Great Britain, 1956.

*Antonio Pacinotti   (1954)   Italia Line.
> Built by Chantiers de la Loire, St. Nazaire, France. Tonnage: 8,086. Dimensions: 502′ x 64′ (506′ o.l.). Twin-screw, 16 knots. Motorship. Two masts and one funnel. Ex-**Edouard Branly** (1957). Sister ships: **Alessandre Volta** and **Galileo Ferraris.**

*Antoniotto Usodimare   (1942)   Italia Line.
Built by Soc. Anon. Ansaldo, Sestri, Genoa, Italy. Tonnage: 9,715. Dimensions: 466' x 62' (485' o.l.). Single-screw, 15½ knots. Motorship. Two masts and one funnel. Launched in 1942.   Commissioned in 1949.   Sister ships: **Amerigo Vespucci, Marco Polo, Paolo Toscanelli** and **Sebastiano Caboto.**

Antony   (1907)   Booth Line.
Built by Hawthorn, Leslie & Co., Newcastle, England. Tonnage: 6,466. Dimensions: 418' x 52'. Twin-screw, 14 knots. Triple expansion engines. Two masts and one funnel. Accommodation for 202 first- and 370 third-class passengers. Torpedoed and sunk on March 17, 1917.   Sister ships: **Hilary** and **Lanfranc.**

Anyo Maru   (1913)   Toyo Kisen Kaisha.
Built by Mitsubishi Dockyard & Engine Works, Nagasaki, Japan.   Tonnage: 9,534.   Dimensions: 466' x 58'.   Twin-screw, 13 knots. Four steam turbines. Two masts and one funnel. Later owned by N. Y. K. Line (Japanese). Service: Japan-United States West Coast-South American West Coast ports. Running mates: **Bokuyo Maru, Ginyo Maru** and **Rakuyo Maru.**

Aquitaine   (1891)   Transport Maritimes (French).
Built by Sunderland Shipbuilding Co., Sunderland, England. Tonnage: 3,161. Dimensions: 350' x 42'. Single-screw, 12½ knots. Triple expansion engines. Two masts and one funnel. Scrapped in France, 1927.

Aragon   (1905)   Royal Mail Line (British).
Built by Harland & Wolff, Ltd., Belfast, Ireland. Tonnage: 9,441.   Dimensions: 513' x 60'.   Twin-screw, 16 knots. Quadruple expansion engines. Two masts and one funnel. Launched, February 23, 1905. Torpedoed and sunk, while being used as a British troopship, in the Mediterranean on December 30, 1917, with the loss of 610 lives. Sister ship: **Amazon.**

*Aragon   (1960)   Royal Mail Line (British).
Built by Harland & Wolff, Ltd., Belfast, Ireland. Tonnage: 20,362. Dimensions: 540' x 78' (584' o.l.). Twin-screw, 17 knots. Motorship. Single mast and one funnel. Passengers: 470. Crew: 200. Sister ships: **Amazon** and **Arlanza.**

Araguaya (1906) Royal Mail Line (British).
Built by Workman, Clark & Co., Belfast, Ireland. Tonnage: 10,196. Dimensions: 515′ x 61′. Twin-screw, 16½ knots. Quadruple expansion engines. Two masts and one funnel. Renamed: **Kraljica Marija** (1930). War loss in 1942.

Arandora Star (1927) Blue Star Line.
Built by Cammell, Laird & Co., Birkenhead, England. Tonnage: 14,690. Dimensions: 512′ x 68′ (535′ o.l.). Twin-screw, 16 knots. Steam turbines. Two masts and two funnels. Rebuilt and altered several times. Torpedoed and sunk, July 2, 1940. Ex-**Arondora.** Sister ships: **Alameda Star, Andalucia Star, Avelona Star** and **Avila Star.** Note: Later these ships were not identical due to alterations.

Araucania (1869) Pacific Steam Navigation Co.
Built by John Elder & Co., Glasgow, Scotland. Tonnage: 2,877. Dimensions: 354′ x 41′. Single-screw. Compound engines. Iron hull. Passengers: 145 first, 75 third. Sold in 1897. Sister ships: **Cordillera, Magellan** and **Patagonia.**

Arcadian (1899) Royal Mail Line (British).
Built by Vickers Sons, & Maxim, Ltd., Barrow, England. Tonnage: 8,939. Dimensions: 500′ x 55′. Twin-screw, 18 knots. Triple expansion engines. Two masts and two funnels. Torpedoed and sunk in the Mediterranean by a German submarine, April 15, 1917, with the loss of 279 lives. She was being used as a British troopship at the time of the disaster. Ex-**Ortona** (1910).

Arcadian (1908) Royal Mail Line (British).
Built by Harland & Wolff, Ltd., Belfast, Ireland. Tonnage: 12,015. Dimensions: 520′ x 62′. Twin-screw, 16½ knots. Quadruple expansion engines. Two masts and one funnel. Scrapped in 1933. Ex-**Asturias** (1923).

Archimede (1881) Navigazione Generale Italiana.
Built by Alexander Stephen & Sons, Ltd., Glasgow, Scotland. Tonnage: 2,837. Dimensions: 350′ x 40′. Single-screw, 12½ knots. Compound engines. Three masts and one funnel. Launched, November 23, 1881. Vessel transferred from the North Atlantic to South American service in 1888. Sunk off Alexandria, March 5, 1905. Sister ships: **Vincenzo Florio** and **Washington.**

Argentina (1905) La Veloce Line.
Built by Cantieri Liguria, Ancona, Italy. Tonnage: 4,985. Dimensions: 394′ x 47′. Twin-screw, 14 knots. Triple ex-

pansion engines. Two masts and two funnels. Renamed:
(a) **Brasile**, (b) **Venezuela**. Lost at Casablanca, March 7,
1920.

Argentina   (1907)   Cosulich Line.
Tonnage: 5,387. In South American service. Sold to Florio
in 1926. *Note: See PART I for details.*

Argentina   (1913)   Spanish Line.
Built by Swan, Hunter & Wigham Richardson, Ltd., Newcastle, England. Tonnage: 10,137. Dimensions: 480' x 61'.
Quadruple-screw, 17 knots. Triple expansion engines and
steam turbines. Two masts and one funnel. Sunk by air
attack at Barcelona in 1937. Later was refloated, sold and
broken up for scrap. Ex-**Reina Victoria Eugenia** (1931).
Sister ship: **Uruguay.** Both in South American service.

Argentina   (1913)   Home Lines.
Built by Cammell, Laird & Co., Birkenhead, England.
Tonnage: 11,015. Dimensions: 511' x 61' (530' o.l.). Twin-
screw, 17 knots. Quadruple expansion engines and steam
turbines. Commenced her first Genoa-South American
voyage in January 1947. Renamed: **Jerusalem** (1953).
Scrapped in 1959. Ex-**Bergensfjord** (1947).

Argentina   (1918)   Hamburg-South American Line.
Built by G. Seebeck, Wesermunde-G, Germany. Tonnage:
5,668. Dimensions: 365' x 51'. Single-screw, 12 knots.
Triple expansion engines. Two masts and one funnel.
Passengers: 800 steerage. Vessel sold to Blohm & Voss in
1932. Dismantled for scrap in Hamburg, 1934.

Argentina   (1929)   (a) American Republic Lines, (b) Moore-
McCormack Line.
Built by Newport News Shipbuilding Co., Newport News,
Va. Tonnage: 20,614. Dimensions: 586' x 80' (613' o.l.).
Twin-screw, 19 knots. Turbo-electric. Two masts and one
funnel. Laid up, 1960. Ex-**Pennsylvania** (1938). Sister
ships: **Brazil** and **Uruguay.**

*****Argentina**   (1949)   Flota Argentina de Navegacion de
Ultramar.
Built by Vickers-Armstrongs, Ltd., Barrow, England. Ton-
nage: 12,459. Dimensions: 509' x 71' (530' o.l.). Twin-
screw, 19 knots. Steam turbines. Two masts and one funnel.
Ex-**Presidente Peron** (1955). Sister ships: **Liberstad** and
Uruguay.

*Argentina   (1958)   Moore-McCormack Line.
Built by Ingalls Shipbuilding Corp., Pascagoula, Mississippi.
Tonnage: 20,614.   Dimensions: 617′ (o.l.) x 84′.   Twin-
screw, 23 knots. Steam turbines. Two masts and one funnel.
Keel laid on October 18, 1956. Launched, March 12, 1958.
Passengers: 553 first-class. Commenced her maiden voyage
from New York to South America on December 19, 1958.
Cost $26,000,000.   Sister ship: **Brasil.**

Argentina Maru   (1939)   Osaka Line.
Built by Mitsubishi Jukogyu K. K., Nagasaki, Japan. Tonnage: 12,755.   Dimensions: 516′ x 68′ (544′ o.l.).   Twin-
screw, 21½ knots. Motorship. Two masts and one funnel.
Passengers, 900. Presumed to be a World War II casualty.
Sister ship: **Brazil Maru.** Note: These ships were built for
round-the-world service, via South American ports.

*Argentina Maru   (1958)   Osaka Line.
Built by Mitsubishi, Ltd., Kobe, Japan. Tonnage: 10,863.
Dimensions: 513′ (o.l.) x 67′.   Single-screw, 16½ knots.
Steam turbines. Two masts and one funnel. Passengers:
12 first, 82 tourist and 960 third. Running mate: **Brasil
Maru.**

*Argentina Star   (1947)   Blue Star Line.
Built by Cammell Laird & Co., Birkenhead, England. Tonnage: 10,716.   Dimensions: 478′ (502′ o.l.) x 68′.   Single-
screw, 16 knots. Steam turbines. Single mast and one funnel.
Passengers: 70 first-class. Service: London-South America,
via Lisbon. Sister ships: **Brasil Star, Paraguay Star** and
Uruguay Star.

Ariguani   (1926)   Elders & Fyffes, Ltd.
Built by Alexander Stephen & Sons, Ltd., Glasgow, Scotland.
Tonnage: 6,746.   Dimensions: 425′ x 54′.   Twin-screw, 14
knots. Triple expansion engines. Two masts and one funnel.
Scrapped in Great Britain, 1956. Sister ships: **Bayano,
Camito, Carare, Cavina** and **Coronado.**

Arlanza   (1912)   Royal Mail Line (British).
Built by Harland & Wolff, Ltd., Belfast, Ireland. Tonnage:
14,930.   Dimensions: 570′ x 65′ (589′ o.l.).   Triple-screw,
17 knots. Triple expansion engines, and steam turbine.
Two masts and one funnel. Scrapped in 1938. Sister ships:
Alcantara, Almanzora and **Andes.**

*Arlanza   (1960)   Royal Mail Line (British).
   Built by Harland & Wolff, Ltd., Belfast, Ireland. Tonnage:
   20,362. Dimensions: 540' x 78' (584' o.l.). Twin-screw, 17
   knots. Motorship. Single mast and one funnel. Passengers:
   470. Crew: 200. Sister ships: **Amazon** and **Aragon.**

*Ascania   (1926)   Grimaldi-Siosa Lines (Italian).
   Built by Ateliers & Chantiers de la Loire, St. Nazaire, France.
   Tonnage: 9,536. Dimensions: 511' x 60'. Twin-screw, 14½
   knots. Steam turbines. Two masts and one funnel. As the
   Florida she had two funnels. Service: Europe-Venezuela-
   Central America. Ex-**Florida** (1955).

Asturias   (1908)   Royal Mail Line (British).
   Built by Harland & Wolff, Ltd., Belfast, Ireland. Tonnage:
   12,015. Dimensions: 520' x 62'. Twin-screw, 16½ knots.
   Quadruple expansion engines. Two masts and one funnel.
   Renamed: **Arcadian** (1923). Scrapped in 1933. Running
   mates: **Amazon, Aragon, Araguaya** and **Avon.**

Asturias   (1925)   Royal Mail Line (British).
   Built by Harland & Wolff, Ltd., Belfast, Ireland. Tonnage:
   22,071. Dimensions: 630' x 78' (655' o.l.). Twin-screw,
   17½ knots. Motorship. Converted to steam turbines in
   1934. Two masts and two funnels. Later had only a single
   mast and one funnel. Note: After World War II was placed
   in service to Australia carrying emigrants. Scrapped in
   Great Britain, 1957. As altered length was 641' (685' o.l.).
   Sister ship: **Alcantara.**

Atenas   (1909)   (a) Tropical Fruit Steamship Co., (b) United
   Fruit Co.
   Built by Workman, Clark & Co., Belfast, Ireland. Tonnage:
   4,962. Dimensions: 378' x 50'. Single-screw, 14 knots. Triple
   expansion engines. Two masts and one funnel. Cabin superstructure was stripped off in the early 1930's and she was
   placed on a 12 passenger basis. Sister ships listed under
   Metapan.

Atlantida   (1924)   Standard Fruit & Steamship Co.
   Built by Workman, Clark & Co., Belfast, Ireland. Tonnage:
   4,191. Dimensions: 350' x 50'. Single-screw, 15½ knots.
   Triple expansion engines. Two masts and one funnel.
   Passengers: 68 first-class. Service: New York-Cuba-Hon-
   duras-Kingston. Scrapped in 1960. Sister ship: **Amapala.**

Atlantique   (1899)   Messageries Maritimes.
Built by Messageries Maritimes, La Ciotat, France. Tonnage: 6,479. Dimensions: 468' x 50'. Twin-screw, 18 knots. Triple expansion engines. Two masts and two funnels. Built for South American trade. Transferred to Far East service in 1912. Complete refit in 1918 and addition of one deck. Renamed: **Angkor.**

Atlantis   (1913)   Royal Mail Line (British).
Built by Harland & Wolff, Ltd., Belfast, Ireland. Tonnage: 15,135. Dimensions: 570' x 67'. Triple-screw, 17 knots. Triple expansion engines and steam turbine. Two masts and one funnel. Mainly used as a cruise ship. Scrapped in Great Britain, 1952. Ex-**Andes** (1930).

Atrato   (1853)   Royal Mail Line (British).
Built by Caird & Co., Greenock, Scotland. Tonnage: 3,467. Dimensions: 315' x 42' (350' o.l.). Paddle-wheels, 14 knots. Three masts and two funnels. Largest merchant ship of that date. Accommodation for 224 first-class passengers. Out of fleet in 1870.

Atrato   (1888)   Royal Mail Line (British).
Built by Robert Napier & Sons, Glasgow, Scotland. Tonnage: 5,366. Dimensions: 421' x 49'. Single-screw, 15 knots. Triple expansion engines. Three masts and two funnels. Note: Altered several times. Wrecked in 1916. Sister ship: **Magdalena.**

Augustine   (1879)   Booth Steamship Co.
Built by Barclay, Curle & Co., Glasgow, Scotland. Tonnage: 3,498. Dimensions: 359' x 43'. Single-screw, 13½ knots. Triple expansion engines. Two masts and one funnel. Scrapped in 1912. Ex-**Grantully Castle** (1896).

Augustus   (1927)   (a) Navigazione Generale Italiana, (b) Italia Line.
Tonnage: 32,650. Commenced her maiden voyage Genoa-Naples-Buenos Aires, November 12, 1927. *Note: See PART I for details.*

*Augustus   (1952)   Italia Line.
Tonnage: 27,226. Entered Italy-Brazil-River Plate service in March 1952. *Note: See PART I for details.*

Auriga   (1909)   Fratelli Grimaldi Armatori (Italian).
Built by Wm. Denny & Bros., Ltd., Dumbarton, Scotland. Tonnage: 10,856. Dimensions: 480' x 60'. Twin-screw,

14 knots. Triple expansion engines. Two masts and one funnel. Service: Italy-Lisbon-Central America. Scrapped in Italy, 1957. Ex-**Ruahine** (1949).

Aurigny (1918) Chargeurs Reunis.
Built by Forges et Chantiers de la Mediterranee, La Seyne, France. Tonnage: 9,589. Dimensions: 481' x 58'. Twin-screw, 13 knots. Triple expansion engines. Two masts and one funnel. Launched on May 23, 1917. Badly damaged by fire at Buenos Aires in December 1941. Repaired by Argentine Government. Renamed: **General San Martin.** Sister ship: **Belle Isle.**

Austrian (1866) Allan Line.
Built by Barclay, Curle & Co., Glasgow, Scotland. Tonnage: 2,682. Dimensions: 319' x 38'. Single-screw, 11 knots. Inverted type engines. Compound engines installed in 1875. Three masts and one funnel. Made her last voyage Glasgow-South America, February 9, 1904. Broken up for scrap in 1905. *Note: See PART I for additional information.*

Avelona Star (1927) Blue Star Line.
Built by John Brown & Co., Clydebank, Glasgow, Scotland. Tonnage: 12,858. Dimensions: 512' x 68'. Twin-screw, 16 knots. Steam turbines. Two masts and two funnels. Later one funnel and a deck were removed, plus other alterations. Became a World War II casualty, June 30, 1940. Sister ships: **Almeda Star, Andalucia Star, Arandora Star** and **Avila Star.**

Avila Star (1927) Blue Star Line.
Built by John Brown & Co., Glasgow, Scotland. Tonnage: 12,872. Dimensions 538' x 68' (550' as lengthened). Twin-screw, 16 knots. Steam turbines. Two masts and two funnels. Second funnel was a dummy. Overall after lengthening was 569' and tonnage increased to 14,443. Torpedoed and sunk by enemy submarine off Portugal, July 5, 1942. Ex-**Avila.** Sister ships: **Almeda Star, Andalucia Star, Arandora Star** and **Avelona Star.**

Avon (1842) Royal Mail Line (British).
Built by William Patterson, Bristol, England. Tonnage: 2,069. Paddle-wheels, 8 knots. Three masts and one funnel. Speed later was increased to 10 knots. Out of fleet in 1862.

Avon (1907) Royal Mail Line (British).
Built by Harland & Wolff, Ltd., Belfast, Ireland. Tonnage: 11,073. Dimensions: 520' x 62'. Twin-screw, 16 knots.

Quadruple expansion engines. Two masts and one funnel. Launched on March 2, 1907. Coal bunker capacity was 4,780 tons. Route: Southampton-Corunna-Vigo-Oporto-Lisbon-Madeira-St. Vincent-Pernambuco-Bahia-Rio de Janeiro-Santos-Montevideo-Buenos Aires. Scrapped in Great Britain, 1930. Similar ships: **Amazon, Aragon, Araguaya** and **Asturias.**

Baden   (1922)   Hamburg-American Line.
Built by Bremer Vulkan, Vegesack, Germany. Tonnage: 8,803. Dimensions: 468' x 58'. Single-screw, 12½ knots. Triple expansion engines. Four masts and one funnel. Service: Germany-South America. Sunk in the Atlantic, December 1940. Similar ships: **Bayern** and **Wurttemburg.**

Baependy   (1899)   Lloyd Brasileiro.
Built by Blohm & Voss, Hamburg, Germany. Tonnage: 4,801. Dimensions: 375' x 46'. Single-screw, 12½ knots. Quadruple expansion engines. Two masts and one funnel. Torpedoed and sunk near Bahia, August 15, 1942. Ex-**Tijuca** (1917).

Bage   (1912)   Lloyd Brasileiro.
Built by Akt. Ges. "Vulkan", Stettin, Germany. Tonnage: 8,235. Dimensions: 439' x 56'. Twin-screw, 13 knots. Triple expansion engines. Two masts and one funnel. In Santos-Hamburg service. Became a World War II casualty. Ex-**Sierra Nevada** (1917).

Bahia   (1898)   Hamburg-South American Line.
Built by Reiherstieg Schiffsw., Hamburg, Germany. Tonnage: 4,817. Dimensions: 375' x 57'. Single-screw, 12½ knots. Quadruple expansion engines. Two masts and one funnel. Vessel seized by Uruguay in 1917, and renamed **Paysandu.** Broken up for scrap in Denmark, 1927.

Bahia   (1910)   Lloyd Brasileiro.
Built by Workman, Clark & Co., Belfast, Ireland. Tonnage: 3,401. Dimensions: 340' x 44'. Twin-screw, 13½ knots. Triple expansion engines. Two masts and one funnel. Accommodation for 118 first, 20 second, 500 third-class passengers. Vessel not listed in 1932.

Bahia Belgrano   (1897)   Hamburg-South American Line.
Built by Reiherstieg Schiffsw., Hamburg, Germany. Tonnage: 4,817. Dimensions: 376' x 46'. Single-screw, 12½ knots. Quadruple expansion engines.

Bahia Blanca   (1912)   Hamburg-South American Line.
Built by Reiherstieg Schiffsw., Hamburg, Germany. Tonnage: 9,349. Dimensions: 491' x 59'. Twin-screw, 13 knots. Triple expansion engines. Two masts and one funnel. Vessel sold to Argentine in 1918; name unchanged. Resold to Italy in 1935 and renamed **Umbria**. Scuttled at Port Sudan in June 1940. Later broken up for scrap. Sister ships: **Bahia Castillo** and **Bahia Laura**.

Bahia Castillo   (1913)   Hamburg-South American Line.
Built by Reiherstieg, Schiffsw., Hamburg, Germany. Tonnage: 9,949. Dimensions: 491' x 59'. Twin-screw, 13 knots. Triple expansion engines. Two masts and one funnel. Vessel surrendered to Great Britain in 1919. She was later sold to A. G. Hugo Stinnes and renamed **General Belgrano**. Sister ships: **Bahia Blanca** and **Bahia Laura**.

Bahia Laura   (1913)   Hamburg-South American Line.
Built by Bremer Vulkan, Vegesack, Germany. Tonnage: 9,791. Dimensions: 491' x 59'. Twin-screw, 13 knots. Triple expansion engines. Two masts and one funnel. Vessel seized by Brazilian Government in 1917. Renamed: (a) **Caxias** (1917), (b) **Ruy Barbosa** (1923). Wrecked near Leixoes, July 31, 1934, while on Hamburg-Brazil voyage. Sister ships: **Bahia Blanca** and **Bahia Castillo**.

Barcelona   (1908)   Pinillos, Izquierdo & Co.
Built by C. Connell & Co., Glasgow, Scotland. Tonnage: 5,574. Dimensions: 415' x 53'. Single-screw, 14 knots. Triple expansion engines. Two masts and one funnel. Sister ship: **Cadiz.**

Baronesa   (1918)   Furness Houlder Line.
Built by Sir Raylton Dixon & Co., Middlesbrough, England. Tonnage: 8,663. Dimensions: 431' x 61'. Twin-screw, 14½ knots. Triple expansion engines. Two masts and one funnel. Service: London-South American East Coast Ports. Running mate: **El Paraguayo.**

Bayano   (1913)   Elders & Fyffes, Ltd.
Built by Alexander Stephen & Sons, Ltd., Glasgow, Scotland. Tonnage: 5,948. Dimensions: 417' x 53'. Twin-screw, 14 knots. Triple expansion engines. Two masts and one funnel. Accommodation for 56 passengers. Sunk by German submarine, while serving as auxiliary cruise, 1915. Sister ships: **Patia** and **Patuca.**

Bayano   (1917)   Elders & Fyffes, Ltd.
   Built by Alexander Stephen & Sons, Ltd., Glasgow, Scotland.
   Tonnage: 6,788. Dimensions: 425′ x 54′. Twin-screw, 14½
   knots. Triple expansion engines. Two masts and one funnel.
   Broken up Belgium shipbreakers in 1956.   Sister ships:
   Ariguani, Camito, Carare, Cavina and **Coronado.**

Bayern   (1921)   North German Lloyd.
   Built by Bremer Vulkan, Vegesack, Germany. Tonnage:
   8,917.   Dimensions: 468′ x 58′.   Single-screw, 13 knots.
   Triple expansion engines.   Four masts and one funnel.
   Service: Germany-France-West Indies. Renamed: **Sontay**
   (1936). Similar ships: **Baden** and **Wurttemburg.**

Bearn   (1881)   Transport Maritimes (French).
   Built by Barrow Shipbuilding Co., Barrow, England. Ton-
   nage: 4,134. Dimensions: 398′ x 40′. Single-screw, 12 knots.
   Compound engines. Two masts and one funnel. Scrapped in
   France, 1901.

Belgrano   (1872)   Chargeurs Reunis.
   Built by Forges & Chantiers de Poc., Havre, France. Ton-
   nage: 2,131. Dimensions: 321′ x 33′. Single-screw. Com-
   pound engines. Three masts and one funnel. Iron hull.
   Vessel purchased prior to launching.   Scrapped in 1894.
   Ex-**Louis XIV.**

Belgrano   (1888)   Hamburg-South American Line.
   Built by Reiherstieg Schiffs-werft, Hamburg, Germany.
   Tonnage: 2,616. Dimensions: 321′ x 39′. Single-screw, 12½
   knots. Triple expansion engines. Two masts and one funnel.
   Renamed: (a) **Adolph Woermann** (1896), (b) **Frieda
   Woermann** (1906), (c) **Macapa** (1917). Vessel was seized
   by Brazil in 1917. Resold to Lloyd Brasileiro in 1927. Later
   scrapped.

Belle Isle   (1918)   Chargeurs Reunis.
   Built by Forge et Chantiers de la Mediterranee, La Seyne,
   France. Tonnage: 9,589. Dimensions: 479′ x 58′. Twin-
   screw, 13 knots. Triple expansion engines. Two masts and
   one funnel. Launched on March 23, 1917. Sunk by aerial
   bombardment in one of Toulon drydocks, November 24,
   1943; subsequently set on fire. Sister ship: **Aurigny.**
   Similar ships: **Jamaique, Kerguelen, Desirade, Eubee,
   Formose** and **Groix.**

Benevente   (1904)   Lloyd Brasileiro.
   Built by J. C. Tecklenborg, Geestemunde, Germany. Tonnage: 4,556. Dimensions: 361' x 46'. Single-screw, 12 knots. Triple expansion engines. Two masts and one funnel. Renamed: **Duque de Caxias** (1926). Ex-**Rio Grande** (1917).

Bermuda   (1927)   Furness-Bermuda Line.
   Built by Workman, Clark & Co., Belfast, Ireland. Tonnage: 19,086. Dimensions: 525' x 74'. Quadruple-screw, 17 knots. Motorship. Two masts and two funnels. Owner listed as: Bermuda & West Indies Steamship Co., Ltd. Liner was completely burnt out in November 1931, while at her builder's yard under-going repairs caused by a previous fire.

Bermudian   (1904)   Quebec Steamship Co.
   Built by Sir James Laing & Sons, Ltd., Sunderland, England. Tonnage: 5,530. Dimensions: 425' x 50' (435' o.l.). Twin-screw, 16½ knots. Triple expansion engines. Two masts and two funnels. Top of funnels 96 feet above furnace grates. Passengers: 240 first, 32 second and 43 third. Renamed: (a) **Fort Hamilton**, (b) **Stella d'Italia**. Scrapped in 1933.

*Biana C   (1944)   "C" Line (Giacomo Costa fu Andrea).
   Built by Provencale de Constructions Navales, La Ciotat, France. Tonnage: 18,427. Dimensions: 565' x 75' (593' o.l.). Twin-screw, 20 knots. Motorship. Two masts and one funnel. Service: Italy-West Indies. Passengers: 200 first, 1,030 tourist. Gutted by fire off St. George's, Grenada, October 22, 1961. Ex-**Arosa Sky** (1958), ex-**La Marseillaise** (1957), ex-**Marechal Petain** (as launched in 1944).

Bilbao   (1905)   Hamburg-South American Line.
   Built by Reiherstieg Schiffsw., Hamburg, Germany. Tonnage: 4,798. Dimensions: 392' x 50'. Single-screw. Triple expansion engines. Two masts and one funnel. Passengers: 800 steerage. Surrendered to Great Britain in 1918. Resold to Hamburg-South American Line in 1922. Renamed: **Bilbao.** Scrapped in Germany, 1932. Ex-**Santa Rita** (1922).

Bluecher   (1901)   Hamburg-American Line.
   Tonnage: 12,334.   Transferred to the South American service in 1911. *Note: See PART I for details.*

Bogota   (1852)   Pacific Steam Navigation Co.
   Built by Robert Napier & Sons, Glasgow, Scotland. Tonnage: 1,461. Dimensions: 258' x 30'. Paddle-wheels. Side

lever type engines. Two masts and two funnels. Iron hull. Hulked after grounding in 1871. Sister ships: **Lima** and **Quito.**

*Boissevain   (1937)   Royal Inter-Ocean Lines (Dutch).
Built by Blohm & Voss, Hamburg, Germany. Tonnage: 14,134. Dimensions: 537' x 72' (560' o.l.). Triple-screw, 17 knots. Motorship. Two masts and one funnel. Service: Far East-South Africa-South America. Sister ships: **Ruys** and **Tegelberg.**

Bokuyo Maru   (1924)   (a) Toyo Kisen Kaisha, (b) N. Y. K. Line.
Built by Asano Shipbuilding Co., Tsurimi, Japan. Tonnage: 8,619. Dimensions: 445' x 58'. Twin-screw, 12 knots. Steam turbines. Two masts and one funnel. In trans-Pacific service to South America, via United States West Coast ports. Burned and sank, July 18, 1939. Running mates: **Anyo Maru, Ginyo Maru** and **Rakuyo Maru.**

Bologna   (1905)   La Veloce Line.
Built by Harland & Wolff, Ltd., Belfast, Ireland. Tonnage: 4,680. Dimensions: 380' x 46'. Twin-screw, 14 knots. Triple expansion engines. Two masts and one funnel. Scrapped in 1928. Sister ship: **Siena.**

Boniface   (1904)   Booth Line.
Built by Barclay, Curle & Co., Ltd., Glasgow, Scotland. Tonnage: 3,506. Dimensions: 355' x 48'. Single-screw, 11 knots. Triple expansion engines. Two masts and one funnel. Passengers: 16 first-class and 100 in steerage. Sunk by German submarine in 1917.

Bonn   (1895)   North German Lloyd.
Built by Germania-werft, Kiel, Germany. Tonnage: 3,969. Dimensions: 355' x 43'. Single-screw, 12½ knots. Triple expansion engines. Renamed: **Gregor.** Stranded in 1920.

Boringuen   (1931)   New York & Porto Rico Line.
Built by Bethlehem Shipbuilding Corp., Quincy, Massachusetts. Tonnage: 7,114. Dimensions 413' x 59' (429' o.l.). Single-screw, 16 knots. Steam turbines. Two masts and one funnel. Renamed: (a) **Puerto Rico** (1949), (b) **Arosa Star** (1954).

Borkum   (1896)   North German Lloyd.
Built by J. L. Thompson & Son, Ltd., Sunderland, England. Tonnage: 5,642. Dimensions: 409' x 50'. Single-screw, 10

knots. Triple expansion engines. Two masts and one funnel. In service to Cuba. Renamed: **Asti** (1916). Torpedoed and sunk in 1917. Ex-**Ellen Rickmers** (1900). Running mates: **Helgoland** and **Norderney.**

Borussia   (1905)   Hamburg-American Line.
Built by Frd. Krupp, Kiel, Germany. Tonnage: 6,951. Dimensions: 421' x 54'. Twin-screw, 12½ knots. Quadruple expansion engines. Two masts and one funnel. Foundered off Portugal in 1907.

Bourgogne   (1865)   Transport Maritimes (French).
Built by James Laing, Sunderland, England. Tonnage: 1,902. Dimensions: 318' x 31'. Single-screw. Compound engines. Iron hull. Ex-**Uitenhage** (1867).

Boyne   (1871)   Royal Mail Line.
Built by Wm. Denny & Bros., Ltd., Dunbarton, Scotland. Tonnage: 3,318.   Dimensions: 372' x 40'. Single-screw. Compound engines. Two masts and one funnel. Out of fleet in 1875.

Brabantia   (1920)   Royal Holland Lloyd.
Built by Akt. Ges. "Weser", Bremen, Germany. Tonnage: 19,821. Dimensions: 590' x 72'. Triple-screw, 17 knots. Triple expansion engines and steam turbine. Two masts and three funnels. Renamed: (a) **Resolute** (1922), (b) **Lombardia** (1935). Ex-**William O'Swald** (1920). Sister ship: **Limburgia.**

Brasil   (1905)   Home Lines.
Built by Alexander Stephen & Sons, Ltd., Glasgow, Scotland. Tonnage: 11,055. Dimensions: 517' x 60' (538' o.l.). Triple-screw, 17 knots. Steam turbines. Two masts and one funnel. Commenced her first voyage from Genoa to South America, July 27, 1948. Note: Also served in Italy-New York trade. Renamed: **Homeland** (1951). Ex-**Drottningholm** (1948), ex-**Virginian** (1920).

*Brasil   (1958)   Moore-McCormack Line.
Built by Ingalls Shipbuilding Corp., Pascagoula, Mississippi. Tonnage: 20,614. Dimensions: 570' x 84' (617' o.l.). Twin-screw, 22 knots. Steam turbines. Two masts and one funnel. Displacement 22,770 tons.   Cost $25,000,000 to build. Accommodation for 553 passengers. Sister ship: **Argentina.**

Brasil Star   (1947)   Blue Star Line.
Built by Cammell Laird & Co., Birkenhead, England.
Tonnage: 10,716. Dimensions: 478' x 68' (502' o.l.). Single-
screw, 16 knots. Steam turbines. Single mast and one funnel.
Passengers: 70 first-class. Sister ships: **Argentina Star,
Paraguay Star** and **Uruguay Star.**

Brasile   (1905)   (a) La Veloce Line, (b) Transoceania Italiana.
Built by Fratelli Orlando, Leghorn, Italy. Tonnage: 5,298.
Dimensions: 394' x 47'. Twin-screw, 14½ knots. Triple
expansion engines. Two masts and two funnels. Renamed:
Venezuela (1912). Lost at Casablanca, March 7, 1920.
Ex-**Argentina.**

Brazil   (1928)   Moore-McCormack Line.
Build by Newport News Shipbuilding & Drydock Co., Newport News, Va. Tonnage: 20,614. Dimensions: 586' x 80'.
Twin-screw, 18½ knots. Steam turbines. Two masts and
one funnel. Laid up in 1960. Ex-**Virginia** (1938). Sister
ships: **Argentina** and **Uruguay.**

Brazil Maru   (1939)   Osaka Line.
Built by Mitsubishi Jukogijo K. K., Nagasaki, Japan.
Tonnage: 12,752. Dimensions: 516' x 68' (544' o.l.). Twin-
screw, 21½ knots. Motorship. Two masts and one funnel.
Sunk by submarine, August 5, 1942. Sister ship: **Argentina
Maru.**

*Brazil Maru   (1954)   Osaka Line.
Built by Mitsubishi Heavy Industries, Kobe, Japan. Ton-
nage: 10,101. Dimensions: 476' x 64' (512' o.l.). Motorship.
Two masts and one funnel. Service: Japan-South America.
Passengers: 12 first, 68 tourist, 902 third. Running mate:
Argentina Maru.

Brazilian   (1890)   Allan Line.
Built by D. & W. Henderson & Co., Glasgow, Scotland.
Tonnage: 3,046. Dimensions: 340' x 42'. Single-screw, 11
knots. Triple expansion engines. Two masts and one funnel.
Commenced her maiden voyage Glasgow-South America,
February 12, 1891. Later transferred to London-Montreal
service. Renamed: **Corcovado** (1910).

Bresil   (1889)   Messageries Maritimes.
Built by Messageries Maritimes, La Ciotat, France. Tonnage: 5,876. Dimensions: 463' x 46'. Single-screw, 16½
knots. Triple expansion engines. Renamed: **Dumbea** (1903).
Scrapped in 1928. Sister ship: **La Plata.**

363

Bretagne   (1877)   Transport Maritimes (French).
Built by Forges & Chantiers de la Mediterranee, La Seyne, France. Tonnage: 2,095. Dimensions: 288′ x 39′. Single-screw. Three masts and one funnel. Wrecked at Bahia in 1903.

Bretagne   (1922)   French Line.
Built by Barclay, Curle & Co., Glasgow, Scotland. Tonnage: 10,171. Dimensions: 450′ x 59′. Twin-screw, 14½ knots. Steam turbines. Two masts and two funnels. Torpedoed and sunk while on voyage to Europe from the West Indies, October 14, 1939. Ex-**Flandria** (1937).

*Bretagne   (1951)   Transport Maritimes (French).
Built by Chantiers & Atel. de St. Nazaire (Penhoet), St. Nazaire, France. Tonnage: 16,355. Dimensions: 554′ x 73′ (580′ o.l.). Twin-screw, 18 knots. Steam turbines. Two masts and one funnel. Largest French liner trading to South America when put in service. Sister ship: **Provence.**

Britannia   (1873)   Pacific Steam Navigation Co.
Built by Laird Bros., Birkenhead, England. Tonnage: 4,129. Dimensions: 411′ x 43′. Single-screw. Compound engines. Three masts and two funnels. Vessel sold to Argentina owners after grounding at Rio de Janeiro. Scrapped at Preston in 1901.

Buenos Aires   (1887)   Spanish Line.
Built by Wm. Denny & Bros., Dumbarton, Scotland. Tonnage: 5,311. Dimensions: 410′ x 48′. Single-screw, 14 knots. Quadruple expansion engines. Two masts and one funnel. Laid up from 1932 to 1939. Sister ship: **Montevideo.**

Buenos Aires   (1912)   Hamburg-South American Line.
Built by Bremer Vulkan Co., Vegesack, Germany. Tonnage: 9,180. Dimensions: 491′ x 59′. Twin-screw, 13 knots. Triple expansion engines. Two masts and one funnel. Vessel turned over to France as a war prize in 1919. Sold to Messageries Maritimes in 1922 and renamed **Cephee.** Scrapped in Great Britain, 1936. Sister ship: **Rosario.**

Buenos Aires Maru   (1930)   Osaka Line.
Built by Mitsubishi Zosen Kaisha, Nagasaki, Japan. Tonnage: 9,626. Dimensions: 461′ x 62′ (473′ o.l.). Two masts and one funnel. Motorship. Sunk by aircraft, November 27, 1943. Sister ship: **Rio de Janeiro Maru.**

Buenos Ayrean   (1879)   Allan Line.
  Built by Wm. Denny & Bros., Ltd., Dunbarton, Scotland.
  Tonnage: 4,005.   Dimensions: 385′ x 42′.   Single-screw,
  12 knots.   Compound engines.   Two masts and one funnel.
  Scrapped in 1911.

Burdigala   (1898)   Compagnie Sud-Atlantique (French).
  Built by F. Schichau, Danzig, Germany. Tonnage: 12,480.
  Dimensions: 581′ x 63′.   Twin-screw, 18 knots.   Quadruple
  expansion engines.   Two masts and three funnels.   Tor-
  pedoed and sunk in the Mediterranean, November 14, 1916.
  Ex-**Kaiser Friedrich** (1912).

Byron   (1901)   Lamport & Holt Co.
  Built by Alexander Stephen & Sons, Ltd., Glasgow, Scotland.
  Tonnage: 3,909.   Dimensions: 371′ x 45′.   Single-screw, 13
  knots.   Triple expansion engines. Two masts and one funnel.
  Clipper bow.   In New York-South American service.   Re-
  named: **Santiago.**   Ex-**Loyalist** (1901).   Sister ship:
  Tennyson.

Cabo de Buena Esperanza   (1921)   Ybarra & Co.
  Built by New York Shipbuilding Co., Camden, N. J.   Tonnage: 12,595.   Dimensions: 516′ x 72′.   Twin-screw, 16
  knots.   Steam turbines. Two masts and one funnel.   Passengers: 824 first and 835 third-class.   Scrapped in 1958.
  Ex-**Maria Del Carmen** (1940), ex-**President Lincoln**
  (1940), ex-**Hoosier State** (1922).   Sister ship: **Cabo de
  Hornos.**

Cabo de Hornos   (1921)   Ybarra & Co.
  Built by New York Shipbuilding Co., Camden, N. J.   Tonnage: 12,599.   Dimensions: 518′ x 72′.   Twin-screw, 16
  knots.   Steam turbines. Two masts and one funnel.   Scrapped
  in Spain, 1959.   Ex-**Maria Pipa** (1940), ex-**President
  Wilson** (1940), ex-**Empire State** (1922). Sister ship: **Cabo
  de Buena Esperanza.**

Cabo Palos   (1927)   Ybarra & Co.
  Built by Cia Euskalduna de Constr., Bilbao, Spain.   Tonnage: 6,342. Dimensions: 397′ x 53′.   Single-screw.   Motorship.   Sunk in 1937 during the Spanish Civil War.   Sister
  ship: **Cabo Quilates.**

Cabo Quilates   (1927)   Ybarra & Co.
  Built by Cia Euskalduna de Constr., Bilbao, Spain. Tonnage:
  6,342   Dimensions: 411′ x 53′.   Single-screw.   Motorship.

During Spanish Civil War was renamed **Ibai.** Sister ship:
Cabo Palos.

Cabo San Agustin   (1931)   Ybarra & Co.
   Built by Soc. Espanola de Constr. Naval, Bilbao, Spain.
   Tonnage: 12,589. Dimensions: 482′ x 63′. Twin-screw, 15
   knots. Motorship. Two masts and two funnels. Renamed:
   Dnepr (Russian). Sister ship: **Cabo Santo Tome.**

Cabo San Antonio   (1930)   Ybarra & Co.
   Built by Soc. Espanola de Constr. Naval, Bilbao, Spain.
   Tonnage: 12,275. Dimensions: 482′ x 63′. Twin-screw, 15
   knots. Motorship. Two masts and one funnel. Damaged by
   fire, December 29, 1939; sank on the following day.

*Cabo San Roque   (1957)   Ybarra & Co.
   Built by Soc. Espanola de Constr. Naval, Bilbao, Spain.
   Tonnage: 14,491.   Dimensions: 556′ (o.l.) x 69′.   Twin-
   screw, 22 knots. Motorship. Single mast and one funnel.
   Sister ship: **Cabo San Vicente.**

*Cabo San Vicente   (1959)   Ybarra & Co.
   Built by Soc. Espanola de Constr. Naval, Bilbao, Spain.
   Tonnage: 14,569.   Dimensions: 556′ (o.l.) x 69′.   Twin-
   screw, 22 knots. Motorship. Single mast and one funnel.
   Sister ship: **Cabo San Roque.**

Cabo Santo Tome   (1931)   Ybarra & Co.
   Built by Soc. Espanola de Constr. Naval, Bilbao, Spain.
   Tonnage: 12,589. Dimensions: 482′ x 63′. Twin-screw, 15
   knots. Motorship. Two masts and two funnels. Destroyed
   by rebel warship during the Spanish Civil War in 1937.
   Sister ship: **Cabo San Agustin.**

Cachar   (1884)   Compagnie Nationale de Navigation.
   Built by Chantiers de la Mediterranee, La Seyne, France.
   Tonnage: 3,485. Dimensions: 344′ x 41′. Single-screw, 12
   knots. Reciprocating engines. Two masts and one funnel.
   Vessel later transferred to Messageries Maritimes. Sister
   ship: **Cachemire.**

Cachemire   (1884)   Compagnie Nationale de Navigation.
   Built by Chantiers de la Mediterranee, La Seyne, France.
   Tonnage: 3,508. Dimensions: 344′ x 41′. Single-screw, 12
   knots. Reciprocating engines. Two masts and one funnel.
   Renamed: **Bithynie** (Paquet Line). Scrapped in Italy,
   1907. Sister ship: **Cachar.** The company wound up their

service to South America in 1891. From 1891 onwards their activities were to Indo-China.

Cadiz (1908)   Pinillos, Izquierdo & Co.
Built by C. Connell & Co., Ltd., Glasgow, Scotland. Tonnage: 5,617. Dimensions: 414′ x 53′. Single-screw, 14 knots. Triple expansion engines. Two masts and one funnel. Sister ship: **Barcelona.**

Calamares (1913)   United Fruit Co.
Built by Workman, Clark & Co., Belfast, Ireland. Tonnage: 7,782. Dimensions: 470′ x 55′. Twin-screw, 15 knots. Quadruple expansion engines. Two masts and one funnel. Accommodation for 143 passengers. Scrapped after World War II. Sister ships: **Pastores** and **Tenadores.**

California (1902)   Pacific Steam Navigation Co.
Built by Caird & Co., Ltd., Greenock, Scotland. Tonnage: 5,547. Dimensions: 400′ x 52′. Twin-screw, 15 knots. Triple expansion engines. Two masts and one funnel. Sunk by submarine off Cape Vilano in October 1917, with the loss of four lives. Sister ship: **Mexico.**

California (1920)   Navigazione Libera Triestina.
Built by Scott's Shipbuilding & Engineering Co., Greenock, Scotland. Tonnage: 13,060. Dimensions: 523′ x 64′. Twin-screw, 15½ knots. Steam turbines. Four masts and one funnel. Became a war casualty, August 11, 1941. Ex-**Albania** (1930).

California (1928)   Panama-Pacific Line (American).
Built by Newport News Shipbuilding Co., Newport News, Virginia. Tonnage: 20,325. Dimensions: 574′ x 80′ (601′ o.l.). Twin-screw, 18 knots. Two steam turbines connected to electric motors. Two masts and two funnels. In service between New York and the west coast of North America, via Panama Canal. Renamed: **Uruguay** (1938). Sister ships: **Pennsylvania** and **Virginia.**

Callao (1858)   Pacific Steam Navigation Co.
Built by John Reid & Co., Port Glasgow, Scotland. Tonnage: 1,062. Dimensions: 235′ x 29′. Paddle-wheels. Diagonal type engines. Iron hull. Hulked about 1870. Sister ship: **Valparaiso.**

Camito (1915)   Elders & Fyffes, Ltd.
Built by Alexander Stephen & Sons, Ltd., Glasgow, Scotland. Tonnage: 6,828. Dimensions: 426′ x 54′. Twin-screw, 14

knots. Triple expansion engines. Two masts and one funnel. Torpedoed and sunk in May 1941. Sister ships: **Ariguani, Carare, Cavina** and **Bayano.**

*Camito   (1956)   Elders & Fyffes, Ltd.
Built by Alexander Stephen & Sons, Ltd., Glasgow, Scotland. Tonnage: 8,687. Dimensions: 427' x 62' (447' o.l.). Single-screw, 17½ knots. Steam turbines. Two masts and one funnel. Passengers: 103 first-class. Sister ship: **Golfito.**

Campana   (1929)   Transport Maritimes (French).
Built by Swan, Hunter & Wigham Richardson, Ltd., New-castle, England. Tonnage: 10,816. Dimensions: 510' x 67'. Twin-screw, 15 knots. Steam turbines. Two masts and two funnels. Renamed: (a) **Rio Jachal** (1943), (b) **Campana** (1946), (c) **Irpinia** (1955). Sister ship: **Florida.**

Canadian   (1872)   Allan Line.
Tonnage: 2,401. Made her first sailing to South America, November 11, 1876. *Note: See PART I for details.*

Canton   (1882)   Compagnie Nationale de Navigation.
Built by Chantiers de la Mediterranee, La Seyne, France. Tonnage: 3,535. Dimensions: 279' x 40'. Single-screw. Compound engines. Two masts and one funnel. Iron hull. In South American service 1887–1891.

Cantuaria Guimaraes   (1907)   Lloyd Brasileiro.
Built by Reiherstieg Schiffsw., Hamburg, Germany. Tonnage: 6,456. Dimensions: 415' x 50'. Twin-screw, 12½ knots. Triple expansion engines. Two masts and one funnel. Renamed: **Siqueira Campos.** Ex-**Curvello**, ex-**Gertrud Woermann.**

Cap Arcona   (1907)   Hamburg-South American Line.
Built by Blohm & Voss, Hamburg, Germany. Tonnage: 9,832. Dimensions: 483' x 55'. Twin-screw, 15½ knots. Quadruple expansion engines. Two masts and one funnel. Vessel was turned over to France as a war prize in 1920. Sold to Messageries Maritimes in 1921 and renamed **Angers.** Scrapped in France, 1938. Running mates: **Cap Blanco, Cap Ortegal** and **Cap Vilano.**

Cap Arcona   (1927)   Hamburg-South American Line.
Built by Blohm & Voss, Hamburg, Germany. Tonnage: 27,561. Dimensions: 643' x 84' (675' o.l.). Twin-screw, 20 knots. Steam turbines. Two masts and three funnels.

Largest and fastest liner to South America when built. Sunk in air attack in Travemunde Bay, May 3, 1945, while serving as a prison ship for political prisoners.

Cap Blanco   (1903)   Hamburg-South American Line.
Built by Reierstieg Schiffsw., Hamburg, Germany. Tonage: 7,523. Dimensions: 440′ x 52′. Twin-screw, 13 knots. Triple expansion engines. Two masts and one funnel. Vessel sold to Hamburg-American Line in 1914 and renamed **Prinz Hubertus.** Surrendered to Great Britain in 1919. Gutted by fire while lying in Thames, 1919. Partially dismantled at Falmouth in 1920, and later hulk towed to Hamburg for complete demolition. Running mates: **Cap Arcona, Cap Ortegal** and **Cap Vilano.**

Cap Finisterre   (1911)   Hamburg-South American Line.
Built by Blohm & Voss, Hamburg, Germany. Tonnage: 14,503. Dimensions: 559′ x 65′. Twin-screw, 17 knots. Quadruple expansion engines. Two masts and two funnels. Vessel seized by United States in 1917. Turned over to Great Britain in 1919. Re-allocated to Japan. Renamed: **Taiyo Maru** (1921). Sunk in China Sea by an American submarine, May 8, 1942.

Cap Frio   (1899)   Hamburg-South American Line.
Built by Reierstieg Schiffsw., Hamburg, Germany. Tonage: 5,732. Dimensions: 411′ x 48′. Single-screw, 13 knots. Quadruple expansion engines. Two masts and one funnel. Wrecked off Barra lighthouse, Bahia, Brazil, August 30, 1908. Sister ships: **Cap Roca** and **Cap Verde.**

Cap Norte   (1922)   Hamburg-South American Line.
Built by Vulcan Werke, Hamburg, Germany. Tonnage: 13,615. Dimensions: 499′ x 64′. Twin-screw, 15 knots. Triple expansion engines. Two masts and one funnel. Renamed: (a) **Sierra Salvada** (1932), (b) **Cap Norte** (1934), (c) **Empire Trooper** (1940) British transport. Note: Vessel was transferred to North German Lloyd in 1932 and renamed **Sierra Salvada.** Reverted back to Hamburg-South American Line in 1934 and name changed back to **Cap Norte.** Captured by British warship **Belfast** near the Faroes on October 9, 1939. Renamed **Empire Trooper** in 1940. Scrapped in Great Britain, 1955. Sister ship: **Antonio Delfino.**

Cap Ortegal   (1903)   Hamburg-South American Line.
Built by Blohm & Voss, Hamburg, Germany. Tonnage: 7,818. Dimensions: 440′ x 52′. Twin-screw, 13½ knots.

Triple expansion engines. Two masts and one funnel. Turned over to France in 1919 as a war prize. Renamed: **Chambord** (1923). Scrapped in France, 1932. Running mates: **Cap Arcona, Cap Blanca** and **Cap Vilano.**

Cap Polonia (1914) Hamburg-South American Line.
Built by Blohm & Voss, Hamburg, Germany. Tonnage: 20,517. Dimensions: 637' x 72'. Triple-screw, 18 knots. Triple expansion engines and steam turbine. Two masts and three funnels. Note: Ran for Union-Castle Line after First World War for a brief period. Later used by P. & O. Line. Sold back to Hamburg-South American Line in 1921. Scrapped in Germany, 1935. Sister ship: **Cap Trafalgar.**

Cap Roca (1900) Hamburg-South American Line.
Built by Reiherstieg Schiffsw., Hamburg, Germany. Tonnage: 5,786. Dimensions: 411' x 48'. Single-screw, 13 knots. Quadruple expansion engines. Two masts and one funnel. Vessel seized by Brazil in 1917. Renamed: (a) **Itu** (1917), (b) **Almirante Alexandrino** (1926). Sister ships: **Cap Frio** and **Cap Verde.**

Cap Trafalgar (1913) Hamburg-South American Line.
Built by Akt. Ges. "Vulkan", Hamburg, Germany. Tonnage: 18,710. Dimensions: 590' x 72'. Triple-screw, 17½ knots. Triple expansion engines. Two masts and three funnels. Service: Hamburg-Vigo-Lisbon-Madeira-Bahia-Rio-Buenos Aires. At start of First World War was fitted out as an armed merchant cruiser by the German warship **Eber** off Bahia, Brazil. She was discovered coaling at Trinidad by the armed Cunarder **Carmania,** September 14, 1914, and was sunk by gunfire during the engagement of action. Sister ship: **Cap Polonia.**

Cap Verde (1900) Hamburg-South American Line.
Built by Flensburger Schiffsb., Flensburg, Germany. Tonnage: 5,909. Dimensions: 410' x 48'. Single-screw, 12½ knots. Quadruple expansion engines. Two masts and one funnel. Vessel was surrendered to Great Britain in 1919. Resold back to Hamburg-South American Line in 1921. Renamed: (a) **Madeira** (1922), (b) **Raul Soares** (1925). Sister ships: **Cap Frio** and **Cap Roca.**

Cap Vilano (1906) Hamburg-South American Line.
Built by Blohm & Voss, Hamburg, Germany. Tonnage: 9,467. Dimensions: 475' x 55'. Twin-screw, 15 knots. Quadruple expansion engines. Two masts and one funnel.

Vessel seized by Brazilian Government in 1917. Renamed:
(a) **Sobral** (1917), **General Metzinger** (1924). Sunk by
German aircraft in Havre roads, June 11, 1940. Broken up
for scrap in 1950. Running mates: **Cap Arcona, Cap
Blanca,** and **Cap Ortegal.**

Carabobo   (1923)   Red "D" Line (American).
Built by New York Shipbuilding Corp., Camden, New
Jersey. Tonnage: 2,916. Dimensions: 305′ x 48′. Twin-screw,
12 knots. Steam turbines. Two masts and one funnel. Sold
to Grace line in 1937. Later to Manila Steamship Company.
Renamed: (a) **North Coast,** (b) **Mayon.**

Caracas   (1889)   Red "D" Line (American).
Built by W. Cramp & Sons, Philadelphia, Pa.   Tonnage:
2,886. Dimensions: 311′ x 40′. Single-screw, 14 knots. Triple
expansion engines. Two masts and one funnel. No longer in
service, 1926.

Caraquet   (1894)   Royal Mail Line (British).
Built by Harland & Wolff, Ltd., Belfast, Ireland. Tonnage:
4,917. Dimensions: 400′ x 47′. Twin-screw, 12 knots. Triple
expansion engines. Three masts and one funnel. Wrecked off
Bermuda, while bound from Halifax to the Antilles, June 25,
1923. Ex-**Guelph** (1913).

Carare   (1925)   Elders & Fyffes, Ltd.
Built by Cammell Laird & Co., Birkenhead, England.
Tonnage: 6,878.   Dimensions: 425′ x 55′.   Twin-screw,
14 knots. Triple expansion engines. Two masts and one
funnel. Became a World War II casualty, May 28, 1940.
Sister ships: **Ariguani, Bayano, Camito, Cavina** and
Coronado.

Cardiganshire   (1913)   Royal Mail Line (British).
Built by Workman, Clark & Co., Belfast, Ireland. Tonnage:
9,426. Dimensions: 500′ x 62′. Twin-screw, 14 knots. Triple
expansion engines. Out of fleet in 1929.

Caribbean   (1890)   Royal Mail Line (British).
Built by Fairfield Shipbuilding Co., Glasgow, Scotland.
Tonnage: 5,625.   Dimensions: 420′ x 49′.   Single-screw,
16 knots. Triple expansion engines. Three masts and two
funnels. Foundered in very heavy weather off Cape Wrath,
September 1915, with the loss of 15 lives. Ex-**Dunottar
Castle** (1913).

371

Caribia   (1932)   Hamburg-American Line.
   Tonnage: 12,049.   Service: Hamburg-West Indies-Central
   America.   *Note: See PART I for details.*

Carl Legien   (1922)   (a) Stinnes Line, (b) Hamburg-American
   Line.
   Built by Marinewerft, Wilhelmshaven, Germany.   Tonnage:
   5,707.   Dimensions: 409′ x 53′.   Single-screw.   Triple expansion engines.   Renamed: (a) **Alba Julia** (1933), (b) **Nicolaev**
   (1947).   Sister ships: **Adolf von Baeyer, Albert Vogler** and
   Emil Kirdorff.

Carmarthenshire   (1915)   Royal Mail Line (British).
   Built by Workman, Clark & Co., Belfast, Ireland.   Tonnage:
   7,823.   Dimensions: 470′ x 58′.   Single-screw, 14 knots.
   Quadruple expansion engines.   Two masts and one funnel.
   Out of fleet in 1929.

Carnarvonshire   (1914)   Royal Mail Line (British).
   Built by Workman, Clark & Co., Belfast, Ireland.   Tonnage:
   9,406.   Dimensions: 500′ x 62′.   Twin-screw, 14 knots.   Triple
   expansion engines.   Two masts and one funnel.   Out of fleet
   in 1933.

Carolina   (1896)   New York & Porto Rico Steamship Co.
   Built by Newport News Shipbuilding Co., Newport News,
   Va.   Tonnage: 5,093.   Dimensions: 381′ x 47′.   Single-screw,
   15 knots.   Triple expansion engines.   Two masts and one
   funnel.   Altered from twin-screw to single-screw in 1914.
   Sunk by submarine in June 1918.   Ex-**City of Savannah**
   (1914), ex-**La Grande Duchesse.**

Coronado   (1915)   Elders & Fyffes, Ltd.
   Built by Workman, Clark & Co., Belfast, Ireland.   Tonnage:
   6,539.   Dimensions: 425′ x 54′.   Twin-screw, 14 knots.   Triple
   expansion engines.   Two masts and one funnel.   Salvaged
   after submarine attacks in 1917.   Scrapped in 1935.   Sister
   ships: **Ariguani, Bayano, Camito, Carare** and **Cavina.**

Carrillo   (1911)   United Fruit Co.
   Built by Workman, Clark & Co., Belfast, Ireland.   Tonnage:
   4,593.   Dimensions: 378′ x 50′.   Single-screw, 14 knots.
   Triple expansion engines.   Two masts and one funnel.   In the
   early 1930's placed in a 12-passenger basis, after alterations.
   Scrapped at Baltimore in 1948.   See **Metapan** for sister ships.

Cartago   (1908)   United Fruit Co.
  Built by Workman, Clark & Co., Belfast, Ireland. Tonnage: 4,732. Dimensions: 378' x 49'. Single-screw, 14 knots. Triple expansion engines. Two masts and one funnel. Carried only 12 passengers from 1937 on. Renamed: (a) **General Lee** (1932), (b) **Cartago** (1937). Scrapped at Tampa in 1949. Sister ships listed under **Metapan.**

Castel Felice   (1930)   "Sitmar" Line (Italian).
  Built by Alexander Stephen & Sons, Ltd., Glasgow, Scotland. Tonnage: 12,150. Dimensions: 471' x 64' (493' o.l.). Twin-screw, 15 knots. Steam turbines. Single-mast and one funnel. Services: Italy-Brazil-Argentina. Also ran in Central America trade. Later in Bremen-Quebec trade. Ex-**Karen** (1952), ex-**Kenya** (1951), ex-**Fairstone** (1950), ex-**Kenya** (1949), ex-**Karen** (1949), ex-**Kenya** (1949).

Castilla   (1927)   United Fruit Co.
  Built by Workman, Clark & Co., Belfast, Ireland. Tonnage: 4,087. Dimensions: 341' x 48'. Single-screw, 15 knots. Triple expansion engines. Two masts and one funnel. Passengers: 34. Became a war casualty in 1942. Sister ships: **Iriona** and **Tela.**

Cavina   (1915)   Elders & Fyffes, Ltd.
  Built by Workman, Clark & Co., Belfast, Ireland. Tonnage: 6,539. Dimensions: 425' x 54'. Twin-screw, 14 knots. Triple expansion engines. Two masts and one funnel. Torpedoed and sunk without warning 45 miles from Fastnet, June 1, 1917.

Cavina   (1924)   Elders & Fyffes, Ltd.
  Built by Alexander Stephen & Sons, Ltd., Govan, Scotland. Tonnage: 6,907. Dimensions: 425' x 54'. Twin-screw, 14 knots. Triple expansion engines. Two masts and one funnel. Renamed: **Catusha** (1957). Sister ships: **Ariguani, Bayano, Camito** and **Carare.** Passengers: 100.

Cavour   (1905)   (a) Ligure Brasiliano Line, (b) Transatlantica Italiana.
  Built by Soc. Esercizio Bacini, Riva Trigoso, Genoa, Italy. Tonnage: 5,156. Dimensions: 381' x 48'. Twin-screw, 14 knots. Triple expansion engines. Two masts and two funnels. Sunk in collision, December 12, 1917. Ex-**Florida** (1912).

Cefalu   (1930)   Standard Fruit Co.
  Built by Workman, Clark & Co., Belfast, Ireland. Tonnage: 5,221. Dimensions: 380' x 53'. Single-screw, 16 knots.

Quadruple expansion engines. Two masts and one funnel. Passengers: 60. Sister ship: **Contessa.**

Cesare Battisti (1920)   Transatlantica Italiana.
Tonnage: 8,331. In South American service. *Note: See PART I for details.*

Centro America (1897)   La Veloce Line.
Built by N. Odero fu A., Sestri Ponente, Italy. Tonnage: 3,522. Dimensions: 358' x 41'. Single-screw, 12 knots. Triple expansion engines. Two masts and one funnel. Clipper bow. Service: Italy-Central America. Renamed: **Solunto** (1911). Scrapped in 1925.

Ceylan (1907)   Chargeurs Reunis.
Built by Swan, Hunter & Wigham Richardson, Ltd., Newcastle, England. Tonnage: 8,430. Dimensions: 483' x 55'. Twin-screw, 14 knots. Triple expansion engines. Two masts and one funnel. Launched: July 30, 1907. Scrapped in 1934. Sister ship: **Malte.**

Chagres (1912)   Elders & Fyffes, Ltd.
Built by Alexander Stephen & Sons, Ltd., Glasgow, Scotland. Tonnage: 5,288. Dimensions: 400' x 51'. Twin-screw, 14 knots. Triple expansion engines. Two masts and one funnel. Sunk by submarine off Crete in 1918.

Chaleur (1893)   Royal Mail Line (British).
Built by Harland & Wolff, Ltd., Belfast, Ireland. Tonnage: 4,758. Dimensions: 400' x 47'. Twin-screw, 12 knots. Triple expansion engines. Two masts and one funnel. Service: Canada-West Indies. Scrapped in 1923. Ex-**Carmarthe-shire** (1913), ex-**Sabor** (1909), ex-**Gaul** (1906). Sister ship: **Chignecto.**

Chandernagor (1882)   Compagnie Nationale de Navigation.
Built by Wm. Denny & Bros., Ltd., Dumbarton, Scotland. Tonnage: 3,056. Dimensions: 341' x 40'. Single-screw. Compound engines. Two masts and one funnel. Commenced service to South America in 1888.

Changuinola (1912)   Elders & Fyffes, Ltd.
Built by Swan, Hunter & Wigham Richardson, Ltd., Newcastle, England. Tonnage: 5,978. Dimensions: 410' x 51'. Twin-screw, 14 knots. Triple expansion engines. Two masts and one funnel. Scrapped in 1935. Ex-**Carl Schurz, ex-Karl Schurz.** Sister ship: **Motagua.**

*Charles Tellier (1952) Chargeurs Reunis.
   Built by Atel. & Chantiers de la Loire, St. Nazaire, France.
   Tonnage: 12,006. Dimensions: 502′ x 64′ (538′ o.l.). Twin-
   screw, 17 knots. Two masts and one funnel. Passengers:
   92 first and 326 second. Sister ship: **Laennec.**

Chateau Yquem (1883) Compagnie Nationale de Navigation.
   Tonnage: 4,211. Chartered in 1888 and used on the service
   to South America. *Note: See PART I for details.*

Chaudiere (1899) Royal Mail Line (British).
   Built by Sir Raylton Dixon & Co., Middlesbrough, England.
   Tonnage: 4,019. Dimensions: 370′ x 46′. Twin-screw, 12
   knots. Triple expansion engines. Two masts and one funnel.
   Out of fleet in 1926. Ex-**Mandingo,** ex-**Philippeville.**

Cheribon (1882) Compagnie Nationale de Navigation.
   Built by Wm. Denny & Bros., Ltd., Dumbarton, Scotland.
   Tonnage: 3,056. Dimensions: 341′ x 40′. Single-screw.
   Compound engines. Two masts and one funnel. Sailed from
   Marseilles on September 26, 1887 for the first voyage in the
   firm's new service to South America. Sister ship: **Cholon.**

Chicago Maru (1910) Osaka Line.
   Built by Kawasaki Dockyard Co., Ltd., Kobe, Japan. Tonnage: 6,182. Dimensions: 419′ x 49′. Twin-screw, 13 knots.
   Triple expansion engines. Two masts and one funnel. Also
   ran in Japan-Tacoma service. Torpedoed and sunk, October
   15, 1943.

Chignecto (1893) Royal Mail Line (British).
   Built by Harland & Wolff, Ltd., Belfast, Ireland. Tonnage:
   4,756. Dimensions: 400′ x 47′. Twin-screw, 12 knots. Triple
   expansion engines. Two masts and one funnel. Scrapped in
   1927. Ex-**Pembrokeshire** (1913), ex-**Segura** (1908), ex-
   Greek (1906).

Chile (1840) Pacific Steam Navigation Co.
   Built in London, England. Tonnage: 682. Dimensions: 190′ x
   29′. Paddle-wheels. Side lever type engines. Wooden hull.
   Launched on April 21, 1840. Commenced her maiden voyage
   from Falmouth, June 27, 1940. Vessel sold in 1852. Sister
   ship: **Peru.** Note: Pioneer vessels of this famous line.

Chili (1894) Messageries Maritimes.
   Built by Messageries Maritimes, La Ciotat, France. Tonnage: 6,097. Dimensions: 462′ x 47′. Single-screw, 16½
   knots. Triple expansion engines. Two masts and two funnels.

Launched on October 14, 1894. Built for South American service. Transferred to Far East trade in 1912. Scrapped in France, 1927. Sister ship: **Cordillere.**

Chimborazo (1871) Pacific Steam Navigation Co.
Built by John Elder & Co., Glasgow, Scotland. Tonnage: 3,847. Dimensions: 384' x 41'. Single-screw, 15 knots. Two compound inverted type D. A. engines. Three masts and one funnel. Iron hull. Note: Transferred along with **Cuzco, Lusitania** and **Garonne** to the Australian trade in 1877. Renamed: **Cleopatra** (1895). Scrapped in Great Britain, 1897. Sister ships: **Cuzco** and **Garonne.**

Chiriqui (1932) United Fruit Co.
Built by Newport News Shipbuilding Co., Newport News, Va. Tonnage: 6,963. Dimensions: 415' x 60'. Twin-screw, 18 knots. Two steam turbines connected to electric motors. Two masts and one funnel. Renamed: (a) **Tarazed** (1941), (b) **Chiriqui** (1945), (c) **Blexen** (1957). Sister ships: **Antigua, Peten, Quirigua, Talamanca** and **Veragua.**

Christopher (1910) Booth Line.
Built by Tyne Iron Shipbuilding Co., Newcastle, England. Tonnage: 4,416. Dimensions: 360' x 50'. Single-screw, 11 knots. Triple expansion engines. Two masts and one funnel. Intermediate type of passenger ship. Renamed: **Obuasi.** Torpedoed and sunk by submarine off England, July 8, 1917.

Chrobry (1939) Gdynia-American Line.
Built by Nakskov. Skibs. A/S, Nakskov, Denmark. Tonnage: 11,442. Dimensions: 477' x 66' (505' o.l.). Twin-screw, 17 knots. Motorship. Two masts and one funnel. Designed for South American service. Torpedoed and sunk during the battle for Narvick, Norway in 1940. Sister ship: **Sobieski.**

Citta di Milano (1897) La Veloce Line.
Built by N. Odero fu A., Sestri Ponente, Italy. Tonnage: 4,041. Dimensions: 364' x 43'. Single-screw, 12 knots. Triple expansion engines. Two masts and one funnel. Built for Central American trade. Placed in New York service in 1901. Made her final voyage to New York in 1907. Sold to Sitmar Line in 1914. Renamed: **Albania** (1914). Acquired by Lloyd Triestino in 1932. Sister ship: **Citta di Torino.**

Citta di Torino (1898) La Veloce Line.
Built by N. Odero & Co., Genoa, Italy. Tonnage: 4,041. Dimensions: 363' x 43'. Single-screw, 12 knots. Triple ex-

pansion engines. Two masts and one funnel. Built for
Central American trade. Later transferred to New York
service. Renamed: **Constantinopoli** (1914) Sitmar Line.
Sister ship: **Citta di Milano.**

City of Alexandria   (1879)   (a) Alexandre Line, (b) Ward Line.
Built by John Roach & Son, Chester, Pennsylvania. Tonnage: 2,480. Dimensions: 307′ x 38′ (338′ o.l.). Single-screw.
Compound engines. Iron hull. Wrecked by an explosion that
took place in its cargo, November 1, 1893, with the loss of
five men.

City of Havana   (1872)   Alexandre Line.
Built at Greenpoint, Long Island, New York. Tonnage:
1,701. Dimensions: 241′ x 37′. Single-screw. Wrecked in
August 1877.

City of Merida   (1870)   Alexandre Line.
Built by John Englis, Greenpoint, Long Island, New York.
Tonnage: 1,492.   Dimensions: 260′ x 36′.   Single-screw.
Destroyed by fire in Havana harbor, September 4, 1884, with
no loss of life.

City of Mexico   (1869)   Alexandre Line.
Built by John Englis, Greenpoint, Long Island, New York.
Tonnage: 1,027.   Dimensions: 215′ x 36′.   Single-screw.
Service: New York-Havana-Mexico. Renamed: **S. Pizzati.**
As a converted barge she foundered previous to March 21,
1901, off Cape Hatteras.

City of New York   (1873)   Alexandre Line.
Built by John Englis, Greenpoint, Long Island, New York.
Tonnage: 1,716.   Dimensions: 280′ x 38′.   Single-screw.
Destroyed by fire in 1880.

City of Puebla   (1881)   Alexandre Line.
Built by W. Cramp & Sons, Philadelphia, Penn. Tonnage:
2,624. Dimensions: 319′ x 38′. Single-screw. Compound
engines. Vessel sold to owners on Pacific coast in 1884.
Scrapped in 1924.

City of Washington   (1877)   Ward Line.
Built by John Roach & Son, Chester, Penn. Tonnage: 2,683.
Dimensions: 300′ x 38′. Single-screw, 15 knots. Compound
engines. Two masts and one funnel. Formerly of Alexandre
Line, as the Ward Line purchased her in 1888. Barge carrier
in 1911. Wrecked on July 10, 1917.

*Claude Bernard   (1950)   Chargeurs Reunis.
Built by Atel. & Chantiers de la Loire, St. Nazaire, France.
Tonnage: 11,969.   Dimensions: 515' x 64'.   Twin-screw,
17½ knots. Motorship. Two masts and one funnel. Originally in service to South America. Transferred to Far East
route in May 1954. Accommodation for 100 first, 226 second
and 326 in third-class. Sister ship: **Lavoisier.** Note: Eight
liners of this type were built in France.

Clement   (1896)   Booth Line.
Built by Robert Napier & Sons, Ltd., Glasgow, Scotland.
Tonnage: 3,445.   Dimensions: 345' x 44'.   Single-screw,
12 knots. Triple expansion engines. Two masts and one
funnel. Renamed: **Freshfield.**   Torpedoed and sunk,
August 5, 1918. Ex-**La Plata.**

Clyde   (1841)   Royal Mail Line (British).
Built by Robert Duncan, Greenock, Scotland. Tonnage:
1,841. Paddle-wheels, 8 knots. Three masts and one funnel.
Wooden hull. First sailing December 18, 1841. Speed later
increased to 10 knots. Out of fleet in 1865.

Clyde   (1890)   Royal Mail Line (British).
Built by Robert Napier & Sons, Glasgow, Scotland. Tonnage:
5,618. Dimensions: 436' x 49'. Single-screw, 15 knots. Triple
expansion engines. Three masts and two funnels. Steel hull.
Disposed of in 1913. Sister ship: **Thames.**

Coamo   (1891)   New York & Porto Rico Line.
Built by Alexander Stephen & Sons, Ltd., Glasgow, Scotland.
Tonnage: 4,384. Dimensions: 377' x 46'. Single-screw, 13½
knots. Triple expansion engines. Two masts and one funnel.
Steel hull. Passengers: 100 first and 40 second-class. Scrapped
in 1925. Ex-**Californian** (1901), ex-**State of California**
(1898).

Coamo   (1925)   New York & Porto Rico Line.
Built by Newport News Shipbuilding Co., Newport News,
Va. Tonnage: 7,057. Dimensions: 429' x 59'. Single-screw,
16½ knots. Steam turbines. Two masts and one funnel.
Listed as missing on voyage from Gibraltar to New York,
December 1942, with the loss of 16 lives.

Cobequid   (1893)   Royal Mail Line (British).
Built by Harland & Wolff, Ltd., Belfast, Ireland. Tonnage:
4,738. Dimensions: 400' x 47'. Twin-screw, 12 knots. Triple
expansion engines. Two masts and one funnel. Totally

wrecked when she struck Trinity Ledge, Newfoundland, January 13, 1914, with no loss of life. Ex-**Goth** (1913).

Coburg   (1908)   North German Lloyd.
Tonnage: 6,750.   *Note: See PART I for details.*

Colombia   (1915)   Panama Mail Steamship Co.
Tonnage: 5,644. Vessel acquired from Pacific Mail Steamship Company in 1925. *Note: See PART II for details.*

Colombia   (1930)   Royal Netherlands Steamship Co.
Built by P. Smit, Jr., Rotterdam, Netherlands. Tonnage: 10,782. Dimensions: 429' x 61'. Twin-screw, 15 knots. Motorship. Two masts and one funnel. Became a war casualty, February 27, 1943.

Colombia   (1932)   Colombian Steamship Co.
Built by Newport News Shipbuilding Co., Newport News, Va. Tonnage: 5,236. Dimensions: 385' x 57' (404' o.l.). Single-screw, 17 knots. Steam turbines. Two masts and one funnel. Renamed: (a) **Mexico** (1938), (b) **Istanbul** (1947) Turkish. Sister ship: **Monterey.**

Colombo   (1917)   Navigazione Generale Italiana.
Built by Palmer's Shipbuilding & Iron Co., Newcastle, England. Tonnage: 12,003. Dimensions: 518' x 64' (536' o.l.). Twin-screw, 17 knots. Quadruple expansion engines. Two masts and two funnels. Transferred to Lloyd Triestino in 1934. Scuttled at Massawa, Eritrea, April 4, 1941. Ex-**San Gennaro** (1921).

Colon   (1899)   Panama Railroad Co.
Built by W. Cramp & Sons Shipbuilding Co., Philadelphia, Pa. Tonnage: 5,667. Dimensions: 360' x 50'. Twin-screw, 15 knots. Triple expansion engines. Two masts and two funnels. Passengers: 182 first-class. Crew numbered 92. In their fleet 1905–1924. Renamed: **Yukon.** Stranded off Alaska, February 3, 1946. Ex-**Mexico** (1905).

Colonial   (1908)   Companhia Colonial (Portuguese).
Built by Frd. Krupp, Kiel, Germany. Tonnage: 8,309. Dimensions: 449' x 54'. Twin-screw, 12½ knots. Quadruple expansion engines. Two masts and one funnel. Sold to British Iron & Steel Corp., in 1950. Renamed: **Bisco 9;** stranded near Campbeltown. Ex-**Assyria** (1929), ex-**Ypiranga** (1921).

Columbia (1917) Panama-Pacific Line.
  Built by Harland & Wolff, Ltd., Belfast, Ireland. Tonnage: 24,578. Dimensions: 670' x 78'. Triple-screw, 17½ knots. Triple expansion engines and steam turbine. Two masts and three funnels. Scrapped in 1936. Ex-**Belgenland** (1934), ex-**Belgic** (1921).

Commewyne (1907) Royal Netherlands Steamship Co.
  Built by Akt. Burmeister & Wain, Copenhagen, Denmark. Tonnage: 2,476. Dimensions: 310' x 40'. Single-screw, 13 knots. Triple expansion engines. Two masts and one funnel. Vessel was purchased in 1912. Renamed: (a) **Progresco** (1932), (b) **Har Carmel** (1935). Burned in Black Sea in 1938. Ex-**St. Thomas.**

Comodoro Rivadavia (1905) Cia Argentina Line. (Delfino, A.M., Y Cia).
  Built by Workman, Clark & Co., Belfast, Ireland. Tonnage: 5,450. Dimensions: 400' x 50'. Single-screw, 14 knots. Triple expansion engines. Two masts and one funnel. Renamed: **Rio Santa Cruz** (1944). Ex-**Anselm.**

Congo (1878) Messageries Maritimes.
  Built by Messageries Maritimes, La Ciotat, France. Tonnage: 3,897. Dimensions: 394' x 39'. Single-screw, 13½ knots. Compound engines. Three masts and one funnel. Launched, March 17, 1878. Later transferred to Far East service. Scrapped in Italy, 1913. Sister ships: **Equateur** and **Parana.**

Conte Biancamano (1925) (a) Lloyd Sabaudo, (b) Italia Line. Tonnage: 24,416. Later transferred to the Far East service of Lloyd Triestino. *Note: See PART I for details.*

Conte Grande (1927) (a) Lloyd Sabaudo, (b) Italia Line. Tonnage: 25,661. *Note: See PART I for details.*

Conte Rosso (1922) (a) Lloyd Sabaudo, (b) Italia Line. Tonnage: 17,048. Later transferred to the Far East service of Lloyd Triestino. *Note: See PART I for details.*

Conte Verde (1923) (a) Lloyd Sabaudo, (b) Italia Line. Tonnage: 18,765. Later employed by Lloyd Triestino in the Far East service. *Note: See PART I for details.*

Contessa (1930) Standard Fruit Co. (British).
  Built by Barclay, Curle & Co., Glasgow, Scotland. Tonnage: 5,512. Dimensions: 381' x 53'. Single-screw, 16 knots.

Quadruple expansion engines. Two masts and one funnel. Renamed: **Leeuwarden** (1959). Sister ship: **Cefalu.**

Copacabana   (1937)   Maritime Belge Lloyd.
Built by Soc. Anon. John Cockerill, Hoboken, Belgian. Tonnage: 7,340. Dimensions: 435' x 61' (459' o.l.). Single-screw, 14 knots. Motorship. Renamed: **Theodore Korner** (1958).

Copiapo   (1937)   Compania Sud Americana de Vap. (Chile).
Built by Nakskov Skibs A/S., Nakskov, Denmark. Tonnage: 7,279. Dimensions: 414' x 58' (440' o.l.). Single-screw. 16 knots. Motorship. Two masts and one funnel. Renamed: **Ordu.** Sister ships: **Aconcagua** and **Imperial.**

Coppename   (1908)   Royal Netherlands Steamship Co.
Built by Workman, Clark & Co., Belfast, Ireland. Tonnage: 3,192. Dimensions: 339' x 42'. Single-screw, 13 knots. Triple expansion engines. Two masts and one funnel. Acquired by Tropical Fruit Company in 1913.

Corcovado   (1872)   Pacific Steam Navigation Co.
Built by Laird Brothers, Birkenhead, England. Tonnage: 3,805. Dimensions: 387' x 43'. Single-screw, 13 knots. Compound inverted D. A. engines. Three masts and two funnels. Vessel sold to Royal Mail Line in 1875. Renamed: **Don** (1875). Scrapped in 1901. Sister ship: **Puno.**

Corcovado   (1907)   Hamburg-American Line.
Built by Frd. Krupp, Kiel, Germany. Tonnage: 8,374. Dimensions: 448' x 55'. Twin-screw, 12 knots. Quadruple expansion engines. Two masts and one funnel. Renamed: (a) **Sueh** (1919), (b) **Corcovado** (1919) French, (c) **Guglielmo Peirce** (1920), (d) **Maria Cristina** (1926), (e) **Mouzinho** (1930). Scrapped in Italy, 1954. Sister ship: **Ypiranga.**

Cordillera   (1869)   Pacific Steam Navigation Co.
Built by John Elder & Co., Glasgow, Scotland. Tonnage: 2,860. Dimensions: 353' x 41'. Single-screw. Compound engines. Iron hull. Lost in Straits of Magellan about 1884. Sister ships: **Araucania, Magellan** and **Patagonia.**

Cordillera   (1932)   Hamburg-American Line.
Built by Blohm & Voss, Hamburg, Germany. Tonnage: 12,055. Dimensions: 497' x 65'. Twin-screw, 17 knots. Motorship. Two masts and one funnel. Service: Hamburg-West Indies-Central America. Suffered heavy damage at Swinemunde in May 1945. Sister ship: **Caribia.**

Cordillere   (1895)   Messageries Maritimes.
    Built by Messageries Maritimes, La Ciotat, France. Tonnage: 6,022. Dimensions: 462′ x 47′. Single-screw, 17 knots. Triple expansion engines. Two masts and two funnels. Launched, October 12, 1895. Built for the South American trade. Transferred to the Far East service in 1912. Sold to French shipbreakers in December 1925. Sister ship: **Chili.**

Cordoba   (1903)   Transport Maritimes (French).
    Built by Blohm & Voss, Hamburg, Germany. Tonnage: 6,375. Dimensions: 417′ x 50′. Twin-screw, 14 knots. Triple expansion engines. Two masts and one funnel. Scrapped in 1932. Ex-**Prinz Regent.**

Corrientes   (1894)   Hamburg-South American Line.
    Built by Blohm & Voss, Hamburg, Germany. Tonnage: 3,720. Dimensions: 342′ x 42′. Single-screw. Triple expansion engines. Two masts and one funnel. In service between Germany and South America. Looked like a freighter. Renamed: **Guaratuba** (1917). Note: Seized by Brazil in 1917 and renamed **Guaratuba.** Sold to Lloyd Brasileiro in 1927. Scrapped at Rio de Janeiro in 1936.

*Corrientes   (1943)   Dodero Line (Argentine).
    Built by Seattle-Tacoma Shipbuilding Corp., Seattle, Wash. Tonnage: 12,053. Dimensions: 468′ x 69′. Single-screw, 16 knots. Steam turbines. Two masts and one funnel. Converted to a passenger ship in 1949. Ex-**Tracker** (1949), ex-**Jamaica.** Note: Vessel designed as "C-3" type cargo ship, but completed as escort carrier, lease-lent to Great Britain. Later purchased on speculation by Newport News Shipbuilding Company and reconstructed in 1949. Sister ship: **Salta.**

Corse   (1908)   Chargeurs Reunis.
    Built by Ateliers et Chantiers de la Loire, St. Nazaire, France. Tonnage: 8,481. Dimensions: 485′ x 56′. Twin-screw, 14½ knots. Triple expansion engines. Two masts and one funnel. Launched, May 16, 1908. Sold to French Line in February 1910; renamed **Niagara.** Sister ship: **Ouessant.** The **Ceylan** and **Malte** were similar.

Costa Rica   (1910)   Royal Netherlands Steamship Co.
    Built by Nederlandsche Schps. Maats, Amsterdam, Netherlands. Tonnage: 8,672. Dimensions: 455′ x 55′. Twin-screw, 22 knots. Quadruple expansion engines. (a) Two masts and two funnels, (b) Only a single funnel. Became a war casualty,

April 27, 1941. Ex-**Prinses Juliana.** Originally was a cargo ship.

Cotopaxi   (1873)   Pacific Steam Navigation Co.
Built by John Elder & Co., Glasgow, Scotland. Tonnage: 4,022. Dimensions: 402′ x 42′. Single-screw, 14 knots. Compound engines. Three masts and one funnel. Clipper bow. Iron hull. Wrecked in the Straits of Magellan, April 15, 1889. Sister ship: **Illimani.**

Cottica   (1927)   Royal Netherlands Steamship Co.
Built by P. Smit, Jr., Rotterdam, Netherlands. Tonnage: 3,989. Dimensions: 315′ x 47′. Single-screw, 12 knots. Triple expansion engines. Two masts and one funnel. Sold to Dutch shipbreakers in 1958.

Crefeld   (1895)   North German Lloyd.
Tonnage: 3,829. In Germany-West Indies service. *Note: See PART I for details.*

Crefeld   (1922)   North German Lloyd.
Built by Flensburger Schiffsb., Flensburg, Germany. Tonnage: 9,620. Dimensions: 474′ x 60′. Single-screw, 12 knots. Triple expansion engines. Four masts and one funnel. Note: This passenger ship was later converted into freighter. Size reduced to 8,045 tons gross. Lost at Massaua in 1941.

Crijnssen   (1919)   Royal Netherlands Steamship Co.
Built by Maats. Fyenoord, Rotterdam, Netherlands. Tonnage: 4,298. Dimensions: 342′ x 47′. Single-screw, 12½ knots. Triple expansion engines. Two masts and one funnel. Passengers: 90 first and 113 second. Became a war casualty, June 10, 1942. Sister ships: **Stuyvesant** and **Van Rensselaer.**

Crispin   (1907)   Booth Line.
Built by Sir Raylton, Dixon & Co., Middlesbrough, England. Tonnage: 3,694. Dimensions: 455′ x 49′. Single-screw, 11 knots. Triple expansion engines. Two masts and one funnel. Intermediate type passenger ship. Sunk by German submarine in 1918.

Cristobal   (1902)   Panama Railroad Co.
Built by Maryland Steel Co., Sparrows Point, Maryland. Tonnage: 9,606. Dimensions: 489′ x 58′. Twin-screw, 13 knots. Triple expansion engines. Two masts and one funnel. Passengers: 172; crew of 74. In fleet 1908–1939. Renamed: (a) **Philippa,** (b) **Esmeralda.** Ex-**Tremont.** Sister ship: **Ancon.**

*Cristobal (1939) Panama Railroad Co.
Built by Bethlehem Steel Co., Shipbuilding Division, Quincy, Mass. Tonnage: 10,021. Dimensions: 474′ x 64′ (493′ o.l.). Twin-screw, 16½ knots. Steam turbines. Two masts and one funnel. Sister ships: **Ancon** and **Panama.**

Cuba (1894) (a) Ward Line, (b) Miami Steamship Co.
Built by Delaware River Co., Chester, Pennsylvania. Tonnage: 2,963. Dimensions: 299′ x 40′ (328′ o.l.). Single-screw, 17 knots. Two masts and one funnel. Renamed: **Seneca.** Burned on January 9, 1928. Ex-**Powhatan**, ex-**Rawlins**, ex-**U.S.N. Resolute**, ex-**Yorktown.**

Cuba (1921) Peninsular & Occidental Steamship Co.
Built by W. Cramp & Sons, Philadelphia, Pennsylvania. Tonnage: 2,472. Dimensions: 325′ x 47′. Twin-screw 17 knots. Triple expansion engines. Two masts and one funnel. Renamed: (a) **Pace,** (b) **Sassari** (Still in service, 1960).

Curvello (1907) Lloyd Brasileiro.
Built by Reiherstieg Schiffsw., Hamburg, Germany. Tonnage: 6,456. Dimensions: 415′ x 50′. Twin-screw, 13 knots. Triple expansion engines. Two masts and one funnel. Renamed: (a) **Cantuaria Guimaraes,** (b) **Sigueira Campos.** Ex-**Gertrud Woermann.**

Cuthbert (1906) Booth Line.
Built by Hawthorn, Leslie & Co., Newcastle, England. Tonnage: 3,563. Dimensions: 355′ x 49′. Single-screw, 11 knots. Triple expansion engines. Two masts and one funnel. Passengers: 16 first and 100 third-class. Out of service in 1934.

*Cuyaba (1906) Lloyd Brasileiro.
Built by Bremer Vulkan, Vegesack, Germany. Tonnage: 6,489. Dimensions: 409′ x 52′. Single-screw, 12½ knots. Quadruple expansion engines. Two masts and one funnel. Service: Santos-Hamburg. Ex-**Hohenstaufen.**

Cuzco (1871) Pacific Steam Navigation Co.
Built by (at) Glasgow, Scotland. Tonnage: 3,845. Dimensions: 384′ x 41′. Single-screw, 15 knots. Compound engines. Three masts and one funnel. Acquired by Orient Steam Navigation Company in 1877 to serve in their new trade to Australia. Scrapped in Italy, 1905. Sister ships: **Chimborazo, Galicia** and **Garonne.**

Cyril   (1883)   Booth Line.
   Built by London & Glasgow Shipbuilding Co., Glasgow, Scotland. Tonnage: 1,190. Dimensions: 235′ x 31′. Single-screw. Compound engines. Iron hull. Renamed: **Braganca.** Wrecked December 28, 1925. Ex-**Pacaxo.**

Cyril   (1883)   Booth Line.
   Built by John Elder & Co., Glasgow, Scotland. Tonnage: 4,380. Dimensions: 380′ x 48′. Single-screw, 14 knots. Triple expansion engines. Two masts and one funnel. Iron hull. Sunk after colliding with the Booth liner **Anselm,** September 5, 1905. Ex-**Hawarden Castle** (1904).

Danube   (1865)   Royal Mail Line (British).
   Built by Millwall Ironworks, London, England. Tonnage: 2,039. Dimensions: 332′ x 34′. Paddle-wheels. Two masts and two funnels. Later converted from Paddle-wheels to screw propulsion and a single funnel. Sold to Union Line (British) in 1871. Sold for scrap in 1888, and was broken up soon afterwards.

Danube   (1893)   Royal Mail Line (British).
   Built by John Elder & Co., Glasgow, Scotland. Tonnage: 5,946. Dimensions: 420′ x 51′. Single-screw, 15 knots. Triple expansion engines. Two masts and one funnel. Out of service, 1920. Sister ship: **Nile.**

Darmstadt   (1890)   North German Lloyd.
   Tonnage: 5,012. In South American service. *Note: See PART I for details.*

Darro   (1912)   Royal Mail Line (British).
   Built by Harland & Wolff, Ltd., Belfast, Ireland. Tonnage: 11,484. Dimensions: 500′ x 62′. Twin-screw, 16½ knots. Quadruple expansion engines. Two masts and one funnel. Launched, May 16, 1912. Scrapped in 1933. Sister ships: **Demerara, Deseado, Desna** and **Drina.**

Dee   (1841)   Royal Mail Line (British).
   Built by J. Scott & Sons, Greenock, Scotland. Tonnage: 1,849. Paddle-wheels, 8 knots. Three masts and one funnel. Commenced first sailing, January 14, 1842. Speed later increased to 10 knots. Out of fleet in 1862.

Dee   (1872)   Royal Mail Line (British).
   Built by Thomas Wingate & Son, Glasgow, Scotland. Tonnage: 1,864. Dimensions: 300′ x 35′. Single-screw, 11 knots.

Compound engines. Three masts and one funnel. Not listed in 1910 register.   Ex-**State of Minnesota** (1875), ex-**Minnesota** (1873).

*Del Mar   (1947)   Delta Line (Mississippi Shipping Co.).
Built by Ingalls Shipbuilding Corp., Pascagoula, Mississippi. Tonnage: 10,074. Dimensions: 466' x 69'. (495' o.l.). Single-screw, 16½ knots.   Steam turbines.   Two masts and one funnel.   Passengers: 120 first-class.   Service: New Orleans-River Plate.   Sister ships: **Del Norte** and **Del Sud.**

*Del Norte   (1946)   Delta Line (Mississippi Shipping Co.).
Built by Ingalls Shipbuilding Corp., Pascagoula, Mississippi. Tonnage: 10,074. Dimensions: 466' x 69' (495' o.l.). Single-screw, 16½ knots.   Steam turbines.   Two masts and one funnel.   Sister ships: **Del Mar** and **Del Sud.**

*Del Sud   (1947)   Delta Line (Mississippi Shipping Co.).
Built by Ingalls Shipbuilding Corp., Pascagoula, Mississippi. Tonnage: 10,074. Dimensions: 466' x 69' (495' o.l.). Single-screw, 16½ knots.   Steam turbines.   Two masts and one funnel.   Sister ships· **Del Mar** and **Del Norte.**   Note: Each has a very wide dummy funnel in front of the real smoke stacks.

Delbrasil   (1939)   Delta Line (Mississippi Shipping Co.).
Built by Bethlehem Steel Co., Shipbuilding Division, Sparrows Point, Maryland. Tonnage: 7,996. Dimensions: 465' x 65' (491' o.l.). Single-screw, 17 knots. Steam turbines. Two masts and one funnel. This was a special type "C-3" passenger ship. She was acquired by the United States Navy in August 1943.   Renamed: (a) **George F. Elliott,** (b) **African Endeavor** (1949).

Demerara   (1851)   Royal Mail Line (British).
Built by William Patterson, Bristol, England. Tonnage: 2,318. Paddle-wheels, 12 knots. Three masts and two funnels. Wooden hull. Our of fleet in 1851. Sister ships: **Amazon, Magdalena, Orinoco** and **Parana.**

Demerara   (1912)   Royal Mail Line (British).
Built by Harland & Wolff, Ltd., Belfast, Ireland. Tonnage: 11,484.   Dimensions: 500' x 62'.   Twin-screw, 16 knots. Quadruple expansion engines. Two masts and one funnel. Launched, December 21, 1911. Scrapped in 1933. Sister ships: **Darro, Deseado, Desna** and **Drina.**

Denis (1911) Booth Line.
Built by Hawthorn, Leslie & Co., Newcastle, England. Tonnage: 4,435. Dimensions: 376' x 50'. Single-screw, 11 knots. Triple expansion engines. Two masts and one funnel. Passengers: 36 first and 100 third-class. Scrapped in 1932.

Derfflinger (1907) North German Lloyd.
Tonnage: 9,144. In South American service. *Note: See PART I for details.*

Derwent (1879) Royal Mail Line (British).
Built by R. Thompson, Jr., Sunderland, England. Tonnage: 2,471. Dimensions: 329' x 36'. Single-screw, 10 knots. Compound engines. Three masts and one funnel. Iron hull. Clipper bow. Renamed: (a) **Lilia,** (b) **Derwent.** Out of fleet in 1902.

Deseado (1912) Royal Mail Line (British).
Built by Harland & Wolff, Ltd., Belfast, Ireland. Tonnage: 11,477. Dimensions: 500' x 62'. Twin-screw, 16 knots. Quadruple expansion engines. Two masts and one funnel. Launched, October 26, 1911. Scrapped in 1934. Sister ships: **Darro, Demerara, Desna** and **Drina.**

Desirade (1921) Chargeurs Reunis.
Built by Ateliers et Chantiers de France, Dunkirk, France. Tonnage: 9,645. Dimensions: 483' x 58'. Twin-screw, 13 knots. Triple expansion engines. Two masts and one funnel. Launched, March 24, 1921. Scrapped in 1950. Sister ship: **Eubee.**

Desna (1912) Royal Mail Line (British).
Built by Harland & Wolff, Ltd., Belfast, Ireland. Tonnage: 11,483. Dimensions: 500' x 62'. Twin-screw, 16 knots. Quadruple expansion engines. Two masts and one funnel. Launched, March 2, 1912. Scrapped in 1933. Sister ships: **Darro, Demerara, Deseado** and **Drina.**

Diolibah (1880) Fabre Line.
Built by A. McMillan & Son, Dumbarton, Scotland. Tonnage: 1,642. Dimensions: 263' x 35'. Single-screw. Compound engines. Iron hull. Later was converted to triple expansion engines. She was rammed and sunk near Las Palmas by the **Liberia,** October 30, 1911, which vessel she was towing.

Divona   (1886)   Compagnie Sud-Atlantique (French).
Built by Fairfield Shipbuilding Co., Glasgow, Scotland.
Tonnage: 6,405.   Dimensions: 465′ x 52′.   Single-screw,
17 knots.   Triple expansion engines.   Four masts and two
funnels.   Later had only two masts.   Steel hull.   Scrapped
in France, 1922.   Ex-**Ormuz** (1912).

Djemnah   (1875)   Messageries Maritimes.
Built by Messageries Maritimes, La Ciotat, France. Tonnage:
3,785.   Dimensions: 394′ x 39′.   Single-screw, 13½ knots.
Compound engines.   Three masts and one funnel.   Iron hull.
Launched, September 27, 1874.   Torpedoed and sunk South
of Crete on July 14, 1918, with the loss of 442 lives.   Sister
ships: **Oxus** and **Yang-Tse.**

Dom Pedro   (1878)   Chargeurs Reunis.
Built by Forges et Chantiers de la Mediterranee, Havre,
France.   Tonnage: 2,999.   Dimensions: 329′ x 39′.   Single-
screw, 12 knots.   Compound engines.   Two masts and one
funnel.   Iron hull.   Sunk on Fraguina Rock, near Cape
Finisterre, May 27, 1895.   Sister ship: **Pampa.**

Dom Pedro I   (1908)   Lloyd Brasileiro.
Built by Alexander Stephen & Sons, Ltd., Glasgow, Scotland.
Tonnage: 6,370.   Dimensions: 400′ x 54′.   Twin-screw, 15
knots.   Triple expansion engines.   Two masts and one funnel.
Ex-**Pedro I** (1935), ex-**Wyreema.** Sister ship: **Dom Pedro II.**

Dom Pedro II   (1910)   Lloyd Brasileiro.
Built by Alexander Stephen & Sons, Ltd., Glasgow, Scotland.
Tonnage: 6,129.   Dimensions: 400′ x 55′.   Twin-screw, 15
knots.   Quadruple expansion engines.   Two masts and one
funnel.   Wrecked off South America in 1927, but was salvaged.
Sister ship: **Dom Pedro I.**

Dominica   (1913)   Bermuda & West Indies Steam Co., Ltd.
Built by Irvine's Shipbuilding Co., West Hartlepool, England. Tonnage: 4,856. Dimensions: 350′ x 50′. Single-screw,
14 knots.   Triple expansion engines.   Two masts and one
funnel.   Owner: Furness Withy & Co., Ltd.   Service: New
York-West Indies.   Renamed: (a) **Baltrover** (1936), (b)
Ionia (1947).   Ex-**Digby** (1925).

Don   (1872)   Royal Mail Line (British).
Built by Laird Bros., Birkenhead, England. Tonnage: 4,028.
Dimensions: 387′ x 43′.   Single-screw, 17 knots.   Compound
engines.   Three masts and two funnels.   Later converted to

triple expansion engines. The alterations included the change to two masts. Her original speed was 13½ knots. Scrapped in Great Britain, 1901. Ex-**Corcovado** (1875). Sister ship: **Para.**

Dorian   (1868)   Anchor Line.
Built by Duncan & Dunlop, Port Glasgow, Scotland. Tonnage: 1,039. Dimensions: 237′ x 30′. Single-screw, 10 knots. Inverted type engines. Three masts and one funnel. Compound engines installed in 1878. In New York-Jamaica service 1888–1892. Vessel sold in 1892. Sister ship: **Tyrian.**

Douro   (1865)   Royal Mail Line (British).
Built by Caird & Co., Greenock, Scotland. Tonnage: 2,824. Dimensions: 326′ x 40′. Single-screw. Inverted D.A. type engines. Two masts and one funnel. Clipper bow. Iron hull. Lost off Cape Finisterre, April 1, 1882.

Dresden   (1889)   North German Lloyd.
Tonnage: 4,580. In Germany-South American service. *Note: See PART I for details.*

Drina   (1913)   Royal Mail Line (British).
Built by Harland & Wolff, Ltd., Belfast, Ireland. Tonnage: 11,483. Dimensions: 500′ x 62′. Twin-screw, 13½ knots. Quadruple expansion engines. Two masts and one funnel. Launched, June 29, 1912. Torpedoed and sunk without warning two miles from Skokham Island on March 1, 1917, with the loss of 15 lives. Sister ships: **Darro, Demerara, Deseado** and **Desna.**

Duca d' Aosta   (1908)   Navigazione Generale Italiana.
Tonnage: 8,169. In South American service. *Note: See PART I for details.*

Duca degli Abruzzi   (1907)   Navigazione Generale Italiana.
Tonnage: 8,249. Transferred to South American service in 1922. *Note: See PART I for details.*

Duca di Galliero   (1883)   La Veloce Line.
Tonnage: 4,304. In South American service. *Note: See PART I for details.*

Duca di Genova   (1907)   (a) Navigazione Generale Italiana, (b) La Veloce Line.
Tonnage: 7,811. Transferred to La Veloce Line in 1913. *Note: See PART I for details.*

Duchessa di Genova   (1884)   La Veloce Line.
　　Tonnage: 4,304. Purchased by La Veloce Line for their
South American service. *Note: See PART I for details.*

Duilio   (1923) (a) Navigazione Generale Italiana, (b) Italia Line.
　　Tonnage: 24,281. In South American service. *Note: See
PART I for details.*

*Duque de Caxias   (1904)   Lloyd Brasileiro.
　　Built by J. C. Tecklenborg, A. G., Geestemunde, Germany.
Tonnage: 4,556.   Dimensions: 361' x 46'.   Single-screw,
12 knots. Triple expansion engines. Two masts and one
funnel. Ex-**Benevente** (1926), ex-**Rio Grande** (1917).

Eastern Prince   (1929)   Furness-Prince Line.
　　Built by Napier & Miller, Ltd., Glasgow, Scotland. Tonnage:
10,926.   Dimensions: 496' x 64' (516' o.l.).   Twin-screw,
17 knots. Motorship. Two masts and one funnel. Renamed:
(a) **Empire Medway** (1950), (b) **Bardic.** Sister ships:
Northern Prince, Southern Prince and **Western Prince.**

Ebro   (1896)   Royal Mail Line (British).
　　Built by Robert Napier & Sons, Ltd., Glasgow, Scotland.
Tonnage: 3,445.   Dimensions: 345' x 44'.   Single-screw,
12 knots. Triple expansion engines. Two masts and one
funnel. Renamed: **Quebec** (1903). Sister ships: **La Plata**
and **Minho.**

Ebro   (1915)   Pacific Steam Navigation Co.
　　Built by Workman, Clark & Co., Ltd., Belfast, Ireland.
Tonnage: 8,480.   Dimensions: 450' x 57'.   Twin-screw, 14
knots. Quadruple expansion engines. Two masts and one
funnel.   Note: In service of Royal Mail Line between
1915–1922.   Renamed: (a) **Princesa Olga** (1935), (b)
Serpa Pinto. Scrapped in Belgian, 1955.   Sister ship:
Essequibo.

Ecuador   (1915)   Panama Mail Steamship Co.
　　Tonnage: 5,544. *Note: See PART II for details.*

Edam   (1921)   Holland-America Line.
　　Tonnage: 8,871. In West Indies service. *Note: See PART I
for details.*

Eider   (1864)   Royal Mail Line (British).
　　Built by Caird & Co., Greenock, Scotland. Tonnage: 1,569.
Dimensions: 296' x 32'. Paddle-wheels. Oscillating engines.
Iron hull. Disposed of in 1883.

Eisenach   (1908)   North German Lloyd.
   Tonnage: 6,757.   In South American service.   *Note: See PART I for details.*

El Paraguayo   (1912)   Houlder Line, Ltd.
   Built by Irvine's Shipbuilding Co., West Hartlepool, England.   Tonnage: 8,508.   Dimensions: 440′ x 58′.   Twin-screw, 15 knots.   Triple expansion engines.   Two masts and one funnel.   Service: London-Monte Video-Buenos Aires.   Running mate: **Baronesa.**

Elbe   (1870)   Royal Mail Line (British).
   Built by John Elder & Co., Glasgow, Scotland.   Tonnage: 3,063.   Dimensions: 350′ x 40′.   Single-screw, 15 knots.   Compound engines.   Two masts and two funnels.   Iron hull.   Clipper bow.   Passengers: 144 first and 22 second.   Scrapped in France, 1902.

Elbe   (1929)   North German Lloyd.
   Built by Deutsche Werke, Kiel, Germany.   Tonnage: 9,179.   Dimensions: 487′ x 60′.   Twin-screw, 17 knots.   Motorship.   Two masts and one funnel.   Service: Germany-West Indies-Mexico.   Sunk in 1941.   Ex-**Wenatchee Star** (1934), ex-**Sud Expreso.**

Elkab   (1904)   Kosmos Steamship Co.
   Built by Blohm & Voss, Hamburg, Germany.   Tonnage: 6,118.   Dimensions: 410′ x 50′.   Single-screw, 12 knots.   Service: West Indies.   Passengers: 40 first, 26 second, 44 third.

*Empire Star   (46)   Lamport & Holt Line.
   Built by Harland & Wolff, Ltd., Belfast, Ireland.   Tonnage: 11,085.   Dimensions: 521′ x 70′ (540′ o.l.).   Twin-screw, 16½ knots.   Motorship.   Single mast and one funnel.   Note: Launched as **Empire Mercia.**   Commenced service as **Empire Star.**   Passengers: 130.

Equateur   (1875)   Messageries Maritimes.
   Built by Messageries Maritimes, La Ciotata, France.   Tonnage: 3,915.   Dimensions: 394′ x 39′.   Single-screw, 13½ knots.   Compound engines.   Three masts and one funnel.   Scrapped in France, 1922.

Erie   (1868)   United States & Brazil Mail Steamship Co.
   Built by Jackman of Newburyport, Massachusetts.   Tonnage: 3,000.   Dimensions: 322′ x 43′.   Single-screw, 11 knots.   Vertical geared type engines.   Three masts and two funnels.

Clipper bow. Wooden hull. In Boston-Liverpool service for only a brief time. Entered South American service in 1870. Destroyed by fire near Pernambuco, January 1, 1873. Sister ship: **Ontario.**

Erlangen   (1901)   North German Lloyd.
Built by Bremer "Vulkan", Vegesack, Germany. Tonnage: 5,285. Dimensions: 378′ x 47′. Single-screw, 12 knots. Triple expansion engines. Two masts and one funnel. In West Indies service. Became a war loss in 1917.

Ermymanthe   (1862)   Messageries Maritimes.
Built by Messageries Maritimes, La Ciotat, France. Tonnage: 1,947. Dimensions: 344′ x 32′. Single-screw. Two masts and one funnel. Iron hull. Clipper bow. In 1888 was lengthened and converted to triple expansion engines. Sold in 1895. Collided with steamer **Berry,** off Cairo, November 19, 1898. Went ashore and broke her back two days later.

Espagne   (1891)   Transport Maritimes (French).
Built by Forges & Chantiers de la Mediterranee, La Seyne, France. Tonnage: 4,144. Dimensions: 398′ x 41′. Single-screw, 14 knots. Triple expansion engines. Three masts and one funnel. Steel hull. Passengers: 17 first, 88 second, 1,204 third. Scrapped in 1924.

Espana   (1921)   Hamburg-South American Line.
Built by Howaldswerke, Kiel, Germany. Tonnage: 7,418. Dimensions: 413′ x 55′. Single-screw, 12 knots. Triple expansion engines. Two masts and one funnel. Vessel taken as a war prize at Sandefjord in May 1945. Allocated to Russia and renamed **General Bagratsion** in 1946. Sister ships: **La Coruna** and **Vigo.**

Esperanza   (1901)   Ward Line.
Built by W. Cramp & Sons Co., Philadelphia, Pennsylvania. Tonnage: 4,702. Dimensions: 341′ x 47′. Twin-screw, 16 knots. Triple expansion engines. Two masts and two funnels. Passengers: 86 first, 60 second, 48 third. Lost by stranding of Mexico in January 1923. Sister ship: **Monterey.**

Essequibo   (1914)   Pacific Steam Navigation Co.
Built by Workman, Clark & Co., Belfast, Ireland. Tonnage: 8,489. Dimensions: 450′ x 57′ (467′ o.l.). Twin-screw, 14 knots. Quadruple expansion engines. Two masts and one funnel. Note: In service of Royal Mail Line, 1914–1922. Transferred to Pacific Steam Navigation Company in 1922.

Renamed: **Neva** (1935) Russian. Still in their service. Sister ship: **Ebro.**

Eubee (1921)   Chargeurs Reunis.
Built by Ateliers & Chantiers de France, Dunkirk, France. Tonnage: 9,645.   Dimensions: 483′ x 58′.   Twin-screw, 13 knots.   Triple expansion engines. Two masts and one funnel. Launched, December 17, 1921. Sunk in collision during fog with steamer **Corinaldo,** August 14, 1936.   Sister ship: **Desirade.**

Europa (1873)   La Veloce Line.
Built by Wigham Richardson, Newcastle, England.   Tonnage: 2,202.   Dimensions: 313′ x 35′.   Single-screw.   Compound engines.   Four masts.   Iron hull.   Service: Italy-South America.   Scrapped in 1894.

Europa (1907)   (a) La Veloce Line, (b) Navigazione Generale Italiana.   Tonnage: 7,910.   Vessel was transferred to Navigazione Generale Italiana in 1922.   *Note: See PART I for details.*

Eva Peron (1950)   Dodero Lines (Argentine).
Built by Vickers-Armstrongs, Ltd., Barrow, England.   Tonnage: 12,627.   Dimensions: 509′ x 71′ (530′ o.l.).   Twin-screw, 19 knots.   Steam turbines.   Two masts and one funnel. Service: Buenos Aires-London.   Renamed: **Uruguay** (1955). Sister ship: **17 de Octobre.**

Evita (1951)   Argentina State Line.
Built by Ansaldo, S. A. Sestri, Genoa, Italy.   Tonnage: 11,317. Dimensions: 525′ x 65′ (549′ o.l.).   Twin-screw, 18 knots. Motorship.   Two masts and one funnel.   Passengers: 116 first-class.   Service: Buenos Aires-New York.   Renamed: **Rio Tunuyan** (1955).   Ex-**Rio Tunuyan** (1952).   Sister ships: **Rio de la Plata** and **Rio Jachal.**

Expresso (1870)   La Veloce Line.
Built by Wigham Richardson & Co., Newcastle, England. Tonnage: 2,009.   Dimensions: 292′ x 35′.   Single-screw. Compound engines.   Iron hull.   In South American trade almost exclusively until 1901.   Renamed: (a) **Colombo,** (b) **Napoli.**

***Federico C** (1958)   "C" Line (Giacomo Costa fu Andrea).
Built by S. A. Ansaldo, Genoa, Italy.   Tonnage: 20,416. Dimensions: 606′ (o.l.) x 78′.   Twin-screw, 21 knots.   Steam turbines.   Single mast and one funnel.   Passengers: 243 first,

300 second, 736 third.   Commenced her maiden voyage Genoa-South America, March 22, 1958.

Finance   (1883)   (a) United States & Brazil Mail Steamship Co., (b) Panama Railroad Co.
Built by John Roach & Son, Chester, Pennsylvania. Tonnage: 2,603.   Dimensions: 2,603.   Dimensions: 300′ x 38′. Single-screw, 12 knots. Compound engines. Two masts and one funnel. Lost by collision, November 26, 1908. Sister ships: **Advance** and **Reliance.**

Flandria   (1922)   Royal Holland Lloyd.
Built by Barclay, Curle & Co., Glasgow, Scotland. Tonnage: 10,171.   Dimensions: 450′ x 59′.   Twin-screw, 14½ knots. Steam turbines. Two masts and two funnels. Renamed: **Bretagne** (1937). Became a war casualty, October 14, 1939. Sister ship: **Orania.**

Florida   (1905)   Lloyd Italiano.
Tonnage: 5,018. *Note: See PART I for details.*

Florida   (1926)   Transport Maritimes (French).
Built by Ateliers & Chantiers de la Loire, St. Nazaire, France. Tonnage: 9,331.   Dimensions: 511′ x 60′.   Twin-screw, 15 knots. Steam turbines. Two masts and two funnels. Renamed: **Ascania** (1955).

Fluminense   (1891)   Booth Line.
Built by Palmers Shipbuilding & Iron Co., Newcastle, England. Tonnage: 2,154. Dimensions: 302′ x 38′. Single-screw, 12 knots. Triple expansion engines. Two masts and one funnel. Steel hull. Clipper bow. Ex-**Il Principe di Napoli.**

Formosa   (1906)   Transport Maritimes (French).
Built by London & Glasgow Shipbuilding Co., Glasgow, Scotland. Tonnage: 4,471.   Dimensions: 408′ x 47′.   Twin-screw, 13 knots. Triple expansion engines. Two masts and one funnel. Scrapped in 1929.

Formose   (1921)   Chargeurs Reunis.
Built by Forges & Chantiers de la Mediterranee, La Seyne, France.   Tonnage: 9,975.   Dimensions: 483′ x 58′.   Twin-screw, 13 knots. Triple expansion engines. Two masts and one funnel. Launched, February 12, 1921. Scrapped in France, 1953. Similar ships: **Aurigny, Belle Isle, Desirade, Jamaique** and **Lipari.**

Fort Amherst   (1936)   Red Cross Line (Furness Withy & Co., Ltd.).
Built by Blythswood Shipbuilding Co., Glasgow, Scotland. Tonnage: 3,489. Dimensions: 314′ x 45′. Single-screw, 13½ knots. Triple expansion engines. Two masts and one funnel. Renamed: **Al Amir Saud** (1952) Arabian. Sister ship: **Fort Townsend.**

Fort Hamilton   (1904)   Furness-Bermuda Line.
Built by Sir James Laing & Sons, Ltd., Sunderland, England. Tonnage: 5,530. Dimensions: 425′ x 50′. Twin-screw, 16 knots. Triple expansion engines. Two masts and two funnels. Renamed: **Stella d'Italia.** Scrapped in 1933. Ex-**Bermudian.**

Fort St. George   (1912)   Furness-Bermuda Line.
Built by Wm. Beardmore & Co., Glasgow, Scotland. Tonnage: 7,785. Dimensions: 411′ x 56′. Twin-screw, 16 knots. Quadruple expansion engines. Two masts and one funnel. Renamed: (a) **Cesarea** (1935), (b) **Arno** (1938). Sunk by a British torpedo bomber 40 miles off Tobruk in September 1942. Ex-**Wandilla** (1920). Sister ship: **Fort Victoria.**

Fort Townsend   (1936)   Red Cross Line (Furness Withy & Co., Ltd.).
Built by Blythswood Shipbuilding Co., Glasgow, Scotland. Tonnage: 3,489. Dimensions: 314′ x 45′. Single-screw, 13½ knots. Triple expansion engines. Two masts and one funnel. Renamed: (a) **Al Amir Saud** (1952), (b) **Mansour** (1956). Sister ship: **Fort Amherst.**

Fort Victoria   (1913)   Furness-Bermuda Line.
Built by Wm. Beardmore & Co., Glasgow, Scotland. Tonnage: 7,784. Dimensions: 411′ x 56′. Twin-screw, 16 knots. Quadruple expansion engines. Two masts and one funnel. Sunk in fog, due to collision with the coastal liner **Algonquin** near Ambrose Lightship, December 1929. There was no loss of life. Ex-**Willochra** (1920). Sister ship: **Fort St. George.**

Forth   (1841)   Royal Mail Line (British).
Built by Robert Menzies, Leith, Scotland. Tonnage: 1,900. Dimensions: 213′ (245′ o.l.). Paddle-wheels, 8 knots. Engines developed 255 horse-power. Breadth over the paddleboxes 60 feet. Three masts and one funnel. Clipper bow. Wooden hull. First sailing from Southampton and Falmouth, December 17, 1841. Out of fleet in 1849.

France (1896) Transport Maritimes (French).
Built by Forges & Chantiers de la Mediterranee, La Seyne,
France. Tonnage: 4,269. Dimensions: 397' x 42'. Single-
screw, 14 knots. Triple expansion engines. Three masts and
one funnel. Sunk by submarine in Mediterranean, 1915.

Francesco Crispi (1925) Transatlantica Italiana.
Built by Ansaldo San Giorgio (near Spezia) Muggiano,
Italy. Tonnage: 7,464. Dimensions: 429' x 52' (447' o.l.).
Twin-screw, 14½ knots. Steam turbines. Two masts and
two funnels. Vessel later was transferred to Lloyd Triestino.
She became a war casualty, April 19, 1943. Sister ship:
Giuseppe Mazzini.

Francis (1910) Booth Line.
Built by Barclay, Curle & Co., Glasgow, Scotland. Tonnage:
3,963. Dimensions: 355' x 49'. Single-screw, 11 knots.
Triple expansion engines. Two masts and one funnel.
Passengers: 17 first and 100 third. Renamed: **Rosalie
Moller.** Sister ships: **Crispin** and **Hubert.**

Frisia (1872) Hamburg-American Line.
Tonnage: 3,256. In West Indies service. *Note: See PART I
for details.*

Frisia (1909) Royal Holland Lloyd.
Built by Kon. Maats de Schelde, Flushing, Netherlands.
Tonnage: 7,442. Dimensions: 421' x 54'. Twin-screw, 12½
knots. Triple expansion engines. Two masts and one funnel.
Renamed: **Holsatia** (1922). Sister ship: **Hollandia.**

Furst Bismarck (1905) Hamburg-American Line.
Built by Fairfield Shipbuilding & Engineering Co., Glasgow,
Scotland. Tonnage: 8,332. Dimensions: 469' x 55' (486,
o.l.). Twin-screw, 14½ knots. Quadruple expansion engines.
Two masts and one funnel. Built for the South American
service. Renamed: (a) **Friedrichsruh,** (b) **Amboise.**
Scrapped in Italy, 1935. Running mate: **Kronprinzessin
Cecilie.**

Galicia (1873) Pacific Steam Navigation Co.
Built by Robert Napier & Sons, Glasgow, Scotland. Ton-
nage: 3,829. Dimensions: 383' x 43'. Single-screw. Com-
pound engines. Three masts and two funnels. Iron hull.
Clipper bow. Renamed: **Gaspesia** (1898). Scrapped in
Italy, 1899.

Galicia   (1901)   Pacific Steam Navigation Co.
Built by Wigham Richardson & Co., Newcastle, England.
Tonnage: 5,896. Dimensions: 400' x 50'. Twin-screw, 14
knots. Triple expansion engines. Two masts and one funnel.
Mined and sunk off Falmouth in May 1917. Sister ship:
Potosi.

Galicia   (1904)   Hamburg-American Line.
Built by Flensburger Schiffsb., Flensburg, Germany. Tonnage: 6,146. Dimensions: 411' x 50'. Single-screw. Quadruple expansion engines. In West Indies service. Ex-**Thessalia.**

*Galileo Ferraris   (1953)   Italia Line.
Built by Chantiers de la Loire, St. Nazaire, France. Tonnage: 8,101. Dimensions: 502' x 64' (535' o.l.). Twin-screw,
16 knots. Motorship. Two masts and one funnel. Ex-**Henri
Poincare**   (1957).   Sister ships: **Alessandro Volta** and
Antonio Pacinotti.

Gallia   (1913)   Compagnie Sud-Atlantique (French).
Built by Forges & Chantiers de la Mediterranee, La Seyne,
France. Tonnage: 14,966. Dimensions: 574' x 62'. Quadruple-screw, 20 knots. Triple expansion engines and steam
turbine. Two masts and three funnels. Passengers: 300
first, 106 second, 80 third and 600 fourth-class. Torpedoed
and sunk by German submarine in the Mediterranean off
Sardinia in 1916, with the loss of over 600 lives. She was
being used as a troopship. Sister ships: **Lutetia** and **Massilia.**

Garibaldi   (1906)   Transatlantica Italiana.
Tonnage: 5,191. *Note: See PART I for details.*

Garonna   (1897)   Compagnie Sud-Atlantique (French).
Built by Fairfield Shipbuilding Co., Glasgow, Scotland.
Tonnage: 5,562. Dimensions: 425' x 50' (440' o.l.). Single-screw, 13 knots. Triple expansion engines. Four masts and
one funnel.   Scrapped in France, 1920.   Ex-**Avondale
Castle** (1912).

Garonne   (1871)   Pacific Steam Navigation Co.
Built by Robert Napier & Sons, Glasgow, Scotland. Tonnage:
3,901. Dimensions: 382' x 41'. Single-screw, 15 knots. Compound engines. Three masts and one funnel. Clipper bow.
Iron hull. Vessel was taken over and operated by the Orient
Steam Navigation Co., Ltd., in 1877. She was sold again in
November 1897. Resold to United States Government in
1898. Wrecked in January 1901. Sister ships: **Chimborazo,
Cuzco** and **Lusitania.** Very similar, but not identical.

Gelria   (1913)   Royal Holland Lloyd.
>   Built by Alexander Stephen & Sons, Ltd., Glasgow, Scotland.
>   Tonnage: 13,868.   Dimensions: 541′ x 65′ (560′ o.l.).   Twin-
>   screw, 16 knots.   Quadruple expansion engines.   Two masts
>   and two funnels.   Renamed: **Gradisca** (1935).   Badly dam-
>   aged after stranding, January 2, 1946.   Sold to Italian ship-
>   breakers at Venice in 1952.   Sister ship: **Tubantia.**

General Artigas   (1923)   (a) Hamburg-American Line,   (b)
Hamburg-South American Line.
>   Built by Howaldtswerke, Kiel, Germany.   Tonnage: 11,343.
>   Dimensions: 473′ x 60′.   Single-screw, 12½ knots.   Steam
>   turbines.   Two masts and one funnel.   Purchased by Hamburg-
>   South American Line in 1936.   Vessel set on fire in British
>   air attack on Hamburg, July 25, 1943, and sank.   Ex-
>   **Westphalia** (1930).   Note: In North Atlantic service only
>   while under name of **Westphalia.**   Sister ship: **General
>   San Martin.**

General Belgrano   (1913)   Hamburg-American Line.
>   Built by Reiherstieg Schiffsw., Hamburg, Germany.   Ton-
>   nage: 10,056.   Dimensions: 491′ x 59′.   Twin-screw, 12½
>   knots.   Triple expansion engines.   Two masts and one funnel.
>   Passengers: 700 first, 202 second and 2,500 third.   Vessel
>   surrendered to Great Britain in 1919.   Sold to Hamburg-
>   American Line in 1926.   Acquired by Akt. zu Seesch in 1928.
>   Scrapped in 1932.   **Ex-Bahia Castillo.**

General Mitre   (1921)   Hamburg-American Line.
>   Built by Bremer Vulkan, Vegesack, Germany.   Tonnage:
>   9,891.   Dimensions: 468′ x 58′ (485′ o.l.).   Single-screw.
>   Triple expansion engines, and steam turbine.   Two masts and
>   one funnel.   Under Hugo Stinnes Line ownership in 1928.
>   Acquired by A. G. fur Seeschf in 1931.   Sold to Italy in 1935.
>   Renamed: **Sannio** (1935).   Sunk in 1941.   Ex-**Artus.**

General Osorio   (1929)   Hamburg-American Line.
>   Built by Bremer Vulkan, Vegesack, Germany.   Tonnage:
>   11,590.   Dimensions: 492′ x 65′.   Twin-screw, 15 knots.
>   Motorship.   Two masts and two funnels.   Purchased by
>   Hamburg-South American Line in 1936.   Always used in the
>   South American trade.   Damaged in air attack on Kiel,
>   April 9, 1945.   Towed to Inverkeithing to be broken up.

General San Martin   (1912)   A. G. Stinnes Line.
>   Built by Reiherstief Schiffsw., Hamburg, Germany.   Tonnage:
>   6,079.   Dimensions: 392′ x 52′.   Single-screw, 13 knots.

Quadruple expansion engines. Two masts and one funnel. Renamed: **Almirante Jaceguay.** **Ex-Edmund Wagen-kneht,** ex-**Professor,** ex-**Professor Woermann.**

General San Martin (1922) (a) Hamburg-American Line, (b) Hamburg-South American Line.
Built by Howaldtswerke, Kiel, Germany. Tonnage: 11,343. Dimensions: 473′ x 60′. Single-screw, 13 knots. Steam turbines. Two masts and one funnel. In North Atlantic service only when under name of **Thuringia.** Note: Taken as war prize at Copenhagen in May 1945. Renamed **Empire Deben** and put under management of Shaw, Savill & Albion Line for the British Government. Scrapped in Great Britain, 1949. Ex-**Thuringia** (1930). Sister ship: **General Artigas.**

General W. C. Gorgas (1902) Panama Railroad Co.
Built by Akt. Ges. "Neptun", Rostock, Germany. Tonnage: 4,636. Dimensions: 370′ x 45′. Single-screw, 12½ knots. Quadruple expansion engines. Two masts and one funnel. Passengers: 93 first-class. Vessel later acquired by Libby, McNeill & Libby Co. Renamed: **Mikhail Lomonosov** (1945). It is quite likely she is still in Russian hands. Ex-**Prinz Sigismund** (1917).

Gera (1890) North German Lloyd.
Tonnage: 5,005. In South American service. *Note: See PART I for details.*

Germania (1871) Hamburg-American Line.
Built by Caird & Co., Greenock, Scotland. Tonnage: 2,876. Dimensions: 329′ x 39′. Single-screw, 11 knots. Compound engines. Two masts and one funnel. Service: Germany-South America. Wrecked off South American coast in 1876.

Ginyo Maru (1921) Toyo Kisen Kabushiki Kaisha.
Built by Asano Shipbuilding Co., Tsurumi, Japan. Tonnage: 8,613. Dimensions: 445′ x 58′. Twin-screw, 12 knots. Steam turbines. Two masts and one funnel. In trans-Pacific service to South America, via United States west coast ports. Sunk by American submarine, December 16, 1943. Running mates: **Anyo Maru, Bokuyo Maru** and **Rakuyo Maru.**

Giulio Cesare (1920) (a) Navigazione Generale Italiana, (b) Italia Line.
Tonnage: 21,657. In South American service. *Note: See PART I for details.*

Giulio Cesare   (1951)   Italia Line.
Tonnage: 27,694.   Service: Italy-Brazil-River Plate ports. Transferred to North Atlantic route in 1957.   *Note: See PART I for details.*

Goethe   (1873)   Hamburg-American Line.
Tonnage: 3,408.   In South American service.   *Note: See PART I for details.*

*Golfito   (1949)   Elders & Fyffes, Ltd.
Built by Alexander Stephen & Sons, Ltd., Glasgow, Scotland. Tonnage: 8,736.   Dimensions: 426′ x 62′.   Twin-screw, 17½ knots.   Steam turbines.   Two masts and one funnel.   Passengers: 101.   Sister ship: **Camito.**

Gotha   (1907)   North German Lloyd.
Built by Bremer Vulkan, Vegesack, Germany.   Tonnage: 6,974.   Dimensions: 428′ x 54′.   Single-screw, 12 knots. Quadruple expansion engines.   Two masts and one funnel. In South American service.   Scrapped in 1932.

Gottardo   (1883)   Navigazione Generale Italiana.
Built by Alexander Stephen & Sons, Ltd., Glasgow, Scotland. Tonnage: 2,847.   Dimensions: 350′ x 40′.   Single-screw, 12 knots.   Compound engines.   Three masts and one funnel. Iron hull.   Vessel laid down for Floria (Italian).   Launched, November 23, 1881.   Transferred to South American service in 1888.   Returned to New York trade in 1899.   Renamed: **Memfi** (1903).   Acquired by Servizi Marittimi in 1910. Sister ship: **Independente.**

Graf Bismarck   (1871)   North German Lloyd.
Tonnage: 2,406.   Built for West Indies service.   *Note: See PART I for details.*

Granada   (1906)   Hamburg-American Line.
Built by Palmer Shipbuilding Co., Newcastle, England. Tonnage: 6,751.   Dimensions: 449′ x 53′.   Single-screw. Quadruple expansion engines.   Surrendered to France in 1919. Later resold to Hamburg-American Line.   Scrapped in 1931. Ex-**Brasilia,** ex-**Granada.**

Great Western   (1838)   Royal Mail Line (British).
Built by William Patterson, Bristol, England.   Tonnage: 1,775.   Dimensions: 212′ x 35′.   Paddle-wheels, 9 knots.   Side lever engines.   Four masts and one funnel.   Vessel originally owned by Great Western Steam Ship Co.   The Royal Mail Line purchased her in 1847.   Scrapped in 1857.

Groix   (1922)   Chargeurs Reunis.
Built by Forges & Chantiers de la Mediterranee, La Seyne, France. Tonnage: 9,975. Dimensions: 483' x 58'. Twin-screw, 13 knots. Triple expansion engines. Two masts and one funnel. Launched, December 19, 1921. Service: (a) Europe-South America; (b) France-Africa. Sold to Bordeaux shipbreakers in May 1951. Broken up in 1952. Sister ship: **Formose.**

Guadalquivir   (1888)   Messageries Maritimes.
Built by Forges & Chantiers de la Mediterranee, Havre, France. Tonnage: 2,620. Dimensions: 334' x 37'. Single-screw, 12 knots. Two masts and one funnel. Sister ship: **Guadiana.**

Guadiana   (1875)   Royal Mail Line (British).
Built by London & Glasgow Engineering & Iron Ship-building Co., Glasgow, Scotland. Tonnage: 2,504. Dimensions: 332' x 36'. Single-screw. Compound engines. Iron hull. Disposed of in 1885.

Guadiana   (1888)   Messageries Maritimes.
Built by Forges & Chantiers de la Mediterranee, Havre, France. Tonnage: 2,614. Dimensions: 334' x 37'. Single-screw, 12 knots. Triple expansion engines. Two masts and one funnel. Scrapped in Italy, 1922. Sister ship: **Guadalquivir.**

Guaruja   (1921)   Transport Maritimes (French).
Built by Forges & Chantiers de la Mediterranee, La Seyne, France. Tonnage: 4,282. Dimensions: 360' x 45'. Single-screw, 13 knots. Steam turbines (Turbo-electric). Two masts and one funnel. Wrecked off Spain in 1938.

Guglielmo Peirce   (1907)   Sicula Americana Line.
Tonnage: 8,512. In South American service. *Note: See PART I for details.*

Guiana   (1907)   Quebec Steamship Co.
Built by Sir James Laing & Sons, Ltd., Sunderland, England. Tonnage: 3,657. Dimensions: 345' x 44'. Single-screw. Two masts and one funnel. In West Indies service. Scrapped in 1925.

Guienne   (1853)   Messageries Maritimes.
Built by Messageries Maritimes, La Ciotat, France. Tonnage: 1,945. Dimensions: 316' x 39'. Paddle-wheels. Two masts and one funnel. Clipper bow. Converted from

paddle-wheels to screw propulsion in 1872; renamed **Gambie**. Lost at Bahia in 1873.

H. H. Meier   (1892)   North German Lloyd.
Tonnage: 5,140.   Laid down as **Lucania;** purchased on the stocks for South American trade.   *Note: See PART I for details.*

Habsburg   (1875)   North German Lloyd.
Tonnage: 3,094.   In South American service.   *Note: See PART I for details.*

Haiti   (1932)   Colombian Mail Steamship Co.
Built by Newport News Shipbuilding Co., Newport News, Virginia. Tonnage: 5,236.   Dimensions: 385' x 57' (404' o.l.). Single-screw, 17 knots.   Steam turbines.   Two masts and one funnel. Renamed: (a) **Puerto Rico** (1938), (b) **Monterey** (1939), (c) **Adana** (1948).

Hakata Maru   (1897)   N. Y. K. Line (Japanese).
Tonnage: 6,241.   Service: (a) Japan-Europe, (b) Japan-Seattle, (c) South America trade.   *Note: See PART II for details.*

Halle   (1895)   North German Lloyd.
Built by Germania-Werft, Kiel, Germany. Tonnage: 3,960. Dimensions: 355' x 43'.   Single-screw, 12½ knots.   Triple expansion engines.   Two masts and one funnel.   Renamed: **Woudrichem.**

Hammonia   (1909)   Hamburg-American Line.
Built by Alexander Stephen & Sons, Ltd., Glasgow, Scotland. Tonnage: 7,291.   Dimensions: 419' x 54'.   Twin-screw, 12½ knots.   Triple expansion engines.   Two masts and one funnel.   Commenced service to South America in 1922. Vessel was purchased by Hamburg-American Line as a replacement, and immediately wrecked in 1922.   Ex-**Hollandia** (1922).   Sister ship: **Holsatia.**

Hannover   (1899)   North German Lloyd.
Built by Wigham Richardson & Co., Newcastle, England. Tonnage: 7,305.   Dimensions: 429' x 54'.   Twin-screw, 12½ knots.   Quadruple expansion engines.   Two masts and one funnel.   Scrapped in 1929.   Sister ships: **Frankfurt** and **Koln**.

Havana (1898) Ward Line.
Built by W. Cramp & Sons Shipbuilding & Engine Building Co., Philadelphia, Pa. Tonnage, 5,667. Dimensions: 360′ x 50′. Twin-screw, 17 knots. Triple expansion engines. Two masts and two funnels. Vessel was purchased from New York & Brazil Mail Steamship Co. in 1894. Renamed: **Panama** (1905).

Havana (1907) Ward Line.
Built by W. Cramp & Sons, Philadelphia, Pa. Tonnage: 6,678. Dimensions: 413′ x 50′. Twin-screw, 17 knots. Triple expansion engines. Two masts and two funnels. Renamed: (a) **Yucatan,** (b) **Shamrock** (U.S. hospital ship). Scrapped in 1947. Sister ship: **Saratoga.**

Heiyo Maru (1930) N. Y. K. Line (Japanese).
Built by Osaka Iron Works, Osaka, Japan. Tonnage: 9,816. Dimensions: 460′ x 60′. Single-screw, 16 knots. Motorship. Two masts and one funnel. Launched, May 5, 1929. Completed on March 15, 1930. Left Kobe on her maiden voyage for Hongkong, April 19, 1930. In trans-Pacific service to South America west coast ports, via United States west coast ports. She replaced the **Anyo Maru** on this route. Sunk by an American submarine, January 17, 1941.

Helgoland (1896) North German Lloyd.
Built by J. L. Thompson & Sons, Ltd., Sunderland, England. Tonnage: 5,666. Dimensions: 409′ x 50′. Single-screw, 10½ knots. Triple expansion engines. In West Indies service. Renamed: **Polyxena** (1914). Ex-**Maria Rickmers.**

Heluan (1908) (a) "Kosmos" Line, (b) Hamburg-American Line.
Built by Reiherstieg Schiffsw., Hamburg, Germany. Tonnage: 7,262. Dimensions: 441′ x 52′. Twin-screw. Triple expansion engines. Two masts and one funnel. In West Indies service. Scrapped in 1931. Ex-**City of Lucknow,** ex-**Heluan.**

Henri IV (1871) Chargeurs Reunis.
Built by Forges & Chantiers de la Mediterranee, La Seyne, France. Tonnage: 1,605. Dimensions: 247′ x 36′. Single-screw. Compound engines. Three masts and one funnel. Iron hull. Sold to Bossiere in 1886. Lost at mouth of Loire in July 1890.

Heredia (1908) United Fruit Co.
Built by Workman, Clark & Co., Ltd., Belfast, Ireland. Tonnage: 4,732. Dimensions: 378′ x 49′. Single-screw, 14½

knots. Quadruple expansion engines. Two masts and one funnel. Renamed: (a) **General Pershing** (1932), (b) **Heredia** (1938). Torpedoed and sunk in Gulf of Mexico, May 19, 1942. Sister ships: Listed under **Metapan.**

Highland Brae (1910)   Nelson Line.
Built by Cammell Laird & Co., Birkenhead, England. Tonnage: 7,634. Dimensions: 413' x 56'. Single-screw, 13 knots. Triple expansion engines. Two masts and one funnel. Captured by the German merchant cruiser **Kronprinz Wilhelm** and scuttle on January 14, 1915. Sister ships: See **Highland Warrior.**

Highland Brigade (1901)   Nelson Line.
Built by Wm. Beardmore & Co., Glasgow, Scotland. Tonnage: 5,662. Dimensions: 384' x 50'. Single-screw, 12½ knots. Triple expansion engines. Two masts and one funnel. Torpedoed and sunk without warning six miles from St. Catherine's, April 7, 1918.

Highland Brigade (1929) (a) Nelson Line, (b) Royal Mail Line.
Built by Harland & Wolff, Ltd., Belfast, Ireland. Tonnage: 14,131. Dimensions: 523' x 69' (544' o.l.). Twin-screw, 16 knots. Motorship. Two masts and two funnels. After funnel a dummy covering dining saloon dome. Renamed: (a) **Henrietta** (1959), (b) **Marianna** (pilgrim work). Sister ships: **Highland Chieftain, Highland Hope, Highland Monarch, Highland Patriot** and **Highland Princess.**

Highland Chieftain (1929) (a) Nelson Line, (b) Royal Mail Line.
Built by Harland & Wolff, Ltd., Belfast, Ireland. Tonnage: 14,131. Dimensions: 523' x 69' (544' o.l.). Twin-screw, 15 knots. Motorship. Two masts and two funnels. Passengers: 766 (500 emigrants). Crew: 180. Renamed: **Calpean Star** (1958). Sister ships: See **Highland Brigade.**

Highland Corrie (1910)   Nelson Line.
Built by Russell & Co., Port Glasgow, Scotland. Tonnage: 7,583. Dimensions: 414' x 56'. Single-screw, 13 knots. Triple expansion engines. Two masts and one funnel. Passengers: 80 first and 40 second-class. Sunk by German submarine off English coast in 1917. Sister ships: See **Highland Warrior.**

Highland Glen   (1910)   Nelson Line.
Built by Russell & Co., Port Glasgow, Scotland. Tonnage: 7,598.   Dimensions: 414′ x 56′.   Single-screw, 13½ knots. Triple expansion engines.   Two masts and one funnel. Renamed: **Jamaica Producer** (1930).   Sister ships: See **Highland Warrior.**

Highland Hope   (1903)   Nelson Line.
Built by Russell & Co., Port Glasgow, Scotland. Tonnage: 5,150.   Dimensions: 384′ x 51′.   Single-screw, 12 knots. Triple expansion engines.   Two masts and one funnel. Captured by the German cruiser **Karlsruhe** and scuttled on September 14, 1914.

Highland Hope   (1929)   Nelson Line. Glasgow, Scotland.
Built by Harland & Wolff, Ltd. Tonnage: 14,129. Dimensions: 523′ x 69′ (544′ o.l.). Twin-screw, 16 knots. Motorship. Two masts and two funnels. Wrecked on the Farilhoes Rocks near Peniche, Portugal, November 19, 1930, with no loss of life. Sister ships: See **Highland Brigade.**

Highland Laddie   (1910)   Nelson Line.
Built by Cammell, Laird & Co., Birkenhead, England. Tonnage: 7,381. Dimensions: 405′ x 56′ (420′ o.l.). Single-screw, 13½ knots.   Triple expansion engines.   Two masts and one funnel.   Renamed: **Jamaica Settler** (1930). Sister ships: See **Highland Warrior.**

Highland Loch   (1911)   Nelson Line.
Built by Cammell, Laird & Co., Birkenhead, England. Tonnage: 7,493. Dimensions: 413′ x 56′. Single-screw, 13 knots.   Triple expansion engines.   Two masts and one funnel. Renamed: **Jamaica Planter** (1929). Sister ships: See **Highland Warrior.**

Highland Monarch   (1928)   (a) Nelson Line, (b) Royal Mail Line.
Built by Harland & Wolff, Ltd., Belfast, Ireland. Tonnage: 14,137. Dimensions: 523′ x 69′ (544′ o.l.). Twin-screw, 16 knots. Motorship. Two masts and two funnels. Scrapped in 1960. Sister ships: See **Highland Brigade.**

Highland Patriot   (1932) (a) Nelson Line, (b) Royal Mail Line.
Built by Harland & Wolff, Ltd., Belfast, Ireland. Tonnage: 14,157. Dimensions: 523′ x 69′ (544′ o.l.). Twin-screw, 16 knots. Motorship. Two masts and two funnels. Torpedoed and sunk by enemy submarine, October 1, 1940. Sister ships: See **Highland Brigade.**

Highland Piper   (1911)   Nelson Line.
　　Built by Cammell, Laird & Co., Birkenhead, England. Tonnage: 7,490. Dimensions: 413′ x 56′. Single-screw, 13½ knots. Triple expansion engines. Two masts and one funnel. Renamed: **Jamaica Merchant** (1930).   Sister ships: **Highland Warrior.**

Highland Pride   (1910)   Nelson Line.
　　Built by Russell & Co., Port Glasgow, Scotland. Tonnage: 7,469. Dimensions: 405′ x 56′. Single-screw, 13½ knots. Triple expansion engines. Two masts and one funnel. Wrecked on the Carallones Rocks, near Vigo in dense fog, September 9, 1929. Sister ships: See **Highland Warrior.**

Highland Princess   (1930)   (a) Nelson Line, (b) Royal Mail Line.
　　Built by Harland & Wolff, Ltd., Belfast, Ireland. Tonnage: 14,157. Dimensions: 523′ x 69′ (544′ o.l.). Twin-screw, 16 knots. Motorship. Two masts and two funnels. She and her sister ships were transferred to Royal Mail Line in 1932. Renamed: **Marianna** (1959). Sister ships: See **Highland Brigade.**

Highland Rover   (1910)   Nelson Line.
　　Built by Russell & Co., Port Glasgow, Scotland. Tonnage: 7,490. Dimensions: 405′ x 56′. Single-screw, 13½ knots. Triple expansion engines. Two masts and one funnel. Scrapped in 1934. Sister ships: See **Highland Warrior.**

Highland Scot   (1910)   Nelson Line.
　　Built by Russell & Co., Port Glasgow, Scotland. Tonnage: 7,604. Dimensions: 414′ x 56′. Single-screw, 13½ knots. Triple expansion engines. Two masts and one funnel. Wrecked on Maricas Island, Brazil, May 6, 1918, and became a total loss. Sister ships: See **Highland Warrior.**

Highland Warrior   (1911)   Nelson Line.
　　Built by Russell & Co., Port Glasgow, Scotland. Tonnage: 7,485. Dimensions: 414′ x 56′. Single-screw, 13½ knots. Triple expansion engines. Two masts and one funnel. Passengers: 80 first and 40 second class. Wrecked north of Cape Prior, Spain, October 3, 1955. Sister ships: **Highland Brae, Highland Corrie, Highland Glen, Highland Laddie, Highland Loch, Highland Piper, Highland Pride, Highland Rover** and **Highland Scot.**

Hilary (1889) Booth Line.
Built by W. B. Thompson & Co., Dundee, Scotland. Tonnage: 1,983. Dimensions: 275' x 37'. Single-screw. Triple expansion engines. Two masts and one funnel. Not many passengers. Renamed: (a) **Misumi Maru,** (b) **Toryu Maru.** Ex-**Red Sea.**

Hilary (1908) Booth Line.
Built by Caledon Shipbuilding & Engine Co., Dundee, Scotland. Tonnage: 6,329. Dimensions: 418' x 52'. Triple expansion engines. Two masts and one funnel. Passengers: 210 first and 372 third. Sunk by German submarine in 10th Cruiser Squadron off Shetland Islands, 1917. Sister ships: **Antony** and **Lanfranc.**

Hilary (1931) Booth Line.
Built by Cammell, Laird & Co., Birkenhead, England. Tonnage: 7,403. Dimensions: 424' x 56'. Single-screw, 15 knots. Triple expansion engines. Two masts and one funnel. In passenger service between Liverpool and Brazil. Passengers: 230. Sailed the well known trip of 1,000 miles up the Amazon River. Scrapped in 1960.

Hildebrand (1893) Booth Line.
Built by Hall, Russell & Co., Aberdeen, Scotland. Tonnage: 1,947. Dimensions: 260' x 36'. Single-screw. Triple expansion engines. Steel hull.

Hildebrand (1911) Booth Line.
Built by Scott's Shipbuilding & Engine Co., Greenock, Scotland. Tonnage: 6,995. Dimensions: 440' x 54'. Twin-screw, 14 knots. Quadruple expansion engines. Two masts and one funnel. Passengers: 218 first and 406 third-class. Scrapped in 1933.

Hildebrand (1951) Booth Line.
Built by Cammell, Laird & Co., Birkenhead, England. Tonnage: 7,735. Dimensions: 420' x 60' (439' o.l.). Single-screw, 15 knots. Single mast and one funnel. Wrecked off Portugal during fog, on September 25, 1957, with no loss of life. Hope to salvage her was given up in December 1958.

Hindoustan (1881) Compagnie Nationale de Navigation (French).
Built by Palmer Shipbuilding Co., Newcastle, England. Tonnage: 2,895. Dimensions: 310' x 40'. Single-screw. Compound engines. Iron hull. Made the second sailing of

the newly opened service by the company to South America in October 1887.

Hoedic   (1922)   Chargeurs Reunis.
Built by Forges & Chantiers de la Mediterranee, La Seyne, France. Tonnage: 9,975. Dimensions: 483′ x 58′. Twin-screw, 14 knots. Triple expansion engines. Two masts and one funnel. Launched, December 21, 1922. Capsized in Bellot Dock at Havre; raised on November 30, 1928. Completely refitted at Rotterdam and renamed **Foucauld** in June 1928. Bombed and sunk on June 20, 1940.

Hohenstaufen   (1874)   North German Lloyd.
Built by Earle's Shipbuilding & Engineering Co., Hull, England. Tonnage: 3,098. Dimensions: 353′ x 39′. Single-screw, 12 knots. Compound engines. Two masts and one funnel. Iron hull. In South American service. Vessel sold in 1900.

Hohenzollern   (1873)   North German Lloyd.
Built by Earle's Shipbuilding & Engineering Co., Hull, England. Tonnage: 3,288. Dimensions: 353′ x 39′. Single-screw, 12½ knots. Compound engines. Triple expansion engines installed in 1890. Two masts and one funnel. Launched, May 24, 1873. Maiden voyage Bremen-Southampton-Panama, December 7, 1873. Made her first Bremen-Southampton-New York sailing, May 6, 1874. Opened Bremen-Antwerp-Brazil River Plate service on March 1, 1875. Sold in 1899 and was broken up for scrap.

Hollandia   (1909)   Royal Holland Lloyd.
Built by Alexander Stephen & Sons, Ltd., Glasgow, Scotland. Tonnage: 7,291. Dimensions: 419′ x 54′. Twin-screw, 12½ knots. Triple expansion engines. Two masts and one funnel. In South American service. Renamed: **Hammonia** (1922). Sister ship: **Frisia.**

Holsatia   (1909)   Hamburg-American Line.
Built by Kon. Maats. de Schelde, Flushing, Netherlands. Tonnage: 7,442. Dimensions: 421′ x 54′. Twin-screw, 12½ knots. Triple expansion engines. Two masts and one funnel. Scrapped in 1928. Ex-**Frisia** (1922). Sister ship: **Hammonia.**

Huayna   (1893)   Booth Line.
Built by Hall, Russell & Co., Aberdeen, Scotland. Tonnage: 1,988. Dimensions: 260′ x 36′. Single-screw. Triple expansion engines. Two masts and one funnel. Renamed: **Manuel Carsi.** Wrecked on May 19, 1921. Ex-**Hildebrande.**

Hubert   (1910)   Booth Line.
   Built by Barclay, Curle & Co., Glasgow, Scotland. Tonnage:
   3,946.   Dimensions: 355' x 49'.   Single-screw, 11 knots.
   Triple expansion engines.   Two masts and one funnel.
   Passengers: 17 first-class and 100 steerage. Scrapped in 1934.

*Hubert   (1956)   Booth Line.
   Built by Cammell, Laird & Co., Ltd., Birkenhead, England.
   Tonnage: 7,898.   Dimensions: 405' x 60' (438' o.l.).   Single-
   screw, 15 knots. Steam turbines. Single mast and one funnel.
   Service: Liverpool - Leixoes - Lisbon - Madeira - Barbados -
   Trinidad - Belem - Manaos. Passengers: 170.

Huron   (1896)   Munson Line.
   Built by Act. Ges. "Vulkan" Co., Stettin, Germany. Tonnage: 10,688.   Dimensions: 523' x 60'.   Twin-screw, 14½
   knots. Quadruple expansion engines.   Two masts and two
   funnels.   Service: New York-South America east coast.
   Renamed: **City of Honolulu** (1922). **Ex-Friedrich der
   Grosse** (1917).

Iberia   (1873)   Pacific Steam Navigation Co.
   Built by John Elder & Co., Glasgow, Scotland. Tonnage:
   4,689.   Dimensions: 433' x 45'.   Single-screw, 15½ knots.
   Originally 14 knots.   Compound engines.   Three masts and
   two funnels.   Triple expansion engines installed in 1899.
   Later was in service in Australia.   Sold to Italian shipbreakers, 1903. Sister ships: **Liguria** and **Potosi.**

Iberia   (1928)   Hamburg-American Line.
   Built by F. Schichau, Danzig, Germany. Tonnage, 9,829.
   Dimensions: 460' x 60'.   Quadruple expansion engines.
   Motorship Two masts and two funnels. Renamed: **Pobeda**
   (Russian). Ex-**Magdalena** (1934).

Ile de France   (1882)   Transport Maritimes (French).
   Built by John Elder & Co., Glasgow, Scotland. Tonnage:
   3,488.   Dimensions: 350' x 39'.   Single-screw.   Compound
   engines.   Two masts and one funnel.   Mainly used as a
   cruising liner.   Sold in 1914.   Renamed: **Urguito.**   Ex-
   Burgermeester Den Tex (1903), ex-**Insulinde.**

Illimani   (1873)   Pacific Steam Navigation Co.
   Built by John Elder & Co., Glasgow, Scotland. Tonnage:
   4,022.   Dimensions: 402' x 42'.   Single-screw, 13 knots.
   Compound engines.   Three masts and one funnel.   Clipper
   bow.   Stranded in July 1879.   Sister ships: **Cotopaxi,
   Aconcagua** and **Sorata.**

Imperial   (1938) Compania Sud Americana de Vapores (Chile).
Built by Nakskov Skibs. A/S, Nakskov, Denmark. Tonnage: 7,279. Dimensions: 414' x 58'. Single-screw, 16 knots. Motorship. Two masts and one funnel. Renamed: **Trabzon** (Turkish). Sister ships: **Aconcagua** and **Copiapo.**

Inanda   (1925) Harrison Line.
Built by Swan, Hunter & Wigham Richardson, Ltd., Newcastle, England. Tonnage: 5,985. Dimensions: 407' x 52' (423' o.l.). Single-screw, 14 knots. Quadruple expansion engines. Two masts and one funnel. Bombed by aircraft, September 7, 1940, and also on the 8th and 9th.

Inca   (1893) Pacific Steam Navigation Co.
Built by Harland & Wolff, Ltd., Belfast, Ireland. Tonnage: 3,593. Dimensions: 360' x 43'. Single-screw, 13½ knots. Triple expansion engines. Two masts and one funnel. Sold to Chile in 1923. Renamed: **Llanguihue.** Same class: **Antisana, Magellan** and **Sarmiento.**

Indiana   (1905)   (a) Lloyd Italiana, (b) Navigazione Generale Italiana.
Tonnage: 5,012. Service: Italy-South America. *Note: See PART I for details.*

Indipendente   (1883) Navigazione Generale Italiana.
Built by Alexander Stephen & Sons, Ltd., Glasgow, Scotland. Tonnage: 2,837. Dimensions: 350' x 40'. Single-screw, 12 knots. Compound engines. Three masts and one funnel. Iron hull. Launched, June 20, 1883. Transferred to South American service in 1888. Renamed: **Tebe** (1903). Acquired by Servizi Marittimi (Italian) in 1910. Sister ships: **Archimede, Gottardo, Vincenzo Florio** and **Washington.**

Infanta Isabel   (1912) Pinillos Izquierdo & Co. (Spanish).
Built by Russell & Co., Port Glasgow, Scotland. Tonnage: 8,182. Dimensions: 459' x 58'. Twin-screw, 15 knots. Quadruple expansion engines. Two masts and one funnel. Renamed: **Midzuho Maru** (Japanese). Sister ship: **Principe di Asturias.**

Ingoma   (1913) Harrison Line.
Built by D. & W. Henderson & Co., Ltd., Glasgow, Scotland. Tonnage: 5,686. Dimensions: 400' x 52'. Single-screw, 14 knots. Triple expansion engines. Two masts and one funnel. Renamed: **San Giovanni Battista** (1937).

Inkosi   (1937)   Harrison Line.
> Built by Swan, Hunter & Wigham Richardson, Ltd., New-castle, England. Tonnage: 6,618. Dimensions: 414′ x 56′. Single-screw, 15 knots. Quadruple expansion engines. Two masts and one funnel. Renamed: (a) **Empire Chivalry** (1941), (b) **Planter** (1946). Scrapped by Belgium ship-breakers in 1958.

Isis   (1841)   Royal Mail Line.
> Built by William Pitcher, Northfleet, England. Tonnage: 1,900. Dimensions: Paddle-wheels, 8 knots. Three masts and one funnel. Wooden hull. Grounded at Porto Rico in September 1842. Refloated quickly, but had been severely damaged. After temporary repairs she was sent back to England, under escort of the **Medway.** However the damaged vessel ran into bad weather off Bermuda, and sank on October 18, 1842, with the loss of one crew member.

Itaba   (1910)   Harrison Line.
> Built by Hall, Russell & Co., Aberdeen, Scotland. Tonnage: 4,835. Dimensions: 386′ x 48′. Single-screw, 13½ knots. Two masts and one funnel. Renamed: **Englestan.**

Italia   (1904)   Peirce Brothers (Italian).
> Built by Cantieri Nav. Siciliani, Palermo, Italy. Tonnage: 6,366. Dimensions: 391′ x 52′. Single-screw. Triple expansion engines. Five masts and one funnel. Renamed: **Masaniello.**

Italia   (1905)   (a) La Veloce Line, (b) Navigazione Generale Italiana.
> Tonnage: 5,203. In South American service. *Note: See PART I for details.*

Italia   (1928)   Home Lines (Italian).
> Tonnage: 16,777. Commenced first voyage Genoa-South America, July 27, 1948. *Note: See PART I for details.*

Italie   (1894)   Transport Maritimes (French).
> Built by Forges & Chantiers de la Mediterranee, La Seyne. France. Tonnage: 4,160. Dimensions: 399′ x 42′. Single-screw, 12½ knots. Triple expansion engines. Three masts and one funnel. Scrapped in Italy, 1929.

Itauri   (1897)   Kosmos Line (German).
> Built by Flensburger Schiffsb. Ges., Flensburg, Germany. Tonnage: 4,591. Dimensions: 368′ x 45′. Single-screw.

12 knots. Triple expansion engines. Passengers: 24 first,
14 second, 34 third.

Jamaica   (1933)   (a) Colombia Line, (b) United Fruit Co.
Built by Newport News Shipbuilding Co., Newport News,
Virginia. Tonnage: 6,968. Dimensions: 415' x 60'. Twin-
screw, 18 knots. Two steam turbines connected to electric
motors. Two masts and one funnel. Renamed: **Blumenthal**
(1958). Ex-**Peten.** Sister ship: See **Peten.**

Jamaica Merchant   (1911)   Jamaica Direct Fruit Line.
Built by Cammell, Laird & Co., Ltd., Birkenhead, England.
Tonnage: 7,490.   Dimensions: 413' x 56'.   Single-screw,
13 knots. Triple expansion engines. Two masts and one
funnel. Scrapped in 1937. Ex-**Highland Piper** (1930).

Jamaica Pioneer   (1931)   Jamaica Banana Steamship Co.
Built by Lithgows, Ltd., Port Glasgow, Scotland. Tonnage:
5,349.   Dimensions: 386' x 54'.   Single-screw, 16 knots.
Quadruple expansion engines. Two masts and one funnel.
Torpedoed and sunk by submarine, August 25, 1940. Sister
ships: **Jamaica Progress** and **Jamaica Producer.**

Jamaica Planter   (1936)   Jamaica Banana Steamship Co.
Built by Lithgows, Ltd., Port Glasgow, Scotland. Tonnage:
4,098.   Dimensions: 356' x 50'.   Twin-screw, 15½ knots.
Motorship. Two masts and one funnel. Lost by collision,
December 27, 1944.

*****Jamaica Producer**   (1934)   Jamaica Banana Steamship Co.
Built by Lithgows, Ltd., Port Glasgow, Scotland. Tonnage:
5,325.   Dimensions: 411' x 54'.   Single-screw, 16 knots.
Quadruple expansion engines. Sister ships: **Jamaica Pioneer**
and **Jamaica Progress.**

Jamaica Progress   (1934)   Jamaica Banana Steamship Co.
Built by Lithgows, Ltd., Port Glasgow, Scotland. Tonnage:
5,351.   Dimensions: 393' x 54'.   Single-screw, 16 knots.
Quadruple expansion engines. Two masts and one funnel.
Torpedoed and sunk by enemy submarine, July 30, 1940.
Sister ships: **Jamaica Pioneer** and **Jamaica Producer.**

Jamaique   (1922)   Chargeurs Reunis.
Built by Swan, Hunter & Wigham Richardson, Ltd., Newcastle, England. Tonnage: 10,123. Dimensions: 484' x 59'.
Twin-screw, 15 knots. Steam turbines. Two masts and one
funnel. Launched, September 3, 1921. Vessel was purchased

from Cie de Navigation Sud Atlantique in May 1928.
Reconditioned in 1947.   Scrapped in 1954.   **Ex-Mosella**
(1928). Sister ship: **Kerguelen.**

Jerome   (1877)   Booth Line.
Built by Robert Napier & Sons, Glasgow, Scotland. Tonnage:
3,056.   Dimensions: 348' x 39'.   Single-screw, 12 knots.
Compound engines.   Triple expansion engines installed in
1891.   Two masts and one funnel. Iron hull. Sold to Turkey
in 1911.   Renamed: (a) **Kerasounde** (1911), (b) **Kiresson**
(1924). Scrapped in 1926. **Ex-Warwick Castle** (1897).

John Elder   (1870)   Pacific Steam Navigation Co.
Built by John Elder & Co., Glasgow, Scotland.   Tonnage:
4,151.   Dimensions: 406' x 41'.   Single-screw, 14 knots.
Compound engines. Three masts and two funnels. Iron hull.
Vessel later in service of the Orient Line to Australia. Lost
on the Chilean coast, January 16, 1877. Ships of this general
class were: **Aconcagua, Britannia, Chimborazo, Cotopaxi, Cuzco, Galicia, Garonne, Iberia, Illimani, Liguria, Lusitania, Potosi, Sorata, Tacora** and **Valparaiso.**

*Juan de Garay   (1928)   Argentina State Line.
Built by Bremer Vulkan Co., Vegesack, Germany. Tonnage:
8,723.   Dimensions: 458' x 60'.   Twin-screw, 15½ knots.
Motorship.   Two masts and two funnels.   **Ex-Olympia**
(1947), ex-**Puebla** (1947), ex-**Orinoco** (1941).

Justin   (1880)   Booth Line.
Built by A. Hall & Co., Aberdeen, Scotland. Tonnage: 1,822.
Dimensions: 278' x 34'.   Single-screw.   Compound engines.
Two masts and one funnel. Iron hull. Not many passengers.
Wrecked, July 28, 1905.   **Ex-Ponca.**

Justin   (1904)   Booth Line.
Built by Barclay, Curle & Co., Glasgow, Scotland. Tonnage:
3,498.   Dimensions: 355' x 48'.   Single-screw, 11 knots.
Triple expansion engines. Two masts and one funnel.   In
1913 she carried 16 first-class and 100 steerage passengers.
Out of service by 1932.

Kanagawa Maru   (1896)   N.Y.K. Line (Japanese).
Tonnage: 6,151. In 1904 she had inaugurated service from
Japan to South America, via South Africa.   Passengers:
29 first, 20 second, 175 third. *Note: See PART II for details.*

Karlsruhe (1889) North German Lloyd.
Tonnage: 5,057. In service to South America. *Note: See PART I for details.*

Karnak (1926) Hamburg-American Line.
Built by Flensburger Schiffsb. Ges., Flensburg, Germany. Tonnage: 7,209. Dimensions: 439' x 55'. Single-screw, 12 knots. Triple expansion engines. Two masts and one funnel. Service: Germany-West Indies. Note: Vessel acquired from Kosmos Line in 1926. As the German Navy supply ship **Hermes** she was scuttled by crew to escape capture, when overtaken in South Atlantic by the P. & O. liner **Canton** in 1941.

Kerguelen (1922) Chargeurs Reunis.
Built by Swan, Hunter & Wigham Richardson, Ltd., Newcastle, England. Tonnage: 10,123. Dimensions: 484' x 59'. Twin-screw, 15 knots. Steam turbines. Two masts and one funnel. Launched, September 30, 1920. Scrapped in Belgium, 1955. Ex-**Meduana** (1928). Sister ship: **Jamaique.**

Klipfontein (1939) Holland-Africa Line.
Tonnage: 10,544. In South American service. *Note: See PART IV for details.*

Koln (1921) North German Lloyd.
Built by Bremer Vulkan, Vegesack, Germany. Tonnage: 9,264. Dimensions: 474' x 60'. Single-screw, 12½ knots. Triple expansion engines. Four masts and one funnel. In South American service. Not listed in 1940.

Konig Friedrich Auguste (1906) Hamburg-American Line.
Tonnage: 9,462. In South American service. *Note: See PART I for details.*

Konig Wilhelm I (1870) North German Lloyd.
Tonnage: 2,453. *Note: See PART I for details.*

Konig Wilhelm II (1907) Hamburg-American Line.
Tonnage: 9,410. *Note: See PART I for details.*

Kosciuszko (1915) Gydnia-American Line.
Tonnage: 6,598. *See PART I for details.*

Krakus (1907) Chargeurs Reunis.
Built by Swan, Hunter & Wigham Richardson, Ltd., Wallsend, England. Tonnage: 8,327. Dimensions: 483' x 56'. Twin-screw, 14 knots. Triple expansion engines. Two masts

and one funnel. Note: Renamed **Krakus** in 1928 for a new
Gdynia-South American service. Ex-**Malte** (1928).

Kronprinz Friedrich Wilhelm   (1871)   North German Lloyd.
Built by Caird & Co., Greenock, Scotland. Tonnage: 2,387.
Dimensions: 318′ x 39′. Single-screw, 12 knots. Inverted
type engines. Compound engines installed in 1875. Then in
1887 quadruple expansion engines replaced the compounds.
Two masts and one funnel. Commenced her maiden voyage
Bremen-Southampton-Panama, April 7, 1871. Disposed of
in 1897–98. Sister ship: **Graf Bismarck.**

Kronprinzessin Cecilie   (1905)   Hamburg-American Line.
Built by Frd. Krupp Akt. Ges., Kiel, Germany. Tonnage:
8,689.   Dimensions: 471′ x 55′.   Twin-screw, 16 knots.
Quadruple expansion engines. Two masts and one funnel.
Fitted with two elevators. One of the finest liners in the
Latin American service of that day. Designed for the South
American trade. Later shifted to the West Indies service.
Served as a cruise ship in 1910. Renamed: **Princess.**

L'Atlantique   (1931)   Compagnie Sud-Atlantique (French).
Built by Chantiers & Ateliers de St. Nazaire (Penhoet), St.
Nazaire, France. Tonnage: 42,512. Dimensions: 713′ x 91′
(742′ o.l.). Quadruple-screw, 23 knots. Twelve steam turbines. Two masts and three funnels. A very impressive
looking liner. Badly gutted by fire in the English Channel,
January 4, 1933, with the loss of 17 of her crew. No passengers were on board at time of the disaster. The vessel was
towed to Havre, France, where she remained tied up to her
pier until 1936, at which time she was towed to Scotland and
broken up for scrap.

La Coruna   (1921)   Hamburg-South American Line.
Built by Reiherstieg Schiffsw., Hamburg, Germany. Ton-
nage: 7,359. Dimensions: 414′ x 55′. Single-screw, 12 knots.
Triple expansion engines.   Two masts and one funnel.
Scuttled east of Iceland to avoid capture by **H.M.S. Maloja,**
April 13, 1940. Sister ships: **Espana** and **Vigo.**

La France   (1871)   Transport Maritimes (French).
Built by Forges & Chantiers de la Mediterranee, La Seyne,
France. Tonnage: 3,572. Dimensions: 426′ x 37′. Single-
screw. Compound engines. Triple expansion engines in-
stalled in 1887. Two masts and two funnels. Iron hull.
Scrapped in 1895.

La Grande Duchesse   (1896)   The Plant Line.
Built by Newport News Shipbuilding & Drydock Co., Newport News, Virginia. Tonnage: 5,018. Dimensions: 381' x 47'. Twin-screw, 20 knots. Quadruple expansion engines. Two masts and one funnel. Services: (a) Boston-Nova Scotia, (b) New York-Charleston, South Carolina, (c) West Indies. Note: One of the first liners ever fitted with a complete telephone system connecting her staterooms. Renamed: (a) **City of Savannah** (1899), (b) **Carolina** (1914). Sunk by a German submarine, June 2, 1918.

La Plata   (1852)   Royal Mail Line (British).
Built by Robert Steele & Co., Greenock, Scotland. Tonnage: 2,404. Dimensions: 285' x 40' (314' o.l.). Paddle-wheels, 12½ knots. Side lever engines. Four boilers. 1,000 H.P. Two masts and two funnels. Launched in December 1851. Had a top speed of 14.35 knots. Commenced her maiden voyage from Southampton, August 17, 1852. Passengers: 116 first and 20 second-class. Crew: 115. Note: She was being built for the Cunard Line, but before completion was purchased by the Royal Mail Line. Considered one of the finest ships in their service of that era. Disposed of in 1871. Ex-**Arabia.**

La Plata   (1882)   Royal Mail Line (British).
Built by J. & G. Thomson, Ltd., Glasgow, Scotland. Tonnage: 4,464. Dimensions: 420' x 45'. Single-screw, 16 knots. Triple expansion engines. Two masts and two funnels. Renamed: **The Viking** (1908). Scrapped in Holland, 1913. Ex-**Moor** (1901).

La Plata   (1889)   Messageries Maritimes.
Built by Messageries Maritimes, La Ciotat, France. Tonnage: 5,807. Dimensions: 462' x 45'. Single-screw, 16½ knots. Triple expansion engines. Three masts and two funnels. In South American service until 1903. Renamed: **Nera** (1903). Scrapped in Italy, 1923. Sister ship: **Bresil.**

La Plata   (1896)   Royal Mail Line (British).
Built by Robert Napier & Sons, Ltd., Glasgow, Scotland. Tonnage: 3,445. Dimensions: 345' x 44'. Single-screw, 12 knots. Triple expansion engines. Two masts and two funnels. Renamed: (a) **Clement** (1900), (b) **Freshfield.** Torpedoed and sunk, August 5, 1918. Sister ships: **Ebro** and **Minho.**

La Plata   (1898)   Hamburg-South American Line.
Built by Reiherstieg Schiffsw., Hamburg, Germany. Tonnage: 4,032. Dimensions: 361' x 44'. Single-screw, 12 knots.

Triple expansion engines. Surrendered to Great Britain in 1919. Resold to Germany in 1922. Renamed: **Guine** (Portuguese). Ex-**Pelotas**. Running mate: **Antonina**.

La Plata　(1922)　Hamburg-South American Line.
Built by Bremer "Vulkan", Vegesack, Germany. Tonnage: 8,109. Dimensions: 468′ x 58′. Single-screw, 12½ knots. Triple expansion engines. Four masts and one funnel. Sunk by United States air attack off Bodo, Norway, April 4, 1943. She was later broken up for scrap. Ex-**Sachsen** (1937).

Lady Drake　(1929)　Canadian National Line.
Built by Cammell, Laird & Co., Birkenhead, England. Tonnage: 7,985. Dimensions: 419′ x 59′. Twin-screw, 14 knots. Steam turbines. Two masts and one funnel. Torpedoed and sunk by submarine, May 5, 1942. Sister ships: **Lady Hawkins, Lady Nelson, Lady Rodney** and **Lady Somers.**

Lady Hawkins　(1929)　Canadian National Lines.
Built by Cammell, Laird & Co., Birkenhead, England. Tonnage: 7,988. Dimensions: 419′ x 59′. Twin-screw, 14 knots. Steam turbines. Two masts and one funnel. Torpedoed and sunk by submarine, January 19, 1942. Sister ships: **Lady Drake, Lady Nelson, Lady Rodney** and **Lady Somers.**

Lady Nelson　(1928)　Canadian National Lines.
Built by Cammell, Laird & Co., Birkenhead, England. Tonnage: 7,970. Dimensions: 419′ x 59′. Twin-screw, 14 knots. Steam turbines. Two masts and one funnel. Renamed: **Gumhuryat Misr** (1953). Sister ships: **Lady Drake, Lady Hawkins, Lady Rodney** and **Lady Somers.**

Lady Rodney　(1929)　Canadian National Lines.
Built by Cammell, Laird & Co., Birkenhead, England. Tonnage: 8,194. Dimensions: 420′ x 60′. Twin-screw, 14 knots. Steam turbines. Two masts and one funnel. Renamed: **Mecca** (1953). Sister ships: **Lady Drake, Lady Hawkins, Lady Nelson** and **Lady Somers.**

Lady Somers　(1929)　Canadian National Lines.
Built by Cammell, Laird & Co., Ltd., Birkenhead, England. Tonnage: 8,194. Dimensions: 420′ x 59′. Twin-screw, 14 knots. Four steam turbines geared to 2 screw shafts. Two masts and one funnel. Torpedoed and sunk in the Caribbean, July 21, 1941, with the loss of 250 lives. Sister ships: **Lady Drake, Lady Hawkins, Lady Nelson** and **Lady Rodney.**

*Laennec (1951) Chargeurs Reunis.
Built by Ateliers & Chantiers de la Loire, St. Nazaire, France.
Tonnage: 12,003. Dimensions: 502' x 64'. Twin-screw, 17
knots. Motorship. Two masts and one funnel. Passengers:
92 first and 326 second. Sister ship: **Charles Tellier.**

Lanfranc (1884) Booth Line.
Built by T. Royden & Sons, Liverpool, England. Tonnage:
1,657. Dimensions: 280' x 34'. Single-screw. Compound
engines. Two masts and one funnel. Renamed: (a) **Olympia,**
(b) **Plan de Guadeloupe,** (c) **St. Charles.**

Lanfranc (1907) Booth Line.
Built by Caledon Shipbuilding & Engine Co., Dundee, Scotland. Tonnage: 6,287. Dimensions: 418' x 52' (433' o.l.).
Twin-screw, 14 knots. Triple expansion engines. Two masts
and one funnel. Passengers: 199 first and 372 third. Torpedoed and sunk 42 miles from Havre, while being used as
a hospital ship, April 17, 1917, with the loss of five lives.
Sister ships: **Antony** and **Hilary.**

ᵉLavoisier (1948) Chargeurs Reunis.
Built by Ateliers & Chantiers de la Loire, St. Nazaire, France.
Tonnage: 11,965. Dimensions: 515' x 64' (538' o.l.). Twin-
screw, 17 knots. Motorship. Two masts and one funnel.
Passengers: 100 first and 226 second-class. Service: North
Europe-Brazil-River Plate ports. Sister ships: **Claude
Bernard** and **Louis Lumiere.**

Leerdam (1921) Holland-America Line.
Tonnage: 8,815. In West Indies service. *Note: See PART I
for details.*

Leonardo da Vinci (1925) Transatlantica Italiana.
Tonnage: 7,432. In South American service. *Note: See
PART I for details.*

Les Alpes (1882) Transport Maritimes (French).
Built by Harland & Wolff, Ltd., Belfast, Ireland. Tonnage:
4,164. Dimensions: 420' x 42'. Single-screw, 12 knots.
Compound engines. Four masts and one funnel. Scrapped
in France, 1910. Ex-**British Princess** (1895). Sister ship:
Les Andes.

Les Andes (1882) Transport Maritimes (French).
Built by Harland & Wolff, Ltd., Belfast, Ireland. Tonnage:
4,150. Dimensions: 420' x 42'. Single-screw, 12 knots.
Compound engines. Four masts and one funnel. Scrapped

in France, 1910. Ex-**British Prince** (1895). Sister ship: **Les Alpes.**

Liban (1882) Fraissinet & Co. (French).
Built by Robert Napier & Sons, Glasgow, Scotland. Tonnage: 2,268. Dimensions: 300' x 36'. Single-screw, 12 knots. Compound engines. Iron hull. In South American service.

*Liberstad (1950) Flota Argentina de Navegacion de Ultramar.
Built by Vickers-Armstrongs, Ltd., Newcastle, England. Tonnage: 12,653. Dimensions: 509' x 71' (530' o.l.). Twin-screw, 18½ knots. Steam turbines. Two masts and one funnel. Service: Buenos Aires-London. Ex-**17 de Octubre** (1955). Sister ships: **Argentina** and **Uruguay.**

Liger (1896) Compagnie Sud Atlantique (French).
Built by Fairfield Shipbuilding Co., Glasgow, Scotland. Tonnage: 5,562. Dimensions: 425' x 50'. Single-screw, 13 knots. Triple expansion engines. Four masts and one funnel. Scrapped in Italy, 1923. Ex-**Tintagel Castle** (1912). Sister ship: **Garonna.**

Liguria (1874) Pacific Steam Navigation Co.
Built by John Elder & Co., Glasgow, Scotland. Tonnage: 4,677. Dimensions: 424' x 45'. Single-screw, 15 knots. Triple expansion engines. Three masts and two funnels. Clipper bow. Iron hull. Later transferred to the service to Australia. Scrapped in 1903. Sister ships: **Iberia** and **Potosi.**

Liguria (1901) Navigazione Generale Italiana.
Tonnage: 5,127. In South American service. *Note: See PART I for details.*

Lima (1851) Pacific Steam Navigation Co.
Built in Glasgow, Scotland. Tonnage: 1,461. Dimensions: 249' x 29'. Paddle-wheels. Two masts and two funnels. Iron hull. Clipper bow. Vessel was lost. Sister ships: **Bogota** and **Quito.**

Limburgia (1920) Royal Holland Lloyd.
Built by J. C. Tecklenborg, Wesermunde-G., Germany. Tonnage: 19,703. Dimensions: 592' x 72'. Triple-screw, 17 knots. Triple expansion engines and one low pressure steam turbine. Two masts and three funnels. In South American service. Renamed: **Reliance** (1922). Ex-**Johann Heinrich Burchard** (1920). Sister ship: **Brabantia.**

Lipari (1922) Chargeurs Reunis.
Built by Ateliers & Chantiers de la Loire, St. Nazaire, France. Tonnage: 9,954. Dimensions: 478' x 59'. Twin-screw, 13½ knots. Six steam turbines. Two masts and one funnel. Launched in September 1921. Sunk in Casablanca harbor, November 8, 1942. Sister ship: **Hoedic.**

Lombardia (1901) Navigazione Generale Italiana.
Tonnage: 5,127. In West Indies service. *Note: See PART I for details.*

*Louis Lumiere (1951) Chargeurs Reunis.
Built by Ateliers & Chantiers de St. Nazaire (Penhoet), St. Nazaire, France. Tonnage: 11,965. Dimensions: 515' x 64' (538' o.l.). Twin-screw, 17 knots. Motorship. Two masts and one funnel. Passengers: 110 first and 326 third. Commenced her maiden voyage from Havre to South America, October 18, 1952. Sister ship: **Claude Bernard.**

*Lucania (1930) Fratelli Grimaldi (Italian).
Built by Cammell, Laird & Co., Birkenhead, England. Tonnage: 6,723. Dimensions: 400' (o.l.) x 57'. Twin-screw, 20 knots. Steam turbines. Two masts and two funnels. Rebuilt in Italy, 1951–52. Service: Italy-Central America. Ex-**Charlton Sovereign** (1952), ex-**Prince Robert** (1948).

Lucerne (1878) Allan Line.
Tonnage: 1,925. Commenced her maiden voyage Glasgow to South America, September 27, 1878. Served much of her time in Glasgow-Quebec-Montreal service. *Note: See PART I for details.*

Luetzow (1908) North German Lloyd.
Tonnage: 8,826. *Note: See PART I for details.*

Luisiana (1906) Lloyd Italiano.
Tonnage: 4,983. In South American service. *Note: See PART I for details.*

Lusitania (1871) Pacific Steam Navigation Co.
Built by Laird Bros., Birkenhead, England. Tonnage: 3,912. Dimensions: 379' x 41'. Single-screw, 13 knots. Compound engines. Triple expansion engines installed in 1886. Three masts and one funnel. Clipper bow. Iron hull. Inaugurated the Orient Line's service to Australia from Plymouth, England, June 28, 1877, arriving at Melbourne, Australia, August 8th. Made the voyage in 40 days, six hours. Commenced her first Liverpool-Halifax-St. John, N. B. sailing

on March 31, 1900. Later was in Liverpool-Quebec-Montreal service. Wrecked near Cape Race, June 26, 1901, with no loss of life. Ships of this general class transferred to the new Australian service between 1877 and 1880 were: **Aconcagua, Chimborazo, Cotopaxi, Cuzco, Garonne, Iberia, John Elder, Liguria, Lusitania, Potosi** and **Sorata.**

Lutetia   (1913)   Compagnie Sud-Atlantique (French).
Built by Chantiers de la Atlantique, St. Nazaire, France. Tonnage: 14,783. Dimensions: 578' x 64'. Triple expansion engines and steam turbines. Two masts and three funnels. Passengers: 462 first, 130 second, 90 third, 450 fourth. Broken up for scrap in 1938. Sister ships: **Gallia** and **Massilia.**

Maasdam   (1921)   Holland-America Line.
Tonnage: 8,812. *Note: See PART I for details.* Built for Rotterdam-Cuba-Mexico.

Madeira   (1900)   Hamburg-South American Line.
Built by Flensburger Schiffsb. Ges., Flensburg, Germany. Tonnage: 6,003. Dimensions: 410' x 48'. Single-screw, 13 knots. Quadruple expansion engines. Two masts and one funnel. Renamed: **Raul Soares** (1925). Ex-**Cap Verde** (1922).

Madeirense   (1891)   Booth Line.
Built by Bonn & Nees, Rotterdam, Netherlands. Tonnage: 2,831. Dimensions: 332' x 40'. Single-screw, 12 knots. Triple expansion engines. Two masts and one funnel. Sold to Norwegian owners. Ex-**Dubbeldam** (1895).

Madrid   (1922)   Hamburg-South American Line.
Built by Vulcan Werke, Stettin, Germany. Tonnage: 8,753. Dimensions: 439' x 56'. Twin-screw, 13½ knots. Triple expansion engines. Two masts and two funnels. Vessel purchased from North German Lloyd in 1934. Sunk off Den Helder by Allied air attack, December 9, 1941. Ex-**Sierra Nevada.**

Magdalena   (1851)   Royal Mail Line (British).
Built by William Pitcher, Northfleet (On-the-Thames), England. Tonnage: 2,943. Paddle-wheels, 12 knots. Three masts and two funnels. Wooden hull. Out of fleet in 1866. Sister ships: **Orinoco** and **Parana.**

Magdalena   (1889)   Royal Mail Line (British).
Built by Robert Napier & Sons, Glasgow, Scotland. Tonnage: 5,373. Dimensions: 421' x 49'. Single-screw, 15 knots.

Triple expansion engines. Three masts and two funnels. Disposed of in 1921. Sister ship: **Atrato.**

Magdalena (1928) Hamburg-American Line.
Tonnage: 9,779. In West Indies service. *Note: See PART I for details.*

Magdalena (1949) Royal Mail Line (British).
Built by Harland & Wolff, Ltd., Belfast, Ireland. Tonnage: 17,547. Dimensions: 551' x 73' (570' o.l.). Twin-screw, 18 knots. Six steam turbines. Two masts and one funnel. Completed in February 1949. Third vessel in Royal Mail Line to have this name. Passengers: 480; crew, 224. During maiden voyage from England to South America, she grounded on a reef a few miles from Rio de Janeiro, April 25, 1949. All the passengers and much of the cargo were saved, but the ship broke in half on April 26th, after refloating, and the bow half sank. She became a total loss. The liner had been insured for 2,500,000 pounds sterling.

Magellan (1868) Pacific Steam Navigation Co.
Built by Randolph, Elder & Co., Glasgow, Scotland. Tonnage: 2,856. Dimensions: 359' x 41'. Single-screw. Compound engines. Iron hull. Scrapped in England, 1893. Sister ships: **Araucania, Cordillera** and **Patagonia.**

Magellan (1893) Pacific Steam Navigation Co.
Built by Harland & Wolff, Ltd., Belfast, Ireland. Tonnage: 3,590. Dimensions: 360' x 43'. Single-screw, 13½ knots. Triple expansion engines. Two masts and one funnel. Torpedoed and sunk in July 1918, with loss of one life. Sister ships: **Antisiana, Inca** and **Sarmiento.**

Magellan (1897) Messageries Maritimes.
Built by Messageries Maritimes, La Ciotat, France. Tonnage: 6,357. Dimensions: 446' x 50'. Twin-screw, 19½ knots. Triple expansion engines. Two masts and single funnel. Originally had two funnels and three masts. Launched, August 29, 1897. Renamed **Magellan** in 1904 when transferred from Far East trade to South American service. Reverted back to Far East service in 1912. Sunk by submarine in Mediterranean, December 11, 1916. Ex-**Indus** (1904).

Magellan (1913) Pacific Steam Navigation Co.
Built by J. C. Tecklenborg, Geestemunde, Germany. Tonnage: 6,706. Dimensions: 461' x 59'. Single-screw. Quad-

ruple expansion engines. Four masts and one funnel. Ex-**Alda**.

Maipu (1951)   Dodero Line (Argentine).
Built by N. V. Konink. Maats "De Schelde", Flushing, Netherlands. Tonnage: 11,500. Dimensions: 480' x 64'. (523' o.l.). Twin-screw, 17 knots. Motorship. Two masts and one funnel. Sunk not long after going into Buenos Aires-North Europe service, off the mouth of the River Weser, after collision with an American transport in November 1951. Sister ships: **Alberto Dodero** and **Yapeyu**.

Malte (1907)   Chargeurs Reunis.
Built by Swan, Hunter & Wigham Richardson, Ltd., Newcastle, England. Tonnage: 8,213. Dimensions: 483' x 56'. Twin-screw, 14 knots. Triple expansion engines. Two masts and one funnel. Launched, May 30, 1907. Renamed **Krakus** for new service between Gdynia and South America in August 1928. Scrapped in 1934. Sister ship: **Ceylan**.

Manchuria (1904)   Panama-Pacific Line.
Tonnage: 13,639. In New York-Panama-California service. *Note: See PART II for details.*

Manco (1908)   Booth Line.
Built by Scott's Shipbuilding & Engine Co., Greenock, Scotland. Tonnage: 2,984. Dimensions: 300' x 45'. Single-screw, 12 knots. Triple expansion engines. Two masts and one funnel. Passengers: 62 first and 92 third-class. Operated by Iquitos Steamship Company, subsidiary of the Booth Line. Vessel sold to Standard Fruit Co. Renamed: **Morazan**.

Manila Maru (1915)   Osaka Shosen Line (Japanese).
Tonnage: 9,518. In South American service. *Note: See PART II for details.*

Manistee (1904)   Elders & Fyffes, Ltd.
Built by Swan, Hunter & Wigham Richardson, Ltd., Newcastle, England. Tonnage: 3,869. Dimensions: 350' x 46'. Single-screw, 12 knots. Triple expansion engines. Torpedoed and sunk in 1917.

Manzanares (1911)   Elders & Fyffes, Ltd.
Built by Alexander Stephen & Sons, Ltd., Glasgow, Scotland. Tonnage: 4,094. Dimensions: 376' x 48'. Single-screw, 14 knots. Triple expansion engines. Two masts and one funnel. Renamed: **Vegesack** (1936).

Mar Del Plata   (1938)   Cie Maritime Belge.
Built by Soc. Anon. John Cockerill, Hoboken, Netherlands.
Tonnage: 7,340. Dimensions: 435' x 61' (459' o.l.). Single-
screw, 14 knots. Motorship. Two masts and one funnel.
Renamed: **Theodor Korner.**

Maracaibo   (1899)   Red "D" Line (American).
Built by Harlan & Hollingsworth Co., Wilmington, Delaware. Tonnage: 1,771. Dimensions: 267' x 37'. Twin-screw,
12 knots. Triple expansion engines. Two masts and one
funnel. Vessel sold to Cia Anonima de Navegacion de
Carenero. Scrapped at Puerto Cabello about 1951.

Marco Minghetti   (1876)   Navigazione Generale Italiana.
Built by J. & G. Thomson, Clydebank, Glasgow, Scotland.
Tonnage: 2,519. Dimensions: 350' x 36'. Single-screw, 13
knots. Triple expansion engines. Three masts and one
funnel. Iron hull. Navigazione Generale Italiana purchased
the vessel about 1888 for their service to South America.
In their Italy-New York trade during 1900–01. Ex-**Loudoun
Castle.**

***Marco Polo**   (1942)   Italia Line.
Built by Soc. Anon. Ansaldo, Genoa-Sestri, Italy. Tonnage:
8,949. Dimensions: 466' x 62' (484' o.l.). Single-screw, 15½
knots. Motorship. Two masts and one funnel. Launched
in 1942, but was not commissioned until August 1948.
Service: Italy-South America. Launched as **Nicolo Giani.**
Sister ships: **Amerigo Vespucci, Antoniotto Usodimare,
Sebastiano Caboto** and **Toscanelli.**

Marowijne   (1908)   K. N. S. M. Line.
Built by Workman, Clark & Co., Ltd., Belfast, Ireland.
Tonnage: 3,192. Dimensions: 339' x 42'. Single-screw, 13
knots. Triple expansion engines. Two masts and one
funnel. Vessel sold to Tropical Fruit Company about 1913.
Later was acquired by the United Fruit Company. Wrecked
in 1914. Class: **Coppename, Saramacca** and **Suriname.**

Martha Washington   (1908)   Cosulich Line.
Tonnage: 8,347. In Italy-South American service. *Note:
See PART I for details.*

Masaniello   (1904)   Peirce Brothers (Italian).
Built by Cantieri Nav. Siciliani, Palermo, Italy. Tonnage:
6,366. Dimensions: 391' x 52'. Single-screw. Triple expansion engines. Five masts and one funnel. Service: Italy-
South America. Ex-**Italia.**

Massilia   (1920)   Compagnie Sud-Atlantique (French).
Built by Forges & Chantiers de la Mediterranee, La Seyne, France. Tonnage: 15,363. Dimensions: 577' x 64'. Quadruple-screw, 20 knots.   Triple expansion engines and two low pressure steam turbines.   Two masts and three funnels. Scuttled by the Germans at Marseilles in August 1944; afterwards salved and broken up for scrap.   Sister ships: **Gallia** and **Lutetia.**   Outstanding French liners to South America of that era.

Matteo Bruzzo   (1882)   La Veloce Line (Italian).
Built by Forges & Chantiers, La Seyne, France.   Tonnage: 3,919.   Dimensions: 390' x 42'.   Single-screw, 12 knots. Compound engines.   Iron and steel hull.   In South American service.   Renamed: **Citta de Genova.**   Scrapped in 1907. Ex-**Golconde.**

Matura   (1901)   Trinidad Shipping & Trading Co., Ltd.
Built by Wm. Denny & Bros., Ltd., Dumbarton, Scotland. Tonnage: 4,550.   Dimensions: 376' x 48'.   Single-screw, 12 knots. Triple expansion engines. Two masts and one funnel. Ex-**Amarapoora.**

Medina   (1841)   Royal Mail Line (British).
Built by T. & J. White, Cowes, Great Britain.   Tonnage: 1,800.   Paddle-wheels, 8 knots.   Three masts and one funnel. Wooden hull.   Grounded on an uncharted reef near Turks Island, May 11, 1842, with no loss of life.   The vessel became a total loss.

Meduana   (1922)   Compagnie Sud-Atlantique (French).
Built by Swan, Hunter & Wigham Richardson, Ltd., Newcastle, England.   Tonnage: 10,123.   Dimensions: 484' x 59'. Twin-screw, 15 knots.   Steam turbines.   Two masts and one funnel.   Renamed: **Kerguelen.**   Sister ship: **Mosella.**

Medway   (1841)   Royal Mail Line (British).
Built by William Pitcher, Northfleet, England.   Tonnage: 1,895.   Paddle-wheels, 8 knots.   Three masts and one funnel. Speed later increased to 10 knots by making changes to the paddle-wheels.   Out of fleet in 1861.

Medway   (1877)   Royal Mail Line (British).
Built by John Elder & Co., Glasgow, Scotland.   Tonnage: 3,730.   Dimensions: 383' x 42'.   Single-screw, 13½ knots. Compound engines.   Triple expansion engines were installed at a later date.   Speed increased to 16 knots.   Three masts

and two funnels. Passengers: 232 first and 30 second-class. Scrapped in Holland, 1899.

Mendoza (1860) Messageries Maritimes.
Built by Forges & Chantiers de la Mediterranee, La Seyne, France. Tonnage: 2,577. Dimensions: 332' x 38'. Single-screw. Iron hull. Saved crew of Allan liner **Germany** wrecked near Gironde entrance in December 1872. Re-named **Mendoza** after being reconditioned and altered in 1872. Scrapped in 1891. Ex-**Estramadure** (1872).

Mendoza (1879) Pacific Steam Navigation Co.
Built by Robert Napier & Sons, Glasgow, Scotland. Tonnage: 2,160. Dimensions: 320' x 40'. Single-screw, 14 knots. Compound engines. Steel hull. First British merchant ship to be fitted with electric lights. Became a hulk in 1904. Sister ship: **Pizarro.**

Mendoza (1904) Lloyd Italiano.
Built by Armstrong, Whitworth & Co., Newcastle, England. Tonnage: 7,028. Dimensions: 420' x 51'. Twin-screw, 14 knots. Triple expansion engines. Two masts and one funnel. Built for the South American service. Renamed: (a) **Caserta** (1914), (b) **Venezuela** (1923). Scrapped in 1928.

Mendoza (1920) Transport Maritimes (French).
Built by Swan, Hunter & Wigham Richardson, Ltd., New-castle, England. Tonnage: 8,199. Dimensions: 450' x 58'. Twin-screw, 15 knots. Steam turbines. Two masts and two funnels. Sunk by German submarine off Durban in 1942. Sister ship: **Alsina.**

Mera (1901) Kosmos Steamship Co.
Built by C. Connell & Co., Glasgow, Scotland. Tonnage: 4,797. Dimensions: 374' x 48'. Single-screw, 12 knots. Triple expansion engines. Passengers: 26 first, 14 second, 30 third.

Merida (1906) Ward Line.
Built by W. Cramp & Sons Shipbuilding & E. B. Co., Philadelphia, Pa. Tonnage: 6,207. Dimensions: 400' x 50'. Twin-screw, 17 knots. Triple expansion engines. Two masts and two funnels. Sunk off Cape Charles by collision with the **Admiral Farragut,** May 12, 1911. Her 197 passengers and crew of 128 were saved. Sister ship: **Mexico.**

Merrimac (1861)   New York & Brazil Steamship Co.
Built by H. Loring, Boston, Massachusetts. Tonnage: 2,199.
Dimensions: 260' x 39'. Single-screw, 12 knots. Compound
engines. Two masts and one funnel. Later changed to three
masts. Iron and wooden hull. Two vertical direct acting
engines. Sold in 1875. Wrecked on the rocks of Little Hope
Island, Nova Scotia, July 10, 1887. Sister ship: **Mississippi.**

Metapan (1909)   United Fruit Steamship Corp.
Built by Workman, Clark & Co., Ltd., Belfast, Ireland.
Tonnage: 5,011.   Dimensions: 379' x 50'.   Single-screw,
14 knots. Triple expansion engines. Two masts and one
funnel. Torpedoed and sunk in the Mediterranean-Black Sea
area, October 1, 1943. Sister ships: **Abangarez, Almirante,
Atenas, Carrillo, Cartago, Heredia, Parismina, Santa
Marta, Sixaola, Tivives, Turrialba** and **Zacapa.**

Mexico (1884)   Conpania Mexicana Transatlantica.
Built by Robert Napier & Sons, Glasgow, Scotland. Tonnage:
4,133.   Dimensions: 400' x 44'.   Single-screw, 14 knots.
Compound engines. Three masts and two funnels. Sister
ships: **Oaxaca** and **Tamaulipas.** This steamship line ran
a passenger ship service between Mexico and Spain during
the 1880's. It is not a little surprising to find a Mexican
company running such distinctive liners during that era.

Mexico (1899)   Ward Line.
Built by W. Cramp & Sons, Philadelphia, Pa.   Tonnage:
5,667.   Dimensions: 360' x 50' (374' o.l.). Twin-screw, 14
knots.   Triple expansion engines.   Two masts and two
funnels. Renamed: (a) **Colon,** (b) **Yukon.**

Mexico (1902)   Pacific Steam Navigation Co.
Built by Caird & Co., Greenock, Scotland. Tonnage: 5,549.
Dimensions: 400' x 52'. Twin-screw, 15½ knots. Triple
expansion engines. Two masts and one funnel. Torpedoed
and sunk, March 23, 1917. Sister ship: **California.**

Mexico (1906)   Ward Line.
Built by W. Cramp & Sons Shipbuilding Co., Philadelphia,
Pa. Tonnage: 6,207. Dimensions: 400' x 50'. Twin-screw,
17 knots. Triple expansion engines. Two masts and two
funnels. Later altered by having her two original funnels
replaced by a single one. Passengers: 189 first, 48 second,
24 third. Renamed: (a) **Aleutian,** (b) **Tradewind.** Broken
up for scrap in Belgium, 1956. Sister ship: **Meridan.**

Mexico (1932)   (a) Colombian Mail Line, (b) Ward Line.
   Built by Newport News Shipbuilding Co., Newport News,
   Virginia. Tonnage: 5,236. Dimensions: 385' x 57' (404' o.l.).
   Single-screw, 17 knots. Steam turbines. Two masts and one
   funnel. Renamed: **Istanbul** (1947) Turkish. Ex-**Colombia**
   (1938).

Mexico Maru (1910)   Osaka Line.
   Built by Mitsubishi Dockyard & Engine Works, Nagasaki,
   Japan. Tonnage: 6,064. Dimensions: 407' x 49'. Twin-screw,
   13 knots. Triple expansion engines. Two masts and one
   funnel. Sunk by American submarine, August 29, 1944.
   Sister ships: **Canada Maru, Chicago Maru, Panama
   Maru, Seattle Maru** and **Tacoma Maru.**

Minas Geraes (1910)   Lloyd Brasileiro.
   Built by Workman, Clark & Co., Belfast, Ireland. Tonnage:
   3,540. Dimensions: 340' x 45'. Twin-screw, 12 knots. Triple
   expansion engines. Two masts and one funnel. Renamed:
   Affonso Penna.

Minho (1872)   Royal Mail Line (British).
   Built by Barclay, Curle & Co., Glasgow, Scotland. Tonnage:
   2,540. Dimensions: 350' x 36'. Single-screw. Compound
   engines. Two masts and one funnel. Iron hull. Out of Royal
   Mail fleet in 1888. Wrecked in 1901. Ex-**Leopold II** (1874)
   Belgium. Sister ship: **Mondego.**

Minho (1896)   Royal Mail Line (British).
   Built by Robert Napier & Sons, Ltd., Glasgow, Scotland.
   Tonnage: 3,445.   Dimensions: 345' x 44'.   Single-screw,
   12 knots. Triple expansion engines. Two masts and one
   funnel. Renamed: (a) **Halifax** (1903), (b) **Montreal** (1912).
   Sister ships: **Ebro** and **La Plata.**

Monarch of Bermuda (1931)   Furness-Bermuda Line.
   Built by Vickers-Armstrongs, Ltd., Newcastle, England.
   Tonnage: 22,424.   Dimensions: 553' x 76' (579' o.l.).
   Quadruple-screw, 19 knots. Turbo-electric. Two masts and
   three funnels. This New York-Bermuda liner was gutted
   by fire on the Tyne in March 1947, while being reconditioned
   after war service. She was later rebuilt as an emigrant ship.
   Renamed: **New Australia.** Sister ship: **Queen of Bermuda.**

Mondego (1874)   Royal Mail Line (British).
   Built by Tod & McGregor, Glasgow, Scotland. Tonnage:
   2,564. Dimensions: 350' x 36'. Single-screw. Compound

engines. Two masts and one funnel. Iron hull. Purchased in 1874. Out of fleet in 1888. Ex-**Santiago.** Sister ship: **Minho.**

Mongolia   (1904)   Panama-Pacific Line.
Tonnage: 13,639. In New York-Panama-California service. *Note: See PART II for details.*

Monte Cervantes   (1927)   Hamburg-South American Line.
Built by Blohm & Voss, Hamburg, Germany. Tonnage: 13,913. Dimensions: 500' x 65'. Twin-screw, 15 knots. Motorship. Two masts and two funnels. Sunk after striking a rock in the Straits of Magellan, near Tierra del Fuego (Beagle Channel), January 22–23, 1930. The Captain of the liner was lost. Sister ships: **Monte Olivia, Monte Pascoal, Monte Rosa** and **Monte Sarmiento.**

Monte Olivia   (1924)   Hamburg-South American Line.
Built by Blohm & Voss, Hamburg, Germany. Tonnage: 13,625. Dimensions: 500' x 65'. Twin-screw, 14½ knots. Motorship. Two masts and two funnels. Damaged by air attack at Kiel on April 3, 1945, while serving as hospital ship. She subsequently capsized. The wreck was broken up for scrap in 1948. Sister ships: **Monte Cervantes, Monte Pascoal, Monte Rosa** and **Monte Sarmiento.**

Monte Pascoal   (1930)   Hamburg-South American Line.
Built by Bremer Vulkan, Vegesack, Germany. Tonnage: 13,870. Dimensions: 500' x 65'. Twin-screw, 14½ knots. Motorship. Two masts and two funnels. Accommodation for 1,800 passengers. Damaged by fire in air attack on Hamburg in February 1944. The burned out liner was scuttled by British wreck disposal group, December 31, 1946, in Skagerrak. Sister ships: **Monte Cervantes, Monte Olivia, Monte Rosa** and **Monte Sarmiento.**

Monte Rosa   (1930)   Hamburg-South American Line.
Built by Bremer Vulkan, Vegesack, Germany. Tonnage: 13,882. Dimensions: 500' x 65' (524' o.l.). Twin-screw, 14½ knots. Motorship. Two masts and two funnels. Served as a hospital ship during World War II. Taken as war prize at Copenhagen in May 1945. The British renamed her **Empire Windrush** in 1946. She was then put under the management of New Zealand Shipping Company, and used as a troopship. The **Empire Windrush** caught fire 32 miles off Cape Caxine on March 28, 1954. The ship was gutted and sank while in tow on the 29th. Sister ships: **Monte Cervantes, Monte Olivia, Monte Pascoal** and **Monte Sarmiento.**

Monte Sarmiento   (1924)   Hamburg-South American Line.
Built by Blohm & Voss, Hamburg, Germany. Tonnage:
13,625. Dimensions: 500′ x 65′. Twin-screw, 14½ knots.
Motorship. Two masts and two funnels. Damaged at Kiel
in air attack, February 26, 1942. Subsequently broken up
for scrap at Hamburg. Sister ships: **Monte Cervantes,
Monte Olivia, Monte Pascoal** and **Monte Rosa.**

Monte Udala   (1948)   Naviera Aznar Soc. Anon. (Spanish).
Built by Cia Euskalduna de Constr., Bilbao, Spain. Tonnage: 10,170. Dimensions: 464′ x 62′ (487′ o.l.). Single-screw,
17½ knots. Motorship. Two masts and one funnel. Passengers: First-class and tourist. Service: Europe-South
America.

Monte Ulia   (1952)   Naviera Aznar Soc. Anon. (Spanish).
Built by Soc. Espanola de Constr. Naval, Bilbao, Spain.
Tonnage: 10,123. Dimensions: 464′ x 62′ (487′ o.l.). Single-
screw, 18 knots. Motorship. Single mast and one funnel.
Service: Spain-West Indies. Ex-**Monasterio de El Escorial**
(1952).

Monte Urbasa   (1949)   Naviera Aznar Soc. Anon. (Spanish).
Built by Soc. Espanola de Constr. Naval, Bilbao, Spain.
Tonnage: 10,142. Dimensions: 464′ x 62′ (487′ o.l.). Single-
screw, 17 knots. Motorship. Two masts and one funnel.
Launched as **Ascorial.** Sister ship: **Monte Urquiola.**

Monte Urquiola   (1948)   Naviera Aznar Soc. Anon. (Spanish).
Built by Soc. Espanola de Constr. Naval, Bilbao, Spain.
Tonnage: 7,723. Dimensions: 464′ x 62′. Single-screw, 17
knots. Motorship. Two masts and one funnel. Passengers:
First-class and tourist. Launched as **Guadalupe.** Sister
ship: **Monte Urbasa.**

Monte Videan   (1887)   Allan Line.
Tonnage: In South American service. *Note: See PART I
for details.*

Monterey   (1901)   Ward Line.
Built by W. Cramp & Sons Shipbuilding Co., Philadelphia,
Pa. Tonnage: 4,702. Dimensions: 341′ x 47′. Twin-screw,
16 knots. Triple expansion engines. Two masts and two
funnels. No longer in commission, 1932. Sister ship:
Esperanza.

Moreno   (1872)   Chargeurs Reunis.
Built by Forges & Chantiers de la Mediterranee, La Seyne,
France. Tonnage: 1,971. Dimensions: 299′ x 34′. Single-

screw. Compound engines. Three masts and one funnel.
Lost on Maricas Islands, October 15, 1874.

Morro Castle   (1900)   Ward Line.
Built by W. Cramp & Sons Shipbuilding Co., Philadelphia,
Pa. Tonnage: 6,004. Dimensions: 400' x 50'. Twin-screw,
18 knots. Triple expansion engines. Two masts and two
funnels. Passengers: 104 first, 60 second, 44 third. Crew: 124.
Not listed in 1929.

Morro Castle   (1930)   Ward Line.
Built by Newport News Shipbuilding Co., Newport News,
Virginia. Tonnage: 11,520. Dimensions: 482' x 70' (508' o.l.).
Twin-screw, 21 knots. Two steam turbines connected to
electric motors. Two masts and two funnels. This luxury
liner was destroyed by fire off New Jersey, September 8,
1934, while bound from Havana to New York. The disaster
caused the loss of 91 passengers and 31 of the crew. Sister
ship: **Oriente.**

Mosella   (1922)   Compagnie Sud-Atlantique (French).
Built by Swan, Hunter & Wigham Richardson, Ltd., Newcastle, England. Tonnage: 10,123. Dimensions: 484' x 59'.
Twin-screw, 15 knots. Steam turbines. Two masts and one
funnel. Renamed: **Jamaique.** Sister ship: **Meduana.**

Moselle   (1871)   Royal Mail Line (British).
Built by John Elder & Co., Govan, Glasgow, Scotland.
Tonnage: 3,298. Dimensions: 358' x 41'. Single-screw.
Compound engines. Two masts and two funnels. Clipper
bow. Iron hull. Wrecked in 1891. Sister ship: **Tagus.**

Motagua   (1912)   Elders & Fyffes, Ltd.
Built by Swan, Hunter & Wigham Richardson, Ltd., New-
castle, England. Tonnage: 5,977. Dimensions: 410' x 51'.
Twin-screw, 14 knots. Triple expansion engines. Two masts
and one funnel. Scrapped in 1935. Ex-**Emil L. Boas** (1914)
Hamburg-American Line. Sister ship: **Changuinola.**

Mouzinho   (1907)   Companhia Colonial (Portuguese).
Built by Frd. Krupp, Kiel, Germany. Tonnage: 8,374.
Dimensions: 448' x 55'. Twin-screw, 12 knots. Quadruple
expansion engines. Two masts and one funnel. Sold to
Italian shipbreakers in December 1954. Ex-**Maria Cristina,**
ex-**Guglielmo Peirce,** ex-**Sueh,** ex-**Corcovado.**

Munargo (1921) Munson Line.
Built by New York Shipbuilding Corp., Camden, New
Jersey. Tonnage: 6,336. Dimensions: 413' x 57'. Single-
screw, 17 knots. Steam turbines. Two masts and one funnel.
Vessel was purchased by United Fruit Company in 1938,
and placed in their New York-Miami-Nassau-Havana
service. Renamed: **Thistle** (U. S. hospital ship). Scrapped
in United States, 1957.

Munorleans (1911) Munson Line.
Built by Bremer Vulkan, Vegesack, Germany. Tonnage:
4,418. Dimensions: 353' x 48'. Single-screw. Quadruple
expansion engines. In New York-South American service.
Scrapped in 1936. Ex-**General G. W. Goethals**, ex-
Grunewald.

Napoli (1870) La Veloce Line.
Built by Wigham Richardson, Newcastle, England. Tonnage: 2,009. Dimensions: 292' x 35'. Single-screw. Compound engines. Iron hull. In Italy-South American service.
Ex-**Colombo**, ex-**Expresso.**

Napolitan Prince (1889) Prince Line (British).
Built by Scott & Co., Greenock, Scotland. Tonnage: 2,900.
Dimensions: 363' x 42'. Single-screw, 15 knots. Triple
expansion engines. Two masts and one funnel. Renamed:
Manouba (Cie de Nav. Mixte). Ex-**Rei de Portugal.**

*Nassau (1923) Incres Nassau Line.
Built by Armstrong Whitworth & Co., Newcastle, England.
Tonnage: 15,044. Dimensions: 551' x 72' (573' o.l.). Twin-
screw, 17 knots. Six steam turbines. Two masts and one
funnel. Passengers: 614 in one class. Service: Cruise ship—
New York-Nassau trade. Ex-**Europa** (1951), ex-**Rimutaka**
(1950), ex-**Mongolia** (1938).

Navarre (1859) Messageries Maritimes.
Built by Forges & Chantiers de la Mediterranee, La Seyne,
France. Tonnage: 1,168. Dimensions: 316' x 38'. Paddle-
wheels. Two masts and one funnel. Clipper bow. Renamed:
Rio Grande (1872).

Nazario Sauro (1921) Transatlantica Italiana.
Tonnage: 8,150. In South American service. *Note: See
PART I for details.*

Neptunia   (1932)   (a) Cosulich Line, (b) Italia Line.
Built by Cantieri Riuniti Dell' Adriatico, Monfalcone, Italy.
Tonnage: 19,475. Dimensions: 555′ x 76′ (589′ o.l.). Twin-
screw, 19½ knots. Motorship. Two masts and one funnel.
In Italy-South American service. Later used in the Far
Eastern trade. Sunk by British submarine in Mediterranean
on August 18, 1941. Sister ship: **Oceania.**

Nerissa   (1926)   Furness-Bermuda West Indies Line.
Built by W. Hamilton & Co., Port Glasgow, Scotland. Tonnage: 5,583. Dimensions: 349′ x 54′. Single-screw. Triple
expansion engines. Two masts and one funnel. Torpedoed
and sunk by submarine, April 30, 1941.

Nerthe   (1874)   Messageries Maritimes.
Built by Alexander Stephen & Sons, Ltd., Glasgow, Scotland.
Tonnage: 3,527. Dimensions: 374′ x 39′. Single-screw, 14
knots. Compound engines. Two masts and two funnels.
Iron hull. Messageries Maritimes purchased the vessel in
1889. Scrapped at Marseilles in 1897. Ex-**Lessing.**

Neva   (1868)   Royal Mail Line (British).
Built by Caird & Co., Greenock, Scotland. Tonnage: 3,025.
Dimensions: 348′ x 40′. Single-screw, 12 knots. Compound
engines. Two masts and one funnel. Passengers: 272 first,
58 second, 42 third. Note: Built as **Rhein** for North German
Lloyd, but was purchased before completion. Out of Royal
Mail Line fleet in 1890.

New Northland   (1926)   Clarke Steamship Co., Ltd.
Built by Swan, Hunter & Wigham Richardson, Ltd., Newcastle, England. Tonnage: 3,445. Dimensions: 287′ x 47′.
Single-screw. Triple expansion engines. Two masts and one
funnel. Service: Canada-Jamaica-Haiti-Havana. Renamed:
Nuevo Dominicano. Capsized on November 27, 1953,
after being refloated. Ex-**Northland.**

Newport   (1880)   Ward Line.
Built by John Roach & Son, Chester, Pennsylvania. Tonnage: 2,735. Dimensions: 326′ x 38′. Single-screw, 13 knots.
Triple expansion engines. Two masts and one funnel. She
was later sold to Pacific Mail Steamship Company. Scrapped
in 1932.

Niagara   (1877)   Ward Line.
Built by John Roach & Son, Chester, Pennsylvania. Tonnage: 2,265. Dimensions: 294′ x 38′. Single-screw. Com-

pound engines. Two masts and one funnel. Vessel taken over by United States Government for war against Spain.

Niger   (1871)   Messageries Maritimes.
Built by Messageries Maritimes, La Ciotat, France. Tonnage: 3,726. Dimensions: 394' x 39'. Single-screw, 13 knots. Compound engines. Three masts and one funnel. Iron hull. Went ashore at Tschemieh, December 24, 1913. Sold for scrap in April 1914. Sister ship: **Senegal.**

Nile   (1870)   Royal Mail Line (British).
Built by Day, Summers & Co., Northam Ironworks, Southampton, England. Tonnage: 3,039. Dimensions: 369' x 40'. Single-screw. Compound engines. Two masts and one funnel. Clipper bow. Out of fleet in 1890. Ex-**Roman** (1890).

Nile   (1893)   Royal Mail Line (British).
Built by J. & G. Thomson, Ltd., Glasgow, Scotland. Tonnage: 5,946. Dimensions: 420' x 51'. Single-screw, 15 knots. Triple expansion engines. Three masts and two funnels. Steel hull. *Note: See PART II for further information.*

Nitokris   (1906)   (a) Kosmos Line, (b) Hamburg-American Line.
Built by Blohm & Voss, Hamburg, Germany. Tonnage: 6,150. Dimensions: 411' x 50'. Twin-screw, 12 knots. Triple expansion engines. Two masts and one funnel. Passengers: 48 first, 20 second, 44 third. Service: Germany-West Indies. Interned in Chile during First World War. Turned over to Great Britain in 1919. Resold to Kosmos Line in 1922. Acquired by Hamburg-American Line in 1926. Scrapped in 1932. Sister ships: **Radames** and **Rhodopis.**

Nivernais   (1882)   Transport Maritimes (French).
Built by Oswald & Co., Sunderland, England. Tonnage: 2,565. Dimensions: 325' x 37'. Single-screw. Compound engines. Three masts and one funnel. Iron hull. Purchased in 1901. Sunk by German submarine in 1918. Ex-**Sumatra** (Dutch). Sister ship: **Orleanais.**

Nord America   (1872)   La Veloce Line.
Built by Wigham Richardson & Co., Newcastle, England. Tonnage: 2,175. Dimensions: 314' x 35'. Single-screw. Compound engines. Service: Italy-South America. Wrecked in January 1883.

Nord America (1882) La Veloce Line.
Tonnage: 4,920. In Italy-South America service. *Note: See PART I for details.*

Norderney (1896) North German Lloyd.
Built by Wigham Richardson & Co., Newcastle, England. Tonnage: 5,497. Dimensions: 410′ x 50′. Single-screw, 10 knots. Quadruple expansion engines. Steel hull. Service: Germany-Cuba. Disposed of in 1916. Ex-**Elisabeth Rickmers** (1900). Running mates: **Borkum** and **Helgoland.**

North America (1862) United States & Brazil Mail Steamship Co.
Built by Jeremiah Simonson, Greenpoint, New York. Tonnage: 2,985. Dimensions: 252′ x 37′. Paddle-wheels, 13½ knots. Vertical beam engines. Two masts and one funnel. Wooden hull. Service: New York-Para-Rio de Janeiro. Made her first sailing to Brazil under charter in October 1865. Second voyage was under their ownership. Scrapped at Boston in 1879. Ex-**Fort Jackson** (1865), ex-**Union** (1863). Running mate: **South America.**

North Star (1930) Clarke Steamship Co.
Built by Cammell, Laird & Co., Birkenhead, England. Tonnage: 6,893. Dimensions: 366′ x 57′. Twin-screw, 22 knots. Six steam turbines. Two masts and three funnels. Renamed: **Empire Parkeston** (1946). Ex-**Prince Henry** (1937).

Northern Prince (1929) Furness-Prince Line.
Built by Lithgows, Ltd., Port Glasgow, Scotland. Tonnage: 10,917. Dimensions: 496′ x 64′ (516′ o.l.). Twin-screw, 16 knots. Motorship. Two masts and one funnel. Passengers: 100; crew: 120. Bombed and sunk by aircraft in Anti-Kithera Channel, Eastern Mediterranean, April 3, 1941. Sister ships: **Eastern Prince, Southern Prince** and **Western Prince.**

Nyassa (1906) Cia Nacional de Navigation Co.
Built by J. C. Tecklenborg, Wesermunde-G., Germany. Tonnage: 8,980. Dimensions: 462′ x 57′ (478′ o.l.). Twin-screw, 14 knots. Quadruple expansion engines. Two masts and one funnel. Scrapped in 1951. Ex-**Tras-os-Montes,** ex-**Bulow.**

Oakland (1929) Hamburg-American Line.
Built by Deutsche Werft, A. G., Hamburg, Germany. Tonnage: 6,757. Dimensions: 433′ x 59′. Single-screw, 14 knots.

Motorship. Two masts and one funnel. Service: Germany-West Indies-Central America. Sunk by Allied air attacks on Brest in 1944. Raised and rebuilt after war as **Alain L. D.** Sister ship: **Roda.**

Oaxaca   (1883)   Compania Mexicana Transatlantica.
Built by Robert Napier & Sons, Glasgow, Scotland. Tonnage: 4,133. Dimensions: 400' x 44'. Single-screw, 14½ knots. Triple expansion engines. Three masts and two funnels. Steel hull. Home port: Vera Cruz, Mexico. In service between Mexico and Spain during the 1880's. Renamed: **Duca di Galliera** (1887). Sister ships: **Mexico** and **Tamaulipas.**

Obidense   (1891)   Booth Line.
Built by T. Royden & Sons, Liverpool, England. Tonnage: 2,380. Dimensions: 300' x 37'. Single-screw, 13½ knots. Triple expansion engines. Two masts and one funnel. Renamed: **Cuneo** (Norwegian). Out of service in 1917.

Ocean Monarch   (1951)   Furness Withy Co., Ltd.
Built by Vickers-Armstrongs, Ltd., Newcastle, England. Tonnage: 13,654. Dimensions: 491' x 72' (516' o.l.). Twin-screw, 18 knots. Steam turbines. Single-mast and one funnel. Launched on July 27, 1950. Commenced her maiden voyage from New York to Bermuda, May 3, 1951. Passengers: 430 in one class. Service: New York-Bermuda; cruising to the West Indies.

Oceana   (1891)   Bermuda & Atlantic Line.
Built by Wm. Denny & Bros., Dumbarton, Scotland. Tonnage: 8,063. Dimensions: 531' x 54'. Twin-screw, 17 knots. Triple expansion engines. Two masts and two funnels. Formerly owned and operated by Hamburg-American Line under name of **Oceana.** Renamed: (a) **Alfonso XIII** (1916), (b) **Vasco Nunez de Balboa** (1923). Scrapped in 1927. Ex-**Scot** (1905).

Oceana   (1903)   Pacific Steam Navigation Co.
Built by Alexander Stephen & Sons, Ltd., Glasgow, Scotland. Tonnage: 7,814. Dimensions: 504' x 55'. Twin-screw, 15 knots. Triple expansion engines. Two masts and one funnel. Later altered to two funnels. Scrapped in 1924. Ex-**Miltiades** (1922). Sister ship: **Oruba.**

Oceania   (1932)   (a) Cosulich Line, (b) Italia Line.
Built by Cantieri Riuniti Dell' Adriatico, Monfalcone, Italy. Tonnage: 19,507. Dimensions: 556' x 76' (589' o.l.).

Quadruple-screw, 20½ knots. Motorship. Two masts and one funnel. In Italy-South American service. Later transferred to Far East trade. Sunk by British submarine in Mediterranean in 1941. Sister ship: **Neptunia.**

Odenwald (1922) Hamburg-American Line.
Built by Deutsche Werft A. G., Hamburg, Germany. Tonnage: 5,098. Dimensions: 399' x 54'. Twin-screw. Motorship. Service: Germany-West Indies. Renamed: (a) **Assuan** (1935), (b) **Odenwald** (1938). Captured by American cruisers off Porto Rico. Renamed: **Blenheim.** Scrapped in 1948.

Ohio (1923) Pacific Steam Navigation Co.
Built by Akt. Ges. "Weser", Bremen, Germany. Tonnage: 18,940. Dimensions: 590' x 72'. Twin-screw, 17 knots. Quadruple expansion engines. Two masts and two funnels. Renamed: **Albertic** (1927). Scrapped in Japan, 1934. Ex-**Munchen** (1923).

Oldenburg (1890) North German Lloyd.
Tonnage: 5,006. Interchangeable in New York, Baltimore and South American services from Germany. *Note: See PART I for details.*

Ontario (1868) American Steamship Company of Boston.
Built by Jackman of Newburyport, Massachusetts. Tonnage: 2,889. Dimensions: 325' x 43'. Single-screw, 11 knots. Vertical geared engines. Three masts and two funnels. Clipper bow. Wooden hull. Made only three voyages to Europe, after which she was employed in the New York-Brazil trade. Destroyed by fire in 1872. Sister ship: **Erie.**

Orania (1922) Royal Holland Lloyd.
Built by Workman, Clark & Co., Belfast, Ireland. Tonnage: 9,763. Dimensions: 450' x 59'. Twin-screw, 15 knots. Four steam turbines. Two masts and two funnels. Sunk after being in collision with the Portuguese steamer **Loanda,** December 19, 1934. Sister ship: **Flandria.**

Oranje Nassau (1911) Royal Netherlands Steamship Co.
Built by Kon. Maats. de Schelde, Flushing, Netherlands. Tonnage: 3,721. Dimensions: 338' x 44'. Single-screw, 12 knots. Triple expansion engines. Two masts and one funnel. Renamed: **Corinthia.** Scrapped in Italy, 1959.

437

*Oranje Nassau   (1957)   Royal Netherlands Steamship Co.
Built by Scheepsbouwwerf Gebroeders Pot, Bolnes, Nether-
lands.   Tonnage: 7,214.   Dimensions: 431' (o.l.) x 56'.
Single-screw, 15 knots.   Motorship.   Two masts and one
funnel.   Accommodation for 116 passengers in one class.
Service: Europe-Caribbean.   Sister   ship: **Prins der
Nederlanden.**

*Oranjestad   (1938)   Royal Netherlands Steamship Co.
Built by Van der Giessen, Krimpen, Netherlands.   Tonnage:
5,091.   Dimensions: 378' (o.l.) x 49'.   Single-screw, 14½
knots.   Motorship.   Two masts and one funnel.   This former
cargo vessel was converted to passenger ship in 1950.   Passengers: 94 in one class.   Service: Europe-Caribbean.   Sister
ship: **Willemstad.**

Oravia   (1897)   Pacific Steam Navigation Co.
Built by Harland & Wolff, Belfast, Ireland.   Tonnage:
5,321.   Dimensions: 421' x 48'.   Twin-screw, 15½ knots.
Triple expansion engines.   Two masts and one funnel.
Wrecked on Falkland Isles in November 1912.   Similar ships:
Orissa and **Oropesa.**

Orazio   (1927)   (a) Navigazione Generale Italiana, (b) Italia Line.
Built by Cantieri ed Officine, Meridionali, Baia, Italy.   Tonnage: 11,669.   Dimensions: 482' x 61' (506' o.l.).   Twin-screw,
14 knots.   Motorship.   Two masts and one funnel.   Passengers: 110 first, 190 second, 340 third.   Burned off French
coast in 1940.   Sister ship: **Virgilio.**

Orbita   (1915)   Pacific Steam Navigation Co.
Built by Harland & Wolff, Ltd., Belfast, Ireland.   Tonnage:
15,495.   Dimensions: 550' x 67' (569' o.l.).   Triple-screw, 15
knots.   Triple expansion engines and one low pressure steam
turbine.   Two masts and one funnel.   Passengers: 190 first,
221 second, 476 third.   Service: Liverpool and West coast of
South America.   Sold to British shipbreakers in 1950.   Sister
ships: **Orca** and **Orduna.**

Orca   (1918)   Pacific Steam Navigation Co.
Built by Harland & Wolff, Ltd., Belfast, Ireland.   Tonnage:
16,063.   Dimensions: 550' x 67'.   Triple-screw, 15 knots.
Triple expansion engines.   Two masts and one funnel.   In
trans-Atlantic service of the Royal Mail Line during 1923–27.
Renamed: **Calgaric** (1927).   Scrapped in 1935.   Sister ships:
Orbita and **Orduna.**

Orcana   (1893)   Pacific Steam Navigation Co.
Built by Harland & Wolff, Ltd., Belfast, Ireland. Tonnage: 4,821. Dimensions: 401' x 47'. Single-screw, 15½ knots. Triple expansion engines. Four masts and one funnel. Vessel sold in 1905. Renamed: **Albingia.** Sister ship: **Orellana.**

Orcoma   (1908)   Pacific Steam Navigation Co.
Built by Wm. Beardmore & Co., Ltd., Glasgow, Scotland. Tonnage: 11,580. Dimensions: 511' x 62'. Twin-screw, 14½ knots. Quadruple expansion engines. Two masts and one funnel. Passengers: 250 first-class. As a new vessel she had accommodation for 1,140 passengers, including 550 in third-class. Commenced her maiden voyage from Liverpool to South America on August 27, 1908. Broken up by British shipbreakers in 1933.

Orduna   (1914)   Pacific Steam Navigation Co.
Built by Harland & Wolff, Ltd., Belfast, Ireland. Tonnage: 15,507. Dimensions: 550' x 67'. Triple-screw, 15 knots. Triple expansion engines and steam turbine. Two masts and one funnel. In North Atlantic service of Royal Mail Line during 1923–1926. Scrapped at Dalmuir in 1951. Sister ships: **Orbita** and **Orca.**

Orellana   (1893)   Pacific Steam Navigation Co.
Built by Harland & Wolff, Ltd., Belfast, Ireland. Tonnage: 4,821. Dimensions: 401' x 47'. Single-screw, 15½ knots. Triple expansion engines. Four masts and one funnel. Vessel sold in 1905. Renamed: **Allemannia.** Sister ship: **Orcana.**

Orenoque   (1874)   Messageries Maritimes.
Built by Messageries Maritimes, La Ciotat, France. Tonnage: 3,833. Dimensions: 393' x 39'. Single-screw, 13½ knots. Compound engines. Three masts and one funnel. Iron hull. Launched, February 22, 1874. Built for the South American service; later transferred to Far East route. Sold for scrap to Saigon shipbreakers in February 1925. Sister ships: **Niger, Saghalien** and **Senegal.**

Oriana   (1906)   Pacific Steam Navigation Co.
Built by Barclay, Curle & Co., Glasgow, Scotland. Tonnage: 8,177. Dimensions: 465' x 56'. Twin-screw, 15 knots. Quadruple expansion engines. Two masts and one funnel. Broken up for scrap in 1927. Sister ships: **Oronsa** and **Ortega.**

Oriente   (1930)   Ward Line.
Built by Newport News Shipbuilding Co., Newport News, Virginia. Tonnage: 11,520. Dimensions: 482' x 70' (508' o.l.).

Twin-screw, 21 knots. Turbo-electric. Two masts and two funnels. Renamed: **Thomas H. Barry** (United States Government). Scrapped in 1957. Sister ship: **Morro Castle.**

Orinoco   (1851)   Royal Mail Line (British).
Built by William Pitcher, Northfleet, England. Tonnage: 2,901. Paddle-wheels, 12 knots. Three masts and two funnels. Wooden hull. Launched, May 17, 1851. Out of fleet in 1859. Sister ships: **Magdalena** and **Parana.**

Orinoco   (1886)   Royal Mail Line (British).
Built by Caird & Co., Ltd., Greenock, Scotland. Tonnage: 4,572. Dimensions: 409′ x 45′. Single-screw, 16 knots. Triple expansion engines. Three masts and two funnels. Reduced to two masts at later date. Scrapped in 1909.

Orinoco   (1928)   Hamburg-American Line.
Built by Bremer Vulkan, Vegesack, Germany. Tonnage: 9,660. Dimensions: 456′ x 61′ (480′ o.l.). Twin-screw, 15 knots. Motorship. Two masts and two funnels. Renamed: **Puebla,** (b) **Olympia,** (c) **Juan de Garay.** Note: Seized by Mexican Government in 1941 and renamed **Puebla.** Later she became the United States transport **Puebla.** Returned to Mexico in 1946. Soon after acquired by Argentine and renamed **Olympia.** Finally renamed **Juan de Garay.**

Orissa   (1895)   Pacific Steam Navigation Co.
Built by Harland & Wolff, Ltd., Belfast, Ireland. Tonnage: 5,360. Dimensions: 421′ x 48′. Twin-screw, 15½ knots. Triple expansion engines. Two masts and one funnel. Torpedoed and sunk without warning 21 miles from Skerryvore, June 25, 1918, with the loss of six lives. Same class: **Oravia** and **Oropesa.**

Orita   (1903)   Pacific Steam Navigation Co.
Built by Harland & Wolff, Ltd., Belfast, Ireland. Tonnage: 9,298. Dimensions: 485′ x 58′. Twin-screw, 16 knots. Quadruple expansion engines. Two masts and one funnel. Scrapped in 1932.

Orizaba   (1886)   Pacific Steam Navigation Co.
Built by Barrow Shipbuilding Co., Barrow, England. Tonnage: 6,298. Dimensions: 460′ x 49′. Single-screw, 16 knots. Triple expansion engines. Four masts and two funnels. Steel hull. Transferred to the Australian mail service of the Orient Line. Wrecked on February 17, 1905. Sister ship: **Oroya.**

Orizaba   (1890)   Ward Line.
Built by Delaware River Shipbuilding Co., Chester, Pennsylvania. Tonnage: 3,497. Dimensions: 336' x 43'. Single-screw, 14 knots. Triple expansion engines. Two masts and one funnel. Steel and iron hull. Passengers: 80 first and 30 second. Renamed: **Northwestern** (Alaska Steamship Co.). Sister ship: **Yumuri.**

Orizaba   (1918)   Ward Line.
Built by W. Cramp & Sons Shipbuilding Co., Philadelphia, Pa. Tonnage: 6,937. Dimensions: 423' x 60'. Twin-screw, 17 knots. Four steam turbines. Two masts and two funnels. Passengers: 306 first, 60 second, 64 third. During 1920 was in trans-Atlantic service. Became an American troopship in 1941. Renamed: **Duque de Caxias** (1946) Brazilian. Sister ship: **Siboney.**

Orleanais   (1882)   Transport Maritimes (French).
Built by John Elder & Co., Glasgow, Scotland. Tonnage: 2,602. Dimensions: 325' x 37'. Single-screw. Compound engines. Three masts and one funnel. Iron hull. Ex-**Lombok** (1903), ex-**Prinses Wilhelmina.**

Oronsa   (1906)   Pacific Steam Navigation Co.
Built by Harland & Wolff, Ltd., Belfast, Ireland. Tonnage: 8,067. Dimensions: 465' x 56'. Twin-screw, 14 knots. Quadruple expansion engines. Two masts and one funnel. Torpedoed and sunk 12 miles from Bardsey Island, April 28, 1918, with the loss of three lives. Sister ships: **Oriana** and **Ortega.**

Oropesa   (1895)   Pacific Steam Navigation Co.
Built by Harland & Wolff, Ltd., Belfast, Ireland. Tonnage: 5,364. Dimensions: 421' x 48'. Twin-screw, 15 knots. Triple expansion engines. Two masts and one funnel. Steel hull. Vessel sunk in 1917. Same class: **Oravia** and **Orissa.**

Oropesa   (1920)   Royal Mail Line (British).
Built by Cammell, Laird & Co., Birkenhead, England. Tonnage: 14,075. Dimensions: 530' x 66' (552' o.l.). Twin-screw, 14 knots. Steam turbines. Two masts and one funnel. Passengers: 141 first, 131 second, 360 third. Began trans-Atlantic crossings to New York in 1921. She was returned to Pacific Steam Navigation Company in 1923 and placed in regular South American service. Torpedoed and sunk in the North Atlantic by German submarine, January 16, 1941.

Orotava (1889) Pacific Steam Navigation Co.
Built by Naval Construction & Arm. Co., Barrow, England.
Tonnage: 5,858. Dimensions: 430' x 49'. Single-screw, 16
knots. Triple expansion engine. Four masts and two funnels.
(Altered later to two masts.) Steel hull. This liner was intended for the direct route to South America. However, she
was subsequently placed in service to Australia by the Orient
Line, with the cooperation of the Pacific Steam Navigation
Co. Vessel sold to Royal Mail Line in 1905, and used in their
service to South America. Sold to the British Admiralty in
1915. Sister ship: **Oruba.**

Oroya (1886) Pacific Steam Navigation Co.
Built by Barrow Shipbuilding Co., Barrow, England. Tonnage: 6,057. Dimensions: 460' x 49'. Single-screw, 16 knots.
Triple expansion engines. Four masts and two funnels. Steel
hull. Tonnage increased to 6,297 at later date. Launched
in September 1886. Commenced her maiden voyage from
London to South America, February 17, 1887. Scrapped in
1909. Sister ship: **Orizaba.**

Oroya (1923) Pacific Steam Navigation Co.
Built by Harland & Wolff, Ltd., Belfast, Ireland. Tonnage:
12,257. Dimensions: 525' x 62'. Twin-screw, 14 knots.
Steam turbines. Two masts and one funnel. Broken up for
scrap in Italy during 1939.

Ortega (1906) Pacific Steam Navigation Co.
Built by Harland & Wolff, Ltd., Belfast, Ireland. Tonnage:
8,058. Dimensions: 465' x 56'. Twin-screw, 15 knots.
Quadruple expansion engines. Two masts and two funnels.
Made a remarkable escape from the German cruiser **Dresden**
in 1914, during which she did 18 knots. Scrapped in Great
Britain in 1927. Sister ships: **Oriana** and **Oronsa.**

Ortona (1899) Pacific Steam Navigation Co.
Built by Vickers, Sons & Maxim, Ltd., Barrow, England.
Tonnage: 8,058. Dimensions: 498' x 55'. Twin-screw, 18
knots. Triple expansion engines. Two masts and two funnels.
She was later employed in the Orient Line service to Aus-
tralia. Sold to Royal Mail Line in 1905; renamed **Arcadian.**

Oruba (1889) Pacific Steam Navigation Co.
Built by Naval & Arm. Co., Ltd., Barrow, England. Ton-
nage: 5,857. Dimensions: 430' x 49'. Single-screw, 16 knots.
Triple expansion engines. Four masts and two funnels.
Altered to two masts at later date. Built for the South

442

American service. However, she was placed along with sister ship **Orotava** in Orient Line service to Australia in 1889. Liner was sold to Royal Mail Line in 1905. Vessel was sold in 1914. Sister ship: **Orotava.**

Oruba   (1903)   Pacific Steam Navigation Co.
Built by Alexander Stephen & Sons, Ltd., Glasgow, Scotland. Tonnage: 7,848. Dimensions: 504′ x 55′. Twin-screw, 15 knots. Triple expansion engines. Two masts and two funnels. In Royal Mail Line service, 1920–1924. Scrapped in 1924. Ex-**Marathon** (1922). Sister ship: **Orcana.**

Ouessant   (1908)   Chargeurs Reunis.
Built by Ateliers & Chantiers de la Loire, St. Nazaire, France. Tonnage: 8,685. Dimensions: 485′ x 56′. Twin-screw, 14 knots. Triple expansion engines. Two masts and one funnel. Launched, in February 1908. Renamed **Swiatovid** in August 1928 for new emigrant between Gdynia and South America. Scrapped in France, 1934. Sister ship: **Corse.**

Pacific   (1865)   Pacific Steam Navigation Co.
Built by Randolph, Elder & Co., Glasgow, Scotland. Tonnage: 1,631. Dimensions: 267′ x 40′. Paddle-wheels. Compound engines. Iron hull. Inaugurated Valparaiso-Liverpool service on May 13, 1868. Made the voyage from Chile to England in 43 days. Vessel was hulked about 1870.

Pampa   (1878)   Chargeurs Reunis.
Built by Forges & Chantiers de la Mediterranee, La Seyne, France. Tonnage: 3,021. Dimensions: 329′ x 39′. Single-screw, 12 knots. Compound engines. Two masts and one funnel. Scrapped in 1905. Sister ship: **Dom Pedro.**

Pampa   (1906)   Transport Maritimes (French).
Built by London & Glasgow Shipbuilding Co., Glasgow, Scotland. Tonnage: 4,471. Dimensions: 408′ x 47′. Twin-screw, 14 knots. Triple expansion engines. Two masts and one funnel. Served as a hospital ship in First World War. Sunk by submarine in the Mediterranean in 1918. Sister ship: **Parana.**

Pan America   (1921)   Munson Line.
Built by Bethlehem Shipbuilding Corp., Sparrow's Point, Maryland. Tonnage: 13,712. Dimensions: 517′ x 72′. Twin-screw, 17 knots. Steam turbines. Two masts and one funnel. In New York-South American service. Renamed: **Hunter**

Liggett. Scrapped in 1948. Ex-**Palmetto State**. Sister
ships: **American Legion, Southern Cross** and **Western
World**.

Panama   (1898)   Panama Railroad Co.
Built by W. Cramp & Sons Shipbuilding Co., Philadelphia,
Pa. Tonnage: 5,638. Dimensions: 360' x 50'. Twin-screw,
14 knots. Triple expansion engines. Two masts and two
funnels. Passengers: 166; crew 95. Renamed: **Aleutian**.
Struck a rock and sank, May 26, 1929. Ex-**Havana**. Sister
ship: **Colon**.

Panama   (1902)   Pacific Steam Navigation Co.
Built by Fairfield Shipbuilding Co., Glasgow, Scotland. Ton-
nage: 5,981. Dimensions: 401' x 52'. Twin-screw, 15½ knots.
Triple expansion engines. Two masts and one funnel.
Passengers: 130 first-class. She became the hospital ship
Maine in 1920. Scrapped in 1948. Sister ship: **Victoria**.

Panama   (1939)   Panama Railroad Co.
Built by Bethlehem Steel Co., Shipbuilding Division, Quincy,
Mass. Tonnage: 10,021. Dimensions: 474' x 64' (493' o.l.).
Twin-screw, 16½ knots. Steam turbines. Two masts and
one funnel. Passengers: 202. Renamed: (a) **James Parker,**
(b) **Panama,** (c) **President Hoover** (1957). Sister ships:
Ancon and **Cristobal**.

Panamanian   (1904)   Cia Transatlantica Centroamericana.
Built by New York Shipbuilding Co., Camden, N. J. Tonnage: 13,639. Dimensions: 600' x 65' (616' o.l.). Twin-screw,
16 knots. Quadruple expansion engines. Four masts and
one funnel. Scrapped at Shanghai in 1946. Ex-**President
Fillmore** (1940), ex-**Mongolia** (1923).

Pancras   (1911)   Booth Line.
Built by Hawthorn, Leslie & Co., Ltd., Newcastle, England.
Tonnage: 4,436. Dimensions: 376' x 50'. Single-screw, 11
knots. Triple expansion engines. Two masts and one funnel.
Passengers: 46 first and 100 third. Broken up for scrap in
1934. Class: **Aidan, Denis** and **Stephen**.

Paolo Toscanelli   (1948)   Italia Line.
Built by Soc. Anon. Ansaldo, Genoa-Sestri, Italy. Tonnage:
9,004. Dimensions: 466' x 62' (485' o.l.). Single-screw,
15½ knots. Motorship. Two masts and one funnel. Sister
ships: **Amerigo Vespucci, Marco Polo, Antoniotto
Usodimare** and **Sebastiano Caboto**.

Para (1873)   Royal Mail Line (British).
   Built by Laird Bros., Birkenhead, England. Tonnage: 4,028.
   Dimensions: 387' x 43'. Single-screw, 13½ knots. Compound
   engines. Three masts and two funnels. Altered to two masts
   at later date. Triple expansion engines installed in 1890.
   Speed increased to 17 knots. Passengers: 245 first and
   26 second. Scrapped at Cherbourg in 1903. Ex-**Puno** (1875).
   Sister ship: **Don.**

Paraense (1871)   Booth Line.
   Built by T. Royden & Sons, Liverpool, England. Tonnage:
   1,697. Dimensions: 270' x 33'. Single-screw, 12½ knots.
   Compound engines. Two masts and one funnel. Iron hull.
   Triple expansion engines installed in 1889. Renamed:
   (a) **Rosina** (1913), (b) **Omoa.**

Paraguay (1888)   Chargeurs Reunis.
   Built by Ateliers & Chantiers de la Loire, St. Nazaire, France.
   Tonnage: 3,563. Dimensions: 360' x 40'. Single-screw,
   13 knots. Triple expansion engines. Three masts and one
   funnel. Steel hull. Scrapped in 1908.

*Paraguay Star (1948)   Blue Star Line.
   Built by Cammell, Laird & Co., Birkenhead, England. Tonnage: 10,722. Dimensions: 478' x 68' (502' o.l.). Single-
   screw, 16 knots. Three steam turbines. Single mast and
   one funnel. Passengers: 70 first-class. Route: London-South
   America, via Lisbon. Sister ships: **Argentina Star, Brasil
   Star** and **Uruguay Star.**

Paramatta (1858)   Royal Mail Line (British).
   Built by Thames Ironworks, Blackwall, England. Tonnage:
   3,439. Paddle-wheels. Three masts and two funnels. Iron
   hull. Out of fleet in 1859.

Parana (1851)   Royal Mail Line (British).
   Built by M. Wigram, Southampton, England. Tonnage:
   2,943. Dimensions: 304' x 42'. Paddle-wheels, 12 knots.
   Three masts and two funnels. Wooden hull. Out of fleet
   in 1876. Sister ships: **Magdalena** and **Orinoco.**

Parana (1882)   Chargeurs Reunis.
   Built by Forges & Chantiers de la Mediterranee, Graville
   (Havre), France. Tonnage: 3,376. Dimensions: 347' x 40'.
   Single-screw, 13 knots. Compound engines. Two masts and
   one funnel. Iron hull. Vessel lost in fog at Cabo Frio, May 15,
   1892. Sister ships: **Rio Negro** and **Uruguay.**

Parana   (1904)   Royal Mail Line (British).
Built by Workman, Clark & Co., Belfast, Ireland. Tonnage: 4,182. Dimensions: 375′ x 48′. Single-screw. Triple expansion engines. Two masts and one funnel. Had a very tall funnel. Scrapped in 1933. Sister ship: **Pardo.**

Parana   (1908)   Transport Maritimes (French).
Built by Forges & Chantiers de la Mediterranee, La Seyne, France. Tonnage: 6,248. Dimensions: 420′ x 50′. Twin-screw, 14 knots. Triple expansion engines. Two masts and one funnel. Sunk by submarine in Mediterranean, 1918. Sister ship: **Pampa.**

Pardo   (1904)   Royal Mail Line (British).
Built by Harland & Wolff, Ltd., Belfast, Ireland. Tonnage: 4,454. Dimensions: 375′ x 48′. Single-screw. Triple expansion engines. Two masts and one funnel. Scrapped in 1934. Sister ship: **Parana.**

Parismina   (1908)   United Fruit Co.
Built by Workman, Clark & Co., Belfast, Ireland. Tonnage: 4,732. Dimensions: 378′ x 49′. Single-screw, 14 knots. Triple expansion engines. Two masts and one funnel. Vessel was chartered to States Steamship Company in 1932. Renamed: **General Sherman** (1932), **Parismina** (1938). Torpedoed and sunk, November 18, 1942. Sister ships listed under **Metapan.**

Pasteur   (1939)   Compagnie Sud-Atlantique (French).
Built by Chantiers & Ateliers de St. Nazaire (Penhoet), St. Nazaire, France. Tonnage: 30,447. Dimensions: 656′ x 87′ (697′ o.l.). Quadruple-screw, 25 knots. Steam turbines. Two masts and one funnel. The huge funnel was placed more forward than usual in a liner. As completed she could accommodate 751 in first, second and third classes. Ran her trials during the summer of 1939. Her maiden voyage from Bordeaux to South America was scheduled for September 1939. However, the sailing was cancelled due to outbreak of World War II. Made her first voyage, Brest to Halifax, August 1940, in role of transport. Troop capacity: 4,500. After World War II was used as a French troopship. She was purchased by the North German Lloyd in 1957, and was refitted at Bremerhaven. Renamed: **Bremen** (1959). Entered North Atlantic passenger service in July 1959.

Pastores   (1912)   United Fruit Co.
Built by Workman, Clark & Co., Belfast, Ireland. Tonnage: 7,242. Dimensions: 470′ x 55′. Twin-screw, 15 knots. Quadruple expansion engines. Two masts and one funnel. Capable of making 17 knots. Passengers: 143 first-class. Scrapped World War II. Sister ships: **Calamares** and **Tenadores.**

Patagonia   (1869)   Pacific Steam Navigation Co.
Built by John Elder & Co., Glasgow, Scotland. Tonnage: 2,866. Dimensions: 353′ x 41′. Single-screw. Compound engines. Iron hull. Lost on coast of Chile about 1895. Sister ships: **Araucania Cordillera** and **Magellan.**

Patagonia   (1890)   Hamburg-South American Line.
Built by Reiherstieg Schibsw., Hamburg, Germany. Tonnage: 2,975. Dimensions: 330′ x 41′. Single-screw, 12½ knots. Triple expansion engines. Two masts and one funnel. Vessel sold to Hamburg-American Line in 1904; name unchanged. Interned in Argentina in 1914. Surrendered to the British in 1920. Sold to Chile in 1922 and renamed **Valdivia.** Wrecked on Chilean coast, October 4, 1933.

Patia   (1913)   Elders & Fyffes, Ltd.
Built by Workman, Clark & Co., Belfast, Ireland. Tonnage: 6,103. Dimensions: 417′ x 53′. Twin-screw, 14 knots. Triple expansion engines. Two masts and one funnel. Sunk by enemy aircraft, May 7, 1941. Sister ships: **Bayano** and **Patuca.**

Patria   (1882)   Fabre Line.
Tonnage: 4,437. Sold to Soc. Italiana di Transp. Marittimi. Renamed: **La Patria.** Quite possible she was in South American service. Broken up by Italian shipbreakers in 1906. Ex-**Rugia** (1895). *Note: See PART I for details.*

Patria   (1938)   Hamburg-American Line.
Built by Deutsche Werft A. G., Hamburg, Germany. Tonnage: 16,595. Dimensions: 562′ x 74′ (589′ o.l.). Twin-screw, 17 knots. Motorship. Two masts and one funnel. Service: North Europe-West Indies-Central America. Renamed: (a) **Empire Welland** (1945), (b) **Rossia** (1946) Russian.

Patuca   (1913)   Elders & Fyffes, Ltd.
Built by Workman, Clark & Co., Belfast, Ireland. Tonnage: 6,103. Dimensions: 417′ x 53′. Twin-screw, 14 knots. Triple expansion engines. Two masts and one funnel. Scrapped in 1935. Sister ships: **Bayano** and **Patia.**

Pembrokeshire (1915) Royal Mail Line (British).
Built by Workman, Clark & Co., Belfast, Ireland. Tonnage: 7,821. Dimensions: 470' x 58'. Single-screw, 14 knots. Quadruple expansion engines. Two masts and one funnel. Scrapped in 1933.

Pennsylvania (1929) Panama-Pacific Line.
Built by Newport News Shipbuilding & Drydock Co., Newport News, Va. Tonnage: 20,526. Dimensions: 586' x 80'. Twin-screw, 19 knots. Turbo-electric. Two masts and two funnels. Rebuilt and altered in 1938. A large single funnel replaced her original two funnels. Renamed: **Argentina** (1938). Sister ships: **California** and **Virginia.**

Peru (1840) Pacific Steam Navigation Co.
Built at London, England. Tonnage: 690. Dimensions: 190' x 29'. Paddle-wheels. Side lever type engines. Two masts and one funnel. Wooden hull. Launched, April 18, 1840. Note: Pioneer vessel of the line. Commenced her maiden voyage from Falmouth, July 10, 1840, calling at Plymouth to embark additional passengers. Placed in South American coastal service. Sold in 1852. Sister ship: **Chile.**

Peru (1861) Pacific Steam Navigation Co.
Built by John Reid, Port Glasgow, Scotland. Tonnage: 1,307. Dimensions: 260' x 32'. Paddle-wheels. Iron hull. Lost near Layerto, July 11, 1863.

Pesaro (1901) Lloyd Sabaudo.
Built by Blohm & Voss, Hamburg, Germany. Tonnage: 12,335. Dimensions: 525' x 62'. Twin-screw, 15½ knots. Quadruple expansion engines. Two masts and two funnels. Made her first Genoa-Naples-New York sailing in 1919. Transferred to the South American service in 1922. Scrapped in 1926. Ex-**Moltke** (1915).

Peten (1933) United Fruit Co.
Built by Newport News Shipbuilding Co., Newport News, Virginia. Tonnage: 6,968. Dimensions: 415' x 60'. Twin-screw, 18 knots. Turbo-electric. Two masts and one funnel. Renamed: **Jamaica** (1937). Sister ships: **Antigua, Chiriqui, Quirigua, Talamanca** and **Veragua.**

Philadelphia (1885) Red "D" Line.
Built by W. Cramp & Sons Shipbuilding Co., Philadelphia, Pa. Tonnage: 2,520. Dimensions: 300' x 35'. Single-screw, 11 knots. Compound engines. Two masts and one funnel. Passengers: 76 first and 30 second. No longer in service, 1929.

Phoenician   (1864)   Allan Line.
Tonnage: 2,356. Placed in regular South American service during 1889–1903. *Note: See PART I for details.*

Picardie   (1864)   Transport Maritimes (French).
Built by Laing of Sunderland, England. Tonnage: 1,371. Dimensions: 305′ x 32′. Single-screw, 10 knots. Compound engines. Three masts and one funnel. Made her first voyage from Marseilles to Panama for French Line, February 6, 1881. Sank off Newfoundland, January 18, 1883, after being taken in tow by French liner **Labrador.** Ex-**Albany** (1867).

Piriapolis   (1938)   Maritime Belge Lloyd.
Built by John Cockerill, Hoboken, Belgian. Tonnage: 7,340. Dimensions: 459′ x 61′. Single-screw, 14 knots. Motorship. Two masts and one funnel. Became a war casualty, June 11, 1940. Sister ships: **Copacanana** and **Mar Del Plata.**

Pizarro   (1879)   Pacific Steam Navigation Co.
Built by Robert Napier & Sons, Glasgow, Scotland. Tonnage: 2,160. Dimensions: 320′ x 40′. Single-screw, 14 knots. Compound engines. Three masts. Steel hull. Converted to hulk in 1907. Sister ship: **Mendoza.**

Plata   (1907)   Transport Maritimes (French).
Built by London & Glasgow Shipbuilding Co., Glasgow, Scotland. Tonnage: 5,577. Dimensions: 420′ x 50′. Twin-screw, 13 knots. Triple expansion engines. Two masts and one funnel. Scrapped in 1931.

*Pocone   (1908)   Lloyd Brasileiro.
Built by Bremer Vulkan, Vegesack, Germany. Tonnage: 6,750. Dimensions: 419′ x 54′. Single-screw, 12 knots. Quadruple expansion engines. Two masts and one funnel. Service: Santos-Hamburg route. Ex-**Coburg.**

Poitou   (1867)   Transport Maritimes (French).
Built by Horn of Waterford. Tonnage: 2,093. Dimensions: 324′ x 34′. Single-screw. Compound engines. Two masts and one funnel. Scrapped in 1893.

Poitou   (1883)   Transport Maritimes (French).
Built by Maats de Schelde, Flushing, Netherlands. Tonnage: 2,679. Dimensions: 319′ x 36′. Single-screw. Quadruple expansion engines. Three masts and one funnel. Ex-**Soembing** (1903), ex-**Batavia.**

Polonia   (1910)   Gdynia-America Line.
Tonnage: 7,890. Transferred to South American service in 1936. *Note: See PART I for details.*

Ponce   (1899)   New York & Porto Rico Steamship Co.
Built by Harlan & Hollingsworth Co., Wilmington, Delaware. Tonnage: 3,506. Dimensions: 317' x 42'. Single-screw, 12 knots. Triple expansion engines. Two masts and one funnel. Passengers: 70 first and 30 second. Renamed: (a) **King Hsing,** (b) **Vest Bay,** (c) **Tai Er Chuang.** Vessel reported sold to Chinese in 1956.

Port Antonio   (1901)   Imperial Direct West India Mail Service Co., Ltd. (Elder, Dempster & Co., Ltd., Managers.)
Built by Sir Raylton Dixon & Co., Middlebrough, England. Tonnage: 4,458. Dimensions: 370' x 46'. Twin-screw, 15 knots. Triple expansion engines. Two masts and one funnel. Renamed: **Rechid Pacha** (Turkish). Sister ship: **Port Royal.**

Port Henderson   (1884)   Imperial Direct West India Mail Service Co. Built by Wm. Denny & Bros., Ltd., Dumbarton, Scotland. Tonnage: 5,167. Dimensions: 439' x 46'. Single-screw, 15 knots. Triple expansion engines. Three masts and two funnels. Steel hull. Renamed: (a) **Anapo** (1912) Italian, (b) **Porto Said** (1913) Italian. Sunk by submarine off Cyrenaica in December 1915. Ex-**Lake Megantic** (1906), ex-**Colon** (1899), ex-**Arawa** (1896).

Port Kingston   (1904)   Imperial Direct West India Mail Service Co. (Elder, Dempster & Co.).
Built by Alexander Stephen & Sons, Ltd., Glasgow, Scotland. Tonnage: 7,585. Dimensions: 460' x 55'. Twin-screw, 17 knots. Triple expansion engines. Two masts and one funnel. Large passenger accommodation. Completed in July 1904. Renamed: **Tahiti** (1910).

Port Maria   (1901)   Imperial Direct West India Mail Service Co. Built by Ramage & Ferguson, Ltd., Leith, Scotland. Tonnage: 2,910. Dimensions: 334' x 40'. Single-screw, 16 knots. Triple expansion engines. Two masts and one funnel. Clipper bow. Passengers: 40 first and 22 second. Renamed: (a) **Mustapha** (1910), (b) **Tocra.** Sister ship: **Port Morant.**

Port Morant   (1901)   Imperial Direct West India Mail Service Co.
Built by Alexander Stephen & Sons, Ltd., Glasgow, Scotland. Tonnage: 2,831. Dimensions: 329' x 40'. Single-screw, 16

knots. Triple expansion engines. Two masts and one funnel.
Renamed: **Sarmiento** (1909). Wrecked in Straits of Magellan in 1912. Sister ship: **Port Maria.**

Port Royal   (1901)   Imperial Direct West India Mail Steamship Co.
Built by Sir Raylton Dixon & Co., Middlesbrough, England.
Tonnage: 4,455.   Dimensions: 370' x 46'.   Twin-screw, 15
knots.   Triple expansion engines.   Two masts and one funnel.
Service: England-Jamaica.   Renamed: **Midhat Pacha.**
Sister ship: **Port Antonio.**

Portena   (1875)   Chargeurs Reunis.
Built by Forges & Chantiers de la Mediterranee, Graville
(Havre), France. Tonnage: 2,321. Dimensions: 333' x 34'.
Single-screw. Compound engines. Two masts and one funnel.
Iron hull. Vessel sold and converted into cable ship; renamed
Contre Caubet.

Portland   (1928)   Hamburg-American Line.
Built by Bremer Vulkan, Vegesack, Germany. Tonnage:
7,132. Dimensions: 462' x 61'. Single-screw, 13½ knots.
Motorship. Two masts and one funnel. Passenger service
between Germany and Central America. Scuttled by crew
in South Atlantic, so as to escape capture by Free French
cruiser, 1943.

Porto Rico   (1903)   New York & Porto Rico Line.
Built by Flensburger Schiffsb., Ges., Flensburg, Germany.
Tonnage: 4,760. Dimensions: 370' x 45'. Single-screw,
12 knots. Quadruple expansion engines. Two masts and
one funnel. Scrapped in 1933. Ex-**Moccasin**, ex-**Prinz
Joachim.**

Potosi   (1873)   Pacific Steam Navigation Co.
Built by John Elder & Co., Glasgow, Scotland. Tonnage:
4,219. Dimensions: 421' x 43'. Single-screw, 14 knots. Compound engines. Three masts and two funnels. Placed in
service of the Orient Line in 1880. Scrapped by Italian
shipbreakers at Genoa in 1897. Sister ships: **Iberia** and
Liguria.

Potosi   (1905)   Pacific Steam Navigation Co.
Built by W. Pickersgill & Sons, Sunderland, England. Tonnage: 4,375. Dimensions: 381' x 49'. Single-screw. Triple
expansion engines. Two masts and one funnel. Note: In 1914
this steamship became the first British owned vessel to pass
through the Panama Canal. Renamed: **Georgios M** (1925).

Presidente Mitre   (1894)   Hamburg-South American Line.
Built by Reiherstieg Schiffsw., Hamburg, Germany. Tonnage: 3,832. Dimensions: 343' x 42'. Single-screw. Triple expansion engines. Two masts and one funnel. Renamed: (a) **Tarapaca** (1923), (b) **Aviles** (1941). Broken up for scrap at Buenos Aires in 1956.   Ex-**Argentina** (1907).

Presidente Peron   (1949)   Dodero Line (Argentina).
Built by Vickers-Armstrongs, Ltd., Barrow, England. Tonnage: 12,459. Dimensions: 509' x 71' (530' o.l.). Twin-screw, 19 knots. Steam turbines. Two masts and one funnel. Passengers: 74 first-class. Service: London-Buenos Aires. Renamed: **Argentina** (1955). Sister ships: **Eva Peron** and **17 de Octubre.**

Presidente Wilson   (1912)   Cosulich Line.
Tonnage: 12,588. In Italy-South American service. *Note: See PART I for details.*

Prince David   (1930)   Canadian National Railways.
Built by Cammell, Laird & Co., Ltd., Birkenhead, England. Tonnage: 6,892. Dimensions: 366' x 57'. Twin-screw, 23 knots. Six steam turbines. Two masts and three funnels. Renamed: **Charlton Monarch.** Scrapped in 1951. Sister ships: **Prince Henry** and **Prince Robert.**

Prince Henry   (1930)   Canadian National Railways.
Built by Cammell, Laird & Co., Birkenhead, England. Tonnage: 6,893. Dimensions: 366' x 57'. Twin-screw, 23 knots. Steam turbines. Two masts and three funnels. Renamed: **North Star** (1937). Sister ships: **Prince David** and **Prince Robert.**

Prince Robert   (1930)   Canadian National Railways.
Built by Cammell, Laird & Co., Birkenhead, England. Tonnage: 6,892. Dimensions: 366' x 57'. Twin-screw, 23 knots. Steam turbines. Two masts and three funnels. Renamed: (a) **Charlton Sovereign** (1948), (b) **Lucania** (1952). Sister ships: **Prince Henry** and **Prince David.**

Principe de Asturias   (1914)   Pinillos Izquierdo & Co. (Spanish).
Built by Russell & Co., Port Glasgow, Scotland. Tonnage: 8,371. Dimensions: 460' x 58'. Twin-screw, 15 knots. Quadruple expansion engines. Two masts and one funnel. Passengers: 144 first, 150 second, 1,750 third. Wrecked off Santos in 1916. Sister ship: **Infanta Isabel.**

Principe di Udine   (1908)   Lloyd Sabaudo Line.
Tonnage: 7,794. In Italy-South American service. *Note: See PART I for details.*

Principe Umberto   (1909)   Navigazione Generale Italiana.
Tonnage: 7,838. Service: Italy-South America. *Note: See PART I for details.*

Principessa Giovanna   (1923)   (a) Lloyd Sabaudo, (b) Italia Line.
Built by Cantieri Nav. Franco Tosi, Taranto, Italy. Tonnage: 8,556. Dimensions: 441' x 59' (460' o.l.). Twin-screw, 13 knots. Steam turbines. Two masts and two funnels. Renamed: **San Giorgio** (1947). Scrapped in 1953. Sister ship: **Principessa Maria.**

Principessa Jolanda   (1908)   Lloyd Italiano.
Built by Societa Esercizio Bacini, Riva Trigosa, Italy. Tonnage: 9,200. Dimensions: 486' x 49'. Twin-screw, 18 knots. Quadruple expansion engines. Two masts and two funnels. She was intended to be used in the Genoa-Buenos Aires service, but capsized when being launched on September 21, 1907. The uncompleted vessel had to be broken up for scrap. Sister ship: **Principessa Mafalda.**

Principessa Mafalda   (1908)   (a) Lloyd Italiano, (b) Navigazione Generale Italiana.
Built by Societa Esercizio Bacini, Riva Trigosa, Italy. Tonnage: 9,210. Dimensions: 485' x 58'. Twin-screw, 18½ knots. Quadruple expansion engines. Two masts and two funnels. Launched in October 1908. Commenced her maiden voyage from Genoa to Buenos Aires in the spring of 1909. Foundered off the coast of Bahia, Brazil, October 25, 1927, with the loss of a number of lives. Sister ship: **Principessa Jolanda.**

Principessa Maria   (1923)   (a) Lloyd Sabaudo, (b) Italia Line.
Built by Cantieri Nav. Franco Tosi, Tarento, Italy. Tonnage: 8,539. Dimensions: 441' x 59' (460' o.l.). Twin-screw, 13 knots. Steam turbines. Two masts and two funnels. Burned off French coast in 1940. Repaired and sold. Renamed: **Rio de La Plata** (1941). Vessel was retired from active service in 1946. Sister ship: **Principessa Giovanna.** Note: As built these ships had only a single funnel.

Prins der Nederlanden   (1902)   Royal Netherlands Steamship Co. Built by Blohm & Voss, Hamburg, Germany. Tonnage: 1,923. Dimensions: 290' x 38'. Single-screw, 10½ knots.

Triple expansion engines. Two masts and one funnel. Passengers: 34 first and 8 second. Scrapped in 1927.

*Prins der Nederlanden   (1957)   Royal Netherlands Steamship Co.
Built by P. Smit, Jr., Rotterdam, Netherlands. Tonnage: 7,220. Dimensions: 431' (o.l.) x 56'. Single-screw, 15 knots. Motorship. Two masts and one funnel. Service: Amsterdam-West Indies. Sister ship: **Oranje Nassau.**

Prins Frederik Hendrik   (1888)   Royal Netherlands Steamship Co.
Built by Kon. Stoom. en Andre Werk, Amsterdam, Netherlands. Tonnage: 1,642. Dimensions: 261' x 36'. Single-screw. Triple expansion engines. Two masts and one funnel. Iron hull. Wrecked off Suriname coast in 1903.

Prins Frederik Hendrik   (1904)   Royal Netherlands Steamship Co.
Built by Nederlandsch Schps. Maats., Amsterdam, Netherlands. Tonnage: 2,164. Dimensions: 317' x 40'. Single-screw, 15 knots. Triple expansion engines. Two masts and one funnel. Passengers: 12 first, 12 second. Renamed: **La Mecque** (Tunis). Scrapped in 1936.

Prins Maurits   (1900)   Royal Netherlands Steamship Co.
Built by Blohm & Voss, Hamburg, Germany. Tonnage: 2,121. Dimensions: 284' x 38'. Single-screw. Triple expansion engines. Two masts and one funnel. Foundered off Cape Hatteras, April 3, 1915, with the loss of 59 lives. Sister ship: **Prins Willem I.**

Prins Willem I   (1884)   Royal Netherlands Steamship Co.
Built by Richardson, Duck & Co., Stockton, England. Tonnage: 1,723. Dimensions: 264' x 36'. Single-screw. Triple expansion engines. Two masts and one funnel. Sunk by collision in English Channel, 1889.

Prins Willem I   (1890)   Royal Netherlands Steamship Co.
Built by Richardson, Duck & Co., Stockton, England. Tonnage: 1,723. Dimensions: 264' x 36'. Single-screw. Triple expansion engines. Two masts and one funnel. Wrecked on July 30, 1900.

Prins Willem I   (1901)   Royal Netherlands Steamship Co.
Built by Nederlandsche Schps. Maats., Amsterdam, Netherlands. Tonnage: 2,121. Dimensions: 284' x 38'. Single-screw,

15 knots. Triple expansion engines. Two masts and one funnel. Passengers: 12 first and 12 second. This steamship line was also known as Royal Dutch West India Mail Line. Renamed: **Ahmedi** (1920). Scrapped in 1935. Sister ship: **Prins Maurits.**

Prins Willem II (1890) Royal Netherlands Steamship Co. Built by Kon. v. Stoom. en Andre Werk, Amsterdam, Netherlands. Tonnage: 1,641. Dimensions: 264' x 36'. Single-screw. Triple expansion engines. Listed as missing in 1910.

Prins Willem III (1890) Royal Netherlands Steamship Co. Built by Nederlandsche Stoom. Maats., Rotterdam, Netherlands. Tonnage: 1,960. Dimensions: 265' x 35'. Single-screw. Triple expansion engines. Renamed: (a) **Elpiniki,** (b) **Georgios Antippa.** Torpedoed and sunk, November 28, 1917.

Prins Willem IV (1894) Royal Netherlands Steamship Co. Built by Richardson, Duck & Co., Stockton, England. Tonnage: 2,047. Dimensions: 270' x 36'. Single-screw, 15 knots. Triple expansion engines. Two masts and one funnel. Passengers: 12 first and 12 second. Renamed: **Sardar** (1913). Wrecked off Italian Somaliland in 1914.

Prins Willem V (1897) Royal Netherlands Steamship Co. Built by Nederlandsch. Schps. Maats., Amsterdam, Netherlands. Tonnage: 2,108. Dimensions: 272' x 36'. Single-screw, 15 knots. Triple expansion engines. Two masts and one funnel. Passengers: 12 first and 12 second. Renamed: **La Dives** (1915). Note: This steamship company was formerly known as Royal Dutch West India Mail Line.

Prinz Adalbert (1902) Hamburg-American Line. Built by Bremer Vulkan, Vegesack, Germany. Tonnage: 6,030. Dimensions: 403' x 49'. Twin-screw, 13 knots. Quadruple expansion engines. Two masts and two funnels. In West Indies service. Placed in Hamburg-Quebec trade in 1909. She also was in the New York-Naples-Genoa service. Seized by British in August 1914. Renamed: (a) **Princetown** (1914), (b) **Alesia** (1917) Cie Sud-Atlantique. Torpedoed and sunk, September 6, 1917. Sister ship: **Prinz Oskar.**

Prinz Auguste Wilhelm (1902) Hamburg-American Line. Built by Flensburger Schiffsb. Ges., Flensburg, Germany. Tonnage: 4,733. Dimensions: 370' x 45'. Single-screw,

13 knots. Quadruple expansion engines. Two masts and one funnel. Burned and scuttled by crew to prevent capture by Colombian Government, 1917.

Prinz Eitel Friedrich (1902) Hamburg-American Line.
  Built by Reiherstieg Schiffsw., Hamburg, Germany. Tonnage: 4,650. Dimensions: 371′ x 45′. Single-screw, 12 knots. Quadruple expansion engines. Two masts and one funnel. Service: Central America. Renamed: (a) **Otsego** (1917), (b) **Ural** (1945).

Prinz Joachim (1903) Hamburg-American Line.
  Built by Flensburger Schiffsb. Ges., Flensburg, Germany. Tonnage: 4,760. Dimensions: 370′ x 45′. Single-screw, 13 knots. Quadruple expansion engines. Two masts and one funnel. Renamed: (a) **Moccasin**, (b) **Porto Rico.**

Prinz Oskar (1902) Hamburg-American Line.
  Built by Bremer Vulkan, Vegesack, Germany. Tonnage: 6,026. Dimensions: 403′ x 49′. Twin-screw, 13 knots. Quadruple expansion engines. Two masts and two funnels. First used in the Genoa-New York trade. After 1906 was employed on Genoa-Buenos Aires service. Renamed: **Orien.** Sister ship: **Prinz Adalbert.**

Prinz Sigismund (1902) Hamburg-American Line.
  Built by Akt. Ges. "Neptun," Rostock, Germany. Tonnage: 4,689. Dimensions: 370′ x 45′. Single-screw, 12½ knots. Quadruple expansion engines. Two masts and two funnels. Originally in Central American service, then later transferred to South American route. Seized by United States in 1917. Renamed: **General W. C. Gorgas** (1917). Afterwards sold to Panama Railroad Co. Somewhat later Libby, McNeill & Libby acquired the vessel. Renamed: **Mikhail Lomonosov** (Russian).

Prinz Waldemar (1903) North German Lloyd.
  Built by Akt. Ges. Seebeck, Bremerhaven, Germany. Tonnage: 3,227. Dimensions: 398′ x 41′. Twin-screw, 12 knots. Triple expansion engines. Two masts and one funnel. Renamed: **Wacouta.**

Provence (1884) Transport Maritimes (French).
  Built by Forges & Chantiers de la Mediterranee, La Seyne, France. Tonnage: 3,874. Dimensions: 387′ x 42′. Single-screw, 14 knots. Compound engines. Three masts and one funnel. Vessel was damaged and sunk in harbor waters by

submarine in First World War. Refloated and reconditioned. Scrapped in 1927.

*Provence   (1950)   Transport Maritimes (French).
   Built by Swan, Hunter & Wigham Richardson, Ltd., Newcastle, England. Tonnage: 15,719. Dimensions: 554′ x 73′ (580′ o.l.). Twin-screw, 18 knots. Six steam turbines. Two masts and one funnel. Passengers: 1,300 in first, tourist and third. Service: France-Italy-South America. Sister ship: **Bretagne.**

Puerto Rico   (1931)   Bull Line (American).
   Built by Bethlehem Shipbuilding Corp., Quincy, Mass. Tonnage: 7,100. Dimensions: 413′ x 59′ (429′ o.l.). Single-screw, 16 knots. Steam turbines. Two masts and one funnel. Service: New York-Porto Rico. Renamed: **Arosa Star** (1954). Ex-**Boringuen** (1949).

Puerto Rico   (1932)   Colombian Steamship Co.
   Built by Newport News Shipbuilding Co., Newport News, Va. Tonnage: 5,236. Dimensions: 385′ x 57′ (404′ o.l.). Single-screw, 17 knots. Steam turbines. Two masts and one funnel. Renamed: (a) **Monterey,** (b) **Adana** (1948). Ex-**Haiti.** Sister ship: **Colombia.**

Pulaski   (1912)   Gdynia-American Line.
   Tonnage: 6,516. Transferred from North Atlantic to South American service. *Note: See PART I for details.*

Puno   (1873)   Pacific Steam Navigation Co.
   Built by Laird Bros., Birkenhead, England. Tonnage: 3,805. Dimensions: 387′ x 43′. Single-screw, 13 knots. Inverted direct acting type engines. Three masts and two masts. Clipper bow. Iron hull. Passengers: 245 first, 26 second. Renamed: **Para** (1875). Scrapped in 1903. Sister ship: **Corcovado.**

Puno   (1881)   Pacific Steam Navigation Co.
   Built by Robert Napier & Sons, Glasgow, Scotland. Tonnage: 2,398. Dimensions: 320′ x 40′. Single-screw, 14 knots. Compound engines. Three masts. Steel hull. Sister ship: **Serena.**

*Queen of Bermuda   (1933)   Furness-Bermuda Line.
   Built by Vickers-Armstrongs, Ltd., Newcastle, England. Tonnage: 553′ x 76′ (579′ o.l.). Quadruple-screw, 21 knots. Two steam turbines connected to electric motors. Two masts

and three funnels. Maximum beam: 83' 6''. Passengers: 730.
Renamed: (a) **New Australia** (1949), (b) **Arkadia** (1958).
Sister ship: **Monarch of Bermuda.**

*Queen of Nassau (1927) Jefferson Steamship Co. (Liberian).
Built by W. Cramp & Sons Shipbuilding Co., Philadelphia,
Pa. Tonnage: 5,002. Dimensions: 379' x 55'. Twin-screw,
19 knots. Steam turbines. Two masts and one funnel. In
Miami-Nassau cruise service. Ex-**Yarmouth Castle** (1957),
ex-**Queen of Nassau** (1957), ex-**Yarmouth Castle** (1954),
ex-**Yarmouth** (1954). Note: Originally this liner was
employed in the Boston-Yarmouth coastal service, along
with sister ship **Evangeline.**

Quillota (1907) Pacific Steam Navigation Co.
Built by Wm. Beardmore & Co., Glasgow, Scotland. Ton-
nage: 3,774. Dimensions: 361' x 46'. Twin-screw, 12½ knots.
Triple expansion engines. Two masts and one funnel.
Renamed: **Chile** (1923). Sister ship: **Quilpue.**

Quilpue (1907) Pacific Steam Navigation Co.
Built by Wm. Beardmore & Co., Glasgow, Scotland. Tonnage: 3,669. Dimensions: 361' x 46'. Twin-screw, 12½ knots.
Triple expansion engines. Two masts and one funnel. Renamed: **Gascoyne** (1922). Sister ship: **Quillota.**

Quirigua (1932) United Fruit Co.
Built by Bethlehem Steel Co., Shipbuilding Division, Quincy,
Mass. Tonnage: 6,982. Dimensions: 415' x 60'. Twin-screw,
18 knots. Turbo-electric. Renamed: **Samala.** Sister ships:
Antigua, Chiriqui, Peten, Talamanca and **Veragua.**

Quito (1852) Pacific Steam Navigation Co.
Built at Glasgow, Scotland. Tonnage: 1,461. Dimensions:
248' x 29'. Paddle-wheels. Two masts and two funnels.
Clipper bow. Iron hull. Wrecked near Huasco, July 10, 1853.
Sister ships: **Bogota** and **Lima.**

Quito (1863) Pacific Steam Navigation Co.
Built at Glasgow, Scotland. Tonnage: 1,388. Dimensions:
271' x 32'. Paddle-wheels. Two masts and one funnel.
Clipper bow. Iron hull. Vessel sold in 1864.

Raimund (1922) (a) Roland Line, (b) North German Lloyd.
Built by Nordsec-werke, Emden, Germany. Tonnage: 3,667.
Dimensions: 369' x 50'. Single-screw. Triple expansion
engines. Service: Bremen-Cuba route. Lost in North Atlantic
in 1941. Ex-**Altair.**

Rakuyo Maru (1921) (a) Toyo Kisen Laisha, (b) N.Y.K. Line. Built by Mitsubishi Zosen Kaisha, Ltd., Nagasaki, Japan. Tonnage: 9,419. Dimensions: 460' x 60'. Twin-screw, 12 knots. Steam turbines. Two masts and one funnel. Service: Trans-Pacific-West Coast of South America, via United States West Coast ports. Sunk by American submarine, September 12, 1944. Sister ships: **Anyo Maru, Bokuyo Maru** and **Ginyo Maru.**

Radames (1901) Kosmos Steamship Co. Built by Blohm & Voss, Hamburg, Germany. Tonnage: 4,756. Dimensions: 380' x 47'. Single-screw, 12 knots. Triple expansion engines. Passengers: 26 first, 20 second, 32 third.

*Raul Soares (1900) Lloyd Brasileiro. Built by Flensburger, Schiffsb. Ges., Flensburg, Germany. Tonnage: 6,003. Dimensions: 410' x 48'. Single-screw, 13 knots. Quadruple expansion engines. Two masts and one funnel. Service: Santos-Hamburg. Ex-**Madeira** (1925), ex-**Cap Verde** (1922).

Ravenna (1901) Soc. di Nav. a Vapore Italia. Built by Odero & Co., Genoa, Italy. Tonnage: 4,252. Dimensions: 363' x 43'. Single-screw, 12 knots. Triple expansion engines. Two masts and one funnel. Service: Italy-South America. Also made sailings between Italy and New York. Vessel lost in 1917. Sister ship: **Toscana.**

Re d' Italia (1907) Lloyd Sabaudo Line. Tonnage: 6,364. Transferred from Italy-New York service to South American route. *Note: See PART I for details.*

Re Vittorio (1907) Navigazione Generale Italiana. Tonnage: 7,977. Transferred from North Atlantic service to South American trade. *Note: See PART I for details.*

Regina d' Italia (1907) Lloyd Sabaudo Line. Tonnage: 6,368. Transferred to South American service on her 4th voyage. *Note: See PART I for details.*

Regina Elena (1907) Navigazione Generale Italiana. Built by Cantieri Ligur. Ancon, Ancona, Italy. Tonnage: 7,865. Dimensions: 476' x 53'. Twin-screw, 16 knots. Quadruple expansion engines. Two masts and two funnels. In Italy-South American service. Torpedoed and sunk in 1918. Sister ships: **Duca d' Aosta, Duca degli Abruzzi** and **Re Vittoria.**

Regina Margherita (1884)   Navigazione Generale Italiana.
Built by A. McMillan & Son, Dumbarton, Scotland. Tonnage: 3,577. Dimensions: 396' x 42'. Single-screw, 16 knots. Compound engines. Two masts and two funnels. A fine looking liner. Clipper bow.

Rei de Portugal (1889)   Hamburg-South American Line.
Built by Scott & Co., Ltd., Greenock, Scotland. Tonnage: 3,236. Dimensions: 363' x 42'. Single-screw. Triple expansion engines. Two masts and one funnel. Renamed: (a) **Napolitan Prince,** (b) **Manouba.**

*Reina del Mar (1956)   Pacific Steam Navigation Co.
Built by Harland & Wolff, Ltd., Belfast, Ireland. Tonnage: 20,225. Dimensions: 560' x 78' (600' o.l.). Twin-screw, 18 knots. Steam turbines. Single mast and one funnel. Launched in June 1955. Passengers: 207 first, 216 cabin, 342 tourist. Route: England-France-Spain to Bermuda-the-Bahamas-Cuba-Jamaica-Panama-Colombia-Ecuador-Peru-Chile.

Reina del Pacifico (1931)   Pacific Steam Navigation Co.
Built by Harland & Wolff, Ltd., Belfast, Ireland. Tonnage: 17,707. Dimensions: 551' x 76' (580' o.l.). Quadruple-screw, 19 knots. Motorship. Two masts and two funnels. The company's first quadruple-screw vessel. Held the speed record for passage between Liverpool and West Coast of South America. Scrapped in Great Britain, 1958.

Renaico (1898)   Cia. Sud Americana de Vapores (Chile).
Built by Sir James Laing, Sunderland, England. Tonnage: 5,961. Dimensions: 431' x 50'. Twin-screw, 15 knots. Triple expansion engines. Three masts and two funnels. In 1929 she was serving as a depot ship at Iquique. Ex-**Nippon Maru.**

Rhaetia (1904)   Hamburg-American Line.
Tonnage: 6,600. In Germany-West Indies service. *Note: See PART I for details.*

Rhakotis (1907)   Kosmos Steamship Co.
Built by Blohm & Voss, Hamburg, Germany. Tonnage: 6,982. Dimensions: 435' x 53'. Twin-screw. Triple expansion engines. Passengers: 48 first, 16 second, 44 third.

Rhein (1925)   Hamburg-American Line.
Built by Akt. Ges. "Weser", Bremen, Germany. Tonnage: 6,013. Dimensions: 453' x 58'. Single-screw. Motorship.

Vessel acquired from Hugo Stinnes Line in 1926. Service: Germany-West Indies. Scuttled by own crew to escape capture by Dutch cruiser in Caribbean in 1940.

Rhodopis (1906) Hamburg-American Line.
Built by Blohm & Voss, Hamburg, Germany. Tonnage: 7,056. Dimensions: 435' x 53'. Twin-screw, 12 knots. Triple expansion engines. Two masts and one funnel. Passengers: 48 first, 16 second, 44 third. Service: Germany-West Indies. Scrapped in 1932. Originally of Kosmos Line.

Rio Bravo (1924) Ozean Line & North German Lloyd.
Built by Frd. Krupp, Akt. Ges., Kiel, Germany. Tonnage: 5,946. Dimensions: 393' x 51'. Twin-screw, 12 knots. Motorship. Two masts and two funnels. Service: Germany-West Indies-Central America. Vessel sold to Burns Philip, Ltd. before World War II. Renamed: **Merkur.** Sister ship: **Rio Panuco.**

Rio de Janeiro (1914) Hamburg-South American Line.
Built by Bremer Vulkan, Vegesack, Germany. Tonnage: 5,261. Dimensions: 401' x 55'. Single-screw. Triple expansion engines. Torpedoed and sunk by Polish submarine off Norway, April 9, 1940. Ex-**Santa Ines** (1921).

Rio de Janeiro Maru (1930) Osaka Line.
Built by Mitsubishi Zosen Kaisha, Ltd., Nagasaki, Japan. Tonnage: 9,627. Dimensions: 461' x 62'. Twin-screw, 17 knots. Motorship. Two masts and one funnel. Service: Round-the-World, via South America. Sunk by American aircraft, February 17, 1944, as a converted submarine tender. Sister ship: **Buenos Aires Maru.**

*Rio de la Plata (1950) Argentina State Line.
Built by Soc. Anon. Ansaldo, Genoa-Sestri, Italy. Tonnage: 11,317. Dimensions: 525' x 65'. Twin-screw, 18 knots. Motorship. Two masts and one funnel. Passengers: 116 first-class. Service: Buenos Aires-New York. Sister ships: **Evita** and **Rio Jachal.**

Rio Grande (1860) Messageries Maritimes.
Built by Forges & Chantiers de la Mediterranee, La Seyne, France. Tonnage: 2,596. Dimensions: 312' x 38'. Single-screw. Triple expansion engines. Two masts and one funnel. Ex-**Navarre** (1872).

Rio Grande   (1904)   Hamburg-South American Line.
   Built by J. C. Tecklenborg, A. G., Geestemunde, Germany.
   Tonnage: 4,556.   Dimensions: 361′ x 46′.   Single-screw, 12
   knots.   Triple expansion engines.   Two masts and one funnel.
   Seized by Brazil in 1917.   Renamed: **Benevente** (1917),
   (b) **Duque de Caxias** (1926).

*****Rio Jachal**   (1950)   Argentina State Line.
   Built by Soc. Anon. Ansaldo, Genoa-Sestri, Italy.   Tonnage:
   11,317.   Dimensions: 525′ x 65′ (549′o.l.).   Twin-screw, 18
   knots.   Motorship.   Two masts and one funnel.   Passengers:
   116 first-class.   Route: Buenos Aires-New York.   Sister ships:
   Evita and **Rio Jachal.**

Rio Janeiro   (1889)   La Veloce Line.
   Built by Wigham Richardson & Co., Newcastle, England.
   Tonnage: 1,916.   Dimensions: 300′ x 35′.   Single-screw.
   Triple expansion engines.   Renamed: **Alsace.**   Ex-**Adelaide
   Lavarello.**

Rio Negro   (1883)   Chargeurs Reunis.
   Built by Ateliers & Chantiers de la Loire, St. Nazaire, France.
   Tonnage: 3,443.   Dimensions: 347′ x 40′.   Single-screw, 13
   knots.   Triple expansion engines.   Two masts and one funnel.
   Service: France-South America.   Sold to Chile-Argentina
   Navigation Co.   Renamed: **Valdivia.**   Sister ships: **Parana**
   and **Uruguay.**

Rio Negro   (1905)   Hamburg-South American Line.
   Built by J. C. Tecklenborg, Geestemunde, Germany.   Tonnage: 4,699.   Dimensions: 361′ x 46′.   Single-screw, 12 knots.
   Triple expansion engines.   Two masts and one funnel.   Purchased by Ellerman Lines in October 1920.   Served as a
   transport for refugees from Yalta and Black Sea Russian ports.
   Renamed: **City of Palermo** (1921).   Sold to Italian shipbreakers in July 1933.

Rio Panuco   (1924)   Ozean Line and North German Lloyd.
   Built by Frd. Krupp, Kiel, Germany.   Tonnage: 5,944.
   Dimensions: 393′ x 52′.   Twin-screw, 12 knots.   Motorship.
   Two masts and two funnels.   Service: Germany-West Indies-
   Central America.   Renamed: (a) **Neptun** (1935), (b) **Nep-
   tuna,** (c) **Merku.**   Sister ship: **Rio Bravo.**

*****Rio Tunuyan**   (1951)   Argentina State Line.
   Built by Ansaldo, Genoa-Sestri, Italy.   Tonnage: 11,317.
   Dimensions: 525′ x 65′ (549′ o.l.).   Twin-screw, 18 knots.

Motorship. Two masts and one funnel. Service: Buenos Aires-New York. Ex-**Evita** (1955), ex-**Rio Tunuyan** (1952). Sister ships: **Rio de la Plata** and **Rio Jachal.**

Rivadavia   (1873)   Chargeurs Reunis.
Built by Forges & Chantiers de la Mediterranee, Graville, France. Tonnage: 2,258. Dimensions: 309' x 34'. Single-screw. Compound engines. Three masts and one funnel. Went ashore in fog near Cape Villano, August 20, 1880, and became a total loss. Sister ship: **San Martin.**

Roda   (1908)   (a) Kosmos Line, (b) Hamburg-American Line.
Built by Reiherstieg Schiffsw., Hamburg, Germany. Tonnage: 7,329. Dimensions: 442' x 52'. Twin-screw, 12 knots. Triple expansion engines. Two masts and one funnel. Passengers: 48 first, 16 second, 44 third. Service: Germany-West Indies. Renamed: **City of Valencia.**

Roland   (1893)   North German Lloyd.
Built by Sir W. G. Armstrong, Whitworth & Co., Newcastle, England. Tonnage: 3,603. Dimensions: 345' x 43'. Single-screw, 12 knots. Triple expansion engines. Two masts and one funnel. Service: Bremen-Cuba. Sold to Turkey in 1911. Renamed: **Bahri Amer.**

Roma   (1926)   (a) Navigazione Generale Italiana, (b) Italia Line. Tonnage: 32,583. Transferred from North Atlantic to South American service. *Note: See PART I for details.*

*Roma   (1943)   Achille Lauro Line.
Tonnage: 14,687. Made her first sailing from Naples to New York in May 1953. Placed in service to South America. *Note: See PART I for details.*

Rosarian   (1887)   Allan Line.
Tonnage: 3,077. Commenced her maiden voyage Glasgow-South America, November 25, 1887. She was also used in North Atlantic service. *Note: See PART I for details.*

Rosario   (1913)   Hamburg-South American Line.
Built by Flensburger Schiffsb. Ges., Flensburg, Germany. Tonnage: 6,079. Dimensions: 449' x 58'. Single-screw, 13 knots. Triple expansion engines. Two masts and one funnel. Fate unknown since World War II. Ex-**Witett**, ex-**Bakara**, ex-**Cannstatt.** Sister ship: Buenos Aires.

Rugia   (1882)   Hamburg-American Line.
Tonnage: 4,053. *Note: See PART I for details.*

Rugia   (1905)   Hamburg-American Line.
   Tonnage: 6,672.   Service: (a) Hamburg-Philadelphia, (b) Germany-South America, (c) Germany-West Indies.   *Note: See PART I for details.*

Saarland   (1924)   Hamburg-American Line.
   Built by Blohm & Voss, Hamburg, Germany.   Tonnage: 6,863.   Dimensions: 449' x 58'.   Single-screw, 12½ knots. Steam turbines.   Two masts and one funnel.   Service: Germany-West Indies.   Renamed: **Teiyo Maru** (1940). Sunk by United States aircraft bombing in 1943.

Sabor   (1893)   Royal Mail Line (British).
   Built by Harland & Wolff, Ltd., Belfast, Ireland.   Tonnage: 4,747.   Dimensions: 400' x 47'.   Twin-screw, 12½ knots. Triple expansion engines.   Two masts and one funnel.   Renamed: (a) **Carmarthenshire** (1913), (b) **Chaleur** (1909), Ex-**Gaul** (1906).

Salier   (1875)   North German Lloyd.
   Tonnage: 3,098.   Commenced Bremen-South American service in 1876.   Made many Bremen-New York voyages. *Note: See PART I for details.*

Salta   (1911)   Transport Maritimes (French).
   Built by Forges & Chantiers de la Mediterranee, La Seyne, France.   Tonnage: 7,284.   Dimensions: 449' x 53'.   Twin-screw.   Triple expansion engines.   Two masts and two funnels. Service: Marseilles-South America (East Coast).   Sank on own mine field off Havre in 1917, while being employed as hospital ship.

*Salta   (1943)   Dodero Line (Argentine).
   Built by Seattle-Tacoma Shipbuilding Corp., Seattle, Washington.   Tonnage: 12,053.   Dimensions: 467' x 69'.   Single-screw, 16 knots.   Steam turbines.   Two masts and one funnel. Vessel converted to passenger liner in 1949.   Service: Italy-Argentine.   Ex-**Shah** (1949).   Sister ship: **Corrientes.**

Samara   (1894)   Compagnie Sud-Atlantique (French).
   Built by Harland & Wolff, Ltd., Belfast, Ireland.   Tonnage: 6,007.   Dimensions: 445' x 49'.   Twin-screw, 13 knots.   Triple expansion engines.   Four masts and one funnel.   Scrapped in 1923.   Ex-**Staffordshire.**

San Francisco   (1928)   Hamburg-American Line.
   Built by Deutsche Werft, Hamburg, Germany.   Tonnage: 6,753.   Dimensions: 432' x 59'.   Single-screw, 13½ knots.

Motorship. Two masts and one funnel. Service: Germany-Central America.

San Giorgio (1886) (a) Navigazione Generale Italiana, (b) Sicula Americana Line.
Tonnage: 2,817. In South American service. *Note: See PART I for details.*

San Giorgio (1907) (a) Sicula Americana Line, (b) Trans-oceanica (Italian). Tonnage: 6,392. In Italy-South American service. *Note: See PART I for details.*

San Giorgio (1923) Italia Line.
Built by Cantieri Nav. Franco Tosi, Taranto, Italy. Tonnage: 8,959. Dimensions: 443' x 59'. Twin-screw, 13 knots. Steam turbines. Two masts and two funnels. In Italy-South American service. Broken up for scrap in Italy in 1954. Ex-**Principessa Giovanna** (1947).

San Giovanni (1907) Sicula Americana Line.
Tonnage: 6,592. Service: Italy-South America. *Note: See PART I for details.*

San Guglielmo (1911) Sicula Americana Line.
Tonnage: 8,341. Service: Italy-South America. *Note: See PART I for details.*

San Jacinto (1903) New York & Porto Rico Steamship Co.
Built by Delaware River Shipbuilding Co., Chester, Pa. Tonnage: 6,069. Dimensions: 380' x 53'. Twin-screw, 15½ knots. Triple expansion engines. Two masts and one funnel. Note: As built had a tall large funnel, but later it was cut down. Torpedoed and sunk in the North Atlantic, April 22, 1942. Note: Vessel was originally owned by Mallory Line.

San Lorenzo (1907) New York & Porto Rico Steamship Co.
Built by Newport News Shipbuilding Co., Newport News, Virginia. Tonnage: 6,576. Dimensions: 401' x 54'. Twin-screw, 16 knots. Quadruple expansion engines. Two masts and one funnel. Scrapped in 1934. Ex-**Brazos** (1926).

San Martin (1873) Chargeurs Reunis.
Built by Forges & Chantiers de la Mediterranee, Graville (Havre), France. Tonnage: 2,258. Dimensions: 294' x 34'. Single-screw. Compound engines. Three masts and one funnel. Iron hull. Went aground in fog and lost near Montevideo, September 4, 1889. Sister ship: **Rivadavia.**

San Nicolas   (1897)   Hamburg-South American Line.
Built by Blohm & Voss, Hamburg, Germany. Tonnage:
4,739. Dimensions: 375′ x 46′. Single-screw, 12½ knots.
Quadruple expansion engines. Two masts and one funnel.
Vessel seized by Brazilian Government in 1917. Renamed·
(a) **Alfenas** (1917), (b) **Campos Salles** (1923). Still in
service in 1957.

San Paulo   (1902)   Soc. di Nav. a Vap. Italia.
Built by Orlando, Leghorn, Italy. Tonnage: 5,021. Dimen-
sions: 401′ x 46′. Single-screw, 14 knots. Quadruple expan-
sion engines. Two masts and one funnel. Service: Italy-
South America. Renamed: **MacGilvray Shiras.** Sunk in
Rio Harbor in 1921. Ex-**Umbria.**

Santa Barbara   (1908)   Hamburg-South American Line.
Built by Akt. Ges. "Neptun", Rostock, Germany. Tonnage:
3,763. Dimensions: 351′ x 50′. Single-screw. Triple expansion engines. Vessel seized by Portugal in 1916. Renamed:
(a) **Sao Thiago** (1916), (b) **Cabo Verde** (1924). Scrapped
in Great Britain, 1950.

Santa Barbara   (1928)   Grace Line (American).
Built by Furness Shipbuilding Co., Haverton-on-Tees, England. Tonnage: 8,060. Dimensions: 466′ x 64′ (486′ o.l.).
Twin-screw, 16½ knots. Motorship. Two masts and two
funnels. Passengers: 150 in single class. Torpedoed and sunk
in 1943. Sister ship: **Santa Maria.**

*****Santa Barbara**   (1946)   Grace Line.
Built by North Carolina Shipbuilding Co., Wilmington, N. C.
Tonnage: 8,357. Dimensions: 441′ x 63′ (459′ o.l.). Single-
screw; 16 knots. Steam turbines. Two masts and one funnel.
Passengers: 52 first-class. Crew: 78. Sister ships: **Santa
Cecilia, Santa Isabel, Santa Luisa, Santa Margarita**
and **Santa Maria.**

Santa Cecilia   (1913)   Grace Line.
Built by W. Hamilton & Co., Port Glasgow, Scotland.
Tonnage: 5,873. Dimensions: 408′ x 55′. Single-screw,
12 knots. Quadruple expansion engines. Four masts and
one funnel. Passengers: 25. Renamed: (a) **Nideros,** (b)
Lyngenfjord. Ex-**Colusa.**

Santa Cecilia   (1918)   Grace Line.
Built by W. Cramp & Sons Shipbuilding Co., Philadelphia,
Pa. Tonnage: 4,870. Dimensions: 360′ x 51′. Single-screw,

14 knots. Quadruple expansion engines. Two masts and one funnel. Note: In service of Panama Mail Steamship Company (Division of Grace Steamship Company). Renamed: (a) **Irwin**, (b) **John L. Clem** (1941). Scrapped in 1948. Ex-**Guatemala**, ex-**Santa Ana.** Sister ships: **Santa Teresa** and **Santa Elisa.**

*Santa Cecilia   (1946)   Grace Line.
Built by North Carolina Shipbuilding Co., Wilmington, N. C. Tonnage: 8,357. Dimensions: 441′ x 63′. Single-screw, 16 knots. Steam turbines. Two masts and one funnel. Passengers: 52. Sister ships: See **Santa Barbara.**

Santa Clara   (1930)   Grace Line.
Built by New York Shipbuilding Co., Camden, N. J. Tonnage: 8,183. Dimensions: 483′ x 63′. Twin-screw, 16½ knots. Turbo-electric. Two masts and two funnels. Passengers: 150. Renamed: **Susan B. Anthony.** Sunk during the invasion of Normandy, without the loss of a soldier.

*Santa Clara   (1946)   Grace Line.
Built by Federal Shipbuilding & Drydock Co., Kearny, N. J. Tonnage: 8,610. Dimensions: 441′ x 63′. Single-screw, 16 knots. Steam turbines. Two masts and one funnel. Passengers: 52. Sister ships: See **Santa Barbara.**

Santa Cruz   (1904)   Tagus Navigation Co. (Portuguese).
Built by New York Shipbuilding Co., Camden, N. J. Tonnage: 16,111. Dimensions: 600′ x 65′. Twin-screw, 16 knots. Quadruple expansion engines. Four masts and one funnel. In service to South America. Scrapped in Italy, 1952. Ex-**President Johnson** (1947), ex-**Manchuria** (1929).

Santa Cruz   (1913)   Grace Line.
Tonnage: 5,081. *Note: See PART II for details.*

Santa Elena   (1907)   Hamburg-South American Line.
Built by Blohm & Voss, Hamburg, Germany. Tonnage: 7,473. Dimensions: 434′ x 54′. Single-screw. Quadruple expansion engines. Two masts and one funnel. Renamed: **Linois.**

Santa Elena   (1933)   Grace Line.
Built by Federal Shipbuilding & Drydock Co., Kearny, N. J. Tonnage: 9,135. Dimensions: 484′ x 72′. Twin-screw, 19 knots. Two steam turbines. Two masts and two funnels. Torpedoed and sunk in the Mediterranean, 1944. The sur-

vivors were rescued by the Matson liner **Monterey**. Sister ships: **Santa Lucia**, **Santa Paula** and **Santa Rosa**.

Santa Elisa   (1919)   Grace Line.
Built by New York Shipbuilding Corp., Camden, N. J. Tonnage: 5,004. Dimensions: 360′ x 51′ (373′ o.l.). Single-screw, 14 knots. Quadruple expansion engines. Two masts and one funnel. Passengers: 114: Renamed: **Baranof** (1936). Sold to Japanese shipbreakers in 1955. Sister ship: **Santa Teresa**.

Santa Fe   (1902)   Hamburg-South American Line.
Built by C. S. Swan & Hunter, Ltd., Newcastle, England. Tonnage: 4,477. Dimensions: 388′ x 47′. Single-screw, 10 knots. Triple expansion engines. Two masts and one funnel. Passengers: 700 steerage. Vessel seized at Antwerp in 1914. Repurchased by Hamburg-South American Line in 1921. Scrapped at Danzig in 1932.

Santa Ines   (1914)   Hamburg-South American Line.
Built by Bremer Vulkan, Vegesack, Germany. Tonnage: 5,261. Dimensions: 401′ x 55′. Single-screw. Triple expansion engines. Two masts and one funnel. Renamed: **Rio de Janeiro** (1921). Torpedoed and sunk by Polish submarine off Norway, April 9, 1940.

*Santa Ines   (1953)   Hamburg-South American Line.
Built by A. G. Howaldtswerke, Hamburg, Germany. Tonnage: 8,995. Dimensions: 473′ x 61′. Single-screw, 14 knots. Motorship. Single mast and one funnel. Passengers: 28. Sister ship: **Santa Teresa**.

Santa Inez   (1929)   Grace Line.
Built by Akt. Burmeister & Wain, Copenhagen, Denmark. Tonnage: 4,691. Dimensions: 370′ x 53′. Twin-screw, 14 knots. Motorship. Two masts and one funnel. Passengers: 75 first and 48 second. Sold as a transport to United States Navy in 1940. Sister ship: **Santa Rita**.

Santa Isabel   (1915)   Grace Line.
Built by Nederlandsch Schps. Maats, Amsterdam, Nether-lands. Tonnage: 5,641. Dimensions: 380′ x 48′. Single-screw, 14 knots. Triple expansion engines. Two masts and one funnel. Scrapped in 1939. Ex-**Venezuela**. Sister ships: **Santa Olivia** and **Santa Columbia**.

*Santa Isabel   (1946)   Grace Line.
Built by North Carolina Shipbuilding Co., Wilmington, N. C. Tonnage: 8,357.   Dimensions: 441′ x 63′.   Single-screw, 16 knots.   Passengers: 52 first-class.   Crew: 9 officers, 74 men. Service: New York and South American west coast ports. Sister ships: See **Santa Barbara.**

Santa Lucia   (1933)   Grace Line.
Built by Federal Shipbuilding Co., Kearny, N. J.   Tonnage: 9,135.   Dimensions: 484′ x 72′.   Twin-screw, 20 knots.   Two steam turbines.   Two masts and two funnels.   Renamed: **Leedstown** (troopship).   Torpedoed and sunk off Algiers in November 1942.   Sister ships: **Santa Elena, Santa Paula** and **Santa Rosa.**

Santa Luisa (1918) Grace Line.
Built by W. Cramp & Sons Shipbuilding Co., Philadelphia, Pa.   Tonnage: 4,847.   Dimensions: 360′ x 51′.   Single-screw, 14 knots.   Quadruple expansion engines.   Two masts and one funnel.   Passengers: 120.   Renamed: (a) **El Salvado,** (b) **Santa Ana,** (c) **Mount McKinley.**

*Santa Luisa   (1946)   Grace Line.
Built by North Carolina Shipbuilding Co., Wilmington, N. C. Tonnage: 8,357.   Dimensions: 441′ x 63′.   Single-screw, 16 knots.   Steam turbines.   Two masts and one funnel.   Passengers: 52.   Sister ships: See **Santa Barbara.**

*Santa Margarita   (1946)   Grace Line.
Built by North Carolina Shipbuilding Co., Wilmington, N. C. Tonnage: 8,357.   Dimensions: 441′ x 63′.   Single-screw, 16 knots.   Steam turbines.   Two masts and one funnel.   Passengers: 52.   Sister ships: See **Santa Barbara.**

Santa Maria   (1907)   Hamburg-South American Line.
Built by Flensburger Schiffsb. Ges., Flensburg, Germany. Tonnage: 7,401.   Dimensions: 426′ x 55′.   Single-screw, 11 knots.   Quadruple expansion engines.   Two masts and one funnel.   Vessel surrendered to Great Britain in 1918.   Resold to Hamburg-South American Line in 1922.   Renamed: **Villa Garcia** (1922).   Scrapped in Germany in 1932.

Santa Maria   (1928)   Grace Line.
Built by Furness Shipbuilding Co., Haverton-on-Tees, England. Tonnage: 8,060.   Dimensions: 466′ x 64′ (486′ o.l.). Twin-screw, 16½ knots.   Two masts and two funnels. Passengers: 158 in one class.   Renamed: **Barnett** (United States transport).   Sister ship: **Santa Barbara.**

*Santa Maria   (1946)   Grace Line.
Built by North Carolina Shipbuilding Co., Wilmington, N. C.
Tonnage: 8,357.   Dimensions: 441′ x 63′.   Single-screw, 16
knots.   Steam turbines.   Two masts and one funnel.   Passengers: 52.   Sister ships: See **Santa Barbara.**

*Santa Maria   (1953)   Companhia Colonial de Navegacao
(Portugal).
Built by Soc. Anon. John Cockerill, Hoboken, Netherlands.
Tonnage: 20,906.   Dimensions: 574′ x 75′ (610′ o.l.).   Twin-
screw, 20 knots.   Six steam turbines.   Single mast and one
funnel.   Launched, June 2, 1951.   Passengers: 1,200 (3 class
ship).   Note: One of the most startling dramas in the history
of marine transportation occurred during the early hours of
January 22, 1961, when this beautiful luxury liner was seized
by an armed band of Portuguese insurgents, who had previously boarded the ship posing as passengers.   After a long
voyage to "no where" (while being hunted by ships and aircraft) the cornered liner landed her passengers at Recife,
Brazil on February 2nd.   She was promptly returned to her
owners, and soon resumed normal service.   Sister ship:
Vera Cruz.

Santa Marta   (1909)   United Fruit Co.
Built by Workman, Clark & Co., Belfast, Ireland.   Tonnage:
4,601.   Dimensions: 378′ x 50′.   Single-screw, 14 knots.
Triple expansion engines.   Two masts and one funnel.
Scrapped at Baltimore in 1948.   Sister ships: See **Metapan.**

*Santa Monica   (1946)   Grace Line.
Built by Federal Shipbuilding & Drydock Co., Kearny, N. J.
Tonnage: 8,610.   Dimensions: 441′ x 63′.   Single-screw,
16 knots.   Steam turbines.   Two masts and one funnel.
Passengers: 52.   Service: New York-Caribbean-South America
(north coast).   Sister ships: **Santa Clara** and **Santa Sofia.**

Santa Olivia   (1915)   Grace Line.
Built by Kon. Maats de Schelde, Flushing, Netherlands.
Tonnage: 5,544.   Dimensions: 360′ x 48′ (380′ o.l.).   Single-
screw, 14 knots.   Triple expansion engines.   Two masts and
one funnel.   Renamed: (a) **David W. Branch** (1937), (b)
Luxor (1947), (c) **Negbah** (1948).   Scrapped in Italy, 1956.
Ex-**Ecuador** (1925).   Sister ships: **Santa Columbia** and
Santa Isabel.

Santa Paula   (1932)   Grace Line.
Built by Federal Shipbuilding Co., Kearny, N. J.   Tonnage:
9,135.   Dimensions: 484′ x 72′ (508′ o.l.).   Twin-screw,

470

19 knots. Two steam turbines. Two masts and two funnels. Note: One of the most active troopships of World War II. Resumed passenger service after the war. Renamed: **Acropolis** (1960). Sister ships: **Santa Elena, Santa Lucia** and **Santa Rosa.**

*Santa Paula (1958)   Grace Line.
Built by Newport News Shipbuilding Co., Newport News, Va. Tonnage: 15,366. Dimensions: 583′ (o.l.) x 84′. Twin-screw, 20 knots. Two steam turbines. Single mast and one funnel. Passengers: 300. Note: This luxury liner made a special sailing up the Hudson River to Albany, N. Y., October 12, 1958. Sister ship: **Santa Inez.**

Santa Rita (1929)   Grace Line.
Built by Akt. Burmeister & Wain, Copenhagen, Denmark. Tonnage: 4,577. Dimensions: 370′ x 53′. Twin-screw, 14 knots. Motorship. Two masts and one funnel. Passengers: 77. Renamed: **William Ward Burrows.** Scrapped in California, 1957. Sister ship: **Santa Rita.**

Santa Rosa (1932)   Grace Line.
Built by Federal Shipbuilding Co., Camden, N. J. Tonnage: 9,135. Dimensions: 484′ x 72′ (508′ o.l.). Twin-screw, 19 knots. Steam turbines. Two masts and two funnels. Renamed: (a) **Santa Paula** (1958), (b) **Athinai.** Sister ships: **Santa Elena, Santa Lucia** and **Santa Paula.**

*Santa Rosa (1959)   Grace Line.
Built by Newport News Shipbuilding Co., Newport News, Va. Tonnage: 15,400. Dimensions: 583′ (o.l.) x 84′. Twin-screw, 20 knots. Steam turbines. Single mast and one funnel. In collision with the oil tanker Valchem on March 26, 1959. None of the 247 passengers on board were injured. The liner did not suffer serious damage. Sister ship: **Santa Paula.**

*Santa Sofia (1947)   Grace Line.
Built by Federal Shipbuilding Co., Kearny, N. J. Tonnage: 8,610. Dimensions: 441′ x 63′. Single-screw, 16 knots. Steam turbines. Two masts and one funnel. Passengers: 52. Route: New York to Caribbean and South American North Coast ports. Sister ships: **Santa Clara** and **Santa Monica.**

Santa Teresa (1918)   Grace Line.
Built by W. Cramp & Sons Shipbuilding Co., Philadelphia, Pa. Tonnage: 5,103. Dimensions: 360′ x 51′. Single-screw, 14 knots. Quadruple expansion engines. Two masts and one funnel. Passengers: 114. Renamed: (a) **Kent,** (b) **Ernest**

Hinds (hospital ship). Scrapped at Baltimore, 1957. Sister ship: **Santa Elisa.**

***Santa Teresa**   (1952)   Hamburg-South American Line.
Built by Howaldtswerke, A. G., Hamburg, Germany. Tonnage: 8,996. Dimensions: 473' x 61'. Single-screw, 14 knots. Motorship. Single-mast and one funnel. Passengers: 28. Sister ship: **Santa Ines.**

Santarem   (1908)   Lloyd Brasileiro.
Built by Bremer Vulkan, Vegesack, Germany. Tonnage: 6,757. Dimensions: 419' x 54'. Single-screw, 12 knots. Quadruple expansion engines. Two masts and one funnel. Passengers: 62 first and 200 third. Service: Santos-Hamburg. Ex-**Eisenach.** Sister ship: **Pocone.**

Santarense   (1891)   Booth Line.
Built by Nederlandsch Stoomvaart, Rotterdam, Netherlands. Tonnage: 2,751. Dimensions: 321' x 40'. Single-screw, 12 knots. Triple expansion engines. Two masts and one funnel. Steel hull. Not listed in 1898 registers. Ex-**Didam** (1895).

Santiago   (1879)   Ward Line.
Built by John Roach & Son, Chester, Pa. Tonnage: 2,359. Dimensions: 369' x 39'. Single-screw, 13 knots. Compound engines. Two masts and one funnel. Sunk by storm off Cape Hatteras on March 11, 1924, with the loss of 25 lives.

Santiago   (1891)   Lloyd del Pacifico (Italian).
Built by Fairfield Shipbuilding Co., Glasgow, Scotland. Tonnage: 4,977. Dimensions: 430' x 47'. Single-screw, 13 knots. Triple expansion engines. Two masts and one funnel. Service: Italy-Chile. Ex-**Weimar** (1909). Sister ship: **Valparaiso.**

Santiago   (1901)   Soc. Anon. Comercial Braun (Chile).
Built by Alexander Stephen & Sons, Ltd., Glasgow, Scotland. Tonnage: 3,909. Dimensions: 371' x 45'. Single-screw, 14 knots. Triple expansion engines. Two masts and one funnel. Clipper bow. Ex-**Byron,** ex-**Loyalist** (1901).

***Santos**   (1898)   (a) Hamburg-South American Line, (b) Lloyd Brasileiro.
Built by Reiherstieg Schiffsw., Hamburg, Germany. Tonnage: 4,855. Dimensions: 375' x 46'. Single-screw, 12½ knots. Quadruple expansion engines. Two masts and one funnel. Vessel was seized by Brazil in 1917; retained same name. Sold to Lloyd Brasileiro in 1927.

Santos Maru   (1925)   Osaka Line.
    Built by Mitsubishi Zozen Kaisha, Ltd., Nagasaki, Japan.
    Tonnage: 7,267.   Dimensions: 430′ x 56′.   Twin-screw, 15
    knots.   Motorship.   Two masts and one funnel.   Service:
    Japan-South Africa-South America.   Sunk by American sub-
    marine, November 25, 1944.

Saramacca   (1908)   (a) Royal Netherlands Steamship Co.,
    (b) Tropical Fruit Co.
    Built by Nederlandsch Schps. Maats, Amsterdam, Nether-
    lands. Tonnage: 3,284. Dimensions: 336′ x 41′. Single-screw,
    13 knots.   Triple expansion engines.   Two masts and one
    funnel.   Similar ships: **Coppename, Marowijne** and
    Suriname.

Saratoga   (1878)   Ward Line.   (Alexander Line.)
    Built by John Roach & Son, Chester, Pa. Tonnage: 2,820.
    Dimensions: 298′ x 38′. Single-screw, 14½ knots. Compound
    engines.   Two masts and one funnel.   Iron hull.   Note: Vessel
    was sold in 1879 by builders to Russia.   Never ran for Ward
    Line.   Renamed: **Africa.**

Saratoga   (1907)   Ward Line.
    Built by W. Cramp & Sons Shipbuilding Co., Philadelphia,
    Pa. Tonnage: 6,391. Dimensions: 413′ x 50′. Twin-screw,
    18 knots.   Triple expansion engines.   Two masts and two
    funnels.   Renamed: **Mercury.**

Sardegna   (1901)   (a) Navigazione Generale Italiana, (b) Soc.
    Italiana di Servizi Marittimi.
    Tonnage: 5,337. Service: Italy-South America. *Note: See
    PART I for details.*

Sarmiento   (1893)   Pacific Steam Navigation Co.
    Built by Harland & Wolff, Ltd., Belfast, Ireland. Tonnage:
    3,603.   Dimensions: 361′ x 43′.   Single-screw, 13½ knots.
    Triple expansion engines.   Two masts and one funnel.   Steel
    hull.   Vessel sold in 1910.   Renamed: **Normand.**   Class:
    Antisana, Inca and **Magellan.**

Saturnia   (1927)   (a) Cosulich Line, (b) Italia Line.
    Tonnage: 23,940. Her maiden voyage was from Trieste to
    South America in 1927. *Note: See PART I for details.*

Savoia   (1897)   La Veloce Line.
    Built by N. Odero & Co., Foce, Genoa, Italy.   Tonnage:
    5,082. Dimensions: 462′ x 45′. Twin-screw, 15 knots. Triple
    expansion engines.   Two masts and one funnel. Note: Her

tall thin funnel was placed somewhat aft. Vessel was lengthened in 1901. Tonnage increased from 4,429 to 5,082. Broken
up for scrap in 1923. Sister ship: **Venezuela.**

Savoie   (1854)   Transport Maritimes (French).
    Built by John Laird, Birkenhead, England. Tonnage: 2,522.
Dimensions: 335' x 36'. Single-screw. Iron hull. Probably
rebuilt in 1867. Renamed: **Savoia** (Italian). Tonnage listed
as 2,883 in 1892. Ex-**Cristobal Colon.**

Savoie   (1889)   Transport Maritimes (French).
    Built by Wigham Richardson & Co., Newcastle, England.
Tonnage: 2,021. Dimensions: 300' x 35'. Single-screw, 13
knots. Triple expansion engines. Two masts and one funnel.
Scrapped in France, 1927. Ex-**Citta di Genova** (1899).

Schleswig   (1903)   North German Lloyd.
    Built by Act. Ges. "Vulkan", Stettin, Germany. Tonnage:
6,955. Dimensions: 450' x 52' (467' o.l.). Twin-screw, 13½
knots. Triple expansion engines. Two masts and one funnel.
Built for South American service, but made some North
Atlantic sailings. Renamed: **General Duchesne** (1919).

Scotia   (1881)   Fabre Line.
    Tonnage: 2,492. Her first Marseilles to South America
voyage was made in December 1882. *Note: See PART I for
details.*

Seattle   (1928)   Hamburg-American Line.
    Built by Deutsche Werft, Hamburg, Germany. Tonnage:
7,369. Dimensions: 461' x 61'. Single-screw, 13½ knots.
Motorship. Two masts and one funnel. Service: Germany-
Central America. Accommodated a few passengers. Lost by
sinking in April 1940.

Seattle Maru   (1909)   Osaka Line.
    Tonnage: 6,182. Service: (a) Trans-Pacific, (b) South
America. *Note: See PART II for details.*

*Sebastiano Caboto   (1947)   Italia Line.
    Built by Soc. Anon. Ansaldo, Genoa-Sestri, Italy. Tonnage:
8,967. Dimensions: 466' x 62' (485' o.l.). Single-screw, 15½
knots. Motorship. Two masts and one funnel. Passengers:
700. Similar ships: **Amerigo Vespucci, Antoniotto Usodimare, Marco Polo** and **Paolo Toscanelli.**

Segura   (1893)   Royal Mail Line (British).
    Built by Harland & Wolff, Ltd., Belfast, Ireland. Tonnage:
4,756. Dimensions: 400' x 47'. Twin-screw, 12 knots. Triple

expansion engines. Two masts and one funnel. Renamed: (a) **Pembrokeshire** (1908), (b) **Chignecto** (1913). Scrapped in 1927. Ex-**Greek** (1906).

Seguranca   (1890)   Ward Line.
Built by Delaware River Co. (Formerly John Roach & Son). Chester, Pa. Tonnage: 4,033. Dimensions: 321′ x 45′. Single-screw, 14½ knots. Triple expansion engines. Steel and iron hull. Two masts and two funnels. Passengers: 100 first and 22 second. No longer in commission, 1929.

Seine   (1860)   Royal Mail Line (British).
Built by Thames Ironworks, Blackwall, England. Tonnage: 3,440. Dimensions: 338′ x 44′. Paddle-wheels. Three masts and two funnels. Iron hull. Out of fleet in 1871. Similar to **Shannon.**

Seneca   (1884)   (a) Clyde Line, (b) Ward Line.
Built by Delaware River Co., Chester, Pa. Tonnage: 2,963. Dimensions: 299′ x 40′. Single-screw, 15 knots. Triple expansion engines. Later converted to turbo-electric. Two masts and one funnel. In Clyde Line service as late as 1926.

Senegal   (1872)   Messageries Maritimes.
Built by Messageries Maritimes, La Ciotat, France. Tonnage: 3,717. Dimensions: 392′ x 40′. Single-screw, 13½ knots. Compound engines. Three masts and one funnel. Sold for scrap after having struck a floating mine at Smyrne in August 1913. Sister ship: **Niger.**

Sequana   (1898)   Compagnie Sud-Atlantique (French).
Built by Workman, Clark & Co., Belfast, Ireland. Tonnage: 4,950. Dimensions: 430′ x 50′. Single-screw, 13 knots. Triple expansion engines. Two masts and one funnel. Not listed in 1919. Ex-**City of Corinth** (City Line).

Serena   (1881)   Pacific Steam Navigation Co.
Built by Robert Napier & Sons, Glasgow, Scotland. Tonnage: 2,398. Dimensions: 320′ x 40′. Single-screw, 14 knots. Compound engines. Steel hull. Converted to a hulk in 1902. Sister ship: **Puno.**

Serpa Pinto   (1915)   Compahia Colonial de Navegacao (Portuguese).
Built by Workman, Clark & Co., Belfast, Ireland. Tonnage: 8,267. Dimensions: 450′ x 57′. Twin-screw, 14 knots. Quadruple expansion engines. Two masts and one funnel. Service:

Lisbon-Santos. Scrapped in 1955. Ex-**Princesa Olga** (1940), ex-**Ebro** (1935).

17 de Octubre   (1950)   Dodero Line (Argentine).
Built by Vickers-Armstrongs, Ltd., Newcastle, England. Tonnage: 12,634. Dimensions: 509' x 71' (530' o.l.). Twin-screw, 18½ knots. Steam turbines. Two masts and one funnel. Passengers: 96 first-class. Service: Buenos Aires-London. Renamed: **Liberstad** (1955). Sister ships: **Eva Peron** and **Presidente Peron.**

Severn   (1842)   Royal Mail Line (British).
Built by William Patterson, Bristol, England. Tonnage: 1,886. Dimensions: 000' x 00'. Paddle-wheels, 8 knots. Speed later increased to 10 knots by alteration of paddle-wheels. Three masts and one funnel. Wooden hull. Out of fleet in 1856.

Seydlitz   (1903)   North German Lloyd.
Tonnage: 7,942. Originally built for Far East/Australia trades. However made a number of North Atlantic crossings. In Bremen-Cuba service in 1924. *Note: See PART I for details.*

Shannon   (1859)   Royal Mail Line (British).
Built by Robert Napier & Sons, Glasgow, Scotland. Tonnage: 3,609. Dimensions: 330' x 44'. Paddle-wheels. Two side lever type engines. Three masts and two funnels. Iron hull. Out of fleet in 1875. Similar to **Seine.**

Shinano Maru   (1900)   N.Y.K. Line (Japanese).
Tonnage: 6,416. In Japan-South American service. *Note: See PART II for details.*

Siboney   (1918)   Ward Line:
Built by W. Cramp & Sons Shipbuilding Co., Philadelphia, Pa. Tonnage: 6,938. Dimensions: 423' x 60' (443' o.l.). Twin-screw, 17 knots. Four steam turbines. Two masts and two funnels. Note: In trans-Atlantic service in 1920. Converted to an American troopship in 1941. Renamed: **Charles A. Stafford** (1944) American hospital ship. Note: As the **Charles A. Stafford** had only a single funnel. Scrapped in United States, 1957. Sister ship: **Orizaba.**

Sicilia   (1900)   Navigazione Generale Italiana.
Tonnage: 5,202. In Italy-South American trade. *Note: See PART I for details.*

476

Sicilia   (1923)   Italia Line.
Built by Akt. Ges. "Weser", Bremen, Germany. Tonnage:
9,646. Dimensions: 458' x 57' (479' o.l.). Twin-screw, 11
knots. Steam turbines. Two masts and one funnel. Vessel
was later transferred to Lloyd Triestino. Became a war loss,
April 23, 1943. Ex-**Coblenz** (1935). Sister ship: **Toscana.**

Sicilian   (1899)   Allan Line.
Tonnage: 6,224. Used in South American service. *Note: See
PART I for details.*

Siena   (1905)   (a) Soc. di Nav. a Vap. "Italia", (b) La Veloce
Line.
Built by N. Odero fu A. & Co., Sestri, Pnente, Italy. Ton-
nage: 4,553. Dimensions: 380' x 46'. Twin-screw, 14 knots.
Triple expansion engines. Two masts and one funnel. Lost
during First World War. Sister ship: **Bologna.** Sold to
La Veloce Line in 1913.

Sierra Cordoba   (1913)   North German Lloyd.
Built by Akt. Ges. "Vulkan", Stettin, Germany. Tonnage:
8,226. Dimensions: 439' x 56'. Twin-screw, 14 knots. Triple
expansion engines. Two masts and one funnel. Renamed:
(a) **Callao** (1917), (b) **Ruth Alexander.** Bombed and sunk
in the Far East, January 9, 1942, with loss of one life. Sister
ships: **Sierra Nevada, Sierra Salvada** and **Sierra Ventana.**
Note: The **Sierra Cordoba** was taken over by Peru in 1917.

Sierra Cordoba   (1923)   North German Lloyd.
Built by Bremer Vulkan, Vegesack, Germany. Tonnage:
11,469. Dimensions: 490' x 61' (511' o.l.). Twin-screw, 14½
knots. Triple expansion engines. Two masts and two funnels.
Transferred to D.A.F. in 1935, under management of North
German Lloyd. Scrapped in 1948. Sister ships: **Sierra
Morena** and **Sierra Ventana.**

Sierra Morena   (1924)   North German Lloyd.
Built by Bremer Vulkan, Vegesack, Germany. Tonnage:
11,430. Dimensions: 490' x 61' (511' o.l.). Twin-screw,
14½ knots. Triple expansion engines. Two masts and two
funnels. Renamed: (a) **Der Deutsche** (1934), (b) **Asia** (1946)
Russian. Sister ships: **Sierra Cordoba** and **Sierra Ventana.**

Sierra Nevada   (1912)   North German Lloyd.
Built by Akt. Ges. "Vulkan", Stettin, Germany. Tonnage:
8,235. Dimensions: 439' x 56'. Twin-screw, 13½ knots.
Triple expansion engines. Two masts and one funnel. Pas-

sengers: 120 first, 80 third, 1,450 steerage. Renamed: **Bage** (1917) Brazilian. Sister ships: **Sierra Cordoba, Sierra Salvada** and **Sierra Ventana.**

Sierra Nevada (1921) Hamburg-South American Line.
Built by Akt. Ges. "Vulkan", Hamburg, Germany. Tonnage: 13,589. Dimensions: 499′ x 64′. Twin-screw, 15 knots. Triple expansion engines. Two masts and one funnel. Renamed: **Antonio Delfino** (1934). Ex-**Antonio Delfino** (1932).

Sierra Nevada (1922) North German Lloyd.
Built by Vulkan Werke, Stettin, Germany. Tonnage: 8,753. Dimensions: 439′ x 56′. Twin-screw, 14 knots. Triple expansion engines. Two masts and two funnels. Maiden voyage Bremen-New York in September 1922. Transferred to South American service. Renamed: **Madrid** (1926). Purchased by Hamburg-South American Line in 1934. Sunk off Den Helder by air attack, December 9, 1941.

Sierra Salvada (1912) North German Lloyd.
Built by Bremer Vulkan, Vegesack, Germany. Tonnage: 8,227. Dimensions: 439′ x 56′. Twin-screw, 13½ knots. Triple expansion engines. Two masts and one funnel. Passengers: 120 first, 80 third, 1,450 steerage. Renamed: (a) **Avare,** (b) **Peer Gynt,** (c) **Neptunia,** (d) **Oceana.** Sister ships: **Sierra Cordoba, Sierra Nevada** and **Sierra Ventana.**

Sierra Salvada (1922) Hamburg-South American Line.
Built by Vulkan Werke, Hamburg, Germany. Tonnage: 13,615. Dimensions: 499′ x 64′. Twin-screw, 15 knots. Triple expansion engines. Two masts and one funnel. Renamed: (a) **Cap Norte** (1934), (b) **Empire Trooper** (1940), Ex-**Cap Norte** (1932). Scrapped in 1955.

Sierra Ventana (1912) North German Lloyd
Built by Bremer Vulkan, Vegesack, Germany. Tonnage: 8,396. Dimensions: 440′ x 55′. Twin-screw, 13½ knots. Triple expansion engines. Two masts and one funnel. Passengers: 120 first, 80 third, 1,450 steerage. Renamed: (a) **Alba,** (b) **Amerique.** Sister ships: **Sierra Cordoba, Sierra Nevada** and **Sierra Salvada.**

Sierra Ventana (1923) North German Lloyd.
Built by Bremer Vulkan, Vegesack, Germany. Tonnage: 11,392. Dimensions: 490′ x 61′ (511′ o.l.). Twin-screw, 14½ knots. Triple expansion engines. Two masts and two funnels. Renamed: **Sardegna** (1935). She became a war

loss, December 29, 1940. Sister ships: **Sierra Cordoba** and **Sierra Morena.**

Silesia   (1869)   Hamburg-American Line.
Built by Caird & Co., Greenock, Scotland. Tonnage: 3,142. Dimensions: 341'. In Germany-West Indies service. *Note· See PART I for details.*

Silesia   (1897)   Hamburg-American Line.
Built by Blohm & Voss, Hamburg, Germany. Tonnage: 4,489. Dimensions: 400' x 46'. Single-screw. Triple expansion engines. Vessel was turned over from Germany to Holland in 1917, so as to replace "Safe Conduct" ship illegally sunk by submarine. Renamed: (a) **Zaandijk,** (b) **Harpon** (1926) Argentine. Ex-**Wally.**

Simon Bolivar   (1927)   Royal Netherlands Steamship Co.
Built by Rotterdamsche Droogdok Maatschappij, Rotterdam, Netherlands. Tonnage: 7,906. Dimensions: 419' x 59'. Single-screw, 13½ knots. Quadruple expansion engines. Two masts and two funnels. Service: Amsterdam-West Indies. Torpedoed and sunk, November 18, 1939.

Siqueira Campos   (1907)   Lloyd Brasileiro.
Built by Reierstieg Schiffsw., Hamburg, Germany. Tonnage: 6,456. Dimensions: 415' x 50'. Twin-screw, 12½ knots. Triple expansion engines. Two masts and one funnel. Service: Santos-Hamburg. In collision and beached, August 25, 1943, and became a total loss. Ex-**Cantuaria Guimaraes,** ex-**Curvello,** ex-**Gertrud Woermann.**

Sirio   (1883)   Navigazione Generale Italiana.
Built by Robert Napier & Sons, Glasgow, Scotland. Tonnage: 4,141. Dimensions: 380' x 42'. Single-screw, 16 knots. Triple expansion engines. Three masts and two funnels. Iron hull. Service: Italy-South America. Wrecked off Cape Palos, August 4, 1906, with the loss of 350 lives. Sister ship: **Orione.**

Sixaola   (1911)   United Fruit Company.
Built by Workman, Clark & Co., Belfast, Ireland. Tonnage: 4,693. Dimensions: 378' x 50'. Single-screw, 14 knots. Triple expansion engines. Two masts and one funnel. Torpedoed and sunk in the Caribbean, June 12, 1942. Sister ships: See **Metapan.** Note: The **Sixaola** and **Santa Marta** continued as active passenger ships when some of their sister ships were converted to 12 passenger capacity.

Sobieski (1939) Gydnia-American Line.
Built by Swan, Hunter & Wigham Richardson, Ltd., Newcastle, England. Tonnage: 11,030. Dimensions: 493′ x 67′ (511′ o.l.). Twin-screw, 17 knots. Motorship. Two masts and one funnel. Built for the Gydnia-South American service. Renamed: **Gruzia** (1953) Russian. Sister ship: **Chrobry.**

Sobral (1906) Lloyd Brasileiro.
Built by Blohm & Voss, Hamburg, Germany. Tonnage: 9,346. Dimensions: 476′ x 55′. Twin-screw, 15 knots. Quadruple expansion engines. Two masts and one funnel. Renamed: **General Metzinger** (1924). Ex-**Cap Vilano** (1917).

Solent (1853) Royal Mail Line (British).
Built by T. & J. White, Cowes, England. Tonnage: 1,804. Dimensions: 000′ x 00′. Paddle-wheels, 14 knots. Three masts and two funnels. Constructed of wood and iron frames. Launched on June 8, 1853. Out of fleet in 1869.

Solent (1878) Royal Mail Line (British).
Built by Oswald Mordaunt & Co., Southampton, England. Tonnage: 1,915. Dimensions: 321′ x 35′. Single-screw, 9 knots. Compound engines. Two masts and one funnel. Passengers: 115 first and 22 second. Scrapped in 1909.

Solway (1841) Royal Mail Line (British).
Built by James MacMillan, Greenock, Scotland. Tonnage: 1,700. Paddle-wheels, 8 knots. Three masts and one funnel. Wooden hull. Made her first sailing, December 18, 1841. Lost due to grounding on reef in April 1843, while outbound from La Coruna. Thirty-six lives were lost, including the Captain.

Sorata (1872) Pacific Steam Navigation Co.
Built by John Elder & Co., Glasgow, Scotland. Tonnage: 4,014. Dimensions: 401′ x 42′. Single-screw, 14 knots. Compound engines. Three masts and one funnel. Iron hull. Clipper bow. Placed in the service of Orient Line to Australia in 1879. Scrapped in 1895. Sister ships: **Aconcagua, Cotopaxi** and **Illimani.**

South America (1861) United States & Brazil Mail Steamship Co.
Built by William H. Webb, New York, N. Y. Tonnage: 2,150. Dimensions: 256′ x 38′. Paddle-wheels, 13½ knots. Vertical beam engines. Two masts and one funnel. Wooden hull. Left New York on her first sailing to Brazil, November

30, 1865. Made her last voyage in September 1875. Laid up and was not listed after 1879. Running mate: **North America.**

Southern Cross (1921) Munson Line.
Built by New York Shipbuilding Corp., Camden, N. J. Tonnage: 13,789. Dimensions: 516′ x 72′ (535′ o.l.). Twin-screw, 17 knots. Steam turbines. Two masts and one funnel. Broken up for scrap at Seattle in 1954. Sister ships: **American Legion, Pan America** and **Western World.**

Southern Prince (1929) Furness-Prince Line.
Built by Lithgows, Ltd., Port Glasgow, Scotland. Tonnage: 10,917. Dimensions: 496′ x 64′ (516′ o.l.). Twin-screw, 16 knots. Motorship. Two masts and one funnel. Owner: Prince Line, Ltd., Managers: Furness, Withy & Co., Ltd. Renamed: **Anna C** (1947). Sister ships: **Eastern Prince, Northern Prince** and **Western Prince.**

Spaarndam (1922) Holland-American Line.
Tonnage: 8,857. In Europe-West Indies-Central America service. *Note: See PART I for details.*

Spreewald (1922) Hamburg-American Line.
Built by Deutsche Werft, Hamburg, Germany. Tonnage: 5,083. Dimensions: 399′ x 54′. Twin-screw, 12½ knots. Motorship. Two masts and one funnel. Service: Germany-West Indies. Renamed: (a) **Anubis** (1935), (b) **Spreewald** (1939). Due to an error she was sunk by a German submarine in 1942, while being employed by German Navy.

Stephen (1910) Booth Line.
Built by Hawthorn, Leslie & Co., Newcastle, England. Tonnage: 4,435. Dimensions: 376′ x 50′. Single-screw, 11 knots. Triple expansion engines. Two masts and one funnel. Passengers: 46 first and 100 third. Scrapped in 1934. Sister ship: **Aidan.**

Stuttgart (1889) North German Lloyd.
Tonnage: 5,048. Service: Germany-South America. *Note: See PART I for details.*

Stuyvesant (1918) Royal Netherlands Steamship Co.
Built by Nederlandsche Schps. Maats., Amsterdam, Netherlands. Tonnage: 4,249. Dimensions: 342′ x 47′ (355′ o.l.). Single-screw, 12 knots. Triple expansion engines. Two masts and one funnel. Renamed: **Aeolia** (1950).

Sud America   (1868)   La Veloce Line.
  Built by Caird & Co., Greenock, Scotland. Tonnage: 3,185.
  Dimensions: 339' x 40'. Single-screw, 13 knots. Compound
  engines installed in 1878. Also two funnels replaced the
  original single one. Scrapped in 1901. Ex-**Mentana** (1890),
  ex-**Provincia di San Paolo** (1889), ex-**Atlantica** (1888),
  ex-**Westphalia** (1887).

Sud America   (1873)   La Veloce Line.
  Built by Wigham Richardson, Newcastle, England. Tonnage: 2,246. Dimensions: 313' x 35'. Single-screw. Two
  compound inverted D.A. type engines. Four masts and one
  funnel. Iron hull. Service: Italy-South America. Lost by
  collision about 1888.

Sully   (1874)   Chargeurs Reunis.
  Built by Forges & Chantiers de la Mediterranee, Graville,
  Havre, France. Tonnage: 1,326. Dimensions: 247' x 30'.
  Single-screw. Compound engines. Three masts and one
  funnel. Iron hull. Launched, March 19, 1874. Service:
  France-South America. Chargeurs Reunis purchased vessel
  in 1880; sold her in 1891.

Suriname   (1908)   (a) Royal Netherlands Steamship Co.,
  (b) Tropical Fruit Company. (Subsidiary of the United Fruit
  Company.)
  Built by Nederlandsch Schps. Maats., Amsterdam, Netherlands. Tonnage: 3,275. Dimensions: 336' x 41'. Single-screw,
  13 knots. Triple expansion engines. Two masts and one
  funnel. Similar ships: **Coppename, Marowijne** and
  Saramacca.

Surriento   (1928)   Achille Lauro Line (Italian).
  Built by Furness Shipbuilding Co., Haverton Hill-on-Tees,
  England. Tonnage: 10,699. Dimensions: 466' x 64'. Twin-
  screw, 16½ knots. Motorship. Two masts and two funnels.
  Passengers: 187 first, 868 tourist. Service: (a) Italy-South
  America, (b) Italy-Australia, via Panama Canal route.
  Ex-**Barnett** (1948), ex-**Santa Maria.**

Swiatowid   (1908)   Chargeurs Reunis.
  Built by Ateliers & Chantiers de la Loire, St. Nazaire, France.
  Tonnage: 8,497. Dimensions: 484' x 55'. Twin-screw, 14
  knots. Triple expansion engines. Two masts and one funnel.
  Note: Renamed **Swiatowid** in 1928 for Gdynia-South American emigrant service. Scrapped in 1934. Ex-**Ouessant**
  (1928).

Sydney   (1944)   Achille Lauro Line (Italian).
Built by Western Pipe & Steel Co., San Francisco, California.
Tonnage: 14,708. Dimensions: 468′ x 69′ (492′ o.l.). Single-
screw, 17 knots. Steam turbines. Single mast and one funnel.
Passengers: 100 first, 670 tourist. Service: (a) Italy-South
America, (b) Genoa-Australia. Ex-**Fencer** (British escort
aircraft carrier on a "C-3" type ship hull). Converted into a
passenger ship for Lauro Line. Renamed **Sydney** in 1953.
Sister ship: **Roma.**

Tacoma   (1930)   Hamburg-American Line.
Built by Deutsche Werft, Hamburg, Germany. Tonnage:
8,268. Dimensions: 477′ x 63′ (499′ o.l.). Single-screw, 13½
knots. Steam turbines. Two masts and one funnel. Service:
Germany-Central America. Vessel now owned by Uruguayan
Government, 1960.

Tacoma Maru   (1909)   Osaka Line.
Tonnage: 6,178. Service: (a) Japan-United States, (b) South
America. *Note: See PART II for details.*

Tacora   (1872)   Pacific Steam Navigation Co.
Built at Glasgow, Scotland. Tonnage: 3,525. Dimensions:
375′ x 41′. Single-screw, 13 knots. Three masts and one
funnel. Clipper bow. Iron hull. Wrecked near Montevideo
in 1872, while on her maiden voyage. Similar ship: **Valparaiso.**

Tagus   (1871)   Royal Mail Line (British).
Built by John Elder & Co., Glasgow, Scotland. Tonnage:
3,298. Dimensions: 358′ x 41′. Single-screw. Two masts and
two funnels. Clipper bow. Iron hull. Out of fleet in 1897.
Sister ship: **Moselle.**

Tagus   (1900)   Royal Mail Line (British).
Built by Robert Napier & Sons, Ltd., Glasgow, Scotland.
Tonnage: 5,545. Dimensions: 410′ x 50′. Single-screw, 15½
knots. Triple expansion engines. Two masts and two funnels.
Out of fleet in 1920. Sister ship: **Trent.**

Takachiho Maru   (1934)   Osaka Line.
Built by Mitsubishi Zosen Kaisha, Ltd., Nagasaki, Japan.
Tonnage: 8,154. Dimensions: 453′ x 59′ (473′ o.l.). Twin-
screw, 16½ knots. Steam turbines. Two masts and one
funnel. In Japan-South America trade. Passengers: 785.
Renamed: **Takatiho Maru** (1938). Became a war casualty,
March 19, 1943.

Talamanca   (1931)   United Fruit Company.
Built by Newport News Shipbuilding Co., Newport News, Va.   Tonnage: 6,963.   Dimensions: 415′ x 60′ (446′ o.l.). Twin-screw, 18 knots.   Two steam turbines connected to electric motors.   Two masts and one funnel.   Renamed: **Sulaco** (Elders & Fyffes, Ltd.).   Sister ships: **Antigua, Chiriqui, Peten, Quirigua** and **Veragua.**

Tamar   (1854)   Royal Mail Line (British).
Built by William Pitcher, Northfleet, England.   Tonnage: 1,850.   Paddle-wheels.   Wooden hull.   Out of fleet in 1871.

Tamar   (1873)   Royal Mail Line (British).
Built by Henderson at Renfrew, Scotland.   Tonnage: 2,923. Dimensions: 349′ x 37′.   Single-screw.   Compound engines. Three masts and one funnel.   Iron hull.   Scrapped in 1898. Ex-**Vancouver** (1878). Sister ship: **Trent.**

Tamaulipas   (1883)   Compania Mexicana Trasatlantica (Mexican).
Built by Robert Napier & Sons, Glasgow, Scotland.   Tonnage: 4,133.   Dimensions: 400′ x 44′.   Single-screw, 14 knots. Compound engines.   Three masts and two funnels.   Steel hull. In Mexico-Spain service during the 1880's.   Renamed: **Vittoria.** Burned on January 11, 1899. Sister ships: **Mexico** and **Oaxaca.**

Tanis   (1902)   Kosmos Steamship Co.
Built by Blohm & Voss, Hamburg, Germany.   Tonnage: 5,950. Dimensions: 410′ x 50′. Single-screw, 11 knots. Triple expansion engines.   Passengers: 32 first, 20 second, 44 third.

Taormina   (1908)   (a) Lloyd Italiano, (b) Navigazione Generale Italiana.
Built by D. & W. Henderson & Co., Glasgow, Scotland. Tonnage: 8,921.   Dimensions: 482′ x 58′ (520′ o.l.).   Twin-screw, 16½ knots. Triple expansion engines. Two masts and one funnel.   Service: (a) Italy-South America, (b) Italy-New York. Sister ships: **Ancona** and **Verona.**

Tartar Prince   (1895)   Prince Line (British).
Built by Short Bros., Sunderland, England. Tonnage: 3,272. Dimensions: 342′ x 43′.   Single-screw, 12 knots.   Triple expansion engines. Two masts and one funnel.   Service: Europe-South America.   Destroyed by fire at sea in 1902.

Tasmanian   (1858)   Royal Mail Line (British).
Built by Hill of Port Glasgow, Scotland. Tonnage: 2,956. Dimensions: 346′ x 39′. Single-screw. Compound engines. Three masts and two funnels. Iron hull. Vessel was purchased from European & Australian Royal Mail Company in 1859. She made a record in 1872 by making the run from Barbados to Plymouth, England in 11 days, 18 hours.

Tay   (1841)   Royal Mail Line (British).
Built by Charles Wood, Dumbarton, Scotland. Tonnage: 1,858. Paddle-wheels, 8 knots. Speed increased to 10 knots by making improvements. Three masts and one funnel. Wooden hull. Commenced her first sailing, December 31, 1841. Out of fleet in 1856.

Tegelberg   (1936)   Royal Inter-Ocean Lines (Dutch).
Built by N. V. Nederlandsch Schps. Maats., Amsterdam, Netherlands. Tonnage: 14,150. Dimensions: 537′ x 72′ (560′ o.l.). Triple-screw, 16½ knots. Motorship. Two masts and one funnel. Passengers: 104 first and 66 second. Service: Far East-South Africa-South America. Sister ships: **Boissevain** and **Ruys.**

Tenadores   (1913)   United Fruit Company.
Built by Workman, Clark & Co., Belfast, Ireland. Tonnage: 7,782. Dimensions: 470′ x 55′. Twin-screw, 15 knots. Quadruple expansion engines. Two masts and one funnel. Passengers: 143. Vessel was lost in First World War. Sister ships: **Calamares** and **Pastores.**

Tennyson   (1900)   Lamport & Holt, Ltd.
Built by Alexander Stephen & Sons, Ltd., Glasgow, Scotland. Tonnage: 3,944. Dimensions: 371′ x 45′. Single-screw, 14 knots. Triple expansion engines. Two masts and one funnel. Renamed: **Valparaiso.** Scrapped in 1932. Ex-**Evangeline** (1901). Sister ship: **Byron.**

Teno   (1896)   Cia Sud Americana de Vapores (Chile).
Built by Caird & Co., Greenock, Scotland. Tonnage: 3,225. Dimensions: 350′ x 43′. Twin-screw. Triple expansion engines. Ex-**Flora** (1936), ex-**Chile.**

Teno   (1922)   Cia Sud-Americana de Vapores (Chile).
Built by Scott's Shipbuilding & Engine Co., Ltd., Greenock, Scotland. Tonnage: 7,289. Dimensions: 422′ x 56′. Twin-screw, 17 knots. Four steam turbines. Two masts and one

funnel.   Passengers: 135 first and 88 second.   Renamed:
Mohamed Ali El-Kiber (1935).   Sister ship: **Aconcagua.**

Teutonia   (1906)   Hamburg-American Line.
   Built by Bremer Vulkan, Vegesack, Germany.   Tonnage:
   6,533.   Dimensions: 409′ x 52′.   Single-screw, 12 knots.   Quadruple expansion engines.   Two masts and one funnel.   Service:
   Germany-West Indies.   Scrapped in 1933.   Ex-**Habsburg.**

Teviot   (1841)   Royal Mail Line (British).
   Built by Robert Duncan, Greenock, Scotland.   Tonnage:
   1,744.   Paddle-wheels, 8 knots.   Three masts and one funnel.
   Wooden hull.   Speed increased to 10 knots by improvements.
   Out of fleet in 1864.

Thames   (1841)   Royal Mail Line (British).
   Built by William Pitcher, Northfleet, England.   Tonnage:
   1,889.   Paddle-wheels, 8 knots.   Three masts and one funnel.
   Wooden hull.   Her speed was increased to 10 knots by feathering paddle-wheels in 1850.   Made her first voyage, December
   29, 1841.   Out of fleet in 1865.   Note: First trans-Atlantic liner
   to cross with feathering paddle-wheels.

Thames   (1890)   Royal Mail Line (British)
   Built by Robert Napier & Sons, Glasgow, Scotland.   Tonnage:
   5,645.   Dimensions: 436′ x 50′.   Single-screw, 15 knots.   Triple
   expansion engines.   Three masts and two funnels.   Steel hull.
   Scrapped in 1914.   Sister ship: **Clyde.**

Theben   (1897)   Kosmos Steamship Co.
   Built by Flensburger Schiffsb., Flensburg, Germany.   Tonnage: 4,614.   Dimensions: 368′ x 45′.   Single-screw.   Quadruple expansion engines.   Passengers: 24 first, 14 second,
   34 third.

Tiber   (1866)   Royal Mail Line (British).
   Built by Lungley of London, England.   Tonnage: 1,591.
   Dimensions: 272′ x 34′.   Single-screw.   Compound engines.
   Two masts and one funnel.   Clipper bow.   Iron hull.   Vessel
   purchased in 1871.   Out of Royal Mail Line fleet in 1882.
   Ex-**Kaikoura** (1871).

Tijuca   (1899)   Hamburg-South American Line.
   Built by Blohm & Voss, Hamburg, Germany.   Tonnage:
   4,801.   Dimensions: 375′ x 46′.   Single-screw, 12½ knots.
   Quadruple expansion engines.   Two masts and one funnel.
   Vessel seized by Brazil in 1917.   She was later sold to Lloyd

Brasileiro. Renamed: **Baependy** (1917). Torpedoed and sunk near Bahia, August 15, 1942.

Tivives (1911) United Fruit Company.
Built by Workman, Clark & Co., Ltd., Belfast, Ireland. Tonnage: 4,596. Dimensions: 378′ x 50′. Single-screw, 14 knots. Triple expansion engines. Two masts and one funnel. Torpedoed and sunk in the Mediterranean, October 21, 1943. Sister ships: See **Metapan.**

*Tjitjalengka (1939) Royal Inter-Ocean Lines (Dutch).
Built by N. V. Nederlandsch Schps. Maats. (Netherland Shipbuilding Co.), Amsterdam, Netherlands. Tonnage: 10,972. Single-screw, 15 knots. Motorship. Two masts and one funnel. Service: Far East-South Africa-South America. Passengers: 225 first and second. Originally operated by Java-China-Japan Line (Dutch).

Toloa (1917) United Fruit Company.
Built by Workman, Clark & Co., Belfast, Ireland. Tonnage: 7,183. Dimensions: 425′ x 54′. Twin-screw, 13½ knots. Triple expansion engines. Two masts and one funnel. Passengers: 131. Scrapped in 1948. Sister ship: **Ulua.**

Tomaso di Savoia (1907) Lloyd Sabaudo Line.
Tonnage: 7,914. Built for the South American service. She was later transferred to North Atlantic trade. Finally was put back on the Italy-South American route. *Note: See PART I for details.*

Toscana (1900) Soc. di Nav. a Vap. "Italia."
Built by N. Odero & Co., Genoa, Italy. Tonnage: 4,252. Dimensions: 363′ x 43′. Single-screw, 12 knots. Triple expansion engines. Two masts and one funnel. Transoceanica (Italian) acquired the vessel in 1917. Lost during First World War. Sister ship: **Ravenna.** Both vessels were built for the Italy-South America service.

*Toscana (1923) Italia Line.
Built by Akt. Ges. "Weser", Bremen, Germany. Tonnage: 9,442. Dimensions: 458′ x 57′. Twin-screw, 11 knots. Triple expansion engines. Two masts and one funnel. Service: Italy-South America. Vessel was later acquired by Lloyd Triestion. Ex-**Saarbrucken** (1935). Sister ship: **Sicilia.**

Tradewind (1906) Caribbean Atlantic Steamship Co.
Built by W. Cramp & Sons Shipbuilding Co., Philadelphia, Pa. Tonnage: 6,361. Dimensions: 416′ x 50′. Twin-screw,

16 knots. Two masts and one funnel. Service: Caribbean cruise trade. Broken up for scrap at Ghent in 1956. Ex-**Aleutian** (1955), ex-**Mexico.**

Trent   (1841)   Royal Mail Line (British).
Built by William Pitcher, Northfleet, England. Tonnage: 1,856. Paddle-wheels, 8 knots. Three masts and one funnel. Wooden hull. The 14 ships of this class were all named after British rivers. Out of fleet in 1866.

Trent   (1873)   Royal Mail Line (British).
Built by Henderson, Coulburn, Ltd., Renfrew, Scotland. Tonnage: 2,912. Dimensions: 349′ x 37′. Single-screw. Compound engines. Three masts and one funnel. Iron hull. Disposed of in 1897. Ex-**Vasco de Gama** (1878). Sister ship: **Tamar.**

Trent   (1901)   Royal Mail Line (British).
Built by Robert Napier & Sons, Ltd., Glasgow, Scotland. Tonnage: 5,525. Dimensions: 410′ x 49′. Single-screw, 15½ knots. Triple expansion engines. Two masts and two funnels. Scrapped in 1922. Sister ship: **Tagus.**

Trinidad   (1884)   Quebec Steamship Co.
Built by James Laing, Ltd., Sunderland, England. Tonnage: 2,592. Dimensions: 310′ x 37′. Single-screw, 15 knots. Triple expansion engines. Two masts and one funnel. Torpedoed and sunk without warning by submarine 12 miles from Codling Light Ship, March 22, 1918, with the loss of 39 lives.

Tubantia   (1913)   Royal Holland Lloyd (Dutch).
Built by Alexander Stephen & Sons, Ltd., Glasgow, Scotland. Tonnage: 14,061. Dimensions: 540′ x 65′ (560′ o.l.). Two masts and two funnels. Torpedoed and sunk in 1916. Sister ship: **Gelria.** Outstanding Dutch liners of that period to South America.

Tubingen   (1900)   North German Lloyd.
Built by Wigham Richardson & Co., Newcastle, England. Tonnage: 5,586. Dimensions: 381′ x 49′. Single-screw, 12½ knots. Quadruple expansion engines. Two masts and one funnel. Service: Second-class and steerage to South America. Renamed: (a) **Manila** (1917), (b) **Seneca,** (c) **Wabash.** Running mates: **Bonn, Halle, Crefeld** and **Erlangen.** Ex-**Wartburg** (1905).

Turrialba   (1909)   United Fruit Company.
Built by Workman, Clark & Co., Belfast, Ireland. Tonnage:
4,538.   Dimensions: 378' x 50'.   Single-screw, 14 knots.
Triple expansion engines. Two masts and one funnel. Placed
on a 12 passenger basis in the early 1930's, after much of
cabin superstructure was removed. Scrapped at Baltimore
in 1948. Sister ships: See **Metapan.**

Tweed   (1841)   Royal Mail Line (British).
Built by Thompson & Spiers, Great Britain. Tonnage: 1,800.
Paddle-wheels, 8 knots.   Three masts and one funnel.
Wooden hull.   Made her first sailing, December 18, 1841.
Out of fleet in 1847.

Tyne   (1854)   Royal Mail Line (British).
Built by Miller & Ravenhill, Newcastle, England. Tonnage:
1,603. Dimensions: 296' x 36'. Paddle-wheels. Two oscillating type engines. Three masts and two funnels. Iron hull.
Out of fleet in 1875. Scrapped in 1878.

Tyrian   (1869)   Anchor Line.
Built by Robert Duncan & Co., Port Glasgow, Scotland.
Tonnage: 1,039. Dimensions: 237' x 30'. Single-screw, 10
knots. Inverted type engines. Compound engines installed in
1879. Service: New York-Jamaica. Converted to Canadian
cable ship in 1913. Sister ship: **Dorian.**

Uberaba   (1911)   Lloyd Brasileiro.
Built by Reiherstieg Schiffsw., Hamburg, Germany. Ton-
nage: 6,062. Dimensions: 393' x 52'. Single-screw, 13 knots.
Quadruple expansion engines. Two masts and one funnel.
Vessel was taken over by Brazil after World War I. Ex-
Henny Woermann.

*Ugolino Vivaldi   (1947)   Italia Line.
Built by Soc. Anon. Ansaldo, Genoa-Sestri, Italy. Tonnage:
8,914. Dimensions: 466' x 62' (485' o.l.). Single-screw, 15½
knots. Motorship. Two masts and one funnel. Launched in
1945. Commissioned in 1947. Vessel transferred to Lloyd
Triestino. Ex-**Ferruccia Buonapace** (1947).

Ulua   (1917)   United Fruit Company.
Built by Workman, Clark & Co., Belfast, Ireland. Tonnage:
7,181. Dimensions: 425' x 54'. Twin-screw, 14 knots. Triple
expansion engines. Two masts and one funnel. Passengers:
131. Scrapped after World War II. Sister ship: **Toloa.**

Umbria (1902) (a) Navigazione Generale Italiana, (b) La
  Veloce Line.
    Built by Orlando, Leghorn, Italy. Tonnage: 5,260. Dimensions: 401' x 46'. Single-screw, 14 knots. Quadruple expansion engines. Two masts and one funnel. Built for Italy-South America service. Made some North Atlantic sailings. Acquired by La Veloce Line in 1913. Renamed: **San Paulo** (1913), (b) **Umbria** (1914) Sitmar Line.

Uruguay (1882) Chargeurs Reunis.
    Built by Ateliers & Chantiers de la Loire, St. Nazaire, France. Tonnage: 3,442. Dimensions: 347' x 40'. Single-screw, 13 knots. Triple expansion engines. Two masts and one funnel. Iron hull. Launched, September 29, 1882. Service: France-South America, later on West African coastal route. Went aground in fog near Contonou, March 4, 1901 and became a total loss. Sister ships: **Parana** and **Rio Negro.**

Uruguay (1913) Spanish Line (Compania Trasatlantica).
    Built by Wm. Denny & Bros., Ltd., Dumbarton, Scotland. Tonnage: 10,348. Dimensions: 481' x 61'. Triple-screw, 17 knots. Triple expansion engines. Two masts and one funnel. Service: Spain-South America. Sunk by air attack at Barcelona during Spanish Civil War; refloated and broken up for scrap. Ex-**Infanta Isabel de Borbon** (1931). Sister ship: **Argentina.**

Uruguay (1928) Moore-McCormack Line.
    Built by Newport News Shipbuilding Co., Newport News, Va. Tonnage: 20,183. Dimensions: 574' x 80'. Twin-screw, 18 knots. Two steam turbines connected to electric motors (turbo-electric). Not in service (1961). Ex-**California.** Sister ships: **Argentina** and **Brazil.**

*Uruguay (1950) Ultramar Line (Argentine).
    Built by Vickers-Armstrongs, Ltd., Newcastle, England. Tonnage: 12,627. Dimensions: 509' x 71' (530' o.l.). Twin-screw, 18½ knots. Steam turbines. Two masts and one funnel. Passengers: 70. Ex-**Eva Peron** (1955). Sister ships: **Argentina** and **Liberstad.**

*Uruguay Star (1947) Blue Star Line.
    Built by Cammell, Laird & Co., Birkenhead, England. Tonnage: 10,723. Dimensions: 478' x 68' (502' o.l.). Single-screw, 16 knots. Three steam turbines. Single mast and one funnel. Passengers: 70 first-class. Service: London-South

America, via Lisbon. Sister ships: **Argentina Star, Brasil Star** and **Paraguay Star.**

Valbanera (1905) Pinillos, Izquierdo & Co. (Cadiz, Spanin).
Built by C. Connell & Co., Glasgow, Scotland. Tonnage: 5,099. Dimensions: 399' x 48'. Single-screw, 12 knots. Triple expansion engines. Two masts and one funnel. Wrecked in 1919.

Valdivia (1911) Transport Maritimes (French).
Built by Chantiers & Steliers de Provence, Port Bouc, France. Tonnage: 7,168. Dimensions: 462' x 54'. Twin-screw, 16 knots. Triple expansion engines. Two masts and two funnels. Scrapped in 1933.

Valparaiso (1873) Pacific Steam Navigation Co.
Built by John Elder & Co., Glasgow, Scotland. Tonnage: 3,757. Dimensions: 379' x 41'. Single-screw, 13 knots. Two compound inverted D.A. engines. Three masts and one funnel. Iron hull. Clipper bow. Lost on February 28, 1887. Similar ship: **Tacora.**

Valparaiso (1890) Lloyd de Pacifico (Italian).
Built by Fairfield Shipbuilding Co., Glasgow, Scotland. Tonnage: 4,930. Dimensions: 430' x 47'. Single-screw, 13 knots. Single-screw, 13 knots. Triple expansion engines. Two masts and one funnel. Service: Italy-Chile. Sunk by submarine during First World War. Ex-**Gera** (1909). Running mate: **Santiago.**

Van Rensselaer (1920) Royal Netherlands Steamship Co.
Built by Nederlandsch Schps. Maats., Amsterdam, Netherlands. Tonnage: 4,299. Dimensions: 342' x 47'. Single-screw, 12 knots. Triple expansion engines. Two masts and one funnel. She became a World War II loss, May 20, 1940. Sister ship: **Crijnssen.**

Vancouver (1930) Hamburg-American Line.
Built by Deutsche Werft, Hamburg, Germany. Tonnage: 8,269. Dimensions: 477' x 63'. Single-screw, 13½ knots. Steam turbines. Two masts and one funnel. Seized by Dutch Government at Curacao, during German invasion of the Netherlands in 1940. Renamed: (a) **Curacao** (1940), (b) **Duivendijk** (1946).

Vandalia (1871) Hamburg-American Line.
Tonnage: 2,815. Service: Germany-West Indies. *Note: See PART I for details.*

491

Vandyck   (1911)   Lamport & Holt Co., Ltd.
   Built by Workman, Clark & Co., Ltd., Belfast, Ireland. Ton-
   nage: 10,328. Dimensions: 495′ x 60′. Twin-screw, 15 knots.
   Quadruple expansion engines. Two masts and one funnel.
   Service: New York-South America. Captured by the German
   cruiser **Karlsruhe** and sunk, October 26, 1914. Sister ships:
   Vauban and **Vestris.**

Vandyck   (1921)   Lamport & Holt Co., Ltd.
   Built by Workman, Clark & Co., Belfast, Ireland. Tonnage:
   13,233. Dimensions: 510′ x 64′ (535′ o.l.). Twin-screw, 14½
   knots. Steam turbines. Two masts and one funnel. Sunk in
   action with enemy aircraft off Norway, June 10, 1940. Sister
   ship: **Voltaire.** Service: New York-South America.

Vasari   (1909)   Lamport & Holt Co., Ltd.
   Built by Sir Raylton Dixon & Co., Middlesbrough, England.
   Tonnage: 10,117. Dimensions: 486′ x 59′. Single-screw,
   14 knots. Quadruple expansion engines. Two masts aud one
   funnel. Service: New York-Brazil River Plate. Renamed:
   (a) **Arctic Queen,** (b) **Pischevaya Industria** (Russian).
   No report on vessel since 1950.

Vauban   (1912)   Lamport & Holt & Co., Ltd.
   Built by Workman, Clark & Co., Belfast, Ireland. Tonnage:
   10,660. Dimensions: 495′ x 60′ (511′ o.l.). Twin-screw, 13½
   knots. Quadruple expansion engines. Two masts and one
   funnel. Scrapped in 1932. Ex-**Alcala** (1913), ex-**Vauban**
   (1913). Sister ships: **Vandyck** and **Vestris.**

Venezuela   (1889)   Red "D" Line (Atlantic & Caribbean
   Steam Navigation Co.). Built by W. Cramp & Sons, Philadelphia, Pa. Tonnage: 2,843. Dimensions: 303′ x 40′. Single-
   screw. Triple expansion engines. Two masts and one funnel.
   Iron hull. Vessel sold to United States Navy in 1898.

Venezuela   (1898)   La Veloce Line.
   Built by N. Odero fu A., Sestri P'nente, Italy. Tonnage:
   3,474. Dimensions: 359′ x 41′. Single-screw, 12 knots.
   Triple expansion engines. Two masts and one funnel.
   Wrecked at Marseilles, February 21, 1909. Similar ships:
   Centro America and **Savoia.**

Venezuela   (1904)   Navigazione Generale Italiana.
   Built by Armstrong Whitworth & Co., Ltd., Newcastle,
   England. Tonnage: 7,028. Dimensions: 420′ x 51′. Twin-
   screw, 14 knots. Triple expansion engines. Two masts and

one funnel. Scrapped in 1928. Ex-**Caserta** (1923), ex-**Mendoza** (1914).

Venezuela (1906) Royal Netherlands Steamship Co.
Built by Reiherstieg Schiffsw., Hamburg, Germany. Tonnage: 6,355. Dimensions: 411' x 50'. Twin-screw, 13 knots. Triple expansion engines. Two masts and one funnel. Vessel was at Rotterdam in August 1914 and remained there until the end of the First World War. She was then surrendered to Great Britain. Used as a troopship for a brief time. Scrapped in 1938. Ex-**Westminster Abbey** (British Government), ex-**Adolph Woermann** (1919).

Venezuela (1915) Royal Netherlands Steamship Co.
Built by Nederlandsch Schps. Maats., Amsterdam, Netherlands. Tonnage: 5,641. Dimensions: 380' x 48'. Single-screw, 14 knots. Triple expansion engines. Two masts and one funnel. Passengers: 111 cabin and 78 steerage. Entered San Francisco-Hong Kong-Manila service in 1917. Vessel transferred to Panama Mail Steamship Company in 1925. Also served in New York-Panama Canal-California inter-coastal trade. Renamed: **Santa Isabel.** Sister ships: **Colombia** and **Ecuador.**

*****Venezuela** (1924) Siousa Line (Italian).
Built by Cammell, Laird & Co., Birkenhead, England. Tonnage: 18,567. Dimensions: 552' x 71' (572' o.l.). Twin-screw, 16 knots. Steam turbines. Two masts and one funnel. Length increased to 597' (o.l.) by new type bow in 1960. Ex-**Empress of Australia** (1956), ex-**De Grasse** (1953).

Vera Cruz (1952) Companhia de Colonial Navegacao (Portuguese).
Built by Soc. Anon. John Cockerill, Hoboken, Belgium. Tonnage: 21,765. Dimensions: 577' x 75' (610' o.l.). Twin-screw, 22 knots. Six steam turbines. Single mast and one funnel. Displacement of 21,500 tons. Launched, June 2, 1951. Passengers: 1,200 in first, second, third and emigrant class. Service: Portugal-South America. Service speed: 20 knots. Sister ship: **Santa Maria.** These beautiful liners are the largest and most important of any built for Portugal to date.

Veragua (1932) United Fruit Company.
Built by Bethlehem Steel Co., Shipyard Division, Quincy, Mass. Tonnage: 6,982. Dimensions: 415' x 60'. Twin-screw, 18 knots. Turbo-electric. Two masts and one funnel. Pas-

sengers: 100.   Renamed: **Sinaloa** (Elders & Fyffes, Ltd.).
Sister ships: **Antigua, Chiriqui, Peten, Quirigua** and
Talamanca.

Verdi   (1907)   Lamport & Holt Co., Ltd.
   Built by Workman, Clark & Co., Belfast, Ireland. Tonnage:
   7,120.   Dimensions: 430' x 53'.   Single-screw, 14 knots.
   Triple expansion engines. Two masts and one funnel. Tor-
   pedoed and sunk without warning 115 miles from Eagle
   Island, August 22, 1917, with the loss of six lives.

Verona   (1908)   "Italia" Societa Anonima di Navigazione.
   Tonnage: 8,886. Service: Italy-South America. Vessel was
   acquired by Navigazione Generale Italiana in 1913. *Note:
   See PART I for details.*

Vestris   (1912)   Lamport & Holt Co., Ltd.
   Built by Workman, Clark & Co., Belfast, Ireland. Tonnage:
   10,494. Dimensions: 495' x 60' (511' o.l.). Twin-screw, 13½
   knots. Triple expansion engines. Two masts and one funnel.
   Service: New York-South America. Foundered after listing
   badly in severe gale off Virginia Capes, November 12, 1928,
   while on voyage to South America. There was a loss of 110
   lives, which included 67 passengers. Sister ships: **Vandyck**
   and **Vauban.**

Victoria   (1902)   Pacific Steam Navigation Co.
   Built by Fairfield Shipbuilding Co., Glasgow, Scotland.
   Tonnage: 5,967. Dimensions: 401' x 52'. Twin-screw, 15½
   knots. Triple expansion engines. Two masts and one funnel.
   Broken up by Dutch shipbreakers in 1923.   Sister ship:
   Panama.

*Victoria   (1936)   Incres Steamship Co. (Liberian).
   Built by Harland & Wolff, Ltd., Belfast, Ireland. Tonnage:
   15,054.   Dimensions: 540' x 71' (560' o.l.).   Twin-screw,
   16 knots. Motorship. Single mast and one funnel. Service:
   Cruise service to the West Indies from United States east
   coast ports. Ex-**Dunnottar Castle** (1958).

Vigilancia   (1890)   Ward Line.
   Built by Delaware River Co., Chester, Pa. Tonnage: 4,115.
   Dimensions: 321' x 45'. Single-screw, 14½ knots.   Triple
   expansion engines. Two masts and two funnels. The Ward
   Line (New York & Cuba Mail Steamship Co.) purchased this
   vessel from New York & Brazil Mail Steamship Company in
   1893. Torpedoed and sunk by German submarine, March 16,
   1917. Sister ship: **Segurana.**

Vigilant (1923) Gdynia-American Line.
Built by Deutsche Werft, Hamburg, Germany. Tonnage: 4,765. Dimensions: 400′ x 54′. Twin-screw. Motorship. Two masts and one funnel. Note: Chartered in 1937–1939 for service between Poland, West Indies and Central America. Ex-**Talisman** (1937). Sister ship: **Vigrid.**

Vigo (1922) Hamburg-South American Line.
Built by Howaldtswerke, Kiel, Germany. Tonnage: 7,418. Dimensions: 413′ x 55′. Single-screw, 12 knots. Triple expansion engines. Two masts and one funnel. Passengers: 600. Renamed: **Sperrbrecher 10** (German). Mined and sunk in Danish waters, April 7, 1943. Sister ships: **Espana** and **La Coruna.**

Vigrid (1923) Gdynia-American Line.
Built by Deutsche Werft, Hamburg, Germany. Tonnage: 4,765. Dimensions: 400′ x 54′. Twin-screw. Motorship. Two masts and one funnel. Chartered from Norwegian ship owners for Poland to West Indies and Central America service. Torpedoed and sunk, June 24, 1941. Sister ship: **Vigilant.**

Villa Garcia (1907) Hamburg-South American Line.
Built by Flensburger Schiffsb., Flensburg, Germany. Tonnage: 7,423. Dimensions: 426′ x 55′. Single-screw, 11 knots. Quadruple expansion engines. Two masts and one funnel. Scrapped in 1932. Ex-**Santa Maria** (1922).

Ville de Bahia (1872) Chargeurs Reunis.
Built by Forges & Chantiers de la Mediterranee, La Seyne, France. Tonnage: 1,515. Dimensions: 292′ x 32′. Single-screw. Compound engines. Three masts and one funnel. Iron hull. Launched, November 14, 1872. Service: France-South America. Vessel sold in 1890. Renamed: **General Gallieni.** Sister ships: **Ville de Rio Janeiro,** and **Ville de Santos.**

Ville de Buenos Ayres (1882) Chargeurs Reunis.
Built by Forges & Chantiers de la Mediterranee, La Seyne, France. Tonnage: 2,119. Dimensions: 305′ x 36′. Single-screw, 12 knots. Compound engines. Two masts and one funnel. Sold to Cie des Bateaux a vapeur du Nord; renamed **Ville de Rochefort.** Lost by collision on October 14, 1910. Sister ships: **Ville de Montevideo, Ville de Pernambuco, Ville de Rosario** and **Ville de San Nicolas.**

Ville de Ceara   (1882)   Chargeurs Reunis.
Built by Schlesinger, Davis & Co., Newcastle, England.
Tonnage: 2,326. Dimensions: 285' x 37'. Single-screw, 12
knots. Compound engines. Two masts and one funnel.
Sold to Dunkirk owners in September 1895. Sister ship:
Ville de Para.

Ville de Maceio   (1883)   Chargeurs Reunis.
Built by Ateliers & Chantiers de la Loire, Nantes, France.
Tonnage: 2,666. Dimensions: 319' x 37'. Single-screw, 13
knots. Triple expansion engines. Two masts and one funnel.
Steel and iron hull. Service: France to South America, later
to West African coastal trade. Sold to British shipbreakers
in 1906. Sister ships: **Ville de Maranhao** and **Ville de
Victoria.**

Ville de Maranhao   (1883)   Chargeurs Reunis.
Built by Ateliers & Chantiers de la Loire, Nantes, France.
Tonnage: 2,548. Dimensions: 319' x 37'. Single-screw, 13
knots. Triple expansion engines. Two masts and one funnel.
Service: France-South America, later in West African
coastal trade. Sold for scrap at Dunkirk in August 1908.
Sister ships: **Ville de Maceio** and **Ville de Victoria.**

Ville de Montevideo   (1881)   Chargeurs Reunis.
Built by Forges & Chantiers de la Mediterranee, La Seyne,
France. Tonnage: 2,119. Dimensions: 305' x 36'. Single-
screw, 12 knots. Compound engines. Two masts and one
funnel. Iron hull. Sold to Cie des Bateaux a vapeur du
Nord in December 1898; renamed **Ville de Lorient.** Sister
ships: See **Ville de Buenos Ayres.**

Ville de Para   (1882)   Chargeurs Reunis.
Built by Schlesinger, Davis & Co., Newcastle, England.
Tonnage: 2,356. Dimensions: 285' x 37'. Single-screw, 12
knots. Two compound inverted type engines. Two masts
and one funnel. Launched, June 1, 1882. Struck a rock and
sunk near Las Palmas, October 11, 1884. Sister ship: **Ville
de Ceara.**

Ville de Pernambuco   (1882)   Chargeurs Reunis.
Built by Forges & Chantiers de la Mediterranee, La Seyne,
France. Tonnage: 2,153. Dimensions: 305' x 36'. Single-
screw, 12 knots. Compound engines. Two masts and one
funnel. Launched, January 10, 1882. Sold to Messageries
Maritimes in May 1905. Scrapped at Marseilles in November 1907. Sister ships: See **Ville de Buenos Ayres.**

Ville de Rio Janeiro   (1872)   Chargeurs Reunis.
   Built by Forges & Chantiers de la Mediterranee, La Seyne,
   France. Tonnage: 1,540. Dimensions: 292′ x 32′. Single-
   screw. Compound engines. Three masts and one funnel.
   In South American service. Sunk in collision in fog with
   French liner La Champagne, off Barfleur, May 7, 1887.
   Sister ships: **Ville de Bahia** and **Ville de Santos.**

Ville de Rosario   (1881)   Chargeurs Reunis.
   Built by Forges & Chantiers de la Mediterranee, La Seyne,
   France. Tonnage: 2,119. Dimensions: 305′ x 36′. Single-
   screw, 12 knots. Compound engines. Two masts and one
   funnel. Sold in December 1898 to Cie des Bateaux a vapeur
   du Nord, renamed **Ville de Constantine.** Name changed to
   Urugne in 1917 (Chargeurs Francais). Sister ships: See
   Ville de Buenos Ayres.

Ville de San Nicolas   (1881)   Chargeurs Reunis.
   Built by Forges & Chantiers de la Mediterranee, La Seyne,
   France. Tonnage: 2,119. Dimensions: 305′ x 36′. Single-
   screw, 12 knots. Compound engines. Two masts and one
   funnel. Sold to Argentine owners in 1905; renamed **Neuquen.**
   Sister ships: See **Ville de Buenos Ayres.**

Ville de Santos   (1873)   Chargeurs Reunis.
   Built by Forges & Chantiers de la Mediterranee, La Seyne,
   France. Tonnage: 1,540. Dimensions: 292′ x 32′. Single-
   screw. Compound engines. Three masts and one funnel.
   Iron hull. Sold to Norwegian owners in February 1890;
   renamed **Vulkan.** Sister ships: **Ville de Bahia** and **Ville
   de Rio Janeiro.**

Ville de Victoria   (1883)   Chargeurs Reunis.
   Built by Ateliers & Chantiers de la Loire, Nantes, France.
   Tonnage: 2,548. Dimensions: 319′ x 37′. Single-screw, 13
   knots. Compound engines. Two masts and one funnel.
   Launched, April 7, 1883. Rammed and sunk at anchor in
   Lisbon harbor, December 24, 1886, **H.M.S. Sultan,**
   dragging her anchors. Sister ships: **Ville de Maceio** and
   Ville de Maranhao.

Vincent   (1895)   Booth Line.
   Built by Armstrong, Mitchell & Co., Newcastle, England.
   Tonnage: 4,561. Dimensions: 360′ x 47′. Single-screw, 13
   knots. Triple expansion engines. Two masts and one funnel.
   Renamed: (a) **Guiarat,** (b) **Gorjistan.** Ex-**Fort Salisbury.**

Vincenzo Florio   (1880)   Navigazione Generale Italiana.
Tonnage: 2,840. Transferred from North Atlantic to South American service. However continued to make an occasional sailing to New York. *Note: See PART I for details.*

Virgilio   (1927)   (a) Navigazione Generale Italiana, (b) Italia Line.
Built by Cantieri Officine Meridionali, Baia, Italy. Tonnage: 11,718. Dimensions: 481′ x 61′ (506′ o.l.). Twin-screw, 14 knots. Motorship. Two masts and one funnel. Service: Genoa-Marseilles-Barcelona-Trinidad-Panama Canal-Callao-Valparaiso. She became a war loss in 1944. Sister ship: **Orazio.**

Virginia   (1906)   Lloyd Italiano.
Tonnage: 5,181. Transferred from North Atlantic to South American service. *Note: See PART I for details.*

Virginia   (1928)   Panama-Pacific Line.
Built by Newport News Shipbuilding Co., Newport News, Virginia. Tonnage: 20,773. Dimensions: 586′ x 80′ (613′ o.l.). Twin-screw, 19 knots. Two steam turbines connected to electric motors. Two masts and two funnels. Service: New York-Panama Canal-California. Renamed: **Brazil** (1938). Sister ships: **California** and **Pennsylvania.**

Vittoria   (1871)   La Veloce Line.
Built by Harland & Wolff, Ltd., Belfast, Ireland. Tonnage: 3,707. Dimensions: 420′ x 40′. Single-screw, 14 knots. Compound engines. Four masts and one funnel. Renamed: **Citta di Napoli.** Scrapped in Italy in 1910. Ex-**Maasdam** (1902), ex-**Republic** (1889).

Vittoria   (1883)   La Veloce Line.
Built by Robert Napier & Sons, Glasgow, Scotland. Tonnage: 4,290. Dimensions: 440′ x 44′. Single-screw, 14 knots. Compound engines. Three masts and two funnels. During Genoa-Buenos Aires voyage, was badly damaged by fire, January 11, 1899, at Alicante. She was subsequently towed to Genoa and broken up for scrap. Ex-**Tamaulipas.**

Vogtland   (1924)   Hamburg-American Line.
Built by Blohm & Voss, Hamburg, Germany. Tonnage: 7,106. Dimensions: 449′ x 58′. Twin-screw, 12 knots. Motorship. Two masts and one funnel. Service: Germany-West Indies-Central America. Vessel seized by Dutch Government at Batavia, when the Germans invaded the

Netherlands in 1940. She was renamed **Berakit.** Torpedoed and sunk by Japanese submarine in the Indian Ocean in 1943.

Voltaire   (1907)   Lamport & Holt Co., Ltd.
Built by D. & W. Henderson & Co., Glasgow, Scotland. Tonnage: 8,618. Dimensions: 485′ x 58′ (501′ o.l.). Triple expansion engines. Two masts and one funnel. Passengers: 60 first-class. Captured by the German raider **Mowe** and sunk on December 2, 1916, when 650 miles west from Fastnet.

Voltaire   (1923)   Lamport & Holt Co., Ltd.
Built by Workman, Clark & Co., Belfast, Ireland. Tonnage: 13,248. Dimensions: 510′ x 64′ (535′ o.l.). Twin-screw, 14½ knots. Quadruple expansion engines. Two masts and one funnel. Torpedoed and sunk, May 3, 1941. Sister ship: **Vandyck.**

Vulcania   (1928)   (a) Cosulich Line, (b) Italia Line.
Tonnage: 24,469.   Mainly employed in North Atlantic service. *Note: See PART I for details.*

Wakasa Maru   (1897)   N. Y. K. Line (Japanese).
Built by D. & W. Henderson, Ltd., Glasgow, Scotland. Tonnage: 6,266. Dimensions: 445′ x 49′. Twin-screw, 14 knots. Triple expansion engines. Two masts and one funnel. Note: First regular ship of the company to be placed in the South American east coast service. Scrapped in 1933.

Waldensian   (1863)   Allan Line.
Tonnage: 2,306. This North Atlantic liner was also used in service to South America from Great Britain. *Note: See PART I for details.*

Washington   (1880)   Navigazione Generale Italiana.
Tonnage: 2,833. Transferred to Italy-South America service in 1888, but made occasional New York voyages 1907. *Note: See PART I for details.*

Weimar   (1891)   North German Lloyd.
Tonnage: 4,996. Interchangeable in North Atlantic and South American services. *Note: See PART I for details.*

Werra   (1922)   North German Lloyd.
Tonnage: 9,476. In Germany-South American service. *Note: See PART I for details.*

Weser   (1922)   North German Lloyd.
   Tonnage: In Germany-South American trade.   *Note: See PART I for details.*

Weser   (1929)   North German Lloyd.
   Built by Deutsche Werke, Kiel, Germany. Tonnage: 9,179. Dimensions: 487′ x 60′. Twin-screw, 17 knots. Motorship. Two masts and one funnel. Note: Vessel was originally built for Norwegian owners, then acquired by Blue Star Line. Finally she was rebuilt and purchased by North German Lloyd.   Lost in 1940.   Ex-**Yakima Star** (1934), ex-**Sud Americano.**

Western Ocean   (1899)   Munson Line.
   Built by Newport News Shipbuilding Co., Newport News, Va. Tonnage: 4,828. Dimensions: 391′ x 48′. Single-screw, 14 knots.   Triple expansion engines.   Two masts and one funnel.   Ex-**Comus.**

Western Prince   (1929)   Furness-Prince Line.
   Built by Napier & Miller, Ltd., Glasgow, Scotland. Tonnage: 10,926.   Dimensions: 496′ x 64′ (516′ o.l.).   Twin-screw, 16 knots.   Motorship.   Two masts and one funnel.   Service: New York-South America (east coast). Torpedoed and sunk, December 14, 1940. Sister ships: **Eastern Prince, Northern Prince** and **Southern Prince.**

Western World   (1921)   Munson Line.
   Built by Bethlehem Shipbuilding Corp., Sparrows Point, Md. Tonnage: 13,712.   Dimensions: 517′ x 72′.   Twin-screw, 17 knots.   Steam turbines.   Two masts and one funnel.   Renamed: **Leonard Wood** (United States transport). Scrapped in 1948. Ex-**Nutmeg State** (1921). Sister ships: **American Legion, Pan America** and **Southern Cross.**

Willehad   (1894)   North German Lloyd.
   Tonnage: 4,761.   In Bremen-South American service.   *Note: See PART I for details.*

*****Willemstad**   (1938)   Royal Netherlands Steamship Co.
   Built by Van der Giessen, Krimpen, Netherlands. Tonnage: 5,088.   Dimensions: 378′ (o.l.) x 49′.   Single-screw, 14½ knots.   Motorship.   Two masts and one funnel.   Converted from freighter to passenger ship in 1950. Ex-**Socrates** (1950). Sister ship: **Oranjestad.** Accommodation for 94 passengers in one class.

Wittekind (1894) North German Lloyd.
Tonnage: 4,755. In Bremen-South American service. *Note: See PART I for details.*

Wittenberg (1895) North German Lloyd.
Built by Flensburger Schiffsb. Ges., Flensburg, Germany. Tonnage: 3,689. Dimensions: 354' x 42'. Single-screw, 12 knots. Triple expansion engines. Vessel sold in 1912. Renamed: **Hochfeld.** Ex-**Thekla.**

Wurttemburg (1921) Hamburg-American Line.
Built by Bremer Vulkan, Vegesack, Germany. Tonnage: 8,894. Dimensions: 466' x 58'. Single-screw, 13 knots. Triple expansion engines. Four masts and one funnel. Service: (a) Germany-West Indies, (b) Germany-South America. Converted into a whaler. Renamed: **Jan Wellem** (1935) German. Sunk in 1940. She was later raised and then broken up for scrap.

Wurzburg (1900) North German Lloyd.
Built by Bremer Vulkan, Vegesack, Germany. Tonnage: 5,085. Dimensions: 402' x 47'. Single-screw, 12 knots. Triple expansion engines. Two masts and one funnel. Service: Germany-Brazil. Passengers: Second-class and steerage. Renamed: **Sao Vicente** (1921) Portuguese.

Yang Tse (1877) Messageries Maritimes.
Built by Messageries Maritimes, La Ciotat, France. Tonnage: 3,803. Dimensions: 394' x 39'. Single-screw, 13½ knots. Compound engines. Three masts and one funnel. Launched, January 21, 1877. Scrapped in France, 1911. Sister ships: **Djemnah** and **Oxus.**

*Yapeyu (1951) Dodero Line (Argentine).
Built by N.V.C. Van der Giessen & Zonen's Schps., Krimpen, Netherlands. Tonnage: 11,540. Dimensions: 490' x 64' (522' o.l.). Twin-screw, 17 knots. Motorship. Two masts and one funnel. Passengers: 800. Service: North Europe-Buenos Aires emigrant trade. Sister ships: **Alberto Dodero** and **Maipu.**

Yorck (1906) North German Lloyd.
Tonnage: 8,976. Service: Germany-South America. *Note: See PART I for details.*

Ypiranga (1908) Hamburg-American Line.
Built by Frd. Krupp, Akt. Ges., Kiel, Germany. Tonnage: 8,309. Dimensions: 448' x 58'. Twin-screw, 12 knots. Quad-

ruple expansion engines. Two masts and one funnel. Renamed: (a) **Assyria** (1921), (b) **Colonial** (1929). Sold to British shipbreakers for scrapping in 1950. Sister ship: **Corcovado.** Note: They were built especially for the Germany-West Indies service.

Yucatan   (1890)   Ward Line.
    Built by Delaware River Co., Chester, Pa. Tonnage: 3,525. Dimensions: 336′ x 43′.   Single-screw, 14 knots.   Triple expansion engines. Two masts and one funnel. Steel hull. Passengers: 80 first and 30 second. Note: This liner carried Col. Theodore Roosevelt and his Routh Riders to Cuba in the Spanish-American War. Vessel sold to Alaska Steamship Company in 1906. Renamed: **Shinkai Maru** (Japanese).

Yucatan   (1907)   Ward Line (Atlantic Gulf, West Indies Steamship Co.).
    Built by W. Cramp & Sons Shipbuilding Co., Philadelphia, Pa. Tonnage: 6,678. Dimensions: 413′ x 50′. Twin-screw, 16 knots. Triple expansion engines. Two masts and one funnel. Renamed: (a) **Agwileon** (1942) troopship, (b) **Shamrock** (1943) U. S. hospital ship. Scrapped in 1947. Ex-**Havana** (1935), ex-**Comfort**, ex-**Havana.**

Yumuri   (1890)   Ward Line.
    Built by Delaware River Co., Chester, Pa. Tonnage: 3,500. Dimensions: 336′ x 43′. Single-screw, 14 knots. Triple expansion engines. Two masts and one funnel. Passengers: 80 first and 30 second. Renamed: (a) **U. S. Lawton,** (b) **Badger,** (c) **Rose City.** Sister ship: **Orizaba.**

Zacapa   (1909)   United Fruit Co.
    Built by Workman, Clark & Co., Belfast, Ireland. Tonnage: 4,568. Dimensions: 378′ x 50′. Single-screw, 14 knots. Triple expansion engines. Two masts and one funnel. Much of cabin superstructure was removed in the early 1930's. She was then placed on 12 passenger basis. Scrapped in America, 1950. Sister ships: See **Metapan.**

Zeelandia   (1910)   Royal Holland Lloyd.
    Built by Alexander Stephen & Sons, Ltd., Glasgow, Scotland. Tonnage: 7,995. Dimensions: 440′ x 55′. Twin-screw, 15 knots. Triple expansion engines. Two masts and one funnel. Passengers: 118 first, 114 second, 998 third. Note: Service speed originally listed as 13½ knots. Scrapped in 1936. Similar ships: **Frisia** and **Hollandia.**

Zulia (1901) Red "D" Line. (Atlantic & Caribbean Steam
Navigation Co.)
Built by Neafie & Levy Co., Philadelphia, Pa. Tonnage:
1,713. Dimensions: 266′ x 37′. Twin-screw, 12 knots. Triple
expansion engines. Two masts and one funnel. Passengers:
35 first and 24 second. Vessel no longer listed in 1925.

Explanation

The numerous passenger ships of the French Line, and also the Spanish Line, which have been used in the West Indies and Central American service are not included in the main list of PART III. However they are listed in full form in PART I, as nearly all were at sometime in the trans-Atlantic trade to New York. In order to keep their Latin American identity clear, these particular French and Spanish liners are noted in brief form following this explanation. This method of handling the information does make for greater compactness.

Europe-West Indies-Central America Service

FRENCH LINE

(Compagnie Generale Transatlantique)

Name of Ship	Year Built	Tonnage
Amerique†	1864	4,517
*Antilles	1952	20,419
Bretagne†	1922	10,171
Californie	1905	5,455
Canada†	1865	4,287
Chicago†	1908	11,127
Colombie†	1862	1,859
Colombie†	1931	13,803
Cuba	1923	11,420
De Grasse†	1924	17,759
De la Salle	1924	8,400
Espagne	1909	11,155
Ferdinand de Lesseps†	1875	2,761
Flandre	1914	8,503
*Flandre	1951	20,459
France†	1865	4,517
Gascogne†	1924	5,195

---

* In service 1961.

† Name change.

FRENCH LINE (*Continued*)
(Compagnie Generale Transatlantique)

Name of Ship	Year Built	Tonnage
Guadeloupe†	1855	1,900
Guadeloupe	1906	6,600
Guadeloupe†	1908	10,502
Haiti†	1913	6,298
Imperatrice Eugenie†	1864	4,517
La Bretagne†	1886	6,766
La Champagne	1885	7,087
La Gascogne	1887	7,090
La Navarre	1892	6,648
La Normandie	1882	6,283
Labrador†	1865	4,612
Lafayette	1865	3,003
Macoris†	1902	5,939
Martinique†	1855	1,900
Martinique†	1883	4,392
Mexique†	1915	12,220
Montreal†	1896	3,342
Niagara†	1908	9,614
Nouveau Monde†	1865	3,200
Olinde-Rodrigues†	1873	3,188
Panama†	1865	3,200
Pellerin de la Touche†	1913	8,848
Pereire	1865	3,950
Perou	1907	6,599
Puerto Rico†	1913	6,127
Quebec†	1896	3,342
St. Germain†	1874	3,641
Saint Laurent	1866	4,067
Saint Simon†	1874	3,133
Tampico†	1855	1,707
Venezuela†	1905	4,772
Vera Cruz†	1855	1,739
Versailles†	1882	4,336
Ville de Bordeaux	1870	2,670
Ville de Brest	1870	2,676
Ville de Marseille†	1874	2,836
Ville de Paris	1866	2,838
Ville de St. Nazaire†	1871	2,634
Winnipeg†	1918	9,802

SPANISH LINE
(Compania Trasatlantica)

Name of Ship	Year Built	Tonnage
Alfonso XII	1875	2,915
Alfonso XII†	1890	6,966
Alfonso XIII	1888	5,000
Alfonso XIII†	1891	8,063
Alfonso XIII†	1923	10,551
Antonio Lopez	1891	5,975
Argentina†	1913	10,137
*Begona	1945	10,139
Buenos Aires	1887	5,311
C. de Elizaguirre†	1904	4,376
C. Lopez-y-Lopez†	1891	4,170
Cataluna	1883	3,665
Ciudad de Cadiz	1878	3,202
Ciudad Condal	1872	2,596
Covadonga†	1884	5,161
*Covadonga	1953	10,226
Cristobal Colon†	1854	2,869
Cristobal Colon	1923	10,833
Espana†	1873	2,679
*Guadalupe	1953	14,540
Habana†	1872	2,678
Habana†	1923	10,551
Infanta Isabel de Borbon†	1913	10,318
Isla de Panay	1882	3,545
Juan Sebastian Elcano†	1928	9,965
Legazpi†	1904	4,349
Leon XIII†	1888	5,087
Leon XIII†	1890	5,206
Magallanes	1928	9,689
Manuel Arnus	1923	7,578
Manuel Calvo†	1892	5,617
*Marques de Comillas	1928	9,922
Meteoro†	1890	6,966
Mexico†	1876	2,113
Montevideo	1889	5,205

SPANISH LINE (*Continued*)
(Compania Trasatlantica)

Name of Ship	Year Built	Tonnage
Montserrat†	1889	4,147
*Montserrat†	1945	9,001
P. de Satrustegui†	1890	4,710
Panama†	1875	2,085
Reina Maria Cristina	1889	4,818
Reina Victoria Eugenia†	1913	10,137
San Augustin†	1882	2,332
San Carlos	1917	2,488
Santa Isabel	1916	2,488
Santiago†	1890	5,206
Santo Domingo†	1877	2,911
*Satrustegui†	1948	6,518
Uruguay	1913	10,348
Vasco Nunez de Balboa†	1891	8,063
*Virginia de Churruca†	1949	6,518

PART IV

PASSENGER SHIPS TO AFRICA

AND THE EASTERN OCEANS

PART IV

PASSENGER SHIPS TO AFRICA
AND THE EASTERN OCEANS

*Asterisk denotes ship in service, 1962.

Aba (1918) Elder, Dempster & Co. (British).
Built by Barclay, Curle & Co., Glasgow, Scotland. Tonnage: 7,937. Dimensions: 450′ x 55′. Twin-screw, 14 knots. Motorship. Two masts and one funnel. Service: England-Africa. Sold in 1947. Renamed: **Matrona.** Ex-**Glenapp.**

Abda (1898) Cie. de Navigation Paquet (French).
Built by Kon. Maats. de Schelde, Flushing, Netherlands. Tonnage: 4,331. Dimensions: 390′ x 45′. Single-screw, 14 knots. Quadruple expansion engines. Two masts and one funnel. Scrapped in 1936. Ex-**Koning Willem I** (1913).

Aberdeen (1881) Thompson's Aberdeen Line (British).
Built by Robert Napier & Sons, Ltd., Glasgow, Scotland. Tonnage: 3,684. Dimensions: 362′ x 44′. Single-screw, 12½ knots. Triple expansion engines. Three masts and one funnel. Clipper bow. Iron hull. Note: Pioneer steamship of the Aberdeen Line (George Thompson & Co., Ltd.). The first ocean liner to be equipped with triple expansion engines. Made a speed of 13.7 knots on her trials. Her appearance was graceful with her trim lines. The Aberdeen Line during previous years had become famous for their clipper type sailing ships that traded to Australia. Service: Liverpool-Australia, via Cape of Good Hope. Vessel sold to Turkey in 1906. Renamed: **Halep.** Not listed after 1919.

Abinsi (1908) Elder, Dempster & Co. (British).
Built by Harland & Wolff, Ltd., Belfast, Ireland. Tonnage: 6,365. Dimensions: 400′ x 53′. Twin-screw, 15 knots. Quadruple expansion engines. Two masts and one funnel. Service: England-Africa. Scrapped in 1933. Ex-**Leopoldville** (1914).

Abosso (1912) Elder, Dempster & Co. (British).
Built by Harland & Wolff, Ltd., Belfast, Ireland. Tonnage: 7,782. Dimensions: 425′ x 57′. Twin-screw, 14 knots. Quadruple expansion engines. Two masts and one funnel. Service: England-West Africa. Torpedoed and sunk without

warning 180 miles from the Fastnet, April 24, 1917, with the
loss of 65 lives.

Abosso (1935) Elder, Dempster & Co. (British).
Built by Cammell, Laird & Co., Birkenhead, England.
Tonnage: 11,330. Dimensions: 460′ x 65′. Twin-screw,
15 knots. Motorship. Two masts and one funnel. Passengers: 550. Service: Liverpool-West Africa. Torpedoed
and sunk by submarine, October 29, 1942. Similar ships:
Accra and **Apapa.**

Achimota (1932) Elder, Dempster & Co. (British).
Built by Harland & Wolff, Ltd., Belfast, Ireland. Tonnage:
9,599. Dimensions: 461′ x 63′ (474′ o.l.). Twin-screw,
15 knots. Motorship. Two masts and two funnels. Note:
This fine liner was sold to Huddart, Parker, Ltd. prior to
completion and fitted out for their Australia-New Zealand
route. Renamed: **Wanganella** (1932).

Accra (1926) Elder, Dempster & Co.
Built by Harland & Wolff, Ltd., Belfast, Ireland. Tonnage:
9,337. Dimensions: 450′ x 62′. Twin-screw, 14½ knots.
Motorship. Two masts and one funnel. Service; Liverpool-
West Africa. Torpedoed and sunk by submarine, July 26,
1940. Sister ship: **Apapa.**

*****Accra** (1947) Elder, Dempster & Co.
Built by Vickers-Armstrongs, Ltd., Newcastle, England.
Tonnage: 11,644. Dimensions: 452′ x 66′ (471′ o.l.). Twin-
screw, 16 knots. Motorship. Two masts and one funnel.
Passengers: 259 first and 24 third. Service: Liverpool-West
Africa. Sister ship: **Apapa.**

Aconcagua (1872) Orient Line (British).
Built by John Elder & Co., Glasgow, Scotland. Tonnage:
4,106. Dimensions: 404′ x 41′. Single-screw, 14 knots.
Compound engines. Three masts and one funnel. This
former South American liner entered the Australian service
in 1880. Vessel owned by Pacific Steam Navigation Co.
Renamed: **Egypte** (1895).

Adda (1922) Elder, Dempster & Co.
Built by Harland & Wolff, Ltd., Greenock, Scotland.
Tonnage: 7,816. Dimensions: 435′ x 57′. Twin-screw,
14 knots. Motorship. Two masts and one funnel. Service:
England-West Africa. Sunk by submarine, June 8, 1941.

Admiral   (1905)   Deutsche Ost Afrika Line.
    Built by Blohm & Voss, Hamburg, Germany. Tonnage: 6,355. Dimensions: 415' x 50'. Twin-screw, 14 knots. Triple expansion engines. Two masts and one funnel. Renamed: **Lourenco Marques** (Portuguese).

Adolph Woermann   (1906)   Woermann Line (German).
    Built by Reiherstieg Schiffsw., Hamburg, Germany. Tonnage: 6,257. Dimensions: 411' x 50'. Twin-screw, 13 knots. Triple expansion engines. Two masts and one funnel. Service: Hamburg-Capetown, via West Africa. Passengers: 102 first, 82 second, 20 third. Renamed: (a) **Westminster Abbey** (British), (b) **Venezuela** (Dutch).

Aeneas   (1910)   Blue Funnel Line (British).
    Built by Workman, Clark & Co., Belfast, Ireland. Tonnage: 10,058. Dimensions: 493' x 60'. Twin-screw, 14 knots. Triple expansion engines. Two masts and one funnel. Service: England-Australia, via the Cape. Passengers: 288 first class. Sunk by bombs from aircraft off Plymouth, England, July 2, 1940. Sister ships: **Anchises** and **Ascanius.**

Afric   (1899)   White Star Line.
    Built by Harland & Wolff, Ltd., Belfast, Ireland. Tonnage: 11,948. Dimensions: 550' x 63'. Twin-screw, 13½ knots. Quadruple expansion engines. Four masts and one funnel. Service: England-Australia, via Capetown. Passengers: 350. Torpedoed and sunk off the Eddystone, February 12, 1917, with the loss of five lives. Sister ships: **Medic** and **Persic.**

Africa   (1903)   (a) Lloyd Austriaco, (b) Lloyd Triestino.
    Built by Lloyd Austriaco, Trieste, Austria-Hungaria. Tonnage: 4,719. Dimensions: 388' x 47'. Twin-screw, 15 knots. Triple expansion engines. 4,400 I.H.P. Two masts and one funnel. Passengers: 82 first and 40 second. Transferred to Lloyd Triestino in 1918. Scrapped in 1929.

***Africa**   (1952)   Lloyd Triestino (Italian).
    Built by Cantieri Riuniti dell' Adriatico, Monfalcone, Italy. Tonnage: 11,427. Dimensions: 493' x 68'. Twin-screw, 19½ knots. Motorship. Single mast and one funnel. Service: Italy-East and South Africa. Passengers: 148 first and 298 tourist. Commenced her maiden voyage in February 1952. Sister ship: **Europa.**

African   (1873)   Union Line (British).
    Built by J. Key, Kinghorn, Scotland. Tonnage: 2,019. Dimensions: 315' x 34'. Single-screw. Compound engines.

Two masts and one funnel. Iron hull. Service: England-South Africa. Employed on South African coastal route after 1881. Sold to F. Stumore & Co., 1885. Wrecked in 1887.

African Comet   (1941)   American-South African Line.
Built by Ingalls Shipbuilding Corp., Pascagoula, Mississippi. Tonnage: 11,812. Dimensions: 465′ x 69′ (489′ o.l.). Single-screw, 16½ knots. Steam turbines. Two masts and one funnel. Service: United States-South Africa. Sister ships: **African Meteor** and **African Planet.** Note: The first all-welded passenger liners in the world.

*African Endeavor   (1940)   Farrell Line (American).
Built by Bethlehem Sparrows Point Shipyard, Maryland. Tonnage: 7,997. Dimensions: 468′ x 66′. Single-screw, 16½ knots. Steam turbines. Two masts and one funnel. Service: United States-South Africa. Passengers: 80 first class. Ex-**George F. Elliot** (1949), ex-**Delbrasil** (1948), ex-**George F. Elliot** (1946), ex-**Delbrasil** (1942). Sister ship: **African Enterprise.**

*African Enterprise   (1940)   Farrell Line (American).
Built by Bethlehem Sparrows Point Shipyard, Maryland. Tonnage: 7,997. Dimensions: 468′ x 66′. Single-screw, 16½ knots. Steam turbines. Two masts and one funnel. Service: New York-South Africa. Passengers: 80 first class. Sister ship: **African Endeavor.**

African Meteor   (1941)   American South African Line.
Built by Ingalls Shipbuilding Corp., Pascagoula, Mississippi. Tonnage: 11,800. Dimensions: 465′ x 69′ (489′ o.l.). Single-screw, 16½ knots. Steam turbines. Two masts and one funnel. Service: United States-South Africa. Sister ships: **African Comet** and **African Planet.**

*African Planet   (1941)   American-South African Line.
Built by Ingalls Shipbuilding Corp., Pascagoula, Mississippi. Tonnage: 11,800. Dimensions: 465′ x 69′ (489′ o.l.). Single-screw, 16½ knots. Steam turbines. Two masts and one funnel. Service: United States-South Africa. Sister ships: **African Comet** and **African Meteor.**

Afrique   (1907)   Chargeurs Reunis (French).
Built by Swan, Hunter & Wigham Richardson, Ltd., Newcastle, England. Tonnage: 5,404. Dimensions: 391′ x 48′. Twin-screw, 14½ knots. Triple expansion engines. Two masts and one funnel. Service: France-West Africa. Lost

in a gale on the Rochebonne bank, during the night of January 11–12, 1920.

Akabo   (1902)   Elder, Dempster & Co.
Built by Sir Raylton Dixon & Co., Middlesbrough, England. Tonnage: 3,814. Dimensions: 352′ x 44′. Single-screw, 13 knots. Triple expansion engines. Two masts and one funnel. Service: England-West Africa. Renamed: **Baltonia.**

Albertville   (1906)   Compagnie Belge Maritime.
Built by Alexander Stephen & Sons, Ltd., Glasgow, Scotland. Tonnage: 4,793. Dimensions: 379′ x 47′. Single-screw, 14 knots. Triple expansion engines. Two masts and one funnel. Renamed: (a) **Elmina**, (b) **Iphigenia**, (c) **Cairo City.**

Albertville   (1912)   Compagnie Belge Maritime du Congo.
Built by Soc. Anon. John Cockerill, Hoboken, Belgium. Tonnage: 7,745. Dimensions: 439′ x 55′. Twin-screw, 14 knots. Triple expansion engines. Two masts and one funnel. Renamed: (a) **Angola**, (b) **Angolia.** Sister ship: **Elisabethville.**

Albertville   (1928)   Compagnie Belge Maritime.
Built by Ateliers & Chantiers de la Loire, St. Nazaire, France. Tonnage: 10,338. Dimensions: 494′ x 62′. Twin-screw, 16½ knots. Motorship. Two masts and two funnels. Service: Antwerp-Belgian Congo. Vessel was later modernized and original funnels replaced by a single streamlined one. Lengthened to 521 feet (11,047 tons). Converted to quadruple expansion engines and low pressure steam turbines. Sunk at Havre, June 11, 1940. Similar ship: **Leopoldville.**

*Albertville   (1948)   Compagnie Belge Maritime.
Built by John Cockerill, Hoboken, Belgium. Tonnage: 10,901. Dimensions: 479′ x 64′ (505′ o.l.). Single-screw, 16½ knots. Motorship. Two masts and one funnel. Service: Antwerp-Congo-Angola. Passengers: 207 in single class. Sister ships: **Charlesville, Elisabethville, Leopoldville** and **Thysville.**

Alnwick Castle   (1901)   Union-Castle Line.
Built by Wm. Beardmore & Co., Glasgow, Scotland. Tonnage: 5,893. Dimensions: 400′ x 50′. Twin-screw, 12 knots. Triple expansion engines. Two masts and one funnel. Torpedoed and sunk 310 miles from Bishop Rock, March 19, 1917, with the loss of 40 lives. The casualties occurred

in life boats after the sinking. Similar ships: **Berwick Castle, Cawdor Castle** and **Newark Castle.**

Alphee   (1861)   Messageries Maritimes (French).
Built by Messageries Maritimes, La Ciotat, France. Tonnage: 1,503. Note: Left Suez on October 27, 1862 to make first Messageries Maritimes sailing for the Far East. Vessel was lengthened and reconditioned in 1888; tonnage increased to 1,939, speed 12½ knots, refitted with triple expansion engines. Scrapped in France, 1899. Sister ship: **Erymanthe.**

Amarapoora   (1920)   Henderson Line (British).
Built by Wm. Denny & Bros., Ltd., Dumbarton, Scotland. Tonnage: 8,012. Dimensions: 465′ x 59′. Single-screw, 14 knots. Triple expansion engines. Two masts and one funnel. Passengers: 150 first class. Service: Great Britain-Burma. Similar ships: **Kemmendie, Pegu, Sagaing** and **Yoma.**

Amazone   (1869)   Messageries Maritimes.
Built by Messageries Maritimes, La Ciotat, France. Tonnage: 3,132. Dimensions: 370′ x 39′. Single-screw, 13½ knots. Compound engines. Three masts and two funnels. Iron hull. She was later converted to single funnel and refitted with triple expansion engines. Tonnage increased to 3,350. Scrapped at Marseilles in 1898. Sister ships: **Ava, Meikong, Pei-Ho** and **Sindh.**

Amazone   (1896)   Messageries Maritimes.
Built by Messageries Maritimes, La Ciotat, France. Tonnage: 6,019. Dimensions: 442′ x 50′. Twin-screw, 18½ knots. Triple expansion engines. Two masts and two funnels. As the **Amazone** commenced service to South America, but was transferred to the Far East trade in 1912. Vessel was reconditioned in 1923. Sold for scrap in February 1932. Ex-**Laos** (1904).

Amboise   (1905)   Messageries Maritimes.
Built by Fairfield Shipbuilding & Engineering Co., Glasgow, Scotland. Tonnage: 8,408. Dimensions: 469′ x 55′ (486′ o.l.). Quadruple expansion engines. Two masts and one funnel. Vessel was purchased in 1921. Sold for scrap at Genoa in September 1935. Ex-**Friedrichsruh,** ex-**Furst Bismarck.**

American   (1873)   Union Line (British).
 Built by Stephen of Dundee, Scotland. Tonnage: 2,126.
 Dimensions: 320′ x 34′. Single-screw. Compound engines.
 Two masts and one funnel. Iron hull. One of five steamers
 built for their England-South African mail service. Wrecked
 near the Equator by broken propeller shaft, April 23, 1880,
 with no loss of life.

Amerique   (1912)   Chargeurs Reunis (French).
 Built by Bremer Vulkan, Vegesack, Germany. Tonnage:
 8,396. Dimensions: 440′ x 55′. Twin-screw, 13 knots.
 Triple expansion engines. Two masts and one funnel.
 Service: France-West Africa. Vessel purchased from Cie de
 Navigation Sud Atlantique. Sold to British shipbreakers in
 February 1936. Ex-**Alba**, ex-**Sierra Ventana.**

*Amra**   (1938)   British India Steam Navigation Co.
 Built by Swan, Hunter & Wigham Richardson, Ltd., Newcastle, England. Tonnage: 8,314. Dimensions: 444′ x 61′
 (461′ o.l.). Twin-screw, 16 knots. Steam turbines. Two
 masts and one funnel. Served as hospital ship during World
 War II. Passengers: 222 first and 737 third. Service: India-
 Africa. Sister ships: **Aska** and **Aronda.**

Anadyr   (1873)   Messageries Maritimes (French).
 Built by Messageries Maritimes, La Ciotat, France. Tonnage: 3,714. Dimensions: 398′ x 39′. Single-screw. Compound engines. Three masts and one funnel. Iron hull.
 Launched, August 31, 1873. Sunk in collision with **Oxus**
 in Aden roads, July 11, 1889. Sister ship: **Iraouddy.**

Anchises   (1911)   Blue Funnel Line (British).
 Built by Workman, Clark & Co., Belfast, Ireland. Tonnage:
 10,046. Dimensions: 493′ x 60′. Twin-screw, 13½ knots.
 Triple expansion engines. 5,500 I.H.P. Two masts and one
 funnel. Passengers: 288. Service: Liverpool-Australia, via
 the Cape. Attacked by aircraft on February 27, 1941, and
 again on the 28th, sunk in Irish Sea. Sister ships: **Aeneas**
 and **Ascanius.**

Ancona   (1879)   P. & O. Line (British).
 Built by Caird & Co., Greenock, Scotland. Tonnage: 3,142.
 Dimensions: 380′ x 38′. Single-screw, 14 knots. Compound
 engines. Three masts and one funnel. Passengers: 93 first
 and 32 second. Sold in 1900. Renamed: **Tabor** (Bombay
 owners). Sister ship: **Verona.**

Andre Lebon (1913)   Messageries Maritimes (French).
 Built by Messageries Maritimes, La Ciotat, France. Tonnage: 13,682. Dimensions: 508' x 61'. Twin-screw, 17 knots. Quadruple expansion engines. Two masts and two funnels. Launched, October 27, 1913. In mail and passenger service between Marseilles and the Far East. Passengers: 500. Broken up for scrap in France, 1953. Sister ship: **Paul Lecat**. Similar ships: **Bernardin de Saint Pierre, Explorateur, Porthos** and **Sphinx**.

Angers (1907)   Messageries Maritimes (French).
 Built by Blohm & Voss, Hamburg, Germany. Tonnage: 9,846. Dimensions: 483' x 55'. Twin-screw, 15½ knots. Quadruple expansion engines. Two masts and one funnel. Vessel was purchased in 1923. Sold for scrap at Marseilles in September 1938. Destroyed by fire while being broken up, April 24, 1939. Ex-**Cap Arcona** (1921).

Angkor (1899)   Messageries Maritimes.
 Built by Messageries Maritimes, La Ciotat, France. Tonnage: 7,357. Dimensions: 468' x 50'. Twin-screw, 13½ knots. Triple expansion engines. Two masts and two funnels. Reconditioned in 1918. Sold for scrap in December 1933. Ex-**Atlantique** (1918).

Anglia (1889)   Anchor Line (British).
 Built by D. & W. Henderson & Co., Glasgow, Scotland. Tonnage: 3,287. Dimensions: 340' x 43'. Single-screw, 12 knots. Triple expansion engines. Two masts and one funnel. Steel hull. In service to Calcutta. Grounded in River Hoogly, August 24, 1892.

Anglian (1873)   Union Line (British).
 Built by Aitken & Mansel, Glasgow, Scotland. Tonnage: 2,159. Dimensions: 314' x 35'. Single-screw. Compound engines. Two masts and one funnel. Iron hull. Service: England-South Africa. Transferred to South African coastal service after 1886. Sold to Huddart, Parker, Ltd. (Australian) in 1894. Converted to hulk at Hobart, Tasmania in 1913.

*Angola (1948)   Companhia Nacional de Navegacao (Portuguese).
 Built by Hawthorn, Leslie & Co., Newcastle, England. Tonnage: 13,016. Dimensions: 528' x 67' (550' o.l.). Twin-screw, 18 knots. Motorship. Two masts and one funnel. Service: Portugal-West Africa-East Africa. Passengers: 80 first, 140 tourist, 98 third, 413 fourth. Sister ship: **Mocambique.**

Annam   (1898)   Messageries Maritimes.
Built by Messageries Maritimes, La Ciotat, France. Tonnage: 6,343. Dimensions: 446′ x 50′. Twin-screw, 19 knots. Triple expansion engines. Two masts and two funnels. Launched, November 6, 1898. Renamed: (a) **Tourane** (1904), (b) **Karnak** (1912). Torpedoed and sunk near Malta by "U-32", November 27, 1916. Sister ships: **Indus, Laos** and **Tonkin.**

Antenor   (1925)   Blue Funnel Line (British).
Built by Palmer's Shipbuilding & Iron Co., Newcastle, England. Tonnage: 11,174. Dimensions: 497′ x 62′. Twin-screw, 15 knots. Four steam turbines. Two masts and one funnel. Service: Liverpool-Far East. Passengers: 190. Crew: 80. Sold to British shipbreakers in 1953. Sister ships: **Hector, Patroclus** and **Sarpedon.**

Anversville   (1899)   Cie. Maritime Belge.
Built by Sir Raylton Dixon & Co., Middlesbrough, England. Tonnage: 4,081. Dimensions: 370′ x 46′ (383′ o.l.). Twin-screw, 13½ knots. Triple expansion engines. Two masts and one funnel. Service: Antwerp-Congo. Renamed: (a) **Dakar,** (b) **Bloemfontein,** (c) **Hong Peng.** Sister ship: **Philippeville.**

Anversville   (1912)   Compagnie Maritime Belge.
Built by Alexander Stephens & Sons, Ltd., Glasgow, Scotland. Tonnage: 8,433. Dimensions: 440′ x 55′. Twin-screw, 14 knots. Quadruple expansion engines. Two masts and one funnel. Service: Antwerp-Congo. Scrapped in 1938. Running mates: **Albertville** and **Elisabethville.**

Aotea   (1895)   Shaw, Savill & Albion Co.
Built by C. S. Swan & Hunter, Ltd., Newcastle, England. Tonnage: 6,364. Dimensions: 430′ x 49′. Single-screw, 12 knots. Triple expansion engines. Two masts and one funnel. Ran ashore at Mouille Point in January 1911, but was refloated two months later. Renamed: **Naneric** (Bank Line). Scrapped in 1925.

Apapa   (1914)   Elder, Dempster & Co.
Built by Harland & Wolff, Ltd., Belfast, Ireland. Tonnage: 7,832. Dimensions: 425′ x 57′. Twin-screw, 14 knots. Quadruple expansion engines. Two masts and one funnel. Service: England-West Africa. Torpedoed and sunk without warning near Lynas Point, November 28, 1917, with the loss of 77 lives.

Apapa   (1927)   Elder, Dempster & Co.
    Built by Harland & Wolff, Ltd., Belfast, Ireland. Tonnage: 9,333. Dimensions: 450′ x 62′. Twin-screw, 14½ knots. Motorship. Two masts and one funnel. Passengers: 400. Crew: 160. Sunk by bombs from enemy aircraft, November 15, 1940. Sister ship: **Accra.**

*Apapa   (1948)   Elder, Dempster & Co.
    Built by Vickers-Armstrongs, Ltd., Barrow, England. Tonnage: 11,651. Dimensions: 452′ x 66′ (471′ o.l.). Twin-screw, 16 knots. Motorship. Two masts and one funnel. Service: Liverpool-West Africa. Passengers: 246 first and 24 third class. Sister ship: **Accra.**

Appam   (1913)   Elder, Dempster & Co.
    Built by Harland & Wolff, Ltd., Belfast, Ireland. Tonnage: 7,781. Dimensions: 425′ x 57′. Twin-screw, 14 knots. Quadruple expansion engines. Two masts and one funnel. In First World War was captured by the famous German raider **Moewe** and sailed to an American port with a prize crew. Passengers: 250. Scrapped in 1936. Ex-**Mandingo,** ex-**Appam.** Sister ships: **Apapa** and **Abosso.**

Aquileja   (1914)   Lloyd Triestino (Italian).
    Built by Nederlandsche Schps. Maats., Amsterdam, Netherlands. Tonnage: 9,448. Dimensions: 481′ x 57′ (498′ o.l.). Twin-screw, 15 knots. Quadruple expansion engines. Two masts and one funnel. Became a war casualty in June 1944. Ex-**Prins der Nederland** (1935).

Arab   (1879)   Union Line (British).
    Built by J. & G. Thomson, Glasgow, Scotland. Tonnage: 3,192. Dimensions: 350′ x 40′. Single-screw, 13 knots. Triple expansion engines. Two masts and one funnel. Served first as a mail steamer from England to South Africa, but later transferred to intermediate service. Scrapped in Germany during 1900.

Arabia   (1898)   P. & O. Line (British).
    Built by Caird & Co., Greenock, Scotland. Tonnage: 7,933. Dimensions: 499′ x 54′. Single-screw, 18 knots. Triple expansion engines. 11,000 I.H.P. Two masts and two funnels. Service: England-Australia-India. Passengers: 314 first and 210 second. Torpedoed and sunk, November 6, 1916, with the loss of eleven lives. Sister ships: **China, Egypt, India** and **Persia.** Note: Outstanding P. & O. liners for that era.

Aramis   (1922)   Messageries Maritimes (French).
Built by Forges & Chantiers de la Gironde, Bordeaux, France.
Tonnage: 14,825. Dimensions: 543' x 65' (576' o.l.). Twin-screw, 14 knots. Triple expansion engines. Two masts and one funnel. Note: Trials of her steam turbines having been a failure, she was converted with two triple expansion engines and renamed **Chenonceaux** (1925).

Aramis   (1932)   Messageries Maritimes (French).
Built by Forges & Chantiers de la Mediterranee, La Seyne, France. Tonnage: 17,537. Dimensions: 543' x 69'. Twin-screw, 18 knots. Motorship. Two masts and two square funnels. Launched, June 30, 1931. Refitted and lengthened in 1935–36; speed increased from 15 to 18½ knots. Sunk by an American submarine, August 18, 1944, while under Japanese control. Sister ships: **Georges Philippar** and **Felix Roussel.**

Arankola   (1911)   British India Steam Navigation Co.
Built by Workman, Clark & Co., Belfast, Ireland. Tonnage: 4,129. Dimensions: 390' x 50'. Twin-screw, 17½ knots. Quadruple expansion engines. Two masts and two funnels. Scrapped in 1937.

Arawa   (1884)   Shaw, Savill & Albion Co.
Built by Wm. Denny & Bros., Ltd., Dumbarton, Scotland. Tonnage: 5,026. Dimensions: 439' x 46'. Single-screw, 13 knots. Triple expansion engines. Four masts and two funnels. Steel hull. Clipper bow. Service: England-Australia-New Zealand. This pioneer steamer made three voyages in the trans-Pacific service from 1893–95. Renamed: (a) **Colon** (1896), (b) **Arawa** (1899), (c) **Lake Megantic** (1900), (d) **Port Henderson** (1905), (e) **Anapo** (1912), **Porto Said** (1913). Torpedoed and sunk by submarine in December 1915. Sister ship: **Tainui.**

Arawa   (1907)   Shaw, Savill & Albion Co.
Built by Swan, Hunter & Wigham Richardson, Ltd., Newcastle, England. Tonnage: 9,372. Dimensions: 459' x 59'. Twin-screw, 14 knots. 5,000 I.H.P. Triple expansion engines. Two masts and one funnel. Passengers: 44 first, 70 second, 200 third. Renamed: (a) **Konigstein** (1928), (b) **Gandia** (1939) Belgian. Became a war loss in January 1942.

Arcadia   (1888)   P. & O. Line (British).
Built by Harland & Wolff, Ltd., Belfast, Ireland. Tonnage: 6,603. Dimensions: 468' x 52'. Single-screw, 16½ knots.

Triple expansion engines. 7,500 I.H.P. Four masts and two funnels. Steel hull. Coal consumption amounted to 110 tons per day. Service: England-Australia. Passengers: 250 first and 160 second class. Scrapped in 1925. Sister ship: **Oceana.** Similar ships: **Britannia** and **Victoria.** Note: These remarkable passenger ships became famous as the "Jubilee" class of 1887.

*Arcadia   (1954)   P. & O. Line (British).
Built by John Brown & Co., Clydebank, Glasgow, Scotland. Tonnage: 29,734. Dimensions: 721′ (o.l.) x 90′. Twin-screw, 21 knots. Six steam turbines. Two masts and one funnel. Launched, May 14, 1953. The largest P. & O. liner ever to be built in Scotland. Services: (a) Great Britain-India-Ceylon-Australia, (b) Great Britain-Australia-California. See PART II. Similar ship: **Iberia.**

Armadale Castle   (1903)   Union-Castle Line.
Built by Fairfield Shipbuilding Co., Glasgow, Scotland. Tonnage: 12,973. Dimensions: 570′ x 64′ (590′ o.l.). Twin-screw, 17 knots. Quadruple expansion engines. Two masts and two funnels. Service: England-South Africa. Passengers: 260 first and 300 second. Scrapped in 1936. Sister ship: **Kenilworth Castle.** The first liners ordered after the merger in February 1900 of the Union Steam Ship Co. with the Castle Mail Packets Co.

Armand Behic   (1892)   Messageries Maritimes (French).
Built by Messageries Maritimes, La Ciotat, France. Tonnage: 6,397. Dimensions: 486′ x 50′. Single-screw, 17½ knots. Triple expansion engines. Three masts and two funnels. Steel hull. Note: Laid down as **Tasmanien;** renamed before being launched, after death of Armand Behic, Chairman of Messageries Maritimes. Service: France-Far East. Scrapped in 1925. Sister ships: **Australien, Polynesien** and **Ville de la Ciotat.**

Arno   (1912)   Lloyd Triestino (Italian).
Built by Wm. Beardmore & Co., Glasgow, Scotland. Tonnage: 8,024. Dimensions: 411′ x 56′ (428′ o.l.). Twin-screw, 16 knots. Quadruple expansion engines. Two masts and one funnel. She became a war loss, September 10, 1942. Ex-**Cesarea** (1938), ex-**Fort St. George** (1935), ex-**Wandilla.**

Aronda   (1912)   British India Steam Navigation Co.
Built by Alexander Stephen & Sons, Ltd., Glasgow, Scotland. Tonnage: 4,062. Dimensions: 390′ x 50′. Twin-screw, 17½

knots. Quadruple expansion engines. Two masts and one funnel. Scrapped in 1939. Sister ship: **Angora.**

*Aronda   (1941)   British India Steam Navigation Co.
Built by Swan, Hunter & Wigham Richardson, Ltd., Newcastle, England. Tonnage: 8,396. Dimensions: 461' x 61'. Twin-screw, 16½ knots. Six steam turbines. Two masts and one funnel. Passengers: 44 first, 22 second, plus 28 interchangeable, 60 intermediate class. Service: Karachi-Colombo-Chittagong.   Sister ships: **Amra** and **Aska.**

Arundel Castle   (1894)   (a) Castle Line, (b) Union-Castle Line.
Built by Fairfield Shipbuilding & Engineering Co., Glasgow, Scotland. Tonnage: 4,588. Dimensions: 415' x 45'. Single-screw, 13½ knots. Triple expansion engines. Four masts and one funnel. Intermediate type of steamer. Vessel sold to Danish East Asiatic Company in 1905. Renamed: (a) **Birma** (1905), (b) **Mitau** (1913), (c) **Joszef Pilsudski** (1920), (d) **Wilbo** (1922). Scrapped in 1924.

Arundel Castle   (1921)   Union-Castle Line.
Built by Harland & Wolff, Ltd., Belfast, Ireland. Tonnage: 19,023. Dimensions: 630' x 75'. Twin-screw, 18 knots. Steam turbines. Two masts and four funnels. Service: Southampton-Cape Town. Passengers: 760. Crew: 440. Lengthened to 661 feet (19,118 tons) in 1938, and also, altered by replacing her original funnels with two of the new streamlined type. Scrapped in Hong Kong, 1959. Sister ship: **Windsor Castle.**

Ascanius   (1910)   Blue Funnel Line (British).
Built by Workman, Clark & Co., Belfast, Ireland. Tonnage: 10,048. Dimensions: 493' x 60'. Twin-screw, 14 knots. Triple expansion engines. 5,500 I.H.P. Two masts and one funnel. Service: England-Australia, via Cape Town. Passengers: 288 first class. Vessel sold in 1949. Renamed: **San Giovannina.** Sold to Italian shipbreakers late in 1952. Sister ships: **Aeneas** and **Anchises.**

*Asia   (1953)   Lloyd Triestino (Italian).
Built by Cantieri Riuniti dell' Adriatico, Trieste, Italy. Tonnage: 11,693. Dimensions: 491' x 68' (522' o.l.). Twin-screw, 21 knots. Motorship. Single mast and one funnel. Passengers: 290 first and 140 tourist. Service: Italy-Far East. Sister ships: **Africa, Europa,** and **Victoria.**

Asie   (1914)   Chargeurs Reunis (French).
Built by Ateliers & Chantiers de France, Dunkirk, France.
Tonnage: 8,561. Dimensions: 439' x 55'. Twin-screw, 14½
knots. Triple expansion engines. Two masts and two
funnels. Service: France-West Africa. Destroyed by aircraft in Genoa harbor, 1945.

Aska   (1939)   British India Steam Navigation Co.
Built by Swan, Hunter & Wigham Richardson, Ltd., Newcastle, England. Tonnage: 8,323. Dimensions: 444' x 61'
(461' o.l.). Twin-screw, 17 knots. Steam turbines. Two
masts and one funnel. Bombed and sunk by enemy aircraft,
September 16, 1940. Sister ships: **Amra** and **Aronda.**

Assyria   (1908)   Anchor Line (British).
Tonnage: 8,072. Service: Great Britain-India. Note: See
PART I for details.

Athenian   (1882)   Union Line (British).
Tonnage: 3,877. Service: England-Cape Town. Sold to the
Canadian Pacific Line in 1897, which was commencing a
new service to handle the passenger business due to the
Klondyke Gold Rush. Note: See PART II for additional
information. The **Athenian** was a sister ship to **Moor.**

Athenic   (1901)   White Star Line.
Tonnage: 12,234. Service: England-Australia, via Cape
Town. Passengers: 93 first, 81 second and 500 third. She
was later operated by Shaw, Savill & Albion Co. Note:
See PART II for details.

*Athlone Castle   (1936)   Union-Castle Line.
Built by Harland & Wolff, Ltd., Belfast, Ireland. Tonnage:
25,564. Dimensions: 696' x 82' (725' o.l.). Twin-screw,
20 knots. Motorship. Two masts and one funnel. Service:
England-South Africa. Passengers: 245 first and 538 tourist.
Sister ship: **Stirling Castle.**

Athos   (1914)   Messageries Maritimes (French).
Built by Ateliers & Chantiers de France, Dunkirk, France.
Tonnage: 12,692. Dimensions: 508' x 61'. Twin-screw, 17½
knots. Triple expansion engines. Two masts and two fun-
nels. Launched, July 25, 1914. Torpedoed and sunk near
Malta, February 17, 1917. Sister ship: **Porthos.**

Athos II   (1925)   Messageries Maritimes (French).
Built by Akt. Ges. "Weser", Bremen, Germany. Tonnage:
15,276.   Dimensions: 543' x 66'.   Twin-screw, 14 knots.

Steam turbines. Two masts and two funnels. Speed increased to 16½ knots in 1937. Also, lengthened to 566 feet (590′ o.l.). A new single stack replaced her original two funnels. Passengers: 84 first, 108 second, 127 third. Converted to transport in 1942. Scrapped in 1960. Sister ship: **D'Artagnan.**

Atlantique (1899) Messageries Maritimes (French).
Tonnage: 6,479. Transferred to Far East service in 1912. Note: See PART III for details.

Atsuta Maru (1909) N. Y. K. Line (Japanese).
Tonnage: 8,523. Sister ships: **Kamo Maru, Hirano Maru, Mishima Maru, Miyazaki Maru** and **Kitano Maru.** This class of liners was built for Japan-European service. Note: See PART II for details.

*__Aurelia__ (1939) Compagnia Genovese di Armamento (Italian).
Built by Blohm & Voss, Hamburg, Germany. Tonnage: 10,480. Dimensions: 487′ x 60′. Single-screw, 17 knots. Motorship. Two masts and one funnel. Passengers: 1,124 tourist. Service: Europe-Australia. Ex-**Beaverbrae** (1954), ex-**Huascaran** (1947).

*__Aureol__ (1951) Elder, Dempster & Co. (British).
Built by Alexander Stephen & Sons, Ltd., Glasgow, Scotland. Tonnage: 14,083. Dimensions: 502′ x 70′ (537′ o.l.). Twin-screw, 18 knots. Motorship. Single mast and one funnel. Service: England-West Africa. Flagship of the line. Passengers: 265 first and 100 tourist. Running mates: **Accra** and **Apapa.**

Ausonia (1928) Lloyd Triestino (Italian).
Built by Soc. Anon. Ansaldo, Sestri-Ponente, Italy. Tonnage: 12,995. Dimensions: 517′ x 66′ (544′ o.l.). Twin-screw, 21 knots. Six steam turbines. Two masts and two funnels. Destroyed by fire at Malta in 1935.

Austral (1881) Orient Line (British).
Built by John Elder & Co., Glasgow, Scotland. Tonnage: 5,524. Dimensions: 456′ x 48′ (474′ o.l.). Single-screw, 16½ knots. Compound engines. Four masts and two funnels. Funnels were lengthened in 1884. An outstanding liner for her era. Service: England-Australia. Scrapped at Genoa in 1903.

Australasian (1884) Aberdeen Line (British).
Built by Robert Napier & Sons, Glasgow, Scotland. Tonnage: 3,662. Dimensions: 361′ x 44′. Single-screw, 13 knots.

Triple expansion engines.   Three masts and one funnel. Iron hull. Clipper bow. Sold to the Turkish Government in 1907, but was not renamed **Scham** until 1912. Converted to hulk in 1924. Broken up at Savona in 1955.

Australasian   (1901)   New Zealand Shipping Co.
Built by Wm. Denny & Bros., Ltd., Dumbarton, Scotland. Tonnage: 8,887. Dimensions: 457′ x 58′. Twin-screw, 13 knots. Triple expansion engines. Two masts and one funnel. Renamed: **Ruapehu.** Scrapped in 1932. Ex-**Ruapehu.**

Australia   (1870)   Anchor Line (British).
Built by Robert Duncan & Co., Port Glasgow, Scotland. Tonnage: 2,243. Dimensions: 324′ x 35′. Single-screw, 12 knots. Compound engines. Three masts and one funnel. Services: (a) Great Britain-India, (b) North Atlantic. Scrapped in 1895.

Australia   (1870)   P. & O. Line (British).
Built by Caird & Co., Greenock, Scotland. Tonnage: 3,666. Dimensions: 381′ x 44′. Single-screw. Compound engines. Three masts and one funnel. Iron hull. Renamed: **Dane** (1889). Scrapped in 1893.

Australia   (1892)   P. & O. Line (British).
Built by Caird & Co., Greenock, Scotland. Tonnage: 6,901. Dimensions: 465′ x 52′. Single-screw, 17 knots.   Triple expansion engines. Four masts and two funnels. Wrecked at Port Phillip Heads, June 20, 1904, and subsequently destroyed by fire. Sister ship: **Himalaya.**

Australia   (1951)   Lloyd Triestino (Italian).
Built by Cantieri Riuniti dell' Adriatico, Trieste, Italy. Tonnage: 13,205. Dimensions: 501′ x 69′ (528′ o.l.). Twin-screw, 18 knots. Motorship. Two masts and one funnel. Note: The first post-war passenger liner to be built for Lloyd Triestino. Passengers: 120 first and 600 tourist. Service: Italy-Australia. Sister ships: **Neptunia** and **Oceania.**

Australien   (1889)   Messageries Maritimes.
Built by Messageries Maritimes, La Ciotat, France. Tonnage: 6,365. Dimensions: 482′ x 49′. Single-screw, 17 knots. Triple expansion engines. Three masts and two funnels. Launched, May 26, 1889.   Torpedoed and sunk in the Mediterranean, July 19, 1918. Sister ships: **Armand Behic, Polynesien** and **Ville de la Ciotat.**

Ava   (1870)   Messageries Maritimes.
Built by Messageries Maritimes, La Ciotat, France. Tonnage: 3,361. Dimensions: 371′ x 39′. Single-screw, 13½ knots. Three masts and two funnels. Later reduced to single funnel. Launched, January 10, 1870. Scrapped in France, 1900. Sister ships: **Amazone, Meikong, Pei-Ho,** and **Sindh.**

Avoca   (1891)   British India Steam Navigation Co.
Built by Wm. Denny & Bros., Ltd., Dumbarton, Scotland. Tonnage: 5,189. Dimensions: 420′ x 48′. Single-screw, 14 knots. Quadruple expansion engines. Three masts and one funnel. Renamed: (a) **San Fernando,** (b) **Avoca,** (c) **Atlanta,** (d) **Avoca,** (e) **Uranium,** (f) **Feltria.** Torpedoed and sunk, May 5, 1917. Sister ship: **Jelunga.**

Avondale Castle   (1897)   Union-Castle Line.
Built by Fairfield Shipbuilding Co., Glasgow, Scotland. Tonnage: 5,531. Dimensions: 425′ x 50′. Single-screw, 13 knots. Triple expansion engines. Four masts and one funnel. Renamed: **Garonna** (1912). Scrapped in 1920. Sister ship: **Tintagel Castle.**

Azay le Rideau   (1910)   Messageries Maritimes (French).
Built by Blohm & Voss, Hamburg, Germany. Tonnage: 7,988. Dimensions: 449′ x 54′. Twin-screw, 12½ knots. Quadruple expansion engines. Two masts and one funnel. Sold for scrap at Marseilles in December 1936. Ex-**General** (1923).

Ballaarat   (1882)   P. & O. Line (British).
Built by Caird & Co., Greenock, Scotland. Tonnage: 4,890. Dimensions: 420′ x 43′. Single-screw, 15 knots. Compound engines. Two masts and two funnels. Steel hull. Scrapped in 1905. Sister ship: **Parramatta.**

Ballarat   (1911)   P. & O. Line (British).
Built by Caird & Co., Greenock, Scotland. Tonnage: 11,120. Dimensions: 500′ x 62′. Twin-screw, 14 knots. Quadruple expansion engines. Two masts and one funnel. Service: England-Australia, via Cape Town. Displayed Lund's "blue anchor" on funnel when first in service. Torpedoed and sunk near Scilly Islands, April 25, 1917. Running mates: **Beltana, Berrima, Benalla** and **Borda.** Passengers: 1,100 one-class.

Ballarat   (1921)   P. & O. Line (British).
Built by Harland & Wolff, Ltd., Belfast, Ireland. Tonnage: 13,033. Dimensions: 519′ x 64′. Twin-screw, 17½ knots.

Quadruple expansion engines. Two masts and one funnel. Scrapped in 1935. Sister ships: **Balranald, Baradine, Barrabool** and **Bendigo.**

Balmoral Castle (1877)   Castle Line (British).
Built by Robert Napier & Sons, Glasgow, Scotland. Tonnage: 2,948. Dimensions: 344' x 39'. Single-screw. Compound engines. Two masts and one funnel. Iron hull. Sold to Spanish owners in 1882. Renamed: (a) **San Augustin** (1882), (b) **Balmoral Castle,** (c) **Madiana** (1892). Wrecked off Bermuda in 1903.

Balmoral Castle (1910)   Union-Castle Line.
Built by Fairfield Shipbuilding Co., Glasgow, Scotland. Tonnage: 13,361. Dimensions: 570' x 64'. Twin-screw, 17 knots. Quadruple expansion engines. Two masts and two funnels. 12,500 I.H.P. Service: Southampton-Cape Town. Passengers: 317 first, 220 second, 268 third. Scrapped in 1939. Sister ship: **Edinburgh Castle.**

Baloeran (1930)   Rotterdam Lloyd.
Built by Maats. Fyenoord, Rotterdam, Netherlands. Tonnage: 16,981. Dimensions: 550' x 70' (574' o.l.). Twin-screw, 18 knots. Motorship. Two masts and one funnel. Service: Holland-Dutch East Indies.   Became a war casualty, September 1, 1943. Sister ship: **Dempo.**

Balranald (1922)   P. & O. Line (British).
Built by Harland & Wolff, Ltd., Greenock, Scotland. Tonnage: 13,039. Dimensions: 519' x 64'. Twin-screw, 15½ knots. Quadruple expansion engines. Two masts and one funnel. Scrapped in 1936. Sister ships: **Ballarat, Baradine, Barrabool** and **Bendigo.**

Banfora (1914)   Fabre Line (French).
Built by Kon. Maats. de Schelde, Flushing, Netherlands. Tonnage: 9,347. Dimensions: 478' x 57'. Twin-screw, 15½ knots. Triple expansion engines. Two masts and one funnel. Service: France-West Africa. Sold to Japanese shipbreakers, arriving at Yokohama under the name of **Banfora Maru,** August 25, 1957 and subsequently broken up. Ex-**Insulinde** (1933).

Baradine (1921)   P. & O. Line (British).
Built by Harland & Wolff, Ltd., Belfast, Ireland. Tonnage: 13,144.   Dimensions: 519' x 64'.   Twin-screw, 15 knots. Quadruple expansion engines. Two masts and one funnel.

Scrapped in 1936. Sister ships: **Ballarat, Balranald, Barrabool** and **Bendigo.**

Barbarossa (1896)   North German Lloyd.
Tonnage: 10,984. Service: Interchangeable between New York and Australian trades. Note: See PART I for details.

Barrabool (1922)   P. & O. Line (British).
Built by Harland & Wolff, Ltd., Belfast, Ireland. Tonnage: 13,148. Dimensions: 519′ x 64′. Twin-screw, 15 knots. Quadruple expansion engines. Two masts and one funnel. Scrapped in 1936. Sister ships: **Ballarat, Balranald, Baradine** and **Bendigo.**

Baudouinville (1939)   Compagnie Belge Maritime.
Built by Soc. Anon. John Cockerill, Hoboken, Belgium. Tonnage: 13,761. Dimensions: 511′ x 67′ (541′ o.l.). Twin-screw, 16 knots. Motorship. Two masts and one funnel. Note: Largest Belgian liner built to date. Passengers: 400. Service: Antwerp-Africa. Sunk at Nantes in 1944. Sister ship: **Grisarville.**

Baudouinville (1950)   Compagnie Belge Maritime.
Built by Soc. Anon. John Cockerill, Hoboken, Belgium. Tonnage: 10,990. Dimensions: 479′ x 64′ (505′ o.l.). Single-screw, 16½ knots. Motorship. Two masts and one funnel. Passengers: 248 single class. Service: Antwerp-Congo and Angola. Renamed: **Thysville** (1957).

***Baudouinville** (1958)   Compagnie Belge Maritime.
Built by Soc. Anon. Cockerill-Ougree, Hoboken, Belgium. Tonnage: 13,921. Dimensions: 558′ (o.l.) x 69′. Single-screw, 16½ knots. Two steam turbines. Two masts and one funnel. Launched in January 1957. Passengers: 300 one class. Service: Antwerp-Congo and Angola. Sold to P. & O. Line in January 1961. Renamed: **Cathay** (1961). Sister ship: **Jadotville.**

Bayern (1886)   North German Lloyd.
Built by "Vulkan", Stettin, Germany. Tonnage: 4,580. Dimensions: 388′ x 45′. Single-screw, 14½ knots. Triple expansion engines. Two masts and one funnel. Steel hull. Lengthened to 440 feet (5,034 tons) in 1894. Sold to Italian shipbreakers in 1909. Sister ships: **Preussen** and **Sachsen.**

***Bayernstein** (1954)   North German Lloyd.
Built by Bremer Vulkan, Vegesack, Germany. Tonnage: 8,999. Dimensions: 492′ x 63′ (537′ o.l.). Single-screw, 19

knots. Motorship. Single-mast and one funnel. Passengers: 86. Crew: 91. Service: Europe-Far East. Sister ships: **Hessenstein** and **Schwabenstein.**

Belgravia   (1882)   Anchor Line.
Tonnage: 4,977. In Bombay service 1884–1889. Note: See PART I for details.

Beltana   (1913)   P. & O. Line (British).
Built by Caird & Co., Greenock, Scotland. Tonnage: 11,120. Dimensions: 500' x 62'. Twin-screw, 14 knots. Quadruple expansion engines. Two masts and one funnel. Passengers: 1,100 single class. Service: England-Australia, via Cape Town. Scrapped in 1930. Running mates: **Ballarat, Benalla, Berrima** and **Borda.**

Benalla   (1913)   P. & O. Line (British).
Built by Caird & Co., Greenock, Scotland. Tonnage: 11,118. Dimensions: 500' x 62'. Twin-screw, 14 knots. Quadruple expansion engines. Two masts and one funnel. Scrapped in 1931. Sister ships: **Ballarat, Beltana, Berrima** and **Borda.**

Bendigo   (1922)   P. & O. Line (British).
Built by Harland & Wolff, Ltd., Greenock, Scotland. Tonnage: 13,039. Dimensions: 519' x 64'. Twin-screw, 15 knots. Quadruple expansion engines. Two masts and one funnel. Service: England-Australia. Scrapped in 1936. Sister ships: **Ballarat, Baradine, Balranald** and **Barrabool.**

Bengal   (1885)   P. & O. Line (British).
Built by Caird & Co., Greenock, Scotland. Tonnage: 4,344. Dimensions: 400' x 45'. Single-screw, 14½ knots. Triple expansion engines. Three masts and one funnel. Steel hull. Served on the Australian and Far East routes. Sold in 1906. Renamed: **Shah Nazam.** Passengers: 118 first and 43 second. Sister ship: **Chusan.**

Bernardin de Saint Pierre   (1925)   Messageries Maritimes.
Built by J. C. Tecklenborg, A. G., Wesermunde, Germany Tonnage: 10,085. Dimensions: 455' x 60'. Twin-screw, 16 knots. Two steam turbines. Two masts and two funnels. Service: Marseilles-Far East. Sunk, October 11, 1943. Similar ships: **Explorateur Gradidier, Porthos, Sphinx** and **Andre Lebon.**

Berrima   (1913)   P. & O. Line (British).
Built by Caird & Co., Greenock, Scotland. Tonnage: 11,137. Dimensions: 500' x 62'. Twin-screw, 14 knots. Quadruple

expansion engines. Two masts and one funnel. Passengers: 1,100 one class. Service: England-Australia, via Cape Town. Scrapped in 1932. Sister ships: **Ballarat, Benalla, Beltana** and **Borda.**

Berwick Castle   (1902)   Union-Castle Line.
Built by Wm. Beardmore & Co., Glasgow, Scotland. Tonnage: 5,891.   Dimensions: 398' x 50'.   Twin-screw, 12½ knots. Triple expansion engines. Two masts and one funnel. Type: Emigrant-cargo.   Gutted by fire at Mombasa in October 1919, but eventually sold to Italian owners. Renamed: **Andorra Castle.** Broken up for scrap at Spezzia in 1925. Similar ships: **Alnwick Castle, Cawdor Castle** and **Newark Castle.**

Bingo Maru   (1897)   N. Y. K. Line (Japanese).
Built by D. & W. Henderson & Co., Glasgow, Scotland. Tonnage: 6,279.   Dimensions: 445' x 49'.   Twin-screw, 13 knots. Triple expansion engines. Two masts and one funnel. Passengers: 35 first, 20 second, 164 third.   Service: Japan-Europe. No longer in commission, 1934. Sister ships: **Inaba Maru** and **Shinano Maru.**

Bloemfontein   (1934)   United Netherlands Steam Navigation Co.
Built by Nederlandsche Scheepsbouw, Amsterdam, Netherlands. Tonnage: 10,081.   Dimensions: 457' x 63' (487' o.l.). Twin-screw, 17 knots. Motorship. Two masts and one funnel. Service: Netherlands-South Africa. Passengers: 93. Scrapped in 1961. Sister ship: **Jagersfontein.**

Bloemfontein Castle   (1950)   Union-Castle Line.
Built by Harland & Wolff, Ltd., Belfast, Ireland. Tonnage: 18,400. Dimensions: 570' x 76' (594' o.l.). Twin-screw, 18½ knots. Motorship. Single mast and one funnel. Service: London-Beira, via Cape Town. Passengers: 727. Renamed: **Patris** (1959) Greek.

*Boissevain   (1937)   Royal Inter-Ocean Lines (Dutch).
Built by Blohm & Voss, Hamburg, Germany. Tonnage: 14,134. Dimensions: 537' x 72' (560' o.l.). Triple-screw, 17 knots. Motorship. Two masts and one funnel. Originally in Far East-South Africa service. Now employed in Far East-Africa-South America trade. Sister ships: **Ruys** and **Tegelberg.**

Borda   (1914)   P. & O. Line (British).
Built by Caird & Co., Greenock, Scotland. Tonnage: 11,136. Dimensions: 500' x 62'.   Twin-screw, 14 knots.   Quadruple

expansion engines. Two masts and one funnel. Route:
England-Australia, via Cape Town.   Scrapped in 1931.
Sister ships: **Ballarat, Beltana, Benalla** and **Berrima.**

Braemar Castle   (1898)   Union-Castle Line.
Built by Barclay, Curle & Co., Glasgow, Scotland. Tonnage:
6,266. Dimensions: 470′ x 52′. Single-screw, 13½ knots.
Quadruple expansion engines. Four masts and one funnel.
Considered Castle Line's finest intermediate type steamship
of that era. Passengers: 70 first and 100 second. Broken up
by Italian shipbreakers in 1924.

*Braemar Castle   (1952)   Union-Castle Line.
Built by Harland & Wolff, Ltd., Belfast, Ireland. Tonnage:
17,029. Dimensions: 556′ x 74′ (576′ o.l.). Twin-screw, 17½
knots. Six steam turbines. Two masts and one funnel.
Service: London-Around Africa route. Passengers: 552
cabin class. Reconditioned in 1960. Sister ships: **Kenya
Castle** and **Rhodesia Castle.**

Braunschweig   (1873)   North German Lloyd.
Tonnage: 3,173. Made a number of Bremen-Australia
voyages. Note: See PART I for details.

Brazza   (1923)   Chargeurs Reunis (French).
Built by Ateliers & Chantiers de la Loire, Nantes, France.
Tonnage: 10,387. Dimensions: 474′ x 59′. Twin-screw,
13½ knots. Motorship. Two masts and two funnels. Note:
Originally built as freighter, but was converted to passenger
ship in 1927. Service: France-West Africa. Torpedoed and
sunk in Atlantic, May 28, 1940. Ex-**Camranh.**

*Brazza   (1947)   Chargeurs Reunis (French).
Built by Swan, Hunter & Wigham Richardson, Ltd., Newcastle, England. Tonnage: 9,066. Dimensions: 458′ x 61′
(479′ o.l.). Twin-screw, 16 knots. Motorship. Two masts
and one funnel. Service: France-West Africa. Passengers:
124 first, 78 second, 38 third, 236 fourth. Sister ship:
Foucauld. The **General Leclerc** is a running mate in this
particular service.

Bremen   (1897)   North German Lloyd.
Tonnage: 11,570. Service: Interchangeable between Australian and New York trades. Note: See PART I for details.

Britannia   (1879)   Anchor Line (British).
Built by D. & W. Henderson, Ltd., Glasgow, Scotland.
Tonnage: 3,069. Dimensions: 350′ x 38′. Single-screw, 11

knots. Compound engines. Two masts and one funnel.
Triple expansion engines in 1895. Service: Interchangeable
between Bombay and New York trades. Sold to Bombay
shipbreakers in February 1908.

Britannia (1887) P. & O. Line (British).
Built by Caird & Co., Greenock, Scotland. Tonnage: 6,525.
Dimensions: 465' x 52'. Single-screw, 16½ knots. Triple
expansion engines. Four masts and two funnels. Steel hull.
Passengers: 250 first and 160 second. Service: England-
Australia, via Suez Canal. Scrapped in 1909. Sister ships:
Arcadia, Oceana and **Victoria.** The largest and finest
P. & O. liners built to date.

Britannia (1926) Anchor Line (British).
Built by Alexander Stephen & Sons, Ltd., Glasgow, Scotland.
Tonnage: 8,802. Dimensions: 460' x 59'. Single-screw, 13
knots. Quadruple expansion engines. Two masts and one
funnel. Passengers: 300. Crew: 175. Service: England-
India. Sunk by enemy raider, March 25, 1941.

Briton (1861) Union Steam Ship Co. (British).
Built by Langley, London, England. Tonnage: 1,167.
Dimensions: 148' x 30'. Single-screw. Two direct acting
engines. Two masts and one funnel. Clipper bow. Iron hull.
Type: Mail steamer. Sold to British Government in 1873.
Renamed: **H.M.T. Dromedary.**

Briton (1897) Union-Castle Line.
Built by Harland & Wolff, Ltd., Belfast, Ireland. Tonnage:
10,248. Dimensions: 530' x 60'. Twin-screw, 17½ knots.
Triple expansion engines. Three masts and two funnels.
Passengers: 270 first and 210 second. Entered service as the
largest mail steamship running between Great Britain and
the Colonies. Scrapped in Italy, 1926.

Bruxellesville (1898) Compagnie Belge Maritime du Congo.
Built by Sir. Raylton Dixon & Co., Middlesbrough, England.
Tonnage: 3,908. Dimensions: 353' x 44'. Single-screw, 12
knots. Triple expansion engines. Two masts and one funnel.
Renamed: (a) **Alexandra Woermann,** (b) **Calypso.**

Bruxellesville (1909) Compagnie Belge Maritime du Congo.
Built by Alexander Stephen & Sons, Ltd., Glasgow, Scotland.
Tonnage: 5,799. Dimensions: 400' x 52'. Twin-screw, 14
knots. Triple expansion engines. Two masts and one funnel.
Renamed: **Mocambique.** Sister ship: **Leopoldville.**

Buluwayo   (1895)   Bucknall Line (British).
Built by Armstrong, Mitchell & Co., Newcastle, England.
Tonnage: 4,412.   Dimensions: 360′ x 47′.   Single-screw, 13
knots.   Triple expansion engines.   Two masts and one funnel.
Passengers: 88 first class.   Renamed: **Kathiawar.**   Sister
ships: **Fort Salisbury** and **Johannesburg.**

Burgermeister   (1902)   Deutsche Ost Afrika Linie.
Built by Flensburger Schiffsb. Ges., Flensburg, Germany.
Tonnage: 5,945.   Dimensions: 411′ x 48′ (425′ o.l.).   Twin-
screw, 13½ knots.   Triple expansion engines.   Two masts
and one funnel.   Passengers: 103 first, 72 second, 58 third.
Renamed: **Macoris** (1920).

Burma   (1914)   Henderson Line (British).
Built by Wm. Denny & Bros., Ltd., Dumbarton, Scotland.
Tonnage: 7,821.   Dimensions: 466′ x 58′ (484′ o.l.).   Single-
screw, 13 knots.   Triple expansion engines.   Two masts and
one funnel.   Renamed: (a) **Florentia** (1949), (b) **Safina-
E-Nusrat** (1953).   Sold to Pakistan shipbreakers in 1957.

Cachar   (1884)   Messageries Maritimes (French).
Built by Forges & Chantiers de la Mediterranee, La Seyne,
France.   Tonnage: 3,645.   Dimensions: 344′ x 41′.   Single-
screw, 13½ knots.   Compound engines.   Two masts and one
funnel.   Iron and steel hull.   Purchased from Cie. Nationale
de Navigation in August 1904.   Scrapped in Italy, 1914.

Caledonia   (1894)   P. & O. Line (British).
Built by Caird & Co., Greenock, Scotland.   Tonnage: 7,558.
Dimensions: 486′ x 54′.   Single-screw, 18½ knots.   Triple
expansion engines.   11,000 I.H.P.   Four masts and two fun-
nels.   Made 19½ knots on her trials.   Broke the London-
Calcutta record by making the run in 24 days, 21 hours.
Passengers: 316 first and 175 second.   Sold to Bombay
shipbreakers in July 1925.

*Caledonia   (1947)   Anchor Line (British).
Built by Fairfield Shipbuilding Co., Glasgow, Scotland.
Tonnage: 11,252.   Dimensions: 483′ x 66′ (506′ o.l.).   Twin-
screw, 16 knots.   Motorship.   Two masts and one funnel.
Service: Great Britain-India-Pakistan.   Passengers: 326.
Sister ships: **Cilicia** and **Circassia.**

Caledonien   (1882)   Messageries Maritimes (French).
Built by Messageries Maritimes, La Ciotat, France.   Tonnage: 4,248.   Dimensions: 413′ x 41′.   Single-screw, 13½
knots.   Three masts and two funnels.   Triple expansion

engines installed. Speed increased to 15 knots. Mined and sunk in Mediterranean, June 30, 1917. Sister ships: **Melbourne, Natal, Oceanien, Salazie, Sydney** and **Yarra.**

Cambodge   (1861)   Messageries Maritimes (French).
Built by Forges & Chantiers de la Mediterranee, La Seyne, France. Tonnage: 2,462. Dimensions: 318' x 38'. Single-screw, 13 knots. Compound engines. Two masts and one funnel. Launched, May 11, 1861. Converted to freighter in 1888. Sold for scrap at Marseilles in December 1902. Sister ships: **Donai, Imperatrice** and **Tigre.**

*Cambodge   (1952)   Messageries Maritimes (French).
Built by Ateliers & Chantiers de France, Dunkirk, France. Tonnage: 13,240. Dimensions: 488' x 72' (532' o.l.). Twin-screw, 21 knots. Six steam turbines. Two masts and one funnel. Service: Marseilles-Far East. Passengers: 117 first, 110 tourist, 120 steerage. Sister ships: **Laos** and **Viet-Nam.**

*Canberra   (1961)   P. & O. Line (British).
Built by Harland & Wolff, Ltd., Belfast, Ireland. Tonnage: 45,000. Dimensions: 820' (o.l.) x 102'. Twin-screw, 27½ knots. Turbo-electric power. 85,000 shaft horsepower. Single mast and twin stacks placed aft. Note: Largest ship to be built in Great Britain since the **Queen Elizabeth.** Launched in March 1960. Commenced her maiden voyage from Southampton on June 2, 1961. Service: England-Australia, then on trans-Pacific route of P. & O.-Orient Lines. Accommodation for 2,250 passengers. See page 292 for further information.

*Canton   (1939)   P. & O. Line (British).
Built by Alexander Stephen & Sons, Ltd., Glasgow, Scotland. Tonnage: 15,784. Dimensions: 541' x 73' (563' o.l.). Twin-screw, 18 knots. Steam turbines. Two masts and one funnel. Tonnage increased to 16,033. Passengers: 298 first and 244 tourist. Service: England-Far East.

Caobang   (1902)   Messageries Maritimes (French).
Built by Forges & Chantiers de la Mediterranee, La Seyne, France. Tonnage: 6,487. Dimensions: 445' x 47'. Twin-screw, 14½ knots. Triple expansion engines. Two masts and one funnel. Launched, July 10, 1902. Purchased from Cie. Nationale de Navigation in August 1904. Lost on Poulo Condor in fog, January 4, 1906.

Cap Lay (1921) Chargeurs Reunis (French).
 Built by Ateliers & Chantiers de la Loire, Nantes, France.
 Tonnage: 8,169. Dimensions: 417′ x 55′. Single-screw, 12
 knots. Three steam turbines. Two masts and one funnel.
 Launched, November 4, 1921. Lost in a typhoon in Bay of
 Along, July 15, 1928. Ex-**Halgan.** Sister ships: **Cap
 Padaran, Cap Saint Jacques, Cap Tourane** and **Cap
 Varella.** Note: These liners were converted from freighters
 to passenger carriers in 1925. Service: France-Far East.

Cap Padaran (1922) Chargeurs Reunis (French).
 Built by Ateliers & Chantiers de la Loire, St. Nazaire,
 France. Tonnage: 8,169. Dimensions: 417′ x 55′. Single-
 screw, 12 knots. Steam turbines. Two masts and one funnel.
 Passengers: 850. Service: France-Far East. Torpedoed and
 sunk near Azores, December 9, 1943. Ex-**D'Iberville.**
 Sister ships: **Cap Lay, Cap Saint Jacques, Cap Tourane**
 and **Cap Varella.**

Cap St. Jacques (1922) Chargeurs Reunis (French).
 Built by Ateliers & Chantiers de la Loire, Nantes, France.
 Tonnage: 8,169. Dimensions: 417′ x 55′. Single-screw, 12
 knots. Three steam turbines. Two masts and one funnel.
 Service: France-Far East. Passengers: 850. Sold to Italian
 shipbreakers in 1954. Ex-**Guichen.** Sister ships: **Cap Lay,
 Cap Padaran, Cap Tourane** and **Cap Varella.**

Cap Tourane (1923) Chargeurs Reunis (French).
 Built by Ateliers & Chantiers de la Loire, Nantes, France.
 Tonnage: 8,169. Dimensions: 417′ x 55′. Single-screw, 12
 knots. Steam turbines. Two masts and one funnel. Service:
 France-Far East. Passengers: 850. Sold to Belgian ship-
 breakers in 1953. Ex-**Jouffroy.** Sister ships: **Cap Lay,
 Cap Padaran, Cap St. Jacques** and **Cap Varella.**

Cap Varella (1921) Chargeurs Reunis (French).
 Built by Ateliers & Chantiers de la Loire, Nantes, France.
 Tonnage: 8,169. Dimensions: 417′ x 55′. Single-screw, 12
 knots. Steam turbines. Two masts and one funnel. Service:
 France-Far East. Passengers: 850. Sunk in 1945. Ex-
 Kersaint (1926). Sister ships: **Cap Lay, Cap Padaran,
 Cap St. Jacques** and **Cap Tourane.**

*****Capetown Castle** (1938) Union-Castle Line.
 Built by Harland & Wolff, Ltd., Belfast, Ireland. Tonnage:
 27,002. Dimensions: 702′ x 82′ (734′ o.l.). Twin-screw, 20
 knots. Motorship. Two masts and one funnel. Launched
 in September 1937. The longest motorship in the world.

Service: Southampton-South Africa. Passengers: 243 first, 553 tourist.

Captain Cook (1925) Owner: British Government.
Built by Fairfield Shipbuilding Co., Glasgow, Scotland. Tonnage: 13,475. Dimensions: 525' x 66' (538' o.l.). Twin-screw, 16 knots. Six steam turbines. Two masts and one funnel. Placed in service as an emigrant ship to Australia, under management of Donaldson Line. Accommodation for 1,000 passengers. Scrapped in 1960. Ex-**Empire Brent** (1951), ex-**Letitia** (1946).

Carisbrook Castle (1898) Union-Castle Line.
Built by Fairfield Shipbuilding Co., Glasgow, Scotland. Tonnage: 7,626. Dimensions: 485' x 56'. Twin-screw, 17½ knots. Quadruple expansion engines. Three masts and one funnel. Passengers: 250 first and 140 second. Service: England-South Africa. Later transferred to East African trade. Scrapped in 1922.

*Carnarvon Castle (1926) Union-Castle Line.
Built by Harland & Wolff, Ltd., Belfast, Ireland. Tonnage: 20,063. Dimensions: 630' x 73'. Twin-screw, 18 knots. Motorship. Two masts and two funnels. First Union-Castle Line motorship. Lengthened to 661 feet (686' o.l.) in 1938. New engines installed and speed increased to 20 knots. She made a record run of 12 days, 13 hours, 38 minutes from Nab Tower to Cape Town in September 1938. Service: Southampton-Capetown. Passengers: 134 first and 450 tourist.

Carthage (1881) P. & O. Line (British).
Built by Caird & Co., Greenock, Scotland. Tonnage: 5,013. Dimensions: 430' x 44'. Single-screw, 15 knots. Compound engines. Four masts and two funnels. Two of her original masts were later removed. Iron hull. Service: England-Australia, via Suez Canal. Out of service by 1903. Sister ship: **Rome.** Note: The first P. & O. liners over 5,000 tons gross.

*Carthage (1931) P. & O. Line (British).
Built by Alexander Stephen & Sons, Ltd., Glasgow, Scotland. Tonnage: 14,182. Dimensions: 522' x 71' (543' o.l.). Twin-screw, 18 knots. Six steam turbines. Two masts and two funnels. Later reduced to single funnel. Service: England-Far East. Passengers: 181 first, 213 tourist. Sister ship: **Corfu.**

Castalia   (1906)   Anchor Line (British).
Built by Barclay, Curle & Co., Glasgow, Scotland. Tonnage: 6,715. Dimensions: 440' x 53'. Single-screw, 12½ knots. Triple expansion engines. Two masts and one funnel. Service: Great Britain-India. Passengers: 135. Sold to Italian owners in January 1949. Sister ship: **Elysia.**

*****Castel Felice**   (1930)   "Sitmar" Line (Italian).
Tonnage: 12,478. Transferred from other services to Europe-Australia trade. Note: See PART III for details.

Cathay   (1925)   P. & O. Line (British).
Built by Barclay, Curle & Co., Glasgow, Scotland. Tonnage: 15,121.   Dimensions: 523' x 70'.   Twin-screw, 16 knots. Quadruple expansion engines. Two masts and two funnels. Service: England-Australia, via Suez Canal. Passengers: 320. Sunk by aircraft off North Africa, November 12, 1942, while being employed as a troopship for the North African invasion. Sister ships: **Chitral** and **Comorin.**

Cawdor Castle   (1901)   Union-Castle Line.
Built by Barclay, Curle & Co., Glasgow, Scotland. Tonnage: 6,243.   Dimensions: 414' x 51'.   Twin-screw, 12½ knots. Triple expansion engines. Two masts and one funnel. Ran aground in Conception Bay, South West Africa, July 30, 1926.   She could not be refloated and was subsequently broken up. Sister ships: **Alnwick Castle, Berwick Castle** and **Newark Castle.**

Celt   (1866)   Union Line (British).
Built by Millwall Shipbuilding Co., London, England. Tonnage: 1,439. Dimensions: 325' x 34'. Single-screw. Two masts and one funnel. Iron hull. Vessel lengthened in 1874. Tonnage increased to 2,112. Type: Mail steamer. Wrecked between Cap Agulhas and Danger Point in February 1875, with no loss of life.

Cephee   (1912)   Messageries Maritimes (French).
Built by Bremer Vulkan, Vegesack, Germany. Tonnage: 9,680. Dimensions: 491' x 59'. Twin-screw, 12 knots. Triple expansion engines. Two masts and one funnel. Purchased in 1922.   Sold to British shipbreakers in December 1935. Ex-**Buenos Ayres.**

Ceramic   (1913)   (a) White Star Line, (b) Shaw, Savill & Albion Co.
Built by Harland & Wolff, Ltd., Belfast, Ireland. Tonnage: 18,495. Dimensions: 655' x 69' (675' o.l.). Triple-screw, 16

knots. Triple expansion engines and one low pressure steam turbine. Four masts and one funnel. Tonnage later increased to 18,713. Service: London-New Zealand, via Cape of Good Hope. Passengers: 480. Crew: 260. Torpedoed and sunk by submarine, December 6, 1942, with the loss of many lives.

Cesarea   (1912)   Lloyd Triestino (Italian).
Built by Wm. Beardmore & Co., Glasgow, Scotland. Tonnage: 7,785. Dimensions: 411′ x 56′ (428′ o.l.). Twin-screw, 16 knots. Quadruple expansion engines. Two masts and one funnel. Renamed: **Arno.** She became a war casualty, September 10, 1942. Ex-**Fort St. George** (1935), ex-**Wandilla.**

Chambord   (1903)   Messageries Maritimes (French).
Built by Blohm & Voss, Hamburg, Germany. Tonnage: 7,562. Dimensions: 440′ x 52′. Twin-screw, 13½ knots. Triple expansion engines. Two masts and one funnel. Scrapped in France, 1932. Ex-**Cap Ortegal** (1923).

Champollion   (1924)   Messageries Maritimes (French).
Built by Soc. Provencale de Construction Navales, La Ciotat, France. Tonnage: 12,262. Dimensions: 508′ x 62′. Twin-screw, 15 knots. Triple expansion engines. Two masts and three funnels. Lengthened to 531 feet (12,546 tons) in 1933–34. At time of rebuilding had a Maier bow installed. Speed increased to 18 knots. Served as a troopship in World War II. Wrecked at entrance to Beyrouth harbor, December 22, 1952. Sister ship: **Mariette Pacha.**

Chantala   (1913)   British India Steam Navigation Co.
Built by Richardson, Duck & Co., Stockton, England. Tonnage: 4,949. Dimensions: 405′ x 52′. Single-screw. Triple expansion engines. Two masts and one funnel. Torpedoed and sunk without warning near Cape Bengut, April 5, 1916, with the loss of 9 lives.

Chantilly   (1923)   Messageries Maritimes (French).
Built by Ateliers & Chantiers de la Loire, St. Nazaire, France. Tonnage: 9,986. Dimensions: 478′ x 59′. Twin-screw, 15½ knots. Steam turbines. Two masts and one funnel. Passengers: 350. Note: Laid down as **Kerguelen** for Chargeurs Reunis. Purchased in June 1923, while fitting out. Scrapped in 1952. Sister ships: **Compiegne** and **Fontainebleau.**

Chaouia   (1896)   Cie. de Navigation Paquet (French).
Built by Kon. Maats. de Schelde, Flushing Netherlands. Tonnage: 4,334. Dimensions: 381′ x 45′. Single-screw, 14

knots. Quadruple expansion engines. Two masts and two funnels. A World War I casualty, 1918. Ex-**Koningin Wilhelmina** (1911).

Charente   (1889)   Messageries Maritimes (French).
Built by Forges & Chantiers de la Mediterranee, Havre, France. Tonnage: 3,835. Dimensions: 371' x 43'. Single-screw, 13½ knots. Triple expansion engines. Steel hull. Sold to Italian shipbreakers in June 1911. Sister ship: **Dordogne.**

Charlesville   (1951)   Compagnie Belge Maritimes.
Built by Soc. Anon. John Cockerill, Hoboken, Belgium. Tonnage: 10,812. Dimensions: 479' x 64' (505' o.l.). Single-screw, 16½ knots. Motorship. Two masts and one funnel. Passengers: 448 in single class.   Service: Antwerp-Congo and Angola.   Sister ships: **Albertville, Elisabethville, Leopoldville** and **Thysville.**

Chenonceaux   (1922)   Messageries Maritimes (French).
Built by Ateliers & Chantiers de la Gironde, Bordeaux, France. Tonnage: 14,825. Dimensions: 543' x 65'. Twin-screw, 15 knots. Two steam turbines. Two masts and one funnel.   Launched, March 30, 1922.   Passengers: 420. Scuttled by Germans on evacuation of Marseilles during World War II. Refloated in April 1948. The wreck was sold for scrap in June 1948. Ex-**Aramis** (1931). Sister ships: **Athos II** and **D'Artagnan.**

Cheshire   (1891)   Bibby Line (British).
Built by Harland & Wolff, Ltd., Belfast, Ireland. Tonnage: 5,775. Dimensions: 445' x 49'. Twin-screw, 14 knots. Triple expansion engines. Four masts and one funnel. Service: Liverpool-Rangoon. Renamed: **Seang Choon.** Sunk by submarine off England in 1917.

Cheshire   (1927)   Bibby Line (British).
Built by Fairfield Shipbuilding Co., Glasgow, Scotland. Tonnage: 15,560. Dimensions: 483' x 60'. Twin-screw, 15 knots. Motorship. Four masts and one funnel. Service: Liverpool-Rangoon. Sold to British shipbreakers in 1957. Sister ships: **Shropshire** and **Staffordshire.**

Chili   (1894)   Messageries Maritimes (French).
Tonnage: 6,097. Built for South American service. Transferred to Far East trade in 1912. Scrapped in 1927. Note: See PART III for details.

Chimborazo   (1871)   Orient Line (British).
Tonnage: 3,847.   Owner: Pacific Steam Navigation Co.
Transferred to Australian service in 1877.   Note: See PART
III for details.

China   (1889)   P. & O. Line (British).
Tonnage: 5,060.   Transferred to the Pacific Mail Steamship
Co.   Note: See PART II for details.

China   (1896)   P. & O. Line (British).
Built by Harland & Wolff, Ltd., Belfast, Ireland.   Tonnage:
7,912.   Dimensions: 500' x 54'.   Single-screw, 18 knots.
Triple expansion engines.   Two masts and two funnels.
Service: England-Australia, via Suez Canal.   Scrapped in
1929.   Sister ships: **Arabia, Egypt, India** and **Persia.**

Chindwin   (1910)   Henderson Line (British).
Built by Wm. Denny & Bros., Ltd., Dumbarton, Scotland.
Tonnage: 6,369.   Dimensions: 445' x 55'.   Single-screw, 12½
knots.   Triple expansion engines.   Two masts and one funnel.
Passengers: 106 first class.   Service: Great Britain-Burma.
Renamed: **Rod-el Farag** (1938).

Chitral   (1925)   P. & O. Line (British).
Built by Alexander Stephen & Sons, Ltd., Glasgow, Scotland.
Tonnage: 526' x 70'.   Twin-screw, 17 knots.   Quadruple ex-
pansion engines.   Two masts and two funnels.   Passengers:
320.   Sold to British shipbreakers in 1953.   Sister ships:
Cathay and **Comorin.**   They were built for the England-
Australian service.

Chodoc   (1898)   Chargeurs Reunis (French).
Built by Forges & Chantiers de la Mediterranee, La Seyne,
France.   Tonnage: 4,686.   Dimensions: 413' x 42'.   Single-
screw.   Triple expansion engines.   Three masts and one fun-
nel.   Launched, August 23, 1898.   Vessel acquired from Cie.
Nationale de Navigation in October 1904.   Service: France-
Far East.   Lost by grounding near Gardafui, June 23, 1905.
Sister ship: **Cholon.**

Cholon   (1897)   Chargeurs Reunis (French).
Built by Forges & Chantiers de la Mediterranean, La Seyne,
France.   Tonnage: 4,665.   Dimensions: 416' x 42'.   Single-
screw, 12 knots.   Triple expansion engines.   Three masts and
one funnel.   Launched, August 3, 1897.   Purchased from Cie.
Nationale de Navigation in October 1904.   Service: France-
Far East.   Transferred to West African route in 1912.
Renamed: **Tchad.**

Christian Huygens (1928) Nederland Royal Mail Line.
Built by Nederlandsche Dok en Scheepsbouw, Amsterdam,
Netherlands. Tonnage: 15,637. Dimensions: 551' x 68'
(570' o.l.). Twin-screw, 18 knots. Motorship. Two masts
and one funnel. Tonnage increased to 16,287. Extremely
small funnel. Service: Netherlands-East Indies. Passengers:
570. Crew: 290. She became a war casualty, August 26,
1945.

Chusan (1852) P. & O. Line (British).
Built in Great Britain. Tonnage: 700. Dimensions: 190' x
29'. Single-screw. Oscillating engines. Three masts and one
funnel. Iron hull. Inaugurated the P. & O. Line service to
Australia, sailing from Southampton on May 15, 1852. The
long voyage took 77 days to reach Melbourne.

Chusan (1884) P. & O. Line (British).
Built by Caird & Co., Greenock, Scotland. Tonnage: 4,636.
Dimensions: 400' x 45'. Single-screw, 14½ knots. Com-
pound engines. Three masts and one funnel. Steel hull.
Sold to Bombay owners in 1906. Scrapped in 1908. Sister
ship: **Bengal.**

*****Chusan** (1950) P. & O. Line (British).
Built by Vickers-Armstrongs, Ltd., Barrow, England. Tonnage: 24,570. Dimensions: 646' x 85' (672' o.l.). Twin-
screw, 22 knots. Six steam turbines. Two masts and one
funnel. Placed in England-Far East service. Transferred to
the extended trans-Pacific service of P. & O.-Orient Lines
in 1959. Passengers: 464 first, 541 tourist.

*****Cilicia** (1937) Anchor Line (British).
Built by Fairfield Shipbuilding Co., Glasgow, Scotland.
Tonnage: 11,250. Dimensions: 485' x 66' (506' o.l.). Twin-
screw, 16 knots. Motorship. Two masts and one funnel.
Passengers: 298 first. Service: Great Britain-India and
Pakistan. Sister ships: **Circassia** and **Caledonia.**

*****Circassia** (1937) Anchor Line (British).
Built by Fairfield Shipbuilding Co., Glasgow, Scotland.
Tonnage: 11,170. Dimensions: 483' x 66' (505' o.l.). Twin-
screw, 16½ knots. Motorship. Two masts and one funnel.
Passengers: 300 first class. Service: Great Britain-India and
Pakistan. Sister ships: **Cilicia** and **Caledonia.**

City of Athens (1901) Ellerman's Line (British).
Built by Workman, Clark & Co., Belfast, Ireland. Tonnage:
5,594. Dimensions: 430' x 50'. Single-screw, 13½ knots.

Triple expansion engines. Two masts and one funnel.
Passengers: 80 first, 16 second class. Sunk by mine laid by
German raider off South Africa in 1917.

City of Barodo   (1918)   Ellerman's Line (British).
Built by Barclay, Curle & Co., Glasgow, Scotland. Tonnage:
7,129. Dimensions: 433' x 57'. Single-screw, 12 knots.
Triple expansion engines. Two masts and one funnel. Torpedoed and sunk by submarine, April 2, 1943.

City of Benares   (1902)   Ellerman's Line (British).
Built by Workman, Clark & Co., Belfast, Ireland. Tonnage:
6,984. Dimensions: 460' x 55'. Single-screw, 13½ knots.
Triple expansion engines. Two masts and one funnel.
Passengers: 47 first and 44 second. Scrapped in 1936.

City of Benares   (1936)   Ellerman's Line (British).
Built by Barclay, Curle & Co., Glasgow, Scotland. Tonnage:
11,081. Dimensions: 486' x 62' (509' o.l.). Twin-screw, 15
knots. Three steam turbines. Two masts and two funnels.
The spacious dining room accommodated 200 passengers.
Note: The only Ellerman liner to be built with two funnels.
Service: Great Britain-India, via Suez. Torpedoed and sunk
by submarine, September 17, 1940.

City of Birmingham   (1911)   Ellerman's Line (British).
Built by Palmer's Shipbuilding Co., Newcastle, England.
Tonnage: 7,498. Dimensions: 452' x 55'. Single-screw, 12
knots. Quadruple expansion engines. Two masts and one
funnel. Passengers: 130 first and 40 second. She became
a war casualty in Mediterranean, 1916.

City of Cairo   (1915)   Ellerman & Bucknall Line.
Built by Earle's Shipbuilding & Engineering Co., Hull,
England. Tonnage: 8,034. Dimensions: 449' x 55' (465' o.l.).
Single-screw, 13½ knots. Quadruple expansion engines. Two
masts and one funnel. Sunk by submarine, November 6, 1942.

City of Calcutta   (1903)   Ellerman's Line (British).
Built by Workman, Clark & Co., Belfast, Ireland. Tonnage:
7,679. Dimensions: 471' x 56'. Single-screw, 14 knots.
Triple expansion engines. Two masts and one funnel. Passen-
gers: 125 first and 18 second. Scrapped in 1934. Sister ship:
City of London.

City of Canterbury   (1922)   Ellerman's Line (British).
Built by Swan, Hunter & Wigham Richardson, Ltd., Newcastle, England. Tonnage: 8,421. Dimensions: 448' x 56'.

Single-screw, 13 knots. Quadruple expansion engines. Two masts and one funnel. Passengers: 178. Service: England-Calcutta, via Suez Canal. Scrapped in 1953.

*City of Durban   (1954)   Ellerman & Bucknall Line.
Built by Vickers-Armstrongs, Ltd., Newcastle, England. Tonnage: 13,350. Dimensions: 516' x 71' (541' o.l.). Twin-screw, 16½ knots. Motorship. Single mast and one funnel. Passengers: 107 first class. Sister ships: **City of Exeter, City of Port Elizabeth** and **City of York.** Note: The largest ships in the Ellerman fleet. The London to Cape-town run is made in 16 days.

City of Exeter   (1914)   Ellerman's Line (British).
Built by Workman, Clark & Co., Belfast, Ireland. Tonnage: 9,623. Dimensions: 486' x 58'. Twin-screw, 15 knots. Quadruple expansion engines. Two masts and one funnel. Passengers: 184 first and 62 second. Scrapped in 1950.

*City of Exeter   (1953)   Ellerman & Bucknall Line.
Vickers-Armstrongs, Ltd., Walker-on-Tyne, England. Tonnage: 13,345. Dimensions: 516' x 71' (541' o.l.). Twin-screw, 16½ knots. Motorship. Single mast and one funnel. Service: London-South and East Africa. Passengers: 107 first class. Sister ships: **City of Durban, City of Port Elizabeth** and **City of York.**

City of Genoa   (1905)   Ellerman's Line (British).
Built by Blohm & Voss, Hamburg, Germany. Tonnage: 6,365. Dimensions: 411' x 50'. Twin-screw, 13 knots. Triple expansion engines. Two masts and one funnel. Renamed: **Joao Belo** (Portuguese).   Ex-**Windhuk**, ex-**Gertrud Woermann.**

City of Harvard   (1907)   Ellerman & Bucknall Line.
Built by Bremer Vulkan, Vegesack, Germany. Tonnage: 7,071. Dimensions: 429' x 54'. Single-screw, 12 knots. Quadruple expansion engines. Two masts and one funnel. Scrapped in 1934. Ex-**Giessen** (North German Lloyd).

City of Hongkong   (1924)   Ellerman & Bucknall Line.
Built by Earle's Shipbuilding Co., Hull, England. Tonnage: 9,678. Dimensions: 470' x 61'. Single-screw, 12 knots. Quadruple expansion engines. Two masts and one funnel. Service: England-South Africa. Renamed: **Centauro** (1951) Grimaldi Bros. Sold to Italian shipbreakers in 1955.

City of Karachi   (1905)   Ellerman & Bucknall Line.
Built by Workman, Clark & Co., Belfast, Ireland. Tonnage:
5,573.   Dimensions: 413′ x 51′.   Single-screw, 13 knots.
Quadruple expansion engines. Two masts and one funnel.
Passengers: 70 first and 24 second. Scrapped in 1934.

City of London   (1907)   Ellerman's Line (British).
Built by Workman, Clark & Co., Belfast, Ireland. Tonnage:
8,956.   Dimensions: 491′ x 57′.   Single-screw, 15 knots.
Quadruple expansion engines. Two masts and one funnel.
Passengers: 200 first and 60 second. Scrapped in 1946.

City of Marseilles   (1913)   Ellerman's Line (British).
Built by Palmer's Shipbuilding Co., Newcastle, England.
Tonnage: 8,317. Dimensions: 469′ x 58′ (483′ o.l.). Twin-
screw, 13 knots. Quadruple expansion engines. Two masts
and one funnel. Passengers: 149 first and 46 second. Became a war casualty in September 1940. Dismantled in 1947.

City of Nagpur   (1922)   Ellerman's Line (British).
Built by Workman, Clark & Co., Belfast, Ireland. Tonnage:
10,136.   Dimensions: 469′ x 59′.   Single-screw, 14 knots.
Quadruple expansion engines. Two masts and one funnel.
Service: England-India, via Suez.   Sunk by submarine,
April 29, 1941.

City of New York   (1930)   American-South African Line.
Built by Sun Shipbuilding & Dry Dock Co., Chester, Pa.
Tonnage: 8,272. Dimensions: 450′ x 61′ (470′ o.l.). Twin-
screw, 14 knots. Motorship. Two masts and one funnel.
Torpedoed and sunk off the American coast in 1942. Note:
A pioneer vessel in the New York-South African service, of
an American shipping firm.

City of Palermo   (1905)   Ellerman & Bucknall Line.
Built by J. C. Tecklenborg, Wesermunde, Germany. Tonnage: 4,699. Dimensions: 362′ x 46′. Single-screw. Triple
expansion engines. Two masts and one funnel. Scrapped in
Italy, 1933. Ex-**Rio Negro** (1921).

City of Paris   (1907)   Ellerman's Line (British).
Built by Barclay, Curle & Co., Glasgow, Scotland. Tonnage:
9,239.   Dimensions: 493′ x 57′.   Single-screw, 15 knots.
Quadruple expansion engines. Two masts and one funnel.
Passengers: 210 first and 80 second. Sunk by a German
submarine in Mediterranean in 1917, with the loss of 122
lives.

City of Paris   (1922)   Ellerman's Line (British).
> Built by Swan, Hunter & Wigham Richardson, Ltd., Newcastle, England. Tonnage: 10,902. Dimensions: 484' x 59'. Single-screw, 14½ knots. Three steam turbines. Two masts and one funnel. Sold to British shipbreakers in 1956.

City of Poona   (1912)   Ellerman's Line (British).
> Built by Swan, Hunter & Wigham Richardson, Ltd., Newcastle, England. Tonnage: 7,474. Dimensions: 452' x 56'. Twin-screw, 13 knots. Quadruple expansion engines. Two masts and one funnel. Scrapped in 1934.

*City of Port Elizabeth   (1952)   Ellerman & Bucknall Line.
> Built by Vickers-Armstrongs, Ltd., Newcastle, England. Tonnage: 13,363. Dimensions: 516' x 71' (541' o.l.). Twin-screw, 16½ knots. Motorship. Single mast and one funnel. Service: England-South Africa. Passengers: 107. Sister ships: **City of Durban, City of Exeter,** and **City of York.**

City of Simla   (1921)   Ellerman's Line (British).
> Built by W. Gray & Co., West Hartlepool, England. Tonnage: 9,468. Dimensions: 476' x 58'. Twin-screw, 13½ knots. Steam turbines. Two masts and one funnel. Torpedoed and sunk by submarine, September 21, 1940.

City of Sparta   (1897)   Ellerman's Line (British).
> Built by Workman, Clark & Co., Belfast, Ireland. Tonnage: 5,415. Dimensions: 430' x 50'. Single-screw, 13 knots. Triple expansion engines. Two masts and one funnel.

City of Valencia   (1908)   Ellerman's Line (British).
> Built by Reiherstieg, Hamburg, Germany. Tonnage: 7,329. Dimensions: 442' x 52'. Twin-screw, 12 knots. Triple expansion engines. Two masts and one funnel. Scrapped in 1934. Ex-**Roda.**

City of Venice   (1924)   Ellerman's Line (British).
> Built by Workman, Clark & Co., Belfast, Ireland. Tonnage: 8,308. Dimensions: 455' x 58' (473' o.l.). Single-screw, 13 knots. Quadruple expansion engines. Two masts and one funnel. Torpedoed and sunk by submarine, July 4, 1943.

City of Vienna   (1890)   Ellerman's Line (British).
> Built by Workman, Clark & Co., Belfast, Ireland. Tonnage: 4,672. Dimensions: 412' x 46'. Single-screw, 13½ knots. Triple expansion engines. Three masts and one funnel. Passengers: 60 first class. Renamed: **Thessaloniki.**

City of York   (1904)   Ellerman's Line (British).
Built by Workman, Clark & Co., Belfast, Ireland. Tonnage:
7,844.   Dimensions: 485′ x 56′.   Single-screw, 14 knots.
Triple expansion engines.   Two masts and one funnel.
Passengers: 100 first and 18 second.

*****City of York**   (1953)   Ellerman & Bucknall Line.
Built by Vickers-Armstrongs, Ltd., Walker-on-Tyne, Eng-
land. Tonnage: 13,345. Dimensions: 516′ x 71′ (541′ o.l.).
Twin-screw, 16½ knots. Motorship. Single mast and one
funnel. Passengers: 107. Service: England-South Africa.
Sister ships: **City of Exeter, City of Durban** and **City of
Port Elizabeth.**

*****Claude Bernard**   (1950)   Chargeurs Reunis (French).
Built by Ateliers & Chantiers de la Loire, St. Nazaire,
France. Tonnage: 11,969. Dimensions: 515′ x 64′ (538′ o.l.).
Twin-screw, 17½ knots. Motorship. Two masts and one
funnel. Entered service to South America in March 1950.
Transferred to Far East route in May 1954. Passengers:
147 first and 296 third. Sister ship: **Lavoisier.**   Note:
Eight liners of this general type were built in France after
World War II.

Claude Chappe   (1909)   Messageries Maritimes (French).
Built by Northumberland Shipbuilding Co., Newcastle,
England. Tonnage: 4,394. Dimensions: 370′ x 47′. Twin-
screw, 14 knots. Triple expansion engines. Two masts and
two funnels. Purchased from Greek National Navigation
Company in April 1925. Sold to Hong Kong shipbreakers
in June 1939. Ex-**Patris.**

Clement Ader   (1953)   Chargeurs Reunis (French).
Built by Ateliers & Chantiers de la Loire, St. Nazaire,
France. Tonnage: 11,300. Dimensions: 515′ x 64′ (538′ o.l.).
Twin-screw, 16½ knots. Motorship. Two masts and one
funnel. Service: Marseilles-Indo China. Passengers: 91
first and 52 second class. Renamed: **Alessandro Volta**
(1956). Sister ships: **Edouard Branly** and **Henri Poincare.**

Cluny Castle   (1903)   Union-Castle Line (British).
Built by Barclay, Curle & Co., Glasgow, Scotland. Tonnage:
5,147.   Dimensions: 419′ x 50′.   Twin-screw, 12½ knots.
Triple expansion engines. Two masts and one funnel. Re-
named: **Umkuzi** (1924). Scrapped in 1938. Sister ship:
Comrie Castle.

Clyde   (1881)   P. & O. Line (British).
  Built by Wm. Denny & Bros., Ltd., Dumbarton, Scotland.
  Tonnage: 4,099.   Dimensions: 390′ x 42′.   Single-screw, 15
  knots.   Compound engines.   Three masts and two funnels.
  Renamed: **Shahnoor** (Essajee Tajbhoy, Bombay, India).
  Scrapped in 1906. Sister ships: **Ganges, Sutlej** and **Thames.**

Coblenz   (1923)   North German Lloyd.
  Tonnage: 9,449.   Service: Bremen-Far East.   Also, in North
  Atlantic service.   Note: See PART I for details.

Colombo   (1882)   Messageries Maritimes (French).
  Built by Forges & Chantiers de la Mediterranee, La Seyne,
  France.   Tonnage: 3,731.   Dimensions: 379′ x 39′.   Single-
  screw, 13½ knots.   Compound engines.   Two masts and one
  funnel.   Purchased from Cie. Nationale de Navigation in
  1904.   Disabled in a typhoon and towed to Tourane, November 1910.   Subsequently broken up for scrap at Saigon.

Commonwealth   (1902)   Blue Anchor Line (British).
  Built by Barclay, Curle & Co., Glasgow, Scotland.   Tonnage:
  6,616.   Dimensions: 450′ x 52′.   Twin-screw, 14 knots.
  Triple expansion engines.   Two masts and one funnel.   Service:
  England-Australia, via Cape Town.   Passengers: 75 first and
  300 third.   Note: The P. & O. Line purchased Lund's Blue
  Anchor Line 1910.   The **Commonwealth** remained in the
  P. & O. Line fleet, until broken up for scrap in 1922.

Comorin   (1925)   P. & O. Line (British).
  Built by Barclay, Curle & Co., Glasgow, Scotland.   Tonnage:
  15,132.   Dimensions: 523′ x 70′.   Twin-screw, 16 knots.
  Quadruple expansion engines.   Two masts and two funnels.
  Service: England-Australia.   Passengers: 320.   Lost by fire
  in the North Atlantic, April 6, 1941.   Sister ships: **Cathay**
  and **Chitral.**

Compiegne   (1923)   Messageries Maritimes (French).
  Built by Ateliers & Chantiers de la Loire, St. Nazaire,
  France.   Tonnage: 9,986.   Dimensions: 478′ x 59′.   Twin-
  screw, 15½ knots.   Steam turbines.   Two masts and one
  funnel.   Launched as **Jamaique** for Chargeurs Reunis,
  November 13, 1922.   Purchased in June 1923, while fitting
  out.   Service: France-Far East.   Passengers: 350.   Scrapped
  in France, 1954. Sister ships: **Chantilly** and **Fontainebleau.**

Comrie Castle   (1903)   Union-Castle Line.
  Built by Barclay, Curle & Co., Glasgow, Scotland.   Tonnage:
  5,167.   Dimensions: 419′ x 50′.   Twin-screw, 12½ knots.

Triple expansion engines. Two masts and one funnel. Re-named: **Umvoti** (1924) Natal Line. Sister ship: **Cluny Castle.**

Congo (1878) Messageries Maritimes (French).
Tonnage: 3,897. Services: (a) Far East, (b) South American. Note: See PART III for details.

Conte Rosso (1922) Lloyd Triestino (Italian).
Tonnage: 17,879. Service: Italy-Far East. Note: Originally owned and operated by Lloyd Sabaudo. See PART I for details.

Conte Verde (1923) Lloyd Triestino (Italian).
Tonnage: 18,765. Service: Italy-Far East. Note: Originally owned by Lloyd Sabaudo. See PART I for details.

Conway Castle (1877) Castle Line (British).
Built by Robert Napier & Sons, Glasgow, Scotland. Tonnage: 2,966. Dimensions: 349' x 39'. Single-screw. Compound engines. Two masts and one funnel. Iron hull. Triple expansion engines in 1892. Wrecked near Madagascar in May 1893. Sister ship: **Warwick Castle.**

Cordillere (1895) Messageries Maritimes (French).
Tonnage: 6,022. Built for the South American service. Transferred to Far East route in 1912. Note: See PART III for details.

Corfu (1931) P. & O. Line (British).
Built by Alexander Stephen & Sons, Ltd., Glasgow, Scotland. Tonnage: 14,170. Dimensions: 522' x 71' (543' o.l.). Twin-screw, 17 knots. Steam turbines. Two masts and two funnels. Later, reduced to single funnel. Service: England-Far East. Passengers: 181 first and 212 tourist. Sister ship: **Carthage.**

Corinthic (1902) White Star Line.
Tonnage: 12,367. Originally in England-Australia trade, via Capetown. She was later transferred to Shaw, Savill & Albion Co. See PART II for details.

Coromandel (1885) P. & O. Line (British).
Built by Caird & Co., Greenock, Scotland. Tonnage: 4,359. Dimensions: 400' x 45'. Single-screw, 14½ knots. Triple expansion engines. Three masts and one funnel. Steel hull. Service: England-Australia/Far East. Sold in 1906. Sister ship: **Bengal.** First P. & O. liners to be fitted with triple expansion engines.

Cotopaxi   (1873)   Orient Line (British).
Tonnage: 4,022.   Owner: Pacific Steam Navigation Co.
Service: England-Australia.   For further details regarding
this former South American ship see PART III.

Cracovia   (1915)   Lloyd Triestino (Italian).
Built by Cantieri San Rocco, San Rocco, Italy.   Tonnage:
8,052.   Dimensions: 430' x 53'   (443' o.l.).   Twin-screw, 13
knots.   Steam turbines.   Two masts and one funnel.   Renamed: **Gerusalemme** (1934).   Sister ship: **Pilsna.**

Cuzco   (1871)   Orient Line (British).
Tonnage: 3,845.   Transferred from South American service
of Pacific Steam Navigation Company to England-Australian
trade.   Note: See PART III for details.

D'Artagnan   (1924)   Messageries Maritimes (French).
Built by Ateliers & Chantiers de la Gironde, Bordeaux,
France.   Tonnage: 15,104.   Dimensions: 543' x 65'.   Twin-
screw, 14 knots.   Triple expansion engines.   Two masts and
two funnels.   Launched, April 23, 1924.   Passengers: 420.
Destroyed by fire at Shanghai in October 1941.   Sister ship:
Athos II.

Dakar   (1899)   Elder, Dempster & Co. (British).
Built by Sir Raylton Dixon & Co., Middlesbrough, England.
Tonnage: 3,987.   Dimensions: 370' x 46'.   Twin-screw, 13½
knots.   Triple expansion engines.   Two masts and one funnel.
Renamed: (a) **Bloemfontein,** (b) **Hong Peng.**   Ex-
Anversville.

Damascus   (1887)   Aberdeen Line (British).
Built by Robert Napier & Sons, Ltd., Glasgow, Scotland.
Tonnage: 3,726.   Dimensions: 362' x 44'.   Single-screw, 13
knots.   Triple expansion engines.   Three masts and one fun-
nel.   Steel hull.   Service: England-Australia, via Capetown.
Sold to Italian owners in 1910.

Dane   (1870)   Union Line (British).
Built by Caird & Co., Greenock, Scotland.   Tonnage: 3,647.
Dimensions: 381' x 44'.   Single-screw.   Compound engines.
Three masts and one funnel.   Iron hull.   Clipper bow.
Scrapped in 1893.   Ex-**Australia** (1889).

Danube   (1866)   Union Steam Ship Co. (British).
Built by Millwall Ironworks, London, England.   Tonnage:
2,039.   Dimensions: 233' x 34'.   Single-screw.   Compound
engines.   Two masts and one funnel.   Purchased from Royal

Mail Line in 1871. Sold in 1888, and subsequently broken up for scrap. Note: See PART III.

Darmstadt   (1890)   North German Lloyd.
Tonnage: 5,012.   Service: Germany-Australia/Far East. Note: See PART I for details.

Delhi   (1905)   P. & O. Line (British).
Built by Caird & Co., Greenock, Scotland. Tonnage: 8,090. Dimensions: 470′ x 56′. Twin-screw, 16 knots. Quadruple expansion engines. Two masts and one funnel. Service: London-Bombay. Wrecked on the African coast, December 13, 1910, with no loss of life. Sister ships: **Delta, Devanha** and **Dongola.**

Delta   (1859)   P. & O. Line (British).
Built by Thames Ironworks & Shipbuilding Co., Blackwall, England. Tonnage: 1,618. Dimensions: 310′ x 35′ (324′ o.l.). Paddle-wheels, 14 knots. Oscillating engines. Two masts and two funnels. Passengers: 126 first and 50 second class. Maiden voyage: Southampton-Alexandria, October 1959. Sold to Japanese in 1874. Renamed: (a) **Takasago Maru,** (b) **Centennial** (1898).

Delta   (1905)   P. & O. Line (British).
Built by Workman, Clark & Co., Belfast, Ireland. Tonnage: 8,089. Dimensions: 470′ x 56′. Twin-screw, 16½ knots. Quadruple expansion engines. Two masts and one funnel. Passengers: 163 first and 180 second. Scrapped in 1930. Sister ships: **Delhi, Devanha** and **Dongola.**

Demosthenes   (1911)   Aberdeen Line (British).
Built by Harland & Wolff, Ltd., Belfast, Ireland. Tonnage: 11,223. Dimensions: 500′ x 62′ (517′ o.l.). Triple-screw, 15 knots. Triple expansion engines. Two masts and one funnel. Passengers: 100 first class. Scrapped in 1931. Sister ship: **Themistocles.** Service: England-Australia, via Capetown.

Dempo   (1930)   Rotterdam Lloyd (Dutch).
Built by Kon. Maats. de Schelde, Flushing, Netherlands. Tonnage: 17,024. Dimensions: 551′ x 70′ (574′ o.l.). Twin-screw, 18 knots. Motorship. Two masts and one funnel. Passengers: 630. Service: Netherlands-East Indies. Became a war casualty, March 17, 1943. Sister ship: **Baloeran.**

Derbyshire   (1897)   Bibby Line (British).
Built by Harland & Wolff, Ltd., Belfast, Ireland. Tonnage: 6,776. Dimensions: 452′ x 52′. Twin-screw, 15 knots. Triple

expansion engines. Four masts and one funnel. Service: England-Rangoon. Passengers: 140 first class. Scrapped in 1932.

*Derbyshire (1935) Bibby Line (British).
Built by Fairfield Shipbuilding Co., Glasgow, Scotland. Tonnage: 11,660. Dimensions: 482' x 66' (501' o.l.). Twin-screw, 15 knots. Motorship. Four masts and one funnel. Service: Liverpool-Rangoon. Passengers: 115 first. Sister ship: **Worcestershire.**

Derfflinger (1907) North German Lloyd.
Tonnage: 9,144. Service: Bremen-Australia/Far East. Note: See PART I for details.

Devanha (1906) P. & O. Line (British).
Built by Caird & Co., Greenock, Scotland. Tonnage: 8,092. Dimensions: 470' x 56'. Twin-screw, 16½ knots. Quadruple expansion engines. Two masts and one funnel. Passengers: 163 first and 180 second. Scrapped in 1928. Sister ships: **Delhi, Delta,** and **Dongola.**

*Devonshire (1939) Bibby Line (British).
Built by Fairfield Shipbuilding Co., Glasgow, Scotland. Tonnage: 11,275. Dimensions: 497' x 63'. Twin-screw, 17 knots. Motorship. Two masts and one funnel. Passengers: 130 first, 96 second, 99 third. Sister ship: **Ettrick.**

Dilwara (1891) British India Steam Navigation Co.
Built by A. & J. Inglis, Ltd., Glasgow, Scotland. Tonnage: 5,378. Dimensions: 425' x 48'. Single-screw, 14 knots. Triple expansion engines. Three masts and one funnel. Passengers: 76 first and 32 second. Sold in 1922. Sister ship: **Dunera.**

Dilwara (1935) British India Steam Navigation Co.
Built by Barclay, Curle & Co., Glasgow, Scotland. Tonnage: 11,080. Dimensions: 496' x 63'. Twin-screw, 17 knots. Motorship. Two masts and one funnel. Tonnage: Increased to 12,555. Passengers: 200. Vessel sold in 1960 to China Navigation Company to carry pilgrims. Renamed: **Kuala Lumpur.** Sister ship: **Dunera.** Note: Specially designed ships for transporting about 800 troops.

Diogenes (1922) Aberdeen Line (British).
Built by Harland & Wolff, Ltd., Belfast, Ireland. Tonnage: 12,351. Dimensions: 500' x 63'. Twin-screw, 15 knots. Four steam turbines. Two masts and one funnel. Service:

England-Australia, via Cape Town. Transferred to Shaw, Savill & Albion Company in 1926. Renamed: **Mataroa** (1926). Scrapped in 1957. Sister ship: **Tamaroa.**

Djemnah (1875)   Messageries Maritimes (French).
Tonnage: 3,785. Services: (a) France-Far East, (b) France-South America. Note: See PART III for details.

*****Djenne** (1931)   Paquet Line (French).
Built by Forges & Chantiers de la Mediterranee, La Seyne, France. Tonnage: 8,790. Dimensions: 426′ x 58′. Twin-screw, 17 knots. Six steam turbines. Two masts and two funnels. Service: France-North West Africa. Sister ships: **Koutoubia, Marechal Lyautey** and **Nicolas Paquet.**

Domala (1921)   British India Steam Navigation Co.
Built by Barclay, Curle & Co., Glasgow, Scotland. Tonnage: 8,441. Dimensions: 450′ x 58′. Twin-screw, 13 knots. Motorship. Two masts and one funnel. Passengers: 130. Bombed and set on fire in 1940. Sister ship: **Dumana.**

*****Dominion Monarch** (1939)   Shaw, Savill & Albion Co.
Built by Swan, Hunter & Wigham Richardson, Ltd., Wallsend, Newcastle, England. Tonnage: 27,155. Dimensions: 657′ x 84′ (682′ o.l.). Quadruple-screw, 20 knots. Motorship. Two masts and two funnels. Note: The world's largest motorship. Service: England-Australia and New Zealand, via Cape Town. Passengers: 508 first class. Served as a troopship in World War II. Resumed regular service in 1948.

Dongola (1905)   P. & O. Line (British).
Built by Barclay, Curle & Co., Glasgow, Scotland. Tonnage: 8,056. Dimensions: 470′ x 56′. Twin-screw, 16 knots. Quadruple expansion engines. Two masts and one funnel. Passengers: 163 first and 80 second. Scrapped in 1927. Sister ships: **Delhi, Delta** and **Devanha.**

Dordogne (1889)   Messageries Maritimes (French).
Built by Forges & Chantiers de la Mediterranee, Havre, France. Tonnage: 3,806. Dimensions: 371′ x 43′. Single-screw, $13\frac{1}{2}$ knots. Triple expansion engines. Steel hull. Sold to Italian shipbreakers in April 1911. Sister ship: **Charente.**

Dorsetshire (1920)   Bibby Line (British).
Built by Harland & Wolff, Ltd., Belfast, Ireland. Tonnage: 9,645. Dimensions: 450′ x 57′. Twin-screw, 13 knots. Motorship. Two masts and one funnel. Passengers: 300.

Troops: 1,400. Crew: 190. After World War II was placed in England-Australia emigrant service. Sister ship: **Somersetshire.** Note: The only two-masted Bibby liner to date.

Doukkala (1900)   Cie. de Navigation Paquet (French).
Built by Maats. Fyenoord, Rotterdam, Netherlands. Tonnage: 4,368. Dimensions: 392' x 45'. Single-screw, 14 knots. Quadruple expansion engines. Two masts and one funnel. Service: France-North West Africa. Passengers: 88 first, 41 second, 30 third. Scrapped in 1935. Ex-**Koning Willem II.**

Doune Castle (1890)   Castle Line (British).
Built by Barclay, Curle & Co., Glasgow, Scotland. Tonnage: 4,046. Dimensions: 396' x 43'. Single-screw, 13½ knots. Triple expansion engines. Two masts and one funnel. Intermediate type of steamer. Vessel was taken back by her builders in 1904, as part payment for new tonnage. She was sold to the East Asiatic Company of Copenhagen. Renamed: **Asia.** Sister ship: **Lismore Castle.**

Dover Castle (1872)   Castle Line (British).
Built by Barclay, Curle & Co., Glasgow, Scotland. Tonnage: 2,341. Dimensions: 327' x 36'. Single-screw. Compound engines. Two masts and one funnel. Iron hull. Note: Donald Currie's pioneer Castle Line steamship. Never in actual service to South Africa, as she was chartered to the Pacific Line for her maiden voyage. On return trip from Callao to Liverpool, caught fire and sunk off Chile, July 1872. Sister ship: **Walmer Castle.**

Dover Castle (1904)   Union-Castle Line.
Built by Barclay, Curle & Co., Glasgow, Scotland. Tonnage: 8,271. Dimensions: 476' x 56' (490' o.l.). Twin-screw, 14 knots. Quadruple expansion engines. Two masts and one funnel. Torpedoed and sunk in the Mediterranean, May 26, 1917, while being employed as a British hospital ship. Sister ships: **Dunluce Castle** and **Durham Castle.** Passengers: 220 first class.

Dresden (1889)   North German Lloyd.
Tonnage: 4,580. Service: Interchangeable between North Atlantic, South America and Australia/Far East. Note: See PART I for details.

Drummond Castle (1881)   Castle Line (British).
Built by John Elder & Co., Glasgow, Scotland. Tonnage: 3,663. Dimensions: 365' x 43'. Single-screw, 13½ knots.

Compound engines. Two masts and one funnel. Iron hull. Triple expansion engines in 1887. Transferred from mail to intermediate service in 1894. Lost off Ushant, June 17, 1896, with liner sinking within six minutes. Only three out of 245 passengers and crew were saved. Sister ship: **Garth Castle.**

Duart Castle   (1878)   Castle Line (British).
Built by Barclay, Curle & Co., Glasgow, Scotland. Tonnage: 1,839. Dimensions: 301' x 33'. Single-screw. Compound engines. Two masts and one funnel. Iron hull. Employed as an extra steamer. Sold to Pickford & Black in 1891. Renamed: **Oruro.** Scrapped in 1925. Ex-**Adjutant** (1879). Similar ship: **Taymouth Castle.**

Dublin Castle   (1877)   Castle Line (British).
Built by Robert Napier & Sons, Ltd., Glasgow, Scotland. Tonnage: 2,805.   Dimensions: 344' x 39'.   Single-screw. Compound engines. Two masts and one funnel. Iron hull. Type: Castle Line mail steamer to South Africa. Sold to Spanish Line in 1882. Renamed: **Santo Domingo.** Scrapped in 1898. Sister ship: **Balmoral Castle.**

Duilio   (1923)   (a) Italia Line, (b) Lloyd Triestino.
Tonnage: 23,635.   Service: Italy-South Africa.   Running mate: **Giulio Cesare.** Note: See PART I for details.

Dumana   (1923)   British India Steam Navigation Co.
Built by Barclay, Curle & Co., Glasgow, Scotland. Tonnage: 8,427.   Dimensions: 450' x 58'.   Twin-screw, 13 knots. Motorship. Two masts and one funnel. Passengers: 130. Torpedoed and sunk by enemy submarine, December 24, 1943. Sister ship: **Domala.**

Dumbea   (1889)   Messageries Maritimes (French).
Built by Forges & Chantiers de la Mediterranee, La Seyne, France. Tonnage: 5,695. Dimensions: 463' x 46'. Single-screw, 16½ knots. Triple expansion engines. Three masts and two funnels. Transferred from South American to Australian/Far East service in 1903. Sold for scrap in September 1928. Ex-**Bresil** (1903). Sister ship: **Nera.**

Dunbar Castle   (1883)   Castle Line (British).
Built by Barclay, Curle & Co., Glasgow, Scotland. Tonnage: 2,608. Dimensions: 335' x 38'. Single-screw. Compound engines. Two masts and one funnel. Iron hull. Sold to Scottish-American Line in 1895. Renamed: **Olympia.**

Ran aground in Prince William Sound, Alaska, December 1910, and became a total loss. Sister ship: **Methven Castle.**

Dunbar Castle (1930) Union-Castle Line.
Built by Harland & Wolff, Ltd., Belfast, Ireland. Tonnage: 10,002. Dimensions: 471′ x 61′. Twin-screw, 14½ knots. Motorship. Two masts and two funnels. Passengers: 440. Sunk by mine in English Channel, January 9, 1940. Similar ship: **Llangibby Castle.**

Dunera (1891) British India Steam Navigation Co.
Built by A. & J. Inglis, Ltd., Glasgow, Scotland. Tonnage: 5,414. Dimensions: 425′ x 48′. Single-screw, 14 knots. Triple expansion engines. Three masts and one funnel. Passengers: 76 first and 32 second. Sold for scrap in 1922. Sister ship: **Dilwara.**

*****Dunera** (1937) British India Steam Navigation Co.
Built by Barclay, Curle & Co., Glasgow, Scotland. Tonnage: 11,162. Dimensions: 496′ x 63′ (516′ o.l.). Twin-screw, 17 knots. Motorship. Two masts and one funnel. Tonnage increased to 12,615. Note: Designed as troopship. During World War II troop capacity was raised to 2,300. Passenger accommodation: 123 first, 95 second, 100 third. Sister ship: **Dilwara.** Similar to **Ettrick.**

Dunluce Castle (1904) Union-Castle Line.
Built by Harland & Wolff, Ltd., Belfast, Ireland. Tonnage: 8,114. Dimensions: 475′ x 56′ (490′ o.l.). Twin-screw, 14 knots. Quadruple expansion engines. Two masts and one funnel. Passengers: 360. Sold to shipbreakers in July 1939. However, was taken over by British Admiralty and converted to depot ship. Sold for scrap in 1945. Sister ships: **Dover Castle** and **Durham Castle.**

Dunnottar Castle (1936) Union-Castle Line.
Built by Harland & Wolff, Ltd., Belfast, Ireland. Tonnage: 15,050. Dimensions: 540′ x 71′ (560′ o.l.). Twin-screw, 16 knots. Motorship. Two masts and one funnel. Passengers: 220 first and 240 tourist. Service: London-Around Africa. Sold to Incres Steamship Co. in 1958. Renamed: **Victoria** (1958). Employed as cruise ship between New York and Nassau, Bahamas. Sister ship: **Dunvegan Castle.**

Dunolly Castle (1897) Castle Line (British).
Built by Barclay, Curle & Co., Glasgow, Scotland. Tonnage: 4,167. Dimensions: 368′ x 46′. Single-screw, 12 knots. Triple expansion engines. Two masts and one funnel. In

Castle Line intermediate service. Sold to Danish owners in 1905. Renamed: (a) **Juliette** (1905), (b) **Arconia** (1906), (c) **Hittfeld** (1908), (d) **Ioannina** (1913). Torpedoed and sunk off the Azores, December 15, 1917. Sister ship: **Raglan Castle.**

Dunottar Castle   (1890)   Union-Castle Line.
Built by Fairfield Shipbuilding Co., Glasgow, Scotland. Tonnage: 5,625. Dimensions: 420' x 49' (433' o.l.). Single-screw, 16 knots. Triple expansion engines. Three masts and two funnels. Steel hull. An outstanding Castle liner for her era. Actually she was Donald Currie's challenge to the opposition line, namely Union Steam Ship Co. She was the first two-funneled vessel built for Castle Line. Launched, May 22, 1890. Broke the speed record for the Cape Town run. Passengers: 160 first, 90 second and 100 third class. Her two 7,000 I.H.P. triple expansion engines gave her a speed of 17 knots. Funnels were lengthened about 6 feet in 1897 during a refit. Chartered to Panama Railroad Company in 1907, for passenger service between New York and Panama. Later, served as a cruise ship. Sold to Royal Mail Line in 1913. Renamed: **Caribbean** (1913). Foundered off Cape Wrath in very heavy weather, September 1915.

Dunrobin Castle   (1875)   Castle Line (British).
Built by Robert Napier & Sons, Glasgow, Scotland. Tonnage: 2,783. Dimensions: 342' x 38'. Single-screw. Compound engines. Two masts and one funnel. Iron hull. Commenced as a mail steamer to South Africa, but later, transferred to intermediate service. Sold to French owners in 1893. Similar ships: **Balmoral Castle, Conway Castle,** and **Warwick Castle.**

Dunvegan Castle   (1896)   Union-Castle Line.
Built by Fairfield Shipbuilding Co., Glasgow, Scotland. Tonnage: 5,958. Dimensions: 450' x 50'. Single-screw, 16 knots. Triple expansion engines. Three masts and one funnel. Service: Southampton-Cape Town. Later employed in East African service. Passengers: 200 first and 170 second. Scrapped in Germany, 1923. Similar ship: **Tantallon Castle.**

Dunvegan Castle   (1936)   Union-Castle Line.
Built by Harland & Wolff, Ltd., Belfast, Ireland. Tonnage: 15,050. Dimensions: 540' x 71' (560' o.l.). Twin-screw, 16 knots. Motorship. Two masts and one funnel. Service: London-South East Africa. Torpedoed and sunk while serving as an armed merchant cruiser, August 1940. Sister ship: **Dunnottar Castle.**

Durban   (1878)   Union Line (Union Steam Ship Co.).
Built by James Laing, Sunderland, England.   Tonnage: 2,875.   Dimensions: 360' x 38'.   Single-screw.   Compound engines.   Two masts and one funnel.   Iron hull.   Service: England-Cape Town.   This mail steamer was later transferred to intermediate service.   Finally converted to cargo carrier.   Wrecked south of Santa Cruz, Teneriffe, June 1893.

*Durban Castle   (1939)   Union-Castle Line.
Built by Harland & Wolff, Ltd., Belfast, Ireland.   Tonnage: 17,388.   Dimensions: 570' x 76' (594' o.l.).   Twin-screw, 17 knots.   Motorship.   Two masts and one funnel.   Service: England-Round Africa route.   Passengers: 180 first and 359 tourist.   Sister ship: **Warwick Castle.** Ex-**Pretoria Castle.**

Durham Castle   (1904)   Union-Castle Line.
Built by Fairfield Shipbuilding Co., Glasgow, Scotland.   Tonnage: 8,217.   Dimensions: 475' x 56' (490' o.l.).   Twin-screw, 14 knots.   Quadruple expansion engines.   Two masts and one funnel.   Prior to First World War had accommodation for 200 first class passengers.   Passenger capacity later increased to 390.   Sold to shipbreakers just before outbreak of World War II, but was soon taken over by British Admiralty.   Sunk off Invergordon in January 1940, while in tow for Scapa.   Sister ships: **Dover Castle** and **Dunluce Castle.**

Edinburgh Castle   (1873)   Castle Line (British).
Built by Robert Napier & Sons, Glasgow, Scotland.   Tonnage: 2,678.   Dimensions: 335' x 37'.   Single-screw.   Compound engines.   Two masts and one funnel.   Iron hull.   In mail service between England and Cape Town.   Sold to Spanish owners in 1880.   Renamed: **Espana.** Scrapped in 1898.   Sister ship: **Windsor Castle.**

Edinburgh Castle   (1910)   Union-Castle Line.
Built by Harland & Wolff, Ltd., Belfast, Ireland.   Tonnage: 13,326.   Dimensions: 570' x 64'.   Twin-screw, 17 knots.   Quadruple expansion engines.   12,500 I.H.P.   Two masts and two funnels.   Service: Southampton-Cape Town.   Passengers: 320 first, 220 second, 250 third.   Fine type of liner for her era.   Withdrawn from service in 1938.   Sold to British Government in 1940.   Served as a base ship at Freetown, Sierra Leone, during World War II.   Sunk by British warships off Freetown in September 1945.   Sister ship: **Balmoral Castle.** Note: Largest Union-Castle liners built to date.

*Edinburgh Castle   (1948)   Union-Castle Line.
Built by Harland & Wolff, Ltd., Belfast, Ireland. Tonnage:
28,705. Dimensions: 717' x 84' (747' o.l.). Twin-screw, 22
knots. Six steam turbines. Two masts and one funnel.
Launched by Princess Margaret, on October 16, 1947. The
first major public engagement for the very individualistic
British Princess. The name of this beautiful liner is linked
to Edinburgh, capital of Scotland. Accommodation for 214
first class and 541 tourist class passengers. Service: England-
South Africa.   In January 1954 the **Edinburgh Castle**
made the Southampton-Cape Town voyage in the record
time of 11 days, 21 hours, 5 minutes. Sister ship: **Pretoria
Castle.**

Edouard Branly   (1951)   Chargeurs Reunis (French).
Built by Ateliers & Chantiers de la Loire, St. Nazaire,
France. Tonnage: 11,968. Dimensions: 525' x 64' (538' o.l.).
Twin-screw, 17 knots. Motorship. Two masts and one fun-
nel. Passengers: 91 first and 52 second class. Troops: 398.
Service: Marseilles-Indo China. Sold to Italia Line in 1957.
Renamed: **Antonio Pacinotti** (1957). Sister ships: **Clement
Ader** and **Henri Poincare.**

Eduard Woermann   (1903)   Woerman Line (German).
Built by Bremer Vulkan, Vegesack, Germany. Tonnage:
5,642.   Dimensions: 403' x 49'.   Single-screw, 12½ knots.
Triple expansion engines. Service: Germany-Africa. Passengers: 44 first, 20 second, 32 third. Ex-**Alabama.**

Egba   (1914)   Elder, Dempster & Co. (British).
Built by Harland & Wolff, Ltd., Glasgow, Scotland. Tonnage: 4,989. Dimensions: 405' x 54'. Single-screw. Triple
expansion engines. Two masts and one funnel. Sister ship:
Ebani.

Egypt   (1897)   P. & O. Line (British).
Built by Caird & Co., Greenock, Scotland. Tonnage: 7,941.
Dimensions: 499' x 54'.   Single-screw, 18 knots.   Triple
expansion engines. Two masts and two funnels. Service:
England-Australia, via Suez Canal. Passengers: 314 first
and 212 second. Sunk in collision with the **Seine** off coast
of France, May 20, 1922, with the loss of 98 lives. She
carried $5,000,000 in gold and several million dollars in
bank notes, most of which was salvaged by divers in 1932.
Sister ships: **Arabia, China, India** and **Persia.**

El Kantara   (1905)   Messageries Maritimes (French).
Built by Messageries Maritimes, La Ciotat, France. Tonnage: 6,888. Dimensions: 447' x 52'. Twin-screw, 12 knots. Triple expansion engines. Two masts and one funnel. Scrapped at Dunkirk in December 1926. Sister ships: **Euphrate, Gange, Louqsor** and **Sontay.**

Elbe   (1881)   North German Lloyd.
Tonnage: 4,897. This famous North Atlantic liner was at a later date transferred to Bremen-Australia service. Note: See PART I for details.

Eleonore Woermann   (1902)   Woermann Line (German).
Built by Blohm & Voss, Hamburg, Germany. Tonnage: 4,624. Dimensions: 364' x 47'. Single-screw. Triple expansion engines. Two masts and one funnel. Passengers: 88 first, 76 second, 50 third. Sunk by British warship in South Atlantic in 1915.

Elisabethville   (1910)   Compagnie Belge Maritime du Congo.
Built by Alexander Stephen & Sons, Ltd., Glasgow, Scotland. Tonnage: 7,017. Dimensions: 415' x 55'. Twin-screw, 14 knots. Quadruple expansion engines. Two masts and one funnel. Torpedoed and sunk by German submarine in 1917. Sister ship: **Albertville.**

Elisabethville   (1921)   Compagnie Belge Maritime.
Built by Soc. Anon. John Cockerill, Hoboken, Belgium. Tonnage: 8,351. Dimensions: 439' x 57' (459' o.l.). Twin-screw, 14 knots. Quadruple expansion engines. Two masts and one funnel. Service: Antwerp-Congo. Renamed: (a) **Empire Bure** (1947), (b) **Charleton Star** (1950), (c) **Maristrella** (1958). Sister ship: **Thysville.**

Elisabethville   (1949)   Compagnie Belge Maritime.
Built by John Cockerill, Hoboken, Belgium. Tonnage: 10,901. Dimensions: 479' x 64' (505' o.l.). Single-screw, 16½ knots. Motorship. Two masts and one funnel. Service: Antwerp-Congo and Angola. Passengers: 207 one class. Sister ships: **Albertville, Charlesville, Leopoldville** and **Thysville.**

Elizabeth Martin   (1872)   Castle Line (British).
Built by Robert Napier & Sons, Glasgow, Scotland. Tonnage: 1,246. Served as a mail steamer to South Africa. Note: Vessel was named after Sir Donald Currie's mother. Sold to Greek owners in 1882. Similar ships: **Gothland, Iceland** and **Courland.**

Elmina   (1906)   Elder, Dempster & Co.
Built by Alexander Stephen & Sons, Ltd., Glasgow, Scotland.
Tonnage: 4,792.   Dimensions: 380′ x 47′.   Single-screw, 14
knots.   Triple expansion engines.   Two masts and one funnel.   Service: England-West Africa.   Renamed: (a) **Iphigenia,** (b) **Cairo City** (Fenton Steamship Co.).   Ex-
Albertville. Sister ship: **Falaba.**

Elysia   (1873)   Anchor Line (British).
Tonnage: 2,714.   Services: (a) North Atlantic, (b) England-
India.   Note: See PART I for details.

Elysia   (1908)   Anchor Line (British).
Built by D. & W. Henderson & Co., Glasgow, Scotland.
Tonnage: 6,757.   Dimensions: 440′ x 53′.   Single-screw, 12½
knots.   Triple expansion engines.   Two masts and one fun-
nel.   Passengers: 100 first class.   Service: England-India.
Torpedoed by two Japanese raiders 350 miles from Durban,
June 5, 1942, while on voyage to India, via South Africa.
Sister ship: **Castalia.**

Empire Trader   (1908)   Shaw, Savill & Albion Co.
Built by Workman, Clark & Co., Belfast, Ireland.   Tonnage:
9,990.   Dimensions: 477′ x 61′.   Twin-screw, 14 knots.   Triple
expansion engines.   Two masts and one funnel.   Torpedoed
and sunk by submarine, February 21, 1943.   Ex-**Tainui**
(1940).

Equateur   (1875)   Messageries Maritimes (French).
Built by Messageries Maritimes, La Ciotat, France.   Ton-
nage: 3,915.   Dimensions: 394′ x 39′.   Single-screw, 13½
knots.   Compound engines.   Three masts and one funnel.
Iron hull.   Confined in Black Sea during First World War.
Scrapped in France, 1922.

Eridan   (1866)   Messageries Maritimes (French).
Built by Messageries Maritimes, La Ciotat, France.   Tonnage: 1,685.   Dimensions: 320′ x 32′.   Single-screw, 13½
knots.   Three masts and one funnel.   Iron hull.   Later, re-
engined with compound engines.   Lengthened (1,825 tons)
in 1888.   Transferred to Saigon shuttle service in 1897.
Sold for scrap at Shanghai in April 1905.   Sister ships:
Niemen, Tanais, Tibre and **Volga.**

Eridan   (1928)   Messageries Maritimes (French).
Built by Soc. Provecale de Const. Nav., La Ciotat, France.
Tonnage: 9,927.   Dimensions: 445′ x 61′.   Twin-screw, 16
knots.   Motorship.   Two masts and two square funnels.

Launched, June 3, 1928. Service: Marseilles-Far East. Passengers: 570. Damaged by fire at Saigon, December 29, 1945. Refitted for service. Sold to French shipbreakers in 1956.

Erna Woermann (1902) Woermann Line (German).
Built by Flensburger Schiffsb., Flensburg, Germany. Tonnage: 5,580. Dimensions: 403′ x 49′. Single-screw, 12 knots. Quadruple expansion engines. Two masts and one funnel. Service: Germany-Africa. Passengers: 56 first, 24 second, 52 third. Renamed: (a) **Huntscastle,** (b) **Sultan.** Ex-**Louisiana.**

Erymanthe (1862) Messageries Maritimes.
Built by Messageries Maritimes, La Ciotat, France. Tonnage: 1,513. Dimensions: 344′ x 32′. Single-screw, Iron hull. Clipper bow. Two masts and one funnel. Lengthened (1,947 tons) and converted to triple expansion engines in 1888. In collision with steamship **Berry,** November 19, 1898. Grounded and wrecked two days later.

Erzherzog Franz Ferdinand (1899) Lloyd Austriaco.
Built by Lloyd Austriaco, Trieste, Austria-Hungary. Tonnage: 6,105. Dimensions: 426′ x 51′. Single-screw, 13 knots. Triple expansion engines. 3,600 I.H.P. Two masts and one funnel. Passengers: 56 first class. Note: This shipping firm became known as Lloyd Triestino after First World War. Renamed: **Fiume-L.** Scrapped in 1931.

Esperance Bay (1922) Aberdeen & Commonwealth Line.
Built by Wm. Beardmore & Co., Glasgow, Scotland. Tonnage: 14,146. Dimensions: 530′ x 68′ (549′ o.l.). Twin-screw, 16 knots. Four steam turbines. Two masts and one funnel. Passengers: 680. Crew: 160. Service: London-Australia. Renamed: **Arawa** (1936). Sister ships: **Hobson Bay, Jervis Bay, Largs Bay** and **Moreton Bay.**

Esperance Bay (1922) Aberdeen & Commonwealth Line.
Built by Vickers, Ltd., Barrow, England. Tonnage: 14,343. Dimensions: 530′ x 68′ (549′ o.l.). Twin-screw, 16 knots. Steam turbines. Two masts and one funnel. Service: London-Australia, via Suez Canal. Scrapped in Scotland, 1955. Ex-**Hobsons Bay** (1936). Sister ships: **Jervis Bay, Largs Bay** and **Moreton Bay.**

Esquilino (1925) (a) Lloyd Triestino, (b) Italia Line.
Built by Cantieri San Rocco S. A., San Rocco, Italy. Tonnage: 8,657. Dimensions: 452′ x 57′ (462′ o.l.). Twin-screw,

13 knots. Motorship. Two masts and no funnel. Passengers: 360. Service: Italy-Australia. Renamed: **Empire Governor** (1942). Sister ship: **Viminale.**

Etolia   (1887)   Elder, Dempster & Co. (British).
Built by Harland & Wolff, Ltd., Belfast, Ireland. Tonnage: 3,270. Dimensions: 345' x 40'. Single-screw. Triple expansion engines. Three masts and one funnel. Steel and iron hull. Service: England-West Africa. Wrecked near Cape Sable, June 10, 1906.

Ettrick   (1938)   P. & O. Line (British).
Built by Barclay, Curle & Co., Glasgow, Scotland. Tonnage: 11,279. Dimensions: 496' x 63' (516' o.l.). Twin-screw, 17 knots. Motorship. Two masts and one funnel. Attractive in appearance with her raked stem. Passengers: 104 first and 90 second class. Torpedoed and sunk during the Allied landings in the North African and Mediterranean campaign, November 15, 1942. Sister ship: **Devonshire.**

Euphrate   (1905)   Messageries Maritimes.
Built by Messageries Maritimes, La Ciotat, France. Tonnage: 6,876. Dimensions: 447' x 52'. Twin-screw, 12 knots. Triple expansion engines. Two masts and one funnel. Grounded at Socotra in September 1951 and became a total loss. Sister ships: **Gange, El Kantara, Louqsor** and **Sontay.**

Euripides   (1914)   Aberdeen Line (British).
Built by Harland & Wolff, Ltd., Belfast, Ireland. Tonnage: 14,947. Dimensions: 550' x 67' (569' o.l.). Triple-screw, 15 knots. Triple expansion engines and one low pressure turbine. Service: Liverpool-Australia, via South Africa. Renamed: **Akaroa** (1932).

*Europa   (1953)   Lloyd Triestino (Italian).
Built by Ansaldo, La Spezia, Genoa, Italy. Tonnage: 11,430. Dimensions: 489' x 68' (522' o.l.). Twin-screw, 21 knots. Motorship. Single mast and one funnel. Passengers: 148 first and 298 tourist. Service: Italy-East and South Africa. Sister ships: **Africa, Asia** and **Victoria.**

Europe   (1905)   Chargeurs Reunis (French).
Built by Chantiers & Ateliers de la Loire, St. Nazaire, France. Tonnage: 4,769. Dimensions: 369' x 46'. Twin-screw, 12½ knots. Triple expansion engines. Launched, December 26, 1905. Service: France-West Africa. Sold to Dunkirk shipbreakers in October 1930.

European (1869)   Union Line (British).
Built by Robert Napier & Sons, Glasgow, Scotland. Tonnage: 2,272. Dimensions: 307′ x 37′. Single-screw. Compound engines. Three masts and one funnel. Iron hull. Vessel purchased in 1872. Served as a mail steamer to South Africa. Lost off Ushant in December 1877. Ex-**Europe** (1872).

Explorateur Grandidier (1924)   Messageries Maritimes.
Built by Chantiers de Penhoet, St. Nazaire, France. Tonnage: 10,267. Dimensions: 455′ x 60′. Twin-screw, 15 knots. Triple expansion engines. Two masts and two funnels. Launched, November 26, 1924. Service: Marseilles-Far East. Passengers: 300. Scuttled by Germans at Marseilles in August 1944. Sister ship: **Bernardin de Saint Pierre.**

*****Fairsea** (1941)   Sitmar Line (Italian).
Built by Sun Shipbuilding & Dry Dock Co., Chester, Pa. Tonnage: 13,432. Dimensions: 492′ (o.l.) x 69′. Single-screw, 17 knots. Motorship. Single mast and one funnel. Passengers: 1,460, one class. Service: Europe-Australia. Ex-**Charger** (1949), ex-**Rio de la Plata.** She was originally one of 4 passenger ships built for Moore-McCormack Line.

Falaba (1906)   Elder, Dempster & Co. (British).
Built by Alexander Stephen & Sons, Ltd., Glasgow, Scotland. Tonnage: 4,806. Dimensions: 380′ x 47′. Single-screw, 14 knots. Triple expansion engines. Two masts and one funnel. Service: England-West Africa. Torpedoed and sunk 38 miles from Smalls Light House, March 28, 1915, with the loss of 104 lives. Sister ship: **Elimina.**

Feldmarschall (1903)   Deutsche Ost Afrika Line.
Built by Reiherstieg Schiffsw., Hamburg, Germany. Tonnage: 6,181. Dimensions: 415′ x 50′ (431′ o.l.). Twin-screw, 14 knots. Triple expansion engines. Three masts and one funnel. Passengers: 113 first, 75 second, 80 third. Renamed: (a) **Field Marshall,** (b) **Hong Kheng.**

Felix Roussel (1930)   Messageries Maritimes (French).
Built by Ateliers & Chantiers de la Loire, St. Nazaire, France. Tonnage: 16,774. Dimensions: 534′ x 68′ (559′ o.l.). Twin-screw, 15 knots. Motorship. Two masts and two square funnels. Launched, December 17, 1929. Note: Refitted and lengthened to 575 feet (17,083 tons) in 1935. Speed increased to 18½ knots. Service: Marseilles-Far East. Passengers: 400. Taken over by the British in July 1940. Reconditioned

for passenger service in 1948, and resumed sailings for Messageries Maritimes. Her square funnels were replaced by single oval one. Vessel was sold in April 1955. Renamed: **Arosa Sun** (1955). Acquired by other owners in 1960. Similar ships: **Aramis** and **Georges Philipar.**

*__Ferdinand de Lesseps__ (1951) Messageries Maritimes (French).
Built by Forges & Chantiers de la Gironde, Bordeaux, France. Tonnage: 10,882. Dimensions: 459' x 64' (492' o.l.). Twin-screw, 17 knots. Motorship. Two masts and one funnel. Service: France-East Africa-Mauritius. Passengers: 88 first, 112 tourist, 40 third. Sister ships: **Jean Laborde, La Bourdonnais** and **Pierre Loti.**

*__Flamina__ (1922) Compagnia Genovese di Armamento (Italian).
Built by Merchant Shipbuilding Corp., Chester, Pa. Tonnage: 8,776. Dimensions: 461' x 59'. Twin-screw, 14½ knots. Motorship. Single mast and one funnel. Converted to diesels in 1955. Originally built as cargo ship. Passengers: 1,024 tourist class. Service: Mediterranean-Australia. Ex-**Genova** (1955), ex-**Capitaine Potie** (1948), ex-**Belgian Freighter** (1946), ex-**Empire Swan** (1942), ex-**Missourian** (American-Hawaiian Steamship Co.).

*__Foch__ (1950) Cie. de Navigation Paquet (French).
Built by Chantiers & Ateliers de St. Nazaire, Penhoet, St. Nazaire, France. Tonnage: 9,504. Dimensions: 448' x 61' (479' o.l.). Twin-screw, 16 knots. Motorship. Two masts and one funnel. Service: France-North and West Africa. Passengers: 126 first, 78 second, 54 third class.

Fontainebleau (1923) Messageries Maritimes (French).
Built by Ateliers & Chantiers de la Loire, St. Nazaire, France. Tonnage: 10,033. Dimensions: 478' x 59'. Twin-screw, 16 knots. Steam turbines. Two masts and one funnel. Launched, November 9, 1923. Note: Laid down as **Islande** for Chargeurs Reunis. Purchased by Messageries Maritimes before launching. Destroyed by fire at Djibouti, July 12, 1926. The gutted hull was used as part of breakwater foundation. Sister ships: **Chantilly** and **Compiegne.**

Fort Salisbury (1895) Bucknall Line (British).
Built by Armstrong, Mitchell & Co., Newcastle, England. Tonnage: 4,404. Dimensions: 360' x 47'. Single-screw, 13 knots. Triple expansion engines. Two masts and one funnel. Service: England-South Africa. Passengers: 90 first class.

Renamed: (a) **Vincent,** (b) **Gujarat,** (c) **Gorjistan.**
Sister ships: **Buluwayo** and **Johannesburg.**

Foucauld   (1922)   Chargeurs Reunis (French).
Built by Forges & Chantiers de la Mediterranee, La Seyne,
France. Tonnage: 11,028. Dimensions: 483′ x 58′. Twin-
screw, 14 knots. Triple expansion engines. Two masts and
one funnel. As originally built had much less superstructure,
tonnage being at that time 9,957. Service: France-West
Africa. Passengers: 450. Sunk on June 20, 1940. Ex-
Hoedic (1929).

*****Foucauld**   (1948)   Chargeurs Reunis (French).
Built by Swan, Hunter & Wigham Richardson, Ltd., Wallsend, England. Tonnage: 9,066. Dimensions: 457′ x 61′
(479′ o.l.). Twin-screw, 16 knots. Motorship. Two masts
and one funnel. Launched, July 17, 1947. Service: France-
West Africa. Sister ship: **Brazza.**

*****Frankfurt**   (1954)   Hamburg-American Line.
Built by Bremer Vulkan, Vegesack, Germany. Tonnage:
8,959. Dimensions: 537′ (o.l.) x 63′. Single-screw, 16½
knots. Motorship. Single mast and one funnel. Service:
Europe-Far East. Passengers: 86 first class. Sister ships:
Hamburg and **Hannover.**

Friedrich der Grosse   (1896)   North German Lloyd.
Tonnage: 10,771. This North Atlantic liner was also used
in Bremen-Australia service. Note: See PART I for details.

Fulda   (1924)   North German Lloyd.
Built by "Weser", Bremen, Germany. Tonnage: 9,492.
Dimensions: 458′ x 57′. Twin-screw, 13 knots. Motorship.
Two masts and one funnel. Service: Germany-Far East.
Later, converted to cargo ship. Sold to Japan in 1940. Re-
named: **Teikoku Maru** (1940). Sister ships: **Coblenz,**
Saarbrucken, Trier, Werra and **Weser.**

Fushima Maru   (1914)   N. Y. K. Line (Japanese).
Tonnage: 10,936. Built for their regular Japan-European
service. Transferred to trans-Pacific service in 1917. Note:
See PART II for details.

Gablonz   (1912)   Lloyd Austriaco (Trieste).
Built by Cantieri San Rocco, Trieste, Austria-Hungaria.
Tonnage: 8,448. Dimensions: 452′ x 53′. Twin-screw, 16
knots. Quadruple expansion engines. Two masts and two
funnels. Vessel taken over by Lloyd Triestino in 1918.

Renamed: **Tevere.** Scuttled in January 1943. Sister ships: **Helouan** and **Wien.**

Gaika   (1897)   Union-Castle Line (British).
Built by Harland & Wolff, Ltd., Belfast, Ireland. Tonnage: 6,287. Dimensions: 430′ x 52′. Twin-screw, 12 knots. Triple expansion engines. Three masts and one funnel. Passengers: 70 first and 110 second. Scrapped in 1928. Sister ships: **Gascon** and **Goorkha.**

Galeka   (1899)   Union-Castle Line.
Built by Harland & Wolff, Ltd., Belfast, Ireland. Tonnage: 6,772. Dimensions: 440′ x 53′. Twin-screw, 12 knots. Triple expansion engines. Two masts and one funnel. Intermediate type of passenger ship. Passengers: 90 first and 120 second. Service: England-South Africa. Sunk by mine off Cape Hogue, October 1916, while serving as hospital ship. Sister ships: **Galician** and **German.** The **Galeka** was the last vessel to be completed for the Union Line.

Galician   (1900)   Union-Castle Line.
Built by Harland & Wolff, Ltd., Belfast, Ireland. Tonnage: 6,757. Dimensions: 440′ x 53′. Twin-screw, 12 knots. Triple expansion engines. Two masts and one funnel. Passengers: 90 first and 120 second. Note: Vessel was completed after the merger of the Union Line and Castle Line in 1900. Renamed: **Glenart Castle** (1914). Sister ships: **Galeka** and **German.**

Galway Castle   (1911)   Union-Castle Line.
Built by Harland & Wolff, Ltd., Belfast, Ireland. Tonnage: 7,988. Dimensions: 452′ x 56′. Twin-screw, 13½ knots. Quadruple expansion engines. Two masts and one funnel. Torpedoed and sunk in the Atlantic, September 12, 1918, with the loss of 189 lives. Sister ships: **Gloucester Castle** and **Guildford Castle.**

Gandia   (1907)   Compagnie Belge Maritime.
Built by Swan, Hunter & Wigham Richardson, Ltd., Newcastle, England. Tonnage: 9,626. Dimensions: 459′ x 59′. Twin-screw, 14 knots. Triple expansion engines. Two masts and one funnel. Became a war casualty, January 22, 1942. Ex-**Konigstein** (1940), ex-**Arawa** (1933).

Gange   (1905)   Messageries Maritimes (French).
Built by Messageries Maritimes, La Ciotat, France. Tonnage: 6,876. Dimensions: 447′ x 53′. Twin-screw, 12 knots.

Triple expansion engines. Two masts and one funnel. Mined and sunk entering Bizerta, April 14, 1917.

Gange   (1912)   Lloyd Triestino (Italian).
Built by Cantieri Nav. Triestino, Monfalcone, Italy, Tonnage: 12,272.   Dimensions: 477′ x 60′.   Twin-screw, 18 knots. Quadruple expansion engines. Two masts and two funnels. Renamed: **Marco Polo** (1936). A World War II casualty.   Ex-**Presidente Wilson** (1929), ex-**Generale Diaz** (1919), ex-**Kaiser Franz Josef I** (1919).

Ganges   (1881)   P. & O. Line (British).
Built by Barrow Shipbuilding Co., Barrow, England. Tonnage: 4,168.   Dimensions: 390′ x 42′.   Single-screw, 14½ knots. Compound engines. Three masts and two funnels. Steel hull. Passengers: 140 first and 60 second. Destroyed by fire at Bombay in 1898. Sister ships: **Clyde, Sutlej** and **Thames.**

Garoet   (1917)   Rotterdam Lloyd (Dutch).
Built by Kon. Maats. de Schelde, Flushing, Netherlands. Tonnage: 7,133.   Dimensions: 446′ x 54′.   Single-screw, 14 knots. Steam turbines. Two masts and one funnel. A war casualty, June 19, 1944.

Garonne   (1871)   Orient Line (British).
Built by Robert Napier & Sons, Glasgow, Scotland. Tonnage: 3,901. Dimensions: 382′ x 41′. Single-screw, 15 knots. Compound engines. Three masts and one funnel. Clipper bow. Iron hull. Vessel was transferred from the Pacific Steam Navigation Company to the newly organized Orient Line in 1877. During this era a number of Pacific Steam Navigation Company ships entered the Orient Line (Orient Steam Navigation Company) service. Namely they were: **Aconcagua, Chimborazo, Cuzco, Iberia, Liguria, Lusitania, John Elder** and **Potosi.** These liners steamed between England and Australia, via Cape of Good Hope, outwards, and by the Suez Canal route homewards. The **Garonne** was wrecked in January 1901.

Garth Castle   (1881)   Castle Line (British).
Built by John Elder & Co., Glasgow, Scotland. Tonnage: 3,660.   Dimensions: 365′ x 43′.   Single-screw, 13½ knots. Triple expansion engines. Two masts and one funnel. Liner was named after the castle Donald Currie purchased in 1880. Sold to Elder, Dempster & Company in June 1901. Resold to Khedival Mail Company. Renamed: **Ismalia,**

(b) **Brunette** (1921).   Scrapped in 1923.   Sister ship: **Drummond Castle.**

Garth Castle   (1910)   Union-Castle Line.
  Built by Barclay, Curle & Co., Glasgow, Scotland. Tonnage: 7,625. Dimensions: 452' x 54'. Twin-screw, 13 knots. Quadruple expansion engines. Two masts and one funnel. Intermediate type of liner. Service: England-South Africa. Taken off the active list in 1930. However, did resume at a later date sailings to Africa. Scrapped in 1939. Sister ship: **Grantully Castle.**

Gascon   (1897)   Union-Castle Line.
  Built by Harland & Wolff, Ltd., Belfast, Ireland. Tonnage: 6,288.   Dimensions: 430' x 52'.   Twin-screw, 12 knots. Triple expansion engines.   Three masts and one funnel. Passengers: 78 first and 118 second class.   Sold to Ward's, the famous shipbreakers, September 1928.   Sister ships: **Gaika** and **Goorkha.**

Gaul   (1893)   Union Line (British).
  Built by Harland & Wolff, Ltd., Belfast, Ireland. Tonnage: 4,745. Dimensions: 400' x 57'. Twin-screw, 12 knots. Triple expansion engines. Two masts and one funnel. Steel hull. Note: First of the famous "G" liners, ten were built. Service: England-Capetown.   Renamed: (a) **Sabor** (1906), (b) **Carmarthenshire** (1909), (c) **Chaleur** (1913). Scrapped in 1923. Sister ships: **Goth** and **Greek.**

Geelong   (1904)   Lund's Blue Anchor Line (British).
  Built by Barclay, Curle & Co., Glasgow, Scotland. Tonnage: 7,954. Dimensions: 450' x 54'. Twin-screw, 14 knots. Triple expansion engines.   Two masts and one very tall funnel. Service: England-Australia, via Capetown.   Passengers: 90 first and 450 third. Transferred to P. & O. Line ownership in 1910, which had been caused by the tragic loss of the **Waratah.**   The **Geelong** was sunk by collision with the **Bonvilston** in the Mediterranean, January 1916.

General Duchesne   (1903)   Messageries Maritimes.
  Built by A. G. "Vulkan", Stettin, Germany.   Tonnage: 7,289.   Dimensions: 450' x 52'.   Twin-screw, 13½ knots. Triple expansion engines. Two masts and one funnel. Purchased the vessel in 1922. Sold for scrap in December 1932. Ex-**Schleswig.**

*General Leclerc   (1951)   Chargeurs Reunis.
Built by Chantiers & Ateliers de St. Nazaire, Penhoet,
France. Tonnage: 9,500. Dimensions: 479' x 62'. Twin-
screw, 16 knots. Motorship. Two masts and one funnel.
Service: France-French West and Equatorial Africa. Passen-
gers: 125 first, 78 second, 48 third, 380 fourth. Similar ships:
Brazza and **Foucauld.**

*General Mangin   (1953)   Cie. de Navigation Fraissinet.
Built by Chantiers & Ateliers de St. Nazaire (Penhoet),
St. Nazaire, France. Tonnage: 12,457. Dimensions: 507' x
64' (531' o.l.). Twin-screw, 16 knots. Motorship. Two
masts and one funnel. Launched in July 1952. Entered
France-North and West African service in spring of 1953.
Passengers: 132 first, 125 second, 101 third. Sister ship:
Jean Mermoz. Largest liners in their fleet.

General Metzinger   (1906)   Messageries Maritimes.
Built by Blohm & Voss, Hamburg, Germany. Tonnage:
9,345. Dimensions: 476' x 55'. Twin-screw, 15 knots.
Quadruple expansion engines. Two masts and one funnel.
Sunk by German bombers in Havre roads, June 11, 1940.
First Messageries Maritimes ship lost by enemy action in
World War II. Ex-**Sobral** (1924), ex-**Cap Vilano** (1917).

General Voyron   (1905)   Messageries Maritimes.
Built by Blohm & Voss, Hamburg, Germany. Tonnage:
6,267. Dimensions: 416' x 50'. Twin-screw, 14 knots. Triple
expansion engines. Two masts and one funnel. Passengers:
64 first, 96 second, 52 third. Sold to French shipbreakers
in April 1933. Ex-**Prinzessin.**

General Werder   (1874)   North German Lloyd.
Tonnage: 3,020. Services: (a) North Atlantic, (b) Far East.
Note: See PART I for detail information.

Georges Philippar   (1930)   Messageries Maritimes.
Built by Ateliers & Chantiers de la Loire, St. Nazaire,
France. Tonnage: 16,990. Dimensions: 542' x 68' (565' o.l.).
Twin-screw, 17½ knots. Motorship. Two masts and two
square funnels. Launched, November 6, 1930. Caught fire
in the Gulf of Aden, Red Sea, while returning from her
maiden voyage, and was abandoned on May 16, 1932.
There was a loss of 41 lives. Sister ships: **Aramis** and
Felix Roussel.

Gera (1890) North German Lloyd.
Built by Fairfield Shipbuilding Co., Glasgow, Scotland.
Tonnage: 5,005. Services: (a) North Atlantic, (b) Latin
America, (c) Far East/Australia. Note: See PART I for
details.

German (1877) Union Line (British).
Built by Wm. Denny & Bros., Dumbarton, Scotland. Tonnage: 3,149. Dimensions: 350' x 39'. Single-screw. Compound engines. Two masts and one funnel. Iron hull.
Employed as a mail steamer in England-South African
service. Broke the speed record for the run. Sold to Navigazione Generale Italiana in 1896. Renamed: **Sempione.**
Converted to hulk in 1902.

German (1898) (a) Union Line, (b) Union-Castle Line.
Built by Harland & Wolff, Ltd., Belfast, Ireland. Tonnage:
6,763. Dimensions: 440' x 53'. Twin-screw, 12 knots.
Triple expansion engines. Two masts and one funnel.
Intermediate steamer. Passengers: 99 first and 126 second.
Renamed: **Glengorm Castle** (1914). Scrapped in 1930.
Sister ships: **Galeka** and **Galician.**

Gertrud Woermann (1905) Woermann Line (German).
Built by Reiherstieg Schiffswerfte, Hamburg, Germany.
Tonnage: 6,365. Dimensions: 411' x 50'. Twin-screw, 12½
knots. Triple expansion engines. Two masts and one funnel.
Renamed: (a) **Windhuk,** (b) **City of Genoa,** (c) **Joao Belo.**

Gertrud Woermann (1907) Woerman Line (German).
Built by Reiherstieg Schiffsw., Hamburg, Germany. Tonnage: 6,456. Dimensions: 415' x 50'. Twin-screw, 12½
knots. Triple expansion engines. Two masts and one funnel.
Passengers: 107 first, 80 second, 90 third. Seized by Brazil
during First World War. Renamed: (a) **Curvello,**
(b) **Cantuaria Guimaraes,** (c) **Siqueira Campos.**

Gerusalemme (1920) Lloyd Triestino (Italian).
Built by Cantieri San Rocco, San Rocco, Italy. Tonnage:
8,052. Dimensions: 430' x 53' (443' o.l.). Twin-screw, 13½
knots. Four steam turbines. Two masts and one funnel.
Transferred to Adriatica Soc. per Azioni di Nav. Scrapped
in Italy, 1952. Ex-**Cracovia** (1934).

Gironde (1869) Messageries Maritimes (French).
Built by Messageries Maritimes, La Ciotat, France. Ton-
nage: 3,261. Dimensions: 367' x 39'. Single-screw, 14 knots.
Compound engines. Three masts and one funnel. Launched,

January 31, 1869. Refitted in 1887. Broken up for scrap at Saigon in 1906.

Giulio Cesare (1920) (a) Italia Line, (b) Lloyd Triestino.
Tonnage: 21,900. Service: Italy-South Africa. Running mate: **Duilio.** Note: See PART I for detail information.

Glenart Castle (1900) Union-Castle Line.
Built by Harland & Wolff, Ltd., Belfast, Ireland. Tonnage: 6,757. Dimensions: 440' x 53'. Twin-screw, 12 knots. Triple expansion engines. Two masts and one funnel. Converted to British hospital ship in 1915. Torpedoed and sunk at the entrance to the Bristol Channel, February 26, 1918, going down within a few minutes with the loss of 153 lives. Ex-**Galician** (1914).

Glengorm Castle (1898) Union-Castle Line.
Built by Harland & Wolff, Ltd., Belfast, Ireland. Tonnage: 6,763. Dimensions: 440' x 53'. Twin-screw, 12 knots. Triple expansion engines. Two masts and one funnel. Scrapped in Holland, 1930. Ex-**German** (1914).

Gloucester Castle (1911) Union-Castle Line.
Built by Fairfield Shipbuilding Co., Glasgow, Scotland. Tonnage: 7,999. Dimensions: 452' x 56'. Twin-screw, 13½ knots. Quadruple expansion engines. Two masts and one funnel. Passengers: 300. Crew: 200. Service: Intermediate. Sunk by a German raider in July 1942. Sister ships: **Galway Castle** and **Guildford Castle.**

Gloucestershire (1910) Bibby Line (British).
Built by Harland & Wolff, Ltd., Belfast, Ireland. Tonnage: 8,124. Dimensions: 467' x 54'. Twin-screw, 15 knots. Quadruple expansion engines. Four masts and one funnel. Passengers: 234 first class. Scrapped in 1937. Sister ship: **Leicestershire.**

Gneisenau (1903) North German Lloyd.
Tonnage: 8,185. Built for Bremen-Australia service, but also, in North Atlantic trade. Note: See PART I for details.

Gneisenau (1935) North German Lloyd.
Built by Deutsche Sch-u-Mschb., A. G. Weser, Bremen, Germany. Tonnage: 18,160. Dimensions: 625' x 74' (652' o.l.). Twin-screw, 21 knots. Steam turbines. Two masts and one funnel. Maier type bow. Service: Bremen-Suez-Far East. Passengers: 300. Struck a mine in the Baltic Sea

in May 1943, as a result capsized. Sister ships: **Scharnhorst** and **Potsdam** (slightly different).

Goeben (1906)   North German Lloyd.
Tonnage: 8,792. Built for Australian and Far East services, but also served in trans-Atlantic trade. Note: See PART I for details.

Goentor (1902)   Rotterdam Lloyd (Dutch).
Built by Kon. Maats. de Schelde, Flushing, Netherlands. Tonnage: 5,891. Dimensions: 425' x 50'. Twin-screw, 14 knots. Quadruple expansion engines. Two masts and one funnel. Passengers: 82 first, 42 second, 24 third, 40 fourth. Service: Netherlands-East Indies. Nice looking passenger liner. Scrapped in 1925.

Golconda (1887)   British India Steam Navigation Co.
Built by Wm. Doxford & Sons, Ltd., Sunderland, England. Tonnage: 5,874. Dimensions: 422' x 48' (438' o.l.). Single-screw, 13 knots. Triple expansion engines. 4,000 I.H.P. Four masts and two funnels. Steel and iron hull. Consumed 50 tons of coal per day. Passengers: 78 first and 24 second class. Service: England-India. Also, served on other routes. Torpedoed and sunk by enemy submarine in the North Sea, June 1916, with the loss of 19 lives.

Goorkha (1897)   Union-Castle Line.
Built by Harland & Wolff, Ltd., Belfast, Ireland. Tonnage: 6,335. Dimensions: 430' x 52'. Twin-screw, 12 knots. Triple expansion engines. Three masts and one funnel. Passengers: 78 first and 118 second. Scrapped in Italy, 1926. Sister ships: **Gaika** and **Gascon.**

Goth (1893)   Union Line (British).
Built by Harland & Wolff, Ltd., Belfast, Ireland. Tonnage: 4,738. Dimensions: 400' x 47'. Twin-screw, 12 knots. Triple expansion engines. Two masts and one funnel. Type: Intermediate steamer. Passengers: 40 first, 50 second. Sold to Royal Mail Line in 1913. Renamed: **Cobequid** (1913). Wrecked in 1914. Sister ships: **Gaul** and **Greek.**

Gothic (1893)   White Star Line (British).
Built by Harland & Wolff, Ltd., Belfast, Ireland. Tonnage: 7,600. Dimensions: 490' x 53'. Twin-screw, 14 knots. Triple expansion engines. Four masts and one funnel. In association with Shaw, Savill & Albion Company, sailed on the England-Australia and New Zealand route, via Capetown.

Renamed: (a) **Gothland** (1907), (b) **Gothic** (1911), (c)
Gothland (1913). Sold for scrap in November 1925.

Gouverneur   (1900)   Deutsche Ost Afrika Line.
Built by Reiherstieg Schiffsw., Hamburg, Germany. Tonnage: 3,336. Dimensions: 321′ x 40′. Single-screw. Triple
expansion engines. Placed in the "Around Africa" service
for a year or two along with **Prasident** and **Markgraf.**
Wrecked near Beira in 1909.

Gradisca   (1913)   Lloyd Triestino (Italian).
Built by Alexander Stephen & Sons, Ltd., Glasgow, Scotland.
Tonnage: 13,870. Dimensions: 541′ x 65′ (560′ o.l.). Twin-
screw, 16½ knots. Quadruple expansion engines. Two masts
and two funnels. Funnels measured 60 feet high from deck
level. Served in various capacities during World War II,
including that of hospital ship. Damaged after stranding
in January 1946. Sold to Italian shipbreakers at Venice in
1952. Ex-**Gelria** (1935) Royal Holland Lloyd.

Grantually Castle   (1879)   Castle Line (British).
Built by Barclay, Curle & Co., Glasgow, Scotland. Tonnage:
3,453. Dimensions: 359′ x 43′. Single-screw. 13½ knots.
Compound engines. Triple expansion engines in 1887. Two
masts and one funnel. Iron hull. Sold to Booth Line in 1896.
Renamed: **Augustine** (December 1896).   Sister ship:
Kinfauns Castle.

Grantully Castle   (1910)   Union-Castle Line.
Built by Barclay, Curle & Co., Glasgow, Scotland. Tonnage:
7,617.   Dimensions: 450′ x 54′.   Twin-screw, 13 knots.
Quadruple expansion engines. Two masts and one funnel.
Service: England-South Africa. Passengers: 100 first, 100
second, 200 third. Sold to shipbreakers in 1939. Sister ship:
Garth Castle.

Greek   (1893)   (a) Union Line, (b) Union-Castle Line.
Built by Harland & Wolff, Ltd., Belfast, Ireland. Tonnage:
4,747.   Dimensions: 400′ x 47′.   Twin-screw, 12 knots.
Triple expansion engines. Two masts and one funnel. Ran
in the intermediate service to South Africa until 1906, when
sold to Royal Mail Line. Renamed: (a) **Segura** (1906),
(b) **Pembrokeshire** (1908), (c) **Chignecto** (1913). Scrapped
in 1927. Sister ships: **Gaul** and **Goth.**

Grosser Kurfurst   (1899)   North German Lloyd.
Tonnage: 13,245. Service: Interchangeable between North
Atlantic and Australian routes. Note: See PART I for details.

Grotius (1907) Nederland Royal Mail Line.
Built by Maats. Fyenoord, Rotterdam, Netherlands. Tonnage: 5,867. Dimensions: 420′ x 48′. Single-screw, 14 knots. Quadruple expansion engines. 4,200 I.H.P. Two masts and one funnel. Passengers: 80 first and 54 second. Service: Amsterdam-Dutch East Indies. Scrapped in 1931. Sister ships: **Rembrandt** and **Vondel.**

Guadiana (1888) Messageries Maritimes (French).
Tonnage: 2,614. Services: (a) South American, (b) Far East. Note: See PART III for details.

Guelph (1894) (a) Union Line, (b) Union-Castle Line.
Built by Harland & Wolff, Ltd., Belfast, Ireland. Tonnage: 4,917. Dimensions: 400′ x 47′. Twin-screw, 12 knots. Triple expansion engines. Three masts and one funnel. Type: Intermediate steamship. Passengers: 50 first and 90 third. Service: (a) West Africa route, (b) London and Durban, via Suez, which she inaugurated in 1910. Sold to Royal Mail Line in 1913. Renamed: **Caraquet** (1913). Wrecked off Bermuda in June 1923. Running mates: **Gaul, Goth** and **Greek.**

Guildford Castle (1911) Union-Castle Line.
Built by Barclay, Curle & Co., Glasgow, Scotland. Tonnage: 7,995. Dimensions: 452′ x 56′. Twin-screw, 14½ knots. Quadruple expansion engines. Two masts and one funnel. Type: Intermediate steamship. Employed as a hospital ship in First World War. Resumed the west coast service to South Africa. Sunk in collision with the **Stentor** in the river Elbe, June 1, 1933, with the loss of two lives. Sister ships: **Galway Castle** and **Gloucester Castle.**

*Gunung Djati (1936) Blue Funnel Line (British).
Built by Blohm & Voss, Hamburg, Germany. Tonnage: 17,891. Dimensions: 547′ x 72′ (578′ o.l.). Twin-screw, 16 knots. Steam turbines. Two masts and two funnels. Converted to pilgrim ship. Service: Indonesia-Jeddah. Passengers: 106 first class and 2,000 pilgrims in lower class quarters. The only Blue Funnel Line ship to have a white painted hull. Ex-**Empire Orwell** (1958), ex-**Empire Doon** (1949), ex-**Pretoria** (1945).

Habsburg (1895) Lloyd Austriaco.
Built by Austrian Lloyd's Arsenal, Trieste, Austria. Tonnage: 4,016. Dimensions: 374′ x 44′. Single-screw, 15½ knots. Triple expansion engines. Steel hull. Passengers: 91

first, 40 second, 28 third. Note: After First World War this line became known as Lloyd Triestino.

Hakata Maru   (1897)   N. Y. K. Line (Japanese).
Built by D. & W. Henderson & Co., Glasgow, Scotland. Tonnage: 6,241. Dimensions: 445′ x 49′. Twin-screw, 13 knots. Triple expansion engines. Four masts and one funnel. Passengers: 29 first, 20 second, 104 third. Service: Japan-Europe, via Suez Canal. Transferred to Japan-Seattle route at later date. Note: See PART II.

Hakone Maru   (1921)   N. Y. K. Line (Japanese).
Built by Mitsubishi Zosen Kaisha, Nagasaki, Japan. Tonnage: 10,420. Dimensions: 495′ x 62′. Twin-screw, 16 knots. Six steam turbines. Two masts and one funnel. Completed on November 1, 1922 for their Japan-European service. Passengers: 175 passengers. Crew: 200. Sunk by aircraft, November 27, 1943. Sister ships: **Hakozaki Maru, Hakusan Maru** and **Haruna Maru.**

Hakozaki Maru   (1922)   N. Y. K. Line (Japanese).
Built by Mitsubishi Zosen Kaisha, Nagasaki, Japan. Tonnage: 10,413. Dimensions: 495′ x 62′. Twin-screw, 16 knots. Steam turbines. Two masts and one funnel. Completed on June 1, 1922. Passengers: 175. Service: Japan-Europe Sunk by submarine, March 9, 1945. Sister ships: **Hakone Maru, Hakusan Maru** and **Haruna Maru.**

Hakusan Maru   (1923)   N. Y. K. Line (Japanese).
Built by Mitsubishi Zosen Kaisha, Nagasaki, Japan. Tonnage: 10,380. Dimensions: 495′ x 62′. Twin-screw, 15½ knots. Steam turbines. Two masts and one funnel. Service: Japan-Europe, via Suez Canal. Passengers: 175. Sunk by submarine, June 4, 1944. Sister ships: **Hakone Maru, Hakozaki Maru** and **Haruna Maru.**

*Hamburg   (1954)   Hamburg-American Line.
Built by Bremer Vulkan, Vegesack, Germany. Tonnage: 9,008. Dimensions: 492′ x 63′ (538′ o.l.). Single-screw, 17 knots. Motorship. Single mast and one funnel. Passengers: 86 first class. Service: Europe-Far East, via Suez Canal. Sister ships: **Frankfurt** and **Hannover.**

*Hannover   (1954)   Hamburg-American Line.
Built by Bremer Vulkan, Vegesack, Germany. Tonnage: 8,974. Dimensions: 492′ x 63′ (537′ o.l.). Single-screw, 16½ knots. Motorship. Single mast and one funnel. Passengers:

86 first. Service: Europe-Far East, via Suez Canal. Sister ships: **Frankfurt** and **Hamburg.**

Hans Woermann   (1900)   Woermann Line (German).
Built by D. J. Dunlop & Co., Port Glasgow, Scotland. Tonnage: 4,059. Dimensions: 340′ x 44′. Single-screw. Triple expansion engines. 1,650 I.H.P. Two masts and one funnel. Passengers: 44 first, 52 second, 30 third. Service: Germany-Africa. Captured by British warship at Duala in 1914. Renamed: **Gold Coast** (Elder, Dempster & Co.). Sunk in 1917.

Harlech Castle   (1894)   (a) Castle Line, (b) Union-Castle Line.
Built by Barclay, Curle & Co., Glasgow, Scotland. Tonnage: 3,264. Dimensions: 350′ x 42′. Single-screw, 12½ knots. Triple expansion engines. Two masts and one funnel. Type: Intermediate steamer. Passengers: 40 first and 250 third class. Service: England-South Africa. Sold to Earl Fitz-william in 1904, and used to convey an expedition to hunt for buried loot on the Island of Cocos. The venture met with no success. Renamed: (a) **Veronique** (1904), (b) **Iquitos** (Beruvian), (c) **Amazonas** (1923).

Haruna Maru   (1922)   N. Y. K. Line (Japanese).
Built by Mitsubishi Zosen Kaisha, Nagasaki, Japan. Tonnage: 10,421. Dimensions: 495′ x 62′. Twin-screw, 15½ knots. Steam turbines. Two masts and one funnel. Completed on January 31, 1922. Service: Japan-Europe, via Suez Canal. Passengers: 175. Sunk on July 7, 1942. Sister ships: **Hakozaki, Hakone Maru,** and **Hakusan Maru.**

Hawarden Castle   (1883)   Castle Line (British).
Built by John Elder & Co., Glasgow, Scotland. Tonnage: 4,380. Dimensions: 380′ x 48′. Single-screw, 14 knots. Compound engines. Two masts and one funnel. Re-engined with triple expansions in 1891. Launched by Mrs. Gladstone in January 1883. She became a very popular passenger liner. Service: England-South Africa. Sold to Booth Line for their Liverpool-Para and Manaos service. Renamed: **Cyril.** Sunk in collision with the **Anselm** in the Amazon, September 5, 1905. Sister ships: **Norham Castle** and **Roslin Castle.**

Hector   (1924)   Blue Funnel Line (British).
Built by Scott's Shipbuilding & Engineering Co., Greenock, Scotland. Tonnage: 11,198. Dimensions: 498′ x 62′. Twin-screw, 15 knots. Steam turbines. Two masts and one funnel. Service: Liverpool-Far East, via Suez Canal. Passengers:

190 passengers. Crew: 80. Bombed and sunk in Colombo Harbor, April 5, 1942. Refloated in 1946, but was broken up for scrap. Sister ships: **Antenor, Patroclus** and **Sarpedon.**

Helouan   (1912)   Lloyd Triestino (Italian).
Built by Lloyd Austriaco, Trieste, Austria. Tonnage: 7,367. Dimensions: 442' x 53'. Twin-screw, 18 knots. Quadruple expansion engines. 10,000 I.H.P. Two masts and two funnels. Passengers: 150 first, 80 second, 60 third. Destroyed by fire in 1937. Sister ships: **Gablonz** and **Wien.** Note: Originally built and operated by Lloyd Austriaco.

Henny Woermann   (1911)   Woermann Line (German).
Built by Reiherstieg Schiffsw., Hamburg, Germany. Tonnage: 6,062. Dimensions: 393' x 52'. Single-screw, 13 knots. Quadruple expansion engines. Two masts and one funnel. Renamed: **Uberaba.**

*Henri Poincare   (1952)   Chargeurs Reunis (French).
Built by Chantiers & Ateliers de St. Nazaire (Penhoet), St. Nazaire, France. Tonnage: 11,965. Dimensions: 515' x 64' (536' o.l.). Twin-screw, 17 knots. Motorship. Two masts and one funnel. Passengers: 91 first, 52 second, 398 third. Renamed: **Galileo Ferraris** (1957) Italian. Sister ships: **Edouard Branly** and **Clement Ader.**

Herefordshire   (1905)   Bibby Line (British).
Built by Harland & Wolff, Ltd., Belfast, Ireland. Tonnage: 7,217. Dimensions: 452' x 54'. Twin-screw, 15 knots. Quadruple expansion engines. Four masts and one funnel. Passengers: 200 first class. Service: England-Rangoon. Scrapped in 1933.

Herminius   (1911)   Aberdeen Line (British).
Built by Workman, Clark & Co., Belfast, Ireland. Tonnage: 9,930. Dimensions: 477' x 63'. Twin-screw, 13 knots. Triple expansion engines. Two masts and one funnel. Renamed: **Waimana** (1932). Scrapped in 1952. Ex-**Waimana.**

Herzog   (1896)   Deutsche Ost Afrika Line.
Built by Blohm & Voss, Hamburg, Germany. Tonnage: 4,946. Dimensions: 401' x 47'. Twin-screw, 12 knots. Triple expansion engines. Two masts and one funnel. Service: Germany-Africa. Renamed: **Beira** (Portuguese). Carried mails between Lisbon and Mozambique, via Capetown.

*Hessenstein   (1954)   North German Lloyd.
Built by Bremer Vulkan, Vegesack, Germany. Tonnage: 8,929. Dimensions: 537' (o.l.) x 63'. Single-screw, 16½ knots. Motorship. Single mast and one funnel. Passengers: 86 first class. Service: Europe-Far East. Sister ships: **Bayernstein** and **Schwabenstein.**

Hilda Woermann   (1914)   Woermann Line (British).
Built by Reiherstieg Schiffsw., Hamburg, Germany. Tonnage: 9,300. Dimensions: 426' x 55' (441' o.l.). Twin-screw, 14 knots. Quadruple expansion engines. Two masts and one funnel. Built for Germany-African trade. Renamed: (a) **Wahehe,** (b) **Marella,** (c) **Captain Marcos,** (d) **Liguria** (1950), (e) **Corsica** (1951). Scrapped in Belgium, 1954.

Himalaya   (1853)   P. & O. Line (British).
Built by Mare's shipyard, Blackwall, England. Tonnage: 3,438. Dimensions: 340' x 46' (372' o.l.). Single-screw, 13 knots. Horizontal direct-acting trunk piston engines. Three masts and one funnel. Iron hull. Clipper bow. Her main mast was about 150 feet high from weather deck. Launched, May 24, 1853. Passengers: 200 first class. Crew: 213. During trials averaged 13.7 knots over the measured mile. Maiden voyage: Southampton-Alexandria, January 20, 1854. The largest ship built to date. Vessel was later sold to British Government. Converted to a coal hulk in 1920. Blasted by German bombs during the "blitz" in 1940.

Himalaya   (1892)   P. & O. Line (British).
Built by Caird & Co., Greenock, Scotland. Tonnage: 6,898. Dimensions: 465' x 52'. Single-screw, 17½ knots. Triple expansion engines. 10,000 I.H.P. Four masts and two funnels. Steel hull. Built for the England-Australia service, via Suez Canal. She had a load draft of 26 feet, which was at that time about the limit allowed for the Suez Canal. She broke the speed record from England to Australia in 1893, by making the voyage in 26½ days. Accommodation for 251 first and 74 second class. Broken up for scrap in 1922. Sister ship: **Australia.**

Himalaya   (1902)   Messageries Maritimes (French).
Built by Messageries Maritimes, La Ciotat, France. Tonnage: 5,620. Dimensions: 427' x 47'. Twin-screw, 13 knots. Triple expansion engines. Service: France-Far East. Torpedoed and sunk in the Mediterranean, June 22, 1917.

*Himalaya   (1949)   P. & O. Line (British).
   Built by Vickers-Armstrongs, Ltd., Barrow, England.
   Tonnage: 27,955. Dimensions: 681' x 90' (708' o.l.). Twin-
   screw, 22 knots. Six steam turbines. Single mast and one
   funnel. Note: A Thornycroft type funnel was installed in
   1953. Attained a speed of 25.13 knots during her trials in
   August 1949. Maiden voyage: England-Australia, October
   1949. Passengers: 743 first and 483 tourist. The first P. &
   O. liner to enter the new extended trans-Pacific service of
   the P. & O.-Orient Lines in 1958. She returned to London
   on June 2, 1958, having completed a voyage of 40,111 miles,
   the longest in the history of the P. & O. Line.

Hindostan   (1842)   P. & O. Line (British).
   Built in Great Britain. Tonnage: 2,018. Dimensions:
   217' x 35' (240' o.l.). Paddle-wheels. Direct acting engines.
   Three masts and two funnels. Wooden hull. First P. & O.
   steamer in China service. Commenced her maiden voyage
   from Southampton on September 24, 1842. Sold in 1856.

Hirano Maru   (1908)   N. Y. K. Line (Japanese).
   Built by Mitsubishi Dockyard & Engine Works, Nagasaki,
   Japan. Tonnage: 8,520. Dimensions: 473' x 54'. Twin-
   screw, 16 knots. Triple expansion engines. Two masts and
   one funnel. Completed, December 3, 1908. Service: Japan-
   Europe, via Suez Canal. Passengers: 83 first, 32 second, 12
   third. Torpedoed and sunk by German submarine 60 miles
   off the Irish coast, October 4, 1918. The second torpedo
   struck her in the middle of the boiler room. Within seven
   minutes she nosedived and went to the bottom. The passengers and crew who were not caught like rats in a trap
   jumped into the sea. An American destroyer came to the
   rescue, but relatively few were saved. Sister ships: **Atsuta
   Maru, Kamo Maru, Kitano Maru, Mishima Maru**
   and **Miyazaki Maru.**

Hitachi Maru   (1898)   N. Y. K. Line (Japanese).
   Built by Mitsubishi Dockyard & Engine Works, Nagasaki,
   Japan. Tonnage: 6,172. Dimensions: 445' x 49'. Twin-screw,
   13 knots. Triple expansion engines. Single funnel. Service:
   Japan-Europe, via Suez Canal. Sunk by the Russians in the
   Russo-Japanese War.

Hobsons Bay   (1922)   Aberdeen & Commonwealth Line.
   Built by Vickers, Ltd., Barrow, England. Tonnage: 14,130.
   Dimensions: 530' x 68' (549' o.l.). Twin-screw, 16 knots.

Four steam turbines. Two masts and one funnel. Passengers: 680. Crew: 160. Service: London-Australia, via Suez Canal. Renamed: **Esperance Bay.** Sister ships: See **Jervis Bay.**

Hohenstaufen   (1874)   North German Lloyd.
Tonnage: 3,098.   Service: Germany-Australia, via Suez Canal. Note: See PART I for details.

Hohenzollern   (1873)   North German Lloyd.
Tonnage: 3,288.   Service: Germany-Australia, via Suez Canal. Note: See PART I for details.

Hohenzollern   (1889)   North German Lloyd.
Tonnage: 6,668.   Service: Germany-Australia, via Suez Canal. Note: See PART I for details.

Horai Maru   (1912)   Osaka Line (Japanese).
Built by Wm. Denny & Bros., Ltd., Dumbarton, Scotland. Tonnage: 9,204. Dimensions: 451' x 60'. Twin-screw, 15 knots. Quadruple expansion engines. Two masts and two funnels. Sunk by aircraft, January 1, 1942. Ex-**Pays de Waes,** ex-**Indarro.**

Hororata   (1914)   New Zealand Shipping Co.
Built by Wm. Denny & Bros., Ltd., Dumbarton, Scotland. Tonnage: 11,243. Dimensions: 511' x 64'. Twin-screw, 14 knots. Quadruple expansion engines. Two masts and one funnel. Renamed: **Waroonga** (1939).

Husimi Maru   (1914)   N. Y. K. Line (Japanese).
Tonnage: 10,936. Service: Japan-Europe, via Suez Canal. Note: See PART II for details listed under her former name **Fushimi Maru.**

Huzi Maru   (1937)   N. Y. K. Line (Japanese).
Built by Mitsubishi Jukogyo K.K., Nagasaki, Japan. Tonnage: 9,138. Dimensions: 452' x 60'. Twin-screw, 18 knots. Steam turbines. Two masts and one funnel. Sunk by submarine, October 27, 1943. Ex-**Fuji Maru** (1938).

Iberia   (1835)   P. & O. Line (British).
Built at Limehouse, London, England.   Tonnage: 516. Dimensions: 155' x 24'.   Paddle-wheels.   Direct acting engines. Three masts and one funnel. Clipper bow. Wooden hull. Note: A pioneer vessel of the P. & O. Line. It is reported that her passenger accommodation in that period was the finest afloat. Sold in 1856.

Iberia   (1873)   Orient Line (British).
  Tonnage: 4,689. This former South American passenger ship was transferred to the England-Australia service in 1880. Note: See PART III for details.

*Iberia   (1954)   P. & O. Line (British).
  Built by Harland & Wolff, Ltd., Belfast, Ireland. Tonnage: 29,614. Dimensions: 687' x 90' (719' o.l.). Twin-screw, 22 knots. Six steam turbines. Two masts and one funnel. Launched, January 21, 1954. During her trials made a speed of 24.9 knots. Passengers: 673 first and 733 tourist. Service originally between England and Australia. Now operated in the extended trans-Pacific service of the P & O-Orient Lines. Similar ships: **Arcadia** and **Himalaya.**

Iceland   (1871)   Castle Line (British).
  Built by J. & G. Thomson, Glasgow, Scotland. Tonnage: 1,474. Dimensions: 251' x 31'. Single-screw. Compound engines. Iron hull. Made the first sailing to South Africa for Donald Currie's Castle Line in 1872. She was built and operated by Leith, Hull & Hamburg Steam Packet Co. She was returned to the North Sea service in 1873. Wrecked off the coast of Holland in December 1876.

Imperator   (1886)   Lloyd Austriaco.
  Built by Lloyd Austro-Ungarico, Trieste, Austria. Tonnage: 4,213. Dimensions: 390' x 45'. Single-screw, 14 knots. Quadruple expansion engines. Three masts and one funnel. Steel hull. Scrapped in 1910.

Imperatrix   (1888)   Lloyd Austriaco.
  Built by Lloyd Austro-Ungarico, Trieste, Austria. Tonnage: 4,194. Dimensions: 390' x 45'. Single-screw, 14 knots. Triple expansion engines. Three masts and one funnel. Wrecked on February 24, 1907, with the loss of 137 lives.

*Imperio   (1948)   Companhia Colonial de Navegacao.
  Built by John Brown & Co., Clydebank, Glasgow, Scotland. Tonnage: 13,186. Dimensions: 508' x 68' (532' o.l.). Twin-screw, 17 knots. Steam turbines. Two masts and one funnel. Passengers: 635. Service: Portugal-West and East Africa. Sister ship: **Patria.**

Inaha Maru   (1897)   N. Y. K. Line (Japanese).
  Built by D. & W. Henderson & Co., Glasgow, Scotland. Tonnage: 6,189. Dimensions: 445' x 49'. Twin-screw, 13 knots. Triple expansion engines. Two masts and one funnel. Passengers: 35 first, 20 second, 156 third. Service: Japan-

Europe.   No longer in commission, 1934.   Sister ships: **Bingo Maru** and **Shinano Maru.**

Inanda   (1904)   Rennie's Aberdeen Line (British).
Built by Hall, Russell & Co., Aberdeen, Scotland. Tonnage: 4,233.   Dimensions: 370' x 46'.   Single-screw, 14 knots. Triple expansion engines. 3,500 I.H.P. Two masts and one funnel. In service to South Africa. Passengers: 64 first and 50 second. Sold to Ellerman's Wilson Line in 1920. Renamed **Orlando.** Scrapped in 1932.

India   (1868)   Anchor Line (British).
Tonnage: 2,477. In Glasgow-Bombay service. Note: See PART I for details.

India   (1896)   P. & O. Line (British).
Built by Caird & Co., Greenock, Scotland. Tonnage: 7,940. Dimensions: 499' x 54'.   Single-screw, 18 knots.   Triple expansion engines. Two masts and two funnels. Largest ship to be built by Caird & Company to that date. Service: England-Australia, via Suez Canal. Passengers: 315 first and 152 second. Blown up in the North Sea, August 11, 1915, while serving as a British auxiliary cruiser. Sister ships: **Arabia, China, Egypt** and **Persia.**

*India   (1951)   Companhia Nacional de Navegacao.
Built by Bartram & Sons, Ltd., Sunderland, England. Tonnage: 7,631. Dimensions: 414' x 59' (431' o.l.). Twin-screw, 14½ knots. Motorship. Two masts and one funnel. Service: Portugal-India-Far East, via Suez Canal. Passengers: 72 first, 29 third and 298 steerage class. Sister ship: **Timor.**

Indrapoera   (1925)   Rotterdam Lloyd (Dutch).
Built by Kon. Maats. de Schelde, Flushing, Netherlands. Tonnage: 10,772. Dimensions: 479' x 60'. Twin-screw, 15½ knots. Motorship. Two masts and one funnel. Lengthened in 1932 and again in 1934. New dimensions: 487' (507' o.l.). Tonnage: 10,825. Service: Netherlands and Dutch East Indies. Passengers: 450. Survived World War II. Converted to cargo-passenger ship in 1947. Renamed: **Assuncion** (1956), (b) **Bianca C** (1957), (c) **Melansien** (1958). Similar ship: **Sibajak.**

Indus   (1897)   Messageries Maritimes.
Built by Messageries Maritimes, La Ciotat, France. Tonnage: 6,357. Dimensions: 446' x 50'. Twin-screw, 17 knots. Triple expansion engines. Three masts and two funnels.

Later reduced to two masts. Launched, April 29, 1897. Service: France-Far East. Transferred to South American service in 1904. Renamed: **Magellan** (1904). Torpedoed and sunk in December 1916. Sister ships: **Annam, Laos** and **Tonkin.**

*Infanta Dom Henrique (1961) Companhia Colonial de Navegacao (Portuguese).
Built by Cockerill-Ougree, Hoboken, Belgium. Tonnage: 23,000. Dimensions: 641′ x 81′. Twin-screw, 22 knots. Steam turbines. Launched, April 29, 1960. Service: Portugal-West and East Africa. Passengers: 150 first, 850 tourist.

Inkosi (1902) Rennie's Aberdeen Line (British).
Built by Hall, Russell & Co., Aberdeen, Scotland. Tonnage: 3,576. Dimensions: 350′ x 43′. Single-screw, 14 knots. 3,000 I.H.P. Two masts and one funnel. South African service. Passengers: 52 first and 36 second. Sunk by submarine off Ireland in 1918.

Insizwa (1899) Rennie's Aberdeen Line (British).
Built by Hall, Russell & Co., Aberdeen, Scotland. Tonnage: 2,984. Dimensions: 330′ x 41′. Single-screw, 14 knots. Triple expansion engines. Two masts and one funnel. Steel hull. Service: South Africa. Passengers: 40 first and 20 second. Renamed: **Tolemaide.** Scrapped in Italy, 1929.

Insulinde (1914) Rotterdam Lloyd (Dutch).
Built by Kon. Maats. de Schelde, Flushing, Netherlands. Tonnage: 9,615. Dimensions: 478′ x 57′. Twin-screw, 15½ knots. Triple expansion engines. Two masts and one funnel. Service: Netherlands-Dutch East Indies. Renamed: **Banfora** (1933). Scrapped in 1957.

Intaba (1910) Rennie's Aberdeen Line (British).
Built by Hall, Russell & Co., Aberdeen, Scotland. Tonnage: 4,832. Dimensions: 386′ x 48′. Single-screw, 14 knots. 4,000 I.H.P. Two masts and one funnel. Note: Last vessel built for Rennie's Aberdeen Line. Passengers: 114 first class. Employed in the South African service until, soon after the outbreak of the First World War. Taken over by British Government for transport duties. Afterwards was transferred to the Harrison Line. Vessel sold to Nemazee of Hongkong in 1927. Renamed: **Englestan.**

Ionic (1882) Shaw, Savill & Albion Co.
Built by Harland & Wolff, Ltd., Belfast, Ireland. Tonnage: 4,748. Dimensions: 427′ x 44′. Single-screw, 14 knots.

Compound engines. Four masts and one funnel. Steel hull. This White Star Line was built for the New Zealand trade. She entered the joint service with Shaw, Savill & Albion Company in 1884. Passengers: 70 first class. Service: England-New Zealand, via Cape of Good Hope outward, and on the home run, via Cape Horn. Quadruple expansion engines installed in 1894, after a mishap to her shaft the previous year. Sold to the Aberdeen Line in 1900. Renamed: **Sophocles.** Scrapped in 1908. Sister ship: **Doric.**

Ionic   (1902)   White Star Line (British).
Tonnage: 12,352. Operated jointly with the management of Shaw, Savill & Albion Company between England and New Zealand. Passengers: 66 first, 81 second, 500 third class. Note: See PART II for details.

Iraouaddy   (1872)   Messageries Maritimes.
Built by Messageries Maritimes, La Ciotat, France. Tonnage: 3,785. Dimensions: 398' x 39'. Single-screw, 13 knots. Three masts and one funnel. Iron hull. Launched, December 1, 1872. Service: France-Far East. Converted to emigrant ship in 1906 for their South American service. Renamed: **Esmeralda.** Scrapped in Italy, 1908. Sister ship: **Anadyr.**

Jadotville   (1956)   Compagnie Maritime Belge.
Built by Chantiers de St. Nazaire, Penhoet, St. Nazaire, France. Tonnage: 13,724. Dimensions: 557' x 70' (583' o.l.). Single-screw, 16½ knots. Two steam turbines. Two masts and one funnel. Launched in November 1955. Passengers: 300 single class. Crew: 200. Service: Antwerp-Congo and Angola. Renamed: **Chitral** (1961). Sister ship: **Baudoiunville.** Both liners sold to P. & O. Line in 1961.

*Jagersfontein   (1934)   United Netherlands Line.
Built by N. V. Nederlandsche Schps. Maats., Amsterdam, Netherlands. Tonnage: 10,083. Dimensions: 457' x 63' (487' o.l.). Twin-screw, 17 knots. Motorship. Two masts and one funnel. Service: Netherlands-South Africa. Passengers: 93. Crew: 80. Became a war casualty, June 26, 1942. Sister ship: **Bloemfontein.**

Jagersfontein   (1948)   Holland-Africa Line.
Built by F. Schichau, Danzig, Germany. Tonnage: 10,574. Dimensions: 499' x 62' (527' o.l.). Twin-screw, 17 knots. Motorship. Two masts and one funnel. Launched in 1940. When nearly completed was seized by the Germans. Recon-

ditioned after the war for her owners African service. Commenced her regular service between the Netherlands and South Africa in March 1950. Passengers: 160. Ex-**Elandsfontein** (1948), ex-**Rielfontein** (1940). Sister ship: **Oranjefontein.**

Jan Pieterszoon Coen (1915)   Nederland Royal Mail Line. Built by Nederlandsche Schps. Maats., Amsterdam, Netherlands. Tonnage: 11,692. Dimensions: 503′ x 60′. Twin-screw, 15 knots. Triple expansion engines. Two masts and two funnels. Service: Between the Netherlands and the Dutch East Indies, via Suez Canal. Passengers: 390. Scrapped in 1940. Similar ship: **Johan de Witt.**

Jean Laborde (1930)   Messageries Maritimes (French). Built by Soc. Provencale de Construction Nav., La Ciotat, France. Tonnage: 11,414. Dimensions: 496′ x 61′. Twin-screw, 17 knots. Motorship. Two masts and two square funnels. Launched in September 1929. Service: France-Far East, via Suez Canal. Passengers: 300. Refitted with new engines and lengthened 27 feet in 1936. Speed increased to 19 knots. Scuttled by Germans at Marseilles in August 1944. Refloated and broken up for scrap in 1946. Sister ship: **Marechal Joffre.**

*****Jean Laborde** (1952)   Messageries Maritimes (French). Built by Forges & Chantiers de la Gironde, Bordeaux, France. Tonnage: 10,944. Dimensions: 459′ x 64′ (492′ o.l.). Twin-screw, 17 knots. Motorship. Two masts and one funnel. Service: Marseilles-Madagascar. Passengers: 88 first, 112 tourist, 40 third. Sister ships: **Ferdinand de Lesseps, La Bourdonnais** and **Pierre Loti.**

*****Jean Mermoz** (1957)   Fraissinet Line (French). Built by Chantiers de l' Atlantique, St. Nazaire, France. Tonnage: 12,460. Dimensions: 527′ x 65′ (527′ o.l.). Twin-screw, 16 knots. Motorship. Two masts and one funnel. Service: France-North and West Africa. Passengers: 142 first, 140 second, 110 third class. Sister ship: **General Mangin.** These very attractive passenger liners have space for 470 troops.

Jervis Bay (1922)   Aberdeen & Commonwealth Line. Built by Vickers, Ltd., Barrow, England. Tonnage: 14,129. Dimensions: 530′ x 68′ (548′ o.l.).   Twin-screw, 16 knots. Four steam turbines. Two masts and one funnel. Service: London-Australia, via Suez Canal. Passengers: 680. Crew:

160. Sunk by gunfire of German warship in the North
Atlantic, November 5, 1940. Sister ships: **Esperance Bay,
Hobson Bay, Largs Bay** and **Moreton Bay.**

Joao Belo (1905) Companhia de Navegacao Colonial.
Built by Blohm & Voss, Hamburg, Germany. Tonnage:
6,365. Dimensions: 411' x 50'. Twin-screw, 13 knots.
Triple expansion engines. Two masts and one funnel.
Service: Portugal-South and East Africa. Ex-**City of
Genoa**, ex-**Windhuk**, ex-**Gertrud Woermann.**

Johan de Witt (1920) Nederland Royal Mail Line.
Built by Nederlandsche Schps. Maats., Amsterdam, Netherlands. Tonnage: 10,519. Dimensions: 482' x 59'. Twin-
screw, 15 knots. Triple expansion engines. Two masts and
two funnels. Lengthened by 23 feet and Maier type bow
fitted in 1933. Service: Netherlands-Dutch East Indies, via
Suez Canal. Passengers: 300. Crew: 226. Renamed:
Neptunia (1948). Damaged by grounding in 1959. Subsequently broken up for scrap.

*****Johan van Oldenbarnevelt** (1930) Nederland Royal Mail
Line.
Built by Nederlandsche Schps. Maats., Amsterdam, Nether-
lands. Tonnage: 19,429. Dimensions: 586' x 74' (605' o.l.).
Twin-screw, 18 knots. Motorship. Two masts and two fun-
nels. Service: Netherlands-Dutch East Indies, via Suez
Canal. Passengers: 680. Placed in round-the-world service,
via Panama Canal in 1958. See PART II. Sister ship:
Marnix van St. Aldegonde.

Johannesburg (1895) Bucknall Line (British).
Built by Armstrong, Mitchell & Co., Newcastle, England.
Tonnage: 4,444. Dimensions: 360' x 47'. Single-screw, 13
knots. Triple expansion engines. Two masts and one fun-
nel. In service to South Africa. Passengers: 90 first class.
Sister ships: **Buluwayo** and **Fort Salisbury.**

John Elder (1870) Orient Line (British).
Tonnage: 4,151. Transferred from the South American
service of Pacific Steam Navigation Company in 1880.
See PART III for details.

Kaiser-i-Hind (1878) P. & O. Line (British).
Built by Caird & Co., Greenock, Scotland. Tonnage: 4,008.
Dimensions: 400' x 42'. Single-screw, 15 knots. Compound
engines. Three masts and one funnel. Iron hull. An out-

standing passenger ship for that era. In service to India.
Passengers: 176 first and 64 second class. Scrapped in India,
1897.

Kaiser-i-Hind   (1914)   P. & O. Line (British).
Built by Caird & Co., Greenock, Scotland. Tonnage: 11,430.
Dimensions: 520' x 61'. Twin-screw, 17 knots. Quadruple
expansion engines. Two masts and two funnels. Service:
England-Bombay. Able to average a speed of 18½ knots.
Made a record run from Plymouth, England to Bombay
of 17 days, 20 hours, 52 minutes. Passengers: 315 first and
233 second. Scrapped in 1938.

Kaiser Wilhelm II   (1889)   North German Lloyd.
Tonnage: 6,990. Services: (a) Bremen-Australia, via Suez
Canal, (b) North Atlantic. Note: See PART I for details.

Kalyan   (1915)   P. & O. Line (British).
Built by Cammell, Laird & Co., Birkenhead, England.
Tonnage: 9,144. Dimensions: 480' x 58'. Twin-screw, 14
knots. Quadruple expansion engines. Two masts and one
funnel. Scrapped in 1932. The P. & O. "K" class ships were:
Khiva, **Khyber**, **Karmala**, **Kashgar** and **Kashmir**.
Service: England-Calcutta and Far East.

Kamakura Maru   (1897)   N. Y. K. Line (Japanese).
Built by Workman, Clark & Co., Belfast, Ireland. Tonnage:
6,126. Dimensions: 445' x 49'. Twin-screw, 14 knots. Triple
expansion engines. Four masts and one funnel. Passengers:
29 first, 20 second, 98 third. Service: Japan-Europe.

Kamo Maru   (1908)   N. Y. K. Line (Japanese).
Built by Mitsubishi Dockyard, Nagasaki, Japan. Tonnage:
8,524. Dimensions: 464' x 54'. Twin-screw, 15½ knots.
Triple expansion engines. 8,500 I.H.P. Two masts and one
funnel. Completed, December 8, 1908. Built for Japan-
European service, via Suez Canal. Passengers: 83 first, 32
second, 12 third. Transferred to trans-Pacific service in
September 1917, because of First World War. Resumed
regular Japan-Europe sailings in 1922. Torpedoed and sunk,
July 3, 1944. Sister ships: **Atsuta Maru, Hirano Maru,
Kitano Maru** and **Miyazaki Maru**.

*Kampala   (1947)   British India Steam Navigation Co.
Built by Alexander Stephen & Sons, Ltd., Glasgow, Scotland.
Tonnage: 10,304. Dimensions: 490' x 66' (507' o.l.). Twin-
screw, 16 knots. Six steam turbines. Two masts and one
funnel. Launched, December 10, 1946. Service: Bombay-

East and South Africa. Passengers: 60 first, 180 second, 800 third. Sister ship: **Karanja.**

Kanagawa Maru   (1896)   N. Y. K. Line (Japanese).
Tonnage: 6,151. Transferred from Japan-European route to the trans-Pacific service in 1904. Note: See PART II for details.

Kanzler   (1892)   Deutsche Ost-Afrika Line.
Built by Blohm & Voss, Hamburg, Germany. Tonnage: 3,136. Dimensions: 321' x 39'. Single-screw, 12 knots. Triple expansion engines. Two masts and one funnel. Passengers: 40 first, 32 second, 42 third. Service: Germany-Africa. Vessel sold to Khandwani of Bombay, India, in 1913.

Karagola   (1917)   British India Steam Navigation Co.
Built by Swan, Hunter & Wigham Richardson, Ltd., Newcastle, England. Tonnage: 7,053. Dimensions: 425' x 55'. Twin-screw, 16 knots. Triple expansion engines. Two masts and one funnel. Passengers: 110. Out of fleet in 1948. Sister ships: **Karapara, Karoa** and **Khandalla.**

Karamea   (1899)   Shaw, Savill & Albion Co.
Built by Hawthorn, Leslie & Co., Newcastle, England. Tonnage: 5,564. Dimensions: 420' x 54'. Single-screw, 12 knots. Triple expansion engines. 4,000 I.H.P. Basically cargo ship, but did have accommodation for 24 first class and 200 third class passengers. Service: England-New Zealand. Renamed: **Mongioia** (1925) Alta Italia. Scrapped in 1929.

Karanja   (1931)   British India Steam Navigation Co.
Built by Alexander Stephen & Sons, Ltd., Glasgow, Scotland. Tonnage: 471' x 64' (486' o.l.). Twin-screw, 18 knots. Six steam turbines. Two masts and one funnel. Passengers: 250. In East African service. Sunk by enemy action during the North African invasion, November 1942. Sister ship: **Kenya.**

*Karanja   (1948)   British India Steam Navigation Co.
Built by Alexander Stephen & Sons, Ltd., Glasgow, Scotland. Tonnage: 10,294. Dimensions: 490' x 66' (507' o.l.). Twin-screw, 16 knots. Six steam turbines. Two masts and one funnel. Launched, March 10, 1948. Service: Bombay-East and South Africa. Passengers: 60 first, 180 second, 800 third. Sister ship: **Kampala.**

Karapara   (1915)   British India Steam Navigation Co.
Built by Swan, Hunter & Wigham Richardson, Ltd., Newcastle, England. Tonnage: 7,117. Dimensions: 425' x 55'.

Twin-screw, 16 knots. Triple expansion engines. Two masts and one funnel. Passengers: 110. Scrapped in 1950. Sister ships: **Karagola, Karoa** and **Khandalla.**

Karlsruhe   (1889)   North German Lloyd.
Tonnage: 5,057. Services: Interchangeable between North Atlantic, South American and Australian routes. Note: See PART I for details.

Karmala   (1914)   P. & O. Line (British).
Built by Cammell, Laird & Co., Birkenhead, England. Tonnage: 8,947. Dimensions: 480′ x 58′. Twin-screw, 14½ knots. Quadruple expansion engines. Two masts and one funnel. Service: England-India and Far East. Scrapped in 1932. "K" class ships were: **Kalyan, Khiva, Khyber, Kashgar** and **Kashmir.**

Karoa   (1915)   British India Steam Navigation Co.
Built by Swan, Hunter & Wigham Richardson, Ltd., Newcastle, England. Tonnage: 7,009. Dimensions: 425′ x 55′. Twin-screw, 16 knots. Triple expansion engines. Two masts and one funnel. Passengers: 110. Scrapped in 1950. Sister ships: **Karagola, Karapara** and **Khandalla.**

Kashgar   (1914)   P. & O. Line (British).
Built by Caird & Co., Greenock, Scotland. Tonnage: 8,840. Dimensions: 479′ x 58′. Twin-screw, 14½ knots. Quadruple expansion engines. Two masts and one funnel. Scrapped in 1932. The "K" class ships were: **Kalyan, Karmala, Kashmir, Khiva** and **Khyber.**

Kashima Maru   (1913)   N. Y. K. Line (Japanese).
Tonnage: 10,559. Built for the Japan-European service, via Suez Canal. Note: See PART II for details.

Kashmir   (1915)   P. & O. Line (British).
Built by Caird & Co., Greenock, Scotland. Tonnage: 8,985. Dimensions: 480′ x 58′. Twin-screw, 14½ knots. Quadruple expansion engines. Two masts and one funnel. Service: England-India and Far East. Scrapped in 1932. The "K" class ships: **Kalyan, Karmala, Kashgar, Khiva** and **Khyber.**

Katori Maru   (1913)   N. Y. K. Line (Japanese).
Tonnage: 10,526. Transferred from Japan-European service to trans-Pacific service in September 1917. Resumed European sailings in 1922. Note: See PART II for details.

Kawachi Maru (1897) N. Y. K. Line (Japanese).
Built by Napier, Shanks & Bell, Glasgow, Scotland. Tonnage: 6,101. Dimensions: 445′ x 49′. Twin-screw, 13 knots. Triple expansion engines. Four masts and one funnel. Service: Japan-Europe. Passengers: 29 first, 20 second, 94 third. Scrapped in 1933.

Kawi (1907) Rotterdam Lloyd (Dutch).
Built by Kon. Maats. de Schelde, Flushing, Netherlands. Tonnage: 4,871. Dimensions: 394′ x 47′. Single-screw, 14 knots. Triple expansion engines. Two masts and one funnel. Renamed: **Izmir.**

Kemmendine (1924) Henderson Line (British).
Built by Wm. Denny & Bros., Ltd., Dumbarton, Scotland. Tonnage: 7,837. Dimensions: 453′ x 59′. Single-screw, 14 knots. Triple expansion engines. Two masts and one funnel. Service: Glasgow-Liverpool-Rangoon. Passengers: 150 first. Crew: 140. Sunk by enemy raider, July 13, 1940. Sister ships: **Amarapoora, Pegu, Sagaing** and **Yoma.**

Kenilworth Castle (1904) Union-Castle Line.
Built by Harland & Wolff, Ltd., Belfast, Ireland. Tonnage: 12,975. Dimensions: 570′ x 64′ (590′ o.l.). Twin-screw, 17 knots. Quadruple expansion engines. Two masts and two funnels. Service: England-South Africa. Passengers: 240 first and 300 second class. Sold for scrap in 1936. Sister ship: **Armadale Castle.** The first two mail steamships ordered for their Capetown service after the merger of the Union-Castle Line.

Kenya (1930) British India Steam Navigation Co.
Built by Alexander Stephen & Sons, Ltd., Glasgow, Scotland. Tonnage: 9,890. Dimensions: 471′ x 64′ (487′ o.l.). Twin-screw, 18 knots. Steam turbines. Two masts and one funnel. Service: England-East Africa, via Suez Canal. Passengers: 250. Transferred to British Navy during World War II. Renamed: (a) **Karen** (1949), (b) **Kenya** (1949), (c) **Fairstone** (1949), (d) **Kenya** (1950), (e) **Keren** (1951), (f) **Castel Felice** (1952). Sister ship: **Karanja.**

*__Kenya__ (1947) British India Steam Navigation Co.
Built by Barclay, Curle & Co., Glasgow, Scotland. Tonnage: 14,434. Dimensions: 516′ x 71′ (539′ o.l.). Twin-screw, 16 knots. Six steam turbines. Two masts and one funnel. Passengers: 194 first and 103 tourist. Service: England-East Africa, via Suez. Sister ship: **Uganda.** Note: These

trim looking passenger liners are the largest that the British India Company have had built to date.

*Kenya Castle   (1952)   Union-Castle Line.
Built by Harland & Wolff, Ltd., Belfast, Ireland. Tonnage: 17,041. Dimensions: 556' x 74' (576' o.l.). Twin-screw, 17½ knots. Six steam turbines. Two masts and one funnel. Passengers: 526 cabin class. Service: England and around Africa trade. Sister ships: **Braemar Castle** and **Rhodesia Castle**.

Khandalla   (1923)   British India Steam Navigation Co.
Built by Swan, Hunter & Wigham Richardson, Ltd., Newcastle, England. Tonnage: 7,018. Dimensions: 425' x 55'. Twin-screw, 16 knots. Triple expansion engines. Two masts and one funnel. Passengers: 110. Sold to British shipbreakers in December 1951. Sister ships: **Karagola, Karapara** and **Karoa**.

Khiva   (1914)   P. & O. Line (British).
Built by Cammell, Laird & Co., Birkenhead, England. Tonnage: 9,135. Dimensions: 480' x 58'. Twin-screw, 14½ knots. Quadruple expansion engines. Two masts and one funnel. Scrapped in 1932. Ships of the "K" class. **Kalyan, Karmala, Kashmir, Khiva** and **Khyber**.

Khyber   (1914)   P. & O. Line (British).
Built by Cammell, Laird & Co., Birkenhead, England. Tonnage: 9,114. Dimensions: 480' x 58'. Twin-screw, 14 knots. Quadruple expansion engines. Two masts and one funnel. Service: England-India and Far East. Passengers: 75 first and 70 second class. Scrapped in 1932. Similar ships: See **Khiva**.

Kiautschou   (1900)   Hamburg-American Line.
Tonnage: 10,911. Built for the Germany-Far East service, via Suez Canal. Note: See PART I for details.

Kigoma   (1914)   Deutsche Ost Afrika Line.
Built by Reiherstieg Schiffsw., Hamburg, Germany. Tonnage: 8,156. Dimensions: 449' x 55'. Twin-screw, 15 knots. Quadruple expansion engines. Two masts and one funnel. The line's finest liner built to date. Completed her first voyage round Africa just prior to the First World War. Renamed: (a) **Algeria** (1921), (b) **Toledo** (1922).

Kildonan Castle   (1899)   Union-Castle Line.
Built by Fairfield Shipbuilding Co., Glasgow, Scotland.
Tonnage: 9,692. Dimensions: 515′ x 59′ (532′ o.l.). Twin-
screw, 17 knots. Quadruple expansion engines. 10,000 I.H.P.
Two masts and two funnels. Note: The last mail steamer
to be laid down for the Castle Line before the merger with
the Union Line. Launched, August 22, 1899. Before entering
service to South Africa, she was taken over by the British
Government for use as a transport during the Boer War.
Afterwards was returned to her builders to be fitted for
regular service. Passengers: 200 first and 230 second class.
Sold to Norwegian shipbreakers in 1931.   Sister ship:
Kinfauns Castle.

Kinfauns Castle   (1880)   Castle Line (British).
Built by John Elder & Co., Glasgow, Scotland. Tonnage:
3,507. Dimensions: 360′ x 43′. Single-screw, 13½ knots.
Compound engines. Two masts and one funnel. Launched
in November 1879. Note: One of the first liners to be constructed of steel. Sold to the Russian Volunteer Fleet in
1883. Renamed: (a) **Moskva,** (b) **Pruth.** Sunk by her own
crew in the Black Sea, October 29, 1914.   Sister ship:
Grantully Castle.

Kinfauns Castle   (1899)   Union-Castle Line.
Built by Fairfield Shipbuilding Co., Glasgow, Scotland.
Tonnage: 9,664. Dimensions: 515′ x 59′ (532′ o.l.). Twin-
screw, 17 knots. Quadruple expansion engines. Two masts
and two funnels. Launched in May 1899. First twin-screw
liner to be built for the Castle Line. Passengers: 250 first
and 100 second. Broken up by Dutch shipbreakers in 1927.
Sister ship: **Kildonan Castle.**

Kitano Maru   (1909)   N. Y. K. Line (Japanese).
Built by Mitsubishi Shipyard, Nagasaki, Japan. Tonnage:
8,512. Dimensions: 473′ x 54′. Twin-screw, 15 knots.
Triple expansion engines. 8,500 I.H.P. Two masts and one
funnel. Service: Japan-Europe. Passengers: 83 first, 32
second, 12 third. Became a World War II casualty, March
27, 1942. Sister ships: **Atsuta Maru, Hirano Maru,
Kamo Maru, Mishima Maru** and **Miyazaki Maru.**

Kleist   (1906)   North German Lloyd.
Tonnage: 8,959. Built for Far East and Australian service.
Note: See PART I for details.

Klipfontein   (1939)   Holland-Africa Line (Dutch).
Built by N. V. Maschinefabriek en Scheepswerf van P. Smit, Jr., Rotterdam, Netherlands. Tonnage: 10,544. Dimensions: 499′ x 62′ (527′ o.l.). Twin-screw, 17 knots. Motorship. Two masts and one funnel. Service: Netherlands-South and East Africa. Passengers: 150. Crew: 90. Lost off Mozambique in January 1953, with no loss of life. Sister ships: **Jagersfontein** and **Orangefontein.**

Koerber   (1904)   Austrian Lloyd (Lloyd Austriaco).
Built by Lloyd Austriaco, Trieste, Austria. Tonnage: 5,440. Dimensions: 399′ x 49′. Twin-screw, 14½ knots. Triple expansion engines. 5,000 I.H.P. Two masts and one funnel. Passengers: 84 first and 43 second class. Service: Trieste-South Africa. Renamed: (a) **Huntspill,** (b) **Asia.** Scrapped in 1933. Running mate: **Africa.**

Konig   (1896)   Deutsche Ost Afrika Line.
Built by Reiherstieg Schiffsw., Hamburg, Germany. Tonnage: 5,034. Dimensions: 401′ x 47′. Twin-screw, 12 knots. Reciprocating engines. Two masts and one funnel. Service: Germany-South Africa. Passengers: 80 first, 60 second, 50 third. Destroyed by British warships at Dar-es-Salaam in 1915.

Konig Albert   (1899)   North German Lloyd.
Tonnage: 10,484. Built for Bremen-Far East service. Also employed in the North Atlantic trade. Note: See PART I for details.

Konigin Luise   (1896)   North German Lloyd.
Tonnage: 10,711. Services: (a) Bremen-Australia, via Suez Canal; (b) North Atlantic. Note: See PART I for details.

Koning Willem I   (1898)   Nederland Royal Mail Line.
Built by Fijenoord Schps. & Wrk. Co., Rotterdam, Netherlands. Tonnage: 4,293. Dimensions: 392′ x 45′. Single-screw, 14 knots. Quadruple expansion engines. 3,700 I.H.P.

Koning Willem I   (1898)   Nederland Royal Mail Line.
Built by Kon. Maats. de Schelde, Flushing, Netherlands. Tonnage: 4,476. Dimensions: 384′ x 45′. Single-screw, 14 knots. Quadruple expansion engines. 3,700 I.H.P. Two masts and one funnel. Passengers: 69 first, 35 second class. Service: Netherlands-Far East. Renamed: **Abda** (1913) French. Scrapped in 1936. Similar ships: **Koning Willem II, Koning Willem III** and **Oranje.**

Koning Willem II   (1900)   Nederland Royal Mail Line.
Built by Fijenoord Schps. & Wrk., Rotterdam, Netherlands.
Tonnage: 4,293.   Dimensions: 392' x 45'.   Single-screw, 14
knots.   Quadruple expansion engines.   Two masts and one
funnel. Loaded draft of 23 feet. Maximum speed 15½ knots.
4,000 I.H.P.   Passengers: 70 first and 32 second class.   A
steady ship in bad weather. Service: Amsterdam-Southampton-Genoa-Port Said-Sabang-Batavia-Singapore-Cheribon-Samarang.   Renamed: **Doukkala** (1912) Paquet Line.
Scrapped in 1935. Similar ships: **Koning Willem I, Koning
Willem III** and **Oranje.**

Koning Willem III   (1900)   Nederland Royal Mail Line.
Built by Kon. Maats. de Schelde, Flushing, Netherlands.
Tonnage: 4,541.   Dimensions: 394' x 45'.   Single-screw, 14
knots.   Quadruple expansion engines.   Two masts and one
funnel. Passengers: 69 first and 35 second. Service: Amsterdam-Dutch Indies, via Suez Canal. Similar ships: **Koning
Willem I, Koning Willem II** and **Oranje.** Note: They
were popular liners in the service to the Dutch East Indies.

Koningin der Nederlanden   (1911)   Nederland Royal Mail
Line.
Built by Nederlandsche Schps. Maats., Amsterdam, Netherlands.   Tonnage: 8,225.   Dimensions: 455' x 55'.   Twin-screw, 15 knots. Quadruple expansion engines. Two masts
and one funnel. Passengers: 128 first, 88 second, 38 third.
Service: Amsterdam-Southampton-Sumatra-Java, via Suez
Canal. Scrapped in 1932. Sister ship: **Prinses Juliana.**

Koningin Emma   (1913)   Nederland Royal Mail Line.
Built by Maats. Fijenoord, Rotterdam, Netherlands.
Tonnage: 9,181.   Dimensions: 470' x 57'.   Twin-screw, 15
knots.   Quadruple expansion engines.   Two masts and one
funnel. Nice looking passenger liner. Service: Netherlands-Dutch East Indies. Sunk by mine off Thames estuary in
1915. Sister ship: **Prins der Nederlanden.**

Koningin Regentes   (1894)   Nederland Royal Mail Line.
Built by Caird & Co., Greenock, Scotland. Tonnage: 3,793.
Dimensions: 376' x 43'.   Single-screw, 14 knots.   Triple
expansion engines. Three masts and one funnel. Renamed:
Koweit (1911) Bombay & Persia Line.

Koningin Wilhelmina   (1896)   Nederland Royal Mail Line.
Built by Kon. Maats. de Schelde, Flushing, Netherlands.
Tonnage: 4,378.   Dimensions: 381' x 45'.   Single-screw, 14

knots. Quadruple expansion engines. Two masts and two funnels. Service: Amsterdam-Dutch East Indies, via Suez Canal. Renamed: **Chaouia** (1911). She became a loss during the First World War, 1918.

Kouang-Si (1904) Messageries Maritimes (French).
Built by Forges & Chantiers de la Mediterranee, Havre, France. Tonnage: 413' x 49'. Triple expansion engines. Two masts and one funnel. Service: France-Far East, via Suez Canal. Broken up by Italian shipbreakers, 1923.

Koutoubia (1931) Compagnie de Navigation Paquet.
Built by Forges & Chantiers de la Mediterranean, La Seyne, France. Tonnage: 8,790. Dimensions: 443' x 58'. Twin-screw, 16½ knots. Steam turbines. Two masts and two funnels. Note: Later altered to single mast and one funnel. Passengers: 136 first, 195 second, 204 third, 654 fourth. Service: France-Canary Islands-West Africa. Renamed: **Phooee** (1961) French. Sister ships: **Djenne, Marechal Lyautey** and **Nicolas Paquet.**

Kronprinz (1900) Deutsche Ost Afrika Line.
Built by Blohm & Voss, Hamburg, Germany. Tonnage: 5,689. Dimensions: 411' x 48'. Twin-screw, 13 knots. Triple expansion engines. 3,200 I.H.P. Two masts and one funnel. Service: Germany-South Africa. Passengers: 100 first, 76 second, 60 third. Renamed: **Quelimane.**

Kumano Maru (1901) N. Y. K. Line (Japanese).
Built by Fairfield Shipbuilding Co., Glasgow, Scotland. Tonnage: 5,076. Dimensions: 400' x 48'. Single-screw, 15 knots. Triple expansion engines. Two masts and one funnel. Launched in June 1901. A fine looking passenger ship. Passengers: 72 first, 24 second, 123 third. Service: Japan-Australia. No longer in commission, 1934.

Kurfurst (1901) Deutsche Ost Afrika Line.
Built by Reiherstieg Schiffsw., Hamburg, Germany. Tonnage: 5,655. Dimensions: 410' x 48'. Twin-screw, 13 knots. Triple expansion engines. Two masts and one funnel. Service: Hamburg-Africa. Wrecked in a fog near Sagres on the coast of Portugal, May 6, 1904, with no loss of life. Sister ships: **Burgermeister** and **Kronprinz.**

La Bourdonnais (1862) Messageries Maritimes.
Built by Messageries Maritimes, La Seyne, France. Tonnage: 1,582. Single-screw. Launched, September 20, 1862. Lengthened in 1872; tonnage increased 1,950. Triple expan-

sion engines installed. Sold to French shipbreakers in August 1896. Sister ship: **Meinam.**

La Bourdonnais   (1951)   Messageries Maritimes.
Built by Arsenal de Lorient, Lorient, France. Tonnage: 10,944. Dimensions: 459' x 64' (492' o.l.). Twin-screw, 17 knots. Motorship. Two masts and one funnel. Service: France-Mauritius. Passengers: 88 first, 112 tourist, 40 third. Sister ships: **Ferdinand de Lesseps, Jean Laborde** and **Pierre Loti.**

La Marseillaise   (1939)   Messageries Maritimes.
Built by Provencale de Construction Nav., La Ciotat, France. Tonnage: 17,321. Dimensions: 565' x 75'. Triple-screw, 20 knots. Motorship. Two masts and one funnel. Launched, June 10, 1944. Note: Scuttled at Port de Bouc by the Germans; raised and reconditioned after World War II. Commenced service under name of **La Marseillaise.** Service: France-Far East, via Suez Canal. Renamed: (a) **Arosa Sky** (1957), (b) **Bianca C** (1958). Destroyed by fire off St. George's, Grenada, October 22, 1961, while cruise trip to the West Indies. Launched as **Marechal Petain.**

La Seyne   (1873)   Messageries Maritimes (French).
Built by Forges & Chantiers de la Mediterranee, La Seyne, France. Tonnage: 312' x 38'. Single-screw, 15 knots. Compound engines. Two masts and one funnel. Iron hull. Refitted in 1888. Sunk in collision with the British steamship **Onda** in Singapore Straits in 1909   Ex-**Etoile du Chili.**

Lamartine   (1914)   Messageries Maritimes (French).
Built by Wm. Denny & Bros., Ltd., Dumbarton, Scotland. Tonnage: 5,152. Dimensions: 381' x 51'. Twin-screw, 13 knots. Triple expansion engines. Two masts and one funnel. Renamed: **Kai Dinh.** Sunk by United States aircraft in Along Bay, November 22, 1942. Ex-**Emperor Alexander II.**

Lancashire   (1889)   Bibby Line (British).
Built by Harland & Wolff, Ltd., Belfast, Ireland. Tonnage: 4,244. Dimensions: 400' x 45'. Single-screw, 14 knots. Triple expansion engines. Four masts and one funnel. Service: England-Rangoon. Renamed: (a) **Kina** (1905), (b) **Lituania** (1907). Sister ship: **Yorkshire.**

Lancashire   (1917)   Bibby Line (British).
Built by Harland & Wolff, Ltd., Belfast, Ireland. Tonnage: 9,445. Dimensions: 482' x 57'. Twin-screw, 15 knots. Quadruple expansion engines. Four masts and one funnel.

Service: England-Colombo-Rangoon.   Passengers: 320.
Tonnage increased to 10,331. Sold to British shipbreakers
in 1956.

Laos   (1896)   Messageries Maritimes (French).
Built by Messageries Maritimes, La Ciotat, France. Ton-
nage: 6,357. Dimensions: 442' x 50'. Twin-screw, 18 knots.
Triple expansion engines. Two masts and two funnels.
Service: France-Far East, via Suez Canal. Vessel trans-
ferred to South American service in 1904.   Renamed:
Amazone (1904). Scrapped in 1932. Sister ships: **Annam,
Indus** and **Tonkin.**

*Laos   (1952)   Messageries Maritimes (French).
Built by Chantiers Navals de la Ciotat, La Ciotat, France.
Tonnage: 12,080. Dimensions: 501' x 72' (532' o.l.). Twin-
screw, 22 knots. Steam turbines. Two masts and one funnel.
Launched, December 21, 1952. Service: Marseilles-Far East.
Passengers: 117 first, 110 tourist, 120 third. Sister ships:
Cambodge and **Viet-Nam.** Nice looking liners.

Largs Bay   (1921)   Aberdeen & Commonwealth Line.
Built by Wm. Beardmore & Co., Glasgow, Scotland. Tonnage: 14,143. Dimensions: 530' x 68' (549' o.l.).   Twin-
screw, 16 knots. Four steam turbines. Two masts and one
funnel. Service: England-Australia, via Suez Canal. Passengers: 680. Sold to British shipbreakers in 1957. Sister
ships: **Esperance Bay, Hobson Bay, Jervis Bay** and
Moreton Bay.

Lavoisier   (1948)   Chargeurs Reunis (French).
Tonnage: 11,965. Services: (a) France-South America, (b)
France-Far East. Note: See PART III for details.

Leasowe Castle   (1916)   Union-Castle Line (Management).
Built by Cammell, Laird & Co., Birkenhead, England.
Tonnage: 9,737. Dimensions: 488' x 58'. Twin-screw, 17
knots. Quadruple expansion engines. Two masts and two
funnels. Owner of vessel: British Government. She was
placed under the management of the Union-Castle Line.
Launched as the Greek liner **Vasilissa Sophia.** Completed
early in 1917. Employed as a troopship, until she was torpedoed and sunk in the Mediterranean, May 26, 1918, when
about 100 miles from Alexandria. There was a loss of 92 lives.

Leconte de Lisle   (1922)   Messageries Maritimes (French).
Built by Soc. Provencale de Construction Nav., La Ciotat,
France. Tonnage: 9,877. Dimensions: 452' x 61'.   Twin-

screw, 15 knots. Steam turbines. Two masts and two funnels. Launched, October 29, 1922. Passengers: 240. Mined
and sunk in Wakasa Bay, July 27, 1944. Raised and repaired before being returned to Messageries Maritimes.
Tonnage increased to: 9,988. Sold to Italian shipbreakers
in 1956. Note: Liner was captured by the Japanese in 1942
and renamed **Teiritu Maru.** Name reverted back to
Leconte de Lisle after the war.

Leicestershire (1909) Bibby Line (British).
Built by Harland & Wolff, Ltd., Belfast, Ireland. Tonnage:
8,059.   Dimensions: 467' x 54'.   Twin-screw, 15 knots.
Quadruple expansion engines. Four masts and one funnel.
Load draft of 27 feet. Commenced her maiden voyage in
September 1909.   Service: England-Ceylon-Burma, via
Suez Canal.   Passengers: 230 first class.   Renamed: (a)
British Exhibitor (1931), (b) **Zamzam** (1933). Served as
a pilgrim ship under the Misr Company ownership. Sunk
by the enemy raider **Tamesis** in the Atlantic during 1941,
with the loss of a number of lives. Sister ship: **Gloucestershire.**

*****Leicestershire** (1949) Bibby Line (British).
Built by Fairfield Shipbuilding Co., Glasgow, Scotland.
Tonnage: 8,908. Dimensions: 480' x 60' (498' o.l.). Single-
screw, 15 knots. Two steam turbines. Single mast and one
funnel. Service: England-Burma. Passengers: 76 first class.
Sister ship: **Warwickshire.**   The line's first post-war
passenger ships.

Leopoldville (1897) Compagnie Belge Maritime.
Built by Sir Raylton Dixon & Co., Middlesbrough, England.
Tonnage: 3,760.   Dimensions: 352' x 44'.   Single-screw, 13
knots. Triple expansion engines. Steel hull. Two masts and
one funnel.   Service: Antwerp-Congo.   Renamed: (a)
Sekondi (1901), (b) **Khosrou** (1910), (c) **Akashi Maru**
(1924).

Leopoldville (1908) Compagnie Belge Maritime.
Built by Harland & Wolff, Ltd., Belfast, Ireland. Tonnage:
6,327.   Dimensions: 400' x 53'.   Twin-screw, 14 knots.
Quadruple expansion engines. Two masts and one funnel.
Service: Antwerp-Congo. Renamed: **Abinsi.** Sister ship:
Bruxellesville.

Leopoldville (1929) Compagnie Belge Maritime.
Built by Soc. Anon. John Cockerill, Hoboken, Belgium.
Tonnage: 11,256. Dimensions: 479' x 62'. Twin-screw, 16½

knots. Quadruple expansion engines. Two masts and two funnels. Passengers: 360. Service: Antwerp-Belgian Congo. Largest Belgian liner built to date. Rebuilt and lengthened to 501 feet (11,509 tons) in 1935. Re-engined and speed increased to $17\frac{1}{2}$ knots. Converted to a single funnel. Served as a British troopship in World War II. Torpedoed and sunk off Cherbourg, December 24, 1944, with the loss of 764 lives. Similar ship: **Albertville.**

*Leopoldville (1948)   Compagnie Belge Maritime.
Built by John Cockerill, Hoboken, Belgium. Tonnage: 10,901. Dimensions: 479' x 64' (505' o.l.). Single-screw, $16\frac{1}{2}$ knots. Motorship. Two masts and one funnel. Service: Antwerp-Congo and Angola. Passengers: 207 single class. Sister ships: **Albertville, Charlesville, Elizabethville** and **Thysville.**

Leopolis (1909)   Lloyd Austriaco.
Built by Lloyd Austriaco, Trieste, Austria. Tonnage: 3,905. Dimensions: 356' x 42'. Single-screw, $14\frac{1}{2}$ knots. Triple expansion engines. Two masts and one funnel. Passengers: 68 first and 30 second. Taken over by Lloyd Triestino in 1918. Sister ship: **Graz.**

Liguria (1874)   Orient Line (British).
Tonnage: 4,677. Built for the Pacific Steam Navigation Co. Vessel was transferred to the newly organized Orient Line in 1880. Note: See PART III for details.

Lismore Castle (1891)   (a) Castle Line, (b) Union-Castle Line.
Built by Barclay, Curle & Co., Glasgow, Scotland. Tonnage: 4,046. Dimensions: 396' x 43'. Single-screw, $12\frac{1}{2}$ knots. Triple expansion engines. Two masts and one funnel. Intermediate type passenger ship. Service: England-South Africa. Passengers: 30 first, 40 second, 80 third. Taken over by builders, as part payment for new tonnage in 1904. Subsequently sold to Spanish Line. Renamed: (a) **Westmount,** (b) **C. Lopez-y-Lopez.** Scrapped at Savona in 1930. Sister ship: **Doune Castle.**

Llandaff Castle (1926)   Union-Castle Line.
Built by Workman, Clark & Co., Belfast, Ireland. Tonnage: 10,799. Dimensions: 471' x 61'. Twin-screw, 14 knots. Quadruple expansion engines. Two masts and one funnel. Service: Around Africa. Passengers: 390. Crew: 230. Torpedoed and sunk by enemy submarine off Zululand coast, November 30, 1942. Sister ship: **Llandovery Castle.**

Llandovery Castle   (1914)   Union-Castle Line.
Built by Barclay, Curle & Co., Glasgow, Scotland. Tonnage:
11,423.   Dimensions: 500′ x 63′.   Twin-screw, 15 knots.
Quadruple expansion engines. Two masts and one funnel.
Designed for the service between London and East Africa,
via the Suez Canal. Torpedoed and sunk off England, June
27, 1918, while on voyage from Halifax to Liverpool in the
role of hospital ship. She went down in less than ten minutes,
causing the loss of 234 lives. Sister ship: **Llanstephan
Castle.**

Llandovery Castle   (1925)   Union-Castle Line.
Built by Barclay, Curle & Co., Glasgow, Scotland. Tonnage:
10,640.   Dimensions: 471′ x 61′.   Twin-screw, 14 knots.
Quadruple expansion engines. Two masts and one funnel.
Employed as an intermediate steamer. Passengers: 390.
Sold to British shipbreakers late in 1952. Sister ship:
Llandaff Castle.

Llangibby Castle   (1929)   Union-Castle Line.
Built by Harland & Wolff, Ltd., Belfast, Ireland. Tonnage:
11,951.   Dimensions: 485′ x 66′.   Twin-screw, 14½ knots.
Motorship. Two masts and two funnels. Service: England-
Africa. Passengers: 450. Sold to British shipbreakers in 1954.

Llandstephan Castle   (1914)   Union-Castle Line.
Built by Fairfield Shipbuilding Co., Glasgow, Scotland.
Tonnage: 11,293. Dimensions: 500′ x 63′.   Twin-screw, 15
knots. Quadruple expansion engines. Two masts and one
funnel. Services: (a) East Africa, (b) Around Africa. Passengers: 440. Crew: 250. Sold to British shipbreakers in 1952.
Sister ship: **Llandovery Castle.**

Lombardia   (1920)   Lloyd Triestino (Italian).
Tonnage: 20,006. The Italian Government purchased this
liner from Germany in 1935, so as to serve as a troopship
during the Ethiopian invasion. Afterwards was used as a
unit in the Lloyd Triestino fleet. Note: See PART I for
details.

Lotus   (1898)   Messageries Maritimes (French).
Built by Messageries Maritimes, La Ciotat, France. Ton-
nage: 6,822. Dimensions: 446′ x 50′. Twin-screw, 18 knots.
Triple expansion engines. Two masts and two funnels.
Vessel was refitted in 1912. Scrapped in Italy, 1932. Ex-
Tonkin (1912).

Louqsor   (1904)   Messageries Maritimes (French).
Built by Messageries Maritimes, La Ciotat, France. Tonnage: 6,879. Dimensions: 447′ x 52′. Twin-screw, 12 knots. Triple expansion engines.   Two masts and one funnel. Scrapped in Belgium, 1930.   Sister ships: **El Kantara, Euphrate, Gange** and **Sontay.**

Lourenco   Marques   (1905)   Companhia   Nacional   de Navegacao (Portuguese).
Built by Blohm & Voss, Hamburg, Germany. Tonnage: 6,298.   Dimensions: 445′ x 50′.   Twin-screw, 14 knots. Triple expansion engines. Two masts and one funnel. This shipping firm was founded in 1918. The Portuguese Government seized this vessel in Delagoa Bay early during the First World War. Ex-**Admiral.**

Luetzow   (1908)   North German Lloyd.
Tonnage: 8,826. Services: (a) Bremen-Far East, (b) North Atlantic, (c) Latin American. Note: See PART I for details.

Lusitania   (1871)   Orient Line (British).
3,912. This Pacific Steam Navigation Company passenger ship inaugurated the Orient Line service from England to Australia in 1877. The voyage from Plymouth, England to Melbourne commenced on June 28, and was made in 40 days, six hours. Note: See PART III for details.

Lusitania   (1906)   Empreza   Nacional   de   Navegacao (Portuguese).
Built by Sir Raylton Dixon & Co., Middlesbrough, England. Tonnage: 5,557. Dimensions: 420′ x 51′. Twin-screw, 14 knots. Triple expansion engines. Two masts and one funnel. Service: Portugal-Africa. Wrecked on Bellows Rock, Cape of Good Hope, in April 1911.

***Lyautey**   (1952)   Compagnie de Navigation Paquet (French).
Built by Forges & Chantiers de la Mediterranee, La Seyne, France. Tonnage: 9,931. Dimensions: 448′ x 63′ (465′ o.l.). Twin-screw, 20 knots. Steam turbines. Single mast and one funnel.   Service: France-Canary Islands-West Africa. Passengers: 730.

Macedonia   (1904)   P. & O. Line (British).
Built by Harland & Wolff, Ltd., Belfast, Ireland. Tonnage: 10,512.   Dimensions: 530′ x 60′.   Twin-screw, 16 knots. Quadruple expansion engines. Two masts and two funnels. Service: England-Australia, via Suez Canal. Sold to Japanese

shipbreakers in June 1931. Sister ship: **Marmora.** Fine type of passenger ships for their era.

Madras   (1852)   P. & O. Line (British).
Built by Tod of Glasgow, Scotland. Tonnage: 1,185. Dimensions: 323′ x 31′. Single-screw. Beam with gearing engines. Three masts and one funnel. Clipper bow. Iron hull. Passengers: 80 first class. Considered a fast vessel for her time. Sister ship: **Bombay.**

Madura   (1921)   British India Steam Navigation Co.
Built by Barclay, Curle & Co., Glasgow, Scotland. Tonnage: 9,032. Dimensions: 465′ x 58′. Twin-screw, 13 knots. Six steam turbines. Two masts and one funnel. Passengers: 175. Service: England-Calcutta, via Suez Canal. Sister ships: **Malda, Mantola, Matiana, Modasa** and **Mulbera.**

*Maetsuycker   (1936)   Royal Interocean Lines (Dutch).
Built by Netherlands Dock Co., Amsterdam, Netherlands. Tonnage: 4,272. Dimensions: 361′ x 52′ (376′ o.l.). Single-screw, 14 knots. Motorship. Two masts and one funnel. Owner originally was the Royal Mail Packet Navigation Co. Service: Malaya-West Australia. Passengers: 55 first class.

Mahia   (1917)   Shaw, Savill & Albion Co.
Built by Workman, Clark & Co., Belfast, Ireland. Tonnage: 10,835. Dimensions: 477′ x 63′ (494′ o.l.). Twin-screw, 14 knots. Quadruple expansion engines. Two masts and one funnel. Service: England-New Zealand. Originally had accommodation for passengers. Sold for scrap in 1953.

Malacca   (1892)   P. & O. Line (British).
Built by Naval Construction & Armaments Co., Barrow, England. Tonnage: 4,045. Dimensions: 385′ x 45′. Single-screw, 14 knots. Triple expansion engines. Two masts and one funnel. Served in the Russo-Japanese War. Later, returned to P. & O. Line. Scrapped in 1910.

Malda   (1913)   British India Steam Navigation Co.
Built by Barclay, Curle & Co., Glasgow, Scotland. Tonnage: 7,884. Dimensions: 450′ x 58′. Twin-screw, 13½ knots. Triple expansion engines. Two masts and one funnel. Service: England-India, via Suez Canal. Torpedoed and sunk without warning 130 miles from Bishop Rock, August 25, 1917, with the loss of 64 lives.

Malda   (1922)   British India Steam Navigation Co.
Built by Barclay, Curle & Co., Glasgow, Scotland. Tonnage: 9,066.   Dimensions: 465′ x 58′.   Twin-screw, 13 knots. Steam turbines. Two masts and one funnel. Passengers: 175. Service: England-Calcutta, via Suez Canal.   Destroyed by enemy warship, April 6, 1942.   Sister ships: See **Madura.**

Maloja   (1911)   P. & O. Line (British).
Built by Harland & Wolff, Ltd., Belfast, Ireland. Tonnage: 12,431. Dimensions: 550′ x 62′ (569′ o.l.). Twin-screw, 18½ knots. Quadruple expansion engines.   16,000 I.H.P.   Two masts and two funnels. Passengers: 450 first and 220 second. Service: England-Australia, via Suez Canal.   Sunk by a mine two miles from Dover Pier, February 27, 1916, with the loss of 122 lives.   Similar ship: **Medina.**

Maloja   (1923)   P. & O. Line (British).
Built by Harland & Wolff, Ltd., Belfast, Ireland. Tonnage: 20,837. Dimensions: 600′ x 73′ (625′ o.l.).   Twin-screw, 17 knots. Quadruple expansion engines.   Two masts and two funnels. Service: London-Australia, via Suez Canal. Passengers: 327 first and 329 second.   Sold to British shipbreakers in 1954. Sister ship: **Mooltan.**   Note: Largest P. & O. liners built to date.

Malta   (1895)   P. & O. Line (British).
Built by Caird & Co., Greenock, Scotland. Tonnage: 6,064. Dimensions: 430′ x 50′.   Single-screw, 14 knots.   Triple expansion engines. 4,500 I.H.P. Two masts and one funnel. Passengers: 81 first and 62 second.   Out of fleet in 1923. Sister ship: **Nubia.**

Malwa   (1908)   P. & O. Line (British).
Built by Caird & Co., Greenock, Scotland. Tonnage: 10,986. Dimensions: 540′ x 61′.   Twin-screw, 16 knots.   Quadruple expansion engines.   13,000 I.H.P. Two masts and two funnels.   Service: England-Australia, via Suez Canal.   Passengers: 350 first and 160 second class.   Sold to Japanese shipbreakers in May 1932. Sister ship: **Mantua.**

Mamari   (1904)   Shaw, Savill & Albion Co. (British).
Built by Harland & Wolff, Ltd., Belfast, Ireland. Tonnage: 8,114.   Dimensions: 455′ x 56′.   Twin-screw, 14 knots. Quadruple expansion engines. Two masts and one funnel. Service: England-New Zealand.   Passengers: 6 first and 200 third class.   Renamed: (a) **Gerolstein** (1929), (b) **Consul Horn** (1939).   Destroyed by mines off Borkum in July 1942.

Mandingo (1899)   African Steamship Co. (Elder, Dempster & Co.).
Built by Sir Raylton Dixon & Co., Middlesbrough, England.
Tonnage: 4,019. Dimensions: 370′ x 46′. Twin-screw, 13½
knots. Triple expansion engines. Two masts and one funnel.
Service: England-West Africa.   Renamed: **Chaudiere.**
Ex-**Philippeville.**

Mandingo (1913)   Elder, Dempster & Co. (British).
Built by Harland & Wolff, Ltd., Belfast, Ireland. Tonnage:
7,781. Dimensions: 425′ x 57′. Twin-screw, 14 knots.
Quadruple expansion engines. Two masts and one funnel.
Service: England-West Africa. Renamed: **Appam.** Scrapped
in 1936. Ex-**Appam.**

Manela (1921)   British India Steam Navigation Co.
Built by Barclay, Curle & Co., Glasgow, Scotland. Tonnage:
8,303. Dimensions: 450′ x 58′. Twin-screw, 13 knots. Steam
turbines. Two masts and one funnel. Service: England-
India, via Suez. Passengers: 130. Scrapped in 1946. Sister
ship: **Mashobra.**

Manila (1892)   P. & O. Line (British).
Built by Caird & Co., Greenock, Scotland. Tonnage: 4,210.
Dimensions: 384′ x 45′.   Single-screw, 14 knots.   Triple
expansion engines. Two masts and one funnel. Steel hull.
Passengers: 30. Renamed: (a) **Maria C** (1910), (b) **Brac-
ciano** (Sitmar Line).

Manora (1913)   British India Steam Navigation Co.
Built by Barclay, Curle & Co., Glasgow, Scotland. Tonnage:
7,876. Dimensions: 449′ x 58′. Twin-screw, 13 knots. Triple
expansion engines. Two masts and one funnel. Scrapped
in 1932.

Mantola (1916)   British India Steam Navigation Co.
Built by Barclay, Curle & Co., Glasgow, Scotland. Tonnage:
450′ x 58′. Twin-screw, 13 knots. Triple expansion engines.
Two masts and one funnel. Torpedoed and sunk without
warning 143 miles from Fastnet, February 8, 1917, with the
loss of 7 lives.

Mantola (1921)   British India Steam Navigation Co.
Built by Barclay, Curle & Co., Glasgow, Scotland. Tonnage:
9,065. Dimensions: 465′ x 58′. Twin-screw, 13 knots. Six
steam turbines. Two masts and one funnel. Service: England-India, via Suez. Passengers: 190. Sold to British ship:

breakers in 1953. Sister ships: **Madura, Malda, Matiana, Modasa** and **Mulbera.**

Mantua   (1909)   P. & O. Line (British).
Built by Caird & Co., Greenock, Scotland. Tonnage: 10,885. Dimensions: 540' x 61'. Twin-screw, 16 knots. Quadruple expansion engines. Two masts and two funnels. Service: England-Australia, via Suez Canal. Sold to Chinese ship-breakers in May 1935. Sister ship: **Malwa.**

Marathon   (1904)   Aberdeen Line (British).
Built by Alexander Stephen & Sons, Ltd., Glasgow, Scotland. Tonnage: 6,795. Dimensions: 454' x 55'. Twin-screw, 15 knots. Triple expansion engines. Two masts and one funnel. Clipper bow. Service: England-Australia, via Capetown. Lengthened to 492 feet (7,827 tons) in 1912. A dummy second funnel was added. After these alterations accommodation was provided for 89 first and 158 third class passengers. Sold later to the Pacific Steam Navigation Company. Renamed: **Oruba** (1922). Scrapped in 1924. Sister ship: **Miltiades.**

Marco Polo   (1912)   Lloyd Triestino (Italian).
Built by Cantieri Nav. Triestino, Monfalcone, Austria. Tonnage: 12,272. Dimensions: 477' x 62' (500' o.l.). Twin-screw, 18 knots. Quadruple expansion engines. Two masts and two funnels. A World War II casualty. Ex-**Gange** (1936), ex-**Presidente Wilson** (1929), ex-**Generale Diaz** (1920), ex-**Kaiser Franz Josef I** (1919).

Marechal Gallieni   (1901)   Messageries Maritimes (French).
Built by J. C. Tecklenborg, Geestemunde, Germany. Tonnage: 7,642. Dimensions: 428' x 54'. Twin-screw, 13 knots. Triple expansion engines. Two masts and one funnel. Sold for scrap in May 1926. Ex-**Cassel** (1919).

Marechal Joffre   (1931)   Messageries Maritimes (French).
Built by Soc. Provencale de Construction Nav., La Ciotat, France. Tonnage: 11,732. Dimensions: 468' x 64' (495' o.l.). Twin-screw, 17 knots. Motorship. Two masts and two square funnels. Service: Marseilles-Far East, via Suez Canal. Passengers: 292. Crew: 350. Taken over by United States at Manila in December 1941; renamed: **Rochambeau.** Name reverted back to **Marechal Joffre** after the war. Sister ship: **Jean Laborde.**

Marechal Lyautey   (1924)   Paquet Line (French).
Built by Forges & Chantiers de la Mediterranee, La Seyne, France. Tonnage: 8,256. Dimensions: 428′ x 56′. Twin-screw, 16 knots. Two masts and two funnels. Service: France-West Africa. Sister ships: **Djenne, Koutoubia** and **Nicolas Paquet.**

Margha   (1917)   British India Steam Navigation Co.
Built by Barclay, Curle & Co., Glasgow, Scotland. Tonnage: 8,278. Dimensions: 450′ x 58′. Twin-screw, 13½ knots. Two masts and one funnel. Scrapped in 1934. Sister ship: **Merkara.**

Marie Woermann   (1916)   Woermann Line (German).
Built by Reiherstieg Schiffsw., Hamburg, Germany. Tonnage: 7,700. Dimensions: 426′ x 55′. Twin-screw, 15 knots. Quadruple expansion engines. Two masts and one funnel. Built for Germany-Africa service. Renamed: (a) **Marie,** (b) **Wadai,** (c) **Tjerimai,** (d) **El Nil.**

Marienbad   (1912)   Lloyd Austriaco.
Built by Cantieri San Rocco, Trieste, Austria. Tonnage: 8,848.   Dimensions: 452′ x 56′.   Twin-screw, 16 knots. Quadruple expansion engines. Two masts and two funnels. Passengers: 200 first, 38 second, 25 third, 282 fourth. Renamed: (a) **General Gallieni,** (b) **Pellerin de Latoche.**

Mariette Pache   (1925)   Messageries Maritimes (French).
Built by Soc. Provencale de Construction Navales, La Ciotat, France. Tonnage: 12,239. Dimensions: 495′ x 62′ (522′ o.l.). Twin-screw, 15 knots. 10,000 I.H.P. Two masts and three funnels. Service: Marseilles-Far East, via Suez. Scuttled by the Germans at Marseilles in August 1944. Sister ship: **Champollion.**

Markgraf   (1893)   Deutsche Ost Afrika Line.
Built by Armstrong, Mitchell & Co., Newcastle, England. Tonnage: 3,680. Dimensions: 364′ x 43′. Single-screw, 13 knots. Triple expansion engines. Two masts and one funnel. Placed in "Round Africa" service. Passengers: 71 first, 43 second, 42 third. Destroyed by British warship at Tanga in 1915. Ex-**Mark** (1902). Running mates: **Gouverneur** and **Prasident.**

Marmora   (1903)   P. & O. Line (British).
Built by Harland & Wolff, Ltd., Belfast, Ireland. Tonnage: 10,509. Dimensions: 530′ x 60′. Twin-screw, 18½ knots.

Quadruple expansion engines. 13,000 I.H.P. Two masts and two funnels. Service: England-Australia, via Suez. Note: First P. & O. vessel to be fitted with quadruple expansion engines. Torpedoed and sunk, July 23, 1918, with the loss of 10 lives. Sister ship: **Macedonia.**

Marnix van St. Aldegonde (1930)   Nederland Line.
Built by Netherland Shipbuilding Co., Amsterdam, Netherlands. Tonnage: 19,355. Dimensions: 586' x 74' (608' o.l.). Twin-screw, 18 knots. Motorship. Two masts and two funnels. Notable for relatively small funnels. Service: Amsterdam-Dutch East Indies, via Suez Canal. Passengers: 683. Crew: 335. Sunk in the Mediterranean, November 6, 1943. Sister ship: **Johan van Oldenbarnevelt.**

Mashobra (1914)   British India Steam Navigation Co.
Built by Barclay, Curle & Co., Glasgow, Scotland. Tonnage: 8,174. Dimensions: 449' x 58'. Twin-screw, $13\frac{1}{2}$ knots. Triple expansion engines. Two masts and one funnel. Service: England-England, via Suez. Torpedoed and sunk without warning 140 miles from Cape Matapan, April 15, 1917, with the loss of 8 lives.

Mashobra (1920)   British India Steam Navigation Co.
Built by Barclay, Curle & Co., Glasgow, Scotland. Tonnage: 8,324. Dimensions: 450' x 58' (465' o.l.). Twin-screw, 13 knots. Triple expansion engines. Two masts and one funnel. Service: England-India, via Suez. Passengers: 130. Lost by enemy action in 1940. Sister ship: **Manela.**

Massilia (1860)   P. & O. Line (British).
Built at London, England. Tonnage: 1,640. Dimensions: 309' x 36'. Paddle-wheels. Oscillating engines. Two masts and two funnels. Clipper bow. Iron hull. Note: The last P. & O. paddle-wheel steamer.

Massilia (1884)   P. & O. Line (British).
Built by Caird & Co., Greenock, Scotland. Tonnage: 4,908. Dimensions: 420' x 45'. Single-screw, 15 knots. Compound engines. Three masts and two funnels. Steel hull. Service: England-Australia, via Suez Canal. Passengers: 154 first and 75 second class. Fitted with electric lights. Scrapped in 1904. Sister ship: **Valetta.** Noted for their steadiness at sea.

Masula (1919)   British India Steam Navigation Co.
Built by Barclay, Curle & Co., Glasgow, Scotland. Tonnage: 7,326. Dimensions: 449' x 58'. Twin-screw, 13 knots.

Triple expansion engines. Two masts and one funnel. Passengers: 69. Scrapped in 1952. Sister ship: **Mundra.**

Matatua   (1904)   Shaw, Savill & Albion Co.
Built by Workman, Clark & Co., Belfast, Ireland. Tonnage: 8,010. Dimensions: 447' x 56'. Twin-screw, 13 knots. Triple expansion engines. Two masts and one funnel. Service: England-New Zealand. Passengers: 6 first and 200 third class. Renamed: **Ilsenstein.** Sunk as a blockship at Scapa Flow in 1940.

Matiana   (1894)   British India Steam Navigation Co.
Built by A. & J. Inglis, Glasgow, Scotland. Tonnage: 5,281. Dimensions: 420' x 49'. Single-screw, 13 knots. Triple expansion engines. Two masts and one funnel. Passengers: 38 first and 25 second. Lost by enemy action in 1918.

Matiana   (1922)   British India Steam Navigation Co.
Built by Barclay, Curle & Co., Glasgow, Scotland. Tonnage: 9,045. Dimensions: 465' x 58'. Twin-screw, 13 knots. Steam turbines. Two masts and one funnel. Service: England-India, via Suez Canal. Passengers: 190. Sold to British shipbreakers in 1952. Sister ships: **Madura, Malda, Mantola, Modasa** and **Mulbera.**

Medic   (1899)   White Star Line (British).
Built by Harland & Wolff, Ltd., Belfast, Ireland. Tonnage: 11,985. Dimensions: 550' x 63'. Twin-screw, 13½ knots. Quadruple expansion engines. Four masts and one funnel. Pioneer of the "Colonial" service of the White Star Line. Route: England-Australia, via Capetown. Passengers: 350. Renamed: **Hektoria.** Sister ships: **Afric** and **Persic.**

Medie II   (1922)   Cie. de Navigation Paquet (French).
Built by Forges & Chantiers de la Mediterranee, La Seyne, France. Tonnage: 5,078. Dimensions: 380' x 45'. Single-screw, 14 knots. Triple expansion engines. Two masts and two funnels. Sold to Italian shipbreakers in 1952.

Medina   (1911)   P. & O. Line (British).
Built by Caird & Co., Greenock, Scotland. Tonnage: 12,358. Dimensions: 550' x 62' (570' o.l.). Twin-screw, 18 knots. Quadruple expansion engines. Three masts and two funnels. One mast was later removed. Passengers: 660 (first and second class). Her bridge was 52 feet above the waterline. Service: England-India-Australia, via Suez Canal. Commenced her first voyage to Australia on June 28, 1912. Torpedoed and sunk by a German submarine in English Channel,

April 28, 1917, with the loss of six lives. Sister ship: **Maloja.** The finest P. & O. liners built to date.

Meikong   (1870)   Messageries Maritimes.
Built by Messageries Maritimes, La Ciotat, France. Tonnage: 3,370. Single-screw, 13½ knots. Compound engines. Three masts and two funnels. Launched, May 1, 1870. Service: France-Far East, via Suez. Lost on Cape Gardafui, June 14, 1877, while on voyage from Hong Kong to France. Passengers and crew were rescued by the British steamship **Glenatney.**   Sister ships: **Amazone, Ava, Pei-Ho** and **Sindh.**

Meinam   (1862)   Messageries Maritimes (French).
Built by Forges & Chantiers de la Mediterranee, La Seyne, France. Tonnage: 1,418. Dimensions: 292′ x 32′. Single-screw. Three cylinder engines. Two masts and one funnel. Launched, November 20, 1862. Sold at Saigon to British owners in 1892. Converted to sail, but retained her name. Sister ship: **La Bourdonnais.**

Melbourne   (1881)   Messageries Maritimes (French).
Built by Messageries Maritimes, La Ciotat, France. Tonnage: 3,998. Dimensions: 413′ x 39′. Single-screw, 13½ knots. Increased to 15 knots. Three masts and two funnels. Launched, December 24, 1881. Service: France-Australia-New Caledonia, via Suez Canal. Sold to Italian shipbreakers in December 1921. Sister ships: **Caledonien, Natal, Oceanien, Salazie, Sydney** and **Yarra.**

Mendi   (1905)   Elder, Dempster & Co. (British).
Built by Alexander Stephen & Sons, Ltd., Glasgow, Scotland. Tonnage: 4,230. Dimensions: 370′ x 46′. Single-screw. Triple expansion engines. Two masts and one funnel. Service: England-West Africa.

Menzaleh   (1865)   Messageries Maritimes (French).
Built by Forges & Chantiers de la Mediterranee, La Seyne, France. Tonnage: 1,912. Dimensions: 347′ x 32′. Single-screw, 11 knots. Three masts and one funnel. Iron hull. Launched, January 12, 1865. Foundered between Shanghai and Yokohama, May 19, 1887, with no loss of life. Sister ship: **Nil.**

Merkara   (1914)   British India Steam Navigation Co.
Built by Barclay, Curle & Co., Glasgow, Scotland. Tonnage: 8,258. Dimensions: 449′ x 58′. Twin-screw, 13 knots. Triple

expansion engines. Two masts and one funnel. Scrapped in 1932. Sister ship: **Margha.**

Methven Castle (1883) Castle Line (British).
Built by Barclay, Curle & Co., Glasgow, Scotland. Tonnage: 2,681. Designed as an intermediate steamship for their African service. Sold to other owners in 1897. Renamed: (a) **Colombia** (Scottish American Line), (b) **Rosecrans** (1903) as converted oil-carrier. Destroyed by fire off California in August 1912, with the loss of 34 lives. Sister ship: **Dunbar Castle.**

Mexican (1882) Union Line (British).
Built by Sir James Laing & Sons, Sunderland, England. Tonnage: 4,661. Dimensions: 378' x 47'. Single-screw, $14\frac{1}{2}$ knots. Triple expansion engines. Three masts and one funnel. Iron hull. Service: England-Capetown. Type: First-class mail steamer. In collision with the cattle steamship **Winkfield** during a dense fog, April 4, 1900. She went down 12 hours later 70 miles from Capetown. Of the 104 passengers and crew, all were transferred to the **Winkfield.**

Miltiades (1903) Aberdeen Line (British).
Built by Alexander Stephen & Sons, Ltd., Glasgow, Scotland. Tonnage: 6,765. Dimensions: 442' x 55'. Twin-screw, 15 knots. Triple expansion engines. Two masts and one funnel. Clipper bow. Lengthened to 492 feet (7,827 tons) in 1912. Also, dummy second funnel added. Service: England-Australia, via Cape of Good Hope. Sold to Pacific Steam Navigation Company for service between England and South America. Renamed: **Orcana** (1922). Scrapped in 1925. Sister ship: **Marathon.**

Min (1913) Messageries Maritimes (French).
Built by Bremer Vulkan, Vegesack, Germany. Tonnage: 7,997. Dimensions: 484' x 62'. Single-screw. Quadruple expansion engines. Vessel seized by Germans at Bizerta in November 1942. Sunk in Sicilian Channel in 1943. Ex-**Java.**

Mishima Maru (1908) N. Y. K. Line (Japanese).
Built by Kawasaki Dockyard Co., Kobe, Japan. Tonnage: 8,500. Dimensions: 474' x 54'. Twin-screw, $15\frac{1}{2}$ knots. Triple expansion engines. Two masts and one funnel. Service: Japan-Europe, via Suez Canal. Passengers: 83 first, 32 second, 12 third. No longer in commission, 1934. Sister ships: **Atsuta Maru, Hirano Maru, Kamo Maru, Kitano Maru** and **Miyazaki Maru.**

Mocambique   (1908)   Portuguese Royal Mail Line.
Built by Alexander Stephen & Sons, Ltd., Glasgow, Scotland.
Tonnage: 5,771.   Dimensions: 400′ x 52′.   Twin-screw, 15
knots.   Triple expansion engines.   Two masts and one funnel.
Service: Lisbon-Africa.   Ex-**Bruxellesville.**

*Mocambique   (1949)   Companhia Nacional de Navegacao.
Built by Swan, Hunter & Wigham & Richardson, Ltd., Newcastle, England.   Tonnage: 12,976.   Dimensions: 528′ x 67′
(549′ o.l.).   Twin-screw, 18 knots.   Motorship.   Two masts
and one funnel.   Passengers: 95 first, 141 tourist, 102 third,
412 emigrants. Service: Portugal-Africa. Sister ship: **Angola.**

Modasa   (1921)   British India Steam Navigation Co.
Built by Swan, Hunter & Wigham Richardson, Ltd., Newcastle, England.   Tonnage: 9,070.   Dimensions: 465′ x 58′.
Twin-screw, 13 knots.   Four steam turbines.   Two masts
and one funnel.   Passengers: 170.   Broken up for scrap in
1954.   Sister ships: **Madura, Malda, Mantola, Matiana**
and **Mulbera.**

Moeris   (1863)   Messageries Maritimes.
Built by Messageries Maritimes, La Ciotat, France.   Tonnage: 1,863.   Dimensions: 311′ x 32′.   Single-screw.   Two
cylinder engines.   Three masts and one funnel.   Iron hull.
Launched, May 31, 1863.   Lengthened in 1869.   Scrapped
in France, 1890.   Sister ships: **Peluse** and **Said.**

Moldavia   (1903)   P. & O. Line (British).
Built by Caird & Co., Ltd., Greenock, Scotland.   Tonnage:
9,500.   Dimensions: 520′ x 58′ (540′ o.l.).   Twin-screw, 18
knots.   Triple expansion engines.   Two masts and two funnels.   Service: England-Australia, via Suez Canal.   Torpedoed and sunk in the English Channel, May 23, 1918,
with the loss of 53 lives. She had been serving as a troopship.
Sister ships: **Mongolia** and **Mooltan** (nearly identical).

Moldavia   (1922)   P. & O. Line (British).
Built by Cammell Laird & Co., Birkenhead, England.
Tonnage: 16,543.   Dimensions: 552′ x 71′ (573′ o.l.).   Twin-
screw, 16 knots.   Steam turbines.   Two masts and two funnels.   Note: Originally had only a single funnel.   Passengers:
840 tourist class.   Scrapped in 1938.   Sister ship: **Mongolia.**

Mombassa   (1889)   British India Steam Navigation Co.
Built by Sir James Laing & Son, Sunderland, England.
Tonnage: 4,662.   Dimensions: 404′ x 47′.   Single-screw, 12

knots. Triple expansion engines. Steel hull. Passengers: 36 first and 20 second. Lost by enemy action in 1915.

Mongara   (1914)   British India Steam Navigation Co.
Built by Swan, Hunter & Wigham Richardson, Ltd., Newcastle, England. Tonnage: 8,205. Dimensions: 450' x 58'. Twin-screw, 13½ knots. Triple expansion engines. Two masts and one funnel. Torpedoed and sunk on July 3, 1917. Sister ship: **Morvada.**

Mongolia   (1903)   P. & O. Line (British).
Built by Caird & Co., Greenock, Scotland. Tonnage: 9,505. Dimensions: 520' x 58' (540' o.l.). Twin-screw, 18 knots. Triple expansion engines. Two masts and two funnels. Service: England-Australia, via Suez Canal. Struck a mine 50 miles from Bombay, June 24, 1917, and subsequently sunk with the loss of 24 lives. Sister ships: **Moldavia** and **Mooltan** (nearly identical).

Mongolia   (1923)   P. & O. Line (British).
Built by Sir W. G. Armstrong, Whitworth & Co., Newcastle, England. Tonnage: 16,576. Dimensions: 551' x 72' (570' o.l.). Twin-screw, 16 knots. Six steam turbines. Two masts and one funnel. Vessel transferred to New Zealand Shipping Company in 1938. Renamed: (a) **Rimutaka** (1938), (b) **Europa** (1950), (c) **Nassau** (1951). Sister ship: **Moldavia.**

Mooltan   (1905)   P. & O. Line (British).
Built by Caird & Co., Greenock, Scotland. Tonnage: 9,621. Dimensions: 520' x 58'. Twin-screw, 18½ knots. Quadruple expansion engines. Two masts and two funnels. Service: England-Australia, via Suez Canal. Passengers: 357 first and 162 second class. Torpedoed and sunk without warning 53 miles from Cape Serrat (Mediterranean Sea), July 26, 1917, with the loss of two lives. Sister ships: **Moldavia** and **Mongolia** (nearly identical).

Mooltan   (1923)   P. & O. Line (British).
Built by Harland & Wolff, Ltd., Belfast, Ireland. Tonnage: 20,952. Dimensions: 600' x 73'. Twin-screw, 17 knots. Quadruple expansion engines and electric drive from low pressure steam turbine. Two masts and two funnels. Service: London-Australia, via Suez Canal. Passengers: 700. Broken up for scrap at Faslane in 1954. Sister ship: **Maloja.** Largest P. & O. liners built to date.

Moor   (1882)   (a) Union Line, (b) Union-Castle Line.
Built by J. & G. Thomson, Ltd., Glasgow, Scotland. Tonnage: 3,688. Dimensions: 365' x 45'. Single-screw, 16 knots.

Triple expansion engines. Three masts and one funnel. Iron hull. Note: Lengthened to 420 feet (4,464 tons) in 1894. Two tall funnels (one a dummy) were installed to replace the original stack. In passenger and mail service between England and South Africa. Sold to Royal Mail Line in 1901. Renamed: (a) **La Plata** (1901), (b) **The Viking** (1908). Sold to Dutch shipbreakers in 1913. Sister ship: **Athenian.**

Moravian   (1899)   Aberdeen Line (G. Thompson & Co.).
Built by Robert Napier & Sons, Ltd., Glasgow, Scotland. Tonnage: 4,573. Dimensions: 390′ x 47′. Single-screw, 14 knots. Triple expansion engines. Three masts and one funnel. Service: England-Australia, via Capetown. Single-class passenger ship. Sold to Bombay & Persia Steam Navigation Company in 1914. Renamed: **Akbar** (1914). Sold to Italian shipbreakers in 1923. Sister ship: **Salamis.**

Morea   (1908)   P. & O. Line (British).
Built by Barclay, Curle & Co., Glasgow, Scotland. Tonnage: 10,890. Dimensions: 540′ x 61′. Twin-screw, 18½ knots. Quadruple expansion engines. Two masts and two funnels. Service: England-Australia, via Suez Canal. Scrapped in 1931. Sister ships: **Malwa** and **Mantua.**

Moreton Bay   (1921)   Aberdeen & Commonwealth Line.
Built by Vickers, Ltd., Barrow, England. Tonnage: 14,145. Dimensions: 530′ x 68′ (549′ o.l.). Twin-screw, 16 knots. Four steam turbines. Two masts and one funnel. Service: London-Australia, via Suez Canal. Sold to British shipbreakers in 1957. Sister ships: **Esperance Bay, Hobsons Bay, Jervis Bay** and **Largs Bay.**

Morvada   (1914)   British India Steam Navigation Co.
Built by Swan, Hunter & Wigham Richardson, Ltd., Newcastle, England. Tonnage: 8,205. Dimensions: 450′ x 58′. Twin-screw, 13½ knots. Triple expansion engines. Two masts and one funnel. Scrapped in 1933. Sister ship: **Mongara.**

Mossamedes   (1895)   Empreza Nacional de Navegacao (Portuguese).
Built by Alexander Stephen & Sons, Ltd., Glasgow, Scotland. Tonnage: 4,615. Dimensions: 400′ x 46′. Single-screw, 14 knots. Triple expansion engines. Two masts and one funnel. Service: Lisbon-Africa. Wrecked at Cape Frio, South West Africa, April 23, 1923, with the loss of 220 lives. Ex-**Sumatra** (P. & O. Line).

Mulbera   (1922)   British India Steam Navigation Co.
Built by Alexander Stephen & Sons, Ltd., Glasgow, Scotland.
Tonnage: 9,100.   Dimensions: 466' x 60'.   Twin-screw, 13
knots.   Six steam turbines.   Two masts and one funnel.
Service: England-Calcutta, via Suez Canal.   Sold to British
shipbreakers in 1954.   Sister ships: **Madura, Malda,
Matiana, Mantola** and **Modasa.**

Munchen   (1889)   North German Lloyd.
Tonnage: 4,801.   Service: Germany-Far East, via Suez
Canal.   Note: See PART I for details.

Mundra   (1920)   British India Steam Navigation Co.
Built by Barclay, Curle & Co., Glasgow, Scotland.   Tonnage:
7,299.   Dimensions: 450' x 58'.   Twin-screw, 13 knots.   Triple
expansion engines.   Two masts and one funnel.   Torpedoed
and sunk by gunfire, July 6, 1942.   Sister ship: **Masula.**
Passengers: 69.

Naldera   (1918)   P. & O. Line (British).
Built by Caird & Co., Greenock, Scotland.   Tonnage: 16,088.
Dimensions: 580' x 67' (605' o.l.).   Twin-screw, 17½ knots.
Quadruple expansion engines.   Two masts and three funnels.
Note: Did not have raised forecastle like sister ship.   Service:
London and Australia, or the Far East.   Passengers: 650.
Scrapped in Great Britain, 1938.   Sister ship: **Narkunda.**

Namur   (1907)   P. & O. Line (British).
Built by Caird & Co., Greenock, Scotland.   Tonnage: 6,694.
Dimensions: 449' x 52'.   Twin-screw, 14 knots.   Quadruple
expansion engines.   Two masts and one funnel.   Limited
passenger accommodation.   Torpedoed and sunk without
warning 55 miles from Gibraltar, October 29, 1917, with the
loss of one life.   Sister ships: **Nile, Nore** and **Nyanza.**

Nankin   (1912)   P. & O. Line (British).
Built by Caird & Co., Greenock, Scotland.   Tonnage: 6,853.
Dimensions: 449' x 52'.   Twin-screw, 14 knots.   Quadruple
expansion engines.   Two masts and one funnel.   Transferred
to the Eastern & Australian Line in 1932.   Sister ships:
Nagoya, Nellore and **Novara.**   Captured by raider in
Pacific, World War II, 1943.

Narkunda   (1920)   P. & O. Line (British).
Built by Harland & Wolff, Ltd., Belfast, Ireland.   Tonnage:
16,572.   Dimensions: 581' x 69' (606' o.l.).   Twin-screw, 17½
knots.   Quadruple expansion engines.   Two masts and three
funnels.   Service: London-Australia, or Far East, via Suez

Canal. Passengers: 650. Bombed, set on fire and sunk, November 14, 1942, when leaving Bougie on her return to Algiers. Sister ship: **Naldera.**

Narrung   (1896)   Lund's Blue Anchor Line.
Built by Sunderland Shipbuilding Co., Sunderland, England. Tonnage: 5,078. Dimensions: 400′ x 47′. Single-screw, 13 knots. Quadruple expansion engines. Two masts and one funnel. Service: England-Australia, via Capetown. Sold to the P. & O. Line in 1910. Renamed: **Mexico City** (Mexico Steamship Co.). Sunk by submarine in 1918. Sister ships: **Wakool** and **Wilcannia.**

Natal   (1881)   Messageries Maritimes (French).
Built by Messageries Maritimes, La Ciotat, France. Tonnage: 4,088. Dimensions: 413′ x 39′. Single-screw, 13½ knots. Compound engines. Three masts and two funnels. Iron hull. Speed increased to 15 knots at later date. Launched, July 3, 1881. Service: France-Australia. Sunk in collision with **Malgache,** August 30, 1917, while in convoy. Sister ships: **Caledonien, Melbourne, Oceanien, Salazie, Sydney** and **Yarra.**

Neckar   (1873)   North German Lloyd.
Built by Caird & Co., Greenock, Scotland. Tonnage: 2,331. Service: Germany-Australia. Note: See PART I for details.

Nellore   (1913)   P. & O. Line (British).
Built by Caird & Co., Greenock, Scotland. Tonnage: 6,942. Dimensions: 450′ x 52′. Twin-screw, 13 knots. Quadruple expansion engines. Two masts and one funnel. Transferred to Eastern Australian Steamship Co. Torpedoed and sunk by submarine, June 29, 1944. Sister ships: **Nagoya, Nankin** and **Novara.**

*****Neptunia**   (1951)   Lloyd Triestino (Italian).
Built by Cantieri Riuniti, dell' Adriatico, Trieste, Italy. Tonnage: 13,212. Dimensions: 501′ x 69′ (528′ o.l.). Twin-screw, 18 knots. Motorship. Single mast and one funnel. Passengers: 136 first and 600 tourist. Service: Italy-Australia, via Suez Canal. Sister ships: **Australia** and **Oceania.**

Nera   (1889)   Messageries Maritimes.
Built by Messageries Maritimes, La Ciotat, France. Tonnage: 5,548. Dimensions: 452′ x 45′. Single-screw, 16½ knots. Triple expansion engines. Three masts and two funnels. Service: France-Far East, via Suez Canal. Passengers:

142 first, 73 second, 97 third. Sold to Italian shipbreakers in April 1923. Ex-**La Plata** (1903). Sister ship: **Dumbea.**

Nestor   (1913)   Blue Funnel Line (British).
Built by Workman, Clark & Co., Belfast, Ireland. Tonnage: 14,629.   Dimensions: 563′ x 68′.   Twin-screw, 14 knots. Triple expansion engines. Two masts and one funnel. Notable for her enormous funnel. Had a straight stem, while her sister ship had a raking one. Service: Liverpool-Australia, via Suez Canal. Passengers: 250. Broken up by British shipbreakers at Faslane in 1950. Sister ship: **Ulysses.**

Neuralia   (1912)   British India Steam Navigation Co.
Built by Barclay, Curle & Co., Glasgow, Scotland. Tonnage: 9,082.   Dimensions: 480′ x 58′.   Twin-screw, 14½ knots. Quadruple expansion engines. Two masts and one funnel. Mined off Southern Italy, May 1, 1945. Sister ship: **Nevasa.**

Nevasa   (1884)   British India Steam Navigation Co.
Built by Wm. Denny & Bros., Ltd., Dumbarton, Scotland. Tonnage: 2,998.   Dimensions: 320′ x 42′.   Single-screw. Compound engines. Steel hull. Out of fleet in 1906.

Nevasa   (1913)   British India Steam Navigation Co.
Built by Barclay, Curle & Co., Glasgow, Scotland. Tonnage: 9,056. Dimensions: 480′ x 58′ (499′ o.l.). Twin-screw, 14½ knots. Quadruple expansion engines. Two masts and one funnel. Launched, December 12, 1912. Maiden voyage: England-Calcutta, March 22, 1913. Passengers: 130 first and 100 second. Their largest liner built to date. Served as a British hospital ship in First World War. Sold to British shipbreakers in 1948. Sister ship: **Neuralia.**

*****Nevassa**   (1956)   British India Steam Navigation Co.
Built by Barclay, Curle & Co., Glasgow, Scotland. Tonnage: 20,527. Dimensions: 609′ (o.l.) x 78′. Twin-screw, 17 knots. Steam turbines. Two masts and one funnel. Launched, November 30, 1955. Passengers: 220 first, 100 second, 180 third, 1,000 troops. Note: Built primarily as a British troopship.

New Australia   (1931)   British Ministry of Transport.
Built by Vickers-Armstrongs, Ltd., Newcastle, England. Tonnage: 20,256. Dimensions: 553′ x 76′ (579′ o.l.). Quadruple-screw, 21 knots. Two steam turbines connected to electric motors. Single mast and one funnel. Note: Due to fire after Second World War, vessel was rebuilt. The reconstruction changed her appearance greatly. Accommodation

was provided for 1,600 passengers. Placed in service between Great Britain and Australia, under the management of Shaw, Savill & Albion Co. Vessel sold to Greek Line. Renamed: **Arkadia** (1958). See PART II. Ex-**Monarch of Bermuda.**

Newark Castle (1901)   Union-Castle Line.
Built by Barclay, Curle & Co., Glasgow, Scotland. Tonnage: 6,253. Dimensions: 414′ x 51′. Twin-screw, 12 knots. Triple expansion engines. Two masts and one funnel. Service: West African and Mauritius. Wrecked off the coast of Zululand, March 12, 1908, shortly after leaving Durban. Sister ships: **Alnwick Castle, Berwick Castle** and **Cawdor Castle.**

*****Niassa** (1956)   Companhia   Nacional   de   Navegacao (Portuguese).
Built by Cockerill-Ougree, Hoboken, Belgium. Tonnage: 10,912. Dimensions: 458′ x 63′ (497′ o.l.). Single-screw, 16 knots. Motorship. Two masts and one funnel. Passengers: 22 first and 284 tourist. Service: Portugal-West Africa.

Nicolas Paquet (1928)   Cie. de Nav. Paquet (French).
Built by Forges & Chantiers de la Mediterranee, La Seyne, France. Tonnage: 8,250. Dimensions: 426′ x 56′. Twin-screw, 16 knots. Triple expansion engines. Two masts and two funnels. Service: France-West Africa. Lost off the Algerian coast in 1933. Sister ships: **Djenne, Koutoubia** and **Marechal Lyautey.**

Nieuw Holland (1928)   Royal   Packet   Navigation   Co. (Dutch).
Built by Nederlandsche Schps. Maats., Amsterdam, Netherlands. Tonnage: 11,066. Dimensions: 540′ x 62′. Twin-screw, 15 knots. Steam turbines. Two masts and two funnels. Service: Dutch East Indies-Australia. Passengers: 155 cabin. Sister ship: **Nieuw Zeeland.**

Nieuw Zeeland (1928)   Royal Packet Nav. Co. (Dutch).
Built by Rotterdamsche Droogdok Maatschappij, Rotterdam, Netherlands. Tonnage: 11,069. Dimensions: 540′ x 62′. Twin-screw, 15 knots. Steam turbines. Two masts and two funnels. Service: Dutch East Indies-Australia. Passengers: 155 cabin. Became a World War II casualty. Sister ship: **Nieuw Holland.**

Niger   (1871)   Messageries Maritimes (French).
Tonnage: 3,726. Service: (a) France-Far East, (b) France-South America. Note: See PART III for details.

Nikko Maru   (1903)   N. Y. K. Line (Japanese).
Built by Mitsubishi Co., Nagasaki, Japan. Tonnage: 5,559.
Dimensions: 428' x 48'.   Single-screw, 16 knots.   Triple
expansion engines. Two masts and one funnel. Considered
a Japanese super-liner for her time. Service: Japan-Australia.
Passengers: 90 first, 24 second, 105 third. Sunk by submarine,
April 9, 1945.

Nil   (1864)   Messageries Maritimes (French).
Built at La Seyne, France. Tonnage: 1,040. Single-screw,
11 knots. Three masts and one funnel. Launched, April 30,
1864. Lost with all hands between Hong Kong and Yoko-hama, March 20, 1874. Sister ship: **Menzaleh.**

Nile   (1906)   P. & O. Line (British).
Built by Caird & Co., Greenock, Scotland. Tonnage: 6,702.
Dimensions: 449' x 52'. Twin-screw, 14 knots. Quadruple
expansion engines. Two masts and one funnel. Limited
passenger accommodation. Wrecked off Japan in 1915.
Sister ships: **Namur, Nore** and **Nyanza.**

Nineveh   (1894)   Aberdeen Line (G. Thompson & Co.).
Built by Robert Napier & Sons, Glasgow, Scotland. Ton-nage: 3,808. Dimensions: 365' x 45'. Single-screw, 13 knots.
Triple expansion engines. Three masts and one funnel.
Steel hull. Service: England-Australia, via Capetown. Sold
to Eastern & Australian Steamship Co. Renamed: **Alden-ham** (1907), (b) **Larne.**

Njassa   (1924)   Deutsche Ost Afrika Line.
Built by Blohm & Voss, Hamburg, Germany. Tonnage:
8,754.   Dimensions: 433' x 58'.   Single-screw, 14 knots.
Four steam turbines. Two masts and one funnel. Service:
Germany-Africa. Badly damaged in German port in 1945.
Broken up for scrap. Sister ships: **Adolph Woermann,
Tanganjika** and **Usambara.**

Nore   (1907)   P. & O. Line (British).
Built by Caird & Co., Greenock, Scotland. Tonnage: 6,703.
Dimensions: 449' x 52'. Twin-screw, 14 knots. Quadruple
expansion engines. Two masts and one funnel. Scrapped in
1926. Sister ships: **Namur, Nile** and **Nyanza.**

Norham Castle (1883)   (a) Castle Line, (b) Union-Castle Line.
Built by John Elder & Co., Glasgow, Scotland. Tonnage:
4,392.   Dimensions: 380′ x 48′.   Single-screw, 15 knots.
Compound engines. Re-engined with triple expansions in
1891.   Two masts and one funnel.   Iron hull.   Service:
England-Africa. Sold to French Line in 1903. Renamed:
Martinique. Sister ships: **Hawarden Castle** and **Roslin
Castle.**

Norman (1894)   (a) Union Line, (b) Union-Castle Line.
Built by Harland & Wolff, Ltd., Belfast, Ireland. Tonnage:
7,537.   Dimensions: 490′ x 53′.   Twin-screw, 17 knots.
Triple expansion engines. 9,000 I.H.P. Two masts and two
funnels.   Coal bunkers held 2,500 tons.   Maiden voyage:
England-Capetown, November 1894. She became a very
popular liner, and regularly made the run to Capetown in
about 16 days. Passengers: 170 first, 100 second, 100 third.
Sold for scrap in the spring of 1926.

Norseman (1866)   Union Line (British).
Built by C. Lungley, London, England. Tonnage: 1,368.
Dimensions: 262′ x 32′. Single-screw. Compound engines.
Two masts and one funnel. Clipper bow. Iron hull. Ran
in the mail service to South Africa. Sold to the West Indies
& Brazil Telegraph Company as a cable ship in 1873. Sold
for scrap in December 1898.

Novara (1912)   P. & O. Line (British).
Built by Caird & Co., Glasgow, Scotland. Tonnage: 6,850.
Dimensions: 449′ x 52′. Twin-screw, 14 knots. Quadruple
expansion engines. 4,500 I.H.P. Two masts and one funnel.
Scrapped in Japan, 1932. Sister ships: **Nankin, Nagoya**
and **Nellore.**

Nubia (1895)   P. & O. Line (British).
Built by Caird & Co., Greenock, Scotland. Tonnage: 5,914.
Dimensions: 430′ x 49′. Single-screw, 13½ knots. Triple
expansion engines. 4,500 I.H.P. Two masts and one funnel.
Passengers: 81 first and 62 second. Wrecked near Colombo
in 1915. Sister ship: **Malta.**

Nubian (1876)   Union Line (British).
Built by C. Mitchell & Co., Newcastle, England. Tonnage:
3,088.   Dimensions: 359′ x 38′.   Single-screw, 10 knots.
Compound engines. Two masts and two funnels. Iron hull.
Clipper bow. Service: England-South Africa. Re-engined
with triple expansions, increasing speed to 14½ knots.

Altered to a single funnel. Wrecked near Lisbon in December 1892, with no loss of life.

Nyanza (1907) P. & O. Line (British).
Built by Caird & Co., Greenock, Scotland. Tonnage: 6,695. Dimensions: 449' x 52'. Twin-screw, 14 knots. Quadruple expansion engines. Two masts and one funnel. Limited passenger accommodation. Scrapped in 1928. Sister ships: **Namur, Nile** and **Nore.**

Oceana (1888) P. & O. Line (British).
Built by Harland & Wolff, Ltd., Belfast, Ireland. Tonnage: 6,188. Dimensions: 468' x 52'. Single-screw, 16½ knots. Triple expansion engines. 7,500 I.H.P. Four masts and two funnels. Steel hull. Service: England-Australia, via Suez Canal. Later transferred to the China and Far Eastern route. Passengers: 250 first and 150 second class. Cargo capacity: 4,000 tons. Sunk as a result of collision with the barque **Pisagua** in the English Channel, near Beach Head, March 16, 1912, with the loss of several lives. Sister ships: **Arcadia, Britannia** and **Victoria.**

Oceania (1932) (a) Cosulich Line, (b) Italia Line.
Built by Cantieri Riuniti dell' Adriatico, Monfalcone, Italy. Tonnage: 19,507. Transferred from South American service to Italy-Far East route. Note: See PART III for details.

*Oceania (1951) Lloyd Triestino (Italian).
Built by Cantieri Riuniti dell' Adriatico, Trieste, Italy. Tonnage: 13,213. Dimensions: 501' x 69' (528' o.l.). Twin-screw, 18 knots. Motorship. Single mast and one funnel. Passengers: 136 first and 536 tourist. Service: Italy-Australia, via Suez Canal. Sister ships: **Australia** and **Neptunia.**

Oceanien (1884) Messageries Maritimes (French).
Built by Messageries Maritimes, La Ciotat, France. Tonnage: 4,162. Dimensions: 416' x 41'. Single-screw, 13½ knots. Triple expansion engines. Three masts and two funnels. Launched, June 22, 1884. Note: First Messageries Maritimes ship to be painted white. Service: France-Australia, via Suez Canal. Refitted in 1895; re-engined with quadruple expansions. Speed increased to 15½ knots. Tonnage raised to 4,657. Scrapped in Italy, 1922. Sister ships: **Caledonien, Melbourne, Natal, Salazie, Sydney** and **Yarra.**

Oder   (1873)   North German Lloyd.
Tonnage: 3,158. Transferred from the North Atlantic to the Far Eastern service in 1886. Note: See PART I for details.

Oldenburg   (1890)   North German Lloyd.
Tonnage: 5,006.   Interchangeable between trans-Atlantic, Latin American and Australian routes. Note: See PART I for details.

Olympia   (1902)   Anchor Line (British).
Built by D. & W. Henderson & Co., Glasgow, Scotland. Tonnage: 5,197. Dimensions: 400′ x 49′. Single-screw, 12 knots. Triple expansion engines. Two masts and one funnel. Passengers: 70 first class. Service: Great Britain-India, via Suez Canal. Scrapped in 1926.

Omar   (1896)   Orient Line (British).
Built by "Vulkan", Stettin, Germany. Tonnage: 11,103. Dimensions: 523′ x 60′. Twin-screw, 15 knots. Quadruple expansion engines. Two masts and two funnels. Service: England-Australia, via Suez Canal. Renamed: **Edison** (1924). Scrapped in 1935. Ex-**Konigin Luise** (1920).

Omrah   (1899)   Orient Line (British).
Built by Fairfield Shipbuilding Co., Glasgow, Scotland. Tonnage: 8,130 (increased to 8,291). Dimensions: 490′ x 56′ (507′ o.l.). Twin-screw, 17 knots. Triple expansion engines. 9,200 I.H.P. Two masts and one funnel. Passengers: 161 first, 162 second, 500 third. Service: England-Australia, via Suez Canal. Tropedoed and sunk 40 miles from Cape Spartivento, Sardinia, May 12, 1918, while serving as a British troopship.

Ophir   (1891)   Orient Line (British).
Built by Robert Napier & Sons, Glasgow, Scotland. Tonnage: 6,910. Dimensions: 465′ x 53′ (482′ o.l.). Twin-screw, 18 knots. Triple expansion engines. 11,400 I.H.P. Two masts and two widely spaced funnels. Steel hull. Note: The first twin-screw ship on the Australian service. During trials made a speed of 18.8 knots. Coal consumption 125 tons per day. Capacity of coal bunkers was 2,000 tons. Scrapped in 1922.

Ophir   (1904)   Rotterdam Lloyd.
Built by Kon. Maats. de Schelde, Flushing, Netherlands. Tonnage: 4,726. Dimensions: 394′ x 47′. Single-screw, 14 knots. Triple expansion engines. Two masts and one funnel. Service: Rotterdam-Dutch Indies, via Suez Canal. Sunk by

a mine at Gibraltar in First World War. Salvaged later and came under ownership of Beaver Steamship Company. No longer in commission after 1924.

Orama   (1912)   Orient Line (British).
Built by John Brown & Co., Glasgow, Scotland. Tonnage: 12,927. Dimensions: 551' x 64'. Triple-screw, 18 knots. Triple expansion engines and steam turbine on center shaft. Two masts and two funnels. Largest Orient Line ship built to date. Service: England-Australia, via Suez. Taken over by British Government in 1914 for war service. Torpedoed and sunk off the South of Ireland, October 19, 1917. Ships of this general class were: **Otway, Orsova, Orvieto, Osterley** and **Otranto.**

Orama   (1924)   Orient Line (British).
Built by Vickers, Ltd., Barrow, England. Tonnage: 19,777. Dimensions: 632' x 75' (658' o.l.). Twin-screw, 19 knots. Six steam turbines. Two masts and two funnels. Passengers: 592 first and 1,244 third. Service: England-Australia, via Suez Canal. Sunk by the German cruiser **Admiral Hipper,** June 8, 1940, during the evacuation of Norway. The Germans rescued about 280 survivors. Sister ships: **Orford, Oronsay, Orontes** and **Otranto.**

Oranje   (1903)   Nederland Royal Mail Line.
Built by Maats. Feyenoord, Rotterdam, Netherlands. Tonnage: 4,419. Dimensions: 397' x 45'. Single-screw, 14 knots. Quadruple expansion engines. Two masts and one funnel. Service: Amsterdam-Dutch East Indies, via Suez Canal. Passengers: 70 first and 35 second class. Renamed: **Anfa.**

*Oranje   (1939)   Nederland Royal Mail Line.
Built by Netherlands Shipbuilding Co., Amsterdam, Netherlands. Tonnage: 20,017. Dimensions: 613' x 83' (656' o.l.). Triple-screw, 21 knots. Motorship. Single mast and one funnel. Built for Amsterdam-Dutch East Indies, via Suez Canal route. Passengers: 700. Reconditioned and transferred to "round-the-world" service, via Panama Canal, 1959. See page 333.

*Oranjefontein   (1940)   Holland-Africa Line.
Built by Van P. Smit, Jr., Rotterdam, Netherlands. Tonnage: 10,549. Dimensions: 499' x 62' (527' o.l.). Twin-screw, 17 knots. Motorship. Two masts and one funnel.

Passengers: 150.   Service: Europe-South and East Africa.
Sister ships: **Jagersfontein** and **Klipfontein.**

Orcades   (1906)   Orient Line (British).
   Built by Akt. Ges. "Vulkan", Stettin, Germany. Tonnage:
   9,764.   Dimensions: 492′ x 57′.   Twin-screw, 15 knots.
   Quadruple expansion engines. 7,000 I.H.P. Two masts and
   two funnels. Service: England-Australia. Passengers: 123
   first and 476 third. Scrapped in Germany, 1925. Ex-**Prinz
   Ludwig** (1920).

Orcades   (1937)   Orient Line (British).
   Built by Harland & Wolff, Ltd., Belfast, Ireland. Tonnage:
   23,456. Dimensions: 639′ x 82′ (664′ o.l.). Twin-screw, 21
   knots.   Six steam turbines. Single mast and one funnel.
   Displacement of 28,400 tons. Steam pressure of 450 lbs. per
   square inch. Two small and four large boilers. Propellers
   of four bladed type and 19 feet in diameter. During her
   trials made a speed of 22.3 knots. Passengers: 463 first and
   605 tourist.   Route: England-Australia, via Suez Canal.
   Torpedoed and sunk in the South Atlantic off Africa, October
   10, 1942, during heavy weather. Of the many on board,
   fortunately few were lost. Similar ship: **Orion.**

*Orcades   (1948)   Orient Line (British).
   Built by Vickers-Armstrongs, Ltd., Barrow, England. Tonnage: 28,396.   Dimensions: 681′ x 90′ (711′ o.l.).   Twin-
   screw, 22 knots. Steam turbines. Single mast and one funnel. Launched, October 14, 1947. Maiden voyage: England-
   Australia, December 14, 1948. Reconditioned at Belfast in
   1959. Passengers: 631 first and 734 tourist. Route: England-
   Australia-New Zealand-California (P & O-Orient Lines
   trans-Pacific). Similar ship: **Oronsay.**

Orenoque   (1874)   Messageries Maritimes (French).
   Tonnage: 3,833. Built for the France-South America route.
   Transferred to the Far East service. Note: See PART III
   for details.

Orford   (1928)   Orient Line (British).
   Built by Vickers, Ltd., Barrow, England. Tonnage: 19,941.
   Dimensions: 632′ x 75′ (659′ o.l.).   Twin-screw, 20 knots.
   Six steam turbines. Two masts and two funnels. Service:
   London-Australia, via Suez Canal. Bombed by aircraft off
   Marseilles during the collapse of France in 1940, and subse-
   quently burned herself out after being beached. Similar
   ships: **Orama, Oronsay, Orontes** and **Otranto.**

*Oriana   (1960)   P & O-Orient Lines. (British).
Built by Vickers-Armstrongs, Ltd., Barrow, England. Tonnage: 41,923.   Dimensions: 804' (o.l.) x 97'.   Twin-screw, 27½ knots.   Steam turbines.   Single mast and one funnel. Launched November 3, 1959.   She has a small stepped-down aft funnel that serves as engine room vent.   Passengers: 688 first and 1,496 tourist.   Entered the England-Australia-New Zealand-California service in December 1960.   This outstanding luxury liner is the first British one to have a bulbous bow.

Orient   (1879)   Orient Line (British).
Built by John Elder & Co., Glasgow, Scotland.   Tonnage: 5,386.   Dimensions: 445' x 46'.   Single-screw, 15 knots. Compound engines.   5,400 I.H.P.   Four masts and two funnels.   Iron hull.   First ship built for the Orient Line.   One of the finest liners of her day.   Made a record voyage from England to Australia of 37 days and 22 hours.   Made the run to Capetown in 17 days, 21 hours.   During her trials made a speed of 17 knots.   Passengers: 120 first, 130 second, 300 steerage.   Re-engined with triple expansions in 1898. Altered to a single tall funnel; reduced to two masts. Scrapped in 1910.

Oriental   (1889)   P. & O. Line (British).
Built by Caird & Co., Greenock, Scotland.   Tonnage: 4,972. Dimensions: 410' x 48'.   Single-screw, 16 knots.   Triple expansion engines.   6,000 I.H.P.   Three masts and one funnel. Steel hull.   Designed for the England-Bombay service. Passengers: 142 first and 96 second.   Renamed: **Hong Kheng**.   Sister ship: **Peninsular.**

*Orion   (1935)   Orient Line (British).
Built by Vickers-Armstrongs, Ltd., Barrow, England. Tonnage: 23,456.   Dimensions: 640' x 82' (665' o.l.).   Twin-screw, 21 knots.   Steam turbines.   Single mast and one funnel.   Commenced her first regular sailing from England to Australia in September 1935.   Converted to troopship in World War II.   Resumed service in 1947.   Passengers: 550 first and 700 tourist.   Similar ship: **Orcades.**

Orlando   (1904)   Ellerman's Line (British).
Built by Hall, Russell & Co., Aberdeen, Scotland.   Tonnage: 4,233.   Dimensions: 370' x 46'.   Single-screw, 14 knots. Triple expansion engines.   Two masts and one funnel. Passengers: 76 first and 594 third.   Scrapped in 1932.   Ex-**Inanda** (1920).

Ormonde   (1917)   Orient Line (British).
Built by John Brown & Co., Glasgow, Scotland. Tonnage: 14,982. Dimensions: 580′ x 66′. Twin-screw, 18 knots. Four steam turbines. Two masts and two funnels. Passengers: 278 first, 195 second, 1,000 third. Service: England-Australia. Converted to troopship in World War II. In 1947 was returned to service as an emigrant ship to Australia. Sold to British shipbreakers late in 1952.

Ormuz   (1886)   Orient Line (British).
Built by Fairfield Shipbuilding Co., Glasgow, Scotland. Tonnage: 6,031. Dimensions: 465′ x 52′. Single-screw, 17 knots. Triple expansion engines. Four masts and two funnels. Note: First Orient Line ship to be given triple expansion engines. 9,000 I.H.P. Passengers: 166 first and 170 second. Sold to French owners in 1912. Renamed: **Divona** (1912).

Ormuz   (1914)   Orient Line (British).
Built by Bremer Vulkan, Vegesack, Germany. Tonnage: 14,588. Dimensions: 550′ x 67′. Twin-screw, 18 knots. Quadruple expansion engines. Two masts and two funnels. Service: England-Australia. Passengers: 293 first and 882 third. Renamed: **Dresden** (1927). Wrecked off the Norwegian coast in 1934. Ex-**Zeppelin** (1920).

Oronsay   (1925)   Orient Line (British).
Built by John Brown & Co., Clydebank, Glasgow, Scotland. Tonnage: 20,001. Dimensions: 633′ x 75′ (658′ o.l.). Twin-screw, 19 knots. Steam turbines. Two masts and two funnels. Passengers: 592 first and 1,244 third. Service: England-Australia, via Suez Canal. Served as a troopship World War II. Torpedoed and sunk by submarine off the West African coast, October 9, 1942. Similar ships: **Orama, Orford, Orontes** and **Otranto.**

*****Oronsay**   (1951)   Orient Line (British).
Built by Vickers-Armstrongs, Ltd., Barrow, England. Tonnage: 27,632. Dimensions: 681′ x 90′ (708′ o.l.). Twin-screw, 22 knots. Six steam turbines. Single mast and one funnel. Launched, June 30, 1950. Entered London-Australia service in May 1951. Passengers: 612 first and 804 tourist. Note: Inaugurated the extended sailings to San Francisco and Vancouver, via the Pacific Ocean in 1954. This extended service is now operated under the merged name of P & O-Orient Lines. Liners now employed in this joint operation are: **Arcadia, Canberra, Chusan, Himalaya, Iberia, Orcades, Oriana, Oronsay** and **Orsova.**

Orizaba   (1886)   Orient Line (British).
Built by Barrow Shipbuilding Co., Barrow, England. Tonnage: 6,077. Dimensions: 460′ x 49′. Single-screw, 16 knots. Triple expansion engines. Four masts and two funnels. Note: Vessel owned by Pacific Steam Navigation Company, but was transferred to the Orient Line for service between England and Australia. Passengers: 126 first, 154 second, 400 third. Tonnage later increased to 6,298. Wrecked on Garden Island near Freemantle, February 17, 1905, due to poor visibility. Sister ship: **Oroya.**

Orontes   (1902)   Orient Line (British).
Built by Fairfield Shipbuilding Co., Glasgow, Scotland. Tonnage: 9,028. Dimensions: 513′ x 54′. Twin-screw, 18 knots. Quadruple expansion engines. Two masts and one funnel. The first Orient Line ship to be fitted with quadruple expansion engines. Two double-ended and four single-ended boilers. 10,000 I.H.P. Steam pressure 215 lbs. per sq. inch. Service: England-Australia, via Suez. Passengers: 320 first and 320 third class. Converted to troopship in 1916 and after the war resumed regular service. Scrapped in 1926. Somewhat similar in appearance to the **Omrah.**

Orontes   (1929)   Orient Line (British).
Built by Vickers-Armstrongs, Ltd., Barrow, England. Tonnage: 20,186. Dimensions: 638′ x 75′ (663′ o.l.). Twin-screw, 20 knots. Steam turbines. Two masts and two funnels. Launched in February 1929. Entered the London-Australia service, via Suez Canal, October 1929. Passengers: 502 first, 1,112 tourist. Crew: 464. Converted to troopship during World War II. Thoroughly reconditioned after performing her war duties. Resumed regular service in June 1948. Accommodation changed to provide for 1,370 in single class. Scrapped in 1962. Similar ships: **Orama, Orford, Oronsay** and **Otranto.**

Orotava   (1889)   Orient Line (British).
Tonnage: 5,858. Passengers: 126 first and 120 second and third class. Vessel was owned by Pacific Steam Navigation Company, but for a time was used by the Orient Line in their service to Australia. Sister ship: **Oruba.** Note: See PART III for details.

Oroya   (1886)   Orient Line (British).
Tonnage: 6,057. Increased later to 6,297 gross tons. This Pacific Steam Navigation Company passenger liner was placed in the Orient Line service to Australia. Sister ship: **Orizaba.** Note: See PART III for details.

Orsova   (1909)   Orient Line (British).
Built by John Brown & Co., Glasgow, Scotland. Tonnage:
12,036. Dimensions: 12,036. Dimensions: 536′ x 63′ (553′
o.l.). Twin-screw, 18 knots. Quadruple expansion engines.
Two masts and two funnels. Passengers: 288 first, 126
second, 660 third.   Maiden voyage: London-Australia,
June 25, 1909.   Route: London-Gibraltar-Marseilles-
Port Said-Aden-Colombo-Adelaide-Melbourne-
Sydney. Sold to British shipbreakers in 1936, after rolling
up a total of 70 round trips to Australia during her life.
Sister ships: **Orvieto, Osterley, Otranto** and **Otway.**

*****Orsova**   (1954)   Orient Line (British).
Built by Vickers-Armstrongs, Ltd., Barrow, England. Tonnage: 28,790.   Dimensions: 668′ x 90′ (722′ o.l.).   Twin-
screw, 22 knots. Steam turbines. Single funnel and no mast.
Launched, May 14, 1953. Commenced service from London
to Australia, via Colombo, in May 1954. Passengers: 1,480
first and tourist class. Similar ship: **Oronsay.**

Ortegal   (1884)   Messageries Maritimes.
Built by Messageries Maritimes, La Ciotat, France. Tonnage: 3,695.   Dimensions: 328′ x 45′.   Single-screw, 13½
knots. Compound engines. Steel hull. Service: France-Far
East, via Suez. Sold for scrap in January 1906.

Oruba   (1889)   Orient Line (British).
Tonnage: 5,857. Vessel owned by Pacific Steam Navigation
Company. This outstanding passenger ship was intended
for the direct line service to South America. However, was
placed along with her sister ship **Orotava,** on the England-
Australia route of the Orient Line in 1889. Note: See PART
III for details.

Orvieto   (1909)   Orient Line (British).
Built by Workman, Clark & Co., Belfast, Ireland. Tonnage:
12,133.   Dimensions: 535′ x 64′.   Twin-screw, 18 knots.
Quadruple expansion engines. Two masts and two funnels.
Passengers: 235 first, 186 second, 696 third. Service: England-Australia, via Suez Canal. After varied service during
World War I, was reconditioned and resumed regular sailings
to Australia. Laid up in 1929. Sold to British shipbreakers
in March 1931. Sister ships: **Orsova, Osterley, Otranto**
and **Otway.**

Osterley   (1909)   Orient Line (British).
Built by London & Glasgow Engineering & Iron Shipbuilding
Co., Glasgow, Scotland. Tonnage: 12,129. Dimensions:

535' x 63'. Twin-screw, 18 knots. Quadruple expansion engines. 14,000 I.H.P. Two masts and two funnels. Service: England-Australia, via Suez Canal. Passengers: 400 first and 700 third class. Sold for scrap in March 1930. Sister ships: **Orsova, Orvieto, Otranto** and **Otway.**

Otranto (1909) Orient Line (British).
Built by Workman, Clark & Co., Belfast, Ireland. Tonnage: 12,124. Dimensions: 535' x 64'. Twin-screw, 18 knots. Quadruple expansion engines. 14,000 I.H.P. Two masts and two funnels. Service: England-Australia, via Suez Canal. Passengers: 235 first, 186 second, 696 third. At later date accommodation altered to: 450 first and 850 third class. Lost due to collision with the **Kashmir** in the Irish Sea, October 6, 1918, with the loss of 431 lives. She had been serving as a transport carrying American troops. Sister ships: **Orsova, Orvieto, Osterley,** and **Otway.** Note: All were not identical.

Otranto (1925) Orient Line (British).
Built by Vickers, Ltd., Barrow, England. Tonnage: 20,032. Dimensions: 632' x 75' (658' o.l.). Twin-screw, 20 knots. Six steam turbines. Two masts and two funnels. Launched, June 9, 1925. Service: London and Australia, via Suez Canal. Converted to troopship in 1939. In 1948 was reconditioned and in 1949 resumed regular sailings to Australia. Accommodation provided for 1,412 tourist class passengers. Sold to British shipbreakers in 1957. Sister ships: **Orama, Orford, Oronsay** and **Orontes.**

Otway (1909) Orient Line (British).
Built by Fairfield Shipbuilding Co., Glasgow, Scotland. Tonnage: 12,077. Dimensions: 535' x 63'. Twin-screw, 18 knots. Quadruple expansion engines. Two masts and two funnels. Fine looking passenger ship for her era. Service: England-Australia, via Suez Canal. Passengers: 400 first and 700 third. As an armed merchant cruiser, she was torpedoed and sunk in the North Sea, July 22, 1917, with the loss of 10 lives. Sister ships: **Orsova, Orvieto, Osterley** and **Otranto.**

Oxfordshire (1912) Bibby Line (British).
Built by Harland & Wolff, Ltd., Belfast, Ireland. Tonnage: 8,646. Dimensions: 474' x 55'. Twin-screw, 15 knots. Quadruple expansion engines. Four masts and one funnel. Service: England-Burma, via Suez Canal. Passengers: 210. Crew: 190. Renamed: **Safina-E-Arab** (1951). Sold to Karachi shipbreakers in April 1958.

*Oxfordshire   (1957)   Bibby Line (British).
   Built by Fairfield Shipbuilding Co., Glasgow, Scotland.
   Tonnage: 20,586. Dimensions: 609′ (o.l.) x 78′. Twin-screw,
   17 knots. Four steam turbines. Single mast and one funnel.
   Attained a speed of 21 knots during her trials in February
   1957. Largest Bibby liner built to date. Passengers: 220
   first, 180 third, 1,000 troops. Service: England-Far East.
   Mainly used as a British troopship.

Oxus   (1879)   Messageries Maritimes.
   Built by Messageries Maritimes, La Ciotat, France. Tonnage: 3,810. Dimensions: 394′ x 39′. Single-screw, 13½
   knots. Compound engines. Three masts and one funnel.
   Fitted with second funnel at later date. Launched, April 27,
   1879. Converted to Russian hospital ship in 1914. Scuttled
   at Novorossisk, June 21, 1918, so as to avoid capture by
   the Germans. The hulk was dismantled in 1919. Sister
   ships: **Djemnah** and **Yang Tse.**

Palawan   (1895)   P. & O. Line (British).
   Built by Caird & Co., Glasgow, Scotland. Tonnage: 4,686.
   Dimensions: 400′ x 46′. Single-screw, 14 knots. Triple
   expansion engines. Two masts and one funnel. Passengers:
   46 first and 44 second. Renamed: **Jeddah.** Sister ship: **Sunda.**

Palermo   (1903)   P. & O. Line (British).
   Built by Barclay, Curle & Co., Glasgow, Scotland. Tonnage:
   7,597. Dimensions: 479′ x 57′. Twin-screw, 14 knots. Triple
   expansion engines. Two masts and one funnel. Scrapped in
   1925. Sister ships: **Palma, Pera, Peshawur** and **Poona.**
   Type: Freighters with limited passenger accommodation.

Papanui   (1899)   New Zealand Shipping Co.
   Built by Wm. Denny & Bros., Dumbarton, Scotland. Tonnage: 6,582. Dimensions: 430′ x 54′. Twin-screw, 14 knots.
   Triple expansion engines. Two masts and one funnel. Service:
   England-New Zealand, via Capetown. Destroyed by fire
   and scuttled near St. Helena in September 1911. Sister
   ship: **Paparoa.**

Paparoa   (1899)   New Zealand Shipping Co.
   Built by Wm. Denny & Bros., Ltd., Dumbarton, Scotland.
   Tonnage: 6,563 (increased to 7,697). Dimensions: 430′ x 54′.
   Twin-screw, 14 knots. Triple expansion engines. 4,000 I.H.P.
   Two masts and one funnel. Service: England-New Zealand,
   via Capetown. Passengers: 34 first and 45 second class.
   Destroyed by fire and scuttled in the South Atlantic, March

17, 1926. Her sister ship met a similar fate near the same spot. A strange coincidence indeed! Sister ship: **Papanui.**

Parramatta   (1882)   P. & O. Line (British).
Built by Caird & Co., Greenock, Scotland. Tonnage: 4,886. Dimensions: 420' x 43'. Single-screw, 14½ knots. Compound engines. Two masts and two funnels. Steel hull. Service: England-Australia, via Suez Canal. Passengers: 153 first and 77 second. Scrapped in 1904. Sister ship: **Ballaarat.**

Patria   (1919)   Rotterdam Lloyd (Dutch).
Built by Kon. Maats. de Schelde, Flushing, Netherlands. Tonnage: 9,891. Dimensions: 480' x 57'. Twin-screw, 15 knots. Steam turbines. Two masts and two funnels. Launched in 1916, but not completed until 1919. Service: Rotterdam-Dutch East Indies, via Suez Canal. Renamed: (a) **Svir** (Russian training ship), (b) **Alexandr Mozhaiski** (Russian).

*Patria   (1947)   Companhia Colonial de Navegacao.
Built by John Brown & Co., Clydebank, Glasgow, Scotland. Tonnage: 13,196. Dimensions: 507' x 68' (531' o.l.). Twin-screw, 17 knots. Four steam turbines. Two masts and one funnel. Service: Portugal-West and East Africa. Passengers: 635 (1st, 2nd and 3rd). Sister ship: **Imperio.** Note: Their largest ships built for their African service to date.

*Patris   (1950)   Greek Australian Line (Piraeus, Greece).
Built by Harland & Wolff, Ltd., Belfast, Ireland. Tonnage: 18,400. Dimensions: 570' x 76' (594' o.l.). Twin-screw, 18½ knots. Motorship. Single mast and one funnel. Service: Greece-Australia. Passengers: 36 first and 1,000 tourist. Ex-**Bloemfontein Castle** (1959).

Patroclus   (1923)   Blue Funnel Line (British).
Built by Scott's Shipbuilding Co., Greenock, Scotland. Tonnage: 11,314. Dimensions: 498' x 62'. Twin-screw, 15 knots. Two steam turbines. Two masts and one funnel. Passengers: 135. Service: Liverpool-Far East, via Suez Canal. Torpedoed and sunk by submarine off Northern Ireland, November 12, 1940. Sister ships: **Antenor, Hector** and **Sarpedon.**

Paul Lecat   (1911)   Messageries Maritimes.
Built by Messageries Maritimes, La Ciotat, France. Tonnage: 12,989. Dimensions: 510' x 61'. Twin-screw, 17 knots. Quadruple expansion engines. Two masts and two

funnels. Launched, March 19, 1911. Service: France-Far
East, via Suez Canal. Passengers: 165 first, 84 second, 100
third. Severely damaged by fire in drydock at Marseilles,
December 31, 1928. The hulk was broken up at Spezia.
Sister ship: **Andre Lebon.**

Pays de Waes   (1912)   Lloyd Belge Royal.
Built by Wm. Denny & Bros., Ltd., Dumbarton, Scotland.
Tonnage: 9,735. Dimensions: 451' x 60'. Twin-screw, 15
knots. Quadruple expansion engines. Two masts and two
funnels. Renamed: **Horai Maru. Ex-Indarro.**

Pegu   (1913)   Henderson Line (British).
Built by Wm. Denny & Bros., Ltd., Dumbarton, Scotland.
Tonnage: 6,348. Dimensions: 445' x 55'. Single-screw, 14
knots. Triple expansion engines. Service: Great Britain-
Rangoon. Sunk by a mine seven miles from Galley Head,
July 8, 1917, with the loss of one life.

Pegu   (1921)   Henderson Line (British).
Built by Wm. Denny & Bros., Ltd., Dumbarton, Scotland.
Tonnage: 8,183. Dimensions: 466' x 59'. Single-screw, 14
knots. Triple expansion engines. Two masts and one funnel.
Service: Glasgow-Liverpool-Rangoon, via Suez Canal.
Passengers: 150 first class. Wrecked in 1929. Similar ships:
Amarapoora, Kemmendie, Sagaing and **Yoma.**

Pei Ho   (1869)   Messageries Maritimes.
Built by Messageries Maritimes, La Ciotat, France. Tonnage: 3,392. Dimensions: 368' x 39'. Single screw, 13½
knots. Three masts and two funnels. Launched, October 17,
1869. Service: France-Far East. Refitted in 1888. Altered
to single funnel. Sold for scrap to Marseilles shipbreakers
in August 1902. Sister ships: **Amazone, Ava, Meikong**
and **Sindh.**

Peluse   (1863)   Messageries Maritimes.
Built by Messageries Maritimes, La Ciotat, France. Tonnage: 1,501. Dimensions: 328' x 32'. Single-screw. Two
cylinder engine. Three masts and one funnel. Iron hull.
Launched, February 2, 1863. Lengthened in 1869. Tonnage
increased to 1,743. Vessel was present at the opening of
Suez Canal in 1869. Scrapped at Singapore in 1891. Sister
ships: **Moeris** and **Said.**

Pembroke Castle   (1883)   Castle Line (British).
Built by Barrow Shipbuilding Co., Barrow, England. Tonnage: (a) 3,946, (b) 4,045. Dimensions: 400' x 42'. Single-

screw, 12½ knots. Compound engines. Four masts and one funnel. Steel hull. Served occasionally as a mail steamer, but often used as an intermediate liner of the route to South Africa. This "odd number" of the Castle Line fleet was sold along with the **Helius,** to the Turkish Government in 1906. Sunk by the Russians near Samsoun in the Black Sea in August 1915.

*****Pendennis Castle**   (1958)   Union-Castle Line.
Built by Harland & Wolff, Ltd., Belfast, Ireland. Tonnage: 28,582. Dimensions: 763′ (o.l.) x 84′. Twin-screw, 22½ knots. Steam turbines. Two masts placed forward of single funnel. Launched, December 24, 1957. Commenced regular service to Capetown on January 1, 1959. Passengers: 187 first and 475 tourist. Crew: 419. A fine type of modern passenger liner.

Peninsular   (1888)   P. & O. Line (British).
Built by Caird & Co., Greenock, Scotland. Tonnage: (a) 4,972, (b) 5,294. Dimensions: 410′ x 48′. Single-screw, 16 knots. Triple expansion engines. Three masts and one funnel. Service: England-India, via Suez Canal. Scrapped in 1909. Sister ship: **Oriental.**

Pericles   (1908)   Aberdeen Line (Geo. Thompson & Co.).
Built by Harland & Wolff, Ltd., Belfast, Ireland. Tonnage: 10,925. Dimensions: 500′ x 62′. Twin-screw, 15 knots. Quadruple expansion engines. Four masts and one funnel. Service: England-Australia, via Capetown. Note: This firm was also known as the "Aberdeen White Star Line". Struck an unknown rock off Cape Leeuwin, West Australia, March 31, 1910, and sank within a few hours. Fortunately the weather was fair and all on board were taken off safely.

Persia   (1900)   P. & O. Line (British).
Built by Caird & Co., Greenock, Scotland. Tonnage: 7,951. Dimensions: 499′ x 54′. Single-screw, 18 knots. Triple expansion engines. Two masts and two funnels. Passengers: 500. Service: England-India-Australia. Torpedoed and sunk 71 miles from Cape Martello, Crete, December 30, 1915, with the loss of 334 lives. Sister ships: **Arabia, China, Egypt** and **India.**

Persia   (1903)   Lloyd Austriaco.
Built by Wigham Richardson & Co., Newcastle, England. Tonnage: 6,283. Dimensions: 424′ x 52′. Single-screw, 12 knots. Quadruple expansion engines. Two masts and one

funnel. Passengers: 40 first class. Note: Came under ownership of Lloyd Triestino in 1918. Destroyed by fire at Bombay in 1926.

Persic   (1899)   White Star Line (British).
Built by Harland & Wolff, Ltd., Belfast, Ireland. Tonnage:
12,042. Dimensions: 550′ x 63′. Twin-screw, 13½ knots.
Quadruple expansion engines. Four masts and one funnel.
Passengers: 350. Service: England-Australia, via Capetown.
Scrapped in 1927. Sister ships: **Afric** and **Medic.**

Peshawur   (1871)   P. & O. Line (British).
Built by Caird & Co., Greenock, Scotland. Tonnage: 3,782
(increased to 4,055). Dimensions: 378′ x 42′. Single-screw,
13½ knots. Compound engines. Three masts and one funnel. Iron hull. Sold in 1900. Renamed: **Ashruf.**

Philippeville   (1899)   Cie. Belge Maritim du Congo.
Built by Sir Raylton Dixon & Co., Middlesbrough, England.
Tonnage: 4,091. Dimensions: 370′ x 46′. Twin-screw, 13½
knots. Triple expansion engines. Two masts and one funnel.
Service: Antwerp-Africa.   Renamed: **Mandingo,**   (b)
Chaudiere.

Pierre Loti   (1913)   Messageries Maritimes (French).
Built by John Brown & Co., Clydebank, Glasgow, Scotland.
Tonnage: 5,114. Dimensions: 381′ x 51′. Twin-screw, 13
knots. Triple expansion engines. Two masts and one funnel.
Passengers: 200. Wrecked near Gabon Estuary, September
2, 1943. Ex-**Emperor Nicholas I.** Sister ship: **Lamartine.**

*Pierre Loti   (1953)   Messageries Maritimes (French).
Built by Direction des Construction & Armes Navales, Brest,
France. Tonnage: 10,944. Dimensions: 492′ x 64′. Twin-
screw, 17 knots. Motorship. Two masts and one funnel.
Passengers: 88 first, 112 tourist, 40 third. Service: France-
Mauritius, via Suez Canal. Sister ships: **Ferdinand de
Lesseps, Jean Laborde** and **La Bourdonnais.**

Pieter Corneliszoon Hooft (1925) Nederland Royal Mail Line.
Built by Ateliers & Chantiers de la Loire, St. Nazaire,
France. Tonnage: 14,642. Dimensions: 521′ x 68′. Twin-
screw, 16 knots. Motorship. Two masts and one funnel.
Service: Amsterdam-Dutch East Indies, via Suez Canal.
Passengers: 253 first, 236 second, 52 third. Destroyed by
fire at Amsterdam in 1932.

Pilsna   (1918)   Lloyd Triestino (Italian).
Built by Cantieri San Rocco S. A., San Rocco, Italy. Tonnage: 8,040. Dimensions: 432' x 51'. Twin-screw, 15 knots. Triple expansion engines. Two masts and one funnel. Renamed: **Galilea.** Sister ship: **Cragovia.**

Po   (1911)   Lloyd Triestino (Italian).
Built by Lloyd Austriaco, Trieste, Austria-Hungaria. Tonnage: 7,367. Dimensions: 442' x 53' (454' o.l.). Twin-screw, 18 knots. Quadruple expansion engines. Two masts and two funnels. A World War II casualty, March 14, 1941. Ex-**Vienna,** ex-**Wien.**

Polynesien   (1890)   Messageries Maritimes (French).
Built by Messageries Maritimes, La Ciotat, France. Tonnage: 6,363. Dimensions: 482' x 49'. Single-screw, 17½ knots. Triple expansion engines. Three masts and two funnels. Steel hull. Launched, April 18, 1890. Service: France-Australia, via Suez Canal. She became a war casualty in the Malta dredged channel, August 10, 1918. Sister ships: **Armand Behic, Australien** and **Ville de la Ciotat.**

Porthos   (1914)   Messageries Maritimes (French).
Built by Ateliers & Chantiers de la Gironde, France. Tonnage: 12,692. Dimensions: 510' x 61'. Twin-screw, 14 knots. Triple expansion engines. Two masts and two funnels. Launched, January 25, 1914. Service: Marseilles-Far East, via Suez Canal. Passengers: 320. Damaged and capsized at Casablanca, November 8, 1942, during the Allied landings. Raised, beached and broken up for scrap in 1945. Sister ship: **Athos.**

Portugal   (1899)   Empreza   Nacional   de   Navegacao (Portuguese).
Built by Sir Raylton Dixon & Co., Middlesbrough, England. Tonnage: 3,998. Dimensions: 365' x 45'. Single-screw, 13 knots. Triple expansion engines. Two masts and one funnel. Inaugurated their Lisbon-African service in 1906.

Potosi   (1873)   Orient Line (British).
Tonnage: 4,230. Passengers: 80 first, 110 second, 350 third. Vessel owned by Pacific Steam Navigation Company. Transferred to the Orient Line service. Note: See PART III for details.

Potsdam   (1935)   North German Lloyd.
Built by Blohm & Voss, Hamburg, Germany. Tonnage: 17,518. Dimensions: 604' x 74' (631' o.l.). Twin-screw, 21

knots. Steam turbines connected to electric motors. Two masts and one funnel. Diameter of funnel 19 feet by 33 feet and height of 36 feet from deck level. Service: Bremen-Far East, via Suez. Passengers: 300. Renamed: (a) **Empire Fowey** (1946) British troopship, (b) **Safina-E-Hujjaj** (1960). Sister ships: **Gneisenau** and **Scharnhorst.** Note: The **Potsdam** had a normal rake bow, while her sister ships had Maier type bows.

Prasident (1900)   Deutsche Ost Afrika Line.
Built by Blohm & Voss, Hamburg, Germany. Tonnage: 3,335. Dimensions: 320′ x 40′. Single-screw, 11 knots. Triple expansion engines. 1,400 I.H.P. Two masts and one funnel. Passengers: 54 first and 42 second. Placed in the "Round Africa" service for a year or two with **Gouverneur** and **Markgraf.** Destroyed by British warships in 1914.

President Doumer (1933)   Messageries Maritimes.
Built by Soc. Provencale de Construction Nav., La Ciotat, France. Tonnage: 11,898. Dimensions: 468′ x 64′ (492′ o.l.). Twin-screw, 18 knots. Motorship. Two masts and one funnel. Launched, January 22, 1933. Service: France-Far East, via Suez. Passengers: 300. Torpedoed and sunk in convoy off Freetown, October 30, 1942, while under Bibby Line management.

Pretoria (1878)   Union Line (British).
Built by Wm. Denny & Bros., Ltd., Dumbarton, Scotland. Tonnage: 3,303. Dimensions: 350′ x 40′. Single-screw, 13 knots. Compound engines. Two masts and one funnel. Iron hull. Originally in the mail service to Capetown. After 1888 in the intermediate service. Re-engined with triple expansions in 1888. Sold to Quebec Steamship Company in 1897, but continued to use same name. Sold to other owners at later date. Renamed: **Saidieh.** Disposed of in 1915.

Pretoria (1936)   German East African Line.
Built by Blohm & Voss, Hamburg, Germany. Tonnage: 16,662. Dimensions: 547′ x 72′ (578′ o.l.). Twin-screw, 18 knots. Six steam turbines. Two masts and two funnels. Service: Germany-East and South Africa. Renamed: (a) **Empire Doon** (1945), (b) **Empire Orwell** (1949), **Gunung Djati** (1958) Blue Funnel Line. Sister ship: **Windhuk.** Owner: Deutsche Ost-Afrika Line.

Pretoria Castle (1939)   Union-Castle Line.
Built by Harland & Wolff, Ltd., Belfast, Ireland. Tonnage: 17,392. Dimensions: 570′ x 76′ (594′ o.l.). Twin-screw, 17

knots. Motorship. Two masts and one funnel. Designed for the intermediate service between London and South East Africa. Passengers: 510. Acquired by the British Admiralty in World War II. Converted into an aircraft carrier. After the war was rebuilt for the Union-Castle Line. Renamed: **Warwick Castle** (1946). Similar ships: **Durban Castle** and **Dunnottar Castle.**

*Pretoria Castle   (1948)   Union-Castle Line.
Built by Harland & Wolff, Ltd., Belfast, Ireland. Tonnage: 28,705. Dimensions: 717' x 84' (747' o.l.). Twin-screw, 22 knots. Steam turbines. Two masts and one funnel. Launched, August 19, 1947. The activation of the launching was performed by Mrs. J. C. Smuts, wife of Field Marshal Smuts, Prime Minister of South Africa, by the means of radio from her home at Irene, in the Transvaal. This unusual method of launching a vessel did much to publicize the noteworthy liner. Service: Southampton-South Africa. Passengers: 214 first and 541 tourist. Sister ship: **Edinburgh Castle.**

Preussen   (1886)   North German Lloyd.
Tonnage: 5,295. Designed for the Bremen-Far East service, but also, made North Atlantic crossings. Note: See PART I for details.

Princess   (1905)   Ellerman & Bucknall Line.
Built by Frd. Krupp, Kiel, Germany. Tonnage: 7,849. Dimensions: 472' x 55'. Twin-screw, 15 knots. Quadruple expansion engines. Two masts and one funnel. Note: Her superstructure was reduced in size. Scrapped in 1926. Ex-**Kronprinzessin Cecilie.**

*Principe Perfeito   (1961)   Companhia Nacional de Navegacao (Portuguese).
Built by Swan, Hunter & Wigham Richardson, Ltd., Newcastle, England. Tonnage: 20,000. Dimensions: 625' (o.l.) x 78'. Twin-screw, 20 knots. Steam turbines. Single mast and one funnel. Launched, September 22, 1960. Passengers: 200 first and 800 tourist. Service: Portugal-West and East Africa. The company's largest ship built to date.

Prins der Nederlanden   (1914)   Nederland Line (Dutch).
Built by Nederlandsche Schps. Maats., Amsterdam, Netherlands. Tonnage: 9,322. Dimensions: 481' x 57' (498' o.l.). Twin-screw, 15 knots. Quadruple expansion engines. Two masts and one funnel. Service: Amsterdam-Dutch East Indies, via Suez Canal. Renamed: **Aquileja** (1935).

Prins Hendrik   (1890)   Nederland Line.
   Built by Caird & Co., Greenock, Scotland. Tonnage: 3,630.
   Dimensions: 360′ x 43′.   Single-screw, 12½ knots.   Triple
   expansion engines. Three masts and one funnel. Steel hull.
   Service: Netherlands-Dutch East Indies, via Suez Canal.
   Sold in 1907. Renamed: **Erna.** Sister ship: **Prinses Sophie.**

Prinses Juliana   (1910)   Nederland Line.
   Built by Nederlandsche Schps. Maats., Amsterdam, Nether-
   lands. Tonnage: 8,000. Dimensions: 455′ x 55′. Twin-screw,
   15 knots. Quadruple expansion engines. Two masts and one
   funnel. Service: Amsterdam-Dutch East Indies, via Suez.
   Passengers: 246 first and 120 second class.   Renamed:
   Costa Rica. Sunk by air attack during evacuation of Crete,
   April 27, 1941.

Prinses Sophie   (1890)   Nederland Line.
   Built by Caird & Co., Greenock, Scotland. Tonnage: 3,591.
   Dimensions: 360′ x 43′.   Single-screw, 12½ knots.   Triple
   expansion engines. Three masts and one funnel.   Service:
   Amsterdam-Dutch East Indies. Sister ship: **Prins Hendrik.**
   Sold in 1907. Renamed: **Ella.** Torpedoed in 1915.

Prinz Eitel Friedrich   (1904)   North German Lloyd.
   Built by "Vulkan", Stettin, Germany.   Tonnage: 8,797.
   Dimensions: 488′ x 55′ (506′ o.l.).   Twin-screw, 16 knots.
   Quadruple expansion engines. 7,500 I.H.P. Two masts and
   two funnels.   Service: Europe-Far East, via Suez Canal.
   Passengers: 166 first, 158 second, 614 third. Renamed: (a)
   De Kalb (1917), (b) **Mount Clay** (1921).   Scrapped in
   1934. Sister ship: **Prinz Ludwig.** Note: These liners were
   specially built for the Far Eastern service.   The **Prinz
   Eitel Friedrich** became famous as a raider during the early
   part of World War I.

Prinz Heinrich   (1894)   North German Lloyd.
   Built by F. Schicahu, Danzig, Germany. Tonnage: 6,636.
   Dimensions: 455′ x 51′.   Twin-screw, 15 knots.   Triple
   expansion engines. Two masts and one funnel.   Service:
   Bremen-Far East. Passengers: 136 first and 72 second.
   Renamed: **Porto** (1916) Portuguese. Sister ship: **Prinz
   Regent Luitpold.**

Prinz Ludwig   (1906)   North German Lloyd.
   Built by "Vulkan", Stettin, Germany.   Tonnage: 9,687.
   Dimensions: 492′ x 57′. Twin-screw, 16 knots. Quadruple
   expansion engines. Two masts and two funnels.   Service:

Europe-Far East, via Suez Canal. Passengers: 100 first, 160 second, 80 third class. Vessel was turned over to the British after First World War. Renamed: **Orcades** (1919). Scrapped in 1925. Sister ship: **Prinz Eitel Friedrich.**

Prinz Regent Luitpold (1894)   North German Lloyd.
     Built by F. Schichau, Danzig, Germany. Tonnage: 6,595. Dimensions: 455′ x 50′. Twin-screw, 15 knots. Triple expansion engines. 5,500 I.H.P. Two masts and one funnel. Service: Bremen-Far East. Also, made some sailings to Australia. Passengers: 76 first and 72 second class. Seized by Italy in First World War. Renamed: **Pietro Calvi** (1916). Sister ship: **Prinz Heinrich.**

Prinzess Alice (1900)   North German Lloyd.
     Tonnage: 10,911. Service: Europe-Far East, via Suez Canal. Note: See PART I for details.

Prinzess Irene (1900)   North German Lloyd.
     Tonnage: 10,881. Service: Europe-Far East, via Suez Canal. Note: See PART I for details.

Prinzessin (1905)   Deutsche Ost Afrika Line.
     Built by Blohm & Voss, Hamburg, Germany. Tonnage: 6,387. Dimensions: 416′ x 50′. Twin-screw, 14 knots. Triple expansion engines. Two masts and one funnel. Service: Hamburg-Africa. Acquired by Messageries Maritimes after First World War. Renamed: **General Voyron.** Scrapped in 1933. Sister ship: **Prinzregent.**

Prinzregent (1903)   Deutsche Ost Afrika Line.
     Built by Blohm & Voss, Hamburg, Germany. Tonnage: 6,375. Dimensions: 416′ x 50′. Twin-screw, 14 knots. Triple expansion engines. Two masts and one funnel. Service: Hamburg-Africa. Passengers: 115 first, 84 second, 80 third. Renamed: **Cordoba** (1919) French. Scrapped in 1932. Sister ship: **Prinzessin.**

Professor Woermann (1903)   Woermann Line (German).
     Built by Bremer Vulkan, Vegesack, Germany. Tonnage: 5,631. Dimensions: 403′ x 49′. Single-screw, 13½ knots. Triple expansion engines. Two masts and one funnel. Service: Germany-Africa. Renamed: **Swakopmund** (1909) Hamburg-American Line, (b) **Arafura** (1920) Eastern & Australian Steamship Co. Ex-**Florida.**

Professor Woermann (1912)   Woermann Line (German).
     Built by Reiherstieg Schiffsw., Hamburg, Germany. Tonnage: 6,079. Dimensions: 392′ x 52′. Single-screw, 13 knots.

Quadruple expansion engines. Two masts and one funnel. Service: Germany-West Africa. One of the line's finest ships of that era. Passengers: 120 first, 94 second, 50 third. Renamed: (a) **Professor,** (b) **Edmund Wagenknecht,** (c) **General San Martin,** (d) **Almirante Jacquay.**

*Prome   (1937)   Henderson Line (British).
Built by Wm. Denny & Bros., Ltd., Dumbarton, Scotland. Tonnage: 7,043. Dimensions: 444′ x 59′ (462′ o.l.). Single-screw, 14 knots. Three steam turbines. Two masts and one funnel. Service: England-Burma. Passengers: 74. Sister ship: **Salween.** Note: The Henderson Line has been controlled by Elder, Dempster & Company since 1952.

*Quanza   (1929)   Cia. Nacional de Navegacao (Portuguese).
Built by Blohm & Voss, Hamburg, Germany. Tonnage: 6,636. Dimensions: 418′ x 52′. Twin-screw, 13½ knots. Triple expansion engines. Two masts and one funnel. Passengers: 111 first, 120 second, 98 third. Ex-**Portugal.**

Raffaele Rubattino   (1882)   Navigazione Generale Italiana.
Built by Palmer's Shipbuilding Co., Newcastle, England. Tonnage: 4,337. Dimensions: 399′ x 44′. Single-screw, 14 knots. Compound engines. Two masts and two funnels. Passengers: 84 first and 40 second class. In the Italy-Far Eastern service, along with **China** (renamed **Domenico Balduino**).

Raglan Castle   (1897)   (a) Castle Line, (b) Union-Castle Line.
Built by Barclay, Curle & Co., Glasgow, Scotland. Tonnage: 4,324. Dimensions: 383′ x 46′. Single-screw, 12 knots. Triple expansion engines. Two masts and one funnel. Type: Intermediate steamer. During the Russo-Japanese war in 1905, she was used as Russian store-ship, but soon re-sold to the Danish East Asiatic Co. Renamed: (a) **Hanna** (1905), (b) **St. Domingo** (1906), (c) **Pythia** (1909), (d) **Ready** (whale) factory ship. Sister ship: **Dunolly Castle.**

Rajputana   (1926)   P. & O. Line (British).
Built by Harland & Wolff, Ltd., Belfast, Ireland. Tonnage: 16,568. Dimensions: 547′ x 71′. Twin-screw, 17 knots. Quadruple expansion engines. Two masts and two funnels. Passengers: 600. Service: England-Far East, via Suez. Torpedoed and sunk by submarine in North Atlantic, April 1941. Sister ships: **Ranchi, Ranpura** and **Rawalpindi.**

*Rajula   (1926)   British India Steam Navigation Co.
Built by Barclay, Curle & Co., Glasgow, Scotland. Tonnage: 8,478. Dimensions: 462′ x 61′ (477′ o.l.). Twin-screw, 13

knots. Triple expansion engines. Two masts and one funnel. Service: Far East. Passengers: 37 first and 133 second. Sister ship: **Rohna.**

Ranchi   (1925)   P. & O. Line (British).
Built by Hawthorn, Leslie & Co., Newcastle, England. Tonnage: 16,650. Dimensions: 548' x 71' (570' o.l.). Twin-screw, 17 knots. Quadruple expansion engines. Two masts and two funnels. Service: England-Far East, via Suez Canal. Passengers: 600. After World War II was converted to a one-class (940 emigrants) ship. Altered to single funnel. Scrapped in Great Britain, 1953. Sister ships: **Rajputana, Ranpura** and **Rawalpindi.**

*Randfontein   (1958)   Holland-Africa Line.
Built by Wilton-Fijenoord, Schiedam, Netherlands. Tonnage: 13,693. Dimensions: 536' x 70' (584' o.l.). Twin-screw, 18½ knots. Motorship. Two masts and one funnel. Entered service in January 1959. Route: Europe-South and East Africa. Passengers: 123 first and 166 tourist. Note: Built to replace the **Klipfontein** lost off the coast of Africa in 1953. Running mates: **Jagersfontein** and **Oranjefontein.**

Ranpura   (1925)   P. & O. Line (British).
Built by Hawthorn, Leslie & Co., Newcastle, England. Tonnage: 16,601. Dimensions: 548' x 71' (570' o.l.). Twin-screw, 17 knots. Quadruple expansion engines. Two masts and two funnels. Passengers: 600. Service: England-Far East, via Suez Canal. Taken over by the British Admiralty early in World War II. She was not returned to the P. & O. Line. Sister ships: **Ranchi, Rajputana** and **Rawalpindi.**

Rawalpindi   (1925)   P. & O. Line (British).
Built by Harland & Wolff, Ltd., Greenock, Scotland. Tonnage: 16,619. Dimensions: 547' x 71' (570' o.l.). Twin-screw, 17 knots. Quadruple expansion engines. Two masts and two funnels. Passengers: 600. Service: England-Far East, via Suez Canal. Converted to an armed merchant cruiser early in World War II. Sunk by gunfire in the North Atlantic during her gallant fight with the German warships **Scharnhorst** and **Gneisenau,** November 23, 1939. Sister ships: **Rajputana, Ranchi** and **Ranpura.**

Razmak   (1925)   P. & O. Line (British).
Built by Harland & Wolff, Ltd., Greenock, Scotland. Tonnage: 10,602. Dimensions: 500' x 63'. Twin-screw, 18 knots. Quadruple expansion engines. Two masts and two funnels. Renamed: **Monowai.**

Re d' Italia   (1907)   Lloyd Sabaudo Line (Italian).
  Tonnage: 6,364.   Services: (a) North Atlantic, (b) Italy-South America, (c) Italy-Australia.   Note: See PART I for details.

Regina d' Italia   (1907)   Lloyd Sabaudo Line.
  Tonnage: 6,368.   Service: (a) North Atlantic, (b) Italy-South America, (c) Italy-Australia.   Note: See PART I for details.

Rembrandt   (1906)   Nederland Royal Mail Line.
  Built by Nederlandsche Schps. Maats., Amsterdam, Netherlands.   Tonnage: 5,876.   Dimensions: 420' x 47'.   Single-screw, 14 knots.   Quadruple expansion engines.   4,200 I.H.P.   Two masts and one funnel.   Service: Amsterdam-Dutch East Indies, via Suez Canal.   Passengers: 80 first and 54 second.   Scrapped in 1928.   Sister ships: **Grotius** and **Vondel.**

Remo   (1927)   (a) Lloyd Triestino, (b) Italia Line.
  Built by Stabilimento Tecnico Triestino, Trieste, Italy.   Tonnage: 9,780.   Dimensions: 484' x 62' (506' o.l.).   Twin-screw, 14 knots.   Motorship.   Two masts and one very small funnel.   Service: Italy-Australia.   Passengers: 250 (680 with emigrants).   Captured at Freemantle in 1940.   Renamed: **Reynella** (Australian Gov't).   Sister ship: **Romolo.**

Remuera   (1911)   New Zealand Shipping Co.
  Tonnage: 11,276.   Service: England-Australia-New Zealand.   Vessels in this service used the Cape of Good Hope route on the outward voyage, and the return trip was made via Cape Horn.   After the completion of the Panama Canal, the **Remuera** used that facility instead of the Cape Horn route.   Note: See PART II for details.

Rewa   (1906)   British India Steam Navigation Co.
  Built by Wm. Denny & Bros., Ltd., Dumbarton, Scotland.   Tonnage: 7,308.   Dimensions: 456' x 56'.   Triple-screw, 17 knots.   Three steam turbines.   Two masts and one funnel.   Torpedoed and sunk 19 miles from Hartland Point, January 4, 1918, with the loss of 4 lives.   Similar ship: **Rohilla.**

Rhein   (1899)   North German Lloyd.
  Tonnage: 10,058.   Services: (a) North Atlantic, (b) Europe-Australia, via Suez Canal.   Note: See PART I for details.

Rhodesia Castle   (1951)   Union-Castle Line.
  Built by Harland & Wolff, Ltd., Belfast, Ireland.   Tonnage: 17,041.   Dimensions: 556' x 74' (576' o.l.).   Twin-screw, 17½

knots. Six steam turbines. Two masts and one funnel. Entered England-Africa service in October 1951. Passengers: 526 cabin class. Sister ships: **Braemar Castle** and **Kenya Castle.**

Rimutaka   (1884)   New Zealand Shipping Co.
Built by John Elder & Co., Glasgow, Scotland. Tonnage: 4,515. Dimensions: 430' x 46'. Single-screw. Compound engines. Three masts and one funnel. Clipper bow. Steel hull. Service: England-Australia-New Zealand. Renamed: **Zamania** (1899) British India Co.   Scrapped in 1911. Sister ship: **Kaikoura.**

Rimutaka   (1900)   New Zealand Shipping Co.
Built by Wm. Denny & Bros., Ltd., Dumbarton, Scotland. Tonnage: 8,997. Dimensions: 457' x 58'. Twin-screw, 13½ knots. Triple expansion engines. Two masts and one funnel. Passengers: 40 first, 50 second, 80 third. Service: England-Australia-New Zealand. Transferred to Panama Canal route at later date. Out of fleet in 1929. Sister ship: **Ruapehu.**

Rindjani   (1906)   Rotterdam Lloyd (Dutch).
Built by Kon. Maats. de Schelde, Flushing, Netherlands. Tonnage: 4,762. Dimensions: 394' x 47'. Single-screw, 14 knots. Triple expansion engines. Two masts and one funnel. Service: Rotterdam-Dutch East Indies, via Suez Canal. Renamed: **Angora,** (b) **Ankara.** Sister ship: **Ophir.**

Ripon   (1846)   P. & O. Line (British).
Built in Great Britain.   Tonnage: 1,508.   Dimensions: 217' x 33'. Paddle-wheels. Oscillating engines. Two masts and two funnels. Clipper bow. Iron hull. An outstanding passenger ship for her day. Service: London-Alexandria-Constantinople. Lengthened to 276 feet (1,903 tons) in 1962.

Rohilla   (1880)   P. & O. Line (British).
Built by Caird & Co., Greenock, Scotland. Tonnage: 3,501 (originally 3,387). Dimensions: 386' x 40' (400' o.l.). Single-screw, 14 knots. Compound engines. Three masts and one funnel. Iron hull. Accommodation for first and second class passengers. Service: (a) England-Bombay, via Suez Canal, (b) England-Australia. Later shifted to minor routes. Renamed: **Rohilla Maru** (1900) Japanese. Wrecked at Ujina in the China Inland Sea, July 1905. Running mates: **Rosetta** and **Ravenna.**

Rohilla (1906) British India Steam Navigation Co.
Built by Harland & Wolff, Ltd., Belfast, Ireland. Tonnage:
7,409. Dimensions: 460′ x 56′. Twin-screw, 17 knots.
Quadruple expansion engines. Two masts and one funnel.
Wrecked near Whitby, October 30, 1914. Sister ship: **Rewa.**

Rohna (1926) British India Steam Navigation Co.
Built by Hawthorn, Leslie & Co., Newcastle, England.
Tonnage: 8,602. Dimensions: 461′ x 61′. Twin-screw, 13
knots. Quadruple expansion engines. Two masts and one
funnel. Sunk by air attack through the means of launching
a guided missile, off Djidjelli, Algeria, November 26, 1943,
and went down within 30 minutes. There was a loss of 1,150
troops and 120 of the crew of 195. This marked one of the
earliest sinkings by this method of attack. Sister ship:
Rajula.

Roman (1863) Union Line (British).
Built by C. Lungley, London, England. Tonnage: 1,282.
Dimensions: 320′ (as lengthened) x 32′. Single-screw. Com-
pound engines installed in 1872. Tonnage increased to:
1,857. Two masts and one funnel. Clipper bow. Iron hull.
In mail service between England and Capetown. Sold to
Turkish owners in 1889. Renamed: **Adana.** Not listed after
1910. Sister ship: **Saxon.**

Roman (1870) Union Line (Union Steam Ship Co.).
Built by Day, Summers & Co., Northam, England. Tonnage:
3,021. Dimensions: 369′ x 40′. Single-screw. Compound
engines. Two masts and one funnel. Clipper bow. Iron
hull. Sold for scrap in 1891. Ex-**Nile** (1890) Royal Mail Line.

Rome (1881) P. & O. Line (British).
Built by Caird & Co., Greenock, Scotland. Tonnage: 5,013.
Dimensions: 430′ x 44′. Single-screw, 16 knots. Compound
engines. Four masts and two funnels. Iron hull. Service:
England-Australia, via Suez Canal. Lengthened to 449 feet
(4,545 tons) in 1892. Re-engined with triple expansions in
1891. Converted to cruise ship in 1904. Renamed: **Vectis**
(1904). Scrapped in Italy, 1912. Sister ship: **Carthage.**

Romolo (1926) (a) Lloyd Triestino, (b) Italia Line.
Built by Stabilimento Tecnico, Triestino, Trieste, Italy.
Tonnage: 9,780. Dimensions: 495′ x 62′ (506′ o.l.). Twin-
screw, 14 knots. Motorship. Two masts and one funnel.
Service: Italy-Australia. Scuttled in mid-Pacific in 1940,
when an Australian cruiser approached. Sister ship: **Remo.**

Roon   (1903)   North German Lloyd.
Tonnage: 8,174. Designed for the Germany-Far East, via Suez Canal, service. Note: See PART I for details.

Rosetta   (1880)   P. & O. Line (British).
Built by Harland & Wolff, Ltd., Belfast, Ireland. Tonnage: 3,502. Dimensions: 390' x 40'. Single-screw, 14 knots. Compound engines. Three masts and one funnel. Built of iron due to the scarcity of steel. Service: England-Australia, via Suez. Vessel sold to Toyo Kisen Kaisha in 1900. Renamed: **Rosetta Maru.** Sister ships: **Rohilla** and **Ravenna.**

Roslin Castle   (1883)   (a) Castle Line, (b) Union-Castle Line.
Built by Barclay, Curle & Co., Glasgow, Scotland. Tonnage: 4,267. Dimensions: 392' x 48'. Single-screw, 15 knots. Compound engines. Two masts and one funnel. Iron hull. Noted as a roller and thus became known as the "Rolling" Castle. In 1888 was lengthened 15 feet (4,487 tons), new stern was fitted and re-engined with triple expansions. These alterations made her the fastest vessel of the line. However, she continued to be a roller! Sold to German owners in 1905 and was chartered to the Russians as a store-ship. Renamed: **Regina.** Ran ashore off Mozambique in March 1905. Subsequently refloated, repaired and in 1907 scrapped at Genoa. Sister ships: **Hawarden Castle** and **Norham Castle.**

Rotorua   (1910)   New Zealand Shipping Co.
Built by Wm. Denny & Bros., Ltd., Dumbarton, Scotland. Tonnage: 11,130. Dimensions: 484' x 62'. Triple-screw, 14 knots. Triple expansion engines and steam turbine. Two masts and one funnel. Service: England-New Zealand. Torpedoed and sunk 24 miles from Star Point (English Channel) on March 22, 1917, with the loss of one life. Sister ships: **Remuera** and **Ruahine.**

Rotorua   (1911)   New Zealand Shipping Co.
Tonnage: 12,184. Service: England-New Zealand. Passengers: 131 first class. Ex-**Shropshire** (1922). Note: See PART II for details.

Ruahine   (1891)   New Zealand Shipping Co.
Built by Wm. Denny & Bros., Ltd., Dumbarton, Scotland. Tonnage: 6,127. Dimensions: 430' x 50'. Single-screw, $13\frac{1}{2}$ knots. Quadruple expansion engines. Two masts and one funnel. Service: England-Australia-New Zealand, via Cape-town outward and by way of Cape Horn on the homeward passage. Renamed: **Antonio Lopez** (Spanish).

Ruahine   (1909)   New Zealand Shipping Co.
Tonnage: 10,839. Service: England-Australia-New Zealand.
Note: See PART II for details.

Runic   (1900)   White Star Line (British).
Built by Harland & Wolff, Ltd., Belfast, Ireland. Tonnage:
12,490.   Dimensions: 550′ x 63′.   Twin-screw, 13 knots.
Quadruple expansion engines. Four masts and one funnel.
Service: England-Australia, via Capetown. Passengers: 350.
Renamed: **New Sevilla.** Sister ship: **Suevic.**

*Ruys   (1936)   Royal Interocean Lines (Dutch).
Built by N. V. Kon. Maats. De Shelde, Flushing, Netherlands. Tonnage: 14,285. Dimensions: 537′ x 72′ (561′ o.l.).
Triple-screw, 17 knots. Motorship. Two masts and one funnel. Passengers: 660. Crew: 230. Service: Far East-Africa-
South America, via Capetown. Sister ships: **Boissevain**
and **Tegelberg.** Note: First large motorships fitted with
triple-screw.

Saarbrucken   (1923)   North German Lloyd.
Built by "Weser", Bremen, Germany. Tonnage: 9,429.
Dimensions: 458′ x 57′ (479′ o.l.). Twin-screw, 11 knots.
Triple expansion engines. Two masts and one funnel.
Service: Bremen-Far East. Renamed: **Toscana** (1935).
Sister ship: **Coblenz.**

Sado Maru   (1898)   N. Y. K. Line (Japan).
Built by Workman, Clark & Co., Belfast, Ireland. Tonnage:
6,227. Dimensions: 445′ x 49′. Twin-screw, 14 knots. Triple
expansion engines. Two masts and one funnel. Service:
Japan-Europe, via Suez Canal. Passengers: 35 first, 20
second, 158 third.

Sagaing   (1925)   Henderson Line (British).
Built by Wm. Denny & Bros., Ltd., Dumbarton, Scotland.
Tonnage: 7,994. Dimensions: 454′ x 61′. Single-screw, 14
knots. Triple expansion engines. Two masts and one funnel.
Service: Glasgow-Liverpool-Rangoon, via Suez Canal.
Passengers: 150 first class. Sunk by aircraft, April 9, 1942.
Running mates: **Amarapoora, Kemmendie, Pegu** and
Yoma.

Saghalien   (1880)   Messageries Maritimes.
Built by Messageries Maritimes, La Ciotat, France. Tonnage: 4,049. Dimensions: 413′ x 39′. Single-screw, 13½
knots. Compound engines. Three masts and one funnel.

Iron hull. Launched, July 25, 1880. Service: France-Australia, via Suez Canal. Scuttled with battleship **Massena** to form a breakwater at Seddul Bahr for the Dardanelles landings, November 10, 1915. Sister ships: **Niger, Orenoque** and **Senegal.**

Said (1863) Messageries Maritimes.
Built by Messageries Maritimes, La Ciotat, France. Tonnage: 1,680. Dimensions: 328' x 32'. Single-screw. Two cylinder engines. Three masts and one funnel. Iron hull. Launched, October 18, 1863. Lengthened in 1869. Scrapped in France, 1890. Sister ships: **Moeris** and **Peluse.**

Salamis (1899) Aberdeen Line (Thompson's).
Built by Hall Russell & Co., Aberdeen, Scotland. Tonnage: 4,508. Dimensions: 392' x 47'. Single-screw, 14 knots. Triple expansion engines. Three masts and one funnel. Clipper bow. Service: England-Australia, via South Africa. Renamed: **Kamarima.** Scrapped in Italy, 1924. Sister ship: **Moravian.** Fine looking passenger ships.

Salazie (1883) Messageries Maritimes.
Built by Messageries Maritimes, La Ciotat, France. Tonnage: 4,147 (increased to 4,255). Dimensions: 413' x 41'. Single-screw, 15 knots. Compound engines. Three masts and two funnels. Iron hull. Launched, April 1883. Service: France-Australia, via Suez Canal. Driven ashore by cyclone North of Vohemar (Madagascar), November 21, 1912, and became a total loss. Sister ships: **Caledonien, Melbourne, Natal, Oceanien, Sydney** and **Yarra.**

Salier (1875) North German Lloyd.
Tonnage: 3,098. Inaugurated regular service to Australia from Germany in 1886. Note: See PART I for details.

Salsette (1909) P. & O. Line (British).
Built by Caird & Co., Greenock, Scotland. Tonnage: 5,842. Dimensions: 440' x 53'. Twin-screw, 20 knots. Quadruple expansion engines. Two masts and two funnels. Designed for the express mail service between Aden and Bombay. Torpedoed and sunk in the English Channel, July 20, 1917, with the loss of 15 lives.

*Salween (1937) Henderson Line (British).
Built by Wm. Denny & Bros., Ltd., Dumbarton, Scotland. Tonnage: 7,063. Dimensions: 444' x 59' (462' o.l.). Single-screw, 15 knots. Three steam turbines. Two masts and one

funnel. Service: Great Britain-Burma. Passengers: 76 first class. Sister ship: **Prome.**

Salzburg (1902)   Austrian Lloyd.
Built by Stabilimente Tecnico, Trieste, Austria. Tonnage: 3,226. Dimensions: 324' x 42'. Single-screw, 12½ knots. Triple expansion engines. 2,450 I.H.P. Two masts and one funnel. Passengers: 44 first and 17 second. Renamed: **Gorizia** (1923). Scrapped in 1931.

Sangola (1901)   British India Steam Navigation Co.
Built by Wm. Denny & Bros., Ltd., Dumbarton, Scotland. Tonnage: 5,184. Dimensions: 410' x 50'. Single-screw. Triple expansion engines. Two masts and one funnel. Out of fleet in 1923. Sister ship: **Santhia.**

*Sangola (1947)   British India Steam Navigation Co.
Built by Barclay, Curle & Co., Glasgow, Scotland. Tonnage: 8,647. Dimensions: 479' x 62'. Twin-screw, 14½ knots. Motorship. Two masts and one funnel. Passengers: 21 first, 64 second, bunks for 335. Service: Bengal-Japan. Sister ships: **Sirdhana** and **Santhia.**

Sannio (1921)   Lloyd Triestino (Italian).
Built by Bremer Vulkan, Vegesack, Germany. Tonnage: 9,834. Dimensions: 468' x 58' (485' o.l.). Single-screw. Triple expansion engines and steam turbine. Four masts and one funnel. Became a war loss, April 10, 1941. Ex-**General Mitre** (1935), ex-**Artus.**

Santhia (1901)   British India Steam Navigation Co.
Built by Wm. Denny & Bros., Ltd., Dumbarton, Scotland. Tonnage: 5,192. Dimensions: 411' x 50'. Single-screw. Triple expansion engines. Two masts and one funnel. Out of fleet in 1923. Sister ship: **Sangola.**

Santhia (1925)   British India Steam Navigation Co.
Built by Swan, Hunter & Wigham Richardson, Ltd., Newcastle, England. Tonnage: 7,754. Dimensions: 436' x 57'. Twin-screw, 13 knots. Triple expansion engines. Two masts and one funnel. Caught fire and capsized in Hooghly River in 1943. Sister ships: **Shirala** and **Sirdhana.**

*Santhia (1950)   British India Steam Navigation Co.
Built by Barclay, Curle & Co., Whiteinch, Scotland. Tonnage: 8,908. Dimensions: 459' x 62' (479' o.l.). Twin-screw, 15 knots. Motorship. Two masts and one funnel. Service: Bombay-Karachi-Persian Gulf ports. Passengers: 25 first,

70 second, 68 third, bunks for 268. Crew: 137. Sister ships: **Sangola** and **Sirdhana.**

Sanuki Maru   (1897)   N. Y. K. Line (Japanese).
Built by Napier, Shanks & Bell, Glasgow, Scotland. Tonnage: 6,164. Dimensions: 445' x 49'. Twin-screw, 13 knots. Triple expansion engines. Four masts and one funnel. Service: Japan-Europe, via Suez Canal. Passengers: 29 first, 20 second, 31 third.

Sarpedon   (1923)   Blue Funnel Line (British).
Built by Cammell, Laird & Co., Birkenhead, England. Tonnage: 11,321. Dimensions: 499' x 62'. Twin-screw, 15 knots. Four steam turbines. Two masts and one funnel. Service: Liverpool-Far East, via Suez Canal. Passengers: 135. Sold to British shipbreakers in 1953. Sister ships: **Antenor, Hector** and **Patroclus.**

Saxon   (1863)   Union Line (British).
Built by Day, Summers, Southampton, England. Tonnage: 1,142. Single-screw. Two masts and one funnel. Clipper bow. Iron hull. Completed her maiden voyage from England to Capetown in 1863 in the record breaking time of 31 days. Sold to Bailley & Leetham in 1876. Renamed: **Benguella.** Lost at sea in June 1890. Sister ship: **Roman.**

Saxon   (1900)   Union-Castle Line (British).
Built by Harland & Wolff, Ltd., Belfast, Ireland. Tonnage: 12,385. Dimensions: 570' x 64' (585' o.l.). Twin-screw, 17 knots. Quadruple expansion engines. Two masts and one funnel. Launched, December 21, 1899. The merger of the Castle and Union Line was completed early in 1900. Maiden voyage: Southampton-Capetown, June 1900. Passengers: 290 first and 200 second class. Vessel laid up off Netley in 1931. Kept as a reserve mail steamer for a time. Sold to shipbreakers in 1935.

Scharnhorst   (1904)   North German Lloyd.
Tonnage: 8,388. Service: (a) Bremen-Far East, (b) North Atlantic. Note: See PART I for details.

Scharnhorst   (1935)   North German Lloyd.
Built by Deutsche Sch-u-Mschb., Flensburg, Germany. Tonnage: 18,184. Dimensions: 625' x 74' (652' o.l.). Twin-screw, 21 knots. Turbo-electric. Two masts and one funnel. Maier type bow. Service: Bremen-Far East, via Suez Canal. Passengers: 300. Taken over by Japanese in 1942. Con-

verted into an aircraft carrier and renamed **Jinyo.** Sunk by submarine in 1944. Running mates: **Gneisenau** and **Potsdam.** Note: These fine passenger ships were built, so as to recapture some of the Far Eastern trade.

*Schwabenstein** (1954) North German Lloyd.
    Built by Bremer Vulkan, Bremen, Germany. Tonnage: 8,955. Dimensions: 492' x 63' (537' o.l.). Single-screw, 16½ knots. Motorship. Single mast and one funnel. Passengers: 86 first class. Service: Europe-Far East, via Suez Canal. Sister ships: **Bayernstein** and **Hessenstein.**

Scindia (1890) Anchor Line (British).
    Built by D. & W. Henderson, Ltd., Glasgow, Scotland. Tonnage: 4,358. Dimensions: 375' x 46'. Single-screw, 12 knots. Triple expansion engines. Two masts and one funnel. Designed for the Great Britain-Calcutta route. Sold to United States Government in 1898. Sister ship: **Algeria.**

Scot (1891) (a) Union Line, (b) Union-Castle Line.
    Built by Wm. Denny & Bros., Ltd., Dumbarton, Scotland. Tonnage: 6,844. Dimensions: 477' x 54' (531' as lengthened). Twin-screw, 18 knots. Triple expansion engines. 12,000 I.H.P. Two masts and two funnels. Launched, December 30, 1890. Note: The most famous of all the steamships built for the Capetown trade prior to 1900. Passengers: 208 first, 100 second, 100 third class. Her clipper bow carried on it a carved figure-head of Sir William Wallace, the "Great Scot". Maiden voyage: Southampton-Capetown, July 25, 1891. She made the long voyage in 15 days, 9 hours, 52 minutes, a record for that day. Her homeward run also broke the speed record. Lengthened by 54 feet (7,815 tons) in 1896. Sold to the Hamburg-American Line in September 1905. Converted to a cruise ship. Renamed: (a) **Oceana** (1905), (b) **Alfonso XIII** (1916), (c) **Vasco Nunez de Balboa** (1923). Scrapped in Italy, 1927.

*Selandia** (1938) The East Asiatic Co. (Danish).
    Built by Nakskov, Skibsvaerft, Nakskov, Denmark. Tonnage: 8,482. Dimensions: 432' x 63' (452' o.l.). Single-screw, 15 knots. Motorship. Four masts and no funnel. Note: Not completed until 1945. Service: Europe-Bagkok-Saigon. Passengers: 64 first class. Sister ship: **Falstria.**

Semiramis (1895) Lloyd Austriaco.
    Built by Wm. Denny & Bros., Ltd., Dumbarton, Scotland. Tonnage: 4,165. Dimensions: 377' x 44'. Single-screw, 16 knots. Triple expansion engines. 5,000 I.H.P. Two masts

and one funnel. Passengers: 91 first, 40 second, 28 third. Ownership transferred to Lloyd Triestino after First World War. Scrapped in 1933.

Senegal   (1872)   Messageries Maritimes (French).
Tonnage: 3,717. Service: (a) France-Far East, via Suez, (b) France-South America. Note: See PART III for details.

Seydlitz   (1903)   North German Lloyd.
Tonnage: 7,942. Service: (a) North Atlantic, (b) Latin American, (c) Bremen-Far East, via Suez. Note: See PART I for details.

Shannon   (1881)   P. & O. Line (British).
Built by Harland & Wolff, Ltd., Belfast, Ireland. Tonnage: 4,189 (increased to 4,362). Dimensions: 400′ x 42′. Single-screw, 15 knots. Compound engines. Two masts and two funnels. Steel hull. Service: England-Australia, via Suez Canal. Passengers: 131 first and 94 second class. Scrapped in 1902.

Shirala   (1901)   British India Steam Navigation Co.
Built by A. & J. Inglis, Glasgow, Scotland. Tonnage: 5,306. Dimensions: 410′ x 50′. Single-screw, 13 knots. Triple expansion engines. Two masts and one funnel. Torpedoed and sunk near Owers Light Vessel, July 2, 1918, with the loss of 8 lives.

Shirala   (1925)   British India Steam Navigation Co.
Built by Hawthorn, Leslie & Co., Newcastle, England. Tonnage: 7,841. Dimensions: 437′ x 57′. Twin-screw, 13 knots. Triple expansion engines. Two masts and one funnel. Scrapped at Blyth in 1951. Sister ships: **Santhia** and **Sirdhana.**

Shropshire   (1891)   Bibby Line (British).
Built by Harland & Wolff, Ltd., Belfast, Ireland. Tonnage: 5,799. Dimensions: 445′ x 49′. Twin-screw, 14 knots. Triple expansion engines. Four masts and one funnel. Steel hull. Service: England-Burma. Renamed: **Seang Bee** (Rangoon). Sunk by submarine off England in 1917. Sister ship: **Staffordshire.**

Shropshire   (1911)   Federal Steam Navigation Co.
Built by John Brown & Co., Glasgow, Scotland. Tonnage: 11,911. Dimensions: 526′ x 61′. Triple-screw, 14 knots. Quadruple expansion engines. Five masts and one funnel.

Service: England-Australia, via Capetown.   Renamed: **Rotorua** (1922).

Shropshire   (1926)   Bibby Line (British).
   Built by Fairfield Shipbuilding Co., Glasgow, Scotland. Tonnage: 10,560. Dimensions: 483' x 60' (502' o.l.). Twin-screw, 15½ knots. Motorship. Four masts and one funnel. Service: Liverpool-Rangoon, via Suez Canal. Passengers: 275. Crew: 200. Renamed: **Salopian.** Torpedoed and sunk, June 1, 1941. Sister ships: **Cheshire** and **Staffordshire.**

Sibajak   (1927)   Rotterdam Lloyd (Dutch).
   Built by Kon. Maats. de Schelde, Flushing, Netherlands. Tonnage: 12,226. Dimensions: 506' x 62' (530' o.l.). Twin-screw, 17 knots. Motorship. Two masts and one funnel. Service: Netherlands-Dutch East Indies, via Suez Canal. Passengers: 520. Converted to emigrant carrier in 1951. Scrapped in 1956. Similar ship: **Indrapoera.**

Sicilia   (1901)   P. & O. Line (British).
   Built by Barclay, Curle & Co., Glasgow, Scotland. Tonnage: 6,696. Dimensions: 450' x 52'. Twin-screw, 14 knots. Triple expansion engines. Two masts and one funnel. Service: Calcutta and Far East. Sister ships: **Sardinia, Somali, Soudan** and **Syria.** Scrapped in 1926.

Simla   (1894)   P. & O. Line (British).
   Built by Caird & Co., Greenock, Scotland. Tonnage: 5,884. Dimensions: 430' x 49'. Single-screw, 14½ knots. Triple expansion engines. 4,500 I.H.P. Two masts and one funnel. Designed for the intermediate service. Passengers: 81 first and 62 second. Torpedoed and sunk by enemy submarine 45 miles from Gezo Island during First World War. Sister ships: **Malta** and **Nubia.**

Sinai   (1898)   Messageries Maritimes (French).
   Built by Forges & Chantiers de la Mediterranee, La Seyne, France. Tonnage: 4,624 (increased to 4,856). Dimensions: 393' x 43'. Twin-screw, 13 knots. Triple expansion engines. Launched, July 19, 1898. Passengers: 24 first and 30 second class. Service: France-Far East. Torpedoed and sunk by submarine in the Mediterranean, December 11, 1916. She had survivors of the **Magellan** on board, which had also just been sunk.

Sindh   (1869)   Messageries Maritimes (French).
   Built at La Ciotat, France. Tonnage: 3,387. Dimensions: 368' x 39'. Single-screw, 13½ knots. Engines developed

2,400 H.P. Three masts and two funnels. Launched, July 25, 1869. Service: France-East of Suez. Scrapped at Marseilles in March 1901. Sister ships: **Amazone, Ava, Meikong** and **Pei-Ho.**

Sindoro   (1899)   Rotterdam Lloyd (Dutch).
Built by Kon. Maats. de Schelde, Flushing, Netherlands. Tonnage: 5,471. Dimensions: 408' x 49'. Twin-screw, 14 knots. Quadruple expansion engines. Two masts and one funnel. Service: Rotterdam-Dutch East Indies, via Suez Canal. Wrecked in 1923.

Sirdhana   (1925)   British India Steam Navigation Co.
Built by Swan, Hunter & Wigham Richardson, Ltd., Newcastle, England. Tonnage: 7,745. Dimensions: 436' x 57'. Twin-screw, 13 knots. Triple expansion engines. Two masts and one funnel. Struck a mine and sank in Singapore Road, November 13, 1939. Sister ships: **Santhia** and **Shirala.**

Sirdhana   (1947)   British India Steam Navigation Co.
Built by Swan, Hunter & Wigham Richardson, Ltd., Newcastle, England. Tonnage: 8,608. Dimensions: 479' x 62'. Twin-screw, 14½ knots. Motorship. Two masts and one funnel. Service: Bengal-Japan. Passengers: 21 first, 62 second, 333 in bunks. Sister ships: **Sangola** and **Santhia.**

Skaubryn   (1951)   Greek Line.
Tonnage: 9,786. Service: Bremen-Australia, via Suez Canal. Originally in North Atlantic service. Note: See PART I for details.

Slamat   (1924)   Rotterdam Lloyd.
Built by Kon. Maats. de Schelde, Flushing, Netherlands. Tonnage: 11,406. Dimensions: 482' x 62'. Twin-screw, 15 knots. Steam turbines. Two masts and two funnels. Lengthened to 510 feet (11,636 tons) in 1931. Maier bow fitted and speed increased to 17 knots. Service: Netherlands-Dutch East Indies, via Suez Canal. Passengers: 420. She became a war loss, April 17, 1941.

Socotra   (1897)   P. & O. Line (British).
Built by Palmer's Shipbuilding Co., Newcastle, England. Tonnage: 6,009. Dimensions: 450' x 52'. Twin-screw, 14 knots. Triple expansion engines. Two masts and one funnel. Stranded near France, while on voyage from Australia to England, November 25, 1915.

Somali   (1901)   P. & O. Line (British).
> Built by Caird & Co., Greenock, Scotland. Tonnage: 6,708. Dimensions: 450' x 52'. Twin-screw, 14 knots. Triple expansion engines. Two masts and one funnel. Designed for Calcutta and Far East services. Scrapped in 1923. Sister ships: **Sardinia, Sicilia, Soudan** and **Syria.**

Somersetshire   (1921)   Bibby Line (British).
> Built by Harland & Wolff, Ltd., Belfast, Ireland. Tonnage: 9,648. Dimensions: 450' x 57' (468' o.l.). Twin-screw, 13 knots. Motorship. Two masts and one funnel. Passengers: 300. Troops: 1,100. Crew: 190. Tonnage originally listed as 7,456. Service: England-Burma, via Suez Canal. Sold to British shipbreakers in 1954. Sister ship: **Dorsetshire.**

Sontay   (1907)   Messageries Maritimes (French).
> Built by Messageries Maritimes, La Ciotat, France. Tonnage: 7,236. Dimensions: 447' x 52'. Twin-screw, 12 knots. Triple expansion engines. Two masts and one funnel. Launched, December 1, 1907. Service: France-Far East, via Suez Canal. Torpedoed and sunk in the Mediterranean (between Sardinia and Sicily) on April 16, 1917. The captain, Commandant Mages went down voluntarily with his ship. Sister ships: **El Kantara, Euphrate, Gange** and **Louqsor.**

Sontay   (1921)   Messageries Maritimes (French).
> Built by Bremer Vulkan, Vegesack, Germany. Tonnage: 8,917. Dimensions: 468' x 58'. Single-screw, 13 knots. Triple expansion engines. Four masts and one funnel. Sold to Panamanian owners in 1955. Ex-**Bayern** (1936) Hamburg-American Line.

Sophocles   (1883)   Aberdeen Line (G. Thompson & Co.).
> Built by Harland & Wolff, Ltd., Belfast, Ireland. Tonnage: 4,673. Dimensions: 439' x 44'. Single-screw, 14 knots. Quadruple expansion engines. Four masts and one funnel. Steel hull. Originally had compound engines. Purchased as a replacement for the **Thermopylae,** which had been wrecked in September 1899. Service: Great Britain-Australia, via Capetown. Scrapped in 1908. Ex-**Ionic** (1900).

Sophocles   (1922)   Aberdeen Line (British).
> Built by Harland & Wolff, Ltd., Belfast, Ireland. Tonnage: 12,360. Dimensions: 500' x 63'. Twin-screw, 15 knots. Four steam turbines. Two masts and one funnel. Service: England-Australia, via Capetown. Vessel transferred to

Shaw, Savill & Albion Line in 1926. Renamed: **Tamaroa** (1926). Sister ship: **Diogenes.**

Sorata (1872) Orient Line (British).
Tonnage: 4,014. This Pacific Steam Navigation Company liner was transferred to the newly formed Orient Line service in 1879. Note: See PART III for details.

Soudan (1901) P. & O. Line (British).
Built by Caird & Co., Greenock, Scotland. Tonnage: 6,680. Dimensions: 450′ x 52′. Twin-screw, 14 knots. Triple expansion engines. Two masts and one funnel. Built for Calcutta and Far East services. Scrapped in 1926. Sister ships: **Sardinia, Sicilia, Somali** and **Syria.**

Spartan (1881) Union Line (British).
Built by J. & G. Thompson, Ltd., Glasgow, Scotland. Tonnage: 3,487. Dimensions: 363′ x 43′. Single-screw, 13½ knots. Triple expansion engines. Two masts and one funnel. Iron hull. Service: England-South Africa. First used as a mail steamer and later placed in the intermediate service. Sold to Italian owners in 1900. Renamed: **Fiume.** Scrapped in 1902. Sister ship: **Trojan.**

Sphinx (1914) Messageries Maritimes (French).
Built by Ateliers & Chantiers de la Loire, St. Nazaire, France. Tonnage: 11,375. Dimensions: 478′ x 60′. Twin-screw, 14 knots. Triple expansion engines. 9,000 I.H.P. Two masts and two funnels. Service: Marseilles-Far East, via Suez Canal. Passengers: 380. Crew: 250. Served as a hospital ship in World War II. She had performed a similar role in the First World War. Captured by the Italians later in World War II. Renamed: **Subiaco.** Sunk by air attack at Genoa, Italy. Very similar to: **Andre Lebon** and **Porthos.**

Staffordshire (1894) Bibby Line (British).
Built by Harland & Wolff, Ltd., Belfast, Ireland. Tonnage: 6,022. Dimensions: 445′ x 49′. Twin-screw, 14½ knots. Triple expansion engines. Four masts and one funnel. Steel hull. Service: Liverpool-Rangoon, via Suez Canal. Renamed: **Samara.** Scrapped in 1923. Sister ship: **Shropshire.**

Staffordshire (1929) Bibby Line (British).
Built by Fairfield Shipbuilding Co., Glasgow, Scotland. Tonnage: 10,595. Dimensions: 483′ x 62′ (502′ o.l.). Twin-screw, 15 knots. Motorship. Four masts and one funnel. Service: Liverpool-Rangoon. Passengers: 275. Crew: 200. After the war was altered to a single new type funnel and

reduced to single mast. Her superstructure was substantially reduced. Sold to Japanese shipbreakers in 1960. Renamed: **Stafford Maru.** Sister ships: **Cheshire** and **Shropshire.** The **Yorkshire** was quite similar, though her funnel was noticeably taller.

Stanleyville   (1899)   Cie. Belge Maritime du Congo.
Built by Sir Raylton Dixon & Co., Middlesbrough, England. Tonnage: 4,051. Dimensions: 370′ x 46′. Single-screw, 13½ knots. Triple expansion engines. Service: Antwerp-Africa.

Stella d' Italia   (1904)   Lloyd Triestino (Italian).
Built by Sir James Laing & Sons, Ltd., Sunderland, England. Tonnage: 5,884. Dimensions: 425′ x 50′. Twin-screw, 16 knots. Triple expansion engines. Two masts and two funnels. Scrapped by Italian shipbreakers in 1934. Ex-**Fort Hamilton,** ex-**Bermudian.**

*Stirling Castle   (1935)   Union-Castle Line (British).
Built by Harland & Wolff, Ltd., Belfast, Ireland. Tonnage: 25,554. Dimensions: 696′ x 82′ (725′ o.l.). Twin-screw, 20 knots. Motorship. Two masts and one funnel. Launched in July 1935. Broke the Southampton-Capetown speed record, by making the passage in the total time of 13 days, nine hours, from August 21, 1936 to September 4. Passengers: 245 first and 538 tourist. Sister ship: **Athlone Castle.** Note: The finest, largest and fastest Union-Castle liners built to date.

*Strathaird   (1931)   P. & O. Line (British).
Built by Vickers-Armstrongs, Ltd., Barrow, England. Tonnage: 22,284. Dimensions: 638′ x 80′ (664′ o.l.). Twin-screw, 22 knots. Two steam turbines connected to electric motors. 28,000 S.H.P. One screw able to drive vessel at 19 knots. At 20 knots fuel consumption (oil) 136 tons per day. Two masts and three funnels. Note: First and third funnels were dummies. Converted to single funnel after World War II. Service: London-Australia, via Suez Canal. Served as a troopship in World War II. Passengers: 1,242 (single class), as of 1960. Sister ship: **Strathnaver.**

Strathallan   (1938)   P. & O. Line (British).
Built by Vickers-Armstrongs, Ltd., Barrow, England. Tonnage: 23,722. Dimensions: 639′ x 82′ (664′ o.l.). Twin-screw, 21 knots. Six steam turbines. Two masts and one funnel. Service: London-Bombay, via Suez Canal. Also, in England-Australia trade. Passengers: 986. Crew: 560.

Torpedoed and sunk by submarine, December 21, 1942, while transporting a large number of troops to North Africa. The torpedo hit the engine room, killing four members of the crew. Sister ship: **Stratheden.** The **Strathmore** was very similar, but had a shorter funnel.

***Stratheden**   (1938)   P. & O. Line (British).
Built by Vickers-Armstrongs, Ltd., Barrow, England. Tonnage: 23,722.   Dimensions: 639′ x 82′ (664′ o.l.).   Twin-screw, 21 knots. Steam turbines. Two masts and one funnel. Service: England-India-Australia, via Suez Canal.   Served as a troopship in World War II.   After the war was under charter to the Cunard Line and used in their trans-Atlantic service during the summer peak seasons.   Reconditioned and resumed England-Australia sailings.   Tonnage now listed as 23,580.   Passengers: 527 first and 453 tourist. Sister ship: **Strathallan.**

***Strathmore**   (1935)   P. & O. Line (British).
Built by Vickers-Armstrongs, Ltd., Barrow, England. Tonnage: 23,428 (increased to 23,580).   Dimensions: 640′ x 82′ (665′ o.l.).   Twin-screw, 21 knots.   Steam turbines.   Two masts and one funnel.   Service: England-Australia, via Suez Canal.   Passengers: 497 first and 487 tourist.   Service speed reduced to 19 knots.   Similar ships: **Strathallan** and **Stratheden.**

***Strathnaver**   (1932)   P. & O. Line (British).
Built by Vickers-Armstrongs, Ltd., Barrow, England. Tonnage: 22,547 (now 22,270).   Dimensions: 638′ x 80′ (664′ o.l.).   Twin-screw, 22 knots.   Turbo-electric. Two masts and three funnels.   Reduced to single funnel after the war. Passengers: 1,252 (one class ship).   Service speed decreased to 17½ knots.   Service: England-Australia, via Suez Canal. Sister ship: **Strathaird.**

Suevic   (1901)   White Star Line (British).
Built by Harland & Wolff, Ltd., Belfast, Ireland. Tonnage: 12,531.   Dimensions: 550′ x 63′.   Twin-screw, 13½ knots. Quadruple expansion engines.   Four masts and one funnel. Displacement of 24,945 tons.   Cargo capacity of 15,435 tons. Coal consumption was at the rate of 80 tons per day at full speed.   Passengers: 400 (one class).   Essentially an emigrant carrier.   Service: England-Australia, via Capetown.   Vessel was completed in March 1901   She grounded near the Lizard on Stag Rock in fog, March 17, 1907, when homeward bound with 382 passengers.   Subsequently she was released from

the rocks, but not until her bow had been severed just forward of the bridge. A new bow was constructed and successfully fitted the main part of the ship. The **Suevic** was back in business by January 1908. Vessel was sold in 1928 and converted into a whale factory ship. Renamed: **Skytteren.** A World War II loss. Sister ship: **Runic.**

Sumatra   (1895)   P. & O. Line (British).
Built by Alexander Stephen & Sons, Ltd., Glasgow, Scotland. Tonnage: 4,607. Dimensions: 400′ x 46′. Single-screw, 14 knots. Triple expansion engines. 3,500 I.H.P. Two masts and one funnel. Passengers: 46 first and 48 second. Renamed: **Mossamedes.** Similar ships: **Borneo, Palawan** and **Sunda.**

Sunda   (1895)   P. & O. Line (British).
Built by Caird & Co., Greenock, Scotland. Tonnage: 4,674. Dimensions: 400′ x 46′.   Single-screw, 14 knots.   Triple expansion engines. Two masts and one funnel. Passengers: 49 first and 49 second class. Renamed: **Hakuko Maru** (1914). Sister ships: **Borneo, Palawan** and **Sumatra.**

Surada   (1902)   British India Steam Navigation Co.
Built by A. & J. Inglis, Glasgow, Scotland. Tonnage: 5,324. Dimensions: 410′ x 50′.   Single-screw.   Triple expansion engines. Torpedoed and sunk, October 2, 1918.

Sutlej   (1881)   P. & O. Line (British).
Built by Barrow Shipbuilding Co., Barrow, England. Tonnage: 4,164.   Dimensions: 390′ x 42′.   Single-screw, 14½ knots. Compound engines. Three masts and two funnels. Steel hull.   Service: England-Australia, via Suez Canal. Passengers: 140 first and 60 second. Scrapped in 1901. Sister ships: **Clyde, Ganges** and **Thames.**

Suwa Maru   (1914)   N. Y. K. Line (Japanese).
Tonnage: 11,780. Built for the Japan-European, via Suez Canal service. Transferred to trans-Pacific service in First World War. Resumed regular European sailings in 1922. Note: See PART II for details.

Sydney   (1883)   Messageries Maritimes.
Built by Messageries Maritimes, La Ciotat, France. Tonnage: 4,128.   Dimensions: 413′ x 41′.   Single-screw, 15½ knots. Triple expansion engines. Three masts and two funnels.   Launched, November 12, 1882.   Service: France-Australia, via Suez Canal. Scrapped in Italy, 1922. Sister

ships: **Caledonien, Melbourne, Natal, Oceanien, Salazie** and **Yarra.**

*Sydney   (1944)   Lauro Line (Italian).
Built by Western Pipe & Steel Co., San Francisco, Cal.
Tonnage: 14,708.   Service: Genoa-Naples-Australia, via
Suez Canal.   Passengers: 119 first, 994 tourist.   Note: See
PART III for details.

Syria   (1863)   Union Line (Union Steam Ship Co., Ltd.).
Built by Day Summers, Southampton, England.   Tonnage:
1,959.   Dimensions: 312′ x 36′.   Single-screw.   Compound
engines.   Originally had oscillating engines.   Two masts and
one funnel.   Iron hull. Vessel was purchased from the P. & O.
Line in 1871. ¡She was a record-breaker in the England-
Capetown service during her early sailings for the Union
Line.   Traded in for new tonnage in 1878.   Foundered in
mid-Atlantic, April 4, 1880.

Syria   (1901)   P. & O. Line (British).
Built by Alexander Stephen & Sons, Ltd., Glasgow, Scotland.
Tonnage: 6,660.   Dimensions: 450′ x 52′.   Twin-screw, 14
knots.   Triple expansion engines.   Two masts and one funnel.
Designed for the Calcutta and Far East routes.   Scrapped in
1925.   Sister ships: **Sicilia, Somali** and **Soudan.**

Tabanan   (1908)   Rotterdam Lloyd (Dutch).
Built by Kon. Maats. de Schelde, Flushing, Netherlands.
Tonnage: 5,271.   Dimensions: 400′ x 49′.   Single-screw, 14
knots.   Triple expansion engines.   Two masts and one funnel.
Service: Netherlands-Dutch East Indies, via Suez Canal.
Renamed: **Ege.**   Similar ships: **Kawi** and **Wilis.**

Tabora   (1912)   Deutsche Ost Afrika Line.
Built by Blohm & Voss, Hamburg, Germany.   Tonnage:
8,022. Dimensions: 449′ x 54′.   Twin-screw, 15 knots.   Quadruple expansion engines.   Two masts and one funnel.   Service:
Germany-Africa.   Destroyed by the guns of the British warship **Hyancinth** at Dares-Salaam in 1916.

Tainui   (1884)   Shaw, Savill & Albion Co. (British).
Built by Wm. Denny & Bros., Ltd., Dumbarton, Scotland.
Tonnage: 5,161.   Dimensions: 439′ x 46′.   Single-screw, 13
knots.   Compound engines.   Four masts and two funnels.
Clipper bow.   Steel hull.   Service: England-New Zealand, via
Capetown (outward); New Zealand-England, via Cape Horn
(homeward bound).   Vessel chartered to Allan Line for 1899
season.   At later date she was refitted for the Anchor Line's

North Atlantic service, as the **Astoria.** Renamed: (a) **Covadonga** (1898), (b) **Tainui** (1899), (c) **Astoria** (1899). Scrapped in 1911. Sister ship: **Arawa.**

Tainui (1908)   Shaw, Savill & Albion Co. (British).
Built by Workman, Clark & Co., Belfast, Ireland. Tonnage: 9,957. Dimensions: 477' x 61'. Twin-screw, 14 knots. 6,500 I.H.P. Two masts and one funnel. Service: England-New Zealand. Passengers: 40 first, 74 second, 300 third. Transferred from the Cape Horn route to, via Panama Canal service at later date. Renamed: **Empire Trader** (1940). A World War II casualty, February 23, 1943. Sister ship: **Arawa.**

Tairea (1924)   British India Steam Navigation Co.
Built by Barclay, Curle & Co., Glasgow, Scotland. Tonnage: 7,933. Dimensions: 450' x 60' (465' o.l.). Triple expansion engines. Two masts and three funnels. Service: India-South Africa. Passengers: 130. Sunk by the famous German warship **Admiral Graf Spee,** December 3, 1939. Sold to British shipbreakers in 1952. Sister ships: **Takliwa** and **Talamba.**

Takliwa (1924)   British India Steam Navigation Co.
Built by Barclay, Curle & Co., Glasgow, Scotland. Tonnage: 7,936. Dimensions: 450' x 60'. Twin-screw, 16 knots. Triple expansion engines. Two masts and three funnels. Service: India-South Africa. Passengers: 130. Stranded and burned out on South Nicobar Islands, in 1945. Sister ships: **Talamba** and **Tairea.** Impressive looking liners for their relatively small tonnage.

Talamba (1924)   British India Steam Navigation Co.
Built by Hawthorn, Leslie & Co., Newcastle, England. Tonnage: 8,018. Dimensions: 450' x 60' (466' o.l.). Twin-screw, 16 knots. Triple expansion engines. Two masts and three funnels. Service: India-South Africa. Passengers: 130. Bombed by enemy aircraft, July 10, 1943, while being used as a hospital ship. Sister ships: **Tairea** and **Takliwa.**

Talma (1923)   British India Steam Navigation Co.
Built by Hawthorn, Leslie & Co., Newcastle, England. Tonnage: 10,000. Dimensions: 451' x 59'. Quadruple expansion engines. Two masts and two funnels. Passengers: 135. Scrapped in 1949. Sister ship: **Tilawa.**

Tamba Maru (1897)   N. Y. K. Line (Japanese).
Built by Napier, Shanks & Bell, Glasgow, Scotland. Tonnage: 6,134. Dimensions: 445' x 49'. Twin-screw, 13 knots.

Triple expansion engines.   Two masts and one funnel.
Service: Japan-Europe, via Suez Canal.   Passengers: 35
first, 20 second, 139 third. Scrapped in 1933.

Tambora   (1909)   Rotterdam Lloyd (Dutch).
Built by Kon. Maats. de Schelde, Flushing, Netherlands.
Tonnage: 5,602. Dimensions: 413′ x 49′. Single-screw, 14½
knots. Triple expansion engines. 4,500 I.H.P. Two masts
and one funnel. Service: Netherlands-Dutch East Indies,
via Suez Canal. Passengers: 77 first, 58 second, 19 third,
40 fourth. Scrapped in 1931.

Tanais   (1867)   Messageries Maritimes.
Built by Messageries Maritimes, La Ciotat, France. Tonnage: 1,682. Dimensions: 319′ x 32′. Single-screw. Compound engines. Three masts and one funnel. Iron hull.
Launched, October 20, 1867. Lengthened in 1886. Service:
East of Suez. Sold to Nagasaki shipbreakers in 1901. Sister
ships: **Eridan, Niemen, Tibre** and **Volga.**

Tanda   (1914)   Eastern & Australian Steamship Co.
Built by Alexander Stephen & Sons, Ltd., Glasgow, Scotland.
Tonnage: 7,174. Dimensions: 430′ x 58′. Twin-screw, 13
knots. Triple expansion engines. Two masts and one funnel.
Note: Originally in P. & O. Line service. Torpedoed and
sunk by submarine, July 15, 1944. Ex-**Madras,** ex-**Tanda.**

Tanganjika   (1922)   Woermann Line (German).
Built by Blohm & Voss, Hamburg, Germany. Tonnage:
8,540. Dimensions: 449′ x 58′. Single-screw, 14 knots.
Four steam turbines. Two masts and one funnel. Service:
Germany-Africa. Passengers: 250. Ownership transferred
to Hamburg-American Line. Sunk by Allied air attack at
Wilhelmshaven in 1943. Salvaged and broken up for scrap
after the war. Similar ships: **Adolph Woermann, Njassa**
and **Usambara.**

Tango Maru   (1905)   N. Y. K. Line (Japanese).
Built by Mitsubishi Drydock & Engine Works, Nagasaki,
Japan. Tonnage: 7,475. Dimensions: 456′ x 50′. Twin-
screw, 14 knots. Triple expansion engines. Two masts and
one funnel. Designed as an improved ship for the European-
Japan service. The largest vessel built by a Japanese ship-
building yard to date. She became a war casualty in the
East China Sea, November 13, 1943.

Tantallon Castle   (1894)   (a) Castle Line, (b) Union-Castle Line.
Built by Fairfield Shipbuilding Co., Glasgow, Scotland.

Tonnage: 5,636. Dimensions: 440' x 50'. Single-screw, 16 knots. Quadruple expansion engines. Three masts and one funnel. First class passengers were quartered aft, which was unusual for this date. In mail service between England and South Africa. Wrecked on Robben Island, Capetown, May 7, 1901. Within a few days nothing remained of the vessel but a mass of junk strewed about the beaches. There had been no loss of life. Similar ship: **Dunvegan Castle.**

Tara   (1902)   British India Steam Navigation Co.
Built by Wm. Denny & Bros., Ltd., Dumbarton, Scotland. Tonnage: 6,322. Dimensions: 446' x 53'. Twin-screw, 14 knots. Triple expansion engines. Two masts and one funnel. Sold for scrap in 1927. Sister ship: **Taroba.**

Taroba   (1888)   British India Steam Navigation Co.
Built by A. & J. Inglis, Ltd., Glasgow, Scotland. Tonnage: 4,793. Dimensions: 410' x 46'. Single-screw, 14 knots. Triple expansion engines. Two masts and one funnel. Steel hull. Renamed: (a) **Isla de Cuba** (1894), (b) **Leon XIII** (1895). Scrapped in 1930.

Taroba   (1902)   British India Steam Navigation Co.
Built by Wm. Denny & Bros., Ltd., Dumbarton, Scotland. Tonnage: 6,322. Dimensions: 445' x 53'. Twin-screw, 14 knots. Triple expansion engines. Two masts and one funnel. Sold for scrap in 1924. Sister ship: **Tara.**

Tartar   (1883)   Union Line (Union Steam Ship Co.).
Built by Aitken & Mansel, Glasgow, Scotland. Tonnage: 4,425. Dimensions: 376' x 47'. Single-screw, 16 knots. Triple expansion engines. Three masts and one funnel. Iron hull. Considered a fast mail liner in the England-South Africa service. Passengers: 160 first, 160 second, 100 third. Sold to the Canadian Pacific Line in 1897, as more tonnage was required to meet the demand of prospective passengers seeking a means during the Klondyke Gold Rush to get to the gold regions. Vessel sold to Japanese owners in 1907, but did not remain long, as she was broken up for scrap in 1908.

Taymouth Castle   (1877)   Castle Line (British).
Built by Barclay, Curle & Co., Glasgow, Scotland. Tonnage: 2,069. Dimensions: 300' x 33'. Single-screw. Compound engines. Two masts and one funnel. Iron hull. Mainly in the intermediate service to South Africa. Sold to Sir

Christopher Furness in 1891. Promptly resold to Pickford & Black of Halifax, Nova Scotia. Renamed: **Ocamo.**

Tchad   (1897)   Chargeurs Reunis (French).
Built by Forges & Chantiers de la Mediterranee, La Seyne, France. Tonnage: 4,317. Dimensions: 416' x 42'. Single-screw. Triple expansion engines. Three masts and one funnel. Steel hull. Refitted for the France-West African service in 1911. Scrapped in Scotland, 1929. Ex-**Cholon** (1912).

Teesta   (1903)   British India Steam Navigation Co.
Built by Sir James Laing & Sons, Ltd., Sunderland, England. Tonnage: 6,295. Dimensions: 446' x 53'. Twin-screw, 14 knots. Triple expansion engines. Two masts and one funnel. Scrapped in 1927. Sister ship: **Thongwa.**

Tegelberg   (1936)   Royal Packet Navigation Co. (Dutch).
Built by N. V. Nederlandsch Schps. Maats., Amsterdam, Netherlands. Tonnage: 14,150. Dimensions: 537' x 72' (560' o.l.). Triple-screw, 16 knots. Motorship. Two masts and one funnel. Passengers: 664. Crew: 231. Service: Far East-South Africa. Transferred to Royal Inter-Ocean Lines (Dutch) after World War II. Sister ships: **Ruys** and **Boissevain.**

Terukuni Maru   (1930)   N. Y. K. Line (Japanese).
Built by Mitsubishi Zosen Kaisha, Nagasaki, Japan. Tonnage: 11,930. Dimensions: 505' x 64' (526' o.l.). Twin-screw, 17 knots. Motorship. Two masts and one funnel. Passengers: 250. Crew: 200. Service: Japan-London, via Suez Canal. Sunk by a mine off the East coast of England, November 21, 1939. Sister ship: **Yasukuni Maru.** Note: The N. Y. K. Line's finest liners built for their European service to date.

Teuton   (1869)   Union Line (British).
Built by London & Glasgow Shipbuilding Co., Glasgow, Scotland. Tonnage: 1,741. Dimensions: 331' x 35'. Single-screw. Compound engines. Three masts and one funnel. Iron hull. Lengthened 46 feet (2,313) in 1875. Service: England-South Africa. Served as a transport during the Zulu War in 1878. Sunk near Quoin Point, Cape of Good Hope, August 30, 1881, with great loss of life. There had been 272 on board, of whom 187 were passengers, when the vessel struck on rocks that day, soon after dark. The dramatic loss of life was caused by the sudden bursting of the watertight compartments at 10:30 P.M., and while the

removal of women, children and men to the lifeboats was taking place. The plunging down into the waters was so swift that she sucked down many that were in the sea. Only 11 passengers and 25 of the crew were saved. Ex-**Glenartney** (1873).

Tevere   (1912)   Lloyd Triestino (Italian).
Built by Cantiere San Rocco, Trieste, Austria. Tonnage: 8,448. Dimensions: 452′ x 56′. Twin-screw, 16 knots. Quadruple expansion engines. Two masts and two funnels. Passengers: 240. Service: Italy-Far East. Scuttled as hospital ship at Tripolis, January 20, 1943. Ex-**Gablonz**.

Thames   (1881)   P. & O. Line (British).
Built by J. & G. Thomson, Ltd., Glasgow, Scotland. Tonnage: 4,101 (increased to 4,258). Dimensions: 390′ x 42′. Single-screw, 14½ knots. Compound engines. Three masts and two funnels. Steel hull. Service: England-Australia, via Suez Canal. Scrapped in France, 1901. Sister ships: **Ganges, Clyde** and **Sutlej.**

Themistocles   (1911)   Thompson's Aberdeen Line.
Built by Harland & Wolff, Ltd., Belfast, Ireland. Tonnage: 11,231. Dimensions: 500′ x 62′ (520′ o.l.). Twin-screw, 15 knots. Quadruple expansion engines. Two masts and one funnel. Service: Great Britain-Australia, via Capetown. Passengers: 103 first and 256 third class. During her life she made a total of 79 voyages to Australia, via Cape of Good Hope. Broken up for scrap at Dalmuir in 1947. Sister ship: **Demosthenes.** Note: The Aberdeen Line of George Thompson remained a private family business until the year 1905, when it became a limited British company in close cooperation with the White Star Line and Shaw, Savill & Albion Co.

Theophile Gautier   (1926)   Messageries Maritimes (French).
Built by Chantiers & Ateliers de France, Dunkirk, France. Tonnage: 8,194. Dimensions: 427′ x 56′ (445′ o.l.). Twin-screw, 12½ knots. Motorship. Two masts and two funnels. Passengers: 280. Note: The first French motorship. Torpedoed and sunk by British submarine in the Aegean Sea, October 4, 1941.

Thermopylae   (1891)   Thompson's Aberdeen Line (British).
Built by Hall, Russell & Co., Aberdeen, Scotland. Tonnage: 3,711. Dimensions: 362′ x 44′. Single-screw. Triple expansion engines. Three masts and one funnel. Steel hull.

Clipper bow. Hull painted green and yellow funnel. The Aberdeen liners of this era were among the most beautiful. Service: Great Britain-Australia, via Capetown. Wrecked at Green Point, Capetown, September 13, 1899, and became a total loss.

Thysville (1922) Compagnie Belge Maritime du Congo.
Built by Soc. Anon. John Cockerill, Hoboken, Belgium. Tonnage: 8,176 (increased to 8,351). Dimensions: 439′ x 57′ (459′ o.l.). Twin-screw, 16 knots. Quadruple expansion engines. Two masts and one funnel. Service: Antwerp-Congo. Renamed: **Empire Test** (1948) British Government. Sister ship: **Elisabethville.**

*****Thysville** (1950) Compagnie Belge Maritime.
Built by Soc. Anon. John Cockerill, Hoboken, Belgium. Tonnage: 10,946. Dimensions: 479′ x 64′ (505′ o.l.). Single-screw, 16½ knots. Motorship. Two masts and one funnel. Service: Antwerp-Congo and Angola. Passengers: 248 single class. Ex-**Baudouinville** (1957). Sister ships: **Albertville, Elisabethville, Leopoldville** and **Charlesville.**

Tibre (1866) Messageries Maritimes (French).
Built at La Ciotat, France. Tonnage: 1,689. Dimensions: 320′ x 32′. Single-screw. Three masts and one funnel. Iron hull. Launched, April 22, 1866. Service: East of Suez. Lengthened in 1890. Tonnage increased to 1,838. Scrapped at Saigon in April 1902. Sister ships: **Eridan, Niemen, Tanais** and **Volga.**

Tigre (1862) Messageries Maritimes (French).
Built by Forges & Chantiers, La Seyne, France. Tonnage: 2,746. Dimensions: 389′ x 38′. Single-screw, 13 knots. Two cylinder engines. Three masts and one funnel. Iron hull. Launched, December 22, 1862. Lengthened in 1870. Tonnage increased to 3,234. Service: France-Far East, via Suez Canal. Converted to freighter in 1889. Scrapped in France, 1904. Sister ships: **Cambodge, Donai** and **Imperatrice.**

Tilawa (1924) British India Steam Navigation Co.
Built by Hawthorn, Leslie & Co., Newcastle, England. Tonnage: 10,006. Dimensions: 451′ x 59′. Single-screw, 12 knots. Quadruple expansion engines. Two masts and two funnels. Passengers: 135. Torpedoed by submarine on November 23, 1942, and again. Sister ship: **Talma.**

*Timor (1951) Companhia Nacional de Navegacao (Portuguese).
Built by Bartram & Sons, Ltd., Sunderland, England. Tonnage: 7,656. Dimensions: 409' x 59' (431' 8" o.l.). Twin-screw, 14½ knots. Motorship. Two masts and one funnel. Service: Portugal-India-Far East, via Suez Canal. Passengers: 76 first and 325 third. Sister ship: **India.**

Tintagel Castle (1896) (a) Castle Line, (b) Union-Castle Line.
Built by Fairfield Shipbuilding Co., Glasgow, Scotland. Tonnage: 5,531. Dimensions: 425' x 50' (440' o.l.). Single-screw, 13 knots. Triple expansion engines. Four masts and one funnel. Service: England-South Africa. Sold to Cie. de Nav. Sud Atlantique in 1912. Renamed: **Liger** (1912). Scrapped in 1923. Sister ship: **Avondale Castle.** Similar to: **Arundel Castle.**

Tjerimai (1916) Rotterdam Lloyd (Dutch).
Built by Reiherstieg Schiffsw., Hamburg, Germany. Tonnage: 7,760. Dimensions: 426' x 55'. Twin-screw, 15 knots. Quadruple expansion engines. Two masts and one funnel. Service: Rotterdam-Dutch East Indies, via Suez. Renamed: **El Nil** (1933) Egyptian. Vessel taken over by British in World War II and placed under Furness, Withy & Company management. Ex-**Waidi,** ex-**Marie,** ex-**Marie Woermann.**

Tjibadak (1929) Java-China-Japan Line (Dutch).
Built by Van der Giessen & Zonen's Schps., Krimpen, Netherlands. Tonnage: 7,803. Dimensions: 433' x 56'. Single-screw, 12 knots. Steam turbines. Two masts and one funnel. Sister ship: **Tjisaroea.**

Tjikarang (1922) Java-China-Japan Line (Dutch).
Built by Nederlandsche Schps. Maats., Amsterdam, Netherlands. Tonnage: 9,505. Dimensions: 483' x 60'. Twin-screw, 12½ knots. Triple expansion engines. Two masts and one funnel. Service: Dutch East Indies and Chinese ports. Accommodation mainly for deck passengers. Became a war casualty in March 1942.

*Tjiluwah (1951) Royal Interocean Lines (Dutch).
Built by Van der Giessen, Krimpen, Netherlands. Tonnage: 8,630. Dimensions: 449' x 62' (479' o.l.). Twin-screw, 16 knots. Motorship. Two masts and one funnel. Service: Australia-Japan-Hong Kong. Passengers: 98 first, 120 second and a number of unberthed. Sister ship: **Tjiwangi.** Fine looking passenger liners.

Tjikarang   (1922)   Java-China-Japan Line (Dutch).
Built by Nederlandsche Schps. Maats., Amsterdam, Netherlands.   Tonnage: 9,505.   Dimensions: 483′ x 60′.   Twin-
screw, 12½ knots.   Triple expansion engines.   Two masts
and one funnel.   Service: Dutch East Indies-Chinese ports.

Tjinegara   (1931)   Java-China-Japan Line (Dutch).
Built by Nederlandsche Schps. Maats., Amsterdam, Netherlands.   Tonnage: 9,227.   Dimensions: 440′ x 62′.   Single-
screw, 15 knots.   Motorship.   Two masts and one funnel.
Service: Dutch East Indies-Chinese ports.   Passengers:
2,000 (including deck accommodation).   She became a war
loss, July 26, 1942.   Sister ship: **Tjisadane.**

*Tjinegara   (1951)   Royal Interocean Lines (Dutch).
Built by P. Smit, Jr., Rotterdam, Netherlands.   Tonnage:
9,067.   Dimensions: 472′ x 63′.   Single-screw, 17 knots.
Motorship.   Two masts and one funnel.   Service: Far East-
Africa-South America, via Capetown.   Passengers: 40 first
class.   Ex-**Straat Makassar** (1956).   Sister ship: **Straat
Banka.**

Tjisaroea   (1926)   Java-China-Japan Line (Dutch).
Built by Nederlandsche Schps. Maats., Amsterdam, Netherlands.   Tonnage: 7,089.   Dimensions: 420′ x 55′.   Single-
screw, 12½ knots.   Steam turbines.   Two masts and one
funnel.   A war casualty, March 4, 1942.   Similar ship:
Tjibadak.

*Tjitjalengka   (1939)   Java-China-Japan Line (Dutch).
Built by N. V. Nederlandsche, Schps. Maats., Amsterdam,
Netherlands.   Tonnage: 10,972.   Dimensions: 454′ x 64′
(475′ o.l.).   Single-screw, 15 knots.   Motorship.   Two masts
and one funnel.   Note: Largest liner built to date for this
line.   The Company is now known as Royal Interocean Lines.
The **Tjitjalengka** is now employed on the Far East-
Africa-South America route.   Passengers: 493 (including
64 first class).

Toledo   (1914)   Hamburg-American Line.
Built by Reiherstieg Schiffswerfte, Hamburg, Germany.
Tonnage: 8,106.   Dimensions: 449′ x 55′.   Twin-screw, 13½
knots.   Quadruple expansion engines.   Two masts and one
funnel.   Sailed in the Germany-South African service of
Deutsch Ost Afrika Line.   Scrapped in 1934.   Ex-**Algeria**
(1922), ex-**Kigoma** (1921).

Tongariro   (1901)   New Zealand Shipping Co.
Built by Hawthorn, Leslie & Co., Newcastle, England.
Tonnage: 8,073.   Dimensions: 457' x 58'.   Twin-screw, 13
knots.   Triple expansion engines.   Two masts and one funnel.
Service: England-South   Africa-Australia-New   Zealand.
Wrecked on Bull Rock, East coast of New Zealand, August
1916.   Similar ships:

Tonkin   (1898)   Messageries Maritimes.
Built by Messageries Maritimes, La Ciotat, France.   Ton-
nage: 6,092.   Dimensions: 446' x 50'.   Twin-screw, 18 knots.
Triple expansion engines.   Two masts and two funnels.
Launched, March 6, 1898.   Service: France-Far East, via
Suez Canal.   Vessel refitted for Mediterranean service in
1912; addition of one deck was constructed.   Renamed:
Lotus (1912). Scrapped in Italy, 1932. Sister ships: **Annam,
Indus** and **Laos.**

Toscana   (1923)   (a) Italia Line, (b) Lloyd Triestino.
Built by Akt. Ges. "Weser", Bremen, Germany.   Tonnage:
9,584.   Dimensions: 458' x 57' (480' o.l.).   Twin-screw, 12
knots.   Triple expansion engines.   Two masts and one funnel.
Service: Italy-Colombo-Australia, via Suez Canal.   Passengers: 819 third class.   Vessel laid up in 1960.   Previously
she had served in the Italy-South American trade.   Scrapped
in 1962.   Ex-**Saarbrucken** (1935).

Tourane   (1898)   Messageries Maritimes (French).
Built at La Ciotat, France.   Tonnage: 6,054.   Dimensions:
446' x 50'.   Twin-screw, 19 knots.   Triple expansion engines.
Two masts and two funnels.   Service: France-Far East, via
Suez Canal.   Refitted in 1912 for the Marseilles-Alexandria
trade.   Renamed: **Karnak** (1912).   Torpedoed and sunk by
submarine near Malta, November 27, 1916.   Ex-**Annam**
(1904).   Running mates: **Indus, Laos** and **Tonkin.**

*Transvaal Castle   (1961)   Union-Castle Line.
Built by John Brown & Co., Clydebank, Glasgow, Scotland.
Tonnage: 33,000.   Dimensions: 760' (o.l.) x 90'.   Twin-
screw, 23 knots.   Steam turbines.   Single mast and one funnel.   Launched, January 17, 1961.   Maiden voyage scheduled
for January 1962.   Passengers: 740.   Service: Southampton-
Capetown.   A single class liner.

Trieste   (1897)   Lloyd Austriaco.
Built by Lloyd Austriaco, Trieste, Austria.   Tonnage: 5,106.
Dimensions: 400' x 48'.   Single-screw, 12½ knots.   Triple

expansion engines. Two masts and one funnel. Vessel transferred to Lloyd Triestino in 1918. Scrapped in 1927.

Trojan   (1880)   Union Line (British).
Built by J. & G. Thomson, Ltd., Glasgow, Scotland. Tonnage: 3,652. Dimensions: 364′ x 42′. Single-screw, 13½ knots. Compound engines. Re-engined with triple expansions in 1887. Two masts and one funnel. Note: The first South African liner to be equipped with electric lights. The **Trojan** was transferred from the mail to the intermediate service in 1889. Served as a hospital ship during the Boer War in 1899. Renamed: (a) **Wassau** (1900), (b) **Islam**. Scrapped at Preston in 1902.

Turakina   (1902)   New Zealand Shipping Co.
Built by Hawthorn, Leslie & Co., Newcastle, England. Tonnage: 8,349. Dimensions: 473′ x 59′. Twin-screw, 14 knots. Triple expansion engines. 5,000 I.H.P. Two masts and one funnel. Service: England-New Zealand. Passengers: 40 first, 50, 105. Torpedoed and sunk without warning 120 miles from Bishop Rock, August 13, 1917, with the loss of two lives.

Ubena   (1928)   Deutsche Ost Afrika Line.
Built by Blohm & Voss, Hamburg, Germany. Tonnage: 9,554. Dimensions: 445′ x 60′. Single-screw, 16 knots. Four steam turbines. Two masts and two funnels. Lengthened to 468 feet in 1934. New bow fitted and speed was increased from 13½ to 16 knots. Service: Germany-South Africa. Passengers: 300. Renamed: **Empire Ken** (British). Scrapped in Great Britain, 1957. Sister ship: **Watussi.**

Uganda   (1898)   British India Steam Navigation Co.
Built by Alexander Stephen & Sons, Ltd., Glasgow, Scotland. Tonnage: 5,431. Dimensions: 410′ x 50′. Single-screw. Triple expansion engines. Two masts and one funnel. Lost by enemy action in 1918. Sister ships: **Ujina, Ula, Umballa, Umta, Upada** and **Urlana.**

*Uganda   (1952)   British India Steam Navigation Co.
Built by Barclay, Curle & Co., Glasgow, Scotland. Tonnage: 14,430. Dimensions: 516′ x 71′ (539′ o.l.). Twin-screw, 16 knots. Steam turbines. Two masts and one funnel. During her trials made a top speed of 19¼ knots. Service: London-East Africa, via Suez Canal. Sister ship: **Kenya.**

*Uige (1954) Companhia Colonial de Navegacao (Portuguese). Built by John Cockerill, Hoboken, Belgium. Tonnage: 10,001. Dimensions: 439′ x 62′ (477′ o.l.). Single-screw, 16 knots. Motorship. Two masts and one extremely short funnel. Passengers: 78 first and 493 third. Service: Portugal-West and East Africa, via Capetown.

Ulysses (1913) Blue Funnel Line (British). Built by Workman, Clark & Co., Belfast, Ireland. Tonnage: 14,626. Dimensions: 563′ x 68′. Twin-screw, 14 knots. Triple expansion engines. 7,750 I.H.P. Two masts and one very large funnel. Service: Liverpool-Australia, via Suez Canal. Passengers: 250. Note: Had a raking stem, while her sister was fitted to a straight one. Torpedoed and sunk by submarine off Palm Beach, Florida, April 10, 1942. Sister ship: **Nestor.**

Umgeni (1938) Bullard, King & Co. (Natal Line). Built by Swan, Hunter & Wigham Richardson, Ltd., Newcastle, England. Tonnage: 8,180. Dimensions: 451′ x 61′ (468′ o.l.). Twin-screw, 15 knots. Triple expansion engines and steam turbines. Two masts and one funnel. Service: England-Durban-Beira. Passengers: 100. Sold to Elder, Dempster Lines in 1957. Renamed: **Winneba** (1957). Sister ship: **Umtali.**

Umhlali (1905) Natal Line (Bullard, King & Co.). Built by Sir James Laing & Sons, Ltd., Sunderland, England. Tonnage: 3,388. Dimensions: 348′ x 43′. Single-screw, 13 knots. Triple expansion engines. Two masts and one funnel. Service: England-South Africa. Wrecked near Cape Point, September 15, 1909, while bound from England to Durban. Sister ship: **Umzumbi.**

Umkuzi (1903) Natal Line (Bullard, King & Co.). Built by Barclay, Curle & Co., Glasgow, Scotland. Tonnage: 5,175. Dimensions: 419′ x 50′. Twin-screw, 12½ knots. Triple expansion engines. Two masts and one funnel. Service: England-South Africa. Passengers: 75. Crew: 100. Scrapped in 1938. Ex-**Cluny Castle** (1924). Sister ship: **Umvoti.**

Umona (1910) Natal Line (Bullard, King & Co.). Built by Sir James Laing & Sons, Ltd., Sunderland, England. Tonnage: 3,735. Dimensions: 356′ x 44′. Single-screw, 13 knots. Triple expansion engines. Two masts and one funnel. Service: England-South Africa. Sunk by enemy submarine off Freetown in 1941.

Umsinga   (1901)   Natal Line (Bullard, King & Co.).
Built by Sir James Laing & Sons, Ltd., Sunderland. Tonnage: 2,958. Dimensions: 340' x 42'. Single-screw, 13 knots. Triple expansion engines. Two masts and one funnel. Service: England-South Africa.   Scrapped in 1928.   Sister ship: **Umvolosi.**

Umtali   (1936)   Natal Line (Bullard, King & Co.).
Built by Swan, Hunter & Wigham Richardson, Ltd., Newcastle, England. Tonnage: 8,158. Dimensions: 451' x 61' (468' o.l.). Twin-screw, 15 knots. Triple expansion engines and steam turbines. Two masts and one funnel. Passengers: 100. Service: England-South Africa. Sold to Elder, Dempster Lines in 1957. Renamed: **Calabar** (1957). Running mates: **Umgeni** and **Umtata.**

Umtata   (1935)   Natal Line (Bullard, King & Co.).
Built by Swan, Hunter & Wigham Richardson, Ltd., Newcastle, England. Tonnage: 8,137. Dimensions: 451' x 61' (468' o.l.). Twin-screw, 15 knots. Triple expansion engines and steam turbines. Two masts and one funnel. Service: England-South Africa, via Capetown.   Passengers: 100. Sunk by submarine, July 7, 1942. Running mates: **Umgeni** and **Umtali.**

Umvolosi   (1902)   Natal Line (Bullard, King & Co.).
Built by Sir James Laing & Sons, Ltd., Sunderland, England. Tonnage: 2,986.   Dimensions: 340' x 42'.   Single-screw, 13 knots. Triple expansion engines. Two masts and one funnel. Service: England-South Africa. Scrapped in Norway, 1930. Sister ship: **Umsinga.**

Umvoti   (1903)   Natal Line (Bullard, King & Co.).
Built by Barclay, Curle & Co., Glasgow, Scotland. Tonnage: 5,183. Dimensions: 419' x 50'. Twin-screw, 12 knots. Triple expansion engines. Two masts and one funnel. Passengers: 75.   Service: England-South Africa.   Ex-**Comrie Castle** (1924). Sister ship: **Umkuzi.**

Umvuma   (1914)   Natal Line (Bullard, King & Co.).
Built by Sir James Laing & Sons, Ltd., Sunderland, England. Tonnage: 4,419. Dimensions: 365' x 49'. Single-screw, 13 knots. Triple expansion engines. Two masts and one funnel. Service: England-South Africa. Passengers: 50. Sunk by submarine, August 7, 1943.

Umzumbi   (1904)   Natal Line (Bullard, King & Co.).
Built by Sir James Laing & Sons, Ltd., Sunderland, England.
Tonnage: 3,388. Dimensions: 348′ x 43′. Single-screw, 13
knots. Triple expansion engines. Two masts and one fun-
nel. Service: England-South Africa. Scrapped in 1932.
Sister ship: **Umhlali.**

Usambara   (1922)   Deutsche Ost Afrika Line.
Built by Blohm & Voss, Hamburg, Germany. Tonnage:
8,690. Dimensions: 433′ x 58′. Single-screw, 14 knots. Four
steam turbines. Two masts and one funnel. Passengers:
250. Service: Germany-West, South and East Africa.
Destroyed by air attack at Stettin in 1945. Sister ship:
Njassa.

Usaramo   (1920)   Deutsch Ost Afrika Line.
Built by Blohm & Voss, Hamburg, Germany. Tonnage:
7,775. Dimensions: 418′ x 56′. Single-screw, 14 knots.
Steam turbines. Two masts and one funnel. Passengers:
250. Service: Germany-West, South and East Africa.
Scuttled by crew at Bordeaux in 1944. Raised and scrapped
after war. **Ussukuma** and **Wangoni.**

Ussukuma   (1920)   Deutsche Ost Afrika Line.
Built by Blohm & Voss, Hamburg, Germany. Tonnage:
7,834. Dimensions: 418′ x 56′. Single-screw, 14 knots.
Steam turbines. Two masts and one funnel. Passengers:
250. Service: Germany-Africa. Scuttled by crew off Bahia
in 1939. Sister ships: **Usramo** and **Wangoni.**

Valetta   (1883)   P. & O. Line (British).
Built by Caird & Co., Greenock, Scotland. Tonnage: 4,911.
Dimensions: 420′ x 45′. Single-screw, 14½ knots. Com-
pound engines. Three masts and two funnels. Steel hull.
Tonnage increased to 5,871 tons at later date. Service:
England-Australia, via Suez Canal. Torpedoed and sunk
without warning, July 8, 1917, when 118 miles from the
Fastnet. Sister ship: **Massilia.**

Varela   (1914)   British India Steam Navigation Co.
Built by Swan, Hunter & Wigham Richardson, Ltd., Newcastle, England. Tonnage: 4,645. Dimensions: 390′ x 53′
(403′ o.l.). Twin-screw, 15½ knots. Triple expansion
engines. Two masts and one funnel. Passengers: 60. Sister
ships: **Varsova, Vasna** and **Vita.**

Vectis   (1881)   P. & O. Line (British).
Built by Caird & Co., Greenock, Scotland. Tonnage: 5,628. Dimensions: 449' x 44'. Single-screw, 16 knots. Compound engines. Four masts and two funnels. Reduced to two masts at later date. Note: The Vectis was employed as a special cruise ship. Sold to the French Government in 1912. At first they intended to use her as a hospital ship, but found the vessel unsuitable and resold to Italian shipbreakers in 1913. Ex-**Rome** (1904). Note: Lengthened to 449 feet.

Verona   (1879)   P. & O. Line (British).
Built by Caird & Co., Greenock, Scotland. Tonnage: 3,069 (increased to 3,246). Dimensions: 380' x 38'. Single-screw, 14 knots. Compound engines. Three masts and one funnel. Iron hull. Service: England-Far East. Scrapped in 1899. Sister ship: **Ancona.**

Viceroy of India   (1929)   P. & O. Line (British).
Built by Alexander Stephen & Sons, Ltd., Glasgow, Scotland. Tonnage: 19,648. Dimensions: 586' x 76' (612' o.l.). Twin-screw, 20 knots. Two steam turbines connected to electric motors. Two masts and two funnels. Note: First turbo-electric P. & O. liner. Service: London-Bombay, via Suez Canal. Made a record run from London to Bombay in 16 days, 1 hour, 42 minutes in September 1932. Passengers: 680. Served as a British troopship in World War II. Torpedoed and sunk off the North African coast, November 11, 1942. Thus, she disappeared beneath the water with bow rising straight into the air.

Victoria   (1887)   P. & O. Line (British).
Built by Caird & Co., Greenock, Scotland. Tonnage: 6,091 (increased to 6,522). Dimensions: 465' x 52'. Single-screw, 16½ knots. Triple expansion engines. 7,000 I.H.P. Four masts and two funnels. Steel hull. Passengers: 250 first and 160 second class. Service: England-Australia, via Suez Canal. Scrapped in 1909. Sister ships: **Arcadia, Britannia** and **Oceana.** Note: Known as the P & O jubilee ships.

Victoria   (1931)   Lloyd Triestino (Italian).
Built by Cantieri Riuniti dell' Adriatico, Trieste, Italy. Tonnage: 13,062. Dimensions: 511' x 68' (540' o.l.). Quadruple-screw, 22 knots. Motorship. 18,900 I.H.P. Two masts and two funnels. Note: Fastest motorship built to date. Service: Trieste-Bombay, via Suez Canal. Passengers: 600. She became a war loss, January 23, 1942.

*Victoria   (1953)   Lloyd Triestino (Italian).
Built by Cantieri Riuniti dell' Adriatico, Trieste, Italy.
Tonnage: 11,695. Dimensions: 491′ x 68′ (522′ o.l.). Twin-screw, 20 knots. Motorship. Single masts and one funnel.
Passengers: 290 first and 141 tourist. Service: Italy-Far East.
Sister ship: **Asia.**

Vienna   (1912)   Lloyd Triestino (Italian).
Built by Lloyd Austriaco, Trieste, Austria. Tonnage: 7,156.
Dimensions: 443′ x 55′ (454′ o.l.). Twin-screw, 17 knots.
Quadruple expansion engines. Two masts and two funnels.
Passengers: 300. Service: Italy-Far East, via Suez Canal.
Renamed: **Po** (1937). World War II casualty. Ex-**Wien.**
Similar ships: **Esperia** and **Tevere.**

*Viet-Nam   (1952)   Messageries Maritimes (French).
Built by Chantiers Navals de la Ciotat, La Ciotat, France.
Tonnage: 13,162. Dimensions: 507′ x 72′ (532′ o.l.). Twin-screw, 21 knots. Steam turbines. Two masts and one funnel. Maiden voyage: Marseilles-Far East, via Suez Canal,
March 30, 1953. Passengers: 117 first, 110 tourist, 120 third.
Sister ships: **Cambodge** and **Laos.**

Ville de la Ciotat   (1892)   Messageries Maritimes.
Built by Messageries Maritimes, La Ciotat, France. Tonnage: 6,378. Dimensions: 485′ x 49′. Single-screw, 17½
knots. Triple expansion engines. Three masts and two funnels. Steel hull. Launched, April 10, 1892. Passengers:
170 first, 70 second, 112 third. Service: France-Australia,
via Suez Canal. Sunk by submarine "U-34", in the Mediterranean (east of Crete) on December 24, 1915, with the loss
of 80 lives. Sister ships: **Armand Behic, Australien** and
Polynesien.

Ville de Strasbourg   (1920)   Messageries Maritimes.
Built by North of Ireland Shipbuilding Co., Londonderry,
Ireland. Tonnage: 7,138. Dimensions: 410′ x 53′. Single-screw. Triple expansion engines. Two masts and one funnel.
Scrapped in December 1952.

Viminale   (1925)   (a) Lloyd Triestino, (b) Italia Line.
Built by Cantieri San Rocco, Trieste, Italy. Tonnage: 8,657.
Dimensions: 452′ x 57′ (467′ o.l.). Twin-screw, 13 knots.
Motorship. Two masts and no funnel. Passengers: 400.
Service: Italy-Australia. World War II casualty, July 25,
1942. Sister ship: **Esquilino.**

Volga   (1864)   Messageries Maritimes (French).
Built by Messageries Maritimes, La Ciotat, France. Tonnage: 1,610. Dimensions: 310′ x 32′. Single-screw. Compound engines. Three masts and one funnel. Iron hull. Sold at Saigon in March 1894; and subsequently used as a hulk at Amboy. Sister ships: **Eridan, Nieumen, Tanais** and **Tibre.**

Volpi   (1931)   Lloyd Triestino (Italian).
Built by Cantieri Riuniti dell' Adriatico, Monfalcone, Italy. Tonnage: 5,292. Dimensions: 423′ x 56′ (440′ o.l.). Single-screw, 14 knots. Motorship. Two masts and one funnel. Passengers: 12. War casualty, December 8, 1941. Sister ship: **Cortellazzo.**

Vondel   (1907)   Nederland Line (Dutch).
Built by Nederlandsche Schps. Maats., Amsterdam, Netherlands. Tonnage: 5,866. Dimensions: 426′ x 47′. Single-screw, 14 knots. Quadruple expansion engines. Two masts and one funnel. Service: Netherlands-Dutch East Indies, via Suez Canal. Passengers: 80 first and 54 second. Scrapped in 1930. Sister ships: **Grotius** and **Rembrandt.**

Wadai   (1922)   Woermann Line (German).
Built by Reiherstieg Schiffsw., Hamburg, Germany. Tonnage: 4,696. Dimensions: 361′ x 50′ (375′ o.l.). Single-screw, 11 knots. Quadruple expansion engines. Two masts and one funnel. Service: Germany-Africa. Passengers: 250. Renamed: **Empire Yare** (1945), (b) **Gogol** (1946) Russian. Still in Russian service, as of 1960. Sister ship: **Wahehe.**

Wahehe   (1922)   Woermann Line (German).
Built by Reiherstieg Schiffsw., Hamburg, Germany. Tonnage: 4,709. Dimensions: 361′ x 50′. Single-screw, 11 knots. Quadruple expansion engines. Two masts and one funnel. Passengers: 250. Service: Germany-Africa. Captured by the British off Vigo in 1940. Renamed: **Empire Citizen.** Sunk by submarine in Atlantic, February 3, 1941. Sister ship: **Wadai.**

Waimana   (1911)   Shaw, Savill & Albion Co. (British).
Built by Workman, Clark & Co., Belfast, Ireland. Tonnage: 10,389. Dimensions: 477′ x 63′. Twin-screw, 13½ knots. Triple expansion engines. Two masts and one funnel. Scrapped in 1952. Ex-**Herminus** (1932), ex-**Waimana.**

Wakasa Maru   (1897)   N. Y. K. Line (Japanese).
Built by D. & W. Henderson, Ltd., Glasgow, Scotland.
Tonnage: 6,266. Service: (a) Japan-Europe, via Suez Canal,
(b) Japan-South America. Note: See PART III for details.

Wakool   (1898)   Lund's Blue Anchor Line (British).
Built by Sunderland Shipbuilding Co., Sunderland, England.
Tonnage: 5,004. Dimensions: 400' x 47'. Single-screw, 13
knots. Triple expansion engines. Two masts and one funnel.
Service: England-Australia, via Cape of Good Hope. Passengers: 50 first class and a number of third class. Ownership
of liner transferred to the P. & O. Line in 1910. Continued
to be used on the same route. The Lund's Blue Anchor
marking on funnel was not removed until 1912. Renamed:
Le Myre de Villers. Sister ships: **Narrung** and **Wilcannia.**

Walmer Castle   (1872)   Castle Line (British).
Built by Barclay, Curle & Co., Glasgow, Scotland. Tonnage:
2,446. Dimensions: 327' x 36'. Single-screw. Compound
engines. Two masts and one funnel. Iron hull. Served as a
mail steamer from England to South Africa for some years.
Sold to Campo Line (Spanish) about 1880. Renamed: (a)
Valencia, (b) **Gaw-Quan-Sia.** Sunk in collision with the
Leerdam off the Belgian coast, December 16, 1889.

Walmer Castle   (1902)   Union-Castle Line (British).
Built by Harland & Wolff, Ltd., Belfast, Ireland. Tonnage:
12,546. Dimensions: 570' x 64' (585' o.l.). Twin-screw, 16½
knots. Quadruple expansion engines. Two masts and two
funnels. Note: The last mail liner ordered by the Union
Line before merging with the Castle Line. As a Union vessel
she was to have been named **Celt.** Made her first voyage to
Capetown in April 1902, and Rudyard Kipling was one of
the many passengers on board. Converted to troopship
during the latter part of World War I. She resumed regular
England-South African sailings in 1919. Scrapped in 1931.

Wandilla   (1912)   Adelaide Steamship Co. (British).
Built by Wm. Beardmore & Co., Glasgow, Scotland. Tonnage: 7,785. Dimensions: 411' x 56' (428' o.l.). Twin-screw,
16 knots. Quadruple expansion engines. Two masts and one
funnel. Note: An excellent type of ocean-going interstate
passenger ship. Passengers: 250 first, 120 second, 60 third
class. Designed for the Australian coastal service. Taken
over during First World War by British Government and
used as a hospital ship. Renamed: (a) **Fort St. George**
(1920), (b) **Cesarea** (1935), (c) **Arno** (1938). She became

a war loss off Tobruk in September 1942. Sister ships: **Warilda** and **Willochra.**

Wangoni   (1920)   Deutsche Ost Afrika Line.
Built by Blohm & Voss, Hamburg, Germany. Tonnage: 7,848.   Dimensions: 418' x 56'.   Single-screw, 14 knots. Steam turbines.   Two masts and one funnel.   Service: Germany-Africa. Passengers: 250. Ownership of vessel was transferred to Woermann Line at later date.   Survived World War II. Renamed: **Chukotka** (1946) Russian. This Russian vessel was still listed as of 1958. Sister ships: **Usaramo** and **Ussukuma.**

Waratah   (1908)   Lund's Blue Anchor Line (British).
Built by Barclay, Curle & Co., Glasgow, Scotland. Tonnage: 9,339.   Dimensions: 465' x 59'.   Twin-screw, 14 knots. Quadruple expansion engines.   Two masts and one funnel. The largest and finest steamship ever built for the Blue Anchor Line. Built as the answer to the newly built **Pericles** of Thompson's Aberdeen Line, which entered service in 1908, only to be lost during the afternoon of March 31, 1910, fortunately with no loss of life. The **Waratah** was named after Australia's most popular wild flower. Maiden voyage: London-Australia, via Cape of Good Hope, November 5, 1908.   Accommodation for 128 first and 160 third class passengers.   Note: The mysterious disappearance of the impressive looking **Waratah** is a sea classic of the highest rank. She left Durban on Sunday, July 26, 1909, bound for Capetown and England. Weather conditions were good as the attractive liner headed out to sea, with 92 passengers and a crew of 119. Captain J. F. Ilbery was in command of the vessel, a veteran of forty years with the Blue Anchor Line and naturally familiar with the route. The last definitely known sighting of the **Waratah** was during the morning of the following day, as she overtook the **Clan MacIntyre,** off the South West coast of South Africa, near Port St. John's. The two vessels flashed signals to each other, in order to make identification. The slower **Clan MacIntyre** soon lost sight of the **Waratah,** which was scheduled to dock at Capetown on July 29. However, the flagship of Mr. William Lund's "Blue Anchor Line" did not arrive at Capetown on that date, nor on any other subsequent day, as she had simply vanished from the face of the earth. The extensive search that was made by the British Government and other interested parties revealed nothing. To this day not a single piece of wreckage, nor one of the missing persons has ever been found. This lack of any tangible

evidence is truly amazing! During the long official inquiry
regarding the loss of the **Waratah,** it was brought out that
the vessel had possibly capsized in rough seas near the area
of Danger Point. Another supposition was the possibility
that the steamship had lost the use of her engines, and in
this helpless condition had drifted toward the Antarctic,
where eventually all on board perished from cold and starv-
ation. It may be well to state that the **Waratah** had two
engines and twin-screws. The number of lifeboats on board
were adequate. One witness during the hearing stated that
he, as commander of the steamer **Harlow,** while sailing
between Port St. John's and East London, had noticed two
bright flashes in the far distance on the evening of July 27,
1909. His observation led to the theory that possibly the
Waratah blew up, as a result of an explosion. It was
extremely unfortunate that the **Waratah** was not equipped
with wireless. This relatively new essential aid to navigation
would have been installed at a later date, but that was part
of the irony of fate. Conjectures continued, as puzzles of
this type have a way of injecting some purely coincidental
elements into the general picture, thus lending a sort of an
imaginative wonderment to the whole account. Perhaps the
story helps to better understand that all people, somehow,
have a niche in the history of the world. The tragic story
of the **Waratah** brings to mind a poem memorized when
I was a boy, titled "The Lost Steamship" by Fitz-James
O'Brien. It may have presented a fairly accurate picture of
the way the people on board the doomed **Waratah** accepted
and met death. The 'blue anchor' emblem on the funnels
of the Blue Anchor Line steamers, soon became a thing of
the past, as Mr. Lund's fleet merged with the P. & O. Line
early in 1910.

Warilda   (1914)   Adelaide Steamship Co. (British).
Built by Wm. Beardmore & Co., Glasgow, Scotland. Tonnage: 7,713. Dimensions: 411′ x 56′ (428′ o.l.). Twin-screw,
16 knots. Quadruple expansion engines. Two masts and one
funnel. This fine passenger ship was designed for the
Australian coastal service. Passengers: 250 first, 120 second,
60 third. Vessel was taken over for government service in
1914. While being used as a hospital ship was torpedoed
and sunk in the English Channel, August 3, 1918, with the
loss of 123 lives. Sister ships: **Wandilla** and **Willochra.**

Waroonga   (1914)   British India Steam Navigation Co.
Built by Wm. Denny & Bros., Ltd., Dumbarton, Scotland.
Tonnage: 9,365. Dimensions: 511′ x 64′. Twin-screw, 14

knots. Quadruple expansion engines. Three masts and one funnel. Torpedoed and sunk by submarine, April 5, 1943. Ex-**Hororata** (1939).

Warwick Castle (1877) Castle Line (British).
Built by Robert Napier & Sons, Ltd., Glasgow, Scotland. Tonnage: 3,056. Dimensions: 348' x 39'. Single-screw, 12 knots. Compound engines. Two masts and one funnel. Iron hull. Service: England-South Africa. Re-engined with triple expansions in 1891. Funnel was lengthened. Sold to Booth Line in 1897. Renamed: (a) **Jerome** (1897), (b) **Kerasounde** (1911), (c) **Kiresson** (1924). Sister ship: **Conway Castle.**

Warwick Castle (1931) Union-Castle Line.
Built by Harland & Wolff, Ltd., Belfast, Ireland. Tonnage: 20,445. Dimensions: 651' x 75' (677' o.l.). Twin-screw, 17 knots. Motorship. Two masts and two funnels. In mail and passenger service between Southampton and Capetown, South Africa. Altered by having a new bow and a single streamlined funnel installed in 1938. Passengers: 262 first, 228 second, 209 tourist. Torpedoed and sunk by submarine in the Atlantic, November 14, 1942, and went down within an hour and a half. Sister ship: **Winchester Castle.**

*****Warwick Castle** (1939) Union-Castle Line.
Built by Harland & Wolff, Ltd., Belfast, Ireland. Tonnage: 17,387. Dimensions: 570' x 76' (594' o.l.). Twin-screw, 18½ knots. Motorship. Two masts and one funnel. Passengers: 180 first and 359 tourist. Service: England-South Africa, via round Africa. Ex-**Pretoria Castle** (1946).

Warwickshire (1902) Bibby Line (British).
Built by Harland & Wolff, Ltd., Belfast, Ireland. Tonnage: 7,980. Dimensions: 470' x 58'. Twin-screw, 15 knots. Quadruple expansion engines. Four masts and one funnel. Passengers: 200. Service: England-Rangoon, via Suez Canal. Scrapped in 1932.

*****Warwickshire** (1948) Bibby Line (British).
Built by Fairfield Shipbuilding Co., Glasgow, Scotland. Tonnage: 8,903. Dimensions: 480' x 60' (498' o.l.). Single-screw, 15 knots. Two steam turbines. Single mast and one funnel. Service: England-Burma, via Suez Canal. Passengers: 76 first. Sister ship: **Leicestershire.**

Watussi   (1928)   Woermann Line (German).
  Built by Blohm & Voss, Hamburg, Germany. Tonnage:
  9,552.   Dimensions: 445' x 60'. Single-screw, 16 knots.
  Four steam turbines. Two masts and two funnels. New
  bow fitted and lengthened to 468 feet in 1934.   Power
  increased and speed raised from $13\frac{1}{2}$ to 16 knots. Service:
  Germany-South Africa. Passengers: 300. Vessel was scuttled
  December 2, 1939. Sister ship: **Ubena.**

Wien   (1911)   Lloyd Austriaco.
  Built by Lloyd Austriaco, Trieste, Austria. Tonnage: 7,367.
  Dimensions: 442' x 53'. Twin-screw, 18 knots. Quadruple
  expansion engines. Two masts and two funnels. Renamed:
  (a) **Vienna,** (b) **Po** (1937). World War II casualty, March
  14, 1941. Sister ships: **Gablonz** and **Helouan.**

Wilcannia   (1899)   Lund's Blue Anchor Line (British).
  Built by Sunderland Shipbuilding Co., Sunderland, England.
  Tonnage: 4,953. Dimensions: 400' x 47'. Single-screw, 13
  knots. Triple expansion engines. Two masts and one funnel.
  Service: England-Australia, via South Africa.   Accommodation for first and third class passengers. Vessel acquired
  by the P. & O. Line in 1910.   Subsequently sold to other
  owners. Renamed: **Dumont d' Urville.** Sister ships:
  Narrung and **Wakool.**

Wilis   (1905)   Rotterdam Lloyd (Dutch).
  Built by Kon. Maats. de Schelde, Flushing, Netherlands.
  Tonnage: 4,738. Dimensions: 394' x 47'. Single-screw, 14
  knots. Triple expansion engines. Two masts and one funnel.
  Service: Rotterdam-Dutch East Indies, via Suez Canal.
  Renamed: **Karadeniz.** Sold to Italian shipbreakers in 1954.
  Sister ship: **Rindjani.**

*Willem Ruys   (1947)   Rotterdam Lloyd (Dutch).
  Built by De Schelde, Flushing, Netherlands.   Tonnage:
  23,114. Dimensions: 580' x 82' (633' o.l.). Twin-screw, 21
  knots. Motorship. Two masts and two funnels. Passengers:
  840. Service: Designed for the Rotterdam-Indonesia route.
  Transferred to round-the-world service in 1959. See PART
  II for listing under Panama Canal route. Note: Tonnage
  originally listed as 21,119.

Willochra   (1913)   Adelaide Steamship Co. (British).
  Built by Wm. Beardmore & Co., Glasgow, Scotland. Tonnage: 7,784. Dimensions: 411' x 56' (428' o.l.). Twin-screw,
  16 knots. Quadruple expansion engines. Two masts and

one funnel. Built for the Australian coastal passenger service. Note: Actually never used in the Australian interstate trade, as upon completion she was chartered by the Union Steamship Company of New Zealand for their New Zealand-Vancouver route. She was later taken over by the British Government for service during World War I. After the war was sold to the Furness-Bermuda Line. Renamed: **Fort Victoria.** Sunk in collision with the **Algonquin** near Ambrose Lightship in December 1929. Sister ships: **Wandilla** and **Warilda.**

Winchester Castle (1930)   Union-Castle Line.
Built by Harland & Wolff, Ltd., Belfast, Ireland. Tonnage: 20,109. Dimensions: 631' x 75'. Twin-screw, 17 knots. Motorship. Two masts and two funnels. New bow installed. Re-engined and speed increased to 20 knots. A new single streamlined funnel replaced the original two short ones. Passengers: 600. Scrapped in 1961. Sister ship: **Warwick Castle.**

Windhuk (1905)   Deutsche Ost Afrika Line.
Built by Blohm & Voss, Hamburg, Germany. Tonnage: 6,365. Dimensions: 411' x 50'. Twin-screw, 12 knots. Triple expansion engines. Two masts and one funnel. Service: Germany-Africa. Renamed: (a) **City of Genoa,** (b) **Joao Belo.** Ex-**Gertrud Woermann.**

Windhuk (1936)   Deutsche Ost Afrika Line.
Built by Blohm & Voss, Hamburg, Germany. Tonnage: 16,662. Dimensions: 547' x 72' (578' o.l.). Twin-screw, 18 knots. Six steam turbines. Two masts and two funnels. Service: Germany-East African ports. Passengers: 500. Crew: 250. Survived World War II. Renamed: **Lejeune** (United States Government). Converted to single funnel. Sister ship: **Pretoria.**

Windsor Castle (1872)   Castle Line (British).
Built by Robert Napier & Sons, Glasgow, Scotland. Tonnage: 2,672. Dimensions: 334' x 37'. Single-screw. Compound engines. Two masts and one funnel. Iron hull. Originally built for the Currie's service to India. Made a record-breaking voyage to Calcutta in September 1872. Transferred to the England-Capetown service in 1873, and also broke the speed record for that particular route. Struck a reef near Dassen Island, Cape Colony, October 19, 1876, and became a total loss. Sister ship: **Edinburgh Castle.**

Windsor Castle   (1920)   Union-Castle Line.
Built by John Brown & Co., Clydebank, Glasgow, Scotland.
Tonnage: 18,967.   Dimensions: 632' x 75'.   Twin-screw, 18
knots.   Steam turbines.   Two masts and four masts.   First
vessel built at the Clydebank shipyard for the Union Castle
Line.   Launched by the Prince of Wales on March 9, 1921.
Entered the Southampton-Capetown service in April 1922.
Passengers: 760 passengers.   Crew: 440.   In 1934 Prince
George traveled from South Africa to England on this
luxury liner.   Reconditioned in 1938.   Lengthened to 661
feet (19,141 tons) in 1938.   Two new streamlined funnels
replaced the original four.   Speed increased to 19 knots.
Torpedoed and sunk by enemy aircraft near Algiers, March
23, 1943.   Sister ship: **Arundel Castle.**

*Windsor Castle**   (1960)   Union-Castle Line.
Built by Cammell, Laird & Co., Birkenhead, England.   Tonnage: 37,640.   Dimensions: 730' x 92' (783' o.l.).   Twin-
screw, 23 knots.   Four steam turbines.   45,000 H.P.   Single
mast and one funnel.   Keel laid on December 9, 1957.
Launched by the British Queen Mother, June 23, 1959.
Maiden voyage: Southampton-South Africa, August 18, 1960.
Passengers: 850.   Crew: 475.   Note: An outstanding passenger
liner for the England-Capetown mail service.   Quite a contrast to the first **Windsor Castle.**

*Winneba**   (1938)   Elder, Dempster Lines (British).
Built by Swan, Hunter & Wigham Richardson, Ltd., New-
castle, England.   Tonnage: 8,355.   Dimensions: 468' x 61'.
Twin-screw, 13½ knots.   Steam turbines.   Two masts and
one funnel.   Passengers: 105 first class.   Service: England-
West Africa.   Ex-**Umgeni** (1957) Natal Line.   Sister ship:
Calabar.

Worcestershire   (1904)   Bibby Line (British).
Built by Harland & Wolff, Ltd., Belfast, Ireland.   Tonnage:
7,160.   Dimensions: 452' x 54'.   Twin-screw, 15 knots.
Quadruple expansion engines.   Four masts and one funnel.
Service: Great Britain-Rangoon.   Passengers: 200 first class.
Sunk by a mine ten miles from Colombo, February 17, 1917,
with the loss of two lives.   Sister ship: **Herefordshire.**

*Worcestershire**   (1931)   Bibby Line (British).
Built by Fairfield Shipbuilding Co., Glasgow, Scotland.
Tonnage: 11,453.   Dimensions: 483' x 64' (501' o.l.).   Twin-
screw, 15 knots.   Motorship.   Four masts and one funnel.
Now has a single modernized funnel and one mast.   Tonnage

reduced to 10,329. Passengers: 115 first class. Originally had accommodation for 280 first class passengers. Service: England-Rangoon, via Suez Canal. Similar ships: **Derbyshire** and **Staffordshire.**

Yamuna (1903) British India Steam Navigation Co.
Built by Sir James Laing & Sons, Ltd., Sunderland, England. Tonnage: 10,606. Dimensions: 510' x 59'. Twin-screw, 13 knots. Triple expansion engines. Two masts and one funnel. Vessel was soon taken over by the Cunard Line and renamed **Slavonia.** Note: See PART I for further information.

Yang Tse (1877) Messageries Maritimes (French).
Built by Messageries Maritimes, La Ciotat, France. Tonnage: 3,803. Dimensions: 394' x 39'. Single-screw, 13½ knots. Compound engines. Three masts and one funnel. Iron hull. Launched, January 21, 1877. Service: France-Far East, via Suez Canal. Sold for scrap to La Rochelle shipbreakers in April 1911. Sister ships: **Djemnah** and **Oxus.**

Yarra (1883) Messageries Maritimes.
Built by Messageries Maritimes, La Ciotat, France. Tonnage: 4,142. Dimensions: 416' x 41'. Single-screw, 13½ knots. Triple expansion engines. Three masts and two funnels. Launched, August 12, 1883. Service: France-East of Suez. Torpedoed and sunk in the Mediterranean on voyage from Port Said to Marseilles, May 29, 1917.

Yasaka Maru (1914) N. Y. K. Line (Japanese).
Built by Kawasaki Dockyard Co., Kobe, Japan. Tonnage: 10,932. Dimensions: 505' x 63'. Twin-screw, 14½ knots. Triple expansion engines. Two masts and one funnel. Service: Japan-Europe, via Suez Canal. Torpedoed and sunk by German submarine without warning near Port Said, December 21, 1915, while bound from Europe to Japan. There was no loss of life among the 120 passengers and 162 crew members. Sister ships: **Kashima Maru, Katori Maru, Fushima Maru, Suwa Maru.**

Yasukuni Maru (1930) N. Y. K. Line (Japanese).
Built by Mitsubishi Co., Nagasaki, Japan. Tonnage: 11,930. Dimensions: 505' x 64' (526' o.l.). Twin-screw, 18 knots. Motorship. Two masts and one funnel. Service: Japan-London, via Suez Canal. Passengers: 250. Crew: 200. She became a victim to a German magnetic mine off the British east coast in November 1939. Sister ship: **Terukuni Maru.**

Note: Finest liners built to date for the N. Y. K. Line's
European service.

Yawata Maru   (1898)   N. Y. K. Line (Japanese).
Built by Robert Napier & Sons, Ltd., Glasgow, Scotland.
Tonnage: 3,817.   Dimensions: 375′ x 44′.   Single-screw, 15
knots.   Triple expansion engines.   Two masts and one funnel.
Service: Japan-Europe, via Suez.   Passengers: 62 first, 24
second, 126 third.   No longer in commission, 1934.

Yoma   (1928)   Henderson Line (British).
Built by Wm. Denny & Bros., Ltd., Dumbarton, Scotland.
Tonnage: 8,139.   Dimensions: 460′ x 61′.   Single-screw, 14
knots.   Quadruple expansion engines.   Two masts and one
funnel.   Service: Great Britain-Rangoon.   Passengers: 150
first class.   Crew: 140.   Torpedoed and sunk by submarine,
June 17, 1943.   Sister ships: **Amarapoora, Kemmendie,
Pegu** and **Sagaing.**

Yorck   (1906)   North German Lloyd.
Tonnage: 8,976.   Service: Germany-Far East, via Suez
Canal.   Note: See PART I for details.

Yorkshire   (1889)   Bibby Line (British).
Built by Harland & Wolff, Ltd., Belfast, Ireland.   Tonnage:
4,269.   Dimensions: 400′ x 45′.   Single-screw, 14 knots.
Triple expansion engines.   Four masts and one funnel.   Steel
hull.   Service: England-Rangoon, via Suez.   Renamed: (a)
Indien (1905), (b) **Estonia** (1907).   Note: See PART I
for other details.   Sister ship: **Lancashire.**

Yorkshire   (1920)   Bibby Line (British).
Built by Harland & Wolff, Ltd., Belfast, Ireland.   Tonnage:
10,184.   Dimensions: 482′ x 58′.   Twin-screw, 15 knots.
Four steam turbines.   Four masts and one funnel.   Only
flushed-decked Bibby liner built to date.   Service: Liverpool-
Rangoon, via Suez Canal.   Passengers: 290 first class.   Crew:
190.   Torpedoed and sunk by German submarine, October
17, 1939.

Yunnan   (1905)   Messageries Maritimes (French).
Built by Chantiers de la Mediterranee, Havre, France.
Tonnage: 6,474.   Dimensions: 414′ x 50′.   Twin-screw, 12
knots.   Triple expansion engines.   Two masts and one funnel.
Service: France-East of Suez.   Renamed: **Ionopolis.**   Torpedoed near Milo, October 4, 1915, but was able to be towed
to anchorage.   However, wreck was abandoned.

Zamzam   (1909)   Societe   Misr   de   Navigation   Maritime
(Egyptian).
Built by Harland & Wolff, Ltd., Belfast, Ireland. Tonnage:
8,299.   Dimensions: 467' x 54'.   Twin-screw, 14 knots.
Quadruple expansion engines. Four masts and one funnel.
Shelled and sunk by German submarine in May 1941. Ex-
British Exhibitor (1933), ex-**Leicestershire** (1931).

Zieten   (1902)   North German Lloyd.
Tonnage: 8,043. Designed for German-East of Suez service.
However, made a number of trans-Atlantic sailings. See
PART I for details.

PART V

FLEET LIST

of

Passenger Ships

NOTES: An asterisk (*) denotes ship in service in 1962.

Gross tonnage equals cubic feet of all enclosed space divided by 100. This form of tonnage (measurement) is given throughout this volume.

ABERDEEN LINE (RENNIE'S)
JOHN T. RENNIE & SON, LTD.
(British)

Dabulamanzi (1882)	1,537	Insizwa (1899)	2,984
Illovo (1890)	1,930	Intaba (1910)	4,832
Inanda (1904)	4,233	Inyati (1896)	2,516
Ingeli (1897)	2,928	Matabele (1885)	1,581
Inkosi (1902)	3,576		

ABERDEEN LINE (THOMPSON'S)
GEORGE THOMPSON & CO., LTD.
(British)

Aberdeen (1881)	3,684	Moravian (1899)	4,573
Australasian (1884)	3,662	Nineveh (1894)	3,808
Damascus (1887)	3,726	Pericles (1908)	10,925
Demosthenes (1911)	11,223	Salamis (1899)	4,508
Diogenes (1922)	12,351	Sophocles (1883)	4,673
Euripides (1914)	14,947	Sophocles (1922)	12,360
Herminius (1911)	9,930	Themistcles (1911)	11,231
Marathon (1904)	6,795	Thermopylae (1891)	3,711
Miltiades (1903)	6,765		

ABERDEEN & COMMONWEALTH LINE
GEORGE THOMPSON & CO., LTD.
(British)

Esperance Bay (1922)	14,146	Hobsons Bay (1922)	14,130
Renamed: Arawa		Jervis Bay (1922)	14,129
Esperance Bay (1922)	14,343	Largs Bay (1921)	14,143
ex-Hobsons Bay		Moreton Bay (1921)	14,145

ADLER (EAGLE) LINE
(German)

NOTE: Hamburg-American Line purchased the fleet in 1875.

Gellert (1874)   3,533
Goethe (1872)   3,408
Herder (1873)   3,494
Klopstock (1874)   3,641

Lessing (1874)   3,527
Schiller (1872)   3,408
Wieland (1874)   3,504

ALCOA STEAMSHIP CO.
(United States)

*Alcoa Cavalier (1947)   8,481
*Alcoa Clipper (1946)   8,481

*Alcoa Corsair (1947)   8,481
Alcoa Polaris (1941)   6,679

ALLAN LINE
ALLAN LINE STEAMSHIP CO., LTD.
(British)

Alsatian (1913)   18,481
Anglo-Saxon (1856)   1,673
Assyrian (1880)   3,317
Austrian (1866)   2,682
Bavarian (1899)   10,376
Belgian (1855)   2,349
Bohemian (1859)   2,190
Brazilian (1890)   3,046
Buenos Ayrean (1879)   4,005
Calgarian (1913)   17,515
Californian (1891)   4,244
Canadian (1854)   1,873½
Canadian (1860)   1,926
Canadian (1872)   2,401
Carthaginian (1884)   4,444
Caspian (1870)   2,747
Castilian (1898)   7,441
Circassian (1872)   3,724
Corean (1881)   3,488
Corinthian (1856)   1,517
Corinthian (1899)   6,229
Corsican (1907)   11,419
European (1866)   2,708
Germany (1868)   3,244
Grampian (1907)   10,920
Grecian (1879)   3,613
Hanoverian (1882)   3,603
Hesperian (1908)   10,920
Hibernian (1861)   1,888
Hungarian (1858)   2,190

Indian (1855)   1,764
Ionian (1901)   8,268
Laurentian (1872)   4,522
Livonian (1881)   4,162
Lucerne (1878)   1,925
Ludgate Hill (1881)   4,063
Manitoban (1865)   1,810
Mongolian (1891)   4,837
Monte Videan (1887)   3,076
Moravian (1864)   2,481
Nestorian (1866)   2,466
North American (1856)   1,715
North Briton (1858)   2,190
Norwegian (1861)   1,888
Norwegian (1865)   3,523
   ex-City of New York
Nova Scotian (1858)   2,190
Numidian (1891)   4,836
Ottawa (1865)   1,810
Parisian (1881)   5,395
Peruvian (1863)   2,549
Phoenician (1864)   2,356
Polynesian (1872)   3,983
Pomeranian (1882)   4,365
Pretorian (1900)   6,436
Prussian (1869)   3,030
Rosarian (1887)   3,077
Roumanian (1882)   4,126
St. Andrew (1861)   1,432
St. David (1864)   1,516

ALLAN LINE (Continued)

St. George (1863)   1,468
St. Patrick (1854)   1,208
Sardinian (1875)   4,376
Sarmatian (1871)   3,647
Scandinavian (1870)   3,068
Scandinavian (1898)   12,116
Scotian (1898)   10,417
Siberian (1884)   3,846

Sicilian (1899)   6,224
State of California (1891)   4,275
Tunisian (1900)   10,576
Turanian (1881)   4,021
Victorian (1904)   10,629
Virginian (1905)   10,754
Waldensian (1863)   2,306

AMERICAN EXPORT LINES
(United States)

*Atlantic (1953)   14,138
*Constitution (1951)   23,750
Excalibur (1930)   9,359
*Excalibur (1944)   9,644
Excambion (1931)   9,360
Excambion (1944)   9,644

Exeter (1931)   9,360
*Exeter (1945)   9,644
Exochorda (1931)   9,359
Exochorda (1944)   9,644
*Independence (1950)   23,719
La Guardia (1944)   17,951

AMERICAN LINE
American Steamship Co.
(United States)

Berlin (1874)   5,526
British Crown (1879)   3,563
British Empire (1878)   3,361
British King (1881)   3,412
British Prince (1882)   3,871
British Princess (1882)   3,864
British Queen (1881)   3,412
Chester (1873)   4,770
Haverford (1901)   11,635
Illinois (1873)   3,104
Indiana (1873)   3,335

Kensington (1894)   8,669
Merion (1902)   11,612
New York (1888)   10,499
Ohio (1873)   3,104
Paris (1889)   10,669
Pennsylvania (1873)   3,126
Philadelphia (1889)   10,786
St. Louis (1895)   11,629
St. Paul (1895)   11,629
Southwark (1893)   8,607

AMERICAN MAIL LINE
(United States)

Established in 1930 and under the control of Dollar Steamship Lines. Ownership was transferred to the newly formed American President Lines in 1938.

President Grant (1921)   14,199
President Jackson (1921)   14,124
President Jefferson (1920) 14,174

President Madison (1921)   14,187
President McKinley (1921) 14,127

AMERICAN PRESIDENT LINES
(United States)

NOTE: At the request of the United States Maritime Commission in 1938, the Dollar Steamship Lines was reorganized as the American President Lines.

President Buchanan (1920) 10,533
  ex-President Monroe
President Cleveland (1921) 14,123
*President Cleveland (1947) 15,359
President Coolidge (1931) 21,936
President Fillmore (1920) 10,533
  ex-President Van Buren
President Grant (1921) 10,533
  ex-President Adams
President Harrison (1921) 10,533
President Hoover (1931) 21,936
*President Hoover (1939) 10,603
President Jackson (1941) 9,273
President Lincoln (1921) 14,187

President Madison (1921) 10,538
  ex-President Garfield
*President Monroe (1940) 9,261
President Pierce (1921) 14,123
*President Polk (1941) 9,260
*President Roosevelt (1944) 18,298
President Taft (1921) 14,123
President Taylor (1921) 10,500
  ex-President Polk
President Tyler (1920) 10,533
  ex-President Hayes
President Van Buren (1941) 9,260
President Wilson (1921) 14,127
President Wilson (1948) 15,359

ANCHOR LINE
(British)

Alexandria (1870) 2,017
Algeria (1891) 4,510
Algeria (1914) 8,156
Alsatia (1876) 2,810
Anchoria (1874) 4,168
Anglia (1869) 2,253
Assyria (1871) 2,023
Assyria (1908) 8,072
Astoria (1884) 5,086
Australia (1870) 2,243
Belgravia (1882) 4,977
Bolivia (1873) 3,999
Britannia (1863) 1,417
Britannia (1879) 3,069
Britannia (1926) 8,802
Calabria (1901) 4,376
Caledonia (1862) 1,681
Caledonia (1863) 1,393
Caledonia (1904) 9,223
Caledonia (1925) 17,046
*Caledonia (1947) 11,252
California (1872) 3,410
California (1907) 8,662

California (1923) 16,792
Cambria (1869) 1,997
Cameronia (1910) 10,963
Cameronia (1920) 16,297
Castalia (1873) 2,201
Castalia (1906) 6,715
*Cilicia (1937) 11,250
Circassia (1878) 4,272
Circassia (1903) 6,861
*Circassia (1937) 11,170
Columbia (1866) 1,698
Columbia (1901) 8,292
Dacian (1868) 1,038
Devonia (1877) 4,270
Dorian (1868) 1,039
Elysia (1873) 2,714
Elysia (1908) 6,757
Ethiopia (1873) 4,005
Europa (1867) 1,746
Furnessia (1880) 5,495
Hesperia (1882) 3,037
Hibernia (1865) 1,615
India (1868) 2,477

ANCHOR LINE (Continued)

Iowa (1864)   1,988
Ismailia (1870)   1,630
Italia (1872)   2,248
Italia (1903)   4,806
John Bell (1854)   1,101
Karamania (1882)   3,148
Macedonia (1864)   2,130
Massilia (1902)   5,156
Olympia (1871)   2,210
Olympia (1902)   5,197
Perugia (1901)   4,348
Scindia (1890)   4,358
Scotia (1889)   2,846

Sidonian (1870)   1,236
Tempest (1855)   866
Transylvania (1914)   14,315
Transylvania (1925)   16,923
Trinacria (1871)   2,051
Tuscania (1915)   14,348
Tuscania (1922)   16,991
Tyrian (1869)   1,039
United Kingdom (1857)   1,264
United States (1860)   1,197
Utopia (1874)   2,731
Victoria (1872)   3,358

ARGENTINA STATE LINE
(Flota Mercante de Estado)

Comodoro Rivadavia (1905)
   5,450
Evita (1951)   11,317
*Juan de Garay (1928)   8,723

*Rio de la Plata (1950)   11,317
*Rio Jachal (1950)   11,317
*Rio Tunuyan (1951)   11,317

AROSA LINE
COMPANIA INTERNACIONAL TRANSPORTADORA
(Panamanian)

Arosa Kulm (1920)   7,572
Arosa Star (1931)   7,114

Arosa Sky (1939)   17,321
Arosa Sun (1930)   20,126

ATLANTIC TRANSPORT LINE
(British)

Boadicea (1898)   7,057
Cleopatra (1898)   6,849
Manitoba (1892)   5,590
Manitou (1898)   6,849
Marquette (1898)   7,057
Massachusetts (1892)   5,590
Mesaba (1898)   6,833
Menominee (1897)   6,919
Michigan (1890)   3,722
Minneapolis (1901)   13,448
Minnehaha (1900)   13,443
Minnekahda (1917)   17,281

Minnesota (1901)   11,667
Minnetonka (1902)   13,440
Minnetonka (1924)   21,716
Minnewaska (1894)   5,713
Minnewaska (1903)   15,801
Minnewaska (1909)   14,317
Minnewaska (1923)   21,716
Mississippi (1903)   7,913
Mobile (1893)   5,780
Mohawk (1885)   4,212
Mohawk (1892)   5,678
Mohegan (1893)   6,889

AUSTRO-AMERICAN LINE
Unione Austriaca di Navigazione
(Austrian)

Alice (1907)   6,122
Argentina (1907)   5,526
Atlanta (1908)   5,387
Canada (1898)   11,440
Carolina (1905)   4,713
Columbia (1908)   5,460
Eugenia (1906)   4,903
Francesca (1905)   4,996
Georgia (1908)   5,380
Gerty (1903)   4,212
Giulia (1904)   4,337

Ida (1906)   4,730
Kaiser Franz Josef I   (1912)
   12,567
Laura (1907)   6,122
Martha Washington (1908) 8,347
Oceania (1907)   5,497
Polonia (1899)   11,464
Sofia Hohenberg (1905)   5,491
Teresa (1900)   3,769
Virginia (1906)   3,563

BALTIC AMERICAN LINE
(Danish)

Estonia (1912)   6,516
Latvia (1908)   8,596

Lituania (1915)   6,598
Polonia (1910)   7,858

BALTIMORE MAIL STEAMSHIP CO.
(United States)

City of Baltimore (1919)   8,378
City of Hamburg (1919)   8,378
City of Havre (1918)   8,378
City of Los Angeles (1918) 8,378
   ex-City of Havre
City of Newport News (1919)
   8,378

City of Norfolk (1918)   8,378
City of San Francisco (1919)
   8,378
   ex-City of Hamburg

BEAVER LINE
Canada Shipping Co., Ltd.
(British)

This line was formed by a group of Montreal merchants in 1867. The company changed hands in 1899 and became the property of Elder, Dempster & Company, who finally sold the Beaver Line to Canadian Pacific Steamship, Ltd. in 1903.

Gallia   (1878)   4,809
Lake Champlain (1874)   2,207
Lake Huron (1881)   4,040
Lake Manitoba (1880)   3,322
Lake Megantic (1875)   2,219

Lake Nepigon (1875)   2,209
Lake Ontario (1887)   4,502
Lake Simcoe (1884)   4,912
Lake Superior (1884)   4,562
Lake Winnipeg (1879)   3,329

BERNSTEIN LINE
(German)

NOTE: Acquired the Red Star liners *Pennland* and *Westernland* in 1935, which were resold to the Holland-America Line in 1939.

Gerolstein (1904)   7,772
Ilsenstein (1904)   8,216
Konigstein (1907)   9,626

Pennland (1922)   16,082
Westernland (1918)   16,231

BIBBY LINE
BIBBY BROTHERS & Co.
(British)

Cheshire (1891)   5,775
Cheshire (1927)   15,560
Derbyshire (1897)   6,776
*Derbyshire (1935)   11,660
*Devonshire (1939)   11,275
Dorsetshire (1920)   9,645
Gloucestershire (1910)   8,124
Herefordshire (1905)   7,217
Lancashire (1889)   4,244
Lancashire (1917)   9,445
Leicestershire (1909)   8,059
*Leicestershire (1949)   8,908
Oxfordshire (1912)   8,646

*Oxfordshire (1957)   20,586
Shropshire (1891)   5,799
Shropshire (1926)   10,560
Somersetshire (1921)   9,648
Staffordshire (1894)   6,022
Staffordshire (1929)   10,595
Warwickshire (1902)   7,980
*Warwickshire (1948)   8,903
Worcestershire (1904)   7,160
*Worcestershire (1931)   11,453
Yorkshire (1889)   4,629
Yorkshire (1920)   10,184

BLUE ANCHOR LINE
WILLIAM LUND & COMPANY
(British)

Commonwealth (1902)   6,616
Geelong (1904)   7,954
Narrung (1896)   5,078

Wakool (1898)   5,078
Waratah (1908)   9,339
Wilcannia (1899)   4,953

BLUE FUNNEL LINE
OCEAN STEAM SHIP COMPANY, LTD.
(British)

Aeneas (1910)   10,058
Anchises (1911)   10,046
Antenor (1925)   11,174
Ascanius (1910)   10,048
*Charon (1936)   3,703
*Gorgon (1933)   3,533
*Gunung Djati (1936)   17,891
Hector (1924)   11,198
Hector (1950)   10,125
Helenus (1949)   10,129

Ixion (1951)   10,125
Jason (1950)   10,125
Nestor (1913)   14,629
Patroclus (1923)   11,314
*Patroclus (1950)   10,109
*Peleus (1949)   10,093
*Perseus (1950)   10,109
*Pyrrhus (1949)   10,093
Sarpedon (1923)   11,321
Ulysses (1913)   14,626

BLUE STAR LINE
(British)

Almeda Star (1926)	14,935		Avila Star (1927)	14,443
Andalucia Star (1927)	14,943		*Brasil Star (1947)	10,716
Arandora Star (1927)	14,690		*Paraguay Star (1948)	10,722
*Argentina Star (1947)	10,716		*Uruguay Star (1947)	10,723
Avelona Star (1927)	12,858			

BOOTH LINE
Booth Steamship Company
(British)

Aidan (1911)	4,545		Hilary (1908)	6,329
Alban (1914)	5,223		Hilary (1931)	7,403
Ambrose (1869)	1,168		Hildebrand (1893)	1,947
Ambrose (1903)	4,594		Hildebrand (1911)	6,995
Anselm (1882)	1,562		Hildebrand (1951)	7,735
Anselm (1905)	5,450		Huayna (1893)	1,988
Anselm (1935)	5,954		Hubert (1894)	1,922
Antony (1907)	6,466		Hubert (1910)	3,946
Atahualp (1894)	1,965		*Hubert (1956)	7,898
Augustine (1865)	1,106		Jerome (1866)	1,090
Augustine (1879)	3,498		Jerome (1877)	3,056
Basil (1871)	1,185		Justin (1880)	1,822
Basil (1895)	3,223		Justin (1904)	3,498
Bernard (1895)	3,280		Lanfranc (1884)	1,657
Boniface (1904)	3,506		Lanfranc (1907)	6,287
Cametense (1891)	2,184		Lisbonense (1871)	1,681
Cearense (1869)	1,381		Madeirense (1891)	2,831
Cearense (1891)	2,766		Mananense (1874)	1,672
Christopher (1910)	4,416		Manco (1908)	2,984
Clement (1877)	1,227		Maranhense (1890)	2,662
Clement (1896)	3,445		Obidense (1891)	2,380
Cuthbert (1906)	3,563		Origen (1886)	1,612
Cyril (1883)	1,190		Oswald (1914)	5,700
Cyril (1883)	4,380		Pancras (1911)	4,436
Denis (1911)	4,435		Paraense (1871)	1,697
Fluminense (1891)	2,154		Santarense (1891)	2,751
Francis (1910)	3,963		Sobralense (1884)	1,982
Grangense (1892)	2,162		Stephen (1910)	4,435
Hilary (1889)	1,983		Vincent (1895)	4,561

BRITISH INDIA STEAM NAVIGATION COMPANY
(British)

*Amra (1938)	8,314		Arratoon Apcar (1896)	4,510
Angora (1911)	4,298		Aska (1939)	8,323
Arankola (1911)	4,129		Avoca (1891)	5,189
Aronda (1912)	4,062		Bagdad (1872)	1,271
*Aronda (1941)	8,396		Bamora (1914)	3,291

BRITISH INDIA STEAM NAVIGATION CO. (Continued)

Bandra (1914)   3,284
Bankura (1912)   3,185
Barala (1912)   3,148
Barjora (1912) 3,172
Baroda (1911)   3,205
Barpeta (1914)   3,194
Berbera (1905)   4,352
Bezwada (1893)   5,001
Bharata (1902)   4,054
Canara (1905)   6,012
Chakdara (1914)   3,080
Chakdina (1914)   3,080
Chakla (1914)   3,081
Chakrata (1913)   5,682
Chanda (1906)   6,169
Chantala (1913)   4,949
Chantala (1920)   3,129
Chilka (1910)   3,952
Chilka (1922)   4,360
Chindwara (1912)   5,192
Chupra (1906)   6,175
Chyebassa (1907)   6,249
Colaba (1906)   6,019
Culna (1907)   6,142
Dacca (1881)   2,545
Dalgoma (1923)   5,953
*Dara (1948)   5,030
*Daressa (1950)   5,180
Dilwara (1891)   5,378
Dilwara (1935)   11,080
Domala (1921)   8,441
Dumana (1923)   8,427
Dumra (1894)   1,695
*Dumra (1946)   4,867
Dunera (1891)   5,414
*Dunera (1937)   11,162
*Dwarka (1947)   4,851
Edavana (1911)   5,284
Egra (1911)   5,108
Ekma (1911)   5,108
Elephanta (1911)   5,292
Ellenga (1911)   5,196
Ellora (1911)   5,201
Erinpura (1911)   5,143
Ethiopia (1922)   5,574
Golconda (1887)   5,874
Gregory Apcar (1902)   4,604
Japan (1906)   6,013
Jelunga (1890)   5,206
*Kampala (1947)   10,304
Karagola (1917)   7,053

Karanja (1931)   9,891
*Karanja (1948)   10,294
Karapara (1915)   7,117
Karoa (1915)   7,009
Kenya (1930)   9,890
*Kenya (1947)   14,434
Khandalla (1923)   7,018
Lalpoora (1885)   3,269
Lama (1905)   2,198
Landaura (1885)   3,308
Lawada (1885)   3,269
Lhasa (1904)   2,184
Lindula (1888)   3,346
Linga (1904)   2,185
Loodiana (1884)   3,269
Lunka (1905)   2,193
Madura (1873)   1,956
Madura (1921)   9,032
Malda (1874)   1,951
Malda (1913)   7,884
Malda (1922)   9,066
Manela (1921)   8,303
Manora (1913)   7,876
Mantola (1916)   8,253
Mantola (1921)   9,065
Margha (1917)   8,278
Mashobra (1914)   8,174
Mashobra (1920)   8,324
Masula (1919)   7,326
Matiana (1894)   5,281
Matiana (1921)   9,045
Mecca (1873)   1,460
Merkara (1914)   8,258
Modasa (1921)   9,070
Mombassa (1889)   4,662
Mongara (1914)   8,205
Morvada (1914)   8,205
Mulbera (1922)   9,100
Mundra (1920)   7,299
Muttra (1891)   4,644
Nerbudda (1882)   3,025
Neuralia (1912)   9,082
Nevasa (1884)   2,998
Nevasa (1913)   9,056
*Nevasa (1956) 20,527
Nowshera (1883)   3,024
Nuddea (1883)   3,005
Obra (1895)   5,462
Okara (1895)   5,291
Okhla (1895)   5,288
Onda (1895)   5,247

BRITISH INDIA STEAM NAVIGATION CO. (Continued)

Onipenta (1896)	5,294	Takliwa (1924)	7,936
Oolobaria (1896)	5,295	Talamba (1924)	8,018
Orissa (1897)	5,436	Talma (1923)	10,000
Queda (1905)	7,703	Tara (1902)	6,322
Querimba (1905)	7,696	Taroba (1888)	4,793
Quetta (1881)	3,302	Taroba (1902)	6,322
Quiloa (1905)	7,697	Teesta (1903)	6,295
*Rajula (1926)	8,478	Tilawa (1924)	10,006
Rewa (1906)	7,308	Torilla (1911)	5,205
Rohilla (1906)	7,409	Uganda (1898)	5,431
Rohna (1926)	8,602	*Uganda (1952)	14,430
Sangola (1901)	5,184	Ujina (1898)	5,310
*Sangola (1947)	8,647	Ula (1898)	5,310
Santhia (1901)	5,192	Umballa (1898)	5,310
Santhia (1925)	7,754	Umta (1898)	5,422
*Santhia (1950)	8,908	Upada (1899)	5,257
Sealda (1902)	5,382	Urlana (1899)	5,253
Shirala (1901)	5,306	Varela (1914)	4,645
Shirala (1925)	7,841	Varsova (1914)	4,691
Sirdhana (1925)	7,745	Vasna (1917)	4,820
*Sirdhana (1947)	8,608	Virawa (1900)	3,360
Sofala (1902)	5,381	Vita (1914)	4,691
Surada (1902)	5,324	Waipara (1904)	6,393
Tairea (1924)	7,933	Waroonga (1914)	9,365
Takada (1914)	6,949	Yamuna (1903)	10,606

"C" LINE
Giacomo Costa fu Andrea
(Italian)

*Andrea C (1942)	8,604	Bianca C (1944)	18,427
*Anna C (1929)	11,736	*Federico C (1958)	20,416

CANADIAN NATIONAL LINE
Canadian National Steamships, Ltd.
(British)

Lady Drake (1929)	7,985	Lady Somers (1929)	8,194
Lady Hawkins (1929)	7,988	Prince David (1930)	6,892
Lady Nelson (1928)	7,970	Prince Henry (1930)	6,893
Lady Rodney (1929)	8,194	Prince Robert (1930)	6,892

ROYAL LINE — URANIUM LINE
Canadian Northern Steamships, Ltd.
(British)

Campania (1902)	9,291	Volturno (1906)	3,602
Campanello (1902)	9,291	Royal Edward (1908)	11,117
Principello (1907)	6,560	Royal George (1907)	11,146

CANADIAN PACIFIC LINE
CANADIAN PACIFIC STEAMSHIPS, LTD.
(British)

Established their trans-Pacific service in 1887. However, it was not until 1903, through the purchase of the Beaver Line fleet from Elder, Dempster & Co., that they entered the trans-Atlantic trade.

Duchess of Atholl (1928) 20,119
Duchess of Bedford (1928) 20,123
Duchess of Richmond (1928) 20,022
Duchess of York (1929) 20,021
Empress of Asia (1913) 16,909
Empress of Australia (1914) 21,833
Empress of Australia (1924) 19,665
Empress of Britain (1906) 14,189
Empress of Britain (1931) 42,348
*Empress of Britain (1955) 25,516
Empress of Canada (1922) 21,517
Empress of Canada (1928) 20,325
*Empress of Canada (1960) 27,500
Empress of China (1890) 5,947
Empress of China (1914) 21,816
*Empress of England (1957) 25,585
Empress of France (1913) 18,357
Empress of France (1928) 20,448
Empress of India (1889) 5,943
Empress of India (1908) 16,992
Empress of Ireland (1906) 14,191
Empress of Japan (1890) 5,940
Empress of Japan (1930) 26,032
Empress of Russia (1913) 16,810
Empress of Scotland (1905) 25,160

Empress of Scotland (1930) 26,313
Grampian (1907) 10,920
Lake Champlain (1900) 7,392
Lake Erie (1900) 7,550
Lake Manitoba (1901) 9,674
Lake Michigan (1901) 9,240
Marburn (1900) 10,743
Marglen (1898) 10,417
Marloch (1904) 10,687
Marvale (1907) 11,438
Melita (1918) 15,183
Metagama (1915) 12,420
Milwaukee (1897) 7,317
Minnedosa (1918) 15,186
Missanabie (1914) 12,469
Monmouth (1900) 4,078
Montclam (1897) 5,505
Montcalm (1921) 16,418
Montclare (1922) 16,314
Monteagle (1899) 6,955
Monterey (1897) 5,478
Montezeuma (1899) 7,345
Montfort (1899) 7,087
Montlaurier (1908) 16,992
Montnairn (1908) 17,282
Montreal (1900) 8,644
Montreal (1906) 9,720
Montrose (1897) 7,207
Montrose (1922) 16,402
Montroyal (1906) 15,646
Mount Royal (1898) 7,998
Mount Temple (1901) 7,656
Ruthenia (1900) 7,392
Tartar (1883) 4,425
Tunisian (1900) 10,576
Tyrolia (1900) 7,535

CASTLE LINE
DONALD CURRIE & CO.
(British)

Arundel Castle (1894) 4,588	Harlech Castle (1894) 3,264
Balmoral Castle (1877) 2,948	Hawarden Castle (1883) 4,380
Conway Castle (1877) 2,966	Iceland (1871) 1,474
Doune Castle (1890) 4,046	Kinfauns Castle (1880) 3,507
Dover Castle (1872) 2,341	Lismore Castle (1891) 4,046
Drummond Castle (1881) 3,663	Methven Castle (1883) 2,681
Duart Castle (1878) 1,839	Norham Castle (1883) 4,392
Dublin Castle (1877) 2,805	Pembroke Castle (1883) 3,946
Dunbar Castle (1883) 2,608	Raglan Castle (1897) 4,324
Dunolly Castle (1897) 4,167	Roslin Castle (1883) 4,267
Dunottar Castle (1890) 5,625	Tantallon Castle (1894) 5,636
Dunrobin Castle (1875) 2,783	Taymouth Castle (1877) 2,069
Edinburgh Castle (1873) 2,547	Tintagel Castle (1896) 5,531
Elizabeth Martin (1872) 1,246	Walmer Castle (1872) 2,446
Garth Castle (1881) 3,660	Warwick Castle (1877) 3,056
Grantully Castle (1879) 3,453	Windsor Castle (1873) 2,672

CHARGEURS REUNIS
COMPAGNIE MARITIME DES CHARGEURS REUNIS
(French)

Afrique (1907) 5,404	Brazza (1923) 10,387
Amerique (1912) 8,396	*Brazza (1947) 9,066
Amiral Aube (1898) 4,026	Cap Lay (1921) 8,169
Amiral Baudin (1898) 4,481	Cap Padaran (1922) 8,169
Amiral Courbet (1899) 4,195	Cap St. Jacques (1922) 8,169
Amiral de Kersaint (1903) 5,570	Cap Tourane (1923) 8,169
Amiral Duperre (1901) 5,037	Cap Varella (1921) 8,169
Amiral Exelmans (1901) 5,029	Ceylan (1907) 8,430
Amiral Fourichon (1901) 5,045	*Charles Tellier (1952) 12,006
Amiral Gueydon (1901) 5,422	Chodoc (1898) 4,686
Amiral Hamelin (1901) 5,041	Cholon (1897) 4,665
Amiral Jaureguiberry (1902) 4,600	*Claude Bernard (1950) 11,969
Amiral Latouche Treville (1903) 5,583	Clement Ader (1953) 11,300
	Corse (1908) 8,481
Amiral Magon (1904) 5,573	Desirade (1921) 9,645
Amiral Nielly (1904) 5,583	Dom Pedro (1878) 2,999
Amiral Olry (1904) 5,567	Dupleix (1914) 7,418
Amiral Ponty (1904) 5,571	Edouard Branly (1951) 11,968
Amiral Villaret de Joyeuse (1912) 5,980	Eubee (1921) 9,645
	Europe (1905) 4,756
Amiral Zede (1912) 5,980	Formose (1921) 9,975
Asie (1914) 8,561	Foucauld (1922) 11,028
Aurigny (1918) 9,589	*Foucauld (1948) 9,066
Belgrano (1872) 2,131	*General Lerclerc (1951) 9,500
Belle Isle (1918) 9,589	Groix (1922) 9,975
	Henri IV (1871) 1,605

CHARGEURS REUNIS (Continued)

Henri Poincare (1952)   11,965
Hoedic (1922)   9,975
Jamaique (1922)   10,123
Kerguelen (1922)   10,123
Krakus (1907)   8,327
*Laennec (1951)   12,003
*Lavoisier (1948)   11,965
Lipari (1922)   9,954
*Louis Lumiere (1951)   11,965
Malte (1907)   8,213
Moreno (1872)   1,971
Ouessant (1908)   8,685
Pampa (1878)   3,021
Paraguay (1888)   3,563
Parana (1882)   3,376
Portena (1875)   2,321
Rio Negro (1883)   3,443
Rivadavia (1873)   2,258
San Martin (1873)   2,258
Sully (1874)   1,326
Swiatowid (1908)   8,497

Tchad (1897)   4,317
Uruguay (1882)   3,442
Ville de Bahia (1872)   1,515
Ville de Buenos Ayres (1882)
   2,119
Ville de Ceara (1882)   2,326
Ville de Maceio (1883)   2,666
Ville de Maranhao (1883)
   2,548
Ville de Montevideo (1881)
   2,119
Ville de Para (1882)   2,356
Ville de Pernambuco (1882)
   2,153
Ville de Rio Janeiro (1872)
   1,540
Ville de Rosario (1881)   2,119
Ville de San Nicolas (1881)
   2,119
Ville de Santos (1873)   1,540
Ville de Victoria (1883)   2,548

COLLINS LINE
New York & Liverpool United States Mail Steamship Co.
(United States)

Adriatic (1857)   3,670
Arctic (1849)   2,856
Atlantic (1849)   2,856

Baltic (1850)   2,856
Ericsson (1853)   1,920
Pacific (1849)   2,856

COLOMBIAN MAIL STEAMSHIP CO.
(United States)

Colombia (1932)   5,236
Haiti (1932)   5,236
Jamaica (1933)   6,968

Mexico (1932)   5,236
Puerto Rico (1932)   5,236
   ex-*Haiti*

COMPAGNIE MARITIME BELGE
Compagnie Belge Maritime du Congo
Lloyd Belge Royal
(Belgian)

Albertville (1906)   4,793
Albertville (1912)   7,745
Albertville (1928)   10,338
*Albertville (1948)   10,901
Anversville (1899)   4,081
Anversville (1912)   8,433
Baudouinville (1939)   13,761

Baudouinville (1950)   10,990
*Baudouinville (1958)   13,921
Bruxellesville (1898)   3,908
Bruxellesville (1909)   5,799
*Charlesville (1951)   10,812
Copacabana (1937)   7,340
Elisabethville (1910)   7,017

COMPAGNIE MARITIME BELGE (Continued)

Elisabethville (1921)   8,351
*Elisabethville (1949)   10,901
Gandia (1907)   9,626
Grisarville (1940)   13,500
*Jadotville (1956)   13,724
Leopoldville (1897)   3,760
Leopoldville (1908)   6,327
Leopoldville (1929)   11,256

*Leopoldville (1948)   10,901
Mar Del Plata (1938)   7,340
Pays de Waes (1912)   9,735
Philippeville (1899)   4,091
Piriapolis (1938)   7,340
Stanleyville (1899)   4,051
Thysville (1922)   8,351
*Thysville (1950)   10,946

COMPAGNIE BORDELAISE DE NAVIGATION A VAPEUR
(French)

Chateau Lafite (1881)   3,467
Chateau Leoville (1881)   3,393

Chateau Marquax (1883)   4,176
Chateau Yquem (1883)   4,211

COMPAGNIE FRANCO-AMERICAINE
(French)

Alma (1856)   2,010
Barcelone (1855)   1,603

Vigo (1855)   1,610

COMPAGNIE DE NAVIGATION SUD-ATLANTIQUE
(French)

Alba (1912)   8,324
Alesia (1902)   6,030
Burdigala (1898)   12,480
*Charles Tellier (1952)   12,006
Divona (1886)   6,405
Gallia (1913)   14,966
Garonna (1897)   5,562
L' Atlantique (1931)   42,512
*Laennec (1951)   12,003

Liger (1896)   5,562
Lutetia (1913)   14,783
Massilia (1920)   15,363
Meduana (1922)   10,123
Mosella (1922)   10,123
Pasteur (1939)   30,447
Samara (1894)   6,007
Sequana (1898)   4,950

COMPAGNIE TRANSATLANTIQUE BELGE
(Belgian Atlantic Line)

Belgique (1855)   2,190
Constitution (1855)   2,160
  Renamed: Princess Charlotte

Leopold I (1957)   2,028

COMPANHIA COLONIAL DE NAVEGACAO
(Portuguese)

Colonial (1908)   8,309
Guine (1905)   2,648
*Imperio (1948)   13,186
*Infanta Dom Herique (1962)   23,000
Joao Belo (1905)   6,365
Loanda (1900)   5,139

Mouzinho (1907)   8,374
*Patria (1947)   13,196
*Santa Maria (1953)   20,906
Serpa Pinto (1915)   8,267
*Uige (1954)   10,001
*Vera Cruz (1952)   21,765

COMPANHIA NACIONAL DE NAVEGACAO
EMPREZA NACIONAL DE NAVEGACAO
(Portuguese)

Angola (1912)   7,884
Angola (1912)   4,297
*Angola (1948)   13,016
Beira (1896)   4,933
Cabo Verde (1908)   4,696
*India (1951)   7,607
Lisboa (1910)   7,700
Lourenco Marques (1905)   6,298
Lusitania (1906)   5,557
Mocambique (1908)   5,771

*Mocambique (1949)   12,976
Mossamedes (1895)   4,615
*Niassa (1956)   10,912
Nyassa (1906)   8,980
Peninsular (1887)   2,744
Portugal (1899)   3,998
Portugal (1929)   6,636
*Principe Perfeito (1961)   20,000
*Quanza (1929)   6,636
*Timor (1951)   7,656

COMPANIA MEXICANA TRANSATLANTICA
(Mexican)

Mexico (1884)   4,133
Oaxaca (1883)   4,133

Tamaulipas (1883)   4,133

COMPANIA SUD AMERICANA DE VAPORES
(Chilean)

Aconcagua (1922)   7,290
Aconcagua (1938)   7,237
Copiapo (1937)   7,279
Imperial (1938)   7,279

Palena (1896)   2,640
Renaico (1898)   5,961
Teno (1896)   3,225
Teno (1922)   7,289

COSULICH LINE
"COSULICH" SOCIETA TRIESTINA DI NAVIGAZIONE
(Italian)

The Cosulich Line fleet originated from the Unione Austriaca di Navigazione (Austro-American Line), which had been founded by the brothers Callisto and Alberto Cosulich.

Argentina (1907)   5,387
Atlanta (1908)   5,387
Belvedere (1913)   7,420
Columbia (1908)   5,460
Martha Washington (1908)
   8,347
Neptunia (1932)   19,475

Oceania (1932)   19,507
Presidente Wilson (1912)   12,588
San Giusto (1890)   8,430
Saturnia (1927)   23,940
Sofia (1905)   5,527
Vulcania (1928)   23,970

CUNARD LINE
CUNARD STEAM SHIP COMPANY, LTD.
Established regular service in 1840. The White Star Line merged with Cunard Line in 1934.

Abyssinia (1870) 3,253	Columbia (1840) 1,155
Acadia (1840) 1,154	Cuba (1865) 2,668
Africa (1850) 2,227	Damascus (1856) 1,214
Alaunia (1913) 13,405	Demerara (1872) 1,904
Alaunia (1925) 14,030	Etna (1855) 2,215
Albania (1900) 7,682	Etruria (1884) 8,127
Albania (1920) 12,768	Europa (1848) 1,834
Aleppo (1865) 2,143	Flavia (1907) 9,291
Algeria (1870) 3,253	Folia (1907) 6,365
Alps (1853) 1,440	Franconia (1911) 18,150
America (1848) 1,825	Franconia (1923) 20,175
Andania (1913) 13,404	Gallia (1878) 4,809
Andania (1922) 13,950	Hecla (1860) 1,784
Andes (1852) 1,440	Hibernia (1843) 1,422
Antonia (1921) 13,867	Ivernia (1900) 14,210
Aquitania (1914) 45,647	*Ivernia (1955) 21,717
Arabia (1852) 2,393	Java (1865) 2,697
Ascania (1911) 9,111	Jura (1854) 2,241
Ascania (1925) 14,013	Kedar (1860) 1,876
Asia (1850) 2,227	Laconia (1912) 18,098
Atlas (1860) 1,794	Laconia (1922) 19,695
Aurania (1883) 7,269	Lancastria (1922) 16,243
Aurania (1915) 13,400	Lebanon (1855) 1,373
Aurania (1924) 13,984	Lucania (1893) 12,950
Ausonia (1909) 8,153	Lusitania (1907) 31,550
Ausonia (1921) 13,912	Malta (1865) 2,244
Australasian (1857) 2,902	Marathon (1860) 1,783
Batavia (1870) 2,553	Mauretania (1907) 30,696
Berengaria (1912) 52,226	*Mauretania (1939) 35,738
Bothnia (1874) 4,556	*Media (1947) 13,345
Britannia (1840) 1,139	Melita (1853) 1,254
Calabria (1857) 3,321	Niagara (1848) 1,825
Caledonia (1840) 1,139	Olympus (1860) 1,794
Cambria (1845) 1,422	Palestine (1858) 2,867
Campania (1893) 12,950	Palmyra (1866) 2,044
Canada (1848) 1,831	Pannonia (1904) 9,851
Carinthia (1895) 5,598 (freighter)	Parthia (1870) 3,502
	*Parthia (1947) 13,362
Carinthia (1925) 20,277	Pavonia (1882) 5,588
*Carinthia (1956) 21,947	Persia (1856) 3,414
Carmania (1905) 19,566	*Queen Elizabeth (1940) 83,673
Caronia (1905) 19,782	*Queen Mary (1935) 80,774
*Caronia (1948) 34,183	Russia (1867) 2,959
Carpathia (1903) 13,603	Samaria (1868) 2,605
Catalonia (1881) 4,841	Samaria (1921) 19,597
Cephalonia (1882) 5,517	Saragossa (1874) 2,166
China (1861) 2,539	Saxonia (1900) 14,197

CUNARD LINE (Continued)

*Saxonia (1954)   21,637
Scotia (1862)   3,871
Scythia (1875)   4,556
Scythia (1920)   19,761
Servia (1881)   7,391
Siberia (1867)   2,498
Sidon (1861)   1,853
Slavonia (1903)   10,606
Sylvania (1895)   5,598

*Sylvania (1957)   21,989
Tarifa (1865)   2,058
Taurus (1853)   1,126
Transylvania (1914)   14,315
Tripoli (1864)   2,058
Tyrrhenia (1922)   16,243
Ultonia (1898)   10,402
Umbria (1884)   8,127
Unicorn (1836)   648

DELTA LINE
Mississippi Shipping Company
(United States)

*Del Mar (1947)   10,074
*Del Norte (1946)   10,074

*Del Sud (1947)   10,074
Delbrasil (1939)   7,996

GERMAN EAST AFRICAN LINE
Deutsche Ost Afrika Linie
(German)

Admiral (1905)   6,355
Burgermeister (1902)   5,945
Feldmarshall (1903)   6,181
General (1910)   8,063
Gouverneur (1900)   3,336
Herzog (1896)   4,946
Kanzler (1892)   3,136
Kigoma (1914)   8,156
Konig (1896)   5,034
Kronprinz (1900)   5,689
Kurfurst (1901)   5,655
Markgraf (1893)   3,680
Njassa (1924)   8,754
Prasident (1900)   3,335

Pretoria (1936)   16,662
Prinzessin (1905)   6,387
Prinzregent (1903)   6,375
Reichstag (1889)   2,202
Somali (1890)   2,550
Tabora (1912)   8,022
Ubena (1928)   9,554
Usambara (1903)   5,999
Usambara (1922)   8,690
Usaramo (1920)   7,775
Ussukuma (1920)   7,834
Wangoni (1920)   7,848
Windhuk (1905)   6,365
Windhuk (1936)   16,662

DODERO LINE
Compania Argentina de Navegacion Dodero
(Argentine)
Now known as: Flota Argentina de Nav. de Ultramar.

*Alberto Dodero (1951)   11,521
Argentina (1949)   12,459
*Corrientes (1943)   12,053
Eva Peron (1950)   12,627
Maipu (1951)   11,500

Presidente Peron (1949)   12,459
*Salta (1943)   12,053
17 de Octubre (1950)   12,634
*Yapeyu (1951)   11,540

DOLLAR STEAMSHIP LINES
(United States)

Founded as the Robert Dollar Company in 1896. Entered the trans-Pacific passenger service in 1924. Inaugurated the first regular round-the-world service in February 1924. The Dollar Line was reorganized as the American President Lines in 1938.

President Adams (1921)	10,533	President Hoover (1931)	21,936
President Cleveland (1921) 14,123		President Johnson (1904)	15,543
		President Lincoln (1921)	14,187
President Coolidge (1931) 21,936		President Monroe (1920)	10,533
		President Pierce (1921)	14,123
President Fillmore (1904) 15,575		President Polk (1921)	10,500
		President Taft (1921)	14,123
President Garfield (1921) 10,538		President Van Buren (1920) 10,533	
President Harrison (1921) 10,533		President Wilson (1921)	14,127
		Ruth Alexander (1913)	8,135
President Hayes (1920)	10,533		

DOMINION LINE
MISSISSIPPI & DOMINION STEAMSHIP CO.
(British)

Brooklyn (1869)	4,215	New England (1898)	12,099
Cambroman (1892)	4,215	Norseman (1882)	4,386
Canada (1896)	9,415	Ontario (1874)	3,175
Columbus (1903)	15,378	Oregon (1883)	3,672
Commonwealth (1900)	12,268	Ottawa (1874)	5,008
Dominion (1874)	3,175	Ottawa (1880)	3,712
Dominion (1894)	7,036	Quebec (1864)	2,621
Kensington (1894)	8,669	Sarnia (1882)	3,726
Labrador (1891)	4,737	Scotsman (1894)	6,041
Mayflower (1902)	13,518	Southwark (1893)	8,607
Memphis (1871)	2,487	Teutonia (1856)	2,546
Mississippi (1871)	2,129	Texas (1872)	2,818
Missouri (1855)	2,259	Toronto (1880)	3,315
Montreal (1879)	3,308	Vancouver (1884)	5,141

DONALDSON LINE
ANCHOR-DONALDSON LINE
DONALDSON ATLANTIC LINE
(British)

Athenia (1904)	9,080	Letitia (1912)	8,991
Athenia (1923)	13,465	Letitia (1925)	13,475
Cassandra (1906)	8,135	*Lismoria (1945)	8,323
*Laurentia (1945)	8,349	Saturnia (1910)	8,611

EAST ASIATIC COMPANY
(Danish

Amerika (1930)   10,218
Boringia (1930)   5,821
Canada (1935)   11,108
Erria (1932)   8,786
Europa (1931)   10,224
*Falstria (1945)   6,993

Fionia (1914)   5,219
*Jutlandia (1934)   8,457
*Lalandia (1927)   5,146
*Meonia (1927)   5,267
Selandia (1938)   8,482
*Selandia (1945)   8,454

ELDER, DEMPSTER & CO., LTD.
(British)

Aba (1918)   7,937
Abinsi (1908)   6,365
Abosso (1912)   7,782
Abosso (1935)   11,330
Accra (1893)   2,826
Accra (1926)   9,337
*Accra (1947)   11,644
Achimota (1932)   9,599
Adda (1922)   7,816
Akabo (1902)   3,814
Apapa (1914)   7,832
Apapa (1927)   9,333
*Apapa (1948)   11,651
Appam (1913)   7,781
*Aureol (1951)   14,083
Bakana (1894)   2,793
Calabar (1935)   1,932
*Calabar (1936)   8,305
   ex-Umtali (1957)
Calgary (1921)   7,275
Calumet (1924)   7,268

Dakar (1899)   3,987
Ebani (1912)   4,862
Egba (1914)   4,989
Elmina (1906)   4,792
Etolia (1887)   3,270
Falaba (1906)   4,806
Loanda (1892)   3,199
Mandingo (1899)   4,019
Mandingo (1913)   7,781
Marino (1895)   3,805
Melrose (1894)   4,038
Mendi (1905)   4,230
Port Antonio (1901)   4,458
Port Henderson (1884)   5,167
Port Kingston (1904)   7,585
Port Maria (1901)   2,910
Port Morant (1901)   2,831
Port Royal (1901)   4,455
*Winneba (1938)   8,355
   ex-Umgeni (1957)

ELDERS & FYFFES, LTD.
(British)

Service: England-Jamaica-Central America.

Ariguani (1926)   6,746
Bayano (1913)   5,948
Bayano (1917)   6,788
Camito (1915)   6,828
*Camito (1956)   8,687
Carare (1925)   6,878
Coronado (1915)   6,539
Cavina (1915)   6,539
Cavina (1924)   6,907

Chagres (1912)   5,288
Changuinola (1912)   5,978
*Golfito (1949)   8,736
Manistee (1904)   3,869
Manzanares (1911)   4,094
Motagua (1912)   5,977
Patia (1913)   6,103
Patia (1922)   5,355
Patuca (1913)   6,103

ELLERMAN LINES
(1) City Line, (2) Ellerman & Bucknall Line, (3) Hall
Line, (4) Ellerman Line
(British)

Buluwayo (1895) 4,412
City of Adelaide (1920) 6,993
City of Athens (1901) 5,594
City of Bagdad (1919) 7,501
City of Barodo (1918) 7,129
City of Benares (1902) 6,984
City of Benares (1936) 11,081
City of Birmingham (1911)
7,498
City of Cairo (1915) 8,034
City of Calcutta (1903) 7,679
City of Canterbury (1922)
8,421
*City of Durban (1954) 13,350
City of Exeter (1914) 9,623
*City of Exeter (1953) 13,345
City of Genoa (1905) 6,365
City of Harvard (1907) 7,071
City of Hongkong (1924) 9,678
City of Karachi (1905) 5,573
City of London (1907) 8,956

City of Marseilles (1913) 8,317
City of Nagpur (1922) 10,136
City of Palermo (1905) 4,699
City of Paris (1907) 9,239
City of Paris (1922) 10,902
City of Poona (1912) 7,474
*City of Port Elizabeth (1952)
13,363
City of Simla (1921) 9,468
City of Sparta (1897) 5,415
City of Tokio (1921) 6,993
City of Venice (1924) 8,308
City of Vienna (1890) 4,672
City of York (1904) 7,844
*City of York (1953) 13,345
Fort Salisbury (1895) 4,404
Johannesburg (1895) 4,444
Orlando (1904) 4,233
Princess (1905) 7,849
Toronto (1900) 6,129

EUROPE-CANADA LINE
(German)

Note: This West German registered line is controlled jointly
by Holland-America Line and Rotterdam Lloyd.

*Seven Seas (1940) 12,575

FABRE LINE
Cyprien Fabre et Cie.
(French)

Alesia (1882) 2,845
Alesia (1906) 9,720
America (1881) 2,403
Asia (1907) 6,122
Banfora (1914) 9,347
Braga (1907) 6,122
Britannia (1881) 2,477
Burgundia (1882) 2,908
Canada (1911) 9,684
Diolibah (1880) 1,642
Europa (1907) 6,122
Gallia (1883) 4,211
Gergovia (1883) 2,024
Germania (1903) 5,103
Iberia (1881) 1,388

Madonna (1905) 5,633
Massilia (1891) 3,097
Neustria (1883) 2,926
Olbia (1873) 2,623
Patria (1874) 1,369
Patria (1882) 4,053
Patria (1913) 11,885
Providence (1915) 11,996
Roma (1902) 5,291
Sant ' Anna (1910) 9,350
Scotia (1881) 2,292
Sinaia (1924) 8,567
Vasconia (1899) 3,281
Venezia (1907) 6,707

FARRELL LINES
(United States)

African Comet (1941)   11,812
African Endeavor (1940)   7,997
African Enterprise (1940)   7,997
African Meteor (1941)   11,800

African Planet (1941)   11,800
City of New York (1930)   8,272
(American-South African Line)

FEDERAL-HOULDER-SHIRE LINE
FEDERAL STEAM NAVIGATION CO.
(British)

Argyllshire (1911)   10,392
Ayrshire (1903)   7,763
Banffshire (1894)   5,736
Baronesa (1918)   8,663
Carmarthenshire (1893)   4,758
Cornwall (1896)   5,490
Dorset (1903)   7,630
El Paraguayo (1912)   8,508
Monmouthshire (1902)   5,091
Morayshire (1898)   6,942

Nairnshire (1899)   5,747
Norfolk (1900)   5,531
Perthshire (1893)   5,550
Shropshire (1911)   11,911
Somerset (1903)   7,150
Suffolk (1902)   7,573
Surrey (1899)   5,980
Sussex (1896)   5,686
Wiltshire (1912)   10,390

FRAISSINET & CO.
CIE. DE NAVIGATION FRAISSINET ET CYPRIEN FABRE
(French)

Amerique (1879)   2,008
Cap Corse (1929)   2,444
Cyrnos (1928)   2,406
*Foch (1950)   9,504
General Bonaparte (1922)   2,796
*General Mangin (1953)   12,457
Hoggar (1923)   5,146
Ile de Beaute (1930) 2,600

*Jean Mermoz (1957)   12,460
Liban (1882)   2,268
Pascal Paoli (1931)   3,200
Sampiero Corso (1936)   3,823
Stamboul (1881)   2,214
Tibet (1883)   2,755
Touareg (1924)   5,135
Ville d'Ajaccio (1929)   2,444

FRENCH LINE
COMPAGNIE GENERALE TRANSATLANTIQUE
(French)

Amerique (1864)   4,585
*Antilles (1952)   20,419
Arkansas (1899)   6,863
Atlantique (1864)   3,200
Bretagne (1922)   10,171
Californie (1905)   5,455
Canada (1865)   4,287
Caravelle (1904)   2,518
Caroline (1908)   6,698

Champlain (1932)   28,124
Carthage (1910)   5,601
Charles Roux (1908)   4,104
Chicago (1908)   9,350
Colombie (1862)   1,859
*Colombie (1931)   13,391
*Commandant Quere (1948)
4,478
Cuba (1923)   11,337

FRENCH LINE (Continued)

De Grasse (1924)   17,759
De la Salle (1924)   8,400
Duc d' Aumale (1912)   4,452
Duc de Bragance (1889)   2,033
Espagne (1909)   11,155
Europe (1864)   3,443
Ferdinand de Lesseps (1875)
  2,920
Figuig (1903)   3,714
Flandre (1914)   8,503
*Flandre (1951)   20,459
Floride (1862)   2,706
Floride (1907)   7,029
France (1865)   3,300
France (1912)   23,769
*France (1961)   66,348
Gascogne (1924)   5,195
General Chanzy (1891)   2,299
*Gouverneur General Chanzy
  (1921)   4,397
Gouverneur General Grevy
  (1922)   4,565
Gouverneur General de Gueydon
  (1922)   4,513
Gouverneur General Jonnart
  4,513
Gaudeloupe (1855)   1,900
Guadeloupe (1906)   6,600
Guadeloupe (1908)   10,502
Haiti (1913)   6,288
Hudson (1904)   5,558
Ile de France (1926)   43,153
Imperatrice Eugenie(1864)
  3,200
Jacques Cartier (1908)   6,693
Jacques Cartier (1918)   8,379
L' Aquitaine (1890)   8,810
La Bourdonnais (1904)   8,287
La Bourgogne (1886)   7,395
La Bretagne (1886)   6,756
La Champagne (1885)   7,087
La Gascogne (1887)   7,090
La Lorraine (1899)   11,146
La Navarre (1892)   6,648
La Normandie (1882)   6,283
La Provence (1905)   13,753
La Savoie (1900)   11,168
La Touraine (1891)   9,047
Labrador (1865)   4,612
Lafayette (1864)   3,394
Lafayette (1915)   11,953

Lafayette (1930)   25,178
Lamoriciere (1921)   4,713
Laperouse (1916)   9,717
Leopoldina (1901)   12,334
Liberte (1930)   51,839
Louisiane (1862)   1,786
Louisiane (1905)   5,399
Macoris (1902)   5,879
*Maroc (1949)   9,544
Marrakech (1913)   6,179
Martinique (1855)   1,900
Martinique (1883)   4,392
Meknes (1913)   6,127
Mexico (1905)   4,885
Mexique (1915)   12,220
Montreal (1896)   3,342
*Napoleon (1960)   5,802
Napoleon III (1866)   3,376
Niagara (1908)   9,614
Normandie (1933)   82,799
Nouveau Monde (1865)   3,200
Olinde-Rodriques (1873)   3,188
Oregon (1929)   7,706
Paimpol (1918)   8,379
Panama (1865)   3,200
Paris (1921)   34,569
Pellerin de la Touche (1913)
  8,217
Pereire (1865)   3,150
Perou (1907)   6,599
Picardie (1865)   1,371
Pologne (1911)   3,112
President Dal Piaz (1929)
  4,929
Puerto Rico (1913)   6,127
Quebec (1896)   3,342
Rochambeau (1911)   12,678
Roussillon (1906)   8,800
St. Germain (1874)   3,641
Saint Laurent (1866)   3,400
Saint Laurent (1905)   5,614
Saint Simon (1874)   3,133
Suffren (1901)   10,622
Tampico (1855)   1,707
Timgad (1911)   5,232
Venezuela (1905)   4,772
Vera Cruz (1855)   1,739
Versailles (1882)   4,336
Ville d' Alger (1890)   2,097
*Ville d' Alger (1935)   10,172
*Ville d' Oran (1936)   10,172

FRENCH LINE (Continued)

*Ville de Bordeaux (1870)   2,670
*Ville de Bordeaux (1940)   6,541
   ex-*Saga* (1956)
 Ville de Brest (1870)   2,676
 Ville de Marseille (1874)   2,836
*Ville de Marseille (1951)   9,576
 Ville de Paris (1866)   3,014
 Ville de St. Nazaire (1870)   2,623
 Ville de Tunis (1884)   1,903

*Ville de Tunis (1952)   9,226
 Ville du Havre (1866)   5,065
 Virginie (1903)   5,330
 Volubilis (1902)   4,747
 Washington (1863)   3,401
 Washington (1929)   7,817
 Winnipeg (1918)   9,802
 Wisconsin (1929)   8,062
 Wyoming (1930)   8,062

FURNESS LINES
FURNESS, WITHY & CO., LTD.
(British)

Digby (1913)   3,960
Dominica (1913)   4,856
Evangeline (1901)   3,944

Fort Amherst (1936)   3,489
Fort Townsend (1936)   3,489
Loyalist (1901)   3,909

FURNESS-BERMUDA LINE

Bermuda (1927)   19,086
Fort Hamilton (1904)   5,530
Fort St. George (1912)   7,785
Fort Victoria (1913)   7,784
Monarch of Bermuda (1931)
  22,424

Nerissa (1926)   5,583
*Ocean Monarch (1951)   13,654
*Queen of Bermuda (1933)
  22,575

FURNESS-PRINCE LINE

Eastern Prince (1929)   10,926
Northern Prince (1929)   10,917

Southern Prince (1929)   10,917
Western Prince (1929)   10,926

FURNESS-WARREN LINE

Newfoundland (1925)   6,791
*Newfoundland (1947)   7,437

Nova Scotia (1926)   6,796
*Nova Scotia (1947)   7,438

GALWAY LINE
(British)

Argo (1852)   2,380
Anglia (1861)   2,913
Columbia (1861)   2,913
Connaught (1860)   2,860
Hibernia (1860)   2,959

Jason (1853)   2,667
Pacific (1854)   1,469
Parana (1851)   2,943
Prince Albert (1857)   2,028

GDYNIA-AMERICA LINE
Polish Transatlantic Shipping Co.
(Polish)

Batory (1936)   14,287
Chrobry (1939)   11,442
Kosciuszko (1915)   6,598
Latvia (1908)   8,596
Pilsudski (1935)   14,294

Polonia (1910)   7,890
Pulaski (1912)   6,516
Sobieski (1939)   11,030
Vigilant (1923)   4,765
Vigrid (1923)   4,765

GRACE LINE
Grace Steamship Company
Panama Mail Steamship Company
(United States)

Santa Barbara (1928)   8,060
*Santa Barbara (1946)   8,357
Santa Cecilia (1913)   5,873
Santa Cecilia (1918)   4,870
*Santa Cecilia (1946)   8,357
Santa Clara (1930)   8,183
*Santa Clara (1946)   8,610
Santa Cruz (1913)   5,081
Santa Elena (1933)   9,135
Santa Elisa (1919)   5,004
Santa Inez (1929)   4,691
Santa Isabel (1915)   5,641
*Santa Isabel (1946)   8,357
Santa Lucia (1933)   9,135

Santa Luisa (1918)   4,847
Santa Luisa (1946)   8,357
*Santa Margarita (1946)   8,357
Santa Maria (1928)   8,060
*Santa Maria (1946)   8,357
*Santa Monica (1946)   8,610
Santa Olivia (1915)   5,544
Santa Paula (1932)   9,135
*Santa Paula (1958)   15,366
Santa Rita (1929)   4,577
Santa Rosa (1932)   9,135
*Santa Rosa (1957)   15,371
*Santa Sofia (1947)   8,610
Santa Teresa (1918)   5,103

GREAT NORTHERN STEAMSHIP COMPANY
(United States)

This steamship line was a subsidiary of the Great Northern Railway. Below are listed the passenger ships which served in their trans-Pacific trade.

Dakota (1904)   20,714   Minnesota (1904)   20,718

GREEK LINES

*Arkadia (1931)   20,256
Athinai (1908)   6,742
Byron (1914)   9,272
Canberra (1913)   7,710
Columbia (1913)   9,424
Constantinople (1896)   11,570
Edison (1896)   11,103
Ioannina (1897)   4,167
King Alexander (1896)   11,455
King Alexander (1908)   16,971
Macedonia (1912)   6,333
Megali Hellas (1914)   9,272
Moraitis (1907)   6,045

Moreas (1901)   8,497
Nea Hellas (1922)   16,991
Neptunia (1920)   10,474
*New York (1922)   16,991
*Olympia (1953)   22,979
Patris (1909)   4,390
Skaubryn (1951)   9,786
Themistocles (1907)   6,045
Thessaloniki (1890)   4,682
Vasilefs Constantinos (1914)
   9,272
Vasilissa Sophia (1914)   9,272

710

GRIMALDI-SIOSA LINES
(Italian)

*Ascania (1926)   9,536
Auriga (1909)   10,856
Centauro (1924)   9,607

*Irpinia (1929)   12,279
*Lucania (1930)   6,723
*Venezuela (1924)   18,567

GUION LINE
LIVERPOOL & GREAT WESTERN STEAMSHIP CO., LTD.
(British)

Alaska (1881)   6,392
Arizona (1879)   5,147
Chicago (1866)   2,866
Colorado (1867)   2,927
Dakota (1872)   4,332
Idaho (1869)   3,132
Louisiana (1858)   2,266

Manhattan (1866)   2,869
Nebraska (1867)   3,985
Nevada (1868)   3,125
Oregon (1883)   7,375
Wisconsin (1870)   3,238
Wyoming (1870)   3,238

Mimesota 1866 2869

HAMBURG-AMERICAN LINE
"HAPAG"
(German)

Abessinia (1900)   5,753
Acilia (1900)   5,656
Adria (1896)   5,472
Albano (1886)   3,736
Albert Ballin (1923)   20,815
Alesia (1896)   5,167
Alexandria (1900)   5,656
Allemannia (1865)   2,619
Altai (1897)   2,480
Amalfi (1881)   2,345
Amasis (1923)   7,129
Amerika (1905)   22,225
Ammon (1922)   7,134
Antonina (1898)   4,010
Arabia (1896)   5,456
Aragonia (1897)   5,446
Arcadia (1896)   5,454
Ariadne (1951)   7,764
Amenia (1896)   5,471
Artemisia (1901)   5,739
Assyria (1898)   6,581
Asturias (1896)   5,500
Athesia (1899)   5,751
Augusta Victoria (1888)   7,661
Australia (1881)   2,119
Austria (1857)   2,383
Baden (1922)   8,803
Batavia (1899)   11,464

Bavaria (1856)   2,273
Belgravia (1899)   11,439
Bermuda (1899)   7,027
Bethania (1899)   7,548
Bismarck (1921)   56,551
Bluecher (1901)   12,334
Bohemia (1881)   3,441
Borussia (1855)   2,349
Borussia (1905)   6,951
Bosnia (1899)   9,683
Brasilia (1897)   10,222
Brisgavia (1899)   6,550
Bulgaria (1898)   11,440
California (1883)   2,690
Caribia (1932)   12,049
Carl Legien (1922)   5,707
Cimbria (1867)   3,037
Cincinnati (1908)   16,339
Cleveland (1908)   16,971
Columbia (1889)   7,383
Corcovado (1907)   8,374
Cordillera (1932)   12,055
Dania (1889)   3,898
Deutschland (1899)   16,502
Deutschland (1923)   20,607
Europa (1879)   1,533
Franconia (1873)   3,181
*Frankfurt (1954)   8,959

HAMBURG-AMERICAN LINE (Continued)

Frisia (1872)   3,256
Furst Bismarck (1905)   8,332
Furst Bismarck (1890)   8,874
Furst Bulow (1910)   7,638
Galicia (1904)   6,146
Gellert (1874)   3,533
General Artigas (1923)   11,343
General Belgrano (1913)   10,056
General Mitre (1921)   9,891
General Osorio (1929)   11,590
General San Martin (1922)
  11,343
Georgia (1891)   3,143
Germania (1863)   2,123
Germania (1871)   2,876
Goethe (1873)   3,408
Gothia (1884)   2,433
Graf Waldersee (1898)   13,102
Granada (1899)   5,144
Granada (1906)   6,751
Habsburg (1906)   6,437
Hamburg (1899)   10,532
Hamburg (1926)   21,133
*Hamburg (1954)   9,008
Hammonia (1855)   2,026
Hammonia (1867)   3,035
Hammonia (1882)   4,247
Hammonia (1909)   7,291
*Hannover (1954)   8,974
Hansa (1899)   16,376
Hansa (1923)   21,131
Heluan (1908)   7,262
Herder (1873)   3,494
Hohenstaufen (1906)   6,489
Holsatia (1868)   3,134
Holsatia (1909)   7,442
Iberia (1928)   9,829
Imperator (1912)   51,969
Italia (1889)   3,564
Kaiserin Auguste Victoria (1905)
  24,581
Karnak (1926)   7,209
Kiautschou (1900)   10,911
Klopstock (1874)   3,641
Konig Friedrich Auguste (1906)
  9,462
Konig Wilhelm II (1907)   9,410
Kronprinzessin Cecilie (1905)
  8,689
La Plata (1898)   4,032

Lessing (1874)   3,527
Magdalena (1928)   9,779
Milwaukee (1929)   16,699
Moltke (1901)   12,335
Moravia (1883)   3,690
Navarra (1905)   5,779
New York (1927)   21,455
Nitokris (1906)   6,150
Normannia (1890)   8,250
Oakland (1929)   6,757
Oceana (1891)   7,815
Oceana (1912)   8,791
Odenwald (1922)   5,098
Palatia (1893)   7,118
Patria (1893)   7,118
Patria (1938)   16,595
Patricia (1899)   13,424
Pennsylvania (1896)   13,333
Persia (1894)   5,713
Phoenicia (1894)   6,761
Pisa (1896)   4,959
Polynesia (1881)   2,171
Pommerania (1873)   3,382
Portland (1928)   7,132
President Grant (1907) 18,072
President Lincoln (1907)   18,162
Pretoria (1897)   13,234
Prinz Adalbert (1902)   6,030
Prinz Auguste Wilhelm (1902)
  4,733
Prinz Eitel Friedrich (1902)
  4,650
Prinz Joachim (1903)   4,760
Prinz Oskar (1902)   6,026
Prinz Sigismund (1902)   4,689
Prinzessin Victoria Luise (1901)
  4,409
Prussia (1894)   7,008
Reliance (1920)   19,802
Resolute (1920)   19,692
Rhaetia (1883)   3,458
Rhaetia (1904)   6,600
Rhein (1925)   6,013
Rhenania (1904)   6,455
Rhodopis (1906)   7,056
Roda (1908)   7,329
Rugia (1882)   4,053
Rugia (1905)   6,598
Russia (1889)   4,017
Saarland (1924)   6,863

HAMBURG-AMERICAN LINE (Continued)

St. Louis (1929) 16,732
San Francisco (1928) 6,753
Santa Barbara (1889) 4,272
Saxonia (1857) 2,404
Scandia (1889) 4,243
Schiller (1872) 3,408
Seattle (1928) 7,369
Silesia (1869) 3,142
Silesia (1897) 4,489
Slavonia (1883) 2,274
Spreewald (1922) 5,083
Suevia (1874) 3,624
Swakopmund (1903) 5,631
Tacoma (1930) 8,268
Tannenberg (1935) 5,504
Taormina (1884) 2,437
Teutonia (1856) 2,034

Teutonia (1906) 6,533
Thuringia (1870) 3,130
Thuringia (1922) 11,343
Tirpitz (1914) 21,833
Toledo (1914) 8,106
Vancouver (1930) 8,269
Vandalia (1871) 2,815
Vaterland (1914) 54,282
Vaterland (1940) 36,000
Victoria Luise (1899) 16,502
Vogtland (1924) 7,106
Westphalia (1868) 3,185
Westphalia (1923) 11,343
Wieland (1874) 3,504
Wurttemburg (1921) 8,894
Ypiranga (1908) 8,309

HAMBURG-SOUTH AMERICAN LINE
(German)

Amazonas (1890) 2,950
Antonio Delfino (1921) 13,589
Argentina (1918) 5,668
Bahia Belgrano (1897) 4,817
Bahia Blanca (1912) 9,349
Bahia Castillo (1913) 9,949
Bahia Laura (1913) 9,791
Belgrano (1888) 2,616
Bilbao (1905) 4,798
Buenos Aires (1912) 9,180
Cap Arcona (1907) 9,832
Cap Arcona (1927) 27,561
Cap Blanca (1903) 7,523
Cap Finisterre (1911) 14,503
Cap Frio (1899) 5,732
Cap Norte (1922) 13,615
Cap Ortegal (1903) 7,818
Cap Polonia (1914) 20,517
Cap Roca (1900) 5,786
Cap Trafalgar (1913) 18,710
Cap Verde (1900) 5,909
Cap Vilano (1906) 9,467
Corrientes (1894) 3,720
Espana (1921) 7,359
General Artigas (1923) 11,343
General San Martin (1922)
  11,343
La Coruna (1921) 7,359
La Plata (1898) 4,032

La Plata (1922) 8,109
Madeira (1900) 6,003
Madrid (1922) 8,753
Monte Cervantes (1927) 13,913
Monte Olivia (1924) 13,625
Monte Pascoal (1930) 13,870
Monte Rosa (1930) 13,882
Monte Sarmiento (1924) 13,625
Patagonia (1890) 2,975
Presidente Mitre (1894) 3,832
Rei de Portugal (1889) 3,236
Rio de Janeiro (1914) 5,261
Rio Grande (1904) 4,556
Rio Negro (1905) 4,699
Rosario (1913) 6,079
San Nicolas (1897) 4,739
Santa Barbara (1908) 3,763
Santa Elena (1907) 7,473
Santa Fe (1914) 4,477
Santa Ines (1914) 5,261
*Santa Ines (1953) 8,995
Santa Maria (1907) 7,401
*Santa Teresa (1952) 8,996
Santos (1898) 4,855
Sierra Nevada (1921) 13,589
Sierra Salvada (1922) 13,615
Tijuca (1899) 4,801
Vigo (1922) 7,418
Villa Garcia (1907) 7,423

HARRISON LINE
T. & J. HARRISON (CHARENTE STEAMSHIP CO.)
(British)

Inanda (1925)	5,985	Inkosi (1937)	6,618
Ingoma (1913)	5,686	Itaba (1910)	4,835

HENDERSON LINE
BRITISH & BURMESE STEAM NAVIGATION CO., LTD.
(British)

Amarapoora (1920)	8,012	Pegu (1913)	6,348
Ava (1895)	3,895	Pegu (1921)	8,183
Bhamo (1908)	5,366	*Prome (1937)	7,043
Burma (1914)	7,821	Sagaing (1925)	7,994
Chindwin (1910)	6,369	*Salween (1937)	7,063
Kemmendie (1924)	7,837	Yoma (1928)	8,139

HOLLAND-AMERICA LINE
NEDERLANDSCH-AMERIKAANSCHE STOOMVAART MAATSCHAPPIJ
(Dutch)

Amsterdam (1879)	3,664	P. Caland (1874)	2,584
Amsterdam (1880)	2,949	Potsdam (1900)	12,522
Damsterdijk (1930)	10,155	Rijndam (1901)	12,529
Delftdijk (1929)	10,220	Rotterdam (1872)	1,694
Didam (1891)	2,751	Rotterdam (1878)	3,329
*Diemerdyk (1950)	11,195	Rotterdam (1897)	8,287
Dinteldijk (1922)	9,399	Rotterdam (1908)	24,149
*Dinteldyk (1957)	11,366	*Rotterdam (1959)	38,645
Dubbeldam (1891)	2,831	*Ryndam (1951)	15,015
Edam (1878)	3,329	Schiedam (1874)	2,236
Edam (1880)	2,950	Spaarndam (1881)	4,539
Edam (1883)	3,130	Spaarndam (1922)	8,857
Edam (1921)	8,871	Statendam (1898)	10,491
Groote Beer (1944)	9,191	Statendam (1917)	32,234
Leerdam (1881)	2,796	Statendam (1929)	29,511
Leerdam (1921)	8,815	*Statendam (1957)	24,294
Maas (1872)	1,703	Veendam (1873)	3,707
Maasdam (1871)	3,984	Veendam (1923)	15,450
Maasdam (1872)	1,703	Volendam (1922)	15,434
Maasdam (1921)	8,812	W. A. Scholten (1874)	2,529
*Maasdam (1952)	15,015	Waterman (1945)	9,177
Nieuw Amsterdam (1906) 17,149		Werkendam (1881)	3,639
*Nieuw Amsterdam (1938) 36,287		*Westerdam (1946)	12,149
		Zaandam (1882)	3,063
Noordam (1902)	12,531	Zaandam (1939)	10,909
*Noordam (1939)	10,726	Zuiderdam (1941)	12,150
Obdam (1880)	3,699	*Zuiderkruis (1944)	9,126

HOME LINES (GENOA, ITALY)
Flag: Panamanian

Argentina (1913) 11,015
Atlantic (1927) 20,553
Brasil (1905) 11,165
Homeland (1905) 11,055

*Homeric (1931) 18,563
*Italia (1928) 21,532
*Queen Frederica (1927) 21,329
    (Under Greek flag)

IMPERIAL DIRECT WEST INDIA MAIL SERVICE CO., LTD.
(British)

See: Elder, Dempster & Co., Ltd.

INCRES LINE
INCRES STEAMSHIP CO.
(United States)

*Nassau (1923) 15,044

*Victoria (1936) 15,054

INMAN LINE
(British)

City of Antwerp (1867) 2,391
City of Baltimore (1854) 2,472
City of Berlin (1875) 5,491
City of Boston (1864) 2,213
City of Bristol (1855) 2,215
City of Brooklyn (1869) 2,911
City of Brussels (1869) 3,081
City of Chester (1873) 4,560
City of Chicago (1883) 5,202
City of Cork (1863) 1,547
City of Dublin (1864) 1,999
City of Glasgow (1850) 1,609
City of Limerick (1855) 1,529

City of London (1863) 2,765
City of Manchester (1851) 1,892
City of Montreal (1872) 4,489
City of New York (1861) 2,360
City of New York (1888) 10,499
City of Paris (1866) 2,651
City of Paris (1889) 10,669
City of Philadelphia (1853)
    2,168
City of Richmond (1873) 4,623
City of Rome (1881) 8,415
City of Washington (1853)
    2,381

"ITALIA" LINE
"ITALIA" SOCIETA ANONIMA DI NAVIGAZIONE
(Italian)

Ancona (1908) 8,210
Bologna (1905) 4,680
Napoli (1899) 9,203
Ravenna (1901) 4,252
San Paulo (1902) 5,021

San Paulo (1902) 5,021
Siena (1905) 4,553
Toscana (1900) 4,252
Verona (1908) 8,886

"ITALIA" LINE
"ITALIA" — FLOTTE RIUNITE COSULICH-LLOYD SABAUDO-NAVIGAZIONE GENERALE ITALIANA
"ITALIA" SOCIETA PER AZIONI DI NAVIGAZIONE*
(Italian)

Formed in January 1931 by the consolidation of Cosulich, Lloyd Sabaudo and Navigazione Generale Italiana Lines.

Alessandro Volta (1954) 8,086	*Marco Polo (1942) 8,949
*Amerigo Vespucci (1949) 9,774	Neptunia (1932) 19,475
Andrea Doria (1953) 29,082	Oceania (1932) 19,507
Antonio Pacinotti (1954) 8,086	Orazio (1927) 11,669
*Antoniotto Usodimare (1942) 9,715	Paolo Toscanelli (1948) 9,004
Augustus (1927) 32,650	Principessa Giovanna (1923) 8,556
*Augustus (1952) 27,226	Principessa Maria (1923) 8,539
Barbarigo (1930) 5,293	Remo (1927) 9,780
Birmania (1930) 5,305	Rex (1932) 51,062
Calabria (1922) 9,515	Roma (1926) 32,583
Conte Biancamano (1925) 24,416	Romolo (1926) 9,780
*Conte Grande (1927) 25,661	San Giorgio (1923) 8,959
Conte Rosso (1922) 17,048	Sardegna (1923) 11,452
Conte Verde (1923) 18,765	*Saturnia (1927) 23,940
*Cristoforo Colombo (1953) 29,083	Sebastiano Caboto (1947) 8,967
Duilio (1923) 24,281	Sicilia (1923) 9,646
Esquilino (1925) 8,657	Toscana (1923) 9,442
Galileo Ferraris (1953) 8,101	Ugolino Vivaldi (1947) 8,914
Giulio Cesare (1920) 21,657	Viminale (1925) 8,657
*Giulio Cesare (1951) 27,694	Virgilio (1927) 11,718
*Leonardo da Vinci (1960) 30,500	*Vulcania (1928) 24,496

JAMAICA BANANA PRODUCERS STEAMSHIP CO., LTD.
(British))

Jamaica Merchant (1911) 7,490	Jamaica Producer (1934) 5,325
Jamaica Pioneer (1931) 5,349	Jamaica Progress (1934) 5,351
Jamaica Planter (1936) 4,098	

JAVA-CHINA-JAPAN LINE
(Dutch))

See: Royal Interocean Lines (Dutch)

Tjibadak (1929) 7,803	*Tjinegara (1951) 9,067
Tjikarang (1922) 9,505	*Tjisadane (1931) 9,228
Tjikembang (1914) 8,000	Tjisalak (1917) 5,787
Tjileboet (1918) 5,760	Tjisaroea (1926) 7,089
*Tjiluwah (1951) 8,630	Tjisondari (1915) 8,000
Tjimanoek (1911) 5,628	*Tjitjalengka (1939) 10,972
Tjinegara (1931) 9,227	*Tjiwangi (1950) 8,624

KHEDIVIAL MAIL STEAMSHIP & GRAVING DOCK CO.
Soc. Misr de Navigation Maritime S.A.E.
(Egyptian)

Abbassieh (1889) 2,784
*Cleopatra (1944) 8,193
El Nil (1916) 7,769
Fouadieh (1923) 1,853
*Gumhuryat Misr (1928) 7,830
Ismailia (1881) 3,704
Kawsar (1923) 7,778
Khedive Ismail (1922) 7,290

Khedive Ismail (1944) 8,193
*Mecca (1929) 8,252
Misr (1947) 7,367
*Mohamed Ali El Kebir (1944) 8,199
Rod-El Farag (1910) 6,369
Zamzam (1909) 8,299

"KOSMOS" STEAMSHIP CO.
(German)

The "Kosmos" fleet was acquired at a later date by the Hamburg-American Line.

Amasis (1896) 4,552
Amasis (1923) 7,129
Ammon (1896) 4,613
Ammon (1922) 7,134
Elkab (1904) 6,118
Heluan (1908) 5,666
Itauri (1897) 4,591

Mera (1901) 4,797
Nitokris (1906) 6,150
Radames (1901) 4,756
Rhakotis (1907) 6,982
Roda (1908) 7,329
Tanis (1902) 5,950
Theben (1897) 4,614

LAMPORT & HOLT, LTD.
(British)

Byron (1901) 3,909
Empire Star (1946) 11,085
Tennyson (1900) 3,944
Vandyck (1911) 10,328
Vandyck (1921) 13,233
Vasari (1909) 10,117

Vauban (1912) 10,660
Verdi (1907) 7,120
Vestris (1912) 10,494
Voltaire (1907) 8,618
Voltaire (1923) 13,248

LAURO LINE
(Italian)

*Roma (1943)
*Surriento (1928) 10,699

*Sydney (1944) 14,708

LEYLAND LINE
Frederick Leyland & Co., Ltd.
(British)

Armenian (1895) 8,825
Bohemian (1900) 8,555
Canadian (1900) 9,309
Cestrian (1896) 8,776
Devonian (1900) 10,418

Devonian (1902) 13,507
Hanoverian (1902) 13,507
Victorian (1895) 8,825
Winifredian (1899) 10,428

LLOYD AUSTRIACO
(Austrian)

After First World War the line became known as Lloyd Triestino and placed under the Italian flag.

Africa (1903)   4,719
Baron Beck (1907)   3,891
Bohemia (1896)   4,284
Cleopatra (1895)   4,024
Dalmatia (1903)   3,184
Elektra (1884)   3,199
Erzherzog Franz Ferdinand
   (1899)   6,105
Gablonz (1912)   8,448
Gastein (1910)   3,817
Graz (1908)   3,905
Habsburg (1895)   4,016
Imperator (1886)   4,213
Imperatrix (1888)   4,194
Innsbruck (1916)   7,039
Karlsbad (1909)   3,819
Koerber (1904)   5,440

Leopolis (1909)   3,905
Maria Teresa (1883)   3,056
Maria Valerie (1892)   4,247
Marienbad (1912)   8,848
Merano (1909)   3,819
Nippon (1902)   6,504
Palacky (1907)   3,891
Persia (1903)   6,283
Prinz Hohenlohe (1908)   2,069
Salzburg (1902)   3,226
Semiramis (1895)   4,165
Silesia (1899)   5,159
Stambul (1910)   3,817
Styria (1900)   2,771
Trieste (1897)   5,106
Urano (1882)   2,627
Wien (1911)   7,367

LLOYD BRASILEIRO
(Brazilian)

Affonso Penna (1910)   3,540
*Almirante Alexandrino (1900)
   5,786
Almirante Jacequay (1912)
   6,079
Baebendy (1899)   4,801
Bage (1912)   8,235
Bahia (1910)   3,401
Benevente (1904)   4,556
*Campos Salles (1897)   4,739
Cantuaria Guimaraes (1907)
   6,456
Cavour (1905)   5,156
Curvello (1907)   6,456

*Cuyaba (1906)   6,489
Dom Pedro I (1908)   6,370
*Dom Pedro II (1910)   6,129
*Duque de Caxias (1904)   4,556
Macapa (1888)   2,523
Minas Geraes (1910)   3,540
*Pocone (1908)   6,750
*Raul Soares (1900)   6,003
*Santarem (1908)   6,757
*Santos (1898)   4,855
Siqueira Campos (1907)   6,456
Sobral (1906)   9,346
Tijuca (1899)   4,801
Uberaba (1911)   6,062

LLOYD ITALIAN
"LLOYD ITALIANO" SOCIETA DI NAVIGAZIONE
(Italian)

Caserta (1904)   6,847
Cordova (1906)   5,000
Florida (1905)   5,018
Indiana (1906)   5,012
Luisiana (1906)   4,983
Mendoza (1904)   7,028

Principessa Jolanda (1908)
   9,200
Principessa Mafalda (1908)
   9,210
Taormina (1908)   8,921
Virginia (1906)   5,181

LLOYD SABAUDO LINE
(Italian)

Conte Biancamano (1925) 24,416
Conte di Savoia (1932) 48,502
Conte Grande (1927) 25,661
Conte Rosso (1922) 17,048
Conte Verde (1923) 18,765
Pesaro (1901) 12,335
Principe di Piemonte (1907) 6,365

Principe di Udine (1908) 7,794
Principessa Giovanna (1923) 8,556
Principessa Maria (1923) 8,539
Re d' Italia (1907) 6,237
Regina d' Italia (1907) 6,560
Tomaso di Savoia (1907) 7,914

LLOYD TRIESTINO
(Italian)

Originally known as Lloyd Austraco, when under the Austrian flag.

Adria (1914) 3,526
Africa (1903) 4,719
*Africa (1952) 11,427
Amazzonia (1916) 7,039
Aquileja (1914) 9,448
Arabia (1926) 7,025
Arno (1912) 8,024
*Asia (1953) 11,693
Ausonia (1928) 12,995
*Australia (1951) 13,205
Aventino (1907) 3,781
Baron Bruck (1913) 2,085
Bulgaria (1908) 3,845
Calabria (1922) 9,515
Calitea (1933) 4,013
Campidoglio (1909) 3,737
Carnaro (1913) 3,802
Celio (1908) 3,872
Cesarea (1912) 7,785
Colombo (1917) 12,003
Conte Rosso (1922) 17,879
Conte Verde (1923) 18,765
Cortellazzo (1931) 5,292
Cracovia (1915) 8,052
Dalmatia (1903) 3,252
Duilio (1923) 23,635
Esquilino (1925) 8,657
*Europa (1953) 11,430
Gange (1912) 12,272
Gerusalemme (1920) 8,052
Giulio Cesare (1920) 21,900
Gorizia (1902) 3,227
Gradisca (1913) 13,870

Graz (1908) 3,905
Helouan (1912) 7,367
Leopolis (1909) 3,905
Liguria (1918) 15,354
Lombardia (1920) 20,006
Marco Polo (1912) 12,272
Marano (1909) 3,754
Nazario Sauro (1921) 8,150
*Neptunia (1951) 13,212
Nippon (1902) 6,443
*Oceania (1951) 13,213
Persia (1903) 6,283
Piemonte (1918) 15,209
Pilsna (1918) 8,040
Po (1911) 7,367
Quirinale (1904) 3,264
Remo (1927) 9,780
Romolo (1926) 9,780
Rosandra (1921) 8,034
Sannio (1921) 9,834
Semiramis (1895) 4,071
Stella d' Italia (1904) 5,884
Tevere (1912) 8,448
*Toscana (1923) 9,584
Tracia (1892) 4,523
Urania (1916) 7,039
Venezia (1901) 7,749
Victoria (1931) 13,062
*Victoria (1953) 11,695
Vienna (1912) 7,156
Viminale (1925) 8,657
Volpi (1931) 5,292

MATSON LINE
MATSON NAVIGATION COMPANY
(United States)

Lurline (1908)	6,509		Matsonia (1913)	9,402
*Lurline (1932)	18,021		Matsonia (1927)	17,226
Malolo (1927)	17,222		*Matsonia (1932)	18,655
Manoa (1913)	6,806		Maui (1917)	9,801
Manukai (1921)	9,547		Maunalei (1921)	7,409
Manulani (1921)	9556		Monterey (1932)	18,017
Mariposa (1883)	3,158		*Monterey (1952)	14,799
Mariposa (1932)	18,017		Wilhelmina (1909)	6,975
*Mariposa (1953)	14,812			

MESSAGERIES MARITIMES
COMPAGNIE DES MESSAGERIES MARITIMES
(French)

Adour (1889)	3,789	Caobang (1902)	6,487
Alphee (1861)	1,240	Cephee (1912)	9,680
Amazone (1869)	3,132	Chambord (1903)	7,562
Amazone (1896)	6,019	Champollion (1924)	12,262
Amboise (1905)	8,408	Chantilly (1923)	9,986
Amiral Pierre (1911)	4,885	Charente (1889)	3,835
Anadyr (1873)	3,714	Chenonceaux (1922)	14,825
Andre Lebon (1913)	13,682	Chili (1894)	6,097
Andromede (1911)	6,037	Claude Chappe (1909)	4,394
Angers (1907)	9,846	Colombo (1882)	3,731
Angkor (1899)	7,357	Commissaire Ramel (1920)	
Annam (1898)	6,343	10,061	
Aramis (1922)	14,825	Compiegne (1923)	9,986
Aramis (1932)	17,537	Congo (1878)	3,897
Arethuse (1864)	1,183	Cordillere (1895)	6,022
Armand Behic (1891)	6,397	D' Artagnan (1924)	15,104
Athos (1914)	12,692	Djemnah (1875)	3,785
Athos II (1925)	15,276	Dordogne (1889)	3,806
Atlantique (1899)	6,479	Dumbea (1882)	5,695
Australien (1889)	6,365	Dupleix (1862)	1,620
Ava (1870)	3,361	Dupleix (1897)	2,394
Aviateur Roland Garros (1902)		El Kantara (1905)	6,879
4,760		Equateur (1875)	3,915
Azay-le-Rideau (1910)	7,988	Eridan (1866)	1,685
Bernardin de Saint Pierre (1925)		Eridan (1928)	9,927
10,085		Ernest Simons (1893)	5,707
Bosphore (1889)	3,200	Erymanthe (1862)	1,947
Bresil (1889)	5,876	Estremadure (1860)	2,132
Cachar (1884)	3,645	Euphrate (1905)	6,876
Caledonien (1882)	4,248	Explorateur Grandidier (1924)	
*Caledonien (1952)	12,712	10,267	
Cambodge (1861)	2,462	Felix Roussel (1930)	16,774
*Cambodge (1952)	13,240		

MESSAGERIES MARITIMES (Continued)

*Ferdinand de Lesseps (1951)
  10,882
Fontainebleau (1923)   10,033
Gange (1905)   6,876
General Duchesne (1903)   7,289
General Metzinger (1906)   9,345
General Voyron (1905)   6,267
Georges Philippar (1930)   10,990
Gironde (1869)   3,244
Guadalquivir (1888)   2,620
Guadiana (1888)   2,614
Guienne (1853)   1,945
Himalaya (1902)   5,620
Hydaspe (1853)
Indus (1897)   6,357
Iraouaddy (1872)   3,785
Jean Laborde (1930)   11,414
*Jean Laborde (1952)   10,944
Kai-Dinh (1914)   5,110
Kouang-Si (1904)   6,472
La Bourdonnais (1862)   1,582
*La Bourdonnais (1951)   10,944
La Marseillaise (1939)   17,327
La Plata (1889)   5,807
La Seyne (1873)   2,379
Lamartine (1914)   5,152
Laos (1896)   6,357
*Laos (1952)   12,080
Laperouse (1911)   4,885
Leconte de Lisle (1922)   9,877
Lotus (1898)   6,822
Louqsor (1904)   6,879
Magellan (1897)   6,357
Manche (1887)   2,395
Marechal Gallieni (1901)   7,642
Marechal Joffre (1931)   11,732
Mariette Pache (1925)   12,239
Meikong (1870)   3,370
Meinam (1862)   1,418
Melbourne (1881)   3,998
Mendoza (1860)   2,577
Menzaleh (1865)   1,912
Min (1913)   7,997
Moeris (1863)   1,863
Natal (1881)   4,088
Navarre (1859)   1,168
Nera (1889)   5,548
Nerthe (1874)   3,527

Niger (1871)   3,726
Nil (1864)   1,040
Oceanien (1884)   4,162
Orenoque (1874)   3,833
Ortegal (1884)   3,695
Oxus (1879)   3,810
Pacifique (1899)   1,938
Paul Lecat (1911)   12,989
Peiho (1907)   5,951
Peluse (1863)   1,743
Pei-ho (1869)   3,392
Pierre Loti (1913)   5,114
*Pierre Loti (1953)   10,944
Polynesien (1890)   6,363
Porthos (1914)   12,692
President Doumer (1933)
  11,898
Rio Grande (1860)   2,596
Saghalien (1880)   4,049
Sagittaire (1929)   7,706
Said (1863)   1,680
Salazie (1883)   4,147
Senegal (1872)   3,717
Si Kiang (1914)   7,014
Sinai (1898)   4,624
Sindh (1869)   3,387
Sontay (1907)   7,236
Sontay (1921)   8,917
Sphinx (1914)   11,375
Sydney (1883)   4,128
Tage (1868)   1,165
*Tahitien (1953)   12,614
Tanais (1867)   1,682
Theophile Gautier (1926)   8,194
Tibre (1866)   1,689
Tigre (1862)   2,746
Tonkin (1898)   6,092
Tourane (1898)   6,054
*Viet-Nam (1952)   13,162
Ville d' Amiens (1924)   7,350
Ville de la Ciotat (1892)   6,378
Ville de Strassbourg (1920)
  7,138
Ville de Verdun (1921)   7,209
Volga (1864)   1,610
Yang Tse (1877)   3,803
Yarra (1883)   4,142
Yunnan (1905)   6,474

MONARCH LINE
ROYAL EXCHANGE SHIPPING COMPANY, LTD.
(British)

Assyrian Monarch (1880)	3,317	Lydian Monarch (1881)	3,987
Egyptian Monarch (1880)	3,916	Persian Monarch (1880)	3,923
Grecian Monarch (1882)	4,364		

MOORE-McCORMACK LINES, INC.
(United States)

Argentina (1929)	20,614	Brazil (1928)	20,614
*Argentina (1958)	20,614	Uruguay (1928)	20,183
*Brasil (1958)	20,614		

MUNSON LINE
(United States)

Aeolus (1899)	12,642	Pan America (1921)	13,712
American Legion (1920)	13,736	Southern Cross (1921)	13,789
Huron (1896)	10,688	Western Ocean (1899)	4,828
Munargo (1921)	6,336	Western World (1921)	13,712
Munorleans (1911)	4,418		

NATAL LINE
BULLARD, KING & COMPANY, LTD.
(British)

Umgeni (1898)	2,662	Umtali (1936)	8,158
Umgeni (1938)	8,180	Umtata (1935)	8,137
Umhlali (1905)	3,388	Umvolosi (1902)	2,986
Umkuzi (1890)	2,057	Umvoti (1903)	5,183
Umkuzi (1903)	5,175	Umvuma (1914)	4,419
Umona (1890)	2,031	Umzumbi (1904)	3,388
Umona (1910)	3,735		

NATIONAL LINE
NATIONAL STEAMSHIP COMPANY, LTD.
(British)

America (1884)	5,528	Holland (1858)	3,847
Canada (1863)	4,276	Italy (1870)	4,341
Denmark (1865)	2,870	Louisiana (1858)	2,266
Egypt (1871)	4,670	Ontario (1864)	3,325
England (1865)	3,440	Pennsylvania (1863)	2,890
Erin (1864)	3,319	Scotland (1865)	3,803
France (1867)	3,572	Spain (1871)	4,512
Greece (1863)	4,310	The Queen (1864)	3,412
Helvetia (1864)	3,325	Virginia (1863)	2,876

NAVIGAZIONE GENERALE ITALIANA
(Italian)

Organized in 1881 by the consolidation of the Italian firms of I. & V. Florio and R. Rubbattino.

America (1908)   8,996
Archimede (1881)   2,837
Augustus (1927)   32,650
Birmania (1882)   2,384
Bormida (1884)   2,304
Caserta (1904)   7,028
Citta di Genova (1903)   7,811
Colombo (1917)   12,003
Domenico Balduino (1882)
   4,365
Duca d' Aosta (1908)   7,804
Duca degli Abruzzi (1907)   7,838
Duca di Genova (1907)   7,811
Duilio (1923)   24,281
Egadi (1872)   1,927
Entella (1883)   2,258
Europa (1907)   7,870
Ferdinando Palasciano (1899)
   10,643
Giulio Cesare (1920)   21,657
Gottardo (1883)   2,847
Indiana (1905)   5,012
Indipendente (1883)   2,837
Lazio (1899)   9,203
Letimbro (1883)   2,202
Liguria (1901)   5,127
Lombardia (1901)   5,127
Manilla (1873)   3,910
Marco Minghetti (1876)   2,489
Marco Polo (1896)   1,664

Marsala (1870)   1,656
Napoli (1907)   6,094
Orione (1883)   4,161
Palermo (1899)   9,203
Palermo (1907)   6,094
Perseo (1883)   4,158
Plata (1878)   1,861
Principe Umberto (1909)   7,838
Principessa Mafalda (1908)
   9,210
Raffaele Rubattino (1882)
   4,337
Re Vittorio (1907)   7,847
Regina Elena (1907)   7,865
Regina Margherita (1884)   3,577
Roma (1926)   32,583
Sannio (1899)   9,210
Sardegna (1901)   5,255
Sempione (1877)   3,149
Sicilia (1900)   5,202
Sirio (1883)   4,141
Stura (1883)   2,238
Taormina (1908)   8,921
Umbria (1902)   5,260
Venezuela (1904)   7,028
Verona (1908)   8,886
Vincenzo Florio (1880)   2,840
Virgilio (1927)   11,718
Washington (1880)   2,833

NAVIGAZIONE LIBERA TRIESTINA
(Italian)

California (1920)   13,060
Duchessa d' Aosta (1921)   7,872
Monte Grappa (1920)   7,434

Piave (1921)   7,565
Rosandra (1921)   7,856
Timavo (1920)   7,549

NEDERLAND ROYAL MAIL LINE
"NEDERLAND" STOOMVAART MAATSCHAPPIJ
(Dutch)

Christian Huygens (1928)
   15,637
Grotius (1907)   5,867

Jan Pieterszoon Coen (1915)
   11,692
Johan de Witt (1920)   10,519

NEDERLAND ROYAL MAIL LINE (Continued)

*Johan van Oldenbarnevelt (1930)
   20,314
Koning Willem I (1898)   4,476
Koning Willem II (1900)   4,293
Koning Willem III (1900)   4,541
Koningin der Nederlanden (1911)
   8,225
Koningin Emma (1913)   9,181
Koningin Regentes (1894)   3,793
Koningin Wilhelmina (1896)
   4,378
Marnix van St. Aldegonde (1930)
   19,355
Oranje (1903)   4,419
*Oranje (1939)   20,551

Pieter Corneliszoon Hooft (1925)
   14,642
Poelau-Bras (1929)   9,278
Poelau-Laut (1929)   9,272
Poelau Roebiah (1928)   9,251
Poelau-Tello (1929)   9,272
Prins der Nederlanden (1914)
   9,322
Prins Hendrik (1890)   3,630
Prinses Juliana (1910)   8,055
Prinses Sophie (1890)   3,591
Rembrandt (1906) 5,876
Sumatra (1907)   5,850
Vondel (1907)   5,866

NELSON LINE
NELSON, HUGH & WILLIAM, LTD.
(British)

The Nelson Line fleet was acquired by the Royal Mail Lines in August 1932.

Highland Brae (1910)   7,634
Highland Brigade (1901)   5,662
Highland Brigade (1929)   14,131
Highland Chieftain (1929)
   14,131
Highland Corrie (1910)   7,583
Highland Glen (1910)   7,598
Highland Hope (1903)   5,150
Highland Hope (1929)   14,129
Highland Laddie (1910)   7,381

Highland Loch (1911)   7,493
Highland Monarch (1928)
   14,137
Highland Patriot (1932)   14,157
Highland Piper (1911)   7,490
Highland Pride (1910)   7,469
Highland Princess (1930)   14,157
Highland Rover (1910)   7,490
Highland Scot (1910)   7,604
Highland Warrior (1911)   7,485

NEW YORK & HAVRE STEAM NAVIGATION CO.
(United States)

Arago (1855)   2,260
Franklin (1848)   2,184
Fulton (1855)   2,307

Humboldt (1850)   2,181
St. Louis (1854)   1,621
Union (1851)   1,650

NEW YORK & PORTO RICO STEAMSHIP CO.
(United States)

Boringuen (1931)   7,114
Carolina (1896)   5,093
Coamo (1891)   4,384
Coamo (1925)   7,057

Ponce (1899)   3,506
Porto Rico (1899)   4,760
San Jacinto (1903)   6,069
San Lorenzo (1907)   6,576

NEW ZEALAND SHIPPING CO., LTD.
(British)

Australasian (1901) 8,887	Rimutaka (1900) 8,997
Hororata (1914) 11,243	Rimutaka (1923) 16,576
Papanui (1899) 6,582	Rotorua (1910) 11,130
Paparoa (1899) 6,563	Rotorua (1911) 12,184
Rangitane (1929) 16,733	Ruahine (1891) 6,127
*Rangitane (1949) 21,867	Riahine (1909) 10,839
*Rangitata (1929) 16,969	*Ruahine (1951) 17,851
*Rangitiki (1929) 16,984	Ruapehu (1901) 8,887
*Rangitoto (1949) 21,809	Tongariro (1901) 8,073
Remuera (1911) 11,276	Turakina (1902) 8,349
Rimutaka (1884) 4,515	

N. Y. K. LINE
NIPPON YUSEN KAISHA
(Japanese)

Established in September 1885, by the amalgamation of Kiodo Unyu Kaisha and Yubin Kisen Mitsubishi Kaisha. This is the oldest and largest Japanese shipping company. The N. Y. K. Line absorbed the Toyo Kisen Kaisha Line in 1926. Their services became world-wide.

Aki Maru (1903) 6,009	Kaga Maru (1901) 6,301
Asama Maru (1929) 16,947	Kamakura Maru (1897) 6,126
Atsuta Maru (1909) 7,974	Kamakura Maru (1930) 17,526
Atuta Maru (1909) 7,983	Kamo Maru (1908) 8,524
Awa Maru (1899) 6,309	Kanagawa Maru (1896) 6,328
Bingo Maru (1897) 6,279	Kashima Maru (1913) 10,559
Bokuyo Maru (1924) 8,619	Kasuga Maru (1898) 3,820
Chichibu Maru (1930) 17,498	Kasuga Maru (1940) 16,500
Fuji Maru (1937) 9,138	Katori Maru (1913) 10,526
Fushima Maru (1914) 10,936	Kawachi Maru (1897) 6,101
Hakata Maru (1897) 6,241	Kinshuiu Maru (1891) 3,967
Hakone Maru (1921) 10,420	Kitano Maru (1909) 8,512
Hakozaki Maru (1922) 10,413	Korea Maru (1901) 11,810
Hakusan Maru (1923) 10,380	Kumano Maru (1901) 5,076
Haruna Maru (1922) 10,421	Miike Maru (1888) 3,308
Heian Maru (1930) 11,616	Mishima Maru (1908) 7,900
Heiyo Maru (1930) 9,816	Nagasaki Maru (1922) 5,268
Hie Maru (1930) 11,621	Miyazaki Maru (1909) 8,500
Hikawa Maru (1930) 11,622	Nikko Maru (1903) 5,559
Hirano Maru (1908) 8,520	Nitta Maru (1939) 16,500
Hitachi Maru (1898) 6,172	Palao Maru (1934) 4,495
Hiye Maru (1930) 11,622	Persia Maru (1881) 4,381
Husimi Maru (1914) 10,936	Rakuyo Maru (1921) 9,419
Huzi Maru (1937) 9,138	Sado Maru (1898) 6,227
Inaba Maru (1897) 6,189	Sanuki Maru (1897) 6,164
Iyo Maru (1901) 6,320	Shanghai Maru (1923) 5,259

N. Y. K. LINE (Continued)

Shidzuoka Maru (1912)   6,568
Shinano Maru (1900)   6,416
Shinyo Maru (1911)   13,039
Siberia Maru (1901)   11,785
Suwa Maru (1914)   10,672
Taiyo Maru (1911)   14,457
Tamba Maru (1897)   6,134
Tango Maru (1905)   7,475
Tatuta Maru (1929)   16,975
   ex-Tatsuta Maru

Tenyo Maru (1908)   13,398
Terukuni Maru (1930)   11,930
Wakasa Maru (1897)   6,266
Yamaguchi Maru (1890)   3,321
Yasaka Maru (1914)   10,932
Yasukuni Maru (1930)   11,930
Yawata Maru (1898)   3,817
Yawata Maru (1939)   16,500
Yokohama Maru (1912)   6,147

NORTH GERMAN LLOYD
NORDDEUTSCHER LLOYD
(German)

North Atlantic service was established in June 1858.

Aachen (1895)   3,833
Aller (1886)   5,217
America (1863)   2,752
Baltimore (1868)   2,321
Barbarossa (1896)   10,984
Bayern (1886)   4,580
Bayern (1921)   8,917
*Bayernstein (1954)   8,999
Berlin (1868)   2,333
Berlin (1908)   17,324
Berlin (1925)   15,286
*Berlin (1925)   18,600
Bonn (1895)   3,969
Borkum (1896)   5,642
Brandenburg (1901)   7,532
Braunschweig (1873)   3,173
Bremen (1858)   2,551
Bremen (1896)   11,570
Bremen (1900)   10,826
Bremen (1929)   51,656
*Bremen (1939)   32,336
Breslau (1901)   7,524
Bulow (1906)   8,980
Cassel (1901)   7,543
Chemnitz (1901)   7,543
Coblenz (1923)   9,449
Coburg (1908)   6,750
Columbus (1914)   34,356
Columbus (1922)   32,354
Crefeld (1895)   3,829
Crefeld (1922)   9,620
Darmstadt (1890)   5,012
Der Deutsche (1924)   11,430
Derfflinger (1907)   9,144
Deutschland (1866)   2,873

Donau (1868)   3,073
Dresden (1889)   4,580
Dresden (1914)   14,690
Eider (1884)   4,719
Eisenach (1908)   6,757
Eble (1881)   4,897
Elbe (1929)   9,179
Ems (1884)   4,933
Erlangen (1901)   5,285
Europa (1930)   49,746
Feldmarschall Moltke (1873)
   3,060
Frankfurt (1869)   2,582
Frankfurt (1899)   7,431
Friedrich der Grosse (1896)
   10,771
Fulda (1882)   4,816
Fulda (1924)   9,492
General von Steuben (1922)
   14,690
General Werder (1874)   3,020
George Washington (1908)
   25,570
Gera (1890)   5,005
Gneisenau (1903)   8,081
Gneisenau (1935)   18,160
Goeben (1906)   8,792
Gotha (1907)   6,974
Graf Bismarck (1871)   2,406
Grosser Kurfurst (1899)   13,245
H. H. Meier (1892)   5,140
Habsburg (1875)   3,094
Halle (1895)   3,960
Hannover (1869)   2,571
Hannover (1899)   7,305

NORTH GERMAN LLOYD (Continued)

Hansa (1861)   2,992
Havel (1890)   6,963
Helgoland (1896)   5,666
Hermann (1865)   2,873
*Hessenstein (1954)   8,929
Hohenstaufen (1874)   3,098
Hohenzollern (1873)   3,288
Hohenzollern (1889)   6,668
Hudson (1858)   2,266
Kaiser Friedrich (1898)   12,481
Kaiser Wilhelm der Grosse (1897)   14,349
Kaiser Wilhelm II (1889)   6,990
Kaiser Wilhelm II (1903)   19,361
Kaiserin Maria Theresa (1890)   7,840
Karlsruhe (1889)   5,057
Karlsruhe (1900)   10,826
Kleist (1906)   8,959
Koln (1871)   2,555
Koln (1899)   7,409
Koln (1921)   9,264
Konig Albert (1899)   10,484
Konig Wilhelm I (1870)   2,550
Konigin Luise (1896)   10,711
Kronprinz Friedrich Wilhelm (1871)   2,387
Kronprinz Wilhelm (1901)   14,908
Kronprinzessin Cecilie (1906)   19,503
Lahn (1887)   5,681
Leipzig (1869)   2,388
Luetzow (1908)   8,826
Madrid (1922)   8,753
Main (1868)   2,893
Main (1900)   10,067
Minister Roon (1873)   3,068
Mosel (1872)   3,125
Munchen (1889)   4,801
Munchen (1922)   13,483
Munchen (1923)   18,940
Neckar (1873)   3,122
Neckar (1901)   9,835
New York (1858)   2,674
Norderney (1896)   5,497
Nurnburg (1873)   3,116
Oder (1873)   3,265
Ohio (1869)   2,394
Oldenburg (1890)   5,006
Potsdam (1935)   17,518

Preussen (1886)   5,295
Prinz Eitel Friedrich (1904)   8,797
Prinz Friedrich Wilhelm (1908)   17,082
Prinz Heinrich (1894)   6,636
Prinz Ludwig (1906)   9,687
Prinz Regent Luitpold (1894)   6,595
Prinz Sigismund (1903)   3,302
Prinz Waldemar (1903)   3,227
Prinzess Alice (1900)   10,911
Prinzess Irene (1900)   10,881
Raimund (1922)   3,667
Rhein (1868)   3,075
Rhein (1899)   10,058
Rio Bravo (1924)   5,946
Rio Panuco (1924)   5,944
Roland (1893)   3,603
Roon (1903)   8,022
Saale (1886)   5,381
Saarbrucken (1923)   9,429
Sachsen (1886)   5,026
Salier (1875)   3,098
Scharnhorst (1904)   8,131
Scharnhorst (1935)   18,184
Schleswig (1903)   6,955
*Schwabenstein (1954)   8,955
Seydlitz (1903)   7,942
Sierra Cordoba (1913)   8,226
Sierra Cordoba (1923)   11,469
Sierra Morena (1924)   11,430
Sierra Nevada (1912)   8,235
Sierra Nevada (1922)   8,753
Sierra Salvada (1912)   8,227
Sierra Ventana (1912)   8,396
Sierra Ventana (1923)   11,392
Spree (1890)   6,963
Steuben (1922)   14,690
Strassburg (1872)   3,025
Stuttgart (1889)   5,048
Stuttgart (1923)   13,387
Trave (1886)   5,262
Trier (1924)   9,415
Tubingen (1900)   5,586
Union (1866)   2,873
Weimar (1891)   4,996
Werra (1882)   5,109
Werra (1922)   9,476
Weser (1858)   2,266

NORTH GERMAN LLOYD (Continued)

Weser (1867) 2,871	Wittenberg (1895) 3,689
Weser (1922) 9,444	Wurzburg (1900) 5,085
Wilhelm Gustolff (1937) 25,484	~Yorck (1906) 8,976
Willehad (1894) 4,761	Zepplelin (1914) 14,588
Wittekind (1894) 4,755	~Zieten (1902) 8,043

NORWEGIAN-AMERICA LINE
DEN NORSKE AMERIKALINJE
(Norwegian)

Established trans-Atlantic service in 1913.

Bergensfjord (1913) 11,013	Oslofjord (1938) 18,372
*Bergensfjord (1956) 18,739	*Oslofjord (1949) 16,844
Kristianafjord (1913) 10,669	*Stavangerfjord (1918) 13,156

OCCIDENTAL & ORIENTAL STEAMSHIP COMPANY
(British)

A subsidiary of the White Star Line. Commenced service between San Francisco and the Orient in 1879 with White Star Line vessels.

Arabic (1881) 4,368	Doric (1883) 4,676
Belgic (1873) 2,652	Gaelic (1872) 2,652
Belgic (1885) 4,212	Gaelic (1885) 4,206
Coptic (1881) 4,352	Oceanic (1870) 3,808

OCEANIC STEAMSHIP COMPANY
(United States)

The Oceanic Steamship Company, also known as the Spreckles Line, was established in 1878. Service was provided between San Francisco and Sydney, Australia, via Honolulu. The Matson Navigation Company acquired control of the line in 1926. However, the Matson Line continued to operate the company, as a subsidiary, under its original name. Included, also, are the Matson Line ships built for this particular service.

Alameda (1883) 3,158	*Monterey (1952) 14,799
Australia (1875) 2,755	Sierra (1900) 6,135
Mariposa (1883) 3,158	Sonoma (1901) 6,279
Mariposa (1932) 18,017	Ventura (1900) 2,282
*Mariposa (1953) 14,812	Zealandia (1875) 2,489
Monterey (1932) 18,017	

ORANJE LINE
Fjell Oranje Lijn
(Dutch)

*Prins Willem Van Oranje (1953) 7,328   *Prinses Irene (1959) 8,526

ORIENT LINE
Anderson, Green & Co., Ltd.
The Orient Steam Navigation Co., Ltd.
(British)

Regular steamship service from England to Australia was established in 1877. In the early days a close association with the Pacific Steam Navigation Company existed.

Aconcagua (1872)	4,106	*Orion (1935)	23,456
Austral (1881)	5,524	Ormonde (1917)	14,982
Chimborazo (1871)	3,847	Ormuz (1886)	6,031
Cotopaxi (1873)	4,022	Ormuz (1914)	14,588
Cuzco (1871)	3,845	Oronsay (1925)	20,001
Garonne (1871)	4,689	*Oronsay (1951)	27,632
John Elder (1870)	4,151	Orontes (1902)	9,028
Liguria (1874)	4,677	*Orontes (1929)	20,186
Lusitania (1871)	3,912	Orotava (1889)	5,858
Omar (1896)	11,103	Oroya (1886)	6,057
Omrah (1899)	8,130	Orsova (1909)	12,036
Ophir (1891)	6,910	*Orsova (1954)	28,790
Orama (1912)	12,927	Oruba (1889)	5,857
Orama (1924)	19,777	Orvieto (1909)	12,133
Orcades (1906)	9,764	Osterley (1909)	12,129
Orcades (1937)	23,456	Otranto (1909)	12,124
*Orcades (1948)	28,396	Otranto (1925)	20,032
Orford (1928)	19,941	Otway (1909)	12,077
*Oriana (1960)	41,923	Potosi (1873)	4,230
Orient (1879)	5,386	Sorata (1872)	4,014

OSAKA LINE
Osaka Mercantile Steamship Co., Ltd.
Osaka Syosen Kabusiki Kaisya
(Japanese)

Africa Maru (1918)	9,476	Atlas Maru (1920)	7,344
*Africa Maru (1951)	8,354	Baikal Maru (1921)	5,266
Aikoku Maru (1939)	10,360	Brazil Maru (1939)	12,752
Alaska Maru (1920)	7,379	*Brazil Maru (1954)	10,101
*America Maru (1950)	8,343	Buenos Aires Maru (1930)	9,626
Arabia Maru (1918)	9,480	Canada Maru (1911)	6,064
Argentina Maru (1939)	12,755	Chicago Maru (1910)	6,182
*Argentina Maru (1958)	10,863	Hawaii Maru (1915)	9,482
Arizona Maru (1920)	9,684	Hokoku Maru (1939)	10,439

OSAKA LINE (Continued)

Horai Maru (1912)   9,204
Huso Maru (1908)   8,199
Kasato Maru (1900)   6,209
Kiturin Maru (1935)   6,783
   ex-Kitsurin Maru
Kokuryu Maru (1937)   7,369
Manila Maru (1915)   9,518
Mexico Maru (1910)   6,064
Naminoue Maru (1936)   4,731
Oryoku Maru (1937)   7,363
Panama Maru (1910)   6,058
Paris Maru (1921)   7,197

Rio de Janeiro Maru (1930)
   9,627
Santos Maru (1925)   7,267
*Santos Maru (1952)   8,516
Seattle Maru (1909)   6,182
Tacoma Maru (1909)   6,178
Takatiho Maru (1934)   8,154
   ex-Takachiho Maru
Toyen Maru (1905)   3,544
Ukisima Maru (1936)   4,730
   ex-Ukishima Maru
Ussuri Maru (1932)   6,386

PACIFIC MAIL STEAMSHIP COMPANY
(United States)

Pacific Mail Steamship Company service was discontinued in 1925. The house flag, good will and trade name were sold to the Dollar Line.

Alaska (1867)   4,011
America (1868)   4,454
Asia (1883)   4,784
Buckeye State (1921)   14,123
China (1866)   3,836
China (1889)   5,060
City of New York (1875)   3,019
City of Peking (1875)   5,080
City of Rio de Janeiro (1878)
   3,548
City of San Francisco (1875)
   3,009
City of Sydney (1875)   3,016
City of Tokio (1874)   5,079
Colima (1873)   2,905
Colombia (1915)   5,644
Colorado (1864)   3,728
Costa Rica (1891)   1,783
Colusa (1913)   6,003
Creole State (1920)   10,533
Dakota (1865)   2,135
Ecuador (1915)   5,544
Empire State (1921)   14,127
Golden Age (1853)   2,181
Golden City (1863)   3,373
Golden Gate (1851)   2,067

Golden State (1921)   14,123
Granite State (1921)   10,500
Great Republic (1866)   3,881
Hawkeye State (1921)   14,123
Henry Chauncey (1865)   2,656
Hoosier State (1921)   14,187
Japan (1867)   4,351
Korea (1901)   11,276
Manchuria (1904)   13,638
Mongolia (1904)   13,635
Montana (1865)   2,676
Moses Taylor (1957)   1,354
Nevada (1867)   2,143
New York (1864)   2,217
Newport (1880)   2,735
Nile (1893)   5,888
Oregon (1848)   1,099
Persia (1881)   4,356
Peru (1892)   3,528
Siberia (1901)   11,785
Sonora (1853)   1,616
Starbuck (1881)   2,157
Vancouver (1873)   2,923
Vasco de Gama (1873)   2,912
Venezuela (1915)   5,641
Wolverine State (1921)   10,533

PANAMA-PACIFIC LINE
AMERICAN LINE STEAMSHIP CORPORATION
(United States)

California (1928)   20,325   Pennsylvania (1929)   20,526
Columbia (1917)   24,578   Virginia (1928)   20,773

PACIFIC STEAM NAVIGATION COMPANY
(British)

Aconcagua (1872)   4,106   Lusitania (1871)   3,912
Amazonas (1874)   2,019   Magellan (1868)   2,856
Andes (1913)   15,620   Magellan (1893)   3,590
Antisana (1893)   3,584   Magellan (1913)   6,706
Araucania (1869)   2,877   Mendoza (1879)   21,160
Atacama (1870)   1,821   Mexico (1902)   5,549
Ayacuacho (1873)   1,916   Ohio (1923)   18,940
Bogota (1852)   1,461   Oravia (1897)   5,321
Britannia (1873)   4,129   Orbita (1915)   15,495
California (1902)   5,547   Orca (1918)   16,063
Callao (1858)   1,062   Orcana (1893)   4,821
Chile (1840)   682   Orcana (1903)   7,814
Chile (1863)   1,672   Orcoma (1908)   11,580
Chile (1896)   3,225   Orduna (1914)   15,507
Chimborazo (1871)   3,847   Orellana (1893)   4,821
Colon (1861)   1,995   Oriana (1906)   8,177
Colombia (1873)   1,823   Orissa (1895)   5,360
Colombia (1899)   3,335   Orita (1903)   9,298
Coquimbo (1870)   1,821   Orizaba (1886)   6,298
Corcovado (1872)   3,805   Oronsa (1906)   8,067
Corcovado (1896)   4,575   Oropesa (1895)   5,364
Cordillera (1869)   2,860   Oropesa (1920)   14,075
Cotopaxi (1873)   4,022   Orotava (1889)   5,858
Cuzco (1871)   3,845   Oroya (1886)   6,057
Ebro (1915)   8,480   Oroya (1923)   12,257
Essequibo (1914)   8,489   Ortega (1906)   8,058
Galicia (1873)   3,829   Ortona (1899)   8,058
Galicia (1901)   5,896   Oruba (1889)   5,857
Garonne (1871)   3,901   Oruba (1903)   7,848
Guatemala (1899)   3,227   Pacific (1865)   1,631
Huanchaco (1907)   4,524   Panama (1866)   1,642
Iberia (1873)   4,689   Panama (1902)   5,981
Illimani (1873)   4,022   Patagonia (1869)   2,866
Ilo (1872)   1,794   Payta (1864)   1,344
Inca (1893)   3,593   Peru (1840)   690
John Elder (1870)   4,151   Peru (1861)   1,307
Junin (1907)   4,536   Peru (1896)   3,225
Kenuta (1907)   5,025   Pizarro (1879)   2,160
Liguria (1874)   4,677   Potosi (1873)   4,219
Lima (1851)   1,461   Potosi (1905)   4,375
Lima (1873)   1,803   Puno (1873)   3,805
Lima (1907)   4,946   Puno (1881)   2,398
Limena (1865)   1,622   Quillota (1907)   3,774

731

PACIFIC STEAM NAVIGATION CO. (Continued)

Quilpue (1907)   3,669
Quito (1852)   1,461
Quito (1863)   1,388
*Reina del Mar (1956)   20,225
Reina del Pacifico (1931)   17,707
Santiago (1871)   1,451
Santiago (1889)   2,953
Sarmiento (1893)   3,603
Serena (1881)   2,398

Sorata (1872)   4,014
Sorata (1897)   4,581
Tacora (1872)   3,525
Truxillo (1872)   1,449
Valdivia (1870)   1,861
Valparaiso (1873)   3,757
Valparaiso (1856)   1,060
Victoria (1902)   5,967

PANAMA MAIL STEAMSHIP COMPANY
(United States)

NOTE: See Grace Steamship Company, which controls this line.

PANAMA RAILROAD COMPANY
(United States)

Advance (1883)   2,603
Alliance (1886)   2,985
Ancon (1902)   9,606
*Ancon (1939)   10,021
Colon (1899)   5,667
Cristobal (1902)   9,606

*Cristobal (1939)   10,021
Finance (1883)   2,603
General W. C. Gorgas (1902)
   4,636
Panama (1898)   5,638
Panama (1939)   10,021

PAQUET, COMPAGNIE DE NAVIGATION
(French)

Abda (1898)   4,331
Anfa (1903)   4,440
Azemmour (1951)   3,921
Azrou (1930)   3,000
Chaouia (1896)   4,334
Chella (1934)   8,920
*Djenne (1931)   8,790
Doukkala (1900)   4,368

*Foch (1950)   9,504
*Koutoubia (1931)   8,790
*Lyautey (1952)   9,931
Marechal Lyautey (1924)   8,256
Medie II (1922)   5,078
Nicolas Paquet (1928)   8,250
Phrygie (1906)   3,884

P. & O. LINE
PENINSULAR & ORIENTAL STEAM NAVIGATION CO.
(British)

The P. & O. Line was founded in 1837. Regular service to Australia was inaugurated by the *Chusan* in 1852. However, the trade to India was opened in 1842 by the *Hindostan*.

Ancona (1879)   3,142
Arabia (1898)   7,933
Arcadia (1888)   6,603

*Arcadia (1954)   29,734
Assaye (1899)   7,376
Australia (1870)   3,666

P. & O. LINE (Continued)

Australia (1892)   6,901
Ballaarat (1882)   4,890
Ballarat (1911)   11,120
Ballarat (1921)   13,033
Balranald (1922)   13,039
Baradine (1921)   13,144
Barrabool (1922)   13,148
Beltana (1913)   11,120
Benalla (1913)   11,118
Bendigo (1922)   13,039
Bengal (1885)   4,344
Berrima (1913)   11,137
Borda (1914)   11,136
Borneo (1895)   4,573
Brindisi (1880)   3,688
Britannia (1887)   6,525
Caledonia (1894)   7,558
*Canberra (1961)   45,000
*Canton (1939)   15,784
Carnatic (1862)   1,776
Carthage (1881)   5,013
Carthage (1931)   14,182
Cathay (1925)   15,121
Ceylon (1858)   2,021
Ceylon (1894)   4,094
China (1889)   5,060
China (1896)   7,912
Chitral (1925)   15,248
Chusan (1852)   700
Chusan (1884)   4,636
*Chusan (1950)   24,570
Clyde (1881)   4,099
Commonwealth (1902)   6,616
Comorin (1925)   15,132
Corfu (1931)   14,170
Coromandel (1885)   4,359
Delhi (1905)   8,090
Delta (1859)   1,618
Devanha (1906)   8,092
Dongola (1905)   8,056
Egypt (1897)   7,941
Ettrick (1938)   11,279
Formosa (1892)   4,045
Ganges (1881)   4,168
Himalaya (1853)   3,438
Himalaya (1892)   6,898
*Himalaya (1949)   27,955
Hindostan (1842)   2,018
Iberia (1835)   516
*Iberia (1954)   29,614
India (1896)   7,940

Isis (1898)   1,728
Japan (1893)   4,319
Java (1892)   4,093
Kaiser-i-Hind (1878)   4,008
Kaiser-i-Hind (1914)   11,430
Kalyan (1915)   9,144
Karmala (1914)   8,947
Kashgar (1914)   8,840
Kashmir (1915)   8,985
Khiva (1914)   9,135
Khyber (1914)   9,114
Macedonia (1904)   10,512
Madras (1852)   1,185
Malacca (1892)   4,045
Maloja (1911)   12,431
Maloja (1923)   20,837
Malta (1895)   6,064
Malwa (1908)   10,986
Manila (1892)   4,210
Mantua (1909)   10,946
Marmora (1903)   10,509
Massilia (1860)   1,640
Massilia (1884)   4,908
Medina (1911)   12,358
Moldavia (1903)   9,500
Moldavia (1922)   16,543
Mongolia (1903)   9,505
Mongolia (1923)   16,576
Mooltan (1905)   9,621
Mooltan (1923)   20,952
Morea (1908)   10,890
Nagoya (1913)   6,874
Naldera (1918)   16,088
Namur (1907)   6,694
Nankin (1912)   6,853
Narkuna (1920)   16,572
Nellore (1913)   6,942
Nemesis (1857)   2,717
Nile (1906)   6,702
Novara (1912)   6,850
Nubia (1895)   5,914
Nyanza (1907)   6,695
Oceana (1888)   6,188
Oriental (1889)   4,972
Osiris (1898)   1,728
Palawan (1895)   4,686
Palma (1903)   7,632
Palermo (1903)   7,597
Parramatta (1882)   4,886
Peninsular (1888)   4,972
Pera (1903)   7,635

P. & O. LINE (Continued)

Persia (1900) 7,951
Peshawur (1871) 3,782
Peshawur (1905) 7,634
Plassy (1901) 7,405
Poona (1905) 7,626
Precursor (1841) 1,817
Rajputana (1926) 16,568
Ranchi (1925) 16,650
Ranpura (1925) 16,601
Rawalpindi (1925) 16,619
Razmak (1925) 10,602
Ripon (1846) 1,508
Rohilla (1880) 3,387
Rome (1881) 5,013
Rosetta (1880) 3,502
Salsette (1909) 5,842
Shannon (1881) 4,189
Shanghai (1889) 3,315
Sicilia (1901) 6,696

Simla (1894) 5,884
Socotra (1897) 6,009
Somali (1901) 6,708
Soudan (1901) 6,680
*Strathaird (1931) 22,284
Strathallan (1938) 23,722
*Stratheden (1938) 23,722
*Strathmore (1935) 23,428
*Strathnaver (1932) 22,547
Sumatra (1895) 4,607
Sunda (1895) 4,674
Sutlej (1881) 4,164
Syria (1901) 6,660
Thames (1881) 4,101
Valetta (1883) 4,911
Vectis (1881) 5,628
Verona (1879) 3,069
Viceroy of India (1929) 19,648
Victoria (1887) 6,091

PINILLOS, IZQUIERDO & CO.
(Spanish)

Barcelona (1908) 5,574
Cadiz (1908) 5,617
Infanta Isabel (1912) 8,182

Principe de Asturias (1914)
  8,371
Valbanera (1905) 5,099

RED "D" LINE
Atlantic & Caribbean Steam Navigation Co.
(United States)

Carabobo (1923) 2,916
Caracas (1889) 2,886
Caracas (1927) 3,365
Maracaibo (1899) 1,771

Philadelphia (1885) 2,520
Venezuela (1889) 2,843
Zulia (1901) 1,713

RED STAR LINE
(Belgian)

Abbotsford (1871) 2,554
Belgenland (1878) 3,692
Belgenland (1917) 27,132
Finland (1902) 12,188
Friesland (1889) 6,409
Gothland (1893) 7,669
Kenilworth (1872) 2,595
Kroonland (1902) 12,760
Lapland (1908) 18,565
Nederland (1873) 2,950

Noordland (1884) 5,129
Pennland (1870) 3,760
Pennland (1922) 16,322
Poland (1898) 8,282
Rhynland (1879) 3,689
Russland (1873) 2,595
Samland (1903) 9,748
Switzerland (1874) 2,957
Vaderland (1873) 2,748
Vaderland (1900) 11,899

RED STAR LINE (Continued)

Waesland (1867) 4,752
Westernland (1884) 5,736
Westernland (1918) 16,289

Zeeland (1865) 2,866
Zeeland (1901) 11,905

ROTTERDAM LLOYD
ROTTERDAMSCHE LLOYD
Wm. Ruys & Zonen
(Dutch)

Baloeran (1930) 16,981
Deli (1912) 6,799
Dempo (1930) 17,024
Djember (1914) 7,057
Garoet (1917) 7,133
Gede (1892) 2,995
Goentor (1902) 5,891
Indrapoera (1925) 10,772
Insulinde (1914) 9,615
Kawi (1907) 4,871
Medan (1908) 5,933
Menado (1907) 5,874
Merauke (1911) 6,674
Oengaran (1883) 2,475
Ophir (1904) 4,726

Palembang (1911) 6,674
Patria (1919) 9,891
Pontianak (1912) 6,675
Rindjani (1906) 4,762
Samarinda (1912) 6,825
Sibajak (1927) 12,226
Sindoro (1899) 5,471
Sitoebondo (1916) 7,057
Slamat (1924) 11,406
Soerakarta (1912) 6,926
Tabanan (1908) 5,271
Tambora (1909) 5,602
Tjerimai (1916) 7,760
Wilis (1905) 4,738
*Willem Ruys (1947) 23,114

ROYAL HOLLAND LLOYD
Koninklijke Hollandsche Lloyd
(Dutch)

Brabantia (1920) 19,821
Flandria (1922) 10,171
Frisia (1909) 7,442
Gelria (1913) 13,868
Hollandia (1909) 7,291

Limburgia (1920) 19,703
Orania (1922) 9,763
Tubantia (1913) 14,061
Zeelandia (1910) 7,995

ROYAL INTEROCEAN LINES
Royal Packet Co. (K. P. M.)
(Dutch)

*Boissevain (1937) 14,134
*Maetsuycker (1936) 4,272
*Ruys (1936) 14,134
*Straat Banka (1952) 9,161
*Tegelberg (1938) 14,281
*Tjiluwah (1951) 8,630

Tjinegara (1931) 9,227
*Tjinegara (1951) 9,067
   ex-Straat Makassar
*Tjisadane (1931) 9,228
*Tjitjalengka (1939) 10,972
*Tjiwangi (1950) 8,624

ROYAL MAIL LINES, LTD.
ROYAL MAIL STEAM PACKET COMPANY
(British)

Agadir (1907) 2,738
Alcala (1912) 10,660
Alcantara (1913) 15,831
Alcantara (1926) 22,181
Almanzora (1914) 15,551
Amazon (1851) 2,256
Amazon (1906) 10,037
*Amazon (1960) 20,348
Andes (1913) 15,620
*Andes (1939) 25,689
Aragon (1905) 9,441
*Aragon (1960) 20,362
Araguaya (1906) 10,196
Arcadian (1899) 8,939
Arcadian (1908) 12,015
Arlanza (1912) 14,930
*Arlanza (1960) 20,362
Asturias (1908) 12,015
Asturias (1925) 22,071
Atlantis (1913) 15,135
Atrato (1853) 3,467
Atrato (1888) 5,366
Avon (1907) 11,073
Avon (1880) 2,225
Balantia (1909) 2,379
Berbice (1909) 2,379
Boyne (1871) 3,318
Caraquet (1894) 4,917
Cardiganshire (1913) 9,426
Caribbean (1890) 5,625
Carmarthenshire (1915) 7,823
Carnarvonshire (1914) 9,406
Chaleur (1893) 4,758
Chaudiere (1899) 4,019
Chignecto (1893) 4,756
City of Glasgow (1841) 1,700
Clyde (1841) 1,841
Clyde (1890) 5,618
Cobequid (1893) 4,738
Danube (1865) 2,039
Danube (1893) 5,946
Darro (1912) 11,484
Dee (1841) 1,849
Dee (1872) 1,864
  ex-State of Minnesota
Demerara (1851) 2,318
Demerara (1912) 11,484
Derwent (1879) 2,471

Deseado (1912) 11,477
Desna (1912) 11,483
Don (1872) 4,028
Douro (1865) 2,824
Drina (1913) 11,483
Ebro (1865) 1,509
Ebro (1896) 3,445
Eider (1864) 1,569
Elbe (1870) 3,063
Forth (1841) 1,900
Great Western (1838) 1,775
Guadiana (1875) 2,504
Humber (1880) 2,371
Isis (1841) 1,900
La Plata (1852) 2,404
La Plata (1882) 4,464
La Plata (1896) 3,445
Liffey (1865) 1,504
Magdalena (1851) 2,943
Magdalena (1889) 5,373
Magdalena (1949) 17,547
Medina (1841) 1,800
Medway (1841) 1,895
Medway (1877) 3,730
Mersey (1859) 1,039
Minho (1872) 2,540
Minho (1896) 3,445
Mondego (1874) 2,564
Moselle (1871) 3,298
Neva (1868) 3,025
Nile (1870) 3,039
Nile (1893) 5,946
Ohio (1923) 18,940
Oneida (1858) 2,293
Orbita (1915) 15,495
Orca (1918) 16,063
Orduna (1914) 15,507
Orinoco (1851) 2,901
Orinoco (1886) 4,572
Oropesa (1920) 14,075
Para (1873) 4,028
Paramatta (1858) 3,439
Parana (1851) 2,943
Parana (1904) 4,182
Pardo (1904) 4,454
Pembrokeshire (1915) 7,821
Rhone (1865) 2,738
Sabor (1893) 4,747

ROYAL MAIL LINES (Continued)

Segura (1893)	4,756	Tay (1941)	1,858
Seine (1860)	3,440	Teviot (1841)	1,744
Severn (1842)	1,886	Thames (1841)	1,889
Shannon (1859)	3,609	Thames (1890)	5,645
Solent (1853)	1,804	Tiber (1866)	1,591
Solent (1878)	1,915	Trent (1841)	1,856
Solway (1841)	1,700	Trent (1873)	2,912
Tagus (1871)	3,298	Trent (1901)	5,525
Tagus (1900)	5,545	Tweed (1841)	1,800
Tamar (1854)	1,850	Tyne (1854)	1,603
Tamar (1873)	2,923	Tyne (1865)	
Tasmanian (1858)	2,956		

ROYAL NETHERLANDS STEAMSHIP CO.
Kon. Nederlandsche Stoomboot Mij. N. V.
(Dutch)

Known, also, as the K.N.S.M. Line, which has served the Europe-West Indies route for a number of years.

Baarn (1928)	5,559	Prins Frederik Hendrik (1904)	
Barneveld (1928)	5,597	2,164	
Bodegraven (1929)	5,593	Prins Maurits (1884)	1,310
Boskoop (1927)	5,620	Prins Maurits (1900)	2,121
Colombia (1930)	10,782	Prins Willem I (1884)	1,723
Commewyne (1907)	2,476	Prins Willem I (1890)	1,723
Coppename (1908)	3,192	Prins Willem I (1901)	2,121
Costa Rica (1910)	8,672	Prins Willem II (1890)	1,641
Cottica (1927)	3,989	Prins Willem III (1890)	1,960
Crijnssen (1919)	4,298	Prins Willem IV (1894)	2,047
Marowijne (1908)	3,192	Prins Willem V (1897)	2,108
Oranje Nassau (1883)	1,304	Saramacca (1908)	3,284
Oranje Nassau (1911)	3,721	Simon Bolivar (1927)	7,906
*Oranje Nassau (1957)	7,214	Stuyvesant (1918)	4,249
*Oranjestad (1938)	5,091	Suriname (1908)	3,275
Prins der Nederlanden (1902)		Van Rensselaer (1920)	4,299
1,923		Venezuela (1906)	6,355
*Prins der Nederlanden (1957)		Willemstad (1938)	5,088
7,220			
Prins Frederik Hendrik (1888)			
1,642			

ROYAL PACKET NAVIGATION COMPANY
Koninklijke Paketvaart Maatschappij
(Dutch)

Note: See Royal Interocean Lines (Dutch).

Barentsz (1915)	4,819	Bontekoe (1922)	5,033
Boissevain (1937)	14,134	Cremer (1926)	4,608

ROYAL PACKET NAVIGATION CO. (Continued)

Houtman (1913) 5,067	Roggeveen (1914) 4,782
Lombok (1907) 5,934	Ruys (1936) 14,155
Maetsuycker (1936) 4,131	Swartenhondt (1922) 4,700
Melchior Treub (1912) 3,458	Tasman (1921) 4,992
Nieuw Holland (1928) 11,066	Tegelberg (1936) 14,150
Nieuw Zeeland (1928) 11,069	Timor (1900) 3,679
Op Ten Noort (1927) 6,076	Van Cloon (1911) 4,519
Ophir (1928) 4,115	Van Heutsz (1926) 4,552
Plancius (1923) 5,955	Van Overstraten (1911) 4,482

RUSSIAN-AMERICAN LINE
RUSSIAN EAST ASIATIC STEAMSHIP CO.
(Russian)

Provided service between Russia and New York during the 1906–1917 period.

Arconia (1897) 4,603	Korea (1899) 6,163
Birma (1894) 4,595	Kursk (1910) 7,890
Czar (1912) 6,503	Lituania (1889) 4,244
Czaritza (1915) 6,598	Mitau (1894) 4,588
Dwinsk (1897) 8,173	ex-Birma
Estonia (1889) 4,250	Russia (1908) 8,596

RUSSIAN VOLUNTEER FLEET
(Russian)

Kherson (1896) 6,707	Saratov (1891) 5,427
Moskva (1890) 8,430	Smolensk (1898) 7,270
ex-Furst Bismarck	Terek (1889) 7,383
Orel (1890) 4,880	Vladimir (1895) 5,621
Petersburg (1894) 5,432	

RUSSIAN PASSENGER SHIPS
(Soviet Union)

Services: Various routes, mainly from Arctic, Baltic, Black Sea and Far Eastern ports.

*Abkhaziya (1927) 4,727	*Asia (1924) 11,453
*Adjaristan (1927) 4,727	ex-Der Deutsche (1946),
ex-Adjaria	ex-Sierra Morena (1934)
*Admiral Nakhimov (1925)	*Baltika (1940) 7,494
15,286	*Beloostrov (1937) 2,916
ex-Berlin	ex-Aarlottar (1946)
Alexandr Mozhaiski (1919)	Chukotka (1920) 7,900
9,686	ex-Wangoni (1946)
ex-Svir, ex-Patria (Dutch)	Dnepr (1931) 12,600
*Armeniya (1960) 4,800	ex-Cabo San Agustin (Spanish)

RUSSIAN PASSENGER SHIPS (Continued)

Estonia (1960)   4,800
*Felix Dzerjinsky (1958)   4,800
*Gregory Ordjonikidze (1959)
   4,800
*Gruzia (1939)   11,030
   ex-Sobieski (1953)
*Gruziya (1928)   4,857
*Ilich (1932)   12,049
   ex-Caribia (1946)
Jakutia (1928)   10,000
   ex-Juan Sebastian Elcano
   (Spanish)
*Krim (1928)   4,867
*Latvia (1960)   4,800
*Lensovet (1939)   6,138
   ex-Marienburg
*Litva (1960)   4,800
*M. Urizkij (1959)   4,800
*Maria Ulyanova (1959)   4,800
*Mikhail Kalinin (1958)   4,800
Neva (1914)   8,489
   ex-Essequibo (1935)
*Norilsk (1951)   3,498
*Petr Veliki (1939)   6,261
   ex-Jagiello   (1949),   ex-Peotr
   Veliki (1947), ex-Empire Ock
   (1946), Duala (1945), ex-Dogu
   (1945)

*Pobeda (1928)   9,829
   ex-Iberia (1946), ex-Magdalena
   (1934)
*Rossia (1938)   17,870
   ex-Empire Welland (1946),
   ex-Patria (1945)
*Russ (1932)   12,055
   ex-Cordillera (1949)
*Sibir (1912)   8,800
   ex-Oceana (1946), ex-Neptunia,
   ex-Peer Gynt, ex-Avare, ex-
   Sierra Salvada (German)
*Sovetsky Sojus (1923)   23,000
   ex-Hansa (1950), ex-Albert
   Ballin (1935)
Svanetija (1937)   4,000
*Tobolsk (1952)   3,498
*Ukraina (1938)   6,672
   ex-Basarabia (1948)
*Vazlav Borovsky (1960)   4,800
*Vladivostok (1960)   4,800

SCANDINAVIAN-AMERICAN LINE
(Danish)

Owned by Det Forenede Dampskibs-Selskab. This well known Danish shipping firm purchased the Thingvalla Line in 1898.

C. F. Tietgen (1897)   8,173
Frederik VIII (1913)   11,850
Hekla (1884)   3,258
Hellig Olav (1902)   9,939
Island (1882)   2,813

Norge (1881)   3,318
Oscar II (1901)   10,012
Thingvalla (1874)   2,547
United States (1903)   10,095

SHAW, SAVILL & ALBION COMPANY, LTD
(British)

The firm of Shaw and Savill was established in 1859. The company consolidated with the Albion Line in 1882. Their steamship service became firmly entrenched when they entered the new beautiful sister ships *Arawa* and *Tainui* on the England-Australia route in 1884. During the same year the company became closely associated with the White Star Line. In 1933 the Australian business of the White Star Line was acquired. It was during this time that the fleet of the Aberdeen Line was purchased.

Akaroa (1914)	15,128	Ionic (1902)	12,352
Aotea (1895)	6,364	Mahana (1917)	10,951
Arawa (1884)	5,026	Mahia (1917)	10,835
Arawa (1907)	9,372	Mamari (1904)	8,114
Arawa (1922)	14,462	Mataroa (1922)	12,390
Athenic (1901)	12,234	Matatua (1904)	8,010
*Athenic (1947)	15,187	New Australia (1931)	20,256
Ceramic (1913)	18,495	Northern Star (1962)	22,000
*Ceramic (1948)	15,896	Pakeha (1910)	10,481
Coptic (1881)	4,448	*Southern Cross (1956)	20,204
Corinthic (1902)	12,367	Tainui (1884)	5,161
*Corinthic (1947)	15,682	Tainui (1908)	9,957
Delphic (1897)	8,273	Tamaroa (1922)	12,405
*Dominion Monarch (1939)		Themistocles (1911)	11,223
	27,155	Waimana (1911)	10,389
Doric (1883)	4,676	Waimarama (1939)	12,843
Empire Trader (1908)	9,990	Waipawa (1934)	10,784
*Gothic (1893)	7,755	Wairangi (1935)	10,779
Ionic (1883)	4,753	Waiwera (1934)	10,782

SICULA AMERICANA LINE
(Italian)

Guglielmo Peirce (1907)	8,512	San Giovanni (1907)	6,592
San Giorgio (1907)	6,392	San Guglielmo (1911)	8,341

SITMAR LINE
"SITMAR", SOC. ITALIANA TRASPORTI MARITTIMA
(Italian)

*Castel Felice (1930)	12,150	*Fairsky (1941)	12,464
*Fairsea (1941)	13,432		

SPANISH LINE
Compania Trasatlantica Espanola
(Spanish)

Compania Trasatlantica was established at Barcelona in 1881, by A. Lopez & Company, steamship owners since 1865.

Alfonso XII (1875)　2,915	Leon XIII (1890)　5,206
Alfonso XII (1890)　6,966	Magallanes (1928)　9,689
Alfonso XIII (1888)　5,000	Manuel Arnus (1923)　7,578
Alfonso XIII (1891)　8,063	Manuel Calvo (1892)　5,617
Alfonso XIII (1923)　10,551	*Marques de Comillas (1928)
Antonio Lopez (1891)　5,975	9,922
Argentina (1913)　10,137	Meteoro (1890)　6,966
*Begona (1945)　10,139	Mexico (1876)　2,113
Buenos Aires (1887)　5,311	Montevideo (1889)　5,205
C. de Elizaguirre (1904)　4,376	Montserrat (1889)　4,147
C. Lopez-y-Lopez (1891)　4,170	*Montserrat (1945)　9,001
Cataluna (1883)　3,665	P. de Satrustegui (1890)　4,710
Ciudad Condal (1872)　2,596	Panama (1875)　2,085
Ciudad de Cadiz (1878)　3,202	Reina Maria Cristina (1889)
Covadonga (1884)　5,161	4,818
*Covadonga (1953)　10,226	Reina Victoria Eugenia (1913)
Cristobal Colon (1866)　2,869	10,137
Cristobal Colon (1923)　10,833	San Augustin (1882)　2,332
Espana (1873)　2,679	San Carlos (1917)　2,488
*Guadalupe (1953)　15,540	Santa Isabel (1916)　2,488
Habana (1872)　2,678	Santiago (1890)　5,206
*Habana (1923)　10,551	Santo Domingo (1877)　2,911
Infanta Isabel de Borbon (1913)	*Satrustegui (1948)　6,518
10,318	Uruguay (1913)　10,348
Isla de Panay (1882)　3,545	Vasco Nunez de Balboa (1891)
Juan Sebastian Elcano (1928)	8,063
9,965	*Virginia de Churruca (1949)
Legazpi (1904)　4,349	6,518
Leon XIII (1888)　5,087	

STANDARD FRUIT & STEAMSHIP CORP.
VACCARO LINE
(United States)

Amapala (1924)　4,148	Cefalu (1930)　5,221
Atlantida (1924)　4,191	Contessa (1930)　5,512

STATE LINE
State Steamship Company, Ltd.
(British)

State of Alabama (1873)　2,313	State of Nebraska (1880)　3,986
State of California (1891)　4,275	State of Nevada (1874)　2,488
State of Florida (1874)　3,155	State of Pennsylvania (1873)
State of Georgia (1873)　2,490	2,472
State of Indiana (1874)　2,528	State of Virginia (1873)　2,472
State of Louisiana (1872)　1,869	

SWEDISH-AMERICAN LINE
Svenska Amerika Linien
(Swedish)

The Swedish-American Line was founded late in 1914.

Drottningholm (1905)	11,182	*Kungsholm (1953)	22,071
Gripsholm (1925)	17,716	Stockholm (1900)	12,835
*Gripsholm (1956)	23,191	Stockholm (1939)	28,000
Kungsholm (1902)	12,528	Stockholm (1940)	28,000
Kungsholm (1928)	20,223	Stockholm (1947)	11,650

THINGVALLA LINE
Dampskibs Selskabet "Thingvalla"
(Danish)

This Danish shipping firm was founded in Copenhagen in 1880. The company was taken over by Det Forenede Dampskibs-Selskab (Scandinavian-American Line) in 1898.

Amerika (1872)	3,867	Island (1882)	2,844
Danmark (1880)	3,414	Norge (1881)	3,318
Geiser (1881)	2,831	Thingvalla (1874)	2,524
Hekla (1884)	3,258		

TOYO KISEN KAISHA
Oriental Steamship Company
(Japanese)

The full name of this old Japanese shipping firm was Toyo Kisen Kisen Kabusiki Kaisha. They opened up their Oriental-United States service in 1898. The amalgamation of Toyo Kisen Kaisha fleet with Nippon Yusen Kaisha took place in 1926.

America Maru (1898)	6,307	Nippon Maru (1898)	6,178
Anyo Maru (1913)	9,534	Persia Maru (1881)	4,356
Bokuyo Maru (1924)	8,619	Rakuyo Maru (1921)	9,419
Chiyo Maru (1908)	13,431	Shinyo Maru (1911)	13,039
Ginyo Maru (1921)	8,613	Siberia Maru (1901)	11,785
Hongkong Maru (1898)	6,185	Taiyo Maru (1911)	14,457
Korea Maru (1901)	11,810	Tenyo Maru (1908)	13,398

TRANSATLANTICA ITALIANA
(Italian)

Ammiraglio Bettolo (1923)	8,139	Francesco Crispi (1925)	7,464
		Garibaldi (1906)	5,191
Cavour (1905)	5,156	Giuseppe Verdi (1915)	9,760
Cesare Battisti (1920)	8,331	Leonardo da Vinci (1925)	7,515
Dante Alighieri (1914)	9,757	Nazario Sauro (1921)	8,150

TRANSPORTS MARITIMES
Societe Generale de Transports Maritimes
(French)

Algerie (1901)   4,035
Alsace (1889)   2,016
Alsina (1921)   8,404
Aquitaine (1891)   3,161
Bearn (1881)   4,134
Bourgogne (1865)   1,902
Bretagne (1877)   2,095
*Bretagne (1951)   16,355
Campana (1929)   10,816
Cordoba (1903)   6,375
Espagne (1891)   4,144
Florida (1926)   9,331
Floride (1908)   9,331
Formosa (1906)   4,471
France (1896)   4,269
Ile de France (1882)   3,488
Italie (1894)   4,160
La France (1871)   3,572
Les Alpes (1882)   4,164
Les Andes (1882)   4,150
Mendoza (1920)   8,199
Nivernais (1882)   2,565

Orleanais (1882)   2,602
Pampa (1906)   4,471
Parana (1908)   6,248
Picardie (1864)   1,371
Plata (1907)   5,577
Poitou (1867)   2,093
Poitou (1883)   2,679
Provence (1884)   3,874
*Provence (1950)   15,719
Russie (1897)   2,015
Salta (1911)   7,284
Savoie (1854)   2,522
Savoie (1889) 2,021
*Sidi-Bel-Abbes (1948)   5,226
Sidi-Bel-Abbes (1929)   4,392
Sidi-Brahim (1910)   2,439
*Sidi-Ferruch (1949)   3,761
Sidi-Mabrouk (1906)   3,883
*Sidi-Mabrouk (1948)   3,988
*Sidi-Okba (1948)   3,988
Valdivia (1911)   7,168

THOMSON LINE
(British)

Cairnrona (1900)   7,682
Gerona (1911)   9,111
   (Sold to Cunard Line before
   completion)

Tortona (1909)   8,153

TURKISH PASSENGER SHIPS
Turkish Maritime Lines

*Akdeniz (1955)   8,809
*Adana (1932)   5,236
   ex-Monterey (1948), ex-Puerto
   Rico (1939), ex-Haiti (1938)
*Ankara (1927)   6,178
   ex-Solace (1948),   ex-Iroquois
   (1948)
Ege (1908)   5,275
   ex-Tabanan
*Ege (1955)   6,042
Egemen (1939)   6,000
*Giresun (1938)   6,790
   ex-Aconcagua (1948)
*Iskenderun (1950)   6,750
*Istanbul (1932)   5,236
   ex-Mexico (1947), ex-Columbia
   (1938)

*Izmir (1955)   6,041
Karadeniz (1905)   4,731
*Karadeniz (1956)   8,809
Kiresson (1877)   3,056
   ex-Kerasounde, ex-Jerome,
   ex-Warwick Castle
*Marmara (1955)   6,041
*Ordu (1937)   6,790
   ex-Copiapo
*Samsun (1951)   6,543
*Tarsus (1931)   9,345
   ex-Harry Lee (1948),
   ex-Exochorda (1948)
*Trabzon (1938)   7,274
   ex-Imperial (1949)

TWIN SCREW LINE
(British)

In trans-Atlantic passenger service between 1883–1887.

Bitterne (1883)	5,085	Richmond Hill (1883)	4,225
Ludgate Hill (1882)	4,162	Saint Ronans (1881)	4,457
Notting Hill (1881)	3,920	Tower Hill (1881)	4,021

ULTRAMAR LINE
Flota Argentina de Navegacion de Ultramar
(Argentina)

Vessels originally built for Cia Argentina de Dodero. See: Dodero Line.

*Alberto Dodero (1951)	11,521	*Uruguay (1950)	12,627
*Argentina (1949)	12,459	*Yapeyu (1951)	11,540
*Liberstad (1950)	12,653		

UNION LINE
Union Steam Ship Company, Ltd.
(British)

African (1873)	2,019	Greek (1893)	4,747
American (1873)	2,126	Guelph (1894)	4,917
Anglian (1873)	2,159	Mexican (1882)	4,661
Arab (1879)	3,192	Moor (1882)	3,688
Asiatic (1873)	2,066	Norman (1894)	7,537
Athenian (1882)	3,877	Norseman (1866)	1,368
Athens (1877)	2,313	Northam (1869)	1,330
Briton (1861)	1,167	Nubian (1876)	3,088
Briton (1897)	10,248	Nyanza (1864)	2,082
Cambrian (1860)	1,055	(Built for P. & O. Line)	
Celt (1855)	514	Phoebe (1857)	613
Celt (1866)	1,439	Pretoria (1878)	3,303
Dane (1855)	530	Roman (1863)	1,282
Danube (1866)	2,039	Roman (1870)	3,021
Durban (1878)	2,875	Saxon (1863)	1,142
European (1869)	2,272	Saxon (1900)	12,385
Gascon (1897)	6,298	Scot (1891)	6,844
Gaul (1893)	4,745	Spartan (1881)	3,487
German (1877)	3,149	Syria (1863)	1,959
German (1898)	6,763	Tartar (1883)	4,425
Goth (1893)	4,738	Teuton (1869)	1,741
Gothland (1872)	1,482	Trojan (1880)	3,652

UNION-CASTLE LINE
Union-Castle Mail Steamship Company, Ltd.
(British)

The Union-Castle Line was founded in February 1900 by the consolidation of the Union Steam Ship Company with the Castle Mail Packets Company (Donald Currie & Co.).

Alnwick Castle (1901)   5,893
Armadale Castle (1903)   12,973
Arundel Castle (1894)   4,588
Arundel Castle (1921)   19,023
*Athlone Castle (1936)   25,564
Avondale Castle (1897)   5,531
Balmoral Castle (1910)   13,361
Berwick Castle (1902)   5,891
Bloemfontein Castle (1950)
   18,400
Braemar Castle (1898)   6,266
*Braemar Castle (1952)   17,029
Briton (1897)   10,248
*Capetown Castle (1938)   27,002
Carisbrook Castle (1898)   7,626
*Carnarvon Castle (1926)   20,063
Cawdor Castle (1901)   6,243
Cluny Castle (1903)   5,147
Comrie Castle (1903)   5,167
Dover Castle (1904)   8,271
Dunbar Castle (1930)   10,002
Dunluce Castle (1904)   8,114
Dunnottar Castle (1936)   15,050
Dunottar Castle (1890)   5,625
Dunvegan Castle (1896)   6,117
Dunvegan Castle (1936)   15,050
*Durban Castle (1939)   17,388
Durham Castle (1904)   8,217
Edinburgh Castle (1910)   13,326
*Edinburgh Castle (1948)   28,705
Gaika (1897)   6,287
Galeka (1899)   6,767
Galician (1900)   6,757
Galway Castle (1911)   7,988
Garth Castle (1910)   7,625
Gascon (1897)   6,288
German (1898)   6,763
Glenart Castle (1900)   6,757
Glengorm Castle (1898)   6,763
Gloucester Castle (1911)   7,999
Goorkha (1897)   6,335
Grantully Castle (1910)   7,617
Greek (1893)   4,747

Guelph (1894)   4,917
Guildford Castle (1911)   7,995
Harlech Castle (1894)   3,264
Hawarden Castle (1883)   4,380
Huntscastle (1902)   5,580
   ex-Erna Woermann
Kenilworth Castle (1904)   12,975
Kenilworth Castle (1946)   9,916
*Kenya Castle (1952)   17,041
Kildonan Castle (1899)   9,692
Kinfauns Castle (1899)   9,664
Leasowe Castle (1916)   9,737
   ex-Vasilissa Sophia
Llandaff Castle (1926)   10,799
Llandovery Castle (1914)
   11,423
Llandovery Castle (1925)
   10,640
Llangibby Castle (1929)   11,951
Llanstephan Castle (1914)
   11,293
Moor (1882)   4,464
Newark Castle (1901)   6,253
Norham Castle (1883)   4,392
Norman (1894)   7,573
Pembroke Castle (1883)   4,045
*Pendennis Castle (1958)   28,582
Pretoria Castle (1939)   17,392
*Pretoria Castle (1948)   28,705
Raglan Castle (1897)   4,324
*Rhodesia Castle (1951)   17,041
Roslin Castle (1883)   4,267
Scot (1891)   7,815
*Stirling Castle (1935)   25,554
Tantallon Castle (1894)   5,636
Tintagel Castle (1896)   5,531
*Transvaal Castle (1961)   30,000
Walmer Castle (1902)   12,546
Warwick Castle (1931)   20,445
*Warwick Castle (1939)   17,387
Winchester Castle (1930)   20,109
Windsor Castle (1920)   18,967
*Windsor Castle (1960)   37,640

UNION STEAMSHIP COMPANY OF NEW ZEALAND, LTD.
(British)

Aorangi (1883)	4,268	Maunganui (1911)	7,527
Aorangi (1924)	17,491	Moana (1897)	3,915
Aotearoa (1915)	15,000	Moeraki (1902)	4,392
Arahura (1905)	1,596	Monowai (1890)	3,433
Arawata (1875)	1,098	Monowai (1925)	10,852
Atua (1906)	3,444	Niagara (1913)	13,413
Awatea (1936)	13,482	Oonah (1888)	1,757
*Hinemoa (1946)	6,911	*Rangatira (1931)	6,152
Loongana (1904)	2,448	Ringarooma (1875)	1,096
Maheno (1905)	5,323	Rotomahana (1879)	1,727
Maitai (1892)	3,393	Ruapehu (1883)	4,163
Makura (1908)	8,075	Ruapehu (1901)	9,018
Manuka (1903)	4,534	Tahiti (1904)	7,898
Maori (1875)	174	Talune (1890)	2,087
first steamer of line		Tamahine (1925)	1,989
Maori (1907)	3,399	*Tofua (1951)	5,299
*Maori (1954)	8,303	Tongariro (1883)	4,163
Marama (1907)	6,437	Wahine (1913)	4,436
Mararoa (1885)	2,598	Wairarapa (1882)	1,786
*Matua (1936)	4,193		

UNITED AMERICAN LINES
American Ship & Commerce Corporation
(United States)

In trans-Atlantic passenger service between 1921 and 1926.

Cleveland (1908)	16,960	Mount Clinton (1921)	7,510
Mount Carroll (1921)	7,469	Reliance (1920)	19,582
Mount Clay (1904)	8,865	Resolute (1920)	19,653

UNITED NETHERLANDS STEAM NAVIGATION CO.
(Dutch)

Amstelkerk (1929)	4,457	Klipfontein (1939)	10,544
Bloemfontein (1934)	10,081	Maaskerk (1929)	4,452
Boschfontein (1928)	7,139	Meliskerk (1919)	6,045
Boschkerk (1928)	6,405	Nijkerk (1915)	5,843
Elandsfontein (1940)	10,500	*Oranjefontein (1950)	10,549
Heemskerk (1919)	6,515	Randfontein (1920)	5,653
ex-Witram		*Randfontein (1958)	13,693
*Jagersfontein (1948)	10,574	Springfontein (1921)	

UNITED FRUIT COMPANY
UNITED FRUIT STEAMSHIP CORP.
UNITED MAIL STEAMSHIP CO.
(United States)

Abangarez (1909)   4,572
Almirante (1909)   5,010
Antigua (1932)   6,982
Atenas (1909)   4,962
Calamares (1913)   7,782
Carrillo (1911)   4,593
Cartago (1908)   4,732
Castilla (1927)   4,087
Chiriqui (1932)   6,963
Heredia (1908)   4,732
Jamaica (1933)   6,968
Metapan (1909)   5,011
Parismina (1908)   4,732

Pastores (1912)   7,242
Peten (1933)   6,968
Quirigua (1932)   6,968
Santa Marta (1909)   4,601
Sixaola (1911)   4,693
Talamanca (1931)   6,963
Tenadores (1913)   7,782
Tivives (1911)   4,596
Toloa (1917)   7,183
Turrialba (1909)   4,538
Ulua (1917)   7,181
Veragua (1932)   6,982
Zacapa (1909)   4,568

UNITED STATES & BRAZIL STEAMSHIP COMPANY
(United States)

Advance (1883)   2,603
Erie (1868)   3,000
Finance (1883)   2,603
Merrimack (1859)   2,199

Mississippi (1859)   2,008
North America (1862)   2,985
Ontario (1868)   2,889
South America (1861)   2,150

UNITED STATES LINES
(United States)

America (1905)   21,145
*America (1940)   33,532
American Banker (1920)   7,430
American Farmer (1920)   7,430
American Importer (1920)
  7,590
American Merchant (1920)
  7,430
American Shipper (1920)   7,430
American Trader (1920)   7,430
American Traveler (1920)   7,555
Blue Hen State (1921)   10,533
Centennial State (1921)   10,533
Ernie Pyle (1945)   12,420
George Washington (1908)
  23,788
Leviathan (1914)   59,957:48,943
Lone Star State (1921)   13,869
Manhattan (1932)   24,289
Marine Falcon (1945)   12,420
Marine Flasher (1945)   12,558

Marine Jumper (1945)   12,420
Marine Marlin (1945)   12,420
Marine Perch (1945)   12,410
Marine Shark (1945)   12,410
Marine Tiger (1945)   12,558
Old North State (1920)   10,533
Panhandle State (1920)   10,533
Peninsula State (1921)   13,869
Potomac (1901)   9,709
President Adams (1921)   10,533
President Arthur (1900)   10,680
President Fillmore (1899)
  10,532
President Garfield (1921)
  10,538
President Harding (1921)
  13,869
President Monroe (1920)   10,533
President Pierce (1922)   14,127
President Polk (1921)   10,500

UNITED STATES LINES (Continued)

President Roosevelt (1922)
  13,869
President Taft (1922)   13,869
President Van Buren (1920)
  10,533
Republic (1907)   17,910

Susquehanna (1899)   9,959
*United States (1952)   53,329
Washington (1933)   24,289
Note: The *MARINE FALCON* class are owned by the United States Department of Commerce.

UNITED STATES MAIL STEAMSHIP COMPANY
(United States)

In trans-Atlantic passenger service during the 1920–1921 period. Due to financial difficulties the fleet was taken over by the United States Shipping Board in August 1921. The service from then on was operated by the United States Lines.

America (1905)   21,145
Blue Hen State (1921)   10,538
Centennial State (1921)   10,533
Creole State (1920)   10,533
George Washington (1908)
  25,570
Hudson (1899)   9,699

Old North State (1920)   10,533
Panhandle State (1920)   10,533
Pocahontas (1900)   10,881
Potomic (1901)   9,709
Princess Matoika (1900)   10,421
Susquehanna (1899)   9,959

VANDERBILT EUROPEAN LINE
(United States)

Commodore Vanderbilt carried on his trans-Atlantic service during the 1855–1861 period.

Ariel (1855)   1,736
Illinois (1851)   2,123
North Star (1853)   1,867

Ocean Queen (1859)   2,801
Vanderbilt (1855)   3,360

VELOCE, LA
"La Veloce" Navigazione Italiana
(Italian)

America (1908)   8,996
Argentina (1905)   4,985
Bologna (1905)   4,680
Brasile (1905)   5,298
Centro America (1897)   3,522
Citta di Genova (1882)   3,919
Citta di Genova (1889)   1,936
Citta di Messina (1894)   2,478
Citta di Milano (1897)   4,041
Citta di Napoli (1871)   4,125
Citta di Torino (1898)   3,836

Duca di Galliero (1883)   4,304
Duca di Genova (1907)   7,811
Duchessa di Genova (1884)
  4,304
Europa (1873)   2,202
Europa (1907)   7,870
Expresso (1870)   2,009
Italia (1905)   5,203
Matteo Bruzzo (1882)   3,919
Napoli (1870)   2,009
Nord America (1872)   2,175

VELOCE, LA (Continued)

Nord America (1882)	4,920	Sud America (1868)	3,185
Oceania (1909)	9,000	Sud America (1873)	2,246
Rio Janeiro (1889)	1,916	Venezuela (1898)	3,474
Savoia (1897)	5,082	Vittoria (1871)	3,707
Siena (1905)	4,553	Vittoria (1883)	4,290
Stampalia (1909)	9,000		

WARD LINE
New York & Cuba Mail Steamship Co.
(United States)

City of Alexandria (1879)	2,480	Oriente (1930)	11,520
City of Washington (1877)	2,683	Orizaba (1890)	3,497
Cuba (1894)	2,963	Orizaba (1918)	6,937
Esperanza (1901)	4,702	Santiago (1879)	2,359
Havana (1898)	5,667	Saratoga (1878)	2,820
Havana (1907)	6,678	Saratoga (1907)	6,391
Merida (1906)	6,207	Seguranca (1890)	4,033
Mexico (1932)	5,236	Seneca (1884)	2,963
Monterey (1901)	4,702	Siboney (1918)	6,938
Morro Castle (1900)	6,004	Vigilancia (1890)	4,115
Morro Castle (1930)	11,520	Yucatan (1890)	3,525
Newport (1880)	2,735	Yucatan (1907)	6,678
Niagara (1877)	2,265	Yumuri (1890)	3,500

WARREN LINE
George Warren & Company
FURNESS-WARREN LINE
(British)

Furness, Withy & Company obtained an interest in the Warren Line in 1912. During 1922 the old Warren Line was liquidated and a new firm was formed, Warren Line (Liverpool), Ltd.

Angloman (1892)	4,892	Nova Scotia (1926)	6,796
Bay State (1898)	6,824	Nova Scotia (1947)	7,438
Bosphorus (1865)	2,045	Ottoman (1890)	4,843
Brazilian (1852)	3,496	Palestine (1858)	2,867
Cambroman (1892)	6,059	Peruvian (1863)	2,304
Concordia (1862)	1,348	ex-Allan liner	
Digby (1913)	3,960	Propontis (1864)	2,132
Iowa (1879)	4,329	Roman (1884)	4,572
Iowa (1903)	8,370	Sachem (1893)	5,204
Kansas (1882)	5,277	Sagamore (1892)	5,197
Massachusetts (1866)	2,869	Sir Francis (1872)	1,833
Michigan (1887)	4,979	Victoria (1867)	3,985
Missouri (1881)	5,146	Fort Victoria (1913)	7,784
Nepthis (1877)	2,010	(Made several trans-Atlantic	
Newfoundland (1925)	6,791	voyages before entering Fur-	
Newfoundland (1947)	7,437	ness-Bermuda Line.)	

WHITE STAR LINE
Oceanic Steam Navigation Company, Ltd.
(British)

The Oceanic Steam Navigation Company was founded in September 1869. The White Star Line commenced trans-Atlantic service in March 1871, with the newly built *Oceanic*. The Cunard and White Star Line merged in 1934.

Adriatic (1872)	3,888	Gaelic (1885)	4,206
Adriatic (1906)	24,563	Georgic (1895)	10,077
Afric (1899)	11,948	Georgic (1932)	27,759
Albertic (1923)	18,940	Germanic (1874)	5,008
Arabic (1881)	4,368	Gothic (1893)	7,700
Arabic (1903)	15,801	Homeric (1914)	34,356
Arabic (1908)	16,821	Ionic (1882)	4,748
Athenic (1901)	12,234	Ionic (1902)	12,352
Atlantic (1870)	3,707	Justicia (1917)	32,120
Baltic (1871)	3,707	Laurentic (1909)	14,892
Baltic (1904)	23,884	Laurentic (1927)	18,724
Belgic (1873)	2,652	Majestic (1890)	9,861
Belgic (1885)	4,212	Majestic (1921)	56,551
Belgic (1903)	9,767	Medic (1899)	11,985
Belgic (1917)	24,547	Megantic (1909)	14,878
Britannic (1874)	5,004	Oceanic (1870)	3,808
Britannic (1914)	48,158	Oceanic (1899)	17,274
Britannic (1930)	28,840	Olympic (1911)	45,324
Calgaric (1918)	16,063	Persic (1899)	12,042
Canopic (1900)	12,268	Pittsburg (1922)	16,322
Cedric (1903)	21,227	Regina (1918)	16,289
Celtic (1872)	3,888	Republic (1871)	3,707
Celtic (1901)	20,904	Republic (1903)	15,378
Ceramic (1913)	18,495	Romanic (1898)	11,394
Coptic (1881)	4,384	Runic (1889)	4,833
Corinthic (1902)	12,367	Runic (1900)	12,490
Cretic (1902)	13,507	Southland (1900)	11,899
Cymric (1898)	13,096	Suevic (1901)	12,531
Delphic (1897)	8,273	Teutonic (1889)	9,686
Doric (1883)	4,676	Titanic (1911)	46,329
Doric (1923)	16,484	Vedic (1918)	9,332
Gaelic (1872)	2,652		

WOERMANN LINE
(German)

Adolph Woermann (1906)	6,257	Erna Woermann (1902)	5,580
Adolph Woermann (1922)	8,577	Frieda Woermann (1888)	2,523
Eduard Bohlen (1891)	2,367	Gertrud Woermann (1885)	
Eduard Woermann (1889)	2,085	1,816	
Eduard Woermann (1903)	5,642	Gertrud Woermann (1905)	
Eleonore Woermann (1902)		6,365	
4,624			

WOERMANN LINE (Continued)

Gertrud Woermann (1907) 6,465
Hans Woermann (1900)   4,059
Henny Woermann (1911)   6,062
Hilda Woermann (1914)   9,300
Irma Woermann (1901)   2,304
Kurt Woermann (1895)   2,263
Jeannette Woermann (1893) 2,229
Lucie Woermann (1902)   4,760

Marie Woermann (1916)   7,700
Professor Woermann (1903) 5,631
Professor Woermann (1912) 6,079
Tanganjika (1922)   8,540
Wadai (1922)   4,696
Wahehe (1922)   4,709
Watussi (1928)   9,552

YBARRA & COMPANY
YBARRA Y CIA
(Seville, Spain)

Cabo de Buena Esperanza (1921) 12,595
Cabo de Hornos (1921)   12,599
Cabo Palos (1927)   6,342
Cabo Quilates (1927)   6,342

Cabo San Agustin (1931)   12,589
Cabo San Antonio (1930)   12,275
*Cabo San Roque (1957)   14,491
*Cabo San Vicente (1959)   14,569
Cabo Santo Tome (1931)   12,589

ZIM LINES
ZIM ISRAEL NAVIGATION COMPANY
(Israel)

Aliya (1913)   11,015
   ex-Jerusalem
Artsa (1930)   3,213
*Israel (1955)   9,831
Jerusalem (1913)   11,015
   ex-Bergensfjord

*Jerusalem (1957)   9,920
Negbah (1915)   5,544
Shalom (building) 23,000
*Theodor Herzl (1958)   9,914
*Zion (1956)   9,855

PART VI

CALIFORNIA-HAWAIIAN PASSENGER SHIPS
Past and Present

Shuttle Service

*Asterisk denotes ship in service, 1962.

Aleutian (1906) Hawaiian Pacific Line.
> Built by Wm. Cramp & Sons Shipbuilding Co., Philadelphia, Pa. Tonnage: 6,361. Dimensions: 400′ x 50′. Twin-screw, 17 knots. Triple expansion engines. Two masts and one funnel. Placed in the California-Hawaii service during the 1953–54 period, but was soon withdrawn from the trade. The **Aleutian** had previously been operated by the Alaska Steamship Company in their coastal trade to Alaska for a number of years. Renamed: **Tradewind** (1955). Scrapped in Belgium, 1956. Ex-**Mexico.**

Calawaii (1893) Los Angeles Steamship Co.
> Built by Harland & Wolff, Ltd., Belfast, Ireland. Tonnage: 7,271. Dimensions: 445′ x 49′. Twin-screw, 13½ knots. Triple expansion engines. Four masts and one funnel. Vessel was laid up in 1932. Broken up for scrap in Japan, 1933. Ex-**Sherman** (1923), ex-**Mobile** (1898).

City of Honolulu (1896) Los Angeles Steamship Co.
> Built by "Vulkan", Stettin, Germany. Tonnage: 10,771. Dimensions: 523′ x 60′ (546′ o.l.). Twin-screw, 15 knots. Quadruple expansion engines. Two masts and two funnels. Commenced her first sailing from Los Angeles to Honolulu, September 11, 1922. Unfortunately on October 12th, while on the return voyage she caught fire at sea. Luckily the passengers and crew were safely removed, after which the gutted vessel was sunk by gun fire. The United States army transport brought the passengers to San Francisco. Ex-**Huron** (1922), ex-**Friedrich der Grosse** (1917).

City of Honolulu (1900) Los Angeles Steamship Co.
> Built by "Vulkan", Stettin, Germany. Tonnage: 10,680. Dimensions: 523′ x 60′. Twin-screw, 15½ knots. Quadruple expansion engines. Two masts and two funnels. Note: Purchased this former German liner in 1926, as a replacement for the earlier **City of Honolulu** that had been lost due to

fire. The reconditioned vessel commenced her first voyage from Los Angeles to Honolulu on June 4, 1927. Accommodation for 279 first class passengers. This second **City of Honolulu** had the misfortune of being badly damaged by fire, while tied to her Honolulu wharf, May 25, 1930. However, the fire-gutted liner was able to return to Los Angeles under her own steam, but was laid up until sold to Japanese shipbreakers in 1933. Ex-**President Arthur** (1924), ex-**Princess Matoika** (1921), ex-**Prinzess Alice** (1917), ex-**Kiautschou** (1903).

City of Los Angeles   (1899)   Los Angeles Steamship Co.
Built by F. Schichau, Danzig, Germany. Tonnage: 12,642. Dimensions: 560' x 62' (580' o.l.). Twin-screw, 16½ knots. Two steam turbines. Two masts and two funnels. Passengers: 446 first class. After being thoroughly reconditioned for the line's Los Angeles-Honolulu service, she commenced her first voyage to Hawaii on September 11, 1922. The white-painted hull added to the attractiveness of this nicely designed ship. Sold for scrap to Japan in February 1937. Ex-**Aeolus** (1922), ex-**Grosser Kurfurst** (1917).

Leilani   (1944)   Hawaiian Steamship Company.
Built by Federal Shipbuilding & Drydock Co., Kearny, N. J. Tonnage: 18,298. Dimensions: 573' x 75' (622' o.l.). Twin-screw, 20 knots. Steam turbines. Two masts and two funnels. Passengers: 600 tourist class. The Hawaiian Steamship Company, which was controlled by Hawaiian Textron, Inc., purchased this vessel from the United States Government in 1956 for their new California-Honolulu passenger service. However, the venture did not prove profitable and the **Leilani** was withdrawn from service. The liner reverted back to the United States Government, but was acquired by the American President Lines in 1961. She was then rebuilt for the new owner's trans-Pacific trade. Renamed: **President Roosevelt** (1961). Ex-**La Guardia** (1956), ex-**General W. P. Richardson** (1949).

Lurline   (1908)   Matson Line.
Built by Newport News Shipbuilding & Drydock Co., Newport News, Virginia. Tonnage: 6,572. Dimensions: 412' x 53' (437' o.l.). Single-screw, 13½ knots. Triple expansion engines. Three masts and single funnel aft. Passengers: 66 first and 25 third class. Prior to World War II this vessel was acquired by Alaska Packers Association, Inc. Renamed: (a) **Chirikof**, (b) **Radnik** (1947). Scrapped in 1952.

*Lurline   (1932)   Matson Line.
   Built by Bethlehem Steel Co., Shipyard Division, Quincy,
   Mass. Tonnage: 18,564. Dimensions: 605' x 79' (631' o.l.).
   Twin-screw, 22 knots. Six steam turbines. 25,000 s.h.p.
   Two masts and two funnels. Passengers: 500 first and 250
   cabin class. Note: Prior to World War II, the **Lurline** and
   Malolo provided weekly sailings in the San Francisco-
   Los Angeles to Honolulu service. The **Lurline** served as an
   American transport during World War II. After the war
   she was thoroughly reconditioned for the California-Honolulu
   trade and re-entered the service in 1948. Accommodation
   was altered to 722 first class passengers. Sister ships: **Mariposa** and **Monterey** (Built for California-Australia service).
   The **Lurline** has had as her running mate since 1957 the
   Matsonia, which was formerly named **Monterey.**

Malolo   (1927)   Matson Line.
   Built by Wm. Cramp & Sons Shipbuilding Co., Philadelphia,
   Pa. Tonnage: 17,222. Dimensions: 554' x 83' (582' o.l.).
   Twin-screw, 21 knots. Eight steam turbines. 25,000 I.H.P.
   Two masts and two funnels. Built at a cost of $7,000,000.
   Passengers: 693 first class. Maiden voyage: San Francisco-
   Honolulu, November 16, 1927. She could make the regular
   run to Hawaii in 4½ days. The earlier liners in this trade
   usually required about 7 days. Renamed: (a) **Matsonia**
   (1937), (b) **Atlantic** (1949), (c) **Queen Frederica** (1955).

Manoa   (1913)   Matson Line.
   Built by Newport News Shipbuilding Co., Newport News,
   Va. Tonnage: 6,806. Dimensions: 422' x 54'. Single-screw,
   14 knots. Quadruple expansion engines. Three masts and
   single funnel aft. Passengers: 100 first class. Renamed:
   Balhash (1943) Russian. Similar ships: **Lurline, Matsonia,
   Maui** and **Wilhelmina.** Note: The somewhat unusual
   arrangement of their engines being placed aft, together with
   funnel being well back of the middle mast, made these
   Matson liners easy to identify.

Matsonia   (1913)   Matson Line.
   Built by Newport News Shipbuilding Co., Newport News,
   Va. Tonnage: 9,402. Dimensions: 480' x 58' (501' o.l.).
   Single-screw, 15 knots. Triple expansion engines. Three
   masts and single funnel aft. Note: Named after Captain
   William Matson, founder of the Matson Navigation Com-
   pany, which became incorporated back in 1901. Service:
   San Francisco-Honolulu. Passengers: 251 first and 58 third
   class. Renamed: **Etolin** (1937). Scrapped in 1957. Similar
   ships: **Lurline, Manoa, Maui** and **Wilhelmina.**

Matsonia (1927) Matson Line.
Built by Wm. Cramp & Sons Shipbuilding Co., Philadelphia, Pa. Tonnage: 17,226. Dimensions: 554' x 83' (582' o.l.). Twin-screw, 21 knots. Steam turbines. Two masts and two funnels. Served as an American troopship in World War II) Re-entered regular service after the war. Sold to Panamanian Lines, Inc. in 1948. Renamed: (a) **Atlantic** (1949). Home Lines, (b) **Queen Frederica** (1955). Ex-**Malolo** (1937).

*****Matsonia** (1932) Matson Line.
Built by Bethlehem Steel Co., Shipyard Division, Quincy, Mass. Tonnage: 18,565. Dimensions: 605' x 79' (631' o.l.). Twin-screw, 22 knots, Steam turbines. Two masts and two funnels. Passengers: 760 first class. Entered Matson Navigation Company's California-Hawaii shuttle service in 1957. Running mate: **Lurline.** Ex-**Monterey** (1956). Note: As the **Monterey** she had been employed during the pre-war days in the San Francisco-Australia service, along with her sister ship the **Mariposa,** now known as the **Homeric** of the Home Lines. In 1952 the Matson Line had sold the liner to the United States Government, but repurchased her in 1956, so as to provide a weekly service to Hawaii.

Maui (1917) Matson Line.
Built by Union Iron Works, San Francisco, California. Tonnage: 9,801. Dimensions: 484' x 58' (501' o.l.). Twin-screw, 16 knots. Steam turbines. Three masts and single funnel aft. Service: San Francisco-Honolulu. Passengers: 300. Served as an American troopship in World Wars I and II. Scrapped in 1946. Similar ships: **Lurline, Manoa, Matsonia** and **Wilhelmina.**

Wilhelmina (1909) Matson Line.
Built by Newport News Shipbuilding Co., Newport News, Va. Tonnage: 6,975. Dimensions: 426' x 54'. Single-screw, 15 knots. Triple expansion engines. Three masts and single funnel in aft position. Passengers: 147 first class. Torpedoed by submarine, December 2, 1940. Similar ships: **Lurline, Manoa, Matsonia** and **Maui.**

PICTORIAL SECTION

PART VII

PICTORIAL SECTION

SHIP PICTURE LIST

Composite list of ship pictures appearing in books by the author.

*Denotes different view of ship.

Code	Book
Page No. in this Edition	Passenger Ships of the World—Past and Present
A	Trans-Pacific Passenger Ships
B	Trans-Atlantic Passenger Ships (1st and 2nd printings)
C	Trans-Atlantic Passenger Ships (3rd printing—Pictorial section revised)

Ship	Code			Page No.
Abangarez (1909) United Fruit Co.............				859
Adriatic (1872) White Star Line...............				779
Aller (1886) North German Lloyd..............	B			
America (1848) Cunard Line..................	B			
America (1884) National Line.................				795
America (1940) United States Lines..........	A*	B	C	919
Amerika (1905) Hamburg-American Line.......		B		
Amerique (1864) French Line.................		B	C	
Andania (1913) Cunard Line..................		B		
Andre Lebon (1913) Messageries Maritimes......				870
Andrea Doria (1952) Italia Line..............	A			933
Aorangi (1924) Union S.S. Co. of N. Z...........	A			
Aquitania (1914) Cunard Line.................		B	C	
Arabic (1903) White Star Line...............				834
Aragon (1905) Royal Mail Line...............				846
Araguaya (1906) Royal Mail Line.............		B	C	
Arandora Star (1927) Blue Star Line...........				897
Arcadian (1899) Royal Mail Line.............				821
Asama Maru (1929) N. Y. K. Line.............	A			901
Ascania (1911) Cunard Line..................				861
Athenia (1923) Anchor-Donaldson Line.........		B		
Atlantic (1927) Home Lines.................				896
Auguste Victoria (1888) Hamburg-American.....		B		
Augustus (1952) Italia Line.................				934
Aurania (1883) Cunard Line..................		B		
Aurania (1924) Cunard Line..................				889
Austral (1881) Orient Line..................				791

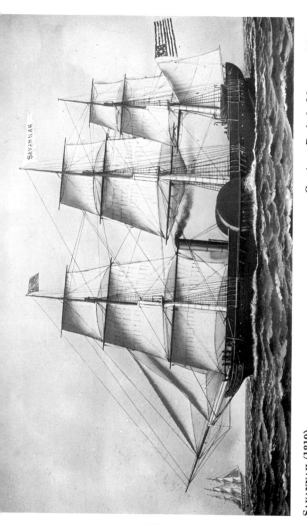

SAVANNAH (1819)
Owner: Colonel John Stevens

Courtesy, Peabody Museum of Salem

BRITANNIA (1840)

Courtesy, Cunard Steam-Ship Co., Ltd.

HIBERNIAN (1861)
Allan Line

Courtesy, Peabody Museum of Salem

WASHINGTON (1863)
French Line

New York (1865)
Pacific Mail Steamship Co.

Courtesy, The Mariners' Museum

Courtesy, Peabody Museum of Salem

CASPIAN (1870)
Allan Line

Courtesy, Peabody Museum of Salem

BATAVIA (1870)
Cunard Line

Courtesy, Peabody Museum of Salem

LUSITANIA (1871)
Orient Line

Cuzco (1871)
Orient Line

Courtesy, Peabody Museum of Salem

CHIMBORAZO (1871)
Orient Line

Courtesy, Peabody Museum of Salem

ADRIATIC (1872)
White Star Line

779

CITY OF MONTREAL (1872)
Inman Line

Courtesy, *Peabody Museum of Salem*

Don (1872)
Royal Mail Line

BOTHNIA (1874)
Cunard Line

CITY OF BERLIN (1875)
Inman Line

MEDWAY (1877)
Royal Mail Line

GALLIA (1878)
Cunard Line

ORIENT (1879)
Orient Line

Photo by N. L. Stebbins

RHYNLAND (1879)
Red Star Line

Courtesy, Peabody Museum of Salem

ELBE (1881)
North German Lloyd

Courtesy, Peabody Museum of Salem

SERVIA (1881)
Cunard Line

Photo by N. L. Stebbins

CITY OF ROME (1881)
Anchor Line

AUSTRAL (1881)
Orient Line

Courtesy, The Mariners' Museum

PERSIA (1881)

Courtesy, Peabody Museum of Salem

PAVONIA (1882)
Cunard Line

LAKE SUPERIOR (1884)

AMERICA (1884)
National Line

Courtesy, Peabody Museum of Salem

UMBRIA (1884)

Courtesy, Peabody Museum of Salem

LA BRETAGNE (1885)
French Line

Courtesy, The Mariners' Museum

ORMUZ (1886)

798

Courtesy, Peabody Museum of Salem

SAALE (1886)
North German Lloyd

TRAVE (1886)

CITY OF NEW YORK (1888)
Inman Line

NEW YORK (1888)
American Line

OROTAVA (1889)
Royal Mail Line

KAISER WILHELM II (1889)

Courtesy, Peabody Museum of Salem

Photo, Nautical Photo Agency

KAISERIN MARIA THERESA (1890)
North German Lloyd

FÜRST BISMARCK (1890)
Hamburg-American Line

EMPRESS OF JAPAN (1890)
Canadian Pacific Line

Courtesy, Peabody Museum of Salem

CLYDE (1890)
Royal Mail Line

Courtesy, Peabody Museum of Salem

THAMES (1890)
Royal Mail Line

LABRADOR (1891)
Dominion Line

Courtesy, Peabody Museum of Salem

MANUEL CALVO (1892)
Spanish Line

CAMPANIA (1893)
Cunard Line

TINTAGEL CASTLE (1896)
Union-Castle Line

KAISER WILHELM DER GROSSE (1897)
North German Lloyd

KAISER FRIEDRICH (1898)
North German Lloyd

NEW ENGLAND (1898)
Dominion Line

Courtesy, Peabody Museum of Salem

DEUTSCHLAND (1899)
Hamburg-American Line

GROSSER KURFURST (1899)
North German Lloyd

La Lorraine (1899)
French Line

Photo by N. L. Stebbins

Photo by N. L. Stebbins

SANNIO (1899)
Navigazione Generale Italiana

ARCADIAN (1899)
Royal Mail Line

Courtesy, *The Mariners' Museum*

SAXONIA (1900)
Cunard Line

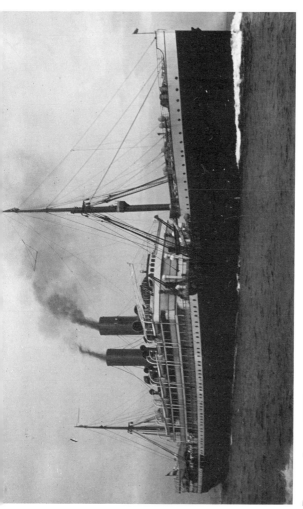

PRINZESS IRENE (1900)
North German Lloyd

Courtesy, The Mariners' Museum

REPUBLIC (1900)

TUNISIAN (1900)
Allan Line

VENTURA (1900)

826

SIERRA (1900)
Oceanic Steamship Co.

COLUMBIA (1901)

Courtesy, The Mariners' Museum

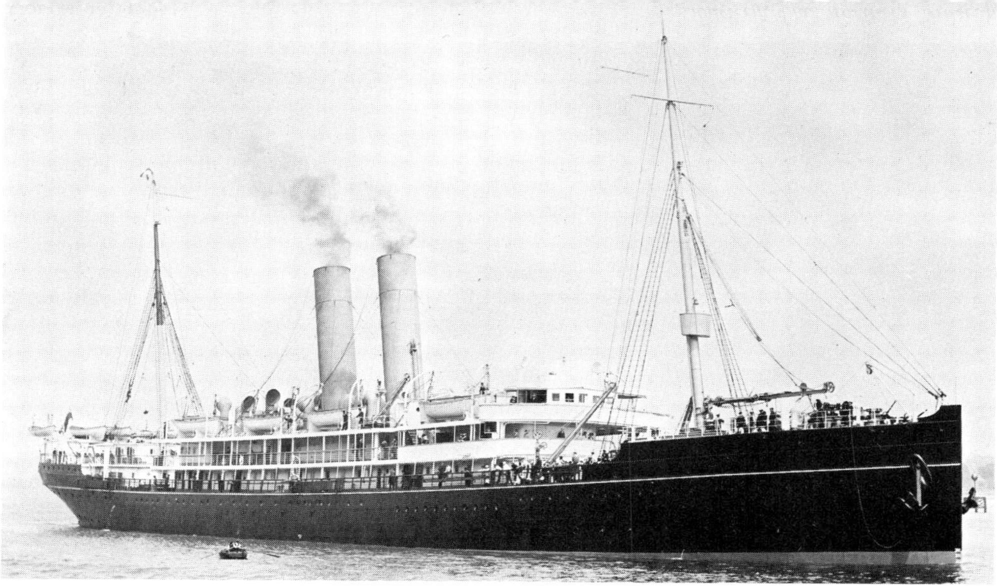

Trent (1901)
Royal Mail Line

Courtesy, Peabody Museum of Salem

ESPERANZA (1901)

830

Courtesy, The Mariners' Museum

FINLAND (1902)
Red Star Line

KUNGSHOLM (1902)

ORONTES (1902)
Orient Line

ARABIC (1903)

Courtesy, Peabody Museum of Salem

CARPATHIA (1903)
Cunard Line

Scandinavian American Line

Courtesy, The Mariners' Museum

Courtesy, Peabody Museum of Salem

ORANJE (1903)
Nederland Line

VICTORIAN (1904)
Allan Line

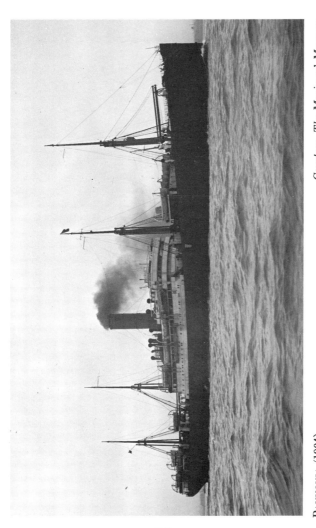

Courtesy, The Mariners' Museum

PANNONIA (1904)
Cunard Line

BALTIC (1904)
White Star Line

CALEDONIA (1904)
Anchor Line

PRINZ EITEL FRIEDRICH (1904)
North German Lloyd

Courtesy, Peabody Museum of Salem

BERMUDIAN (1904)
Quebec Steamship Co.

KAISERIN AUGUSTE VICTORIA (1905)
Hamburg-American Line

Courtesy, Peabody Museum of Salem

Courtesy, Peabody Museum of Salem

CARONIA (1905)
Cunard Line

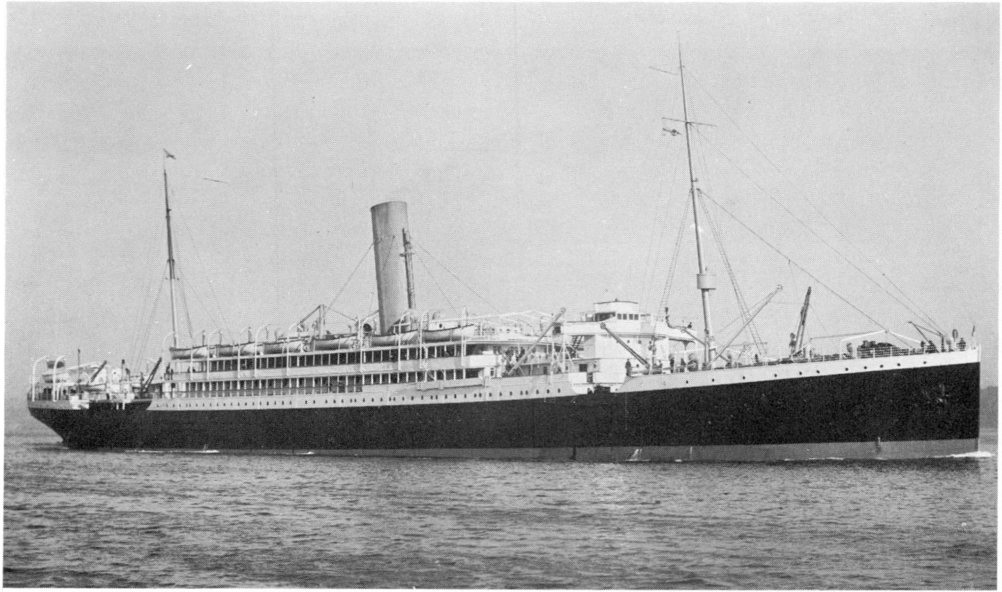

ARAGON (1905)
Royal Mail Line

Courtesy, Peabody Museum of Salem

Courtesy, The Mariners' Museum

EMPRESS OF BRITAIN (1906)
Canadian Pacific Line

NIEUW AMSTERDAM (1906)
Holland-America Line

Courtesy, Peabody Museum of Salem

YORCK (1906)
North German Lloyd

MAURETANIA (1907)
Cunard Line

DUCA DI GENOVA (1907)
Navigazione Generale Italiana

Photo by N. L. Stebbins

851

PRINCIPELLO (1907)
Canadian Northern Line

Avon (1907)
Royal Mail Line

LAPLAND (1908)
Red Star Line

EMPRESS OF INDIA (1908)
Canadian Pacific Line

Courtesy, Peabody Museum of Salem

MALWA (1908)

856

Courtesy, Peabody Museum of Salem

OSTERLEY (1909)
Orient Line

857

OTRANTO (1909)

ABANGAREZ (1909)
United Fruit Co.

TITANIC (1911)

ASCANIA (1911)
Cunard Line

IMPERATOR (1912)

862

Photo by N. L. Stebbins

LACONIA (1912)
Cunard Line

FRANCE (1912)

864

Courtesy, Peabody Museum of Salem

DESEADO (1912)
Royal Mail Line

PASTORES (1912)

866

Courtesy, Peabody Museum of Salem

INFANTA ISABEL (1912)
Pinillos, Izquierdo & Co.

Courtesy, Peabody Museum of Salem

GALLIA (1913)

Compagnie de Navigation Sud Atlantique

KONINGIN EMMA (1913)
Nederland Line

ANDRE LEBON (1913)
Messageries Maritimes

Courtesy, Peabody Museum of Salem

FORT VICTORIA (1913)
Furness-Bermuda Line

473

LEVIATHAN (1914)
United States Lines

ORDUNA (1914)
Pacific Steam Nav. Co.

DANTE ALIGHIERI (1914)
Transatlantica Italiana

PROVIDENCE (1915)
Fabre Line

Courtesy, Peabody Museum of Salem

JAN PIETERSZOON COEN (1915)
Nederland Line

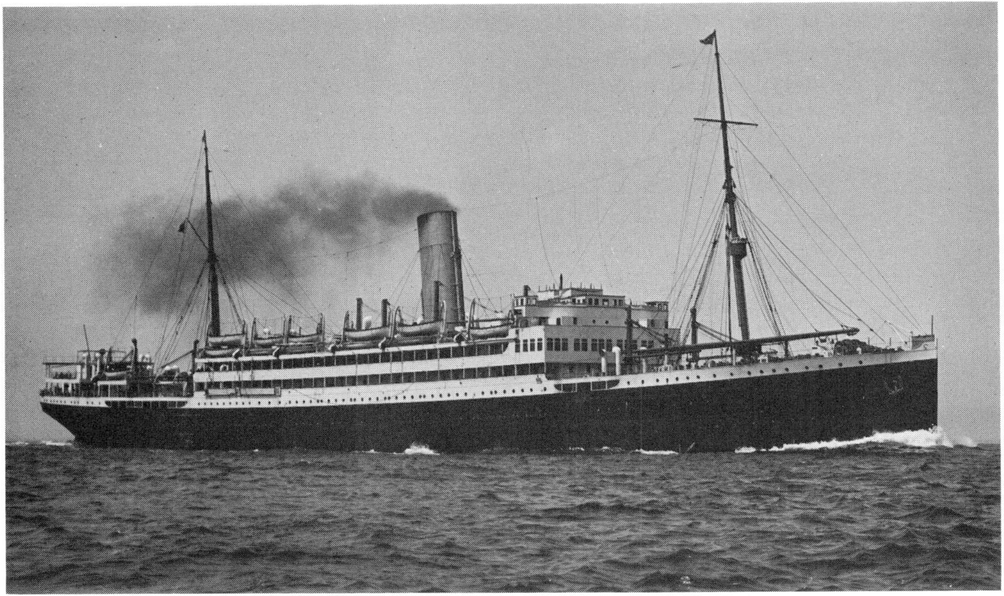

ORBITA (1915)
Royal Mail Line

Courtesy, The Mariners' Museum

BELGENLAND (1917)
Red Star Line

Toloa (1917)
United Fruit Co.

879

OROPESA (1920)
Pacific Steam Navigation Co.

CENTENNIAL STATE (1921)
United States Mail Steamship Co.

PRESIDENT POLK (1921)
Dollar Steamship Lines

Courtesy, Dollar Steamship Lines

PRESIDENT TAFT (1921)
Dollar Steamship Lines

CAP LAY (1921)
Chargeurs Reunis

Courtesy, Peabody Museum of Salem

Photo by Wm. B. Taylor

LACONIA (1922)
Cunard Line

VOLENDAM (1922)
Holland-America Line

Courtesy, The Mariners' Museum

LECONTE DE LISLE (1922)
Messageries Maritimes

MOOLTAN (1923)

Courtesy, Peabody Museum of Salem

Courtesy, Peabody Museum of Salem

AURANIA (1924)
Cunard Line

Courtesy, Italia Line

CONTE BIANCAMANO (1925)

Photo by R. Loren Graham

CALEDONIA (1925)
Anchor Line

ILE DE FRANCE (1926)
French Line

Courtesy, Peabody Museum of Salem

CARNARVON CASTLE (1926)
Union-Castle Line

Courtesy, Peabody Museum of Salem

CAP ARCONA (1927)
Hamburg-South American Line

SATURNIA (1927)
Italia Line

ATLANTIC (1927)
Home Lines

Eugene W. Smith Collection

ARANDORA STAR (1927)
Blue Star Line

CHRISTIAN HUYGENS (1928)
Nederland Line

Courtesy, Nederland Line

BRAZIL (1928)
Moore-McCormack Lines

Courtesy, Moore-McCormack Lines

Courtesy, Grace Line

SANTA MARIA (1928)

ASAMA MARU (1929)
Nippon Yusen Kaisha

Photo, Nautical Photo Agency

SANTA INEZ (1929)
Grace Line

Courtesy, Grace Line

LADY HAWKINS (1929)
Canadian National Line

BRITANNIC (1930)
Cunard-White Star Line

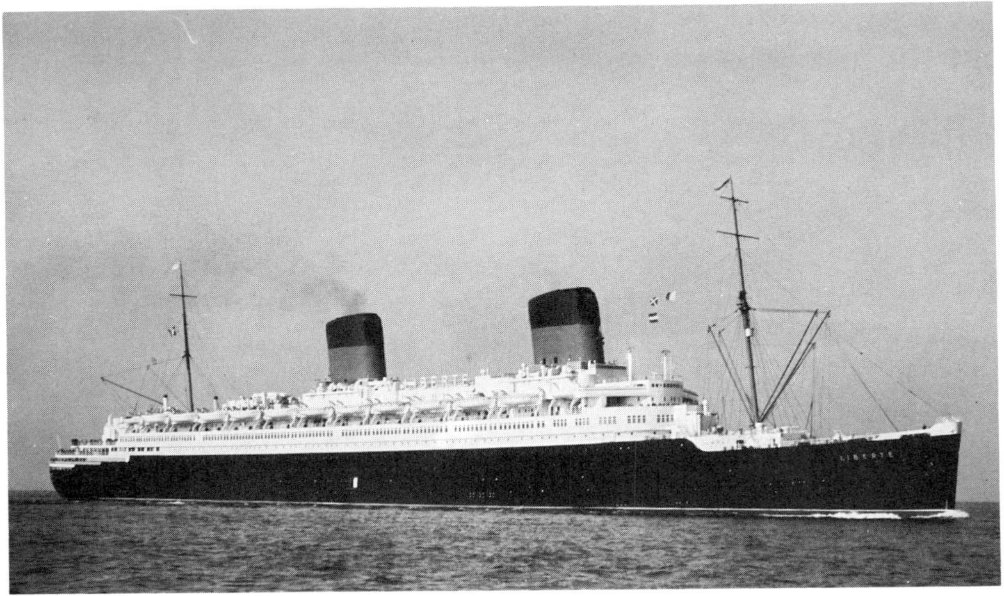

LIBERTE (1930)
French Line

Courtesy, French Line

MARNIX VAN ST. ALDEGONDE (1930)
Nederland Line

MONTE ROSA (1930)
Hamburg-South American Line

MORRO CASTLE (1930)
Ward Line

CHAMPLAIN (1932)
French Line

LURLINE (1932)
Matson Lines

Courtesy, Grace Line

SANTA ROSA (1932)
Grace Line

NORMANDIE (1933)
French Line

QUEEN OF BERMUDA (1933)
Furness-Bermuda Line

ORION (1935)
Orient Line

QUEEN MARY (1936)
Cunard Line

PASTEUR (1939)
Compagnie de Navigation Sud-Atlantique

916

BREMEN (1939)
North German Lloyd

Courtesy, North German Lloyd

917

QUEEN ELIZABETH (1940)
Cunard Line

Courtesy, Cunard Steam-Ship Co., Ltd.

AMERICA (1940)
United States Lines

EXCALIBUR (1944)

Courtesy, American Export Lines

MEDIA (1947)
Cunard Line

WILLEM RUYS (1947)
Rotterdam Lloyd

CARONIA (1948)
Cunard Line

Courtesy, Cunard Steam-Ship Co., Ltd.

PRESIDENT WILSON (1948)
American President Lines

Courtesy, Peabody Museum of Salem

GOTHIC (1948)
Shaw, Savill & Albion Co.

HIMALAYA (1949)
P & O Line

CONSTITUTION (1951)
American Export Lines

Courtesy, American Export Lines

GIULIO CESARE (1951)
Italia Line

Courtesy, Italia Line

Courtesy, French Line

FLANDRE (1951)
French Line

RYNDAM (1951)
Holland-America Line

ORONSAY (1951)
Orient Line

UNITED STATES (1952)
United States Lines

ANDREA DORIA (1952)
Italia Line

AUGUSTUS (1952)
Italia Line

SAXONIA (1954)
Cunard Line

Courtesy, Orient Line

ORSOVA (1954)
Orient Line

IBERIA (1954)
P. & O. Line

Courtesy, P. & O. Line

Courtesy, Canadian Pacific Line

EMPRESS OF BRITAIN (1955)
Canadian Pacific Line

ISRAEL (1955)
Zim Lines

BERGENSFJORD (1956)
Norwegian-America Line

Courtesy, Holland-America Line

STATENDAM (1957)
Holland-America Line

JERUSALEM (1957)
Zim Lines

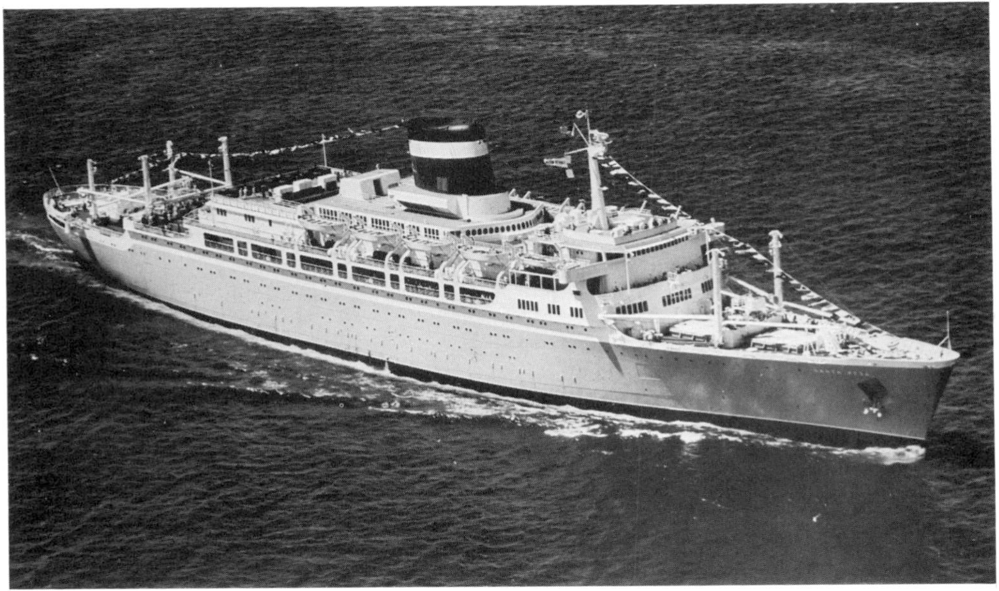

SANTA ROSA (1957)
Grace Line

Courtesy, Grace Line

ORANJE NASSAU (1957)
Royal Netherlands Steamship Co.

Courtesy, Grace Line

SANTA PAULA (1958)
Grace Line

BRASIL (1958)
Moore-McCormack Lines

PENDENNIS CASTLE (1958)
Union-Castle Line

947

ROTTERDAM (1959).
Holland-America Line

948

Courtesy, P & O-Orient Lines

CANBERRA (1961)
P & O-Orient Lines

Courtesy, French Line

FRANCE (1961)
French Line

APPENDIX

DISTANCES BETWEEN PORTS

NOTE: The Panama Canal was officially opened to commerce in August 1914.

The Suez Canal was opened to navigation in November 1869.

	Nautical Miles
Boston to Liverpool	2,898
Capetown to Durban	800
Capetown to Fremantle, Australia	4,808
Capetown to Wellington, N. Z.	8,375
Capetown to Adelaide	5,786
Liverpool to Buenos Aires	6,400
Liverpool to Colon, Panama	4,530
Liverpool to Cape Horn	7,350
Liverpool to Halifax	2,509
Liverpool to Montreal, via Cape Race	2,947
Liverpool to Sydney, via Panama Canal	12,600
Liverpool to Valparaiso, via Panama Canal	7,191
Liverpool to Wellington, via Panama Canal	11,200
London to Bombay, via Suez Canal	6,300
London to Hong Kong	9,688
London to Sydney, via Suez Canal	12,000
London to Port Said	3,214
Marseilles to Port Said	1,516
New York to Antwerp	3,350
New York to Barcelona	3,750
New York to Bermuda	700
New York to Bremen	3,590
New York to Buenos Aires	5,870
New York to Colon, Panama	1,974
New York to Durban, via Cape of Good Hope	7,565
New York to Genoa	4,045

New York to Gibraltar	3,192
New York to Goteborg, Sweden	3,738
New York to Hamburg	3,536
New York to Havana	1,186
New York to Havre	3,170
New York to Liverpool	3,058
New York to London	3,282
New York to Queenstown	2,840
New York to Rio de Janeiro	4,770
New York to Southampton	3,120
San Francisco to Auckland, N. Z.	5,680
San Francisco to Hong Kong	6,404
San Francisco to Honolulu	2,091
San Francisco to Manila	6,221
San Francisco to Melbourne	6,970
San Francisco to Suva, Fiji Islands	4,749
San Francisco to Sydney	6,448
San Francisco to Wellington, N. Z.	5,905
San Francisco to Yokohama	4,536
Vancouver to Auckland, N. Z.	6,205
Vancouver to Yokohama	4,262
Vancouver to Sydney	6,840

Conversion table of knots into miles per hour

NOTE: The sea mile equals 6,080 feet. The land mile equals 5,280 feet.

```
10 knots equal 11.515 miles per hour
15 knots equal 17.27  miles per hour
20 knots equal 23.03  miles per hour
25 knots equal 28.787 miles per hour
30 knots equal 34.53  miles per hour
35 knots equal 40.287 miles per hour
40 knots equal 46.04  miles per hour
```

APPENDIX

LONGEST PASSENGER SHIPS IN THE WORLD

Past and Present

NOTE: *Denotes in service, 1962.

Length Over-all	Length Between Perpendiculars	Beam	Gross Tonnage	Year Built	Name of Ship	Owners
1035'	951'	110'	66,348	1961	*France	French Line
1031'	987'	118'	83,673	1940	*Queen Elizabeth	Cunard Line
1027'	981'	117'	82,799	1933	Normandie	French Line
1018'	975'	118'	81,237	1935	*Queen Mary	Cunard Line
990'	916'	101'	53,329	1952	*United States	United States Lines
956'	915'	100'	56,551	1921	Majestic	White Star Line
					ex-Bismarck	Hamburg-American Line
950'	907'	100'	59,957	1914	Leviathan	United States Lines
			54,282		ex-Vaterland	Hamburg-American Line
937'	898'	101'	51,656	1929	Bremen	North German Lloyd
936'	893'	101'	51,839	1930	Liberte	French Line
			49,746		ex-Europa	North German Lloyd
919'	883'	98'	52,226	1912	Berengaria	Cunard Line
			51,969		ex-Imperator	Hamburg-American Line
903'	870'	94'	48,158	1914	Britannic	White Star Line
901'	868'	97'	45,647	1914	Aquitania	Cunard Line
882'	852'	92'	46,439	1911	Olympic	White Star Line
882'	852'	92'	46,329	1911	Titanic	White Star Line

953

Length Over-all	Length Between Perpendiculars	Beam	Gross Tonnage	Year Built	Name of Ship	Owners
879'	833'	97'	51,062	1932	Rex	Italia Line
818'		102'	45,270	1961	*Canberra	P. & O. Line
814'	785'	96'	48,502	1932	Conte di Savoia	Italia Line
804'		97'	41,923	1960	*Oriana	Orient Line
791'	763'	92'	43,153	1926	Ile de France	French Line
790'	762'	88'	30,696	1907	Mauretania	Cunard Line
790'	762'	87'	31,550	1907	Lusitania	Cunard Line
783'		92'	37,640	1960	*Windsor Castle	Union-Castle Line
776'	751'	83'	34,356	1914	Homeric	White Star Line
775'	749'	83'	32,354	1922	Columbus	North German Lloyd
771'	739'	89'	35,738	1939	*Mauretania	Cunard Line
763'		83'	28,582	1958	*Pendennis Castle	Union-Castle Line
763'	735'	83'	34,569	1921	Paris	French Line
761'	676'	92'	33,340	1960	*Leonardo da Vinci	Italia Line
760'		90'	32,697	1961	*Transvaal Castle	Union-Castle Line
758'	713'	88'	36,287	1938	*Nieuw Amsterdam	Holland-America Line
748'	680'	94'	38,645	1959	*Rotterdam	Holland-America Line
747'	717'	84'	28,705	1948	*Pretoria Castle	Union-Castle Line
747'	717'	84'	28,705	1948	*Edinburgh Castle	Union-Castle Line
758'	733'	97'	42,348	1931	Empress of Britain	Canadian Pacific Line
742'	713'	91'	42,512	1931	L'Atlantique	Cie. Sud-Atlantique
734'	702'	82'	27,002	1938	*Capetown Castle	Union-Castle Line
726'	709'	75'	24,563	1906	Adriatic	White Star Line
726'	709'	75'	23,884	1904	Baltic	White Star Line
725'	696'	82'	25,564	1936	*Athlone Castle	Union-Castle Line

954

Length Over-all	Length Between Perpendiculars	Beam	Gross Tonnage	Year Built	Name of Ship	Owners
725'	696'	82'	25,550	1935	*Stirling Castle	Union-Castle Line
723'	660'	93'	33,532	1940	*America	United States Lines
722'	668'	90'	28,790	1954	*Orsova	Orient Line
722'	699'	78'	23,788	1908	George Washington	United States Lines
			25,570		ex-German liner	North German Lloyd
721'		90'	29,734	1954	*Arcadia	P. & O. Line
720'	690'	75'	23,769	1912	France	French Line
718'	687'	90'	29,614	1954	*Iberia	P. & O. Line
715'	683'	91'	34,183	1948	*Caronia	Cunard Line
712'	683'	82'	27,759	1932	*Georgic	White Star Line
712'	681'	82'	26,840	1930	Britannic	White Star Line
711'	666'	90'	27,955	1948	*Orcades	Orient Line
710'	681'	82'	32,650	1927	Augustus	Italia Line
708'	681'	90'	27,955	1949	*Himalaya	P. & O. Line
708'	685'	90'	27,632	1951	*Oronsay	Orient Line
706'	684'	74'	19,503	1906	Kronprinzessin Cecilie	North German Lloyd
706'	666'	72'	19,361	1903	Kaiser Wilhelm II	North German Lloyd
705'	668'	82'	32,583	1926	Roma	Italia Line
705'	668'	86'	24,289	1932	Manhattan	United States Lines
705'	685'	86'	24,289	1933	Washington	United States Lines
704'	656'	68'	17,274	1899	Oceanic	White Star Line
700'	677'	90'	29,082	1953	Andrea Doria	Italia Line
699'		77'	25,160	1905	Empress of Scotland	Candian Pacific Line
			24,581		ex-Kaiserin Auguste Victoria	(German)
698'	670'	81'	29,510	1929	Statendam	Holland-America Line

955

Length Over-all	Length Between Perpendiculars	Beam	Gross Tonnage	Year Built	Name of Ship	Owners
697'	656'	87'	32,336	1939	*Bremen	North German Lloyd
			30,447		ex-Pasteur	Cie. Sud-Atlantique
697'	656'	89'	29,083	1953	*Cristoforo Colombo	Italia Line
697'	680'	75'	20,904	1901	Celtic	White Star Line
697'	680'	75'	21,227	1903	Cedric	White Star Line
696'	670'	78'	27,132	1917	Belgenland	Red Star Line
691'	680'	82'	18,915	1858	Great Eastern	British
687'	668'	74'	21,145	1905	America	United States Lines
			22,225		ex-Amerika	Hamburg-American Line
686'	660'	67'	16,502	1899	Deutschland	Hamburg-American Line
686'	661'	73'	20,141	1926	*Carnarvon Castle	Union-Castle Line
683'	637'	89'	23,719	1950	*Independence	American Export Line
683'	637'	89'	23,719	1951	*Constitution	American Export Line
682'	657'	84'	27,155	1939	*Dominion Monarch	Shaw Savill Line
680'	649'	87'	27,226	1952	*Augustus	Italia Line
680'	649'	87'	27,694	1951	Giulio Cesare	Italia Line
678'	650'	72'	19,566	1905	Carmania	Cunard Line
678'	650'	72'	19,782	1905	Caronia	Cunard Line
676'	648'	72'	21,131	1923	Hansa	Hamburg-American Line
			20,815		ex-Albert Ballin	Hamburg-American Line
675'	645'	72'	21,046	1923	Deutschland	Hamburg-American Line
675'	645'	72'	22,117	1926	Hamburg	Hamburg-American Line
675'	645'	72'	22,337	1927	New York	Hamburg-American Line

INDEX

960

Atlantic (1849) 16, 21, 26, 198, 699
Atlantic (1870) 22, 26, 191, 750
Atlantic (1927) 22, 219, 715, 755, 756
Atlantic (1953) 22, 689
Atlantica (1868) 255, 280, 482
Atlantida (1924) 345, 354, 741
Atlantique (1864) 11, 22, 123, 707
Atlantique (1899) 355, 518, 525, 720
Atlantis (1913) 348, 355, 736
Atlas (1860) 22, 117, 133, 161, 194, 246, 702
Atlas Maru (1920) 729
Atrato (1853) 355, 736
Atrato (1888) 355, 422, 736
Atsuta Maru (1909) 297, 309, 525, 580, 588, 593, 611, 725
Atua (1906) 746
Atuta Maru (1909) 725
Audacious (1913) 30
Augusta Victoria (1888) 22, 187, 711
Auguste Victoria (1888) 23, 67, 101, 711
Augustine (1865) 694
Augustine (1879) 355, 574, 694
Augustus (1927) 23, 226, 355, 716, 723
Augustus (1952) 23, 107, 355, 716
Aurania (1883) 23, 702
Aurania (1915) 23, 702
Aurania (1924) 3, 12, 14, 19, 24, 702
Aurelia (1939) 525
Aureol (1951) 705, 525
Auriga (1909) 337, 355, 711
Aurigny (1918) 356, 359, 394, 698
Ausonia (1909) 24, 260, 702
Ausonia (1921) 12, 14, 19, 24, 702
Ausonia (1928) 525
Austral (1881) 24, 525, 729
Australasian (1857) 24, 42, 702
Australasian (1884) 525, 687
Australasian (1901) 337, 526, 725
Australia (1870) 13, 25, 44, 526, 690
Australia (1870) P. & O. Line 526, 550, 732
Australia (1875) 297, 330, 728
Australia (1881) 25, 711
Australia (1892) 526, 579, 733
Australia (1951) 526, 616, 621, 719
Australien (1889) 522, 526, 635, 674, 720
Austria (1857) 241, 711
Austrian (1866) 25, 178, 182, 205, 356, 688
Ava (1870) 516, 527, 610, 632, 653, 720
Ava (1895) 714, 720
Avare (1912) 478, 739
Avelona Star (1927) 344, 348, 356, 694, 351
Aventino (1907) 719
Aviateur Roland Garros (1902) 720
Avila Star (1927) 344, 348, 356, 694, 351
Aviles (1884) 452
Avoca (1891) 25, 266, 527, 694
Avon (1842) 356
Avon (1880) 736
Avon (1907) 354, 356, 736

Avondale Castle (1897) 397, 527, 666, 745
Awa Maru (1899) 307, 725
Awatea (1936) 746
Ayacuacho (1873) 731
Ayrshire (1903) 707
Azay-le-Rideau (1910) 527, 720
Azemmour (1951) 732

Baarn (1926) 737
Baden (1922) 357, 359, 711
Badger (1890) 502
Badger Mariner (1953) 22
Baependy (1899) 357, 487, 718
Bagdad (1872) 694
Bage (1912) 357, 478, 718
Bahama Star (1931) 19
Bahia (1910) 357, 718
Bahia Belgrano (1897) 357, 713
Bahia Blanca (1912) 358, 713
Bahia Castillo (1913) 358, 398, 713
Bahia Laura (1913) 358, 713
Bahri Amer (1893) 463
Baikal Maru (1921) 729
Bakana (1894) 705
Bakara (1913) 463
Balantia (1909) 736
Balhash (1913) 755
Ballarat (1882) 527, 631, 733
Ballarat (1911) 527, 531, 532, 733
Ballarat (1921) 527, 528, 529, 530, 733
Balmoral Castle (1877) 528, 555, 557, 698
Balmoral Castle (1910) 528, 558, 745
Baloeran (1930) 528, 551, 735
Balranald (1922) 528, 529, 733
Baltic (1850) 16, 21, 26, 198, 699
Baltic (1871) 2, 22, 26, 191, 222, 269, 750
Baltic (1904) 2, 26, 52, 53, 222, 750
Baltika (1940) 738
Baltimore (1868) 26, 31, 149, 726
Baltonia (1902) 515
Baltrover (1913) 78, 388
Bamora (1914) 694
Bandra (1914) 695
Banffshire (1894) 707
Banfora (1914) 528, 584, 706
Bankura (1912) 694
Baradine (1921) 528, 733
Barala (1912) 695
Baranof (1919) 468
Barbarigo (1930) 716
Barbarossa (1840) 37
Barbarossa (1896) 26, 529, 726
Barcelona (1855) 271
Barcelona (1896) 14
Barcelona (1908) 358, 367, 734
Barcelone (1855) 27, 700
Bardic (1929) 390
Barentsz (1915) 737
Barjora (1912) 695
Barnett (1928) 469, 482
Barneveld (1928) 737

961

Calabar (1935) 671, 682, 705
Calabar (1936) 705
Calabria (1857) 24, 42, 702
Calabria (1901) 42, 690
Calabria (1922) 278, 716, 719
Calamares (1913) 367, 447, 485, 747
Calawaii (1893) 172, 753
Caledonia (1840) 1, 37, 42, 67, 702
Caledonia (1862) 42, 690
Caledonia (1863) 37, 42, 690
Caledonia (1894) 534, 733
Caledonia (1904) 43, 45, 690
Caledonia (1921) 32, 158
Caledonia (1925) 43, 261, 690
Caledonia (1947) 534, 542, 690
Caledonien (1882) 534, 610, 616, 621,
    659, 720
Caledonien (1952) 293, 332, 338, 647,
    720
Calgarian (1913) 7, 43, 688
Calgaric (1918) 43, 438, 750
Calgary (1921) 705
California (1872) 43, 270, 690
California (1883) 711
California (1902) 367, 427, 731
California (1907) 43, 44, 45, 690
California (1920) 4, 367, 723
California (1923) 44, 263, 690
California (1928) 367, 448, 490, 498, 731
Californian (1891) 44, 250, 378, 688
Californie (1905) 504, 707
Calitea (1933) 719
Callao (1858) 367, 731
Callao (1913) 477
Calumet (1924) 705
Calypso (1898) 533
Cambodge (1861) 535, 665, 720
Cambodge (1952) 535, 598, 674, 720
Cambrai (1920) 10
Cambria (1845) 44, 118, 702
Cambria (1869) 13, 25, 44, 690
Cambrian (1860) 744
Cambroman (1892) 45, 704, 749
Cameronia (1910) 43, 44, 45, 690
Cameronia (1920) 45, 147, 690
Cametense (1891) 694
Camito (1915) 353, 359, 367, 371, 372,
    373, 705
Camito (1956) 368, 400, 705
Campana (1929) 126, 368, 743
Campanello (1902) 38, 45, 46, 96, 696
Campania (1893) 45, 153, 702
Campania (1902) 38, 45, 46, 96, 237,
    696
Campidoglio (1909) 719
Campos Salles (1897) 466, 718
Camranh (1923) 532
Canada (1848) 7, 46, 91, 184, 199, 702
Canada (1863) 46, 110, 202, 203, 722
Canada (1865) 46, 504, 707
Canada (1896) 47, 704
Canada (1898) 40, 47, 692
Canada (1911) 47, 237, 706
Canada (1935) 705

Canada Maru (1911) 428, 729
Canadian (1854) 47, 124, 688
Canadian (1860) 47, 688
Canadian (1872) 47, 368, 688
Canadian (1900) 48, 717
Canara (1905) 695
Canarias (1855) 69
Canberra (1913) 48, 710
Canberra (1961) 290, 535, 626, 733
Cannstatt (1913) 463
Canopic (1900) 48, 68, 750
Cantigny (1920) 9, 18, 216
Canton (1882) 368
Canton (1939) 414, 535, 733
Cantuaria Guimaraes (1907) 368, 384,
    479, 571
Caobang (1902) 535, 720
Cap Arcona (1907) 368, 369, 518, 713
Cap Arcona (1927) 368, 371, 713
Cap Blanco (1903) 368, 369, 371, 713
Cap Corse (1929) 707
Cap Finisterre (1911) 327, 369, 713
Cap Frio (1899) 369, 370, 713
Cap Lay (1921) 536, 698
Cap Norte (1922) 369, 478, 713
Cap Ortegal (1903) 368, 369, 371, 539
    713
Cap Padaran (1922) 536, 698
Cap Polonia (1914) 370, 713
Cap Roca (1900) 344, 369, 370, 713
Cap St. Jacques (1922) 536, 698
Cap Tourane (1923) 536, 698
Cap Trafalgar (1913) 49, 370, 713
Cap Varella (1921) 536, 698
Cap Verde (1900) 369, 370, 421, 459,
    713
Cap Vilano (1906) 368, 369, 370, 480,
    570, 713
Capetown Castle (1938) 536, 745
Capitaine Potie (1922) 565
Capo Manara (1921) 179
Captain Cook (1925) 150, 537
Captain Marcos (1914) 579
Carabobo (1923) 371, 734
Caracas (1889) 371, 734
Caracas (1927) 734
Caramanie (1874) 197
Caraquet (1894) 371, 575, 736
Carare (1925) 353, 359, 368, 371, 372,
    373, 705
Caravelle (1904) 707
Cardiganshire (1913) 371, 736
Caribbean (1890) 371, 557, 736
Caribia (1932) 48, 71, 372, 381, 711, 739
Carinthia (1895) 48, 702
Carinthia (1925) 48, 99, 142, 235, 702
Carinthia (1956) 49, 128, 241, 256, 702
Carisbrook Castle (1898) 537, 745
Carl Legien (1922) 341, 372, 711
Carl Schurz (1912) 374
Carmania (1905) 49, 50, 274, 370, 702
Carmarthenshire (1893) 374, 464, 569,
    707
Carmarthenshire (1915) 372, 736

City of San Francisco (1875) 300, 730
City of San Francisco (1919) 60, 692
City of Savannah (1896) 372, 416
City of Simla (1921) 546, 706
City of Sparta (1897) 546, 706
City of Sydney (1875) 300, 730
City of Tokio (1874) 299, 300, 301, 730
City of Tokio (1921) 706
City of Valencia (1908) 463
City of Venice (1924) 546, 706
City of Vienna (1890) 259, 546, 706
City of Washington (1853) 58, 64, 715
City of Washington (1877) 377, 749
City of York (1904) 547, 706
City of York (1953) 544, 546, 547, 706
Ciudad Condal (1872) 506, 741
Ciudad de Cadiz (1878) 64, 506, 741
Clan Macintyre (1903) 677
Claris (1860) 117
Claude Bernard (1950) 378, 418, 420,
    547, 698
Claude Chappe (1909) 202, 547, 720
Clement (1877) 694
Clement (1896) 378, 416, 694
Clement Ader (1953) 344, 547, 559, 578,
    698
Cleopatra (1852) 64
Cleopatra (1871) 376
Cleopatra (1895) 718
Cleopatra (1898) 5, 32, 64, 173, 691
Cleopatra (1944) 65, 134, 717
Cleveland (1908) 56, 65, 134, 711, 746
Cluny Castle (1903) 547, 549, 670, 745
Clyde (1841) 378, 736
Clyde (1881) 548, 568, 658, 664, 733
Clyde (1890) 378, 486, 736
Coalgacondor (1848) 7
Coamo (1891) 44, 250, 378, 724
Coamo (1925) 378, 724
Cobequid (1893) 378, 573, 736
Coblenz (1923) 65, 101, 278, 477, 548,
    566, 646, 726
Coburg (1908) 65, 84, 379, 449, 726
Colaba (1906) 695
Colima (1873) 301, 730
Colombia (1873) 731
Colombia (1883) 611
Colombia (1899) 731
Colombia (1915) 301, 302, 328, 379, 493,
    730
Colombia (1930) 379, 737
Colombia (1932) 379, 428, 457, 699
Colombie (1862) 65, 96, 504, 707
Colombie (1931) 66, 707
Colombo (1870) 393, 432
Colombo (1882) 66, 548, 720
Colombo (1917) 66, 236, 379, 719, 723
Colon (1861) 731
Colon (1884) 145, 150, 521
Colon (1899) 379, 427, 444, 732
Colonial (1908) 20, 282, 379, 502, 700
Colorado (1864) 287, 301, 730
Colorado (1867) 55, 66, 159, 170, 711
Colorado (1887) 66
Columbella (1901) 67

Columbia (1840) 1, 37, 42, 66, 702
Columbia (1854) 218
Columbia (1861) 67, 69, 119, 709
Columbia (1866) 67, 119, 690
Columbia (1889) 23, 67, 101, 187, 711
Columbia (1901) 43, 44, 45, 67, 178, 690
Columbia (1908) 67, 104, 692, 701
Columbia (1913) 68, 710
Columbia (1917) 29, 380, 731
Columbia (1932) 743
Columbus (1903) 68, 222, 704
Columbus (1914) 68, 120, 726
Columbus (1922) 68, 726
Colusa (1913) 301, 466, 730
Comfort (1907) 502
Commandant Quere (1948) 707
Commewyne (1907) 380, 737
Commissaire Ramel (1920) 333, 720
Commonwealth (1900) 48, 68, 704
Commonwealth (1902) 548, 693, 733
Comodoro Rivadavia (1905) 348, 380,
    691
Comorin (1925) 538, 541, 548, 733
Compiegne (1923) 539, 548, 565, 720
Comrie Castle (1903) 547, 548, 671, 745
Comus (1899) 500
Concordia (1862) 42, 749
Conde de Vilana (1860) 117
Congo (1878) 380, 549, 720
Congress (1913) 315
Connaught (1860) 67, 69, 119, 709
Connemara (1881) 54
Constantinople (1896) 35, 69, 134, 710
Constantinopoli (1888) 57, 377
Constantinoupolis (1903) 226
Constitution (1855) 69, 213, 700
Constitution (1951) 69, 123, 689
Consuelo (1900) 3, 69
Consul Horn (1904) 106, 604
Conte Biancamano (1925) 69, 70, 380,
    716, 719
Conte di Savoia (1932) 70, 224, 719
Conte Grande (1928) 70, 380, 716, 719
Conte Rosso (1922) 70, 71, 380, 549,
    716, 719
Conte Verde (1923) 71, 380, 549, 716,
    719
Contessa (1930) 380, 741
Continental (1901) 71, 347
Contre Caubet (1875) 451
Conway Castle (1877) 549, 557, 679,
    698
Copacabana (1937) 381, 449, 699
Copiapo (1937) 341, 381, 410, 701, 743
Coppename (1908) 381, 424, 473, 482,
    737
Coptic (1881) 71, 301, 317, 728, 740, 750
Coquimbo (1870) 731
Corcovado (1872) 381, 389, 457, 731
Corcovado (1890) 35, 363
Corcovado (1896) 731
Corcovado (1907) 71, 112, 282, 381,
    431, 502, 711
Cordillera (1869) 351, 381, 422, 447, 731
Cordillera (1932) 48, 71, 381, 711, 739

967

973

975

977

Jura (1854) 91, 130, 702
Jurio Dolgoruki (1926) 114
Justicia (1917) 130, 252, 750
Justin (1880) 413, 694
Justin (1904) 413, 694
Jutlandia (1934) 130, 705

Kaga Maru (1901) 309, 725
Kai-Dinh (1914) 597, 721
Kaijo Maru (1873) 95
Kaikoura (1866) 288, 486
Kaikoura (1884) 643
Kaiser Franz Josef I (1912) 130, 212, 568, 606, 692
Kaiser Friedrich (1898) 131, 365, 727
Kaiser-i-Hind (1878) 587, 733
Kaiser-i-Hind (1914) 588, 733
Kaiser Wilhelm der Grosse (1897) 131, 132, 137, 727
Kaiser Wilhelm II (1889) 120, 131, 588, 727
Kaiser Wilhelm II (1903) 131, 137, 727
Kaiserin Auguste Victoria (1905) 88, 132, 712
Kaiserin Maria Theresa (1890) 132, 249, 727
Kalyan (1915) 588, 590, 592, 733
Kamakura Maru (1897) 299, 307, 588, 725
Kamakura Maru (1930) 309, 725
Kamarima (1899) 647
Kamo Maru (1908) 297, 309, 525, 580, 588, 593, 611, 725
Kampala (1947) 588, 589, 695
Kanagawa Maru (1896) 307, 309, 413, 589, 725
Kangaroo (1854) 132
Kansas (1882) 132, 749
Kanzler (1892) 589, 703
Karadeniz (1890) 75, 193
Karadeniz (1905) 680, 743
Karadeniz (1956) 743
Karagola (1917) 589, 590, 592, 695
Karamania (1882) 691
Karamea (1899) 589
Karanja (1931) 589, 591, 695
Karanja (1948) 589, 695
Karapara (1915) 589, 590, 592, 695
Karen (1930) 52, 373, 591
Karl Schurz (1912) 374
Karlsbad (1909) 718
Karlsruhe (German cruiser) 405, 492
Karlsruhe (1889) 75, 105, 133, 193, 255, 414, 590, 727
Karlsruhe (1900) 36, 133, 207, 216, 727
Karmala (1914) 588, 590, 592, 733
Karnak (1898) 519, 668
Karnak (1926) 414, 712
Karoa (1915) 589, 590, 592, 695
Kasato Maru (1900) 730
Kashgar (1914) 588, 590, 733
Kashima Maru (1913) 305, 310, 326, 590, 683, 725
Kashmir (1915) 588, 590, 592, 629, 733

Kasima Maru (1913) 306, 310
Kasshu Maru (1908) 104
Kasuga Maru (1898) 725
Kasuga Maru (1940) 316, 329, 725
Kate Dyer 243
Kathiawar (1895) 534
Katoomba (1913) 68
Katori Maru (1913) 305, 310, 326, 590, 683, 725
Kawachi Maru (1897) 307, 591, 725
Kawi (1907) 591, 659, 735
Kawsar (1923) 347, 717
Kedar (1860) 22, 117, 133, 161, 194, 246, 702
Kehrwieder (1871) 267
Kemmendine (1924) 516, 591, 632, 646, 684, 714
Kenilworth (1872) 1, 734
Kenilworth Castle (1904) 522, 591, 745
Kenilworth Castle (1946) 745
Kenmore (1921) 319, 321
Kensington (1894) 133, 249, 689, 704
Kent (1918) 471
Kenuta (1907) 731
Kenya (1930) 52, 373, 589, 591, 695
Kenya (1947) 532, 591, 669, 695
Kenya Castle (1952) 592, 643, 745
Kerasounde (1877) 413, 679, 743
Kerguelen (1922) 359, 413, 414, 425, 539, 699
Kerlew (1906) 273
Kersaint (1921) 536
Keystone State (1921) 322
Khandalla (1923) 589, 590, 592, 695
Khedive Ismail (1922) 341, 707
Khedive Ismail (1944) 65, 133, 172, 717
Kherson (1896) 738
Khiva (1914) 588, 590, 591, 592, 733
Khosrou (1897) 599
Khyber (1914) 588, 590, 592, 733
Kiautschou (1900) 134, 209, 213, 592, 712, 754
Kigoma (1914) 6, 592, 667, 703
Kildonan Castle (1899) 593, 745
Kilpatrick (1890) 2, 167
Kina (1889) 146, 152, 597
Kinfauns Castle (1880) 574, 593, 698
Kinfauns Castle (1899) 593, 698, 745
King Alexander (1896) 35, 69, 134, 710
King Alexander (1908) 65, 134, 710
King George V (1900) 231
King Hsing (1899) 450
Kinshiu Maru (1891) 725
Kirby Hall 59
Kiresson (1877) 413, 679
Kitano Maru (1909) 297, 309, 525, 580, 588, 593, 611, 625, 725
Kitsurin Maru (1935) 730
Kiturin Maru (1935) 730
Kleist (1906) 108, 134, 593, 727
Klipfontein (1939) 414, 594, 624, 641, 746

978

982

Mayflower (1902) 73, 78, 115, 164, 704
Mayon (1923) 371
McPherson (1880) 40, 190
Meade (1875) 31, 58
Mecca (1873) 695
Mecca (1929) 113, 717
Medan (1908) 735
Media (1947) 164, 201, 702
Medic (1899) 513, 609, 634, 750
Medie II (1922) 609, 732
Medina (1841) 425, 736
Medina (1873) 252
Medina (1911) 604, 609, 733
Medina Victory (1945) 147
Meduana (1922) 414, 425, 431, 700
Medway (1841) 411, 425, 736
Medway (1877) 425, 736
Megali Hellas (1914) 41, 164, 268, 710
Megantic (1909) 148, 165, 750
Meikong (1870) 516, 527, 610, 632, 653, 721
Meinam (1862) 597, 610, 721
Mekke (1874) 251
Meknes (1913) 165, 217, 708
Melansien (1925) 583
Melbourne (1881) 535, 610, 616, 621, 647, 659, 721
Meliskerk (1919) 746
Melita (1853) 165, 702
Melita (1918) 165, 169, 697
Melrose (1894) 705
Memfi (1883) 108, 400
Memphis (1871) 165, 270, 704
Menado (1907) 735
Mendi (1905) 610, 705
Mendoza (1860) 426, 721
Mendoza (1879) 426, 449, 731
Mendoza (1904) 51, 166, 426, 493, 718
Mendoza (1920) 345, 426, 743
Menominee (1897) 5, 160, 162, 166, 173, 691
Mentana (1856) 258
Mentana (1868) 255, 280, 482
Menzaleh (1865) 610, 619, 721
Meonia (1927) 705
Mera (1901) 426, 717
Merano (1909) 718
Merauke (1911) 735
Mercury (1907) 473
Merida (1906) 426, 427, 749
Merion (1902) 116, 166, 689
Merkara (1914) 607, 610, 695
Merkur (1924) 461, 462
Merrimac (1859) 427, 747
Mersey (1859) 736
Mesaba (1898) 160, 162, 166, 173, 280, 691
Metagama (1915) 166, 171, 697
Metapan (1909) 341, 345, 354, 372, 404, 427, 446, 470, 479, 487, 489, 502, 747
Meteoro (1890) 5, 116, 167, 506, 741
Methven Castle (1883) 556, 611, 698
Mexican (1882) 611, 744

Mexico (1876) 167, 506, 741
Mexico (1884) 82, 167, 189, 427, 436, 484, 701
Mexico (1899) 379, 427
Mexico (1902) 367, 427, 731
Mexico (1905) 708
Mexico (1906) 426, 753
Mexico (1932) 379, 428, 699, 743, 749
Mexico City (1896) 616
Mexico Maru (1910) 428, 730
Mexique (1915) 143, 167, 505, 708
Michigan (1887) 167, 749
Michigan (1890) 2, 167, 691
Michigan (1898) 126
Midbat Pacha (1901) 451
Midnight Sun (1874) 103
Midzuho Maru (1912) 411
Miike Maru (1888) 313, 725
Mikado (1873) 313
Mikhail Kalinin (1958) 739
Mikhail Lomonosov (1902) 216, 399, 456
Milano (1889) 127
Miltiades (1903) 436, 606, 611, 687
Milwaukee (1897) 168, 179, 697
Milwaukee (1929) 168, 234, 712
Min (1913) 611, 721
Minas Geraes (1910) 428, 718
Minho (1872) 428, 736
Minho (1874) 430
Minho (1896) 176, 390, 416, 428, 736
Minister Roon (1873) 168, 727
Minneapolis (1901) 168, 169, 171, 691
Minnedosa (1918) 165, 168, 697
Minnehaha (1900) 168, 169, 171, 691
Minnekahda (1904) 319
Minnekahda (1917) 169, 691
Minnesota (1866) 55, 66, 73, 159, 169
Minnesota (1872) 286
Minnesota (1901) 170, 283, 691
Minnesota (1904) 302, 313, 710
Minnetonka (1902) 168, 169, 170, 171, 691
Minnetonka (1924) 170, 171, 691
Minnewaska (1894) 170, 205, 691
Minnewaska (1903) 15, 170, 691
Minnewaska (1909) 168, 169, 171, 691
Minnewaska (1923) 170, 171, 691
Minsk (1884) 117
Miowera (1892) 289, 311, 313, 329
Miramar (1874) 242
Mishima Maru (1908) 297, 309, 525, 580, 593, 611, 725
Misr (1947) 717
Missanabie (1914) 167, 171, 697
Mississippi (1859) 427
Mississippi (1871) 171, 704
Mississippi (1903) 171, 235, 691
Missouri (1855) 29, 114, 172, 704
Missouri (1881) 75
Missourian (1922) 565
Misumi Maru (1889) 407
Mitau (1894) 32, 129, 172, 523, 738

983

984

Munargo (1921) 432, 722
Munchen (1889) 179, 615, 727
Munchen (1922) 4, 179, 192, 253, 727
Munchen (1923) 180, 255, 437, 727
Mundra (1920) 609, 615, 695
Munorleans (1911) 432, 722
Munster (1861) 13
Mustapha (1901) 450
Muttra (1891) 695

Nagasaki Maru (1922) 725
Nagoya (1913) 616, 620, 733
Nairnshire (1899) 707
Naldera (1918) 615, 616, 733
Naminoue Maru (1936) 730
Namur (1907) 615, 619, 621, 733
Naneric (1895) 519
Nankin (1912) 615, 616, 620, 733
Nanking (1913) 315
Nansemond (1896) 204
Nantucket (Lightship) 194
Napoleon III (1866) 180, 272, 708
Napoletano (1873) 55, 59
Napoli (1870) 393, 432, 748
Napoli (1899) 39, 180, 237, 715
Napoli (1907) 180, 236, 723
Napolitan Prince (1889) 246, 432, 460
Narkunda (1920) 615, 733
Narrung (1896) 616, 676, 680, 693
Nassau (1923) 92, 336, 432, 613, 715
Natal (1881) 525, 610, 616, 621, 647, 659, 721
Natale (1898) 160, 270
Nautique (1864) 60, 218
Navarra (1905) 712
Navarre (1860) 461, 432, 721
Nazario Sauro (1921) 180, 347, 432, 719, 742
Nea Hellas (1922) 181, 183, 262, 263, 710
Nebraska (1865) 315
Nebraska (1867) 181, 711
Neckar (1873) 178, 181, 191, 616, 727
Neckar (1901) 158, 181, 224, 727
Nederland (1873) 181, 256, 266, 734
Negbah (1915) 470, 751
Nellore (1913) 616, 620, 733
Nelly (1940) 245
Nemesis (1857) 733
Nepthis (1877) 749
Neptun (1924) 462
Neptuna (1924) 462
Neptunia (1912) 478, 739
Neptunia (1920) 182, 587, 710
Neptunia (1932) 433, 437, 701, 716, 719
Neptunia (1951) 526, 616, 621
Nera (1889) 555, 616, 721
Nerbudda (1882) 695
Nerissa (1926) 433, 709
Nerthe (1874) 150, 433, 721
Nestor (1913) 617, 670, 693
Nestorian (1866) 25, 178, 182, 205, 688
Neuquen (1881) 497
Neuralia (1912) 617, 695

Neustria (1883) 182, 706
Neva (1868) 433, 736
Neva (1914) 393, 739
Nevada (1867) 315, 730
Nevada (1868) 122, 182, 711
Nevasa (1884) 617, 695
Nevasa (1913) 617, 695
Nevasa (1956) 617, 695
Neville (1918) 63
New Australia (1931) 18, 428, 458, 617, 740
New England (1898) 182, 226, 242, 704
New Northland (1926) 433
New Rochelle (1899) 114, 121
New Sevilla (1900) 646
New York (1851) 183
New York (1858) 35, 121, 183, 278, 727
New York (1864) 730
New York (1888) 62, 183, 200, 206, 222, 689
New York (1922) 181, 183, 263, 710
New York (1927) 4, 77, 114, 183, 712
Newark Castle (1901) 516, 531, 538, 618 745
Newfoundland (1925) 184, 189, 709, 749
Newfoundland (1947) 184, 189, 709, 749
Newport (1880) 433, 730, 749
Niagara (1848) 7, 46, 91, 184, 702
Niagara (1877) 433, 749
Niagara (1908) 184, 382, 505, 708
Niagara (1913) 287, 315, 746
Niassa (1956) 618, 701
Nicolaev (1922) 372
Nicolas Paquet (1928) 553, 596, 607, 618, 732
Nicolo Giani (1942) 424
Nideros (1913) 466
Nieman (1865) 561, 661, 665, 675
Nieuw Amsterdam (1906) 184, 714
Nieuw Amsterdam (1938) 185, 714
Nieuw Holland (1928) 618, 738
Nieuw Zeeland (1928) 618, 738
Niger (1871) 434, 439, 475, 619, 647, 721
Nijkerk (1915) 746
Nijni Novgorod (1857) 241
Nikko Maru (1903) 619, 725
Nikolaieff (1893) 198
Nil (1864) 610, 619, 721
Nile (1870) 434, 644, 736
Nile (1893) 316, 385, 434, 730, 736
Nile (1906) 619, 621, 733
Nineveh (1894) 619, 687
Nippon (1902) 718, 719
Nippon Maru (1898) 296, 308, 316, 460, 742
Nitokris (1906) 434, 712, 717
Nitta Maru (1939) 316, 329, 725
Nivernais (1882) 434, 743
Njassa (1924) 619, 661, 672, 703
Normand (1921) 473
Noordam (1902) 138, 185, 209, 225, 714
Noordam (1939) 185, 279, 283, 714
Noordland (1884) 185, 279, 734

Orama (1924) 623, 624, 626, 627, 629, 729
Orania (1922) 394, 437, 735
Oranje (1903) 594, 595, 623, 724
Oranje (1939) 291, 335, 623, 724
Oranje Nassau (1883) 737
Oranje Nassau (1911) 437, 737
Oranje Nassau (1957) 438, 454, 737
Oranjefontein (1940) 586, 594, 623, 641, 746
Oranjestad (1938) 438, 500, 737
Oravia (1897) 438, 440, 441, 731
Orazio (1863) 8, 10
Orazio (1927) 438, 498, 716
Orbita (1915) 195, 438, 439, 731, 736
Orca (1918) 43, 195, 196, 438, 439, 731, 736
Orcades (1906) 624, 639, 729
Orcades (1937) 624, 625, 729
Orcades (1948) 292, 624, 626, 729
Orcana (1893) 439, 731
Orcana (1903) 611, 443, 731
Orcoma (1908) 439, 751
Ordu (1937) 381, 743
Orduna (1914) 195, 438, 439, 731, 736
Oregon (1848) 730
Oregon (1883) 195, 711
Oregon (1883) Dominion Line 196, 197, 239, 704
Oregon (1929) 708
Orel (1890) 738
Orellana (1893) 439, 731
Orenoque (1874) 439, 624, 647, 721
Orford (1928) 623, 624, 626, 627, 629, 729
Oriana (1906) 439, 441, 442, 731
Oriana (1960) 292, 625, 626, 729
Orien (1902) 456
Orient (1879) 625, 729
Oriental (1889) 625, 633, 733
Oriente (1930) 431, 439, 449, 749
Origen (1886) 694
Orinoco (1851) 386, 421, 440, 446, 736
Orinoco (1886) 440, 736
Orinoco (1928) 157, 413, 440, 712
Orion (1902) 215
Orion (1935) 624, 625, 729
Orione (1883) 196, 204, 479, 723
Orissa (1895) 438, 440, 731
Orissa (1897) 441, 696
Orita (1903) 440, 731
Orizaba (1886) 440, 442, 627, 731
Orizaba (1890) 441, 749
Orizaba (1918) 441, 476, 749
Orlando (1904) 583, 625, 706
Orleanais (1882) 434, 441, 743
Ormonde (1917) 626, 729
Ormuz (1886) 388, 626, 729
Ormuz (1914) 80, 284, 626, 729
Oronsa (1906) 439, 441, 442, 731
Oronsay (1925) 623, 624, 626, 629, 729
Oronsay (1951) 288, 290, 624, 626, 627, 628, 729
Orontes (1902) 627, 729

Orontes (1929) 623, 624, 626, 627, 629, 729
Oropesa (1895) 438, 440, 441, 731
Oropesa (1920) 195, 196, 441, 731, 736
Orotava (1889) 442, 443, 627, 729, 731
Oroya (1886) 440, 442, 627, 729, 731
Oroya (1923) 442, 731
Orsova (1909) 623, 628, 629, 729
Orsova (1954) 292, 626, 628, 729
Ortega (1906) 439, 441, 442, 731
Ortegal (1884) 628, 721
Ortona (1899) 351, 442, 731
Oruba (1889) 442, 627, 628, 729, 731
Oruba (1903) 436, 443, 606, 731
Oruro (1878) 555
Orvieto (1909) 623, 628, 629, 729
Oryoku Maru (1937) 730
Oscar II (1901) 117, 196, 265, 739
Osiris (1898) 733
Oslofjord (1938) 196, 728
Oslofjord (1949) 197, 728
Osterley (1909) 623, 628, 729
Oswald (1914) 694
Otranto (1909) 623, 628, 629, 729
Otranto (1925) 624, 626, 627, 629, 729
Otsego (1902) 215, 456
Ottawa (1865) 160, 688
Ottawa (1874) 106, 197, 704
Ottawa (1880) 196, 197, 704
Ottoman (1890) 749
Otway (1909) 623, 628, 629, 729
Ouessant (1908) 382, 443, 482, 699
Ourcq (1920) 9
Oxenholme (1865) 6
Oxfordshire (1912) 629, 693
Oxfordshire (1957) 630, 693
Oxus (1879) 388, 501, 517, 630, 683, 721
P. Caland (1874) 197, 275, 714
P. de Satrustegui (1890) 197, 507, 741
Pacaxo (1883) 385
Pace (1921) 384
Pacific (1849) 16, 21, 26, 198, 699
Pacific (1854) 709
Pacific (1865) 443, 731
Pacific Glory (1929) 335
Pacifica (1869) 247
Pacifique (1881) 61
Pacifique (1899) 721
Paimpol (1918) 281, 708
Pak Ling (1890) 327
Pakeha (1910) 740
Palacky (1907) 718
Palao Maru (1934) 725
Palatia (1893) 198, 201, 206, 712
Palawan (1895) 630, 658, 733
Palembang (1911) 735
Palena (1896) 701
Palermo (1899) 39, 148, 198, 723
Palermo (1903) 630, 733
Palermo (1907) 148, 198, 236, 723
Palestine (1858) 702, 749
Palma (1903) 630, 733
Palmetto State (1921) 444

Palmyra (1866) 4, 159, 198, 257, 262, 702
Pampa (1878) 388, 443, 699
Pampa (1906) 443, 446, 743
Pan America (1921) 347, 443, 481, 500, 722
Panama (1865) 46, 123, 199, 505, 708
Panama (1866) 731
Panama (1875) 199, 507, 741
Panama (1898) 403, 444, 732
Panama (1902) 444, 494, 731
Panama (1939) 292, 320, 347, 384, 444, 732
Panama Maru (1910) 428, 730
Panamanian (1904) 314, 318, 444
Pancras (1911) 444, 694
Panhandle State (1920) 53, 199, 211, 318, 322, 747, 748
Pannonia (1904) 199, 247, 702
Paolo Toscanelli (1948) 347, 350, 424, 444, 474, 716
Paou Shan (1867) 315
Papanui (1899) 630, 631, 725
Paparoa (1899) 630, 725
Para (1873) 389, 445, 457, 736
Paraense (1871) 445, 694
Paraguay (1888) 445, 699
Paraguay Star (1948) 353, 363, 445, 491, 694
Paramatta (1858) 445, 736
Parana (1851) 386, 421, 440, 445, 736
Parana (1852) 199, 709
Parana (1876) 380
Parana (1882) 445, 462, 490, 699
Parana (1904) 446, 736
Parana (1908) 443, 446, 743
Pardo (1904) 446, 736
Paris (1889) 63, 199, 200, 206, 689
Paris (1921) 92, 151, 200, 708
Paris Maru (1921) 730
Parisian (1881) 200, 688
Parismina (1908) 306, 427, 446, 747
Parramatta (1882) 527, 631, 733
Parthia (1870) 27, 200, 288, 317, 702
Parthia (1947) 164, 200, 702
Pascal Paoli (1931) 707
Pasteur (1939) 36, 446, 700
Pastores (1912) 367, 447, 485, 747
Patagonia (1869) 351, 381, 422, 447, 731
Patagonia (1890) 447, 713
Patia (1913) 358, 447, 705
Patia (1922) 705
Patria (1882) 201, 229, 447, 706
Patria (1893) 198, 201, 206, 712
Patria (1913) 201, 217, 706
Patria (1919) 631, 735, 738
Patria (1938) 201, 447, 712, 739
Patria (1947) 582, 631, 700
Patricia (1899) 109, 201, 204, 212, 712
Patriota (1890) 138, 187
Patris (1909) 202, 547, 710
Patris (1950) 531, 631
Patroclus (1923) 519, 578, 631, 649, 693
Patroclus (1950) 693
Patuca (1913) 358, 447, 705
Paul Lecat (1911) 518, 631, 721
Pavonia (1882) 52, 53, 202, 702
Pays de Waes (1912) 581, 632, 700
Paysandu (1898) 357
Payta (1864) 731
Pedro I (1908) 388
Pedro Tercero (1860) 117
Peer Gynt (1912) 478, 739
Pegu (1913) 632, 714
Pegu (1921) 516, 591, 632, 646, 684, 714
Pei-ho (1869) 516, 527, 632, 653, 721
Pelagos (1901) 332
Peles (1922) 341
Peleus (1949) 693
Pellerin de la Touche (1913) 202, 505, 607, 708
Pelotas (1905) 417
Peluse (1863) 612, 632, 647
Pembroke Castle (1883) 632, 698, 745
Pembrokeshire (1893) 375, 475, 574
Pembrokeshire (1915) 448, 736
Pendennis Castle (1958) 633, 745
Peninsular (1888) 625, 633, 733
Peninsular (1887) 701
Peninsular State (1921) 202, 211, 747
Pennland (1870) 6, 202, 734
Pennland (1922) 203, 207, 279, 693, 734
Pennsylvania (1863) 46, 722
Pennsylvania (1873) 123, 124, 192, 203, 252, 689
Pennsylvania (1896) 109, 202, 212, 712
Pennsylvania (1929) 352, 367, 448, 498, 731
Peotr Veliki (1939) 739
Pera (1903) 630, 733
Pereire (1865) 204, 272, 505, 708
Pericles (1908) 633, 677, 687
Permanente (1902) 71, 347
Perou (1907) 112, 204, 505, 708
Perseo (1883) 196, 204, 723
Perseus (1950) 693
Persia (1856) 204, 702
Persia (1881) 71, 301, 317, 730
Persia (1894) 170, 205, 217, 712
Persia (1900) 541, 559, 583, 633, 734
Persia (1903) 520, 633, 718, 719
Persia (1881) 71, 301, 317, 725, 742
Persia Maru (1881) 301, 317
Persian Monarch (1880) 84, 155, 205, 722
Persic (1899) 513, 609, 634, 750
Perthshire (1893) 707
Peru (1840) 375, 448, 731
Peru (1861) 448, 731
Peru (1892) 317, 730
Peru (1896) 731
Perugia (1901) 205, 691
Peruvian (1863) 25, 178, 182, 205, 688, 749
Pesaro (1901) 173, 205, 206, 448, 719
Peshawur (1871) 634, 734
Peshawur (1905) 630, 734

Santa Barbara (1928) 466, 710
Santa Barbara (1946) 466, 467, 469, 470, 710
Santa Cecilia (1913) 466, 710
Santa Cecilia (1918) 466, 710
Santa Cecilia (1946) 467, 710
Santa Clara (1930) 467, 710
Santa Clara (1946) 467, 470, 471, 710
Santa Columbia (1915) 68, 470
Santa Cruz (1904) 311, 321, 467
Santa Cruz (1913) 324, 467, 710
Santa Elena (1907) 467, 713
Santa Elena (1933) 467, 469, 471, 710
Santa Elisa (1919) 467, 468, 472, 710
Santa Fe (1902) 468, 713
Santa Ines (1914) 461, 468, 713
Santa Ines (1953) 468, 472, 713
Santa Inez (1929) 468, 471, 710
Santa Isabel (1915) 328, 468, 470, 493, 710
Santa Isabel (1916) 235, 237, 507, 741
Santa Isabel (1946) 469, 710
Santa Lucia (1933) 468, 469, 471, 710
Santa Luisa (1918) 469, 710
Santa Luisa (1946) 469, 710
Santa Margarita (1946) 469, 710
Santa Maria (1907) 469, 495, 713
Santa Maria (1928) 466, 469, 482, 710
Santa Maria (1946) 470, 710
Santa Maria (1953) 470, 493, 700
Santa Marta (1909) 427, 470, 479, 747
Santa Monica (1946) 470, 471, 710
Santa Olivia (1915) 302, 468, 470, 710
Santa Paula (1932) 468, 469, 470, 471, 710
Santa Paula (1958) 471, 710
Santa Rita (1905) 360
Santa Rita (1929) 468, 471, 710
Santa Rosa (1921) 179
Santa Rosa (1932) 468, 469, 471, 710
Santa Rosa (1957) 471, 710
Santa Sofia (1947) 470, 471, 710
Santa Teresa (1918) 467, 468, 471, 710
Santa Teresa (1952) 468, 472, 713
Santarem (1908) 84, 472, 718
Santarense (1891) 78, 472, 694
Santhia (1901) 647, 648, 651, 696
Santhia (1925) 648, 653, 696
Santhia (1950) 648, 653, 696
Santiago (1871) 732
Santiago (1874) 429
Santiago (1879) 472, 749
Santiago (1889) 732
Santiago (1890) 149, 237, 507, 741
Santiago (1891) 277, 472, 491
Santiago (1901) 153, 365, 472
Santo Domingo (1877) 237, 555, 741
Santos (1898) 472, 713, 718
Santos Maru (1925) 473, 730
Santos Maru (1952) 293, 331, 337, 730
Sanuki Maru (1897) 307, 649, 725
Sao Thiago (1908) 466
Sao Vicente (1900) 501
Saragossa (1874) 237, 702

Sarah Sands (1846) 238
Saramacca (1908) 424, 473, 482, 737
Saratoga (1878) 473, 749
Saratoga (1907) 403, 473, 749
Saratov (1891) 206, 248, 738
Sardar (1894) 455
Sardegna (1901) 238, 473, 723
Sardegna (1923) 238, 246, 478, 716
Sardinia (1902) 652, 654
Sardinian (1875) 208, 238, 689
Sarmatian (1871) 238, 239, 689
Sarmiento (1893) 349, 410, 422, 473, 732
Sarmiento (1901) 451
Sarnia (1882) 196, 197, 239, 704
Sarpedon (1923) 519, 578, 631, 649, 693
Sarvistan (1899) 99
Satrustegui (1948) 273, 507, 741
Saturnia (1910) 150, 239, 704
Saturnia (1927) 239, 275, 473, 701, 716
Savannah (1819) 239, 240
Savannah (1961) 240
Savoia (1954) 73, 473, 474
Savoia (1897) 240, 473, 492, 749
Savoie (1854) 73, 474, 743
Savoie (1889) 743
Saxon (1863) 644, 649, 744
Saxon (1900) 649, 744
Saxonia (1857) 25, 240, 713
Saxonia (1900) 128, 241, 702
Saxonia (1954) 49, 128, 241, 256, 703
Scandia (1889) 75, 241, 713
Scandinavian (1870) 217, 241, 689
Scandinavian (1898) 183, 226, 242, 689
Scanmail (1919) 242
Scanpenn (1919) 242
Scanstates (1919) 242
Scansyork (1919) 242
Scham (1884) 526
Scharnhorst (1904) 108, 139, 226, 242, 245, 649, 727
Scharnhorst (1934) 641
Scharnhorst (1935) 573, 636, 649, 727
Schiedam (1874) 242, 714
Schiller (1872) 103, 108, 118, 134, 150, 242, 688, 713
Schleswig (1903) 242, 474, 569, 727
Schwabenstein (1954) 530, 579, 650, 727
Scindia (1890) 6, 650, 691
Scot (1891) 5, 190, 267, 436, 650, 744, 745
Scotia (1862) 205, 243, 703
Scotia (1881) 8, 37, 243, 474, 706
Scotia (1889) 243, 691
Scotian (1898) 161, 243, 252, 689
Scotland (1865) 89, 213, 243, 722
Scotsman (1894) 244, 704
Scotstoun (1925) 43
Scythia (1875) 34, 244, 703
Scythia (1920) 49, 142, 235, 244, 703
Sealda (1902) 696
Seang Bee (1891) 651
Seang Choon (1891) 540
Seattle (1928) 474, 713

994

Volendam (1922) 269, 274, 714
Volga (1864) 561, 661, 665, 675, 721
Volga (1928) 130
Volkerfreundschaft (1947) 254
Volpi (1931) 675, 719
Voltaire (1907) 499, 717
Voltaire (1923) 492, 499, 717
Volturno (1906) 274, 696
Volubilis (1902) 709
Von Steuben (1901) 136
Vondel (1907) 575, 642, 675, 724
Vulcain (1894) 206
Vulcania (1928) 239, 275, 499, 701, 716
Vulkan (1873) 497

W. A. Scholten (1874) 197, 275, 714
Wabash (1900) 488
Wacouta (1903) 456
Wadai (1916) 607
Wadai (1922) 675, 751
Waesland (1867) 230, 275, 735
Wahehe (1914) 579
Wahehe (1922) 579, 675, 751
Wahine (1913) 746
Waidi (1916) 666
Waimana (1911) 578, 675, 740
Waimarama (1939) 740
Waipara (1904) 696
Waipawa (1934) 740
Wairangi (1935) 740
Wairarapa (1882) 746
Waiwera (1934) 740
Wakasa Maru (1897) 307, 499, 676, 726
Wakefield (1932) 159
Wakool (1898) 616, 676, 680, 693
Waldensian (1863) 232, 275, 499, 689
Wally (1879) 479
Walmer Castle (1872) 554, 676, 698
Walmer Castle (1902) 676, 745
Wandilla (1912) 395, 522, 539, 676, 678, 681
Wanganella (1932) 512
Wangoni (1920) 672, 677, 703, 738
Waratah (1908) 569, 677, 678, 693
Warilda (1914) 677, 678, 681
Waroonga (1914) 581, 678, 696
Warren (1889) 241
Warrimoo (1892) 311, 313, 329
Wartburg (1900) 488
Warwick Castle (1877) 413, 549, 557, 679, 698
Warwick Castle (1931) 679, 681, 745
Warwick Castle (1939) 558, 637, 679, 745
Warwickshire (1902) 679, 693
Warwickshire (1948) 599, 679, 693
Washington (1847) 118, 275
Washington (1863) 93, 123, 142, 709
Washington (1880) 15, 108, 124, 273, 351, 410, 499, 723
Washington (1890) 2, 167
Washington (1929) 337, 709
Washington (1933) 159, 748
Wassau (1880) 669

Waterman (1945) 277, 284, 714
Watussi (1928) 669, 680, 751
Wayland (1921) 14
Weimar (1891) 75, 105, 133, 193, 255, 277, 472, 499, 727
Wenatchee (1920) 320
Wenatchee Star (1929) 391
Werkendam (1881) 39, 190, 277, 714
Werra (1882) 84, 101, 277, 727
Werra (1922) 65, 101, 278, 499, 566, 727
Weser (1858) 35, 121, 183, 278, 727
Weser (1867) 8, 77, 118, 264, 278, 728
Weser (1922) 65, 101, 278, 500, 728
Weser (1929) 500
West Point (1940) 9
Westerdam (1946) 185, 278, 279, 714
Western Metropolis (1863) 279
Western Ocean (1899) 500, 722
Western Prince (1929) 390, 435, 481, 500, 709
Western World (1921) 320, 347, 444, 481, 500, 722
Westernland (1884) 279, 735
Westernland (1918) 203, 220, 279, 693, 735
Westminster Abbey (1906) 493, 513
Westmount (1891) 41, 600
Westphalia (1868) 120, 247, 255, 279, 482, 713
Westphalia (1923) 280, 259, 398, 713
Whampoa (1873) 159
Wieland (1874) 103, 108, 118, 134, 150, 242, 280, 688, 713
Wien (1911) 567, 578, 635, 674, 680, 712
Wilbo (1894) 32, 129, 172, 523
Wilcannia (1899) 616, 676, 680, 693
Wilhelm Gustloff (1938) 727
Wilhelmina (1909) 720, 755, 756
Wilis (1905) 659, 680, 735
Willard A. Holbrook (1921) 323
Willehad (1894) 280, 500, 727
Willem Ruys (1947) 293, 338, 680, 735
Willemstad (1938) 438, 500, 737
William O'Swald (1920) 223, 362
William P. Biddle (1919) 60
William Penn (1866) 93
William Ward Burrows (1929) 471
Willochra (1913) 97, 395, 677, 678, 680
Wiltshire (1912) 707
Winchester Castle (1930) 679, 681, 745
Windhuk (1905) 544, 571, 587, 681, 703
Windhuk (1936) 636, 681, 703
Windsor Castle (1872) 558, 681, 698
Windsor Castle (1920) 523, 682, 745
Windsor Castle (1960) 682, 745
Winifreda (1898) 166, 280
Winifredian (1899) 78, 281, 717
Winkfield (1882) 611
Winneba (1938) 670, 682, 705
Winnipeg (1918) 281, 505, 709
Wisconsin (1870) 281, 711
Wisconsin (1929) 709
Witett (1913) 463
Wittekind (1894) 280, 281, 501, 728

Note: The longest passenger ships in the world are listed on pages 953 to 956. These particular pages are not posted in the general index.